GO

■ THE RESOURCE FOR THE INDEPENDENT TRAVELER

"The guides are aimed not only at young budget travelers but at the indepedent traveler; a sort of streetwise cookbook for traveling alone."

—*The New York Times*

"Unbeatable; good sight-seeing advice; up-to-date info on restaurants, hotels, and inns; a commitment to money-saving travel; and a wry style that brightens nearly every page."

—*The Washington Post*

"Lighthearted and sophisticated, informative and fun to read. [Let's Go] helps the novice traveler navigate like a knowledgeable old hand."

—*Atlanta Journal-Constitution*

"A world-wise traveling companion—always ready with friendly advice and helpful hints, all sprinkled with a bit of wit."

—*The Philadelphia Inquirer*

■ THE BEST TRAVEL BARGAINS IN YOUR PRICE RANGE

"All the dirt, dirt cheap."

—*People*

"Anything you need to know about budget traveling is detailed in this book."

—*The Chicago Sun-Times*

"Let's Go follows the creed that you don't have to toss your life's savings to the wind to travel—unless you want to."

—*The Salt Lake Tribune*

■ REAL ADVICE FOR REAL EXPERIENCES

"The writers seem to have experienced every rooster-packed bus and lunar-surfaced mattress about which they write."

—*The New York Times*

"A guide should tell you what to expect from a destination. Here Let's Go shines."

—*The Chicago Tribune*

LET'S GO PUBLICATIONS

TRAVEL GUIDES

Alaska & the Pacific Northwest 2003
Australia 2003
Austria & Switzerland 2003
Britain & Ireland 2003
California 2003
Central America 8th edition
Chile 1st edition **NEW TITLE**
China 4th edition
Costa Rica 1st edition **NEW TITLE**
Eastern Europe 2003
Egypt 2nd edition
Europe 2003
France 2003
Germany 2003
Greece 2003
Hawaii 2003 **NEW TITLE**
India & Nepal 7th edition
Ireland 2003
Israel 4th edition
Italy 2003
Mexico 19th edition
Middle East 4th edition
New Zealand 6th edition
Peru, Ecuador & Bolivia 3rd edition
South Africa 5th edition
Southeast Asia 8th edition
Southwest USA 2003
Spain & Portugal 2003
Thailand 1st edition **NEW TITLE**
Turkey 5th edition
USA 2003
Western Europe 2003

CITY GUIDES

Amsterdam 2003
Barcelona 2003
Boston 2003
London 2003
New York City 2003
Paris 2003
Rome 2003
San Francisco 2003
Washington, D.C. 2003

MAP GUIDES

Amsterdam
Berlin
Boston
Chicago
Dublin
Florence
Hong Kong
London
Los Angeles
Madrid
New Orleans
New York City
Paris
Prague
Rome
San Francisco
Seattle
Sydney
Venice
Washington, D.C.

LET'S GO

AUSTRALIA
2003

CHRISTINE A. MONTA EDITOR
SHEENA LEE ASSOCIATE EDITOR
JAY PENDSE ASSOCIATE EDITOR

RESEARCHER-WRITERS
MEGAN CREYDT   **BRYN LOVEJOY-GRINNELL**
HOLLY FLING   **GRETCHEN PUTTKAMER**
NICK HORBACZEWSKI   **SCOTT ROY**
LUCY IVES   **ABBY SCHLATTER**
TIM SOHN

NICHOLAS DONIN MAP EDITOR
CHRISTOPHER BLAZEJEWSKI MANAGING EDITOR
CHRIS CLAYTON TYPESETTER

ST. MARTIN'S PRESS ⚘ NEW YORK

Maps by David Lindroth copyright © 2003 by St. Martin's Press.

Distributed outside the USA and Canada by Macmillan.

Let's Go: Australia Copyright © 2003 by Let's Go, Inc. All rights reserved. Printed in the United States of America. No part of this book may be used or reproduced in any manner whatsoever without written permission except in the case of brief quotations embodied in critical articles or reviews. Let's Go is available for purchase in bulk by institutions and authorized resellers. For information, address St. Martin's Press, 175 Fifth Avenue, New York, NY 10010, USA.

ISBN: 0-312-30561-3

First edition
10 9 8 7 6 5 4 3 2 1

Let's Go: Australia is written by Let's Go Publications, 67 Mount Auburn Street, Cambridge, MA 02138, USA.

Let's Go® and the LG logo are trademarks of Let's Go, Inc.
Printed in the USA on recycled paper with soy ink.

WHO WE ARE

A NEW LET'S GO FOR 2003

With a sleeker look and innovative new content, we have revamped the entire series to reflect more than ever the needs and interests of the independent traveler. Here are just some of the improvements you will notice when traveling with the new *Let's Go.*

MORE PRICE OPTIONS

Still the best resource for budget travelers, *Let's Go* recognizes that everyone needs the occassional indulgence. Our "Big Splurges" indicate establishments that are actually worth those extra pennies (pulas, pesos, or pounds), and price-level symbols (❶ ❷ ❸ ❹ ❺) allow you to quickly determine whether an accommodation or restaurant will break the bank. We may have diversified, but we'll never lose our budget focus—"Hidden Deals" reveal the best-kept travel secrets.

BEYOND THE TOURIST EXPERIENCE

Our Alternatives to Tourism chapter offers ideas on immersing yourself in a new community through study, work, or volunteering.

AN INSIDER'S PERSPECTIVE

As always, every item is written and researched by our on-site writers. This year we have highlighted more viewpoints to help you gain an even more thorough understanding of the places you are visiting.

IN RECENT NEWS. *Let's Go* correspondents around the globe report back on current regional issues that may affect you as a traveler.

CONTRIBUTING WRITERS. Respected scholars and former *Let's Go* writers discuss topics on society and culture, going into greater depth than the usual guidebook summary.

THE LOCAL STORY. From the Parisian monk toting a cell phone to the Russian *babushka* confronting capitalism, *Let's Go* shares its revealing conversations with local personalities—a unique glimpse of what matters to real people.

FROM THE ROAD. Always helpful and sometimes downright hilarious, our researchers share useful insights on the typical (and atypical) travel experience.

SLIMMER SIZE

Don't be fooled by our new, smaller size. *Let's Go* is still packed with invaluable travel advice, but now it's easier to carry with a more compact design.

FORTY-THREE YEARS OF WISDOM

For over four decades *Let's Go* has provided the most up-to-date information on the hippest cafes, the most pristine beaches, and the best routes from border to border. It all started in 1960 when a few well-traveled students at Harvard University handed out a 20-page mimeographed pamphlet of their tips on budget travel to passengers on student charter flights to Europe. From humble beginnings, *Let's Go* has grown to cover six continents and *Let's Go: Europe* still reigns as the world's best-selling travel guide. This year we've beefed up our coverage of Latin America with *Let's Go: Costa Rica* and *Let's Go: Chile;* on the other side of the globe, we've added *Let's Go: Thailand* and *Let's Go: Hawaii.* Our new guides bring the total number of titles to 61, each infused with the spirit of adventure that travelers around the world have come to count on.

CONTENTS

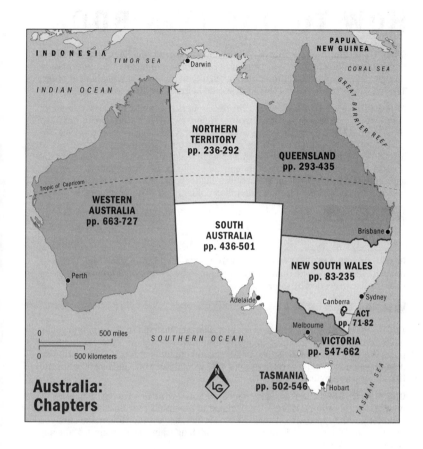

Australia: Chapters

- INDONESIA
- TIMOR SEA
- INDIAN OCEAN
- Darwin
- PAPUA NEW GUINEA
- CORAL SEA
- GREAT BARRIER REEF
- NORTHERN TERRITORY pp. 236-292
- QUEENSLAND pp. 293-435
- Tropic of Capricorn
- WESTERN AUSTRALIA pp. 663-727
- SOUTH AUSTRALIA pp. 436-501
- Brisbane
- NEW SOUTH WALES pp. 83-235
- Perth
- Adelaide
- Canberra
- Sydney
- ACT pp. 71-82
- Melbourne
- VICTORIA pp. 547-662
- SOUTHERN OCEAN
- 0   500 miles
- 0   500 kilometers
- TASMANIA pp. 502-546
- Hobart
- TASMAN SEA

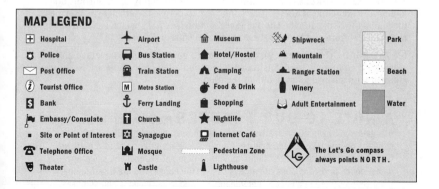

MAP LEGEND

✚ Hospital	✈ Airport	🏛 Museum	🎏 Shipwreck
✪ Police	🚌 Bus Station	🏨 Hotel/Hostel	⛰ Mountain
✉ Post Office	🚆 Train Station	⛺ Camping	🏕 Ranger Station
ⓘ Tourist Office	M Metro Station	🍎 Food & Drink	🍷 Winery
$ Bank	⚓ Ferry Landing	🛍 Shopping	👙 Adult Entertainment
⚑ Embassy/Consulate	⛪ Church	★ Nightlife	
▪ Site or Point of Interest	✡ Synagogue	💻 Internet Café	
☎ Telephone Office	☪ Mosque	⋯ Pedestrian Zone	
🎭 Theater	♜ Castle	🕯 Lighthouse	

Park

Beach

Water

The Let's Go compass always points NORTH.

HOW TO USE THIS BOOK

ORGANIZATION. Australia has six states and two territories. Each chapter of this book corresponds to a state or territory of Australia and begins with information on that region or state's capital city. The chapters are listed in alphabetical order. The black tabs on the side of the book should help you navigate your way through.

PRICE RANGES AND RANKINGS. Our researchers list establishments in order of value from best to worst. Our absolute favorites are denoted by the Let's Go thumbs-up (🖑). Since the best value does not always mean the cheapest price, we have incorporated a system of price ranges in the guide. Symbols are based on the lowest cost for one person, excluding special deals or prices. Many accommodations in Australia offer a range of lodging all in one locale. Read listings carefully, as accommodations listed as ❶ may offer higher-range options as well. The table below lists how prices (listed in Australian dolllars) fall within each bracket.

AUSTRALIA	❶	❷	❸	❹	❺
ACCOMMODATIONS	under $15	$16-25	$26-40	$41-60	over $60
FOOD	under $10	$11-15	$16-20	$21-25	over $25

PHONE CODES AND TELEPHONE NUMBERS. Area codes for each region appear opposite the name of the region and are denoted by the ☎ icon. Phone numbers in text are also preceded by the ☎ icon.

WHEN TO USE IT

TWO MONTHS BEFORE. The first chapter, **Discover Australia** (p. 31), contains highlights of the region, including Suggested Itineraries (see p. 35) that can help you plan your trip. The **Essentials** (see p. 40) section contains practical information on planning a budget, making reservations, renewing a passport, and has other useful tips about traveling in Australia.

ONE MONTH BEFORE. Take care of insurance and write down a list of emergency numbers and hotlines. Make a list of packing essentials (see **Packing**, p. 33) and shop for anything you are missing. Read through the coverage and make sure you understand the logistics of your itinerary (catching trains, ferries, etc.). Make any reservations if necessary.

TWO WEEKS BEFORE. Leave an itinerary and a photocopy of important documents with someone at home. Take some time to peruse the **articles** (p. 385), near the end of the book, and the **Life and Times** section (see p. 7), which has info on history, culture, flora and fauna, recent political events, and more.

ON THE ROAD. The **Appendix** (p. 728) contains a guide to Aussie beverage lingo, a glossary of commonly used Australian terms, and a temperature chart. Now, arm yourself with a travel journal and hit the road.

A NOTE TO OUR READERS The information for this book was gathered by *Let's Go* researchers from May through August of 2002. Each listing is based on one researcher's opinion, formed during his or her visit at a particular time. Those traveling at other times may have different experiences since prices, dates, hours, and conditions are always subject to change. You are urged to check the facts presented in this book beforehand to avoid inconvenience and surprises.

ACKNOWLEDGMENTS

Oz Thanks: Our amazing RWs, Anne, Frzulie, Mollie, and Allison, Team SEAS, Nick D., Prod, Poland Springs man, Adam and Car Talk, Bertucci's, Elvis Costello, Jesse's Girl, Plamen, Kris, Amelia, our beloved proofers, Alex, Cody, and Jude and Stu.

Chrissy Thanks: Sheena and Jay, Viactiv Chews will reign forever; RWs for the awesome work; Donin, for teaching me that "sick" can be a good thing; Michelle B. for being ever helpful; Aine, Jennie, and Fleur, my international inspirations; Kris, for love, support, and late-night calls (and of course the creatures); Angela, for almost persuading me to get the donkey; Mom and Dad, for a much-needed vacation and, of course, for everything else; Matt, for letting me pick on you; Niki, for distracting me; the boys, for all the late-night HH sings; Amy D., for Palestrina and friends; Kevin, come sing to me in Mexico; Sredmond, for being yourself; Mare, for all the laughs, for cooking with Josh, and for euchre; Laura, Leila, and Ange, you guys are my heart, can't wait for the RA reunion tour.

Sheena Thanks: Chrissy and Jay for a great summer; the RWs for hard work; my parents for keeping me sane; Jeff for driving me around; Char for the emails; Melissa for the moral support; Cass for being there always; Ryan for rescuing me from boredom and sketchy locals; Birgit for putting things in perspective; Derek and his basement; Cody, Qian, Beth, and Ken for housing me; Hawaii for laughs and pie.

Jay Thanks: Sheena for tenacity; Chrissy for trust; Nick for patience; Chris for irrelevant talks; Team Southeast Asia for sparing me; Team Hawaii for care; the R-Ws for inspiring awe. Dael et al.; Douglas Adams; a nonexistent little thimble. To roommates and a Crew that will be. Thanks beyond words and icons to my family for support and understanding.

Nick Thanks: Tracy for Hugs and Polar Bears, The Seeders for salt and tunes, and the Burlington 4 for funk and melody.

Editor
Christine A. Monta
Associate Editors
Sheena Lee, Jay Pendse
Managing Editor
Christopher Blazejewski
Map Editor
Nicholas Donin

Publishing Director
Matthew Gibson
Editor-in-Chief
Brian R. Walsh
Production Manager
C. Winslow Clayton
Cartography Manager
Julie Stephens
Design Manager
Amy Cain
Editorial Managers
Christopher Blazejewski,
Abigail Burger, D. Cody Dydek,
Harriett Green, Angela Mi Young Hur,
Marla Kaplan, Celeste Ng
Financial Manager
Noah Askin
Marketing & Publicity Managers
Michelle Bowman, Adam M. Grant
New Media Managers
Jesse Tov, Kevin Yip
Online Manager
Amélie Cherlin
Personnel Managers
Alex Leichtman, Owen Robinson
Production Associates
Caleb Epps, David Muehlke
Network Administrators
Steven Aponte, Eduardo Montoya
Design Associate
Juice Fong
Financial Assistant
Suzanne Siu
Office Coordinators
Alex Ewing, Adam Kline,
Efrat Kussell

Director of Advertising Sales
Erik Patton
Senior Advertising Associates
Patrick Donovan, Barbara Eghan,
Fernanda Winthrop
Advertising Artwork Editor
Leif Holtzman
Cover Photo Research
Laura Wyss

President
Bradley J. Olson
General Manager
Robert B. Rombauer
Assistant General Manager
Anne E. Chisholm

RESEARCHER-WRITERS

Megan Creydt   *Victoria, Southern and Western New South Wales*

A former associate editor for *Let's Go: Peru, Bolivia, and Ecuador 2001*, Megan spent a semester in the Canary Islands before bringing her love for the outdoors to the parks and refuges of Victoria. Armed with Vegemite behind the ears, her favorite '80s tunes, and the blessing of her family, Megan set out to beef up national park coverage and did so beautifully, braving both the Victorian winter and a temperamental laptop in the name of *Let's Go*.

Nick Horbaczewski   *Northern Territory, Pilbara, and the Kimberley*

Our resident stunt artist took to the rugged North with an untiring spirit of adventure. After completing an eight-week whirlwind tour of Europe and Northern Africa, Nick sought refuge among crocs, kangaroos, and carnivorous bats in the dusty Land Down Under. His attention to safety, cultural respect, and environmentally responsible travel shone through in his diligent reorganization, and he consistently wowed us with his immeasurable tenacity.

Lucy Ives   *Sydney, Melbourne, and the South Coast of NSW*

Former Berlin researcher for *Let's Go: Germany 2000* and editor of *Let's Go: Paris 2001*, Lucy knows her cities, and her nose for gourmet restaurants and hot clubs led to some great finds. Prior to this book, Lucy spent three weeks in Oz working on a traveling Monet exhibition, and her flair for aesthetics did not go unnoticed in her copy. Always a poet, Lucy has contributed to publications such as *Ploughshares*, *The Colorado Review*, *3rd Bed*, and *Fence*.

Bryn Lovejoy-Grinnell   *New South Wales and Canberra*

A veteran researcher for *Let's Go: California 2002*, Bryn's experiences in the Sierra Nevada proved invaluable as she trekked through the wilderness of New South Wales. While she initially found herself a platypus out of water in Canberra, Bryn was quickly won over by Oz's charms, facing her obstacles with determination and an unsinkable smile. Never afraid to engage in political debate, this *Let's Go* ambassador represented the guide with charm.

Gretchen Puttkamer   *Northern Queensland*

Tired of office life after associate editing *Let's Go: Australia 2002* and *Southeast Asia 2002* and editing *Let's Go: Middle East and Egypt 2003*, Gretchen ventured to Oz for a third time. Impressing locals with her determination to brave Queensland's far north, this marathon runner handled her 4WD like a pro, even pausing to share an evening meal with a horde of wallabies. She brought endless energy to rural goldfield towns, and her copy reflected nothing less.

Scott Roy   *Central and Southern Western Australia*

Scott professed early his love of driving in unpopulated spaces, and Oz's wild wild west was happy to oblige. Armed with a faulty laptop, a second-hand guitar, and a backpack full of molecular evolutionary biology articles, our amateur geologist-botanist put his extensive experience in the great outdoors to good use. Though a trick foot provided a minor setback, Scott never failed to find the most interesting folks, stopping only to thank the stromatolites along the way.

Abby Schlatter   *Southern Queensland*

After exploring ancient empires for *Let's Go: Mexico 2001*, Abby traded in her *español* for a surfboard and a dictionary of 'strine. Comfortable on any terrain, this midwestern farm girl combined flawless prose, unfailing enthusiasm, and a love of all things adventure to produce new coverage editors only dream about. Abby's no-fear attitude that brought us a collection of quirky interviews will serve her well in her anticipated career as an outdoor writer.

Tim F. Sohn   *South Australia and the Great Ocean Road*

Simultaneously intrepid explorer and literary luminary, Tim gave life to the desolate Outback with his expressive prose. Beyond researching for *Let's Go: Central America 2001*, this proficient outdoorsman has worked across the globe, from commercial fishing in Alaska to English instruction in Spain. His keen eye for subtle detail and deep appreciation of natural beauty will prove a great asset as he assumes a position at *Outdoor Magazine* this year.

Holly Fling   *Tasmania and Gippsland, VIC*

After editing *Let's Go: New Zealand 2002*, Holly returned to her first love, having researched for *Let's Go: Spain, Portugal, and Morocco 2000* and *Let's Go: New Zealand 2001*. A fearless, self-sufficient, to-the-point researcher, she made Tassie's Overland Track her backyard, then went back for more. Though conciseness is her forte, her experience is endless, with outdoor adventures in Iberia, Southeast Asia, and across the continental United States.

CONTRIBUTING WRITERS

Kristofer M. Helgen is a research scientist at the South Australian Museum and is currently pursuing his Ph.D in mammalogy at the University of Adelaide. His work focuses on the mammals of Australia, New Guinea, and the Pacific.

Plamen Jordanoff was a Researcher-Writer for *Let's Go: Germany* in 1994. He now lives in Sydney, Australia, working as a strategy consultant.

Amelia Lester is from Sydney, Australia, and is a contributing writer to Australian *Vogue*. She has also worked on *The Sun Herald*, a major Australian newspaper.

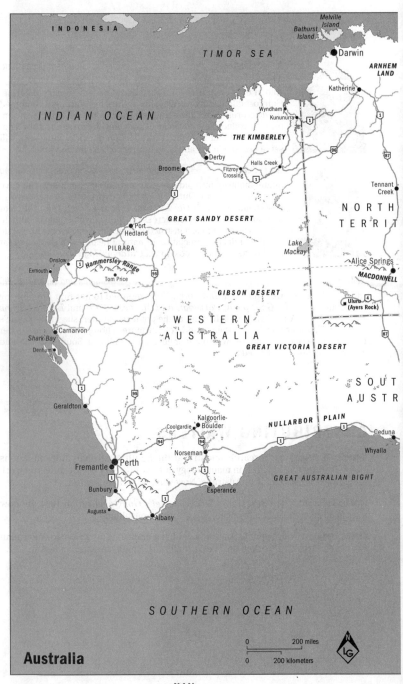

Australia

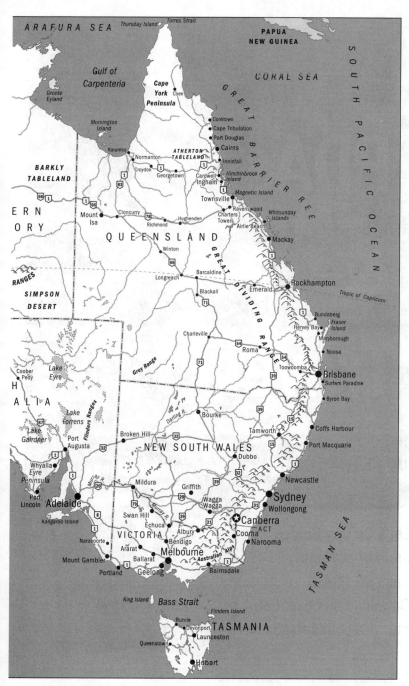

DISCOVER
AUSTRALIA

The Aborigines who arrived 40,000 years ago, and later, the British convicts sent against their will, somehow succeeded in creating a home on this far flung island at the edge of the earth. Today it's easy to see why they didn't give up: the continent enjoys a greatly varied but consistently stunning landscape, a dazzling array of outdoor adventure activities, a rich (though not always pleasant) history, and a vibrant blossoming of cultural diversity thanks to the gold rushes of old and recent waves of immigration. Shaped by the geography of the land and its spatial isolation, the uniqueness and sheer diversity of this nation-continent-island does not go unnoticed by its denizens or visitors. Where else are you presented a choice among wine tasting, getting dangerously close to a saltwater crocodile, fashioning yourself a didge, snorkeling in vast expanses of ancient coral reef, and dancing the night away in the largest club in the Southern Hemisphere? What other continent offers the bustling metropolis of Sydney on the same platter as the vastness of the Outback, the rainforests of Cape York, and the sands of Fraser Island? It is by no means a stretch to say that Australia is a place like no other, and any Aussie (or wide-eyed tourist for that matter) will tell you they'd have it no other way.

FACTS AND FIGURES

CAPITAL: Canberra

HUMAN POPULATION: 19.4 million

LENGTH OF COASTLINE: 25,760km

WEST-TO-EAST DISTANCE: 4000km

PERCENT LARGER THAN BRITAIN, ITS FORMER COLONIAL RULER: 3152%

PERCENT OF THE WORLD'S OPALS: 90%

BEER PER AUSTRALIAN: 94L beer/yr.

KINDS OF KANGAROOS: 60

AMOUNT OF FOLIAGE KOALAS MUST EAT EACH DAY TO SURVIVE: 9kg (about 20 lb.)

NUMBER OF JARS OF VEGEMITE CONSUMED PER YEAR: 22 million.

MOST VALIANT ATTEMPT TO SAVE THE SHEEP: World's longest fence (5,531km/ 3,435 mi.) keeps Queensland's dingoes in the north away from sheep in the south.

NUMBER OF REPORTED SNAKEBITES PER YEAR: 3000

WHEN TO GO

Australia is big. Really big. When to travel depends on where you want to go and what you want to do. Crowds and prices of everything from flights to hostel bunks tend to be directly proportional to the quality of the weather.

In the south, the **seasons** of the temperate climate zone are reversed from those in the Northern Hemisphere. Summer lasts from December to February, autumn from March to May, winter from June to August, and spring from September to November. In general, Australian winters are mild, comparable to the southern

U.S. or southern Europe, but while snow is infrequent except in the mountains, in winter it's far too cold to have much fun at the beach. In the south, peak season falls rougly between November and April.

The north, however, is an entirely different story—many people forget that over one-third of Australia is in the sweltering tropics. Seasons here are defined wildly varying precipitation rather than the generally constant temperature. During **"The Wet"** (November to April), heavy downpours and violent storms plague Australia, especially on the north coast. During **"The Dry"** (May to October), nearly every section of Australia endures a drought. Traveling in the Wet is not recommended for the faint of heart; the heavy rains, washing out unsealed roads, make driving a challenge in non-urban areas.

Diving on the Great Barrier Reef is seasonal as well; January and February are rainy months, and the water is clearest between April and October. The toxic **box jellyfish** is most common around the east coast between October and April.

Ski season in New South Wales, Victoria, and Tasmania runs from late June to September, and the famous wildflowers of Western Australia bloom from September to December. For help planning when and where to go, read below, and see the chart of **temperature and rainfall** (p. 730) data and the list of major **holidays and festivals** (p. 23).

THINGS TO DO

SAND AND SURF. Great beaches are everywhere—Australia is an island continent, after all. Beachlife can mean lounging in the sun with cool drinks and swarms of happy sunbathers or quiet solitude among expansive dunes and gently lapping waves. **Bondi** and **Coogee** beaches in Sydney (p. 86) are crowded and glamorous. The ocean off Queensland's **Fraser Island** (p. 352) offers pristine beauty, but mind the sharks. **Whitehaven Beach** in the Whitsunday Islands (p. 380) paints perfect white sand against azure waters. The green hills at Broome's **Cable Beach** (p. 711) tumble softly into the Indian Ocean.

Surf's up in the land down under, and the east coast takes center stage. The waves at **Surfers Paradise** (p. 322) are perfect for beginners, and a little farther south, **Coolangatta** (p. 319) is the place for pros, Duranbah for fast waves, Kirra and Snapper Rocks for some of the best all around. In New South Wales, **Byron Bay** (p. 183) and **Newcastle** (p. 150) are among the country's most popular spots, whereas **Lennox Head** (p. 190) is home to one of the longest right-hand breaks in the world. On the southern coast, Victoria's **Bell's Beach** in Torquay (p. 596) hosts the annual Rip Curl Classic. Though not as popular as the east coast's veritable surfing carnivals, the crowds love **Yallingup** (p. 681) in Western Australia and Bruny Island's **Cloudy Bay** (p. 517) in Tasmania.

SCUBA DIVING. Whether you're a seasoned scuba diver or a determined beginner, you've probably got "see the Great Barrier Reef" scrawled on your list of things to do in your lifetime. And for good reason—off the coast of Queensland, the 2000km reef system encompasses hundreds of islands and cays and thousands of smaller coral reefs, rendering the marine wonderland available to anyone. Most choose to venture out from **Cairns** (p. 400), the main gateway to the reef. Further south, on the reef's doorstep, the sunken *S.S. Yongala* near **Townsville** (p. 384) is among the best wreck dives in the world. **Airlie Beach** (p. 375) draws backpackers ready to leave the bars for the thrill of the reefs. Though the Great Barrier Reef is quintessential, most coasts have good diving spots. In New South Wales, the diving in **Batemans Bay** (p. 206) is second only to the Reef. In South Australia, **Innes National Park** (p. 482) yields access to the Southern

Ocean's depths. In Western Australia, giant whale sharks patrol **Ningaloo Reef** in Exmouth (p. 705), making for an exhilarating dive. For those looking to learn how to dive, the cheapest certification courses can be found in Queensland at **Hervey Bay** (p. 348), **Bundaberg** (p. 357), and **Magnetic Island** (p. 390). For additional diving information, see **The Great Barrier Reef** (p. 296).

THE OUTBACK. Geographically confined by the continent's more developed coasts, Australia's outback seems like the most never-ending place on earth. Every year, both travelers and Aussies take on the *never never*, hoping to find an adventure or peace of mind. During the Dry season, the **Kimberley** (p. 710) opens to those brave souls who dare to rumble along the rough but stunning **Gibb River Road** (p. 718). In the Northern Territory, **Kakadu National Park** (p. 249) is a gateway to another world of thundering waterfalls, snapping crocs, and mystical beauty. While the Aboriginal homeland **Arnhem Land** (p. 260) captures the essence of the outback, it is virtually inaccessible. In Australia's Red Centre, imposing **Uluru (Ayers Rock)** (p. 288) and its cousin **Kata Tjuta** (p. 290) keep a dignified 360° watch over the rest of the outback. Down into South Australia, **Coober Pedy** (p. 492) playfully affirms the Down Under mentality—scorching temperatures force residents to carve their homes underground. The **Nullarbor** (p. 500 and p. 697), as its name suggests, is a vast stretch of empty plain. For travelers who won't make it out of the east, Queensland's outback mining towns (p. 429) and New South Wales's **Broken Hill** (p. 230) are on the fringe but offer a taste of what lies within.

NATIONAL PARKS AND UNTAMED WILD. Australia has a national park around every corner. The parks preserve all types of terrain—from rainforest to desert, from mountain to coast. Hands-down, the Northern Territory has the best national parks in Australia. The itinerary-topping **Uluru (Ayers Rock)** (p. 288) and timeless **Kakadu** (p. 249) ensure the other (some say better) Territory parks stay more pristine and untrammeled. The **Macdonnell Ranges** (p. 280) have some of the continent's best hiking, and just next door is the spectacular **Kings Canyon** (p. 285). Up the track, the write-home-to-Ma lookouts of **Nitmiluk (Katherine Gorge)** (p. 266) are equalled by the surprising waterfalls of **Litchfield** (p. 261). In Queensland, lush rainforest complements the nearby reef from the tip of **Cape York** (p. 426) all the way down to **Eungella** (p. 373). In New South Wales, the **Blue Mountains** (p. 131) attract avid abseilers and in winter **Kosciuszko** (p. 208) becomes a haven for skiers. **Wilsons Promontory** (p. 648) is a gorgeous stretch of southern coast. Tasmania is Australia's hiking mecca; the **Overland Track** (p. 524) is among the best bushwalks in the world. South Australia's **Flinders Ranges** (p. 483) cater to the truly hardcore. Western Australia showcases marine life, including the whales and dolphins that call **Bunbury** (p. 680) and **Monkey Mia** (p. 702) home.

ABORIGINAL CULTURE. Aborigines traditionally see a strong connection between the earth and its inhabitants. During the "Dreaming," spirits are believed to have carved the canyons and gorges and come to life as animals and trees. In New South Wales, **Mungo National Park** (p. 234) records the earliest Aboriginal presence. Sacred regions and timeless rock art sites are found from Tasmania (p. 502) in the far south to **Kakadu National Park** (p. 249) in the Northern Territory's Top End. Though lore in a glitzier, commercialized form has become popular among tourists, **Tjapukai** (p. 410) near Cairns, **Brambuk Living Cultural Centre** (p. 611) in Grampians National Park, and **Warradjan Aboriginal Cultural Centre** (p. 250) in Kakadu National Park attempt to present accurate representations of "Dreaming" stories and European interaction. Modern Aboriginal art can be found in small galleries in larger cities, but the **National Gallery of Australia** in Canberra (p. 71) has the continent's best collection.

4 ■ THINGS TO DO

CITY SIGHTS. Australia's outback spirit and rugged beauty might have made it easy for travelers to bypass city life altogether, but Australia's cosmopolitan meccas shine nonetheless. **Sydney** (p. 86) thrives under several influences—the city center demonstrates European roots, Haymarket is the city's fast-growing Chinatown, bohemian Glebe speaks up for university life, and the sands of Bondi play home to the beach crowd. Melding international culture with a typical Aussie laid-back attitude, **Melbourne** (p. 549) offers more style than Sydney with less hype, boasting incredible nightlife, a chill daytime cafe society, and a bustling budget food scene. Smooth as the jazz in its clubs, **Brisbane** (p. 297) eases coastal backpackers into urban culture. **Hobart** (p. 505) is a civilized bastion in the Tasmanian wild. The antithesis of a tourist trap, the country town of **Adelaide** (p. 438) lives at a slower pace. Farther from the east, **Perth** (p. 665) and **Darwin** (p. 239) grant relaxing coastal stretches and hopping nightlife on the other edge of the *never never*.

WINE. Though not known for its cuisine, Australia has recently acquired an international reputation for the quality of its victual spirits. All throughout Australia, scores of tiny boutique vineyards dot random small towns and river banks. Just follow your nose and keep your wallet in your pocket—most wine tastings are absolutely free. The premier, and most touristed, wine region is New South Wales's **Hunter Valley** (p. 145). West across the Victoria border, **Rutherglen** (p. 641) is smaller but its proximity to the **Milawa Cheese Region** (p. 639) will whet your *fromage*-inclined palate. Just south, the **Yarra Valley** (p. 588) is Victoria's contribution to the scene. At the end of the wine trail, South Australia's **Barossa** (p. 467) and **Clare Valleys** (p. 472) offer the quality of the Hunter without the hype.

◪ LET'S GO PICKS

HARDEST TOWN TO FIND ON A MAP: The asbestos-ridden "town" of **Wittenoom, WA** (p. 708) or the cartoon city of **Ettamogah Pub, NSW** (p. 201).

BEST PLACE TO FIND MINERS: Mount Isa, QLD (p. 433) or the Toy Museum in The Rocks, **Sydney, NSW** (p. 102).

BEST PLACE TO GET A BITE: The gourmet mecca of **Adelaide, SA** (p. 405) or with a shark at Scuba World, in **Maroochy, QLD** (p. 337).

BEST UNDERGROUND SCENE: The underground city of **Coober Pedy, SA** (p. 492) or the mosh pits of the **Melbourne Fringe Festival** (p. 581).

BEST PLACE FOR DREAMING: Under the stars along the **Gibb River Road, WA** (p. 718) or in the Aboriginal art galleries of **Kakadu National Park, NT** (p. 297).

MOST UNDERRATED: Perth, WA (p. 665) or **Tasmania** (p. 502).

BEST PLACE TO PONDER YOUR OWN INSIGNIFICANCE: The surreal emptiness of the **Nullarbor Plain, SA** (p. 500) or the thumping dancefloor of Metro, **Melbourne, VIC** (p. 585).

BEST PLACE TO GET WRECKED: At the best wreck dive in the world, the *S.S. Yongala*, off **Townsville, QLD** (p. 384), or for free in the wine vineyards of the **Hunter Valley, NSW** (p. 145).

BEST DRIVE: The winding seaside cliffs of the **Great Ocean Road, VIC** (p. 594) or off your very own plot of astroturf in the **Outback, SA** (p. 492).

BEST PLACE TO ROCK OUT: The amazing formations of **Devil's Marbles, NT** (p. 272) or in front of the webcam at Bojangles, **Alice Springs, NT** (p. 273).

BEST COUNTRY: Hut River Province (p. 642), a principality in Western Oz, or **Australia,** that big continent in the South Pacific.

SUGGESTED ITINERARIES

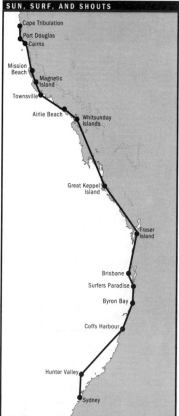

SUN, SURF, AND SHOUTS

Cape Tribulation
Port Douglas
Cairns
Mission Beach
Magnetic Island
Townsville
Airlie Beach
Whitsunday Islands
Great Keppel Island
Fraser Island
Brisbane
Surfers Paradise
Byron Bay
Coffs Harbour
Hunter Valley
Sydney

Magnetic Island (p. 390) promise sunshine and great diving. Bounce over to the sparkling white sands of **Mission Beach** (p. 395) before tropical **Cairns** (p. 400) puts it all together with unlimited diving and adventure opportunities, along with hearty backpacker nightlife. Those with extra time can daytrip to the rainforests, roads, and reef of nearby **Port Douglas** (p. 416) and **Cape Tribulation** (p. 420).

BEST OF AUSTRALIA (3 WEEKS). Cosmopolitan **Sydney** (p. 86) begins this tour of the continent's highlights. Heading north up the coast, get a taste of the surf in **Newcastle** (p. 150) before having your aura read in **Byron Bay** (p. 183). Hop into Queensland, to the ever-shifting sand dunes of **Fraser Island** (p. 352). Dive the Great Barrier reef from **Magnetic Island** (p. 390) before heading farther north to **Cairns** (p. 400). Snorkel a day or two or check out the World Heritage rainforest before catching a flight to the Northern Territory's laid-back **Darwin** (p. 239). From there, experience the wonder of **Kakadu National Park** (p. 249) before heading to **Alice Springs** (p. 273). From this famous Outback town,

SUN, SURF, AND SHOUTS (3-4 WEEKS). Start your coastal journey in **Sydney** (p. 86), getting a taste of the city's beaches and nightlife before touring the vineyards of the **Hunter Valley** (p. 145). Grab a coldie with your mates in **Coffs Harbour** (p. 171) and head to **Byron Bay** (p. 183) for surfing and relaxation. For those who want to learn how to party, **Surfers Paradise** (p. 322) offers a crash course that will serve you well farther up the coast. Nurse your hangover at **Brisbane's** (p. 297) smoky jazz clubs or the gorgeous beaches of **Fraser** (p. 352) and **Great Keppel Islands** (p. 366). After recuperating from a big night in **Airlie Beach** (p. 366), go scuba diving or sail to the **Whitsunday Islands** (p. 380). **Townsville** (p. 384) and

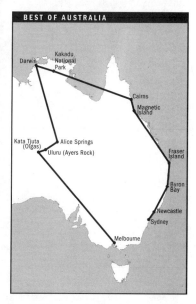

BEST OF AUSTRALIA

Darwin
Kakadu National Park
Cairns
Magnetic Island
Kata Tjuta (Olgas)
Alice Springs
Uluru (Ayers Rock)
Fraser Island
Byron Bay
Newcastle
Sydney
Melbourne

it's just a short trip to the most famous of Australian icons: **Uluru (Ayers Rock)** (p. 288) and **Kata Tjuta (the Olgas)** (p. 288). From Alice, fly to **Melbourne** (p. 549), the cultural heart of Oz. To make a loop, bus directly back to Sydney or reverse the All Points South itinerary.

WILD WILD WEST (2-3 WEEKS). This itinerary is particularly stunning between August and November, when Western Australia is carpeted in wildflowers. Base yourself in **Perth** (p. 663). Get lost in the history of **Fremantle** (p. 675), then bike around beautiful **Rottnest Island** (p. 678). Daytrip out to the eerie limestone pillars rising from the dunes at the **Pinnacles** (p. 699). Heading north, learn to windsurf in **Geraldton** (p. 699) before frolicking with the dolphins of **Monkey Mia** (p. 702) in Western Australia's only World Heritage Area, **Shark Bay** (p. 702). Dive into the ocean off of **Exmouth** (p. 705), then swim in the plunge pools within the red gorges of **Karijini National Park** (p. 709). The wayward tourist destination of **Broome** (p. 711) entices backpackers with pristine beaches and serves as a gateway to the indescribable wilderness adventure that is **The Kimberley** (p. 710), starting from the incomparable **Gibb River Road** (p. 718).

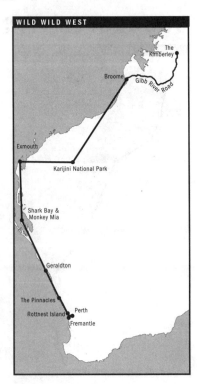

WILD WILD WEST

ALL POINTS SOUTH (2-3 WEEKS).

After exploring **Sydney** (p. 86), head out for some abseiling and sightseeing in the **Blue Mountains** (p. 131). Observe Aussie politics in action at the nation's capital of **Canberra** (p. 71). Do some hiking in the rugged **Snowy River National Park** (p. 657) on your way to the coastal wonders of **Wilsons Promontory National Park** (p. 648). Squeal at the adorable little penguins at **Phillip Island** (p. 589) before sliding west into **Melbourne** (p. 549) for an injection of funk, nightlife, and cafe culture. From Melbourne, venture out by ferry to **Devonport** (p. 529) and embark on Tasmania's breathtaking **Overland Track** (p. 524). Back on the mainland, fall in love with the **Great Ocean Road** (p. 594) before breaking for another natural high atop the jagged peaks of **Grampians National Park** (p. 611).

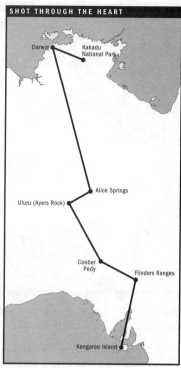

SHOT THROUGH THE HEART

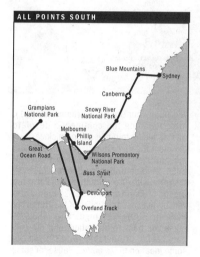

ALL POINTS SOUTH

SHOT THROUGH THE HEART (3-4 WEEKS).

Start your trek among the caves and happy creatures of **Kangaroo Island** (p. 459) before heading inland to the dusty hills and majestic peaks of the **Flinders Ranges** (p. 483). Descend into the curious subterranean opal town of **Coober Pedy** (p. 492), surfacing to drop your jaw at **Uluru (Ayers Rock)** (p. 288), a site sacred to Aboriginal cultures and local tourism alike. Recharge in the Red Centre's surprisingly cosmopolitan **Alice Springs** (p. 273) before setting out to the Northern Territory's tropical backpacker playground of **Darwin** (p. 239), from where you can reach the breathtaking landscape and Aboriginal art of **Kakadu** (p. 249).

DISCOVER

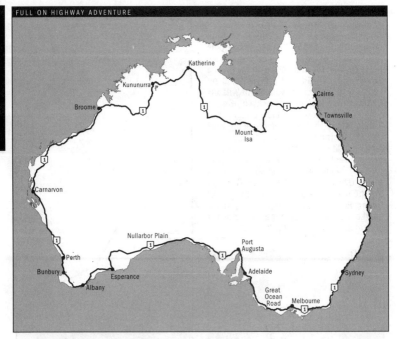

FULL ON HIGHWAY ADVENTURE

FULL ON HIGHWAY ADVENTURE (UP TO A LIFETIME). Highway 1 conveniently circles our favorite continent, providing an epic itinerary catering to only the truly hardcore. Begin your odyssey among the creature comforts of **Sydney** (p. 86). Eat up, honey—it's gonna be a long ride. Surf your way up the Queensland coast to the diving mecca of **Townsville** (p. 384), making a detour to **Cairns** (p. 400) for a quick skydive and a bungy jump before heading west. Let a miner show you how it's done in **Mount Isa** (p. 433), then head toward **Katherine** (p. 270) to take a dip in the hot springs before continuing your journey to the oasis of **Kununurra** (p. 724), in the eastern **Kimberley** (p. 710). Lines of Indian Ocean surf and outdoor cafes greet you upon your arrival in **Broome** (p. 711). After rounding the continent's desolate west, pausing to make some quick cash on the plantations of **Carnarvon** (p. 703), tour the parks and pubs of mellow **Perth** (p. 663); keep on truckin' to **Bunbury** (p. 679) to frolic with the dolphins. Take a deep breath in **Esperance** (p. 692) before traversing the vast emptiness of the **Nullarbor Plain** (p. 500). **Port Augusta** (p. 483) will nurse you back to animation, and the culinary capital of **Adelaide** (p. 438) will put some meat on those bones. Pause for some photo-ops along the amazing **Great Ocean Road** (p. 594) before It's back to the big city with **Melbourne** (p. 549). Get reaccustomed to human interaction before closing the loop back in Sydney. Good on ya.

LIFE AND TIMES

ENVIRONMENT

When plants and animals landed on an isolated continent nearly devoid of competition, they grew quickly, exploding from a limited number of ancestral groups to become some of the world's most peculiar plants and animals. Australia's inevitable contact with the outside, however, has presented an enormous challenge, upsetting Australia's delicate ecology; it is estimated that 13 species of mammals and one species of bird have already become extinct since European settlement. In recent years, environmental policy has begun to recognize the importance of protecting Australia's precious biodiversity.

PLANTS

STRANGE GROWTHS IN SECRET PLACES. There is one plant you are guaranteed to find in Australia. Dominating forests from coast to coast, the **eucalypts,** also known as **gum trees,** amaze biologists with their successful adaptation to diverse environments, taking on many different shapes and sizes across the continent. The majestic **karri** soars to over 50m in ancient stands along well-watered valleys, while the **mallee** gum tends to grow in stunted copses across scrubland, like that of western Victoria. The characteristically bulging trunk and splayed branches of the **boab** mark the horizon, particularly in the arid Kimberley of Western Australia. In the drier areas of the southeast, a common species of the **acacia** tree known as the **golden wattle** is distinguished by its fragrant blooms, which also happen to be Australia's national flower. Perhaps the most unusual—and most rare—tree is the **Wollemi pine.** The pine was discovered by scientists a few years ago, who had previously thought that the species was extinct (see **Wollemi National Park,** p. 143).

BRING ME A SHRUBBERY. Gums aren't the only plant dominating the landscape. Other regulars in the bush and coastal thickets include **banksias, tea trees,** and **grevillias.** Feathery and almost pine-like in appearance, **casuarinas** also exist in multiple habitats. In temperate, rain-fed stretches of Victoria and Tasmania, valleys of tall, dinosaur-era **tree ferns** are dwarfed by towering **mountain ash,** the tallest flowering plant in nature. The **mangrove,** found along parts of Australia's tropical coasts, has adapted readily to its unfavorable environment, its stilt-like trunks clinging tenaciously to the briny mud of alluvial swamps. Australia also has wide swaths of land that grow nary a tree. The arid outback is dominated by dense tufts of **spinifex** grasses. Another common plant is the **saltbush,** a hearty shrub pivotal in converting harsh habitats to livestock pastures.

FLOWER POWER. Although Australia has a tough plant life, wildflowers are abundant in more fertile areas. Western Australia is home to **swamp bottlebrush, kangaroo paw,** and **Ashby's banksia,** along with nearly 10,000 other species. Yellow and pink **everlastings** cover fields across the country, to the delight of casual wildflower viewers, but rare **spider orchids** hidden in the forests reveal themselves only to the most dogged of investigators. The **Sturt pea** adds a distinctive splash of red and black to the inland deserts of South Australia and Western Australia. Elsewhere, **orchids** and **begonias** provide extra visual garnish.

LAND ANIMALS

The kangaroos and cuddly koalas of postcard fame represent only two of the 300,000 species of animals that call Australia home. While most of these are insects, many larger and more exotic creatures make the island continent their breeding ground. Most of these critters are generally harmless when unprovoked, but see p. 60 for important info on dangerous wildlife.

MAMMALS. Kangaroos, often synonymous with Australia, have thrived on the fringes of human communities since colonization. The kangaroo's look-alike cousin, the **wallaby,** is another common outback critter. Australia's other best loved marsupial, the **koala,** lives on and among the leaves of certain eucalypt trees. Other native marsupials include **wombats, possums, bandicoots,** and **quolls.** Two families of monotremes, or egg-laying mammals, call Australia home. **Echidnas** are small ant-eaters that resemble porcupines with protruding snouts. The **platypus** sports a melange of zoological features: the bill of a duck, the fur of an otter, the tail of a beaver, and webbed claws. So outrageous did this anatomy seem to colonists that early naturalists refused to consider stuffed specimens real. For more information on Australia's unique mammals, see **Of Monotremes and Men,** p. 747.

REPTILES. The most fearsome reptiles, saltwater crocodiles **("salties")** actually live in both brine and freshwater and grow to lengths of 7m. In addition to crocodiles, Australia's reptiles include aggressive **goannas** and a wide array of **poisonous snakes,** including the **taipan, smooth snake, tiger snake, brown snake,** and **death adder** (for advice on what to do in the case of a meeting with these nasties, see p. 60).

BIRDS. Outshining Australia's mammals in vividness of color is the continent's tremendous diversity of **birds.** The **emu** is related to other flightless birds such as the African ostrich and the extinct moa of New Zealand. Flightless hordes of **little** (or **fairy) penguins** can be spotted at sites on the south coast, where they wade ashore each night. Australia's flight-endowed birds include noisy flocks of **galahs,** colorful **rainbow lorikeets,** and large **cassowaries.** Songs and poems have immortalized the unmistakable laugh of the **kookaburra.** Both **crimson rosellas** and **cockatoos** are common in the southeast.

MEGAFAUNA. Giant marsupials once roamed the landscape of prehistoric Australia. Now extinct, these megafauna included towering relatives of kangaroos called diprotodons. The megafauna died off soon after the arrival of humans (see **Megafauna to Megamen,** p. 235). The **thylacine,** or **Tasmanian tiger,** is a more recent loss. Resembling a large wolf with stripes, the predator was driven to the edge of extinction by competition with dingoes, then hunted by white settlers who feared for livestock. One infamous marsupial carnivore has survived, however. Fierce in temperament, **Tasmanian devils** are nocturnal scavengers, known to hunt small prey and kill livestock with their powerful jaws (see **Marsupials from Hell,** p. 522).

PESTS. Humans have been responsible for the introduction of animals to Australia since prehistoric times, and many of these introduced species are now consid-

---

I'M-A GOANNA GET YA! Goannas are large lizards, growing up to 3 or 4 meters. Should you encounter one, the old maxim applies: it's more afraid of you than the other way around. Be aware, however, that goannas protect themselves from danger by scurrying up trees, and if a scared goanna comes running toward you (away from whatever scared it), there's the off-chance that it will try to seek refuge on you! Crouch down or lie flat to avoid being climbed. Once your pursuer realizes you're not a tree and offer no protection, it should leave you alone.

ered pests. The **dingo,** a lithe, wild canine with a vicious bite but no bark, crossed the Timor Sea with ancestors of Aboriginal populations several thousand years ago. The creatures mainly hunt small, wild prey, but may also menace livestock (ranchers detest them and kill those they encounter near their flocks). Although dingoes pose little threat to adults, they are can injure and even kill children. Accidental introductions such as European **rats** and **Cane toads** present serious threats to native fauna as well. The massive overpopulation of **rabbits,** purportedly introduced to Australia to provide practice targets for marksmen, has become one of Australia's gravest wildlife problems. **Foxes** also present a serious problem to endemic wildlife, particularly in Tasmania (see **In Recent News,** p. 518). Environmental efforts have since emerged to protect native wildlife.

LIVESTOCK. These more recent arrivals accompanied European colonists to help settle the land. With ranches across the continent, domesticated **cattle** and **sheep** have always been of tremendous economic importance in Australia. Vast tracts have been converted to pasture to support the meat industry, creating a dramatic impact on the landscape and ecological balance of the nation. The farming of non-native **honeybees** has also become a growing part of the economy.

MARINE LIFE

THE GREAT BARRIER REEF. Fur seals, elephant seals, and sea lions populate Australia's southern shores during summer breeding seasons, but it's the Great Barrier Reef that makes Australia's sea life unique. It's also one of Australia's biggest tourist draws and a diving wonderland (see **The Great Barrier Reef,** p. 293). The longest coral formation in the world, it is actually a series of many reefs that stretches more than 2000km along the eastern coast of Queensland from the Tropic of Capricorn to Papua New Guinea. Although adult **coral polyps** are sedentary, corals actually belong to the animal kingdom. Thus, the Great Barrier Reef is the only community of animals visible to the eye from space.

CORAL. Coral reefs take a number of different forms. Closest to the shore are **patch reefs,** comprising patches of **hard** and **soft coral.** Soft corals, such as slender **sea whips** and delicate, intricate **fan corals,** lose their shape and turn to sludge when taken out of water, but hard coral is often dried, bleached, and sold to tourists in shops. Beware of national marine park rules against removing living creatures from the sea and customs **fines up to $500** for removing any piece of a coral reef. Hard corals come in hues ranging from purple to emerald to red, and are mostly categorized as either branched, boulder, or plate coral. The fast-growing **branched coral** is named for its appearance; its most common varieties are the thin, brittle **needle coral,** the antler-like **stag coral,** and **finger coral. Boulder coral** is sturdier and slower-growing, including the **honey-comb, golfball,** and **brain boulders;** in areas where cyclones are frequent, these are the species that tend to survive. **Plate corals,** such as **sheet** and **table corals,** are named appropriately for their shapes.

Farther out than the patch reefs are **fringe reefs,** which contain the same types of coral. Their arrangement in circular patterns deeply entrenched in the sea floor means that they frequently fill with silt, clouding visibility for divers. The far outer reef is made up of 710km of **ribbon reef;** this includes some of Australia's best diving, but is accessible only to boats that venture out for four days or longer.

FISH AND MAMMALS. The reef also houses a spectacular variety of colorful, sometimes otherworldly fish, from the enormous **potato cod** to the **fusaleres,** a family of fish that change color at night. The **parrotfish** eats bits of coral by cracking it in its beak-like mouth, and at night envelops itself in a protective mucus sac, a phenomenon that might be a highlight of a night dive. If you're diving, taking a **briefing**

course on marine life is an excellent way to familiarize yourself with what you'll see. While it's impossible to memorize every species, many shops sell **fish identification cards** that you can take down with you. A few terms to know: the **wrasse** is a long, slender, cigar-like fish; **angel** and **surgeon fish** have similar oblong shapes, but the surgeon has a razor-sharp barb close to its tail; the **butterfly** and **bat fish** are round, but the latter is larger and has a black stripe across the eye. Despite Australia's reputation for **sharks**, only gray **reef sharks** (and the very occasional **tiger shark**) are seen around the reef and are typically harmless when unprovoked. Besides fish, the reef houses **turtles, porpoises, dolphins,** and **whales,** as well as **echinoderms:** sea cucumbers, sea stars, feather stars, and brittle stars.

POISONOUS SEA CREATURES. If an Aussie is somewhat scared of something, that means you should probably be terrified. If you're told that the unidentified creature you're holding is a **nasty**—drop it. Better yet, **don't touch unfamiliar objects.** Many benign-looking creatures are poisonous, some even deadly. The most infamous nasty is the **box jellyfish,** a near-transparent creature which tends to live near the coast, particularly near river mouths or estuaries. Its up-to-3m tentacles contain a toxin that can kill you within three minutes; carrying a vinegar-based antivenom is wise. The best option is to avoid coastal diving (and swimming) altogether during box jellyfish season (Oct.-Apr.) and to obey all posted warnings. The **cone shell** has brightly patterned shells that look as though they would make excellent souvenirs, but the stingers inside are packed with enough venom to kill an adult human. The **stone fish** lies motionless and camouflaged against the coral, waiting for prey. If you're unlucky enough to step on its poison-filled spines, seek medical attention pronto. It takes a lot of weight to step on one of these and get hurt, so it is dangerous only in shallow water. **Sting rays, lion fish,** and **sea snakes** are all poisonous as well, but aren't likely to attack except in retaliation. Some nasties are irritating but not deadly. If you pick up the inert **sea urchin,** you may get small pieces of its spines embedded in your skin, causing swelling and pain. A prick from the **crown of thorns,** a type of sea star, will send a low-grade poison into your bloodstream. However, its effects on the reef itself are far worse, as it feeds on coral. A recent population explosion has led to the legalized removal of sea stars by dive boats.

HISTORY

ABORIGINAL AUSTRALIA

THE PEOPLE. By some estimates, the **Aboriginal** people have inhabited the island continent for as long as 100,000 years and had settled across most of the continent by 30,000 years ago. Archaeologists have unveiled evidence of ancient art, complex burial practices, and Stone Age boomerangs. Estimates of the Aboriginal population of Australia just prior to European colonization vary widely, from 300,000 to over one million. Aborigines were **hunters and gatherers,** migrating seasonally in search of food and increasing the land's productivity by setting controlled fires (see **Burn, Baby, Burn,** p. 251).

TRIBAL LIFE. The Aborigines formed tribes largely based on territorial claims. While language did not determine tribal boundaries, it has been estimated that more than 200 languages, with up to 600 dialect groups, were spoken. Within their tribes, Aborigines divided into smaller groups, called bands, made up of two or three different families. Aborigines were generally accepting of polygamy, and inter-band marriages were used to solidify communities.

In place of a system of private land ownership, a sort of unwritten charter tied together a particular tribe and the territory they covered in their travels, known as a "range." The relationship between these caretakers and their areas was considered one of reciprocal responsibility. Along with strong ties to the land, there was a strong cultural emphasis on expansion through personal relationships such as kinship, marriage, and ceremony.

THE DREAMING. Aborigines believe the world was created during the Dreaming, or Creation Time, a mythological period of time with no beginning or end, when the acts and deeds of powerful ancestral beings shaped the land and populated it with humans, animals, and plants. There are three categories of land in Aboriginal culture: ceremonial sites, *djang* (Dreaming), and *djang andjamun* (Sacred Dreaming). Ceremonial sites are now used for burials, rites of passage, and other events. At *djang* sites, a creator passed through, took shape, or entered or exited the Earth, leaving the site safe to visit. *Djang andjamun* sites, however, where the ancestor still lingers, are considered spiritual hazard zones. Laws prohibit entry to the latter group of sites. Because features of these areas are linked to the ancestors, they are considered sacred sites rather than inherited possessions.

EUROPEAN SETTLEMENT

COLONIZATION

UNKNOWN LAND. Chinese explorers were among the first non-Aborigines to arrive, and **Dutch** explorers included a misshapen Australia on 16th-century maps, leaving a memorial at Shark Bay (see p. 702) in 1616. In 1642, **Abel Tasman,** a Dutch explorer, sailed south to spot the rest of Australia—a "new" southern island which came to be known as Tasmania. Though he explored Australia's coast, a settlement was never established. In 1770, the English captain **James Cook,** in his ship *Endeavour,* explored the eastern coast of what would become Australia. With the other sides of the island continent already mapped, the Great Barrier Reef continued to deter explorers from the east. Cook and his crew of astronomers and scientists discovered and named **Botany Bay,** and returned to England with stories of strange animals and plants.

SETTLING DOWN. The motives for the British colonization of Australia have been a matter of debate. The traditional explanation is that Britain needed to solve its prison overcrowding problem, and another explanation suggests that the English hoped to establish a base for a global navy with plentiful natural resources and an available work force, particularly prisoners. In any case, the prisons in London were full, and on May 13, 1787, the 11-ship **First Fleet** left from England. Led by **Arthur Phillip,** appointed to command the fleet by British Home Secretary **Lord Sydney,** the fleet arrived with about 730 convicts in Botany Bay after a grueling eight-month voyage. After local resources were deemed insufficient, Commander Phillip headed north to Port Jackson. The English flag was raised on January 26, on the spot where Sydney stands today.

CONVICT(ION)S AND PERSISTENCE

LET'S GO AGAINST OUR WILL. Upon arrival in Australia, the convicts and their guards faced a foreign, inhospitable land. The colony saw little success: half the workforce was occupied guarding the other half; livestock escaped into the bush; relations with Aborigines deteriorated; most subsequent supply ships wrecked. The convicts themselves were mostly undesirables with no agricultural experience from the slums of London, deported to Australia for small crimes. The seeds and cuttings that the fleet had so carefully carried across the sea failed in the local climate. Captain Phillip's grand plans for 200-foot-wide streets had to be scrapped; no mill or team of cattle would be available for another eight years.

EARLY ABORIGINAL INTERACTION. Australia's history of white settlement is, as often is the case, partly a history of genocide. When the British landed in Australia and claimed the land for the Crown, they did so under a doctrine of **terra nullius** (empty land), which meant either that there were no people on the continent, or that inhabitants were mere occupants rather than landowners. This doctrine gave the British free rein (or so they rationalized) to take what land they wished, without the hassle of treaties or agreements. Most Aborigines were displaced, if not eradicated; European settlement disrupted hunting territories, destroyed watering holes, and brought numerous diseases. Many Aboriginal children were kidnapped and forced into assimilation programs, a practice not officially ended until the twentieth century. Some Europeans even took to deliberately and savagely killing the Aborigines. The history of Aboriginal and white interaction in Tasmania, where the Aborigines had remained isolated for over thousands of years, is particularly horrid; systematic genocide of the Aboriginal population caused their near-complete disappearance within 70 years of contact.

EXPANSION

THE NEVERENDING STORY. After 1815, as more convicts continued arriving, the government began hiring convicts to private employers to lighten the load. Abolitionist crusades in the 1830s convinced some that the practice smelled suspiciously of **slavery.** In 1840, the practice was abolished, and almost no more convicts were sent to the continent, except in Tasmania and Western Australia. January 1868 marked the arrival of the last convict ship, ending an era in which approximately 160,500 convicts had been sent to Australia.

WORTH A SHOT. England also encouraged settler migration with **land grants** and offered cheap passage for women to equalize the gender imbalance. **Wool** was Australia's major export, and by 1845, **sheep farming** was the most profitable business in the country. But despite land grants and economic improvements, the population remained stagnant. The discovery of **gold** in 1851 accomplished what the promise of land could not. At the end of 1851, the non-Aboriginal population numbered around 450,000, eight times that of a quarter-century earlier. Ten years later, the number was 1,150,000. The fierce competition for gold inevitably led to conflict, Australia's closest brush with civil war (see **Our Proudest Defeat,** p. 622).

TWENTIETH CENTURY

UNIFICATION AND SEGREGATION

FEDERATION. Four of the six states were formed between 1829 and 1859, bringing **self-government** to Australia for the first time. Before the formation of a central government, each individual colony had little to do with other colonies and instead communicated directly with London. The **Commonwealth of Australia** was founded on January 1, 1901. Federation had been a difficult process for Australia; the new constitution was only ratified after a decade of debate among the six colonies. The six states of Australia are New South Wales, Victoria, Queensland, South Australia, Western Australia, and Tasmania. The Northern Territory and the Australian Capital Territory are self-governing territories that still do not have state status.

SUFFRAGE. The year after federation, Australia became the second country in the world, after New Zealand, to grant federal **suffrage to women.** In 1921, **Edith Dircksey Cowan** of Western Australia became the first female in a state parliament in Australia, after Lady Astor served in the British House of Commons in 1919.

RACE. When convicts stopped arriving, Europeans encouraged the immigration of Chinese laborers. However, race-based immigration restrictions were soon adopted, especially when **Chinese immigrants** started working the goldfields. By 1888, the "Chinese question" had emerged onto center stage, and a Queensland journal coined the rallying cry **"White Australia."** In 1896, immigration restrictions were extended to include all non-whites. With federation came the **Immigration Restriction Act of 1901,** which required immigrants to pass a 50-word dictation test in any European language chosen at the discretion of the immigration officers.

WORLD WAR

At the outset of **World War I,** Australia's prime minister declared support for the mother country, saying: "Our duty is quite clear—to gird up our loins and remember that we are Britons." About 330,000 Australians girded up their loins and 60,000 lost their lives. 165,000 more soldiers were wounded. While these figures pale in comparison to casualties from other countries, they were a shocking percentage of the country's relatively small population. The single worst day of battle was April 25, 1915, when 2000 members of the **Australian and New Zealand Army Corps** (ANZAC) were killed at **Gallipoli,** Turkey, initiating a campaign that eventually took 8500 Australian lives and forced evacuation of the troops. Australia celebrates **Anzac Day** (April 25) each year to remember the heroism of these troops.

A generation later, The Royal Australian Air Force reiterated its commitment to Great Britain and its allies in **World War II**, and other troops enjoyed victories at Tobruk and El-Alamein in North Africa. After the Japanese attack on Hawaii's Pearl Harbor (Dec. 7, 1941) and the fall of British-protected Singapore (Feb. 15, 1942), Australian citizens became increasingly concerned about safety on their own shores. On February 19, 1942, **Darwin,** the capital of the Northern Territory, suffered the first of many bombings by the Japanese. The US, committed to the Pacific theater, became a closer ally to Australia than the more distant Britain. About 30,000 Australian soldiers were lost over the course of the war.

TODAY

No traveler should venture into Australia without brushing up on certain news stories that shook the nation. Below are a few examples of current events having a marked impact on Australia and the world.

ENVIRONMENT. For the most part, Australia has shown an intense commitment to preservation of the environment. In 1995, when French President Jacques Chirac decided to sponsor **nuclear weapons testing** in the South Pacific, protesters fire-bombed the French consulate in Perth and demonstrations were held all over the country. In May 1997, the Australian government funded a $1.3 billion project to clean up the Murray and Darling Rivers by selling **Telstra,** the previously state-owned telecommunications company. Recent protests about a **uranium mining** project on Aboriginal lands in Kakadu National Park reveal two central issues in contemporary Australian politics: race and the environment. The controversy has put the spotlight on native land rights and government intervention, in addition to environmental policy.

ELECTION OF JOHN HOWARD. In August 2001, the Norwegian freighter *Tampa,* carrying 460 mostly Afghan refugees, was denied entrance to the country by conservative Prime Minister John Howard. Thanks in large part to his hardline stance against asylum seekers, Howard managed a surprise win that following November, thus securing him a third three-year term in office while revealing a strong anti-refugee sentiment among Australian voters.

DETENTION CENTER RIOTS. Curtin Detention Centre, in Western Australia, has had a long history of refugee hunger strikes and protests. Video footage of one such outbreak last June was leaked to the media, causing quite a stir. On April 22, 2002, about 300 detainees set fire to a building, brandishing cleavers and sharpened broomsticks to protest substandard conditions and demand asylum for their families. The detainees eventually surrendered, but Canberra responded by allowing 10 UN inspectors to conduct random checks on detention centers. Around the same time, demonstrations at **Woomera Detention Centre,** in South Australia, brought refugee conditions to national attention (see **In Recent News,** p. 490).

PEOPLE

The Commonwealth of Australia is home to 19.3 million people. Immigration has defined the narrative of the Australian population, as more than 20% of the current population was born overseas. The **White Australia Policy** (see p. 15) created a fairly homogenous population. In 2001, whites made up 92% of the population while Aborigines comprised less than 1%. In recent years, Asian immigration has accelerated. Asians now account for about 7% of the Australian population.

Australia's population density is 2.5 people per square kilometer. In comparison, the United States squeezes 28.2 people in an average square kilometer, and, for a particularly tight fit, the United Kingdom has 243.6 people per square kilometer. Eighty-five percent of Australians live in urban areas, and the suburbs are still growing. The vast majority live on or relatively near the coasts, particularly the east coast—some theories point to the vast, inhospitable desert in the center of the country as the reason for this coastal population concentration.

English (better known as **'Strine**; see p. 728) is Australia's only national language, spoken in 85% of Australian homes. Virtually 100% of the population is **literate.** The religious composition of the population generally reflects immigrant backgrounds. Just over 75% of Australians declare themselves **Christians.** Roman Catholics make up about 26% of the population, Anglicans account for 26.1%, and other Christian denominations make up 24.3%. **Non-Christian** religions comprise 11%, with Buddhism, Islam, and Judaism leading the list. Roughly 10% of Australians reject organized religion.

CULTURE

FOOD AND DRINK

Australians eat four meals a day: breakfast, lunch, dinner, and beer. Aussies hardly ever eat their **"brekkie"** out, and most restaurants don't open until noon except in the larger cities. An interesting part of brekkie that Aussies enjoy is spaghetti, along with the traditional eggs, toast, and sausage. Not to be confused with the diminutive British version, the evening meal of **"tea"** is the largest meal of the day. Beware of ordering only an **"entree,"** an appetizer in Australia. A **"cuppa"**—tea or coffee—should tide you over between meals. The pub is the place to go to relax and grab a quick bite to eat. And whatever the country may lack in gourmet cuisine it makes up for in delectable beer. **Tipping** in Australian restaurants and pubs is rare and never expected. **Vegetarians** shouldn't go hungry despite Australia's meat-hungry reputation. Trendy urban eateries frequently cater to special diets, but traditional establishments rarely will.

AUSTRALIAN "CUISINE"

WATCH WHAT YOU EAT. Australia's origin as a convict colony didn't endow the country with a subtle palate. **Meat pies** are the ultimate Australian fare. Inexplicably popular, these doughy shells contain meat of dubious origin and often a mushy vegetable filling. Most consumers douse them in **tomato sauce** (a sweet ketchup-like concoction) to disguise the taste. Let us say again—*tomato sauce is not ketchup.* Use Australian condiments sparingly until you are familiar with them. Aussie mustard delivers a horseradishy kick, and the infamous **Vegemite,** a yeasty by-product of the beer-brewing process, should be scraped thinly rather than spread liberally.

Seafood is a favorite on this island-continent, but all meats can be found. From the British come cholesterol-heavy **pub meals,** such as steak and eggs, and the Aussie institution of **fish 'n' chips.** The fish is fried, battered, rolled in newspaper, and served with British-style chips (thick french fries). **Chook** (chicken) is often substituted for fish to create much-needed variety. **"Chippers"** are the quintessential Aussie eateries, and most specialize in **takeaway** (take-out).

SPICE UP YOUR DIET. Australia may suffer from a reputation of having a notoriously dull national cuisine, but it has been remarkably successful at adding layers of flavor with each wave of immigration. Recent European and Middle Eastern arrivals have spiced up Australian menus with Greek souvlaki, Italian pasta, and Lebanese tabbouleh. The cheapest way to sample these flavors is at any of numerous takeaway joints. Influxes of immigrants from Asian and Pacific countries have added further variety. Chinese dishes first arrived with Chinese gold prospectors in the 1850s and have so infiltrated the menu that even their names have taken a uniquely Australian twist: **"dim sims"** are Australian *dim sum.* Japanese, Thai, Malay, and Vietnamese restaurants also are abundant, particularly in Darwin and cosmopolitan centers in the southeast.

NOT UNTIL YOU FINISH DINNER. Australia has plentiful pickings when it comes to fruit for desserts; its tropical north supports fruit industries that other western countries can only fantasize about. Travelers from fruit-deprived countries will encounter exotic offerings such as custard apples, lychees, passionfruit, star fruit, coconuts, mangoes, quandong, and pineapples. Queensland is the main fruit-producing region. Of the typical prepared desserts, there's the ubiquitous **lamington**—a coconut-covered chunk of pound cake dipped in chocolate, and the festive **pavlova** meringue.

BUSH TUCKER. Coastal Aborigines have eaten crayfish, **yabbies** (freshwater shrimp), and fish for centuries. **Witchetty grubs** are the most well known of the bush foods that make some first-timers twinge. Australia has recently discovered a taste for its "exotic" indigenous food. And with "bush tucker" as the new urban catch phrase, menus are increasingly inclined to incorporate Aboriginal wild foods like bunya nuts, Kakadu plums, and wild rosella flowers with specialty meats such as kangaroo filet, crocodile meat, Northern Territory buffalo, and wild magpie geese. If you want to sample **goanna** or **ants,** however, you might have to catch dinner yourself or join one of the Red Centre tours that feature real bush tucker.

MORE THAN JUST DRINKIN'

COFFEE. It might sound bizarre to some, but ordering "just coffee" is nearly impossible. Though they are a long way from Italy, Australia's major cities harbor a cappuccino culture that can deliver caffeine into your bloodstream in an infinite number of ways. If you need some help ordering, see **Cool Beans,** p. 728.

BEER. Let's move on to the more important skill of choosing a **beer.** Australia produces some of the world's best brews, and Australians over the legal drinking age of 18 consume it readily (we can't speak for those under the legal age). The best place to share a coldie with your mates is the omnipresent Aussie **pub.** Traditional payment etiquette is the **shout,** in which drinking mates alternate rounds. If the beach is more your style, throw a **slab** (24 containers of beer) in the **Esky** (ice chest). For more beer terminology and information on the types of beer available, consult **Terms of Embeerment,** p. 728.

WINE. Australian **wines** rival the best wines in the world. Overseas export started soon after the first vineyards began to produce wine in the early 1800s, and the industry has gained renown after a post-WWII influx of European talent. The **Hunter Valley** (see p. 145), the **Barossa** and **Clare Valleys** (see p. 467), the **Swan** and **Margaret Rivers** (see p. 681), and the **Derwent** and **Tamar Valleys** (see p. 519) possess some of the best Aussie vineyards. Many cafes and low-end restaurants advertise that they are **BYO,** or "bring your own." Though typically not licensed to serve alcohol, these establishments permit patrons to furnish their own bottle of wine with the meal and charge only a small **corkage fee,** if anything.

CUSTOMS & ETIQUETTE

MEETING, GREETING, AND EATING. Australians are known for their friendly informality, and most people are on a first-name basis right off the bat. This lack of pretension also renders rank largely irrelevant. While Australians are generally laid-back, keep an eye on your watch—**punctuality** is of the utmost importance. When eating, most people find **loud chewing, burping, and talking** with a full mouth rude. **Tipping** in restaurants and bars is rare and never expected.

THE UNWRITTEN RULES. Holding hands or **hugging** in public is common, but kissing is generally frowned upon. Although most cities are tolerant of **homosexuality,** gay or lesbian couples should be aware that they may receive unwanted attention for public displays of affection. **Littering** in this environmentally conscious society is not taken lightly.

THE UNSPOKEN WORDS. Extending your **middle finger** at someone (otherwise known as "giving the finger" or "flipping off" someone) is considered very rude and might get you into trouble. Beware the **"thumbs up"** sign, which is the equivalent of "up yours." **Winking** at women is also considered offensive.

WHAT YOU WEAR. For women, almost any clothing is acceptable as long as it covers the essential parts—tube tops, halters, and tank tops are all common in summer, but **conservative dress** in rural areas, especially those near the Outback or in Tasmania, might be a good idea. For men, pants or shorts are the norm. In most cases, neither gender should go topless, bottomless, or barefoot, and a swimsuit is usually appropriate only at the beach.

THE ARTS

While Australians might identify better with a national athlete than a native artist, art in Australia is slowly becoming part of a strong national identity, with Aboriginal art becoming one of Australia's cultural icons. Historically, European arts exerted a strong influence on non-Aboriginal Australian artists and writers, and the artists responded by focusing particularly on their relationship with their unique landscape and climate. Though modern artists are branching out to explore new themes, the most popular national arts are still those that depict traditional themes, sustain an Australian mythology, or explore some facet of the nation's cultural and natural heritage.

LITERATURE

Most of the works among newly settled Europeans were in the form of short written histories and accounts of pioneer life. During the 1870s, popular poet **Adam Lindsay Gordon** wrote *Bush Ballads and Galloping Rhymes*, evoking Australian camaraderie and stoicism. Possibly the first uniquely Australian literature was the **bush ballad,** a form of poetry that celebrated the working man and the superiority of life in the bush. The most famous of these ballads is **Banjo Paterson's** *Waltzing Matilda*, a song often considered more representative of the independent Australian pride than the national anthem (see p. 221). **Henry Savory** wrote the first Australian novel, *Quintus Servinton*, in 1831. The most famous Australian work is *Voss* (1957), by Nobel Prize-winner **Patrick White,** a love story about the idiosyncrasies of Australia 150 years ago, many of which still occupy authors and readers today.

The tradition and misogyny in early bush ballads and short stories provoked conflict between male and female writers in the 20th century. Among the better-known female writers is **Miles Franklin,** author of *My Brilliant Career* (1901). **Peter Carey** is best known as the author of *Bliss* (1981), a humorous exploration of the Australian national character, as well as his particularly dark satire, the Booker Prize-winning *Oscar and Lucinda* (1988). The attention given to "ethnic" writing, Aboriginal literature, and song-cycles has also been growing in the 20th century. A growing number of **Aboriginal writers** are beginning to gain national recognition.

POPULAR MUSIC

Australia's early colonial period relied heavily on British folk music, with lively fiddle and drum bushdances held in cleared-out sheep-shearing sheds. You can now find virtually any music from around the world in Australia. Oz's youth radio, **Triple J,** plays contemporary local music, and is always promoting new acts. Many of the nightlife spots mix everything from top-40 hits to alternative music to the European electronica.

HARD ROCK AND NEW WAVE. Refusing to emulate American and English sounds, **Cold Chisel, Goanna,** and **Australian Crawl** gained local fame with Aussie-themed hits that still get radio airtime. The '80s saw the advent of bands like **Midnight Oil,** a group borne out of hard rock pub culture and known for its support of social causes. **Men At Work** broke into the American music scene for a short while, and **Crowded House** briefly became a well-known international band at the height of New Wave. **INXS** became one of the most successful Australian bands.

Today's Australian music is very diverse, influenced by grunge and world music. **Savage Garden** flew to the moon and back, leaping onto the international pop scene, while **Nick Cave and the Bad Seeds** carry a fair-sized European following. Both **Kylie Minogue** and **Natalie Imbruglia** graduated from the Australian TV show *Neighbours* to take a shot at pop music. In August 2002, Sydney-based grunge band **The Vines** hit the Billboard Modern Rock Top 10 with their single, "Get Free."

BUSH ROCK. Yothu Yindi, a band out of Arnhem Land, has combined Aboriginal musical styles with dance music and rock. Other similarly politicized Aboriginal "bush rock" groups are the **Coloured Stones,** the **Warumpi Band,** and **Archie Roach,** whose country-influenced tunes reflect on his background as a "stolen child" and the problems of Aborigines in urban Australia.

AUSTRALIA

AUSTRALIA

VISUAL ARTS

ABORIGINAL PAINTING. Aboriginal art has become iconoclastic, in both authentic portrayals and in the world of marketing tourism. Before the 1970s, public perception of Aboriginal art was restricted to "bark paintings"—paintings on strips of eucalyptus that were traditionally ceremonial and generally destroyed during or after the ceremony. During the 1970s, other forms of Aboriginal art, such as mural art, body painting, and rock painting, were rediscovered and became popular, partly because of government support.

ART IN MODERN TIMES. Sidney Nolan's series on Ned Kelly illustrates the folk hero's exploits, final capture, and execution. Other prominent contemporary artists include **John Perceval,** expressionist **Albert Tucjer,** abstract artist **John Colburn,** and **Arthur Boyd,** who depicts popular figures of Australian legend. Younger Australian painters such as **Mandy Martin, Susan Norrie,** and **Neil Taylor** have flooded the scene with eclectic collections and explorations of post-industrial Australia.

FILM

In the last few decades, the rest of the world has begun giving greater respect to Australian talent in the film industry. While Australia has jumped into the international movie-scene, with Sydney sometimes being referred to as "the next Hollywood," domestic hits continue to attract large audiences. Check out *Chopper,* a true story about an Aussie who literally got away with murder, or *The Dish,* about Australia's own involvement in the US's achievement of putting man on the moon (visit the real 'dish' in Parkes, NSW, p. 221). *Bootmen,* starring the extremely talented **Adam Garcia** (of *Coyote Ugly* fame), has a great mix of love, drama, tears, and extreme dance. (For a chronicle of Australian cinematics in the past century, see **Hollywood Downunder,** p. 749.)

AUSSIE STARS Australian movie stars with recent international success include: **Geoffrey Rush** (*Shine, Shakespeare in Love, Quills, The Tailor of Panama*), **Cate Blanchett** (*Elizabeth, The Shipping News, Lord of the Rings: The Fellowship of the Ring, Lord of the Rings: The Two Towers*), **Nicole Kidman** (*Eyes Wide Shut, Moulin Rouge, The Others*), **Russell Crowe,** born a Kiwi but raised an Aussie (*Gladiator, A Beautiful Mind*), **Guy Pierce** (*Memento*), **Heath Ledger** (*10 Things I Hate About You, A Knight's Tale*), **Hugh Jackman** (*X-Men, Kate and Leopold, X-Men2,* to be released July 2003), and **Mel Gibson** (*Signs*).

SPORTS AND RECREATION

Often referred to as the national identity, Australians take sport very seriously. You can't walk into a bar without a sports event from somewhere in Oz on TV. In winter, Western Australia, South Australia, and Victoria catch **footy fever** for **Australian Rules Football,** while New South Wales and Queensland traditionally follow **rugby.** In summer, **cricket** is the spectator sport of choice across the nation. Star Aussie Rules football players and top cricketers enjoy hero status. Tune in to H. G. Nelson and Roy Slaven's Sunday afternoon Triple-J radio show *This Sporting Life* for a taste of Aussie sport culture, or check out the ridiculously popular *Footy Show,* on television's Channel 9.

CRICKET. The uninitiated may have trouble making sense of a sport where people can "bowl a maiden over of five flippers and a googly," but visitors won't be able to avoid the enthusiasm. Two teams of 11 players face off in a contest that can last anywhere from an afternoon to five days. Each summer, **international cricket** overshadows the national competition. Not just a scrimmage, a "test match" is the most lengthy and serious form of international cricket. In 1877, Australia's cricket team headed to England for its first international test against the mother country, emerging victorious. The Australians, as a shocked English reporter wrote, had "taken off with the ashes" of English cricket. Ever since then, British and Australian Test teams have been in noble contest for **"the Ashes"** (the trophy is a small, symbolic urn) with other former British colonial countries such as India, Pakistan, and South Africa joining in the competition. In December and January, international teams arrive for a **full tour**, consisting of five test matches, one each in Melbourne, Sydney, Perth, Adelaide, and Brisbane. The five-day tests, accompanied by smaller one-day matches, are over by February, just in time for the country to turn its attention to **national cricket** and the Sheffield Shield finals in March.

AUSTRALIAN RULES FOOTBALL. In Victoria, South Australia, and Western Australia, the **Australian Football League (AFL)** teams fill the winter void that the end of the cricket season leaves. Played on cricket ovals, the game was originally designed to keep cricket players in shape in the off-season. The **AFL grand final,** in early September, is a marvelous spectacle at the home of Australian sport, the **MCG** (see p. 573). For more information on footy, see **Footy 101,** p. 22.

RUGBY. According to legend, **rugby** was born one glorious day in 1823 when one inspired (or perhaps frustrated) student in Rugby, England, picked up a soccer ball and ran it into the goal. Since then, rugby has evolved (or devolved) into an intricately punishing game with two variants: **rugby union** involving 15-man teams, and **rugby league** with 13-man teams. Despite the international reputation of the national union team, the **Wallabies,** rugby union sometimes carries a muted following. Since they defeated France to win the World Cup in 1999, though, rugby union has grown in popularity. Matches such as the **Super 12** tournament and **Tri-nation** series (Australia, South Africa, and New Zealand) often pack stadiums and pubs. Part of the Tri-nation series, the **Bledisloe Cup** (first played in 1931) perpetuates a healthy animosity with Australia's down-under cousin, New Zealand.

Rugby league attracts a much larger following, especially in New South Wales and Queensland. The national league competition culminates in the **National Rugby League (NRL) final** in September. The only match that comes close to the intensity or popularity of the NRL final is the **State of Origin** series in June, when Queensland takes on New South Wales. Both games promise a mix of blood, mud, and plenty of drinking. For more info, check out www.rugbyworld.com.

 RUGBY WORLD CUP. From October 10 to November 22, 2003, Australia will host the Rugby World Cup for the first time since 1987. The games will be played in 12 stadiums across ten cities (Adelaide, Brisbane, Canberra, Gosford, Launceston, Melbourne, Perth, Sydney, Townsville, and Wollongong) and are expected to attract over 40,000 visitors.

OTHER SPORT. While the Australian team hasn't entered the World Cup since 1974, **soccer** is widely played, and Australia's **National Soccer League** has a fierce fanbase. Melbourne hosts one of **tennis'** Grand Slam events, the **Australian Open,** each January. Grassy tennis courts, bowling greens, and golf courses pepper the cities coast-to-coast. Most towns also have a horse racing track, and on the first Tuesday in November, the entire country stops to watch jockeys jockey for the prestigious **Melbourne Cup,** where fashionable and outlandish attire some-

AUSTRALIA

FOOTY 101. Below is a quick interpretive guide to the three most popular footy sports in Australia.

Footy #1: Rugby union, union, rugger, "You mean I can tread on him?"

Die-hard electorate: New South Wales and Queensland; the national team, "The Wallabies," have a country-wide following

Traditional Crowd: Students and alumni from male private schools

Rules: Played on a field bounded by touch lines on each side and goal lines on each end. In the middle of each goal line are two raised goal posts connected by a horizontal crossbar. Ten meters behind each goal line is the **dead-ball line,** which marks the end of the in-goal areas. Two teams of 15 try to score a **try** by placing the ball in the other team's in-goal area. Five points are awarded for a try, and the team that scores also gets to kick a goal, thus adding another two points to its credit; alternatively, if the goal is kicked during play, it is worth three points. A **scrum** takes place after a foul (such as a forward pass), and involves a **pack** of players from each team binding together to restart play. The **lineout** is how the ball is returned to play after being out of bounds. In a **ruck,** players group together to take possession of the ball, after a player carrying the ball has been tackled to the ground, while during a **maul,** the player carrying the ball is blocked but still standing,and a number of his teammates band around him to continue the advance of the ball and ensure possession.

Footy #2: Rugby league, league, football, "Why only five tackles?"

Die-hard electorate: New South Wales and Queensland

Traditional Crowd: Blue-collar working males and outer suburbs

Rules: League differs from union in a three major ways. First, the number of players on each team is reduced to thirteen. Second, when a player is tackled, play stops until the ball is put back into play by the tackled player, and each team is allowed to be tackled only five times before turning over possession to the other team. Finally, tries in league count for 4 points, while conversions count for 2 points and goals during play are awarded 1 point.

Footy #3: AFL, Aussie Rules, football, aerial ping pong, "That sport in Victoria"

Die-hard electorate: Victoria, South Australia, Western Australia

Traditional crowd: Everyone in the above locales and transplants from the above locales in New South Wales and Queensland

Rules: Eighteen players play four 20min. quarters on a cricket oval with 4 goal posts at each end. The basic move in AFL is the **punt,** used for both passing and scoring; good players can punt the ball over 70m. Kicking **goals** through the middle two posts counts for 6 points, while the ball passing on either side of the two main posts and the two outer posts, brings a **behind** or 1 point. Players can only pass the ball by kicking or hitting it with their fists. Once a player catches a kick from a teammate, he makes a **mark,** and the opposing team leaves him unobstructed to pass the ball or shoot at goal. A player in possession of the ball who has no mark can be tackled on any part of the body between shoulders and knees. Players within 5m of the ball can also be blocked and pushed (called **shepherding**) which, coupled with the rule that players are never disciplined during the course of the game, can sometimes lead to truly spectacular brawls.

Plamen Jordanoff was a Researcher-Writer for Let's Go: Germany in 1994. He now lives in Sydney, Australia, working as a strategy consultant.

times appears more important than the race. On Boxing Day, even as the Melbourne Cricket Test gets underway, half of Australia's amateur sailing community fills Sydney Harbour with billowing white sails to begin the **Sydney-to-Hobart yacht race**, the highlight in a full calendar of water sports. Australia is famous for its **surfing,** which for some is a competitive sport in addition to a great way to spend a summer morning.

HOLIDAYS AND FESTIVALS

Major regional festivals are also included within the state capitals. Banks, museums, and other public buildings are often closed or operate with reduced hours during these times. Vacations differ between schools and regions, but as a general rule, tourism peaks when school is out of session. **Summer holidays** for primary and secondary schools generally include December and January; for universities, they're from the end of November to the middle of February. **Winter break** runs from the end of June through early July. From Christmas to New Year's is ultra-peak season.

AUSTRALIA'S HOLIDAYS & FESTIVALS (2003)

DATE	NAME & LOCATION	DESCRIPTION
Jan. 1	New Year's Day	National holiday
Jan. 17-27	Carlton Country Music Festival (Tamworth, NSW)	One of the Top 10 Festivals of the World in the country music capital of Australia (www.tamworth.nsw.gov.au)
Jan. 26	Australia Day	National celebration of t Captain Arthur Phillip's landing in present-day Sydney (www.australiaday.com.au)
Feb. 21-23	WOMAdelaide	World Music Art Dance Adelaide; 2003 marks the 10th anniversary; theme is Sounds of the Planet (www.womadelaide.ozemail.com.au)
Mar. 3	Sydney Gay and Lesbian Mardi Gras (NSW)	2003 marks Sydney's 25th celebration of pride (www.mardigras.com.au)
Mar. 7-11	Melbourne Moomba Festival (VIC)	Primarily geared toward families; features multicultural performances and food, fireworks, and rides (www.melbournemoombafestival.com.au)
Apr. 17-23	National Folk Festival (Canberra ACT)	Over 1200 performers in 17 venues; theme for 2003 is music of South Australia (www.folkfestival.asn.au)
Apr. 25	ANZAC Day	Day of national commemoration; marks the anniversary of the WWI ANZAC landing in Gallipoli (www.anzacday.org.au).
June 9	Queen's Birthday	National holiday
July 12	Camel Cup Carnival (Alice Springs, NT)	Includes a Miss Camel Cup competition (www.camelcup.com.au)
Mid-July to early Aug.	Melbourne International Film Festival (VIC)	Once a year, buffs, stars, and critics flock to this showcase of world film (www.melbournefilmfestival.com.au).
Nov. 4	Melbourne Cup Races	"A horse race that stops a nation" (www.vrc.net.au)
Dec. 25	Christmas Day	National holiday
Dec. 26	Boxing Day	National holiday

ADDITIONAL RESOURCES

GENERAL HISTORY

Prehistory of Australia, by John Mulvaney and Johan Kamminga (1999). Offers a detailed account of the development of Aboriginal culture over the course of the last 40,000 years, from the continent's initial colonization to current issues of Aboriginal control over archaeological fieldwork.

Australia's Gold Rushes, by Robert Coupe (2001). Illustrated with maps and engravings, Coupe's book describes the story of Australia's explosive development through the lens of life in the goldfields.

Why Weren't We Told? by Henry Reynolds (1999). A shocking account of a nation's selective amnesia regarding Aborigines. Reynolds uncovers the truth behind the sugar-coated brand of history fed to generations of Australians.

A History of Australia, by Manning Clark (1999). Both acclaimed and controversial, this six-volume classic traces the history of Australia from the Aborigines to WWII.

Belonging: Australians, Place and Aboriginal Ownership, by Peter Read (2000). Read explores the nature of non-Aboriginal Australian identity and reconciliation in the face of past injustice toward indigenous peoples, consulting members of just about every demographic group imaginable while throwing in a healthy dose of daringly candid introspection.

FICTION AND NON-FICTION

Subhuman Redneck Poems, by Les Murray (1998). Murray is often considered Australia's premier poet, and it was this collection that won him the T.S. Eliot Prize in 1997.

Riders in the Chariot, by Patrick White (2002 reprint). This novel, written by Australia's Nobel laureate in literature, follows the stories of four friends in 1960's Sydney who do some serious soul-searching.

True History of the Kelly Gang, by Peter Carey (2001). Carey's Pulitzer Prize-winning imaginative account of the life and times of outlaw and Australian folk hero Ned Kelly.

Wise Women of the Dreamtime: Aboriginal Tales of the Ancestral Powers, compiled by K. Langloh Parker (1993). A collection of myths, creation stories, and ceremonial accounts, told from the perspective of Aboriginal female elders.

TRAVEL BOOKS

Tracks: A Woman's Solo Trek Across 1,700 Miles of Australian Outback, by Robyn Davidson (1995). Armed with four camels, a National Geographic photographer, and one hell of a mission, Robyn Davidson crosses the desert and lives to tell the tale.

The Confessions of a Beachcomber, by E. J. Banfield (2001). Following Thoreau's example, Banfield ditches a life of constant stress and heads for the sands of Dunk Island.

Cold Beer and Crocodiles: A Bicycle Journey into Australia, by Roff Martin Smith (2001). Smith, a *Time* magazine correspondent born in the United States, packs his bags on an impulse and embarks on the adventure of his life: an epic bicycle tour of the continent punctuated by surprises, close calls, and dazzling new insights.

In a Sunburned Country, by Bill Bryson (2001). Peppered with amusing anecdotes and witty cynicism, this entertaining travelogue relates Bryson's journey to the Land Down Under.

ESSENTIALS

FACTS FOR THE TRAVELER

ENTRANCE REQUIREMENTS. Unlike during the convict era, a criminal record is no longer required for entry into Australia.
Passports (p. 26). Required for all visitors.
Visas (p. 27). Required for all visitors except holders of Australian and New Zealand passports.
Working Visa (p. 27). Required for all foreigners planning to work in Australia.
Inoculations (p. 34). Only necessary for those who come from or have just visited yellow fever-infected areas (parts of South America and Central Africa).
Driving Permit (p. 47). Recommended; required for most car rental agencies.

E S S E N T I A L S

EMBASSIES AND CONSULATES

AUSTRALIAN CONSULAR SERVICES ABROAD

Canada: High Commission, 50 O'Connor St. #710, **Ottawa,** ON K1P 6L2 (☎613-236-0841; fax 236-4376; www.ahc-ottawa.org).

Ireland: Fitzwilton House, 2nd Fl., Wilton Tce., **Dublin** 2 (☎01 676 1517; fax 661 3576; www.australianembassy.ie).

New Zealand: High Commission, 72-78 Hobson St., P.O. Box 4036, **Wellington** (☎04 473 6411; fax 498 7135; www.australia.org.nz). Consulate, Union House, 7th-8th fl., 132-138 Quay St., Private Bag 92023, **Auckland** (☎09 303 2429; fax 377 0798).

South Africa: High Commission, 292 Orient St., Arcadia, **Pretoria** 0083; Private Bag X150, Pretoria 0001 (☎012 342 3781; fax 342 8422; www.australia.co.za).

United Kingdom: High Commission, Australia House, The Strand, **London** WC2B 4LA (☎171 379 4334; fax 465 8217; www.australia.org.uk). Consulate, Melrose House, 69 George St., **Edinburgh** EH2 25G (☎131 624 3333; fax 624 3701).

United States: Visa requests should go to Washington, D.C. or Los Angeles. Embassy, 1601 Massachusetts Ave. NW, **Washington, D.C.** 20036-2273 (☎202-797-3000; fax 797-3168; www.austemb.org). Consulate, 150 E. 42nd St., 34th fl., **New York,** NY 10017-5162 (☎212-351-6500; fax 351-6501). Consulate, 2049 Century Park E, 19th fl., **Los Angeles,** CA 90067-3121 (visas ☎310-229-4840, general 229-4800; fax 277-5620).

CONSULAR SERVICES IN AUSTRALIA

Canada: High Commission, Commonwealth Ave., **Canberra** ACT 2600 (☎02 6270 4000; fax 6273 4081). Consulate, Level 5, Quay West Building, 111 Harrington St., **Sydney** NSW 2000 (☎02 9364 3000; fax 9364 3098). Consulate, 267 St. George's Tce., **Perth** WA 6000 (☎08 9322 7930; fax 9261 7706).

Ireland: Embassy, 20 Arkana St., Yarralumla, **Canberra** ACT 2600 (☎02 6273 3022; fax 6273 3741). Consulate, Aberdeen St., P.O. Box 20, **Perth** WA 6865 (☎/fax 08 9385 8247). Consulate, Level 30, 400 George St., **Sydney** NSW 2000 (☎02 9231 6999; fax 9231 6254).

New Zealand: High Commission, Commonwealth Ave., **Canberra** ACT 2600 (☎02 6270 4211; fax 6273 3194). Consulate, Level 10, 55 Hunter St., GPO Box 365, **Sydney** NSW 2000 (passport ☎02 9223 0222, visa 9223 0144; fax 8256 2056).

South Africa: High Commission, State Circle, Yarralumla, **Canberra** ACT 2600 (☎02 6273 2424; fax 6273 3543).

United Kingdom: High Commission, Commonwealth Ave., Yarralumla, **Canberra** ACT 2600 (☎02 6270 6666; fax 6273 3236). Consulate, 17th fl., 90 Collins St., **Melbourne** VIC 3000 (☎03 9650 4155; fax 9650 3699). Consulate, Level 26, Allendale Sq., 77 St. George's Tce., **Perth** WA 6000 (☎08 9221 5400; fax 9221 2344). Consulate, Level 16, The Gateway, 1 Macquarie Pl., **Sydney** NSW 2000 (☎02 9247 7521; fax 9251 6201).

United States: Embassy, Moonah Pl., Yarralumla, **Canberra** ACT 2600 (☎02 6214 5600; fax 6214 5970). Consulate, Level 59, MLC Ctr., 19-29 Martin Pl., **Sydney** NSW 2000 (☎02 9373 9200; fax 9373 9184). Consulate, 553 St. Kilda Rd., **Melbourne** VIC 3004 (☎03 9526 5900; fax 9510 4646). Consulate, 13th floor, 16 St. George's Tce., **Perth** WA 6000 (☎08 9202 1224; fax 9231 9444).

TOURIST OFFICES

The government-sponsored **Australian Tourist Commission (ATC)** promotes tourism internationally, distributing literature and sponsoring helplines. The ATC carries books, magazines, and fact sheets for backpackers, younger people, disabled travelers, and others with special concerns. For more information on events and domestic travel, check out www.australia.com and www.atc.net.au. Contact these office affiliates in the nearest location:

Australia (Head Office): Level 4, 80 William St., **Wolloomooloo** NSW 2011; GPO Box 2721, **Sydney** NSW 1006 (☎02 9360 1111; fax 9331 6469).

New Zealand: Level 13, 44-48 Emily Pl., P.O. Box 1666, **Auckland** 1 (☎09 915 2826 or 0800 65 03 03; fax 307 3117).

United Kingdom: Gemini House, 10-18 Putney Hill, **London** SW15 6AA (☎20 8780 2229; fax 8780 1496).

U.S./Canada: 2049 Century Park E, Ste. 1920, **Los Angeles**, CA 90067 (☎310-229-4870 or 800-333-4305; fax 310-552-1215).

DOCUMENTS AND FORMALITIES

PASSPORTS

REQUIREMENTS. Citizens of Canada, Ireland, New Zealand, South Africa, the UK, and the US need valid passports to enter Australia and to re-enter home countries. Returning home with an expired passport is illegal and may result in a fine.

NEW PASSPORTS. Citizens of Canada, Ireland, New Zealand, the UK, and the US can apply for a passport at any post office, passport office, or court of law. Citizens of South Africa can apply for a passport at any office of Home Affairs. Any new passport or renewal applications must be filed well in advance of the departure date, though most passport offices offer rush services for a very steep fee. Citizens living abroad who need a passport or renewal should contact the nearest passport office of their home country.

PASSPORT MAINTENANCE. See **Identification** (p. 27), and make sure to keep copies of your passport handy as described. If you lose your passport, immediately notify the local police and the nearest embassy or consulate of your home govern-

ment. To expedite its replacement, you need to know its information an
and proof of citizenship. In some cases, a replacement may take weeks t(
and it may be valid only for a limited time. Visas stamped in your old pas:
be hard to verify; in Australia, you must visit a regional office of the Depai
Immigration and Multicultural and Indigenous Affairs, and you may incur
an emergency, ask for immediate emergency traveling papers that will pei ..... you
to re-enter your home country.

 Since April 8, 2002, US embassies and consulates no longer issue American passports abroad. Applying for a passport in a foreign consulate now takes longer because it needs to be printed in the US. In the case of lost or stolen passports, consulates will only issue temporary passports, which cannot be extended. For more information regarding lost and stolden passports, see the Australian US Embassy website (www.usis-australia.gov/consular/newpassportproc.html).

VISAS AND ETA

Australia **requires all visitors** except Australian citizens and New Zealand passport holders to have a visa. You can obtain an **Electronic Travel Authority (ETA)** while purchasing your ticket at a travel agency, at the airport ticket counter, or over the Internet (www.eta.immi.gov.au). Quick and simple, the fully electronic ETA replaces a standard visa. It allows three months on each visit within a one-year period and is free for those staying less than three months. To extend a visit over three months, contact the nearest office of the Department of Immigration and Multicultural and Indigenous Affairs in Australia before the end of your three-month stay period. There is no provision for obtaining a further ETA when you are in Australia. For more info, contact the nearest Australian Tourist Commission branch (see p. 26). Standard visas (US$40) may be obtained from the nearest Australian high commission, embassy, or consulate. If you register in person, it will take two days to process; allow 21 working days by mail. Rates on extending your ETA or visa depend on length of stay and type of visa; an application to extend a standard visa is AUS$150. Contact the Department of Immigration and Multicultural and Indigenous Affairs at their inquiries line (☎ 13 18 81) before your stay period expires. Otherwise, contact an Australian consulate or embassy (see p. 25). It is also possible to enter Australia for a working holiday or for scholarship; see **Alternatives to Tourism,** p. 66.

US citizens can take advantage of the **Center for International Business and Travel (CIBT; ☎** 800-929-2428), which secures visas for travel to most countries for a variable service charge. Between the hours of 8:30am and 8pm EST Monday through Friday, email to customerservice@cibt.com will be returned within two hours.

Be sure to double-check on entrance requirements at the nearest embassy or consulate of Australia for up-to-date info before departure. US citizens can also consult www.pueblo.gsa.gov/cic_text/travel/foreign/foreignentryreqs.html.

IDENTIFICATION

Always carry two or more forms of identification on your person, including at least one photo ID; a passport combined with a driver's license or birth certificate is usually adequate. Never carry all your forms of ID together; separate them in case of theft or loss, and keep photocopies of them in your luggage and at home. Be sure to copy any visas and the page of your passport with your photo; consulates also recommend that you carry an expired passport or an official copy of your birth certificate in your baggage, separate from other documents.

STUDENT, YOUTH, & TEACHER IDENTIFICATION. The **International Student Iden-tity Card (ISIC)**, the most widely accepted form of student ID, provides discounts on sights, accommodations, food, and transport (typically around 10%); access to 24hr. emergency helpline (in North America ☎877-370-ISIC, elsewhere US collect +1 715-345-0505); and insurance benefits for US cardholders (see **Insurance,** p. 36). The ISIC is preferable to a specific university's or other institution's ID because it is more likely to be recognized and honored abroad. Applicants must be degree-seeking students of a secondary or post-secondary school and must be of at least 12 years of age. Because of the proliferation of fake ISICs, some services (particularly airlines) require additional proof of student identity, such as a school ID or a letter attesting to your student status, signed by your registrar and stamped with your school seal.

For travelers who are under 26 but are not students, the **International Youth Travel Card (IYTC)** offers many of the same benefits as the ISIC. The **International Teacher Identity Card (ITIC)** offers teachers the same insurance coverage as the ISIC as well as similar but limited discounts. Each of these identity cards costs US$22 or equivalent. ISIC and ITIC cards are valid for roughly one and a half academic years; IYTC cards are valid for one year from the date of issue. Many student travel agencies (see p. 38) issue the cards. For a listing of issuing agencies, or for more information, contact the **International Student Travel Confederation (ISTC),** Herengracht 479, 1017 BS Amsterdam, Netherlands (☎ +31 20 421 28 00; fax 421 28 10; istcinfo@istc.org; www.istc.org).

DISCOUNTS. "Concessions" is the Australian catch-all phrase for discounts always given to specific groups, most often students and senior citizens. However, it may be limited to holders of specific Australian concession cards. "Pensioners" are Australian senior citizens, and discounts for pensioners may not apply to non-Australians who otherwise fit the bill. Student discounts often require that you show an ID and may only apply to Australian university students, or even to university students within the particular state. Discounts on accommodations are regularly given to VIP, YHA, ISIC, or NOMADS card holders.

CUSTOMS

Thanks to its isolation as an island nation, Australia has managed to avoid some of the pests and diseases that plague other countries. But burgeoning tourism increases the risk of contamination from imported goods, and the Customs Bureau takes the need to protect Australia's shores seriously. Articles not automatically forbidden but subject to a **quarantine inspection** may include camping equipment, live animals, food, animal products, plants, plant products, and protected wildlife. Don't risk large fines or hassles when entering Australia—throw out questionable items in the big customs bins as you leave the plane, and declare anything about which you have the slightest suspicion. The beagles in orange smocks know their stuff, and they *will* find you out. If you must bring your **pets** with you, contact the **Australian Quarantine and Inspections Service,** GPO Box 858, Canberra ACT 2601 (☎02 6272 3933; animalimp@aqis.gov.au) to obtain a permit. Pick up *Customs Information for Travellers* at an Australian consulate or any travel agency for more info. Australia expressly forbids the entry of drugs, steroids, and weapons.

Visitors over 18 may bring into Australia up to 1125ml alcohol and 250 cigarettes (or 250g tobacco) **duty-free.** For other goods, whether or not intended as gifts, the allowance is AUS$400 (over 18) or AUS$200 (under 18). Upon returning home, you must declare articles acquired abroad and pay a **duty** on the value of articles that exceeds the allowance established by your country's customs service. Goods bought at **duty-free** shops abroad are not exempt from duty tax at your return; you must declare these items as well. "Duty-free" merely means that you need not pay a tax in the country of purchase. On the bright side, Australia recently implemented a **Tourist Refund Scheme** (TRS) that refunds the **Goods and Services Tax** (GST) on items bought in Australia (see **Tipping and Taxes,** p. 32). For more information on customs requirements, contact the following information centers:

Australia: Australian Customs Service (in Australia ☎ 1300 363 263, elsewhere ☎ 02 6275 6666; www.customs.gov.au).

Canada: Canadian Customs and Revenue Agency, 2265 St. Laurent Blvd., Ottawa, ON K1G 4K3 (24hr. in Canada ☎ 800 461 9999, elsewhere ☎ 204 983 3500; www.ccra-adrc.gc.ca).

Ireland: Customs Information Office, Irish Life Ctr., Lower Abbey St., Dublin 1 (☎ 01 878 8811; fax 878 0836; ceadmin@revenue.iol.ie; www.revenue.ie).

New Zealand: New Zealand Customhouse, 17-21 Whitmore St., Box 2218, Wellington (☎ 04 473 6099, general 09 300 5399 or 0800 428 786; fax 04 473 7370; www.customs.govt.nz).

South Africa: Customs and Excise, P.O. Box 13802, Tramshed, Pretoria 0001 (☎ 012 334 6400; fax 328 6478; www.sars.gov.za).

United Kingdom: Her Majesty's Customs and Excise, Passenger Enquiry Team, Wayfarer House, Great South West Rd., Feltham, Middlesex TW14 8NP (☎ 020 8910 3744; National Advice Service: 0845 010 9000; www.hmce.gov.uk).

United States: US Customs Service, 1300 Pennsylvania Ave. NW, Washington, D.C. 20229 (☎ 202-927-1000; fax 354-1010; www.customs.gov).

MONEY

No matter how low your budget, you should keep a large amount of cash handy. Carrying it around is risky but necessary; personal checks are seldom accepted, and even traveler's checks may not be accepted in some locations.

> **LET'S GO: AUSTRALIA LISTS ALL PRICES IN AUSTRALIAN DOLLARS UNLESS OTHERWISE STATED.**

CURRENCY AND EXCHANGE

The Australian currency comes in dollars ($) and cents (¢). Notes come in $5, $10, $20, $50, and $100 denominations, and coins in 5¢, 10¢, 20¢, 50¢, $1, and $2 denominations. The currency chart below is based on August 2002 exchange rates between local currency and US dollars (US$), Canadian dollars (CDN$), British pounds (UK£), New Zealand dollars (NZ$), South African Rand (ZAR), and European Union euros (EUR€). Check a large newspaper or the currency calculator on our website (www.letsgo.com) for the latest exchange rates.

CURRENCY	
US$1 = AUS$1.84	AUS$1= US$0.54
CDN$1 = AUS$1.18	AUS$1= CDN$0.85
UK£1 = AUS$2.83	AUS$1= UK£0.35
NZ$1 = AUS$0.86	AUS$1= NZ$1.16
ZAR1 = AUS$0.17	AUS$1= ZAR5.78
EUR€ = AUS$1.81	AUS$1= EUR€0.55

As a general rule, it's cheaper to convert money in Australia. It's good to bring enough foreign currency to last for the first 24-72 hours of a trip to avoid being penniless after banking hours or on a holiday. In the U.S., **International Currency Express** (☎ 888-278-6628; www.foreignmoney.com) will deliver foreign currency for over 120 countries or traveler's checks to your home overnight (US$15) or second-day (US$12) at competitive exchange rates.

Watch out for commission rates, and check newspapers for the standard rate of exchange. When changing money abroad, try to go only to banks or *bureaux de change* that have at most a 5% margin between their buy and sell prices. The largest and most widespread banks in Australia are ANZ, Commonwealth, National, and Westpac. Since you lose money with every transaction, **convert large sums** (unless the currency is depreciating rapidly, as is not likely to be the case in Australia in the near future), **but no more than you'll need.** In fact, using an ATM (see p. 46) or a credit card (see p. 31) often gets you the best possible rates.

When you use traveler's checks or bills in your home currency, carry some in small denominations (the equivalent of US$50 or less) for times when you are forced to exchange money at disadvantageous rates, but bring a range of denominations, since charges may be levied per check cashed. Store your money in a variety of forms; ideally, you will at any given time be carrying some cash, some traveler's checks, and an ATM card and/or credit card (see p. 31).

TRAVELER'S CHECKS

Traveler's checks are one of the safest and least troublesome means of carrying funds, since they can be refunded if stolen or lost. Several agencies and banks sell them, usually for face value plus a small commission. Sometimes you can even escape the commission: for instance, members of the American Automobile Association and some banks and credit unions can get American Express checks commission-free (see **International Driving Permits**, p. 47). Each traveler's check agency provides refunds if checks are lost or stolen, and many provide additional services, like toll-free refund hotlines, emergency message services, and stolen credit card assistance. The most recognized brands are listed below.

While traveling, keep check receipts and a record of which ones you've cashed (separate from the checks themselves). Also, leave a list of check numbers with someone at home. Never countersign checks until you're ready to cash them, and when you do cash them, always have your passport with you. If your checks are lost or stolen, immediately contact one of your agency's refund centers to be reimbursed; they may require a police report verifying the loss. Less touristed, rural areas may not have refund centers at all, so you might have to wait to be reimbursed. Ask about toll-free refund hotlines and the location of refund centers when purchasing checks, and always carry emergency cash.

American Express: Checks available with commission at select banks and all AmEx offices. US residents can also purchase checks by phone (☎ 888-887-8986) or online (www.aexp.com). AAA (see p. 48) offers commission-free checks to its members. Checks available in US, Australian, British, Canadian, Japanese, and Euro currencies. *Cheques for Two* can be signed by either of 2 people traveling together. For purchase locations or more information, contact AmEx's service centers: In the US and Canada ☎ 800-221-7282; in the UK 0800 521 313; in Australia 800 25 19 02; in New Zealand 0800 441 068; elsewhere US collect +1 801-964-6665.

Visa: Checks available (generally with commission) at banks worldwide. For the location of the nearest office, call Visa's service centers: In the US ☎ 800-227-6811; in the UK 0800 89 50 78; elsewhere UK collect +44 020 7937 8091. Checks available in US, British, Canadian, Japanese, and Euro currencies.

Travelex/Thomas Cook: In the US and Canada ☎800-287-7362; in the UK 0800 62 21 01; elsewhere UK collect +44 1733 31 89 50.

CREDIT, ATM, AND DEBIT CARDS

Credit cards are generally accepted in all but the smallest businesses in Australia. Where they are accepted, credit cards often offer superior exchange rates—up to 5% better than the retail rate used by banks and other currency exchange establishments—but some credit cards will then charge you a special fee for the service, so check beforehand. Credit cards may also offer services such as insurance or emergency help and are sometimes required to reserve hotel rooms or rental cars. **MasterCard** and **Visa** are the most welcomed; **American Express** cards work at some ATMs and at AmEx offices and major airports.

ATM CARDS

ATM cards are widespread in Australia. Depending on the system that your home bank uses, you can most likely access your personal bank account from abroad. ATMs get the same wholesale exchange rate as credit cards, but there is often a limit on the amount of money you can withdraw per day (around US$500), and computer networks sometimes fail. There is typically also a surcharge of US$1-5 per withdrawal. Be sure to memorize your PIN code in numeric form since machines often don't have letters on their keys. Also, if your PIN is longer than four digits, ask your bank whether you need a new number.

ELECTRONIC BANKING. The two major international money networks are **Cirrus** (US ☎800-424-7787) and **PLUS** (US ☎800-843-7587). To locate ATMs around the world, call the above numbers, or consult www.mastercard.com/cardholderservices/atm or http://visaatm.infonow.net/bin/findNow?CLIENT_ID=VISA. **Cirrus** is the most widespread ATM network in Australia; **PLUS** is almost as frequent, and **Visa,** though probably third best, is still fairly common. **Mastercard** and **American Express** are found less often and **NYCE** not at all. Though ATMs are increasingly prevalent in smaller towns and rural areas, they are scarce in northern Western Australia and more remote interior areas.

Visa TravelMoney (for emergency assistance in Australia ☎0800 450 346) is a system allowing you to access money from any Visa ATM, common throughout Australia. You deposit an amount before you travel (plus a small administration fee), and you can withdraw up to that sum. The cards, which give you the same favorable exchange rate for withdrawals as a regular Visa, are especially useful if you plan to travel through many countries. Check with your local bank or AAA chapter to see if it issues TravelMoney cards.

EFTPOS. Electronic Funds Transfer at Point Of Sale (EFTPOS) is an extremely common way for Australians to pay for goods. ATM cards (from Australian banks only) swiped at the register double as debit cards, withdrawing money directly from your bank account. What's more, most establishments offer EFTPOS with a **cash-back** option, cutting down on the number of transactions you must perform and thereby saving you time and per-transaction bank fees. EFTPOS is useful for travelers because it means they can carry less cash and not have to worry about credit card bills, so if you'll be in Australia for a while, it might make sense to open an Australian bank account. A permanent Australian address and two or three forms of identification are required to open an account—your home driver's license and your passport are the most sure-fire bets—and you can expect a routine check on your credit history. Bringing along bank statements from home for the last three months can expedite the process enormously; accounts can be ready in as little as an hour. Banks accept cash or traveler's checks as initial deposits.

ESSENTIALS

GETTING MONEY FROM HOME

If you run out of money while traveling, the easiest and cheapest solution is to have someone back home make a deposit to your credit card or ATM card. Failing that, consider one of the following options.

WIRING MONEY. It is possible to arrange a **bank money transfer,** which means asking a bank back home to wire money to a bank in Australia. This is the cheapest way to transfer cash, but it's also the slowest, usually taking several days or more. Note that some banks may only release your funds in local currency, potentially sticking you with a poor exchange rate; inquire about this in advance. Money transfer services like **Western Union** are faster and more convenient than bank transfers, but also much pricier. Western Union has many locations worldwide. (To find one, visit www.westernunion.com, or call in Australia ☎ 800 501 500, in the US ☎ 800-325-6000, in Canada ☎ 800-235-0000, in the UK ☎ 0800 83 38 33, in New Zealand ☎ 800 27 0000, or in South Africa ☎ 0860 100031.) Money transfer services are also available at **American Express** and **Thomas Cook** offices.

US STATE DEPARTMENT (US CITIZENS ONLY). In dire emergencies only, the US State Department will forward money within hours to the nearest consular office, which will then disburse it according to instructions for a US$15 fee. If you wish to use this service, you must contact the Overseas Citizens Service division of the US State Department (☎ 202-647-5225; nights, Sundays, and holidays ☎ 202-647-4000).

TIPPING AND TAXES

In Australia, tipping is not required at restaurants, bars, taxis, or hotels—service workers do not rely on tips for income. Tips are occasionally left at pricier restaurants, when the service is exceptionally good. In this case, 10% is more than sufficient. Taxes are already included in the bill, so only pay the advertised price.

The New Tax System of 2000 provides for a **10% Goods and Services Tax (GST)**. Some goods such as basic foods and medicines are not subject to this tax. However, the System also implemented a **Tourist Refund Scheme (TRS)** whereby tourists and Australian overseas retailers may be entitled to a refund of the GST and of the **Wine Equalisation Tax (WET)** on purchases of goods bought from Australian retailers. The refund is only good for GST or WET paid on purchases of $300 or more. Travelers can claim the refund from customs officers when departing Australia by presenting tax receipts from retailers along with a valid passport and proof of travel at TRS booths in the international airports or cruise terminals. For more information on the TRS, see the Australian Customs web page (www.customs.gov.au).

SAFETY AND SECURITY

EMERGENCY PHONE NUMBER   Anywhere in Australia, dial ☎ **000.**

Although Australia is a relatively safe country, it is always important to keep personal safety in mind. Tourists are particularly vulnerable to crime because they often carry large amounts of cash and are not as street-savvy as locals. To avoid unwanted attention, try to blend in as much as possible. The gawking camera-toter is a more obvious target than the low-profile traveler. Familiarize yourself with your surroundings before setting out; if you must check a map on the street, duck into a cafe or shop. If you are traveling alone, be sure that someone at home knows your itinerary and *never admit that you're traveling alone.* The **Australian Department of Foreign Affairs and Trade** (☎ 02 2261 1111) offers travel information and advisories at their website (www.dfat.gov.au).

PERSONAL SAFETY

EXPLORING. Extra vigilance is always wise, but there is no need for panic when exploring a new city or region. Find out about unsafe areas from tourist offices, from the manager of your hotel or hostel, or from a local whom you trust. You may want to carry a **whistle** to scare off attackers or attract attention; memorize the emergency number of the city or area. Anywhere in Australia, **dial ☎000 for emergency medical help, police, or fire.** Whenever possible, *Let's Go: Australia* warns of unsafe neighborhoods and areas.

SELF DEFENSE. There is no sure-fire way to avoid all the threatening situations you might encounter when you travel, but a good self-defense course will give you concrete ways to react to unwanted advances. **Impact, Prepare, and Model Mugging** can refer you to local self-defense courses in the US (☎800-345-5425). Visit the website at www.impactsafety.org for a list of nearby chapters. Workshops (2-3hr.) start at US$50; full courses run US$350-500.

DRIVING. If you are using a **car,** learn local driving signals and wear a seatbelt. Children under 40 lbs. should ride only in a specially-designed carseat, available for a small fee from most car rental agencies. Study route maps before you hit the road, and if you plan on spending a lot of time on the road, you may want to bring spare parts. If your car breaks down, wait for the police to assist you. For long drives in desolate areas, invest in a cellular phone and a roadside assistance program. Be sure to park your vehicle in a garage or well traveled area, and use a steering wheel locking device in larger cities. **Sleeping in your car** is one of the most dangerous ways to get your rest (and often illegal to boot). For info on the perils of **hitchhiking,** see p. 49.

TERRORISM. Australia has been fairly safe from terrorism as of August 2002, but be aware of violence against foreigners in parts of nearby Indonesia and Timor. The box on **travel advisories** below refers to offices and webpages that provide the most updated list of your home government's warnings about travel.

TRAVEL ADVISORIES. The following government offices provide travel information and advisories by telephone, by fax, or via the web:

Australian Department of Foreign Affairs and Trade: ☎1300 555 135; faxback service 02 6261 1299; www.dfat.gov.au.

Canadian Department of Foreign Affairs and International Trade (DFAIT): In Canada and the US call ☎800-267-6788, elsewhere call +1 613-944-6788; www.dfait-maeci.gc.ca. Call for their free booklet, *Bon Voyage...But.*

New Zealand Ministry of Foreign Affairs: ☎04 494 8500; fax 494 8506; www.mft.govt.nz/trav.html.

United Kingdom Foreign and Commonwealth Office: ☎020 7008 0232; fax 7008 0155; www.fco.gov.uk.

US Department of State: ☎202-647-5225; faxback service 202-647-3000; http://travel.state.gov. For their free booklet, *A Safe Trip Abroad,* call 202-512-1800.

FINANCIAL SECURITY

PROTECTING YOUR VALUABLES. There are a few steps you can take to minimize the financial risk associated with traveling. First, **bring as little with you as possible.** Second, buy a few combination **padlocks** to secure your belongings either in your pack or in a hostel or train-station locker. Third, **carry as little cash as possible.** Keep your traveler's checks and ATM/credit cards in a **money belt**—not a "fanny pack"—along with your passport and ID cards. Fourth, **keep a small cash reserve separate from your primary stash.** This should be about US$50 (US$ is best) sewn into or stored in the depths of your pack, along with your traveler's check numbers and important photocopies.

ACCOMMODATIONS AND TRANSPORTATION. Never leave your belongings unattended; crime occurs in even the most demure-looking hostel or hotel. Bring your own **padlock** for hostel lockers, and don't ever store valuables in any locker.

Be particularly careful on **buses** and **trains;** horror stories abound about determined thieves who wait for travelers to fall asleep. Carry your backpack in front of you where you can see it. When traveling with others, sleep in alternate shifts. When alone, use good judgement in selecting a train compartment: never stay in an empty one, and use a lock to secure your pack to the luggage rack. Try to sleep on top bunks with your luggage stored above you (if not in bed with you), and keep important documents and other valuables on your person. If traveling by **car,** don't leave valuables (such as radios or luggage) in it while you are away.

DRUGS AND ALCOHOL

Australia has fairly strict drug laws. There is a debate currently ensuing over whether or not to legalize marijuana, but for now it remains illegal. Australia does not differentiate between illicit substances; all are illegal to possess in any quantity. If you carry **prescription drugs,** take a copy of the prescription with you.

Very strict **drunk-driving** (or "drink-driving," as Aussies say) laws apply, and most states operate frequent random breath-testing. The maximum legal blood-alcohol limit for drivers is .05%. For learner drivers, P-plate holders, and drivers under 25 who have had their license for less than three years, the maximum blood-alcohol limit is .02%. You must be 18 to purchase alcohol or consume it in public.

Smoking is prohibited in most enclosed buildings and on most public transportation in Australia, including domestic and international flights. Furthermore, there is currently discussion about whether to toughen anti-smoking laws, so check before lighting up. See **In Recent News,** p. 388, for more information.

HEALTH

In the event of a serious illness or emergency, call ☎**000 from any phone**—this is a free call—to connect to police, an ambulance, or the fire department. Common sense is the simplest prescription for good health while you travel. Drink lots of fluids to prevent dehydration and constipation, and wear sturdy, broken-in shoes and clean socks.

BEFORE YOU GO

In your **passport,** write the names of any people you wish to be contacted in case of a medical emergency, and list any allergies or medical conditions. Matching a prescription to a foreign equivalent is not always easy, safe, or possible, so carry up-to-date, legible prescriptions or a statement from your doctor stating the medication's trade name, manufacturer, chemical name, and dosage. While traveling, be sure to keep all medication with you in your carry-on luggage. For tips on packing a basic **first-aid kit** and other health essentials, see p. 34.

IMMUNIZATIONS. Travelers over two years old should make sure that the following vaccines are up to date: MMR (for measles, mumps, and rubella); DTaP or Td (for diptheria, tetanus, and pertussis); OPV (for polio); HbCV (for haemophilus

INOCULATION REQUIREMENTS. Vaccinations are not required unless you have visited a yellow fever-infected country or zone within six days prior to arrival. See http://www.health.gov.au/pubhlth/strateg/communio/fact sheets/yellow.htm for more information. You do not need any other health certificate to enter Australia.

influenza B); and HBV (for hepatitus B). For recommendations on immunizations and prophylaxis, consult the CDC (see below) in the US or the equivalent in your home country, and check with a doctor for guidance.

USEFUL ORGANIZATIONS & PUBLICATIONS. The US **Centers for Disease Control and Prevention** (**CDC;** ☎877-FYI-TRIP; fax 888-232-3299; www.cdc.gov/travel) maintains an international travelers' hotline and an informative website. The CDC's comprehensive booklet, *Health Information for International Travel*, an annual rundown of disease, immunization, and general health advice, is free online or US$25 via the Public Health Foundation (☎877-252-1200). Consult the appropriate government agency of your home country for consular information sheets on health, entry requirements, and other issues for various countries (see the listings in the box on **Travel Advisories,** p. 33). For quick information on health and other travel warnings, call the **Overseas Citizens Services** (☎202-647-5225; after-hours 202-647-4000), or contact a passport agency, embassy, or consulate abroad. US citizens can send a self-addressed, stamped envelope to the Overseas Citizens Services, Bureau of Consular Affairs, #4811, US Department of State, Washington, D.C. 20520. For information on medical evacuation services and travel insurance firms, see the US government's website at http://travel.state.gov/medical.html or the **British Foreign and Commonwealth Office** (www.fco.gov.uk).

For detailed information on travel health, including a country-by-country overview of diseases, try the **International Travel Health Guide** (US$20; www.travmed.com). For general health info, contact the **American Red Cross** (☎800-564-1234; www.redcross.org).

MEDICAL ASSISTANCE ON THE ROAD. If you are concerned about obtaining medical assistance while traveling, you may wish to employ special support services. The *MedPass* from **GlobalCare, Inc.,** 2001 Westside Pkwy., #120, Alpharetta, GA 30004 (☎800-860-1111; fax 770-677-0455; www.globalems.com), provides 24hr. international medical assistance, support, and medical evacuation resources. The **International Association for Medical Assistance to Travelers** (**IAMAT;** US ☎716-754-4883, Canada ☎416-652-0137, New Zealand ☎03 352 20 53; www.sentex.net/~iamat) has free membership, lists English-speaking doctors worldwide, and offers detailed info on immunization requirements and sanitation. If your regular **insurance** policy does not cover travel abroad, you may wish to purchase additional coverage (see p. 36)

ONCE IN AUSTRALIA

ENVIRONMENTAL HAZARDS

Since there is so much outdoor fun in Australia, apply **sunscreen** liberally and often to avoid burns and lower the risk of skin cancer, a disease which is no stranger to Australia. Queensland has the highest rate of skin cancer cases in the world. The sun is very strong; if you don't usually burn, still wear sunscreen, at least for the first few days of exposure. If you are planning on spending time near water, in the desert, or in the snow, you are at risk of getting burned, even when it is cloudy. If sunburned, drink more fluids than usual and apply an aloe-based lotion.

ESSENTIALS

INSECT-BORNE DISEASES

Many diseases are transmitted by insects—mainly mosquitoes, fleas, ticks, and lice. Be aware of insects in wet or forested areas (such as northern Queensland and Kakadu, NT), especially while hiking and camping. Wear long pants and long sleeves, tuck your pants into your socks, and buy a mosquito net. Use insect repellents such as DEET, and soak or spray your gear with permethrin (licensed in the US for use on clothing). **Ticks**—responsible for Lyme and other diseases—can be particularly dangerous in rural and forested regions. While walking, pause periodically to brush off ticks from exposed parts of your body using a fine-toothed comb. Do not attempt to remove ticks by burning them. Natural repellents can be useful: taking vitamin B-12 pills regularly can make you smelly to insects, as can garlic pills. Calamine lotion or topical cortisones (like Cortaid) may stop insect bites from itching, as can a bath with a half-cup of baking soda or oatmeal.

The following insect-borne diseases occur in parts of Australia; consult the **Communicable Diseases Network Australia** (http://www.health.gov.au/pubhlth/cdi/cdihtml.htm) for a more complete list.

Dengue fever: An "urban viral infection" transmitted by *Aedes* mosquitoes, which bite during the day rather than at night. Causing periodic epidemics in parts of northern Queensland and the Torres Strait Islands, Dengue is often indicated by a rash 3-4 days after the onset of fever. Symptoms for the first 2-4 days include chills, high fever, headaches, swollen lymph nodes, muscle aches, and, in some instances, a pink rash on the face. If you experience these symptoms, see a doctor, drink plenty of liquids, and take fever-reducing medication such as acetaminophen

Murray Valley Encephalitis: A rarely occurring viral infection of the central nervous system, transmitted by mosquitoes in regions of Western Australia, Queensland, and the Northern Territory. Carriers breed annually north of Port Hedland between Feb. and Apr. Symptoms include headaches, neck stiffness, and nausea.

Ross River and Barmah Forest Virus (epidemic polyarthritis): A disease transmitted by mosquitoes in regions of Victoria. Symptoms include fever, aching joints and sometimes small purple blotches that look like bruises. Full recovery can take up to several months.

WOMEN'S HEALTH

Women travelers may be vulnerable to **urinary tract** and **bladder infections,** common and uncomfortable bacterial diseases that cause a burning sensation and painful and frequent urination. To minimize risk, drink plenty of vitamin-C-rich juice and clean water and urinate frequently, especially after intercourse. Untreated, these infections can lead to kidney infections, sterility, and even death.

Tampons and **pads** are sometimes hard to find when traveling, especially in Australia's less populated areas like parts of the Northern Territory, so it may be advisable to take supplies along. **Reliable contraceptive devices** may also be difficult to find. Women on the pill should bring enough to allow for possible loss or extended stays. Bring a prescription, since forms of the pill vary a good deal.

INSURANCE

Travel insurance generally covers four basic areas: medical/health problems, property loss, trip cancellation/interruption, and emergency evacuation. Although your regular insurance policies may well extend to travel-related accidents, you may consider purchasing travel insurance if the cost of potential trip cancellation/interruption is greater than you can absorb. Prices for travel insurance purchased separately generally run about US$50 per week for full coverage, while trip cancellation/interruption may be purchased separately at a rate of about US$5.50 per US$100 of coverage.

Medical insurance (especially university policies) often covers costs incurred abroad; check with your provider. **US Medicare** does not cover foreign travel. Canadians are protected by their home province's health insurance plan for up to 90 days after leaving the country; check with the provincial Ministry of Health or Health Plan Headquarters for details. **Homeowners' insurance** (or your family's coverage) often covers theft during travel and loss of travel documents (passport, plane ticket, railpass, etc.) up to US$500.

ISIC and **ITIC** (see p. 27) provide basic insurance benefits, including US$100 per day of in-hospital sickness for up to 60 days, US$3000 of accident-related medical reimbursement, and US$25,000 for emergency medical transport. Cardholders have access to a toll-free 24hr. helpline (run by the insurance provider **TravelGuard**) for medical, legal, and financial emergencies overseas (US and Canada ☎ 877-370-4742, elsewhere US collect +1-715-345-0505). **American Express** (US ☎ 800-528-4800) grants most cardholders automatic car rental insurance (collision and theft, but not liability) and ground travel accident coverage of US$100,000 on flight purchases made with the card.

PACKING

Pack light: lay out only what you absolutely need, then take half the clothes and twice the money. The less you have, the less you have to lose (or store, or carry on your back). Save any extra space left for souvenirs or items you pick up along the way. If you plan to do a lot of hiking, see **Camping And The Outdoors,** p. 57.

LUGGAGE. Toting a suitcase or trunk is fine if you plan to stay in one or two cities and explore from there, but a very bad idea if you're going to be trekking through the Kimberly or hiking through the rainforest. A small backpack, rucksack, or courier bag may be useful as a daypack for sight-seeing expeditions; it doubles as an airplane carry-on. An empty, lightweight duffel bag packed inside your luggage may also be useful. Once abroad, you can fill your luggage with purchases and keep your dirty clothes in the duffel.

CLOTHING. No matter if it's the Wet or the Dry, it's always a good idea to bring a **warm jacket** or wool sweater, a **rain jacket** (Gore-Tex® is both waterproof and breathable), sturdy shoes or **hiking boots,** and **thick socks. Flip-flops** or waterproof sandals are crucial for grubby hostel showers. You may also want to add one outfit beyond the jeans and t-shirt uniform, and maybe a nicer pair of shoes if you plan to do any clubbing in the bigger cities.

SLEEPSACKS. Many hostels require that you either provide your own linen or rent sheets from them. Save cash by making your own sleepsack: fold a full-size sheet in half the long way, then sew it closed along the long side and one of the short sides. Keep in mind that some hostels in larger cities prohibit sleeping bags.

WASHING CLOTHES. *Let's Go* attempts to provide info on laundromats in the Practical Information and hostel listings. Most cities have laundromats, but sometimes it may be cheaper and easier to use a sink. Bring a small bar or tube of detergent soap, a small rubber ball to stop up the sink, and a travel clothesline.

ELECTRIC CURRENT. In Australia, electricity is 220/240 volts, and AC is 50Hz, enough to fry 110V North American appliances. Hardware stores sell adapters (to change the shape of the plug) and converters (to change the voltage). Don't make the mistake of using only an adapter (unless instructions state otherwise).

FIRST-AID KIT. For a basic first-aid kit, pack: contact lenses, bandages, pain reliever, antibiotic cream, a thermometer, a Swiss Army knife, tweezers, moleskin,

ESSENTIALS

decongestant, motion-sickness remedy, diarrhea or upset-stomach medication (Pepto Bismol), an antihistamine, sunscreen, insect repellent, and burn ointment.

OTHER USEFUL ITEMS. For safety purposes, you should bring a **money belt** and small **padlock.** Basic **outdoors equipment** (plastic water bottle, compass, waterproof matches, pocketknife, sunglasses, sunscreen, hat) may also prove useful. **Quick repairs** of torn garments can be done on the road with a needle and thread; also consider bringing electrical tape for patching tears. If you want to do laundry by hand, bring detergent, a small rubber ball to stop up the sink, and string for a makeshift clothes line. **Other things** you're liable to forget: an umbrella; sealable **plastic bags** (for damp clothes, soap, food, shampoo, and other spillables); an **alarm clock;** safety pins; rubber bands; a flashlight; earplugs; garbage bags; and a small **calculator.**

GETTING TO AUSTRALIA

When it comes to airfare, a little effort can save you a bundle. The key is to hunt around, to be flexible, and to ask persistently about discounts. Students, seniors, and those under 26 should never pay full price for a ticket.

AIRFARES

Airfares to Australia peak between December and February; holidays (see p. 23) are also expensive. The cheapest times to travel are between September and November. Midweek (M-Th morning) round-trip flights run US$40-50 cheaper than weekend flights, but they are generally more crowded and less likely to permit frequent-flier upgrades. Traveling with an "open return" ticket can be pricier than fixing a return date when buying the ticket. Round-trip flights are by far the cheapest; "open-jaw" (arriving in and departing from different cities, e.g. Los Angeles-Sydney and Melbourne-Sydney) tickets tend to be pricier. Patching one-way flights together is the most expensive way to travel. Flights between Australia's regional hubs—Sydney, Brisbane, Melbourne—will tend to be cheaper.

If Australia is only one stop on a more extensive globe-hop, consider a round-the-world (RTW) ticket. Tickets usually include at least 5 stops and are valid for about a year; prices range US$1200-5000. Try **Northwest Airlines/KLM** (US ☎ 800-447-4747; www.nwa.com) or **Star Alliance,** a consortium of 22 airlines including United Airlines (US ☎ 800-241-6522; www.star-alliance.com).

The privilege of spending 24 hours or more on a plane doesn't come cheap. Full-price round-trip **fares** to Australia from the US or Canada (depending upon which coast of each continent you are heading to and from) can be US$900-2000; from the UK, £500-1100; from New Zealand, NZ$400-700.

BUDGET AND STUDENT TRAVEL AGENCIES

While knowledgeable agents specializing in flights to Australia can make your life easy and help you save, they may not spend the time to find you the lowest possible fare—they get paid on commission. Travelers holding **ISIC and IYTC cards** (see p. 27) qualify for big discounts from student travel agencies. Most flights from budget agencies are on major airlines, but in peak season some may sell seats on less reliable chartered aircraft.

CTS Travel, 44 Goodge St., **London,** UK W1T 2AD (☎0207 636 0031; fax 637 5328; ctsinfo@ctstravel.co.uk).

STA Travel, 7890 S. Hardy Dr., Ste. 110, **Tempe,** AZ 85284, USA (24hr. reservations and info ☎800-781-4040; www.sta-travel.com). A student and youth travel organization with over 150 offices worldwide (check their website for a listing of all their offices). Ticket booking, travel insurance, railpasses, and more.

ESSENTIALS

Travel CUTS (Canadian Universities Travel Services Limited), 187 College St., **Toronto, ON** M5T 1P7 (☎416-979-2406; fax 979-8167; www.travelcuts.com). 60 offices across Canada. Also in the UK, 295-A Regent St., **London** W1R 7YA (☎0207 255 1944).

usit world (www.usitworld.com). Over 50 **usit campus** branches in the UK, including 52 Grosvenor Gardens, **London** SW1W 0AG (☎0870 240 10 10); **Manchester** (☎0161 273 1880); and **Edinburgh** (☎0131 668 3303). Nearly 20 **usit NOW** offices in Ireland, including 19-21 Aston Quay, O'Connell Bridge, **Dublin** 2 (☎01 602 1600; www.usit-now.ie), and **Belfast** (☎02 890 327 111; www.usitnow.com).

FLIGHT PLANNING ON THE INTERNET.

Many airline sites offer special last-minute deals on the Web. Other sites do the legwork and compile the deals for you—try www.bestfares.com, www.flights.com, www.hotdeals.com, www.onetravel.com, and www.travelzoo.com.

StudentUniverse (www.studentuniverse.com), **STA** (www.sta-travel.com), and **Orbitz.com** provide quotes on student tickets, while **Expedia** (www.expedia.com) and **Travelocity** (www.travelocity.com) offer full travel services. **Priceline** (www.priceline.com) allows you to specify a price, and obligates you to buy any ticket that meets or beats it; be prepared for inconvenient hours and odd routes. **Skyauction** (www.skyauction.com) allows you to bid on both last-minute and advance-purchase tickets.

An indispensable resource on the Internet is the *Air Traveler's Handbook* (www.cs.cmu.edu/afs/cs/user/mkant/Public/Travel/airfare.html), a comprehensive listing of links to everything you need to know before you board a plane.

Just one last note—to protect yourself, make sure that the site you use has a secure server before handing over any credit card details. Happy hunting!

COMMERCIAL AIRLINES

Commercial airlines' lowest regular offer is the **APEX** (Advance Purchase Excursion) fare, which provides confirmed reservations and allows "open-jaw" tickets. Generally, reservations must be made seven to 21 days ahead of departure, with seven- to 14-day minimum-stay and up to 90-day maximum-stay restrictions. These fares carry hefty cancellation and change penalties (fees rise in high season). Book peak-season APEX fares early; by October you may have a hard time getting your desired departure date. Use **Microsoft Expedia** (msn.expedia.com) or **Travelocity** (www.travelocity.com) to get an idea of the lowest published fares, then use the resources outlined here to try to beat them.

Popular carriers to Australia include **Air New Zealand** (www.airnewzealand.co.nz), **British Airways** (www.britishairways.com), **Cathay Pacific** (www.cathaypacific.om), **South African Airlines** (www.saa.co.za), and **United Airways** (www.united.com), most of which have daily nonstop flights from Los Angeles to Sydney. **Qantas** (www.qantas.com.au) is Australia's main airline and has the most international connections.

GETTING AROUND

BY PLANE

Because Australia is so large, many travelers, even many budget travelers, take a domestic flight at some point while touring the country. Oz Experience (p. 44) and Qantas offer an **Air-Bus Pass** with which travelers can fly one-way, and bus back (or vice versa) around Australia. Passes are valid for six months with unlimited stops;

all dates can be changed. **Flight Centre** (www.flightcentre.com.au) offers a plethora of Internet-only deals, including group rates.

Qantas: Reservations ☎ 13 13 13 in Australia, 800-227-4500 in the U.S. and Canada, 0845 7 747 767 in the UK; www.qantas.com.au. Qantas "boomerang passes" allow travelers to change flight dates free of charge on domestic flights; cities can be changed for $50. For international travelers (with the exception of New Zealanders and Fijians, who are not eligible), a boomerang pass may be the best domestic flight option (min. 2 flights, max. 10). One-way passes within zones are US$160, between zones starts at US$190. The first two segments must be purchased before arriving in Australia.

Regional Express (Rex): Reservations ☎ 13 17 13; www.regionalexpress.com. Formed from the acquisition and merger of Kendell and Hazelton Airlines in August, 2002. Offers service to much of South Australia, New South Wales, Victoria, and Tasmania.

VirginBlue: Reservations ☎ 13 67 89 in Australia, 7 3295 2296 outside Australia; www.virginblue.com.au. Service between all coastal cities.

BY TRAIN

The **Austrail Pass** (www.train-ticket.net/austral/austrail.htm) allows unlimited travel over consecutive days within a given period (14 days AUS$721, 21 days $934, 30 days $1130). The **Austrail Flexipass** allows you to purchase eight (US$599), 15 (AUS$852), 22 ($1217), or 29 ($1573) traveling days to be used over a six-month period. Both passes are only available to non-Australians and must be bought overseas. **Rail Australia** has agents in the US (☎ 800-423-2880), Canada (☎ 416-322-1034), New Zealand (☎ 09 639 0515), South Africa (☎ 021 419 9382), Japan (☎ 03 3818 5671), and the UK (☎ 87075 002 22). The **East Coast Discovery Pass** allows unlimited stops in one direction on the Eastern Seaboard within six months (Sydney-Cairns AUS$270, Melbourne-Cairns $359). For information on more passes, go to www.railpage.org.au/pass.html.

Each state runs its own rail service, and transfers between services may require a bus trip to the next station. For reservations and ticketing from the US, call ☎ 800 423 2880. Wheelchair access on interstate trains can be poor, as the corridors are often too narrow. Some but not all larger stations provide collapsible wheelchairs. Also, some stations have platforms that make it difficult to disembark. The main rail companies are:

Countrylink (☎ 13 22 32; www.countrylink.nsw.gov.au), based in New South Wales. Ages 4-15 and ISIC/concession card holders 50% discount.

V/Line (☎ 13 61 96; www.vline.vic.gov.au) in Victoria. Off-peak fares up to 30% discount. Children and concesions 50% discount on interstate travel.

Queensland Rail (☎ 13 22 32; www.qr.com.au) in Queensland. The cheapest and fastest way to travel Queensland's coast. Students 50% discount.

Westrail (☎ 13 10 53; www.wagr.wa.gov.au) in Western Australia. Pensioners, seniors, and children 50% discount.

Great Southern Railways (☎ 13 21 47; www.gsr.com.au) in South Australia and the Northern Territory. Consists of the *Indian Pacific*, the *Overland*, and *The Ghan*. Students and backpackers 50% discount, children and pensioners 55%..

BY BUS

Buses cover more of the rural landscape of Australia than do trains. Buses run regularly to major cities, but journeys off the beaten track may require a wait of a few days. It may be more cost efficient to buy a kilometer or multi-day pass if you are planning on doing a large amount of travel by bus. **Contiki Travel** (☎ 1-888-CONTIKI; www.contiki.com), offers comprehensive tour packages that include accommodations, transportation and some meals. They run 3-26 day tours starting at $295.

MCCAFFERTY'S/GREYHOUND. While Greyhound (☎ 13 20 30; www.greyhound.com.au) was recently acquired by McCafferty's (☎ 13 14 99; www.mccaffertys.com.au), the two lines generally operate under the name Greyhound and honor each other's tickets and passes.

Greyhound's 7- to 21-day passes allow you to travel on any route within 30 to 60 days, depending on the length of your pass; days of travel do not have to be consecutive. These passes cost between AUS$672 and AUS$1325. The **Aussie Explorer Pass** allows you to predetermine a route and take up to 12 months to get there, while an **Aussie Kilometer Pass** lets you choose a number of kilometers to be used on any Greyhound route (minimum 2000km, AUS$281). Most of these passes can be used to take **Greyhound Pioneer Tours,** which offer combinations of tours for National Parks and scenic spots in Central Australia, Western Australia, and the Top End.

McCafferty's **Travel Australia** passes are valid for 6-12 months (up to AUS$1116), and let travelers ride with unlimited stops one way along any of seven predetermined routes. A 10% discount is available for international students, pensioners, and backpacker card holders; the discount is 15% if the purchase is made outside of Australia. McCafferty's also offers an **Australian Roamer** pass, which allows long-distance travelers to pay by the kilometer (2000km AUS$239, 10,000km AUS$915); the Roamer pass is available only to backpacker card and ISIC card holders. Non-Australians can also get the **Discover Australia Day Pass,** but it must be purchased before arrival in Australia. The pass allows for unlimited travel on the McCafferty's network for an allotted time; you can choose between 7 (AUS$693) and 30 (AUS$1643) days worth of travel, to be redeemed within a range of 30 to 60 days.

OZ EXPERIENCE. This popular bus company offers backpacker packages with a lot of flexibility and charismatic drivers who double as tour guides. The packages must be purchased for predetermined routes (cheaper if bought outside of Australia), and travelers can usually take up to six months to finish with unlimited stopovers. Be prepared for a younger, more party-heavy crowd. (☎ 02 8356 1766 or 1300 30 00 28; www.ozexperience.com. YHA discount 5%.)

BY CAR

Some regions of Australia are virtually inaccessible without a car, and in many sparsely populated areas, public transportation options are simply inadequate. One of the major dilemmas of traveling in Australia, at least beyond the main coastal cities, is that the road system is in many areas basic and often poorly maintained. To travel on most outback roads and in many national parks, you will often need a **four-wheel-drive (4WD),** which unfortunately can double the cost of renting or buying. Shopping around well ahead of time is advisable.

RENTING

Although the cost of renting a car can be prohibitive for an individual traveler, rentals can become cost-efficient when traveling with a group.

RENTAL AGENCIES

You can generally make reservations before you leave by calling their offices in your home country. However, occasionally the price and availability information they give doesn't jive with what the local offices in Australia will tell you. Try

checking with both numbers to get the best price and most accurate information. Australia numbers and web addresses are listed below:

Avis (☎ 02 9353 9000, nationwide 13 63 33; www.avis.com). YHA member discounts available; quote code P081600 when making reservations.

Britz (☎ 800 331 454; www.britz.com) offers super saver 4WD discounts; rents to under 25 with no surcharge.

Budget (☎ 03 9915 3322, nationwide ☎ 1300 36 28 48; www.budget.com.au). YHA discounts available; quote code E013609.

Delta Europcar (☎ 03 9330 6160; www.deltaeuropcar.com.au).

Hertz (☎ 03 9698 2555, nationwide ☎ 13 30 39; www.hertz.com). YHA discounts available; quote CDP code 317961.

Thrifty (☎ 1300 36 72 27; www.thrifty.com.au).

To rent a car from most establishments, you need to be at least 21 years old. Some agencies require renters to be 25, and most charge those aged 21-24 an additional insurance fee (around AUS$15-25 per day). Policies and prices vary greatly. Small local operations occasionally rent to people under 21, but be sure to ask about the insurance coverage and deductible, and always read the fine print.

COSTS AND INSURANCE
Rental car prices start at around AUS$45 a day from national companies and AUS$30 from local agencies. Expect to pay more for larger cars and for 4WD. Cars with **automatic transmission** can cost up to AUS$15 a day more than standard manuals (stick shift), and in Western Australia, Northern Territory, and more remote areas of the eastern states, automatic transmission is hard to find at all. It is virtually impossible to find an automatic 4WD.

Many rental packages offer unlimited kilometers, while others offer 100-200km per day with a surcharge of approximately AUS25¢ per kilometer after that. Return the car with a full tank of petrol to avoid high fuel charges at the end. Be sure to ask whether the price includes **insurance** against theft and collision. Remember that if you are driving a conventional vehicle on an **unsealed road** (Australian for unpaved) in a rental car, you are almost never covered by insurance; ask about this before leaving the rental agency.

Beware that cars rented on an **American Express** or **Visa/Mastercard Gold or Platinum** credit cards in Australia might *not* carry the automatic insurance that they would in some other countries; check with your credit card company. Insurance plans almost always come with an **excess** (or deductible) of around AUS$1000 for conventional vehicles; excess ranges up to around AUS$2500 for younger drivers and for 4WD. This means you pay for all damages up to that sum, unless they are the fault of another vehicle. The excess you will be quoted applies to collisions with other vehicles; collisions with non-vehicles, such as trees or kangaroos ("single-vehicle collisions"), will cost you even more. The excess can often be reduced or waived entirely if you pay an additional charge, between AUS$5-20 per day.

National chains often allow one-way rentals, picking up in one city and dropping off in another. However, there is usually a minimum hire period and sometimes an extra drop-off charge of several hundred dollars.

BUYING AND SELLING USED CARS

Buying used cars and then reselling them is popular among long-term travelers or those too young to rent. Automotive independence costs around AUS$1600-5000. However, used car dealers have been known to rip off foreigners, especially backpackers. Research prices, or ask a trustworthy Aussie about reasonable prices; some people recommend bringing an Aussie along when purchasing the car. Buying from a private owner or fellow traveler is often a cheaper alternative. In many cities, hundreds of private sellers rent space at used car lots, as buyers stroll around and haggle. Hostel or university bulletin boards are another good bet. In Sydney, check the *Weekly Trading Post* on Thursdays for used car advertisements, and the *Daily Telegraph Mirror* and *Sydney Morning Herald* on Saturdays. When selling a car back, consider the high tourist season for the region you're in. Vehicles are also easier to sell if they are registered in the state where they are being sold—new owners need to register the car, and some states don't allow registration transfer by mail. If you buy a car privately, check the registration papers against the license of the person who is selling the car.

WHAT TO LOOK FOR. Before buying a used car, check with the local branch of the AAA, as states have varying requirements for a transfer of ownership, and local organizations can advise you on how to get your money's worth. The NRMA in New South Wales publishes *International Tourists Car Buying Advice* and *Worry-free Guide to Buying a Car*. In Victoria, all cars are required to carry a Road Worthiness Certificate. Local auto clubs also do mechanical inspections (NRMA inspections ☎ 1300 362 802).

BEFORE YOU BUY. When buying a car, call the **Register of Encumbered Vehicles** or check online at www.revs.nsw.gov.au to confirm that a vehicle is unencumbered—that it has not been reported as stolen and has no outstanding financial obligations nor traffic warrants. For cars registered in NSW, VIC, ACT, QLD, or NT, ☎ 02 9600 0022 or ☎ 1800 42 49 88; in TAS, ☎ 03 6233 5201; in SA, ☎ 13 10 84; in WA, ☎ 1300 30 40 24. You'll need to provide the registration-, engine-, and VIN/chassis-numbers of the vehicle. In New South Wales, a car must have a pink inspection certificate to guarantee that it is roadworthy. It is valid for 20 days and available at most service stations.

REGISTRATION. Within two weeks after purchase, you'll need to **register** the car in your name at the Motor Vehicle Registry. Although requirements vary between states, re-registration costs about AUS$15, and must be completed within about two weeks. The local automobile organization can always help.

INSURANCE AT A GLANCE
Third-party personal injury insurance (a.k.a. green slip): automatically included with every registered vehicle. Covers any person who may be injured except the driver at fault; does not cover damage or repairs to cars or property.
Third-party property damage insurance: covers cost of repair to other people's cars or property if you're responsible for an accident.
Full comprehensive insurance: covers damage to all vehicles.
International Insurance Certificate: proof of liability insurance, required of all rented, leased, and borrowed cars.

INTERNATIONAL DRIVING PERMITS

If you plan to drive a car while in Australia, your home country's driver's license will suffice. If your home country's driver's license is not printed in English, you must have an English translation with you. After driving in the same state for three months, you must have an International Driving Permit (IDP). Your IDP, valid for one year, must be issued in your own country before you depart; AAA affiliates cannot issue IDPs valid in their own country. You must be 18+ to receive the IDP. A valid driver's license from your home country must always accompany the IDP. An application for an IDP usually needs to include one or two photos, a current local license, an additional form of identification, and a fee. To apply, contact the national or local branch of your home country's Automobile Association.

Canada: www.caa.ca/CAAInternet/travelservices/internationaldocumentation/idp-travel.htm. Permits CDN$13.

Ireland: www.aaireland.ie/travel/id_permit.htm. Permits €5.08.

New Zealand: www.nzaa.co.nz/cg/MainMenu. Permits NZ$12.

South Africa: www.aasa.co.za/holiday/perm.html. Permits ZAR45.

UK: www.theaa.co.uk/motoringandtravel/idp/. Permits UK£4.

US: www.aaa.com/aaa/240/sne/travel/idpc.html. Permits US$10.

ON THE ROAD

Australians drive on the **left side** of the road. In unmarked intersections, a driver must yield to vehicles entering the intersection from the right. In some big cities, right turns often must take place from the farthest left lane, after the light has already turned red—keep your eyes peeled for signs to that effect. By law, **seat belts** must be worn. Children under 40 lb. should ride only in a special kind of carseat, available for a small fee at most car rental agencies. The speed limit in most cities is 60kph (35mph) and on highways 100 or 110kph (62 or 68mph). Radar guns are often used to patrol well-traveled roads; sly speed cameras nab offenders on less populated paths. **Petrol (gasoline)** prices vary by state, but average about AUS80¢-$1 per liter in cities and from AUS90¢-$1.05 per liter in outlying areas.

PRECAUTIONS. When traveling in the summer or in the outback, bring substantial amounts of water (a suggested 5L of **water** per person per day) for drinking and for the radiator. For long outback drives, travelers should register with police before beginning the trek, and again upon arrival at the destination. Check with the local automobile club for details. In the north, **four-wheel-drive (4WD)** is essential for seeing the parks, particularly in the Wet, when dirt roads turn to mud. When traveling in the outback or for long distances, make sure tires are in good repair and have enough air, and get good maps. A **compass** and a **car manual** can also be very useful. You should always carry a **spare tire** and **jack, jumper cables, extra oil, flares, a torch (flashlight),** and **heavy blankets** (in case your car breaks down at night or in the winter). If you don't know how to **change a tire,** learn before heading into the outback. Blowouts on dirt roads are exceedingly common. If you do have a breakdown, **stay with your car;** if you wander off, it's less likely that trackers will find you.

DANGERS. Australia's highway system can be tough, and road conditions are not consistent. Find out ahead of time whether roads are sealed, especially if you're driving a conventional vehicle. **Unsealed** roads dominate rural Australia, ranging from smooth, hard-packed sand to an eroded mixture of mud, sand, and stones. Locals are a good source of information on the road conditions in the immediate vicinity. When driving on unsealed roads, call regional tourist boards ahead of time for road conditions, especially in the North, as the Wet sometimes makes roads impassible for months after the rains stop. Furthermore, you should allow at least twice as much time as you would for travel on paved roads. One can skid on gravel almost as badly as on ice. **Kangaroos are a serious danger** to drivers; they may be cute, but they are large and will jump in front of or into the side of cars. Dusk and dawn are particularly dangerous times when 'roos are usually hopping about.

ASSISTANCE. The **Australian Automobile Association (AAA)** is the national umbrella organization for all of the local automobile organizations. You won't often see it called the AAA, though; in most states, the local organization is called the **Royal Automobile Club (RAC).** In New South Wales and the ACT, it's the **National Royal Motorist Association (NRMA).** In the Northern Territory, it's the **Automobile Association of the Northern Territory (AANT).** Services—from breakdown assistance to map provision—are similar to those offered by automobile associations in other countries. Most overseas organizations have reciprocal membership with AAA (includ-

GET CARD. TRAVEL HARD.

There's only one way to max out your travel experience and make the most of your time on the road: The International Student Identity Card.

 Packed with travel discounts, benefits and services, this card will keep your travel days and your wallet full. Get it before you hit it!

Visit **ISICUS.com** to get the full story on the benefits of carrying the ISIC.

90 minutes, wash & dry (one sock missing).
5 minutes to book online (Detroit to Mom's).

Save money & time on student and faculty travel at **StudentUniverse.com**

 StudentUniverse.com   **Real Travel Deals**

ing AAA in the US; AA and RAC in the UK; NZAA in New Zealand; AASA in South Africa). Bring proof of your membership to Australia, and you'll be able to use AAA facilities free of charge. **AAA roadside assistance** can be reached at ☎ 13 11 11, and 08 8941 0611 in the Northern Territory. It's possible to join AAA through any state's organization. *Let's Go* lists the location of the state automobile organization in each state introduction.

BY BICYCLE

Australia has many **bike tracks** to attract cyclers. Much of the country is flat, and road bikers can travel long distances without needing to huff and puff excessively. In theory, bicycles can go on **buses and trains,** but most major bus companies require you to disassemble your bike and pay a flat AUS$15 fee. You may not be allowed to bring your bike into train compartments. Safe and secure cycling requires a quality helmet and lock. A good **helmet** costs about AUS$40—much cheaper than critical head surgery. Helmets are required by law in Australia. Travel with good **maps** from the state Automobile Associations.

The **Bicycle Federation of Australia (BFA),** GPO Box 3222, Canberra ACT 2601 (☎ 03 9827 4453; www.bfa.asn.au), a nonprofit bicycle advocacy group, publishes *Australian Cyclist* magazine and has a list of regional bicycling organizations on its web page.

BY THUMB

LET'S GO DOES NOT RECOMMEND HITCHHIKING. *Let's Go* strongly urges you to seriously consider the risks before you choose to hitch. We do not recommend hitching as a safe means of transportation, and none of the information printed here is intended to do so.

Given the infrequency of public transportation to several popular destinations, travelers often need to find other ways to get where they're going. Hostels frequently have message boards where those seeking rides and those seeking to share the cost of gas can meet up. On the east coast, backpacker traffic moves from Sydney to Brisbane (and possibly as far north as Cairns, see p. 400), and those who go with the flow are sure to make friends who have wheels.

Standing on the side of the highway with your thumb out is much more dangerous than making a new friend at your hostel. Safety issues are always imperative, even when you're traveling with another person. **Hitching** (Australian for hitchhiking) means risking assault, sexual harassment, and unsafe driving, all while entrusting your life to a random person who happens to stop beside you on the road. If you're a woman traveling alone, don't hitch. A man and a woman are a safer combination; two men will have a harder time finding a ride, as drivers also must be careful. Avoid getting in the back of a two-door car (there is little chance of escape if in trouble), and never let go of your backpack. Hitchhiking at night can be particularly dangerous. Don't accept a ride that you are not entirely comfortable with. If you ever feel threatened, insist on being let off, but keep in mind that the vast distances between towns on some stretches of highway increase your chance of being left literally in the middle of nowhere.

If you decide to hitch, choose a spot on the side of the road with ample space for a car to pull over, where traffic is not moving too fast. The edges of town are ideal as people have not yet accelerated to highway speed. Dress nicely and keep your backpack in full view, as it tells people you're a backpacker and justifies your reason for hitching. A sign with your destination marked in large letters can also help.

KEEPING IN TOUCH

BY MAIL

SENDING MAIL HOME FROM AUSTRALIA

Airmail is the best way to send mail home. **Aerogrammes,** printed sheets that fold into envelopes and travel via airmail, are available at post offices. Write "par avion" or "air mail" on the front. Most post offices will charge exorbitant fees or simply refuse to send aerogrammes with enclosures. **Surface mail** is by far the cheapest and slowest way to send mail. It takes one to three months to cross the Atlantic and two to four to cross the Pacific—good for items you won't need to see for a while, such as souvenirs or other articles you've acquired along the way that are weighing down your pack. The **Australia Post** website (www.auspost.com) has a postage calculator for international deliveries. These are standard rates for mail from Australia to:

Canada: Allow 5-7 days for regular airmail home. Postcards/aerogrammes cost AUS$1. Letters up to 50g cost $1.50; packages up to 0.5kg $11.50, up to 2kg $38.50.

Ireland: Allow 4-5days for regular airmail home. Postcards/aerogrammes cost AUS$1. Letters up to 50g cost $1.50; packages up to 0.5kg $13, up to 2kg $46.

New Zealand: Allow 3-4 days for regular airmail home. Postcards/aerogrammes cost AUS$1. Letters up to 50g cost $1; packages up to 0.5kg $7.50, up to 2kg $22.50.

UK: Allow 4-5 days for regular airmail home. Postcards/aerogrammes cost AUS$1. Letters up to 50g cost $1.50; packages up to 0.5kg $13, up to 2kg $46.

US: Allow 4-6 days for regular airmail home. Postcards/aerogrammes cost AUS$1. Letters up to 50g cost $1.50; packages up to 0.5kg $11.50, up to 2kg $38.50.

SENDING MAIL TO AUSTRALIA

Mark envelopes "air mail" or "par avion" or your letter or postcard will never arrive. In addition to the standard postage system whose rates are listed below, **Federal Express** (Australia ☎ 13 26 10; US and Canada ☎ 800-247-4747; New Zealand ☎ 0800 73 33 39; UK ☎ 0800 12 38 00; www.fedex.com) handles express mail services from most of the above countries to Australia; they can get a letter from New York to Sydney in three business days for US$33.15. Rates among non-US locations are prohibitively expensive (e.g. London to Sydney costs UK£31.80).

Canada: www.canadapost.ca. Allow 4-10 days for regular airmail to Australia. Postcards and letters up to 30g cost CDN$1.25; packages up to 0.5kg CDN$10.00, up to 2kg CDN$38.55.

Ireland: www.letterpost.ie. Allow 5-7 days for regular airmail to Australia. Postcards and letters up to 25g cost €0.57. Add €3.40 for Swiftpost International (1 day faster).

Japan: www.post.yusei.go.jp. Allow 4-5 days for regular airmail to Australia. Postcards 70¥; letters up to 25g 90¥, up to 50g 160¥; packages up to 0.5kg 780¥, up to 2kg cost 2,150¥.

New Zealand: www.nzpost.co.nz/nzpost/inrates. Allow approximately 7 days for regular airmail to Australia. Postcards NZ$1.50. Letters up to 20g cost NZ$1.50-2; small parcels up to 0.5kg NZ$6.89-24, up to 2kg NZ$15.09-39.

UK: www.consignia-online.com. Allow 4-8 days for airmail to Australia. Letters up to 20g cost UK£0.65; packages up to 0.5kg UK£5, up to 2kg UK£19.20. UK Swiftair delivers letters a day faster for an extra UK£2.85.

US: http://ircalc.usps.gov. Allow 7-10 days for regular airmail to Australia. Postcards/aerogrammes cost US70¢; letters under 1 oz. US80¢; packages under 1 lb. cost US$14.50. **US Global Priority Mail** delivers small/large flat-rate envelopes to Australia in 4 business days for US$5/$9.

RECEIVING MAIL IN AUSTRALIA

There are several ways to arrange pick-up of letters sent to you by friends and relatives while you are abroad. Mail can be sent fairly reliably via **Poste Restante** (General Delivery) to almost any city or town in Australia with a post office. Address *Poste Restante* letters like so:

Croc O'DOYLE

C/- Poste Restante

City STATE Postcode

The mail will go to a special desk in the central post office unless you specify a post office by street address. It's best to use the largest post office, since mail may be sent there regardless. Bring passport (or other photo ID) for pick-up.

BY TELEPHONE

CALLING HOME FROM AUSTRALIA

A **calling card** is probably your cheapest bet. You can frequently call collect without even possessing a company's calling card just by calling their access number and following the instructions. See the **Inside Back Cover** of this book for calling card access numbers in Australia.

Let's Go has recently formed a partnership with ekit.com to provide a calling card that offers a number of services, including email and voice messaging services. Before purchasing any calling card, always be sure to compare rates with other cards, and to make sure it serves your needs. For more information, visit www.letsgo.ekit.com.

You can usually make **direct international calls** from pay phones, but if you aren't using a calling card you may need to drop your coins as quickly as your words. Prepaid phone cards and occasionally major credit cards can be used for direct international calls, but they are less cost-efficient. Although incredibly convenient, in-room hotel calls invariably include an arbitrary and sky-high surcharge.

The expensive alternative to dialing direct or using a calling card is using an international operator to place a **collect call;** sometimes in an emergency, though, this is the only way to reach home.

 PLACING INTERNATIONAL CALLS. To call Australia from home or to call home from Australia, dial:

    1. The **international dialing prefix.** To dial out of: **Australia,** dial 0011; **Canada** or the **US,** 011; **Ireland, New Zealand,** or the **UK,** 00; **South Africa,** 09.

    2. The **country code** of the country you want to call. To call **Australia,** dial 61; **Canada** or the **US,** 1; **Ireland,** 353; **New Zealand,** 64; **South Africa,** 27; the **UK,** 44;

    3. The **city/area code.** *Let's Go* lists the city/area codes for cities and towns in Australia opposite the city or town name, next to a ☎. If the first digit is a zero (e.g., 02 for Sydney), omit the zero when calling from abroad (e.g., dial 2 from Canada to reach Sydney).

    4. The **local number.**

ESSENTIALS

ESSENTIALS

CALLING WITHIN AUSTRALIA

Public phones are easy to find nearly everywhere you go in Australia. Some phone booths in Australia are coin-operated, some are phone-card operated, and some accept either coins or phone cards. Local calls from phone booths cost AUS40¢. In addition to phone booths, public phones (often small blue or orange boxes) can sometimes be found in bars and hotels, and local calls on these often cost AUS50¢. **Long-distance calls** within Australia use STD (Subscriber Trunk Dialing) services. You must dial an **area code** (listed next to towns) before the eight-digit number.

Australia has two main telecommunications companies: **Optus** and **Telstra.** Telstra rules every local market and much long-distance, while Optus concentrates on mobile phone service and long-distance. Most phone cards have a toll-free access telephone number and a personal identification number (PIN), though some must be inserted into the phone. As phone cards have grown in popularity, so have the number of booths accepting cards only. Therefore, if heading to a remote area, it might be best to have both types of cards. A few public phones (at airports, city center locations, and major hotels) even take **credit cards.**

For **directory assistance,** you can call toll-free ☎013. Six-digit phone numbers beginning with **13** are information numbers that can be dialed from anywhere in Australia for the price of a local call. Numbers beginning with **1300** operate similarly. Numbers beginning **1800 or 0800** are **toll-free.**

Mobile phones are everywhere in urban Australia. Mobile phone numbers are either nine or 10 digits; the nine-digit phone numbers begin 01* and ten-digit numbers begin 04**. Usually the caller picks up the charges when calling a mobile phone, and charges run about AUS80¢ per minute. Some hotel owners ask guests to register their mobile phones when they check in.

EMAIL AND INTERNET

Finding Internet access in Australia is simple. Most big cities have **Internet shops** that also offer discounted international calling. These coffee-less counterparts to **cybercafes** offer access from as low as **free** to as high as $8 per hour. Coin-operated Internet kiosks are an expensive (usually $2 per 10min.) yet common options in cities and many hostels. In addition, virtually all public libraries now offer free access to the web, though sometimes you are restricted from checking email or must have a prior reservation. *Let's Go* lists Internet access options in the **Practical Information** section of towns and cities. Other Internet access points in Australia can be found at www.gnomon.com.au/publications/netaccess.

TIME ZONES

Time zones in Australia can be a bit confusing, especially when only certain states across the continent observe Daylight Savings Time (late October to late March), marking the official beginning of summer. This means that Australia's times zones follow state borders both vertically and horizontally. Greenwich Mean Time (GMT) is not affected by **Daylight Savings Time (DST),** providing a standard to calculate differences in time zones. In the table below, the rows on the left represent where you are. The columns across the top represent where you wish to know the time. To calculate the time in a different zone, simply add or subtract the difference in hours between the two places. For example, if it is noon in GMT, then it is 10pm in Victoria. Remember that the date is affected in some cases—Australia is ahead of the Western Hemisphere, so Monday evening in New York is Tuesday morning in Sydney. All regions that observe DST have an asterisk. Therefore, during DST, if you start in a row with an asterisk, you must subtract one hour. If you end in a column with an asterisk, you must add one hour. For example, during DST if it is noon in GMT, then it is 11pm in Victoria. In 2003, all states except Tasmania begin DST at 2am on October 26, while Tasmania begins its observation on October 5. DST ends on March 28, 2004, in all states.

London is 1 hour ahead of GMT from the last Sunday in March to the last Sunday in October due to DST. **New York City** is normally 5 hours behind GMT. However, from the first Sunday in April to the last Sunday in October, NYC is only 4 hours behind GMT due to DST.

	GMT	WA	NT	SA*	QLD	ACT, NSW, TAS, VIC*
Greenwich Mean Time		+8	+9.5	+9.5	+10	+10
Western Australia	-8		+1.5	+1.5	+2	+2
Northern Territory	-9.5	-1.5		0	+0.5	+0.5
Southern Australia*	-9.5	-1.5	0		+0.5	+0.5
Queensland	-10	-2	-0.5	-0.5		0
ACT, NSW, Tasmania, Victoria*	-10	-2	-0.5	-0.5	0	

E S S E N T I A L S

ACCOMMODATIONS

HOSTELS

In Australia, a "youth hostel" is more commonly known as a "backpackers." Hostels are generally dorm-style accommodations, often in single-sex large rooms with bunk beds, although most hostels do offer private rooms or doubles for families and couples. Some have kitchens and utensils for your use, bike rentals, storage areas, and laundry facilities. Remember that crime occurs in even the most demure-looking hostel; bring your own **padlock** for your storage locker. Many hostels allow guests to leave valuables in a safe at the front desk. Some hostel owners provide transportation to and from bus stations and airports. In Australia, a bed in a hostel will average around AUS\$15-20. A **VIP** discount card offered by Backpackers Resorts International gets AUS\$1 off per night at many hostels. *Let's Go* designates these hostels with a VIP at the end of the listing. The two most common hostel chains in Australia are YHA and NOMADS (see below). A list of many hostels, regardless of affiliation, can be found at www.hostels.com.

 A HOSTELER'S BILL OF RIGHTS. There are certain standard features that we do not include in our hostel listings. Unless we state otherwise, you can expect that every hostel has: no lockout, no curfew, free hot showers, secure storage, and no key deposit.

HOSTELLING INTERNATIONAL

Joining the youth hostel association in your own country (listed below) automatically grants you membership privileges in **Hostelling International (HI)**, a federation of national hosteling associations. The Australian branch of HI, **Youth Hostel Association (YHA)**, has hostels and agencies throughout Australia that are typically less expensive than private hostels. Many accept reservations via the **International Booking Network** (Australia ☎02 9261 1111; Canada ☎800-663-5777; England and Wales ☎1629 58 14 18; Northern Ireland ☎1232 32 47 33; Republic of Ireland ☎01 830 1766; NZ ☎03 379 9808; Scotland ☎8701 55 32 55; US ☎800-909-4776; all international reservations ☎202-783-6161; www.hostelbooking.com). HI's umbrella organization's web page (www.iyhf.org) lists the websites and phone numbers of all national associations.

Most HI hostels also honor **guest memberships**—you'll get a blank card with space for six validation stamps. Each night you'll pay a nonmember supplement (one-sixth the membership fee) and earn one guest stamp; get six stamps, and you're a member. Most student travel agencies (see p. 38) sell HI cards, as do all of the national hosteling organizations listed below. All prices listed below are valid for **one-year memberships** unless otherwise noted.

Australian Youth Hostels Association (AYHA), Level 3, 10 Mallett St., Camperdown NSW 2050 (☎02 9565 1699; fax 9565 1325; www.yha.org.au). AUS$52, under 18 AUS$16.

Hostelling International-Canada (HI-C), 400-205 Catherine St., Ottawa, ON K2P 1C3 (☎800-663-5777 or 613-237-7884; fax 613-237-7868; info@hostellingintl.ca; www.hihostels.ca). CDN$35, under 18 free.

An Óige (Irish Youth Hostel Association), 61 Mountjoy St., Dublin 7 (☎01 830 4555; fax 830 5808; anoige@iol.ie; www.irelandyha.org). €15, under 18 €7.50.

Youth Hostels Association of New Zealand (YHANZ), 193 Cashel St., 3rd Fl. Union House, P.O. Box 436, Christchurch 1 (☎03 379 9970; fax 365 4476; info@yha.org.nz; www.yha.org.nz). NZ$40, under 17 free.

Hostels Association of South Africa, 73 St. George's House, 3rd fl., P.O. Box 4402, Cape Town 8000 (☎021 424 2511; fax 424 4119; info@hisa.org.za; www.hisa.org.za). SAR45.

Scottish Youth Hostels Association (SYHA), 7 Glebe Crescent, Stirling FK8 2JA (☎01786 89 14 00; fax 89 13 33; www.syha.org.uk). UK£6.

Youth Hostels Association (England and Wales) Ltd., Trevelyan House, Dimple Rd., Matlock, Devonshire DE4 3YH, UK (☎01629 59 26 00; fax 59 27 02; www.yha.org.uk). UK£13, under 18 UK£6.50; families UK£26.

Hostelling International Northern Ireland (HINI), 22-32 Donegal Rd., Belfast BT12 5JN, Northern Ireland (☎02890 31 54 35; fax 43 96 99; info@hini.org.uk; www.hini.org.uk). UK£10, under 18 UK£6.

Hostelling International-American Youth Hostels (HI-AYH), 733 15th St. NW, #840, Washington, D.C. 20005 (☎202-783-6161; fax 783-6171; hiayhserv@hiayh.org; www.hiayh.org). US$25, under 18 free.

NOMADS

Another large hosteling chain in Australia is NOMADS Backpackers (www.nomadsworld.com). Though it has only about one third as many locations as YHA, the services and amenities are similar. You don't have to be a member to stay at a NOMADS hostel. The NOMADS Adventure Card (AUS$29) offers discount international calling, cheaper rates at many Internet cafes, and either $1 off per night or seventh night free at NOMADS. For reservations, call ☎1800 819 883 (from overseas, +8 8363 7633; fax 8363 7968), or write to bookings@nomadsworld.com.

HOTELS

While **hotels** in large cities are similar to those in the rest of the world, "hotels" in rural Australia, particularly in Victoria and New South Wales, are simple furnished rooms above local pubs. Some resemble fancy Victorian-era lodging with grand back staircases, high tin ceilings, and wrap-around verandas. A simple breakfast may be included and there's occasionally a common kitchen. Others have been converted to long-term worker housing, and are thus less conducive to brief overnight stays. Singles in these hotels usually cost AUS$15-30. This generally includes a towel, a shared bathroom, and a private bedroom (no bunks, usually). The pubs are fully functional downstairs, so it's a good idea to choose a quieter one if you're fond of tucking in early. **Motels** in Australia are accommodations with parking.

BED AND BREAKFASTS

For a cozy alternative to impersonal hotel rooms, B&Bs (pri\
rooms available to travelers) range from the acceptable to the su\
sometimes go out of their way to be accommodating by giving pe\
or offering home-cooked meals. On the other hand, many B&Bs\
phones, TVs, or private bathrooms. Rooms in B&Bs generally cost A\
single and AUS$60-100 for a double but are more expensive in touri\

Several travel guides and reservation services specialize in B&B\
www.babs.com.au for a list of Australian B&Bs. **Bed and Breakfast Australia,** P.O. Box 448, Homebush St., Sydney NSW 2140 (☎02 9763 5833; fax 9763 1677; www.bedandbreakfast.com.au) can plan itineraries and make advance bookings.

UNIVERSITY DORMS

Many colleges and universities open their residence halls to travelers when school is not in session; some do so even during term-time. Getting a room may take a couple of phone calls and require advanced planning, but rates tend to be low, and many offer free local calls. *Let's Go* lists colleges that rent dorm rooms among the accommodation listings for appropriate cities.

Typical university holidays include most of September and the summer break from late November to late February. Easter break lasts for two weeks, while winter break encompasses the first two weeks of July. No one policy covers all institutions. Contact the universities directly; the Australian Tourist Commission has contact info at www.australia.com, under "Traveller's Resources," then "Special Interest Fact Sheets," then "Student Travel." Demand is high, so book ahead.

CAMPING AND THE OUTDOORS

If your travels take you to Australia when the weather is agreeable, camping is by far the cheapest way to go. The ubiquitous caravan parks offer sites without power for campers, and some hostels have camping facilities or at least allow guests to pitch tents in the yard. Unpowered campsites can vary in price from free to AUS$20 for a prime spot during Christmas holidays, and powered sites go for about $3-5 more. Caravan parks also offer unpowered sites, and some hostels either have camping facilities or will allow guests to pitch tents in the yard. The flexibility of camping allows you to access the more remote corners of the country's numerous wilderness areas.

USEFUL PUBLICATIONS & RESOURCES

A variety of publishing companies offer hiking guidebooks to meet the educational needs of novice or expert. For information about camping, hiking, and biking, write or call the publishers listed below to receive a free catalog.

Automobile Association, Contact Ctr., Car Ellison House, William Armstrong Dr., Newcastle-upon-Tyne, UK NE4 7YA. (☎0870 600 0371; fax 0191 235 5111; www.theaa.uk).

Sierra Club Books, 85 Second St., 2nd fl., San Francisco, CA 94105 (☎415-977-5500; www.sierraclub.org/books). Publishes general resource books on hiking, camping, and women traveling in the outdoors.

The Mountaineers Books, 1001 SW Klickitat Way #201, Seattle, WA 98134 (☎800-553-4453 or 206-223-6303; fax 800-568-7604; www.mountaineersbooks.org). Over 400 titles on hiking, biking, mountaineering, natural history, and conservation.

Other publications about camping and hiking are available from the **NSW National Parks and Wildlife Service Head Office,** Level 1, 43 Bridge St., Hurstville NSW 2220 (☎02 9585 6444; fax 9585 6555; www.npws.nsw.gov.au; open M-F 8:30am-5pm). **Australia Outdoor Connection** (http://flinders.com.au/home.htm), sponsored by 's Camping in Adelaide, provides camping and environmental information inks. For **topographical maps of Australia**, contact the **Australian Surveying & and Information Group (AUSLIG;** ☎ 02 6201 4201 or 0800 80 01 73; www.auslig.gov.au), or write to P.O. Box 2, Belconnen ACT 2616. AUSLIG publishes over 500 maps (most $7.50, plus shipping).

NATIONAL PARKS

A major source of pride for Australians—and a highlight for many visitors—is the number and variety of national parks across the continent. From the jagged ranges of the far northwest to the scrub plains of the Red Centre to the great sandy beaches of the east coast and the mountains of the southwest, Australia offers a dramatically changing landscape, much of which, thanks to government protection, is accessible to campers, climbers, and bushwalkers of all levels.

Most national parks require visitor fees; day passes are usually around AUS$10 per vehicle, while Parks Passes allow you to make unlimited visits to selected parks within a given period. Some parks require camping permits (usually around AUS$5) which can be obtained from the local ranger station. The list below contains contact information for each state's parks service, most of whom provide free publications on state and national protected areas. For direct links to individual parks across Australia, visit www.ea.gov.au/pa/contacts.html.

Australian Bushwalking & Camping (www.galactic.net.au/bushwalking) offers a list of walks and parks, along with valuable tips and links to national parks.

New South Wales National Parks Centre, 102 George St., The Rocks, Sydney NSW 2000 (☎ 02 9253 4600; fax 9251 8482; www.npws.nsw.gov.au).

Northern Territory Visitors Centre, 22 Cavenagh St., Darwin NT 0800 (☎ 08 8941 2167; fax 8941 2815; www.northernterritory.com).

Queensland Parks and Wildlife Service, Dept. of Environment, P.O. Box 155, Brisbane QLD 4002 (☎ 07 3227 8185; www.epa.qld.gov.au).

Nature Foundation South Australia, P.O. Box 448, Hindmarsh SA 5007 (☎ 1300 366 191; fax 08 8340 2506; www.naturefoundationsa.asn.au).

Tasmania Parks & Wildlife Service, GPO Box 44, Hobart, TAS 7001 (☎ 1300 368 550; www.parks.tas.gov.au).

Parks Victoria, Level 10, 535 Bourke St., Melbourne VIC 3000 (☎ 03 8627 4699; fax 9629 5563; www.parkweb.vic.gov.au).

Conservation and Land Management, Western Australia, Locked Bag 104, Bentley Delivery Ctr. 6983 (head office ☎ 08 9442 0300, general enquiries 9334 0333; fax 9334 0466; www.calm.wa.gov.au).

CAMPING AND HIKING EQUIPMENT

WHAT TO BUY...

Good camping equipment is both sturdy and light. Camping equipment is generally more expensive in Australia, New Zealand, and the UK than in North America.

Sleeping Bag: Most sleeping bags are rated by season ("summer" means 30-40°F at night; "four-season" or "winter" often means below 0°F). Prices range US$80-210 for a summer synthetic to US$250-300 for a good down winter bag. **Sleeping bag pads** include foam pads (US$10-20), air mattresses (US$15-50), and Therm-A-Rest self-inflating pads (US$45-80). Bring a **stuff sack** to store your bag and keep it dry.

Tent: Good 2-person tents start at US$90, 4-person at US$300. Seal the seams of your tent with waterproofer, and make sure it has a rain fly. Other tent accessories include a **battery-operated lantern,** a **plastic groundcloth,** and a **nylon tarp.**

Backpack: Any serious backpacking requires a pack of at least 4000 in^3 (16,000cc), plus 500 in^3 for sleeping bags in internal-frame packs. Sturdy backpacks cost anywhere from US$125-420–this is one area where it doesn't pay to skimp. Either buy a **waterproof backpack cover,** or store all of your belongings in plastic bags inside your pack.

Boots: Be sure to wear hiking boots with good **ankle support.** They should fit snugly and comfortably over 1-2 pairs of wool socks and thin liner socks. Break in boots over several weeks first in order to spare yourself painful and debilitating blisters.

Other Necessities: Synthetic layers, like those made of polypropylene, and a **pile jacket** will keep you warm even when wet. A **"space blanket"** will help you to retain your body heat and doubles as a groundcloth (US$5-15). Plastic **water bottles** are virtually shatter- and leak-proof. Bring **water-purification tablets** for when you can't boil water. In Australia, fires are only permitted in designated fireplaces; to cook elsewhere you'll need a **camp stove** (the classic Coleman starts at US$40) and a propane-filled **fuel bottle** to operate it. Also, don't forget a first-aid kit, pocketknife, insect repellent, calamine lotion, and waterproof matches or a lighter.

...AND WHERE TO BUY IT

The mail-order/online companies listed below offer lower prices than many retail stores, but a visit to a local camping or outdoors store will give you a good sense of the look and weight of certain items.

Campmor, 28 Parkway, P.O. Box 700, Upper Saddle River, NJ 07458 (US ☎800-525-4784; outside US ☎+1 201-825-8300; www.campmor.com).

Discount Camping, 880 Main North Rd., Pooraka, SA 5095 (☎08 8262 3399; fax 8260 6240; www.discountcamping.com.au).

Eastern Mountain Sports (EMS), 1 Vose Farm Rd., Peterborough, NH 03458 (☎888-463-6367 or 603-924-7231; www.shopems.com).

L.L. Bean, Freeport, ME 04033 (US and Canada ☎800-441-5713; UK ☎0800 891 297; elsewhere, call US ☎+1 207-552-3028; www.llbean.com).

Mountain Designs, 51 Bishop St., Kelvin Grove, QLD 4059 (☎07 3856 2344; fax 3856 0366; info@mountaindesigns.com; www.mountaindesigns.com).

Recreational Equipment, Inc. (REI), Sumner, WA 98352 (☎800-426-4840 or 253-891-2500; www.rei.com).

YHA Adventure Shop, YHA Adventure Shop, 152-160 Wardour St., London, W1F 8YA (☎020 7025 1900; www.yhaadventure.com). The flagship store of one of Britain's largest outdoor equipment suppliers.

WILDERNESS SAFETY

Stay warm, stay dry, and stay hydrated. The vast majority of life-threatening wilderness situations result from a breach of this simple dictum. On any hike, however brief, you should pack enough equipment to keep you alive should disaster befall. This includes **raingear, a hat, mittens, a first-aid kit, a reflector, a whistle, high energy food,** and extra **water.** Dress in warm layers of **synthetic materials** designed for the outdoors, or **wool.** Pile fleece jackets and Gore-Tex® raingear are excellent choices. Never rely on **cotton** for warmth. This "death cloth" will be absolutely useless should it get wet. Make sure to check all equipment for any defects before setting out, and see **Camping and Hiking Equipment,** p. 58, for more information.

Check **weather forecasts** and pay attention to the skies when hiking. Weather patterns can change suddenly. Whenever possible, let someone know when and where you are going hiking—either a friend, your hostel, a park ranger, or a local hiking organization. Do not attempt a hike beyond your ability—you may be endangering your life. See **Health,** p. 34, for info on outdoor ailments as well as basic medical concerns and first aid. For information on **dangerous wildlife,** see p. 60. For **further reading,** consult *How to Stay Alive in the Woods* by Bradford Angier (Macmillan, US$8).

ESSENTIALS

DANGEROUS WILDLIFE: If bitten or stung, it is best to take the offending creature to the hospital with you (if you are not in danger of being bitten or stung again) so that doctors can administer the correct anti-venom. The following list contains some dangerous creatures found in Australia.

Box jellyfish: large with multiple trailing tentacles. *Warnings to stay out of the water should be strictly observed*—if stung, chances of surviving are virtually zero; the pain alone causes immediate shock. Box jellyfish that have washed up on shore are still dangerous, so walking barefoot at the water's edge is discouraged. Box jellyfish inhabit the waters on the Top End Oct.-Apr., and the northern shores on the west and east coasts Nov.-Apr. Beware also the **stonefish** and **blue-ringed octopus**.

Cassowaries: birds characterized by brown crests and dagger-like claws, found mainly in Queensland. Have been known to attack during mating season.

Crocodiles: "Salties" are found in fresh and saltwater; they are hard to see and attack without provocation. Heed local warning signs; don't swim or paddle in streams, lakes, the ocean, or other natural waterways, and keep kids away from the water's edge. **"Freshies,"** the saltie's freshwater counterpart; they will not attack unless provoked but are also hard to see.

Dingoes: pose little threat to adults; can injure or even kill children. Pack away all food and keep fish and bait off the ground.

Sharks: Lifeguards at heavily visited beaches generally keep a good look out—don't swim outside the red and yellow flagged areas.

Snakes: most species are scared enough of humans that they will slide away at the sound of footsteps. If cornered, though, a few might attack in self-defense. Wear boots and long pants when walking through the wilderness, and never approach, attempt to step over, or try to kill a snake. Instead, walk around it at a safe distance. If bitten, tightly wrap the wounded area and work the bandage down to the tip of the limb and back up to the next joint to help slow the spread of venom. If possible, keep the infected area immobile, and seek medical attention immediately. Do not try to suck out the venom or clean the bite. Don't panic—most snake bites can be treated effectively.

Spiders: The **funnel-web** (found in eastern Australia including Tasmania) and the **redback** (common throughout Australia, particularly in urban areas) are among the most dangerous.

Stinging insects: bull-ants, wasps, bees, and bush-ticks may hurt a lot, but they are not life-threatening. If allergic to bee stings or other insect bites, carry your own epinephrine kit. Check for lumps on your skin to remove bush-ticks.

CAMPERS AND RVS

Caravanning is popular in Australia, where most campgrounds double as caravan parks, consisting of both tent sites and powered sites for caravans. On-site caravans (also called on-site vans) are a frequent feature at caravan parks and are anchored permanently to the site and rented out. "Cabins" at caravan parks are often analogous to an on-site van, with a toilet inside.

There is a distinction between **caravans** and **campervans (RVs)**. The former is pulled as a trailer, while the latter has its own cab. Renting a caravan is more expensive than tenting or hosteling, but cheaper than renting a car and staying in hotels. The convenience of bringing along your own bedroom, bathroom, and kitchen makes it an attractive option, especially for older travelers and families.

It's not difficult to arrange a campervan rental, although you should start gathering information several months before departure. Rates vary widely by region, season (December through February are the most expensive), and type of van. It pays to contact several different companies to compare vehicles and prices. **Hertz** (☎ 800-654-3001) is a US firm which arranges caravan rentals in Australia. **Maui Rentals** (☎ 02 9556 6100; fax 9556 3900; www.maui-rentals.com) and **Britz Campervan Rentals and Tours** (☎ 03 8379 8890; www.britz.com) rents RVs in Australia. Check out **Family Parks of Australia** (www.fpa.org.au) for a list of caravan and cabin parks across their Australian chain.

ORGANIZED ADVENTURE TRIPS

Organized adventure tours offer another way of exploring the wild. Activities include hiking, biking, skiing, canoeing, kayaking, rafting, climbing, and photo safaris. Tourism bureaus can often suggest parks, trails, and outfitters; other good sources for info are stores and organizations that specialize in camping and outdoor equipment like REI and EMS (see above).

Companies such as **Adventure Tours Australia** (within Australia ☎ 1300 654 604; ☎ 08 8309 2277; www.adventuretours.com.au) and the award-winning **Adventure Company Australia** (☎ 07 4051 4777; fax 4051 4888; www.adventures.com.au) provide educational programs on ecology and Aboriginal culture in addition to adventure activities.

SPECIFIC CONCERNS

WOMEN TRAVELERS

Women exploring on their own inevitably face some additional safety concerns, but it's easy to be adventurous without taking undue risks. If you are concerned, consider staying in hostels which offer single rooms that lock from the inside or in religious organizations with rooms for women only. Communal showers in some hostels are safer than others; check them before settling in. Stick to centrally located accommodations and avoid solitary late-night treks or metro rides.

Conditions for women in Australia have improved greatly in recent years, but vestiges of a male-dominated culture remain. Outback pubs, especially, can be chauvinistic and uncomfortable places to some. In general, though, it is safe for women to travel alone in Australia.

Always carry extra money for a phone call, bus, or taxi. **Hitchhiking** is never safe for lone women, or even for two women traveling together. When on overnight or long train rides, if there is no women-only compartment, choose one occupied by women or couples. Look as if you know where you're going and approach older women or couples for directions if you're lost or uncomfortable.

For general information, contact the **National Organization for Women (NOW)**, 733 15th St. NW, 2nd fl., Washington, D.C. 20005 (☎ 202-628-8669; www.now.org), which has branches across the US that can refer women travelers to rape crisis centers and counseling services.

TRAVELING ALONE

There are many benefits to traveling alone, including independence and greater interaction with locals. On the other hand, any solo traveler is a more vulnerable target of harassment and street theft. As a lone traveler, try not to stand out as a tourist, look confident, and be especially careful in deserted or very crowded areas. If questioned, never admit that you are traveling alone. Maintain regular contact with someone at home who knows your itinerary. For more tips, pick up *Traveling Solo* by Eleanor Berman (Globe Pequot Press; US$17) or subscribe to **Connecting: Solo Travel Network,** 689 Park Road, Unit 6, Gibsons, BC V0N 1V7, Canada (☎ 604-886-9099; www.cstn.org; membership US$35). **Travel Companion Exchange,** P.O. Box 833, Amityville, NY 11701, USA (☎ 631-454-0880, or in the US ☎ 800-392-1256;

www.whytravelalone.com; US$48), will link solo travelers with companions with similar travel habits and interests.

OLDER TRAVELERS

Senior citizens are eligible for a wide range of discounts on transportation, museums, movies, theaters, concerts, restaurants, and accommodations. If you don't see a senior citizen price listed, ask, and you may be delightfully surprised. The books *No Problem! Worldwise Tips for Mature Adventurers*, by Janice Kenyon (Orca Book Publishers; US$16) and *Unbelievably Good Deals and Great Adventures That You Absolutely Can't Get Unless You're Over 50*, by Joan Rattner Heilman (NTC/Contemporary Publishing; US$15) are both excellent resources. For more information, contact one of the following organizations:

Elderhostel, 11 Ave. de Lafayette, Boston, MA 02111, USA (☎877-426-8056; www.elderhostel.org). Organizes 1- to 4-week "educational adventures" in Australia on varied subjects for those 55+.

The Mature Traveler, P.O. Box 15791, Sacramento, CA 95852, USA (☎800-460-6676). Deals, discounts, and travel packages for the 50+ traveler. Subscription$30.

Walking the World, P.O. Box 1186, Fort Collins, CO 80522, USA (☎800-340-9255; www.walkingtheworld.com), organizes trips for 50+ travelers to Australia.

BISEXUAL, GAY, AND LESBIAN TRAVELERS

The profile of bisexual, gay, and lesbian community in Australia has risen in recent years, most notably in the popularity of the **gay and lesbian Mardi Gras** in Sydney each year, which is now the largest gay and lesbian gathering in the world (see p. 122). Though pockets of discrimination exist everywhere, the east coast is especially gay-friendly—Sydney ranks in the most gay-friendly cities on earth. The farther into the country you get, the more homophobia you may encounter. Homosexual acts are now legal in every state except Tasmania.

Gay and Lesbian Tourism Australia (GALTA) is a nonprofit nationwide network of tourism industry professionals who are dedicated to the welfare and satisfaction of gay and lesbian travelers to, from, and within Australia. They can be reached at ☎08 8379 7498 or on the web at www.galta.com.au. Listed below are contact organizations, mail-order bookstores, and publishers that offer materials addressing some specific concerns. **Out and About** (www.outandabout.com) offers a bi-weekly newsletter addressing travel concerns and a comprehensive site addressing gay travel concerns.

FURTHER READING: BISEXUAL, GAY, & LESBIAN.
Spartacus International Gay Guide 2002-2003. Bruno Gmunder Verlag (US$33).
Odysseus: The International Gay Travel Planner (17th Edition). Odysseus Enterprises (US$31).
Gay Travel A to Z, Ferrari Guides' Men's Travel in Your Pocket, and *Ferrari Guides' Inn Places.* Ferrari Publications (US$16-20).

TRAVELERS WITH DISABILITIES

Travelers with disabilities should inform airlines and hotels of their disabilities when making arrangements for travel; some time may be needed to prepare special accommodations. Call ahead to restaurants, hotels, parks, and other facilities to find out about the existence of ramps, the widths of doors, the dimensions of elevators, etc. **Guide dog owners** should inquire as to the quarantine policies of each destination country. At the very least, they will need to provide a certificate of immunization against rabies. After the 2000 Sydney Olympics and Paralympics, many locations in Australia (particularly the east) became wheelchair accessible, and budget options for the disabled are increasingly available. The following organizations provide information or publications that might be of assistance:

National Information Communication Network (NICAN), P.O. Box 407, Curtin ACT 2605 (☎02 6285 3713; fax 6285 3714; www.nican.com.au). National database of accommodations, recreation, tourism, sport and arts for the disabled.

Australian Quadriplegic Association, Letterbox 40 184 Bourke Rd., Alexandria NSW 2015 (☎02 9661 8855; fax 02 9661 9598; www.aqa.com.au). Network of community services for individuals with spinal cord injuries.

Accessibility.com.au, the access information supermarket, provides information about accessible opportunities in Sydney.

Wheelabout Van Rental, P.O. Box 3180, Erina NSW 2250 (☎02 4367 0900; fax 4365 5840; www.wheelabout.com). Wheelchair accessible van rentals and sales.

Mobility International USA (MIUSA), P.O. Box 10767, Eugene, OR 97440, USA (☎541--343-1284, voice and TDD; www.miusa.org). Sells *A World of Options: A Guide to International Educational Exchange, Community Service, and Travel for Persons with Disabilities* (US$35).

Society for Accessible Travel and Hospitality (SATH), 347 5th Ave., #610, New York, NY 10016, USA (☎212-447-7284; www.sath.org). An advocacy group that publishes free online travel information and the travel magazine *OPEN WORLD* (US$18, free for members). Annual membership US$45, students and seniors US$30.

MINORITY TRAVELERS

Australia is a generally tolerant and diverse country, but fear of losing jobs to **Asian** immigrants has inflamed racism in some areas. This may well extend to Asian travelers. White Australians are often described as racist in their attitudes toward the **Aborigines,** and this assessment is not unfounded. Black travelers are likely to get a few stares in smaller towns and may encounter some hostility in outback areas, but will probably not be discriminated against in cities. As always, cities tend to be more tolerant; don't let this dissuade you from venturing off the beaten track. *Let's Go* asks that its researchers exclude from the guides establishments that discriminate. Contact us if you encounter discrimination in any establishment we list.

TRAVELERS WITH CHILDREN

Family vacations often require that you slow your pace, and always require that you plan ahead. If you rent a car, make sure the rental company provides a car seat for younger children. **Be sure that your child carries some sort of ID** in case of an emergency or in case he or she gets lost. Finding a private place for **breast feeding** is often a problem while traveling, so plan accordingly. For more information, consult one of the following books:

Backpacking with Babies and Small Children, Goldie Silverman. Wilderness Press (US$12).

How to take Great Trips with Your Kids, Sanford and Jane Portnoy. Harvard Common Press (US$5).

Have Kid, Will Travel: 101 Survival Strategies for Vacationing With Babies and Young Children, Claire and Lucille Tristram. Andrews McMeel Publishing (US$9).

Adventuring with Children: An Inspirational Guide to World Travel and the Outdoors, Nan Jeffrey. Avalon House Publishing (US$15).

Trouble Free Travel with Children, Vicki Lansky. Book Peddlers (US$9).

ESSENTIALS

ESSENTIALS

DIETARY CONCERNS

Despite the prevalence of meat pies, **vegetarians** should have little problem finding suitable cuisine in Australia. *Let's Go* notes restaurants with vegetarian selections in city listings. For more information, visit the **Australian Vegetarian Society,** (www.moreinfo.com.au/avs). For a vegetarian shopping guide and restaurant listings, consult *The Vegetarian Traveler:Where to Stay If You're Vegetarian, Vegan, Environmentally Sensitive,* by Jed and Susan Civic (US$16). Travelers who keep **kosher** should contact synagogues in larger cities for information on kosher restaurants and lists of Jewish institutions in Australia. If your observance is strict, you may have to prepare your own food on the road. A good resource is the *Jewish Travel Guide,* by Michael Zaidner (Vallentine Mitchell; US$17).

OTHER RESOURCES

Let's Go tries to cover all aspects of budget travel, but we can't put *everything* in our guides. Listed below are books and websites that can serve as jumping off points for your own research.

USEFUL PUBLICATIONS

Hunter Publishing, 470 W. Broadway, 2nd Fl., Boston, MA 02127, USA (☎617-269-0700; www.hunterpublishing.com). Has an extensive catalog of travel guides and diving and adventure travel books.

Rand McNally, P.O. Box 7600, Chicago, IL 60680, USA (☎800 275 7263; www.randmcnally.com), publishes road atlases.

Adventurous Traveler Bookstore, P.O. Box 2221, Williston, VT 05495, USA (☎800-282-3963; www.adventuroustraveler.com).

Travel Books & Language Center, Inc., 4437 Wisconsin Ave. NW, Washington, D.C. 20016, USA (☎800-220-2665; www.bookweb.org/bookstore/travelbks). Over 60,000 titles from around the world.

UBD, P.O. Box 1530, Macquarie Park NSW 2113 (☎02 9857 3700; fax 9888 9074; www.ubd.com.au). Incredibly helpful street directories and motoring atlases.

THE WORLD WIDE WEB

Almost every aspect of budget travel (with the most notable exception, of course, being experience) is accessible via the web. Listed here are some budget travel sites to start off your surfing; other relevant web sites are listed throughout the book. Because website turnover is high, use search engines (such as www.google.com) to strike out on your own.

 WWW.LETSGO.COM Our newly designed website now features the full online content of all of our guides. In addition, trial versions of all nine City Guides are available for download onto Palm OS™ PDAs. Our website also contains our newsletter, links for photos and streaming video, online ordering of our titles, info about our books, and a travel forum buzzing with stories and tips.

THE ART OF BUDGET TRAVEL

How to See the World: www.artoftravel.com. A compendium of great travel tips, from cheap flights to self defense to interacting with local culture.

Travel Library: www.travel-library.com. A fantastic set of links for general information and personal travelogues.

Lycos: http://travel.lycos.com. General introductions to cities and regions thro Australia, accompanied by links to applicable histories, news, and local tourism

INFORMATION ON AUSTRALIA

Atevo Travel: www.atevo.com/guides/destinations. Detailed introductions, travel tips, and suggested itineraries.

Australia Tourist Commission: www.australia.com. Information about Australia and travel including climate, economy, health, and safety concerns.

Australian Tourism Net: www.atn.com.au. Has tons of service listings and Oz facts.

Australian Whitepages: www.whitepages.com.au. If you ever need a phone number or address, this is the place.

CIA World Factbook: www.odci.gov/cia/publications/factbook/index.html. Tons of vital statistics on Australia's geography, government, economy, and people.

Embassy of Australia: www.austemb.org. Facts about Australia and travel information related to Australian law and politics.

MyTravelGuide: www.mytravelguide.com. Country overviews, with everything from history to transportation to live web cam coverage of Australia.

PlanetRider: www.planetrider.com. A subjective list of links to the "best" websites covering the culture and tourist attractions of Australia.

TravelPage: www.travelpage.com. Links to official tourist office sites in Australia.

World Travel Guide: www.travel-guides.com/navigate/world.asp. Helpful practical info.

INTERNET DOWN UNDER The state web abbreviations in Australia are *act, nsw, nt, qld, sa, tas, vic,* and *wa*. Many cities, towns, and shires in Australia have websites, and they generally follow the address format: www.*town*.*state*.gov.au. Thus, the site for Ballarat VIC is www.ballarat.vic.gov.au, Townsville QLD is www.townsville.qld.gov.au, and so on.

ALTERNATIVES TO TOURISM

Traveling from place to place around the world may be a memorable experience. But if you are looking for a more rewarding and complete way to see the world, you may want to consider Alternatives to Tourism. Working, volunteering, or studying for an extended period of time can be a better way to understand life in Australia. This chapter outlines some of the different ways to get to know a new place, whether you want to pay your way through or just get the personal satisfaction that comes from studying and volunteering. In most cases, you will feel that you partook in a more meaningful and educational experience—something that the average budget traveler often misses out on.

While Australia offers amazing tourist attractions, its study, work, and volunteer opportunities are second to none. It boasts a large and vibrant international academic community, as well as a welcoming network of employers looking to hire friendly and eager backpackers. If organized thoughtfully and approached with a positive attitude, these opportunities will not replace the tourist experience but instead will augment it and in turn create a wealth of friendships and memories.

VISA INFORMATION
See the Department of Immigration and Multicultural and Indigenous Affairs website (www.immi.gov.au) to apply for visas. The following visas are required for temporary work and study in Australia.

Working Holiday Visa. For 18-30 year old citizens of Canada, China, Denmark, Germany, Ireland, Japan, Korea, Malta, the Netherlands, Norway, Sweden, and the UK. Valid for 12 months. Requirements include application and US $84 fee, valid passport, and proof of medical coverage and adequate funds.

Special Program Visa. For 18-30 year old United States citizens. Allows up to 4 months of temporary work with an approved exchange program. Requirements include application and US$84 fee, valid passport, flight itinerary, proof of funds, and letter from employment program (see p. 68 for eligible programs).

Student Visa. All student visas require application and US$158 fee, valid passport, and Electronic Confirmation of Enrollment (eCoE)/Acceptance Advice Form from Australian institution. Students enrolling for over 12 months need a signed medical report. Citizens of the US, Sweden, and Norway visiting for 12 months or less can get a visa online at www.immi.gov.au/e_visa/index.htm.

STUDYING ABROAD

Study abroad programs range from high school cultural exchanges to college-level classes, often for credit. In order to choose a program that best fits your needs, you will want to find out what kind of students participate in the program and what sort of accommodations are provided. In programs that have large groups of students who speak the same language, there is a trade-off. You may feel more comfortable in the community, but you will not have the same opportunity to befriend other international students. Dorm life provides a better opportunity to mingle with fellow students, but there is less of a chance to experience the local scene. If you live with a family, there is potential to build lifelong friendships with natives and to experience day-to-day life in more depth, but conditions can vary greatly from family to family.

A good resource for finding programs that cater to your particular interests is www.studyabroad.com, which has links to various semester abroad programs based on a variety of critera, including desired location and focus of study. The following is a list of organizations that can help place students in university programs abroad, or have their own branch in Australia.

AMERICAN PROGRAMS

American Institute for Foreign Study, College Division, River Plaza, 9 West Broad St., Stamford, CT 06902, USA (☎ 800-727-2437, ext. 5163; www.aifsabroad.com). Organizes programs for study at Macquarie University in Sydney.

Arcadia University for Education Abroad, 450 S. Easton Rd., Glenside, PA 19038, USA (☎ 866-927-2234; www.arcadia.edu/cea). Operates summer, semester, and graduate programs in Australia. Costs range from $3000 (summer) to $20,000 (full-year).

School for International Training, College Semester Abroad, Admissions, Kipling Rd., P.O. Box 676, Brattleboro, VT 05302, USA (☎ 888-272-7881 or 802-257-7751; www.sit.edu). Semester- and year-long programs in Australia run US$10,600-13,700. Also runs the **Experiment in International Living** (☎ 800-345-2929; fax 802-258-3428; www.usexperiment.org), a 5-week summer program that offers high-school students cross-cultural homestays and ecological adventures in Australia for US$5000.

Center for International Studies, 17 New South St. #105, Northampton, MA, 01060, USA (☎ 877-617-9090 or 413-582-0407; www.studyabroad-cis.com). Offers semester and year programs in Australian universities for $6000-9000.

Council on International Educational Exchange (CIEE), 633 3rd Ave., 20th fl., New York, NY 10017-6706 USA (☎ 800-407-8839; www.ciee.org/study) sponsors university study in Sydney, Melbourne, Perth, and Wollongong.

International Association for the Exchange of Students for Technical Experience (IAESTE), 10400 Little Patuxent Pkwy., Suite 250, Columbia, MD 21044-3519, USA (☎ 410-997-2200; www.aipt.org/iaeste.html). 8- to 12-week programs for college students who have completed 2 years of technical study. US$25 application fee.

Institute for Study Abroad, Butler University (ISA), 1000 W. 42nd St., Suite 305, Indianapolis, IN 46208-3345 USA (☎ 800-858-0229 or 317-940-9336; www.isabutler.org). A semester abroad program that is affiliated with the major universities of Australia. The ISA program takes care of applications to the universities, visas, housing, and provides personal guidance while abroad. US$40 application fee.

PROGRAMS IN AUSTRALIA

Start by visiting the Australian government's website, www.studyinaustralia.gov.au, which contains comprehensive information about requirements, programs, and fees. High school students can usually find exchange programs. For university courses, most American undergraduates enroll in programs sponsored by US universities. However, applying directly through Australian schools can be much cheaper than an American university program, though it can be hard to receive academic credit (and sometimes housing). Services that connect foreigners to study abroad programs are listed below. For a more complete list of schools and services, check out www.studyabroadlinks.com/search/Australia.

Association of Commonwealth Universities (ACU), John Foster House, 36 Gordon Sq., London WC1H OPF, UK (☎+44 020 7380 6700; www.acu.ac.uk). Publishes information about Commonwealth universities including Australian National University, University of Sydney, University of Melbourne, and all state universities.

IDP Education Australia, 1 Geils Court, Deakin, ACT 2600 (☎02 6285 8222; www.idp.com). An independent organization offering information about Australian institutions, access to IDP counsellors, and a free application and enrollment processing service.

International Student Exchange Australia, Unit 16, 172 Redland Bay Rd., Capalaba, QLD 4157 (☎07 3390 3838, fax 07 3390 3446; www.i-s-e.com.au). Arranges voluntary work experience, individual homestays, and high school exchange programs (1-4 terms, AUD$3000-13,000) for a AUD$100 application fee.

University of New South Wales, Level 16 Matthews Building, UNSW Kensington, Sydney NSW (☎02 9385 3179; www.studyabroad.unsw.edu.au). UNSW, aside from semester offerings, hosts 6-week study programs during Northern Hemisphere summer for undergraduates, graduate students, and adults. Subjects include Australian history, Outback art, biogeography, conservationism, and mass media, among others.

WORKING

Working in Australia provides two major benefits: it can help fund your further travels, and it can allow you to experience Aussie culture far more in depth. However, obtaining legal working permits can be difficult, especially for U.S. citizens. See the box on p. 66 for specific **visa requirements** to work in Australia.

If you plan to work in Australia, you should apply for a **tax file number (TFN)** from the Australian Taxation Office (www.ato.gov.au). Without a TFN, you may be taxed at a higher rate than necessary. You also may consider opening a **bank account,** which is easier to do within Australia than before arriving.

Though most programs and employers hire travelers carrying a 12-month Working Holiday Visa, United States citizens must obtain a Special Program visa in order to work. The Special Program Visa is valid for 4 months and only applies to the following organizations (which also accept Working Holiday Visas).

Council Exchanges, 633 Third Ave., New York, NY 10017 USA (☎888-268-6345; http://councilexchanges.org). The US$475 program fee includes document assistance, overseas and emergency aid, arrival orientation, and one night free accommodation; fee does not include visa application fee and mandatory US$40/month insurance cost.

International Exchange Programs, P.O. Box 4096, Sydney NSW 2001 (☎02 9299 0400; www.iep-australia.com). Helps organize working holidays; arranges visas, bank accounts, and tax file numbers; forwards mail; and helps find jobs and accommodations. For application and fees, contact the partner organization in your home country.

Visitoz, Springfield Farm, Goomeri QLD 4601 (☎07 4168 6106; www.visitoz.org). Arranges jobs, English language instruction, farm holidays, and agricultural training. Job options range from pubs and hostels to domestic work to teaching in the outback. Farm and station work requires introductory agricultural courses at a Visitoz training farm.

Work Experience Down Under, 2330 Marinship Way, Suite 250, Sausalito, CA 94965 USA (☎800-999-2267 or 415-339-2728; www.ccusa.com). The US$750 cost includes visa processing, comprehensive work and travel insurance, two nights accommodation, arrival and city orientation, Sydney Harbour Cruise, and access to a Job Search Centre.

SHORT-TERM WORK

Traveling for long periods of time can get expensive; therefore, many travelers try their hand at odd jobs for a few weeks at a time to make some extra cash to carry them through another month or two of touring around. Seasonal fruit-picking is a widespread and popular option in Australia. The climatic diversity across the continent ensures that picking jobs are available year-round, and the popularity of the work has created a sort of fruit-picking subculture. Many hostels in picking areas cater specifically to workers, offering transportation to worksites and other such amenities. In cities and highly touristed areas, hostels often contain employment boards and sometimes even employment services to help lodgers find temporary work. One popular option is to work several hours a day at a hostel in exchange for free or discounted room and/or board. Most often, these short-term jobs are found by word of mouth, or simply by talking to the owner of a hostel or restaurant. Many places, especially due to the high turnover in the tourism industry, are always eager for help, even if only temporary.

While word of mouth is generally an effective method of finding work, many employers join networks that connect workers to jobs nationwide. These services usually charge a membership fee, but often their websites alone can be helpful. The following resources provide information and access to job networks.

Employment National, (Harvest Hotline ☎ 1300 720 126; www.employmentnational.com.au, click on "Go Harvest"). Features a "Go Harvest" jobs board with up-to-date harvesting opportunities.

Workabout Australia, 8 White St., Dubbo NSW 2830 (☎(02) 6884 7777; www.workaboutaustralia.com.au). Joining the club costs $27.50, but the website offers a list of employment vacancies by state, including employers' contact information. Also sells *Workabout Australia,* a book containing seasonal and casual employment info by state.

WorldWide Workers, 234 Sussex St., Sydney NSW 2000 (☎(02) 8268 6001; www.worldwideworkers.com). Also locations in Melbourne and Cairns. $99 club membership includes 6 month membership in WorldWideWorkers, 12-month membership in WorldWidePickers, travel and social discounts, free Internet access at store locations, and access to job network with opportunities in labor, hospitality, sales, fruit-picking, nursing, accounting, and clerical work.

Let's Go tries to list temporary job opportunities whenever possible. Check the practical information sections in larger cities, or look under "work" in the index.

VOLUNTEERING

Volunteering can be one of the most fulfilling experiences you can have in life, especially if you combine it with the wonder of travel in a foreign land. Many volunteer services charge you a fee to participate in the program and to do work. These fees can be surprisingly hefty (although they frequently cover airfare and most, if not all, living expenses). Try to do research on a program before committing—talk to people who have previously participated and find out exactly what you're getting into, as living and working conditions can vary greatly. Different programs are geared toward different ages and levels of experience, so make sure that you are not taking on too much or too little. The more informed you are and the more realistic expectations you have, the more enjoyable the program will be.

Most people choose to go through a parent organization that takes care of logistical details and frequently provides a group environment and support system. Generally these organizations' program fees do not include flight costs, and tourist visas are sufficient for participation. You can sometimes avoid the high application fees charged by the organizations that arrange placement by contacting the individual workcamps directly; check with the organizations.

Amizade, Ltd., 367 S. Graham St., Pittsburgh, PA 15232, USA (☎888-973-4443; fax 412-648-1492; www.amizade.org). Volunteers spend two weeks in an Aboriginal community, working to promote culture and provide opportunities for economic self-sufficiency. Must be 18+. $1800 program fee, $350 deposit required.

Conservation Volunteers Australia, P.O. Box 423, Ballarat VIC 3353 (☎03 5333 1483 or nationwide ☎1800 032 501; www.conservationvolunteers.com.au). Offers travel volunteer packages (AUS$23 per day) that include service opportunity as well as accommodations, meals, and project-related transport.

Earthwatch, 3 Clocktower Pl., Suite 100, Box 75, Maynard, MA 01754, USA (☎800-776-0188 or 978-461-0081; www.earthwatch.org). Arranges 1- to 3-week programs in Australia to promote conservation of natural resources. Fees vary based on program location and duration, costs average $1800 plus airfare.

Elderhostel, Inc., 11 Avenue de Lafayette, Boston, MA 02111-1746, USA (☎877-426-8056; fax 877-426-2166; www.elderhostel.org). Seniors age 55 and over can experience Australia through 2-5 week learning tours. Costs $4500-7500, including international airfare, but not domestic connections.

Habitat for Humanity International, 121 Habitat St., Americus, GA 31709, USA (☎229-924-6935 x2551; www.habitat.org/intl). Offers volunteer opportunities in Australia to live and build houses in a host community. Short-term program costs range from US$1200-4000.

International Volunteers for Peace (IVP), 499 Elizabeth St., Surry Hills NSW 2010 (☎(02) 9699 1129; www.ivp.org.au). Arranges placement in Australian community work camps for those 18+. Membership $35. If you are not in Australia, contact **Service Civil International (SCI)**, IVP's affiliate, in your home country (www.sciint.org).

Involvement Volunteers, P.O. Box 218, Port Melbourne VIC 3207 (☎03 9646 5504; www.volunteering.org.au). Offers volunteering options in Australia ranging from social service, research, education, conservation, and farmwork. Registration fee AUS$242.

Volunteers for Peace, 1034 Tiffany Rd., Belmont., VT 05730, USA (☎802-259-2759; www.vfp.org). Affiliated, but not synonymous, with IVP (above). Arranges placement in work camps in Australia. Membership required for registration. Annual *International Workcamp Directory* US$20. Programs average US$200-500 for 2-3 weeks

Willing Workers on Organic Farms (WWOOF), Buchan VIC 3885 (☎03 5155 0218; www.wwoof.com.au). Exchange your labor for food, accommodation, and local culture. There can be stipulations on minimum stays and work expected from a WWOOFer, but each site has its own expectations. Membership (AUS$45 or AUS$50 for two people) includes a guide to hosts in Australia and can be purchased from many outlets throughout Australia (see www.wwoof.com.au/agents.html).

FOR FURTHER READING ON ALTERNATIVES TO TOURISM

How to Live Your Dream of Volunteering Overseas, by Collins, DeZerega, and Heckscher. Penguin Books, 2002 (US$17).

International Directory of Voluntary Work, by Whetter and Pybus. Peterson's Guides and Vacation Work, 2000 (US$16).

International Jobs, by Kocher and Segal. Perseus Books, 1999 (US$18).

Overseas Summer Jobs 2002, by Collier and Woodworth. Peterson's Guides and Vacation Work, 2002 (US$18).

Work Abroad: The Complete Guide to Finding a Job Overseas, by Hubbs, Griffith, and Nolting. Transitions Abroad Publishing, 2000 ($16).

Work Your Way Around the World, by Susan Griffith. Worldview Publishing Services, 2001 (US$18).

AUSTRALIAN CAPITAL TERRITORY

Carved out of New South Wales in 1908, the Australian Capital Territory (ACT), designed and constructed at the beginning of the 20th century, was a geographic and political compromise between Sydney and Melbourne in the competition to host the capital of the newly federated Australia. Although it is not a fully qualified state, the center of the territory—Canberra—is the political heart of the country. Home to commuters and suburban shopping areas, neatly designed satellite towns creep outward from Canberra into the bush. The ACT's combination of a cosmopolitan center and outlying natural refuges promises visitors a capital look at high culture and government at an easygoing pace.

CANBERRA ☎ 02

For a city that is home to 320,000 people and the government of an entire continent, Canberra's streets are, for the most part, amazingly quiet. Wide avenues, huge tracts of green spaces, and modern architecture offer a utopian vision of metropolis, yet the city feels empty, as if someone expected a lot more people to show up. The city houses a myriad of beautifully planned tourist attractions from space centers to dinosaur museums, but there is a shortage of tourists to see it all. The unique city was designed by Walter Burley Griffin, student of Frank Lloyd Wright. The American architect's proposal was selected from a pool of 137 competitors before construction began in 1913. The first Canberra Parliament convened in 1927; since then, the pace has picked up a bit, but even today's Canberra keeps a low profile and a refined lifestyle to match. Regardless of its dull reputation, Canberra's blend of culture and class qualifies it as one of Australia's most underrated destinations.

CANBERRA HIGHLIGHTS

QUESTION TIME. Don't miss the political antics that ensue when the Parliamentary floor is opened to lively debate (p. 77).

NATIONAL SCREEN AND SOUND ARCHIVE. Mix entertainment with education at this audiovisual extravaganza (p. 80).

GYPSY BAR. Catch a local band, shoot some pool, or down schooners all night at this Canberra institution (p. 81).

◼ INTERCITY TRANSPORTATION

BY PLANE. Located in Pialligo, 7km east of the city center, the **Canberra International Airport** is an easy ride by car. From Commonwealth Ave., take Parkes Way east past the roundabout at Kings Ave. The name of the road changes first to Morshead Dr., then to Pialligo Ave., en route to the airport. On weekdays, **Deane's Buslines** (☎ 6299 3722; http://deansbuslines.com.au) operates the **Air Liner,** a shuttle service that transports passengers between the airport and the City Interchange (20min., 14 per day, $5). For weekend transit, a **taxi** (☎ 13 22 27) is your best bet. ($17 one-way from the city center.) The airport only handles domestic flights to four cities; all international travel requires a stop in Sydney. **Virgin Blue Airlines** (☎ 13 67 89; www.virginblue.com.au) is a new major player in the Canberra travel market, offering competitive service and super low prices to Brisbane (2hr., 1 per day, $248). **Qantas** (☎ 13 13 13; www.qantas.com.au) connects Canberra to: Adelaide (1½hr., 2-4 per day, $375); Brisbane (2hr., 4 per day, $350); Melbourne (1hr., 10 per day, $250); and Sydney (50min., 24 per day, $198). To get the best fares, book at least 14 days in advance or check for special deals on the Internet.

BY TRAIN. The **Canberra Railway Station,** on the corner of Wentworth Ave. and Mildura St. in Kingston, 6km from the city center, is on ACTION bus route #39 (bus to Civic 25min., at least 1 per hr.). Alternatively, a taxi ride from the station to the city will cost $12-14. The station houses little more than a **Countrylink** office. (☎ 13 22 32 or 6239 7053. Open M-Sa 6:20am-5:30pm, Su 10:30am-5:30pm.) **Trains** leave for Brisbane (24hr., 2 per day, $110) via Sydney (4hr., 3 per day, $47). **Train/coach** runs to: Bega (3½hr., 1 per day, $33); Cooma (1¼hr., 1-2 per day, $16); Goulburn (1¼hr., 3 per day, $11); Melbourne (8½hr., 1 per day, $90); and Wollongong via Moss Vale (4hr., 1 per day, $37). Discounts for advanced bookings: 7-14 day 40%, 15+ day 50%.

BY BUS. Intercity **buses** converge at **Jolimont Tourist Centre,** 65-67 Northbourne Ave., just north of Alinga St. in Civic. (Open daily 6am-10:30pm; in winter 5am-10:30pm.) Self-service coin lockers cost $4 per day. The McCafferty's/Greyhound ticketing office stores bags for the day ($2 per piece of luggage). Several bus companies, both major domestic airlines, and Countrylink have desks in the building.

McCafferty's/Greyhound (☎ 13 14 99 or 13 20 30) provides **bus** service to: Adelaide (17hr., 2 per day, $127); Albury (5-6hr., 4 per day, $34); Goulburn (1hr., 4 per day, $24); Griffith (6hr., 1 per day, $48); Gundagai (1¾hr., 3 per day, $27); Melbourne (8-10hr., 4 per day, $62); Parramatta (3½hr., 5 per day, $37); Sydney (3-4hr., 10 per day, $35); and Wagga Wagga (3hr., 2 per day, $34). From June to October buses run to: the snowfields at Cooma (1½hr., 2 per day, $37); Perisher Blue via the **Skitube** (3hr., 2 per day, $51); and Thredbo (3½hr., 2 per day, $54) via Jindabyne (2¼hr., 2 per day, $43). **Murrays** (☎ 13 22 51) also runs to: Bateman's Bay (2½hr., 1 per day, $24); Goulburn (1¼hr., 1 per day, $16); Narooma (4¼hr., 1-2 per day, $38); Sydney (4hr., 4 per day, $37); Wollongong (3½hr., 1 per day, $25). Murrays also has ski-season service to: Cooma (1¼hr., 1-2 per day, $29); Jindabyne (3¼hr., 1-2 per day, $28); Perisher Blue (3hr., 1-2 per day, $27); and Thredbo (3hr., 1-2 per day, $33). McCafferty's and Murray's offer great deals on **ski packages,** which include return transport, lift tickets, ski rental, and park entrance for $100. **Transborder Express** (☎ 6241 0033) runs to Yass (1hr., 1-4 per day, $12).

BY CAR. The **NRMA automobile club,** 92 Northbourne Ave., is the place to turn for road service or car problems. (☎ 6243 8880. Open M-F 9:30am-5pm.) For 24hr. **emergency road service, call** ☎ 13 11 11. **Avis,** 17 Lonsdale St. (☎ 6249 6088; open M-F 8am-6pm, Sa 8am-2pm, Su 8am-1pm); **Budget** (☎ 13 27 27; open M-F 8am-5pm, Sa 8am-noon), on the corner of Mort and Girraween St.; **Delta Europcar,** 74 Northbourne Ave. (☎ 13 13 90; open M-F 8am-5:30pm, Sa 8am-4pm); **Hertz,** 32 Mort St. (☎ 6257 4877; open M-F 8am-6pm, Sa 8am-3pm); and **Thrifty,** 29 Lonsdale St. (☎ 6247 7422; open M-F 8am-5:30pm, Sa-Su 8am-5pm) all have offices in Braddon and at the airport. Local outfit **Value Rent-a-Car,** in the Rydges Capital Hill Hotel on Canberra Ave. and National Circuit, charges $35 per day and $195 weekly. (☎ 1800 629 561. Open M-F 8am-6pm, Sa-Su for pickup and drop-off only.)

▨ ORIENTATION

Lake Burley Griffin, formed by the damming of the Molonglo River, splits Canberra in two; on each side is a central hill with concentric roads leading outwards. **Commonwealth Ave.** spans the lake to connect these points.

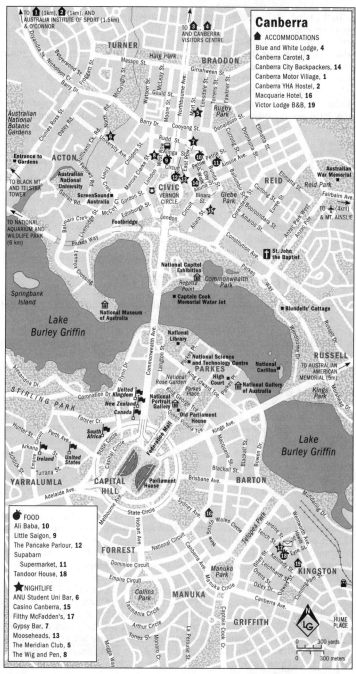

TO ■1 (1km), ■2 (1km), AND
AUSTRALIA INSTITUTE OF SPORT (1.5km)
& O'CONNOR

TO ■3 ■4
AND CANBERRA
VISITORS CENTRE

Canberra

■ ACCOMMODATIONS
Blue and White Lodge, **4**
Canberra Carotel, **3**
Canberra City Backpackers, **14**
Canberra Motor Village, **1**
Canberra YHA Hostel, **2**
Macquarie Hotel, **16**
Victor Lodge B&B, **19**

TURNER
BRADDON
ACTON
REID
CIVIC
VERNON
CIRCLE
Australian
National
Botanic
Gardens
Entrance to
Gardens
TO BLACK MT.
AND TELSTRA
TOWER
Australian
National
University
ScreenSound
Australia
TO NATIONAL
AQUARIUM AND
WILDLIFE PARK
(6 km)
Footbridge
Australian
War
Memorial
Reid Park
TO ■ (4km)
& MT. AINSLIE
Glebe
Park
St. John
the Baptist
National Capitol
Exhibition
Commonwealth
Park
Regatta
Point
Captain Cook
Memorial Water Jet
Blundells' Cottage
Springbank
Island
Lake
Burley Griffin
National Museum
of Australia
National
Library
National Science
and Technology Centre
National
Carillon
RUSSELL
TO AUSTRALIAN
AMERICAN
MEMORIAL (5m)
PARKES
High
Court
National Gallery
of Australia
Kings
Park
STIRLING PARK
National
Rose Garden
National
Portrait
Gallery
Old Parliament
House
United
Kingdom
New Zealand
Canada
South
Africa
Ireland
United
States
Lake
Burley Griffin
YARRALUMLA
CAPITAL
HILL
Parliament
House
BARTON
FORREST
Manuka
Park
KINGSTON
Collins
Park
MANUKA
GRIFFITH
HUME
PLACE
0   300 yards
0   300 meters

ACT

■ FOOD
Ali Baba, **10**
Little Saigon, **9**
The Pancake Parlour, **12**
Supabarn
  Supermarket, **11**
Tandoor House, **18**

★ NIGHTLIFE
ANU Student Uni Bar, **6**
Casino Canberra, **15**
Filthy McFadden's, **17**
Gypsy Bar, **7**
Mooseheads, **13**
The Meridian Club, **5**
The Wig and Pen, **8**

To the north of the lake is **Vernon Circle,** marking the center of Canberra and the southern edge of the area known as **Civic.** Civic serves as the city's social center and bus interchange. Restaurants, shops, pubs, and nightclubs crowd the pedestrian mall known as **City Walk**—the area between Northbourne Ave., Akuna St., Bunda St., and London Circuit. Immediately north of Vernon Circle, Commonwealth Ave. becomes Northbourne Ave.

To the south of the lake is **State Circle** and the governmental part of the capital. Within State Circle, **Capital Hill's** huge four-pronged flagpole reaches up from the new Parliament House. One corner of the area known as **Parliamentary Triangle** encloses most of the city's museums and government-related attractions. Commonwealth Ave., Kings Ave., and Parkes Way form the three sides of the triangle.

The key to understanding the city plan is the system of roundabouts, the multiple concentric streets ("circuits"), and the wheel-spoke offshoots. If you drive, a good map is absolutely essential. Roundabouts are well marked, but signs often refer to districts rather than to streets. **O'Connor** is a northern suburb beginning at Dyandra St. and accessible by the #34 and #35 buses. The railway station and an assortment of budget lodging are in **Kingston,** southeast of Capital Hill. The embassies populate **Yarralumla,** west of Capital Hill. **Dickson,** northeast of Civic via Northbourne Ave. and Antill St., and **Manuka** (MINE-icka), southeast of Capital Hill, have clusters of reasonably priced restaurants.

◧ LOCAL TRANSPORTATION

The primary hub for Canberra's public transit system, **ACTION** (☎ 13 17 10), centers on the city bus interchange, located at the junction of East Row, Alinga St., and Mort St. Full maps and timetables for all routes are available, free of charge, at the ACTION information office, next to the Civic Library on East Row, between Alinga St. and London Circuit. Route maps are also clearly posted near the passenger shelters at the city bus interchange. Relevant timetables are posted at individual bus stops. Buses generally run M-Sa 6am-12:30am and Su 7am-8:15pm, though some routes have more limited hours.

ACTION bus fares are based on a zone system, but the airport and the majority of the city's attractions and budget accommodations fall within the central zone, so you'll probably only need the **one-zone fare** ($2.30, concessions $1.20). These are valid for a single trip; if you ask for a **transfer ticket** from the bus driver, the single ticket is good for one hour. **Fare-saver tickets** ($19.80, concessions $9.90) are available for ten one-zone rides. To make the most of a single day, purchase an all-zone **Shopper's Off-Peak Daily ticket** ($5.40, concessions $4.70), valid weekdays 9am-4:30pm and after 6pm, and all day weekends and public holidays. Purchase tickets on the bus or at most news agencies.

Though considerably more expensive than an ACTION off-peak daily ticket, City Sightseeing's less logistically complex **Canberra Tour** makes 14 stops in a red double-decker bus, covering all major tourist attractions. The ticket is valid for 24hr. with unlimited stops. Tickets can be purchased on the bus, in most hotels, or at the visitors center. (☎ 6257 3423 or 0500 505 012. $25 per person.) **Canberra Cabs** (☎ 13 22 27) covers the city and suburbs 24hr.

Thanks to a superb system of **bicycle paths,** the capital can also be covered easily on a bike. A ride along the shores of Lake Burley Griffin is an excellent way to take in Parliamentary Triangle without having to find parking. For **bike rental,** the best deal is through the **YHA** in O'Connor. (☎ 6248 9155. Open daily 7am-10pm. Full-day $25, YHA guests $6; includes helmet and bike lock.) Closer to the city center is **Mr. Spokes Bike Hire and Cafe,** on Barrine Dr. in Acton Park, near the ferry terminal. (☎ 6257 1188. Open daily in summer 9am-6pm; in winter 9am-5pm. $10 per hr.)

☑ PRACTICAL INFORMATION

TOURIST AND FINANCIAL SERVICES

Tourist Offices: Canberra Visitors Centre, 330 Northbourne Ave. (☎6205 0044, accommodations booking 1800 100 660; www.canberratourism.com.au), about 3km north of Vernon Circle. Take bus #30, 31, 32, 39, 50, or 80. Open M-F 9am-5:30pm, Sa-Su 9am-4pm. Wheelchair accessible. Smaller volunteer-staffed **Canberra Tourism Booth,** inside Jolimont Tourist Centre, is 2 blocks from the city bus interchange. Open M-F 9am-5pm, Sa-Su 11am-3pm.

Budget Travel: STA Travel, 13 Garema Pl. (☎6247 8633), on the corner of City Walk. Open M-Th 9am-5pm, F 9am-7pm, Sa 10am-2pm.

Embassies: Unless specified, all locations are in Yarralumla. **Canada** (☎6270 4000; fax 6273 3285), on Commonwealth Ave. south of the lake. Open for consular services M-F 8:30am-12:30pm and 1-4:30pm. **Ireland,** 20 Arkana St. (☎6273 3022; fax 6273 3741). Open M-F 9:30am-12:45pm and 2-5pm. **New Zealand** (☎6270 4211; fax 6273 3194), on Commonwealth Ave., south of the lake. Open M-F 8:45am-5pm. For consular services, contact the consulate in Sydney (☎02 8256 2000; fax 9221 7836). **South Africa** (☎6273 2424; fax 6273 3543), on the corner of State Circle and Rhodes Pl. Open M-F 8:30am-5pm. The consular section is open M-F 8:30am-1pm. **United Kingdom** (☎6270 6666, emergency 6285 6171; fax 6270 6606), on Commonwealth Ave. Open M-F 9am-5pm. Consular services downtown, SAP building, Level 10, corner of Bunda and Akuna St. Open M-F 9am-3pm. **United States,** 21 Moonah Pl. (☎6214 5600, emergency 6214 5900). Open M-F 8am-5pm. For routine consular services, contact the consulate in Sydney (☎02 9373 9200).

Currency Exchange: American Express, Shop 1, Centrepoint, 185 City Walk (☎6247 2333). Cardholders and travelers check users can have mail held for 3 weeks at no charge. Send mail Attn: Client Mail, P.O. Box 153, Civic Square ACT 2608. No fee for AmEx Traveler's Cheque transactions. Currency exchange 1% fee. Open M-F 9am-5pm, Sa 9am-noon. **Thomas Cook** (☎6247 9984), Canberra Centre shopping mall, Bunda St., corner of Petrie Plaza, offers free cashing of Thomas Cook checks and a flat fee of $7 on other checks and currency exchange. Open M-F 9am-5pm, Sa 9:30am-12:30pm.

LOCAL SERVICES

Library: Civic Library (☎6205 9000; www.act.gov.au/library), on East Row between Alinga St. and London Circuit. One of 9 branches within the ACT. Open M-Th 10am-5:30pm, F 10am-7pm, Sa 9:30am-5pm. See **National Library of Australia,** p. 79.

Ticket Agencies: Ticketek, GIO building, 11 Akuna St., Civic (☎6219 6666; www.ticketek.com). Tickets to sport and music events and **Royal Theatre.** Open M-F 9am-5pm, Sa 9am-noon. **Canberra Ticketing** (☎6257 1077), on London Circuit, covers the **Canberra Theatre** and **Playhouse.** Open M-Sa 9am-5:30pm, later on the nights of shows.

Travel Books and Maps: Map World (☎6230 4097), inside the Jolimont Tourist Centre. Open M-F 9am-5:30pm, Sa 9am-3pm.

Public Markets: Gorman House Markets (☎6249 7377), on Ainslie Ave. between Currong and Doonkuma St., vend crafts, clothing, and miscellany. Open Sa 10am-4pm. The **Old Bus Depot Markets,** 49 Wentworth Ave., Kingston (☎6292 8391), feature many food and arts-and-crafts stalls. Open Su 10am-4pm.

EMERGENCY AND COMMUNICATIONS

Emergency: ☎000.

Police Attendance: ☎1 1444.

Police: On London Circuit opposite University Ave., Civic (☎6245 7208).

Crisis Lines: Drug and Alcohol Crisis Line (☎6205 4545; 24hr.). **Poison Info Centre** (☎13 11 26; 24hr.). **Gay/Lesbian Info and Counseling Service** (☎6247 2726; daily 6-10pm, after-hours recording). **Women's Info and Referral Service** (☎6205 1075; M-F 9am-5pm).

MEDIA AND PUBLICATIONS
Newspapers: The main newspaper is the *Canberra Times* ($1.10). They also put out a local newspaper, *The Chronicle*.
Entertainment: *bma* (bands music action) is Canberra's free, alternative, entertainment bimonthly. *Good Times*, released on Thursdays in the Canberra Times, also has a list of entertainment options.
Radio: Easy Listening, 106.3FM; Mix, 104.7FM; Rock, Triple J 101.5FM; News, 1440AM; Tourist Info, 88FM.

Late-Night Pharmacy: O'Connor Capital Chemist, 9 Sargood St. (☎6248 7050), in the O'Connor Shopping Ctr. Open daily 9am-11pm.

Hospital/Medical Services: Canberra Hospital (☎6244 2222, emergency 6244 2611), on Yamba Dr., Garren. Follow signs to Woden southwest from Capital Hill.

Internet Access: Cheap access is not common. The **ACT Library Service** (see **Local Services,** p. 75) and the **National Library** (see **National Library of Australia,** p. 79) offer free 1hr. sessions; book ahead. **KC's Cafe,** 11 East Row (☎6257 5558), charges $2.50 per 15min. and $6 per hr. Open M-Sa 9am-late, Su 11am-late.

Post Office: General Post Office (GPO), 53-73 Alinga St. (☎6209 1680). Open M-F 8:30am-5:30pm. **Australia Post** at Civic Square, outside Canberra Centre mall, has stamps and counter service. Open M-F 8:45am-5:15pm. **Postal Code:** 2601.

ACCOMMODATIONS

■ **Canberra City Backpackers,** 7 Akuna St., Civic (☎1800 300 488). This centrally located, swanky hostel-hotel puts travelers within easy reach of downtown cafes, shops, and nightlife. Multiple kitchens and common areas, rooftop BBQ, small gym, heated pool, pool tables, laundry, bike rentals ($16 per day), security cameras, in-room lockers ($10 deposit), and in-room TVs with free movies. 24hr. reception. Dorms $26; singles $70; twins $80; doubles with bath $95; family rooms from $95. AmEx/MC/V. ❸

■ **Canberra YHA Hostel,** 191 Dryandra St., O'Connor (☎6248 9155). Not to be confused with the YHA office in the city center. Bus #35 travels to and from the city interchange, stopping directly out front. By car, follow Northbourne Ave. north from the city center. Turn left on Macarthur Ave., go 2km, then turn right on Dryandra. Situated away from the urban jungle along the eastern edge of a Canberra nature park, 5km northwest of the city center, this pleasant, family-friendly hostel is impeccably clean and has a wonderfully helpful staff. A great place for watching birds and meeting other travelers. Multiple kitchens, 3 daily shuttles to the city (free), TV/pool room, great movie selection, bike rental (full-day $6), small store, laundry, and Internet kiosks ($2 per 20min.). Key deposit $10. Reception daily 7am-10pm. Dorms 10-bed $18, 4-bed $20; doubles $50; ensuite twins $54; family room $85. ❷

■ **Victor Lodge Bed and Breakfast,** 29 Dawes St., Kingston (☎6295 7777; www.victorlodge.com.au), 6 km south of the city center. Free pickup in Civic at Jolimont Tourist Centre by arrangement. Bus #38 or 39 from the city bus interchange stops 2 blocks away on Eyre St. Within biking distance of Parliamentary Triangle, this quiet lodge/hostel is only a block from the shops and restaurants of Kingston. Kitchen, TV, laundry, Internet ($1 per 7min.), bike hire ($15 per day), and free all-you-can-eat continental breakfast (7-9am). Key deposit $10. Linens included. Reception daily 7:30am-9:30pm. Dorms $23; 2-bed dorms $49, weekly $245; doubles $65. VIP. ❷

Blue and White Lodge, 524 Northbourne Ave., Downer, and **Canberran Lodge,** 528 Northbourne Ave., Downer (both ☎6248 0498). It's hard to differentiate between the two B&Bs. Each guesthouse offers TV, fridge, and kettle in a large, clean, floral-smelling room. Some rooms have verandas; all have bath. Breakfast included. Reception daily 7am-9pm. Singles $83; doubles $88. ❺

ACT

Canberra Motor Village (☎ 6247 5466 or 1800 026 199), on Kunzea St., O'Connor, 4km northwest of the city center, along the eastern edge of a Canberra nature park. Take Bus #34 or 35 to Miller and Macarthur Ave. By car, follow Northbourne Ave. north from Civic, turn left on Macarthur, right on Dryandra, and take an immediate left on Kunzea. Toilets, showers, laundry, BBQ, pool, tennis courts, store, restaurant, and playground. Key deposit $10. Reception daily 7am-10:30pm. Sites for 1 $15, with power and water $21, extra person $6; $3.30 extra on weekends and public holidays. ❶

Canberra Carotel (☎ 6241 1377), on Federal Hwy., Watson, 7km north of the city center, on the #36 bus line. By car, follow Northbourne Ave. until it becomes Federal Hwy. Swimming pool, store, playground, BBQ, toilets, showers, and laundry. Reception M-F 7am-9pm, Sa-Su 7am-8pm. Sites for 2 $14, powered $17, extra person $2.50; on-site caravans for 2 $39, extra person $4; bungalows for 2 $55, extra person $6 (5 person max.); cabins with cooking facilities for up to 3 $80; family cabins with cooking facilities for up to 10 $115. Prices rise during public holidays. ❶

◨ FOOD

In a city populated by government officials, cheap food is never easy to find. Inexpensive cafes near the city bus interchange, along with the food court at Canberra Centre (☎ 6247 5611), a three-story mall with main entrances off either City Walk or Bunda St., between Petrie Plaza and Akuna St., provide welcome exceptions. On Bunda St., opposite the Canberra Centre, the **City Market** complex packs in fruit stands, butcher shops, and prepared food stalls. You'll also find a vast Supabarn **supermarket.** (☎ 6257 4055. Open M-F 8am-10pm, Sa-Su 8am-9pm.)

Tandoor House, 39 Kennedy St., Kingston (☎ 6295 7318). Sit back and savor the flavorful Indian curries, vindaloos, masalas ($11-16), and yummy breads ($2-3). Numerous vegetarian options. Open daily 5:30-11pm, also M-Sa noon-2:30pm. ❷

Ali Baba (☎ 6257 2538), at the corner of Bunda St. and Garema Pl., Civic. Don't be put off just because this Lebanese eatery is part of a chain. The lamb, beef, or chicken kabobs and falafels are hot and filling ($5-6) and can be customized with an assortment of sauces. Open Su-Th 9am-10pm, F-Sa 24hr. ❶

Little Saigon Restaurant (☎ 6230 5003), on Alinga St. in the Novotel, Civic. Popular Vietnamese restaurant has traditional food at tantalizing prices. Mains $9-13. Lunch box deal (any menu item plus rice $5). Open daily 10am-3pm and 5-10:30pm. ❷

The Pancake Parlour, 121 Alinga St., Civic (☎ 6247 2982), downstairs. Despite its slightly multiple-franchise feel, late night munchies and early-morning cravings are easily satisfied, whether you opt for fruit pancakes ($7-10) or more standard steak and fish fare ($11-16). YHA discount 10%. Daily early bird dinner specials 5-7pm. Open Su-Th 7am-10:30pm, F-Sa 7:30am-2:30am. ❷

Silo Bakery and Cheese Room, 36 Giles St., Kingston (☎ 6260 6060). Known by locals as the best bakery in Canberra. Although only offering a few dishes each day, Silo creates delicate and intense appetizers and mains that feature their quality imported cheeses, freshly made breads, and other authentic ingredients. Mains $13-20. Open Tu-Sa for breakfast and lunch. ❸

◉ SIGHTS

LOOKOUTS

A stop at one of the city's lookouts can give you a general idea of what's in store on a sightseeing tour. On a hill in Commonwealth Park at Regatta Point, on the north shore of Lake Burley Griffin, the **National Capital Exhibition** provides a panorama of Canberra with a ten-minute film and displays on the planning and growth of the city. (☎ 6257 1068. Open daily 9am-5pm. Free. Wheelchair accessible.)

IN RECENT NEWS

SEX IN THE CITY

The ACT is a veritable island of sin in this otherwise relatively conservative nation, with legal fireworks and firearms and lenient penalties for possessing, using, and even selling drugs. But among the most popular of Canberra's unregulated underworlds is the sex industry. While most sex publications are restricted in other parts of Australia, all are allowed to be sold in the ACT (albeit in specially-zoned areas), and adult shops and X-rated videos have also been completely decriminalized within the territory. The largest deviation from the national norm, however, is in sex work itself—within the ACT, brothels and independent escorts are fully legal. Their activities must take place within industrial zones, and the workers must be licensed, but for the most part, the selling of sex is legal here. Before setting out to see the sights on your own, consider taking a tour with the **"Love Bus"** (bookings ☎6262 9266; www.lovebus.com.au). Tour stops include the **National Museum of Erotica,** 37a Northbourne Ave. (☎6230 5022; www.nationalmuseumoferotica.com), a sex shop, two "entertainment spaces" with peep shows and live reviews, and an honest-to-goodness brothel. For more information about sex laws and practices, as well as worker contacts and sex shop details, contact the **Eros Foundation** (www.eros.com.au).

Farther back from the city's center, Mt. Ainslie and Black Mountain offer broader views of the city and are—for the energetic—within walking distance. North of Lake Burley Griffin and east of the city center, **Mt. Ainslie** rises 845m above the lake, the Parliamentary Triangle, and the Australian War Memorial, providing the classic postcard view down Anzac Pde. To reach the summit by car, turn right onto Fairbairn Ave. from the Memorial end of Anzac Pde., to Mt. Ainslie Dr. Hiking trails lead to the top from directly behind the War Memorial.

Two lookout points above the city on **Black Mountain** are a vigorous walk away. The first, on Black Mountain Dr., accessible by taking Barry Dr. to Clunies Ross St. and heading left, faces southeast and takes in the Parliamentary Triangle and Lake Burley Griffin. The second viewpoint faces north toward the surrounding countryside and the **Australian Institute of Sport** (see p. 80). From the peak of Black Mountain, **Telstra Tower** climbs 195m to ensure viewers an unobstructed gaze in every direction. Exhibits in the tower catalogue the history of Australian telecommunications. (☎6248 1991 or 1800 806 718. Open daily 9am-10pm. $3.30.)

PARLIAMENTARY TRIANGLE

A showpiece of grand architecture and cultural attractions, Canberra's Parliamentary Triangle is the center of the capital. The triangle is bordered by Commonwealth Ave., Kings Ave., and, across the lake, Parkes Way.

■**PARLIAMENT HOUSE.** The focal point of the triangle, Parliament House takes the ideal of unifying architecture and landscape to a new level. The building is actually built *into* Capital Hill so that two sides jut out of the earth, leaving the grassy hilltop on its roof undisturbed and open to the public 24hr. The design intentionally places the people above Parliament. Perched on this landmark is a four-pronged stainless steel flagpole visible from nearly every part of Canberra. Inside the building, free guided tours *(every 30min., daily 9am-4pm)* give an overview of the unique features of the building and the workings of the government housed inside. Visitors can even observe both houses of Parliament in action from viewing galleries. The House of Representatives, which meets more often than the Senate, allows advance bookings. The televised **Question Time** provides some viewer-friendly acrimony. Every day when the House and the Senate are sitting *(M-Th in approximately 2-week blocks, except during recess in Jan. and July)*, the floor is opened up at 2pm for on-the-spot questioning of the Prime Minister and other ministers. *(☎6277 5399, reservations 6277 4889; www.aph.gov.au/house. Open daily 9am-5pm, as late as 11pm when either chamber is in session. Free. Wheelchair accessible.)*

OLD PARLIAMENT HOUSE AND THE NATIONAL PORTRAIT GALLERY. This building, aligned with the front of Parliament House, served as Australia's seat of government from 1927 to 1988, when the current Parliament House was completed. It is now a political history museum and home to the National Portrait Gallery. (☎ 6270 8222, gallery 6270 8236. Daily "Behind the Scene" tours of Old Parliament House every 45min. 9:30am-3:15pm. Tours of the Portrait Gallery daily 11:30am and 2:30pm. Open daily 9am-5pm. $2, concessions $1, families $5. Wheelchair accessible.)

NATIONAL GALLERY OF AUSTRALIA. The third side of the Parliamentary Triangle is comprised of the four large modern buildings on Parkes Pl., just off King Edward Tce. On the southeastern end, nearest Kings Ave., the National Gallery displays an extensive Australian art collection, Aboriginal works spanning more than 30,000 years of indigenous culture, and a good contemporary collection. Keep your eyes out for a few big-name French impressionists, too. The surrounding sculpture garden is free and open 24hr. (☎ 6240 6502, info 6240 6501; www.nga.gov.au. Open daily 10am-5pm. 1hr. guided tours daily 11am and 2pm. Aboriginal art tour Th and Su 11am. Free; separate fees for special exhibits $12-18. Wheelchair accessible.)

HIGH COURT OF AUSTRALIA. Next door to the National Gallery, Australia's highest court is encased in a seven-story wall of seemingly impregnable glass and steel. When court is in session—two weeks every month—visitors may watch proceedings from public galleries in the courtrooms. (☎ 6270 6811. Open M-F 9:45am-4:30pm. Free. Wheelchair accessible.)

NATIONAL LIBRARY OF AUSTRALIA. The nation's largest library (six million volumes) is the final stop on Parkes Pl. Open for research and visitation, it houses copies of Australian publications on over 200km of shelving. The library also features alternating exhibits on Australian topics. Free **Internet** and printing. (☎ 6262 1111, exhibition schedule 6262 1156; www.nla.gov.au. Free tours Tu and Th 12:30pm. Open M-Th 9am-9pm, F 9am-6pm, Sa 9am-5pm, Su 1:30-5pm. Wheelchair accessible.)

LAKE BURLEY GRIFFIN. The last two attractions in the Parliamentary Triangle are actually located in the middle of the lake. The **Captain Cook Memorial Jet** blows a six-ton column of water to heights of up to 147m to commemorate Captain James Cook's arrival at the east coast of Australia. The bell tower of the **National Carillon** is located on Aspen Island at the other end of the lake's central basin. A gift from Britain on Canberra's 50th birthday in 1963, the Carillon, one of the largest musical instruments in the world, is rung several times a week. (Concert schedule www.nationalcapital.gov.au/visiting/carillon.htm)

OTHER GOVERNMENT BUILDINGS. West of Capital Hill, on the south side of the lake, Yarralumla is peppered with embassies of over 70 nations, displaying a multicultural melange of architecture. **The Lodge,** home to the Australian Prime Minister, is on the corner of Adelaide Ave. and National Circuit, but hecklers be warned—it's closed to the public. Farther down Adelaide Ave., at the **Royal Australian Mint,** on Denison St. in Deakin, you can watch coins being minted. Push a button to "press your own" dollar coin…for $2. (☎ 6202 6819. Open M-F 9am-4pm, Sa-Su 10am-4pm; coin production M-F 9am-noon and 1-4pm. 45min. tours available upon request. Free. Wheelchair accessible.)

NORTH OF THE LAKE

▨ NATIONAL MUSEUM OF AUSTRALIA. Opened in 2001, this attraction, just a short trip from the city center, provides an excellent introduction to the history of the nation's land and people. Highlights include *Circa*, a futuristic rotating multimedia theater, and the First Australians exhibit. (Take bus #32 from Civic. ☎ 6208 5000 or 0800 026 132. Open daily 9am-5pm. Free; fees for special exhibitions.)

PENNY FOR YOUR THOUGHTS No, that waitress isn't stiffing your change; the 1-cent and 2-cent pieces were removed from circulation starting in 1992. Their introduction dates back to Valentine's Day 1966, when Australia moved from the British currency system to a decimal-based one. Officials were so concerned with the smooth transition between systems that they composed the "Decimal Change Over Song": *In come the dollar and in come the cents / To replace the pounds and the shillings and the pence / Be prepared for change when the coins begin to mix / on the 14th of February 1966.* Chorus: *Clink go the coins clink clink clink / Change over day is closer than you think / Learn the value of coins and the way that they appear / And things will be much smoother when the decimal point is here.*

AUSTRALIAN WAR MEMORIAL. The popular crucifix-shaped memorial, with artifacts, photos, and depictions of wartime life by Australian artists, makes a moving tribute. The Hall of Memory holds the tomb of an unknown Australian soldier beneath a beautiful handmade mosaic dome. *(Anzac Pde., on bus route #33 from Civic. ☎ 6243 4211. Tours daily; call for times. Open daily 10am-5pm. Free. Wheelchair accessible.)*

SCREENSOUND AUSTRALIA. Formerly the **National Screen and Sound Archive,** Screensound is one of Canberra's least-known but most enjoyable attractions. The bonanza of sight-and-sound relics of Australian radio, film, and television ranges from the 19th century to today. *(On McCoy Circuit in Acton. Take bus #34 to Liversidge St. ☎ 6248 2000. Open M-F 9am-5pm, Sa-Su 10am-5pm. Free. Wheelchair accessible.)*

AUSTRALIAN INSTITUTE OF SPORT (AIS). After Australia left the 1976 Olympics empty-handed, the disgruntled nation took action and established the AIS as a training facility for the nation's top athletes in 1981. Tours led by resident athletes take regular humans through the world of the aerobically superhuman, with a stop at the hands-on Sportex exhibit where you can try rowing, wheelchair basketball, or golf. A pool and several tennis courts are open for your muscle-toning pleasure. *(On Leverrier Crescent just northwest of O'Connor. Take bus #80 from Civic. ☎ 6214 1010. Open M-F 8:30am-5pm, Sa-Su 10am-4pm. Tours M-F 10:20, 11:30am and 2:30pm; Sa-Su 10, 11:30am, 1, and 2:30pm. $12, children $6, families $33. Outdoor Tennis Courts $10 per hr. Pool $4; swimcap mandatory.)*

AUSTRALIAN NATIONAL BOTANIC GARDENS. Designed in the 1950s and opened to the public in 1970, the park is a living monument to the vast and unique biodiversity of the nation. Planting groups highlight the diversity within both species, as in the Eucalypt Lawn, and ecosystems, as in the Rainforest Gully. *(Take bus #34 to Daley Rd.; walk 20min. toward the lake along Clunies Ross Rd. ☎ 6250 9540. Free guided walks daily 11am and 2pm. Open daily 9am-5pm. Visitors Center open 9:30am-4:30pm. Free.)*

NATIONAL AQUARIUM AND WILDLIFE SANCTUARY. Unless you're a kid (or have one), you may have trouble justifying the trip from the city center. The nearly seven-hectare sanctuary for native Australian fauna does have some redeeming features, but it's little more than your average animal park. *(From Parkes Way, heading out of the city to the west, Lady Denman Dr. branches south toward the aquarium at Scrivener Dam. ☎ 6287 1211. Open daily 9am-5pm. $16, concessions $12.50, children $9.50, families $46.)*

☑ ENTERTAINMENT

Casino Canberra, 21 Binara St., can help you strike it rich, or not. *(☎ 6257 7074. Open daily noon-6am.)* In addition to the usual first-run cinemas, Canberra has some funky art-house alternatives, including **Electric Shadows,** on Akuna St. near City Walk. *(☎ 6247 5060. $13.50, students $8.50; before 5pm $8.50/$7.)*

Housing several venues in varying shapes and sizes, the **Canberra Theatre** on London Circuit is the best place to start looking for live entertainment. Register for the free Under 27 Club and take advantage of great savings on tickets. (☎6257 1077. $30-65, ages 18-27 $25.)

Canberra's calendar is packed with minor **festivals,** but a few annual events temporarily transform the city. Easter weekend (Apr. 17-21, 2003) brings the **National Folk Festival** (www.folkfestival.asn.au), with music, dance, poetry, and art exhibitions. For 16 days in April, the **Canberra Festival** (www.canberrafestival.org.au) brings musical productions, a hot-air balloon show, and street parties to the captial. The last day of the festival is a public holiday, Canberra Day. **The Floriade** (Sept. 13-Oct. 12, 2003) paints the shores of Lake Burley Griffin with thousands of springtime blooms and relieves the city of all accommodations; book ahead. See www.floriadeaustralia.com for details and future dates.

NIGHTLIFE

Canberra's after-hours scene is surprisingly vibrant. The student population supports a solid range of bars and clubs, while relaxed licensing allows boozing to continue until 4am. Most places claim to close "late," meaning midnight on slow nights and until whenever people stop partying on busier nights. On weekend nights, just wander around Civic and follow the pounding music and scurrying clubgoers. The clientele at hot spots can usually be characterized as one of three different crowds: raging uni students, posh government officials, or unwinding defense school students. Check out the city's entertainment publications, p. 76.

■ **The Wig and Pen** (☎6248 0171), on Alinga St., 2 blocks west of the bus interchange. This cozy, laid-back pub, named for its location in the solicitors' district, is the perfect place to sample some incredible, prize-winning homebrews and catch up with friends. After a few schooners ($5), you'll be primed for crazier clubs and bars. Bands (jazz, folk, blues) every night. No cover. Open M-F noon-late, Sa 2pm-late, Su 3pm-late.

■ **Gypsy Bar,** 131 City Walk (☎6247 7300). A Canberra institution. One of the few places where you'll find ripped jeans, black turtlenecks, and government suits partying in the same place. The unpretentious Gypsy books both local talent and big names, from laid-back acoustic to full-on hardcore, and pulls it off with style. Tu all-night Happy Hour and free pool. Th-Sa cover $5-15. Open Tu-F 5pm-late, Sa 8pm-late.

Filthy McFadden's (☎6239 5303), in the far corner of Green Square at the intersection of Jardine and Eyre St., Kingston. Frequented by loyal backpackers and regulars, "Filthy's" epitomizes the Irish country pub. Pints of Guinness will set you back $6, but you can bring in pizza from the shop next door. Largest whiskey collection in the southern hemisphere (200+). Live music Su nights. No cover. Open daily noon-late.

Mooseheads, 105 London Circuit (☎6257 6496). A rare Canadian bar with rare Canadian paraphernalia. Very popular with uni students. The adjacent nightclub, **The Moose Upstairs,** gyrates Th-Sa with retro dance (70s to early 90s) and Top-40 until 5am. Sa cover $5. Bottle of the bar's Canadian namesake beer $5. Open M-Sa 11am-late.

The Meridian Club, 34 Mort St., Braddon (☎6248 9966). A short walk north from the city bus interchange in Civic. Canberra's only exclusively gay/lesbian club. The dance floor, a large raised platform, grooves and grinds, especially on F-Sa nights. Cover F-Sa $5, students $3. Open Tu-Th 7pm-midnight, F 7pm-late, Sa 8pm-late, Su 6-10pm.

ANU Student Uni Bar (☎6249 0786), in the student union building, near the corner of North Rd. and University Ave., Acton. A popular student hangout and the cheapest pub in Canberra, hosting some of the biggest names in music. Check *bma* (see p. 76) for a comprehensive gig listing. Open M-Sa noon-late, except during uni holidays.

ACT

⚡ DAYTRIPS FROM CANBERRA

SOUTH OF CANBERRA

Bushland pushes on Canberra's borders with the promise of an easy retreat from urban refinement. The Tourist Drive 5 hits the major southern attractions on a long, full day of sightseeing.

CANBERRA DEEP SPACE COMMUNICATIONS COMPLEX. One of the most powerful antenna centers in the world, the Complex will awe novices and serious space cadets alike. The 70m radio dish tracks signals from an orbiting spacecraft. The **Canberra Space Centre** has displays on the history of space exploration. An old Telstra phone booth now serves as the NASA hotline, a visitors' link to the latest space mission info. *(Off Paddy's River Rd., 40km southwest of Civic. ☎6201 7800; www.cdscc.nasa.gov. Open daily 9am-5pm. Free.)*

TIDBINBILLA NATURE RESERVE. Dedicated to preserving the natural gum-forest habitat of the kangaroos, wallabies, koalas, emus, and other animals that roam the area, the reserve loosely monitors its residents to better your chances of encountering them. Thirteen marked bushwalks in the park range from 30min. strolls to full-day outings. The walk to **Gibraltar rock** (3hr.) rewards not-so-easy rock climbing with stupendous views. The **Birrigai Time Trail** (3km) is an easy trail that allows bushwalkers to see a 21,000-year-old rock shelter. The **Tidbinbilla Visitor Centre,** a 40min. drive southwest of Civic off Paddy's River Rd., has info on bushwalks and ranger-led activities throughout the 5500-hectare park. *(☎6205 1233; www.environment.act.gov.au. Park open daily 9am-6pm. $9 per car per day, full-year pass $16.50. Visitor Centre open M-F 9am-4:30pm, Sa-Su 9am-5:30pm. M-F Bushbird Feed 2:30pm; Sa-Su Koala Walk 1pm, Bushbird Feed and Wetland tour 2:30pm. Other programs offered throughout the week as staffing permits.)*

NAMADGI NATIONAL PARK. The expansive Namadgi National Park is the western border of Tidbinbilla Nature Reserve and fills almost all of the southern arm of the ACT with preserved alpine wilderness traversed by only one major paved route, the Naas/Bobayan Rd. Though the park has walking tracks for all experience levels, it is most famous for its untrammeled recesses accessible only to serious hikers. **Campsites ❶** at Orroral River and Mt. Clear, each with parking nearby, have firewood, untreated water, and toilets. The **Namadgi Visitor Centre,** on the Naas/Bobayan Rd. 3km south of **Tharwa,** sells maps and has info about Aboriginal rock painting and camping options. *(☎6207 2900. Park open 24hr. Sites $3.30 per person. Register at Visitor Centre. Open M-F 9am-4pm, Sa-Su 9am-4:30pm.)*

LANYON HOMESTEAD. Built in the 1800s, the buildings at Lanyon Homestead survey Canberra's European architectural history, from the days of convict labor through Federation. An Aboriginal canoe tree gives evidence of earlier habitation at the same site. Lanyon's greatest draw may be the **Nolan Gallery,** which has many of Sidney Nolan's paintings of bushranger Ned Kelly. *(Tharwa Dr., 30km south of Canberra. Homestead ☎6237 5136, gallery 6237 5192. Open Tu-Su 10am-4pm. Homestead buildings $6.50, gallery $3, both $7. Wheelchair accessible.)*

NORTH OF CANBERRA

NATIONAL DINOSAUR MUSEUM. The privately-run museum includes over 300 fossils, ten full-sized dinosaur skeletons, and three reconstructions, complete with skin and teeth. *(Barton Hwy. at the corner of Gold Creek Rd. Follow Northbourne until the turn-off to Barton Hwy. ☎6230 2655. Open daily 10am-5pm. $9, families $26.)*

GINNINDERRA FALLS AND GORGE. Just over the New South Wales border on the Murrumbidgee River, 20km from Civic, a privately-owned park holds the Ginninderra Falls, which spill 200m down into the Ginninderra Ravine. The park is also known for its **rock-climbing** faces. *(☎6278 4222. Open daily 10am-5pm. $4.50, children $2.50; $10 per vehicle.)*

NEW SOUTH WALES

From a historical perspective, there's no disputing that New South Wales is Australia's premier state. It was here that British convicts lived through the first bitter years of colonization, dreaming of what might lie beyond the impassable Blue Mountains, and here that explorers first broke through the Great Dividing Range, opening the interior of the country for settlement and ensuring the stability of the colony. In the central plains and on the rich land of the Riverina, Merino wool and agricultural success provided the state with its first glimpses of prosperity. Then, in 1851, prospectors struck gold just west of the mountains, and Australia's history changed forever. No longer the desolate prison of exiled convicts, New South Wales became a place that promised a new life and a chance to strike it rich. Although the gold rush days are long gone, New South Wales has continued to grow. Today, it's the most populous state and—thanks largely to Sydney—the diverse and sophisticated center of modern Australia.

The country's biggest and flashiest city, Sydney sits midway along the coast. North and south of Sydney, sandy surfing and swimming beaches string together in an almost unbroken chain. The trip up the coast is the be-all-and-end-all of backpacker party routes, with the large coastal towns of Port Macquarie and Coffs Harbour whetting appetites for the full-on delights awaiting in the legendary counterculture of Byron Bay. The south coast is colder but refreshingly far less crowded and every bit as beautiful. Directly west of Sydney's suburban reaches, the Blue Mountains encompass some of the state's favorite getaways and separate the coastal strip from the expansive Central West and outback regions. The New England Plateau, along the Great Dividing Range north of the wineries of the Hunter Valley, achieves an unusually lush and high-altitude setting for a cozy collection of small Australian towns and stunning national parks. Just below the carved-out enclave of the Australian Capital Territory, the Snowy Mountains offer winter skiing and superb summer hiking.

The attractions of New South Wales are as varied as the terrain. Whether it's the cosmopolitan buzz of Sydney, the challenging bushwalks of the Blue Mountains, the laid-back surf culture of Byron, or the post-apocalyptic simplicity of the outback, most visitors find plenty to write home about.

NEW SOUTH WALES HIGHLIGHTS

NAMBUCCA HEADS. Relax and soak up the rays on the peaceful beaches of Nambucca Heads or paint your own masterpiece on the V-Wall. (p. 168.)

SYDNEY. 'nuff said. (p. 86.)

BLUE MOUNTAINS. Escape urban life in the great outdoors of the Blue Mountains. Venture to the Three Sisters outcropping at Echo Point or go on a walkabout. (p. 131.)

HUNTER VALLEY. Tour the vineyards and taste the fine red and white wines of the Hunter Valley. (p. 145.)

THREDBO. Fly down the long runs on Thredbo's black diamond slopes. (p. 214.)

NIMBIN. Inhale the counterculture and wily ways of Nimbin. (p. 180.)

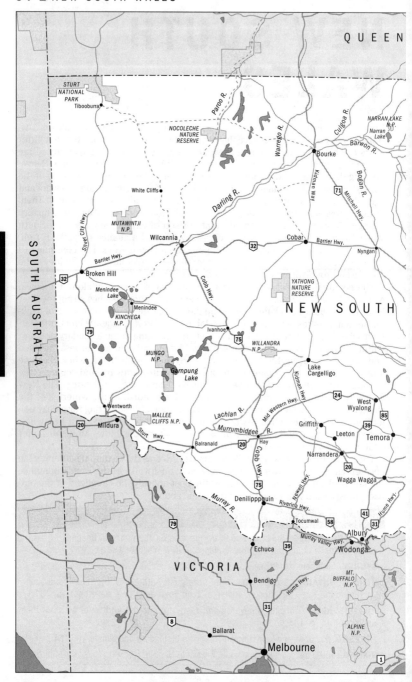

NEW SOUTH WALES

QUEEN

SOUTH AUSTRALIA

NEW SOUTH

VICTORIA

STURT NATIONAL PARK
Tibooburra

NOCOLECHE NATURE RESERVE

Paroo R.

Warrego R.

Culgoa R.

NARRAN LAKE N.P.
Narran Lake

Barwon R.

Bourke

Kidman Way

71

Mitchell Hwy.

Bogan R.

White Cliffs

Darling R.

MUTAWINTJI N.P.

Wilcannia

Cobar   Barrier Hwy.

32

Nyngan

Silver City Hwy.

Barrier Hwy.

32

Broken Hill

Menindee Lake
Menindee

KINCHEGA N.P.

Cobb Hwy.

YATHONG NATURE RESERVE

79

Ivanhoe

75

WILLANDRA N.P.

MUNGO N.P.
Garnpung Lake

Lake Cargelligo

Kidman Hwy.

24

West Wyalong

85

Wentworth

MALLEE CLIFFS N.P.

Lachlan R.

Mid Western Hwy.

Griffith

Leeton

39

Temora

20

Mildura

Sturt Hwy.

Murrumbidgee R.

Balranald

20   Hay

75

Cobb Hwy.

Narrandera

20

Wagga Wagga

79

Murray R.

Denilippppquin

Riverina Hwy.

Newell Hwy.

Tocumwal

58

41

Hume Hwy.

31

Albury

Murray Valley Hwy.

Wodonga

Echuca

39

MT. BUFFALO N.P.

Bendigo   Hume Hwy.

31

8

Ballarat

ALPINE N.P.

Melbourne

1

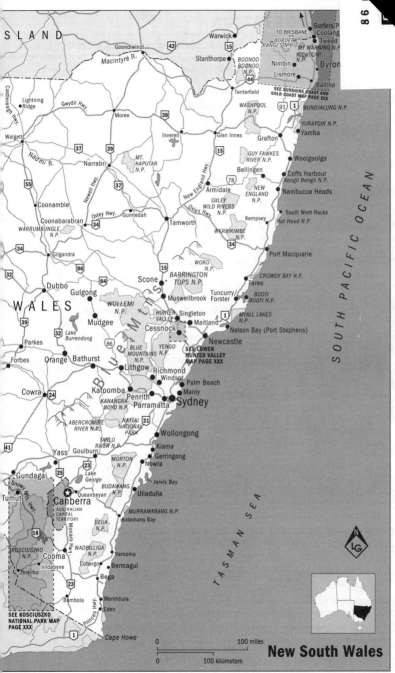

NEW SOUTH WALES

New South Wales

SLAND

QUEENSLAND
Goondiwindi
Macintyre R.
42
Warwick
15
Stanthorpe
BOONOO
BOONOO
N.P.
44
Nimbin
Lismore
TO BRISBANE
BORDER
RANGES N.P.
MT WARNING N.P.
NIGHTCAP
N.P.
Surfers P.
Coolang
Tweed
Byron
Ballina

Lightning
Ridge
Castlereagh Hwy.
Gwydir Hwy.
Moree
38
Tenterfield
WASHPOOL
N.P.
91 1 BUNDJALUNG N.P.
SEE SUNSHINE COAST AND
GOLD COAST MAP PAGE XXX

Walgett
37
39
Inverell
Glen Innes
15
Grafton
YURAYGIR N.P.
Yamba

Naomi R.
55
Narrabri
MT.
KAPUTAR
N.P.
37
Armidale
GUY FAWKES
RIVER N.P.
Bellingen
78
NEW
ENGLAND
N.P.
Woolgoolga
Coffs Harbour
Bongil Bongil N.P.
Nambucca Heads

Coonamble
Coonabarabran
34
WARRUMBUNGLE
N.P.
Oxley Hwy.
Gunnedah
Tamworth
OXLEY
WILD RIVERS
N.P.
Oxley Hwy.
Kempsey
WERRIKIMBE
N.P.
34
South West Rocks
Hat Head N.P.

34
Gilgandra
86
32
Dubbo
Gulgong
84
WALES
39
32 Lake
Burrendong
Mudgee
WOLLEMI
N.P.
Scone
WOKO
N.P.
BARRINGTON
TOPS N.P.
Muswellbrook
Singleton
HUNTER
VALLEY
Cessnock
Maitland
Port Macquarie
CROWDY BAY N.P.
Taree
Tuncurry/
Forster
BOOTI
BOOTI N.P.
MYALL LAKES
N.P.
1
Nelson Bay (Port Stephens)

Parkes
Forbes
Orange
Bathurst
BLUE
MOUNTAINS
N.P.
YENGO
N.P.
Newcastle
SEE LOWER
HUNTER VALLEY
MAP PAGE XXX
Lithgow
Richmond
Windsor
Katoomba
KANANGRA
BOYD N.P.
Penrith
Parramatta
Palm Beach
Manly
Sydney
Cowra
24
ABERCROMBIE
RIVER N.P.
NATTAI
NATIONAL
PARK
31
Wollongong

41
Yass
Goulburn
TARLO
RIVER N.P.
MORTON
N.P.
Kiama
Gerringong
Nowra
25
23
Lake
George
Jervis Bay

Gundagai
Snowy Mts Hwy.
Tumut
Canberra
AUSTRALIAN
CAPITAL
TERRITORY
Queanbeyan
BUDAWANG
N.P.
Ulladulla
DEUA
N.P.
MURRAMARANG N.P.
Batemans Bay

18
KOSCIUSZKO
N.P.
Cooma
Monaro Hwy.
WADBILLIGA
N.P.
Narooma
Jindabyne
Cobargo
Bermagui
Thredbo
23
Bega

Bombala
SEE KOSCIUSZKO
NATIONAL PARK MAP
PAGE XXX
Princes Hwy.
Merimbula
Eden
1
Cape Howe

SOUTH PACIFIC OCEAN

TASMAN SEA

Blue Mtns.

N
LG

0   100 miles
0   100 kilometers

_ TRANSPORTATION

New South Wales has an excellent **public transportation** system, especially in the coastal part of the state. For timetables or route info regarding bus, rail, or ferries in Sydney and throughout the state, call **CityRail** (☎ 13 15 00) or **Countrylink** (☎ 13 22 32; www.countrylink.nsw.gov.au), New South Wales' sole rail transport. The major bus companies are **McCafferty's/Greyhound** (☎ 13 14 99 or 13 20 30; www.mccaffertys.com.au or www.greyhound.com.au) and **Premier** (☎ 13 34 10).

SYDNEY ☎ 02

At times elegant, at times almost American in its commercialism, at times other-worldly, unusually optimistic, and always amazing, Sydney pulses with self-assurance as only one of the world's great cities can pulse. Nearly four million Sydney-siders (about 20% of the national population) inhabit Australia's unofficial capital, and most international visitors first touch Australian soil here—even if only to find themselves swept up in a cosmopolitan whirlwind of finance and culture.

Still basking in the glow of the tourism boom of its Olympic moment, Sydney reveals a history as old as any Australian city's in its sights and museums. In 1788, the city's stupendous natural harbor, then called Port Jackson, drew the First Fleet of colonists and convicts north of their intended settlement at Botany Bay. Today, the iconic Harbour Bridge and Sydney Opera House occupy the foreshores of Sydney Cove and draw visitors to the water's edge for a few photo-framing moments...which easily become hours on sunny days when sailboats skim across the water and the Quay rings with conversations in multiple languages.

Sydney refuses to be culturally contained, even on a more permanent basis. The city is currently home to an Asian population (Indian, Thai, Korean, Japanese, and Chinese) who have not just influenced the fashion and cuisine but also set the standard in Sydney for what comes "next." Sydney is also one of the most gay-friendly cities in the world. The annual Mardi Gras attracts enormous crowds of all persuasions, and *Priscilla, Queen of the Desert*, was partially filmed here. Some Aussies find Sydney's future-forward perspective intimidating (or perhaps just prefer the euro-stylings of more laid-back Melbourne), but for visitors, Sydney isn't as fast-paced as other international cities of equal size. Remember, this, after all, is Australia, the land of "no worries."

After the urban preening and momentary price-hikes brought on by the 2000 Olympics, spirits here are high. The world's greatest perspiration-celebration couldn't have found a more appropriate home than multi-ethnic, athlete-worshipping, environmentally conscious Sydney. Eager to serve as a springboard to the continent, the locals are glad you came; after raging at the clubs, relaxing by the water, and marvelling at the taste of Down Under history and culture, you will be ready to relocate Sydney-side for the long haul.

SYDNEY HIGHLIGHTS

SYDNEY HARBOUR. Mrs. Macquaries Point has grand views of the Harbour. (p. 114)

DARLING HARBOUR. This popular tourist area holds the Sydney Aquarium and Powerhouse Museum. (p. 116)

BONDI BEACH. The world-renowned backdrop for countless surf movies. You've seen the glitz and glamour on postcards, now see it in real life. (p. 92)

SYDNEY OPERA HOUSE. Defining the Sydney skyline, the Opera House is not to be missed. If you're lucky enough to catch a show, make sure to be on time. (p. 113)

KINGS CROSS. This is the place for non-stop partying. (p. 124)

■ INTERCITY TRANSPORTATIO

BY PLANE. Sydney's **Kingsford-Smith Airport,** 10km southw
ness District, serves most major international carriers. **Qar**
most domestic destinations. For security reasons, long-terr
available; however, 24hr. "temporary baggage storage" i
bag. The **New South Wales Tourism Centre** (a.k.a the **Sydney I**
international terminal, offers a booking service and free
tels. (☎9667 6058. Open daily from 5:30am until after the
Transportation into the city is available directly outside the termin...
Express runs to the city center (#300), Kings Cross (#350), and the northern and
eastern beaches. (☎13 15 00. Daily 5:30am-11pm. $7 one-way, $12 return.) **Kings-ford-Smith Transport** runs to city and inner suburb accommodations. (☎9667 3221.
Daily every 20min. 5am-10pm. $7 one-way, $11 return.) A variety of independent
shuttles run to the city for around $7. **Airport Link,** part of the Cityrail network, effi-
ciently shuttles passengers to Circular Quay (15min.; trains run every 10min.) and
the city suburbs. (☎13 15 00; www.airportlink.com.au. Trains operate daily 5am-
midnight. $10, students $7.) Many hostels offer free pickup. A **taxi** to the city center
costs about $20 from the domestic terminal and $25 from the international area;
the drive takes 20-45min., depending on traffic.

BY TRAIN. Countrylink (☎13 22 32) **trains** depart from the **Central Railway Station** on
Eddy Ave. Branch offices at **Town Hall Station, Bondi Junction Station,** in the **Coun-trylink New South Wales Travel Centre** next door to Wynyard Station, and on **Alfred St.**
at Circular Quay also sell tickets. Fares include all meals. To Perth, Adelaide, or
Alice Springs, holiday class is about twice as expensive as coach and includes a
sleeping berth, while a luxurious first-class trip is about three times as much as
coach. First class for daytrips, however, is generally 30% more expensive than
coach, and return fares for all trips are generally double the price of one-way.

BY TRAIN, FROM SYDNEY TO:

DESTINATION	COMPANY	DURATION	TIMES	PRICE
Adelaide	Great Southern	25hr.	M, Th	$176
Alice Springs	Great Southern	45hr.	Su, W	$390
Brisbane	Countrylink	14½-15hr.	2 per day	$110
Byron Bay	Countrylink	12½hr.	2 per day	$98
Canberra	Countrylink	4hr.	3 per day	$47
Coffs Harbour	Countrylink	8hr.	3 per day	$79
Melbourne	Countrylink	10½hr.	2 per day	$110
Surfers Paradise	Countrylink	14-15hr.	2 per day	$105
Perth	Great Southern	3 days	M, Th	$459

BY BUS. Fifteen bus companies operate from the **Sydney Coach Terminal,** Central
Station, on the corner of Eddy Ave. at Pitt St. (☎9281 9366. Open daily 6am-10pm.)
Luggage storage is available ($6-9 per day). Because special rates and concessions
vary, consult a travel agent for the lowest rate on any given itinerary—the folks at
the Central Station coach terminal are well-informed. The major national company, **McCafferty's/Greyhound** (☎13 14 99 or 13 20 30; www.mccaffertys.com.au or
www.greyhound.com.au) generally offers more frequent trips to major destinations than the smaller regional carriers, but their rates are often not the best. Be
sure to shop around. The Table below refers to McCafferty's/Greyhound.

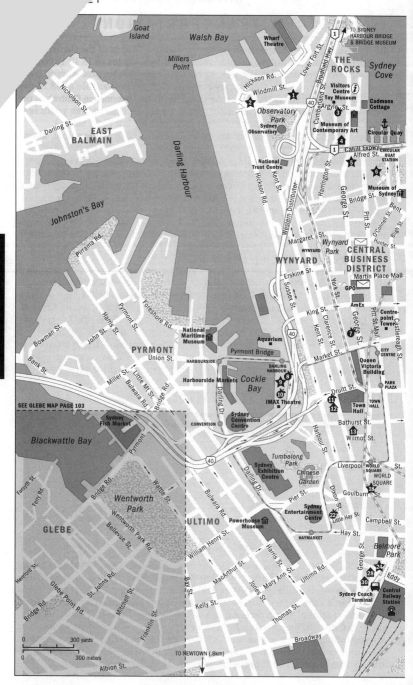

Goat
Island

Walsh Bay

Wharf
Theatre

TO SYDNEY
HARBOUR BRIDGE
& BRIDGE MUSEUM

THE
ROCKS

Sydney
Cove

Millers
Point

Hickson Rd.

Lower Fort St.

Cumberland St.

Bradfield Hwy.

Windmill St.

Visitors
Centre
Toy Museum

Argyle St.

Cadmans
Cottage

2

Observatory
Park

Museum of
Contemporary Art

Circular Quay

Sydney
Observatory

3

4

EAST
BALMAIN

Nicholson St.

Darling St.

Hickson Rd.

Kent St.

Harrington St.

Cahill EXPWY

Alfred St.

CIRCULAR
QUAY
STATION

National
Trust Centre

5

Darling Harbour

George St.

Bridge St.

6

Museum of
Sydney

Pitt St.

Bent St.

Johnston's Bay

O'Connell St.

Bligh St.

Hunter St.

Margaret St.

WYNYARD

Erskine St.

Sussex St.

Wynyard
Park

CENTRAL
BUSINESS
DISTRICT

Martin Place Mall

GPO

Pirrama Rd.

Foreshore Rd.

Pyrmont St.

Harris St.

Bowman St.

John St.

York St.

King St.

Clarence St.

Kent St.

AmEx

Centre-
point
Tower

George St.

Pitt St. Mall

Castlereagh St.

Bank St.

Miller St.

Little Mt St.

Bulwara Rd.

Bridge Rd.

PYRMONT

Union St.

National
Maritime
Museum

Aquarium

Pyrmont Bridge

HARBOURSIDE

Market St.

7

CITY
CENTRE

Queen
Victoria
Building

PARK
PLAZA

SEE GLEBE MAP PAGE 103

Harbourside Markets

Cockle
Bay

DARLING
HARBOUR

8

9

Druitt St.

11

12

Town
Hall

TOWN
HALL

Bathurst St.

13

Wilmot St.

Sydney
Fish Market

CONVENTION

10

IMAX Theatre

Sydney
Convention
Centre

Darling Dr.

Blackwattle Bay

Wentworth Park

GLEBE

Forsyth St.

Ferry Rd.

Hereford St.

Bridge Rd.

Glebe Point Rd.

St. Johns Rd.

Mitchell St.

Franklin St.

Bellevue St.

Wentworth Park Rd.

Pyrmont

Wattle St.

Bulwara Rd.

Darling Dr.

Sydney
Exhibition
Centre

Tumbalong
Park

Chinese
Garden

Pier St.

Sydney
Entertainment
Centre

Liverpool St.

WORLD
SQUARE

WORLD
SQUARE

Goulburn St.

15

Dixon St.

Little Hay St.

22

Campbell St.

ULTIMO

William Henry St.

Bay St.

MacArthur St.

Harris St.

Jones St.

Mary Ann St.

Ultimo Rd.

Powerhouse
Museum

HAYMARKET

Hay St.

George St.

Belmore
Park

28

24

Eddy Ave.

30

Sydney Coach
Terminal

Central
Railway
Station

Kelly St.

Thomas St.

Broadway

0   300 yards

0   300 meters

TO NEWTOWN (.8km)

Albion St.

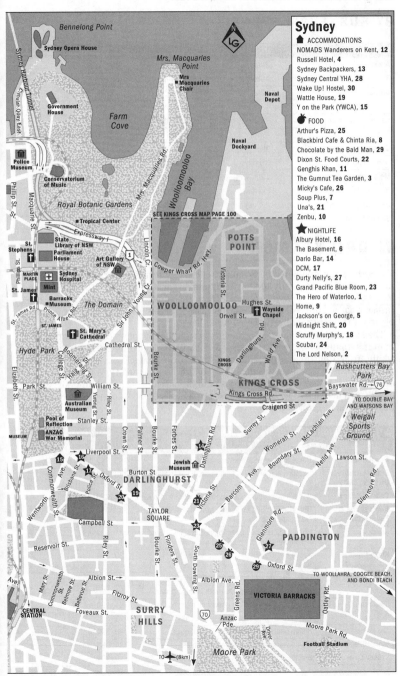

Sydney

🏠 **ACCOMMODATIONS**

NOMADS Wanderers on Kent, **12**
Russell Hotel, **4**
Sydney Backpackers, **13**
Sydney Central YHA, **28**
Wake Up! Hostel, **30**
Wattle House, **19**
Y on the Park (YWCA), **15**

🍴 **FOOD**

Arthur's Pizza, **25**
Blackbird Cafe & Chinta Ria, **8**
Chocolate by the Bald Man, **29**
Dixon St. Food Courts, **22**
Genghis Khan, **11**
The Gumnut Tea Garden, **3**
Micky's Cafe, **26**
Soup Plus, **7**
Una's, **21**
Zenbu, **10**

⭐ **NIGHTLIFE**

Albury Hotel, **16**
The Basement, **6**
Darlo Bar, **14**
DCM, **17**
Durty Nelly's, **27**
Grand Pacific Blue Room, **23**
The Hero of Waterloo, **1**
Home, **9**
Jackson's on George, **5**
Midnight Shift, **20**
Scruffy Murphy's, **18**
Scubar, **24**
The Lord Nelson, **2**

SEE KINGS CROSS MAP PAGE 100

BY BUS, FROM SYDNEY TO:

DESTINATION	DURATION	TIMES	PRICE
Adelaide	24hr.	2 per day	$133
Alice Springs (via Adelaide)	40hr.	2 per day	$289
Brisbane	17hr.	6 per day	$93-98
Byron Bay	13hr.	4 per day	$89
Cairns (via Brisbane)	2½ days	6 per day	$271
Canberra	4¾hr.	11 per day	$36
Coffs Harbour	9hr.	5 per day	$74
Darwin (via Alice Springs)	3½ days	2 per day	$473
Melbourne	12hr.	5 per day	$62
Mt. Isa (via Brisbane)	3½ days	2 per day	$355
Perth (via Adelaide)	2½ days	1 per day	$359
Surfers Paradise	15hr.	5 per day	$89

■ ORIENTATION

The Sydney metropolitan area is immense. The city seems to be contained only by the forces of nature, with **Ku-Ring-Gai Chase National Park** to the north, the **Blue Mountains** to the west, **Royal National Park** to the south, and the **Pacific Ocean,** the **Tasman Sea,** and **Sydney Harbour** to the east. Much of this area, however, is made up of largely quiet, residential outer suburbs.

The standard city map creates the impression that Sydney's center is far larger than it actually is. In truth, the walk to Circular Quay along Pitt St. takes only 30min. from Central Station and only 15min. from Kings Cross. Within the city proper are areas that Sydney-siders call "suburbs"—don't worry, you haven't wandered out of Sydney—others might just call these really big neighborhoods. Each has its own distinctive *je-ne-sais-quoi*. For a bird's eye view of it all, ascend **Centrepoint Tower** (see p. 115).

SYDNEY'S NEIGHBORHOODS AT A GLANCE		
NEIGHBORHOOD	FEATURES	BY BUS
Bondi Beach	Home to most of Sydney's celebrity types.	380, 382, L82
Central Business District (CBD)	Includes Martin Place, Chinatown, Paddy's Market.	380, 394
Coogee Beach	Bondi's rival; youthful energy and a vibrant nightlife.	314, 372, 373, 374
Darlinghurst & Paddington	Hip neighborhood for young, fashionable, creative types; hot nightlife.	380, 394
Glebe	Home to cafes, pubs, and bookstores; influenced by neighboring student population.	431, 432, 433, 434
Kings Cross	Seedy center of Sydney backpacker culture, with hostels, cafes, and strip shows.	380, 394
Kirribilli	Quiet upscale neighborhood, excellent cafes.	151, 190
Manly	Friendly holiday resort area with great beaches.	151, 190/155, 247/144
Mosman	Taronga Park Zoo, other parks and gardens.	151, 190, 247
Newtown	Bohemian; vintage clothing, used books.	423
The Rocks	Historic neighborhood, upscale boutiques.	380, 394, 423
Surry Hills	Multicultural; cafes and clothing stores.	394, 380, 373
Sydney Cove	Sydney Opera House and Sydney Harbour.	380, 394

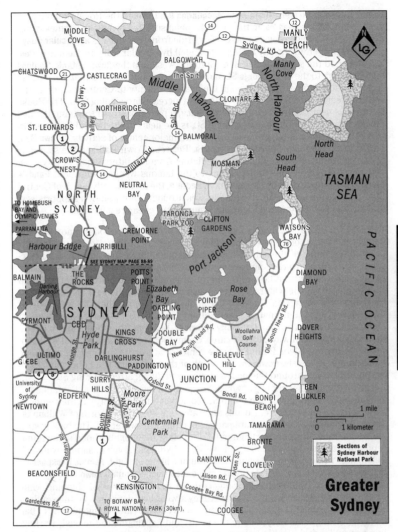

Greater Sydney

0 ___ 1 mile
0 ___ 1 kilometer

Sections of Sydney Harbour National Park

SYDNEY COVE AND THE CITY CENTER. Sydney's most famous sights lie on the Harbour at **Sydney Cove,** directly north of the city center. On the Cove and at the southern end of the **Sydney Harbour Bridge** is **The Rocks,** a historic neighborhood with upscale boutiques. Drivers entering downtown Sydney from the north can enter over the **Harbour Bridge** or through the **Harbour Tunnel,** which enters the city east of the Cove (southbound toll for either $2). Though less scenic, the tunnel is a more convenient route for anyone heading into the eastern suburbs. The **Sydney Opera House** is located prominently on Bennelong Point, east of the cove, and north of the sprawling **Royal Botanic Gardens** and an emerald gem of a park called the **Domain** just south of the Gardens. For the best views of the Harbour Bridge and

Opera House, take a stroll via **Mrs. Macquaries Rd.** through the Royal Botanic Gardens to **Mrs. Macquaries Point,** the tip of the peninsula that forms the northeast corner of the Botanic Gardens; or take a ferry ride from the wharves at **Circular Quay.**

Sydney proper, or the **city center,** is bounded by Circular Quay to the north, **Central Station** to the south, **Darling Harbour** to the west, and the **Royal Botanic Gardens** and **Hyde Park** to the east. **George St.** and **Pitt St.** are major avenues that run parallel from Circular Quay straight through the heart of the city to Central Station in the south. Street numbers begin at the water and increase proceeding from The Rocks to the 800s near Central Station. **Martin Place,** a pedestrian mall spanning the five blocks between George and Macquarie St., is the heart of the **Central Business District (CBD).** Farther south in the CDB, the next major center of activity is **Town Hall,** on Druitt St. between George and Kent St. Between Town Hall and the station is Sydney's rapidly growing **Chinatown,** radiating from the intersection of Hay, Sussex, and George St. This area is home to the famous weekend-discount **Paddy's Market,** also known locally as **Haymarket. Redfern,** the area directly south of Central Station, *may be unsafe at night.* The area around Central Station supports several backpacker accommodations and a number of cheap restaurants.

INNER SUBURBS. Many tiny municipalities (or "neighborhoods") known as the **inner suburbs** compose the rest of Sydney's central urban area. Despite their proximity to one another, the suburbs maintain distinct characters and special attractions. Many areas overlap, and some are known by more than one name. West of the city center, **Pyrmont** covers the point of land between Darling Harbour and Blackwattle Bay. The waterside here is also called **Darling Harbour** and is serviced by the Sydney Monorail. South of Pyrmont, **Ultimo** approaches the west side of Central Station and ultimately reaches the Chinatown area. **Glebe,** southwest of Ultimo and just north of the **University of Sydney,** benefits from the presence of students in all the usual ways: casual cafes, cheap food, crowded pubs, and well-supplied bookstores. Glebe Point Rd. is the center of activity in this district and home to a number of hostels. **Newtown,** just south of the university, is a bohemian neighborhood centered around the main shopping and dining artery of King St.

The infamous inner suburb of **Kings Cross,** east of the city center at the far end of William St., once reigned (and continues to, albeit half-heartedly) as the center of Sydney backpacker culture. Hostels and cafes line Victoria St. north of William St. and busy nightclubs and pubs are packed in along Bayswater Rd. The bawdy strip shows and solicitors on Darlinghurst Rd. explain the neighborhood's newfound reputation as the center of all that is seedy in Sydney. Travelers should watch all belongings while in the Cross and avoid walking alone at night. **Female backpackers on their own should probably steer clear of the area from dusk until dawn.**

Near Kings Cross, **Woolloomooloo** gets down to the business of shipping while **Potts Point** and **Elizabeth Bay** nourish Sydney's wealthier denizens. To the south of Kings Cross, **Victoria St.** goes chic with the city's coolest cafes lining the way to **Darlinghurst.** Along with **Surry Hills** to the south and **Paddington** to the east, Darlinghurst provides fashionable housing for young, creative types. Sydney's nightlife revolves around the outrageous clubs along **Oxford St.,** the main road through Darlinghurst, Paddington, and Woollahra to the east. Just south of the army's stately Victoria Barracks, **Moore Park** and **Centennial Park** to the east form the city's largest swath of greenery and house Sydney's major athletic facilities, including the **Sydney Football Stadium** and the **Cricket Ground.**

FAR EAST AND SOUTHERN BEACHES. Outside of these central areas, surroundings get less urban. East of Paddington, **Woollahra's** terrace houses provide a nice change of scenery. To the north, **Double Bay** and **Rose Bay** are among Sydney's most exclusive residential areas and are the location of Sydney's elegant resort shopping areas. **Bondi Junction** (BOND-eye), south of Woollahra, is the last train stop on the eastern end of the subway system. Ten minutes east by bus or subway is the famous **Bondi Beach,** model of many a surf movie and home to some of Sydney's "A-list." Farther south, the beaches of **Tamarama, Clovelly,** and **Bronte** offer low-key alternatives for families and quieter sunbathers. **Coogee Beach** lies farthest south and rivals Bondi with its popular beachlife and young residents. Decide for yourself by taking the hour-long ☐walk along the coastline between Bondi and Coogee Beaches, sampling all the beaches in between.

NORTH SHORE. The second half of Sydney's professional district fronts the **north shore** of Sydney Harbour at the other end of Harbour Bridge. **North Sydney** was originally settled by wealthy merchants and its upper-class heritage gleams through today. It's the playground of wealthy urbanites and posh business people. While tourist attractions on the north shore are essentially limited to **Taronga Park Zoo** in Mosman and the beach communities of **Manly** and **Collaroy** (all accessible by ferry), the beautiful, more secluded north shore beaches are worthy escapes from the city proper. The meandering ferry rides to Manly and Taronga (see p. 118) are interesting enough in themselves to justify the trip on a pleasant day.

▐ LOCAL TRANSPORTATION

Sydney's well-oiled public transportation machine makes for simple traveling. The **Sydney Transit Authority (STA)** is comprised of **Sydney Buses, CityRail Trains,** and **Sydney Ferries;** the network stops just about anywhere. For information or route advice on any part of the STA system, call ☎ 13 15 00. A **bus information kiosk** is at Circular Quay, on the corner of Alfred and Loftus St. (Open M-F 8am-8pm, Sa-Su 9am-2pm.) There's a **ferry kiosk** near Wharf 4, on Circular Quay, dispensing maps and advice (open M-F 7am-6pm, Sa-Su 8am-6pm) and a **train kiosk** at Central Station (open daily 6:30am-10:30pm).

Check out various passes, frequently cheaper than paying individual fares. For $13 per day, the **DayTripper** grants unlimited use of Sydney ferries, local buses, and central CityRail lines. The **TravelPass** for the four centermost zones includes unlimited seven-day access to buses, trains, and ferries for just $29. The **Sydney Pass** includes unlimited bus, train, and ferry use within the basic TravelPass zone, return Airport Express service, access to both Explorer Buses, and passage on Sydney Harbour cruises and the higher-speed ferries to Manly and Parramatta. (3-day pass $90, ages 4-16 $45, families $225; 5-day pass $120/$60/$300; 7-day pass $140/$70/$350.)

BY BUS. Buses don't automatically stop at bus stops; hail them as you would a taxi. Fares range from $1.50 to $4.60 (children half-price, seniors $1-3; ask for student concessions). Pay when boarding. Color-coded **TravelTen** passes cover 10 trips at a significant discount and can be purchased from most news agencies. (Blue TravelTen for 10 trips within the city and inner suburbs $11.30, children $5.60.) The **Bus Tripper** ($9.70, children $5.60; bus and ferry $13.40/$6.70) covers one day of bus travel or bus and ferry travel. Most buses run between 5am and 11:30pm, but there is 24hr. service between the city center, Kings Cross, and other central locales. The STA info line (☎ 13 15 00) has schedule details, or visit the info kiosk sandwiched between McDonald's and Circular Quay on Alfred St.

In addition to local commuter bus service, the STA operates two sightseeing buses, the **Sydney Explorer** and the **Bondi & Bay Explorer,** which allow passengers to get on and off at major attractions along designated routes. The Sydney Explorer covers sights between the Harbour and Central Station, moving as far east as Woolloomooloo Bay and as far west as Darling Harbour, originating in Circular Quay every 18min. between 8:40am and 5:22pm. The Explorer services are expensive but can be an excellent way to do concentrated touring. ($30 for a 1-day pass for either route, ages 4-16 $15, families $75; tickets combining both routes over 2 non-consecutive days $50/$25/$125. Purchase tickets on a bus at any stop along the route.) The Bondi & Bay Explorer service visits the eastern bays and southern beaches down to Coogee, departing from Circular Quay every 30min. between 9:15am and 4:15pm. Start early to get the most bang for your buck.

BY SUBWAY AND TRAIN. Sydney's **CityRail** subway system rumbles 24hr. from Bondi Junction in the east to the most distant corners of the suburban sprawl in the north, west, and south. Service is fast, frequent, and easy to navigate. CityRail's lowest one-way fare is $2.20, but most trips cost a little bit more. Return fares are double the one-way price weekdays before 9am. At all other times, the purchase of a round-trip "off-peak return" ticket gets you a sizeable discount. The combined service **TravelPass** is generally a bargain for regular subway users. (Good for 1 week beginning on day of validation; Red Pass for city center and beaches $30, concessions $15.50.)

Both the **Monorail** and **Light Rail** (☎8584 5288; www.metromonorail.com.au), operated by the same company, provide futuristic methods of transportation. Riding above the city bustle is a nice change if you are going from one point directly to another and don't mind the slightly heftier fee. The Monorail links the City Centre with Darling Harbour and Chinatown. (Every 3-5min. M-Th 7am-10pm, F-Sa 7am-midnight, Su 8am-10pm. $4, seniors $ 2.20, under 6 free; day passes with unlimited transport $8, families $24.) The somewhat more practical Light Rail connects Chinatown, Darling Harbour, Glebe, Star City, and Ultimo. (Daily every 10-15min. 6am-midnight; every 30min. midnight-6am. $2.50-4.80, seniors and ages 4-15 $1.30-3.50; unlimited day pass $8, concessions $6, families $24. Signal the driver from designated stopping areas.)

BY FERRY. STA green and gold **ferries** (www.sydneyferries.nsw.gov.au) provide passengers with a magnificent view of the harbor. Ferries embark from the **Circular Quay** wharves between the Opera House and the Harbour Bridge daily 5am-midnight. The **information office** (☎9207 3170) is opposite Wharf 4. Short one-way trips in the harbor cost $4.20; a **FerryTen** pass for the same area costs $26.30 and works much like the TravelTen bus pass. The fare for the high-speed JetCat to Manly is $6.60 (FerryTen pass $54.70). The STA's fastest commuter ferry services its most distant port: take the RiverCat to Parramatta for $6.30, or FerryTen for $44.60. Children ages 4-16 and concession card-carriers ride all these ferries for half-price.

STA has several **Sydney Ferries Harbour Cruises:** the Morning Cruise (1hr.; daily 10:30am; $15, ages 4-16 $7.50, families $37.50); the Afternoon Cruise (2½hr.; M-F 1pm, Sa-Su 1:30pm; $22/$11/$55); and the after-dark Evening Harbour Cruise (1½hr.; M-Sa 8pm; $19/$9.50/$47.50). The Sydney Ferries **information line** has details. (☎9207 3170. Operates M-F 7am-6pm, Sa-Su 8am-6pm.) Posher private ships offer tea time and have slightly more comprehensive harbor cruises (read: live narration). Browse along East Circular Quay for the lowest fare; fares typically range from $20 to $40, and ships depart from mid-morning to evening.

BY CAR. The **National Royal Motorist Association (NRMA),** Level 2, 430 Forest Rd., Hurstbille, is a comprehensive driver's resource. Anyone doing extensive driving should consider joining—benefits include roadside and accident assistance, knowledgeable staff, accurate maps, and emergency passenger transport and accommodation. (☎13 21 32. Open daily 7am-10pm. $99 first-time annual membership, $46 renewal or if a member of an international agency.)

All major **car rental** companies have desks in Kingsford-Smith Airport, and most appear again on William St. near Kings Cross. The big names include: **Avis,** 214 William St. (☎ 13 63 33 or 9357 2000); **Budget,** 93 William St. (☎ 13 27 27 or 8255 9600); **Hertz** (☎ 13 30 39 or 9360 6621), corner of William and Riley St.; **Thrifty,** 78 William St. (☎ 9331 1385 or 1300 367 227); and **Dollar** (☎ 9223 1444), on Sir John Young Crescent. All rent cars starting around $55 per day, with surcharges for 21- to 25-year-olds and airport pickup. Dollar is a bit cheaper than the others, with small, manual transmission cars starting at $40 per day with unlimited kilometers ($28 per day with longer rentals) and automatic transmission cars for $45 per day. However, it is a smaller chain, which can make interstate travel and drop-off more difficult.

In general, local and regional outfits offer much better monetary deals than the big companies, but consider the possible downsides: again, fewer locations translates to more difficult interstate travel and drop-off. **Delta Car Rentals,** 77 William St., has small manual cars from $39 per day. (☎ 9380 6288 or 13 13 90; www.deltacar.com.au. Open daily 8am-5pm. Ages 21-24 $12 surcharge.) **Bayswater Car Rental,** 180 William St., at corner of Dowling, Kings Cross, is cheap ($10 per day for a week or longer) and has the lowest age limit at 20. (☎ 9360 3622; www.bayswatercarrental.com.au. Open M-F 8am-6pm; Sa 8am-noon. Credit cards accepted.) All companies offer reduced long-term rental rates, and most offer free pickup from the airport or Central Station.

Hostel notice-boards overflow with fliers for privately owned cars, campers, and motorcycles **selling** for as little as several hundred dollars. When purchasing a car this way, it's a good idea to make sure it's registered to the seller so the registration can be transferred. For more information on car sales, see **Buying and Selling Used Cars,** p. 46. **Kings Cross Backpackers Car Market,** Level 2, Kings Cross Car Park, on the corner of Ward Ave. and Elizabeth Bay Rd., brings buyers and sellers together. They offer third-party insurance for travelers (see **Insurance at a Glance,** p. 47) and their knowledgeable staff has valuable information on registration and other matters for car-buyers. (☎ 9358 5000 or 1800 808 188; www.carmarket.com.au. Open daily 9am-6pm. Weekly charge from $40. Required vehicle inspection $26.) **Travellers Auto Barn,** 177 William St., offers guaranteed buy-back agreements on cars over $3000. Minimum buy-back rates are 30-50% of purchase price, depending on the length of time you take the car. Cheaper cars are also available but do not come with warranties and buy-back guarantees, whereas purchases over $3000 include 5000km engine warranties and free NRMA Service membership. (☎ 9360 1500. Open M-Sa 9am-6pm, Su 10:30am-3pm.)

BY TAXI. Taxis can be hailed from virtually any street. Initial fare is $2.25 ($1.10 surcharge with call-in request), plus $1.32 per km. Tipping is not expected, though rounding up the fare is appreciated. Some companies are: **Legion Cabs** (☎ 13 14 51 or 9211 2300); **Premiere Taxi** (☎ 13 10 17); **RSL Cabs** (☎ 13 22 11 or 9698 3511); **St. George Cabs** (☎ 13 21 66); and **Taxis Combined** (☎ 9332 8888).

BY BICYCLE. For taking in lots of scenery at a manageable pace, cycling is hard to beat; by complementing cycling with ferries and trains, it's possible to tour the Harbour and northern and eastern beaches in a single day, or even venture out to Royal or Ku-Ring-Gai Chase National Park. **Bicycles in the City,** 722 George St., near Chinatown, hires bikes from $20 per day in-season and provides cycling maps and comprehensive information for day and longer adventure tours. (☎ 9280 2229. Open daily 9am-6pm.) **Inner City Cycles,** 151 Glebe Point Rd., rents bikes starting at $33 per day. (☎ 9660 6605. Open M-W and F-Su 9am-6pm, Th 9am-8pm.) For a coastal ride, visit **Manly Cycle Centre,** 36 Pittwater Rd., at Denison St. in Manly. (☎ 9977 1189. Open M-W and F 9am-6pm, Th 9am-7pm, Su 9am-5pm. $12 per hr., $18 per 2hr., full-day $25.) **Bicycle NSW,** Level 2, 209 Castlereagh St., has 10,000 members and organizes weekly rides. (☎ 9283 5200. Annual dues $59.)

⁊ PRACTICAL INFORMATION

TOURIST AND TRAVEL INFORMATION

Tourist Office: Sydney Visitors Centre, 106 George St. (☎9255 1788 or 1800 067 676; www.sydneyvisitorcentre.com), in the white, historic sailors' building in the Rocks. The 17min. presentation on the Rocks area is an entertaining introduction to the city's history. Friendly staff and mountains of brochures provide enough information for even the most enthusiastic traveler. Open daily 9am-6pm.

Travel Offices: Sydney is riddled with Travel Offices, including:

Travellers Contact Point, Level 7, 428 George St. (☎9221 8744; fax 9221 3746; sydney@travellers.com.au), between King and Market St. Free 30min. **Internet** access. Mail forwarding and holding in Australia, including your own email address, $50 per year. Employment board with recruiting officers for travelers with work visas. Open M-F 9am-6pm, Sa 10am-4pm. MC/V.

Student Uni Travel, Level 8, 92 Pitt St. (☎9232 8444; www.sut.com.au), near Martin Pl. Free 15min. email and **Internet** access. Mail forwarding. Luggage storage $1 per day. Job agency and visa assistance. Open M-F 9am-6pm, Sa 10am-5pm. ISIC/NOMADS/VIP/YHA. MC/V.

Australian Travel Specialists, Jetty 2 and Jetty 6, Circular Quay (24hr.☎ 9555 2700; fax 9555 2701), on the waterfront. Comprehensive information on trips around Sydney and beyond. Locations also at Manly Ferry Wharf, Harbourside Shopping Centre (Darling Harbour), and Centrepoint Shopping Centre. Open daily 7am-9pm.

YHA Travel Center, 422 Kent St. (☎9261 1111; www.yha.com.au), behind Town Hall, between Market and Druitt St. ,or 11 Rawson Pl. (☎9281 9444). Open M-W and F 9am-5pm, Th 9am-6pm, Sa 10am-2pm. MC/V.

Consulates: Canada, Level 5, 111 Harrington St. (☎9364 3000). Open M-F 8:30am-4:30pm. **New Zealand,** Level 10, 55 Hunter St. (passport ☎9223 0222, visa 9223 0144; fax 9221 7836 or 9223 0166). **United Kingdom,** Level 16, 1 Macquarie Pl. (☎9247 7521; fax 9251 1201). Open M-F 10am-12:30pm and 1:30-4:30pm. **United States,** 59th fl., 19-29 Martin Pl., MLC Centre (☎9373 9200). Open M-F 8am-12:30pm; phones answered 8am-4:30pm.

FINANCIAL SERVICES

Banks and exchange offices are crammed on the streets of Sydney, particularly in the Central Business District **(CBD).** They are generally open M-F 9am-5pm. **ATMs** are equally ubiquitous and usually accept Cirrus, MasterCard, Plus, and Visa.

Singapore Money Exchange: 304-308 George St. (☎9223 6361), opposite Wynyard Station. 5% commission on traveler's checks. Other locations include: 401 Sussex St., Chinatown (☎9281 0663); on Eddy Ave. near Central Station, Shop #10 by the Greyhound office (☎9281 4118); in Darling Harbour's Harbourside Mall ☎(9212 7124); Centrepoint Tower's Castlereagh St. level ☎(9223 9222). All open daily 9am-5:30pm.

Thomas Cook: (☎1800 801 002). Several locations in the international terminal (☎9317 2100) of the airport. $7 charge on traveler's checks and currency exchanges. Open daily 5am-9:30 or 10pm. There are dozens of other offices, including 175 Pitt St. (☎9231 2877). Open M-F 8:45am-5:15pm, Sa 10am-1pm.

Money Change: On the mall at Darlinghurst Rd. and Springfield Ave., Kings Cross. 5% commission on traveler's checks and currency. Open daily 8am-11:45pm.

American Express Office: (☎1300 139 060). Dozens of locations around the city, including Level 3, 130 Pitt St. (☎9236 4200), around the corner from Martin Pl. Traveler's Cheques cashed and currency changed with no commission; $3.20 minimum or 1.1% commission to buy cheques. Mail held for card and Traveler's Cheque holders up to a month. Open M-F 8:30am-5pm, Sa 9am-noon.

LOCAL SERVICES

Bookstores: Dymocks Booksellers, 424-430 George St. (☎1800 688 319; www.dymocks.com.au). Open M-W 9am-6pm, Th 9am-9pm, F 9am-6pm, Sa-Su 9am-5pm. Australia's largest bookstore has franchise locations all over the city center.

Library: Sydney City Library, Town Hall House, 456 Kent St. (☎9265 9470), at the corner of Kent and Druitt St. Open M-F 8am-7pm, Sa 9am-noon. The **State Library of New South Wales** (☎9273 1414), part of the former hospital complex on Macquarie St., houses galleries and research facilities. Open M-F 9am-9pm, Sa-Su 11am-5pm.

Ticket Agencies: Ticketek (☎9266 4800; www.ticketek.com.au), has offices in retail stores and an information kiosk at 195 Elizabeth St., or you can buy online. Full-price advance booking for music, theater, sports, and selected museums. Phone lines are open for credit card purchases M-Sa 9am-9pm, Su 8am-8pm. **Ticketmaster** (☎13 61 00; www.ticketmaster7.com), covers many concert and theatrical venues. Phones answered M-Sa 9am-9pm, Su 9am-5pm.

EMERGENCY SERVICES

MEDIA AND PUBLICATIONS.

Newspapers: The main papers are the (more white-collar) *Sydney Morning Herald* and *The Australian* ($1.10) and (more blue-collar) *Daily Telegraph* (90¢).

Nightlife: *Streetpress, The Revolver,* or *3-D World* (www.threedworld.com.au). For gay nightlife, check out *Sx* (www.sxnews.com.au) or *Sydney Star Observer* (www.ssonet.com.au). All free. See **Nightlife,** p. 123.

Entertainment: The *Metro* section of Friday's *Sydney Morning Herald,* as well as free weeklies *Beat* and *Sydney City Hub.*

Radio: Rock, Triple J 105.7FM and Triple M 104.9FM; News, ABC 630AM; Tourist Info, 88FM.

Emergency: ☎000 anywhere in Australia for police, ambulance, or fire assistance.

Police: 570 George St. (☎9265 6595). Kings Cross police station, 1-15 Elizabeth Ba Rd. (☎8356 0099), on Fitzroy Gardens.

Crisis Lines: Alcohol and Drug Information Service 24hr. ☎9361 2111. **Rape Crisis Centre** 24hr. ☎9819 6565, outside Sydney ☎1800 424 017. **HIV/AIDS Information Line** ☎9332 4000; phones answered M-F 8am-7pm, Sa 10am-6pm. **Suicide prevention** ☎9331 2000 or 1300 360 980. **Gay & Lesbian Counselling Service** ☎9207 2800 or 1800 805 379, daily 4pm-midnight.

Late-Night Pharmacy: 24hr. Prescription and Delivery Service ☎9966 8397. **Crest Hotel Pharmacy,** 60A Darlinghurst Rd., Kings Cross (☎9358 1822), opposite the rail station. Open Su-M 8:30am-midnight, Tu-Sa 8:30am-2am. **Wu's Pharmacy,** 629 George St., Chinatown (☎9211 1805). Open M-Sa 9am-9pm, Su 9am-7pm.

Medical Services: Sydney Hospital (☎9382 7111 or 9382 7009), on Macquarie St. opposite the Martin Pl. station. **Traveller's Medical and Vaccination Centre,** Level 7, 428 George St. (☎9221 7133). Consultation fee $40. Open M-F 9am-6pm, Th until 8pm, Sa 9am-1pm. **Kings Cross Travellers' Clinic,** 13 Springfield Ave. (☎9358 3066). Provides travel medical services and vaccinations. Consultation fee $40. Open M-F 9am-1pm and 2-6pm, Sa 10am-noon. **Contraceptive Services,** Level 3, 195 Macquarie St. (☎9221 1933). Open M-F 8:30am-4:30pm, Sa 8:30am-1pm.

POST AND COMMUNICATION

Internet Access: Internet cafes are as copious as pubs and McDonald's. Cheap rates abound, especially near Chinatown and Kings Cross; common charges in the city center are $3 per hr. and $4 for unlimited use, but rates fluctuate. **Global Gossip** (☎9212 1466) shops are franchised across the city and offer 3min. free access. 770 George St., near Sydney Central YHA. Internet $3.25 per hr. Open daily 9am-midnight. Other locations include: 111 Darlinghurst Rd., Kings Cross (☎9326 9777); 108 Oxford St., Darlinghurst (☎9380 4588); 14 Wentworth, Sydney City (☎9263 0400); 37 Hall St.,

Bondi Beach (☎9365 4811); and 317 Glebe Point Rd. (☎9552 6966). Hours and rates vary by location. They also offer postboxes and mail-forwarding ($9.95 per month) and super-cheap **international call rates** in their on-site phone booths. There are also a few competitively priced places on George St. near Chinatown and the Sydney YHA.

Directory Assistance: ☎013.

Post Office: Sydney General Post Office (GPO), 1 Martin Pl. (☎13 13 18), corner of George St. Open M-F 8:15am-5:30pm, Sa 10am-2pm. Poste Restante available at 310 George St., inside Hunter Connection across from Wynyard Station. They will hold mail for up to a month. Enter up the ramp with the "Hunter Connection" sign and go up the escalator. Open M-F 8:15am-5:30pm. Many hostels will also hold mail for up to a month. **Postal Codes:** 2000 for city center, 2001 for *Poste Restante.*

CYBER-SYDNEY ;-)

www.cityofsydney.nsw.gov.au The homepage of Sydney. Visitor guide and information on services provided by the local government.

http://sydney.citysearch.com.au A comprehensive business directory, entertainment listings, shopping, restaurants, and gay/lesbian info.

www.ninemsn.com.au/sydneyguide The website for "the official guide" pamphlet to Sydney, with attractions, restaurants, etc. by region

www.sydney.com.au Sydney's sights, accommodations, and transportation.

http://australia.craigslist.org/syd This newcomer is a community notice board, with work, housing, and events listings.

www.eatstreetsatnight.com.au Listings of restaurants open late into the night for late-night munchies.

www.sydneyforchildren.com.au Information on a wide range of activities and services for children and families.

⬏ WORKING IN SYDNEY

Sydney is bursting with backpackers seeking jobs, especially young Brits taking advantage of working holiday visas (for info on **work permits,** see p. 66). Fortunately, in economically optimistic Sydney, there is generally plenty of work available for the persistent. Those who arrive without prior arrangements report a two- to three-week or shorter lag before finding semi-permanent employment. Virtually all Sydney hostels have services to help guests find work (NOMADS Wanderers on Kent and Sydney Central YHA distribute lists of employment agencies at their employment desks, provide listings of available jobs, and help with issues like taxes, Medicare, and visas). Travel magazines like *TNT* and *OVG* also have work advice and listings of work agencies (*Wanderers' Chantal* is especially helpful).

It pays to start preparing before leaving home. Have a resume typed and saved on a disk; you can print it at most Internet shops and at some hostels. The best way to prepare for job hunting in Sydney is to do research and establish contacts before arriving. Qualified applicants in computer fields enjoy the most success in landing high-quality positions. If you don't have the opportunity to set up house before commencing your search, it is advisable *not* to list hostel numbers as contact information—you'll look transient. Instead, use a friend, get a cellular phone, or set up a mailbox at **Global Gossip** (see **Internet,** p. 52) or **Travellers Contact Point** (☎9221 8744); both are good sources for job search ideas and allow you to receive incoming faxes. **Student Uni Travel** (☎9232 8444) is another useful job agency. Newspapers are always an essential resource. The *Sydney Morning Herald* is stuffed with job classifieds on Wednesday and Saturday. *The Australian* is especially strong for computer opportunities in its Tuesday listings.

WORK RESOURCES ON THE WEB. Monster (www.monster.com.au) gives access to thousands of job listings while allowing you to post your resume for potential employers. A personalized search agent will deliver new job listings fitting your criteria. **Cowley's Job Centre** (www.cowleys.com.au) allows you to advertise yourself as well and provides access to employment news groups and links to other employment-related packages. Also try the following sites: www.**seek**.com.au, www.**webwombat**.com.au, www.**mycareers**.com.au, www.**jobwire**.com.au, www.**sydneycareers**.com.au.

For tax info, visit the **Australian Taxation Office,** 100 Market St., GPO Box 9990, at the Centrepoint shopping plaza in the Central Business District. There you can grab the annual *TaxPack.* (☎ 13 28 61; www.ato.gov.au. Open M-F 8:30am-4:45pm.) The helpful officers at this office report that the biggest misunderstanding for foreigners is that they believe they will be charged the 47% income tax while their tax number is being processed by immigration. In fact, travelers are given a 28-day grace period and are taxed starting at the 29% non-resident rate. However, it is essential to apply for a **tax file number** (after you have a work visa), and many employers will not even consider your application until you've file the paperwork. For more info on working in Australia, see **Alternatives to Tourism,** p. 66.

⚑ ACCOMMODATIONS

As the travelers' gateway to Australia, Sydney supports a thriving budget accommodation market. The best way to choose an accommodation is according to the neighborhood you'd most like to stay in—you will almost certainly be able to find a nice place in any one of them. The second question most travelers must answer when looking for a bed in Sydney is whether or not to stay in Kings Cross. Well-located, traveler-friendly, and party-ready, Kings Cross is an established back-packer mecca, and the high concentration of steadily improving hostels ensures that beds are almost always available. However, the omnipresence of prostitutes and go-go bars make many travelers uncomfortable. In addition, tales of theft are rampant. If you do opt to stay in the Cross, be sure you feel comfortable with your hostel's security measures before letting your valuables out of sight.

While staying in the Central Business District brings the benefit of convenient transportation, many travelers sing the praises of slightly more remote suburbs, as the CBD's crowds, skyscrapers, and dearth of culture can be a bit alienating. Good suburban bets include Glebe, which offers a high concentration of very safe, super laid-back backpacker accommodations in proximity to excellent cafes, student nightlife, and Coogee Beach.

Unless stated otherwise, hostels accept major credit cards, have 24hr. access, no linen fee, and a 10am check-out. Laundry, when available, is generally $3 per wash. Prices listed are **winter rates** and most dorm beds increase in price by a few dollars ($2-5) during peak season (Nov.-Feb.). The most expensive time to travel, by far, is during late December and April.

KINGS CROSS AND AROUND

If you decide to take up residence in the Cross, Sydney's one-time answer to Greenwich Village, expect good nightlife, lots of backpacking company, and seedy, seedy streets. Some accommodations here can be pretty run-down, but plenty of clean, well-maintained rooms exist: Victoria St. locations are rather stately as hostels go. **CityRail** runs from Martin Pl. in the city to Kings Cross Station. **Buses** run from Circular Quay (#324, 325, or 327) and Chatswood (#200) to the Cross as well. You've arrived when you reach the world's largest Coca-Cola sign.

NEW SOUTH WALES

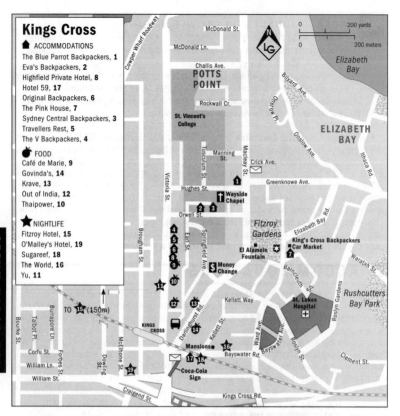

Kings Cross

🏠 ACCOMMODATIONS
The Blue Parrot Backpackers, **1**
Eva's Backpackers, **2**
Highfield Private Hotel, **8**
Hotel 59, **17**
Original Backpackers, **6**
The Pink House, **7**
Sydney Central Backpackers, **3**
Travellers Rest, **5**
The V Backpackers, **4**

🍴 FOOD
Café de Marie, **9**
Govinda's, **14**
Krave, **13**
Out of India, **12**
Thaipower, **10**

⭐ NIGHTLIFE
Fitzroy Hotel, **15**
O'Malley's Hotel, **19**
Sugareef, **18**
The World, **16**
Yu, **11**

■ **The Pink House,** 6-8 Barncleuth Sq. (☎9358 1689 or 1800 806 384; thep-inkh@qd.com.au), off Ward Ave. Unlike most other Kings Cross hostels, the Pink House feels like a house—a big, fun, light-pink house. Copious group activities (daytrips, pub outings, skydiving, inter-hostel soccer) promote a family atmosphere and get you discounts. Brick kitchen, garden terraces, and BBQ. All rooms have TVs and couches; most have fireplaces and large mirrors; each is unique. Luggage storage $5 per week, $15 per month. Laundry $5. Free 20min. Internet. Book ahead. Reception daily 8:30am-9pm. Dorms $20-22, weekly $120-130; twins and doubles $52-56/$270-300; triples $69/$405. 7th night free. Discounts for long-term stays. VIP/YHA. MC/V. ❷

■ **Original Backpackers,** 160-162 Victoria St. (☎9356 3232; www.originalbackpackers.com.au). Wraparound front porch, 2 kitchens, and dining area make for the most spacious hostel common area in the Cross. Cable TV, Internet ($2 per 15min.), a safe for valuables, and laundry ($4.40). Luggage storage free first day, $2 per day after. Every room has a TV and fridge and some boast baths, kitchens, and balconies at no extra cost. Linen $3. Key deposit $20. Reception 24hr. Dorms $20, weekly $120; singles $35/$210; twins and doubles $55/$300. Discounts for long-term stays. MC/V. ❷

■ **The V Backpackers,** 144 Victoria St. (☎9357 4733). A swank, tight-knit hostel, with one of the best common rooms in the city. Comes with jukebox, pool table, free Internet, free BBQ M and F, and (most importantly) free beer. Internet cafe and travel desk downstairs. Continental breakfast included. Free airport or city pickup. Luggage storage $2.

Laundry $4. Reception daily 7:30am-8pm. 6
$139; doubles $50/$300. AmEx/MC/V. ❷

The Blue Parrot Backpackers, 87 Macleay
llnghurst Rd. turns into Macleay St. past Fi
Cross scene, the electric blue Parrot Bac
sweet, with a great outdoor terrace for BE
discerning need apply. Dorms from $20.

Highfield Private Hotel, 166 Victoria St.
for less hectic, comfortable long-term s
room, security-coded lock, and a safe f
$10. Reception M-F 7:30am-7pm, Sa
weekly $130; singles $45/$270; doul

Sydney Central Backpackers, 16 Orv
packers.com.au). Clean bedrooms v
rooftop offers a BBQ, pool table, anu g..
Fridges in every room. Free pickup from airport or Ueı.u..
deposit $20, blanket deposit $10. Reception daily 8am-10pm. Dorms ₊₂,
doubles $52. 7th night free. MC/V. ❷

Eva's Backpackers, 6-8 Orwell St. (☎9358 2185; www.evasbackpackers.com.au).
Cozy, homey feel, with tidy rooms and family management. Mesmerizing view. Daily
security patrols. Free storage. Laundry $6. Internet $2 per 30min. Key deposit $10.
Book ahead. Reception daily 7am-2pm and 5-8pm. Bunks in 4- to 10-bed dorms $20;
twins and doubles $50; triples $60. 7th night free. MC/V ($50 minimum charge). ❷

Travellers Rest, 156 Victoria St. (☎9358 4606). This friendly, job-oriented hostel provides lists of potential employers and employment agency contacts. TV, fridge, sink,
and phone in every room. Outdoor seating area. Laundry $2. Key deposit $10. Reception daily 8am-noon and 4:30-6pm. Check-out 9am. Dorms $20, weekly $124; twins
$45/$262; doubles $50/$288. No advance bookings or credit cards. ❷

Hotel 59, 59 Bayswater Rd. (☎9360 5900; www.interspace.net.au/inns/hotel59.html).
A brothel less than a decade ago, Hotel 59 now offers 8 nicely-arranged family rooms
with TV and bath. Breakfast included. Reception daily 7:30am-6pm. Check-out 11am.
Singles $88; doubles $99-132; extra adult $15, extra child $10. No credit cards. ❺

CENTRAL BUSINESS DISTRICT AND THE ROCKS

The number-one choice for airport layovers and springbreakers, these accommodations are close to Central Station and other main transportation lines. The CBD
has no pretensions toward charm, or anything, really, other than rampant commercialism—opportunities for (mall) shopping abound. Excluding the first three
listings, nicer accommodation can generally be found in Kings Cross or Glebe, but
sometimes sheer convenience can't be beat.

Russell Hotel, 143A George St., The Rocks (☎9241 3543; www.therussell.com.au). A
small, inviting hotel with exquisitely furnished, brightly painted rooms and a rooftop garden overlooking The Rocks. Relaxing sitting room is well-suited for reading or socializing.
Continental breakfast included. Reception daily 6am-10pm. Check-in from 1pm. Check-
out 11am. Singles $125-165, ensuite $200-275; doubles $140-180/$215-290; suite
or studio $300. Extra person $15, under 2 free. ❺

Sydney Central YHA, 11 Rawson Pl. (☎9281 9111; sydneycentral@yhansw.org.au), at
the corner of Pitt St. and Rawson Pl. Visible from Central Station's Pitt St. exit: it's the
"historic" brick building. Pool, sauna, game room, employment and travel desks, TV
rooms, Internet ($2 per 30min.), parking ($11 per night), multiple kitchens, arranged
activities, bar and cafe, and more. Its size is amazing but a little alienating. No sleeping
bags allowed. Lockers $3. Linen free, towels $1. Laundry $5. No key deposit. 14-day
max. stay. Reception 24hr. Check-in from noon. Dorms $28-33; twins $77, ensuite doubles $87. Under 18 half-price. YHA discount $3. Wheelchair accessible. ❸

Wake up! Hostel, 50 Pitt
as the Central YHA, in a
the set of MTV's Tota
backpacker accom
travel desk, and
Daly? Well, if
raspberry-co
tion 24h
$28/$
NOM
d

St. (☎9288 7888; www.wakeup.com.au), in the same block
nearly identical brick low-rise. Ever dream of waking up inside
Request Live? Well, now you can, at this brand-new, independent
modation: subterranean cafe and bar, Internet access ($3 per hr.),
multiple TVs in the lobby. Ever dream of waking up next to Carson
e's staying here, you'll be sharing a pristine room with new furniture and
lored walls. Walking tours and guest DJs make the dream complete. Recep-
. 10-bed dorms $25, weekly $161; 8-bed dorms $26/168; 6-bed dorms
82; quads $30/$196; singles $42; doubles $79-88. ❸

DS Wanderers on Kent, 477 Kent St. (☎9267 7718 or 1800 424 444; www.wan-
erersonkent.com.au), between Druitt and Bathurst St., a block from Town Hall. A stone's
throw from Darling Harbour, the Rocks, and CBD nightlife. In addition to being the best-
located, swipe-card access and the security cameras on every floor make this hostel one
of the most secure as well. Clean, contempo rooms with 320 beds and much, much
more: tanning booth $3 per 3min., employment and travel desks, TV and pool rooms,
Internet $6 per hr. Attached **Zambezi bar and cafe** has daily breakfast, lunch, and dinner
specials ($3-6) and crazy Happy Hour games. No sleeping bags. Lockers $4-8 per day,
linen deposit $20, laundry $6. Key deposit $10. 28-day max. stay. Free airport shuttle
with 2-night stay. Reception 24hr. 6- to 10-bed dorms $24-30; quads $33; twins and
doubles $42. Ask for a room that do\esn't face the air-shaft. NOMADS $1 discount for
most rooms or 7th night free. Wheelchair accessible. No credit cards. ❸

Sydney Backpackers, 7 Wilmot St. (☎9267 7772 or 1800 887 766; www.sydneyback-
packers.com). Turn onto Wilmot off George St. at the Planet Hollywood. Incredibly large
and clean 2- to 8-bed dorms have satellite TV and fridge. Common spaces are cozy but
never cramped. Astro-turfed rooftop BBQ, keycard room access, Internet $2 per 10min.,
laundry $4.40. Reception 6:30am-11pm. Dorms $25 ($21 off-season), weekly $159;
doubles $84/$504. AmEx/DC/MC/V. ❸

Y on the Park (YWCA), 5-11 Wentworth Ave. (☎9264 2451 or 1800 994 994;
www.ywca-sydney.com.au), on the southeastern corner of Hyde Park; Wentworth Ave. is
at the junction of Liverpool and Oxford St. Barracks à la Martha Stewart—carpeting,
closet space, and pastels. Everything's sparkling and spacious. Women-only floor. A/C,
heat, TVs, kitchen. Free short-term luggage storage. Laundry $4. Internet $2 per 30min.
Open daily 7am-7:30pm. Key deposit $20. Reception 24hr. Check-in from 1pm. Dorms
$30; singles $70, ensuite $108; twins $95/$132; doubles $85; triples $108/$142;
family rooms $118. 10% YWCA discount. Wheelchair accessible. AmEx/MC/V. ❸

Hotel Bakpak Westend, 417 Pitt St. (☎9211 4588 or 1 800 813 522; www.hotelbak-
pak.com), near Haymarket. Balances its somewhat stark, recently refurnished rooms
with a great dining area and tons of organized activities including free yoga sessions
and pub crawls. Laundry $6. Airport pickup and breakfast included. Lockers $2-5 per
day. Reception 24hr. Ensuite dorms $22-24, weekly $125-135; doubles $55/$320;
twins $54/$280; triples $85; family rooms $85. MC/V. ❷

GLEBE

To get to Glebe Point Rd., your main artery for all Glebian antics, take bus #431,
432, 433, or 434. Or, from Central Station, follow George St., and then Broadway,
west 15min. to Victoria Park and turn right onto Glebe Point Rd.

Wattle House, 44 Hereford St. (9552 4997; www.wattlehouse.com.au), a 5min. walk
from Glebe Point Rd. A hostel with a B&B feel, this is Sydney's smallest—and one of its
nicest—backpackers. Restored Victorian decor includes lace curtains, brick kitchen, and
manicured garden. Plush bean bags fill the small TV room, where guests get acquainted
over complimentary hot chocolate, tea, coffee, and soup. Laundry $4. 2-week max.
stay. Book way ahead. Reception M-F 9am-6pm, Sa-Su 10am-noon; reservations 8am-
7pm. 4-bed dorms from $25; doubles $70. Weekly rates available. MC/V. ❸

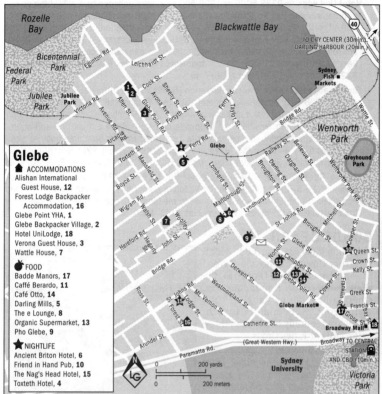

Glebe

🔺 ACCOMMODATIONS
Alishan International
   Guest House, **12**
Forest Lodge Backpacker
   Accommodation, **16**
Glebe Point YHA, **1**
Glebe Backpacker Village, **2**
Hotel UniLodge, **18**
Verona Guest House, **3**
Wattle House, **7**

🍎 FOOD
Badde Manors, **17**
Caffé Berardo, **11**
Café Otto, **14**
Darling Mills, **5**
The e Lounge, **8**
Organic Supermarket, **13**
Pho Glebe, **9**

⭐ NIGHTLIFE
Ancient Briton Hotel, **6**
Friend in Hand Pub, **10**
The Nag's Head Hotel, **15**
Toxteth Hotel, **4**

🏠 **Glebe Backpacker Village,** 256 Glebe Point Rd. (☎9660 8133 or 1800 801 983). Beautiful frontyard with bamboo plots, picnic tables, and strings of patio lights is complemented by hardwood-floored dorms, cozy brick-walled reception, and a big ol' kitchen. The atmosphere outdoors is somehow simultaneously romantic and party-ready. Internet $2 per hr. Laundry $6. Also promises "heaps of work contacts." Quiz night with free wine and cheese, Th night BBQ, tours and pub crawls. Free pickup. 10- to 12-bed dorms $22, weekly $132; 6-bed dorms $23/$138; 4-bed dorms $24/$144; doubles $60/$360; triples $27/$162. VIP discount $1 per night. ❷

Alishan International Guest House, 100 Glebe Point Rd. (☎9566 4048; www.alishan.com.au). Neat Victorian house, managed by an award-winning gardener, features new rooms with TVs and fridges. The dorms are a bit less sparkling than the private rooms, but both are great values. Parking. Key deposit $10. Laundry $4. Reception daily 8am-10:30pm. Dorms $27-33; ensuite singles $88-99; ensuite twins and doubles $99-115; ensuite family room for 4 $154, each extra person $16. Wheelchair accessible room available. AmEx/DC/MC/V. ❸

Glebe Point YHA, 262-264 Glebe Point Rd. (☎9692 8418; glebe@yhansw.org.au). Guests hang out on the roof for BBQs and in the subterranean lounge to play pool. Spacious, social kitchen and dining area. Sinks in rooms. Bus service to the airport and city center $10. No sleeping bags allowed. Luggage storage $2 per bag per week. Laundry $4.20. Key deposit $10. Internet $2 per 20min. Reception daily 7am-10:45pm. Dorms $26-30, weekly $154; twins and doubles $35. YHA discount $3.50. MC/V. ❸

Hotel UniLodge (☎9338 5000 or 1800 500 658; www.unilodge.com.au), at the corner of Broadway and Bay St. Just when you thought budget accomodation had to be weird, UniLodge comes along to prove you wrong. A large, standard hotel on the edge of Glebe, complete with gym and indoor pool, UniLodge has spotless ensuite motel-modern rooms, each with TV and kitchenette. Includes bare-bones continental breakfast. Parking $6 per day. Singles $120; doubles $170; triples $195; family rooms for 4 $220, extra person $25. AmEx/MC/V. ❺

Forest Lodge Backpacker Accommodation (NOMADS), 117 Arundel St. (☎9660 1873 or 1800 688 815; flhotel@bigpond.net.au). From Victoria Park, walk along Broadway/ Parramatta Rd. to the fork it makes with Arundel. A small, reliable hotel with some dorm rooms, with kitchen facilities and TV lounge one story above a local pub and bistro. Family-run and friendly, with complimentary schooner Th after 8pm, free pool Su afternoons, and $6 pasta in the bistro every night. Key deposit $20. Reception M-Sa 6:30am-midnight, Su 6:30am-10pm. Dorms $20; singles $45; doubles $55. MC/V. ❷

Verona Guest House, 224 Glebe Point Rd. (☎9660 8975; www.verona-guest-house.com). This beautifully restored Victorian manor has gleaming hardwood floors and elegant furniture in every room, not to mention A/C and private bathrooms. Hot breakfast included. Singles $125; doubles $145. MC/V. ❺

BONDI BEACH

Take bus #380, 382, or L82, which run from Circular Quay via Oxford St., or drive east along Oxford St. **CityRail** trains run to Bondi Junction, where a bus can be caught to the waterfront. Accommodations in Bondi are generally better than those in the CBD or Kings Cross.

Noah's Bondi Beach, 2 Campbell Pde. (☎9365 7100, reservations 1800 226 662), up the hill on the beach's south end. It can get a bit rowdy. Two rooftops' worth of balcony with BBQ, a great view, and (if renovations go according to plan) an outdoor movie-screen. Free surf and boogie board use. Pool table, TV. Breakfast included. Dinners in connected bar/restaurant $2-10. Female-only ensuite dorm available. Laundry $5. Key deposit $20. Dorms $19-22, weekly $114-132; twins and doubles $50/$300; beachside doubles $55/$330. VIP. AmEx/DC/V. ❷

The Biltmore Private Hotel, 110 Campbell Pde. (☎9130 4660 or 1800 684 660), as close as you can get to Bondi's waves without a houseboat. Comfy common room with big TV, kitchen, storage, activities, and free boogie board use. Laundry $4. Internet $2 per 20min. Key deposit

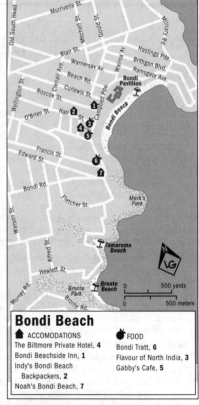

Bondi Beach

▲ ACCOMODATIONS
The Biltmore Private Hotel, **4**
Bondi Beachside Inn, **1**
Indy's Bondi Beach
   Backpackers, **2**
Noah's Bondi Beach, **7**

● FOOD
Bondi Tratt, **6**
Flavour of North India, **3**
Gabby's Cafe, **5**

$20. Reception daily 7:30am-10:30pm. Dorms $22, weekly $120; singles $36/$169; doubles $49/$299; triples $66/$420. MC/V. ❷

Bondi Beachside Inn, 152 Campbell Pde. (☎9130 5311; www.bondiinn.com.au). Seven stories of rooms over the beach; ideal for families or couples. Rooms have kitchenette, TV, balcony, and phone. No laundry. Parking. Key deposit $5. Reception 24hr. Cots $10; oceanview singles and doubles $110-120, land-side $100. Discounts for stays of over one week. Wheelchair accessible. AmEx/DC/MC/V. ❺

Indy's Bondi Beach Backpackers, 35A Hall St. (☎9365 4900; www.indysbackpackers.com.au). One and a half blocks inland from Campbell Pde. Extensive surfboard exchange program. Large TV, Nintendo 64, and video library. Free use of bikes, inline skates, wetsuits, and boards. Breakfast included. Laundry $4. Internet $2 per 30min. Key deposit $25. Reception daily 8am-10pm. A less social location is at 252 Campbell Pde. Book through main office. Free transfers to other locations in Surry Hills and Coogee. Large dorms $17-19, weekly $116-133; doubles at 252 Campbell Pde. $49 (4-6 day stay $45), weekly $299. VIP. AmEx/MC/V. ❷

COOGEE BEACH

Take bus #373 or 374 from Circular Quay, #372 from Central Station, or #314 from Bondi Junction.

Surfside Backpackers, 186 Arden St. (☎9315 7888; www.surfsidebackpackers.com.au). Entrance off street behind McDonald's; buzz to be let in. You couldn't ask for a better location. Balconies connecting the sunny rooms encourage socializing. The bigger dorms, especially the 16-bed dinosaur, are somewhat cramped, but that's par for the beachside hostels. Female-only dorm available. Laundry $4. Internet $2 per 30min. Key deposit $20. Reception M-F 8am-12:30pm and 5-8pm, Sa-Su 8:30am-12:30pm and 5-8pm. Check-out 9:30am. Dorms $20-23, weekly $110-140; doubles $50-52/$320. No doubles in summer. VIP. No credit cards. ❷

Coogee Beach Wizard of Oz, 172 Coogee Bay Rd. (☎9315 7876 or 1800 013 460; www.wizardofoz.com.au), 1½ blocks from the center of the beach. Hardwood floors, fresh paint, and lots of open common space allow for relaxation and socializing with the Munchkins. Free Th BBQs in summer. Free pickup. No smoking. Laundry. Key deposit $20. Reception daily 8am-1pm and 5-8pm. Check-out 9:30am. Dorms $22, weekly $126; doubles $55/$350. VIP. MC/V. ❷

MANLY

To get to Manly from Circular Quay, take the **ferry** (30min.; M-F 6am-7pm, Sa-Su 8am-7:30pm; $10.60 return) or **Jetcat** (15min; M-Sa 6am-midnight, Su 7:15am-11pm; $13.20 return, $10 when ferry is not operating). See **Local Transportation,** p. 94.

Manly Bunkhouse, 35 Pine St. (☎9976 0472 or 1800 657 122; www.bunkhouse.com.au). From the ferry, cross the Esplanade to Belgrave St., which becomes Pittwater St., then turn left onto Pine St. (10min.). This small and quiet hostel is one of the best-kept in Manly; each 4-bed dorm has its own kitchenette, bathroom, TV, heater, lockers, and closet space. Free wharf pickup. Key deposit $20. Dorms $20, weekly $100; twins $50/$300. Wheelchair accessible. VIP. ❷

Manly Beach Resort, 6 Carlton St. (☎9977 4188; www.manlyview.com.au). From the ferry, walk 10min. down Belgrave St., which becomes Pittwater St., and turn right onto Carlton St. A nicer-than-budget accommodation that also has backpackers dorms and apartments. Free pickup from the wharf 9am-noon. Heated pool, TV room, laundry. Key deposit $20. Reception 24hr. All rooms have bath. Dorms $20; doubles $50, weekly $315. Motel rooms: singles $115; twins $140; studios $160; interconnecting family rooms $215; 10% off weekly stays. Advance motel room bookings require $100 deposit. VIP. AmEx/DC/MC/V. ❷

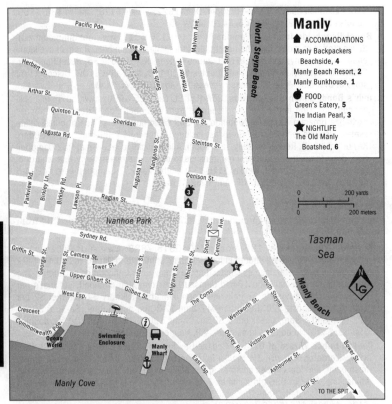

Manly

🏠 ACCOMMODATIONS
Manly Backpackers
  Beachside, **4**
Manly Beach Resort, **2**
Manly Bunkhouse, **1**

🍎 FOOD
Green's Eatery, **5**
The Indian Pearl, **3**

⭐ NIGHTLIFE
The Old Manly
  Boatshed, **6**

Manly Backpackers Beachside, 28 Raglan St. (☎9977 3411; www.manlybackpack-ers.com.au). From the ferry, cross the Esplanade to Belgrave St., which becomes Pittwa-ter St., and turn right onto Raglan St. Despite the blank, narrow hallways, the hostel manages to have an open, friendly atmosphere and cozy dorms. Enormous TV room/kitchen with skylights. Safe for valuables at reception; small lockers not in rooms. Free body boards and Su BBQs. Laundry $4. Key deposit $30. Max. stay 2 weeks. Reception M-F 9am-7pm, Sa-Su 9am-6pm. Dorms $21, weekly $119-133; twins and doubles $48-70/$294. VIP. MC/V. ❷

Manly Lodge, 22 Victoria Pde. (☎9977 8655). Luxurious rooms with bath are a steal for families or couples. All rooms have A/C, TV, VCR, and fridge; some have hot tubs and kitchens. Sauna, spa, and gym. Laundry $6. Breakfast included. Twins from $120-159; doubles $110-144; deluxe $130-168, extra person $35, under age 10 $20. For Sa only bookings, rates increase $30. Lower weekly rates in winter. ❺

COLLAROY

To get to Collaroy, take bus #L90, L88, or any of the Northern Beach expresses that originate at Wynyard Station (Carrington St. side), or take the ferry to Manly and catch bus #151, 155, or 156.

🏠 Sydney Beachouse/Collaroy Beach YHA, 4 Collaroy St. (☎9981 1177; www.sydney-beachouse.com.au). A chic contemporary house 100m from the water, with tons of activities (such as free didgeridoo lessons) and free surfboards, snorkeling gear, skateboards, and bikes. Buses to bushwalks, national parks, and Palm Beach. Free luggage storage. Laundry $4. Key deposit $20. Reception daily 8am-9pm. Dorms $20-25, weekly $140-147; family rooms for 5 $104. MC/V. ❷

KIRRIBILLI

Kirribilli is a quiet, residential neighborhood. Most travelers who stay here are older, and many others are students or people on working holidays. Kirribilli is most easily accessed by taking the Neutral Bay ferry (6 min. from Wharf 4, Circular Quay). Alternately, the train stops at nearby Milson's Point. From Milson's Point, walk down Ennis Rd. toward the harbor, turn left onto Kirribilli St., and then left onto Carabella St.

Glenferrie Lodge, 12A Carabella St. (☎9955 1685; mail@glenferrielodge.com). From the ferry, walk up Holbrook St., and take a left onto Carabella St. A stately house with balconies aplenty and a pleasant garden-courtyard out back. Breakfast included. Dinner served Su-Th ($7 each night, 5 nights $30). TV hire weekly $20, deposit $80. Laundry $4. Key deposit $50. Reception daily 24hr. Dorms $28, 2 nights or more $25 per night, weekly $145; singles $38/$34/$170; doubles $61/$55/$290. MC/V. ❸

Tremayne Private Hotel, 89 Carabella St. (☎9955 4155). From the Neutral Bay ferry, walk up Holbrook St., turn right, and take a 5min. walk up Carabella St. Rooms with balconies and fridges. Breakfast and M-F dinner included. TV room and kitchen. Reception 8am-10pm. $15 airport shuttle. Laundry $5. Key deposit $10. Dorms $20; singles $170, ensuite $220; twins and doubles $260/$280. No credit cards. ❷

DARLINGHURST

Many of the "hotels," those old-school Australian pubs, in Darlinghurst, Paddington, and nearby Surry Hills, are actually… hotels. That is, they have a few reasonably priced rooms to let (generally $50-120 per night). Check around in the off-season and you may find a good deal.

Wattle Private Hotel, 108 Oxford St., Darlinghurst (☎9332 4118; www.wsydneyhotel.com), on the corner of Palmer St. Cozy, bright and chintzily elegant rooms with TV and fridge, some with balcony, living room, and extensive furniture. Reception daily 8am-8pm. Singles $88, weekly $490; twins $110; doubles $99, weekly $560; studio $350 weekly. Extra person $10. MC/V. ❺

⬚ FOOD

Sydney's streets overflow with eateries of every flavor for any budget. Asian options, most notably Thai and Chinese cuisine, rank highly among the international selections. The Central Business District is rife with quick lunch stops for the professional masses still dreaming of three-martini lunch status. Sandwiches, meat pies, and focaccias run $2.50-6 at sandwich counters throughout these blocks. Slightly south, the feeding frenzy of **Chinatown** lurks west of Central Station, around Hay St., Little Hay St., and the Dixon St. Plaza. Just east of the center, the Oxford St. social artery runs between Surry Hills in the south (where many of the city's best **Thai** kitchens line up on Crown St.), and the (very) **Little Italy** on Stanley St., between Crown and Riley St., in Darlinghurst. Cafes in Little Italy serve excellent **coffee** and hearty hot sandwiches. Continuing east through Darlinghurst, the strip of restaurants on Oxford St. near St. Vincent's Hospital (at Victoria St.) is known for a quality variety of **Asian** and **European flavors.** Victoria St. runs north from Oxford at the hospital into the land of high **cappuccino chic** before depositing the last of its cafe class amidst the hostels of Kings Cross. In the Cross, Darlinghurst Rd. and Bayswater Rd. offer fare abiding by the local atmosphere of **late-night cheap bites** and fast-food chains.

As usual, a large student population means good, **cheap cafes** and restaurants on both Glebe Point Rd. in Glebe and Kings St. in Newtown. Blues Point Rd. on McMahons Point and Fitzroy St. in Kirribilli lead the North Shore's attempts at affordability with style, featuring several cafes well-loved by the locals. **Breakfast** is big on the beachfront drives of Manly, Bondi, and Coogee. At most coastal cafes, $6-7 buys a large cooked breakfast and an excuse to appreciate the view over the morning paper. Manly offers even less expensive food counters along the Corso. Though the neighborhoods vary in their offerings, none disappoint. Unless otherwise noted, major credit cards are accepted.

THE ROCKS

The Rocks has some of Sydney's best and most tourist-targeted eating. That said, plenty of the food is still cheap, and (of course) all the restaurants are extremely aesthetically pleasing. Should you desire, you may pay dearly for an evening dining at the harbor's edge, but even the budget traveler will find splendor: the Rocks is gorgeous all lit-up at night, and every place comes with a view.

▨ **The Gumnut Tea Garden,** 28 Harrington St. Tucked away on the corner of Harrington and Argyle St., the Gumnut charms customers with assorted cakes and puddings all day ($3-7) and tasty, inexpensive breakfasts ($7-10, until 11:30am) and lunches ($13-16). The front room is lit by a fireplace and the leafy garden terrace has views of the CBD. Open daily 9am-7pm. ❷

The Rocks Cafe, 99 George St. An enormous selection of breakfasts ($11) and lunch specials (from $17). Pastries ($3-7) can be found in its main shop, or eat outdoors on the terrace across George St., overlooking Circular Quay. Open daily 9am-7pm. ❸

La Renaissance Patisserie Francaise, 47 Argyle St. (☎9241 4878). All confections are made on the premises by a "master chef" and can be devoured right before his eyes or in the courtyard out back. Breakfast pastries ($2-3) and the devil's own profiteroles ($2) begin the creation of a new, lusher you. Open daily 8:30am-6pm. ❶

Wok on Inn Noodlebar (☎9247 8554), in the Rocks Square above George St. Makes up for its silly name with oodles of noodles, prepared fresh and to order ($9-12). Outdoor seating only, with splendid views of Circular Quay. Open daily 11:30am-10pm. ❷

Wolfie's Grill, 17-21 Circular Quay W (☎9241 5577). Two levels of dining for lovers of Australian prime beef and fresh seafood. Casual atmosphere, with less-than-casual prices (grill items start at $28)--but the supremely good eating and priceless harbor view make up for it. Open daily 11:30am-late. ❺

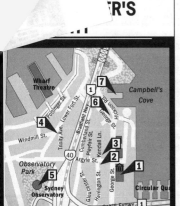

THE ROCKS

In one of Sydney's most eclectic and best-loved suburbs, it's all about the little things.

1 The Museum of Contemporary Art boasts an excellent Aboriginal art collection, along with scores of more trendoid pieces (☎9252 4033)

2 Enjoy a lovely view of the CBD with your pudding at the **Gumnut Tea Garden** (☎9247 9591)

3 Indulge your inner child at the **Toy Museum** (☎9251 9793)

4 A local favorite since 1845, **The Hero of Waterloo Pub** offers live Irish music(☎9252 4553)

5 Enjoy some little gardens and big views at the **Sydney Observatory** (☎9217 0485)

6 With something to accommodate all tastes, the **Rocks Market** serves all your local art-and-craft, homeware, and collectible needs

7 Smaller is better! **The Italian Village** is a miniaturized version of a typical Tuscan village...complete with life-sized fresh homemade pasta (☎9247 6111)

Italian Village, 7 Circular Quay W (☎9247 6111). Proof that Las Vegas lives in Sydney, this working reproduction of a Tuscan village market includes fountains, an outdoor dining plaza, and 3 levels of cries of "Eh! That's a spicy meat-a-ball!" But seriously folks, the fresh pasta ($15-17) and steaming mains ($25-49) are meltingly good. $20 lunch special includes a glass of wine. Open daily 11:30am-late. ❺

KINGS CROSS

▨ **Govinda's,** 112 Darlinghurst Rd. (☎9380 5155). A unique, can't-miss restaurant and cinema. $16 covers a mostly Indian, wholly vegetarian, all-you-can-eat buffet, and a current (artsy) movie in the upstairs theater, where cushy sofas recline for total viewing bliss or dark room flirtation. Open daily 6-10:30pm. ❸

▨ **Café de Marie,** 166 Victoria St. (☎9358 2343). Squeeze into this tiny 20-seat cafe for its famous French toast ($7). Sandwiches $6-7. Open daily 9am-3pm, M-Sa 6-9:30pm. No credit cards. ❶

Thaipower, 146 Victoria St. (☎8354 0434). Build your own spicy noodle mound ($9-13) or inhale some "special Thai foods," like ginger prawns ($14) or fresh basil vegetables and tofu ($9). Mighty lunch specials offered noon-4pm bring everything on the menu down to a measley, puny, quivering $7. BYO. Open daily noon-10:30pm. ❷

Out of India, 178 Victoria St. (☎9357 7055). "The only place for lovers of Indian food" has 3 balconied floors, free wine with eat-in meals, to-go only specials ($10), a $10 "Thali Meal" for an evening snack (5-7pm), and, last but not least, a "Special Banquet" deal ($20 per person). BYO. Open daily noon-10pm. ❸

Krave, 37 Darlinghurst St. (☎9358 6436). Brekkie ($5) and pasta ($7) make this 24hr. diner an affordable stop for dinner or a post-partying recharge. BYO. Open daily. ❶

CITY CENTER

Cheap food is everywhere in the many malls of the CBD and Chinatown. Trust us, you won't really need our help, but here are a few listings just in case.

Dixon St. Food Courts, in Chinatown. The **Dixon House Food Court,** 80 Dixon St., downstairs, on the corner of Little Hay St., boasts cheap Asian meals ($6-10). Open daily 10:30am-8:30pm. The **Sussex House Food Court,** 60 Dixon St., has more variety and fresh fruit and vegetable options. Open daily 10:30am-9:30pm. The **Harbour Plaza Food Court,** at the corner of Dixon and Goulburn St., is chaotic but slightly cheaper: several restaurants offer hearty $5 meals. Open daily 10am-10pm. No credit cards. ❶

Zenbu, 31 Wheat Rd., Darling Harbour, in the IMAX Complex (☎9211 9888). This date-ready restaurant has many candles and a menu of Japanese fusion cuisine, the "usual in an unusual way," including tasty saki-tails ($9) and an extensive sushi bar. Mains like the tuna with green tea noodles run $15-20, but that includes complementary 5min. head and neck massages given right at your table. Open Su-W 11:30am-1am, Th-Sa 11:30am-2am. ❸

Soup Plus, 383 George St., in the CBD (☎9299 7728). With a $25 cover on F-Sa nights, this smoky jazz bar is an expensive dinner option, but the value-per-dollar is unbeatable. The price covers entertainment and a 2-course dinner; mains include mousaka, lasagna, and stuffed pumpkin. Cover M-Th $5 from 7:30pm. ❹

Blackbird Cafe, on Balcony Level, Cockle Bay Wharf (☎9283 7385). Very trendy eatery with a great view of Darling Harbour. Coffee, cakes, and a wide variety of alcohol with an ambience posh enough to justify the price. Board games, comfy leather couches, outside heaters, and books make for an unbeatable lounging atmosphere. Open daily 8am-1am. ❸

Spanish Terrazas, 541 Kent St. (☎9283 3046). Affordable tapas ($6-9) and paella ($32-35 for 2) in the pricey Spanish Quarter. Wash it all down with a pitcher of sangria while you enjoy the live Latin music. Open for lunch M-Sa 11:30am-3:30pm, for dinner M-Th 5:30-10pm, F-Sa 5:30pm-midnight. ❸

Chinta Ria: Temple of Love (☎9264 3211), Roof Tce., Cockle Bay Wharf. A fantastic spot for soaking in the trendy wharf neighborhood amongst stunning Malaysian decor. Yummy, if pricey, Malaysian fare from $14-20. Live music outside Tu. Open daily noon-2:30pm and 6-11pm (10:30pm on Su). No reservations. ❸

Genghis Khan, 469 Kent St. (☎9264 3863). Diners crowd around the central grill to watch the chef cook their self-selected Mongolian BBQ. 1-serve lunch $9.20, dinner $13; all-you-can-eat $15.20/$18.20. Open for lunch M-F noon-3pm; for dinner Su-W 6-10pm, Th-Sa 6-10:30pm. ❷

GLEBE

Let's Go says students know best—we are pleased to present the invention of our Sydney University brethren. **Glebe Point Rd.** has one-stop shopping for all meals cheap, tasty, and Asian or Italian (or some interesting combination thereof) and perhaps the highest concentration of coffeeshops per block in the entire universe.

▨ **The e Lounge,** 92 Glebe Point Rd. (☎9518 6002). A cafe offering street-side seating and pleasant indoor tables as well as rich pasta dishes ($12-15), woodfired pizzas ($9-15), and the traditional Glebian assortment of intense coffees and evil desserts. Open Tu-Th noon-10pm, F noon-11pm, Sa 8am-11pm, Su 8am-10pm. AmEx/MC/V. ❷

Badde Manors, 37 Glebe Point Rd. (☎9660 3797), the one on the corner with plastic angels on the roof. World music plays in the background as the scent of freshly ground coffee permeates the air in this vegetarian cafe. Gourmet coffee, fresh sorbet, and smoothies. Tofu or lentil burger $9. Delicious daily soup specials $6.50. Open M-F 7:30am-midnight, Sa 8am-1am, Su 9am-midnight. No credit cards. ❶

Caffé Berardo, 119 Glebe Point Rd. (☎9518 4443; www.berardocaffe.com). The world's only distributor of a delectable Roman wood-fired "Berardo" roast. A cozy, funky place to kick back with a cuppa. Live music and spoken word F night, Sa DJ. Open Tu-Sa 8am-6pm, Su 9:30am-5pm. No credit cards. ❶

Darling Mills, 132 Glebe Point Rd. (☎6605 5666). Where locals go for a nice candlelit dinner for two. Fireplaces, brick walls, and hanging plants complement traditional Australian fare. $27 menu includes a glass of wine. Open for dinner M-Sa; also for lunch F. Reservations recommended. AmEx/DC/MC/V. ❹

Pho Glebe, 97 Glebe Point Rd. (☎9660 3888). Beautiful rock pool with live goldfish and blue-tiled chairs and tables. Lunch specials $8; meals from $12. Open daily 6-10:30pm, Sa-Su noon-3:30pm. No credit cards. ❷

Cafe Otto, 79 Glebe Point Rd. (☎9552 1519). High-ceilinged diner with insulated, heated outdoor courtyard. Everything from popular pastas ($12-21) and pizza ($12-16) to pricier meat dishes. Separate kids menu. For dessert, try the local fave: sticky date pudding ($9). BYO. Open Su-Th 9am-11pm, F-Sa 9am-midnight. AmEx/MC/V. ❸

Organic Supermarket, 53-55 Glebe Point Rd. An alternative to the markets inside the Broadway Mall, offering organics, both animal and vegetable. And don't forget the power crystals. Open M-W 9:30am-7pm, Th 9:30am-8pm, F 9:30am-7pm, Sa 9am-6pm, Su 10am-5pm. AmEx/MC/V.

NEWTOWN

King St. bisects Newtown and provides backpacker-style cheap eats, from Indian and Thai takeaways to filling espresso-shop breakfast deals. Newtown is a very young and bohemian place—cheap and tasty options are endless. Shop around to find good deals in the various produce and fish markets that crop up along King St.

▨ **Kilimanjaro African Eatery,** 280 King St. (☎9557 4565). Re-creates the flavors of several African nations with meals cooked in glazed clay pots and served in a simple dark-wood setting. Lots of couscous dishes. Filling entrees from $10. Appetizers and sides $6. Try a delicious ginger drink for $1.50. BYO. Open daily noon-late. ❷

Green Gourmet, 115-117 King St. (☎9519 5123; www.greengourmet.com). A veritable cornucopia of Thai-style vegan cuisine awaits. Try a pair of delicious Kumera Ginger Purses (sweet potato pastry with ginger and vegetable filling, $3) or the Lion King's Clay Pot, a great warmer-upper in cold months ($15). Open Su-Th noon-3pm and 6-10pm, F-Sa noon-3pm and 6-11pm. Also check out the neighboring **Vegan's Choice Grocery,** 113 King St. (☎9519 7646). ❷

Paros Taverna, 135 King St. (☎9516 5972). A fine brick floor and an inviting outdoor courtyard are only a few of the pleasures this Greek taverna has to offer. Oysters (half-dozen $13-15) and seafood pasta ($20) come fresh, as does the fantastic menu-deal ($20 for choice of entree, main course, dessert, and glass of retsina or shot of ouzo). Open W-Su 6pm-late. ❸

Tamana's North Indian Diner, 196 King St. (☎9519 2035), with smaller location at 236 King St. It's rare to find a fast-food joint with such a faithful following. Tamana's keeps local favor with its generous curry portions for under $7 and a wide variety of dishes labeled with degrees of spiciness. Open daily 11:30am-10:30pm. No credit cards. ❶

DARLINGHURST AND PADDINGTON

Oxford St. addresses start at the street's origin on Hyde Park, but confusingly *begin again* at the intersection with Victoria and Dowling St., the dividing line between Darlinghurst and Paddington. Noting whether an address is in Darlinghurst or Paddington is the easiest way to locate an Oxford St. property.

▨ **Una's,** 340 Victoria St., Darlinghurst (☎9360 0885). Austrian food in a delightful wood and brick enclave, with cafe seating on the street. The locals have been coming here for over 30 years. Try the strawberry pancakes for a great breakfast. Vienna schnitzel ($13) and bratwurst ($11). Daily pasta special $15. Open daily 7:30am-10:30pm. Licensed and BYO $1.50. No credit cards. ❷

▨ **Chocolate by the Bald Man,** 447 Oxford St., Paddington (☎9357 5055). Enough chocolate to overwhelm the most diehard cacao bean fanatic, from ice cream to whole beans. Try the hot chocolate ($4) with a pastry or fudge ($6-10). Popular strawberry fondue plate $7. Mobbed on the weekends. Open M-F 10am-6pm, Sa-Su 10am-6:30pm. AmEx/MC/V. ❶

▨ **Bill & Toni's Restaurant,** 74 Stanley St., E. Sydney (☎9360 4702). Heaping 1st courses of pasta only $7.50. For the hungrier, mains include schnitzel, casseroles, and veal ($11), and a full meal is $17. Free bread and orange punch complete the feast. Take-away sandwiches at the cafe downstairs are a super deal ($2-5). Open daily noon-2:30pm and 6-10:30pm. BYO. No credit cards. ❸

Micky's Cafe, 268 Oxford St., Paddington (☎9361 5157). Every combination under the sun in this dim bistro: stir-fry, burgers, burritos, cheesecakes, pasta, risotto, chicken satay, and Caesar salad. Meals from $10-16. Open daily 9am-midnight, F-Sa 9am-1am. MC/V. ❷

Arthur's Pizza, 260 Oxford St., Paddington (☎9331 1779). Arthur's hits the spot with gourmet pizza options like lamb and marinated chicken. Be prepared for waits of 1hr. or more in peak hours. Pizzas from $12-20, family size $26. Open daily 5-10pm; also F-Sa noon-3pm. AmEx/MC/V. ❸

Burgerman, 116 Surrey St., Darlinghurst (☎9361 0268), off Victoria St., near Willam St. Also at 249 Bondi Rd. (☎9130 4888). Sort of like a little '70s-style American burger joint—except it's a trendy cafe. For an Aussie treat, get a burger with beetroot ($7). Other world-burgers $6.40-9. Open daily noon-10pm. Licensed and BYO $4 corkage. ❶

SURRY HILLS

Formerly an industrial wasteland serving Sydney's once more locally supplied Central Business District, Surry Hills is now a pleasant residential area inhabited by student-artist types, working-class oldsters, and recent immigrants. Walk down

◠ St. from Oxford for a panoply of eating delights, a few tattoo parlors, and ℯ funkalicious boutiques.

Prasits Northside Thai Take Away, 395 Crown St. (☎9332 1792). A 10min. walk south of Oxford St. Fresh, creative, dishes such as the flavorful green peppercorn stir-fry ($12). Vegetarian mains $11, other mains $15-19. Limited seating. Open Tu-Su noon-3pm and 5:30-10pm. ❸ For a pricier sitdown meal, go a few storefronts down to **Prasits Northside Restaurant,** 401 Crown St (☎9319 0748). Open Tu-F noon-3pm and M-Sa 6-10pm. AmEx/MC/V. ❹

Mehrey Da Dhaba Indian Street Restaurant, 466 Cleveland St. (☎9319 6260). Mehrey Da, the oldest *dhaba* in Sydney, brings a tradition of inexpensive and filling East Indian food. Whole tandoori chicken $10. Vegetarian meals from $6-10; meat dishes $10-18. *Naan* or *roti* $1.20. Open Su-Tu 5:30-11pm, W-F noon-3pm and 5:30-11pm, F noon-3pm and 5:50pm-midnight, Sa noon-midnight. BYO. No credit cards. ❷

Haru Haru, 660 Crown St. (☎9699 3999). Japanese and Korean cuisine, with steals (noodles $9-12) and succulent splurges (BBQ barramundi $24). Sushi and sashimi combinations $20-21. Open daily 5:30-11pm. ❸

BONDI BEACH

Bondi Tratt, 34b Campbell Pde. (☎9365 4303). Mostly Italian with occasional mod-Oz twists. Try some kangaroo: it's supposed to be low-fat, if chewy. High on the hill, with a gorgeous view. Mains from $13. BYO. Open daily 7am-11pm. AmEx/MC/V. ❷

Gabby's Cafe, 94 Campbell Pde. (☎9130 3788). Gabby's has served its all-day filling breakfasts ($6) for more than 20 years. Soup special $6. Open daily 7am-5pm. No credit cards. ❶

Flavour of North India, 138 Campbell Pde. (☎9365 6239). Warm and ready curries $6-8. Fresh *naan* ($2) tempers the spicier options. Open Su-Th noon-10:30pm, F-Sa noon-11:30pm. MC/V. ❶

COOGEE BEACH

Coogee is no thrill for the gourmet, but Coogee Bay Rd. provides a more than a few doable lunch options: small, slightly trendy cafes and fish eateries.

Cozzi Cafe, 233 Coogee Bay Rd. (9665 6111). The Cozzi has wraps ($6), salads ($10), and an extensive selection of more complex lunch specials ($11-16). Happy Hour (that is, $2 coffee, tea, and cakes) daily 4-5pm. Open daily 8am-10pm. ❷

Barzura (☎9665 5546), at the end of Carr St. at the south end of the beach. Outdoor seating. Breakfast until 1pm ($8-10), modern Australian mains $20 and up. Open daily 7am-11pm. Licensed and BYO wine only; corkage $2.50 per person. AmEx/MC/V. ❹

MANLY

Cheap cafes, takeaways, and American imperialist fast-food chains colorfully line the Corso, which connects the harbor to the Pacific. More expensive, image-conscious bars and cafes can be found on Steyne St., which runs parallel to the ocean.

Green's Eatery, 1-3 Sydney Rd. (☎9977 1904), on the pedestrian stretch of Sydney Rd. near the ocean. Sunny, vegetarian cafe serves amazingly hearty meals, with rice and interesting vegetable combos for $4-7. Try the chickpea casserole or the sauteed veggies with tofu. Roll-ups $4-5; salads $3-7. Open daily 8am-6:30pm. No credit cards. ❶

The Indian Pearl, 26-28 Pittwater Rd. (☎9977 2890), north of the town center. Savory curry and tandoori dishes include chicken, lamb, and beef from $13. Goan fish curry comes highly recommended ($17). Takeaway $2 cheaper. BYO wine only. Free delivery. Live music F-Sa. Open daily 5:30-11pm. AmEx/DC/MC/V. ❸

◙ SIGHTS

The main sights of Sydney are truly the city's two **harbors** (Sydney Cove and Darling Harbor) and the **green spaces** of the Botanical Gardens and the Domain, near the Central Business District. Each of these merits a day of strolling and perusal. Sydney's neighborhoods do not have specific "sights" per se—their attraction lies in their tasty cafes, off-beat stores, and local nooks and crannies. There's architecture to appreciate in Paddington, markets to rummage through in Glebe and Newtown, and tanned and toned beach action on Bondi and Coogee. Find adrenaline-fixes and pulse-quickeners in **Activities** (p. 118) and the best spots for retail-therapy in **Capitalist Capers** (p. 120).

THE ROCKS AND CIRCULAR QUAY

The southern base of the harbor bridge, The Rocks is the site of the original Sydney Town settlement, where living spaces were, at one time, literally chiseled out of the face of the shoreline rock. Built up slowly during the lean years of the colony's founding, the area remained rough-and-tumble into the 1900s. In the 70s, when plans to raze the slums which had grown up here were revealed, a movement to preserve the area began. Street performers and live bands now liven up the Rocks Market (every Sa-Su; see **Capitalist Capers**, p. 120). The **Sydney Visitors Centre** and the **Rocks Walking Co.** share the white, three-story Sailors' Home at 106 George St. The former has info on local attractions and displays on the history of the Rocks, and the latter conducts informative walking tours of The Rocks. (Visitors Centre: ☎9255 1788 or 1800 067 676. Open daily 9am-6pm. Walking Co.: ☎9247 6678. 90min. tours depart M-F 10:30am, 12:30, and 2:30pm; Sa-Su 11:30am and 2pm. $16, ages 10-16 and seniors $10.70, under 10 free.)

⬛ SYDNEY OPERA HOUSE. Like a fleet of sails full of wind, the Opera House defines all harbor views of Sydney. Designed by Danish architect Jørn Utzon, Sydney's pride and joy took 14 years to construct. A saga of bureaucracy and broken budgets (planned at $7 million, the building ended up costing $102 million) plagued the construction, eventually leading the architect to leave the project. In 1973, Queen Elizabeth opened the building, despite strong winds, a false fire alarm, and 1400 spectator seats initially set up facing the wrong way. The Opera House has recovered from a rocky start by starring in thousands of tourist photographs daily and hosting operas, ballets, classical concerts, plays, and films, eventually coming to symbolize Sydney itself. (*On Bennelong Point, opposite the base of the Harbour Bridge. ☎9250 7250; www.soh.nsw.gov.au. For box office info, see* **Entertainment,** *p. 121. 45min. tours every hr. daily 8:30am-5pm. $15.40, concessions $10.60, families $41.45.*)

⬛ SYDNEY HARBOUR BRIDGE. Spanning the harbor, the arching steel latticework of the massive Harbour Bridge has been a visual symbol of the city, and the best place to get a look at the Harbour and the cityscape, since its opening in 1932. Pedestrians can enter the bridge walkway from a set of stairs on Cumberland St. just south of Argyle St. in The Rocks. At the bridge's southern pylon, there is an entry on the walkway which leads up to solid photo-ops. The **Harbour Bridge Museum** inside the pylon tells the baffling story of the bridge's construction. (*☎9247 7833 for more info. Open daily 10am-5pm. Lookout and museum $5, children 4-12 $3, families $12.*) For high adventure, **Bridgeclimb** will take you up to the apex for a gut-wrenching view of the city and Harbour. Only mildly strenuous and hyper-safe, this has maximum bragging potential with minimum stress—though it will noticeably lighten your wallet. All potential climbers must first take a breathalizer test, so don't hit the pubs beforehand. (*5 Cumberland St., off of Argyle St. ☎8274 7777; www.bridgeclimb.com. Open daily 7am-4:30pm. 3hr. climbs every 10min. Day climbs M-F $125, ages 12-16 $100; Sa-Su $150/$125. Night climbs M-F $150/$125, Sa-Su $170/$150.*)

CIRCULAR QUAY. Of course it's pronounced "key." How else would you say it? Between Dawes Point and Bennelong Point is the departure point for both the city ferry system and numerous private cruise companies. The Quay becomes a lively hub of tourist activity on weekends, with street performers, souvenir shops, and easy access to many major sights. It's also a prime place for those sun-worshippers who find that the concrete jungle of the CBD blocks their rays.

DER'S

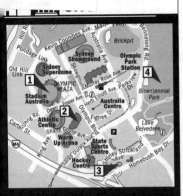

HOMEBUSH BAY

The September 2000 Olympic Games marked the second time Australia hosted the event (the first was in Melbourne in 1956). The impressively **huge** Homebush Bay Olympic Site, 14km west of the city center along the **Parramatta River**, is where most events took place. To get to Homebush Bay, take a CityRail train to the **Olympic Park Station**; *do not take the train to "Homebush."* Contact the Homebush Bay Visitors Centre **for information on tours (business hours ☎ 9714 7545, 24hr. ☎ 9714 7888; www.oca.nsw.gov.au).**

1 Take a tour or catch a rugby match at **Telstra Stadium,** the largest Olympic Stadium to date, with 110,000 seats (☎ 8765 2000)

2 Swim laps at the **Aquatic Centre,** where Aussie swimmer Ian Thorpe won 3 gold and 2 silver medals (☎ 9752 3666)

3 Dry off with a round of tennis (watching or playing) at the sprawling **Tennis Centre** (☎ 8746 0777)

4 End with a picnic and a hike at the 100-hectare **Bicentennial Park** (☎ 9714 7300)

MUSEUM OF SYDNEY. Even history has succumbed to the technology age. Located in the site of the first Government house, this new and stylish museum celebrates the city's past through films, high-tech multimedia, and interactive exhibits. *(37 Phillip St., at the corner of Bridge St. ☎ 9251 5988; www.mos.nsw.gov.au. Open daily 9:30am-5pm. $7, concessions $3, families $17.)*

ROYAL BOTANIC GARDENS. All of the city center's greenery is concentrated in charmingly landscaped plants, flowers, and trees filling 30 hectares around Farm Cove. Not for the heartsick—couples shamelessly lounge everywhere. Within the gardens, attractions such as the Aboriginal plant trail and the formal rose garden are free, but the **Tropical Center** greenhouses charge admission. *(Open daily 10am-4pm. $2.20, concessions $1.10, families $5.50.)* **Government House,** in the northwest corner of the Gardens, served as the home of the governor of New South Wales as recently as 1996. *(☎ 9931 5222. Grounds open daily 10am-4pm; house tours every 30min. F-Su 10:30am-3pm. Free.)* On the eastern headland of Farm Cove, the Botanic Gardens end at **Mrs. Macquaries Chair.** The chair, carved from the stone at the point, was fashioned for the wife of Governor Lachlan Macquarie and is now a classic Sydney photo-op. Daily guided walks begin at a Visitors Center, in the southeast corner of the park near Art Gallery Rd. *(Open daily 7am to sunset. Free. Palm Grove Centre: ☎ 9231 8125; www.rbg-syd.nsw.gov.au. Open daily 9:30am-5pm. 2hr. guided walks daily 10:30am; 40min. lunchtime walks M-F 1pm.)*

THE HARBOUR

The **Sydney Harbour National Park** preserves four Harbour islands, several south shore beaches, a few green patches on the northern headlands, and North and South Head. Float around the waterways on **Captain Cook Cruises.** *(☎ 9206 1111; www.captain-cook.com.au. More than 20 departures per day from 9:30am. Departs from Jetty no. 6, Circular Quay.)* Guided visits to the Harbour islands themselves must be booked ahead through the **National Park Information Centre,** 110 George St., The Rocks, in **Cadman's Cottage.** *(☎ 9247 5033. Open M-F 9am-4:30pm, Sa-Su 10am-4:30pm. Tours depart from the Cottage.)* **The Heritage Tour** focuses on history (M and F-Su 12:30pm; $20, concessions $15.40). **The Water Rats** tour visits the sets of the popular TV show (M and F-Su 11:45am; $20, concessions $15.40). **The Gruesome Tales Tour** focuses on the grisly aspects of convict history. (Sa 5:45pm, daylight savings 6:45pm. $24; not suitable for children).

ISLANDS. The early colony's most troublesome convicts were isolated on Pinchgut Island, off Mrs. Macquaries Point. The name came from the habit of punishing unruly convicts by isolating them on the exposed rock with a diet consisting of only bread and water. The island was later renamed Fort Denison for the fort that was built to protect the city from a feared Russian invasion. On Goat Island, west of the city center, near the shore at Balmain, the sandstone gunpowder station and barracks were the site of cruel punishments for the convicts who built them.

BEACHES. The park's south shore beaches—**Nielson Park, Camp Cove,** and the nude beach **Lady Jane**—are situated on Vaucluse Bay, accessible by bus #325, which runs to Watsons Bay. Popular North Shore Harbour beaches include **Balmoral Beach,** on the north side of Middle Head, a 15min. walk from Military Rd.; **Chinaman's Beach,** north of Balmoral, a seven-minute walk from Spit Rd.; and **Manly Cove,** at the Manly Wharf ferry port. To get to Balmoral Beach, take bus #244 to Balmoral. To get to Manly, take a ferry or Jetcat or bus #143 or 144 from Spit Junction. Up the coast from Manly are **Freshwater, Coogee,** and **Narrabeen**—all of which are less commercial and less crowded.

CITY CENTER, HYDE PARK, AND THE DOMAIN

▧ SYDNEY CENTREPOINT TOWER. Rising 325m above sea level (and containing four floors of shopping mall), the tower affords a stunning panoramic view of the city and surroundings. The 40-second ride to the top of Australia's highest building is steep in grade and price, so don't waste the trip on a cloudy day. When the sky is clear, views extend as far as the Blue Mountains to the west, the New South Wales central coast to the north, and Wollongong to the south. **Sydney Tower Restaurants ❺,** the city's only revolving restaurants, spin on the second-highest floor. *Let's Go* does not recommend looking down from the top after eating—it could get messy. *(100 Market St. ☎9229 7444; www.sydneyskytour.com.au. Open Su-F 9am-10:30pm, Sa 9am-11:30pm. $20, concessions $16, families $55. Restaurant reservations ☎8223 3800. Buffet lunch $40, dinner $49. Fixed price menu also available.)*

TOWN HALL. Sydney's age insures that architecture in the center is far from uniformly modern. The French Renaissance-style Town Hall was built in the prosperity of the late 1800s; the building's ostentation merits at least a passing look. The wood-lined concert hall fields an 8000-pipe organ; free recitals are held periodically. *(483 George St. ☎9265 9007. Open daily 9am-5pm. Free admission. Tours with Centrepoint Touring Company ☎8223 3815.)*

QUEEN VICTORIA BUILDING. The imposing statue of Queen Victoria, visible from the north corner of Town Hall, guards the entrance to her namesake's lavish building. The Byzantine edifice was constructed in 1898 as a home for the plebeian city markets, but recent renovations have brought in ritzier shopping venues. Fortunately, a stroll in the fantastic wood and brass interior still doesn't cost a cent. *(455 George St. ☎9264 9209; www.qvb.com.au. Free guided tours M-Sa 11:30am and 2:30pm, Su noon and 2:30pm. Open M-Sa 9am-6pm, Su 11am-5pm.)*

SYDNEY HOSPITAL AND NEW SOUTH WALES PARLIAMENT HOUSE. The 1814 hospital building is a landmark of colonial architecture. In 1854, with new wealth coming in from the recent gold rush, Sydney Hospital's south wing became a branch of the Royal Mint. The central section of the building is still Sydney's main medical facility, while the **NSW Parliament House** occupies the north wing. Visitors are welcome in the building, with access to public viewing galleries during parliamentary sessions and free tours. *(Parliament faces Macquarie St. between Martin Pl. and Hunter St. ☎9230 2637. Open M-F 9:30am-4pm. Free admission. Book ahead for tours when Parliament is not in session or for Parliamentary session viewing.)*

BARRACKS MUSEUM. An unusual display of artifacts from the days of convict immigration is housed in the Hyde Park Barracks, a former prison, women's immigration depot, and asylum. The defunct barracks were going to pot in the late 1980s, when a group of enterprising curators got together and organized an archeological dig on the grounds of the barracks and inside the house itself. The number

NEW SOUTH WALES

of rat corpses turned up from between the floorboards is astounding, but so are the rare fragments of the history of this building, a structure once built by convicts for their own containment. *(In Queens Sq., on Macquarie St. ☎9241 5866; www.hht.nsw.gov.au. Open daily 9:30am-5pm. $7, concessions $3, families $17.)*

ART GALLERY OF NEW SOUTH WALES. Sydney's major art museum's strength lies in its contemporary Australian works, Asian collections, and its extensive Aboriginal and Torres Strait Islander gallery. Bonnard, Picasso, and other big names are also represented. *(Northeast corner of the Domain, on Art Gallery Rd. ☎9225 1744; www.artgallery.nsw.gov.au. Open daily 10am-5pm. Free.)*

AUSTRALIAN MUSEUM. The creatively titled museum houses a unique mix of natural and cultural history. Stuffed re-creations of prehistoric Australian mega-fauna cast shadows over popular Aussie animals such as the koala and kangaroo. Though the science exhibits are fun for kids, the museum's treatment of the cultures of indigenous Australian peoples, both historically and as part of Australian society today, is superb for all ages. *(6 College St., on the east side of Hyde Park. ☎9320 6000; www.austmus.gov.au. Open daily 9:30am-5pm. $8, students $4, ages 5-12 $3, Aussie seniors and under 5 free, families $19. Special and temporary exhibits cost extra, up to $5.)*

HYDE PARK. Between Elizabeth and College St. at the eastern edge of the city center, Hyde Park was set aside in 1810 by Governor Lachlan Macquarie and is still Sydney's most structured public green space, complete with fountains and stately trees. A buzzing urban oasis during the day, the park warrants some caution for those strolling at night. In the southern half, below Park St., the Art Deco-style **ANZAC Memorial** commemorates the service of the Australian and New Zealand Army Corps in WWI, as well as that of the Australians who have fought in the nation's eight other overseas conflicts. *(☎9267 7668. Open M-Tu and Th-Su 9am-4:30pm, W 1-4:30pm.)* On the park's east sits **St. Mary's Cathedral,** a Neo-Gothic structure. The original structure was erected in 1833, burned to the ground in 1865, and completed again in 1928. The originally-planned two Gothic towers on the southern end were constructed in 2000. An exhibit placed awkwardly in the crypt gives an informative and thoughtful account of the cathedral's place in a modern city. *(☎9220 0400. Crypt open daily 10am-4pm. Admission $3, photography permit $2. Tours Su noon after mass or by arrangement. Tourists not permitted during masses.)*

THE DOMAIN. Behind the buildings on Macquarie St., the unmanicured, grassy expanse of the Domain stretches east along the south edge of the Royal Botanic Gardens. Concerts fill the area during January's **Sydney Festival** (see p. 122). During the rest of the year, the park is most popular for corporate weekday lunch breaks and Sunday-morning rabble-rousing at **Speakers' Corner,** modeled after London's traditional weekly public speaking in the park.

DARLING HARBOUR

The site of several events of the XXVII Olympiad, Darling Harbour, on the west side of the city center, is a popular tourist stop reminiscent of Disneyland, with its immaculate brick walkways, trams, squealing children, and opportunities to spend money. The concentration of tourist attractions in this small area makes it a perfect outing for afternoon sightseeing and a popular spot for families.

On foot, Darling Harbour is only ten minutes from Town Hall Station. Follow George St. north, then turn left on Market St. to Pyrmont Bridge. Bus #888 approaches Darling Harbour from Circular Quay by way of Town Hall, and ferries run from Circular Quay to the Aquarium steps. For transport as tourist-oriented as the destination, hop on the **monorail** from Pitt St., at Park or Market St. in the CBD (see p. 101). For more info on 2000 Olympic sites, see **Homebush Bay,** p. 114.

■ **SYDNEY AQUARIUM.** Over 11,000 marine animals from Australia's many aquatic regions inhabit the tanks on the pier at Darling Harbour's eastern shore. If you need more evidence that Australia has the weirdest fauna on earth, stop at the mudskipper containment where these freaks of the fish world display their ability to live out of water by absorbing moisture from the air. More conventional attractions include the recently-opened Great Barrier Reef exhibit, a penguin pool, a seal pool, and a small touching pool. The underwater Oceanariums, three plexiglass walking tunnels below street level through huge enclosures of fish, sharks, and stingrays help justify the pricey admission. (*On Aquarium Pier.* ☎ *9262 2300; www.sydneyaquarium.com.au. Open daily 9am-10pm; last entry 9pm. Seal sanctuary closes at sunset. $22, concessions $13, ages 3-15 $10, under 3 free, families of 5 $48. Wheelchair accessible.*)

POWERHOUSE MUSEUM. The largest museum in the Southern Hemisphere explores the breadth of human ingenuity. Its exhibits, interactive displays, and demos focus on technology and applied science. From decorative arts to space exploration, communication to transportation advances, the museum's astounding variety makes it popular with visitors of all ages. (*500 Harris St., just south of Darling Harbour between Ultimo and Haymarket St.* ☎ *9217 0444; www.phm.gov.au. Open daily 10am-5pm. $10, students $3, ages 5-15 $3, families $23, Australian seniors and under 5 free.*)

CHINESE GARDEN. This serene garden was a bicentennial gift to New South Wales from her sister province in Guangdong, China. The delicately manicured plot in traditional southern Chinese style provides a sheltered break from the hubbub of the city. There are admission packages which include Devonshire tea or lunch from $8-14. (*On the corner of Harbour and Pier St.* ☎ *9281 6863. Open daily 9:30am-5pm; teahouse until 4:30pm. $4.50, concessions $2, families $10, wheelchair-bound persons free.*)

INNER EAST

The suburbs just east of the city center are some of Sydney's most vibrant areas for shopping, eating, and meandering. Although Kings Cross tends to be a bit seedy, the neighborhood is not without a certain vibrance and charm. Oxford St. slides through Surry Hills, Darlinghurst, and Paddington in an endless string of cafes, boutiques, and hip houseware outlets. Sydney's large, outgoing gay community inhabits much of this strip. Buses #378, 380, and 382 run the length of Oxford St., connecting the city center to the inner eastern suburbs.

FOX STUDIOS AUSTRALIA. This state-of-the-art theme park and studio only opened in Moore Park in late 1999. *The Matrix II* was filmed on location here, as will be the next prequel of *Star Wars*. The park features 16 movie screens, pubs, and restaurants, not to mention a **backlot tour** with interactive exhibits on the film and TV industry. (☎ *9383 4000 or 9383 4333; www.foxstudios.com.au. Open daily 10am-midnight. Backlot access $25, concessions $20, ages 6-15 $15.*)

MOORE PARK. South of Paddington, Moore Park contains the **Sydney Football Stadium** and the city's major **cricket oval** (see **Sports and Recreation,** p. 20). For a tour of the Stadium and a small museum of Aussie sports history, call **Sportspace.** (☎ *9380 0383. Tours M-F 10am and 1pm on non-game days. $19, concessions $15.*)

CENTENNIAL PARK. The city's largest park abuts Moore Park's east side and stretches north to meet Oxford St. between Paddington and Woollahra. The park includes eight small lakes, a bird sanctuary, athletic fields, and cycling tracks.

SYDNEY JEWISH MUSEUM. This moving and informative museum is a remarkable exhibition of Australia's Jewish heritage and the horrors of the Holocaust. (*148 Darlinghurst Rd., at the corner of Burton St.* ☎ *9360 7999. Open Su-Th 10am-4pm, F 10am-2pm. $10, concessions $7, children $6, families $22.*)

NEW SOUTH WALES

PLAYING WITH FIRE As with all modern Olympic Games, the Sydney 2000 games were preceded by the relay of the Olympic torch around the country. With over 10,000 torchbearers and a route in excess of 27000km, the 2000 Torch Relay was the longest in history. The lighted torch arrived in Yulara, NT, and zig-zagged across the continent for 100 days before reaching the opening ceremonies in Sydney. The route was designed to run within an hour's drive from the homes of 85% of the Australian population.

NORTH SHORE

Coastal amusements at the northern beach resort of **Manly** have a tacky boardwalk feel unusual for an Australian beach. For less contrived pleasure, the **Manly to Spit Bridge walk** (9½km; 3hr.) offers uncluttered harbor coastline, sandy beaches, national park, and bayside homes. The walk begins at the **Manly Visitors Centre** next to the wharf. (☎9977 1088. Open M-F 9am-5pm, Sa-Su 10am-4pm.) From the Spit Bridge, bus #144 and 143 return to Manly and run to Sydney.

TARONGA PARK ZOO. The koalas, kangaroos, and tigers at Taronga Zoo enjoy million-dollar harbor views. The impressive collection contains animals from all over Australia and the world. Admission includes an enclosed chair-lift safari ride, widely considered the best part of a visit. (At the end of Bradley's Head Rd. in Mosman. To reach the zoo, take a 12min. ferry ride from Circular Quay. ☎9969 2777. Open daily 9am-5pm. $22, students $15.50, ages 4-15 $12, families $56. A Zoopass, purchased at Circular Quay, covers admission, ferry, and bus. $27.20, children $13.60. Parking $5.50.)

OCEAN WORLD. This aquatic playground earns rave reviews for its strange and rare specimens of tropical fish. There is a snake show three times daily, and weekends bring an extensive array of tours and presentations geared especially toward children. (On the West Esplanade at Manly Cove. ☎9949 2644. Open daily 10am-5:30pm. $16, concessions $11, children $8, families of 5 $40; reduced admission after 3:30pm. Shark feeding M, W, and F 11am.)

🎣 🔱 ACTIVITIES

NAUTICAL DIVERSIONS

SAILING. On any sunny day, white sails can be seen clipping across the waters. **East Sail Sailing School,** at D'Albora Marina on Rushcutters Bay, caters to all experience levels and offers intimate courses and trips. (Follow William St. until it merges with Bayswater Rd., then turn left on Beach Rd. ☎9327 1166; www.eastsail.com.au. Open daily 8am-6pm. 2½hr. sailing trips depart daily 10am; 2-12 passengers. $86, includes morning tea.) **Sydney by Sail** runs intro sailing lessons from the National Maritime Museum. (☎9280 1110 or 0419 367 180; www.sydneybysail.com. Trips daily depending on weather and demand; 8-12 person max. 1½hr. lesson, 11am, $54; 3hr. lesson, 1pm, $98; full intro course $420. Book ahead.)

DIVING. Sydney's rocky shores include several worthwhile spots for both shore and boat diving. With over 20 different dive sites, it's possible to dip in all along the coast. **ProDive** has excellent advice on local diving spots and all the gear you'll ever need. They also offer certification courses. (City center: Level 7, 428 George St. ☎9264 6177 or 1800 820 820. Coogee: 27 Alfreda St. ☎9665 6333. Both open M-W and F-Su 8:30am-5pm, Th 8:30am-6pm. 4-day courses from $295; trips and courses for other Australian locations can be arranged. Full-day boats and gear $120; gear alone $75.)

SURFING. Surfing at **Bondi Beach** makes all the postcards, but Sydney has other beaches with equally appealing waves and smaller crowds. **Coogee** can be just as crowded as Bondi, and **Tamarama** is smaller but with trickier rips. The locals are protective of **Maroubra,** south of Coogee, and to an extent the beaches north of the Harbour. Up north, **Manly** ranks with Bondi and Coogee as a popular city beach. Farther up the coast, **Curl Curl, Dee Why, North Narrabeen, Newport Reef,** and **Palm Beach** are well worth the relative seclusion they offer. To get to the northern beaches, take bus #183, 187, 188, 189, 190, 151, or any of the northern beach expresses that originate at Wynyard Station (Carrington St. side); or take the ferry to Manly and catch bus #151, 155, or 157. The **Manly Surf School,** at North Steyne Surf Club, gives surf lessons to everyone from beginners to more experienced surfers. (☎9977 6977; www.manlysurfschool.com. Open for lessons M-F 11am-3pm, Sa-Su 9-11am, 11:30am-1:30pm, and 2-4pm. 2hr. $45, 4hr. $80, 5-day $150; private lessons 1hr. $55, 2hr. $100.; prices include wetsuit and board. Bookings essential.) In Manly, **Aloha Surf,** 44 Pittwater Rd., rents boards and wetsuits. (☎9977 3777. Open M-W and F-Su 9am-6:30pm, Th 9am-9pm. Short and long boards half-day $20, full-day $40; bodyboards $20.) **Bondi Surf Co.,** 72-76 Campbell Pde., rents surfboards and bodyboards with wetsuits. (☎9365 0870. Open daily 9am-6pm. 2hr. $30, full-day $60; credit card or passport required.)

FISH AND WHALES. A number of charter boats run guided deep-sea **fishing** trips; groups get cheaper rates. **Whale watching season** is from June to July and September to October. **Halicat,** 410 Elizabeth St., Surry Hills., has both fishing and whale watching tours for up to 23 people running from Rose Bay and Cremorne. (☎9280 3043 or 1800 679 629. Trips depart 6:30am and return mid-afternoon. Reef fishing $110. Sport fishing trips go farther out and find bigger fish $200. Whale watching 3½hr. Weekend trips $85, seniors and students $75, children $55.) **Zane Grey** offers similar rates. (☎9565 4949 or 0412 225 201. Trips depart 7am and return mid-afternoon. Reef fishing $100; sport fishing $160.) Award-winning **Broadbill** runs a smaller operation (their boat holds six) at competitive prices from Sans Souci Wharf. (☎9534 2378. Trips depart 7am and return 5-6pm. Sport fishing $170-200.)

CRUISES. Ferry cruises are a great way to take in the harbor. In addition to those offered by Sydney Ferries (see p. 94), **Australian Travel Specialists,** Jetty 6, Circular Quay, books a number of one- to three-hour Harbour cruises that run from Circular Quay and Darling Harbour. (☎9247 5151. Depart 9:30am-8pm. From $19-116.) **Matilda Cruises,** at Pier 26 near the Aquarium, has lots of options: ferries between Darling Harbour and Circular Quay; the **Rocket Harbour Express** between Sydney Aquarium, Circular Quay, the Opera House, Taronga Zoo, Watson's Bay, and back to Darling Harbour; and sailing tours. (☎9264 7377. Harbour to Quay: $4, concessions $2. Express: $21, families $50. Sail from $27, seniors $22.)

AERIAL EXPLOITS

SKYDIVING. Skydiving in Australia is cheaper than almost anywhere else. **Simply Skydive Australia** throws people out of planes from 4300 ft.—with an instructor and parachute attached. (☎9970 5037. With Sydney pickup $295.) **Skydive Tandem** does the same from Bankstown Airport. (☎9791 9056. $325, backpackers $275.)

SCENIC FLIGHTS. For aerial views of Sydney without having to plummet towards it, a couple places offer scenic flights around Sydney and environs. **Sydney Air Scenic Flights** runs from the Bankstown Airport. (☎9790 0628. Blue Mountains 1hr. $185; Sydney Harbour 1hr. $185; coastal tour 1¼hr. $340; day tours also available to Hunter Valley, Snowy Mountains, and Coffs Harbour.) **Dakota National Air** also operates out of the Bankstown airport. (☎9791 9900 or 1800 246 747; www.dakota-air.com. F night Sydney Harbour with champagne supper 1hr. $149; Su morning Harbour 1hr. $105. Other tours available.)

EXTRA TERRESTRIAL ADVENTURES

WALKING TOURS. Walking tours of The Rocks depart from the Visitors Center, 106 George St. (☎9247 6678; see p. 96.) Additionally, **Unseen Sydney** conducts 1½hr. walking tours entitled "History, Convicts, and Murder Most Foul," which include a complimentary drink from the historic Hero of Waterloo's cellar. (☎9907 8057. Tu and Th-Sa 6:30pm. $19, students $15.) The **Original Sydney Walking Tours** runs five different tours delving into the sensational past of The Rocks and Kings Cross. (☎9380 2059 or 0413 139 162. $14, concessions $10.)

SELF-GUIDED WALKS. They don't cost a cent and are a better way for the purist to enjoy Sydney's beautiful landscape. The walk from the Opera House to Mrs. Macquaries Chair through the Royal Botanic Gardens is deservedly popular, while the one from Watson's Bay to the Gap provides equally beautiful serenity with even more isolation from the urban center. The walk from Manly to Spit Bridge is a bit rigorous and provides views and lush flora from the other side of the Harbour, while that from Bondi to Coogee Beach has a city beach at every valley and a breathtaking Pacific view at every peak.

RAW POWER. Australian Travel Specialists (☎9555 2700) books a number of chauffeured Harley-Davidson motorcycle tours, ranging from a Harbour tour (1hr., $99) to a mammoth tour of the Hunter Valley and Blue Mountains (8hr., $345).

OTHER RENTALS. Several places rent **in-line skates** or **skateboards.** In Bondi Junction, visit **Bondi Boards and Blades,** 230 Oxford St. (☎9369 2212. Open daily 10am-6pm. $11 1st hr., $5.50 per hr. afterwards, $22 per day. Group discounts.) In Manly, try **Manly Blades,** 49-53 North Steyne St. (☎9976 3833. Open M-W 9am-7pm, Th 9am-9pm, F-Sa 9am-7pm, Su 9am-6pm. $12 per hr., full-day $25, 24hr. $30. Scooters $20 per hr.) Paddington's **Total Skate,** 36 Oxford St., Woollahra, is close to Centennial Park. (☎9380 6356. $10 first hr., $5 each additional hr., $30 per day.)

CAPITALIST CAPERS

Sydney has numerous year-round weekend markets, all of which tend to specialize in arts, crafts, and souvenirs. Haggling is fun, the food is reasonably priced, and there's generally at least one cart selling fresh fruit.

MARKETS. Paddington Markets, 395 Oxford St., is Sydney's best known and liveliest market, featuring entertainment, food, and a variety of clothing and crafts. (Take buses #380 or L82 from Circular Quay. ☎9331 2923; www.paddington-market.com.au. Open Sa 10am-4pm.) **Paddy's Markets,** on Ultimo Rd. at Hay St, is legendary and as old as the city itself. The goods on sale here are always cheap but only sometimes quality. Check out the 2nd level, home to a food court and a handful of brand name factory outlets. (☎1300 361 589; www.paddysmarkets.com.au. Open rain or shine Th 10am-6pm, F-Su 9am-4:30pm.) **Paddy's Flemington,** run by Paddy's Markets, is off Parramatta Rd. in the Sydney Markets across from the Homebush Bay Olympic Site. (Open F 10am-4:30pm, Su 9am-4:30pm; see p. 114.) **The Rocks Market,** at the north end of George St. under the bridge, is more touristy and upmarket, with antiques, jewelry, and collectibles, as well as street performers and live musicians. (Take the monorail to Haymarket. Open rain or shine Sa-Su 9am-5pm.) **Glebe Markets,** at Glebe Public School, on the corner of Glebe Point Rd. and Derby Pl., sells new and second-hand crafts and amazing clothes by talented young designers. (Sa 10am-4pm, weather permitting.) The hip **Bondi Beach Market,** at Bondi Beach Public School on Campbell Pde., features locally made arts and crafts. (☎9315 8988. Open Su 10am-4pm, weather permitting.)

▣ ENTERTAINMENT

The iconic **Sydney Opera House** is the lynchpin of Sydney's creative culture and its primary venue. With five stages (described below), the Opera House nimbly hosts a variety of the city's artistic endeavors. (Box office for all venues ☎9250 7777; www.soh.nsw.gov.au; bookings@soh.nsw.gov.au. Open M-Sa 9am-8:30pm, Su 2hr. prior to show only for ticket pick-up. Doors close at showtime. Student rush ticket policy differs from company to company; contact each one for information.)

▨ **Opera Theatre.** The excellent **Opera Australia** (☎9699 1099, tickets 9319 1088; www.opera-australia.org) performs here. Reserved seats range from $83-180 and sell out fast, even though there are 1547 of them. Partial-view seats (blocking more than a quarter of the stage) start at $43. Standing room and listening-only (totally obstructed stage "view") are $33 and are available over-the-counter only at 9am the morning of the performance; limit 2 per person. Leftover tickets are sometimes sold 30min. before showtime on performance night as student rush tickets for $33 (ISIC required). Doors close promptly at showtime—be sure to arrive on time. The **Australian Ballet Company** (☎1300 36 97 41; www.australianballet.com.au) and the **Sydney Dance Company** (☎9221 4811; www.sydneydance.com.au) share the same theater space. Call for ticket prices and info.

▨ **Concert Hall.** The 2678-seat Concert Hall, the most majestic of the Opera House's stages, is the one-stop shop for symphony, chamber, and orchestral music performances. **Sydney Symphony Orchestra** (☎9334 4644; www.symphony.org.au) and the **Australian Chamber Orchestra** (☎9357 4111; www.aco.com.au) perform here throughout the year. Call for ticket info.

Drama Theatre. Most frequently stars the **Sydney Theatre Company** (☎9250 1777; www.sydtheatreco.com/~exstce). Theater seats 544. Advance seating from $50, standing room tickets $25 available 1hr. prior to show, student rush tickets from $15 available 30min. prior to show.

Playhouse Theatre. A traditional round-stage forum with 398 seats. Contact the **Bell Shakespeare Company** (☎9241 2722; bellshakespeare@orangemail.com.au) for information on which of Will's classics they might be presenting.

Studio Stage. This catch-all, transformable stage seats 300 and exhibits less traditional Opera House offerings, including cabaret shows and contemporary performances.

SPECTATOR SPORTS

Australia is a land of beer-guzzling, meatpie-gorging, obscenity-hurling mega-fans (see **Sports**, p. 20). Check out a sports match for an unforgettable lesson in social psychology, mob action, and VB-induced testosterone rituals. All events below sell tickets through **Ticketek** (☎9266 4800; www.ticketek.com.au) and are played in stadiums in Moore Park, accessible by bus #349, 373, 393, and 395.

Rugby League. The **Sydney Football Stadium** (☎9360 6601), on the corner of Driver Ave. and Moore Park Rd., is home to the **South Sydney** and **Sydney City Side** teams. It draws rowdy, fiercely loyal fans throughout the winter season and in Sept. for the Wynfield Cup. Tickets $17-25. Children receive discounts.

Australian Rules Football. This head-crushing, uniquely Aussie game is also held at the Sydney Football Stadium. Root, root, root for the home team: the **Sydney Swans.** It's a silly name for some very big boys. Tickets cost more and are harder to get than rugby tickets ($20-60).

Cricket. To some, the games feel perpetual, the rules are maddeningly complicated, and the "athletes" are men wearing white straw hats and sweater vests. To others, games are suspense-thrillers and the players are gods. Either way, head to the **Sydney Cricket Ground** (☎9360 6601), on Moore Park Rd. Tickets $10-40, depending upon the game.

CINEMAS

Don't get too excited about the film possibilities in Sydney: the American schlock-busters marketed around the world make their way here too, to be advertised on buses and subways and kiosks and little children's hearts. But take heart, ye lovers of indie celluloid! The city also hosts a variety of independent movie houses and small festivals. Tuesdays are **bargain day**—tickets are half price. The rest of the week, prices hover around $13-14 and $10-11 for children. Call **Movieline** (☎13 27 00) for showtimes at all cinemas. For info on the **Sydney Film Festival,** see p. 122.

■ **Valhalla,** 166d Glebe Point Rd. (☎9660 8050). Possibly the best independent cinema in the city. Formerly a 1980's den of mary jane and trip-flicks, Valhalla's got two theaters and a busy schedule. Hosts the **International Animation Festival** in mid-July and sometimes has concerts.

■ **Dendy Cinemas,** 2 East Circular Quay (☎9247 3800;www.dendy.com.au); 261-263 King St. (☎9550 5699); 19 Martin Pl. (☎9233 8166). All locations show quality films of artsy ilk. Martin Pl. location focuses on anime and has a bar and bistro. Open daily noon-9pm; bar closes at midnight.

Govinda's, 112 Darlinghurst Rd., Darlinghurst (☎9360 7853). Reaps cult, classic, and contemporary films and throws in an all-you-can eat buffet (see **Food,** p. 107).

Hoyts Centre, 505-525 George St. (☎9273 7431). The largest mainstream cinema, located midway between Chinatown and the CBD.

Reading Cinemas, Level 3, Market City Mall, Hay St., (☎9280 1202), Chinatown. Undercuts other cinemas by $1-2; Su double-features.

Chauvel Cinema, (☎9361 5398), at Oxford and Oatley St., Paddington Town Hall, Paddington. Specializes in indie and foreign films.

Panasonic IMAX Cinema (☎9281 3300), Southern Promenade, Darling Harbour. The eight-story-high movie screen is the largest in the world. A different film is shown every hour. Open daily 10am-10pm.

GAMBLING

Okay, so gambling destroys marriages, depletes hard-saved nest eggs, and is a tax on people who are bad at math. But games of chance can't be all bad: public lottery revenues financed the Sydney Opera House, after all. Australia, with just 1% of the world's population, fields 20% of its gaming machines (known locally as "pokies"). These video poker machines allow you to compete against a computer very effectively programmed to kick your ass. New South Wales lays claim to more than half of the continent's collection; pokies fill pub rooms across the state. But it might be the state governments that are the real gambling addicts. The New South Wales treasury takes a healthy cut from Sydney's $1.2 billion **Star City Casino,** 80 Pyrmont St., Pyrmont (☎9777 9000), in West Darling Harbour. The twinkling complex entices the punters 24hr. with lucky seven restaurants, seven bars, a nightclub, plastic trees, an indoor waterfall, 5-star hotel, and an endless (okay, a mere 145,000 square meters) gaming room with 1500 poker machines and 160 gaming tables. The casino, in existence since 1997, can be accessed by light rail or shuttle bus to the casino or monorail to Harbourside.

⚡ FESTIVALS

Sydney-siders aren't as gung-ho as Melbournians when it comes to flaunting random festivals, but they still know how to party.

Sydney Festival, throughout Jan. (☎8248 6500; www.sydneyfestival.org.au). Features arts and entertainment events. Check the *Daily Telegraph* for details on free concerts in The Domain, street theater in The Rocks, and fireworks in Darling Harbour.

Tropfest, Feb. 2-24, 2003 (☎9368 0434; www.tropfest.com.au). World's largest short film festival screens in The Domain, Royal Botanic Gardens, and cafes along Victoria St.

Gay and Lesbian Mardi Gras, Mar. 1, 2003 (☎9557 4332; www.mardigras.com.au). Brings the rip-roaring, no-holds-barred festivities of this huge international event. The festival climaxes on its final day with a parade attended annually by over 500,000 people and a gala party at the RAS Show Ground in Moore Park. Though the party is restricted and the guest list fills up way, way ahead of time, travelers can get on the list by becoming "International Members of Mardi Gras" well in advance. Intl. Membership $60, tickets around $110, concession $55.

Royal Agricultural Society's Easter Show, Apr. 11-24, 2003 (☎9704 1111; www.eastershow.com.au). Held at the Homebush Olympic Site. The carnival atmosphere and rides make it fun even for those with no interest in farming.

Sydney Film Festival, mid-June 2003 (☎9660 3844; www.sydfilm-fest.com.au). The ornate State Theatre, 49 Market St., between George and Pitt St., and Dendy Opera Quays showcase documentaries, retrospectives, and art films from around the world. The festival tours Australia throughout the year.

City to Surf Run, Aug. 10, 2003 (☎9282 3606). Draws 50,000 contestants for a semi-serious 14km trot from Park St to Bondi Beach. Some are world-class runners; others treat the race as a lengthy pub crawl. Entries ($25) are accepted up to race day.

Manly Jazz Festival, Oct. 3-5, 2003 (☎9977 1088; www.pcn.com.au/manlyjazz). Oz's biggest jazz festival, featuring all types of national and international artists.

Bondi Beach Party, Dec. 25 each year. Bondi sets the pace for debauchery all along the coast as people from around the world gather for a foot-stomping Christmas party.

Sydney-to-Hobart Yacht Race, Dec. 26 each year. Brings the city's hungover attention (see above) back to civilized entertainment.

▌ NIGHTLIFE

Whether they're out on the town for drinks and dancing or huddling around a TV for the latest crucial sports telecast, many Sydney-siders hit the pub and club scene four or five times per week. Different neighborhoods have distinctly different scenes, and the scenes vary from night to night. Bars in Kings Cross attract a large, **straight male crowd,** which quickly spills over from the strip joints into the pubs and dance clubs. **Backpackers** round out the mix in this neighborhood, giving several spots an international feel. Outside Kings Cross, travelers generally congregate in pubs to avoid the high cover charges and inflated drink prices of Sydney's high-profile dance venues. Gay Sydney struts its stuff on Oxford St. in Darlinghurst, Paddington, and Newtown, where some establishments are specifically **gay or lesbian** and many others are mixed. Because the gay clubs provide much of the city's best dance music, flocks of young, beautiful club scenesters of all persuasions fill any extra space on their vibrant, vampy dance floors. Taylor Square, at the intersection of Oxford, Flinders, and Bourke St., is the heart of this district. **Suits** clog the bars in the Central Business District, and night spots in The Rocks tend toward the **expensive.** For more **casual pub crawling,** wander on Bourke and Flinders St. in Surry Hills. Large **student populations** in Glebe and Newtown make for a younger crowd and cheaper drinks on special nights at pubs here.

Major concerts are held in the **Sydney Entertainment Centre,** on Harbour St., Haymarket (☎9320 4200; www.sydentcent.com.au; box office open M-F 9am-5pm, Sa 10am-1pm); the **Hordern Pavilion,** in Moore Park; and the **Enmore Theatre,** 130 Enmore Rd., Newtown (☎9550 3666).

Sydney's daily **live music** scene consists largely of local cover bands casting their pearls before pub crowds. The *Metro* section of the Friday *Sydney Morning Herald* and free weeklies such as *Beat* and *Sydney City Hub* contain listings for upcoming shows, along with info on art showings, movies, theater, and DJ appearances city-wide. The bible of the Sydney clubber is *3-D World* (www.threedworld.com.au), a free Tuesday publication that can be found in hostels, music stores, and trendy clothing stores. It gives the lowdown on special events for each night of the week. Look for the free *Streetpress* or *The Revolver*, which highlight the weekly hotspots for shaking your groove thang; *Drum Media* covers music. *Sx News* (www.sxnews.com.au) and *Sydney Star Observer* (www.sonet.com.au) focus on the gay community.

BARS AND PUBS

KINGS CROSS

▨ **Fitzroy Hotel,** 129 Dowling St. (☎9356 3848), on the corner of Cathedral St., 3 blocks west of Victoria St. A neighborhood pub comfortably sequestered from the more hectic Cross. Upstairs is popular with backpackers for its casual atmosphere and pool tables ($2 per game). Frequent discounts through local hostels. Schooners $3.40. Happy Hour M 5:30-7:30pm. Tu free pool. Open M-Sa 10:30am-midnight, Su 3-10pm.

O'Malley's Hotel, 228 William St. (☎9357 2211), on the corner of Brougham St. Upscale style in a casual pub atmosphere. The row of TVs makes O'Malley's into something of an Irish sports bar, but its nightly live music (local rock bands) is the best in the Cross. Eclectic crowd proves that backpackers, business-types, and locals can, will, and must integrate. Schooners of Toohey's $3.30. Open M-Th 11am-2am, F-Su 11am-3am.

The World, 24 Bayswater Rd. (☎9357 7700; www.theworldbar.com). Infamous daily Happy Hours make the World go 'round (and 'round, and 'round, and... 6-7pm, schooners $2; 10-11pm, schooners and wine $1.50). Or, try the teapot full of shots, premixed with as many or as few cups as you like ($15). W free pool; Th live music; F classic house; Sa top-100; live DJs every night. Open M-Th 5pm-2am, F-Su 5pm-6am.

Bourbon and Beefsteak, 24 Darlinghurst St. (☎9358 1144). It's 7am and there is nowhere that you *haven't* had a drink, but you can still stomach the neon and excessive Australian flag regalia. A bit of a bottom-feed, but somehow everybody ends up here at one time or another while carousing in the Cross. Open 24hr. for breakfast.

PADDINGTON

Durty Nelly's, 9-11 Glenmore Rd. (☎9360 4467), off Oxford St. at Gipps St. Even wedged in on a street of frou-frou Paddington shops, Nelly takes her Guinness very seriously; those in the know claim hers is the best around (schooners $4.20). Even on weekends when it's packed, the dark wood decor and jovial staff create a relaxing refuge from the nearby Oxford St. melee. Open M-Sa 11am-midnight, Su noon-10pm.

Darlo Bar, 306 Liverpool St. (☎9331 3672), on the corner of Darlinghurst Rd. A mixed crowd, old and young, come here to booze on down to a tune slightly cheaper than the usual (schooners $3.40). Open M-Sa 10am-midnight, Su noon-10pm.

Grand Pacific Blue Room (☎9331 7108), on the corner of Oxford and S Dowling St. A very cool lounge bar with live acoustic performances and the occasional DJ. Shed the backpack for a night to join a young sophisticated crowd wearing clothes purchased just across the street. DJs Th-Su (Th jazz/funk, F hip-hop, Sa R&B, Su hip-hop). Cover F $8, Sa $10. Open Tu-W and Su 5:30pm-1am, F-Sa 5:30pm-3am.

Albury Hotel, 6 Oxford St. (☎9361 6555). A classic drag venue: a bit touristy, but when you go to Rome, you see the Vatican, right? Two large rooms provide separation between the drag show and the bar scene. Together, these halves comprise a fully functioning meat market—surely you will leave with a story to tell your friends. A mixed gay-and-straight crowd revel in the debauchery. Schooners $4.10. Shows at 10 and 11pm; main performance at midnight. Happy Hour daily 2-8pm. Cover F-Sa $5. Open M-Sa 2pm-2am, Su 2pm-midnight.

THE ROCKS

■ **The Lord Nelson,** 19 Kent St. (☎9251 4044), on the corner of Argyle St. west of The Rocks center. Nautical flags drape from sturdy wooden beams in this colonial building. Sydney's oldest hotel and pub, first licensed in 1841 to a former convict landlord, shelters a young crowd. A very chill place for an after-work pint from one of Sydney's only micro-breweries. Try the award-winning Old Admiral (pints $6). Open daily 11am-11pm.

■ **The Hero of Waterloo,** 81 Lower Fort St. (☎9252 4553), 1 block off Argyle St. west of The Rocks center. Since 1845, this pub has been an Australian favorite; its underground tunnels were once used for rum smuggling. The older group of regulars has been drinking here since before you were born (so they should be pretty drunk by now). Live entertainment (Irish and folk music) W-Su. Open M-Sa 10am-11pm, Su 10am-10pm.

CITY CENTER

■ **The Basement,** 29 Reiby Pl. (☎9251 2797). Arguably the hottest live music venue in the CBD, with acts ranging from jazz to rock. Schooners $5.50. Cover ranges from $10 to $50 for the most exclusive acts. Open daily noon-3pm for lunch and 7:30pm-late.

Jackson's on George, 176 George St. (☎9247 2727), near Circular Quay. 4 swanky levels: danceclub, pool bar, games, and restaurant. "Stik" drinks ($9) pack a punch with fresh fruit, ice, and spirits. Happy Hour F-Sa 5-7pm. Schooners $4. Cover F-Sa $10 after 10pm. Open M-Th 11am-3am, F-Su 11am-6am.

Scubar, 4 Rawson Pl. (☎9212 4244; www.scubar.com.au), in the YHA basement, 1min. west of Central Station. Pool competitions, big screen cable TVs, and periodic jug-and-pizza dinner deals bring backpackers over from next door in droves. Not really a place to meet Sydney-siders, but a mecca for international travelers. M $6.50 jugs of beer. Open M-F noon-late, Sa-Su 5pm-late.

Scruffy Murphy's, 43-44 Goulburn St. (☎9211 2002), on the corner of George St. It may not be the most authentic Irish pub, but it's a decent live music venue in the city center. And it's always chockers. Pub, disco dance, and terrace. Schooners $3.50. Tu $7 jugs. No cover. Open 24hr.

GLEBE

■ **Toxteth Hotel,** 345 Glebe Point Rd. (☎9660 2370), on the corner of Ferry Rd. Lively and always packed with a crew of unusually attractive young folk, right near Glebe Village Backpackers and the YHA. Flirt, if you must, over pokies and pool. Schooners of VB $3.50. M and W free movies in the beautiful courtyard. Open M-Sa 11am-midnight, Su 11am-11:45pm.

The Nag's Head Hotel, 162 St. John's Rd. (☎9660 1591; www.nagshead.com.au), at the corner of Lodge St. A relaxed English-style pub with a rooftop garden and a giant chessboard. Princess Diana's ex-chef whips up excellent dishes in the bistro next door. Within stumbling distance of the Forest Lodge Hotel. Schooners $3.40. W Uni night with $8 jugs, 3 spirits for $10. Open daily 11am-midnight.

Ancient Briton Hotel (☎9660 1417), at the corner of Glebe Point Rd. and Lyndhurst St. Local students and ancients gather 'round the kegs where the AB won "coldest beer on tap" from the *Sydney Telegraph*. Schooners $3.20. Pool $1 per game. 2-for-1 cocktails Th-Sa 8pm-11pm. Happy Hour (beer $2.30) Su-W 6:30-8:30pm. Tu-W pool contests. Free Internet access with purchase of a drink. Video jukebox upstairs in the funky pool lounge. Open daily 8am-midnight, Su 8am-10pm.

Friend In Hand Pub, 58 Cowper St. (☎9660 2326), off Glebe Point Rd. The name is ripe for jokes, so we'll just skip to the skinny. Tu poetry competition; W legendary crab races and eating contests prove that it's possible to earnestly bet on pretty much anything; Th trivia night, promising "absolutely pathetic prizes." Somewhat tamer on weekends. Schooners $3.25. Open M-Sa 10am-midnight, Su noon-10pm.

NEW SOUTH WALES

NEWTOWN

Kuletos Cocktail Bar, 157 King St. (☎9519 6369). Deliciously fruity liqueurs go down smooth during Kuletos' Happy Hour (M-Sa 6-7:30pm), with 2-for-1 mixed drinks ($10). The Toblerone, an essence of everyone's favorite pointy chocolate, is by far the best. Extra Happy Hour Th 9:30-10:30pm. Open M-Sa 4pm-late, Su 3-10pm.

Marlborough Hotel, 145 King St. (☎9519 1222). The Marley is the place to be after Happy Hour at Kuletos for pokies, pool, much boozin', and some decent local musical talent. Tu comedy night; Th-F DJ; Sa band night. Schooners $3.30, before 6pm $2.80. No sandals. Open M-Sa 10am-late, Su noon-midnight.

NORTH SHORE

Sydney-siders call going to the North Shore "OTB"—over the bridge.

The Old Manly Boatshed, 40 The Corso, Manly (☎9977 4443; www.manlyboat-shed.com.au). Cozy and subterranean. A nice alternative to DJs and clubbin'. Cityslick-ers deem it a must-stop during a night out OTB. Live music most weeknights. M comedy. Open daily 6pm-3am.

Coogee Bay Hotel (☎9665 0000), on the corner of Coogee Bay Rd. and Arden St., Coo-gee Beach. Large enough to supply the juice for the Coogee scene single-handedly. Backpackers and UNSW students swarm to the cheap drinks. Multiple bars, beer gar-den, and a nightclub with no cover. **Selina's Entertainment Center,** in the hotel, is one of Sydney's more popular concert venues and gets international acts. Schooners $3.50. Happy Hour M-Sa 9am-6pm. Open Su-W 9am-midnight, Th-Sa 9am-3am or later.

NIGHTCLUBS

Home, 101 Cockle Bay Wharf, Darling Harbour (☎9266 0600). Looks like the ruby slip-pers finally worked. The scene is ultra-trendy and very happening—be prepared for huge lines to get in. The cover charge is steep, but hey, it's popular. Get schooled in the Beat-fix room every Th. F-Sa 4 dance floors and 15 DJs have the place grinding with every-thing from disco to break-beat 10pm-7am. Cover F $20, Sa $25. Discounts for members. Absolutely 18+; photo ID required.

Imperial Hotel, 35 Erskineville Rd., Erskineville (☎9519 9899). Take a train to Erskinev-ille, take a taxi, make the hike. The costumes at the outrageous weekend drag shows make it well worth it. The "Priscilla: The New Generation" show adds one more layer to the parody and homage surrounding Swedish super-group ABBA; scenes from *Priscilla* were filmed here. The crowd is straight, gay, lesbian, and huge by showtime. Schooners of VB $2.50. M free pool; Happy Hour 5-9pm. Shows W-Th 12:30 and 1:30am; F-Sa 10:30, 11:30pm, 1:15, and 2:15am; Su 10:30 and 11:15pm. Th-Sa dance music until 7am. No cover. Open M-Tu 4pm-2am, W 2pm-3am, Th 4pm-6am or later, F-Sa 1pm-8am, Su 4pm-midnight.

Yu, 171 Victoria St., Kings Cross (www.yu.com.au). A funny-delicious mix of classic and contemporary hip-hop and soul, irreverent breaks and intellectual sampling: intelligent DJs only. Dress to look too cool to care about impressing anyone, and then sneakily impress them like that (oh yeah). Full of cuties of all makes and models. F is "Ear Candy," a popular night to pretend to be casual, promising "tasty treats for your danc-ing feets." Cover $15, members $10 (join the "club" online). Cover sometimes jumps up to $20 on Sa. Open W-Sa 10pm-early morning, Su 9pm-3am.

Tank, 3 Bridge Ln., CBD (☎9240 3094). Next door to **The Est@blishment.** A bar con-stantly stuffed with suits and their trendoid honeys, Tank provides you with a subterra-nean cube in which to get tanked and dance around to tres chic disco, sophisticated house, and some damn slippery beats. Dress to impress, then try again. So, did we mention there's attitude at the door? Cover $20. Open Th-Su 10pm-6am.

Sugareef (☎9638 0763), on Bayswater Rd, Kings Cross. *You will dance here.* Th trance. F and Sa funk, break-beats, and dark 'n' evil house vocals. No cover W and Th; cover F-Sa after 11pm $10. Open W-Sa 9pm-early morning.

Obar, 156 Devonshire St., Surry Hills (☎9319 6881). Always a new lounge-y groove for sexy you and yours: come with friends, discard them on the couches, and then leave with a few brand-new ones. The decor must be an attempt to attract and capture George Michael, but so far he hasn't appeared. No cover. Open W-Sa 8pm-3am.

The Roxbury, 182 St. Johns Rd., Glebe (☎9692 0822). Don't you want to see that hottie from the coffeeshop once he lets his dreds down? He's a lot friendlier when he's imbibing wine coolers instead of caffeine. Lounge action Th, many varieties of music not likely to annoy you F-Sa. Cover $15, members $10; often free before 11pm. Hours vary, depending on DJs and acts; generally open Tu-Su from 8pm.

DCM, 31-33 Oxford St., Darlinghurst (☎9267 7036 or 9267 7380; www.dcmsydney.com). Once voted the best club in the Southern Hemisphere by *Harper's Bazaar*, trendy twenty-somethings still "dress to impress" in order to get by the door and get their freak on. Cover $22. Open F-Su 10pm-late.

Gas, 477 Pitt St., Haymarket (9211 3088; www.gasnightclub.com.au). Come on and get funky at the only "bohemian gas company" in all the CBD, with hip-hop, heavy house, schwingin' soul, and a smidge of disco. Cover Th $12, F $15, Sa $20; before 11pm $8-10. Open Th-F 10pm-5am, Sa 10pm-6am.

Midnight Shift, 85 Oxford St., Darlinghurst (☎9360 4463). While the door policy is not strictly male-only, the "no open shoes under any circumstances" sifts out most curious women. The showy, sexual atmosphere gets deeper and dirtier as the night progresses, attracting a very mixed mob—testimony to the club's 20+ years of popularity. Draft beers $3-4. Open daily noon-6am or later.

▣ DAYTRIPS FROM SYDNEY

Sydney's attractions are not just limited to the city proper. The surrounding hills and valleys contain a sampling of the greater natural beauty for which the continent is known. The small towns outside Sydney give a feel for small town life that the lights of the big city often drown. If your stay in Oz is confined to Sydney, each of these daytrips give at least a flavor of the rest of the continent.

ROYAL NATIONAL PARK. Just 30km south of Sydney's city center, Royal National Park is an easy and glorious escape from city life. The national park, Australia's oldest and the world's second-oldest (after the United States's Yellowstone), consists of over 16,000 hectares of beach, heath, rainforest, swamp, and woodland. The range of activities available in the park is as diverse as its habitats—bushwalkers, birdwatchers, swimmers, and surfers all find favorite getaways in different corners of the park. Across the Princes Hwy. on the west side of the park, the smaller, often-forgotten **Heathcote National Park** contributes another 2000 hectares of heathland to those aching to lose themselves in green.

BOTANY BAY NATIONAL PARK. Straddling the two headlands at the entrance to Botany Bay, this national park has a unique combination of natural and cultural heritage features. The site of first contact between Aboriginal people and the crew of James Cook's *Endeavour* in 1770, the park is also the place where the Comte de Laperouse, France's famous explorer, arrived within a week of the British First Fleet in 1788. Beneath the park's sandstone cliffs, there are rich marine environments. Above them are remnants of the heathland vegetation that Cook's botanists first studied in 1770.

PARRAMATTA ☎02

In April 1788, Governor Phillip led an expedition to discover what lay upriver from the new settlement of Sydney, and Australia's second town was established as a result. Parramatta is now a suburban extension of the city, complete with a nearby theme park for daytripping Sydney-siders. The five-floor **Westfield mall** is said to be the largest in the Southern Hemisphere. Parramatta also has several buildings from the early days of colonization, including the **Old Government House** in Parramatta Park at the west end of town. The oldest public building in Australia, it contains the country's largest collection of pre-1855 colonial furniture. (☎9635 8149. Open M-F 10am-4pm, Sa-Su 11am-4pm. $7, concessions $5; combo ticket with Experiment Farm $10/$7.) **Elizabeth Farm,** 70 Alice St., in Rosehill, east of the town center, was home to John and Elizabeth Macarthur, founders of the Australian merino wool industry. (☎9635 9488. Open daily 10am-5pm. $7, concessions $3, families $17.) In 1789, the colonial government made its first land grant to convict James Ruse at the site of **Experiment Farm Cottage,** 9 Ruse St. (☎9635 5655. Open Tu-F 10:30am-3:30pm, Sa-Su 11:30am-3:30pm. $5.50, concessions $4, families $14.) **The Sushi Train ❷,** 188 Church St., whirls plates of sushi around on a conveyor belt tempting customers to taste the color-coded samples. (☎9891 1399. Samples $2-4.50. Open daily 11:30am-8pm. No credit cards.)

West of Parramatta, in Doonside, **Featherdale Wildlife Park,** 217 Kildare Rd., provides wonderful interactive animal fun that allows visitors to cuddle koalas, feed kangaroos, and see the country's largest collection of native Australian animals up close. (☎9622 1644. Open daily 9am-5pm. $16, students $13, families $40.) The park is 40min. from Sydney by car (Reservoir Rd. exit from M4) and also accessible by bus #725 from the Blacktown train station ($5 return from Central Station). Attractions at **Wonderland Sydney** range from wombats to waterslides to rollercoasters galore. (☎9830 9100. Open daily 10am-5pm. $46.20, children $31.) Take the Wallgrove Rd. exit from the M4 or catch Busways bus #738 (return $5) from the Rooty Hill train station (from Central Station off-peak return $6).

Parramatta is 20min. from Sydney along Parramatta Rd. Before reaching Parramatta, the road becomes the M4 Tollway at Strathfield, the most direct route to the Blue Mountains. Both **trains** and **ferries** make the trip to Sydney. The one-hour cruise on the sleek RiverCat pontoon (1 per hr. from Wharf 2; $5.50) is preferable to the 30min. train ride ($4). **CityRail** also runs to: Blackheath ($10, concessions and children $5); Katoomba ($10/$5); Lithgow ($13/$6.30); and Penrith ($4.20/$2.10). The **Parramatta Visitors Centre,** 346 Church St., is within the Parramatta Heritage Center. (☎9630 3703; fax 9630 3243. Open M-F 10am-5pm, Sa-Su 10am-4pm.) Parramatta's accommodations scene does not cater to budget travelers, but Sydney is close enough to allow commuting.

PENRITH ☎02

The town of Penrith, 35km west of Parramatta along the Great Western Hwy. (M4 Motorway), hovers on the edge of Sydney's sphere of suburban influence at the base of the Blue Mountains. Running through the west half of town, the **Nepean River,** a wide, placid corridor, is one of Penrith's best features. The **Nepean Belle** paddlewheel riverboat makes leisurely trips through the Nepean Gorge in **Blue Mountains National Park.** (☎4733 1274. Departs Tench Reserve Park, off Tench Ave., with morning, afternoon, and dinner cruises. Shortest cruise 90min. $18.) Just 5km north of town along Castlereagh Rd., the **Sydney International Regatta Centre** and ◪**Penrith Whitewater Stadium** served as the **Olympic** venues for all rowing and canoeing events. The landscaped grounds around the Regatta Centre's water course are good for picnicking or frolicking in the grass (open daily 9am-5pm). Alternatively, test your inner champion with a go at the actual Olympic whitewater course. (☎4730 4333; www.penrithwhitewater.com.au. Book ahead. 90min. rafting $55; guides available. Paddling $25. Canoe or kayak instruction $66 per half-day, $110 per full-day. $25 deposit for all rentals. Guided 45min. stadium tour $5.50, seniors $4.40, children $3, families $14.) On the way back from the stadium, celebrate your bravado with a visit to the **Sun-Masamune Sake Brewery**, 29 Cassola Pl., off Lugard St. (☎4732 2833; www.sun-masamune.com.au. Open daily 2-4pm.)

CityRail trains (ticket office at railway; open M-F 5am-9pm, Sa 5:45am-8:30pm, Su 6:45am-8:30pm) run to: Blackheath (1½hr., 15-21 per day, $8); Katoomba (1hr., 15-21 per day, $6); Lithgow (2hr., 12-14 per day, $10); Parramatta (30min., 23-34 per day, $4.20); and Sydney (1hr., 23-33 per day, $6.40). The **Penrith Valley Visitors Center**, on Mulgoa Rd., in the carpark of the Panther's World Entertainment Complex, provides info on Penrith and the Blue Mountains. (☎4732 7671; www.penrithvalley.com.au. Open daily 9am-4:30pm.) ◙**Explorers Lodge ❸**, 111 Station St., often houses herds of athletes frequenting the area and accordingly provides extra long beds, a rock climbing machine, a small gym, and laundry facilities for all those sweaty workout clothes (wash $5.40). The young owners keep a laid-back atmosphere in this spacious and convenient house. (☎4731 3616; www.explorerslodge.com. Linen included. Reception daily 9am-9pm. Flexible check-in time. Check-out 11am. 6-bed dorms $27.50, weekly $165; singles $44/$264; twins and doubles $66/$330.) **Nepean River Caravan Park ❷**, on MacKellar St., in Emu Plains just a short drive over the river, provides inexpensive sleeping arrangements. Creature comforts include kitchen, swimming pool, games room, and a TV lounge. (☎4735 4425. Reception M-F 8am-7pm, Sa-Su 8-11am and 4-7pm. Linen $10. Sites for 2 $16, powered $20; dorms $17; cabins for 2 $50, ensuite $55. MC/V.)

KU-RING-GAI CHASE NATIONAL PARK

The second oldest national park in NSW (after Royal National Park, founded 1879), Ku-Ring-Gai Chase covers some 15,000 hectares in the lands traditionally owned by the Guringai Aboriginal people. Founded by zealous local Eccleston du Faur (yes, that was his real name) in 1894, the park is now visited by about two million people every year, though it came close to serving a far more central role in the new nation's development as the site of the capital city. However, the proposal to build the city on the park land in medieval English style—as a moated fortress to be called **Pacivica**—was eventually passed over in favor of the plan that led to the creation of Canberra. Waterways leading out to the ocean carve their way through the park's sandstone rock landscape giving the park a rugged beauty. Many Sydney-siders come for the peace, the quiet, the numerous Aboriginal rock engravings, and the bright winter wildflowers that bloom early in August.

▐▀ **TRANSPORTATION.** Gates to West Head, Bobbin Head and Appletree Bay are locked at 8pm during daylight savings (roughly Nov-Mar.) and 5.30pm outside daylight savings (Apr.-Oct.). The park entrance fee is $9.90 per car. Entrances are open from sunrise to sunset. Ku-Ring-Gai Chase is split in two by access roads. **Ku-Ring-Gai Chase Rd.** from the Pacific Hwy. and **Bobbin Head Rd.** from Turramurra provide access to the southwest area of the park. From Sydney, you can reach the Bobbin Head Rd. entrance by first taking the **train** to Turramurra (35min., $4) and then catching bus #577 of **Shorelink Bus Company** (☎9457 8888 or 13 15 00, www.shorelink.com.au; 15min.; M-Sa every 30min., Su every hr.; $3) from North Turramurra Station to just outside the park gates. A three-hour hike then brings you to the Visitors Center. Another option is to take **bus** L90 or L85, which run from Circular Quay in Sydney (1½hr.) to Church Point, where it's possible to catch a **ferry** (☎9498 3382; $4.50 one-way, $7.50 return) or **water taxi** (Pink Water Taxi ☎0428 238 190; www.pinkwatertaxi.com.au; max. 6 passengers; available 24hr.;

$12 one-way) across Broken Bay to Halls Wharf where the YHA hostel is located, with free and direct hiking access to the park. **Palm Beach Ferry Service** (☎9918 2747), accessible from Sydney by bus L90 or L85, departing from Palm Beach, which is farther north along the Church-Point side of Broken Bay, stops at **The Basin,** the park's sole camping area (8 per day, $8 return). **Palm Cruises** (☎9997 4815) also run from Palm Beach to Bobbin Head inside the park (scenic cruise departs daily 11am, returns 3:30pm; $30) and stop at Patonga along the way (at least 1 per day, $13), though this service is not a very practical means of entering the park itself for an extended stay, as Bobbin Head is over a half-day's walking distance from any camping or accommodation.

⋔ PRACTICAL INFORMATION. The Bobbin Head area in the southwest is home to the main **Visitors Center,** a picnic area, lush views of the valley, and peaceful headwaters of Cowan Creek. The volunteer-run **Kalkari Visitors Centre,** on Ku-Ring-Gai Chase Rd, 4km inside the park gates, distributes free hiking maps and offers educational information on the park's wildlife. (☎9457 9853. Open daily 9am-5pm.) **Bobbin Head Information Centre,** inside the Wildlife Shop at the bottom of the hill at Bobbin Head, is the official information outlet for the park. (☎9472 8949. Open daily 10am-4pm.) General inquiries can be made to **The Rocks Visitors Center** (☎1300 361 967 or 9253 4600; www.npws.nsw.gov.au) in Sydney.

⌂ ACCOMMODATIONS. The only place you can camp in Ku-Ring-Gai Chase National Park is at **The Basin ❶.** You can get there on foot along The Basin Track, by car on West Head Rd., or by the hourly ferry from Palm Beach ($2.20, children $1.10). Campsites have cold showers, toilets, gas BBQs, and a public phone, but all supplies other than bait and drinks must be carried in. Vehicles staying overnight require a day pass ($10). Bookings are required and must be arranged through the NPWS 24hr. automated reservation service; your call will be returned within 3 days. (☎9974 1011. Max. 8 per site. Sites Sep.-Apr. $9 per person, $4.50 per child; May-Aug. $7.50/$4.)

If camping's not your scene, you can spend a weekend at **Towlers Bay House ❺,** accessible from Church Point via the ferry to Halls Wharf. The four-bedroom house is self-contained and fully furnished and can accommodate up to eight people. Its facilities include showers, toilets, a kitchen, a BBQ, and a swimming pool. Bookings are essential and the house is available only on weekends. (☎9974 1011. Weekends $400, during school holidays $500.) Certainly the most refreshing and remote hostel in the greater Sydney area and possibly one of the most gorgeous cheap stays in the entire known universe, the nearby ⧉ **Pittwater YHA Hostel ❷** enjoys lush green scenery from its lofty, terraced perch over Pittwater. Take bus #156 from Manly (1hr.), bus E86 from Wynyard (1¼hr.), bus L85 or L90 from Sydney (departs Central, Circular Quay, Wynyard every 30min.; 1¼hr.), or follow Pittwater Rd. to the ferry at Church Point Wharf ($6.50 return). The open, outdoorsy hostel provides a retreat without TV or radio, though you may be a bit distracted by all the singing birds that inhabit the area. (☎9999 2196; fax 9997 4296. Canoe hire $10. Linen $2. No laundry. Bookings required. Reception daily 8-11am and 5-8pm. Dorms $22, YHA $19; twins $51/$46. MC/V.)

⋔ HIKING. Ku-Ring-Gai Chase has **bushwalks** for any level of expertise. The **Discovery Walk** (20min.; wheelchair accessible) just outside the Kalkari Visitors Centre is a quick, easy way to spot a few kangaroos, emus, and some native plant life. An easily accessible bushwalk (10km) begins at the Bobbin Head Rd. entrance to the park and follows the **Sphinx-Warrimoo Track** (6½km) to Bobbin Head. The hike can be made into a circuit by taking the Bobbin Head Track (3½km) back to the park entrance. The bushwalk passes through mangroves, along a creek, and near an Aboriginal engraving site. The **Basin Bay Track** and **America Track** (3½km) at West Head are both moderately difficult hikes which incorporate stunning Aboriginal engraving sites, accessible by West Head Rd. Rock engravings in the park include mythical beings and whales up to 8m long. For the best views of the **Hawkesbury River** as it feeds into **Broken Bay,** proceed north along West Head Rd. until you reach a picnic lookout area.

BLUE MOUNTAINS

The motto of the Blue Mountains region, "Come up for air," bespeaks the getaway-from-it-all attitude of this tourist wonderland. Although a variety of adventure activities such as abseiling and canyon rafting have become popular in recent years, the major attractions of the Blue Mountains remain their excellent hiking trails and lookouts. The remarkable color of the hazy valleys and ridges in this area results from sunlight filtering through the eucalyptus oil in the air, which is also responsible for the blue tint of most eucalypt forests within Australia. From lookout points all along canyon edges, the earth falls away into endless blue foliage speckled with white bark and bordered by distant sandstone cliffs. Whether you have the urge to take a dip in drenching waterfalls, hike through serene rainforest and Aboriginal ceremonial grounds, abseil into a deep canyon, or enjoy jaw-dropping panoramic views, you'll find your passion here.

Because the so-called mountains are actually a series of canyons separated by several high plateaus, colonial explorers found impassable cliffs at the edges of the valleys instead of hills. Although several Aboriginal groups traveled the mountains for thousands of years, white explorers struggled for decades with the crossing until finally asking the indigenous tribes for help in 1813. Today, the mountains are an easy getaway for Sydney-siders and the first stop on most backpacker trips west from Sydney. The short trip inland, a 1½hr. drive or a two-hour train ride, grants summertime visitors a reprieve from the oppressive heat that hangs over the coast. In winter, crisp sunny days, occasional snowfalls, and Yulefest (Christmas in July) festivities draw travelers.

▐ TRANSPORTATION

BY CAR. The Blue Mountains are an easy 1½hr. drive west of Sydney. The M4 Motorway goes to Penrith and meets the **Great Western Hwy.,** the main route through the mountains. All service centers and attractions lie on or near this road. Alternatively, the northern route, **Bells Line of Road** (see p. 142), roams west from Windsor, northeast of Parramatta, providing a more beautiful passage.

BY TRAIN. CityRail trains stop throughout the Blue Mountains at most of the towns along the Great Western Hwy., offering the least expensive option for travelers who are willing to walk sizable distances from rail stations and bus stops to trailheads. Within the towns, most distances are walkable, and local bus companies cover those that aren't (for bus info, see **Katoomba,** p. 133). There is **no public transportation** to Kanangra-Boyd National Park or Wollemi National Park.

BY TOUR. There are three above-par companies running **smaller-bus tours** into the Blue Mountains from Sydney. **Wonderbus** offers a tour that includes stops at Euroka Clearing Campground, Wentworth Falls, Katoomba's Echo Point, and Blackheath's Govetts Leap. The aim is to allow time for wilderness bushwalks with the experienced driver-guide. Participants who wish to adopt a more leisurely touring pace can arrange for an overnight stay in the mountains. (☎9555 9800. Departs daily 7:30am, returns 7pm. $70, ISIC/NOMADS/VIP/YHA $65.) The **OzTrails** tour takes you

BLUE MOUNTAIN BUSHFIRES

The fires that burned through the Blue Mountains region during the summer of 2001-2002 were started as a children's prank on Christmas Day and continued through mid-January. Ravenous fires seemed to consume the entire region. Many towns were threatened and over 120 homes destroyed. Many animals were killed in the fires; the heat was so intense that snakes and iguanas were burned when rocks heated up in the flames, and wombats, wallabies, and possums had no place to hide. Most birds lost their homes in the trees when they burned, and many probably continue to be displaced as a result of slow regrowth in some areas. Lake Burragorang, Sydney's primary water supply, was threatened when ash from burning trees fell into it. Luckily, the Wollemi pine grove was unaffected by the blazes, as it is safely north of the park. Regeneration is well underway, with some species of eucalypt able to sprout new branches within 24hr. of being burned, and rangers say that the majority of the area devastated by this fire will recover within seven to ten years.

The Blue Mountains National Park was shut down intermittently due to the continued fire risk, and parts of the Great Western Hwy. and Bells Line of Road were closed as well. Parts of the park continue to remain off-limits to the public—particularly wilderness campsites—as the NPWS rebuilds structures and trails and allows animals and plants time to repopulate the burned areas.

to the highlights of the region with a group of ten or more. (☎9387 8390. $85.) **Wildframe Ecotours** provides similar services and offers a trip into the challenging Grand Canyon, a tremendous rainforest-filled gorge in Blackheath. (☎0500 505 056. Daytrip $74, concessions $62; with 1 night at the Katoomba YHA $110, 2 nights $125.) Both companies offer other trips as well, including **spelunking** and **abseiling.**

Several companies run **large-bus tours** to the mountains from Sydney. **AAT Kings**, Jetty 6, on Circular Quay, offers several options. (24hr. ☎9518 6095. Basic tour $94, concessions $89; bushwalking package with cattleman's lunch $125/$116; bushwalking with horseriding or 4WD $115/$105. Tours depart 8:30am, return 5:45pm. Jenolan Caves tour with 6:45pm return $109/$99. YHA discount 10%.)

✈ ORIENTATION

Three national parks divide the wild stretches of the region. **Blue Mountains National Park** (see p. 140), the largest and most accessible of the three, spans most of the Jamison Valley (south of the Great Western Hwy. between Glenbrook and Katoomba), the Megalong Valley (south of the Great Western Hwy. west of Katoomba) and the Grose Valley (north of the Great Western Hwy. and east of Blackheath). The Grose and Jamison Valleys appeal primarily to hikers, while horseback riders favor the Megalong Valley (for more information on horse-riding, see **Blackheath,** p. 138). **Kanangra-Boyd National Park** (see p. 144), tucked between two sections of Blue Mountains National Park in the southwest reaches of the mountains, is reserved for skilled bushwalkers. The park, accessible by partially paved roads from Oberon and from Jenolan Caves, has only one 2WD road. **Wollemi National Park** (see p. 143) contains the state's largest preserved wilderness area. It's a place so unspoiled and untrafficked that a species of pine tree thought to be long extinct was found here in 1994, alive and well. Access to Wollemi, the southern edge of which abuts the north side of **Bells Line of Road,** is possible at Bilpin and at several points north of the central Blue Mountains.

The national parks of the Blue Mountains region are administered by different branches of the **National Parks and Wildlife Services (NPWS).** If you are planning to bushcamp or even to drive into these parks, contact the appropriate NPWS office (see specific park listings) a few days in advance to ensure that roads are drivable and that no bushfire bans are in place. Additionally, it is recommended that you leave a bushwalk plan filed with the appropriate NPWS office before you go.

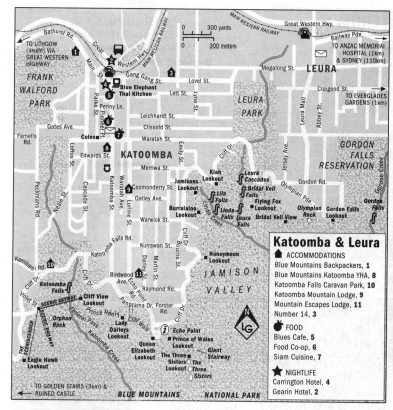

Katoomba & Leura

▲ ACCOMMODATIONS
Blue Mountains Backpackers, **1**
Blue Mountains Katoomba YHA, **8**
Katoomba Falls Caravan Park, **10**
Katoomba Mountain Lodge, **9**
Mountain Escapes Lodge, **11**
Number 14, **3**

🍅 FOOD
Blues Cafe, **5**
Food Co-op, **6**
Siam Cuisine, **7**

★ NIGHTLIFE
Carrington Hotel, **4**
Gearin Hotel, **2**

KATOOMBA

☎ 02

A main gateway to the Blue Mountains National Park, Katoomba (pop. 9000) offers excellent hiking, climbing, and biking opportunities and a very convenient rail-accessible location. The result is an outdoor enthusiast's dream. Though Katoomba is touristy, the town retains a distinctively liberal flavor, replete with VW vans, vegetarian eateries, and dredlocks galore. The image most widely associated with the Blue Mountains is that of the Three Sisters, a trio of towering stone outcroppings jutting out into the Jamison Valley, silently holding vigil over the dark blue-green valley below. One of the most accessible places to marvel at the formation is found at Echo Point, at the south end of Katoomba.

▐ TRANSPORTATION

Trains: Katoomba Railway Station (☎ 4782 1902) is on Main St., at the north end of Katoomba St. **CityRail** trains and **Countrylink** (☎ 13 22 32) trains and buses run to: Bathurst (2hr., 7 per day, $13-19); Blackheath (13min., 17-23 per day, $3); Dubbo (5hr., 1 per day, $52); Glenbrook (50min., 18-28 per day, $6); Lithgow (45min., 12-15 per day, $6); Mt. Victoria (20min., 12-15 per day, $3); Orange (3hr., 1 per day, $29); Parramatta (1½hr., 20-29 per day, $10); Penrith (1hr., 19-26 per day, $6); Sydney (2hr., 20-29 per day, $12); and Zig Zag Railway (45min., 2 per day, $6), but make sure

FROM THE ROAD

A WALK TO REMEMBER

Evan Gallard is the one-man proprietor of Blue Mountains Walkabout. A walkabout is traditionally undertaken after an Aboriginal initiation rite; a new initiate journeys to ceremonial grounds, followed at a distance by a tribe elder. I met him early on a Saturday morning and we set off. He immediately led us off any semblance of a track. Our first stop was an ancient initiation site where Evan interpreted a Dreamtime story carved into sandstone. We stopped on a sunny rock in a stream, cooked up wild kangaroo, and brewed tea from the sarsaparilla leaves we picked on the walk. After a brief rest, we started moving again, stopping at a breathtaking waterfall, gazing at stalactites dripping from sandstone caves, and trying our hands at ochre painting in traditional hues of rich browns, reds, and white. We scrambled up rock faces, pausing at an amazing rock outcropping at the top of a ridge to hear traditional musical instruments and try throwing a boomerang. As we hiked, Evan appeared never to notice how I was coming along, and after one particularly difficult climb down a rock face, I asked him if he would please pay more attention to make sure that I was safe. He replied that he had been keeping a close eye on me but wanted to avoid worrying me by glancing back. By the time we stopped at the pub for a drink at the trip's end, I couldn't believe all that I had done and all that I had learned.

—Bryn Lovejoy-Grinnell

you request this stop with the guard at the rear of the train (see p. 143). **Mountainlink** (☎ 4782 3333) runs to Leura ($3), Blackheath ($5), and Mt. Victoria ($5.30). 50% discount for concessions.

Buses: Greyhound Pioneer (☎ 13 20 30) runs from opposite the Gearin Hotel, 273 Great Western Hwy., to: Adelaide (21½hr., 1 per day, $129); Bathurst (2hr., 1 per day, $35); Broken Hill (14hr., 1 per day, $131); Dubbo (4¾hr., 1 per day, $58); Lithgow (40min., 1 per day, $17); Orange (3hr., 1 per day, $35); Penrith (40min., 1 per day, $15); and Sydney (2½hr., 1 per day, $34).

Local and Park Transportation: Blue Mountains Bus Company (☎ 4782 4213) runs between Katoomba and Wentworth Station, with stops at Woodford, near Echo Point, the Edge Cinema, Leura Mall, the Valley of the Waters trailhead, the Scenic Skyway, and Wentworth Falls. $1.80-3; unlimited day-pass $7.50. Regular service M-F approx. 7:30am-6pm, Sa-Su 7:30am-3pm. For day-touring at your own pace, the **Blue Mountains Explorer Bus** (☎ 4782 4807) runs a 27-stop circuit allowing passengers to get on and off as often as they choose. $25, concessions $22, students through high school $12. All prices include a ticket to see *The Edge* movie. Buses run daily every hr. May-Sept. 9:30am-5:30pm.; Oct.-Apr. 9:30am-6:30pm. Timetables for both services are available at the Blue Mountains Tourism Authority center on Echo Point. All pickups from the **Carrington Hotel** on Main St. **Mountainlink Trolley Tours** (☎ 1800 801 577) runs the cheapest bus tours in the area, with all-day access and unlimited stops for just $12, stopping a throughout the Leura and Katoomba areas.

Taxis: Katoomba Leura Radio Cars (☎ 4782 1311) picks up 24hr. anywhere between Wentworth Falls and Mt. Victoria. Initial fare $4, plus $1.07 per km.

Automobile Clubs: NRMA (road service ☎ 13 11 11).

Bike Rental: Cycletech, 182 Katoomba St. (☎ 4782 2800). Mountain bikes half-day $28, full-day $50. Non-front suspension bikes half-day $19, full-day $28. Helmets, locks, and repair kits included. YHA/backpacker discount 10%. Open M-F 9am-5:30pm, Sa 9am-5pm, Su 9am-4pm.

PRACTICAL INFORMATION

Katoomba sits just south of the Great Western Hwy., 2km west of Leura and 109km from Sydney. The town's main drag, **Katoomba St.,** runs south from the Katoomba Railway Station through town toward Echo Point. Echo Point Rd. brings visitors to the Blue Mountains' most famous sight, the Three Sisters.

Tourist Office: Blue Mountains Tourism (☎1300 653 408; fax 4739 6787; www.blue-mountainstourism.org.au), at the end of Echo Point Rd., on Echo Point. Take Lurline St. south and veer left onto Echo Rd. when Lurline St. ends. Open daily 9am-5pm. For hiking advice from park rangers, try the **NPWS Blue Mountain Heritage Center** In Blackheath (see p. 138).

Work Opportunities: Backpackers can usually find hospitality-related work in the Blue Mountains region; check with hostels about hiring. **Quindalup Permaculture Farm and Education Centre** (☎6355 5800), 60km northeast of Katoomba in Portland, hires farm workers. Fruit-picking work is often available at the **Fruit Shack** (contact Michael ☎0417 655 984; fruitshack@hotmail.com), in Leeton, near Narrandera.

Hospital: Blue Mountains District Anzac Memorial Hospital (☎4780 6000), on the Great Western Hwy., 1km east of the railway station.

Internet Access: Blue Elephant Thai Kitchen, 6 Katoomba St. (☎4782 6896). Snacks and coffee available. $3 per 30min, $5 per hr. Open daily 9am-9pm.

Post Office: (☎4782 1005), on Pioneer Pl. Open M-F 9am-5pm. **Postal Code:** 2780.

▛ ACCOMMODATIONS

Katoomba provides a range of accommodations for travelers on any budget, but the hostel and guesthouse offerings are more diverse than elsewhere. Although beds here are plentiful, so are the vacationers that swamp the town November through April and on winter weekends. Advance bookings are highly recommended, especially on school holidays and long weekends.

▧ **Blue Mountains Katoomba YHA,** 207 Katoomba St. (☎4782 1416; bluemountains@yhansw.org.au), a 5-10min. walk south of the train station via Katoomba St. This fully renovated Art Deco guesthouse just opened in 2001. You may initially feel like a kid in a candy store, overwhelmed by the all the amenities. Spacious kitchen, relaxed dining area, huge commons area, gas fireplace, pool table, Internet, TV/video lounge, activity-planning room, outside terrace, laundry, lockers, and ample parking. The amazingly helpful staff provides heaps of information. Linen included. Reception daily 7am-10pm. Dorms $16-20; doubles $60, ensuite $68; family rooms $60-80. ❷

▧ **Number 14,** 14 Lovel St. (☎4782 7104; www.bluemts.com.au/no14), a 5min. walk east of the train station via Gang Gang St. If the mix of slate and rare Baltic Pine floors, the outstanding kitchen, the sunny side-porch, and the comfortable furnishings don't convince you to stay in this small home-away-from-home, the quiet and friendly atmosphere will. No TV. Reception daily 8am-noon and 4:30-9:30pm. Dorms $20-22; twins and doubles $55-59; ensuite doubles $60-65. MC/V. ❷

Blue Mountains Backpackers, 190 Bathurst Rd. (☎4782 4226; kac@kacadventures.com.au), a 5min. walk west of the train station. It's a fun, friendly, mellow accommodation aimed at a young crew. Small kitchen, dining area with TV/video, common room, outdoor spa, and BBQ/patio. Free luggage storage. Bikes $21 per half-day, $29 per day. Linen $1. Laundry $6. Key deposit $10. Reception daily 9am-noon and 5-8pm. Occasionally closes Tu-Th in winter; call ahead. Sites $12 per person, weekly $63; dorms $15-19/$91; twins and doubles $48-54/$294. VIP/YHA. ❶

Mountain Escapes Lodge, 77 Darley St. (☎1800 357 577; www.bluemts.com.au/escapes), a 15min. walk from the train station and a 5min. walk to Echo Point. Colorful walls, abundant windows, and wood floors add to the homey feel of this small, gracious hostel. TV/video, kitchen, BBQ, laundry, and off-street parking. Linen and continental breakfast included. Reception 24hr. Dorms $22; doubles with veranda $60. MC/V. ❷

Katoomba Mountain Lodge, 31 Lurline St. (☎4782 3933; kmtlodge@pnc.com.au), accessible through alley off Katoomba St. The closest hostel to the center of town, this lodge has great views. Cramped kitchen, large TV/video lounge with fireplace, BBQ patio area, and free Internet. Dining room serves lunch ($6) and dinner ($16). Reception 9am-6pm. Dorms $12-16; singles $39; twins and doubles $48. MC/V. ❶

Katoomba Falls Caravan Park (☎4782 1835), on Katoomba Falls Rd., south of town via Katoomba St. Well-positioned for bushwalks and the Scenic Skyway, Sceniscender, and Scenic Railway. Toilets, hot showers, indoor BBQ, laundry, and children's playground. No linen. Key deposit $20. Reception daily 8am-7pm. Sites for 2 $22, families $26; powered for 2 $26.40, families $30; ensuite cabins for 2 $81, extra adult $11, extra child $6. MC/V. ❷

🚹 🎵 FOOD AND ENTERTAINMENT

Katoomba St. is littered with cafes, takeaways, and nicer restaurants serving a variety of cuisines at all price levels. One of several popular cafes clustered at the top of the hill near the train station, the **Blues Cafe ❶**, 55-57 Katoomba St., prepares excellent, high-class veggie cuisine for dine-in or takeaway. (☎4782 2347. Mains $8-13. YHA discount 10%. Open daily 9am-5pm.) **Siam Cuisine ❷**, 172 Katoomba St., has delicious, authentic Thai food. (☎4782 5671. Lunch specials $6, mains $10-14. BYO. Open Tu-Su 11:30am-2:30pm and 5:30-10pm.) Coles **supermarket** is next to K-Mart on Parke St. (Open daily 6am-midnight.) The **Food Co-op**, on Hapenny Ln. (pedestrian access only), off Katoomba St., sells organic and bulk foods. (Open M-W and F-Sa 9am-5pm, Th 9am-6:30pm. YHA discount 10%.)

Katoomba's nightlife revolves around two main downtown pubs. The historic **Carrington Hotel**, 15-47 Katoomba St., oversees three separate establishments. There's a small piano bar at the hotel, a mellow watering hole at the top of Katoomba St., and a large pub with an upstairs nightclub on Main St. (☎4782 1111. DJs F-Sa. Nightclub open Th-Sa until 4am. Open daily 11am-late. Cover Th $25, includes all drinks; cover Sa $5.) The **Gearin Hotel**, 273 Great Western Hwy., can get rowdy and smoky. The crowd varies in age but tends to be more alternative than other nightspots in town. On Wednesdays, the Gearin hosts a popular local band Jam Night. (☎4782 6028. Open daily 11am-late.)

The **Edge Maxvision Cinema**, 225 Great Western Hwy., projects *The Edge*, a 38min. film on the Blue Mountains, onto a six-story screen. The movie takes viewers to several places in the mountains that cannot be accessed by visitors, including the secret grove where the recently-discovered Wollemi pine species grows. The cinema also shows other giant-format films and recent feature films. (☎4782 8900. *The Edge*: 6 shows daily 10:30, 11:20am, noon, 1:30, 2:25, and 5:30pm. $13.50, concessions and YHA $11.50, seniors and children $9. Other films: M and W-Su $10.50/$9.50/$8, Tu $8.)

Outdoor markets run year-round in the Blue Mountains region. In Katoomba, they are held on the 1st and 4th Saturday of each month at the Civic Leura, on the 1st Sunday of each month at the public school on the Great Western in Mt. Victoria, on the 2nd Sunday of each month at Imperial Park in the town center, on the 3rd Sunday of each month at the public school on the Great Western in Springwood, and on the 2nd Saturday of each month on Macquarie Rd.

🔳 LOOKOUTS, WALKS, AND ACTIVITIES

ECHO POINT. Nearly everyone who visits Katoomba ventures out to Echo Point, at the southernmost tip of town, to take in the geologic grandeur of the **Three Sisters.** According to Aboriginal legend, the Three Sisters are more than just pretty rocks; they are beautiful maidens trapped since the Dreamtime (the Aboriginal time of creation) in stone pillars. Even after sunset, strategically placed floodlights lend a surreal brilliance to these three golden dames (dusk-10:30pm). There are numerous short trails and dramatic overlooks in the Echo Point area, but if you're up for a longer, more demanding circuit, descend the steep and taxing 860-step **Giant Stairway Walk** (4-5hr.) down the back of the Three Sisters and connect up with the **Federal Pass Trail.** At the trail junction, turn right and follow Federal Pass as it snakes its way through the Jamison Valley and past the base of **Katoomba Falls,** and the beautiful, free-standing pillar known as **Orphan Rock.** Just beyond the base of Orphan Rock are two ways out of the valley. You can either hike the seemingly endless **Furber Steps** and ascend through overhanging sandstone and clay rock formations, past the spray of waterfalls, and through rainforest foliage; or you can buy a ticket to ride the harrowing, mechanized **Scenic Railway** (see below) or walk ten minutes along the boardwalk to the sleek, steady **Sceniscender** (see below). From the top of the canyon, it's possible to return to Echo Point via the **Prince Henry Cliff Walk.**

SCENIC RAILWAY STATION. At the corner of Violet St. and Cliff Dr., this transportation hub offers three unique perspectives on the Blue Mountains region. The **Scenic Railway,** the world's most steeply inclined railway, is a tourist attraction in its own right. Originally designed for hauling unappreciative chunks of coal, its 52° pitch now thrills white-knuckled tourists and hikers during its seven-minute trip in or out of the Jamison Valley (one-way $5). The large, brand-new **Sceniscender** cable car, Australia's steepest cable car, smoothly travels a similar route as the railway, from clifftop to valley floor (one-way $10). The **Scenic Skyway** is a cable gondola suspended high over the Katoomba Falls Gorge. Though you only travel out and back, the views looking down are tremendous. (☎4782 2699; www.scenicworld.com.au. Open daily 9am-5pm. Trips depart approx. every 10min. 9am-4:50pm. $8.)

NARROW NECK PLATEAU. Jutting out and separating the Jamison Valley and the Megalong Valley, the Narrow Neck Plateau offers short and long **walks,** excellent **mountain biking,** panoramic views, and spectacular sunsets. To reach the plateau by car, follow Cliff Dr. west out of Katoomba. Just past the Landslide Lookout, turn right onto the gravel **Glen Raphael Dr.** You can drive about 1½km along Narrow Neck up to a locked gate, but the next 7km is for walkers or bicyclists only. One kilometer after the Cliff Dr. turnoff is the trailhead for the **Golden Stairs.** This track runs steeply down the cliff face and intersects the Federal Pass track. To get to the Scenic Railway (1½hr. one-way), turn left at the bottom of the stairs. To get to **Ruined Castle** (5-6hr. return), a distinctive rock formation reminiscent of crumbling turrets, turn right at the bottom and follow the path to the Ruined Castle turn-off on the right. At the Ruined Castle, a short climb to the top yields views straight across the valley to distant parts of the Blue Mountains and Kanangra-Boyd National Parks. Because of the grueling ascent back up the Golden Stairs, many walkers on the return from Ruined Castle continue east, past the Golden Stairs junction, to the Scenic Railway (see above). If you do this, add another hour onto your itinerary.

TOURS. Several companies in Katoomba organize adventure trips throughout the Blue Mountains, from guided **bushwalking** to **abseiling** to **canyoning.**

▨ **Blue Mountains Walkabout** (☎0408 443 822). A new and unique full-day bushwalking experience with Evan, a part-Aboriginal member of the Darug Custodians. The challenging hike traverses uneven and often difficult terrain on its way to Aboriginal ceremonial and living spaces, with ochre body painting, sampling bush tucker, and learning to boomerang along the way. Trips leave June W-Sa 9:15am; July-Aug. Sa only. Book in advance. $66, concessions $59. Food and transportation to base not provided.

High 'n' Wild Mountain Adventures, 3/5 Katoomba St. (☎4782 6224; www.high-n-wild.com.au). Mountain bike tours half-day from $75, full-day $130; abseiling $75/$119; year-round canyoning courses from $129; rock climbing course $129. Student and backpacker discount $10. Open daily 8:30am-5:30pm.

Katoomba Adventure Centre, 1 Katoomba St. (☎1800 624 226). Offers similar packages as High 'n' Wild, but has recently imported the New Zealand whitewater sport known as "River Bugging" and introduced it to the narrow rivers of the region. Rafting from $130, summer only. Open daily 9am-6pm.

Australian School of Mountaineering, 166B Katoomba St. (☎4782 2014; www.ausmtn.com.au), inside the Paddy Pallin outdoor shop. Offers both introductory and advanced technical courses from 1-10 days. 4hr. abseiling trip $89, with lunch $119. YHA discount $10. Open daily 8:30am-5:30pm.

Tread Lightly Eco-Tours, (☎4788 1229; www.treadlightly.com.au). One of the few tour operators in Australia with national *Advanced Ecotourism* accreditation, focuses on the ecology, flora and fauna, history, and Aboriginal culture of the Blue Mountains. Wilderness walks from $25; "Rocks to Rainforest" 4WD from $85; Glowworm night walk $39. YHA discount 10%.

Fantastic Aussie Tours, 283 Main St. (24hr. ☎4782 1866 or 1300 300 915; www.fantastic-aussie-tours.com.au), at the top of the railway stairs. Arranges a variety of coach-based excursions. "Blue Mountains Highlights" M-F 11:30am-3:15pm or 2-5:15pm; $44, concessions $32, families $103. Jenolan Caves daily 10:30am-5:15pm; from $80/$57/$40; YHA discount $16. Daylight tour daily 7:15-10:15am; $92/$85/$46.

BLACKHEATH ☎02

Behind the facade of restaurants, pubs, and upscale shops lining the Great Western Hwy., Blackheath is primarily a small, friendly, residential town in a great location. To the northeast, the beautiful Grose Valley offers many of the area's best lookouts and most challenging walks. To the south is the Megalong Valley, a popular spot for horseback riding. Given its prime position and its easy accessibility, Blackheath is a natural choice as a Blue Mountains gateway, though its services are more limited than Katoomba's.

⊡ TRANSPORTATION. The Great Western Hwy. snakes 11km west and north from Katoomba to the town of Blackheath on the way to Mt. Victoria and Lithgow. **Mountainlink** runs **buses** from Katoomba to Mt. Victoria by way of Blackheath and comes as close as possible to the town's major trailheads. (☎4782 3333. Service M-F 7:30am-6pm, Sa 6:30am-4:30pm; from $4.80.) **CityRail train** service connects Blackheath to: Glenbrook (1hr., 15-22 per day, $6); Katoomba (11min., 15-23 per day, $3); Lithgow (30min., 12 per day, $5); Parramatta (2hr., 15-20 per day, $10); Penrith (1¼hr., 15-20 per day, $8); and Sydney (2½hr., 15-20 per day, $13). Hikers, keep in mind that Blackheath Station is 3km from the trailhead at Govetts Leap.

⁊ PRACTICAL INFORMATION. Regional tourist information falls under the auspices of **Blue Mountains Tourism,** at Echo Point, Katoomba (☎1300 653 408). Questions concerning Blue Mountains National Park, Wollemi National Park, and Kanangra-Boyd National Park are best handled by the NPWS-run **Blue Mountains Heritage Centre,** at the end of Govetts Leap Rd. Staffed by park officials who know their stuff, the center also has exhibits, detailed trail guides ($2-4), and refreshments. (☎4787 8877. Open daily 9am-4:30pm.)

⌐⌐ ACCOMMODATIONS AND FOOD. The **New Ivanhoe Hotel ❺,** at the corner of the Great Western Hwy. and Govetts Leap Rd., has clean, tasteful, and not-at-all-pub-like rooms. (☎4787 8158. Light breakfast included. Reception at bar Su-Th

6am-midnight, F-Sa 6am-2am. Twins and doubles $66, ensuite $88. MC/V.) The tent camping area at **Blackheath Caravan Park ❶**, on Prince Edward St. off Govetts Leap Rd., lies in a tree-covered grove down a steep hill, secluded from the rest of the park. (☎4787 8101. Toilets, showers, and BBQ. Key deposit $10. Reception daily 8am-7pm. Sites $9 per person, powered $12; ensuite cabins for 2 $42, extra adult $12, extra child $6. MC/V.)

There are two **NPWS camping areas ❶** accessible from Blackheath: **Perrys Lookdown,** 8km from the Great Western Hwy. at the end of the mostly unpaved Hat Hill Rd. (5 walk-in sites; 1-night stay only), and **Acacia Flat,** on the floor of the Grose Valley, a hefty four-hour hike from Govetts Leap and a two- to three-hour hike from Perrys Lookdown. Both sites are free and lack facilities other than pit toilets. Campfires are not permitted. Water from Govetts Creek is available at Acacia Flat, but it must be treated. There is no reliable water source at Perrys Lookdown.

If small Blackheath is too big for you, head 7km west on the Great Western Hwy. to **Mt. Victoria,** a quiet village that serves as an alternate Blue Mountains base. It has several historic buildings, including **Manor House,** on Montgomery St., built in 1876. The **Victoria and Albert Guesthouse ❺**, 19 Station St., is a beautiful restored home with a pool, spa, and sauna. (☎4787 1241; victoria.alber@nepean.net.au. Reception daily 8am-8pm. B&B room for 1-2 $120-160, extra person $60.)

🏵 **HIKES AND LOOKOUTS.** Walks in the Blackheath area vary widely in length and level of difficulty. The **Fairfax Heritage Track** (30min. one-way) is wheelchair accessible and leads to the **Govetts Leap,** one of the most magnificent lookouts in Blue Mountains National Park. From Govetts Leap, the moderate **Pulpit Rock Track** (3hr. return) follows the cliff line north for spectacular views along the way of Horseshoe Falls and a 280° view of the Grose Valley from the Pulpit Rock lookout. The **Cliff Top Walk** travels the other direction to **Evans Lookout** (2hr. return) past the majestic **Bridal Veil Falls,** a thin and wispy stream that takes nearly ten seconds to tumble all the way into the valley below.

The **Grand Canyon Walking Track** (5km; 3-4hr. circuit) is undoubtedly one of the most popular hikes in all the Blue Mountains. You can start either at **Neates Glen** or **Evans Lookout,** but if you need to park a car, leave it at the Grand Canyon Loop Car Park, along the Evans Lookout Rd. On a misty day or after a rainstorm, the steps leading from there can be slippery; be cautious and consider beginning at Evans. The circuit passes through sandstone cliffs, wet rainforest, and exposed heathland. Anthropologists speculate that the Grand Canyon was probably a route long used by Aboriginal people to gain access to the deposits of chert (a quartzite rock

---

WORLD HERITAGE WHAT? In the Blue Mountains, the term "World Heritage" gets thrown around quite a bit. The National Parks and Wildlife Service tosses it into nearly every piece of literature it creates, and the Blue Mountains Tourism people seem required to say it at least once every ten minutes. But with the term on everyone's lips, it's easy to forget how remarkable the honor actually is. The label was created by a world convention nearly thirty years ago, and since that time more than 160 nations have ratified its agreement to protect those places and sites throughout the world that they deem valuable to all people. Other places listed under World Heritage status are: Auschwitz Concentration Camp, Poland; Yosemite National Park, United States; and the Taj Mahal, India. Within Australia there are 14 such sites, including Kakadu National Park; Shark Bay, Western Australia; and the Australian Fossil Mammal Sites in Riversleigh and Naracoorte. The World Heritage classification ensures that this area will be left to change according to the tools of evolution and natural erosion, instead of those of humankind, and that the resources are available to preserve the Blue Mountains for generations to come.

used in cutting tools) at the base of Beauchamp Falls. Archaeological evidence suggests that Aborigines occupied the Grand Canyon at least 12,000 years ago.

Six kilometers north of Blackheath along the Great Western Hwy. is **Hat Hill Rd.**, a mostly dirt route that bumps and bounces to an excellent lookout and a popular trailhead for the **Blue Gum Forest.** Near the end of the road, the turn-off leading to the parking area for **Anvil Rock** and the magical features of the misnamed **Wind Eroded Cave** (the feature is the result of water) is well worth the side trip. At the end of the road, the trail from **Perrys Lookdown** steeply descends 600m and leads to a forest with parrots, cockatoos, and lyrebirds (5hr. walk).

The **scenic drive** into the **Megalong Valley** begins on Shipley Rd., across the Great Western Hwy. from Govett's Leap Rd. Cross the railroad tracks from the highway and take an immediate left onto Station St., following it until it turns right to become Shipley Rd. Megalong Rd. is a left turn from Shipley Rd., leading down to a picturesque farmland area that contrasts nicely with the surrounding wilderness. In the valley, outfitters supply horses or conduct guided **trail rides. Werriberri Trail Rides** is 10km along Megalong Rd. near Werriberri Lodge. (☎4787 9171. Open daily 9am-3:30pm; reservations 7:30am-8:30pm. 30min. $19; 3hr. $57.) The **Megalong Australian Heritage Centre,** a bit farther south on Megalong Rd., has longer guided rides, unguided outings, livestock lassoing shows, and 4WD bush trips on their 2000 acres. (☎4787 8188; www.megalong.cc. Open daily 9am-5pm. Horse rides daily 10am-4pm. 3hr. ride with lunch $82, full-day $95. Unguided: $25 for first hr., $22 each additional hr. 4WD $25 per hr.)

BLUE MOUNTAINS NATIONAL PARK

The largest and most touristed of the Blue Mountain region national parks, Blue Mountains National Park is one of eight protected areas making up the World Heritage site collectively known as the Greater Blue Mountains Area. This World Heritage status was awarded only two years ago. (See **World Heritage What?,** p. 139.)

BLUE MOUNTAINS AT A GLANCE

AREA: 208,756 hectares.

FEATURES: Govetts Leap, Three Sisters, Wentworth Falls.

HIGHLIGHTS: Over 140km bushwalking trails, horseback riding, canyoning, and riding the world's steepest railway.

GATEWAYS: Glenbrook (p. 141), Katoomba (p. 133), Blackheath (p. 138).

CAMPING: Minimum impact camping allowed; see individual regions.

FEES: Vehicles $6 (Glenbrook only).

✱🛈 ORIENTATION AND PRACTICAL INFORMATION

Blue Mountains National Park lies between Kanangra-Boyd National Park to the south and Wollemi National Park to the north. Two east-west highways partition the park into three sections: the section north of the **Bells Line of Road,** the section south of the **Great Western Hwy.,** and the small section between the two highways. Three gateway towns lie along the Great Western Hwy: from east to west, **Glenbrook** (p. 141), **Katoomba** (p. 133), and **Blackheath** (p. 138).

Blue Mountains Tourism (☎1300 653 408; fax 4780 5729; www.bluemountainstourism.org.au) operates offices in Glenbrook (open M-F 9am-5pm, Sa-Su 8:30am-4:30pm) and Katoomba (open daily 9am-5pm). The NPWS-run **Blue Mountains Heritage Centre,** at the end of Govetts Leap Rd. in Blackheath, handles questions regarding Blue Mountains, Kanangra-Boyd, and Wollemi National Parks. (☎4787 8877. Open daily 9am-4:30pm.)

⛰ BLUE MOUNTAINS: A TOWN BY TOWN GUIDE

ALONG THE GREAT WESTERN HIGHWAY

Leaving Sydney, the Great Western Hwy. passes Penrith just before the entrance to the Blue Mountains National Park. It extends to Lithgow, passing Katoomba (p. 133) and Blackheath (p. 138) on its way through the park.

GLENBROOK. Glenbrook is a gateway town just north of the easternmost entrance to the park. From the highway, take Ross St. until it ends, turn left on Burfitt Pde. (later named Bruce Rd.), and follow it to the park. The walking track to **Red Hands Cave** starts at the NPWS Visitors Center and runs an easy 8km circuit through patches of open forest, leading ultimately to a gallery of **hand stencils** attributed to the Daruk Aborigines. Along the way to the cave, the trail passes the turn-off for **Jellybean Pool,** a popular swimming hole near the park's entrance. You can reduce the length of the hike to a mere 300m stroll (one-way) if you drive to the Red Hands carpark and begin there.

Four kilometers beyond the Bruce Rd. entrance of the park, over mostly paved roads, is the **Euroka Clearing Campground ❶.** The site has pit toilets and BBQ plates, but no water. Kangaroos congregate close by at dawn and dusk. The park entrance is locked in the evenings (summer 7pm-8:30am; winter 6pm-8:30am); campers are advised to bring ample firewood, food, and drinking water. Call the **NPWS** in Richmond to arrange permits in advance. (☎4588 5247. Open M-F 9am-5pm. Sites $5, children $3.) Bushcamping is free.

BLAXLAND. At **Blaxland,** roughly 4km west of Glenbrook, Layton Ave. turns off onto a pleasant 2km detour towards **Lennox Bridge,** the **oldest bridge** on the Australian mainland. West of Blaxland (and the towns of Warrimoo, Valley Heights, and Springwood) lies **Faulconbridge,** site of the National Trust-owned **Norman Lindsay Gallery,** at 14 Norman Lindsay Crescent. The gallery displays a large collection of work by the controversial and multitalented artist who once inhabited the house. To get to the gallery by car from Sydney, turn right off the Great Western Hwy. onto Grose Rd., in Falconbridge, and follow the well-posted signs for the next 9km. (☎4751 1067. Open daily 10am-4pm. $8, concessions $5.50.) Public transportation to the site is limited to a **taxi** ($10-12) from the Springwood Railway Station.

WOODFORD. Woodford, about 15km east of Katoomba on the Great Western Hwy., serves as a turn-off to a few popular campgrounds. A left off the highway onto Park Rd., a left onto Railway Pde., and a right onto Bedford Rd., lead to the **Murphys Glen Campground ❶,** 10km south of Woodford. Located within a forest of tall eucalypts, turpentines, and angophoras, the campground has pit toilets but lacks drinking water. (No permits required. Free.) Also within Blue Mountains National Park is the **Ingar Campground ❶.** To get there, drive west past Woodford (and the towns of Hazelbrook, Lawson, and Bullburra), turn left off the highway onto Tableland Rd., travel 2km, turn left at Queen Elizabeth Dr., and proceed 11km along an unpaved road to Ingar. The campground has pit toilets but lacks drinking water and cooking facilities. (No permits required. Free.) Nearby, a small pond and creek make the spot popular for picnics and camping.

WENTWORTH FALLS. The town of **Wentworth Falls,** 14km beyond Woodford, is renowned for its picturesque waterfall walks and foliage diversity—more varieties of plants exist in the Blue Mountains than in all of Europe. To find the trailhead at the **Wentworth Falls Picnic Area,** turn off the Great Western Hwy. onto Falls Rd. and continue to the end of the road. From this area, several viewpoints are within easy reach. The 15min. walk to **Princes Rock** ends at a lookout with views of Wentworth

Falls, Kings Tableland, and Mt. Solitary. The 30min. walk to **Rocket Point Lookout** wanders through open heathland and has views into the Jamison Valley. To find the trailhead at the **Conservation Hut,** turn off the highway at either Falls Rd. or Valley Rd., turn right onto Fletcher St., and continue straight to the parking area. Perched on the rim of the valley, the hut is both a Blue Mountains information kiosk and a cafe with a killer view. (☎ 4757 3827. Open daily 9am-5pm.)

For an ambitious and stunning loop hike, begin at the hut off Fletcher St. and follow the **Valley of the Waters Track** to **Empress Lookout,** head down the metal stairs, then follow the trail along the Valley of Waters Creek. Take the Wentworth Pass through the valley to Slacks Stairs, where the steep steps take you up to Wentworth Falls and the **Wentworth Falls Picnic Area.** From the carpark, you can head back to the hut via the **Shortcut Track** (5hr. circuit) or the **Undercliff-Overcliff Track** (6-7hr. circuit). Spectacular scenery and lush hanging swamps will reward the extra effort. **National Pass,** an alternate route through the valley between Empress Lookout and Slacks Stairs, is closed until mid-2003; check with the NPWS for info on its re-opening. On starry nights, visit the **Kings Tableland Observatory,** 55 Hordern Rd. A local astronomer-extraordinaire shows you constellations, globular clusters, and distant planets. (☎ 4757 2954. Open M-Su 7-9pm; daylight savings 8-11pm. 2hr. $10, children $8, families $28.)

LEURA. The pleasant and affluent town of Leura (pop. 8500), 5km west of Wentworth Falls and adjacent to Katoomba, offers shops, cafes, and galleries along its central street, Leura Mall. **Everglades Gardens,** 37 Everglades St., is a lush example of the former floral cultivation for which the town is known. Designed by Dutch master gardener Paul Sorensen, this immaculate 5.2-hectare estate in the Jamison Valley is now owned and run by the National Trust. (☎ 4784 1938. Open daily Sept.-Feb. 10am-5pm, Mar.-Aug. 10am-4pm. $6, concessions $4.) Near the gardens, Fitzroy St. intersects Everglades Rd. and leads east to Watkins Rd., which soon turns into Sublime Point Rd. and ends at the breathtaking overlook at **Sublime Point,** a great spot for watching the sunrise. For travelers continuing west toward Katoomba, the 8km **Cliff Drive,** beginning at Gordon Rd. near the south end of Leura Mall, provides a scenic escape from the highway. The loop passes many lookouts and several trailheads. In Katoomba, Cliff Dr. turns into Echo Point Rd.

ALONG THE BELLS LINE OF ROAD

The difference between taking the Great Western Hwy. through the Blue Mountains and taking Bells Line of Road through the same region is similar to the difference between setting out to get drunk with a tumbler of cheap gin and going so with a bottle of fine wine. You eventually wind up in the same place, but one route allows you to savor the experience a bit more along the way. This 87km drive between Windsor and Lithgow provides bucolic passage through the mountains, perfect if you have the luxury of time.

BILPIN. The town of Bilpin, 5km west of Kurrajong Heights, has several active orchards and roadside fruit stands that sell fresh-picked produce most of the year.

MT. TOMAH BOTANIC GARDEN. A few kilometers west of Berambing, Mt. Tomah Botanic Garden is the cool-climate and high-altitude plant collection of Sydney's Royal Botanic Garden. The plants thrive on the rich volcanic soil and grow in naturalistic arrangements, with the exception of the herbs and roses in the formal terrace garden. The garden's best moments are in spring (Sept.-Oct.), when the large collection of rhododendrons and other flowers bloom, and in autumn (Apr.-May), when the deciduous forest areas change their colors. Free tours depart the Visitors Center during the week. (☎ 4567 2154. Open daily Mar.-Sept. 10am-4pm; Oct.-Feb. 10am-5pm. $4.40, concessions $2.20, families $8.80.)

MT. WILSON. People come from far and wide to see the formal, European-style gardens and unspoiled rainforest of the small town of Mt. Wilson, 8km north of Bells Line of Road, between Mt. Tomah and Bell. For a sample of the fern-laden rainforest, turn right onto Queens Ave. off the main road through town and proceed about 500m until you reach a park area on the left. From there, follow signs to a moderate 45min. **circular walk** (with steep steps) that leads to the base of two small waterfalls. Three gardens in and around town stay open throughout the year: **Sefton Cottage,** on Church Ln. (☎4756 2034; open daily 10am-6pm; $3); **Merry Garth,** on Davies Ln., 500m from Mt. Irvine Rd. (☎4756 2121; open daily 9am-6pm; $3); and **Lindfield Park,** on Mt. Irvine Rd., 6km northeast of Mt. Wilson (☎4756 2148; open daily 10am-dark; $3).

ZIG ZAG RAILWAY. The Zig Zag Railway, 10km east of Lithgow at Clarence, is a functional train operating on a piece of the 1869 track that first made regular travel possible across the Blue Mountains and down into the Lithgow Valley. (☎6351 4826. 1½hr. tours depart daily at 11am, 1, and 3pm. $17 return, concessions $14, ages 5-18 $8.50.) By request, **CityRail** trains from Sydney's Central Station stop near the bottom of the track ($13).

LITHGOW. The Great Western Hwy. and Bells Line of Road meet on the west side of the Blue Mountains at Lithgow, a medium-sized, vaguely industrial town, at the end of the Sydney's CityRail train line. The town provides a good base from which to explore nearby wilderness areas such as Wollemi National Park to the north and the Jenolan Caves and Kanangra-Boyd National Park to the south.

Blackfellows Hands Reserve, 24km north of Lithgow, off Wolgen Rd. to Newnes, was a meeting place for Aboriginal tribes, and paintings adorn the walls of the cave. **Gardens of Stone National Park,** 30km north of Lithgow, features pagoda-like formations from millions of years of erosion. The highest lookout in the Blue Mountains (1130m) is indisputably worth the five minute detour along the **Hassans Walls Link** drive. The spectacular granite formations of **Evans Crown Nature Reserve** (☎6354 8155), 32km west of Lithgow, is a climbers' playground.

Several hotels line Main St., but the **Grand Central Hotel ❷,** 69 Main St., is the pick of the litter with its spacious singles, TV lounge, **pub** and adjacent **bistro.** Take a left out of the train station and walk two blocks. (☎6351 3050. Bistro open daily noon-2pm and 6-9pm. Singles $23; continental breakfast included.) The **Blue Bird Cafe ❶,** 118 Main St., prepares basic sandwiches ($3-7) and tasty milkshakes. (☎6352 4211. Open daily 6:30am-7:30pm.) The Food For Less **grocery store** is on Railway Pde. (☎6352 2011. Open M-Sa 7am-7pm, Su 7am-6pm.)

WOLLEMI NATIONAL PARK

Covering 4875 square kilometers, Wollemi (WOOL-em-eye) National Park is the second largest park in New South Wales. It extends north of Blue Mountains National Park all the way to the Hunter and Goulburn River valleys. Because 2WD access is extremely limited, the park still has many pockets of undiscovered land. One such area yielded an amazing find in 1994, when scientists found a species of pine tree known previously only through the fossil record. Only around 40 adult **Wollemi Pine** trees have been found in three remote locations in the region, but these few trees provide a view to the past that have already helped researchers retrace evolutionary steps back to the era of dinosaurs. The location of the grove is a closely-guarded secret, and scientists studying the trees must have their instruments sterilized to avoid introducing disease to the grove.

NEW SOUTH WALES

The southernmost entrance point to the park is at Bilpin on Bells Line of Road. In this corner of the park, also accessible from Putty Rd. north of Windsor, the **Colo River** slices the landscape along the 30km Colo Gorge. The picturesque, car-accessible camping area at **Wheeny Creek ❶** lies near good walking tracks and swimming holes. Entrance and campgrounds are free. Additional information is available at the **NPWS** office, 370 Windsor Rd. (☎4588 5247. Open M-F 9:30am-12:30pm and 1:30-5pm.) The NPWS office in Mudgee (☎6372 7199; mudgee@npws.nsw.gov.au; open M-F 9am-5pm) services the northwest section of the park.

Farther west, a 37km unsealed road from Lithgow takes starry-eyed observers within 1½km of **Glow Worm Tunnel**, an abandoned railway tunnel housing hundreds of tiny bioluminescent worms. Keep in mind that what you're looking at is not a beautiful constellation but a wall plastered with shining excrement. Be sure to bring a flashlight. The **Visitors Center,** 1 Cooerwull Rd., off the Great Western Hwy. in Lithgow, has maps and info. (☎6353 1859; fax 6353 1851. Open daily 9am-5pm.) There are no marked trails in the northern section of Wollemi National Park.

KANANGRA-BOYD NATIONAL PARK

Southwest of the Blue Mountains National Park, the 680km^2 that comprise Kanangra-Boyd National Park awe visitors with stark wilderness punctuated by rivers and creeks, still-developing caves, and the dramatic sandstone cliffs that mark the edges of the Boyd Plateau. The park's remote location and rugged terrain attract serious bushwalkers looking for long-term solitude.

The park is nonetheless worthwhile for the casual visitors who follow its only 2WD access, the unpaved Kanangra Walls Rd., across the **Boyd Plateau** to the famous lookouts at **Kanangra Walls.** From the east via Mt. Victoria, drive to Jenolan Caves off the Great Western Hwy. (see p. 141). From there, a 5km stretch of dirt road will lead to the park and the junction with Kanangra Walls Rd. Turn left at the intersection. The Kanangra Walls carpark is another 26km farther. From the west, drive to the town of Oberon and follow the unpaved Jenolan Caves Rd. south to the junction with Kanangra Walls Rd. Turn right to reach the lookouts.

The **NPWS** office, 38 Ross St., Oberon (northeast of the park), has details on the park's longer tracks. Be sure to call before visiting or you may find the branch unattended. Cave exploration permits must be obtained at least four weeks in advance. (☎6336 1972. Open M-F 9am-4:30pm.)

The **Boyd River Campground ❶,** on Kanangra Walls Rd. 6km before Kanangra Walls, has the park's only car-accessible camping. There are pit toilets and fireplaces. Bring your own wood and/or a camp stove. Potable water is available from the Boyd River but it should be treated before consumption. Camping is free, but park fees apply ($6 per vehicle per day).

Three **scenic walks** begin at the Kanangra Walls carpark. **Lookout Walk** (20min. return) is a wheelchair accessible path leading to two viewpoints. The first gazes out across the Kanangra Creek gorge towards **Mt. Cloudmaker,** and the other peers into the ravines at the head of the eight-tiered, 400m **Kanangra Falls.** The **Waterfall Walk** (20min. one-way with steep return) leads from the second lookout to the deep pool at the bottom of **Kalang Falls.** The moderate **Plateau Walk** (2-3hr.) branches from the Lookout Walk between the parking lot and the first lookout, descending briefly from the plateau before ascending to Kanangra Tops for views of Kanangra Walls. Along the way, **Dance Floor Cave** contains indented floors and other signs of old-time recreation in the park. A water container placed in the cave in 1940 catches pure, drinkable water dripping from the cave ceiling. Longer walks, like the three- or four-day **hike** from Kanangra Walls to Katoomba via Mt. Stormbreaker, Mt. Cloudmaker, the Wild Dog Mountains, and the Narrow Neck Plateau, should be planned in advance with help from the Oberon NPWS.

JENOLAN CAVES

Known by the Aborigines as *Binoomea*, meaning "dark places," the amazing limestone and crystal formations of Jenolan (Je-NO-lan) Caves, 46 km south of the Great Western Hwy. (on the northwestern edge of the park) from Hartley following Jenolan Caves Rd., have beguiled visitors since they were opened to the public in 1838. The caves can be reached by bus from Katoomba (see p. 133). Nine different ent areas within the massive cave system, overseen by the **Jenolan Caves Reserve Trust,** at the Jenolan Caves turn-off, offer **guided tours. (☎** 6359 3311; www.jenolan-caves.org.au. Ticket office open daily in summer 9am-5pm; in winter 9am-4:30pm. M-F 11 tours per day, Sa-Su 25; $14.50-27.50. YHA discount 10%.)

    Lucas Cave (1½hr., $15) displays a broad range of features and is generally the place to start, but the large crowds can seriously detract from the experience. Cello concerts are given once a month; call ahead for dates. ($33, children $20; includes admission.) **Orient Cave** (1½hr., $22) and **Imperial Cave** (1hr., $15) both have a more tolerable flow of visitors as well as several eye-catching stalactites and stalagmites. The **Temple of Baal** (1½hr., $22) and the **River Cave** (2hr., $28) are also exciting options. Orient Cave and **Chifley Cave** (1hr., $15) are partially wheelchair accessible. **Adventure tours,** run by the Trust, take small groups of people who want to get down and dirty through some of the cave system's less accessible areas. These trips involve moderate to strenuous climbing, some crawling, and a healthy dose of darkness. Spelunkers heading into the **Plughole** (2hr., $55) must be at least ten years old; those venturing into **Aladdin Cave** (3hr., $61) must be at least 12; and those exploring **Mammoth Cave** (6hr., $155) must be at least 16. The Trust also offers theme tours such as ghost tours and off-track adventures with miner's lights and overalls (2hr., from $28). For those not wanting to head underground, well-defined pathways amble along the surface and lead to **Carlotta Arch,** the **Devils Coachhouse, McKeown's Valley,** and the **Blue Lake.**

    Overnight **camping ❶** is available at Jenolan Caves. Each site has a fireplace, and the campground has a shared amenities block (sites $11). Serious outdoor enthusiasts might want to head off for two to three days of hiking along the original dirt roadway that once connected Katoomba and Jenolan Caves back in the late 1800s. Today the **Six Foot Track** is a 42km trail from Jenolan Caves to Nellies Glen Rd. off the Great Western Hwy., at the west end of Katoomba. The trail is steep in places, and hikers must bring their own water. Overnight **camping ❶** is available at four primitive sites along the way. One-way transfers to Katoomba are available from Jenolan Caves ($47, concessions $32).

HUNTER VALLEY

Located within just a few hours' drive of Sydney and known for its famous worldwide wine exports, the Hunter Valley is a popular holiday destination for international travelers and Sydney-siders alike. Over 100 wineries take advantage of the region's warm, dry climate and sandy loam creek soils, and many guesthouses and B&Bs dot the landscape to cater to the mostly weekend tourist onslaught. Though only 8-10% of all Australian wines are made from Hunter Valley fruit, local vintages claim more than their share of national wine trophies and medals. Chief among the varieties produced in the area are the spicy, peppery **Shiraz** and the crisp **Semillon** with its strong citrus character. Using the terms "world-premier wine region" and "budget travel" in the same sentence can seem suspicious, but the area can be cheaply explored via free wine tastings, a hired car, and a designated driver. Most of the vineyards are clustered in **Pokolbin** in the lower Hunter Valley at the base of the Brokenback Mountains, but several notable labels are situated in the upper Hunter, centered around the small town of **Denman.** For other Aussie wine regions, see Barossa Valley SA, p. 405; Rutherglen VIC, p. 552; Yarra Valley VIC, p. 504. For more information on vineyard touring, see **A Quick Wine Primer,** p. 471.

📧 ⚡ TRANSPORTATION AND TOURS

The best time to visit wine country is mid-week, when the number of people is fewer and the prices of tours and accommodations are lower. **Countrylink** (☎ 13 22 32) departs daily from Sydney to Scone (4½hr., $47) via Muswellbrook (3½hr., $41). **Keans Travel Express** (☎ 6543 4688 or 1800 043 339) departs from Bay 14 in Sydney Central Station's coach terminal (M-Sa 3pm, F 3pm and 6pm, Su 6:40pm) en route to: Cessnock (2¼hr., $28); Singleton (2¾hr., $33); Muswellbrook (3½hr., $36); and Scone (3¾hr., $45). **Rover Motors,** 231 Vincent St., in Cessnock (☎ 4990 1699 or 1800 801 012), directly connects Cessnock and Newcastle (1¼hr., M-Sa 4-6 per day, $10). On Sundays, take the bus to Maitland (45min., 5 per day, $7) and then catch the **CityRail** train to Newcastle (50min., 5 per day, $4). **Bicycle rental** is available from **Grapemobile Bicycle Hire** in Pokolbin, at the corner of McDonalds Rd. and Palmers Ln. (☎ 4991 2339. Half-day $20, full-day $25.) **Hertz,** 1A Aberdare Rd., is the only car rental company in Cessnock. (☎ 4991 2500. Open M-F 8am-5pm, Sa 8-noon.) If you're not on a tour and your Bacchanalian revelries have gotten the best of you, **Cessnock Radio Cabs** (☎ 4990 1111) can get you home safely.

Unless you have a car to get you to the individual wineries, and a responsible designated driver who can resist all the tempting free tastings, you'll need to book a tour. If you're starting in Newcastle or Maitland, the standard 10- to 20-person tour generally lasts from 9am to 5pm (or 10am-4pm if you're in Cessnock) and visits four to five wineries. The **Vineyard Shuttle Service** is cheapest and is run by an entertaining and informative tee-totaler who lets his passengers suggest wineries rather than following a strict itinerary. (☎ 4991 3655. M-F $33, Sa-Su $35-40; with evening restaurant transfer add $8.) **Shadows** visits both boutique and large, commercial wineries. Book ahead to arrange door-to-door transfers for Newcastle and surrounding addresses. (☎ 4990 7002. $35, with lunch $55.) **Hunter Vineyard Tours** (☎ 4991 1659) picks up from Cessnock ($38, with lunch $55), Newcastle ($43), and Maitland ($60). **Trekabout** creates a more intimate setting by limiting tours to six. (☎ 4990 8277. M-F half-day $28, daily full-day $44.) **Horse-drawn carriage tours** are available through **Paxton Brown** (☎ 4998 7362; from $53 with gourmet lunch) and **Pokolbin Horse Coaches** (☎ 4998 7305; 2hr. ride $35, with lunch $45).

Several tour companies offer daytrips from Sydney. **Wonderbus** runs 20-person groups straight to the Hunter Valley, and also offers a full-day trip to Port Stephens for a dolphin-watching excursion followed by a trek to the Hunter Valley for a half-day wine tour. (☎ 9555 9800. Departs 7:30am, returns 7:30pm. $130, ISIC/NOMADS/VIP/YHA $120; includes lunch.) **Oz Trails** caters to groups of two to ten and visits the valley via Lake Macquarie and the Hawkesbury River for morning and afternoon tea. (☎ 9387 8390. Pickup 8am, drop-off 6:30pm. $108, with tea and lunch.)

🍷 WINERIES

Most wineries are open for free tastings and occasional tours daily 10am-5pm (some 9:30am-4:30pm), although some of the smaller ones are only open on weekends. Of the 100-plus wineries, the largest are **McGuigan's, Lindemans, Tyrrell's, Drayton's, Rothbury Estate, Wyndham Estate,** and **McWilliams-Mount Pleasant Estate.** Smaller boutiques, such as **Ivanhoe, Pokolbin Estate, Rothvale,** and **Sobel's,** only sell their wines on their private premises. While not as glitzy, they are generally more relaxed. Check with the Cessnock Visitors Center about free tours of individual wineries. Wine prices vary widely but typically start around $10 per bottle.

THE LOWER HUNTER VALLEY   ☎ 02

The best and most popular launching point to see the vineyards is the centrally-located town of Cessnock, and the vast majority of the lower Hunter Valley vineyards are just north of the town in the Pokolbin and Rothbury shires.

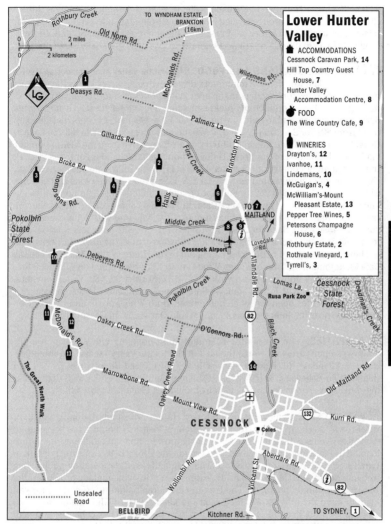

Lower Hunter Valley

🏠 ACCOMMODATIONS
Cessnock Caravan Park, **14**
Hill Top Country Guest
  House, **7**
Hunter Valley
  Accommodation Centre, **8**

🍎 FOOD
The Wine Country Cafe, **9**

🍷 WINERIES
Drayton's, **12**
Ivanhoe, **11**
Lindemans, **10**
McGuigan's, **4**
McWilliam's-Mount
  Pleasant Estate, **13**
Pepper Tree Wines, **5**
Petersons Champagne
  House, **6**
Rothbury Estate, **2**
Rothvale Vineyard, **1**
Tyrrell's, **3**

NEW SOUTH WALES

■■ 🛈 **ORIENTATION AND PRACTICAL INFORMATION.** Most visitors to the
Hunter stay in the lower valley, the most accessible part of the valley to Sydney
and Newcastle. By car, Cessnock is approximately two hours from Sydney and
30km west of the Sydney-Newcastle Fwy. along Aberdare Rd. **Hunter Valley Wine
Country Tourism,** 6km north of Cessnock, on the tourist route from Branxton, is
stuffed with helpful information about the region. The friendly staff will book vineyard tours and accommodations, and a daily specials board highlights cheaper
standby rates at guesthouses and B&Bs. The indispensable (and free) *Hunter Valley Wine Country Visitors Guide* includes area maps, a calendar of events, and
info on wineries, cellar doors, attractions, restaurants, and accommodations.
(☎ 4990 4477; www.winecountry.com.au. Open M-F 9am-5pm, Sa 9:30am-5pm, Su

9:30am-3:30pm.) The town of **Maitland** is 30min. east of Cessnock along the Hunter River. A historic city, it once rivaled Sydney as a potential state capital. The **Visitor Information Centre** is in Ministers Park, near the junction of High St. and the New England Hwy. (☎4933 2611; www.visitmaitland.com.au. Open daily 9am-5pm.)

⌂⌂ ACCOMMODATIONS AND FOOD. The **Hunter Valley Accommodation Centre ❷**, 210 Allandale Rd., about a ten-minute drive north of Cessnock, has the greatest number of options for travelers in the area. Ask about discounts on skydiving next door. (☎4991 4222. Continental breakfast included for motel guests. Heated dorms $25; motel ensuite doubles with TV Su-Th $66, F-Sa $99; family rooms that sleep up to 13 from $99 for 2, extra person $17. Wheelchair accessible.) The **Hill Top Country Guest House ❺**, 81 Talga Rd., in Rothbury, is a 20min. drive from the Visitors Center via Lovedale Rd. and offers horse riding, a pool, billiards, and a gorgeous view of the surrounding countryside. (☎/fax 4930 7111; www.hilltopguesthouse.com.au. Twins and kings with shared bath Su-Th $88, F-Sa $165; ensuite twins and doubles $110/$186; spa suite $154/$240. Full hot breakfast included. 2-night min. on weekends, but negotiable.) The **Cessnock Caravan Park ❶** is 3km north of the town center on the main tourist route and has a pool, BBQ, and one wheelchair accessible cabin. (☎4990 5819. Sites for 2 Su-Th $16, F-Sa $18; on-site caravans $35/$65; cabins $45/$85; special access cabin $80/$95.) **Pubstays** are also available in Cessnock.

There are few cheap options for eating out in the Hunter Valley. **The Wine Country Cafe ❶**, adjoining the Hunter Valley Wine Country Tourism office on Allendale Rd., offers delicious gourmet sandwiches ($7-13), hot drinks ($3-5), and sweets. (☎4990 9208. Open M-F 9am-5pm, Sa-Su 8:30am-5pm.) Many vineyards have restaurants and cafes open for lunch and dinner. Both Woolworth's and Coles **supermarkets** lie near the intersection of Cooper and Darwin St. in Cessnock.

▨ ACTIVITIES. The adrenaline rush and mind-boggling views (once you pry your eyes open) are well worth the cost at the **Hunter Valley Tandem Skydiving Centre**, 210 Allendale Rd. **Balloon Aloft** (☎4938 1955), **Cloud Nine** (☎9686 7777), and **Hunter Valley Ballooning** (☎1800 818 191) all have sunrise hot air balloon flights lasting roughly one hour. ($220-270; usually includes a champagne breakfast.)

▨ WINERIES. The vineyards of the lower Hunter are situated along a tangle of rural roads, so the free map from the Cessnock Visitors Center is the best way to navigate. Even so, the entire area is well-signposted, and large billboard maps are located at the major intersections. You couldn't ask for a better starting point than **Tyrrell's** (☎4993 7000), on Broke Rd. The enigmatic, self-deprecating guides give free one-hour tours (M-Sa 1:30pm) revealing the entire wine-making process of the 142-year-old family business. The free tastings aren't skimpy, so make sure you keep in mind the other stops. **McGuigan's** (☎4998 7402), on McDonalds Rd., is an all-purpose stop. In addition to the great wines, they also have a cheese shop with free tastings. **Wyndham Estate** (☎4938 3444), on Dalwood Rd., is the oldest winery in Australia, first planting vines in 1828. Today, it has an excellent tasting room along with a huge space filled with wine casks for tables. **Petersons Champagne House** (☎4998 7881), at the corner of Broke and Branxton Rd., is the only place in New South Wales strictly devoted to the bubbly, including an interesting selection of sparkling red wines.

Of the smaller boutique wineries in the lower valley, **Rothvale** (☎4998 7290), on Deasys Rd., consistently receives high praise. Another notable boutique, **Ivanhoe** (☎4998 7325), on Marrowbone Rd., is owned and operated by a member of the distinguished wine-making Drayton family. The vineyard produces a deliciously sweet-and-fruity dessert wine. If you'd like some tips on the art of wine tasting, take a lesson at the **Hunter Valley Wine School.** The tour finishes with an evaluation of three whites and three reds. (☎ 4998 7777. Daily 9-11am. $25. Book ahead.)

THE UPPER HUNTER VALLEY   ☎ 02

A few towns well northwest of Cessnock are great bases from which to explore the Upper Hunter Valley vineyards. **Singleton** (pop. 12,500), on the New England Hwy., is the home of the world's largest **sundial.**

MUSWELLBROOK. On the New England Hwy., Muswellbrook (MUSCLE-brook) is closest to the action. The small town (pop. 12,000) has an abundance of historical buildings, many of them visible on the 4½km **Muswellbrook Heritage walk** beginning at the Old Tea House on Bridge St. (New England Hwy.). The highway is also the site of a living **Vietnam Memorial,** a grove of 519 trees that represent each of the Australian casualties in the conflict. The **Tourist Office,** 87 Hill St., just off Bridge St., shares a building with the Upper Hunter Wine Centre. (☎ 6541 4050; www.muswellbrook.org.au. Open daily 9:30am-5pm.) **Eatons Hotel ❷,** 188 Bridge St., has basic rooms. (☎ 6543 2403. Singles $20; twins $30; doubles $30.) **Pinaroo Caravan Park ❶** is 3km south on the New England Hwy. (☎ 6543 3905. Pool, laundry, BBQ, and social room. Sites for 2 $13, powered $17; cabins $47-60.)

SCONE. A more charming alternative for Upper Hunter Valley accommodation is Scone, 26km north on the New England Hwy., a small but pretty town which prides itself on being the horse capital of Australia. The distinction is owed to the annual, week-long Scone Horse Festival in mid-May, which includes an air show featuring WWII fighter jets. The week culminates in three days of thoroughbred racing for the Scone Cup. The race course is five minutes from the town center. The **Scone Visitor Information Center** is at the corner of Kelly St. (New England Hwy.) and Susan St., in front of the train station. (☎ 6545 1526; www.horsecapital.com.au. Open daily 9am-5pm.) The peaceful and remote **Scone YHA ❷,** 1151 Segenhoe Rd., is a converted country schoolhouse surrounded by horse stud farms and has a kitchen, BBQ, warm fireplace, and friendly hosts. Take Gundy Rd. 7km south from the southern end of town. (☎/fax 6545 2072. Dorms $21, YHA $17; twins and doubles $43/$36; family rooms $45, non-YHA members add $3.50 per person). The **Highway Caravan Park ❶,** 248 New England Hwy., is a place to pitch a tent next to the humming of road noise. (☎/fax 6545 1078. Sites for 2 $11, powered $17; ensuite caravans $22-42.)

WINERIES OF THE UPPER HUNTER VALLEY. Though the Upper Hunter Valley has fewer wineries, is more spread out, and has less tourists, it has many fabulous wines. Pick up the *Vineyards of the Upper Hunter Valley* brochure with listings and a map from any area tourist centers. The well-marked trail starts off the New England Hwy. a few kilometers north of Muswellbrook. Unfortunately, no tour groups operate here, so you need your own car. All the wineries can easily be visited in one day, but be sure to keep tabs on how much wine you're drinking. **Rosemount Estate** (☎ 6549 6400), on Rosemount Rd., is the largest vineyard and has extraordinary varieties from a light Sauvignon Blanc to a mild Shiraz to a more peppery Cabernet Sauvignon. Since it exports 70% of its 2.5 million cases, you may be familiar with this label from home. **Arrowfield** (☎ 6576 4041), on Denman Rd., is also a large winery worth visiting. It prides itself on producing affordable, approachable wines. **Cruickshank Callatoota Estate,** 2656 Wybong Rd. (☎ 6547 8149), specializes in Cabernet Sauvignon and Cabernet Franc wines. **James Estate** (☎ 6547 5168), 951 Bylong Valley Way, in Sandy Hollow, produces a delicious Shiraz.

NEW SOUTH WALES

NORTH COAST

Called the Holiday Coast by Sydney-siders, the sandy fantasyland of the northern New South Wales coast caters to meandering backpackers, die-hard surfers, and swarms of families. Existing somewhere between the rat-race of the big city and the permanent-vacation attitude of points north, this area offers locals easy access to both bright lights and holiday hot-spots, with a slightly slower pace of life. Newcastle and Port Macquarie draw travelers itching to sunbathe, water-ski, or hang-ten. At the other end of the spectrum, inland eco-activist centers Lismore and Bellingen thrive on highly productive agricultural land punctuated by scenic national parks and fast-flowing rivers. With virtual cult status, Byron Bay synthesizes these two distinct flavors, magnetically pulling sunburned, party-ready mobs and detaining them for a spell (or a bender) before they head for the Queensland beaches. For coverage of Tweed Heads, see **Coolangatta and Tweed Heads,** p. 319.

NEWCASTLE   ☎ 02

Newcastle, originally a colony to which the most troublesome convicts were sent (pop. 265,000), is a city with a complex. As the world's largest coal exporter, Newcastle ships out over one and a half million tons each week, giving it a historical reputation as a smokestack-ridden industrial metropolis. But as the second-largest city in NSW, Newcastle stubbornly insists that it has balanced its industrial roots with a pleasantly livable (and visitable) environment. It isn't just talk: Newcastle offers high-adrenaline surfing, a spectacular view of the Pacific, and easy access to the nearby Hunter Valley wineries and wetland reserves.

▐ TRANSPORTATION

Trains: Newcastle Railway Station (☎ 13 15 00), on Wharf Rd., Queen's Wharf. **CityRail trains** chug often to Sydney (3hr., at least 1 per hr. 2:45am-11:15pm, $17). The main transfer station for **CountryLink** access to the northern coast is **Broadmeadow,** a 5min. train ride on CityRail. From Broadmeadow, Countrylink runs to: Brisbane (12hr., 2 per day, $98); Coffs Harbour (6-7hr., 3 per day, $57); and Surfers Paradise (12hr., 2 per day, $98). Luggage storage $1.50 (open daily 8am-5pm). Broadmeadow station open daily 6am-7:15pm; after hours use ticket machines. Ask for student discounts.

Buses: The bus depot abuts the wharf side of the railway station. Several bus lines including **McCafferty's/Greyhound** (☎ 13 14 99 or 13 20 30) zip to: Sydney (3½hr., at least 5 per day, $27); Brisbane (14½hr., 4 per day, $74); Byron Bay (10hr., 2 per day, $73); Cairns (42½hr., 4 per day, $247); Coffs Harbour (7hr., 3 per day, $52); Port Macquarie (4hr., 2 per day, $38); Surfers Paradise (12hr., 3 per day, $74); and Taree (3hr., 3 per day, $37). **Rover Motors** (☎ 4990 1699) goes to Cessnock (1¼hr., M-F 6 per day, $10). **Port Stephens Coaches** (☎ 4982 2940; www.psbuses.nelsonbay.com) shuttles to Port Stephens (1hr.; M-F 11 per day, Sa-Su 4 per day; $9). Be sure to ask for backpacker and student discounts. The depot has no ticket offices, so tickets should be purchased in advance from a Newcastle travel agency; the CountryLink office in the train station also sells bus tickets.

Public transportation: City **buses** (☎ 4961 8933) run along Hunter St. every few minutes during the day, less frequently at night; some run as late as 3:30am. Tickets allow unlimited travel (1hr. ticket $2.40, concessions $1.40).

Ferries: Passenger ferries (☎ 4974 1160) depart from the tip of the wharf, just west of the train station, and cross the river north to **Stockton** (15min.). The ferry leaves at least once every 30min. Operates M-Sa 5:15am-midnight, Su and holidays 8:30am-10:05pm. Tickets $1.70, children and students 85¢; purchase onboard.

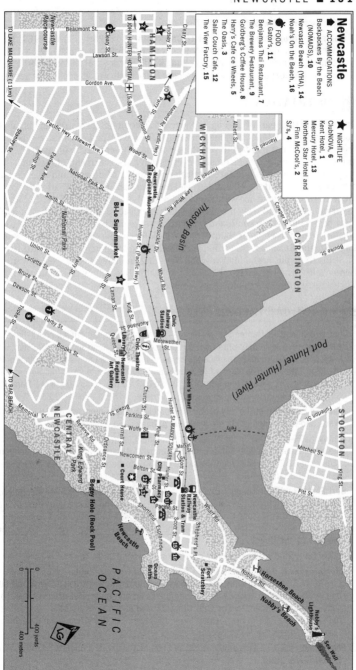

Newcastle

ACCOMMODATIONS
Backpackers By the Beach
(NOMADS), **10**
Newcastle Beach (YHA), **14**
Noah's On the Beach, **16**

◆ **FOOD**
Al Gator's, **11**
Benjamas Thai Restaurant, **7**
The Brewery Restaurant, **9**
Goldberg's Coffee House, **8**
Harry's Cafe ce Wheels, **5**
The Oasis, **3**
Salsa Couch Cafe, **12**
The View Factory, **15**

★ **NIGHTLIFE**
ClubNOVA, **6**
Kent Hotel, **1**
Mercury Hotel, **13**
Northern Star Hotel and
Finn McCool's, **2**
SJ's, **4**

NEW SOUTH WALES

Taxis: Newcastle Taxi Services (☎ 4979 3000). MC/V.

Car and Motorcycle Rental: Thrifty Car Rental, 113 Parry St. (☎ 4961 1141; www.thrifty.com.au), rents from $44 per day (under 25 $11 surcharge). Get a $10 discount voucher from the tourist office. **Budget,** 107 Tudor St., Hamilton (☎ 4913 2727; www.budget.com.au), has comparable rates. Check both websites for online specials.

ORIENTATION

Hunter St., at the heart of the city, is Newcastle's commercial district and is (as one hostel owner put it) "not very inspirational." The mostly pedestrian street, south of the harbor and parallel to the wharf, is overrun with chintzy mall-inspired stores and gangs of pimply toughs on skateboards. On the eastern end of the main drag, atop a peninsular hill, lies **Fort Scratchley,** a number of hostels and seaside bars, crashing waves, and the emerald-green **Foreshore Park. Queen's Wharf** runs the distance of the city, starting with the Convict Lumberyard on east Scott St., next to the train station and near the shore. Climb the **Queen's Wharf Tower** to get a 360° view of the city to the south and the harbor to the north. Follow the wharf to the western end of town, near Hamilton, and look for the perpendicular (north-south) **Darby St.** and **Beaumont St.** to find Newcastle's hip happenings. Westward Hunter St. leads to a split in the highway; the New England Hwy. heads west toward the **Hunter Valley** wineries (see p. 192) and the Pacific Hwy. climbs north up the coast. Take a ferry from Newcastle's town center to cross the river to **Stockton.**

PRACTICAL INFORMATION

Tourist Office: 363 Hunter St. (☎ 4974 2999; www.newcastletourism.com). From the train station, take a right onto Scott St. and continue as Scott merges onto Hunter St. Walk past Darby St. and the office will be on your left after a couple blocks (right before the Civic Theatre). Free maps of Newcastle and the Macquarie area; free accommodation location service and tour bookings. Internet $3.75 per 30min. Open M-F 9am-5pm, Sa-Su 10am-2pm.

Currency Exchange: In the city center on Hunter St. (store numbers 49-101), between Watts and Newcomen, there are a number of **banks** and 24hr. **ATMs.**

Library: (☎ 4974 5300), in the Newcastle Memorial Cultural Centre on Laman St., next to the Newcastle Art Gallery at the corner of Darby St. **Internet** access free for non-email sites, email $2.75 per 30min. Call ☎ 4974 5340 to book ahead. Open M-F 9:30am-8pm, Sa 9:30am-2pm.

Surf Shop: Pacific Dreams, 7 Darby St. (☎ 4926 3355; www.pacificdreams.com.au), is the only place in town that rents boards. Boogie boards and short boards from $20 per day, $100 per week; long boards $30/$160. Open M-Th 9am-5:30pm, F 9am-8pm, Sa 9am-4pm, Su 10am-3pm. Credit card and driver's license required. Also see **Backpackers by the Beach,** p. 153.

Police: (☎ 4929 0999; emergency ☎ 000), on the corner of Church and Watt St.

Internet Access: Backpackers by the Beach has speedy computers at only $4 per hr. (see p. 153). **Newcastle Regional Museum,** 787 Hunter St., has 3 free terminals, although they're slow and often have a wait. Also see public **library** and **tourist office** above. For a snack while you email, try **The Last Drop,** 37 Hunter St. (☎ 4926 3470), an espresso bar with access ($6 per hr.). Open M-F 8am-11pm, Sa 8am-4pm. **Salar Couch Cafe** (see **Food,** p. 153) has free access.

Post Office: (☎ 13 13 18), on the corner of Scott and Market St. Open M-F 8:30am-5pm. **Postal Code:** 2300.

ACCOMMODATIONS

With tourism (and a hankering for backpackers' business) on the rise, budget accommodations have flourished in Newcastle. Inquire about negotiable long-term rates, especially in winter. Other than the listings below, pub rooms abound (in summer from $40; in winter from $30). Remember to book ahead in summer, on weekends, and around national holidays.

Newcastle Beach (YHA), 30 Pacific St. (☎4925 3544). Just around the corner from the breaking surf and local train station lies this crown jewel of hostels in a breezy, bricked, and retro-feeling remodeled heritage building. This hostel offers cavernous accommodations, compulsively cleaned facilities, steaming hot showers, and a common area reminiscent of a country club with a TV, pool table, and fireplaces for chilly winter months. Inexpensive winery tour for $35. Kitchen. Occasional BBQ. Internet access $2 per 20min. Linen free. Laundry $4. Reception 7am-10:30pm. Book at least a month ahead in summer. Dorms $23-25, YHA $20-22; twins and doubles $60/$54. MC/V. ❷

Backpackers by the Beach (NOMADS), 34-36 Hunter St. (☎4926 3472; backbeach@nobbys.net.au). Less than a 5min. walk north of the train station, this hostel occupies its own yellow corner of Hunter and Pacific St. Modern but small dorms, with heaps of bright light and high ceilings. All-female/male dorm rooms have single-sex bathrooms. Unbeatable access to beaches, transportation, and the wharf. Lobby-reception also doubles as kitchen. A young and friendly staff makes for an easygoing atmosphere. Free surfboard loans. Free linen, TV room, and weekly BBQ. Speedy Internet $4 per hr. Key deposit $15. Reception 7am-11pm. Make reservations a week ahead in summer. Dorms $23, weekly $125; twins and doubles $51/$325. NOMADS/VIP/YHA discount $3. MC/V. ❷

Anne's B&B, 3 Stevenson Pl. (☎4929 5376 or 0416 285 376). From the train and bus station, turn left onto Hunter St., then left on Zarra Ave., and right onto Stevenson St. This 1911 townhouse was converted into a warm and elegant B&B by owner Anne Creevey. Gleaming hardwood, polished period antiques, fine linen, and an open fire complete the picture of perfect comfort. 3 sets of accommodations, guest lounge with TV/video, formal dining room, private balcony/sunroom, laundry, and kitchenette. Continental breakfast included; more extensive morning spread $10. Kingsize ensuite room with sunroom $132-176; double with "spa" bathroom and kitchenette $121-$156; ensuite double with kitchenette and veranda $121-156, extra person $44-66. MC/V. ❸

Noah's on the Beach (☎4929 5181; www.noahsonthebeach.com.au), on the Esplanade. A big, standard hotel right next to the schoolbus-yellow Holiday Inn. Rooms have stunning views of the Pacific. All motel-pristine rooms come with A/C and heat, TV, data ports, mini-fridges, bars, and coffee and tea. Free parking, pool, laundry services. Reception 24hr. Harborside singles, doubles, and twins $116-130; oceanview singles, doubles, and twins $138-220. AmEx/MC/V. ❺

FOOD

Popular with locals for its diverse options, **Darby St.** is by far the best place in town to hunt for eateries. **Hunter St.** has $5-6 lunch specials, but stick to the Pacific St. end if you're looking for atmosphere. If you're trying to sneak a cheap dinner, go early, as many places close at 6pm. Though a 20min. walk southwest of city center, over 80 restaurants line Hamilton's **Beaumont St.,** a popular hangout for students and home to tasty, cheap, and bustling restaurants favored by Newcastle's lunching number-crunchers. Monday through Wednesday nights in Newcastle bring dinner specials at many restaurants. Cheap food-court options can also be found at

Market Square, in the center of a pedestrian mall on Hunter St. running from New-comen to Perkins Sts., and **The Oasis,** on the corner of Beaumont and Cleary St. The huge **Bi-Lo supermarket** (☎ 4926 4494), in the Marketown shopping center at the corner of National Park and King St., is open 24hr.

▨ **Salar Couch Cafe,** 54 Watt St. (☎ 4927 5329). Draped in comfortable colors, a good old-fashioned *Lady and the Tramp* candle-in-a-bottle and mismatched-table-and-chair kind of place—with a touch of the exotic. Enjoy Peruvian-inspired $6 lunch specials while perusing their book collection in the "boudoir," a socks-only area of comfortable floor pillows, or surfing the Net for free. Luscious $8 Su brekkie; Su YHA dinner soup deal. Kept toasty in winter by an open fire. Open daily 11am-late. No credit cards. ❶

▨ **Benjamas Thai Restaurant,** 100 Darby St. (☎ 4926 1229). Pastel decor and sparkling table settings. Heaps of seafood specialties (squid $14, king prawns $14-16, whole fish $19), all Thai-style and incorporating local catches. Great vegetarian menu ($5-13) and oodles of noodles ($11-16). Weekday $6.50 lunch special. BYO. Open W-F 11:30am-2:30pm; also M-Su 5:30-10pm. MC/V. ❷

Goldberg's Coffee House, 137 Darby St. (☎ 4929 3122). Early in the evening, this place is where everybody meets up for dinner or drinks before heading out for the night. Dark interior with hardwood and a classy soundtrack. Swing in for a late cup of coffee ($3-5) or a glass of wine to scope and be seen at this Euro-style coffeehouse. Open 8am-midnight or later. ❶

Harry's Cafe de Wheels, 672 Hunter St. (☎ 4926 2165). What better place to sample a famous Australian meat pie than the oldest takeaway joint in the nation? Follow in the footsteps of Bill Cosby, Shirley MacLaine, Pamela Anderson, and repeat customer Elton John. The "Tiger" presents brave souls with a pie smothered in mushy peas, mashed potatoes, and gravy. A quick and historic snack or light meal only $2-4. Open daily 9am-late (ranging from 10pm to 4am). ❶

Al Gator's, 38 Hunter St. (☎ 4929 1386). Across the street from Bogie Hole Cafe is possibly the best bang for your lunch buck in the city. A tasty variety of sandwiches is nearly all under $4 and includes a number of vegetarian options. Limited outdoor seating lets you catch some rays while you chow down. Open Su-F 6am-4pm. ❶

The View Factory (☎ 4929 4580), at the corner of Telford and Scott St., on the eastern part of town. High ceilings, screened lanterns on every table, and specialty salads, pastas, and lighter lunches. Mains $6-18. Buy-1-get-1-free Tu dinner deal. YHA discount. Open M-Sa 11am-midnight, Su 11am-6pm. AmEx/MC/V. ❸

The Brewery Restaurant, 150 Wharf Rd. (☎ 4929 6333; www.qwb.com.au). On the water, this is the neighborhood drink spot. A gourmet menu with mains from $6-20. Bar has three house-crafted beers and gets to be something of a scene once the sun sets. Management hosts free BBQ, beer, and trivia contests for hostelers on advertised nights. Live music Su-W; W "uni night," Sa live bands or DJ. Restaurant open daily 11am-9pm; bar open Su-Tu and Th 10am-midnight, W and F-Sa 10pm-3am. ❸

◉ ◕ SIGHTS AND ACTIVITIES

Newcastle's public image problems are nothing new: the city was established in 1804 as a settlement for the most egregious of convicts and was dubbed "Sydney's Siberia." However, looking closely, one finds that this hard-luck town has a number of redeeming aspects. Its ornate **heritage buildings,** built by convicts, are the architectural highlights of the town, along with the **cathedral** in the city center. But people don't come to Newcastle for Victorian balconies—they come for the seaside parks, the gut-wrenching crash of the sea against the rocky shore, and the hardcore surf where four-time world champ Mark Richards got his start.

▨ NEWCASTLE'S TRAM. The famous tram offers a delightful, informative city overview and tells of the devastation that resulted from a freak earthquake in 1989. The ride is a great way to get a quick feel for the city's sights, from the historic architecture to whales breaching off the coastline. (☎ 4963 7954; 45min.; *departs from Newcastle Railway Station M-F every hr. 10am-1:45pm, Sa-Su 10am-noon and 2pm; extra ride 3pm on school holidays. $10, children $6.50, families $29.)*

FORT SCRATCHLEY. Climb the hill for the best view in the city. Play around on the cannons (don't they look like faces with very long noses?) and explore the underground tunnel system for $2.50. The fort has been an inactive military site since the 1970s and now houses the Military Museum and, next door, the Maritime Museum. Jumbly Boat Gallery just outside the walls has a big pile of boats. *(Military Museum open Sa-Su noon-4pm. Free. Maritime Museum ☎ 4929 2588. Open Tu-F 10am-4pm, Sa-Su noon-4pm. Free.)*

BEACHES. Newcastle's shore is lined with white sand beaches, tidal pools, and landscaped parks. At the tip of Nobby's Head peninsula is a walkable seawall, and **Nobby's Lighthouse,** surrounded by (you guessed it) **Nobby's Beach,** a terrific surfing spot. Walking clockwise around the peninsula from Nobby's leads to a surf pavilion, then to the **Ocean Baths,** a public saltwater pool on the cliffs overlooking the surf; keep walking to find its predecessor **Bogey Hole,** a convict-built ocean bath at the edge of the manicured **King Edward Park.** Farther along, you'll see a cliffside walk leading to the **Susan Gilmore nude beach;** farther still is the large **Bar Beach,** popular with surfers.

BLACKBUTT RESERVE. A 182-hectare tree sanctuary with five walking trails over 20km and many animals along the way. There's a koala enclosure as well as kangaroo and emu reserves. If you're lucky, you can pet a koala (Sa-Su 11:30am and 2:30pm). It may be stoned, but it's not stupid; definitely don't stick your finger in its mouth. Bring your own picnic food; no food is available. *(Catch bus #232 or 363 in the city center for 45min. to Lookout Rd., Cardiff Heights, and follow signs down the hill. ☎ 4952 1449; www.ncc.nsw.gov.au. Open daily 7am-5pm; wildlife exhibits 9am-5pm. Free.)*

WETLANDS CENTRE. Founded in 1980 to provide sanctuary to birds and reptiles, these "rehabilitated wetlands" also offer respite to city-weary humans with its walking paths, a creek, and a swamp for canoeing. Every Sunday brings activities like wilderness wine tastings and "Billabong" breakfasts at sunrise by canoe. *(Take the CityTrain to Sandgate, in the suburb of Shortland, and then walk 10min. on Sandgate Rd. ☎ 4951 6466; www.wetlands.org.au. Canoe rental $7.50-10.50 per 2hr., $11-20 per 4hr. Bikes $6 per hr. Open M-F 9am-3pm, Sa-Su 10am-3pm. Entry $4.50, families $9.)*

FESTIVALS. Surfest rides into town in late February for a two-week international surfing spectacular, drawing crowds from all of Oz. The **Newcastle Jazz Festival** plays out in late August at Club NOVA. The **King St. Fair** is a city-wide carnival in early December. **Newcastle Maritime Festival's** boat races and watersports are the last week of January.

🎵 🍸 ENTERTAINMENT AND NIGHTLIFE

The Post, a free Newcastle newspaper, publishes a guide to the next week's live music around the area each Wednesday. For info on clubs and pubs, peruse the free local guide *TE (That's Entertainment)* at the tourist office. **SJ's,** 8 Beaumont St. (☎ 4961 2537), is 65% gaming room, 30% pub, and 5% Australian mystery meat: it has rock bands Wednesday through Sunday and is swamped Saturday and Sunday nights. The **Northern Star Hotel,** 112 Beaumont St. (☎ 4961 1087; www.northernstarhotel.com.au), is a popular jazz spot, which houses the blarnier-than-Ireland pub, **Fin McCools.** The more straightforward **Kent Hotel,** 59-61 Beaumont St. (☎4961 3303), fronts more mainstream bands. Check out fortress-like **ClubNOVA** (☎4926 2700; www.clubnova.com.au) at the corner of King and Union St. for regular rock concerts, the Newcastle Jazz Festival, and a Las Vegas-themed gaming lounge; or head to **Mercury Hotel,** 23 Watt St. (☎4926 1119), for the most effectively trendy dance club in town. (Open W and F-Sa until 3am, cover varies $6-10.) The solid **Clarendon Hotel,** 347 Hunter St. (☎4927 0966), offers signature cocktails for only $2.50 during its uni Happy Hours (W 9-11pm). Attracting a backpacker and student crowd, the **Brewery** (see **Food,** p. 153) packs it in with homemade brews. .

■ DAYTRIPS FROM NEWCASTLE

Fifteen minutes south of Newcastle and 1½hr. north of Sydney, **Lake Macquarie** is one of Australia's largest coastal saltwater lakes (four times the size of Sydney Harbour) and a weekend-vacation hot spot. The shore is popular with surfers and families on holiday, with hefty waves, deep caverns at **Caves Beach,** and a mining village at **Catherine Hill Bay.** Spelunkers must go at **low tide** so as not to get trapped in the caves. Find tide tables at the **Lake Macquarie Information Center,** 72 Pacific Hwy., in the Blacksmiths. The lake is not easily accessible without a car; detailed driving directions can be found on the info center's website. (☎4972 1172; www.lakemac.com.au. Open M-F 9am-5pm, Sa-Su 9am-4pm.)

The mountainous **Watagans National Park** separates Lake Macquarie from the Hunter River. An hour from Newcastle and the Hunter Valley, it's ideal for hikes, picnics, and camping. There are seven **campsites ●,** most with firewood, grills, toilets, and water. Call the **NPWS Hunter** office (☎4358 0400; www.npws.nsw.gov.au) for more info. Many visitors use Newcastle as a "gateway to the Hunter" or as a springboard to wine sampling at the many nearby vineyards (see **Wineries,** p. 146).

PORT STEPHENS BAY AREA   ☎02

North of Newcastle, Port Stephens is a placid, secluded bay and sleepy rural townships defined by blue-green water and **Tomaree National Park.** Most of the region's activities, restaurants, and facilities are in Nelson Bay. Anna Bay and Shoal Bay offer beautiful and somewhat isolated beaches. During the summer, surfing beaches and luxury resorts draw backpackers and families alike, clogging central shopping areas with traffic. The ocean beyond the surf also attracts visitors of the aquatic kind. Bottlenose dolphins are visible year-round in the harbor and are quite cheeky—they'll come right up and tag along with the daily dolphin cruises. Locals say the dolphins do more people-watching than vice-versa. The whale-watching season runs from June to October, after which the giants head north to warmer waters in order to breed. On the coastal edge of the national park, abandoned Australian-American forts stand as remnants of WWII training camps. Port Stephens also boasts some of the most spectacular sand dunes in the country, an attraction growing to rival the sealife in popularity.

▐ TRANSPORTATION

Port Stephens Buses (☎4982 2940 or 1800 045 949; www.psbuses.nelsonbay.com) run from Newcastle (1½hr.; M-F 11 per day, Sa-Su 4 per day; return $9, students $4.50) to four of the townships and Sydney (3hr., 1 per day, $25). The main stop in Nelson Bay is at the **Bi-Lo** on Stockton St. **Local buses** run hourly on weekdays, every two hours on Saturday and Sunday (around $3; 1-day unlimited travel $11). It may be more convenient to rent a car from Newcastle to avoid being stranded in one township for a few hours. The **Port Stephens Ferry Service** (☎4981 3798) makes

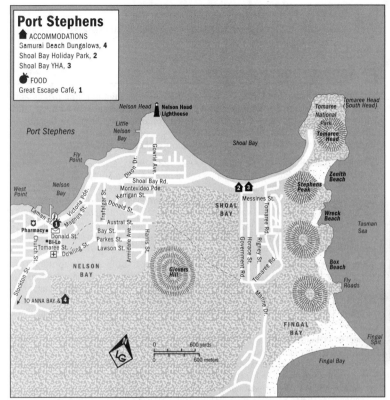

Port Stephens

🏠 ACCOMMODATIONS
Samurai Beach Dungalows, **4**
Shoal Bay Holiday Park, **2**
Shoal Bay YHA, **3**

🍎 FOOD
Great Escape Café, **1**

three trips daily to **Tea Garden,** across the water from Nelson Bay (8:30am, noon, and 3:30pm; $17 roundtrip, families $40). **Shoal Bay Bike Hire,** 63 Shoal Bay Rd., near the YHA, is a cheap bike option. (☎ 4981 4121. $10 per 2hr.; $20 per day. Open daily 9am-5pm; hours vary in winter.) For a **taxi,** call ☎ 4984 6699.

🔆 🛈 ORIENTATION AND PRACTICAL INFORMATION

Nelson Bay Rd. leads from Newcastle to four local residential townships of the Port Stephens area. The road forks onto **Gan Gan Rd.,** which leads to the seaside township of **Anna Bay,** home to **Stockton Bight,** the largest sand dune area in the southern hemisphere, and close to the popular surfing destination of **One Mile Beach,** known simply as "The Big Beach" to locals. Gan Gan and Nelson Bay Rd. rejoin en route to three other townships: **Nelson Bay** (the largest), **Shoal Bay,** and the rural **Fingal Bay.** The marina, shopping complex, and cafes are on **Victoria Parade** and **Stockton Street** in Nelson Bay. The **tourist office,** on Victoria Pde. by the wharf, arranges bookings for local attractions. (☎ 4981 1579; www.portstephens.org.au. Open daily 9am-5pm.) The **Salamander Shopping Centre,** a five-minute bus ride west, is home to the Tomaree public **library,** where you can access the **Internet.** (☎ 4982 0670. Open M, W, F 10am-6pm; Tu and Th 10am-8pm; Sa 9:30am-2pm. Access free; email $2.75 per 30min. Book ahead for both.) **Terrace Cafe** also offers Internet access in a convenient shopping arcade on Victoria Pde. overlooking the tourist office. (☎ 4981 0750. Open Su-Th 8am-5pm, F-Sa 8am-9pm. $2 per 15min.)

WATCH YOUR STUFF. Travelers are advised not to keep valuables in unattended cars—vandals have been known to break into vehicles, especially those parked along the beach in Port Stephens.

ACCOMMODATIONS

Winter often brings great deals, while summer usually means rising prices and fewer available beds. Book four to six weeks ahead on weekends, in summer, and around holidays. Beware of significant price spikes on weekends in the hotel/ motel market. The following are on the Port Stephens local bus route. Check with the tourist office for a full listing of local motels and caravan parks.

Samurai Beach Bungalows Backpackers (☎/fax 4982 1921; samurai_backpackers@nelsonbay.com). On Robert Connell Cir., reached by Frost Rd. off of Nelson Bay Rd., just outside Anna Bay. Solidly located in the bush, this is a city-weary traveler's dream. Volleyball court, outdoor kitchen, TV, pool table, free surfboards and boogie boards, and a campfire at night. Ask the owner about "sandboarding" the local dunes. Linen included. Bike rentals $12 per day; free for those staying 3 or more days. Sparse 5-bunk dorms with shared bath $17; doubles with TV, bath, coffee maker, and mini-kitchen from $44; family room $60. MC/V. VIP. ❷

Shoal Bay Holiday Park (☎4981 1427 or 1800 600 200; shoal@portstephens.nsw.gov.au). On Shoal Bay Rd. on the way to Fingal Bay, within earshot of the ocean. New kitchen, 2 common TV areas, pool and ping-pong tables, tennis court, trivia contests, and movie nights. Laundry $2. Reception daily 8:15am-6pm. Powered tent and caravan sites for 2 $18-22, additional adult $7.50. 4-person budget bungalows $30-60; ensuite family cabins for 5 $44-126. Discount for 7-night stay. ❷

Shoal Bay YHA, 59-61 Shoal Bay Beachfront Rd. (☎4981 0982). In the Shoal Bay Motel, across from the beach and a 15min. walk west of the Tomaree trails. Rooms have TV, fridge, heat, and A/C. The 6-bed women's dorm has an attached bathroom, as does the 6-bed men's dorm, which is separated from the common room only by partitions and a curtain. Kitchen, TV lounge, sauna, and BBQ. $20 key deposit includes linen rental. Laundry machines $6. Reception 7:45am-10pm. Dorms $26, YHA $18; twins and doubles $32, $23; ensuite family rooms $64, $52. ❸

FOOD

Nelson Bay—the Port Stephens hub—is the best place to find cheap food, particularly on Magnus and Donald St., both parallel to Victoria Pde. For a generous breakfast for little over $10, try the **Great Escape Cafe** ❷, 19 Stockton St., Nelson Bay (☎4984 3322), at the corner of Stockton and Victoria Pde and near the water. Upstairs from the Great Escape is the **Greek Village Restaurant** ❸; bring along a bottle of wine and enjoy a romantic evening of Greek cuisine. (☎4984 3388. Mains $20.) Trusty supermarket **Bi-Lo** has locations on the corner of Stockton and Donald St. (☎4981 1666) and in the Salamander Shopping Center, which also offers a **Woolworth's** and a number of fast-food joints.

SIGHTS AND ACTIVITIES

You've probably seen sport-utility-vehicle ads on TV and wondered if anyone really drives off-road like that. Now's your chance to find out. The fun-loving folks at Port Stephens Council (☎4980 0255) will let you buy a day pass for $5 so you and your 4WD can go play on **Stockton Bight,** the biggest sand dune in the Southern

Hemisphere; passes are available at the Mobil station in Anna Bay. Follow signs to Anna Bay from Nelson Bay Rd.; the Mobil is past the beach access sign. For renting or participating in more organized group-duning, try the **6-Wheeler Bushmobile Dune Adventure** and conquer the deserts for just $20 per person (☎ 4038 5744; www.bushmobile.com.au). ⬛**Sand Safaris** offers a pricey but worthwhile adventure activity. For $99 a head, you get two hours on your very own ATV and an award-winning guided trip at 40kph over dunes nearly 100m high. (☎ 4965 0215 or 0418 209 747; www.sandsafaris.com.au. 4-5 trips daily; pickup from Newcastle Airport.) For tamer sand activities, ask about camel rides at the Nelson Bay tourist office or join **Sahara Trails** on spectacular two hour dune and beach horse rides and one hour beginners bush rides starting at $15. (☎ 4981 9077; www.saharatrails.com. Open daily. Bookings required.)

Whale watching and **dolphin cruise boats** depart five times per day in the summer (winter trips are weather-permitting). The cheapest of the lot is the large **Tamboi Queen,** which cruises the harbor for sightings of the over 150 dolphins that live there year-round. (☎ 4981 1959. 2-4 trips daily. 1½hr. dolphin cruise $18, winter special $13.50.) On the ocean side, try **Moonshadow Cruises** (☎ 4984 9388) for daily whale watching trips. **Blue Water Sea Kayaking** (☎ 4981 5177 or 0409 408 618; www.seakayaking.com.au) offers daily two-hour trips at around $30. Book a high speed jet **boat ride** at the tourist office or call ☎ 4984 9811 (15min. for $33).

For second-to-none views of the bay's rippling blue-green waters, stark headlands, and the expanse of the South Pacific horizon, make the 30min. walk to the summit of **Tomaree Head** at the end of Shoal Bay. Follow Shoal Bay Rd. until it ends at the Tomaree National Park; signs direct you to the tracks. You can find opportunities for **surfing** and **nude bathing** on the Anna Bay shore; inquire at the Nelson Bay tourist office for information.

MYALL LAKES NATIONAL PARK

If you consider yourself an ecotourist, you may well find paradise in the Myall Lakes National Park among over 10,000 hectares of lakes, 40km of beaches, and walking tracks traversing coastal rainforest, heath, and paperbark swamp. With only two major vehicular access points ($6 vehicle entry fee per day), the area provides endless opportunities for undisturbed recreation and relaxation. Pick up the park notes at the **Visitors Center** and explore the various ways to access the park from The Lakes Way. Most people enter via **Bulahdelah,** 83km north of Newcastle, 70km south of Taree along the Pacific Hwy., and 60km southwest of Forster by The Lakes Way. **Bulahdelah Visitor Centre** (☎ 4997 4981), at the corner of Pacific Hwy. and Crawford St., is the park's only "interpretive center," with comprehensive maps and information. (Open daily 9am-5pm.) From Bulahdelah, take the Myall Way (Lakes Rd.), a one-lane partly-paved road with an absurd 100kph speed limit. Beware of cars, caravans, and boat tugs barreling along.

Lakes Rd. finishes at **Bombah Point,** a center of activity for both Myall Lakes and Bombah Broadwater. Here, the **Myall Shores Ecotourism Resort ❷** (☎ 4997 4495) office distributes maps and some supplies, rents canoes ($14 per hr.) and outboards ($40 per 2hr.), and also sells **petrol.** The **campground's** facilities include BBQs, laundry, a store, and a restaurant. (Sites $17-22, powered $20-26; prices vary seasonally.) A **toll ferry** carries vehicles over to the Mungo Brush area of the park. (5 min., every 30min. 8am-6pm, $3.) The almost-all-paved **Mungo Brush Rd.** extends 25km along the coast to the park's southern edge. The lake side of the road has various entrances to the usually-crowded **Mungo Brush campgrounds ❶** that have toilets, BBQs, and access to the shallow lake, but **no water.** (NPWS office ☎ 4987 3108. Sites for 2 $10, not including $6 daily vehicle fee. First come first served. Pay a ranger if one comes by, or use the honesty box.) On the other side of the park the secluded **Yagon park campsite** on the ocean headland is accessible via Seal Rocks Rd. (turnoff after Bungwahl on The Lakes Way).

Access points all along the road lead to the **beach.** The poorly signposted **Mungo Brush Rainforest Walking Track,** a 1½km loop through a rainforest that is unusually fertile for this stretch of coast, begins at the northern end of Mungo Brush. Pick up a trail map at the **Visitors Center** before heading out. This track has its share of interestingly large and intimidating vegetation, and koalas snooze in the trees year-round. Other tracks on this side of the ferry can be walked consecutively to make up the hardy **Mungo Track,** which will take the day if you're moving reasonably quickly; pick up the trail map before setting out. Trees have been known to fall without warning throughout the park—take care walking and hiking, and obey all park warning signs.

FORSTER   ☎02

Situated on twin isthmuses, the small towns of Forster (FOS-ter) and Tuncurry are the height of civilization in the popular Great Lakes region, Aussie holiday spots frequently passed over by international travelers. Blessed with a temperate climate and close to endless stretches of empty beaches, the Forster area makes for a nice stop on the way to Sydney or Byron Bay.

▐▐▌ TRANSPORTATION AND PRACTICAL INFORMATION. From the south via the Pacific Hwy., take the Failford Rd. exit east and then **The Lakes Way** south. For a more scenic route, The Lakes Way turn-off heads east right after Buladelah, and Forster is one hour down the road. From the north, The Lakes Way turn-off is east at Rainbow Flat, and Forster is a 15min. drive away. **Great Lakes Coaches** (☎4983 1560) connects to Bluey's Beach (2 per day; $9.40, concessions $4.70) and Sydney (5½hr.; 1-2 per day; $45, concessions $31) via Newcastle (3hr.; 5 per day M-F, 2 per day Sa-Su; $29, concessions $24). **Eggins Comfort Coaches** (☎6552 2700) goes to Taree (1hr.; 2-4 per day M-Sa; $10, 50% student and YHA discounts). The **Great Lakes Visitors Centre,** on Little St. by the wharf, is the **coach terminal** and a booking agency. Tickets can also be purchased on the bus. (☎6554 8799 or 1800 802 692. Open daily 9am-5pm.) The **post office** is on the corner of Wallis Ln. and Beach St. in the center of Forster. **Postal Code:** 2428.

▐▐▌ ACCOMMODATIONS AND FOOD. The owners of the **Dolphin Lodge (YHA)** ❷, 43 Head St., treat their guests to surf and boogie boards, a kitchen, and a TV lounge with cable and videos, all just a block from the beach and four blocks from town. They offer pre-arranged pickup at the bus stops in Nabiac on the Pacific Hwy., bike rentals, and Internet access. (☎/fax 6555 8155; dolphin_lodge@hotmail.com. Internet $2 per 20min. $10 key deposit. Dorms $20; singles $32; ensuite doubles $46.) **Smugglers' Cove Holiday Village ❷,** 45 The Lakes Way, has top-notch facilities, including a pool, mini-golf, a kitchen, and $5 canoe hire. (☎6554 6666. Sites $23-29, powered $30-37; in winter $15, $21; economy cabins $63-86, ensuite $78-105; in winter $46, $58.) The tourist office can provide you with a list of budget motel clones around the area. For food, Wharf St. has small **markets** and restaurants serving burgers, pizza, and Chinese food. **Fat Ant Cafe ❶,** 32 Wharf St. (☎6555 3444), transforms into a groovy nightclub Friday at 10pm.

▐▐▌ SIGHTS AND ACTIVITIES. Tobwabba, 10 Breckenridge St., means "place of clay" to the Worimi Aborigines who welcome visitors to this studio and art gallery. The beautiful prints and canvasses are a unique alternative to the ubiquitous stuffed kangaroos and koalas. (☎6554 5755; www.tobwabba.com.au. Open M-F 9am-5pm.) At the north end of **Forster Beach,** at the end of West St. off Head St., there's a gas BBQ, a saltwater swimming pool, and a beach. For stunt skiing, seaplane flights, fishing cruises, or diving, consult the visitors center. Boat and tackle rental sheds line the lake shore. Near Forster, **Eureka Trails** offers **horseriding.** (☎6554 1281. $20 per hr., $35 per 2hr.) **Forster's Dive School** at Fisherman's Wharf opposite the post office, runs a variety of trips, including a **swim with dolphins** cruise (2hr.; $38, 10% Dolphin Lodge YHA discount) and a dive with gray nurse sharks near Seal Rock. (☎6554 7478. Rates vary; two dives with equipment $127.)

NEAR FORSTER: GREAT LAKES REGION

BOOTI BOOTI NATIONAL PARK. For a piece of Booti Booti, follow The Lakes Way south of Forster along the coastline of Elizabeth Beach. Wallis Lake, the forest between the road and beach, and the hinterland on the road's other side make up **Booti Booti National Park** (NPWS Office ☎6591 0300; greatlakesarea@npws.nsw.gov.au). **Biking** from Forster to the park's beaches is the best way to go (at least an hour each way). Bike hire is available from the Dolphin Lodge YHA (see above; $10 per 4hr., $16 per day; guests $8, $12). **Cape Hawke** is a climb by bike but provides both a spectacular view from the newly-built tower and access to a significant part of NSW's coastal rainforest. **Tiona Park ❷,** 15min. south of Forster, rents sites on both the lake and beach sides of the road. (☎6554 0291. Sites $18; cabins $38-67.) Tiona Park is also home to the popular **Green Cathedral,** set along the lake's edge. The sheltered waters of Lake Wallis can be enjoyed affordably with **Lakeside Family Boat Hire,** off The Lakes Way. (☎6554 0309. Sea buggies $5 per hr., paddle boats $5 per 30min., double canoes $10 per hr., motor boats $25 per hr.) A one-hour walk around the lake through cabbage tree palms and eucalyptus leads you to the ocean and **Elizabeth Beach** (see below). You can camp with less clutter at **The Ruins Camping Area ❶** by the soft white sand of **Seven-Mile Beach,** next to a mangrove forest. (BBQ, toilets, and showers. Pay camping fees in slots at the entrance to camping area; $7.50 per person per night.) Good **surfers** should travel 1km north to **Janice's Corner.**

PACIFIC PALMS AND NEARBY BEACHES. Approximately 20min. along The Lakes Way south of Forster, a sign appears for Bluey's Beach. Boomerang Dr., passes several beaches and continues through the small town of Pacific Palms before rejoining The Lakes Way a few kilometers south. **Elizabeth Beach** is the first turn-off on the left. Patrolled by pelicans and lifeguards, the waves usually die down in summer, making the safe surf ideal for swimmers. Farther along Boomerang Dr. is **Shelly's Beach,** a calm secluded stretch with clothing-optional bathing. **Boomerang Beach,** home of myriad **surfer** dudes, is just a couple minutes farther. From here, Boomerang Dr. loops through **Pacific Palms,** which has a small strip of shops selling junk food, sundries, and magazines. At its end is the **info center.** (☎6554 0123. Open daily 9am-4pm.) A bit farther on, you can camp in style at the **Oasis Caravan Park ❷,** with petrol, a market, and a small pool on premises. (☎6554 0488. Reception daily 8am-8pm; in summer open later. Sites $14-18; cabins $73-125.) **Great Lakes Sea Planes** (☎6555 8771) offers scenic flights departing from Forster Marina and Pacific Palms for as low as $40 per person. Pacific Palms is also home to the 6500 hectare **Wallingat State Forest,** which adjoins the Wallis Lake system. A 15km drive on an uneven dirt road from The Lakes Way, **Whoota Whoota lookout** is spectacular, featuring panoramic views of the endless coastline and lakes region. A kilometer south of the southern end of Boomerang Dr. along The Lakes Way is the turn-off for a dirt road that takes you 2km to **Celito Beach.** The 300m boardwalk leads through dry littoral forest to a beach to drool over, whether you're a surfer or a sunbather. Take a left off on the main dirt road to the **Sandbar Caravan Park ❶,** to reach a wilderness site on **Smith's Lake.** (☎6554 4095. Sites $10-30; cabins without bath $40-85; prices vary seasonally.)

NEW SOUTH WALES

TAREE
☎ 02

Taree, on the Manning River off the Pacific Hwy., is a small base for nearby beaches, state parks, and forests. The many budget hotels, motels, and caravan parks outside Taree and surrounding areas make it a convenient stop on long road trips. Though northbound travelers usually push on a little farther to the welcoming arms of Port Macquarie, Taree has a growing B&B and "country retreat" industry, particularly in nearby Wingham, allowing for a more comfortable pit stop.

Taree's main street, **Victoria St.**, conveniently feeds directly to the Pacific Hwy. Most shops, food, and bus stations are on Victoria St. or the streets between Pulteney and Macquarie St. **Countrylink** (☎13 22 32), **McCafferty's/Greyhound** (☎13 14 99 or 13 20 30), **Premier** (☎13 34 10), **Eggins Comfort Coaches** (☎6552 2700), and **Great Lakes Coaches** (☎1800 043 263) run **buses** to: Brisbane (10-11hr., 7 per day, $54-66); Byron Bay (7½hr., 6 per day, $54-65); Coffs Harbour (3½hr., 7 per day, $37-40); Forster (1hr.; 2-4 per day; $10, YHA $5); Port Macquarie (1½hr., 6 per day, $26-35); Sydney (5-6hr., 10 per day, $44-59). The **Manning Valley Visitors Information Centre** on Manning River Dr., 4km north of town, is just past the Big Oyster car dealership (☎1800 801 522 or 6552 1900. Open daily 9am-5pm). The **post office** is on Albert St. (parallel to Manning River Dr.), near the corner of Manning St.

Taree is 200km south of Coffs Harbour, 83km south of Port Macquarie, and 310km north of Sydney. **Beaches** near Taree are gorgeous and inviting, but have unexpected currents; swim only where patrolled. The closest is **Old Bar Beach** in the little village of Old Bar, a 15min. drive southeast from the town center on Old Bar Rd. **Wallabi Point,** to the south, offers great surfing and has a swimming lagoon. **Diamond Beach** and **Hallidays Point,** two well-known beaches farther south, offer camping. A 40min. drive to the north is **Crowdy Head,** site of a lighthouse lookout.

Accommodations are cheap and plentiful. **Exchange Hotel ❷**, on the corner of Victoria and Manning St., offers basic but clean rooms. (☎6552 1160. Reception at bar 10am-late. Singles $20; doubles $30.) Motel after indistinguishable motel line the Old Pacific Hwy. with doubles starting at $45. **Twilight Caravan Park ❶**, 3km south of the city on Manning River Dr., has laundry ($5), BBQ, and kitchen facilities. (☎0500 854 448; twilight@tsn.cc. Linen $1.20 per item. Powered sites for 2 $18; caravans for 2 $33-64; cabins $40-45, ensuite $55-64. Extra adult $5, teenager $4, child $3. Wheelchair accessible.) Those looking to camp might also consider trekking to one of the nearby national parks rather than staying in town.

FROM TAREE TO PORT MACQUARIE

CROWDY BAY NATIONAL PARK. Crowdy Bay is home to some of the area's most popular beaches, bushwalks, picnic areas, and a healthy supply of kangaroos. The park supposedly derives its name from Captain Cook's passing observation that the headland was crowded with Aborigines. Coralville Rd., at Moorland on the Pacific Hwy., leads into the southern entrance of the park. Wild eastern grey kangaroos live at all three of the camping sites: **Diamond Head, Indian Head,** and **Kylie's Rest Area** (named for Australian author Kylie Tennant, not Top-40 diva Kylie Minogue). There are septic toilets and cold showers at Diamond Head; all other sites have squat toilets. Whereas groups of **kangaroos** hop within feet of astounded visitors, and **whales** can be spotted off the headlands, it often takes an expert to spot more elusive **koalas** at Indian Head and Kylie's Hut. There are three reasonably tame **bushwalks** in the park which pass through delicate habitats stunted from exposure to wind and subject to harsh salt sprays. The shortest walk is along the base of the cliff of the headland, accessible from Diamond Head at low tide. During low tide, the **Cliff Base Walk** passes rock pools abounding with marine life. The longer **Diamond Head Loop Track** (4.8km) links Diamond Head and Indian Head, while a third, short track goes from Kylie's Hut to the beach at Crowdy Bay.

Visitors must bring their own fresh water into the park. The roads are 2WD-accessible dirt tracks. (Daily vehicle fee $6; one-time camping fee for 2 $10.)

BULGA STATE FOREST. A 50km daytrip from Taree and the site of a 99km tourist drive, the Bulga Forests are actually four separate forests: the Bulga, Doyles River, Dingo, and Knorrit. The Bulga is home to **Tirrill Creek Flora Reserve,** with walking trails, picnic areas, and the **Blue Knob Lookout,** from which even Taree is sometimes visible. **Maxwells Flat,** with toilet and BBQ facilities, has camping.

The most spectacular sight of the Bulga drive is **Ellenborough Falls,** an hour's drive from Taree. Created by a fault line 30 million years ago, it's one of the largest drops in the southern hemisphere (200m). There are multiple walking tracks, the most difficult of which leads to the bottom of the gorge. At the top of the Falls, there are picnic tables, restrooms, and a refreshment kiosk. (Open Sa-Su 10am-4pm). The falls can be reached without the Bulga drive by an east-west trip through **Comboyne.** This route also gives access to the **Boorganna Nature Reserve.** Both this and the Bulga drive are along rough, unsealed roads. For more info, call the **Manning Valley Visitors Centre** in Taree (see **Practical Information,** p. 162).

PORT MACQUARIE   ☎02

Travelers en route to Sydney and Byron Bay often make the sad mistake of bypassing Port Macquarie (ma-KWAR-ie; pop. 40,000), once a lock-up for Sydney's worst offenders. Today, the coastal town is a veritable action-sport capital and a haven for weary partiers and nature enthusiasts.

▐ TRANSPORTATION

Major bus lines including **McCafferty's/Greyhound** (☎13 14 99 or 13 20 30) and **Premier** (☎13 34 10) pass through town once per day. Check to make sure your bus stops at Hayward St. rather than out on the highway. **Budget** (☎13 27 27), at the corner of Gordon and Hollingsworth St.; **Hertz,** 102 Gordon St. (☎6583 6599); and **Thrifty** (☎6584 2122), at the corner of Horton and Hayward St., hire cars.

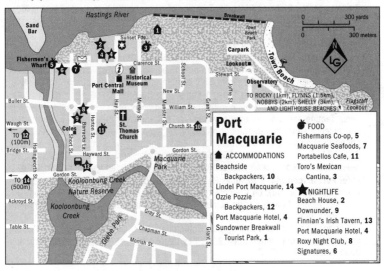

Port Macquarie

▲ ACCOMMODATIONS
Beachside
    Backpackers, **10**
Lindel Port Macquarie, **14**
Ozzie Pozzie
    Backpackers, **12**
Port Macquarie Hotel, **4**
Sundowner Breakwall
    Tourist Park, **1**

◆ FOOD
Fishermans Co-op, **5**
Macquarie Seafoods, **7**
Portabellos Cafe, **11**
Toro's Mexican
    Cantina, **3**

★ NIGHTLIFE
Beach House, **2**
Downunder, **9**
Finnian's Irish Tavern, **13**
Port Macquarie Hotel, **4**
Roxy Night Club, **8**
Signatures, **6**

NEW SOUTH WALES

✈ ℹ ORIENTATION AND PRACTICAL INFORMATION

Port Macquarie's town center is bordered on the north by the Hastings River and on the west by a narrow, bridged section of Kooloonbung Creek. **Horton St.** is the main commercial drag, and the area in the surrounding two-block radius comprises the central business district. Perpendicular to Horton St., and running along the river to the Marina, is **Clarence St.,** along which you'll find numerous restaurants and cafes. The well-organized **Visitors Center** is at the corner of Clarence and Hay St. (☎ 6581 8000 or 1300 303 155. Open in summer M-F 8:30am-5pm, Sa-Su 9am-4pm; in winter M-F 8:30am-5pm, Sa-Su 9am-2pm.) Other services include: **police** (24hr. ☎ 6583 0199), on the corner of Hay St. and Sunset Pde.; **banks** with **ATMs** on both sides of Horton St. between Clarence and William St.; **Internet** access at the **library,** on the corner of Grant and Gordon St. (☎ 6581 8723; open M-F 9:30am-6pm, Sa 9am-noon; $4 per hr., bookings essential); and a **post office** on the corner of Clarence and Horton St. **Postal Code:** 2444.

🏠 ACCOMMODATIONS

Port Macquarie has a range of good budget options; most offer the 7th night free. During peak season (summer, school holidays, and Easter), when motels and caravan parks sometimes double their prices, booking ahead is essential.

▨ **Ozzie Pozzie Backpackers (NOMADS),** 36 Waugh St. (☎ 6583 8133 or 1800 620 020; ozziepozzie@bigpond.com), off Gore St. between Buller and Bridge St. Friendly owners go beyond the call of duty, creating an activities board and arranging surfing and camel trips. Bright rooms (with lockers) open onto a cozy inner courtyard with hammocks. Kitchen open noon-10:30pm. W vegetarian chili dinner (summer) and daily muesli cereal for breakfast included. Free use of bikes ($50 deposit) and boogie boards. Laundry, Internet ($1 per 15min). Free pickup from bus stop. Reception daily 8am-noon and 3-8pm. Dorms from $20; twins and doubles from $46; 1 ensuite double from $50. ISIC/ NOMADS/VIP/YHA. ❷

Beachside Backpackers (YHA), 40 Church St. (☎/fax 6583 5512 or 1800 880 008; portmacqyha@hotmail.com). The closest hostel to the beaches and a 5min. walk from the town center. Clean and friendly. Free use of bikes, boogie boards, and fishing rods. W night BBQs $5. Common area has lights-out at 11pm. Free pickup from bus stop. Laundry $4, Internet $2 per 20min., TV, and free videos. No linen deposit. Reception daily 8am-10pm. Dorms from $20; twins $44. ❷

Port Macquarie Hotel (☎ 6583 1011), at the corner of Horton and Clarence St. In the middle of downtown, only a half-block from the beach, this old-style hotel is outfitted in Art Deco design. Basic singles from $33, ensuite with TV $55; doubles $50/$66. ❸

Sundowner Breakwall Tourist Park, 1 Munster St. (☎ 6583 2755 or 1800 636 452; www.sundowner.net.au). A huge waterfront park adjacent Town Beach and the Hastings River. Tenting area doesn't offer much shade, but you can't beat the view. Pool, BBQ, convenience store, free Internet at office, tackle shop, and food stand. No linen. Book ahead in summer. Sites off-peak $19, holidays and long weekends $22-32; powered $21/$24-35; 5-person cabins $55/$72-100; 4-person ensuite cabins $66/$95-130; 5-person 2-bedroom ocean view cottages $106/$182-230; additional person $8. ❷

Lindel Port Macquarie, 2 Hastings River Dr. (☎/fax 6583 1791 or 1800 688 882; lindel@midcoast.com.au), on the heavily-trafficked corner of Hastings River Dr. and Gordon St., 10min. from the town center. The closest backpackers to the bus terminal. Pool, BBQ, TV room, billiards, Internet $5 per hr., laundry $4, kitchen, and pickup. Free use of boogie boards and fishing gear. Limited parking. Quiet time at 11pm, but kitchen and common room remain open 24hr. Key deposit $10. Dorms from $18; twins and doubles from $40. VIP. ❷

FOOD

Clarence St. is lined with a number of affordable cafes and takeaway shops. The **Port Central Mall,** left of the tourist office, has a food court, delis, and a **supermarket.**

Portabellos Cafe and BYO Restaurant, 124 Horton St. (☎6584 1171), prepares handmade dishes using regional foods. Try a mouth-watering sandwich, foccacia or wrap ($5-9) for lunch, or savor one of their innovative salads or pastas ($8-15) for dinner, followed by one of their fantastic desserts. Choose between bright indoor or sunny patio dining. Open Tu-Th 8am-3pm, F-Sa 8am-late. ❷

Macquarie Seafoods (☎6583 8476), at the corner of Clarence and Short St. The best bet for fresh seafood takeaway. Fish 'n' chips $5.30. Open daily 11am-8pm. ❶

Fishermans Co-op (☎6584 7399), at the marina at the bottom of Clarence St. The catch comes in right off the boat. Open M-F 9:30am-5:30pm, Sa-Su 9:30am-5pm. ❶

Toro's Mexican Cantina (☎6583 4340), on Murray St. between Sunset Pde. and Clarence St. Serves up filling burritos and enchiladas ($12-15), and yummy, if not authentic, desserts. Open 5pm-late. BYO. ❷

⊙ SIGHTS

CREEPY CHURCH. The **St. Thomas Church** was built by convicts between 1824 and 1828 and is one of the oldest churches in Australia. The jail's former superintendent is buried under one of the pews because he feared that if he was buried in the cemetery, he would be exhumed by vengeful convicts. *(On the corner of Hay and William St. ☎6584 1033. Open M-F 9:30am-noon and 2-4pm. Donation $2, children $1.)*

KOALAS. Like koalas? The Port Macquarie area has the biggest urban population in the country. The secret to spotting them in the wild is to look through the trees rather than at individual forks in the trees. The town also provides a home for two of the best koala facilities in New South Wales. At one of Australia's few **Koala Hospitals,** there are usually four or more injured or sick koalas on site. *(20min. from the town center on Lord St. ☎6584 1522. Feedings daily at 8am and 3pm. Gold coin donation requested.)* At the **Billabong Koala Breeding Centre,** you can pet and feed koalas, wallabies, and kangaroos on the landscaped grounds. This is an unparalleled opportunity to interact with Australia's most-loved marsupials. *(61 Billabong Dr., west of the intersection of the Oxley and Pacific Hwy. 10km from Port Macquarie. ☎6585 1060. Feedings 10:30am, 1:30, and 3:30pm. $9.50, backpackers $7.50, children $6.)*

BEACHES. Starting at the **Lighthouse Beach** lookout, at the end of Lighthouse Rd. south of town, follow an 8km track back to Port Macquarie to all eight area beaches. Hostels are usually willing to drop you off at the lookout. From the viewpoint, retrace your steps back up Lighthouse Rd. (5-10min.) to the sign for **Miners Beach** (a nude beach). The forest path leads to the beach and then continues up along the cliffs. North of Harry's Lookout is **Shelly Beach,** home to huge **goannas.** Next in line is **Nobby's Beach,** immediately north of Nobby's Hill (the obelisk here stands in memory of those who died swimming in the dangerous blowhole—don't even think about trying). After Nobby's, you'll find **Flynns Beach** (popular with surfers), **Rocky Beach,** and **Oxley Beach.** The walking track ends at **Town Beach,** a good spot for swimming, "sunbaking," and fishing. From the headlands overlooking Town Beach, you can see **North Beach** and across the inlet to the Hasting River.

PARKS. The **Sea Acres Rainforest Center,** at Shelly's Beach, preserves the largest and southernmost stretch of coastal rainforest in Australia. A 1.3km raised boardwalk circles through a portion of the 72-hectare reserve and allows glimpses of brush turkeys and flying foxes. Guided walks, led by volunteers, head out roughly every 45min. The last tour leaves at 3pm. The **Visitors Center** has a 20min. film and ecological displays. (☎6582 3355. Open daily 9am-4:30pm. $10.) At the end of Horton St. is one of several entrances that lead into **Kooloonbung Creek Nature Reserve,** a 52-hectare conservation area of peaceful bushland. Several kilometers of footpaths wind through mangroves and rainforest. At the northern tip of North Beach is **Point Plomer** and **Limeburner Creek Nature Reserve,** the site of Aboriginal artifacts and the **Big Hill walking track.** A vehicle ferry runs across the river from Settlement Point in Settlement City. The 16km coastal road to Point is unsealed and rough but bike-able. **Campsites ❶** are available at Melaleuca near Big Hill and Barries Bay at Point Plomer. The campgrounds provide toilets and cold showers. Bring drinking water. (☎6583 8805. Sites for 2 $6; extra person $3. Check-in at campground kiosk daily 8am-4pm. Book ahead in summer.)

◤ ACTIVITIES

BY LAND. Aussie extraordinaire Greg leads **Port Macquarie Camel Safaris.** Caravan along Lighthouse Beach and perhaps even spot a wild koala. Pickup in the camel car can be arranged. (☎6583 7650. 20min. $15, children $10; 1hr. $28/$18. Book 1hr. tours in advance.) **Bicycles** can be rented from **Graham Seers Cyclery.** (In Port Marina on Park St. ☎6583 2333. $6.60 per hr., $22 per day, $55 per week.) **Macquarie Mountain Tours** visits four nearby **vineyards** for free tastings. (☎6582 3065. www.atotaladventure.com.au. Th and Sa-Su afternoons. $29.)

BY BOAT. Port Macquarie Sea Kayak takes paddlers out in 2-person boats to play in the surf. (☎0438 847 058. Open Tu, Th, and Sa 10am-2pm. $35; includes BBQ lunch.) Built in 1949, *The Pelican* is the second oldest wooden boat still in service, operating on the Hastings River. You don't travel fast, but you do cruise in style. (☎6582 3328 or 0418 652 171. 2½hr. Explorer cruise M, W, and F 2pm; $18, children $10. 5hr. BBQ cruise Tu and Th 10am; $36/$18.) **Port Venture** has the largest boat. (☎6583 3058. 2hr. tea and dolphin cruise Tu and Th-Su 10am and 2pm; $20, back-packers $15. 4-5hr. BBQ cruise M and W 10am; from $35.) **Everglade Tours** offers similar trips. (☎6582 5009. 2hr. tea and dolphin-spotting cruise daily 10am and 2pm; $22. 3½hr. oyster farm lunch cruise Th 11am; $32. 5½hr. Everglades lunch cruise Tu 9:30am; $50.) **Ocean Star** runs half-day reef and game fishing charters, as well as cruises to look for whales and dolphins. (☎6584 6965. 6hr. fishing trips depart daily 6:30am; $95, includes lunch and tea. Free pickup locally.) **Gypsy Boat Hire,** 52 Settlement Point Rd., can provide many water vehicles for your recreation pleasure. (☎6583 2353. Fishing boats $20 per 2hr.; runabouts $25 per 2hr.; half-cabin cruisers $30 per 2hr.; BBQ pontoon boats $45 per 2hr.) **Settlement Point Boat-shed,** next to Settlement Point Ferry, has similar deals along with canoe hire. (☎6583 6300. Canoes $15 per 4hr.)

SURF AND SCUBA. If you've had enough of staring out at the crashing waves from the beach, give **Learn to Surf** a call. Level I surf coach, Debbie, will have you laughing and ripping the curl in no time. (☎6584 4189 or 0413 282 932. Boards and wetsuits provided. M-Tu and Sa. 1-1½hr. $25 per person.) **Port Macquarie Dive Centre** can help you create personalized adventure weekends, whether you want to snorkel, scuba, or ski tube. (☎6583 8483; www.portdive.tsn.cc.)

IN THE SKY. Coastal Skydivers has one of the cheapest backpacker prices for tandem skydiving in NSW. (☎6584 3655. 3000m jumps $290, backpackers $250.) **High Adventure Air Park** offers a variety of tandem flights. (☎6556 5265. 30min. hang-gliding $175; 30min. paragliding $165; 30min. motorized microlight $140.)

NIGHTLIFE

The local watering hole is the **Port Macquarie Hotel,** on the corner of Clarence and Horton St. (☎ 6583 1011. Open Su-Th 10am-midnight, F-Sa 10am-2am.) Partygoers in their Saturday best flock to the **Beach House** nightclub, on the town green just down the street from the Port Macquarie Hotel. (☎ 6584 5692. Cover $5 after 10pm. Open until 3am.) Look for the **Roxy Night Club** on William St. between Horton and Short St. (☎ 6583 5466. Cover F-Sa after 11pm.) **Downunder** (☎ 6583 4018), on Short St., next to the Coles supermarket, has karaoke on Wednesday and rocking music on weekends. **Signatures,** 72 Clarence St. (☎ 6584 6144), has Happy Hour daily from 5-6pm. **Finnian's Irish Tavern** (☎ 6583 4646), on the corner of Gordon and Horton St., attracts a slightly older crowd. Live bands perform on the weekends. A free entertainment guide, *Hastings Happenings*, is published on Wednesdays.

SOUTH WEST ROCKS   ☎ 02

Because South West Rocks is *way* off the typical backpacker trail and is a tough place to get to without a car, it is often bypassed in the frenetic rush to travel up and down the coast to more mainstream destinations. Although the lack of nightlife might be a drawback, you can easily fill your days with spectacular scuba diving, leisurely bushwalks, and quiet beaches.

⁊ PRACTICAL INFORMATION. The turn-off for South West Rocks and **Hat Head National Park,** off the Pacific Hwy., is about 10km north of Kempsey. After crossing the Macleay River and Spencers Creek, the twisting rural route becomes Gregory St. To visit the national park and the **Smoky Cape Lighthouse,** turn right onto Arakoon Rd., drive 6km, and then turn right onto Lighthouse Rd. To find the **tourist information center,** housed in the old Boatman's Cottage, drive to the end of Gregory St. and turn left on Ocean St. The volunteer staff there knows the area's trails and beaches inside and out. (☎ 6566 7099. Open daily 10am-4pm.) **Cavanagh's Coaches** (☎ 6562 7800) has **buses** departing from Kempsey (30min., 2 per day, $8).

⁊⁊ ACCOMMODATIONS AND FOOD. Next door to the tourist office, **Horseshoe Bay Beach Park ❷** is just paces from a surf and swim beach. (☎/fax 6566 6370. Powered sites $23, in winter $20; vans $47/$39; cabins $68/$65. Call ahead for reservations in summer. Christmas-New Years holiday reservations should be made more than a year in advance.) **Lighthouse Bed and Breakfast ❺,** Lighthouse Rd., Arakoon, is a heritage-listed, fully-restored lighthouse keeper's home with two beautifully-appointed bedrooms; guests are well-cared-for with four-poster beds, three-course breakfasts on the lawn, and sweeping vistas of the beach and ocean far below. There are also two self-contained cottages that were originally assistant lighthouse keeper's homes, both of which sleep eight. (☎ 6566 6301; www.smokycapelighthouse.com. Main house singles $110; doubles $165; includes 3-course breakfast. Cottages for 2 nights $350-465, weekly $580-1450 depending on season; no 2-night rentals Apr., Sept-Oct., and Dec.-Jan.) **Arakoon State Recreation Area,** a five- to ten-minute drive from the town center, features **campsites ❷** at the Trial Bay Gaol. The sites are cheap and right next to Front Beach. (☎ 6566 6168. Toilets, water, coin-operated hot showers. Powered sites for 2 $20-27.) The full spectrum of food service is available in South West Rocks. Some of the best is served up at **Geppy's Seaside Restaurant ❸,** at the corner of Livingstone St. and Memorial Ave. The gregarious owner, Geppy, will amaze your palate with modern Italian made from the freshest ingredients. (☎ 6566 6196. Open daily 6pm-late. Entrees from $6.50, mains from $17.)

◪ **ACTIVITIES.** The best **surfing** waves break northwest of the tourist office at **Back Beach.** Sunbathers will enjoy **Front Beach,** which surrounds Trial Bay, a warm-water swimming hole. To see what's under the waves, visit Fish Rock Cave, considered one of the ten best dives in Australia. Contact the **Fish Rock Dive Center,** 328 Gregory St. Though their prices are higher than elsewhere, courses range from beginner to instructor and the center offers technical expertise in rebreathers, nitrox blending, and underwater photography. (☎ 6566 6614; www.fish-rock.com.au. 4-5 day open water course with on-site accommodation $525; double boat-dive $80, including 2nd cylinder; full set of gear $40.) **South West Rocks Dive Centre,** Shop 5, 98 Gregory St., also takes divers out to Fish Rock Cave and offers certification classes for similar prices. (☎ 6566 6474. Open daily 7:30am-5pm. Book in advance.) A good spot for bushwalking is **Little Bay.** Drive to the end of Wilson St. and into the Arakoon Recreation Area. From the Overshot Dam carpark, you can follow the **Gap Beach Track** into **Hat Head National Park,** around Little Smoky in the Cape Range, to Gap Beach (45min. one-way). From Gap Beach, it's possible to continue on to **North Smoky Beach** and the **Smoky Cape Lighthouse.** The lighthouse promontory is a great vantage point for spotting migrating humpback and southern right whales. Pick up a trail map from the park office at the Trial Bay Gaol.

NAMBUCCA HEADS ☎ 02

For the traveler in need of a break from relentless tourist attractions and constant activities, peaceful Nambucca Heads (nam-BUH-kuh; pop. 6500) provides a welcome respite. Nambucca's allure is its Nambucca River, which winds lazily through lush hills on its way to the Pacific, and its dazzling beaches. The friendly residents often refer to the area as "our paradise."

▐ TRANSPORTATION

The **railway station** is a few kilometers out of town. From Mann St., bear right at the roundabout to Railway Rd. **Countrylink** (☎ 13 22 32) goes to Coffs Harbour (1hr., 3 per day, $5.50). **King Bros** (☎ 6568 1296 or 1300 555 611) runs **buses** to Coffs Harbour (45min., 4 per day, $5), and **Joyce's** (☎ 6655 6330) serves Bellingen (1hr., 3 per day, $5.60). **McCafferty's/Greyhound** (☎ 13 14 99 or 13 20 30) and **Premier** (☎ 13 34 10) stop daily on their Sydney-Brisbane route. **Radio Cabs** (☎ 6568 6855) run 24hr.

◪ ▐ ORIENTATION AND PRACTICAL INFORMATION

Heading north, the Pacific Hwy. splits off to the right and joins the multiple-personality **Riverside Dr.,** the main road in Nambucca Heads. As Riverside Dr. climbs the hill at the RSL club, it becomes **Fraser St.;** at the town center, it becomes **Bowra St.;** on the way back out to the Pacific Hwy., it's **Mann St.;** and then **Old Coast Rd.** To get to the beaches, follow **Ridge St.** until it forks upon leaving town. **Liston St.,** to the left, leads to the **Headland** and **Surf Beach. Parkes St.,** to the right, leads to **Shelly Beach.** Use caution when driving in Nambucca Heads—the roads are like roller coasters, and it's often hard to see past the crest of the next hill. For general information, visit the brand-new **Nambucca Valley Visitor Information Centre,** at the intersection of the Pacific Hwy. and Riverside Dr. (☎ 6568 6954; fax 6568 5004; www.nambuccatourism.com. Open daily 9am-5pm.) The **bus stops** for travelers heading north and south from Nambucca Heads are also along the highway, near the info center. Behind the northbound bus stop is a shopping center with a Woolworth's **supermarket** and a movie theater. Another supermarket is located on Back St., up the hill from the RSL Club. For an **Internet** fix, head for **The Bookshop and Internet Cafe** ($9 per hr.; see **Food and Entertainment,** p. 169). **Commonwealth Bank** and the **post office** are on Bowra St. **Postal Code:** 2448.

ACCOMMODATIONS

Nambucca and the surrounding townships of Bowraville, Scotts Head, and Valla Beach are "chock-a-block" with accommodations situated near the beaches or along the Pacific Hwy. near the tourist office. Book ahead for summer holidays.

Beilby's Beach House, 1 Ocean St. (☎6568 6466; beilbys@midcoast.com.au). From downtown, take Ridge St. toward the beaches, turn left on Liston St., and follow the signs. This romantic guesthouse with private verandas, hardwood floors, and a large pool is ideal for families, couples, and hostel-weary backpackers. Less than a 5min. walk to the beach. Free bikes, surfboards, and boogie boards. Kitchen, Internet ($6 per hr.), laundry, and off-street parking. Arrange for pickup. Breakfast included. Twins and doubles $46; ensuite doubles $60; triples $60; ensuite queen $70; ensuite double with connecting twin from $77. MC/V. ❹

Nambucca Heads Backpackers, 3 Newman St. (☎6568 6360 or 1800 630 663; www.midcoast.com.au/~jpilgrim). After the 2nd speed bump on Bowra St., turn right onto Rosedale St., continue 2 long blocks to Newman St., and turn right. Free boogie boards, snorkeling gear, bikes, and paint for the V-Wall stones (ask inside). A 15min. walk through state forest to secluded beaches. 2 kitchens, common lounge, TV, laundry, and Internet. Pickup during business hours. Reception daily 7am-11pm. Dorms from $18, off-peak 3-night special $54; twins and doubles from $38; 6-person self-contained units $50. VIP. ❷

White Albatross Holiday Resort (☎6568 6468; www.white-albatross.com.au), at the ocean end of Wellington Dr., next to the Wall Tavern. A sprawling caravan park with a gorgeous setting near a swimming lagoon and the Nambucca River. Picnic and BBQ areas, camp kitchen, laundry, small game room, convenience store, takeaway cafe. Linen $5.50. Sites from $19; on-site vans from $27.50; flats and homes from $47; service units from $80. All prices for two people; extra adult $11, extra child $5.50. Call ahead during summer. MC/V. ❷

FOOD AND ENTERTAINMENT

Bowra St. has an assortment of quick, cheap food possibilities. **The Bookshop and Internet Cafe ❶,** on the corner of Bowra and Ridge St., is the perfect place to trade in your old books and have a delicious lunch. The cafe serves mouth-watering sandwiches ($6-9) and unusual juices ($4.50), including spinach, celery, and watermelon. (☎6568 5855. Open daily 9am-5pm. Internet $9 per hr.) For an upscale meal at a moderate price, try **Spices Cafe ❸,** 58 Ridge St., for a caesar salad ($7), spring rolls ($8), or fresh seafood ($9-17), and great ambience. (☎6568 8877. Open daily for dinner.) The **V-Wall Tavern ❶,** at the mouth of the Nambucca River on Wellington Dr., has unbeatable views and an active night scene, with discos on Saturdays. (☎6568 6344. Open daily 10am-midnight. Meals $7-9.) The **White Albatross Kiosk ❶,** the holiday park's takeaway and general store, is adjacent to the tavern and has the cheapest prices. (☎6568 9160. Open daily 7:30am-7:30pm.)

SIGHTS AND ACTIVITIES

Nambucca is full of delightful and spontaneous artwork. Don't miss the **mosaic wall** in front of the police station on Bowra St., a glittering, 3-D, 60m long sea serpent scene made completely of broken crockery and a toilet. Many of the town's lampposts are painted with colorful underwater scenes. Hundreds of rocks along the breakwater **V-Wall,** named for its shape, are painted with dates and rhyming ditties from years of tourists, honeymooners, and families. It's one of the few places where graffiti artists are welcomed and even provided with an outdoor gallery;

NEW SOUTH WALES

travelers are encouraged to contribute. Hostel owners typically provide paint packets. Supplies are also available at **Valley Community Arts,** in the Seascape Shopping Centre at the corner of Ridge St. and Estuary Ln. (☎ 6568 7645. Open M-F 9am-4pm, Sa 8:30-11:30am.)

The **Nambucca Boatshed Boathire,** 1 Wellington Dr. (☎ 6568 5550), and **Beachcomber Marine** (☎ 6568 6432), on Riverside Dr., both have a good selection of motor boats. **Got Lost Kayak Tours** can set you up with touring sea kayaks. (☎ 6564 7346; gotlostinnambucca@hotmail.com. Half-day self-guided $44; full-day escorted $120 per person.) **East Coast Adventures,** 5 Mann St., has on-site **scuba** certification courses (PADI), with accommodation, and runs trips to the Solitary Islands and Fishrock Cave. (☎ 6569 4422. Double boat-dive with all equipment $95; Learn-to-Dive course $165, with 4 nights accommodation $219.)

There are **walks** of varying difficulty throughout the beach and bush areas of Nambucca, some of which pass by the gorgeous **Rotary, Captain Cook,** and **Lions Lookouts.** For more structured exploring, contact **Kyeewa Bushwalkers** (☎ 6569 5627). The group organizes walks on Wednesdays, Saturdays, and Sundays.

To get the inside on surfing, call the president of the **Loggerheads Malibu Board Riding Club** (☎ 6568 7314) or try **Surf Beach** for yourself. The 16km beach separating Nambucca Heads and **Scotts Head,** to the south, is also a great surfing beach.

BELLINGEN ☎ 02

Bellingen (BELLIN-gin; pop. 2600), is a laid-back town situated cozily on the banks of the Bellinger River, 30min. from the World Heritage-listed **Dorrigo National Park** (see p. 171), roughly halfway between Coffs Harbour and Nambucca Heads. Although its heyday was 50 years ago, when it was the financial and commercial center for the Coffs Harbour region, Bellingen has reinvented itself. Reputedly having more artists per capita than anywhere down under, locals claim to live in the second-most alternative town in Australia (after Nimbin, of course).

🖅 🛂 TRANSPORTATION AND PRACTICAL INFORMATION. Running parallel to the Bellinger River, **Hyde St.** cuts right through the center of town. Travel east to reach Urunga and Coffs Harbour. Drive west to explore the rainforests of Dorrigo National Park and streets of Armidale. Buses stop at Hyde and Church St. **King Bros** (☎ 1300 555 611) services Coffs Harbour (1hr., 3 per day, $5.20) and Nambucca Heads (1hr., M-F 5 per day, $5.60). **Keans** (☎ 1800 043 339) travels to: Coffs Harbour (45min., 1 per day, $11.50); Port Macquarie (3hr.; M, W, and F 1 per day; $28) via Nambucca Heads (1hr., $21); and Tamworth (5hr.; Tu, Th, and Su 1 per day; $49) via Armidale (3hr., $26). **Traveland,** 42 Hyde St. (☎ 6655 2055), books seats on various bus services. Local travel is easily accomplished through **Bellingen Taxi** (☎ 6655 9995). As of August 2002, the permanent location of the **Bellingen Tourist Information Centre** had yet to be determined; ask locally for an update when you arrive in town. The **library,** in the park across from the post office, has **Internet** access. (☎ 6655 1744. $2 per 10min. Book ahead. Open Tu-W 10:30am-5:30pm, Th-F 10:30am-12:30pm and 1:30-5:30pm.)

🖬 🖸 ACCOMMODATIONS AND FOOD. Winner of the 2001 NSW Tourism Board award for "Best Budget Accomodation," 🏠**Bellingen Backpackers (YHA) ❶,** 2 Short St., can't help but impress with its huge verandas, awesome tree-fort, and terraced sites that overlook the Bellinger River. Turn at the driveway for the Lodge 214 Gallery Cafe, off the Pacific Hwy. on the north end of town. The lounge/kitchen has oversized floor pillows, musical instruments and a small, hidden TV. Be sure to check out all the photographs, especially the upstairs "Nude Wall of Fame." The super-friendly owners and staff pick up guests from the Urunga train or bus stations and arrange group day-trips to Dorrigo National Park ($15). Bike rentals ($5), laundry, and Internet are available. (☎6655 1116; belloyha@mid-coast.com.au. Sites for 2 $14; dorms $22; twins and doubles $50. YHA discount $2.)

The delicious **Cool Creek Cafe ❹**, 5 Church St., books local and national musicians. Call or check the website for events. (☎6655 1886; www.coolcreek-cafe.com.au. Open M and Th-F 5-10pm, Sa-Su 11am-3pm and 5-10pm; holidays and festivals daily 11am-10pm. Lunch from $7.50, dinner $13-24.) The **Lodge 241 Gallery Cafe ❷**, 117-121 Hyde St., on the western edge of town, combines panoramic views, displays of local art, and generous portions of freshly prepared dishes. (☎6655 2470. Open Su-Th 8am-5pm, F-Sa 8am-late.) The **Natural Lifestyles and Produce Market ❶**, held the 2nd and 4th Saturday of every month at the **showgrounds** on Black St., specializes in eco-friendly foods and has healthy breakfast for $5. (☎6655 2924. Open daily 8am-1pm.)

⬛◫ SIGHTS AND ACTIVITIES. Even if you're not in the market for a "didg" and have no idea how to circular breathe, **Heartland Didgeridoos**, 25 Hyde St., has an outstanding collection of instruments. The owners are incredible players and offer lessons. (☎6655 9881; www.heartdidg.com. Open M-F 9am-5pm, Sa 10am-2pm. Didgeridoos from $100. Lessons $15 per 30min., $20 per hr.) Just across the Bellinger River on Hammond St., behind the Bellingen Caravan Park, is the entrance to **Bellingen Island**, a year-round home to an active colony of "flying foxes," or **fruit bats**, which have a one-meter wingspan. A forest trail loops through the surprisingly open understory for excellent views. The **Promised Land** and the **Never Never River,** both lovely spots with BBQs and excellent, crocodile-free **swimming holes,** are easier to reach than their names imply; they are an easy 10-15km bike ride from town. Cross the Bellinger on Bridge St. and take a left at the first rotary onto Wheatley St. Continue straight until you see a sign for Gleniffer. Bear right at this sign and continue for another 6km. The route passes the humble abode of David Helfgott, the inspiration for the movie *Shine*, and the house of Serge Cockburn, the young actor from *Crocodile Dundee 3*. You'll find the Never Never behind the church in Gleniffer. To get to the Promised Land, cross the bridge and take the first right. Shy and elusive platypuses live in the Never Never.

Bellingen Canoe Adventures has rentals and tours. (☎6655 9955. $11 per hr.; $33 per 4hr.; half-day tour with 3 rapids $44.) To see the sights from the top of a saddle, contact **Valery Trails** (see p. 176). **Gambaarri Tours** offers half-day local tours with an Aboriginal guide and an introduction to traditional dance and spear throwing. (☎6655 4195. $50, children $25.)

Though it may seem surprising for such a small town, Bellingen hosts several major festivals during the year. The annual **Jazz Festival** (www.bellingenjazzfestival.com.au), held Aug. 15-17 2003, features scheduled, ticketed concerts as well as free street jams. The **Global Carnival and World Music Festival** (www.globalcarnival.com), happening Oct. 5-7, 2002, attracts a diverse group of musicians, dancers, and artists, along with enthusiastic crowds.

NEAR BELLINGEN: DORRIGO NATIONAL PARK

Begin your exploration of Dorrigo National Park, part of the World Heritage-listed "Central Eastern Rainforest Reserves," at the **Rainforest Centre,** complete with a cafe and newly renovated educational and audio-visual displays. Keep your eyes open; red-necked **pademelons** (they look like mini-wallabies) and brush turkeys often hop through the picnic area. (☎6657 2309. Open daily 9am-5pm.) Allow 35min. to drive from Bellingen (29km east) or one hour from Coffs Harbour (64km east). Dorrigo is lush rainforest, with sections of multi-layered canopy and wet eucalypt forest. When the rain makes things sloppy (not usually a problem on the fully sealed trails), the **leeches** have a field day. Pick them off, or buy a cream stick from the Centre that repels them. Do *not* rub them with salt—this is bad for the rainforest. The 75m long **Skywalk** extends out and over the steep slope behind the Rainforest Centre up in the tree canopy, 21m above the forest floor. For a more relaxed stroll, try the **Walk with the Birds** (2½km; 45min. return). On the **Wonga Walk** (6.6 km; 2½hr. return), you'll soak your shoes as you journey past waterfalls. Take the trail only as far as Crystal Shower Falls for a chance to walk behind a waterfall and through the plunging water (3.3km; 1hr. return). Drive the well-maintained, gravel **Dome Rd.** from the Rainforest Centre to the **Never Never Picnic Area** (10km) for several hiking tracks. From the park, follow Megan Rd. through the town of Dorrigo to visit the spectacular **Dangar Falls** overlook. A sealed pathway leads from the viewpoint to the base of the falls if you want to go for a swim. Numerous picnic areas and varied walks and attractions make this a good day excursion.

COFFS HARBOUR   ☎02

Situated along a coastline backed by the hills of the Great Dividing Range and covered in lush banana plantations, Coffs Harbour (pop. 60,000) is a popular spot for partiers, scuba divers, and adrenaline-junkies, partly for its proximity to Solitary Islands National Marine Park. Coffs' rapid expansion in the past decade has come at the expense of its coastal charm, but four social and tight-knit hostels make it a worthwhile stop.

▐ TRANSPORTATION

Trains: The **railway station** is at the end of Angus McLeod St. by the jetty. From High St., turn right on Camperdown St. and take your first left. **Countrylink** (☎ 13 22 32) goes to: Brisbane (6-7hr., 2 per day, $72); Byron Bay (4hr., 4 per day, $42); Nambucca Heads (35min., 3 per day, $5.50); and Sydney (9hr., 3 per day, $79). Discounts of up to 40% for booking more than 1 week ahead, 50% for more than 2 weeks.

Buses: The long-distance bus stop is on Elizabeth St., near the corner of High and McLean St. **McCafferty's/Greyhound** (☎ 13 14 99 or 13 20 30) and **Premier** (☎ 13 34 10) go to: Byron Bay (5hr., 4 per day, $53); Brisbane (7hr., 5 per day, $56); Newcastle (6½hr., 4 per day, $56); Port Macquarie (2½hr., 4 per day, $36); and Sydney (9hr., 5 per day, $76). ISIC/VIP/YHA 10% discount. **King Bros** (☎ 1300 555 611) runs locally to Bellingen (1hr., M-F 3 per day, $5.40) and Nambucca Heads (1hr., M-F 4 per day, $5.60). **Keans** (☎ 1800 043 339) travels once per Tu, Th, and Su to: Armidale (4hr., $29); Dorrigo (1½hr., $16); and Tamworth (5hr., $53). Return trips once per M, W, and F.

Car Rental: Coffs Harbour Rent-A-Car (☎ 6652 5022), at the Shell Service Station, on the corner of Pacific Hwy. and Marcia St., rents from $44 per day. **A Little Car and Truck Hire,** 32 Alison St. (☎ 6651 3004), rents cars from $29 and 4WD from $90; 5-day minimum hire required. National companies such as **Budget** (☎ 13 27 27) and **Delta Europcar** (☎ 13 13 90) are also available.

Taxi: ☎ 6658 8888.

◢◤ ▐ ORIENTATION AND PRACTICAL INFORMATION

The Pacific Hwy., as it passes through Coffs Harbour, takes on two new names: **Grafton St.** and **Woolgoolga Rd.** Three large shopping centers divide the focus of the town: the **Palms Centre Mall** on Vernon St. in the center of town, the **Jetty Village Shopping Centre** on High St. near the water, and the **Park Beach Plaza** on the Pacific Hwy. in the northern part of town. The NPWS **Muttonbird Island Nature Reserve** is accessible by walking along the breakwater boardwalk at the end of Marina Dr. The city can be difficult to maneuver without a car, but hostels will often provide rides to attractions and the beaches more than a 15min. walk from any of them.

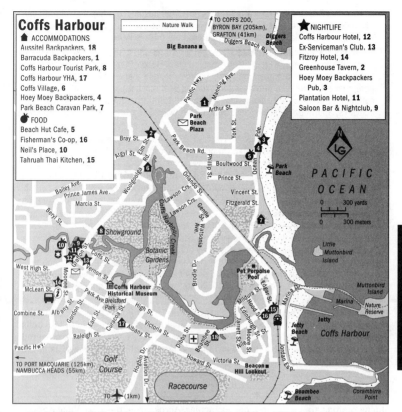

Coffs Harbour

♠ ACCOMMODATIONS
Aussitel Backpackers, 18
Barracuda Backpackers, 1
Coffs Harbour Tourist Park, 8
Coffs Harbour YHA, 17
Coffs Village, 6
Hoey Moey Backpackers, 4
Park Beach Caravan Park, 7

🍴 FOOD
Beach Hut Cafe, 5
Fisherman's Co-op, 16
Neil's Place, 10
Tahruah Thai Kitchen, 15

★ NIGHTLIFE
Coffs Harbour Hotel, 12
Ex-Serviceman's Club, 13
Fitzroy Hotel, 14
Greenhouse Tavern, 2
Hoey Moey Backpackers Pub, 3
Plantation Hotel, 11
Saloon Bar & Nightclub, 9

NEW SOUTH WALES

Tourist Office: Visitor Information Centre (☎6652 1522 or 1300 369 070; www.coffs-tourism.com), on the corner of Elizabeth and McClean St. Open daily 9am-5pm.

Currency Exchange: ANZ bank, on the corner of Moonee and High St. Other banks with 24hr. international **ATMs** are in the Palms Centre Mall and the Park Beach Plaza.

Police: 16 Moonee St. (☎6652 0299). **Water Police** (☎6652 0257), on the wharf.

Internet: Coffs Harbour City Library (☎6648 4905), on the corner of Coffs and Duke St. Free 30min. sessions; try to book in advance. Open M-F 9:30am-6pm, Sa 9:30am-3pm.

Post Office: (☎6652 2022), in the Palms Centre Mall; (☎6652 7499), in the Park Beach Plaza. Both open M-F 8:30am-5pm, Sa 9am-noon. **Postal Code:** 2450.

🏠🏕 ACCOMMODATIONS AND CAMPING

Many motels are clustered along the Pacific Hwy. and Park Beach Rd. All caravans and hostels provide a 7th night free during off-peak.

🛏 **Aussitel Backpackers,** 312 High St. (☎6651 1871 or 1800 330 335; www.aussitel.com), a 20min. walk from the town center; 10min. walk from the beach. Social, clean, and wholesome. The busy open kitchen/lounge area includes Internet and a TV. Features include BBQ, pinball machine, darts, heated pool, luggage storage, and laundry. Surfboards, boogie boards, wetsuits, bikes, and canoes available. **East Coast**

Adventures Scuba Crew (see p. 174) runs out of the hostel and offers a great PADI certification. Quiet time after 11pm. Free pickup and drop-off. Dorms $20, in winter $22, 3-night winter special $54; twins and doubles from $48. NOMADS/VIP/YHA. MC/V. ❷

Barracuda Backpackers (NOMADS), 19 Arthur St. (☎6651 3514 or 1800 111 514; barracud@key.net.au), a 2min. walk from the Park Beach Plaza; 5min. walk from the beach. Each 4- and 6-bunk dorm has linen, lockers, and a small fridge. Internet, BBQ, pool, and spa. Free use of didgeridoos, fishing gear, cricket bats, boogie boards, and surfboards. Courtesy 1hr. orientation van tour of town on request, frequent organized activities, and rides to local sights. Dorms $22; twins $46; doubles $50, ensuite $54. ISIC/VIP/YHA. MC/V. ❷

Coffs Harbour YHA, 110 Albany St. (☎/fax 6652 6462; coffsyha@ozemail.com.au), a 10min. walk from the town center; 20min. walk from the beach. This laid-back 2-story feels like a beach house. A chalkboard downstairs lists local activities. Kitchen, common area, TV, Internet, laundry, and pool. Bikes available for $5; $15 deposit. Bus runs to the beaches twice daily (10am and 3pm) and on request to local attractions. Breakfast $3-7. Dorms $22; twins and doubles from $48; family rooms for 4-6 from $64. ❷

Hoey Moey Backpackers (☎6651 7966 or 1800 683 322; hoey@hoeymoey.com.au), at the corner of Park Beach Rd. and Ocean Pde. A 10min. walk from the Park Beach Plaza; 1min. walk to the beach. Hoey Moey, slang for "Hotel Motel," is a backpackers, motel, and pub all rolled into one. The lively pub has weekly bands, a beer garden, and meals starting at $5.50. Kitchen, BBQ, and TV lounge. Free bikes, surfboards, and boogie boards. All rooms have bath, TV, and small fridge. Shuttle to town available. Reception 7:30am-7:30pm. Key deposit $10. Hostel-style dorms $18; doubles $38. Motel singles $37. ISIC/VIP/YHA. MC/V. ❷

Park Beach Caravan Park ❷, near the Surf Club on Ocean Pde., is the closest to the beach. (☎6648 4888. Sites $16, powered $19; on-site vans $35; cabins $44-68.) **Coffs Harbour Tourist Park ❷** is at 123 Pacific Hwy. (☎6652 1694. Sites $15.40, powered $17; on-site caravans $29; cabins $44.) **Coffs Village ❶,** 215 Pacific Hwy., is in the Clog Barn complex. (☎6652 4633. Sites $14, powered $17; cabins $44.)

FOOD

Dining options are, in general, unspectacular. Across from the Jetty Village Shopping Centre, on High St. near the harbor, is a row of popular restaurants. A local favorite is **Tahruah Thai Kitchen ❷,** 366 High St. (☎6651 5992. Open daily 6-10pm. Mains from $9.) The **Fisherman's Co-op ❶,** at the end of Marina Dr. by the breakwater boardwalk, serves hot seafood straight off the boat. (☎6652 2811. Fish counter open daily 9am-6pm; cooked counter open daily 11am-early evening.) Head for the **Beach Hut Cafe ❶** on Ocean Pde. just down the street from the Hoey Moey Backpackers. Eggs and hotcakes are served all day. (☎6651 2773. Breakfast from $6. Open daily 7:30am-3pm; dinner served Sept.-Mar. daily 6-9pm.) For vegetarian options, stroll on over to **Neil's Place ❶,** 40 Moonee St. (☎6652 5922. Open M-F 7:30am-5pm.) The **Palms Centre Mall** and **Park Beach Plaza** each have **supermarkets,** cheap takeaways, and sit-down cafes. The Hoey Moey Hotel, Plantation Hotel, and Greenhouse Tavern (see **Nightlife,** p. 177) all have cheap pub meals.

DIVING OFF THE SOLITARY ISLANDS

Solitary Islands Marine Reserve stretches 70km from Coffs Harbour to the Sandon River and encompasses nearly 100,000 hectares. It is composed of at least 19 protected beaches, headlands, creeks, and rocky islands. Because of the unique mixing of warmer, tropical waters from the north and cooler, temperate waters from the south, the area has some of the most diverse marine life. Species common to the Great Barrier Reef mingle with species typically found near Tasmania. The marine park is well-respected as a top diving spot. Visibility is often better during the winter, but the water gets chilly. Luckily, you can swim with harmless gray nurse sharks year-round. Contact the **NSW Fisheries and Marine Parks Office,** 32 Marina Dr., for more info. (☎6652 3977. Open M-F 8:30am-4:30pm.) Coffs has two dive shops that rent equipment and run trips to the Solitary Islands. A third company offers only courses and trips.

East Coast Adventures, 312 High St. (☎6569 4422 or 1800 330 335), at the Aussitel Backpackers. This company offers a 4-day PADI course and a 4-night Aussitel dorm package for $229. No minimum amount of people required to dive. Charter double boat-dive $95, with advanced certification $120. Open daily 9am-5pm.

Jetty Dive Centre, 398 High St. (☎6651 1611). The 4-day PADI course, including all boat-dives, costs $185 for backpackers staying at any Coffs hostel, min. 6 people. Double boat-dive with gear from $107; single intro-dive $109, double intro-dive $137. Snorkeling charters $45. Open daily 9am-5pm.

Pacific Blue Dive Center, 40 Marina Dr. (24hr. ☎6652 2759). Courtesy pickup available. Double boat-dive with gear $105; double intro-dive $135. 4-day PADI course $165, min. 4 people required. Open daily 7am-6pm.

SIGHTS

The Coffs Harbour **jetty,** built in 1890, was the center of a busy marine industry at the start of the 20th century. Commercial fishing boats continue to take refuge in the protected harbor but the area's emphasis has shifted somewhat to recreation in recent years. The jetty foreshore has BBQ facilities and is an easy walk from **Jetty Beach.** The breakwater boardwalk, near the marina, connects the mainland to **Muttonbird Island** (named after the wedge-tailed shearwaters that nest there), a terrific lookout for spotting **whales.** The island was sacred to the region's Aborigines, whose adolescent males would swim out to the island for several weeks of initiation into manhood. **Park Beach,** and the beach immediately north of the marina, are also popular hang-outs but have dangerous currents. The best **surfing** is at **Diggers Beach,** north of Macauleys Headland, accessible off the Pacific Hwy. From the Big Banana, turn onto Diggers Beach Rd. and follow it to the end.

The **Botanic Gardens,** one block north at the corner of High and Hardacre St., displays colorful native and exotic plants and endangered species. (☎6648 4188. Open daily 9am-5pm. Donation requested.) The 4km-long **Coffs Creek Walk** connects Rotary Park, at the intersection of Gordon and Coffs St. in the city center, and the Coffs Creek inlet, near Orlando St., and also has a detour to the gardens. You can make the hike a 10km circuit by following the 6km-long **Coffs Creek Habitat Walk** that edges the northern side of the creek.

At the **Pet Porpoise Pool (Oceanarium),** on Orlando St. by Coffs Creek, dolphins and seals perform tricks daily at 10:30am and 2:15pm in the Sea Circus. (☎6652 2164. Open daily 9am-5pm. $18, backpackers $14, concessions $11, children $7, families $47.) The **Coffs Zoo,** 12km north of Coffs along the Pacific Hwy. past Moonee Beach, offers daily presentations on koalas (11am and 3pm), wombats (10:30am), and echidnas (10:45am). (☎6656 1330. Open daily 8:30am-4pm, later during holidays. $14.50, concessions $10.50, children $7, families $36.)

The **Coffs Harbour Historical Museum,** 191 High St., documents the history of the area with a model banana plantation, the optic from South Solitary Island Lighthouse, and other displays. (☎6652 5794. Open daily 10am-4pm. $2.) The **Bunker Cartoon Gallery,** at the corner of Hogbin Dr. and Albany St. near the airport, is Australia's first and only black-and-white collection of contemporary and classic original cartoons. (☎6651 7343. Open daily 10am-4pm. $2.) Meanwhile, the **Big**

NEW SOUTH WALES

Banana, on the Pacific Hwy. 4km north of town, is quintessential kitsch. Zoom around the plantation on a monorail and learn more than you need to know about banana cultivation methods ($12), try your luck at ice-skating ($12) or tobogganing (5 rides $15), or just gawk at the giant banana out front. (☎6652 4355. Open daily 9am-4pm. Admission to shops, banana, and feelings of inadequacy free.)

ACTIVITIES

There's no shortage of activities and the variety is ever-increasing. Hostels can offer good rates, but don't hesitate to call companies and ask about commission-free fun. Some companies may offer cheaper rates during the winter months.

WATER SPORTS

WHITEWATER RAFTING AND JET SKIING. The **Nymboida River,** two hours west of Coffs, is the most popular place to raft. The rapids, mostly grade 3 to 4 with some grade 5 sections, pass through dense rainforest. The **Goolang River,** a man-made kayaking course, is a steady grade 3. **Liquid Assets Adventure Tours,** the pioneers of sea rafting, runs unbeatable whitewater rafting on the Goolang. (☎6658 0850. Half-day $80. 3hr. sea kayaking $45; 3hr. surf-rafting $50.) **Rapid Rafting** also plunges down the Goolang. (☎6652 1741 or 1800 629 797. Full-day $125, half-day $80.) Award-winning **Wildwater Adventures,** 754 Pacific Hwy. (☎6653 3500), 7km south of Coffs, and **WOW Rafting Professionals** (☎6654 4066 or 1800 640 330), lead one- and multi-day trips down the Nymboida, complete with BBQ dinner. (Full-day $153, 2-day with camping $325, 4-day with camping $560.) **Wild Scenic Rivers** will also take you down the Nymboida for slightly cheaper. (☎6652 1741 or 1800 629 797. Full-day 7am-5pm $150.) **Coffs Water Sports** offers jet skiing. (☎0418 665 656. Single-seat jet ski 15min. $38, 30min. $65; double-seat 15min. $48, 30min. $85.)

SURFING. With the sand as its chalkboard, **East Coast Surf School** has a remarkable success rate with novices. Classes for advanced surfers are also available. Call to arrange pickup from hostels. (☎6651 5515. One 2hr. group lesson $35 per person, five 2hr. group lessons $175 per person; 1hr. private lesson $50.) Most hostels provide surfboards and boogie boards for trying out the waves on your own.

FISHING AND WHALE WATCHING. The fishing boats **Adriatic III** (☎6651 1277) and **Cougar Cat 12** (☎6651 6715) will set you up with bait, line, and tackle. (Half-day reef fishing $65; game fishing by appointment.) Whales swim north past Coffs from June to July and again from September to November. The catamaran **Pacific Explorer** (☎6652 7225 or 0418 663 815) and the **Spirit of Coffs Harbour II** (☎6650 0155) lead whale-watching cruises. (At the Marina. 2-2½hr. cruise $45, concessions $35.)

OTHER ACTIVITIES

ON HORSE. Valery Trails, 25 min. south of Coffs on Valery Rd. off the Pacific Hwy., offers two-hour horseback rides. (☎6653 4301. Daily 10am and 2pm. $35; $10 extra for pickup—call ahead.) **Bushland Trail Rides,** 217 Grays Rd., Halfway Creek, 35min. north of Coffs off the Pacific Hwy., goes to Newfoundland State Forest. (☎6649 4487. 2hr. $38; 3½hr. $68; full-day $120.)

ON WHEELS. 4WD Discovery Tours (☎6651 1223 or 0419 993 965) and **Mountain Trails 4WD Tours** (☎6658 3333) both offer a variety of guided trips to see rainforest, waterfalls, and glowworms. (Half-day $55; full-day $85-88; night tour $48.) **Bob Wallis Bicycle Centre,** at the corner of Collingwood and Orlando St., rents mountain bikes. (☎6652 5102. Open Jan.-Sept. M-F 8:30am-5pm, Sa 8:30am-1pm; Oct.-Dec. also Su 9am-1pm. $20 per 24hr., plus $50 deposit.)

IN THE SKY. Coffs City Skydivers offers tandem skydiving from 10,000 and 8000 ft. (☎6651 1167. 10,000 ft. $304, backpackers $231; 8000 ft. $275/$205. Free pickup.)

ENTERTAINMENT AND NIGHTLIFE

Coffs nightlife, focused around Grafton St., isn't quite as pumping as the daytime scene, but finding the party crowd isn't too difficult; hostels sometimes organize nights out for their guests. Most pubs have cover bands or DJs on weekends.

The popular **Saloon Bar & Nightclub,** 76 Grafton St. (☎6658 0877), is a pick-up scene lacking subtlety, but it does have frequent drink specials and money-saving three-drinks-for-$10 backpacker and student cards available at the coat check; no cover until 11pm. **Hoey Moey Backpackers Pub** (☎6652 3833), on Ocean Pde., has hard rock a few nights a week and a pool competition with free pizza Monday nights. **Coffs Harbour Hotel,** at the corner of Grafton and W. High St. across from the Palms Centre Mall, pours the best drink in town—$5 pints of Guinness. (☎6652 3817. W karaoke, Th-Su live bands.) Some of the cheapest drinks in town are at the state-subsidized **Ex-Serviceman's Club** (☎6652 3888), on the corner of Grafton and Vernon St. You need a passport or laminated driver's license to get in. Friday nights are the most happening, but non-members must arrive before 10:30pm. Many people start their evenings at the club. The **Fitzroy Hotel** (☎6652 3007), on Grafton St. one block south of the Coffs Hotel, has a 24hr. license and often doesn't close until the last person leaves. The **Plantation Hotel** (☎6652 3855), on Grafton St., half a block north of the Coffs Hotel, has a relaxed sports bar and live music on weekends with an occasional cover. The **Greenhouse Tavern** (☎6651 5488), on the Pacific Hwy. across from the Park Beach Plaza, has two bars and live music weekly.

WOOLGOOLGA   ☎02

On its edges, Woolgoolga is an intriguing coastal town. It is flanked to the south by a strikingly-white Indian temple, **Guru Nanak Sikh Gurdwara,** indicating a thriving Punjabi Sikh community, and to the north by a mini-replica of the Taj Mahal, complete with large artificial elephants in the front lawn announcing an Indian restaurant. If you leave the Pacific Hwy. and continue to the town center, however, the novelty disappears but beautiful coastline remains. The views from the **Woolgoolga Headland** of the **Solitary Islands Marine Reserve** (see p. 174), an aquatic sanctuary with marine biodiversity approaching that of the Great Barrier Reef, are fantastic. Dolphin and whale sightings are common from May to October. From the headland, the surfing- and fishing-friendly **Back Beach** stretches to the south and the pristine, patrolled **Front Beach** extends to the north. To stroll in the rainforest, go to the roundabout on the Pacific Hwy. near the elephants and exit onto Pullen St. Drive 3km, veer left at the fork, and then continue another 1km until you reach a locked gate. A short walk along an old forestry road leads to a waterfall.

Ryans buses (☎6652 3201) run to Coffs Harbour (40min.; M-F 5-7 per day; $8.30, concessions $4.60) and Grafton (1½hr., M-F 2 per day, $13). The **Tourist Information Centre** is at the corner of Boundary Rd. and Beach St., the main drag. (☎6654 8080. Open M-F 9:30am-4pm, Sa 9:30am-1pm, Su 11am-1:30pm.) **Internet** is at **Access.Net,** 66 River St. (☎6654 9999. Open M-F 9am-6pm, Sa 10am-5pm. $2 per 20min.)

To sleep in the bush—or near it, anyway—turn left at the town center onto Wharf St. and drive 1km to the end of the road where you'll find the peaceful **Lakeside Holiday Park ❶,** with direct access to the beach and a lake. (☎6654 1210. Sites for 2 from $11-16, powered from $16-22; on-site vans from $24-44; cabins from $40-66.) To sleep in the middle of town, look for a spot at **Sunset Caravan Park ❷,** also right on the beach. (☎6654 1499. Sites for 2 $16-23, powered $19-28; 5-person cabins $45-83.) The ornate, but weary-looking **Raj Mahal ❸** restaurant, behind the artificial elephants, has very good food. (☎ 6654 1149. Open daily 5:30pm-late; also Tu-Su noon-3pm. Meals $9-16.) Though not in Woolgoolga, **Coffs Harbour Dive Centre,** 15min. north of Coffs Harbour, conducts trips to both the north and south Solitary Islands. (☎ 6654 2860. Double boat-dive $80, full-gear hire $33; 2hr. snorkeling $50.)

BALLINA   ☎ 02

Technically an island, Ballina (pop. 18,750) is a peaceful port and beach town 30min. south of Byron Bay. Getting around is surprisingly easy considering the extensive **network of bike paths** linking Ballina and Lennox Head; pick up a *Bike Safe* booklet and map from the Visitors Center. **Lighthouse Beach** and **Pat Morton Lookout** are two great vantage points for whale watching. The 68-hectare reserve at **Angels Beach,** in East Ballina, features playful dolphins, dune ecology, and ocean invertebrates. **Flat Rock,** in particular, has fantastic surfing and an incredible array of marine life occupying three distinct intertidal zones, home to sea anemones, sea stars, octopi, and neptune's necklace (an algae also known as "sea grapes").

■🛈 **TRANSPORTATION AND PRACTICAL INFORMATION. McCafferty's/Greyhound** (☎ 13 14 99 or 13 20 30) and **Premier** (☎ 13 34 10) stop in Ballina on their Sydney-Brisbane runs. The long-distance **bus stop** at the **Transit Centre** is a good 4km from town center, in a large building complex known affectionately as **The Big Prawn** for the enormous pink shrimp nailed to its roof; tickets can be purchased inside the restaurant. **Ballina Taxi Service** (☎ 6686 9999) will take you into town for $10-12. Regional bus companies stop in town at the Tamar St. bus zone. **Blanch's Bus Company** (☎ 6686 2144) travels daily to **Lennox Head** (20min., 7 per day, $4.60) and **Byron Bay** (50min., 7 per day, $7.40).

The **Visitor Information Centre,** on the eastern edge of town at the corner of Las Balsa Plaza and **River St.** (the main drag), has details on area and regional activities. (☎ 6686 3484; balinfo@balshire.org.au. Open M-F 9am-5pm, Sa-Su 9am-4pm.) **Internet** access is at the **Ballina Ice Creamery Internet Cafe,** 178 River St. (☎ 6686 5783. Open daily in summer 9:30am-9pm, in winter 9:30am-6pm. $6 per hr.) The **post office** is at 85 Tamar St. (☎ 13 13 18. Open M-F 9am-5pm.) **Postal Code:** 2478.

■🛈 **ACCOMMODATIONS AND FOOD.** The ⊠**Ballina Travelers Lodge (YHA) ❷,** 36-38 Tamar St., is a motel and hostel combo. Go one block up Norton St. from the tourist office, then turn left. The friendly owners keep the lodge quiet and meticulously clean. The YHA part of the complex has four basic rooms, a separate communal kitchen/TV area, BBQ, and laundry. The larger motel rooms have TVs and lots of amenities. There's a small saltwater pool, bikes (for a nominal fee), limited fishing gear, and free boogie boards. (☎ 6686 6737. Courtesy pickup from the Transit Centre by arrangement. Dorms from $18; twins and doubles $48-56; YHA discount $3.50. Motel rooms $70-109.) The **Ballina Central Caravan Park ❷,** 1 River St., is just north of the info center. (☎ 6686 2220. Open daily 7am-7pm. Sites $16-20, powered $18-22; cabins $38-72). **Paddy McGinty's ❶,** 56 River St., is the local Irish pub and serves counter lunches and dinners. (☎ 6686 2135. Mains from $9. Open daily 11am-3pm and 6-9pm.) Delicious deli food awaits at **Sasha's Gourmet Eatery ❶,** in the Wigmore Arcade off River St. Takeaway selections such as pasta salads, quiches, and fancy sandwiches ($4-7) make for a perfect picnic. (☎ 6681 1118. Open M-F 9am-5pm, Sa 9am-1pm.) Woolworth's **supermarket** is at 72 River St. (Open M-F 8am-9pm, Sa 8am-6pm, Su 8:30am-6pm.)

🖪 **ACTIVITIES. Ballina Ocean Tours** offers 2½-3hr. dolphin and whale-watching tours at 9am and 1pm (☎ 6686 3999. $45-55). Learn to surf or just perfect your technique with **Ballina & Evans Head Surf School.** (☎ 6682 4393. Private 1½hr. lessons in

Ballina $45, in Evans Head $35.) **Forgotten Country,** in Byron Bay, leads half-day to multi-day tours to nearby rainforests, waterfalls, and even an ancient shield volcano. (☎6687 7845. $55-330. Student discount 10%.) **MV Bennelong** conducts cruises along the Richmond River. (☎6688 8266. 2hr. $16.) For self-guided exploring, **Jack Ransom Cycles,** 16 Cherry St., just off River St., rents bikes. (☎6686 3485. Half-day $12; full-day $18, plus $50 deposit.)

NEAR BALLINA: BUNDJALUNG NATIONAL PARK

From the south, take Woodburn-Evans Head Rd. 11km east to **Evans Head,** between Broadwater and Bundjalong National Parks. There is camping at the beachside **Koinina recreation park ❶,** on Terrace St. at the north end of Evans Head. (☎6682 4329. Sites $10, powered $12.)

At Evans Head is a little-known entrance to **Bundjalung National Park;** cross the Evans River Bridge and turn right. The road narrows into dirt track, and several turn-offs lead to rest stops and boat launches on the estuary. Continue 2km to the road's end at the **Gumma Garra Picnic Area.** Three walks begin across the footbridge next to the park and finish at an Aboriginal midden. The **Dirrawong Track** hugs the river and passes through swamp and dry littoral forest. The **Jenna Jenna Track** crosses an Aboriginal campsite, and the **Guweean** leads through a dry forest. Camping is forbidden in these sections of the park. Two kilometers south of the river is **Chinamans Beach,** a favorite among serious surfers.

LISMORE   ☎02

Lismore (pop. 46,000) is a large country town. Wide, tree-bordered boulevards, brick sidewalks, and well-preserved buildings give the town the charm of a slower era, while students at nearby Southern Cross University help to sustain Lismore's cultural venues. A legacy of environmental protection follows naturally from Lismore's surroundings: three World Heritage-listed rainforests and the volcanic remains of Mt. Warning National Park. The disproportionately high number of rainbows (due to the position of local valleys) earn the area the nickname "Rainbow Region." Lismore is refreshingly normal. It's one of the few places where you can walk through the business district without feeling like a tourist target.

⊟ TRANSPORTATION. The **railway station** is on Union St., across the river. **Countrylink** (☎13 22 32) hugs the rails to Sydney (12hr., 2 per day, $98) and Brisbane (4hr., 1 per day, $33). The new **Transit Centre** (☎6621 8620) is on the corner of Molesworth and Magellan St. **Kirkland's** (☎1300 367 077) runs **buses** to: Brisbane (4½hr., 5 per day, $33) via Byron Bay (1hr., $12) and Surfers Paradise (3hr., 2 per day, $31); Murwillumbah (2hr., 4 per day, $17); and Tenterfield (3 hr., M-F 1 per day, $27). Local operator **Marsh's** (☎6689 1220) services Nimbin (45min., M-F 3 per day, $7.50). **McCafferty's/Greyhound** (☎13 20 30) and **Premier** (☎13 34 10) **buses** run once per day to Brisbane (5½hr., $39) and Sydney (11½hr., $81- 92). The best way to get around may be to rent a car. Options include **Hertz,** 49 Dawson St. (☎13 30 39), and **Thrifty,** 147 Woodlark St. (☎1300 367 227). For a **taxi,** call ☎13 10 08.

▇▐ ORIENTATION AND PRACTICAL INFORMATION. In the hinterlands west of Ballina, Lismore lies off the Bruxner Hwy. (called **Ballina St.** in town) just east of the **Wilson** (or **Richmond**) **River.** Approaching the river from the east, Ballina St. crosses **Dawson, Keen,** and **Molesworth St.,** the busiest part of town. Perpendicular to these streets in the town center are small **Conway** and **Magellan St.** and the main thoroughfare **Woodlark St.,** accessible from the Dawson St. roundabout and leading across the river to **Bridge St.** and Nimbin.

NEW SOUTH WALES

At the corner of Molesworth and Ballina St., the **Lismore Visitor Information Centre** has a small indoor tropical rainforest and social history exhibit. (☎6622 0122; www.liscity.nsw.gov.au. Exhibit $1. Open M-F 9:30am-4pm, Sa-Su 10am-3pm.) Other services include: **ATMs** everywhere; **police** (☎6623 1599) on Molesworth St.; **Internet** access at **Lismore Internet Services,** 172 Molesworth St. (☎6622 7766; open M-F 9am-5pm; $5.50 per hr.) and, in the near future, at the visitors center; **Lismore Base Hospital,** 60 Uralba St (☎6621 8000); **post office** on Conway St. between Molesworth and Keen St. (☎6622 1855. Open M-F 8:30am-5pm.) **Postal Code:** 2480.

▐ ACCOMMODATIONS. Currendina Lodge/Lismore Backpackers ❷, 14 Ewing St. (☎6621 6118; currendi@nor.com.au), has neat rooms, TV lounge, kitchen, and a shaded porch. From the info center, go left on Ballina St., cross Keen St., and turn left on Dawson St. Ewing is the 2nd right off Dawson. (Laundry $4. Reception daily 8am-10pm. Dorms $20, weekly $105; singles $28-30/$125; doubles $42/$165.) **Lismore City Motor Inn ❹,** 129 Magellan St. (☎6621 4455), on the corner of Dawson St., features comfy ensuite motel-style rooms with TV, fridge, and A/C. (Pool and laundry. Reception daily 7:30am-9pm. Singles $50; twins and doubles $60; extra person $10.) The **Lismore Palms Caravan Park ❶** is at 42 Brunswick St. (☎6621 7067) and offers basic rooms with kitchen and laundry access. Follow Dawson St. north and turn right onto Brunswick St. (Sites $14, powered $17; cabins $46.)

▐ FOOD. The demand by uni students for cheap vegetarian eats has resulted in some terrifically funky cafes. The cheapest **supermarket** in town is Woolworth's on Keen St., with a back entrance on Carrington St. (Open M-Sa 7am-10pm, Su 9am-6pm.) Many pubs offer cheap lunch and dinner meals.

▨ **20,000 Cows,** 58 Bridge St. (☎6622 2517). No cows are served at this vegan restaurant, with wild tablecloths pinned down by tall candlesticks and comfy sofas. Fresh pasta, Indian, and Middle Eastern food (mains $8-15). Open W-Su from 6pm. ❷

▨ **Dr. Juice Bar,** 142 Keen St. (☎6622 4440). A vegetarian/vegan student haunt. The Doctor prescribes marvelous fresh smoothies, veggie burgers, and wildly popular tofu cheesecake, all for less than $7. Open M-F 9:30am-4pm, Sa 10am-2pm. ❶

Caddies Coffee, 20 Carrington St. (☎6621 7709). The indoor deck, outdoor patio, and beautiful stained glass make this a sure shot, with sandwiches, pasta, and focaccia. Open M-F 8am-6pm, Sa 8am-1:30pm. ❷

◎ SIGHTS

The fabulous **Richmond River Historical Society,** 165 Molesworth St., in the Municipal Building houses a natural-history room with preserved baby crocs and mummified tropical birds as well as a hallway with Aboriginal boomerangs. (☎6621 9993. Open M-Th 10am-4pm. $2.) For a breath of fresh air, there are many parks nearby. **Rotary Park,** in the center of town, is a hoop pine and giant fig rainforest with an easy boardwalk. The **Boatharbour Nature Reserve,** 6km northeast of Lismore on Bangalow Rd., sports 17 hectares of rainforest trees, the remnants of the "Big Scrub Forest." The original 75,000 hectares of lowland forest throughout northern New South Wales has been almost completely deforested. **Tucki Tucki Nature Reserve,** which doubles as a koala sanctuary, is 15min. from Lismore on Wyrallah Rd. Lismore's water supply comes from the **Rocky Creek Dam,** home to a waterfront boardwalk and a platypus lagoon.

NIMBIN ☎02

A popular daytrip from Byron, Nimbin is an experience you won't forget, though as Australia's Cannabis Capital, maybe you will. Galleries and psychedelic streetscape facades attest that the area's artistic talents are as rich as the soil. Since thousands of university students descended on Nimbin Village (pop. 800) for the 1973 Aquarius Festival, Australia's answer to America's Woodstock, the community has retained an image as Australia's hippie and drug capital. Along with their famous relaxed attitude toward drugs, Nimbin's residents also support numerous other liberal causes, including environmentalism, animal rights, and a return to natural living. More than 350 shared communities, some open to the public, are sheltered by the volcanic valley around the town. WWOOF (see **Volunteering**, p. 69) has a strong presence here, and many area farms accept travelers for farmstays and organic farming. Residents' lives are closely intertwined with the land and its fruits, most of which are legal. Life here is, well, interesting.

⌕ TRANSPORTATION. The Nimbin **Shuttle Bus** (☎6680 9189) is the only direct public transportation to the village. It departs daily from Byron Bay at 10am, returning at 2:30pm; in summer a second trip leaves at 1pm and returns at 5:30pm ($25, one-way $13). For visitors who just want a glimpse of the spectacle, Byron-based **Jim's Alternative Tours** stops in town for an hour or two as part of a day-long trip including the area's national parks. (☎6685 7720. Trips M-F 9:30am-6pm. $30.)

⚑ PRACTICAL INFORMATION. Nimbin's commercial district and center is on **Cullen St.**, between the police station and the corner hotel—you can't miss the vivid murals, wild storefront displays, and thin wisps of smoke. **The Nimbin Connexion,** 80 Cullen St., at the north end of town, has info on national parks and regional WWOOFing opportunities, sells WWOOF memberships, and serves as a booking agency for buses and trains; it also has the cheapest **Internet** access in town. (☎6689 1764. Open daily 10am-5:30pm. $4.50 per hr.) The **police** station is on the south end of Cullen St., as is the **hospital,** 35 Cullen St. (☎6689 1400). The **post office** is at 43 Cullen St. (Open M-F 9am-5pm, Sa 9am-noon.) **Postal Code:** 2480.

⌂⌂ ACCOMMODATIONS AND FOOD. Though many visitors to Nimbin come for just the day, the town's hostels are eager to welcome those who wish to take a few days to sample all that Nimbin has to offer. ◼**Nimbin Rox YHA ❷,** 74 Thorburn St., is worth the 20min. walk from town for the fabulous view from the landscaped gardens and decks, not to mention its pool, Internet, laundry, art workshops, and massage center. Take a left onto Thorburn from Cullen St., just across a green stream; the hostel is up a rocky, unpaved driveway through a horse pasture. (☎6689 0022; www.nimbinroxhostel.com.au. Dorms $20-22; doubles and twins $45; 4-person cabins $50.) **Nimbin Backpackers at Granny's Farm ❶** is a 10min. walk from the town center north on Cullen St.; turn left just before the bridge. The creekside lodge has two pools, showers, a large kitchen and TV room, frequent BBQs, and free-roaming horses; platypuses frolic in the creek. Nightly outdoor fires and free breakfast are great icebreakers. (☎6689 1333. Laundry $4. Sites $10 per person; dorms $18; doubles $45. VIP.) For pure living, the **Rainbow Retreat ❶,** 75 Thorburn St., is a 20min. hike from the town center and miles from anywhere else. (☎6689 1262; www.skybusiness.com/rainbowretreat. Free bus from Byron M, W, and F 2pm. Sites $8 per person; dorms $15; brightly colored VW $30; doubles, including the "Love Shack" $40.)

Nimbin eateries, like everything else, are all along Cullen St. The **Rainbow Cafe ❶,** 64A Cullen St., was the first alternative cafe in Nimbin, with focaccia sandwiches ($7) and a sunny garden patio out back. (☎6689 1997. Open daily 8am-5pm.) **Choices Cafe ❶,** 45 Cullen St., grills tofu burgers and meat kebabs for around $6. (☎6689 1698. Open daily 9am-4pm.) A nearby **grocery** store, the Nimbin Emporium, 58 Cullen St., sells health and bulk foods and rents videos. (☎6689 1205. Open M-F 8:30am-7:30pm, Sa-Su 8:30am-6:30pm.) **Bush Theatre/Picture Factory ❷,** just outside the village center on Cullen, has put together a $13 movie/meal deal with wine. (☎6689 1111. Open F-Su, special backpackers nights Tu-W through Granny's Farm. Movies $7.) The **Ellora Vegetarian Cafe ❶**, 81 Cullen St., behind the community center, doubles as a vegetarian Indian cafe and the groovy nightclub **Cave** in summer. (☎6689 1183. Cafe open daily 9am-11:30pm. Lunch special $5.)

◙ ▣ SIGHTS AND FESTIVALS. The mural-covered **Nimbin Museum,** on Cullen St., redefines creativity and historical interpretation. It's complete drug-induced strangeness but at the same time ingenious (or is that redundant?). The rooms relate the founders' version of regional history, with proportionate coverage of all three major historical periods: the first room is about Aborigines, the second about European settlers, and the next five about the hippies. (☎6689 1123. $2 donation.) The **HEMP (Help End Marijuana Prohibition) Party,** which must be one raging party, has its base at the **Hemp Embassy,** 51 Cullen St. (☎6689 1842; www.nimbinaustralia.com/hemp. Open daily 9am-6pm.) The attached **Hemp Bar** offers "refreshments." (☎6689 1842; www.hempbar.nimbinaustralia.com.) On the first weekend of every May, crowds flock to the tiny town for the annual **Mardi Grass.** Events include the Hemp Olympics, where contestants battle it out in everything from a bong-throwing competition to a joint-rolling contest (both artistic and speed). The **Cannabis Cup** lets lucky judges test local growers' products in categories including aroma, size, and effect.

In 1973, the Australian Union of Students created the **Aquarius Festival** as a forum for a new future. An indirect outcome of the festival, and a major employer in Nimbin, is the **Rainbow Power Company,** a 10min. walk from the city center down Cullen St. to Alternative Way, on the right. The building, made of mud bricks, is a remarkable achievement in solar and wind energy production; they even sell their excess generated power to the electricity grid for general consumption. (☎6689 1430; www.rpc.com.au. Open M-F 9am-5pm, Sa 9am-noon. Group tours by advance arrangement; 1hr., $2.) For a hands-on look at earth-conscious living, trek to **Djanbung Gardens Permaculture Centre,** 74 Cecil St. Take a left onto Cecil St. at the southern end of Cullen; the gardens are just after Neem Rd. A resource center offers insights and workshops on organic gardening, permaculture design, village and community development, and more. Ask about accommodations for long-term workshop and class stays. (☎6689 1755; www.earthwise.org.au. Guided tours of the garden Tu and Th 10:30am. In-depth farm tour Sa 11am, other times by appointment. Open Tu-Sa 10am-4pm.)

NEAR NIMBIN: NIGHTCAP NATIONAL PARK

An 8000-hectare park with the highest rainfall in the state and containing the southern rim of the 20-million-year-old **Mt. Warning** volcano crater, Nightcap has two main areas: **Mt. Nardi,** 12km out of Nimbin, and the **Terania Creek/Protestors Falls** area, 15km out of **The Channon** (20km from Nimbin). Mt. Nardi, one of the highest peaks, is accessible on sealed roads and has BBQ and picnic facilities. The viewing platform has info on the walk to nearby **Mt. Matheson** (1½km) and the **Pholi's Walk** (2km), with a lookout to the **Tweed Valley.**

Gravel Terania Creek Rd. leads to Protestor's Falls in the Terania Creek basin and to a picnic area with BBQ, toilets, wood, and shelter. **Camping ❶** is limited to one night. The track to Protestor's Falls (1.4km return) passes **Waterfall Creek** on the way. **Tuntable Falls** in the Tuntable Falls commune is a 120m waterfall (from the parking lot, 3-4hr. return). From Nimbin, the turn-off is 6km down Sibley St., then another 6km. The **Nimbin Rocks,** an Aboriginal sacred site, are another way out of town, toward Lismore. **Hanging Rock Falls** is just 25min. from Nimbin near Wadeville. The natural swimming hole, bordered by basalt columns, is perfect for picnics.

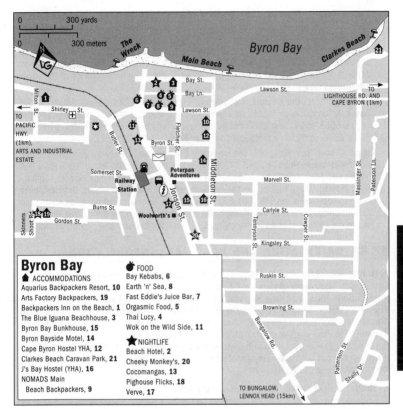

Byron Bay

🏠 ACCOMMODATIONS
Aquarius Backpackers Resort, 10
Arts Factory Backpackers, 19
Backpackers Inn on the Beach, 1
The Blue Iguana Beachhouse, 3
Byron Bay Bunkhouse, 15
Byron Bayside Motel, 14
Cape Byron Hostel YHA, 12
Clarkes Beach Caravan Park, 21
J's Bay Hostel (YHA), 16
NOMADS Main
 Beach Backpackers, 9

🍴 FOOD
Bay Kebabs, 6
Earth 'n' Sea, 8
Fast Eddie's Juice Bar, 7
Orgasmic Food, 5
Thai Lucy, 4
Wok on the Wild Side, 11

⭐ NIGHTLIFE
Beach Hotel, 2
Cheeky Monkey's, 20
Cocomangas, 13
Pighouse Flicks, 18
Verve, 17

NEW SOUTH WALES

BYRON BAY

☎ 02

The "come for a day, stay for a week" coastal malaise that infects a wandering traveler on the Holiday Coast of Australia hits its peak in Byron Bay, one of the most popular stops on the Sydney-to-Cairns route. With Byron's excellent family and surfing beaches and refreshing lack of high-rises and mass consumerism, it's not hard to see why. While Byron feeds its happy, muesli-eating masses with palm reading, massage classes, and bead shops, it's more than just commercialized karma. The relaxed, rejuvenating coastal town with a famously "alternative" attitude is nirvana for its devotees: aged hippies, dreadlocked backpackers, bleached surfers, young families, sharp businessmen, and yoga gurus. Passion for vegetarianism and sunshine is manifest here.

▐ TRANSPORTATION

Trains: Countrylink (☎ 13 22 32) runs to: Brisbane (5hr., 1 per day, $28); Coffs Harbour (4hr., 3 per day, $45); Surfers Paradise (4½hr., 1 per day, $17); and Sydney (13hr., 2 per day, $102).

Buses: Among **McCafferty's/Greyhound** (☎ 13 14 99 or 13 20 30), **Kirkland's** (☎ 1300 367 077), **Blanch's Coaches** (☎ 6686 2144), and **Premier** (☎ 13 34 10), **buses** run to:

Ballina (50min., 5 per day, $8); Brisbane (4hr., at least 10 per day, $35); Coffs Harbour (4-5hr., 8 per day, $53); Lennox Head (20min., 3-7 per day, $5); Lismore (1hr., 2-4 per day, $12); Murwillumbah (1hr., 2-6 per day, $13); Port Macquarie (6-7hr., 4 per day, $68); Surfers Paradise (2hr., at least 6 per day, $29); and Sydney (11-13hr., 8 per day, $93). McCafferty's/Greyhound offers 10% discounts for backpackers. Buses depart from the Bus Depot in the center of town. Tickets can be purchased at **Peterpan Adventures** (see **Practical Info, p. 184**.)

Car Rental: Earth Car Rentals, 4 Middleton St. (☎6685 7472 or 6680 9708). **JetSet Travel,** at the corner of Marvell and Jonson St., hires small, manual cars from $44 per day (☎6685 6554; bustop@lis.net.au). International chains include **Thrifty,** 67 Shirley St. (☎6685 8966; www.thrifty.com.au), and **Hertz,** 11-21 Butler St. (☎6685 6522).

Tours: All tours provide shuttle service to the Channon and Bangalow Sunday markets. **Jim's Alternative Tours** (☎6685 7720; www.byron-bay.com/jimstoursa) offers a great 9hr. trip through Minyon Falls and Nimbin, with a route along Cape Byron for dolphin spotting. $30. Named "Party Tour of the Year" by The International Party Guide. **Grasshoppers Eco-Explorer Tours** (☎0500 881 881; www.rockhoppers.com.au) offers an all-day trip to subtropical rainforest, waterfalls, koala and platypus sighting spots, and Nimbin. In season, they also have whale-watching. $35; includes tree planting and BBQ lunch.

■ 🛈 ORIENTATION AND PRACTICAL INFORMATION

Byron is not on the Pacific Hwy., but is accessible from it through nearby Bangalow. From Bangalow, **Bangalow Rd.** enters Byron Bay from the south. Turn off a roundabout onto Browning St., which leads to **Jonson St.,** the southern boundary of the city center. **Lawson St.** is to the north of town, running at times along **Main Beach.** To the east, Lawson St. becomes **Lighthouse Rd.,** running past Clarkes Beach, The Pass surfing spot, Wategos Beach, the lighthouse, and the Cape Byron lookout. To the west, Lawson becomes **Shirley St.** and curves off to **Belongil Beach.** Farther west it becomes **Ewingsdale Rd.** and passes the **Arts and Industrial Estate** before reaching the Pacific Hwy.

Tourist Office: Byron Visitor Centre, 80 Jonson St. (☎6680 9271; info@visitbyron-bay.com.au), in front of the bus station on the southern edge of town. Friendly staff will book local adventure activities and separate accommodations desk will search the options with you and help you book. Open M-F 9am-5pm.

Budget Travel: Most hostels book activities. At **Peterpan Adventures,** 87 Jonson St. (☎6880 8926 or 1800 252 459; www.peterpans.com), the friendly staff will book most local activities for free. Luggage storage $5 per day. Open daily 9am-7pm.

Currency Exchange: Banks on Jonson St. are open M-Th 9:30am-4pm, F 9:30am-5pm. Other **ATMs** are across the street from the tourist office.

BLOODY HELL! Certain beachfront properties in Byron Bay that are currently worth millions couldn't be *given* away less than 20 years ago. An acre near Clarks Beach that cost only $100 in 1970 is now worth a thousand times that. Why? Byron used to be the home of a whaling station that dumped truckloads of whale blood and parts into the water, transforming the bay into a shark extravaganza during the 1960s. Without tourists coming to stick their toes in the water, the town subsisted on the rather unpleasant business of pig slaughtering. All in all, Byron was a somewhat rough, disagreeable place. Then, whaling became illegal and the piggery closed. Now, too cool for its own good, Byron is an exploding tourist destination, trying to balance its granola goodness with the bucks and backpackers that are scrambling in droves up the coast from Sydney. The lesson? Always buy cheap property on the water. Always.

Taxis: Byron Bay Taxis (☎ 6685 5008). 24hr. wheelchair access and minibuses available.

Police: (☎ 6685 9499), on the corner of Butler and Shirley St.

Internet Access: Internet cafes literally line the streets of backpacker-ready Byron Bay. **The Gossip Shop,** 33 Byron St. (☎ 6680 9556; www.thegossipshop.com.au), is the cheapest in town at $2 per hr. Open daily 9am-7pm. **Global Gossip,** 84 Jonson St. (☎ 6680 9140), at the bus stop, is open late. $4 per hr. Open daily 9am-11pm. Some Internet shops pass out vouchers on the street for cheaper-than-average access. Most activity-booking offices also offer free Internet access with bookings.

Post Office: 61 Jonson St. (☎ 13 13 18). Open M-F 9am-5pm. **Postal Code:** 2481.

ACCOMMODATIONS

In summer, especially around Christmas, Byron floods with thousands of tourists; everything gets packed, and some accommodation prices go up as much as twofold. The best advice is to book early, but demand is so high that some hostels do not take reservations in summer. Many unlucky would-be Byron dwellers make do in Ballina (see p. 178) or Lennox Head (see p. 190).

HOSTELS

Byron has numerous hostels, and the standard of quality is amazingly high, with common amenities like free shuttles from the bus station, activity booking desks, luggage storage, and pools. Most of the hostels have strict 11pm lights-out in the common room and 10am check-out.

▩ **Backpackers Inn on the Beach,** 29 Shirley St. (☎ 6685 8231; www.byron-bay.com.au/backpackersinn). Follow Jonson St., veer left onto Lawson St., cross the railroad tracks, and continue on Shirley St. to the corner of Milton St. A 5-10min. walk to town. The only hostel in Byron with direct beach access. Large, functional, and social. Loft kitchen, volleyball, heated pool, BBQ, pool table, free bus shuttle, cable TV, and Internet ($6 per hr). Free luggage storage, bikes, and boogie boards. Small cafe sells food like veggie burgers and chicken sandwiches for under $6. Reception daily 8am-8pm. Reserve 2-3 days ahead. Dorms $22-24; doubles $56-64. Rates drop $1 nightly after 3 days, another $1 after one week. ISIC/VIP/YHA. Wheelchair accessible. MC/V. ❷

▩ **Arts Factory Backpackers Lodge** (☎ 6685 7709; www.artsfactory.com.au), on Skinners Shoot Rd. Cross the railroad tracks behind the bus stop and take a right on Burns St. to Skinners Shoot Rd. A 10min. walk to town; 10min. walk to beach. Sprawling 5-acre grounds with "funky abodes" ranging from teepees to island bungalows in a lake. Free daily activities include didgeridoo-making, yoga, fire-twirling, massage classes, and drum workshops. Volleyball courts, pool, sauna, laundry ($4), Internet ($4.50 per 30min.), bikes ($8 per day), large shop, cinema, and day spa. Surfboard and bodyboard $15 per day. Weekly talent shows and $7 BBQ. Cafe open for breakfast and lunch; pizzeria and Hare Krishna restaurant open for dinner. Reception daily 7am-noon and 4-9pm. Sites $9-15; dorms $20-26; twins and doubles $42-70; 3- and 5-night and winter discounts. ISIC/VIP/YHA. MC/V. ❶

▩ **Aquarius Backpackers Resort,** 16 Lawson St. (☎ 6685 7663 or 1800 028 909; www.aquarius-backpack.com.au), at the corner of Middleton St., 2 blocks off Jonson St. Formerly a luxury motel. Many of the spacious rooms have 2 levels, porches, and fridges; all have beautiful rosewood beds. Poolside bar with Happy Hours, fully licensed travel desk, parking, kitchen, and cafe where guests receive discounts (pancakes $6). Free boogie boards and shuttle bus. Linen $1, blanket deposit $10. Laundry $4. Key deposit $10. Internet $4 per hr. Bikes and surfboards $35 per day. Reception daily 7am-9pm. Check-in 24hr. Ensuite dorms $23-25; doubles $55-65; self-contained motel units, 2 with spa, $120-220. 3- and 7-day discounts. MC/V. ❷

J's Bay Hostel (YHA), 7 Carlyle St. (☎6685 8853 or 1800 678 195; jbay@nor.com.au). Clean, colorful, and cozy, J's has one of the best all-you-can-eat-and-drink BBQ deals with live music Th ($6). Billiards and picnic tables in an upstairs covered pavilion, very large kitchen, heated pool, and secure parking. Family-friendly. Free use of bikes and boogie boards. Laundry $5. Reception daily 8am-9pm. Book 1 week ahead. Dorms $25-28; twins and doubles $59-73; ensuite doubles $68-88; separate family building $73-88. YHA discount $3. MC/V. ❸

Cape Byron Hostel YHA, (☎6685 8788 or 1800 652 627; www.capebyronhostel.com.au), on the corner of Middleton and Byron St. From the bus stop, go 2 blocks down Byron St. and take a left on Middleton. Pinball machines, TV/VCR, a pool table, and video games in the living room. Upstairs deck and eating area overlooks a heated pool bordered by palm trees. $10 BBQ and wine Tu and F. YHA travel office open 10am-6pm. Free bikes and boogieboards ($20 deposit). Family-friendly. Secured parking. Laundry $4. Internet $1.15 per 10min., $4 per hr. Lockers $4 per day. Reception daily 6:45am-10pm. Dorms $20-29; twins and doubles $60-80; ensuite doubles $70-110. MC/V. ❷

The Blue Iguana Beachouse, 14 Bay St. (☎6685 5298), opposite the Surf Club, on the corner of Bay and Fletcher St. Relaxation in an intimate beachhouse near the town center. Sundeck and screened front porch with couches and TV. Free bodyboards. Off-street parking. Reception daily 9am-noon and 4-9pm. Book 1 week ahead. Linen $2. Ensuite dorms from $28; doubles from $80. 7th night free. No credit cards. ❸

Byron Bay Bunkhouse, 1 Carlyle St. (☎6685 8311 or 1800 241 600; www.byronbaybunkhouse.com.au), opposite the Jonson St. Woolworth's. Crowded and loud, but with $4 dinners that can be eaten on the candle-lit terrace. Live entertainment and BBQ W. Pancake breakfast included. Free linen and boogie boards. Laundry $4. Free Internet 1hr. per day. Key deposit $15. Reception daily 7:30am-10pm. Dorms $19-23; doubles $50-60, ensuite $54-60. Weekly rates available. MC/V. ❷

NOMADS Main Beach Backpackers (☎6685 8695 or 1800 150 233), at the corner of Lawson and Fletcher St. Take a right on Lawson from the beach end of Jonson St. High ceilings, wood paneling, fireplace, rooftop deck, patio, saltwater pool, secured parking, and a common room with TV and pool table. Clean bedrooms have individual lockers. BBQ twice a week in summer, once a week in winter. Laundry $4. Reception daily 8am-9:30pm. Key deposit $20. Book at least 1 week ahead. Dorms $17-25; doubles $45-100. Winter and multiple night discounts. ISIC/NOMADS/VIP/YHA. Wheelchair accessible. MC/V. ❷

MOTELS AND CAMPING

Byron Bayside Motel, 14 Middleton St. (☎6685 6004). Take Byron St. from Jonson St. Great location near the town center and beaches. Large, clean rooms with beautiful furniture, full kitchen, TV, laundry, and sparkling private bathroom; many feature balconies with flowerbeds. Secure parking garage locked 9pm-7am. Off-season singles $70-165; doubles $75-175, extra person $15. Wheelchair accessible. AmEx/MC/V. ❺

Clarkes Beach Caravan Park (☎6685 6496; www.bshp.com.au/clarkes), on Clarkes Beach, off Massinger St. Well-kept sites, some right on the beach's edge. Quiet time after 9:30pm. Reception 7am-7pm. Sites for 2 $20-34, weekly $120-238; powered sites for 2 $23-38/$138-266; ensuite cabins $80-115/$480-805. ❷

◖ FOOD

◪ **Thai Lucy** (☎6680 8083), on Bay Ln., the alley opposite Hog's Breath Cafe on Jonson St. You'll have to wait to get in, but the food is fantastic. Indoor and outdoor seating. Every savory bite worth the price (mains $12-18). Takeaway available. Open daily noon-3pm and 5:30-10pm. BYO. ❷

▓ **Orgasmic Food** (☎6680 7778), on Bay Ln. behind the Beach Hotel . Word is spreading throughout NSW about the self-titled "best falafels in Australia" ($6). When you sample their Middle Eastern fare along with some freshly crushed sugarcane juice, you'll see why. Outdoor seating. Open daily 10am-late. No credit cards. ❶

Earth 'n' Sea, 11 Lawson St. (☎6685 6029). Cheesy, doughy comfort food. The surfer decor and the friendly banter between waiters make this long-running, family-friendly joint a great place to unwind. It caters to "pastaholics," hitting a nerve with anyone who wants to stuff their face with carbo-goodness. Try their original "Beethoven" pizza, a surprisingly delicious combo of prawns, banana, and pineapple. Pastas from $10, 20 different pizza pies from $15. Delivery available. Open daily 5:30-9pm; also in summer for lunch and later hours. AmEx/MC/V. ❸

Fast Eddie's Juice Bar, 7 Jonson St. (☎6685 8805). Fast Eddie's serves up stylish and healthy full meals and iced juicy nectars. The soy-dominated menu has a wide range of veggie options, including tofu burgers ($9) and daily salad specials ($8-10). Ask about upcoming concerts and parties; an informal network of local DJs circulates through. Open daily in summer 8am-10pm; in winter 8am-6pm. ❶

Bay Kebabs (☎6685 5596), at the corner of Jonson and Lawson St. Try the traditional *doner* (lamb and beef), or the highly addictive marinated chicken ($6). Meal deal ($6) gets you a sizable "small" kebab and a drink. Open daily 10am-late. ❶

Wok on the Wild Side, 18 Jonson St. (☎6685 6220). Choose from 5 different noodles and 9 choices of meat and vegetarian options to make your own pasta stir-fry in Malay, Chinese, or Thai sauces. Large portions at $9-12 make this a great dinner option. Open daily noon-midnight. No credit cards. ❷

Supernatural Food (☎6685 5833), at the Arts Factory. Hare Krishna staff prepares "karma free" vegetarian dinners including Indian curries and samosas ($8-15). Candles cast flickering shadows on the lofty ceiling; long wooden tables are surrounded by stone statues, sculptures, and a splashing waterfall. Open daily from 6pm. ❷

◉ SIGHTS

Built in 1901, the **Byron Bay Lighthouse,** at the end of Lighthouse Rd., is Cape Byron's crowning glory and the most powerful lighthouse in Australia. Its steadily rotating beam pierces through 40km of darkness every night. The last lighthouse keeper left in 1988, long after the lighthouse became fully automated. The keepers' cottages are still standing, however; one is a small museum and the other is available for private holiday rental. (Grounds open daily 8am-5:30pm. Tours during school holidays.) A boardwalk leads to the lighthouse, a one-hour walk passing along Main Beach to Clarks Beach and **Captain Cook Lookout.** From here, a walking circuit follows the beach to **The Pass** and winds up a steep gradient past Wategos Beach to the **Headland Lookout,** the easternmost point in Australia and an excellent place for spotting dolphins and whales. The lighthouse is just a short distance farther; the track then heads through forest back to Captain Cook Lookout.

Byron's artistic community is flourishing; the best example is **The Cape Gallery,** 2 Lawson St., which exhibits primarily local artists and a fine pottery collection. (☎6685 7658; www.capegallery.com.au. Open daily in summer 10am-6pm, in winter 10am-5pm. AmEx/MC/V). **Gondwana Gifts,** 7-9 Byron St., has Aboriginal art and free weekly didgeridoo and fire-twirling lessons. (☎6685 8866; info@ozarts.net. Open M-F 10am-5pm, Sa 10am-4pm. AmEx/MC/V.) West of town, the **Arts and Industrial Estate,** off Ewingsdale Rd. (called Shirley Rd. in town), houses a number of stores hawking industrial glass and metals, paintings, sculptures, crafts, and shoes. Colin Heaney **blows glass** at 6 Acacia St. (☎6685 7044. Gallery open M-F 9am-5pm, Sa-Su 10am-4pm; glass-blowing M-Th 9am-4pm, F 9am-2:30pm.)

NEW SOUTH WALES

ACTIVITIES

Many activities offer extended packages up to a week or more for those who wish to sharpen their skills beyond the first stumbling day. Nearly all have free pickup from and return to your accommodation.

SURFING

Boards slung over their shoulders, herds of bleach-blonde surfers trudge dutifully to Byron's beaches every morning at sunrise. Surf schools entice novices by providing all equipment and soliciting through hostels; most have a stand-up guarantee. Byron has excellent surfing spots all around the bay, so no matter the wind conditions there are always good waves somewhere. Just off Main Beach, **The Wreck** is known for waves that break close to the beach. Working down the shore toward the lighthouse, **The Pass** promises long, challenging rides, but can be dangerous because of overcrowding, sharp rocks, and boats. The water off **Wategos Beach,** close to The Pass, is best for longer surfboards, since the waves are slow and rolling. Again, the rocks can be dangerous. **Cosy Corner,** on the other side of the headland from Wategos, has great northern-wind surfing. On the western side of Main Beach, southern winds bring **Broken Head** and **Belongil Beach** alive.

Byron Bay Surf School (☎ 1800 707 274; www.byronbaysurfschool.com). The original surf school in the area. 4hr. lesson $45, 3-day course $110, 5-day course $150. All-female lessons available.

Black Dog Surfing (☎ 6680 9828, after hours 0412 804 970; www.byronbay.com/black-dog). Has multi-day packages. 3hr. lesson $45; 3-, 5-, and 10-day courses and private lessons available. Surfboards full-day $22, weekly $66; wetsuits $10/$40; boogie boards $15/$45. Lessons can be booked through **Bay Action,** 14 Jonson St. (☎ 6685 7819).

DIVING

Most diving is done at **Julian Rocks Marine Park,** 2½km off Main Beach, widely considered one of the best dive sites in Australia. Julian Rocks has both warm and cold currents and is home to 500 species of fish, including the occasional grey nurse shark. Required medical clearances cost $50. Dive certification courses can go up by $70-100 or more during the summer.

Sundive (☎ 6685 7755), on Middleton St. next to the Cape Byron YHA. Has an on-site pool and offers many types of dives. Courses usually start on Tu, but certification courses over two weekends are sometimes offered. 4-day PADI certification $350, in winter 20% discount; intro dives $130, day dives $75, additional trips $55; snorkeling $45.

Byron Bay Dive Centre, 9 Marvel St. (☎ 6685 8333 or 1800 243 483; www.byronbaydivecentre.com.au), between Middleton and Fletcher St. 4-day SSI certification courses start M and Th $450, winter $350; intro dives $135, day dives $75, additional trips $55; snorkeling $45.

KAYAKING AND RAFTING

Byron Bay Sea Kayaking (☎ 6685 7651). Half-day trips along the coast from Main Beach to the Lighthouse allow plenty of time for wave riding. $45.

Dolphin Kayaking (☎ 6685 8044). Half-day guided tour of Byron's marine life, taking guests right up to a school of local dolphins or whales in season. $40.

Wildwater Rafting (☎ 6653 3500). Trips on the nearby Goolang, Nymboida, and Gwydir rivers, with pickup in Byron Bay and Coffs Harbour. From $70.

OUT OF THE SKY

Byron Air Charter (☎ 6684 2753 or 6684 4976). Scenic flights over Cape Byron and Mt. Warning starting at $40 per seat.

Skylimit (☎6684 3711). Motorized ultralight tours from $70. 1½hr. trip to view Mt. Warning $270.

Flightzone Hanggliding School (☎6685 8768 or 0408 441 742). 30min. tandem flights $105. Multi-day courses available.

Byron Airwaves (☎6629 0354 or 0427 615 950). Tandem flights $105.

Skydive Cape Byron (☎6685 5990 or 1800 666 770; www.skydive-cape-byron.com). Half-day tandem dive trips directly over Cape Byron from $229.

Byron Bay Skydiving Centre (☎6684 1323). Dives $229-343. Price depends on height.

New Dimensions Trapeze (☎6680 4104), on Bayshore Dr. Trapeze classes; also squeezes in some tumbling, juggling, trampoline jumping, and sundry circus skills. 2hr. lesson Tu and F-Sa $35; includes pickup.

RUBBED DOWN

Samadhi Flotation Centre (☎6685 6905), opposite Woolworth's. Massages and great-value massage classes. Full-day intro massage classes with breakfast and lunch $50; 1hr. massage $55, backpackers $50. Open M-Sa 9am-6pm, Su 10am-6pm. Book ahead. MC/V.

Relax Haven (☎6685 8304), at the rear of Belongil Beachhouse on Childe St., 2km from town. Much smaller but offers great value. 1hr. float and 1hr. massage $40.

Vision Studios (☎0414 368 057; www.zenshiatzu.com), on Jonson St. where it turns into Browning. Open 9am-3:30pm. Full-day courses in zen shiatsu massage every Tu and Th $45; includes breakfast/lunch.

OTHER ACTIVITIES.

▓ **Rockhoppers,** 87 Jonson St. (☎0500 881 881; www.rockhoppers.com.au), across from Woolworth's. Package deals combine trips and can save you money if you're planning several adventures. All equipment and food included, with vegetarian options. Mt. Warning sunrise trip with champagne breakfast at the top $55; departs 2:30am. Full-day mountain biking $69. "Extreme Triple Challenge" includes abseiling and caving; full-day $119. Learn-to-wakeboard trips $129.

Byron Bay Bicycles, 93 Jonson St. (☎6685 6067). Half-day $12, full-day $26, weekly $85.

Pegasus Park Equestrian Centre (☎6687 1446), 15min. west of Byron. Leads horseback rides and canoe rows along Byron Creek ($35 per hr., $55 per 2hr.) and along the beach ($55 per hr., $75 per 2hr.). Beach rides not offered weekends or holidays.

Seahorses (☎6680 8155), 20min. west of Byron. Offers a 1½hr. forest horseback ride.

▓▓ NIGHTLIFE AND ENTERTAINMENT

Cheeky Monkey's (☎6685 5886), on the corner of Jonson and Kingsley St. Packed with backpackers dancing on the tables and generally being rowdy. Dinner specials $5-7. Open daily 7pm-3am.

Beach Hotel (☎6685 6402), on Jonson St., overlooking the beach. A local favorite of slightly older drinkers, with a garden bar and huge patio. Large indoor stage hosts both local and nationally recognized bands. Live music W-Su. No cover. Open until 3am.

Verve (☎6685 6170; www.vervenightclub.com), on Jonson St., in the Woolworth's parking lot. The new kid on the block, with a movie theater that converts into a stylish nightclub at 9:30pm. Free Internet access and a cafe offering Japanese snacks add respite from shaking your booty. Cover $3-5; no cover before 11pm. Open until 3am.

Cocomangas, 32 Jonson St. (☎6685 8493). Has a slightly calmer and smaller dance floor and affordable drinks. Try the tasty Jam Jar, a mix of juices, gin, malibu, and triple sec for $3.50. M '70s night; Tu R&B; W 1 free drink for the first 75 women; Th R&B and hip-hop. Cover $3-5; no cover before 10pm, in winter before midnight. Open until 3am.

Pighouse Flicks (☎6685 5828), at the Piggery on Skinners Shoot Rd. by the Arts Factory. Shows art and foreign (read: American) films 3 times nightly. Opens at 5pm. 4 shows Sa $11. Movie-and-dinner deal with nearby vegetarian restaurant $16.

NEAR BYRON BAY: LENNOX HEAD   ☎02

Lennox Head (pop. 2300) lies between Ballina and Byron Bay. It's renowned for its excellent **surf**—it has one of the longest right-hand surf breaks in the world, and from June to August it's rated one of the top 10 surfing areas in the world. Lennox is also a great spill-over location if Byron gets too crowded. The highway enters the town on Tourist Rd. The town center is accessible by taking the roundabout to coastal Ballina St., which becomes Pacific Pde. and runs along **Seven Mile Beach,** prime dolphin-spotting territory. The freshwater **Lake Ainsworth** is at the north end of Pacific Pde. **Lennox Point,** 2km south, is an excellent but crowded surf area. **Blanch's Coaches** run through Lennox Head a few times daily to Byron Bay; the bus stop is on Ballina St. near the town center, but you can also flag buses down along Pacific Pde. (☎6686 2144. $5.)

ATMs, food stores, eateries, police, the **post office,** and the local pub are clustered within one minute's walk of each other at the southern end of Ballina St. **All Above Board,** 68 Ballina St. (☎6887 7522), rents surfboards and Malibus (half-day $10) and body boards (half-day $5).

The ▓**Lennox Head Beach House YHA ❷,** 3 Ross St., is north of the town center, just off Pacific Pde. and a short walk from Lake Ainsworth. The intimate beachhouse has free surfboards, boogie boards, bicycles, and fishing rods; unlimited use of windsurfers and catamarans is just $5, and lessons are free. Aspiring gourmets can help themselves to the herb garden and dine in the open courtyard. Once a week, enjoy a massage from their "natural healing center." Bedrooms are small but tidy. (☎6687 7636. Internet $1 per 10min. 4-bed dorms $23; doubles $52. YHA discount $2. Ask about weekly rates.) **Lake Ainsworth Caravan Park ❷** is across Ross St. next to the lake. (☎6687 7249. Sites $14-17, powered $17-20; cabins $33-61.)

MURWILLUMBAH   ☎02

Located in a mountain valley halfway between Byron Bay and Tweed Heads, Murwillumbah (mur-wuh-LUM-buh) is a small country town bisected by the mud-colored **Tweed River**. The town's name (often shortened by locals to "MUR-buh") has several suggested Aboriginal meanings, including "place of high mountain that catches sun" and "place of many possums and people." There are several national parks near Murwillumbah including **Springbrook, Lamington, Mebbin, Border Ranges, Nightcap, Mt. Jerusalem, Mooball,** and **Mt. Warning** (see **Mt. Warning and Border Ranges,** p. 191). Approaching Murwillumbah from the east on the Pacific Hwy., the ancient volcanic plug that forms Mt. Warning dominates the skyline.

Though the majority of town lies west of the Tweed River, you'll find the Pacific Hwy., the tourist office, and the **railway station** on its east bank. **Kirkland's** (☎1300 367 077) buses stop at the corner of Main and Queen St. and continue on to: Brisbane (2¼ hr., 4 per day, $24); Byron Bay (1hr., 2-4 per day, $15); and Surfers Paradise (1¼ hr., 1-2 per day, $18). Southbound **McCafferty's/Greyhound buses** stop at the railway station on the Pacific Hwy.; northbound buses stop outside the tourist info center. In **Budd Park,** at the corner of the Pacific Hwy. and Alma St., is the **Tourist Information Centre,** in the **World Heritage Rainforest Centre.** (☎6672 1340 or 1800 674 414; www.tweed-coolangatta.com.au. Open M-Sa 9am-4:30pm, Su 9:30am-4pm.) To find the town center, cross the Tweed River on the **Alma St.** bridge. Alma St. crosses Commercial Rd. and becomes **Wollumbin St.** A 24hr. Coles **supermarket** is in the Sunnyside Shopping Center at the end of the block. Parallel to Wollumbin St. one block north is **Main St.** (also called Murwillumbah St.), along which are a handful of eateries. **Internet** is at **Precise PCs,** 8 Wharf St. (☎6672 8300. $6 per hr. Open M-F 9am-5pm.)

The ▦**Mt. Warning/Murwillumbah YHA** ❷, 1 Tumbulgum Rd., is a well-kept, color-fully painted lodge. From the info center, cross the Alma St. bridge, turn right on Commercial St., and follow the river less than 1km. The lodge sits on the river-bank, with a fabulous deck directly facing Mt. Warning, and offers free use of inner tubes and a canoe for lazing in the river. There's also a small pontoon moored to the riverbank that sports comfy hammocks and serves as a swimming platform. (☎6672 3763. Kitchen, laundry, separate TV lounge. M, W and F trips to Mt. Warn-ing. Bike rental $5 per day, $50 deposit. Reception daily 8-10am and 5-10pm, and whenever the manager is around. Dorms $23; twins and doubles, including the "penthouse," $48.) The **Hotel Murwillumbah** ❶, 17 Wharf St., offers cheap pubstays on the newly-renovated and clean second floor. Meals downstairs are an unbeat-able $5. (☎6672 1139; www.murwillumbahhotel.com.au. Dorms $15; twins and doubles $30.) Just past the YHA, the small but excellent ▦**Tweed River Regional Art Gallery,** 5 Tumbulgum Rd., awards the world's biggest portraiture prize, a whop-ping $100,000. Past prizewinners hang proudly on the walls alongside moving national and international exhibits. (☎6670 2790. Open W-Su 10am-5pm. Free.) **Stokers Siding Pottery,** 8km south of Murwillumbah in Stokers Siding, offers unique "reduced lustre" work by resident artist Bob Connery and other local artists. (☎6677 9208. Open daily 9:30am-5pm.)

WHIAN WHIAN AND MULLUMBIMBY ☎02

Surrounded by Nightcap National Park, the **Whian Whian State Forest** (WHY-an WHY-an) is another rainforest and waterfall showcase, easily accessible from Dunoon, Mullumbimby, or some of the small villages around Lismore. One of the best ways to see the park is by following the **Whian Whian Forest Drive** (30km; 2hr.). Traveling roughly east to west, the first highlight along the drive is the view of **Minyon Falls.** A bit farther along, a short detour to the right onto **Peates Mountain Rd.** leads to **Rummery Park** (200m), a popular picnic and camping spot, and **Peates Mountain Lookout** (3½km). The lookout is a five- to ten-minute walk from the road. Beyond the junction with Peates Mountain Rd., the Forest Drive continues through logged areas replanted with blackbutt trees, the **Gibbergunyah Roadside Reserve** (a 40m strip of unlogged forest), and the **Big Scrub Flora Reserve.** The drive ends near the **Rocky Creek Dam,** a favorite family picnic stop.

The town of **Mullumbimby** (MUH-lum-BIM-bee; pop. 2700) is so small it doesn't even have a tourist office. It is, however, a convenient stopping place when travel-ling to Whian Whian as well as the **Border Ranges National Park.** Mullumbimby has a string of motels on Dalley St. The **Mullumbimby Motel** ❹, 121 Dalley St., is popular and nicely landscaped. (☎6684 2387. Singles $50; twins and doubles $60.) **Brun-swick Valley Coaches** (☎6685 1385) runs to Brunswick Heads (30min., 2 per day, $4.50), the transfer point for **Kirkland's** (☎1300 367 077), serving Byron Bay (30min., 4 per day M-F, $9). Tucked in the hills, 7km beyond Mullumbimby on Monet Dr. off Coolamon Scenic Dr., is the harmonious, tranquil **Crystal Castle.** If you ever wonder what kind of aura you are radiating, find out here. A photograph and interpretation of your aura costs $25. (☎6684 3111. Open daily 10am-5pm.)

MT. WARNING AND BORDER RANGES ☎02

From a distance, the stony spire of **Mt. Warning** greatly resembles a gigantic thumb extending towards the heavens. Named by Captain Cook in 1770 in an effort to warn mariners of dangerous offshore reefs, and known to the area's Aboriginal people as *Wollumbin* (meaning "fighting chief of the mountains"), **Mt. Warning National Park** today attracts hikers and geology-enthusiasts alike. Formerly a shield volcano with twice the height, most of the ancient lava flows have eroded away, leaving behind an enormous bowl-shaped landform known as a **caldera**—the larg-est in the Southern Hemisphere. The prominent spire in the middle of the caldera

NEW SOUTH WALES

represents the volcano's erosion-resistant central chamber. The summit of Mt. Warning is the first place on the continent to greet the dawn. The climb to the peak offers a fantastic 360° view of the coast and surrounding forest, but in summer the view can sometimes be blocked by clouds. The **Summit Track** (8.8km return; 4-5hr.) is moderately strenuous; the last segment is a vertical rock scramble with a necessary chain handrail. Watching the sunrise is spectacular, especially during the Dry (June-Nov.), although you'll need a flashlight for the climb. Bring your own water, and keep in mind the only toilets are at the start of the walk. To reach the Summit Track from Murwillumbah, take Kyogle Rd. 12km west, turn on Mt. Warning Rd., and go about 6km to Breakfast Creek. *Let's Go* does not recommend hitchhiking, but it is a popular way to get from town to the mountain. The nearest hostel to Mt. Warning is the **Murwillumbah YHA** (see **Murwillumbah,** p. 190). The **Mount Warning Caravan Park ❶** also makes a great base for exploring the mountain. (☎6679 5120. TV room, pool, BBQ, and a few friendly wallabies. No kitchen. Reception daily 8am-5pm. Sites for 2 $15, powered $18; 6- to 8-person vans $33; cabins $44, ensuite $66.)

If you find Mt. Warning too touristed, the gorgeous **Border Ranges National Park** is an ideal getaway. It takes some work to get there, but its seclusion rewards you with the shade of a lush canopy and a great vantage point for viewing the volcano region. Take the Kyogle Rd. west from Murwillumbah for 44km; the Barker Vale turn-off leads 15km along gravel road to the park entrance. Inside the park, the road becomes the **Tweed Range Scenic Drive** (60km; 4-5hr.). The drive exits the park at **Wiangaree,** 13km from Kyogle and 66km from Murwillumbah.

The first picnic area in the park is **Bar Mountain,** with a lovely beech glade. Less than 1km farther is the even more remarkable **Blackbutts** picnic area, with striking views of Mt. Warning and the basin. If heights don't scare you, try the **Pinnacle Lookout,** another 8km north. To reach the **Forest Tops** camping area, travel 4km past the lookout, turn left at the junction, go another 4km, and turn left again. If you turn right instead of left at this last junction, you'll wind up at the **Brindle Creek** picnic area, the departure point for the **Brindle Creek Walk** (10km return; 3-4hr.), a track that winds among rainforests and waterfalls and ends at the **Antarctic Beech** picnic area, home to 2000-year-old trees.

NEW ENGLAND

The **New England Hwy.** is a north-south route that takes you the 566km from Newcastle to Brisbane but through much different terrain than the coastal drive. The numerous inviting country towns dotting its length exude a simple beauty and boast a cooler year-round climate than towns along the coast, and most are serviced by the area's major bus lines. The highway traverses the Hunter Valley, cruising slightly west of Maitland (but tantalizingly close to the vineyards), past Singleton's army base, and through Muswellbrook's coal mines and Scone's horse stud farms. Just beyond Tenterfield, the road begins the climb up and over the Dividing Range, from Tamworth to Armidale, and into New England proper. The **Oxley Hwy.** ventures coastward from Bendemeer, 41km north of Tamworth, and meets Port Macquarie at the coast, 178km east of Walcha. The Oxley comprises a stretch of raw and remote national parks that are nothing short of spectacular. The national parks in New England (clustered in southern Queensland and northern New South Wales) are worth re-routing an itinerary. Unfortunately, most are only accessible by vehicle (some only by 4WD), although **Gumnuts Wilderness Adventures** (☎6775 3990) and **Waterfall Way Tours** (☎6772 2018), both based in Armidale, lead half-, full-, and multi-day trips into the surrounding natural areas. Call the Armidale Visitors Center (☎6772 4655) for an update.

TENTERFIELD AND NEARBY PARKS ☎02

It was in Tenterfield in 1889 that Sir Henry Parkes made his "one nation" speech that foresaw Australian federation. Although it clings to its history with preserved buildings and the Sir Henry Parkes Festival—a celebration of nationhood and community achievements—travelers today know Tenterfield as a base for exploring nearby parks and a stop on the way into Queensland's Southern Downs region.

Tenterfield lies near three national parks; a great map ($8) is available at the Visitors Center or the **NPWS**, 68 Church St. (☎6732 5133), in Glen Innes. **Boonoo Boonoo National Park** (BUNner BER-noo) is 27km north; take Rouse St. south, turn right on Nas St., then quickly bear left on Mt. Lindsay Rd. The next 27km to the park entrance is mostly unsealed. From the entrance, 14km of gravel leads to the stunning, carved-granite **Boonoo Boonoo Gorge and Falls,** the park hub and overnight **camping ❶** area (no water; $5). There is a swimming hole surrounded by wildflowers and grasses upstream from the falls; take the path left of that to the falls. For a less touristy and nearly as impressive look at a giant rock monolith, skip Ayers Rock and head to **Bald Rock National Park,** which showcases the largest exposed granite rock in Australia. To confuse matters, the rock is known to Aborigines as Boonoo Boonoo, but since the name was already taken when the national park was created, founders called it by its white settler name. To reach it, head down Mt. Lindsay Rd. for 29km to a paved road that runs 5km to the park's camping and picnic areas. The **Burgoona Walk** (5km return) is the less steep of two hiking routes to the 1277m summit that provides amazing views of the McPherson Ranges and the Clarence River. **Girraween National Park** (see p. 324) is just west of Bald Rock but is located in Queensland, 9km down a paved road 11km north of Wallangara on the New England Hwy. **Tenterfield Traveller Tours** runs out of the Tenterfield Lodge and provides personalized tours of the area's national parks. (☎6736 1477; call for details and bookings.)

GLEN INNES ☎02

Glen Innes (pop. 10,000), one hour from both Armidale and Tenterfield on the New England Hwy., has a Celtic heritage and constantly finds cause to celebrate it. A full slate of annual festivals complement the changing seasons. Glen Innes' most striking monument is a collection of vertical megalithic **Standing Stones** overlooking the town and valley, an homage to an ancient Celtic form of timekeeping. Resting solemnly on **Martins Lookout,** 1km east of the Visitors Center on Meade St. (Gwydir Hwy.), the Stones bear an uncanny resemblance to Stonehenge.

The main commercial street in town is **Grey St.,** parallel to and one block west of the **New England Hwy.** (called **Church St.** as it runs through town). The **Gwydir Hwy.,** known in town as **Meade St.** and **Ferguson St.,** runs west 65km to Inverell and east 160km to Grafton and the Pacific Hwy. **Countrylink** (☎13 22 32) has **bus** service to: Armidale (1¼hr., 1 per day, $14); Byron Bay (6hr., 1 per day, $14); Grafton City (1¾hr., 1 per day, $27); Sydney (9¾hr., 1 per day, $87); Tamworth (3½hr., 1 per day, $31); and Tenterfield (1¼hr., 1 per day, $27). **McCafferty's/Greyhound** (☎13 14 99 or 13 20 30) send buses to: Armidale (1hr, 3 per day, $35); Brisbane (5hr., 2 per day, $65); Sydney (9hr., 1 per day, $72); and Tenterfield (1hr., 3 per day, $27). Buses stop at various local service stations; contact individual companies for details. Call **taxis** at ☎6732 1300. The **Visitors Center,** 152 Church St., is near the intersection of the New England Gwydir Hwys. (☎6732 2397; www.gleninnestourism.com.au. Open M-F 9am-5pm, Sa-Su and public holidays 9am-3pm.) Grey St. is home to several **banks** with **ATMs, supermarkets,** pubstays, greasy eateries, and the **library** with free **Internet** access. (Library ☎6732 2302. Open M-F 10am-5pm.)

Cheap rooms are available at the **pubs ❷** on Grey St. (Singles $20-25; twins and doubles $35-40.) **New England Motor Lodge ❺,** on the northern end of town at 160 Church St., has much nicer rooms and a swimming pool for a bit more coin. (☎6732 2922. Singles $80-90; doubles $85-95; family rooms $150-160.)

ARMIDALE ☎02

The town of **Armidale** (pop. 22,270) has two claims to fame: it has four distinct seasons and it is the highest city in Australia (elevation 980m). It's also a great base from which to explore the varied and magnificent countryside. The **University of New England** is the oldest regional uni in Australia, and its campus, 5km from the city center, brings energy and business to a healthy number of pubs. The town is also conveniently positioned at the start of Waterfall Way (see p. 195).

Armidale's main drag is **Beardy St.** The **Visitors Center,** 82 Marsh St., is attached to the bus terminal and next to the Pizza Hut. (☎6772 4655 or 1800 627 736. Open M-F 9am-5pm, Sa 9am-4pm, Su 10am-4pm.) **McCafferty's/Greyhound** (☎13 14 99 or 13 20 30) runs to Sydney (10hr., 1 per day, $74) and Brisbane (7hr., 1 per day, $68). **Countrylink** (☎13 22 32) provides limited train service south to Sydney (8hr., daily 9am, $79.20). One block up Marsh St. is **Beardy St. Mall,** Armidale's cluster of shops and cafes. **New England Travel Centre,** 188 Beardy Mall, is helpful for booking trips, buses, and trains in the area. (☎6772 1722; www.newengland.tvl.com.au. Open M-F 9am-5pm, Sa 9am-noon.) For a **taxi,** call ☎13 10 08 or 6766 1111. The Armidale **NPWS office** (☎6776 0000), at 85-87 Faulkner St., has info on area parks. The cheapest **Internet** access in town is at **Armidale Computers,** 100 Jessie St. (☎6771 2712. Open M-F 9am-5pm, Sa 9am-12:30pm. $4.50 per hr.)

The ▨**Pembroke Caravan Park ❶,** 39 Waterfall Way (also known as Grafton Rd. and Barney St. in town), is 2km east of town and has an adjoining **YHA hostel ❷** with a huge recreation room and TV lounge area. (☎6772 6470 or 1800 355 578; www.pembroke.com.au. Free linen. Kitchen attached to dorms. Laundry. Reception 7:30am-6pm. Sites $15; dorms $24, YHA $20; cabins $50-78. MC/V.) **Tattersall's Hotel ❸,** 174 Beardy St. Mall, is a central pubstay with small, quiet rooms. (☎6772 2247. Breakfast included. Singles $28; doubles $44; extra person $11. MC/V.)

The tourist center provides a free two-hour daily tour of Armidale; call to book. Following Marsh St. south and up the hill to the corner of Kentucky St. leads to the much-praised ▨**New England Regional Art Museum.** (☎6772 5255. Open daily 10:30am-5pm. Free.) As you exit the art museum, the **Aboriginal Cultural Centre and Keeping Place** is on your right. (☎6771 1249; www.home.bluepin.net.au/acckp. Open M-F 10am-4pm. Free.) **Waterfall Way Tours,** 5 Canambe St., travels by 4WD to up to six national parks along Waterfall Way and focuses on natural history as well as Aboriginal and European history. (☎6772 2018; www.waterfallway.com.au. Half-day trip $50; full-day trip with lunch $100; overnight tours available.) Horseback riding and fishing are also popular; the Visitors Center has details.

EAST FROM ARMIDALE

APSLEY AND TIA GORGES. The highlights of the eastern end of **Oxley Wild Rivers National Park** (see p. 195) are the must-see waterfalls of the Apsley and Tia Gorges, which are most easily accessed from the Oxley Hwy. The larger part of the park is usually accessed from Waterfall Way, closer to Armidale (see p. 194). About 20km east of Walcha and 83km from Armidale is the turn-off for the **Apsley Gorge,** 1km off the highway. This mighty gorge will take your breath away, even when the dry season reduces the falls to a trickle. At the far end of the carpark is a stairway leading partway into the gorge with a good view of the falls. Swimming in the pool is permitted at your own risk. Beware of sometimes-submerged boulders just in front of the falls. The **Oxley Walk** (2km; 45min.) takes you around the rim of the gorge and across a bridge over the Oxley River. Camping and fresh water are available. Nineteen kilometers south of the Apsley Falls entrance is the small picnic and camping area of **Tia Falls.** A nearby walk shows off the **Tia Gorge.**

Small and unexciting, **Walcha** is still a useful jumping-off point for Apsley and Tia Gorges and the rest of Oxley Wild Rivers National Park. You'll find the **tourist infor-**

mation center and **NPWS outpost** in the Fenwicke House Bed and Breakfast on the Oxley Hwy. (☎6777 1400. Open daily 8am-5pm.) The **Commercial Hotel ❸**, on Churchill Lane off the highway, has food and rooms. (☎6777 2551. Singles $28.)

WERRIKIMBE NATIONAL PARK. Remoteness and poor access roads have preserved the rugged wilderness of Werrikimbe National Park. This is a camper's paradise, gleefully veering from the paths into the depths of temperate and subtropical rainforest, eucalypt forest, and snow gum woodlands. District managers in Armidale (☎6776 0000) or Port Macquarie (☎6586 8300) have info on expeditions beyond the western section of the park. Look closely for the sign for Werrikimbe National Park and Mooraback Rd., which appears 40km south of Walcha. The first 15km of this track isn't bad, but the twisting, climbing, and loose gravel may wear on conventional vehicles. Inside the park, the tracks crumble but remain flat and direct. You can either go left a few kilometers to Mooraback Rest Area or right to Cobcroft's Rest Area. **Mooraback** is set amid snow gum woodlands and by the Mooraback Creek. Walks meander along the creek and deeper into the forest. Campsites at **Cobcroft** are set in open eucalypt forest with a few tree ferns for seasoning. The **Carrabeen Walk** (1hr.) passes through an adjacent warm temperate rainforest. The vivid passage crosses through gullies of Antarctic beeches with gnarled, web-like bases that take on astounding shapes. The **campsites ❶** have pit toilets and firewood.

WATERFALL WAY   ☎02

Waterfall Way (Rte. 78) runs east-west between Armidale and the north coast of New South Wales. Along the way, the aptly-named tourist route passes four excellent national parks with accessible campgrounds, several tiny hamlets, and the charming town of Bellingen (see p. 170). The 169km route is worth the trip, but be cautious on the sometimes steep highway. In addition to the parks below, are the Ebor Falls, approximately 42km west of Dorrigo and 600m off the highway, are an excellent photo-op. A 600m walk from the carpark leads to a scintillating lookout. **Waterfall Way Tours** (☎6772 2018) runs to the national parks (see Armidale, p. 194).

OXLEY WILD RIVERS NATIONAL PARK. World Heritage-listed Oxley is an extensive park of rough, rocky terrain with a network of gorges, campsites, bushwalks, and appropriately wild rivers. Useful pamphlets with photos and maps can help you choose a site to camp or picnic; contact the Armidale **NPWS** (☎6776 0000; armidale@npws.nsw.gov) or **Armidale Visitors Center** (☎1800 627 736; visit@northnet.com.au). For info on **Apsley** and **Tia Gorges** at the more remote eastern end of the park, see p. 194.

Dangars Gorge is an easy 22km trip from Armidale, with the 120m Dangars Falls as the centerpiece. Take Dangarsleigh Rd. (Kentucky St.) from Armidale for about 11km, then go left at the Perrott's War Memorial; 10km of gravel lead to the gorge. The rest area there is equipped with BBQ, firewood, and pit toilets and is the trailhead for a series of walks ranging from the Gorge Lookout path (100m) to 10-14km half-day treks. An eroding, unofficial path from the rest area leads down to the Gorge riverbed and a deep pool, zig-zagging along a steep gradient (2hr.).

Long Point is a secluded wilderness area in an open eucalypt forest adjacent to a rare dry rainforest, a fact that has earned it World Heritage status. The turn-off for Long Point appears 40km east of Armidale along Waterfall Way. A 7km stretch of sealed track passes through Hillgrove, where a left turn skips onto a dirt track that reaches the park 20km down. The attached **campsite ❶** has pit toilets, picnic tables, and fresh water and is the trailhead for the excellent **Chandler Walk** (5km; 2-2½hr.), leading through a grove of mosses, vines, and yellow-spotted Hillgrove Gums, which are found only in this area. A tremendous lookout along the walk surveys the valley and Chandler River.

The **Wollomombi Falls** gorge is severe and the surrounding forest rugged and dry. Turn-off 40km east of Armidale onto a 2km bitumen road leading to the Falls. The strenuous **Chandler River Track** (5.6km; 4hr.) starts here. Alternately, a moderately strenuous 1.2km walk leads to the river, or a 700m path heads to a gorge lookout. There is a bushcamping site near the entrance to the gorge area.

NEW ENGLAND NATIONAL PARK. New England National Park, also World Heritage-listed, offers some fabulous bushwalking trails. Its densely vegetated basalt cliffs flows from several lava flows from the Ebor volcano over 18 million years ago. The park gets chilly in summer and downright cold in winter. Near the park entrance, 85km from Armidale and 75km from Dorrigo, is the **Thungutti Campground ❶**. Nearby begin the Wright's **Lookout Walk** (2½hr.) and **Cascades Walk** (3½hr.). Most people skip these outskirts to head for the **Point Lookout Picnic Area**, the park's hub, with toilets, fire pits, and ample parking. Point Lookout Rd. heads up to the area; about 11km is gravel and 2½km of it is sealed. Point Lookout marks the start of nine walks ranging from 5min. to 3½hr., all of which can be linked for nearly a full day of walking. **The Point Lookout,** a vertical escarpment rising 1564m from sea level, surveys dense forest often shrouded in mist. **Eagles Nest Track** (2hr.) passes straight down and along the steep cliffside. It takes ingenuity to negotiate the rocky areas through moss-covered beeches, snow gum woodland, and water sprays that turn to icicles in winter. The difficult **Lyrebird Walk** links with the Eagles Nest Track and can be made a 2km (1hr.) route or a 7km (3½hr.) circuit. The NPWS also rents three cabins within the park, including **The Residence ❺** ($60-70; sleeps 10); contact the Dorrigo **NPWS** office for details and booking (☎6657 2309).

TAMWORTH ☎02

Coo-ee! Welcome to the country, folks. Tamworth (pop. 38,000) annually hosts the **Country Music Festival,** which brings famous crooners and hordes of people to town (Jan. 17-27, 2003; www.countrymusic.asn.au). The country spirit is otherwise maintained by gallon-hatted city slickers and cheesy tourist attractions such as a giant golden guitar and a concrete slab with handprints of country artists.

▐ **TRANSPORTATION.** The **train station,** at the corner of Brisbane and Marius St., has a travel center that books all buses and trains. (☎6766 2357. Open M-F 8:30am-5:30pm, Sa 8:30am-noon.) **Countrylink** (☎13 22 32) runs express trains to Sydney (6hr., 1 per day, $72). All buses run from the **coach terminal** next to the tourist information center. **McCafferty's/Greyhound** (☎13 14 99 or 13 20 30) travels to: Brisbane (10hr.; daily 10:55pm, also Tu, Th, and Sa-Su 6:50am; $68); Coonabarabran (2hr.; Su-M, W, and F 8:50pm; $17); and Sydney (8hr., daily 5am, $66). **Kean's Travel Express** (☎6543 1322) goes to Port Macquarie (8hr.; M, W, and F; $65); and Scone (2½hr.; Tu, Th, and Su; $17). **Budget** (☎13 27 27) hires cars from $39 per day. **Avis** (☎6760 7404) sometimes offers deals for multi-day car hire. Call **Tamworth Radio Cabs** for a taxi (☎13 10 08 or 6766 1111).

▐ **PRACTICAL INFORMATION.** Tamworth is 412km north of Sydney on the New England Hwy. (which enters the town from the east and departs south) and is a convenient rest stop on a journey to Brisbane (578km). The town center lies along **Brisbane St.,** which crosses the Peel River, becoming **Bridge St.** in West Tamworth. The **Visitors Center** is at the corner of Peel and Murray St. (☎6755 4300; www.tamworth.nsw.gov.au. Open daily 9am-5pm.) The **library**, 203 Marius St., has free **Internet** access. (☎6755 4460. Open M-Th 10am-7pm, F 10am-6pm, Sa 9am-2pm. Book ahead.)

⚑◻ ACCOMMODATIONS AND FOOD. Most rooms for January's Country Music Festival are booked by the previous March, and numerous places will not take reservations for that week; throughout the rest of the year, beds are plentiful. The ☒**YHA Country Backpackers ❷**, 160 Marius St., is opposite the train station and has a well-equipped kitchen and clean, bright rooms with A/C. (☎6761 2600. No heat, but blankets are provided in winter. Linen and breakfast included, towels $1. Laundry $6. Free pickup from the bus station. Internet $1 per 15min. Dorms $20-22; doubles $46.) **Tamworth Hotel ❸**, 147 Marius St., also opposite the train station, is the most upscale pubstay. The downstairs **restaurant ❶** has breakfast deals from $6-9. (☎6766 2923. Singles $30. AmEx/MC/V.) **Paradise Caravan Park ❶**, next to the Visitors Center along the creek, has grills and a playground. (☎/fax 6766 3120. Linen $5 per single, $7 per double; laundry $4.40. Key deposit $5. Reception 7am-7pm. Sites for 2 $14, powered $19; budget cabins for 2 $44; cabins with A/C, kitchen, and TV $55. Off-season 7th night free. MC/V.)

Each end of Peel St. is marked by locally beloved cafes. The **Inland Cafe ❷**, 407 Peel St., is cosmopolitan and chic in its decor and atmosphere. (☎6761 2882. Open M-W 7am-6pm, Th-Sa 7am-11pm, Su 9am-5pm; in winter M-W and F-Sa 7am-6pm, Th 7-11am, Su 9am-4pm. MC/V.) The **Old Vic Cafe ❷**, 261 Peel St., frequented by a relaxed local clientele, is a bit more laid-back and sells its own homemade sauces and vinaigrettes. (☎6766 3435. Open M-F 8am-5:30pm, Sa 8am-4pm, Su 9am-noon. BYO. MC/V.) Both serve up gourmet mains ($15) like grilled tiger prawns and goat cheese frittata to the delight of locals who pack them both at mealtime. **The Coffee Bean ❶**, Shop 18, Tamworth Arcade at 345 Peel St., takes coffee-brewing seriously; they also have a more whimsical line of pastries and cakes, as well as **Internet** access. (☎6766 3422. Open M-W and F 8am-5pm; Th 8am-7pm; Sa 8am-3pm. Internet $7 per hr. MC/V.) There are a number of Thai and Chinese eateries on the main drag. Coles **supermarket** is at 436-444 Peel St. in the K-Mart shopping plaza. (Open 24hr., except Sa noon to Su 8am, Su 8pm to M 6am. AmEx/MC/V.)

◪ SIGHTS AND ACTIVITIES. You don't have to be a country music fan to enjoy Tamworth—you just need a high tolerance for kitsch. The turn-off for **The Golden Guitar Complex,** south of town on the New England Hwy., is marked by, predictably enough, a gaudy 12m golden guitar. Inside, a realistic "Gallery of Stars" **wax museum** dresses 22 replicas in the donated clothes of the crooning stars themselves, including Slim Dusty. In an odd juxtaposition, a large gem and mineral display shares the complex. (☎6765 2688; www.big.goldenguitar.com.au. Open daily 9am-5pm. $6, children $3, families $14.) The popular **Hands of Fame Cornerstone** is on the corner of the New England Hwy. and Kable Ave. This cement memorial holds the imprints of country music celebrities. Also check out **Joe Macguires' Noses of Fame,** 148 Peel St. (☎6766 2114), a 15min. walk west of town, for a more comical monument to country. For real devotees, the **Australian Country Music Foundation,** 93 Brisbane St., is an archive with a small museum. (☎6766 1577. Open M-Sa 10am-2pm. $5.50, concessions $3.30)

Bring out your inner cowboy or cowgirl at one of the **"Jackaroo and Jillaroo schools"** in the Tamworth area, with crash courses on how to ride horses, train dogs, milk cows, lasso, operate farm equipment, and muster cattle from the saddle. Certificates and help finding **jobs** are given upon completion. ☒**Leconfield** runs a highly recommended school of this type about an hour out of Tamworth. If you're lucky, they'll even let you castrate a baby lamb the old fashioned way—with your teeth. (☎6769 4328; www.leconfield.com. 5-day course from $375, begins M. Free Tamworth pickup at the YHA.) For an insider's perspective on Jackaroo school, see **The Local Story,** p. 224.

Parallel to Peel St., one block south along the river, is **Bicentennial Park,** a reclusive stretch of greenery, ponds, and picnic tables. (Open daily 8am-4:45pm.) The **Oxley Scenic Lookout** at the top of White St. gives a bird's-eye view of the bustling city. It also marks the start of the **Kamilaroi Walking Track** (6.2km), a scenic tour that passes by the **Endeavour Drive Marsupial Park,** past the top end of Brisbane St., with its free-roaming 'roos, echidnas, and red-necked wallabies. (Open daily 8am-5pm.) A lighter **Heritage Walk** (4.7km) loops through town, starting at the corner of Kable and Brisbane St.

■■ **ENTERTAINMENT AND NIGHTLIFE.** Tamworth is a backcountry town, and nightlife here has a very local flavor. Local teens too young to drink cruise the streets on weekend nights, but their older siblings fill the pubs most nights of the week. Most establishments close after 2am, but the standard 1 or 1:30am curfews mean that if you want to stay later, you better be in the door by that time. The **RSL Club,** behind Peel St. on Kable Ave., is really the only constantly country live venue. (☎6766 4661. Th "country music jamboree." Generally no cover. Open Th-Sa 7:30pm, Su 2:30pm.) The **Imperial Pub,** on the corner of Marius and Brisbane St., draws a mix of ages. (☎6766 2613. Live mainly rock music Th-Sa. Curfew 1:30am.)

SOUTH COAST

Princes Hwy., south of Sydney, is the string that links the pearls of the South Coast. All of New South Wales' undiscovered seaside treasures—towns such as Kiama and Narooma, and natural areas such as Booderee National Park—reward those who seek them out. Exploring this coast can be a refreshing escape from the hectic pace of the city and other tourist-mobbed places.

WOLLONGONG   ☎02

Directly down the coastline, about 80km from Sydney, Wollongong (WOOLEN-gong) suffers from the city-versus-town identity crisis that plagues many of Australia's mid-sized cities. New South Wales' third-largest metropolitan area (pop. 230,000), Wollongong has a city center small enough to be walkable yet urban enough to be unattractive. The easy view of Port Kembla's steel, coal, and grain plants, collectively labeled "Australia's Industry World," showcases the most concentrated industrial area in the entire country. Still, it's close enough to the peaks of the Illawarra Escarpment and the waters of the Tasman Sea to allow for adrenaline-pumping activities, and some of the best surfing is within easy reach.

■ **TRANSPORTATION. CityRail trains** (☎13 15 00) stop at Wollongong City Station on Station St. and run to: Bomaderry, near Nowra (1½hr., 4-10 per day, $9); Kiama (45min., 11-16 per day, $5.20); and Sydney (1½hr., 12-28 per day, $9). **Buses** arrive at Wollongong City Coach Terminus (☎4226 1022), on the corner of Keira and Campbell St., and run to: Batemans Bay (3-3¾hr., 2-3 per day, $32); Bermagui (6hr., 1 per day, $44); Melbourne (15hr., 1 per day, $67); Narooma (4½-5¼hr., 2-3 per day, $43); Sydney (1½-2hr., 1-3 per day, $13); and Ulladulla (2¾hr., 2-3 per day, $25). **Murrays** (☎13 22 57) runs to Canberra (3½hr., 1 per day, $32).

■■ **ORIENTATION AND PRACTICAL INFORMATION.** The Princes Hwy. leads directly into Wollongong, becoming **Flinders St.** just north of the city center and merging into **Keira St.** downtown. The **pedestrian shopping mall** on Crown St., between Keira and Kembla St., is the city's commercial heart. **ATMs** are abundant here. **Tourism Wollongong,** 93 Crown St., is on the corner of Crown and Kembla St.

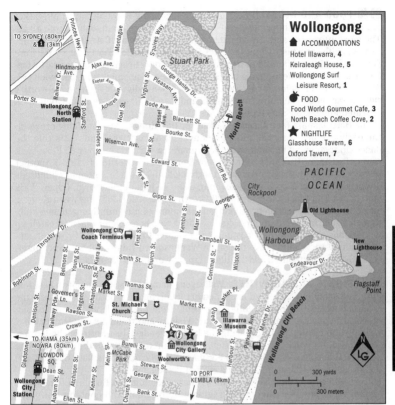

(☎4227 5545 or 1800 240 737; fax 4226 6629. Open M-F 9am-5pm, Sa 9am-4pm, Su 10am-4pm). **Network Cafe,** 176 Keira St., has **Internet** access. (☎4228 8686. Open M-W 10am-6pm, Th 10am-10pm, F 10am-midnight, Sa 9:30am-midnight, Su 10am-5pm. $6 per hr.) The **post office** is at 324 Crown St. (☎4229 1609. Open M-F 6am-5:30pm, Sa 6am-noon, Su 6-11am.) **Postal Code:** 2500.

⌐ ACCOMMODATIONS. Keiraleagh House ❷, 60 Kembla St., between Market and Smith St., is Wollongong's cheapest and friendliest option, though the house and backyard show their age. (☎4228 6765; backpack@primus.com.au. Light breakfast included. Laundry, kitchen, and TV lounge. Key deposit $10. Bunks $17; singles $25, ensuite $35; doubles $45; family rooms $50-60.) Rooms in the **Hotel Illawarra ❸,** on the corner of Market and Keira St., are not as swanky as the nightclub downstairs, but they're tidy and easy to crawl home to after an evening of your favorite schooners. Rooms get noisy on weekends due to the bar below. (☎4229 5411; fax 4229 5140. Laundry $2. Key deposit for 1st-floor rooms $50, for 2nd-floor rooms $20. Singles $35; doubles $65-70.) **Wollongong Surf Leisure Resort ❷,** on Pioneer Rd. in Fairy Meadow, is the nearest campground, 4½km north of downtown, a 15min. walk from Fairy Meadow CityRail station. Inquire at Tourism Wollongong for directions. (☎4283 6999. Laundry, pool, spa, and indoor tennis courts. Hot shower 10¢ per 5min. Bicycle hire $5 per 1hr. Key deposit $20. Reception M-Sa 8am-9pm, Su 8am-6pm. Sites for 2 $16.50, powered $20; extra person $5.50.)

🔲🔳 **FOOD AND NIGHTLIFE.** The restaurants lining Keira St., north of Market St., cover an astonishing variety of Asian cuisines with main dishes from $9-12. The most affordable and always packed **Food World Gourmet Cafe ❶**, 148 Keira St., serves healthy and tasty Chinese dishes from $6-9. (☎ 4225 9655. Open Su-W 11am-8pm, Th-Sa 11:30am-9pm.) For a picnic lunch at North Beach, stop in at nearby **Coffee Cove ❶**, on Bourke St. half a block from the ocean, and pick up a sandwich ($3-6) or a fresh fruit salad for $3. (☎ 4229 7876. Open daily 7am-4pm.) Woolworth's **supermarket** is on the corner of Kembla and Burelli St. (☎ 4228 8066. Open M-Sa 7:30am-midnight, Su 8am-10pm.)

The **Hotel Illawara** (see **Accommodations,** p. 199) draws a 20-something crowd in the early evening for cocktails and conversation. On weekends, DJs rule the dance-floor spinning music into the wee hours. (☎ 4229 5411. Cover $5 F-Sa; back room after 1am $10. Open 24hr., except from Su midnight to M 11am.) Another favorite night spot, the **Bourbon Street Night Club,** 150 Kiera St., often has hundreds of party-goers lined up as early as 8pm, eager to join the in-crowd. (Open W-Sa 8pm-3am.) The **Glasshouse Tavern,** 90 Crown St. (☎ 4226 4305), between Kembla and Corrimal St., has recently changed into more of a tavern than a dance club, though good times still abound. Its late-night cafe is a quieter place to catch up with friends. At the alternative, student-dominated, **Oxford Tavern,** 47 Crown St., up-and-coming rock bands take the stage Wednesday, Friday, and Saturday night. (☎ 4228 3892. Open Su-Tu and Th 10am-11pm, W and F-Sa 10am-3am.)

🔳🔲 **SIGHTS AND ACTIVITIES. Wollongong Harbour** is by far the city's best feature. The small cove, created using convict labor, shelters both sailboats and the local fishing fleet. The old lighthouse, visible from the beach, adds an air of old-time charm absent from the city's center. Visitors and residents enjoy a beautiful walking and cycling path following the harbour's edge. Just north of the harbor, surfers wait for waves at North Beach. If you want to break into the surfing scene or just refine your technique, **Pines Surfriders School** can help. (☎ 0500 824 860. $39 per hr., students $33; group booking $22 per person, min. 3.)

The 🔳**Wollongong City Gallery,** on the corner of Kembla and Burelli St., creatively displays a fabulous collection of regional, Aboriginal, and contemporary art. (☎ 4228 7500. Open Tu-F 10am-5pm, Sa-Su noon-4pm. Free.) **Hangdog Climbing Gym,** 130 Auburn St., offers both outdoor rock-climbing courses and 100 different indoor climbs on 40 ropes. (☎ 4225 8369. Open M-F 10am-9pm, Sa-Su 9am-6pm. Entry $14, harness included.) South of Port Kembla, **Lake Illawarra** draws crowds from Wollongong in good weather. CityRail **trains** run to Port Kembla station, just a short walk from the lake. (10min., 18-31 per day, $2-3.)

🔳 **DAYTRIPS FROM WOLLONGONG.** The winding Bulli Pass road twists inland to the Southern Fwy., 12km north of Wollongong, and leads to a magnificent panoramic view of the area. Down at sea level, Wollongong's biggest attractions await at **Bulli Point** (also know as **Sandion Point Headland**), and farther north, **Austinmer Beach.** Beach bums flock to Bulli or Thirroul for some of the area's best surfing. CityRail runs from Wollongong ($2). English writer D.H. Lawrence resided in **Thirroul,** between Bulli and Austinmer, for several months in 1922 and described the area in his novel *Kangaroo.* The home is privately owned and inaccessible to the public, but the beach is open for strolling and literary speculation. North of Bulli Pass, **Lawrence Hargrave Dr.** winds along the coast, providing tantalizing glimpses of the shore below, before reaching the lookout at **Bald Hill,** north of **Stanwell Park,** perhaps the best view on this stretch of coast.

The **Illawarra Escarpment** defines Wollongong's inland border. The nearest peak, **Mt. Keira,** is a short drive from town on Mt. Keira Rd. Take bus #39 to get within

8km of Mt. Keira's peak. Bushwalking trails lead to a fantastic view from the top. In the southern suburb of **Berkeley,** on the north shore of Lake Illawarra, **Nan Tien Temple,** the largest Buddhist Temple in the Southern Hemisphere, towers above the horizon and welcomes visitors. (☎ 4272 0600. Open Tu-Su 9am-5pm. Donation for entry to museum and offerings. Wheelchair accessible.) **Rutty's bus** #34 goes from the bus terminal on Marine Dr. to the temple ($3.20). The **Cockatoo Run,** a scenic mountain railway, stops at Wollongong City Station and offers day-long excursions that climb over the escarpment into the highlands and back. (☎ 1300 653 801. Operates W and Su 1 per day most of the year; departs Wollongong 10:55am, returns 4:35pm. Bookings required in summer. $40, children $30, families $110.)

KIAMA
☎ 02

Under the right conditions, when the wind is high and the waves surge from the southeast, water washing into a sea cave in Kiama (KAI-amma) is forced noisily upward through a hole in the rocks to heights of 20-35m. Reminding visitors of a whale spouting, the oceanic "geyser" attracts onlookers from miles around. Stand well back from **Kiama's Blowhole,** as a surprising blast of water could potentially knock the overzealous into the turbulent surf below the craggy cliffs. Appropriately, the word *Kiama* means "sound of the sea." Even if the wind and waves don't comply, Kiama and the surrounding area make for a worthwile coastal stop. Situated 40km south of Wollongong via the Princes Hwy., Kiama and the nearby beaches at Gerringong and Gerroa lie within a reasonable daytrip of Sydney.

▛▌ TRANSPORTATION AND PRACTICAL INFORMATION. From the **CityRail** station, on Bong Bong St., just west of Blowhole Point, **trains** (☎ 13 15 00) run to: Bomaderry/Nowra (30min., 10-15 per day, $4); Sydney (2hr., 12-16 per day, $13); and Wollongong (45min., 13-17 per day, $5). From the Bombo Railway Station, **Premier Motor Service** (☎ 13 34 10) runs **buses** to: Batemans Bay (2½-3¼hr., 2-3 per day, $32); Bega (5-5½hr., 2-3 per day, $47); Bermagui (5¼hr., 1 per day, $44); Melbourne (15hr., 1 per day, $67); Narooma (4-4¼hr., 2-3 per day, $43); Nowra (40min., 2-3 per day, $14); Sydney (2½hr., 2-3 per day, $19); Ulladulla (2¼hr., 2-3 per day, $14); and Wollongong (35min., 2-3 per day, $13). **Ilawara Buslines** (☎ 4271 1322) often has cheaper rates to similar destinations. Dotted with trees, historic buildings, and takeaways, Manning St. is the main street in town. The center of tourist life is **Blowhole Point,** down Terralong St., toward the coast. The **Visitors Center** is on Blowhole Pt. (☎ 4232 3322 or 1300 654 262. Open daily 9am-5pm.) **Internet** access is available in the Kiama **Library,** 7 Railway Pde. (☎ 4233 1133. Bookings required. Open M and W-F 9:30am-5:30pm, Tu 9:30am-8pm, Sa 9:30am-2pm. $3.30 per hr.) The **post office** is at 24 Terralong St. (☎ 13 13 13. Open M-F 9am-5pm.) **Postal Code:** 2533.

▛▐ ACCOMMODATIONS AND FOOD. The **Kiama Backpackers Hostel ❷,** 31 Bong Bong St., a few steps downhill from the CityRail Station, feels a bit like a university dormitory but manages to preserve the backpackers spirit. (☎/fax 4233 1881. TV, kitchen. Internet $5 per hr. Key deposit $10. Free use of bikes, fishing reels, and surfboards. Dorms $16; singles $21, F-Sa $23; twins and doubles $37/$42.) Behind the Visitors Center on Blowhole Point, the **Blowhole Point Holiday Park ❷** reveals picturesque views of the harbor. (☎ 4232 2707. Sites for 2 $22, powered $25; caravans and motor homes $55-72.)

For a bite to eat with a view of the ocean, locals recommend the fish 'n' chips ($6.50) at the **Kiama Harbour Takeaway ❶,** below the Blowhole Point Holiday Park, in the beige building nearest the mainland. (☎ 4232 1138. Open daily 10:30am-6:30pm, later during summer.) The **Coffee Table Bookshop ❶,** 2/3 Railway Pde., serves up delicious breakfasts and an assortment of gourmet sandwiches for $7-10. (☎ 4233 1060. Open M-Sa 9am-5pm, Su 10am-4pm.)

NEW SOUTH WALES

◼ ◪ **SIGHTS AND ACTIVITIES.** Every visitor to Kiama should give the **Blowhole** a chance to do its trick. It's an impressive show. At **Marsden Head,** at the end of Tingira Crescent, near the Endeavour Lookout, the **Little Blowhole** erupts more regularly than its highly celebrated larger sibling. It's worth the extra trip if Big Brother proves to be a disappointment. For swimming, check out either the **natural rock pool** on the northern side of Blowhole Point or the deeper rock pool, north of Kiama Harbour at Pheasant Point. To the north of Pheasant Point, experienced **surfers** brave the riptides at **Bombo Beach.** Slightly north of Bombo Beach, just around the next headland, sightseers will discover the striking rock formation known as **Cathedral Rock.** Surfers refer to this same area as the **Boneyard,** but despite the menacing nickname, it's a popular spot for catching waves. Don't be fooled, though—it's still no place for novices. To the south of Blowhole Point, surfers and swimmers frequent the patrolled **Surf Beach.** The next stop on a surfer's tour of the Kiama area lies 8km south at **Werri Beach** in Gerringong. For those who get tired of just idly gazing out across the ocean, **Kiama Charter Service** (☎ 4237 8496), **Kiama Harbour Game and Reef Fishing Charter** (☎ 4232 1725), and **Signa Charter** can send you out on the deep sea for some sport fishing. (☎ 4233 1020. 7hr. $65-70, including bait and gear.)

The **Saddleback Mountain Lookout** offers a vista that can extend from Wollongong to Jervis Bay on clear days. Follow Manning St. south until it bends inland, then proceed straight onto Saddleback Mountain Rd. at the edge of town. The steep path up the mountain is signposted from Saddleback Mountain Rd. Farther west, the **Barren Grounds Nature Reserve** is accessible by Jamberoo Mountain Rd. by way of Tourist Dr. 9 through Jamberoo. The reserve contains several moderate **hiking trails,** from 2km to 19km. The area is known as the home to over 160 species of birds. Turning off Jamberoo Mountain Rd. leads nature-lovers to **Minnamurra Rainforest** (☎ 4236 0469) in **Budderoo National Park,** a rare tract of subtropical rainforest with two delightful bushwalks originating from the Visitors Center. The **Rainforest Walk** (1.6km; 2hr.), a looping, boardwalked track, tours the unusual plant life in the park. The longer, steeper walk to the **Minnamurra Falls** (2.6km; 3hr.) branches off from the Rainforest Walk and rewards hikers with gorgeous falls. (Open daily 9am-4pm. Rainforest access until 3pm, waterfall access until 4pm. $10 per car.)

NOWRA AND BOMADERRY ☎ 02

Every sign in the Shoalhaven directs you to Nowra. Smaller sibling Bomaderry lies immediately north, across the Shoalhaven River. Together, they are the population centers of the shire. Rock climbers come from all over for what many claim to be the best sport climbing in Australia.

◼ ◪ **TRANSPORTATION AND PRACTICAL INFORMATION. CityRail's** (☎ 13 15 00) last stop is in Bomaderry on Railway St. **Trains** run to: Kiama (30min., 12-15 per day, $4); Sydney (2¾hr., 12-15 per day, $15); and Wollongong (1½-2hr., 9 per day, $8.50). **Premier** (☎ 13 34 10) **buses** run to: Batemans Bay (1¾hr., 2-3 per day, $20); Bega (4¼hr., 2-3 per day, $35); Bermagui (4hr., 1 per day, $32); Kiama (40min., 2-3 per day, $12); Melbourne (13½hr., 1 per day, $63); Narooma (2¾hr., 2-3 per day, $30); Sydney (3-3¼hr., 2-3 per day, $18); Ulladulla (1hr., 2-3 per day, $13); and Wollongong (1¼hr., 2-3 per day, $12). **Kennedy's Coaches** (☎ 4421 7596 or 0411 232 101) services Fitzroy Falls (1hr., 1 per day, $10) and Kangaroo Valley (30-60min., 2 per day, $7). The **Shoalhaven Shuttle** (☎ 4422 8333) runs door-to-door express service to Sydney Airport (1-2 per day, $45). The **police station** (☎ 4421 9699) is on Kinghorn St. The **post office** (☎ 4421 3155) is at 59 Junction St. (Open M-F 9am-5pm, Sa 9am-noon.) **Postal Code:** 2541.

The new **Shoalhaven Visitors Centre** lies on the corner of Princes Hwy. and Pleasant Way, south of the bridge to Nowra, on the left. (☎ 4421 0778 or 1800 024 261; www.shoalhaven.nsw.gov.au. Open daily 9am-4:30pm.) The **National Parks and**

Wildlife Service, 55 Graham St., Nowra, has info on parks in the area. (☎ 4423 2170; fax 4423 3122. Open M-F 8:30am-5pm.) **Flatearth Internet Cafe,** Level 1, Nowra Mall, has **Internet** access (☎ 4423 7771; open M-F 9am-5pm; $6 per hr.) as does the **Nowra Public Library** on Berry St. (☎ 4429 3705. $2 per hr.) For ideas about what to do in Nowra and throughout the South Coast, visit www.nowrabackpackers.com.

⌂ ACCOMMODATIONS. Due to its proximity to Berry, Kangaroo Valley, and Jervis Bay, many choose to stay in Nowra when exploring the area. The historic, 1920s bungalow-style **M&M's Guesthouse ❷,** 1A Scenic Dr., on the right just across the bridge into Nowra, transports lodgers back to a bygone era. (☎ 4422 8006; www.mmguesthouse.com. Laundry, TV, pool table, and kitchen. Internet access $2 per hr. Dorms $20, with brekkie $25; doubles $60, includes breakfast.) For scenic camping sites, head for **Nowra Animal Park ❶.** From Bomaderry, take a right on Illaroo Rd., just before the grey metal bridge to Nowra; follow McMahon's Rd. left from the roundabout, and take a left on Rockhill Rd. The owner can also direct travelers to local rock climbing sites. (☎/fax 4421 3949. Toilets and hot showers. Reception 8am-5pm. Sites $5.50 per person; powered $8.) Separate from the campground is a rehabilitation center for wombats, koalas, and other animals; the park is open to the public ($10, campers $7.50; children $5/$4; families $26.)

⚠ ROCK CLIMBING AND OTHER ACTIVITIES. Most area climbers recommend **Thompson's Point,** on the southern shore of the Shoalhaven river and find PC, Grotto, and South Central to be challenging. Climbers must supply their own gear. **The Gym** (☎ 4421 0587), at the corner of McMahons and Illaroo Rd., offers indoor rock climbing. On weekends, the more adventurous can try flying sail planes at the Nowra Naval Air Station, Braidwood Rd. Contact the **Royal Australian Naval Gliding Association** (☎ 4421 1333). **Skydive Nowra** (☎ 0500 885 556) offers tandem skydives ($360 with video) and freefall courses ($380). Book in advance.

NEAR NOWRA

KANGAROO VALLEY   ☎ 02

The fading Caltex petrol station in the middle of Kangaroo Valley's main thoroughfare is probably the last vestige of the original one-marsupial town. Today, Kangaroo Valley (pop. 280) has gone decidedly arts-and-crafts touristy, but the area is still remote, pleasant, and rightfully popular for B&B and camping retreats.

At the northwest end of town, the **Hampden Bridge** spans the Kangaroo River. Built in 1898, it is Australia's oldest suspension bridge. With two locations on the north side of the bridge, **Kangaroo Valley Safaris,** 2210 Moss Vale Rd., organizes canoe camping trips to Kangaroo River and Shoal Haven, including a 25km overnight canoe trip. A shuttle picks up from the rail station. (☎ 4465 1502. Open daily 7am-7pm. Canoes $45 per day, kayaks $25-55 per day, sea kayaks $65 per day, tents $25 per day.) **Kennedy's Coaches** (☎ 4421 7596 or 0411 232 101) goes to the park from the Kangaroo Valley post office en route to Moss Vale (25min., 1 per day, $5); a bus does not return until the following morning. Tourist information is available at **News Agents** (☎ 4465 1150).

The **Bendeela Picnic Area ❶,** 7km outside town, provides plenty of free **camping,** toilets, BBQ, and water. Reach it by driving north out of town and turning left on Bendeela Rd., following signs to the entrance. For campers looking for showers or a roof, there is **Glenmack Caravan Park ❶** on the main road just east of town. (☎ 4465 1372. Reception 8am-6pm. Sites $8 per person, powered $12; cabins for 2 $55-75.) At one of **Morton National Park's** entrances, 20km from Kangaroo Valley on Moss Vale Rd., **Fitzroy Falls** greets visitors. Run by the NPWS, the **Fitzroy Falls Visitors Center** has maps for bushwalking trails. (☎ 4887 7270. Open daily 9am-5:30pm.) By **car,** avoid the steep, winding Kangaroo Valley Rd. leading west from Berry and opt for the Moss Vale Rd., which leads northwest from Bomaderry, off the Princes Hwy. Check road conditions ahead of time for both routes. **Prior's** (☎1800 816 234) runs **buses** (M-F and Su 1 per day) to: Batemans Bay (2¼hr., $20); Narooma (4hr., $26); Parramatta (3hr., $20); and Ulladulla (1½hr., $15).

JERVIS BAY   ☎02

Almost entirely enclosed by its northern headland, Jervis Bay is a serene body of water surrounded by the strikingly white beaches of **Beecroft Peninsula.** It teems with marine life and contains underwater rock formations that make for arguably the best **diving** in Australia outside of the Great Barrier Reef. To take in the bay, stop at any of the towns—**Huskisson** is the largest—along the shore and wander down to the water's edge even if you decide not to don a mask and fins.

Underwater, Jervis Bay is an exquisite natural meeting place for tropical marine life from the north as well as a variety of southern species not found in the Great Barrier Reef. Divers rave about the massive archways and rock shelves; spots such as Cathedral Cave and Smuggler's Cave are perfect for **cave diving.** The Arch, Stoney Creek Reef, and the Ten Fathom Dropoff are known for **deep diving.** Steamers Beach Seal Colony is great for **open-water dives** and **snorkeling.** Despite chillier waters, visibility is best from April to early August. **Jervis Bay Sea Sports,** 47 Owen St., takes certified divers out for a day. Ask about the 4-day PADI course ($420) if you're not certified and wish to be. (☎4441 5012. Two dives $130, including equipment and lunch.) **Pro-Dive,** 64 Owen St. (☎4441 5255), offers similar services.

For those content to enjoy marine life from a drier vantage point, **Dolphin Watch Cruises,** 50 Owen St. (☎1800 246 010), and **Dolphin Explorer Cruises,** 62 Owen St. (☎1800 444 330), offer 3hr. whale watching trips ($40) during peak whale migrations (June-Nov.) and 2½hr. dolphin cruises daily at 1pm ($25, concessions $22).

Fishermen work for their dinner at nearby Currambene Creek, and **Husky Hire-a-Boat** rents and delivers boats. (☎4441 6200. Open dawn-4:30pm. $40 per 2hr.; $55 per 3hr.; $50 deposit required.) If you just want to paddle around, **Jervis Bay Kayak Company** allows you to stretch your arms in sleek style. (☎4443 3858. Rentals $50 per day; half-day guided tours $77; full-day tours $110.) Tour cost includes transport, snack, and park user fees.

HUSKISSON. Twenty-four kilometers southeast of Nowra along the coast of Jervis Bay lies Huskisson. **Nowra Coaches** (☎4423 5244) goes to Huskisson (35min., 2-4 per day, $10) and Jervis Bay Village in **Booderee National Park** (1¼hr.; Tu and Fr; $9). For tourist info, visit the **Huskisson Trading Post** on the corner of Tomerong and Dent St. (☎4441 5241. Open daily 9:30am-5pm.) **Leisure Haven Caravan Park ❷,** 1.5km outside of town along Currambene Creek on Woollamia Rd., provides sites with free hot showers and laundry. (☎4441 5046. Key deposit $20. Reception 8am-6pm. Sites for 2 $16-20, powered $18-28. 7th night free.) **The Husky Pub ❸,** on Owen St. overlooking the Bay, is the town's pubstay. The rooms are basic and have shared toilets. (☎4441 5001; fax 4441 6754. Bar and reception M-F 11am-10pm, Sa-Su 11am-11pm. Singles $30, doubles $55.)

BOODEREE NATIONAL PARK. On the southern end of the bay, **Booderee National Park,** which is under joint Aboriginal management, has three **camping** areas: **Greenpatch ❷,** on Jervis Bay (hot showers, toilets, and water; sites $14-20); **Cave Beach ❶,** near Wreck Bay to the south (cold showers, no electricity; max. 5 people; sites $9-11); **Bristol Point ❷** is intended for larger groups and has toilets, hot showers, fireplaces, and very, very big sites. (Sites $69, peak $87.) The **Visitors Center,** just beyond the park entry gates, accepts campsite bookings and can provide maps to the various hiking tracks. (☎4443 0977. Open daily 9am-4pm. $10 per car per day.) The **Botanic Gardens** are inside the park as well. (☎4442 1122. Open M-F 8am-4pm,

Sa-Su 10am-5pm. No additional charge.) The beach at **Green Patch,** often a good place to see rainbow lorikeets and eastern gray kangaroos, is a popular **snorkeling** spot. ▧**Murrays Beach,** staggering in its beauty, is a popular place for **swimming.**

ULLADULLA   ☎02

Moving south through the Shoalhaven, the next major service center is Ulladulla (uh-luh-DUH-luh; pop. 12,000), given this name back in 1828 because it was thought to sound like its original Aboriginal name, *Woolahderrah.* Off the coast between Jervis Bay and Ulladulla Harbour are a fair number of shipwrecks for divers to explore, including the famous 1870 wreck of the *Walter Hood.* Still, the best known—and most beautiful—draw is the Pigeon House Bushwalk.

🖃🔁 **TRANSPORTATION AND PRACTICAL INFORMATION. Premier** (☎13 34 10; www.premierms.com.au) **buses** stop at the Marlin Hotel (southbound) and the Traveland Travel Agency (northbound) on route to: Batemans Bay (45min., 2-3 per day, $11); Bermagui (3hr., 1 per day, $25); Kiama (2hr., 2-3 per day, $14); Melbourne (12½hr., 1 per day, $65); Narooma (1¾hr., 2-3 per day, $20); Nowra (1hr., 2-3 per day, $14); Sydney (5hr., 2-3 per day, $27); and Wollongong (3hr., 2-3 per day, $26). The **Visitors Center** is on the Princes Hwy., in the Civic Centre. (☎4455 1269. Open M-F 10am-5pm, Sa-Su 9am-5pm.) **Internet** is available there and at the adjacent **library.** (Open M-F 10am-6pm, Sa 9am-2pm. Access free; email $1.10 per 30min.) The **police station** is at 73 Princes Hwy. (☎4454 2542).

🝖 **ACCOMMODATIONS.** The local hostel, ▧**South Coast Backpackers ❷,** 63 Princes Hwy., between Narrawallee and North St., is a small, friendly operation with laundry, TV, kitchen, beautiful hardwood floors, brightly-colored walls, off-street parking, and a great sundeck and hammock area. (☎4454 0500. Key deposit $10. Dorms $20; twins $42; doubles $45. VIP.) For some top-notch pampering—think free champagne and fresh fruit upon arrival—a relaxing lounge by the pool or spa, and hallways and rooms filled with brilliant local art, check into the multi-award-winning ▧**Ulladulla Guest House ❺,** 39 Burrill St., just down South St. off the Princes Hwy. (☎4455 1796; www.guesthouse.com.au. Rooms start at $179; occasionally rates reduced to as little as $99 for same-day standby.) At the end of South St., **Ulladulla Tourist Park ❶** has camping space, though the site area slopes slightly. (☎1300 733 021. Showers, toilets, laundry, BBQs, pool, and access to a secluded beach. Sites $8-14 per person, powered $11-16; cabins $100-165, off-peak $44-89.)

🝖🗺 **SIGHTS AND ACTIVITIES.** The people at the **Ulladulla Dive Shop,** 150 Princes Hwy., at the corner of Deering St., can give seasoned advice on **reef diving** in the area, or they can take you out themselves. (☎4455 5303. Open Nov.-Apr. daily 7am-6pm; May-Oct. M-F 9am-5pm, Sa-Su 8am-5pm. Gear $55 per day; intro dives $85.) Or try the **Ulladulla Dive and Adventure Centre,** 211 Princes Hwy. (☎4455 3029), for snorkeling, canoe, and kayak lessons, or a shot at kite surfing. Bushwalkers generally stop in Ulladulla on the way out to the **Pigeon House Walk.** Turn off the Princes Hwy. onto Wheelbarrow Rd. 3km south of Burrill Lake. The trailhead is 27km farther at a picnic area. The walk, which involves some ladder climbing, is a strenuous 5km affair—allow three hours—but the view at the top is a knock-out. ▧**One Track for All** is an awe-inspring 2km trail dotted with hand-carved stumps, statues, and logs depicting the Aboriginal and post-settlement history of the land; the trail, which winds about the North Head cliffs near Ulladulla Harbour, affords several staggering ocean lookouts. (Turn off Princes Hwy. onto North St., across from the Police Station, take a left onto Burrill St., then a right onto Dolphin St. The trailhead is at the end of Dolphin St. Wheelchair accessible.) Noel and Jenny Butler, the folks who created the track, are also in the process of

NEW SOUTH WALES

creating an **Aboriginal bush and sea camp,** situated deep within a private tract of pristine rainforest, where they will teach hardy backpackers traditional Aboriginal song, dance, weapon-making, fishing, and gathering techniques. (budawang-galanj@shoal.net.au. Expected to be open Nov. 2002.) Nearby **Lakes Burrill** and **Conjola** have nice **swimming** beaches, and **Mollymook Beach,** just north of town, is good for **surfing.** Dolphins have been known to ride the waves along with surfers.

MURRAMARANG NATIONAL PARK   ☎ 02

With expansive views of the Pacific and tame kangaroos all over, the coastline in the Murramarang National Park makes a great detour from the highway and a superb spot to check out (and pet) the 'roo beach bums who lazily congregate on ▨**Pebbly Beach.** If you've any leftover carbs, and feel like being mobbed by beautiful parrots, then the world is your petting zoo (but don't feed the 'roos—processed bread can kill them). The shore itself is at the far end of a 15min. drive over mostly unpaved roads. A number of worthy campgrounds and caravan parks are speckled throughout the park, but tent **camping ❶** sites are cheapest at the Pebbly Beach camping area. (☎4478 6006. Sites $11 per person; includes park fee.) At the southernmost point in the Shoalhaven half of Murramarang National Park, **Durras North** looks onto Durras Lake and a beautiful windswept ocean beach. Pick up a brochure for a self-guided bushwalk from the tourist office in Batemans Bay. **Durras Lake North Caravan Park ❷,** approximately 16km south of Durras North by car, the first of several caravan parks at the end of Durras Rd., is clean and quite a kangaroo gathering place. (☎4478 6072. Reception daily 8:30am-9:30pm. Powered sites $16; caravan for 2 $35, extra adult $10.)

SOUTH FROM BATEMANS BAY

Batemans Bay, 10km south of Durras Lake on the Princes Hwy., and just inland from Murramarang National Park, has some spectacular diving spots. On the way out of Shoalhaven and into the Eurobodalla shire, the larger towns center around industries like fishing and dairy farming and are less touristed. Smaller, quieter villages hidden in the countryside, such as Mogo and Central Tilba, are the most compelling reasons to follow the Princes Hwy. along the coast.

BATEMANS BAY   ☎ 02

Situated south of the junction at the mouth of Clyde River, the town begins where the Kings Hwy. from Canberra (152km inland) meets the Princes Hwy. at the coast. Though you won't see any threatening fins from shore, dozens of grey nurse sharks—comprising one of Australia's largest colonies—circle the islands offshore, making Batemans Bay a popular dive spot. Or, if you're not easily impressed by zombie-eyed fauna, join the dozens of other backpackers who migrate to this laid-back fishing village for its proximity to the 'roos and parrots at Murramarang National Park.

◨▨ TRANSPORTATION AND PRACTICAL INFORMATION. Buses leave from outside the Promenade Plaza on Orient St. **Premier** (☎ 13 34 10) goes to: Bega (2½-3½hr., 2-3 per day, $22); Bermagui (2½hr., 1 per day, $18); Kiama (3hr., 2-3 per day, $33); Melbourne (12hr., 1 per day, $59); Narooma (1-1¾hr., 2-3 per day, $14); Nowra (2hr., 2-3 per day, $21); Sydney (5½hr., 2-3 per day, $35); Ulladulla (45min., 2-3 per day, $11); and Wollongong (3½hr., 2-3 per day, $33). **Murrays** (☎ 13 22 57) offers a 10% YHA discount and goes to Canberra (2½hr., 1-2 per day, $24). The staff at **Batemans Bay Tourist Information Centre,** on Princes Hwy. at Beach Rd., will book your accommodations in town at no charge as well as supply you with a stack of brochures and suggestions. (☎4472 6900 or 1800 802 528; fax 4472 8822. Open daily 9am-5pm.) The **police station** is at 28 Orient St. (☎4472 0044). The **post office** is on Orient St., adjacent to the bus stop. (Open M-F 9am-5pm.) **Postal Code:** 2536.

▐▐ **ACCOMMODATIONS AND FOOD.** Copious motels fringe Orient St. and Beach Rd.; rooms usually start at $60-70 in winter. The **Batemans Bay Backpackers (YHA) ❷,** inside a caravan park on the corner of Old Princes Hwy. and South St., off the new Princes Hwy., offers tidy facilities as well as daily trips to Pebbly Beach ($11) and Mogo ($5) when there is enough interest. The hostel rents bikes ($12 per day) and lends boogie boards. (☎4472 4972; www.shadywillows.com.au. Laundry, kitchen, TV, and pool. Call to arrange pickup from the bus stop in town. Dorms $23, YHA $19; twins and doubles $62/$58.) Small and friendly, **Beach Road Backpackers ❷,** 92 Beach Rd., is a flat 1km walk from town. (☎4472 3644; fax 4472 7208. Trips to Pebbly Beach $15. TV, kitchen, free pickup and drop-off at bus stop. Bike hire $7.50 per day. Dorms $19; doubles $40. VIP.) Fish and chips seems to be the town's favorite meal; try **The Boat Shed ❶,** next to the bus stop on Orient St., with a back porch overlooking the waterfront, for eat-in or takeaway seafood. (☎4472 4052. Open in summer daily 9am-8pm; in winter M-W 9am-4pm, Th-Su 9am-7pm.)

▨▨ **SIGHTS AND ACTIVITIES.** The 1880 wreck of the Lady Darling is considered a fantastic dive and is suitable for all levels of diving and snorkeling. Other dives include the Burrawarra Wall, the Maze, and, for scoping the nurse sharks, Montague Island. The **Dive Shop,** 33 Orient St., can be your link to the water world. (☎4472 9930. Single boat dive $38; double $66; full equipment hire $50-88.) The compact **Opal and Shell Museum,** 142 Beach Rd., owned and operated by a veteran opal miner, showcases an extensive display of opals and shells from Australia and around the world; for those interested in buying a token opal, prices are much more affordable here than in larger cities. (☎4472 7248. Open M and W-Su 10am-6pm. Closed Aug. $1.50, families $3.) Buy or rent a surfboard at **Kaffir Surfboards.** (☎4472 3933. Single fin $25; 3-fin thrusters $35.)

To indulge in a spot of bushwalking, join the locals from **Batemans Bay Bushwalkers** ($2). Contact Len Tompkins (☎4472 3113) or ask the tourist office for a schedule. Traveling south on the coastal road, Malua Bay and Broulee have good **surf. U-Canoe** has canoe and kayak hire. (☎4474 3348; www.sci.net.au/ucanoe. $30 per day for 1 person, $40 for 2, $50 for 3; includes pickup and delivery.)

NAROOMA ☎02

With several parks and other protected natural areas nearby, the town of Narooma is a good basecamp for outdoor exploration. Only 7km offshore, fur seals, crested terns, and some 10,000 pairs of fairy penguins inhabit the ▨**Montague Island Nature Reserve.** The island, of volcanic origin, was used by Aborigines for food and ceremony for over 4500 years. In 1770, Captain Cook was the first European to discover the island; years later settlers introduced goats and rabbits to Montague for shipwreck victims. When the lighthouse was built, horses and cows, and subsequently grasses to feed them, continued a gradual destruction of the island's original habitat. Today, National Parks and Wildlife Service (NPWS) is working hard to preserve the island's amazing range of wildlife by restoring the natural habitat and managing the *kykuya* grass, which has choked much of the original vegetation, making it difficult for fairy penguins and other birds to nest. The reserve is only accessible through official NPWS-sanctioned tours; watch for whales on your trip out to the island. (3½hr.; 1-2 per day; $69, families $198; 90 people allowed per day). Book through NPWS or the Visitors Centre (see below). **Eurobodalla National Park** (☎4476 2888), a popular 2WD-accessible destination, protects a 30km stretch of coastline, from Moruya Head in the north to Tilba Tilba Lake in the south. Featuring, among other things, lush spotted gum forest, this park has one **campground ❶** at Congo ($5 per person), near the town of **Moruya.**

On Wagonga Head, off Bar Rock Rd., ocean waves, coastal winds, and a bit of chiseling have left one rock, known as **Australia Rock,** with a hole, amazingly enough, in the shape of Australia, minus a bit of the Cape York peninsula. The resemblance is uncanny. **Glasshouse Rocks,** another locally famous rock formation, lies at the south end of Narooma Beach. Depending on the winds, **surfers** will head out to Handkerchief, Bar, Carter's, or Josh's Beaches.

Premier Motor Service (☎ 13 34 10) stops in Narooma and goes to: Batemans Bay (1hr., 2-3 per day, $14); Bega (1½hr., 2-3 per day, $15); Kiama (4-5hr., 2-3 per day, $44); Melbourne (11hr., 1 per day, $53); Nowra (3-3½hr., 2-3 per day, $32); Sydney (6½-7½hr., 2-3 per day, $46); Ulladulla (2-2½hr., 2-3 per day, $20); and Wollongong (4¾-5½hr., 2-3 per day, $44). **Murrays** (☎ 13 22 51) runs from Narooma Plaza to Canberra (4½hr., 1-2 per day, $36.25).

The **Narooma Visitors Centre,** on Princes Hwy., handles advance bookings for some campgrounds and tours. (☎ 4476 2881. Open daily 9am-5pm.) The **National Parks and Wildlife Service (NPWS)** office is a block away on the corner of Princes Hwy. and Field St. (☎ 4476 2888. Open M-F 9am-4pm.) The **post office** is just up the hill on Princes Hwy. (☎ 4476 2049. Open M-F 9am-5pm.) **Postal Code:** 2546.

The **Bluewater Lodge (YHA) ❷,** 8 Princes Hwy., is clean and comfortable. The knowledgeable and gracious owner has lived in the area his whole life. (☎ 4476 4440; naroomayha@narooma.com. Breakfast included. Laundry, kitchen, TV. Bikes and canoes $6 per day. Internet $5 per hr. Reception daily May-Aug. 8am-noon and 3-9pm; Sept.-April 8am-9pm. Dorms $24, YHA $21; twins $23; family rooms $55.) **Easts Narooma Shores Holiday Park ❷** is off the Princes Hwy. just after the bridge into town. (☎ 4476 2046. Reception 8am-8pm. Sites $18-28, powered $20-30.) **Narooma Golf Club and Surfbeach Resort ❷,** on Ballingala St., has fine views of the water and good facilities. (☎ 4476 2522. Reception 8:30am-5:30pm. Sites for 2 $20, powered $24.)

SNOWY MOUNTAINS

While skiers and snowboarders make the Snowies their playground during the winter, the warmer months attract swarms of hikers to Australia's highest mountains. Kosciuszko National Park, home of **Mount Kosciuszko** (2228m), Australia's highest peak, covers most of this area. The Snowy Mountains Hwy. and the Alpine Way ramble past the boulder-strewn countryside where the skiing industry is king, though compared to other mountain ranges around the world, the runs are shorter and less challenging. Conditions on each mountain vary wildly: **Thredbo** is a black diamond paradise; **Perisher,** despite its ominous-sounding name, is a favorite of hikers; and **Mt. Selwyn** offers unbeatable deals and easier slopes.

KOSCIUSZKO NATIONAL PARK

Named after the heroic Polish nationalist, Thadeus Kosciuszko (kaw-zee-AW-sko), Kosciuszko National Park contains Australia's **tallest mountains,** several stunning **wilderness areas,** and NSW's premier **ski fields.** While the park may forever be associated with ski resorts, outdoor enthusiasts appreciate the year-round beauty of **Yarrongobilly Caves** and the wildflower-strewn alpine walks in summer that lead to the rooftop of Australia. Numerous **hiking tracks** and **camping** areas are available throughout the park. There's an entry fee for Kosciuszko ($15 per car per 24hr.), though motorists passing through non-stop are exempt. During ski season (June 1-Oct. 10), snow chains must be carried. The Shell stations along the Alpine Way,

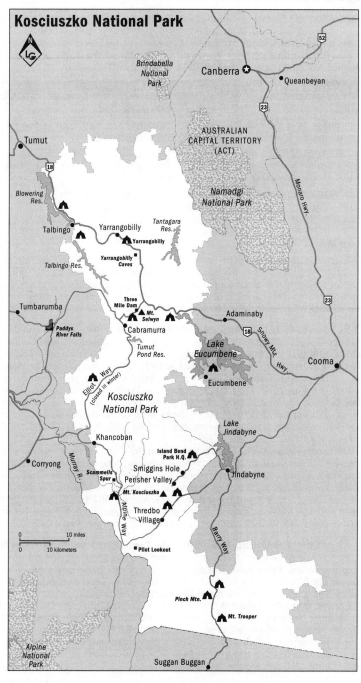

Kosciuszko National Park

Khancoban, and Jindabyne, allow one-way chain rental and drop-off ($20). Trail maps, camping information, guide books, and park stickers can be obtained at the **Snowy Region Visitors Centre** in Jindabyne (see p. 211), the entrance station on the way to Perisher Blue (stickers only), or the **NPWS office** at the corner of Scott and Mitchell Ave. in Khancoban. (☎6076 9373. Open daily 8:30am-4pm.)

KOSCIUSZKO NATIONAL PARK AT A GLANCE	
AREA: 6494km².	**GATEWAYS:** Cooma and Jindabyne.
HEIGHTS: Mount Kosciuszko: 2228m. Mount Selwyn: 1520m.	**CAMPING:** Free, although a few privately-run sites charge various fees.
FEATURES: Australia's tallest mountain, for which the park is named, the Snowy River, Yarrongobilly Caves, Mount Selwyn.	**FEES:** $15 per day vehicle fee, though motorists passing through non-stop are exempt.
HIGHLIGHTS: Skiing some of Australia's best slopes; camping and hiking during the warmer months.	**SKI SEASON:** Approximately June to October 10.

COOMA ☎02

The self-proclaimed "Capital of the Snowy Mountains," Cooma links Canberra and the coast with the mountains. Because of its peripheral location on the eastern edge of the Snowy Mountains region, Cooma is far enough from the price-inflated snowfields to permit bargain accommodation and reasonable rental rates during the ski season for those willing to make the commute.

⌨🗺 TRANSPORTATION AND PRACTICAL INFORMATION. The main drag through Cooma is **Sharp St.**, flanked on either side by Massie St. and Commissioner St. **Buses** come through frequently during ski season, but service is severely curtailed the rest of the year. **Countrylink** (☎13 22 32) and **McCafferty's/Greyhound** (☎13 20 30) run to: Canberra (1½-2hr., 2 per day, $30); Jindabyne (50min., 2 per day, $20); Sydney (6hr., 2 per day, $66); and Thredbo (1¾hr., 2 per day, $26). **Snowliner Coaches,** 120 Sharp St. (☎6452 1584), services Jindabyne (50min.; M-F 2 per day; $13.20, correct change required). **Harvey World Travel,** 114 Sharp St., opposite the Visitors Center, arranges reservations. (☎6452 4677. Open M-F 9am-5pm, Sa 9am-noon.)

The **Cooma Visitors Centre,** 119 Sharp St., is in the center of town. (☎6450 1742; fax 6450 1798. Open daily mid-Oct. to May 9am-5pm, June to mid-Oct. 7am-5pm.) You can book accommodations through the Visitors Center, but beware: some hotel owners charge extra for this. **Internet** access can be found at the Visitors Center (see above; $3 per 30min.) or at **Percy's News Agency,** 158 Sharp St. (☎6452 2880. Open M-F 6am-6:30pm, Sa 6am-3pm, Su 6am-2pm. $3 per 30min.) The **post office,** on the corner of Massie St. and Vale St., is open M-F 9am-5pm. **Postal Code:** 2630.

⌨🍴 ACCOMMODATIONS AND FOOD. The **Cooma Bunkhouse Backpackers ❷,** 30 Soho St., on the corner of Commissioner St., has great year-round hostel accommodation. Every room is equipped with a private bathroom, kitchen, and TV. (☎/fax 6452 2983; www.bunkhousemotel.com.au. Reception 24hr. Heated dorms $20; singles in adjacent motel $35; doubles $44-55; family rooms $60. VIP.) The pricier **White Manor Motel ❺,** 252 Sharp St., has rooms with color TV, A/C, heat, and electric blankets. (☎6452 1152; fax 6452 1627. Reception daily 9am-10:30pm. Ensuite singles in winter $85, in summer $62; doubles $77/$68; family units available.) On Sharp St., 1.6km west of the town center, **Snowtels Caravan Park ❶** provides a kitchen, laundry, and BBQ. (☎6452 1828; fax 6452 7192. Sites $15, powered $20; caravans $33-$55; ensuite cabins $45-90.)

Organic Vibes ❶, 82A Sharp St., is a beacon of hope to road-weary travelers surviving on fish 'n' chips and meat pies. The mother-daughter team sells organic produce, gluten and wheat-free pastas, and fresh juices. Try the dried mangoes or the homemade lunch specials. (☎/fax 6452 6566. Open M-F 9am-5:30pm, Sa 9am-noon.) **Grumpy's Diner ❶**, across from the Visitors Centre on Sharp St., has traveler-friendly staff and tummy-friendly meals. Focaccias, sandwiches, and veggie options are tasty and filling and run $5-10. (☎ 6452 1002. Open M-F 7am-4pm, Sa-Su 7am-2:30pm.) Stock up on **groceries** at Woolworth's, on the corner of Vale and Massie St., as well as at 228 Sharp St. (Open daily 7am-10pm.)

⛷ **SKIING.** Because the ski resorts of Thredbo, Perisher, and Mt. Selwyn lie within 100km of Cooma, **rental shops** clutter the town's streets. Flashing signs advertising "round-the-clock" rentals resemble a casino town dependent on gambling for its livelihood. Rates are comparable to those closer to the mountains. Skis, poles, and boot rentals run about $30 the first day and $10-15 per day thereafter; snowboard and boot rental cost about $45 for the first day. The visitors center (see p. 213) has brochures with 10-15% discount coupons.

JINDABYNE ☎ 02

On the scenic shores of man-made **Lake Jindabyne,** the town of Jindabyne is a logical stopping point for those who can't afford chalets at the foot of the Thredbo chairlifts, and a great place to be (or encounter) a true ski bum who alternates between the northern and southern hemispheres in pursuit of snow and slopes. During ski season, "Jindy" acts as a satellite ski town, with the corresponding services and high seasonal prices. After the ski season, bushwalkers and backpackers stop through while exploring the vast Kosciuszko National Park. The original town was flooded as part of the hydroelectric scheme (see **In Recent News,** p. 212); when the water level is low, visitors can swim to the old church.

📞 **TRANSPORTATION AND PRACTICAL INFORMATION.** During the ski season, **Jindabyne Coaches** (☎ 6457 2117 or 0411 020 680) runs four shuttles to the Skitube. From there, it's possible to catch a train up to Perisher Blue ($13 return). Transport into Jindabyne from the northeast passes through Cooma (see p. 210). **Greyhound Pioneer** (☎ 13 20 30) operates limited service in the winter and **Mushwan-dry Bus Service** (☎ 6452 3802 or 1800 636 525) offers limited service in the summer. The **Snowy Region Visitors Centre,** on the Alpine Way at the east end of town, combines a NPWS office and a tourist center. (☎ 6450 5600; fax 6456 1249. Road conditions ☎ 6450 5551, snow reports 6450 5553, weather 6450 5550. Open daily in winter 8am-5:30pm, in summer 8:30am-5pm.)

To get to the slopes from Jindabyne, follow the **Alpine Way.** It leads to the Skitube station (23km from town), which services **Perisher Blue** resorts, and then continues on to **Thredbo** (30km farther). From Thredbo, the Alpine Way extends its sometimes treacherous path through the mountains to **Khancoban,** a full-service town on the western edge of Kosciuszko National Park. Cars traveling to Khancoban are required to carry **snow chains.** The **Shell station** at the Perisher/Thredbo junction, outside of Jindabyne, rents snow chains for $20 and has a drop-off program with the Khancoban's Shell station.

Job opportunities are everywhere in Jindabyne; many of the skiiers and snowboarders who worship the Australian shrines of Thredbo and Perisher arrive in Jindabyne without work or housing and find both through postings and word of mouth. Two great places to find postings are outside the IGA **supermarket** in Nuggets Crossing shopping center and in the windows of **Snowy River Continental Butchery** in Snowy Mountains Plaza. **Snowy Mountain Backpackers** (see below; $10 per hr.) and **Leading Edge Video,** Lakeview Plaza on Snowy River Ave., have **Internet** access (☎ 6456 2665; open Su-Th 9:30am-9pm, F-Sa 9:30am-9:30pm; $10 per hr.).

IN RECENT NEWS

DAM STRAIGHT

Since the 1967 construction of the Jindabyne Dam, Australia's great Snowy River has been a mere shadow of its former self. The Snowy Mountains Hydroelectric Scheme—one of the greatest engineering feats in the world—was created to provide hydroelectric power and irrigation for the Murray River system by diverting 99% of the Snowy River's water to the west. This has meant a reduction in its wetland habitat and in aquatic biodiversity, a spreading of vegetation such as willows and blackberries over the former riverbed, and an increased salinity in the lower river, causing (according to one source) an annual loss of $4 million in agricultural production. While the benefits to the Murray River system are significant, Snowy River locals had hoped for a more balanced arrangement.

Locals began protesting the scheme over ten years ago and have convinced federal and state governments to implement a new plan for the river, which will benefit both the natural habitat and the region's options for tourist activity.

Beginning in 2003, the Australian governments will orchestrate a corporatization of the Snowy River Hydroelectric Scheme and slowly restore the river to what has been agreed upon as a sustainably healthy level (28% of its original volume). Though many fighting for the river remain skeptical of the plan's success and there exists little hope of returning the Snowy River to its original volume, this recent move seems to be a step in the right direction.

ACCOMMODATIONS. Even in the height of ski madness, affordable accommodation in Jindabyne does exist, but availability may be a problem. Be sure to book well in advance. ⚑**Snowy Mountain Backpackers ❸**, 7 Gippsland St., behind the Nuggets Crossing shopping center, combines an unbeatable location with new facilities, laundry, Internet, and kitchen. (☎6456 1500 or 1800 333 468; backpackers@snowy.net.au. Key deposit $10. Reception daily June-Oct. 8am-8pm; Nov.-May 9am-6pm. Bunks $25-35; doubles $60-100. VIP. Wheelchair accessible.) The **Jindy Inn ❹**, 18 Clyde St., has private ensuite rooms with TV's and fridges. There's a well-equipped kitchen downstairs and a nice adjoining restaurant. During ski season the inn functions more as a B&B. Bookings are essential and single-night stays are rare. (☎6456 1957; fax 6456 2057. Breakfast included. Reception 24hr. Bunks in winter $45-95, in summer from $25.) **Jindabyne Holiday Park ❶** is in the center of town on a choice stretch of Lake Jindabyne shoreline. (☎6456 2249. Laundry, camp kitchen. Key deposit $20. Ski-and-boot rental $30; snowboard-and-boot $40. Sites for 2 $15, powered $18; extra person $5. On-site caravans Oct.-June from $30, July-Aug. from $65.) The **Station Resort ❺** is in a self-contained village 6km south of Jindabyne, at the corner of Barry Way and Dalgety Rd., and is popular for cheap lodging with little hassle. Bars, restaurants, and bus services are all on the premises. (☎6456 2895 or 1300 369 9090. Laundry, TV, Internet, and small fridge. Reception 24hr. During ski season, F-Sa 2 nights including breakfast and 2-day lift tickets $369; Su-F 5 nights including 5-day lift tickets $559; packages vary.)

FOOD AND NIGHTLIFE. Cheap food is hard to come by. Preparing a flavorful range of traditional and multicultural dishes, the newly-opened **Mad Az Cafe ❷**, 8 Gippsland St., adjacent to the Snowy Mountain Backpackers, has decent prices and a relaxed, funky interior. (☎6456 1503. Open daily June-Oct. 8am-9pm; Nov.-May 8am-4pm. Meals $5-20.) **Wrap A Go-Go ❷**, in Lakeview Plaza on Snowy River Ave., features spicy Mexican meals and tasty wraps. (☎6457 1887. Open daily noon-9pm; in summer closed M. Mains $10-14.) The **Cactus Cafe ❶**, in Nuggets Crossing shopping center, serves meals from $5. (Open daily 8am-5pm.) Across from it is an IGA **supermarket**. In the evenings, people relax at the **Lake Jindabyne Hotel**, on Kosciuszko Rd. in the center of town. Entertainment ranges from drinking and shooting pool to rock concerts. On Wednesday night, LJH is the first stop for many locals. (☎6456 2203. Open M-Sa 10am-late, Su 10am-midnight. Schooners of VB $3.30.)

🔲 **ACTIVITIES.** The experts at **Wilderness Sports,** in Nuggets Crossing, organize cross-country skiing, back-country snowboarding, snowshoe, and alpine touring adventures from $70 per day in the Thredbo area. (☎6456 2966; www.wildernesssports.com.au. Open daily June-Oct. 8am-6pm, Nov.-May Th-Tu 9am-5pm. Prices generally depend upon group size.) Their **Backcountry Centre** is at the top of the Kosciuszko Express chairlift at Thredbo and offers a myriad of rentals—including snowshoes, telemark and cross-country skis, and snowcamping gear—and courses on topics like snowcamping and rock climbing. (☎6457 6955. Open daily 9am-4pm. Snowshoe hire $25-35 per day; half-day abseiling $69; full-day Mt. Kosciuszko tour $110, includes lunch.) **Paddy Pallin,** next to the Shell station at the Perisher-Thredbo junction, offers similar services as well as mountaineering courses and mountain bike and kayak rental. (☎6456 2922 or 1800 623 459. 4-day intro to mountaineering $850; mountain bikes $16 per hr., full-day $50; kayaks half-day $33, full-day $48.) **Upper Murray White Water Rafting** organizes thrill-ride rafting down the Murray River in spring and summer. Book in advance. (☎6452 7998 or 1800 677 179. Sept.-Apr. full-day $140.)

THE MOUNTAINS

THE SKI SLOPES	THE LOWDOWN	FEATURES	PRICES
PERISHER BLUE	Australia's premier resort, with Perisher Valley, Blue Cow, Smiggens, and Guthega alpine villages.	7 peaks, 51 lifts, and over 95 trails.	$77 per day, under 14 $42; night skiing (Tu and Sa) $16/$11. Lift pass and lesson $77/$59.
MT. SELWYN	Lacks the difficulty of other mountains in the park, but has 45 hectares of marked trails.	Beginner runs and a few expert; draws families.	$48 per half-day, under age 15 $24; full-day $58/ $29. Cross-country skiing free.
THREDBO	Home to Australia's longest slopes. Outdoor activities abound year-round.	12 lifts and a majority of intermediate runs.	$77 per day, under age 15 $42; night ski (Tu and Sa) free with valid lift pass. 2hr. group lessons $41.

PERISHER BLUE

New South Wales's premier ski resort, Perisher Blue (☎1300 655 822; www.perisherblue.com.au), is actually four resorts in one. One lift ticket buys entry to the interconnected slopes leading down to the **Perisher Valley, Blue Cow, Smiggens,** and **Guthega** alpine villages. Surprisingly, access between the seven peaks is relatively easy. Situated above the natural snow line, with a slightly higher elevation than its competitors, Perisher offers some of the best snow around. **Zali's Run,** named after Zali Steggall, the female Australian World Cup skier, is a popular intermediate slope. **Kamikaze** and **Double Trouble** will really put snowbunnies to the test.

All **lift tickets** include unlimited use of the Perisher-Blue Cow segment of the Skitube. Purchase tickets at Bullocks Flat or at the **Perisher Blue Jindabyne Ticket Office** in the Nuggets Crossing shopping center. (☎6456 1659. Open daily 7am-7pm.) **Murrays** (☎13 22 51) and **Lever Coachlines** (☎6262 3266; www.transboarderexpress.com.au) offer daytrip skiing and snowboarding packages from Canberra from $100. (Includes return bus, park entry, lift ticket, and equipment hire.)

Perisher is not a full-service village and has neither budget accommodation nor overnight parking. On busy days, the Perisher Valley day lot fills up quickly and is often entirely inaccessible due to road conditions, but the **Skitube** (☎6456 2010) is an all-weather train that makes the 8km journey into the Perisher Valley Alpine Village from **Bullocks Flat,** located along the Alpine Way. You can either start your adventures in the Village or keep riding the Skitube halfway up the mountain to the Blue Cow terminal. There, chairlifts take more advanced skiers and boarders to the blue and black runs atop **Guthega Peak** and **Mount Blue Cow**. To get to the Ski-tube station at Bullocks Flat, take **Jindabyne Coaches** (☎6457 2117), which runs shuttles from **Jindabyne** (4 per day, $13 return). By **car,** drive along the Alpine Way from Jindabyne until you reach the station; there's plenty of parking. Once at the Perisher Station, follow your nose to the Bullocks Flat platform, on the lower level, to **Lil' Orbits Donuts ❶,** where you can grab a dozen cinnamon mini-donuts for $3. If donuts aren't enough, **Gingers ❶** (☎6457 5558), on the main floor, serves up hot cheese and tomato melts for $4.

THREDBO

Thredbo was recently named the NSW Tourist Destination of the Decade. Though it does not have as many slopes as Perisher, it does sport the longest slope, at 5.9km. Many skiers and boarders eat, sleep, and party in nearby Cooma and Jindabyne, though an extensive resort lies at the base of Thredbo's slopes.

🖫🖬 TRANSPORTATION AND PRACTICAL INFORMATION. Thredbo-bound hitchhikers stand at the roundabout outside Jindabyne; *Let's Go* does not recommend hitchhiking. **Greyhound Pioneer** (☎13 20 30) also runs June-Oct. from Cooma (1½hr., 2 per day, $29). **Thredbo Information Centre** is at 6 Friday Dr. (☎6459 4198 or 1800 026 333; www.thredbo.com.au. Open daily in winter 8am-6pm, in summer 9am-5pm.) Charges for ski and snowboard rentals at **Thredbo Sports** (☎6459 4176), at the base of the Kosciuszko Express chairlift, and at the east end of the village near the Friday Flat lift, are $10-20 higher than in Jindabyne or Cooma. (Skis, stocks, and boots $50; snowboard and boots $58.)

🖫🖬 ACCOMMODATIONS AND FOOD. With its nearest competitors charging hundreds of dollars more per night, the 🖬**Thredbo YHA Lodge ❸,** 8 Jack Adams Path, is the best deal in town. Though less luxurious than its neighbors, the lodge has a comfortable chalet feel with ample common space, a big kitchen, and an Internet kiosk. (☎6457 6376; thredbo@yhansw.org.au. Reception 7-10am and 4:30-9pm. Singles June $24; July-Oct. $48-58; Nov.-May $21. During ski season, 2-night F-Sa $117; 5-night Su-Th $242; 7-night Su-Sa $358.) Other lodges can be booked through **Thredbo Resort Centre.** (☎1800 020 589. Open daily Mar.-Aug. 9am-6pm; Sept.-Feb. 9am-5pm, though hours can vary.)

Eating on the mountain is pricey. 🖬**Altitude 1380 ❷,** on Mowamba Pl., has lunches ($8-13), super-friendly servers, and famous coffee. (☎6457 6190. Open daily 10am-3:30pm and 6:30-9pm.) **Alfresco Pizzeria ❸,** just below the Thredbo Alpine Hotel, serves pastas and pizza that will satisfy even the biggest appetite. (☎6457 6327. Open Th noon-9pm, F-Su noon-1pm. Large pies from $14.) After a tiring day on the slopes, collapse at the **Schuss Bar,** in Palmers Lodge, for an afternoon of live entertainment. The bar can be so much fun that many skiers don't make it to the slopes the next day.

🖪 ACTIVITIES. **Kosciuszko Express** chairlift runs year-round for hikers and wanderers. (All-day summer pass $21. Operates daily 8:30am-4:30pm.) Several excellent walks depart from the top of the chairlift, leading to sweeping views of Kosciuszko National Park. The **Mt. Kosciuszko Walk** (12km return) leads to the mountain's summit, though the easy walk to Kosciuszko Lookout (4km return) also provides sweeping views. Another option is the **Dead Horse Gap and Thredbo River Track** (10km), which ends in the village. Free maps of all trails are available throughout Thredbo. **Alternative Adventures** (☎0417 422 198) offers year-round diversions such as mountaineering, snowcamping, climbing, and abseiling. For more info, inquire at **Thredbo Sports** (see p. 214).

MOUNT SELWYN

Along the Snowy Mountains Hwy., halfway between Cooma and Tumut, the **Selwyn Snowfields** offers beginner and budget skiing. (☎ 6454 9488; www.selwyns-now.com.au.) Primarily a family resort, Selwyn has a small number of trails, minimal amenities, and only a couple advanced runs. Elevation at the base is 1492m, and the summit is only 122m higher. When natural snowfall is scarce, Mt. Selwyn relies on its 80% snowmaking coverage. **Lift tickets** are inexpensive. (Half-day valid 8:30am-12:45pm or 12:45-4:30pm $48, under 15 $24; full-day $58/29. Over 65 and under 6 free.) Forty-five hectares of marked trails and no lift fee make **cross-country skiing** another attractive option.

Equipment hire for alpine or cross-country skis and snowboards is pretty reasonable on the mountain. (Skis half-day $29, full-day $35; snowboards $37/$45.) **Toboggans** are available for $9 per day (toboggan lift ticket $15 per 20 rides) with a 1½hr. lift and lesson package ($68, under 15 $45; includes full-day lift ticket). There is no accommodation at Mt. Selwyn, but Cooma (see p. 210) is an hour away.

NEAR KOSCIUSZKO: YARRANGOBILLY CAVES

Hidden near a valley floor in the beautiful northern scrub wilderness of the Kosciuszko National Park, the Yarrangobilly Caves attract curious visitors and hardcore spelunkers alike. The **Yarrangobilly River**, off the Snowy Mountains Hwy. 77km south of Tumut and 109km northwest of Cooma, runs through a 12km long stretch of limestone, riddled with caves. The caves are a well-signposted 6½km from the highway, downhill on a windy unsealed road. There is a $3 per car site fee for the Yarrangobilly Caves precinct. Only **South Glory Cave** is open for a **self-guided tour** (45min.), but you'll need a token from the visitor center to explore beyond the unusual "glory arch" entrance. (Open daily 9:30am-4:30pm. $9, children $5.50, families $22.) The remaining caves are open to **guided tours.** (1-1½hr. daily 11am, 1, and 3pm; other times with advance scheduling. $11, children $8, families $33.) **Jillabenan Cave** is the only **wheelchair-accessible** cave. Its stalactites and stalagmites amid crystal-lined nooks are spectacular. **Jersey Cave** and **North Glory Cave** contain equally stellar sights. After wandering around underground, head to the surface and try a short bushwalk on a maintained trail, or take a load off in the 27°C (81°F) **thermal pools** near the river, a 700m steep downhill walk from the carpark (free). The **NPWS Visitors Center** at the site is an essential first stop. (☎ 6454 9597. Open daily 9:30am-5pm. $3 car site fee.)

RIVERINA

Dry, brown, and flat, much of the Riverina's terrain looks ill-suited for farming. Heavy irrigation, however, has turned the land into fertile plains. Two rivers supply water to the region: the Murrumbidgee, which starts as a trickle in the Snowy Mountains, and the Murray. While the area is not a prime sightseeing destination, the Riverina does attract budget travelers seeking seasonal farm or fruit-picking work in order to save up for more exciting destinations.

ALBURY   ☎ 02

Spanning the Murray River, which marks the border between New South Wales and Victoria, the Albury-Wodonga metropolitan area (pop. 90,000) belongs to both states. Right on the Hume Hwy., it breaks the transit between Sydney and Melbourne and provides an excellent base for daytrips to nearby wineries, alpine retreats, and the neighboring Riverina. The preponderance of quality budget accommodations and cheap eats makes Albury the most backpacker-friendly pitstop along the Hume. Many linger a while, especially during the summer months when the river is high and ripe for outdoor excursions.

NEW SOUTH WALES

216 ■ RIVERINA

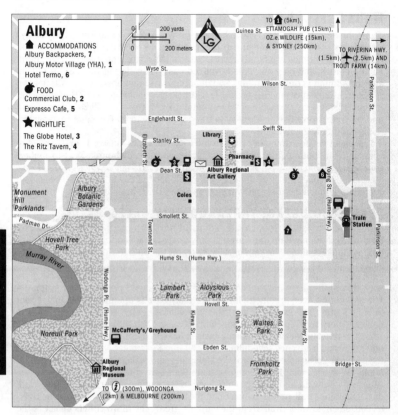

PICKING WORK. Seasonal picking jobs abound in the Riverina year-round, although December to April is the easiest time to find work. Conditions can be tough—even the basics such as water and toilets are unusual, and pay is typically based on how much you pick, not how long you work. To find out more about seasonal work, check out **Employment National** (www.employmentnational.com.au), call the toll free **Harvest Hotline** (☎ 1300 720 126) or check out the "Seasonal Work" section of the **Australian Jobsearch** website (http://jobsearch.deetya.gov.au). Riverina tourist offices keep copies of the useful *Working Holidays in the Riverina*, also available online at www.riverinatourism.com.au.

■ TRANSPORTATION

The impressive Albury railway station is at the eastern end of Dean St.

> **Trains: Countrylink Travel Centre,** in the railway station, books Countrylink and V/Line transport. (☎ 6041 9555. Open M-F 9am-5pm.) **Countrylink** (☎ 13 22 32) trains run to: Goulburn (5hr., 2 per day, $66); Melbourne (3hr., 2 per day, $56.10); Sydney (7½hr., 2 per day, $85.80); Wagga Wagga (1¼hr., 2 per day, $22); Wangaratta (45min., 2 per day, $13.20); and Yass (4hr., 2 per day, $47.30).

Buses: V/Line (☎ 13 61 96) services destinations in Victoria far more frequently and cheaply; they run buses to: Echuca (3-4hr., 1-2 per day, $23.70); Melbourne (3-3½hr., 4-6 per day, $44); Mildura (10hr.; M, W, Th, Sa mornings; $62); Wangaratta (45min., 4-6 per day, $11); Rutherglen (40min; M, W, Th, Sa mornings; $6.90); and Swan Hill (5½-7hr., 1-2 per day, $39.10). **McCafferty's/Greyhound** (☎ 13 20 30) runs from the corner of Ebden St. and Wodonga Pl. to: Adelaide (16½hr., 3 per day, $118); Brisbane (26½hr., 5 per day, $141); Canberra (5hr., 4 per day, $34); Melbourne (4½hr., 5 per day, $41); Sydney (9½hr., 5 per day, $48); and Wangaratta (45min., 2 per day, $24).

✈ 🛈 ORIENTATION AND PRACTICAL INFORMATION

The **Hume Hwy.** (Hwy. 31) from Sydney enters Albury from the northeast, runs through town, and then turns sharply west to bypass Wodonga. The **Murray Valley Hwy.** (Hwy. 16) runs along the Victorian side and enters Wodonga from the southeast, running through town before uniting with the Hume Hwy. Along the river on the New South Wales side, the **Riverina Hwy.** (Hwy. 58) runs west to Corowa. Albury's main street, **Dean St.,** runs east to west from the railroad tracks and is crossed by (the easternmost) **Young St.,** Macauley, David, Olive, Kiewa, and Townsend St. **Smollett St.** runs parallel to Dean St. one block south.

Tourist Office: Gateway Visitors Information Centre (☎ 1300 796 222; fax 6051 3759) is located in the Gateway Village between Albury and Wodonga just south of the Murray on the Hume Hwy. A bus goes back and forth between Albury (Dean St.) and Wodonga (High St.), passing by the info centre every 30min. 24hr. computer information station outside. Open daily 9am-5pm.

Currency Exchange: Several banks and 24hr. **ATMs** line Dean St. Bank hours M-Th 9:30am-4pm and F 9:30am-5pm.

Police: 539-543 Olive St. (☎ 6023 9299), near Swift St.

Internet Access: Albury City Library (☎ 6041 6633), in the city block behind the Regional Art Centre, has 2 terminals. Free for research, but email costs $2.75 per 30min. Book ahead. Open M-F 9am-7pm, Sa 9am-2pm. **Cyberheaven** (☎ 6023 4320), across from the post office on Kiewa St., has more terminals. ($5.50 per 30min., $8.80 per hr. Open M-F 9am-6pm, Sa 10am-2pm.)

Post Office: (☎ 6051 3633), at the corner of Dean and Kiewa St. Open M-F 9am-5pm. Poste Restante. **Postal Code:** 2640.

⌂ ACCOMMODATIONS

■ **Albury Backpackers,** 452 David St. (☎ 6041 1822; www.alburybackpackers.com.au). Just south of Smollett St. Recently renovated, this comfy hostel has laundry facilities, kitchen, dining hut, and mosaic-tiled hall bath. Laid-back travelers bond through town pub crawls, varied regional daytrips, and renowned overnight canoe trips run by the affable owner (1-day Murray trip $26, 2-day $59). Linens included. Internet $5 per hr. Check-out 11am. Dorms $17; twins and doubles $38. VIP. Wheelchair accessible. ❷

Albury Motor Village (YHA), 372 Wagga Rd., Hume Hwy (☎ 6040 2999; albury@motor-village.com.au), 5km north of the city center in Lavington just beyond Kaylock Rd. McCafferty's/Greyhound will drop off here; $10 cab ride from train station. Quiet, clean, and family-friendly. Pool, kitchenette, TV lounge, parking, and laundry. Internet $2 per 20min. Key deposit $10. Reception 8am-8pm. Book ahead in summer. Dorms $18; powered sites for 2 $19; self-contained cabins for 2 $68-120 (all but deluxe cabins are BYO linens). AmEx/DC/MC/V. ❷

Hotel Termo, 47 Dean St. (☎ 6041 3544), 1 block from the train station. Basic pub accommodations upstairs and popular nightspot. Linens included. Singles $22.50; doubles $33. AmEx/DC/MC/V. ❷

NEW SOUTH WALES

◖◗ FOOD AND NIGHTLIFE

Commercial Club ❷, 618 Dean St., serves an $11 all-you-can-eat lunch and dinner with a rich variety of vegetables, meat dishes, and surprisingly gourmet desserts—the best deal in town. The casino is downstairs. (☎6021 1133. Open daily for lunch noon-2pm, dinner 6-9pm. Sign in at the lobby desk; bring photo ID to prove you're just visiting—locals must have club membership.) **Expresso Cafe ❶,** 449c Dean St., with comfortable indoor and outdoor seating, is a popular local destination that serves full breakfasts, focaccias and sandwiches ($4-7), and great coffee ($2.50-3). Internet access ($6 per 30min., $8 per hr.) is an added bonus. (☎6023 4730. Open Su-W 9am-4pm, Th-Sa 9am-10pm.) Coles **supermarket** is in the West End Plaza on Kiewa St. between Dean and Smollett St. (Open M-Sa 7am-midnight, Su 7am-8pm.)

The Globe Hotel is a few doors down from the Commercial Club on Dean St. Monday "Hospitality Nights" feature live cover bands and Happy Hour prices, with $2 beer and $4-5 spirits. Wednesday is Uni Night; F-Sa DJs spin. (☎6021 2622. Open Su until midnight, M and W 3am, Tu and Th 1am, F-Sa 4am.) **The Ritz Tavern,** 480 Dean St., features DJs until dawn. (☎6041 4484. F-Sa cover $5 after midnight. Open W 7pm-1am, Th 7pm-4am, F-Sa 7pm-5am.)

◉ ◪ SIGHTS AND ACTIVITIES

On Wodonga Pl. between Smollett and Dean St., the **Albury Botanic Gardens** (☎6023 8241) have diverse arboreal displays and plenty of grassy picnic space. To take in a sweeping view of the region, climb to the top of the **Monument Hill Bushlands** and gaze out onto Albury-Wodonga from the base of the Deco obelisk Albury War Memorial. Walk uphill from Dean St. or follow the street up and around the back of the hill. On the Riverina Hwy. 14km east of Albury, the **Hume Weir Trout Farm** raises rainbow trout for commercial and recreational purposes. You can catch trout (rod and bait free, fish caught $10 per kg) and sample smoked trout. (☎6026 4334. Open daily 9am-5pm. $6, students $5, children $3.50.)

◪ DAYTRIP FROM ALBURY: ETTAMOGAH PUB

Just 15km north of Albury along the Hume Hwy., the **Ettamogah Pub** (☎6026 2366) explodes in goofy fun as it caters to gawking tourists and satirizes and stereotypes all things Aussie. The late cartoonist Ken Maynard had been drawing the place for the *Australia Post* for years before someone decided to actually construct it. The amusement-park-style village is composed of eye-popping, off-kilter buildings decorated with a running stream of witticisms. The centerpiece is the hilariously constructed and fully operational Ettamogah Pub itself, capped with a vintage Fosters beer truck on the roof and a crashed airplane next door. (Pub open M-Th 10am-9pm, F-Su 10:30am-10pm. Bistro open F-Sa 6-9pm.) The **Ettamogah Winery** predates the pub but is now part of the complex, and it features free tastings and wine sales. Next door is a restaurant and souvenir shop. (Open daily 9am-4pm.) There's no admission to tour the site, and signs will clearly direct you from the highway.

FOLLOW THAT MOTH Occurring in late November, the annual **Ngan Girra festival** is a cultural celebration held in Mungabareena Reserve near Albury. The festival celebrates the traditional confluence of several local Aboriginal groups, who gathered to follow the springtime Bogong moth migration. The moths, after being smoked out and cooked, are a high-nutrient feast. The indigenous term for this particular "meeting place" is *ngan girra*, or *kamberra*, which was only altered slightly when it was used to create the name of the Australian capital city, Canberra.

Had enough booze? Time to see the animals! **oz.e.wildlife,** formerly the Etta-mogah Sanctuary, allows visitors to hand-feed kangaroos and wallabies and get close to penguins and koalas. A parade (daily 11am, 1, and 3pm) will ensure you get your money's worth. (☎ 6040 3677. $10, concessions $8, children $5, families $25, under 4 free. Open daily 9am-5pm.)

WAGGA WAGGA ☎ 02

New South Wales' largest inland city (pop. 58,000), Wagga Wagga (WAH-guh) derives its name from the local Aboriginal tribe, for whom repetition implied plu-rality. *Wagga* means crow. Hence *wagga wagga* means a place of many crows. Charles Sturt University is just outside the city.

Baylis St. is the town's main drag, becoming **Fitzmaurice St.** once it crosses the bridge over Wollundry Lagoon. The bus stop is at the railway station, on the south end of Station Pl. **Countrylink** (☎ 13 22 32) and **Fearnes Coaches** (☎ 1800 029 918) operate **bus** and **train** service to Gundagai (1hr., 1 per day, $20) and **Sydney** (6½-7¼hr., 3 per day, $48). **Greyhound** (☎ 13 20 30) runs to: Canberra (3hr., 2 per day, $34); Griffith (2hr., 1 per day, $34); Gundagai (1hr., 2 per day, $27); and Sydney (8¼hr., 2 per day, $48). The **Visitors Center** is at 20 Tarcutta St. (☎ 6926 9621; www.tourismwaggawagga.com.au. Open daily 9am-5pm.) A **post office** is in the Wagga Wagga Marketplace. (Open M-F 8:30am-5pm.) **Postal Code:** 2650.

For inexpensive accommodations, try the **Wagga Wagga Guesthouse (NOMADS) ❸**, 149 Gurwood St., a popular spot with seasonal workers because of its amenities: kitchen, TV, laundry, lockers, Internet, and wheelchair accessibility. (☎ 6931 8702. Sin-gles $25; doubles $45; weekly rates available.) **Billy's Cafe ❶**, 35 Gurwood St., serves popular breakfasts for $10 and under. (Open daily 6am-3:30pm.) A Woolworth's **super-market** is directly across from Billy's Cafe on Gurwood St. (Open daily 7am-10pm.)

The attractive **Botanic Gardens,** with an entrance near the intersection of Urana and Macleay St., are arranged across nine hectares. Pathways wind pleasantly among the trees. (☎ 6925 4065. Open daily 7:30am-dusk. Free.) The **Wiradjuri Walk-ing Track** meanders for 30km, covering many of the city's natural highlights. The trail runs through the Botanic Gardens, along the Murrumidgee River, past Lake Albert to many panoramic views of the region.

For fun on the river, check out **Murrumbidgee River Cruises** (☎ 6925 8700). Cruises take passengers to see nearby islands and inform them of the history and natural wonders of the region. (Depart M and W-Su 2pm. Adults $12, concessions $10, chil-dren $6. Call to book.) If you'd prefer to row your own boat, you can hire canoes from **Action Outdoors,** 140 Hammond Ave. (☎ 6931 8681. 1-day canoe hire $39; pick-up and drop-off programs available for multi-day hire. Open M-F 9:30am-5:30pm, Sa 9am-1pm.) In the summertime, **Wagga Beach,** at Cabriata Park, is filled with sun-bathers and water fanatics of all kinds.

NARRANDERA ☎ 02

Downtown Narrandera (na-RAN-dra) feels refreshingly like an intimate Anytown, Australia. This low-key transportation hub (pop. 5000) doesn't trip over itself in an attempt to nab tourists. About halfway between Adelaide and Sydney off the Sturt Hwy., and a day's drive from Melbourne en route to Brisbane along the Newell Hwy., Narrandera provides excellent budget beds for commuters.

The main street, **East St.,** runs north-south, one block east of Cadell St. The **Tour-ist Information Centre** is on Cadell St., right on Narrandera Park. (☎ 6959 1766 or 1800 672 392. Open daily 9am-5pm.) While inside the info center, you can't miss the world's second-largest playable guitar—Bristol, England recently reclaimed the title with one slightly larger. There is **Internet** access at the **library,** 39-51 East St. (☎ 6959 2128. Open M-F 10am-5:30pm, Sa 9:30am-noon. $3.30 per hr., min. charge $1.10.) The **post office** is at 140 East St. **Postal Code:** 2700. For a good bed above the liveliest pub in town, the **Charles Sturt Hotel ❷**, 77 East St., on the corner of East and Douglas St., offers nicely furnished rooms. (☎ 6959 2042. TV lounge, BBQ. Reception at bar 10am-late. Singles $20; doubles $25.)

Narrandera is an excellent place to look for koalas relaxing in river red gum trees, thanks to the ◪**Narrandera Koala Regeneration Reserve,** established in 1972, on the southeast edge of town along the Murrumbidgee River. See the **Tourist Information Centre** for details about walking tracks and driving possibilities or contact retired resident Roy Russell, who is happy to show visitors around the reserve. (☎ 6959 2441. Free, though donations to support the koalas are welcomed.)

CENTRAL WEST

The cities and towns of the Central West lie between the rugged plateaus of the Blue Mountains and the stark dryness of outback New South Wales. The major route into the region from the east is the Great Western Hwy., which crosses through the Blue Mountains to Bathurst. From Bathurst, the Mitchell Hwy. heads northwest to Dubbo, Bourke, and beyond, and the Mid Western Hwy. runs southwest to Cowra and eventually Hay. Both of these roads intersect the Newell Hwy., the major route between Melbourne and Brisbane, which cuts a long path across the Central West. Most towns of the Central West, surrounded by miles of rolling agriculture, are regarded as pitstops between grander destinations. Even with a short stay in this region, you'll notice an extraordinary degree of hospitality in locals who have chosen to live the less hectic life.

BATHURST   ☎ 02

Bathurst (pop. 30,800) features wide avenues and large, ornate lampposts, suggesting it was once slated for greatness. But it is an unadorned route on the southwest corner of town that has brought the city notoriety. Originally built in 1938 as a scenic drive, the 6km loop road up Mt. Panorama and back down doubles as a public road and the track for the annual touring car races for **V-8 Supercars** and the **2-litre class,** held in early October and mid-November, respectively. During these events, over 150,000 people swamp the usually low-profile town, and thanks to the races and the population of students at Charles Sturt University, Bathurst has a certain vibrance that the industrial towns of the region lack.

◪◪ **TRANSPORTATION AND PRACTICAL INFORMATION.** Bathurst is 101km west of Katoomba on the Great Western Hwy. **Trains** and **buses** leave the **Railway Station** at the corner of Keppel and Havannah St. **Countrylink** (☎ 13 22 32) goes to: Cowra (1½hr.; M, W, and F-Sa 1 per day; $19); Dubbo (3hr., 3 per day, $35); Forbes and Parkes (3½hr., M-Sa 1 per day, $33); Katoomba (2hr., 2 per day, $19); Lithgow (1-1¼hr., 3-7 per day, $13); Orange (1hr., 1-2 per day, $24); Parramatta and Penrith (3hr., 2 per day, $28-31); and Sydney (4hr., 2 per day, $38). **McCafferty's/Greyhound** (☎ 13 14 99 or 13 20 30) runs to: Dubbo (3hr., 3 per day, $49); Katoomba (2hr., 2 per day, $32); Lithgow (1hr., 3-7 per day, $32); Parramatta and Penrith (2½-3½hr., 2 per day, $32); and Sydney (3½-4½hr., 2 per day, $35). The **Bathurst Visitors Center,** 28 William St., has brochures and free maps. (☎ 6332 1444 or 1800 681 000. Open daily 9am-5pm.) The **post office,** 230 Howick St., is between George and William St. (☎ 6339 4813. Open M-F 9am-5pm.) **Postal Code:** 2795.

◪◪ **ACCOMMODATIONS AND FOOD.** Bathurst has a few pubstays downtown. Rates for all accommodations skyrocket during the races. Outside of town, the **Bathurst Explorer's Hotel ❹**, 357 Stewart St., offers luxurious rooms with TV, fridge, heat, A/C, and a $12 dinner coupon for area restaurants. (☎ 6331 2966 or

WALTZING MATILDA No song—not even Australia's official national anthem—is as deeply ingrained in the hearts of Aussies as *Waltzing Matilda*. The folk ballad originated in the social upheaval of the shearing disputes between unionist woolworkers and wealthy landowners during the late 19th century. Conflict erupted in September 1894 at Dagworth Station (Orange, NSW), when laborers and police fired at each other, and a shed containing 100 "jumbucks" (colloquial for sheep, derived from an Aboriginal term) with hundreds of bales of wool was burned to the ground. Banjo Paterson, a wealthy man who sided with the workers, adapted an old Scottish folk song to commemorate the event. Completed in 1895, the song still strikes a chord in the Australian psyche, recalling the tough frontier spirit of the bushmen and shearers.

1800 047 907. Reception 7am-9pm. Singles $59; twins and doubles $69, extra person $10. $6 weekend surcharge. MC/V.) **East's Bathurst Holiday Park ❷** is on Sydney Rd. (the Great Western Hwy.), 4km east of town. (☎6331 8286 or 1800 669 911. Showers, laundry, BBQ, and TV room. Reception daily 8am-6pm. Sites for 2 $17, powered $20; cabins $50, ensuite $62-93. MC/V.)

Ziegler's Cafe ❷, 52 Keppel St., has a range of salads, grilled veggie dishes, and burgers. (☎6332 1565. Lunches $10-20, dinners $12-22. BYO. Open M-F 10am-9pm, Sa 9am-9pm, Su 10am-3pm. AmEx/DC/MC/V.) Coles **supermarket,** 47 William St., has a **deli ❶** with sandwiches ($3) and pizza for $6.50. (☎6332 9566. Open M-Sa 6am-midnight, Su 8am-10pm.)

🔲 **SIGHTS.** A trip to Bathurst would be incomplete without a spin round the **Mt. Panorama circuit,** southwest on William St. until it becomes Panorama Ave. As you twist your way up and down the steep hills, you'll gain an appreciation for the pros who do it in excess of 200kph. Don't let the banner ads and tire piles seduce you; local police patrol the area frequently, looking for drivers who edge above the 60kph speed limit. The recently expanded **National Motor Racing Museum,** near the starting line, keeps the thrill of the race alive year-round. (☎6332 1872. Open daily 9am-4:30pm. $7, concessions $5, families $16.) The **courthouse** on Russell St. was considered so grand when it was built in 1880 that residents of the town thought there must have been a mistake when it was put in Bathurst. Rumors circulated that the building had been meant for a more prominent colony in India or Africa, as the massive railings encircling the building would easily have kept elephants out. (Open M-F 9am-5pm, but hours vary when in use.) Don't miss the **Abercrombie Caves,** part of the Jenolan Caves Trust, 70km south of Bathurst via Trunkey Creek. The majestic Grand Arch is the largest limestone archway in the southern hemisphere. (☎6368 8603. Open daily 9am-4pm. $12, concessions $8. Guided tour daily 2pm; $15, concessions $10.)

FORBES AND PARKES ☎02

A feeling of timelessness and the nearby Parkes Radio Telescope, famous for its involvement with putting the first man on the moon, compensate for a lack of compelling sights. Once the stomping grounds of renowned bushranger **Ben Hall,** Forbes (pop. 10,000) shows little evidence of its checkered past. The **Newell Hwy.** runs through Forbes, with Dubbo 153km to the northeast, Orange 93km to the east, and Cowra 90km to the southeast. The downtown, anchored by Lachlan St., is surrounded by the flood-prone **Lake Forbes,** which looks suspiciously like a river to the untrained eye. From the old **railway station** on Union St., **Countrylink** (☎13 22 32) runs **buses** to: Dubbo (2hr., 3-4 per week, $21); Orange (2hr., 13 per week, $18); Parkes (30min., 1-3 per day, $6); and Sydney (7hr., M-Sa 1 per day, $77); ISIC discount 50%. **McCafferty's/Greyhound** (☎13 14 99 or 13 20 30) handles services to

Coonabarabran (5hr., 3 per day, $57) and Parkes (30min., 2 per day, $45). **Harvey World Travel,** 6 Templar St., sells all bus tickets with $5 service fee. (☎6852 2344. Open M-F 9am-5pm, Sa 9am-noon.) The old railway station on Union St. is now the **Forbes Railway Arts and Tourist Centre.** (☎6852 4155. Open daily 9am-5pm.)

Pubstays in Forbes are some of the best and cheapest in the area. Everything's huge at the **Albion Hotel** ❸, 135 Lachlan St., from the clean rooms to the men's showers that could house a town meeting. (☎6851 1881. Reception at bar. Singles $25; doubles $50.) **Apex Caravan Park** ❶, 86 Reymond St., 2km south of the town center via Bridge and Flint St., is along the river. (☎6851 1929. Showers, laundry, and BBQ. Sites for 2 $15, powered $18; cabins from $41, ensuite from $66. Holiday surcharges.) Buy **groceries** at Woolworth's, on the corner of Rankin and Grenfell St. (☎6852 2421. Open M-Sa 7am-9pm, Su 8am-8pm.)

The **64m satellite dish,** visible from the Newell Hwy., 55km northeast of Forbes (20km north of Parkes) on the road to Dubbo, belongs to the **Parkes Radio Telescope.** The combination of low radio interference, relative proximity to Sydney, and expert staff and visiting scientists puts Parkes at the forefront of research. A major contributor to astronomy since its opening in 1961, the Parkes Telescope has participated in high-profile projects including the televising of the first moon walk, portrayed in the movie *The Dish* and the rescue of NASA's Apollo 13. The Visitors Discovery Centre is a surprisingly low-tech facility with extensive displays on the telescope, but visitors don't have an opportunity to look at the dish any closer than from the Centre. The knowledgeable staff and two 20min. films (one about the Centre for $3 and another about the solar system for $5) make it interesting even for non-scientists. (☎6861 1777; www.parkes.atnf.csiro.au/visitors_centre. Open daily 8:30am-4:15pm. Free.)

MUDGEE   ☎02

A land of wine and honey cradled in the foothills of the Great Dividing Range, Mudgee (from the Aboriginal for "nest in the hills"; pop. 18,000) has over 20 vineyards and not much else to offer the tourist, though locals proudly proclaim that Mudgee is "tasting better each year."

Mudgee is a 3½hr. drive from Sydney on Hwy. 86, between Lithgow (159km) and Dubbo (109km). **Countrylink** (☎13 22 32) runs one to two times per day to: Coonabarabran (3hr., $33); Lithgow (2½hr., $24); and Sydney (5hr., $49). Book at **Harvey World Travel,** Shop 28-29, Town Centre, Church St. (☎6372 6077. Open M-F 8:30am-5:30pm, Sa 8:30am-noon.) For **taxis,** call ☎13 10 08. The **Mudgee Visitors Centre,** 84 Market St., is armed with maps and advice. (☎6372 1020 or 1800 816 304. Open M-F 9am-5pm, Sa 9am-3:30pm, Su 9:30am-2pm.) The **NPWS office,** 160 Church St., administers the northwest section of Wollemi National Park (☎6372 7199; mudgee@npws.nsw.gov.au. Open M-F 9am-5pm. See p. 144.)

Pubstay accommodations are the most readily available in town. **The Woolpack Hotel** ❷, 67 Market St., is near the Visitors Center; turn left and go one block down Market St. (☎6372 1908. Reception 7am-midnight at bar. Singles and doubles $25 per person. MC/V.) The **Mudgee Riverside Caravan and Tourist Park** ❶, 22 Short St., behind the Visitors Center, has showers and laundry. (☎6372 2531; rivside@winsoft.net.au. Linen $10. Laundry $4. Reception daily 8am-8pm. Sites for 2 $14, powered $17; ensuite cabins with A/C $55-66. AmEx/MC/V.)

▧**Red Heifer Grill and Carvery** ❸, 1 Church St., inside the Lawson Park Hotel, is a great spot for good grub—grill your own steak dinner ($14-17) and enjoy it with a bottle of local wine (from $10). Mains ($16-18) come with all-you-can-eat salad bar for only $5 extra. (☎6372 2183. Open daily 10am-10pm; lunch noon-2:30pm, dinner 6-9pm.) A Bi-Lo **supermarket** is on Church St., in the cavernous Town Centre shopping plaza next to Harvey World Travel. (Open M-Sa 7am-10pm, Su 8am-8pm.

Mudgee's selling point is its victual offerings, ranging from small, communal vineyards to large, self-sufficient **wineries.** There are many vineyards in the area; consult the tourist office for extensive information. Travelers passing through in September will find the streets hopping with the **Mudgee Wine Festival.** If you want to do the wine-tasting circuit but also wish to avoid running afoul of stringent drink-driving laws, a number of companies offer tours. Try **Mudgee Transit Wine Tours** (☎ 6372 0091 or 1800 779 997; half-day $45, full-day $60) or **Mudgee Valley Tours** (☎ 0721 0121; 4hr. tour Su-F $45; full-day Sa with lunch $50.). **Poet's Corner Wine Cellar,** a conglomeration of Craigmoor, Montrose, and Poet's Corner labels, has been making tawny Rummy Port for 70 years. To reach the winery, bike or drive 7km northwest of Mudgee on Henry Lawson Dr., then turn onto Craigmoor Rd. (☎ 6372 2208. Open M-Sa 10am-4:30pm, Su 10am-4pm.) **Huntington Estate Wines,** 8km from town past the airport on Cassilis Rd., has an array of reds for sample on a free self-guided tour. (☎ 6373 3825. Open M-F 9am-5pm, Sa 10am-5pm, Su 10am-3pm.) **Botobolar,** 89 Botobolar Rd., 16km northeast of town, is an organic winery with daily tastings. (☎ 6373 3840. Open M-Sa 10am-5pm, Su 10am-3pm.)

DUBBO   ☎ 02

The hub of the Central West region, Dubbo is a busy, blue-collar service city filled with down-to-earth Australians. In the midst of the town's bustling center, it's possible to forget how close you are to the Outback, but a drive after dark in any direction will demonstrate just how isolated you really are. Dubbo's headline attraction is the Western Plains Zoo, an amazingly well-developed and modern attraction for being in the middle of nowhere, and no visit to the city would be complete without a stop here.

▐ TRANSPORTATION. Countrylink (☎ 13 22 32) **trains** and **buses** depart from the **railway station** on Talbragar St. to: Albury (7hr.; Su, Tu, and Th 1 per day; $71.50); Broken Hill (8½hr.; 1 per day; $86); Forbes (2hr.; Su, Tu, and Th 1 per day; $19); Melbourne (10½hr.; Su, Tu, and Th 1 per day; $98); Orange (2hr., 1 per day, $22); Sydney (7-11hr., 1 per day, $66); and Wagga Wagga (5½hr.; Su, Tu, and Th 1 per day; $47.30). The Shell Station at the intersection of the Newell and Mitchell Hwy. is the drop-off point for **McCafferty's/Greyhound** (☎ 13 14 99 or 13 20 30) and **Rendell Coaches** (☎ 1800 023 328 or 6884 4199). They service: Adelaide (15hr., 2 per day, $115); Brisbane (11½-14hr., 3 per day, $95-105); Broken Hill (8hr., 1 per day, $112); Coonabarabran (2hr., 2 per day, $46); Bathurst (2¾hr, 1 per day, $38); and Melbourne (11½-13hr., 2 per day, $97-114). All tickets can be booked at the railway station. (Open M-F 8am-5pm, Sa-Su 8-9:30am and 10:30am-2pm.) Drop-off in Dubbo frequently occurs in the wee hours of the morning as coaches ramble on to further destinations. To reach accommodations, rely on 24hr. **taxis** (☎ 6882 1911). **Darrell Wheeler Cycles,** 25 Bultje St., hires bikes for $15 per day. (☎ 6882 9899. Open M-F 8:30am-5:30pm, Sa 8:30am-1pm.) Bike trails cross town and head out to the zoo.

▐▐ ORIENTATION AND PRACTICAL INFORMATION. Dubbo sits at the intersection of the **Newell Hwy.,** which runs between Melbourne and Brisbane, and the **Mitchell Hwy.,** which leads from Sydney and Bathurst to points west. The town's sprawling layout could make life difficult for those without a car, but major sights cluster around the zoo or the town center. **Talbragar St.** runs east-west, parallel to the two major highways that sandwich the town. The intersection of Talbragar and **Macquarie St.** marks the town center, with most of the action, including **banks, ATMs,** and **pharmacies** running down Macquarie St.

The **Dubbo Visitors Centre,** on the corner of Erskine and Macquarie St. in the northwest corner of the small downtown area, has maps of biking trails and

OUTBACK JACK

Kelvin Murphy is a Jackaroo student at the Western Institute TAFE Rural Skills and Environment Centre in Dubbo. Interview July 21, 2002.

Q: What kind of things do you learn at jackaroo school?

A: At jackaroo school, the one I'm going to, we're learning all about husbandry of all different animals, but mainly cattle and sheep, and we learn horse skills and how to drive and maintain our four-wheel drives and motorbikes, chainsaws, mechanics of all those things I just mentioned. Also tractors and the safety of tractors and how to use them, water supplies and farm chemicals we're going through as well. Those are the main things—sometimes we might go through little bits of first aid, but those are the main details.

Q: What are the skills that you're learning that are most interesting to you?

A: Most interesting to me would be the horse skills, and probably the first aid and the farm chemicals. I haven't had very much background at all with those. Like, most people know a little bit about cattle and sheep, but those things I don't know much about at all.

Q: Where are you expecting or planning that these skills will take you?

A: The course itself helps me get job work within the jackaroo sort of trade, and other than that the only other idea that I've had is actually buying my own property. With this course I'll have the basic skills needed to run a farm myself.

books river cruises. (☎6884 1422; www.dubbotourism.com.au. Open daily 9am-5pm.) The **police station** is on Brisbane St. across from the Grape Vine Cafe. Find **Internet** access at the **Dubbo Regional Library,** on the southwest corner of Macquarie and Talbragar St. ($5.50 per hr.; open M-F 10am-6pm, Sa 10am-3pm, Su noon-4pm), or the **Grape Vine** cafe ($2.50 per 30min.; see **Food,** p. 224). The **post office** is on Talbragar St. between Brisbane and Macquarie St. **Postal Code:** 2830.

⌐⌐ ACCOMMODATIONS AND FOOD. Plenty of hotels cluster around Talbragar St. in the city center, with singles from $20; motels in the area generally run $50-80 for a single and $60-90 for a double. The cheapest beds are at the **Dubbo YHA Hostel ❷,** 87 Brisbane St., close to the old intercity bus station. The talking pet cockatoo and verandahs off of every room add flavor to an otherwise unglamorous place, as do nightly fire-front gatherings to watch sports on the telly. (☎/fax 6882 0922; yhadubbo@lisp.com.au. Washer $2, no dryer. Bikes $7 per day. Reception 7:30am-10:30pm. Dorms $24, YHA $20; twins and doubles $45/$38; family rooms $56/$47. MC/V.) The upscale **Amaroo Hotel ❺,** 83 Macquarie St., is in the middle of town. (☎6882 3533. Breakfast included. Singles $59; doubles $80. MC/V.) The excellent **Dubbo City Caravan Park ❶,** on Whylandra St. just before it becomes the Newell Hwy., has shaded sites overlooking the Macquarie River and the most beautiful bathrooms of any NSW caravan park. (☎6882 4820; dccp@dubbo.nsw.gov.au. Bikes $15 per day, $10 per half-day. Linen $10. Laundry $4. Reception daily 7:30am-7:30pm. Check-in 1pm. Curfew 10pm. Sites from $14, powered $18, ensuite $25; caravans $28; cabins from $42, ensuite $49. 10% surcharge on cabins during school holidays. AmEx/DC/MC/V.)

Sandwich shops and bakeries are plentiful in the city center, but there is no truly cheap restaurant. For the best coffee concoctions, pastries, and light meals, seek out the **Grape Vine Cafe ❶,** 144 Brisbane St. (☎6884 7354. Lunch $8-11. Internet $2.50 per 30min. Open M-Sa 8:30am-10:30pm, Su 9am-6pm.) A food court with a cafe, Asian noodles, and Subway sandwich shop is inside **Riverdale Shopping Centre,** 49 Macquarie St., as is Woolworth's **supermarket** (open M-Sa 7am-10pm, Su 8am-8pm); the attached movie theater provides a quick flick. (☎6881 8600. $12.50, concessions $9.80, children $8.70; all Tu shows $7.60.) There are **local markets** at the showground on Wingewarra St. every 2nd and 4th Saturday of the month. (Open 2nd Sa 9am-1pm with crafts, produce, and bric-a-brac; 4th Sa 8am-noon with fresh produce, cheese, and flowers.)

◙ **SIGHTS.** Dubbo's premier tourist attraction is the ▨**Western Plains Zoo,** on Obley Rd., 4km south of the city center off the Newell Hwy. In addition to Australian native species, the zoo houses Bengal tigers, black rhinoceri, and Australia's only **African elephants;** exhibits are arranged by continent around a paved track suitable for driving or biking with BBQ and picnic areas along the way. Many of the animals wander unrestrained through loose enclosures. Don't miss the nursery for injured and orphaned animals; the sight of infant joeys snuggling together under baby blankets is priceless. On weekends, and Wednesdays and Fridays during school holidays, 6:45am zoo walks provide a behind-the-scenes look at the animals for an additional $3. (☎6882 5888; www.zoo.nsw.gov.au. Open daily 9am-5pm; last entry 3:30pm. 2-day pass $23, students $16, ages 4-16 $12.50. 4hr. bike rental $11 plus $10 deposit.) **Macquarie River Cruises** offers trips on one of the biggest riverboats in outback New South Wales. Some trips stop for tea or lunch at the Homestead before a hay ride and trip down the river. (1hr. cruise leaves 1:30pm: $16, ages 4-16 $8. 2hr. lunch cruise leaves 12:45pm: $25, ages 4-16 $12.50. Book through the Visitors Center.) The dough-faced animatronic models of **Old Dubbo Gaol,** on Macquarie St. between Commonwealth and State Banks, tell the bygone convicts' sad, macabre stories that prove any subject (including the hanging of eight men) can be funny if you add enough goofy talking mannequins. (☎6882 8122. Open daily 9am-5pm; last admission 4:30pm. $7, students $5.50, ages 5-18 $3.50.) Down the street at the **Dubbo Observatory,** on Camp Rd. off the Newell Hwy., you can see the three galaxies visible only in the Southern Hemisphere. (☎6885 3022. 2 shows nightly; book ahead. $13.50, families $38.50.)

If you want a taste (and smell) of the real Central West Australia, don't miss the ▨**livestock markets** 4km north on the Newell Hwy. towards Gilgandra; look for the sign. Entering, watching, and mingling with the *cockies* (farmers) is free of charge. (Auction M, Th, and some F; cattle 8am-noon or 1pm, sheep noon-3 or 4pm.)

Learn about aerodynamics, Aboriginal history, woodcraft, and flying sticks (that only come back to you with a little skill) at **Jedda Boomerangs,** on Minore Rd., White Pines. As you head southwest toward the zoo, turn right onto Minore; it's 4km down Minore Rd. The excellent, informative hourly tour culminates in burning your own design on a boomerang ($7 extra to take it home) and learning how to throw one. (☎6882 3110. Open daily 10am-4pm. Free. Tours $7, children $5.)

Inquire at the Visitors Center about local wineries. There are two tours that go to the zoo and other local attractions: **Langley's Dubbo Day Tours** (☎6884 5333) and **Jolly Swagman Tours** (☎6884 9984).

COONABARABRAN ☎02

For folks living in a tiny town in the middle of nowhere, the lifestyle of Coonabarabran (coon-a-BAR-a-bran, Aboriginal for "an inquisitive person"; pop. 3000) embodies all that is good about the laid-back and friendly country life. As the astronomy capital of Australia, thanks to low levels of urban light pollution, a large number of clear night skies, and relative proximity to major urban areas—Sydney and Brisbane are only a day's drive—it draws many visitors.

▐ **TRANSPORTATION.** Coonabarabran lies 159km northeast of Dubbo on the Newell Hwy. It's accessible from the northeast through Gunnedah on the Oxley Hwy., which joins the Newell and enters from the north. **Countrylink** (☎13 22 32) runs **buses** from the Visitors Center to Sydney (8hr, Su-F 1 per day, $82). **McCafferty's/Greyhound** (☎13 14 99 or 13 20 30) leave from the Caltex Service Station outside of town heading toward: Bendigo (12½hr., 1 per day, $122); Brisbane (9hr., 3 per day, $96); Dubbo (2hr., 3 per day, $47); Echuca (11hr., 1 per day, $119); Melbourne (13-15hr., 2 per day, $121); Narrabri (1½hr., 1 per day, $54); and Sydney

NEW SOUTH WALES

(10hr., 1 per day, $128) via Dubbo. **Harvey World Travel,** 79 John St. (☎6842 1566), makes transport bookings for a $5 service fee. Inquire at the Visitors Center about local car hire for Warrumbungle National Park, 30km from town.

⚡ PRACTICAL INFORMATION. The main drag is **John St.** (the Newell Hwy.), home to several motels and crossed by **Dalgarno, Cassilis,** and **Edwards St.** Warrumbungle National Park and the observatories are both west of town. The **Visitors Center** is at the south end of town on the Newell Hwy. It has a display on **Australian megafauna,** including the skeleton of a 33,000-year-old giant diprotodon, the largest marsupial ever to roam the earth. (☎6842 1441 or 1800 242 881; www.coonabarabran.com. Open daily 9am-5pm.) Other services include: **NPWS office,** 30 Timor St. (☎6842 1311), with info on Warrumbungle National Park; 24hr. **ATMs** on John St.; **Internet** at the library, on John St. (☎6842 1093; $2.75 per 30min.; open M-F 9am-5pm); and a **post office,** 71a John St., in the center of town. (☎6842 1197. Open M-F 9am-5pm.) **Postal Code:** 2357.

🏠🍴 ACCOMMODATIONS AND FOOD. Book ahead for accommodations during school holidays. The **Imperial Hotel ❷,** at the corner of John and Dalgarno St., is over a pub with thin walls and floors through which the cries (and crying) of pokies-players downstairs can be heard. (☎6842 1023. Reception 8:30am-11pm. Check-out 9am. Singles $22, with breakfast $29; ensuite doubles $41/$55; extra person $12. AmEx/MC/V.) The other two pubstays are smaller but similar. At **John Oxley ❶,** 1km north of town on the Oxley Hwy., the affable hosts tend a shop, playground, and gas grill. (☎6842 1635. Reception in summer 8am-8pm; in winter 8am-7pm. Linen $11. Sites for 2 $12, powered $16; on-site vans for 2 $29; ensuite cabins for 2 $43-48; large family ensuite cabins $53-60.) A number of **B&Bs** and **farmstays** are also available in Coonabarabran and within the Warrumbungle area, with singles starting at $40; ask at the Visitors Center.

The **Golden Sea Dragon Restaurant ❷,** next to the Visitors Center at 8 John St., features a golden Buddha and instrumental Bette Midler but serves fantastic Chinese fare. (☎6842 2388. 2-course traveler's special $12. Open daily noon-2:30pm; also Sa-Su 5-10 or 11pm.) **Woop Woop Cafe ❶,** 38a John St., lets you brag to friends about discovering the "hole-in-the-wall" eatery with the best coffee in town. (☎6842 4755. Sandwiches $5-14. Open Tu-Sa 10am-6pm, Su 10am-4pm. BYO. MC/V.) The **Jolly Cauli Coffee Shop ❶,** 30 John St., has reasonable prices and **Internet** access. (☎6842 2021. Open M-F 8am-5pm, Sa 9am-1pm. Devonshire tea and scone $5.50. Internet $6 per hr. No credit cards.) The IGA **supermarket** is on Dalgarno St. (Open M-W 8:30am-6pm, Th-F 8:30am-6:30pm, Sa 8:30am-4pm, Su 9am-1pm.)

📷 SIGHTS. The highlight of Coonabarabran is the ⭐**Skywatch Night and Day Observatory,** 2km from town on the road to Warrumbungle National Park. The effusive staff guides night viewing sessions that clarify the jumbled stars. (☎6842 3303; www.skywatchobservatory.com. Open daily 2-5pm. Night session daily Nov.-Jan. 9 and 10pm; Feb. 9pm; Mar. 8:30 and 9:30pm; Apr.-Sept. 7 and 8pm; Oct. 7:30 and 8:30pm. Display only or golf $7.70, ages 5-16 $5.50, families $22; display and nightshow $12.10/$7.15/$33.) Australia's largest optical telescope (3.9m long) resides at **Siding Spring Observatory,** 28km from Coonabarabran on the road to Warrumbungle National Park. The observatory's Visitors Center offers an interactive, multimedia window onto the work of the resident astronomers but no public viewing of the night sky. You'll see groundbreaking research here but might have more laughs at Skywatch. (☎6842 6211. Special tours by arrangement. Open daily 9:30am-4pm. $5.50, concessions $3.30, families $13.20.) The **sandstone caves** within the **Pilliga Nature Reserve** were hollowed out by wind and water erosion and are tricky to locate, but the Visitors Center has explicit directions.

BETTER THAN A LET'S GO MAP! Down Under, the night sky is an entirely different panorama from the world's flip-side, yielding hours of neck-crimping stargazing. The Milky Way is a clear beacon, cutting a fiery swath directly through the center of the sky, and three galaxies are visible only in the Southern Hemisphere. Whereas *Polaris*, the North Star, guided European explorers for centuries, lost travelers in Australia have a trickier task. First, find the Southern Cross (which really looks more like a kite), its four points vibrantly marked. Check out the pattern on the Australian flag to get an idea of what you're looking for. Two bright "pointer" stars guide the way from their left side, if you're having trouble. Now gauge the distance of the long axis of the cross and extend it down and to the left one, two, three times. Fix that point and drag your finger down to the skyline. That point is due south. Got it? Neither do we.

WARRUMBUNGLE NATIONAL PARK   ☎02

The jagged spires and rambling peaks of the Warrumbungle Mountains, at the juncture of the lush east and the barren west, are the result of volcanic activity millions of years ago. Softer sandstone worn away under hardened lava rock has left unusual shapes slicing into the sky above the forested hills. Kangaroos and wallabies have long called the area home, while hikers, rock-climbers, and campers have more recently discovered its splendor.

A 75km **scenic drive** (approximately 12km unsealed) branches off from the Newell Hwy. 39km north of Gilgandra and runs through the park, circling back to the highway at Coonabarabran. The park entry fee can be paid at the **Warrumbungle National Park Visitors Centre,** on the park road 33km west of Coonabarabran. They have $3 bushcamping and free rock climbing permits; climbing is not permitted on Breadknife. (☎6825 4364. Open daily 9am-4pm; outside drop-box for after hours fees. Entry $6 per car; pedestrians free.) The **NPWS** (☎6842 1311) has a district office at 30 Timor St., Coonabarabran.

Of the park's serviced **camping ❶** areas, only four are open to individual travelers (sites for 2 $12, extra person $2). **Camp Blackman** is car-accessible and has toilets, rainwater, showers, and a pay phone (powered sites $17, extra person $4). **Camp Pincham** lies a short walk from the nearest carpark, while **Burbie Camp** is a 4km hike from the park road (both areas have toilets and showers). **Gunneemooroo** ("place of snakes") is reached by car on the unsealed road from **Tooraweenah** (bushcamping only). Firewood cannot be collected in the park, so bring a fuel stove. Pets are also not allowed. Contact the NPWS office in Coonabarabran (see p. 226) about group campsite information.

The **Gurianawa Track** (1km; 15min.) runs an easy circle around the Visitors Center, passes fields of kangaroos, and includes views of the Siding Spring Observatory and the area's extinct volcanoes. The short walk (1km return) to **Whitegum Lookout,** 27km from Coonabarabran at the east end of the park, offers striking views of the surrounding mountains. The most popular of the park's longer walks, the hike to **Grand High Tops** (12½km; 5-6hr.) starts at a carpark 1km south of the main park road and 500m west of the Visitors Center turn-off. The steep circuit through the southern half of the park passes stunning views of **Breadknife,** an imposing 90m stone tower, and turn-offs for most of the park's other major sights. The walk back via West Spiney adds 2km and provides a chance to see the eagles that often fly around **Bluff Mountain.**

NARRABRI   ☎02

Equidistant from Sydney and Brisbane (560km), Narrabri (NEHR-uh-BRYE, meaning "forked waters"; pop. 7900) is a wheat and cotton-growing center that has

NEW SOUTH WALES

three major attractions: the six-dish Australia Telescope complex, the brand-new Cotton Centre, and the beautifully rugged scenery of Mt. Kaputar National Park.

⌨️📱 TRANSPORTATION AND PRACTICAL INFORMATION. Countrylink (☎ 13 22 32) **trains** run to Sydney (8hr., 1 per day, $81) from the train station at the east end of Bowen St., four blocks from Maitland St. **McCafferty's/Greyhound** (☎ 13 14 99 or 13 20 30) **buses** depart from the corner of Bowen and Maitland St., two blocks south of the **post office.** They leave for Brisbane (8hr., 2 per day, $68) and Melbourne (14-16hr., 2 per day, $129) via Coonabarabran (1¼hr., 2 per day, $54) and Dubbo (4hr., 2 per day, $69). Tickets can be booked through **Harvey World Travel,** 60 Maitland St., for a $5 service fee. (☎ 6792 2555. Open M-F 8am-5:30pm, Sa 8:30-11:30am.) **Thrifty,** 39 Maitland St. (☎ 6792 3610), and **Budget,** 121 Barwan St. (☎ 13 27 27), rent cars. The main drag is **Maitland St.,** which runs parallel to Tibbereena one street farther from the creek. The **Narrabri Visitors Center** is opposite Lloyd St. on the Newell Hwy. (Tibbereena St.), which veers north in town along Narrabri Creek. (☎ 6792 3583 or 1800 659 931. Open M-F 9am-5pm, Sa-Su 9am-noon.) The **NPWS** office, Level 1, 100 Maitland St., offers info about outdoor activities. (Enter around the corner on Dewhurst St. and go up the stairs. ☎ 6799 1740. Open M-F 8:30am-4:30pm.) The **post office** is at 140 Maitland St., at the corner of Dewhurst St. (☎ 6799 5999. Open M-F 9am-5pm.) **Postal Code:** 2390.

📷🏠 ACCOMMODATIONS AND FOOD. Many of the pubs along the central three-block stretch of Maitland St. offer inexpensive accommodation, and there are a number of motels on the highway leading into town. Camping is also a great option (see **Sights,** below). A few dollars more than its competitors, but in the best location, the **Tourist Hotel ❷,** 142 Maitland St., has comfortable beds in small, tidy rooms with shared bathrooms. (☎ 6792 2312. Singles $23; twins and doubles $35, ensuite $50. MC/V.) The cheapest motel and camping are both at the **Narrabri Motel and Caravan Park ❶,** 52 Cooma Rd., on the Newell Hwy. toward Coonabarabran. (☎ 6792 2593. Pool, grill, and free linen and breakfast. Sites for 2 $12, powered $16; singles $45; doubles $53; ensuite cabins $45-53; luxury motel rooms for 2 $95, extra person $10.) Woolworth's **supermarket** is on the corner of Lloyd and Maitland St. (Open M-F 7am-10pm, Sa 7am-9pm, Su 8am-8pm.)

◼️ SIGHTS. Narrabri's newest tourist attraction is the **Australian Cotton Centre,** located next to the Visitors Center on the Newell Hwy. (☎ 6792 6443; www.australiancottoncentre.com.au. Open daily 9am-5pm. $10, children $8.) Signs on the Newell Hwy. heading toward Coonabarabran lead to the **Australia Telescope,** 24km west of Narrabri, a set of six large radio dishes that comprise the largest, most powerful telescope array in the Southern Hemisphere. The Visitors Center has a helpful staff, and its videos and displays are fun and simplified to layman's terms. (☎ 6790 4070. Open daily 8am-4pm; staffed M-F. Free.)

East of Narrabri, the peaks of the **Nandewar Range** beckon travelers to leave the paved road behind (either by hiking or unsealed driving) and scale the summit of **Mt. Kaputar,** whose views encompass one-tenth of New South Wales. The entrance to the central section of **Mt. Kaputar National Park** lies 31km east of Narrabri heading south on Maitland St. and Old Gunnedah Rd. **Bark Hut Camping Area ❶** is 14km inside the park, and **Dawsons Spring Camping Area ❶** is 21km inside near the Mt. Kaputar summit. Both have hot showers, toilets, electricity, and BBQs (sites $3, children $2); be sure to bring your own firewood. The two **cabins ❺** at Dawson's Spring, each with four beds, a full kitchen, and a shower, are a great deal for families or groups. (Book well in advance at NPWS office ☎ 6799 1740. $55; 2 night min.) The park's most famous attraction is **Sawn Rocks,** an amazing basalt rock formation, in the northern section accessible from the Newell Hwy. north of Narrabri

(30min. drive northeast, 15min. walk from the parking lot). The eerie organ-pipe geometry is best seen from down in the creek bed. There is an excellent pamphlet available from the NPWS office in Narrabri with hiking info on 13 tracks of varying difficulties, including Mt. Kaputar, Sawn Rocks, and **Waa Gorge** ($2.50). The roads to and within the park are mostly unsealed and unstable after rain; call the NPWS office (☎6799 1740) for updates.

OUTBACK NEW SOUTH WALES

The empty stretches of northwest New South Wales are sparsely populated, difficult to reach, and largely untouched by the typical traveler. What's that you say? You're not the typical traveler? You want to explore and embrace the arid western lands—the dusty brown hills, dusty brown roads, and dusty brown cows? What deep knowledge you will have gleaned when you have stepped one toe past Bourke's city limits merely for the sake of being able to say to your typical-traveler friends Sydneyside, "Yes, I have been Back O' Bourke. I have seen desolation not unlike a nuclear winter. I know what life looks like after the road ends."

BOURKE   ☎02

On a blistering hot day, Bourke (BURK) can be eerie. It's dead quiet. Haze covering the unusually wide, naked streets distorts distance. Bourke is a study in racial division of the sort that is often hidden beneath the surface of Australian society. At one end of Oxley St., the main drag, white office workers stroll past the immaculately restored Federation-style courthouse, post office, and banks. At the other end, Aboriginal kids in worn clothing loiter beside the pub, convenience store, and public housing office. That shouldn't scare you away; visiting Bourke is an educational experience in this and many other ways. An important inland port town in the 19th century, Bourke is rich with history, and today it's both a symbolic (as per the idiom "Back o' Bourke") and a real gateway to the Outback.

Bourke lies on the Mitchell Hwy. (Hwy. 71), 367km northwest of Dubbo and 142km south of the Queensland-NSW border. The Mitchell Hwy. becomes Anson St. through town; Richard St. branches off to the north and runs all the way to the Darling River. Oxley St. runs off Richard St. to the left, and should be avoided at night. Mitchell St. crosses Richard St. a half block from Oxley St. The **Tourist Information Center,** on Anson St., a block west of Richard St., can suggest farms for **year-round work.** (☎6872 1222; tourinfo@lisp.com.au. Open daily 9am-5pm.) The **library,** 29 Mitchell St., has **Internet** access. (☎6872 2751. $2.50 per hr. Open M-F 9am-5pm, Sa 9:30am-12:30pm.)

Port of Bourke Hotel ❸, 32 Mitchell St., has large rooms with hardwood floors, shared baths, A/C, and heaters; many open onto balcony. (☎6872 2544; pobh@bigpond.com. Singles $34; doubles $61; family rooms $57, ensuite $83.) For a real "Outback" experience, contact **Comeroo Camel Station ❺,** in the red desert of Comeroo, where you can bushcamp, take a camel safari, or stay in cottages. You need 4WD to reach the 100,000-acre family-run station. (☎/fax 6874 7735. Cottages with brekkie and dinner $60 per person; with activities $100.) A **supermarket** is at the corner of Warraweena and Darling St. (☎6872 2613. Open daily 8am-8pm.)

The all-purpose guide *Back o' Bourke Mud Map Tours,* free at the tourist office, details trips beyond the town borders or several thousand kilometers into the Outback. Trips include **Mt. Oxley's** eagles, **Gundabooka National Park's** Aboriginal rock art (NPWS ☎6872 2744), and **Brewarrina's** Aboriginal cultural museum. (☎6839 2868. Open M-F 9am-5pm. $6, concessions $3.) The manly **Darling River Run,** billed as "the last of the Great 4WD Adventures," is a 439km route tracing the Darling to its junction with the Murray at Wentworth and passes famous bush pubs, camping spots, and fishing holes.

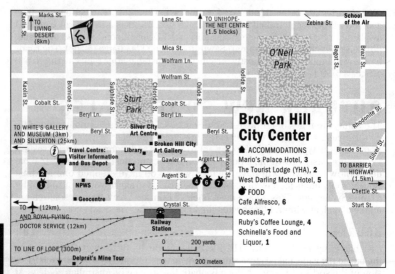

Broken Hill
City Center
♠ ACCOMMODATIONS
Mario's Palace Hotel, **3**
The Tourist Lodge (YHA), **2**
West Darling Motor Hotel, **5**
🍴 FOOD
Cafe Alfresco, **6**
Oceania, **7**
Ruby's Coffee Lounge, **4**
Schinella's Food and
Liquor, **1**

BROKEN HILL   ☎08

Broken Hill sits at the extreme western end of New South Wales, right on the edge of nowhere. In 1883, Charles Rasp, a German-born boundary rider, discovered that the misshapen hill known locally as the "hog's back" was in fact the biggest lode of silver-lead ore in the world. Rasp and his associates attracted thousands of people, transforming seemingly worthless scrubland into a booming expanse almost overnight. Like Victoria's Goldfield boom towns, Broken Hill's burgeoning tourism board hopes to lure visitors with the area's rich history. Local mining continues to this day, on the same giant lode of silver, zinc, and lead discovered by Rasp. However, as the last operational mine is expected to shut its shafts in 2006, the town's other markets now silently battle for the position of leading industry. At the same time, the city supports a thriving art scene that has century-old roots in miners' "naive art," attracting a broadening international renown. This odd conjunction of commercialism, contemporary artistry, and a history of gritty labor has imbued Broken Hill with a character unlike other towns in Australia.

▐ TRANSPORTATION

Trains: The train station (☎8087 1400) is on Crystal St. near the intersection with Chloride St. **Great Southern** (☎13 21 47) runs the *Indian-Pacific* to Sydney (16½hr.; W and Su 4:30pm; $99, ISIC $59) and Perth (48hr., Tu and F 9:20am, $343/$172) via Adelaide (6½hr., Tu and F 9:30am, $59/$30). Great Southern also runs the *Ghan* to Alice Springs (27hr.; Su 5:50am; $250, ISIC $125) via Adelaide (6¼hr., M 5:55am, $59/ $30). **Countrylink** (☎13 22 32) trains go to Sydney (16¼hr.; daily 1-2 per day; $117/ $59; booked 15 days in advance $59/$30).

Buses: The bus depot (☎8087 2735; open M-F 9am-4pm) is in the Visitors Center, at the corner of Blende and Bromide St. **McCafferty's/Greyhound** (☎13 14 99 or 13 20 30) goes to: Melbourne (17hr.; $142, ISIC $128) via Adelaide (7hr., daily 10:30am, $83/ $75); other destinations are accessible via Dubbo (9hr.; daily 3:35pm; $119/$107), including Sydney (16hr., $133/$120) and Brisbane (24hr., $185/$167).

Local Buses: Murton's Citybus runs 4 routes throughout greater Broken Hill M-F 8am-5:30pm and Sa roughly 9am-noon. Timetable available at the Visitors Center.

Taxi: Yellow Radio Cabs (☎ 13 10 08).

Car Rental: Sundry around-town rentals can go as low as $58 per day. **Thrifty,** 190 Argent St. (☎ 8088 1928), and **Hertz** (☎ 8087 2719) are at the Visitors Center.

Bike Rental: The **YHA Tourist Lodge** (☎ 8088 2086) hires bikes for $15 per day.

ORIENTATION AND PRACTICAL INFORMATION

Rather than use the points of the compass, Broken Hill's streets are aligned with the line of lode upon which the mining city has long depended. Most shops and services congregate in the walkable rectangle bounded by **Bromide** (W), **Mica** (N), **Iodide** (E), and **Crystal** (S) St. Cutting west-to-east, one block above Crystal St., Argent St. is the main thoroughfare, with most of the food and lodging. Several outlying attractions require motorized transport (particularly **Silverton, Mutawintji National Park,** and the **Living Desert**), but rental cars are extremely expensive. Organized tours are a reasonable option for seeing the sights.

> Broken Hill has adopted the phone code of South Australia (☎ 08) as well as its **time zone,** Central Standard Time (CST), 30min. behind the rest of NSW.

Tourist Office: Broken Hill Visitors Center (☎ 8087 6077; www.murrayoutback.org.au), on the corner of Blende and Bromide St. From the railway station, turn left onto Crystal and walk 2 blocks west, then turn right onto Bromide; the office is 2 blocks down on the left. Tune in to 88FM for a recorded replay of the town's history. Open daily 8:30am-5pm.

Tours: Many tour operators offer similarly priced daytrips to **Silverton** ($45-60), **Mutawintji National Park** ($125-150), the **Living Desert Sculptures** ($20-25), and multi-day outback safaris (hundreds of dollars). Though pricey, the tours are the best option for lone risk-averse travelers and for those without their own vehicle.

National Parks Information: New South Wales National Parks and Wildlife Service (NPWS), 183 Argent St. (☎ 8088 5933; fax 8088 4448).

Bank: ANZ, 357 Argent St. (☎ 13 13 14), is right next to **Commonwealth,** 338-340 Argent St. (☎ 13 22 21). Both open M-Th 9:30am-4pm, F 9:30am-5pm. 24hr. **ATMs.**

Library: Broken Hill Library (☎ 8088 3317), on Blende St. Free **Internet access.** Open M-W 10am-8pm, Th-F 10am-6pm, Sa 10am-1pm, Su 1-5pm.

Police: 252 Argent St. (☎ 8087 0299).

Internet Access: Slow but free at the library (see above). **Unihope—The Net Centre,** on Oxide St. between Chapple and Williams St., located in a church building, has many computers and great rates. (☎ 8087 8506. Internet $3.30 per hr. Open M-F 10am-6pm, Sa 10am-4pm.)

Post Office: 260 Argent St. (☎ 8087 7071). Open M-F 9am-5pm. Poste Restante available; pickup at the window around side of building. **Postal Code:** 2880

ACCOMMODATIONS

If everything is full, try a pubstay on Argent St. Campers have also been known to set up in the dry creekbed near the Pinnacles Mine, southwest of town.

Mario's Palace Hotel, 227 Argent St. (☎ 8088 1699). Visitors stay here not for the quality of the rooms but for the sheer experience. Foyer, corridor, and lounge walls beam with waterfall murals painted by a local Aborigine. One wildly-decorated 6-person bedroom was featured in *Priscilla, Queen of the Desert.* All rooms have fridge, TV, A/C, heat, and electric blankets. Reception 7am-late. Key deposit $10. Singles $32, ensuite $45; doubles $45-65/$53; *Priscilla* room $95-145. AmEx/MC/V. ❸

The Tourist Lodge (YHA), 100 Argent St. (☎8088 2086; mcrae@pcpro.net.au). This sprawling hostel has a swimming pool to beat the desert heat. A/C and heat cost extra. The tourist center and bus depot are at the back door. Kitchen with TV, common room with ping-pong table, and laundry. Reception 7:30am-noon and 3-9pm. Key deposit $10. Dorms and twins $17; singles $30; doubles 44. AmEx/MC/V. ❷

West Darling Motor Hotel, 400 Argent St. (☎8087 2691), on the corner of Oxide St. The favorite of ore magnates back in the day, now a quality pub accommodation. Plain, neat rooms, some with fridge and veranda, all with A/C, heat, and washbasin. TV lounge, parking, and continental breakfast. Reception open M-Sa 11am-midnight, Su 11am-10pm. Singles $28, weekly $168; twins and doubles $55/$330, ensuite $60/$360; families $55-60/$330-360, ensuite $66/396. AmEx/DC/MC/V. ❸

◖ FOOD

Broken Hill's numerous hotels, service clubs, and takeaways, most on or near Argent St., offer a fair amount of cheap chow. **Cafe Alfresco ❷,** on the corner of Argent and Oxide St., serves up big portions of quality pasta ($12). The funky pizzas (from $11) are decent but depressingly small. There's sidewalk dining for those who prefer their meals, well, *al fresco.* (☎8087 5599. Open 8am-11:30pm or midnight.) To beat the heat, try a fruit smoothie ($3.50) at **Ruby's Coffee Lounge ❶,** 393 Argent St. (☎8087 1188. Open M-F 8am-4pm.) **Oceania ❶,** 423 Argent St., has an $8 all-you-can-eat Chinese buffet. (☎8088 4539. Open daily 5-9:30pm.) **Schinella's Food and Liquor,** on Argent St. across from the YHA hostel, has a solid variety of **groceries** and booze. (Open M-Sa 8:30am-6pm, Su 9am-1pm.)

◉ SIGHTS

▨ DELPRAT'S MINE TOUR. Gain insight into the city's rugged history with a tour of the original Broken Hill Proprietary mine. The fantastic two-hour trip—all 130m underground—features equipment demonstrations and an insightful comparison of the mining labor system through time, with former miners-*cum*-annotative tour guides. Don your miner's hat and marvel at how they did it with only a candle 100 years ago. *(The BHP mine site is on the Broken Hill. Follow the gravel road off Iodide St. just past the train tracks; it's a mildly steep 10-15min. walk. ☎8088 1604. Tours M-F 10:30am, Sa 2pm; during school holidays daily 10:30am and 2pm. $34, concessions $30, children $26, families from $80; book ahead during school holidays.)*

LINE OF LODE VISITORS CENTRE. The pinnacle of Broken Hill's tourism movement, on the pinnacle of the hill itself. This shiny new complex runs daily surface tours of the South Mine as well as special night tours throughout the week. Just outside, the **Miners' Memorial,** dedicated April 21, 2001, pays homage to the hundreds of individuals who have died mining the Lode from the 1850s to the present. The center also contains a macabre touchscreen database of fallen miners, as well as a cafe with panoramic views of the city. *(The entire complex is on Broken Hill's highest point, a 5-10min. walk past Delprat's up the hill. ☎8088 1318; www.lineoflodebrokenhill.org.au. Tours 3½hr.; daily 10am and 2pm; $28, concessions $24, under 16 $10, families $60. Sunset BBQ tour Su 3:30-8pm; $39/$35/$15/$87; book ahead. Miners' Memorial $2.50/$2/free. Night tours Su from 3:30-8pm; $39/$35/$15/$87. Open daily 9am-10pm. AmEx/DC/MC/V.)*

BUSHY WHITE'S MINING MUSEUM. Former miner Bushy White teaches the history of Broken Hill mining through creative dioramas and demonstrations. The dedicated owner uses insightful methods of instruction to reenact the real mining experience in his own house. Over 250 of White's original mineral art works depict mining equipment and techniques as well as landscapes and assorted Australiana. *(1 Allendale St., off of Brookfield Ave., about 2km west of the city center. ☎8087 2878. Tours upon request. Open daily 9am-5pm. $4, families $10. Wheelchair accessible.)*

ROYAL FLYING DOCTOR SERVICE. The Flying Doctors provide health care to outback residents in over 80% of Australia (see **What's Up, Doc,** p. 697). A museum and film detail the history of this noble institution. *(At the Broken Hill Airport. ☎8080 1717. Open M-F 9am-5pm, Sa-Su 11am-4pm. 1hr. session $3.30, children $2.20.)*

SCHOOL OF THE AIR. The School of the Air provides remote education for distant schoolchildren (see **The World's Largest Classroom,** p. 279). Visitors can observe the lessons being broadcast on weekdays but must book at the tourist office the day before and be seated by 8:20am (demerits for tardiness). The worthwhile proceedings give a real feel for the quirks of life in the bush and Outback. *(On Lane St., 2 blocks east of Iodide St. $3.30, children $2.20.)*

LIVING DESERT RESERVE. In 1993, the Broken Hill Sculpture Symposium commissioned a group of local and international sculptors to create sandstone works atop a hill. The masterful pieces blend Aboriginal with modern and international influences and are best viewed at sunrise and sunset, when the light plays upon the colors. A 1½hr. walking trail from the sculpture site leads past gullies, ledges, and plenty of outback critters back to the carpark. *(Head north 8km along the northern segment of Kaolin St. From Argent St., turn left onto Bromide, left onto Williams, then right onto Kaolin St. You can drive all the way up the hill by obtaining a gate key from the tourist office for $6 with a $10 deposit, but the 15min. hike from a nearby carpark is more fun and free.)*

BROKEN HILL CITY ART GALLERY. Both excellent local work and 20th-century Australian painting makes up this small collection. The signature piece, *Silver Tree,* is a delicately wrought arboreal centerpiece commissioned by Charles Rasp for the 1882 Melbourne Exhibition. *(At the corner of Blende and Chloride St. ☎8088 5491. Open M-F 10am-5pm, Sa-Su 1-5pm. $2, concessions $1, families $5.)* Across Chloride St., the **Silver City Art Centre** houses **The Big Picture.** Local artist Peter Andrew Anderson created the largest canvas painting in the world at 100m long and 12m high. The work depicts the attractions of the Broken Hill Outback. *(☎8088 6166. Gallery free; admission to The Big Picture $5.)*

NEAR BROKEN HILL: SILVERTON

Silverton makes Broken Hill, 25km to the south, look like a metropolis. The 1876 discovery of silver, zinc, and lead ore at Thackaringa brought Silverton into existence. Prospectors arrived in droves, and the population peaked at around 3000 in 1885. Unfortunately for Silverton, most of the ore was gone by this point, just as Broken Hill's lode was revealing its precious potential. This combination of circumstances rendered Silverton a ghost town, home today to fewer than 60. Silverton has been used in numerous films, including the classic *Mad Max II.* But don't let fear of post-nuclear desert mutants keep you away from Silverton; it is an experience like no other.

Silverton's handful of buildings ranges from old brick ruins that have stood abandoned since the 1800s to some good art galleries specializing in outback naturalism. The main social activity 'round these parts is getting sloshed, making the legendary **Silverton Hotel ❶** (☎8088 5313) the most important building in town. Filled to the rafters with a huge diversity of beer cans and signs with naughty sayings, the hotel serves simple food and drink until 8 or 9pm. Try the hot quandong pie, made from a staple fruit in local bush tucker.

Penrose Park ❶, a five-minute walk north of town, offers powered and unpowered sites with toilet blocks, livable 6- to 8-person bunkhouses with kitchen, A/C, BBQ, and fridge, and six tennis courts free for day use but $4 at night. (☎8088 5307. Sites $4 per person or $10 per family, powered $6/$12; bunkhouses $25-35; showers $1; BYO linen.) The **Silverton Camel Farm,** on the road from Broken Hill, grants rides on the temperamental humped beasts. (☎8088 5316. $5 per 15min.; $25 per hr.; 2hr. sunset safari $50; day rides including BBQ lunch $100.)

During the Ice Age, glaciers scraped the plains 6km west of Silverton until they were as level as a freshly zambonied ice rink. After years of government deforestation, the **Mundi Mundi Plains** are one of the largest stretches of flat plains on Earth. Looking out 400km to the horizon, you'll understand why the plains were named after the Aboriginal word for "never-ending."

MUTAWINTJI (MOOTWINGEE) NATIONAL PARK

The 130km drive from Broken Hill to Mutawintji National Park is worth every bump in the dirt road: the park offers an array of wildlife (including the only known colony of the endangered yellow-footed rock wallaby), beautiful hikes, and an extensive network of Aboriginal rock art. A vast seabed over 400 million years ago, Mutawintji is now an area full of gorges, rock pools, and fossil remains. The Malyankapa and Pandjikali Aboriginal peoples have occupied the region for over 8000 years, and formally reclaimed ownership of the land in 1998.

Today, visitors can explore the park through designated **walks,** many of which pass the park's unique land features as well as Aboriginal rock engravings. The walks vary in length and difficulty. Many begin from the Homestead Creek camping area. **Camping ❶** facilities are basic and include fireplaces (but no firewood), toilets, cold showers, and water. ($5, children $3. Vehicles free.)

The **Historic Site Tours** cover restricted areas such as the Mutawintji Historic site, once the location of Aboriginal ceremonies. Book ahead with Mutawintji Heritage Tours. (☎8088 7000. Tours Apr.-Nov. depart from the Homestead Creek campground W and Sa 11am. $20, concessions $15, families $40). **Discovery Ranger Guided Activities,** held on school holidays, include a Kuluwirru Dreaming tour, the Ngalkirrka tour of the Amphitheater Gorge, and billy tea and damper campfire activities. For more info, contact **NPWS** (☎8088 5933) in Broken Hill.

MUNGO NATIONAL PARK

Fascinating **Mungo National Park** lies 110km northeast of Mildura on the **Arumpo-Ivanhoe Rd.** Ages ago, before the pyramids at Giza were even a twinkle in the eye of world history, hunter-gatherer communities flourished on the banks of Lake Mungo, in the extreme southwest corner of present-day New South Wales. Forty thousand years and 1600 Aboriginal generations later, life continues at one of the oldest continually inhabited sites in the world. Today, the lake is dry (and has been for 15,000 years), and Mungo has undergone some spectacular weathering. Sand dunes on the edges of the lake bed have been sculpted into strange, otherworldly landforms by erosion, accelerated over the course of the past hundred years by settlers' unwitting introduction of harmful foreign species: grazing sheep and foraging rabbits. Known as the **Walls of China,** their erosion has revealed countless fossils and artifacts, including **Mungo Three,** a skeleton of a human male that is, at an estimated 40,000 years, the oldest remaining *Homo sapiens* relic in the world. (The skeleton was buried again in a secret location so that it wouldn't be plundered.) The colored layers of sand clearly demarcate periods of water change up to 120,000 years ago. The archaeological information uncovered here has earned the **Willandra Lakes** region status as a **World Heritage Site.**

MEGAFAUNA TO MEGAMEN Evidence collected throughout Australia strongly suggests that the early Aborigines shared the continent with some fearsome beasts: giant mammals now termed megafauna. *Zygomaturus trilobus*, for example, was sized like a buffalo, built much like a wombat, and had either a horn similar to a rhinoceros's or a short, flexible trunk. *Procoptodon goliah*, a kangaroo twice as big as the largest red 'roos, climbed trees and ate leaves. Its skull was flattened and its eyes were set forward, giving it a snub-nosed, eerily humanoid visage. Unlike regular kangaroos, *Goliah*'s arms and shoulders allowed it to manipulate objects and even reach overhead, much like the ancestors of human beings.

Roads to and within Mungo National Park are unsealed and subject to weather conditions; call ahead to the **NPWS** (☎03 5021 8900). In addition, visitors are advised to carry their own food, drinking water, and petrol.

The park's **Visitors Center** offers info on the park's history, visitor rules and regulations, and the incredible 70km **self-guided drive tour** that allows visitors to see the diverse wonders of the park at their own pace. This is also the place to pay vehicle fees ($6 per night). Camping facilities are available at the **Main Camp ❶** (near the park entrance) and at **Belah Camp ❶** (farther into the park along the drive tour). Both sites have toilets and tables, but wood fires are only allowed at the Main Camp—be warned that in the winter months, you're going to want a campfire! (Both sites $3, children $2.) The old, unheated **Shearers Quarters ❷**, next to the Visitors Center, have been converted into basic bunk accommodations and provide access to the kitchen next door. (Book ahead with the Lower Darling Area Office in Buronga ☎5021 8900. Bunks $17, children $5.50.) The **Mungo Lodge ❺**, on the park road just before the park entrance, has heated ensuite cabins. (☎5029 7297. Reception daily 8am-6pm. Book ahead. Singles $78; doubles $88.)

NEW SOUTH WALES

NORTHERN
TERRITORY

Against the backdrop of a pastel sky, silver eucalyptus trees contort their limbs into ghost-like curves and cockatoos squawk noisily from their branches. Sparse foliage and palm trees break the otherwise dry woodland. The thick smoke of a bush fire bruises the horizon. A well-worn 4WD rumbles down an endless road toward a fiery sunset, bellowing pumpkin-colored dust behind its growling motor. The mud-caked license plate says "Northern Territory: Outback Australia." And if it's Outback Australia that you're after, you've come to the right place.

The Northern Territory (NT) stretches into the country's most extreme regions. In its 1.3 million km² area, the 200,000 inhabitants could enjoy 6½km² of land apiece. Instead, nearly 60% choose to settle in the cities of Darwin in the tropical Top End or Alice Springs in the desert-like Red Centre. The rest scatter among three or four substantially sized towns such as Katherine or Tennant Creek or upon the cattle stations and Aboriginal homelands that lend droplets of human life to the vast outback. The stretches between such outposts can be a day's drive, giving rise to the notion that most of the NT is simply empty. The wonderfully wide-open spaces, however, truly reveal the Australian landscape at its best.

Thirty percent of the Territory's population is indigenous, with whites and Aborigines living together in relatively mild, if indifferent, peace. Separatism is rampant, however, and most businesses and services are predominantly run and staffed by whites. Though colonization began in the 17th century, the Territory's European population was slow to grow. Only telegraph and railway construction and the gold rushes brought an influx of white Australians to this frontier land.

Apart from the residents of protected Aboriginal land, Territorians are anything but territorial. In fact, traveling through the NT is getting easier as the tourism infrastructure keeps building. Kakadu and Litchfield National Park in the Top End and Uluru and the MacDonnells in the Red Centre are accessible once the vast distances between them are overcome. While being a tourist in the NT is certainly more adventurous than participating in the overcrowded beach culture of the east coast, it is most rewarding (and highly recommended) to stay for longer than a whirlwind tour of the NT's greatest hits.

As a land that stands for independence, it is not surprising that the NT has not pushed for statehood. A Territory referendum for statehood in 1998 was voted down by a substantial margin. For now, it will continue to be financially run by Canberra, but in spirit and in reality, the region grasps firmly to its political status. The spectacular sunsets and overwhelming starscapes in the Northern Territory have a way of making governmental dictums and daily minutiae unimportant in the face of the realization that life goes on as it will.

⊏ TRANSPORTATION

The NT's vast expanses make transportation a significant issue. Darwin, Alice Springs, and Yulara (Ayers Rock Resort) are most commonly reached by air. Smaller planes often fly to smaller destinations, but prices are high. There is as yet **no train system** traversing the Territory, except from Alice heading south to Adelaide, but one is on the way (see **In Recent News,** p. 274). **McCafferty's/Greyhound** (☎ 13 14 99 or 13 20 30) **buses** offer service to most major tourist centers but not to

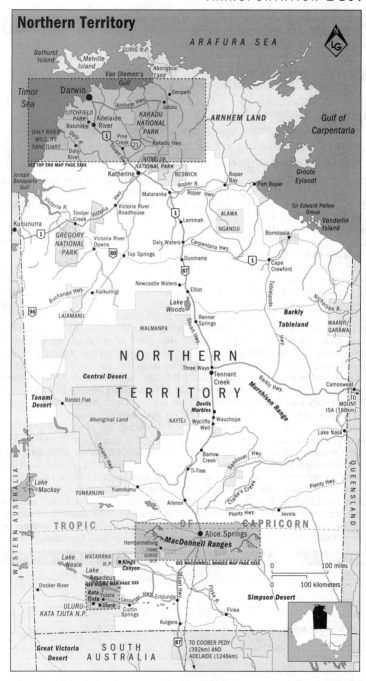

Northern Territory

ARAFURA SEA

Bathurst Island
Melville Island
GURIG N.P.

Van Diemen's Gulf

Aboriginal Land

Timor Sea

Darwin
Oenpelli

Arnhem Hwy.
Jabiru

LITCHFIELD PARK
Adelaide River
Batchelor
KAKADU NATIONAL PARK
ARNHEM LAND

Gulf of Carpentaria

DALY RIVER WILDLIFE SANCTUARY
Daly R.
Pine Creek
Kakadu Hwy.

Daly River

NITMILUK NATIONAL PARK

SEE TOP END MAP PAGE XXXX

Katherine
BESWICK
Roper Bay
Port Roper
Groote Eylandt

Joseph Bonaparte Gulf

Victoria R.
Mataranka
Roper R.
Roper Hwy.

Victoria River Roadhouse

Kununurra

Timber Creek
Victoria

Larrimah
ALAWA
NGANDJI

Sir Edward Pellew Group
Vanderlin Island

GREGORY NATIONAL PARK

Victoria River Downs

Daly Waters
Carpentaria Hwy.
Borroloola

Top Springs

Dunmarra

Cape Crawford

Buchanan Hwy.
Kalkuringi

Newcastle Waters
Elliot

LAJAMANU

Lake Woods

Renner Springs

Tablelands

Barkly Tableland

WAANYI GARAWA

WALMANPA

N O R T H E R N

Three Ways
Tennant Creek

Murchison Range

Camooweal
TO MOUNT ISA (188km)

Central Desert

T E R R I T O R Y

Tanami Desert
Rabbit Flat

Devils Marbles

Barkly Hwy.

Lake Nask

Aboriginal Land

KAYTEJ
Wycliffe Well
Wauchope

Tanami Hwy.

Barrow Creek

Sandover Hwy.

Plenty Hwy.

Lake Mackay

YUNKANJINI
Yuendumu

Ti-Tree

Clarke's Creek

QUEENSLAND

Aileron

Plenty Hwy.
Jervois

TROPIC
OF
CAPRICORN

WESTERN AUSTRALIA

Alice Springs
Hermannsburg
MacDonnell Ranges
FINKE GORGE N.P.

SEE MACDONNELL RANGES MAP PAGE XXXX

Lake Neale
WATARRKA N.P.
Kings Canyon

Lake Amadeus

SEE ULURU MAP PAGE XXX

Kata Tjuta
Yulara
Lassetter Hwy.
Erldunda

Finke R.

Simpson Desert

0   100 miles

0   100 kilometers

Docker River
ULURU-KATA TJUTA N.P.
Uluru
Curtin Springs

Finke

Kulgera

Great Victoria Desert

S O U T H
A U S T R A L I A

TO COOBER PEDY (392km) AND ADELAIDE (1246km)

NORTHERN TERRITORY

NORTHERN TERRITORY HIGHLIGHTS

MINDIL BEACH MARKET. Experience Darwin at its best as crafts, culture, and delicious food come out in festive form to greet the Top End twilight. (p. 245)

TWIN FALLS. Hike across white sand then swim in croc territory to reach this tropical earthly paradise in Kakadu National Park. (p. 257)

ABORIGINAL ART. Visit some of Australia's best-preserved rock art galleries in the Jawoyn-owned Nitmiluk National Park. (p. 266)

DEVIL'S MARBLES. Ponder the origin of these stunning rock formations. (p. 272)

ULURU. The rock never disappoints. (p. 288)

VALLEY OF THE WINDS. Free your mind in at Kata Tjuta National Park. (p. 290)

the farther reaches of the national parks. **Renting a car** is the best way to retain freedom and flexibility, but it's also the most expensive, and you must be at least 21. There are many national chains that have offices all over the NT; **Territory-Thrifty Car Rental** (☎ 1800 891 125) and **Budget** (☎ 13 27 27) are the cheapest but limit kilometers (100km per day, each additional km 25-32¢), whereas **Britz** (☎ 1800 331 454) offers unlimited kilometers and rents 4WD to customers under 25. Each company does one-way rentals, but for a one-way fee, usually $300-400.

Major tourist centers are accessible by sealed or gravel roads. You'll need a 4WD only to venture into the bush on dirt tracks; however, this is necessary to see many of the spectacular sights of Kakadu National Park and the MacDonnell Ranges. Furthermore, conventional vehicles are not insured on unsealed or gravel roads. Rental companies determine their own restrictions, even for 4WD vehicles; explain your itinerary before you rent. If going to remote areas, ask for a **high-clearance 4WD** with **two petrol tanks;** trendier vehicles are often too low to the ground. Also, make sure the 4WD you rent is not so top-heavy that it could flip over in rough terrain driving. There are many safari tours that operate in national parks and the bush which usually run about $100-130 per day. **Wilderness 4WD Adventures** (☎ 1800 808 288) or **Gondwana** (☎ 1800 242 177) are good for Top End tours, and **Wayoutback Desert Safaris** (☎ 8953 4304) hits the Uluru area. These companies center around small groups and try to get off the beaten path.

If going beyond the highways, make sure to bring lots of extra water, food, emergency materials (tire, tools, rope, jack, etc.), and check in with a friend, Visitors Center, or ranger station. Avoid driving at dusk and dawn, when **kangaroos** and **wild camels** loiter in the road. There are many sections of unfenced ranch land along the highways; beware of **wandering cattle. Road trains** (multi-part trucks) can be up to 50m long, often generating dust storms behind them. *It is dangerous to pass road trains.* When venturing onto unsealed roads, be sure to call ahead to find out **road conditions** (☎ 1800 246 199); some tracks may be washed out entirely. For **weather reports,** call ☎ 8982 3826. The **Automobile Association of the Northern Territory (AANT;** ☎ 8941 0611) can provide valuable assistance (see **Essentials,** p. 48).

FROM DARWIN TO:	KILOMETERS	APPROX. TIME
Alice Springs	1491km	15hr.
Batchelor	98km	1¼hr.
Kakadu National Park	257km	3hr.
Katherine	314km	3½hr.
Litchfield National Park	129km	1½hr.
Pine Creek	226km	2½hr.
Tennant Creek	986km	10hr.

FROM ALICE SPRINGS TO:	KILOMETERS	APPROX. TIME
Darwin	1491km	15hr.
Kata Tjuta (Mt. Olga)	500km	5¼hr.
Katherine	1177km	12hr.
Tennant Creek	504km	5hr.
Uluru (Ayers Rock)	461km	4¾hr.
Watarrka (King's Canyon)	331km	4hr.
Yulara	444km	4½hr.

THE TOP END

A lush tropical crown atop a vast interior desert, the winterless Top End enjoys perpetually warm weather; as in other extreme northern parts of Australia, seasons here are divided only into the **Wet** monsoonal season (Nov.-May) and the semi-desert-like **Dry** season (June-Oct.). In the latter season, backpack-toting pilgrims descend on Darwin and use this island of civilization as a base to explore the region's prime natural wonders—Kakadu, Litchfield, and Nitmiluk National Parks.

The very few brave souls who venture to the Top End during the Wet season will be rewarded with views of the region at its most dramatic. Torrential rains drench the reddish dust, sparking the growth of velvet green vegetation and clouds of mozzies (mosquitoes). Top Enders are willing to share their vast home for half the year, but they also seem to rejoice when the rain drives the trespassers out and Mother Nature once again puts their fierce outback spirit to the test.

DARWIN ☎ 08

Anywhere else in the world it would be just another small city, but Darwin (pop. 80,000) is not anywhere else—it is the gateway to the rugged natural playground of the Top End. Compared to the natural wonders that draw tourists here, the capital of the Northern Territory is a pit stop before bigger adventures, but its location makes it an oasis. From its incessant sunshine and azure beaches to its thumping nightlife and mouth-watering food, Darwin can fill every minute of a visit with much needed stimulation after time in the isolating outback.

Those who visit during the Dry will encounter mobs of midriff-baring backpackers who come to Darwin to play under the palm trees and stars, with each other at the bars, and with the didgeridoos. Darwin's character, however, has not always been so footloose and fancy-free. Darwin suffered nearly two years of intense Japanese bombing as Australia's hardest-hit target in WWII. After rebuilding over the following decades, the city was decimated a second time by Cyclone Tracy on Christmas Eve, 1974. With true Territory grit, Darwin started from scratch once again, creating the convenient city center, manicured parks, and touristy outdoor mall that exist today. Still, visitors don't come to Darwin looking for refined, urban pleasures. They're on their way to explore the natural splendors of the Top End, even if they may forget that for a few days while under Darwin's spell.

⊠ INTERCITY TRANSPORTATION

BY PLANE. Darwin International Airport (☎ 8920 1850) is about 10km northeast of the city center on McMillans Rd.; from the city center, take a left on Bagot Rd. off the Stuart Hwy. **Qantas,** 16 Bennett St. (☎ 13 13 13), runs to: Adelaide ($260); Alice Springs ($200); Ayers Rock ($230); Brisbane ($242); Broome ($414); Cairns ($300);

NORTHERN TERRITORY

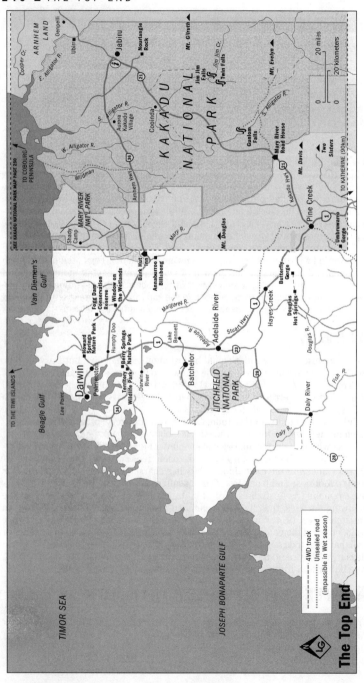

The Top End

4WD track
Unsealed road
(impassible in Wet season)

TIMOR SEA

JOSEPH BONAPARTE GULF

TO THE TIWI ISLANDS

Beagle Gulf

Lee Point

Darwin
Palmerston

Howard Springs
Nature Park

Territory
Wildlife Park

Berry Springs
Nature Park

Darwin
River

Batchelor

LITCHFIELD
NATIONAL
PARK

Daly R.

Van Diemen's
Gulf

Fogg Dam
Conservation
Reserve

Window on
the Wetlands

Humpty Doo

Lake
Bennett

Adelaide River

Margaret R.

Annaburroo
Billabong

Bark Hut
Inn

Adelaide R.

Stuart Hwy.

Hayes Creek

Butterfly
Gorge

Douglas
Hot Springs

Douglas R.

Fish R.

Daly River

MARY RIVER
NAT'L PARK

Shady
Camp

Mt. Douglas

Maty R.

Pine Creek

Umbrawarra
Gorge

Mt. Davis

Two
Sisters

TO KATHERINE (90km)

Kakadu Hwy.

Mary River
Road House

Gunlom
Falls

S. Alligator R.

K A K A D U   N A T I O N A L   P A R K

Jim Jim
Falls

Twin Falls

Jim Jim Cr.

Mt. Evelyn

Mt. Gilruth

Nourlangie
Rock

Jabiru

Cooinda

Aurora
Kakadu
Village

S. Alligator R.

W. Alligator R.

Wildman

Arnhem Hwy.

ARNHEM   LAND

Cooper Cr.

E. Alligator R.

Ubirr

Genpelli

TO COBOURG
PENINSULA

SEE KAKADU NATIONAL PARK MAP PAGE 250

20 miles

20 kilometers

0

0

Melbourne ($310); Perth ($250); and Sydney ($300). Numerous airlines offer service to Southeast Asia, Singapore, and Bali. Other airline offices include **Royal Brunei Airlines,** 22 Cavenagh St. (☎8941 0966); **Merpati Nusantara,** 6 Knuckey St. (☎8981 5229); and the Territory-carrier **Airnorth** (☎8945 2866), at the airport. For transport between the city and the airport, the **Darwin Airport Shuttle** is your best bet. (☎8981 5066 or 1800 358 945. $7.50 one-way, return $13.) Many accommodations will reimburse patrons for the ride. **Taxis** (☎13 10 08) run to the airport for $20.

BY BUS. The **Transit Centre,** is at 67-69 Mitchell St., between Peel and Nuttall St. (☎8941 0911. Open daily 6am-7:45pm.) **McCafferty's/Greyhound** (☎13 14 99 or 13 20 30) run to: Adelaide (39hr., 1-2 per day, $365); Alice Springs (20hr., 2 per day, $195); Broome (24hr., 1 per day, $260); Cairns (41hr., 1 per day, $400); Katherine (4hr., 4 per day, $50); Melbourne (51hr., 1 per day, $425); Sydney via Alice Springs and Adelaide (67hr., 1 per day, $500); and Tennant Creek (12hr., 3 per day, $138).

ORIENTATION

Darwin is on a peninsula, with the city center in the southeastern corner. The tree-lined **Esplanade** and the rocky **Lameroo Beach** run along the western edge of the peninsula. The center of the backpacker district is the Transit Centre on **Mitchell St.**, which runs parallel to The Esplanade. The **Smith Street Mall**, a pedestrian zone occupying the block between Knuckey and Bennett St., is home to many shops and services and runs parallel to Mitchell St. at the southern end of the city. At the tip of the peninsula, **Stokes Hill** and the **Wharf** area hold several sights.

Moving northeast out of downtown, **Daly St.** eventually becomes the **Stuart Hwy.** and heads out to the airport. Smith St. and Mitchell St. both continue north of the city center for 500m before converging with Gilruth Ave. at **Lambell Tce.**, which leads to the **MGM Casino, Mindil Beach,** and the **Museum and Art Gallery of the Northern Territory.** Gilruth Ave. becomes **East Point Rd.**, eventually leading to the **East Point Reserve,** 6km from the city center.

LOCAL TRANSPORTATION

Public Transit: Darwinbus (☎8924 7666) runs to suburbs and beaches along the major thoroughfares. Terminal is between Harry Chan Ave. and Bennett St., with stops along Mitchell and Cavenagh St. Fares $1.40-2.40. **Tourcards** allow unlimited travel for 1 day ($5, concessions $2.50) or 1 week ($25, concessions $12.50). **Territory Shuttle** (☎8928 1155) will take you anywhere downtown for $2.

Taxis: Darwin Radio Taxis (☎13 10 08). $1.26 per km.

Car Rental: Rental companies abound but availability decreases in the Dry, so book ahead. Sedans start around $55 per day and 4WD from $100 per day, including 100km per day and 23-33¢ per extra km. Damage liability can usually be reduced at an additional rate of $15-45 per day. Large chains include: **Avis,** 145 Stuart Hwy. (☎8981 9922); **Budget** (☎8981 9800), at the corner of Daly St. and Doctors Gully Rd.; **Hertz** (☎8941 0944), at the corner of Smith and Daly St.; and **Territory Rent-a-Car,** 64 Stuart Hwy. (☎8981 4796). **Nifty,** 39 Cavenagh St. (☎8941 7090), specializes in small vehicles. For short distances, **Port** (☎8981 8441), at Fisherman's Wharf, and **Europcar,** 77 Cavenagh St. (☎13 13 90), offer rates from $39 per day and charge for each km, while unlimited km are available at Nifty, **Britz,** 44-66 Stuart Hwy. (☎8981 2081), and **Advance,** 86 Mitchell St. (☎8981 2999). The minimum age for rental is 21 at Britz and **Apollo,** 93 McMinn St. (☎8981 4796); the rest require renters to be at least 25. Most major chains offer 4WD options, and Britz rents 4WD with sleeper compartments ideal for long treks into the bush.

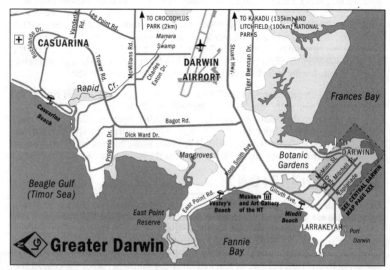

Greater Darwin

NORTHERN TERRITORY

Buying and Selling Used Cars: Travelers Car Market (☎0418 600 830), at Peel and Mitchell St. caters to backpackers. Sellers pay $40 per week to cram into the lot, but buyers browse for free. Cars sell fastest May-Oct. Open daily 8am-4pm. Also check bulletin boards at hostels and Internet shops. Registration requirements vary for each state. Also, see **Buying and Selling Used Cars**, p. 46.

Automobile Club: The **Auto Association of the Northern Territory (AANT),** 79-81 Smith St. ☎8981 3837. Open M-F 8am-5pm.

Bike Rental: Available through most hostels ($4 per hr., $16 per day)

🛈 PRACTICAL INFORMATION

TOURIST AND FINANCIAL SERVICES

Tourist Office: Tourism Top End (☎8936 2499), at the corner of Mitchell and Knuckey St. Open M-F 9am-5:45pm, Sa 9am-12:45pm, Su 10am-1:45pm. Main office of the **Parks & Wildlife Commission of the Northern Territory** (☎8999 5511; www.nt.gov.au/pawis) is in Palmerston, but info can be found at the tourist office.

Travel Offices: Tours can be booked from many locations on Mitchell St. or the Smith St. Mall. **STA,** Shop T-17 in Galleria, Smith St. Mall (☎8941 2955), sells ISIC ($16.50) and VIP ($29) cards. Open M-F 9am-5pm. **Flight Centre,** 24 Cavenagh St. (☎13 16 00), guarantees to beat any quoted current airfare price. Open M-F 9am-5:30pm, Sa 9am-4pm.

Currency Exchange: Bank South Australia, 13 Knuckey St. (☎13 13 76). Open M-Th 9:30am-4pm, F 9:30am-5pm. **ANZ Bank** (☎13 13 14), on Knuckey St. by the Smith St. Mall. Open M-Th 9:30am-4pm, F 9:30am-5pm.

American Express: Travellers World, 18 Knuckey St. (☎8981 4699). Holds mail (no packages) for 30 days for card holders or Traveler's Cheque holders. Address mail "ATTN: Client Mail, GPO Box 3728, Darwin NT 0801." Open M-F 8:30am-5pm, Sa 9am-noon. Not to be confused with **Travel World,** also on Knuckey St.

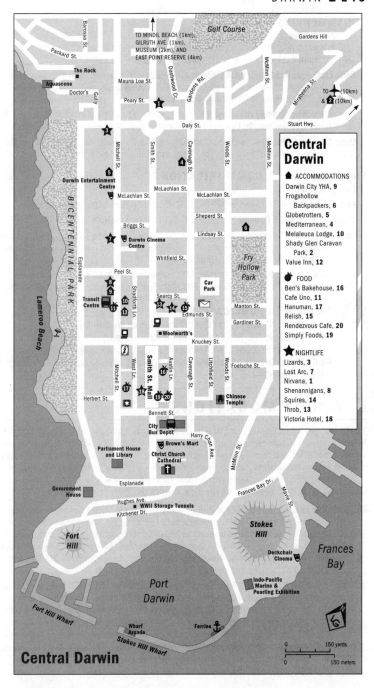

Central Darwin

Central Darwin

▲ ACCOMMODATIONS
Darwin City YHA, **9**
Frogshollow
    Backpackers, **6**
Globetrotters, **5**
Mediterranean, **4**
Melaleuca Lodge, **10**
Shady Glen Caravan
    Park, **2**
Value Inn, **12**

♦ FOOD
Ben's Bakehouse, **16**
Cafe Uno, **11**
Hanuman, **17**
Relish, **15**
Rendezvous Cafe, **20**
Simply Foods, **19**

★ NIGHTLIFE
Lizards, **3**
Lost Arc, **7**
Nirvana, **1**
Shenannigans, **8**
Squires, **14**
Throb, **13**
Victoria Hotel, **18**

NORTHERN TERRITORY

LOCAL SERVICES

Backpacking Supplies: NT General Store, 42 Cavenagh St. (☎8981 8242), at Edmunds St., has everything you need for the outdoors and a large selection of good maps. Open M-W 8:30am-5:30pm, Th-F 8:30am-6pm, Sa 8am-1pm.

Book Exchange: Read Back Book Exchange (☎8981 8885), Darwin Plaza off Smith St. Mall. Open M-F 9am-5:30pm, Sa 9am-3pm. **Dusty Jackets,** Shop 3, 29 Cavenagh St. (☎8981 6772). Open M-F 10:30am-5pm, Sa 9am-noon.

Library: Northern Territory Library (☎8999 7410), in the Parliament building at the corner of Mitchell and Bennett St. Open M-F 10am-6pm, Sa-Su 1-5pm.

Gym: Carlton Hotel Gym (☎8980 0800), in the Carlton Hotel on the Esplanade. The best-equipped gym in Darwin city. Free for guests, but anyone can use it for $8 per visit.

EMERGENCY AND COMMUNICATIONS

Emergency: ☎000.

Police: 24 Mitchell St. (24hr. ☎8927 8888). Open M-F 8am-11pm, Sa-Su 8-11pm.

Crisis Lines: NT AIDS Council (☎1800 880 899). **Sexual Assault** (24hr. ☎8922 7156).

Internet Access: Didjworld Internet Shop, 60 Smith St. (☎8981 3510), in the Harry Chan Arcade, which charges 9¢ per min. (7-10pm 8¢ per min.) and has a fast connection. Open M-Sa 9am-10pm, Su 10am-8pm.

Post Office: General Post Office Darwin, 48 Cavenagh St. (☎13 13 18), at Edmunds St. Poste Restante held 30 days. Open M-F 8:30am-5pm, Sa 9am-noon. **Postal Code:** 0800.

MEDIA AND PUBLICATIONS

Newspapers: *NT News* (90¢) daily; *Darwin Sun* on Wednesday.

Entertainment: *The Top End Visitors' Guide* monthly; *Arts Darwin* monthly; Entertainment section of *NT News* on Wednesday and Friday.

Radio: Rock, Triple J 103.3FM and HOT-100 101.1FM; News, ABC 105.7FM; Tourist info, 88FM.

⌐ ACCOMMODATIONS

There are plenty of hostels in Darwin. Most are clumped on Mitchell St. Darwin hostels pump backpackers in and out again as quickly as possible, so prepare yourself to feel like a number and check your standards at the city limit. The highest-end accommodations can be found along the Esplanade, but most are drastically overpriced. For better prices (and often nicer facilities), try Smith and Cavenagh St. Book ahead during the Dry; during the Wet, prices are lower.

■ **Darwin City YHA,** 69 Mitchell St. (☎8981 3995), next to the Transit Centre. Large, clean, and efficient—the king of Darwin hostels sets the standard. International crowd and competent staff. Large lockers in every room, A/C, pool, kitchen, dining area, Internet ($8 per hr.), sun deck, 2 TV rooms, and luggage storage ($2 per day). All-you-can-eat BBQ F $5. Free airport shuttle. Linen and key deposit $15. Laundry $4.20. Reception 24hr. Dorms $23; singles and doubles $52. VIP/YHA. MC/V. ❷

Frogshollow Backpackers, 27 Lindsay St. (☎8941 2600 or 1800 068 686; www.frogshollow.com.au), at Woods St., 10min. from the Transit Centre. Exceptional facilities under overhanging palm trees. Friendliest hostel staff in Darwin. Airport shuttle reimbursed for 2-night stay or longer. Lockers, luggage storage and safe, pool, spa, laundry, spacious kitchen, TV room, and Internet ($7 per hr.). Breakfast included. Key, linen, and cutlery deposit $20. Reception daily 6am-9pm. Dorms $21; twins and doubles $48, with A/C $50, ensuite $55. VIP/YHA. MC/V. ❷

Melaleuca Lodge, 50 Mitchell St. (☎8936 1092; info@melaleucalodge.com). Patios, pool, palms, social environment, and great location. A/C, lockers, 2 kitchens, TV rooms, Internet ($6 per hr.), and laundry. Free storage, pickup, and breakfast. Reception 24hr. Dorms $22; twins $60; doubles $65. NOMADS/VIP. Wheelchair accessible. MC/V. ❷

Globetrotters, 97 Mitchell St. (☎8981 5385). A party hostel and pub in one. Madness ensues around the clock and around the big-screen TV. Rooms are somewhat crowded, with 6-8 beds. Pool, kitchen, and laundry. Key and linen deposit $20. Dorms $21; twins and doubles $58. NOMADS/VIP/YHA. MC/V. ❷

Mediterranean, 81 Cavenagh St. (☎8981 7771 or 1800 357 760). Newly renovated and luxurious, the Mediterranean offers guests spacious ensuite rooms with huge sitting areas, full kitchens, A/C, and satellite TV. Parking. Tours desk. Rooms from $130 in the Dry, from $95 in the Wet. Wheelchair accessible. AmEx/MC/V. ❺

Value Inn, 50 Mitchell St. (☎8981 4733), across from the Transit Centre. The most centrally located motel in Darwin. Clean and simple ensuite rooms with TV, fridge, and A/C. Pool. Reception daily 10am-11pm. Book ahead. $50 deposit. Rooms from $85 in the Dry, from $59 in the Wet. Wheelchair accessible. AmEx/MC/V. ❺

Camping options in Darwin are limited. With harsh weather half the year and no campgrounds in central Darwin, die-hard campers must head out of town. Camping or sleeping in cars is strictly forbidden in the Mindil Beach area. The **Shady Glen Caravan Park** ❶ is closest to the city, about 10km from central Darwin at the intersection of the Stuart Hwy. and Farrell Crescent. Patrons are treated to pool, kitchen, BBQ, and laundry. (☎8984 3330. Sites $10 per person; van sites $23.)

◖ FOOD

Darwin has a variety of options to feed the onslaught of budget travelers. The food stalls inside the **Transit Centre** and in the side arcades off Smith St. Mall offer hot, relatively cheap, mostly Asian cuisine. The **Mindil Beach market** offers cheap, delicious pan-Asian food (full meals $6-8) and fresh fruit in a great atmosphere. (Open Th and Su 5-9pm.) The **Parap market** is smaller and more mellow but popular with locals. Take bus #4 to Parap Shopping Plaza. (Open Sa 8am-2pm.) Woolworth's **supermarket** is at the corner of Knuckey and Smith St. (Open M-Sa 6:30am-midnight, Su 8am-10pm.)

Rendezvous Cafe, Shop 6, Star Village (☎8981 9231), at Smith St. Mall. Asian dishes cheaper than at other restaurants in town but just as tasty. A local favorite. Mains $9-16. Open M-W 9am-2:30pm, Th-F 5:30-9pm, Sa 9am-2pm and 5:30-9pm. MC/V. ❷

Cafe Uno (☎8942 2500), on Mitchell St. next to the Transit Centre. While it serves everything from gourmet pizzas ($13-16) to huge burgers ($10), Cafe Uno's specialty is breakfast. Try any of their fabulous egg breakfasts served with thick-cut toast ($9), while soaking up the sun in their outdoor cafe seating. Open daily 7am-late. MC/V. ❷

Relish (☎8941 1900), on Cavenagh St. across from the post office. The best sandwich joint in town. Devour one of their wild creations or invent one of your own for $6. Try it toasted on foccacia bread, on one of their melt-in-your-mouth rolls, or wrapped and ready to go as a beach snack. Lots of vegetarian options. Open M-F 6:30am-5pm. ❶

Ben's Bakehouse, Shop 4, Anthony Plaza (☎8981 1561), at Smith St. Mall. Tempting pies, pastries, and other sinful delights, and it's all baked fresh daily. Don't miss their hot pumpkin rolls ($2). Open M-F 6am-6:30pm, Sa-Su 6am-3pm. ❶

Simply Foods (☎8981 4765), Star Village at the Smith St. Mall. Wholesome veggie-friendly meals. Creative sandwiches and salads for $4-6. Open M-F 9am-3pm. ❶

Hanuman, 28 Mitchell St. (☎8941 3500). For those looking to indulge a little in Darwin's famously good Asian food, Hanuman is a must. In a dark purple setting that's elegant but relaxed and hip, it serves Thai, Indian, and Nonya dishes. Mains average $17. Open M-F noon-2:30pm and daily from 6:30pm until late. AmEx/MC/V. ❸

◎ SIGHTS

Though its visitors are often aiming to hit Kakadu and Litchfield, some of Darwin's own attractions justify a diversion. Most sights are accessible by foot, bike, or a short public bus ride. The **Tour Tub,** popular with seniors, rounds up passengers at major accommodations or at the corner of Smith and Knuckey St. and herds them to ten popular sights from Stokes Hill Wharf to East Point Reserve. (☎8981 5233. Operates daily 9am-4pm. Full-day pass $25. Half-day pass valid 1-4pm $15.)

◪**MINDIL BEACH SUNSET MARKET.** A celebration of arts, crafts, and food, the Mindil night market is where Darwin really shines. Outback goods, pottery, and clothes from Bali are on sale, while musicians and street performers vie for your attention. Grab a dinner of samosa, laksa, and ice cream for $8-10, and watch the setting sun with the rest of Darwin. *(Open May-Oct. Th 5-9pm, also June-Sept. Su 4-9pm.)*

THE MUSEUM AND ART GALLERY OF THE NORTHERN TERRITORY. A great general introduction to Darwin and the NT. Exhibits include: a thorough introduction to Aboriginal art, a documentary film on Cyclone Tracy, a maritime annex, and many displays of Territorial wildlife, including "Sweetheart," a gargantuan 5m croc famous for sinking fishing boats (though he never killed anyone). Also part of the museum is the **Fannie Bay Gaol,** which served as Darwin's main jail from 1883-1979. The marked self-tour leads through eerie rooms where prisoners once slept and two were executed. *(Museum is along the shore toward Vestey's Beach; turn left on Conacher St. off Gilruth Ave. Gaol is on the right farther up Gilruth, which becomes East Point Rd. ☎8999 8201. Open M-F 9am-5pm, Sa-Su 10am-5pm. Free. Wheelchair accessible.)*

MINDIL BEACH AND VESTEY'S BEACH. Prime locales for soaking up UV rays are north of the city, just off Gilruth Ave. Mindil Beach is on the left behind the casino, and Vestey's Beach is just north of the museum. Box jellyfish warnings (see **Dangerous Wildlife,** p. 60) apply from October to March, but stings have been recorded all months of the year. *(Heading away from downtown, take Smith St. past Daly St. and turn right onto Gilruth Ave. at the traffic circle. 30min. walk, or catch bus #4 or 6.)*

AQUASCENE. Darwin's most unusual sight lets you share an intimate moment with a warm and friendly...fish. Each high tide, you can wade into the water and hand-feed bread to an enormous horde of surprisingly large fishies—watch those fingers—or take in the scene from the concrete bleachers. Fishing punishable by $10,000 fine. *(28 Doctors Gully Rd. North off Daly St. ☎8981 7837. Call ahead for the feeding schedule or check "Darwin and the Top End Today" guide. $6, under 15 $3.60.)*

PARK IT. The area around Darwin is full of tranquil parks. Just north of Daly St., the shaded paths of the **Botanic Gardens** wind through a series of Australian ecosystems: rainforest, mangroves, and dunes. The gardens survived cyclones in 1897, 1937, and 1974. *(Entrances on Geranium St. off the Stuart Hwy., and just past Mindil Beach on*

BISEXUAL BARRAMUNDI The premier fish of Top End, the illustrious barramundi, is served on almost every street corner in Darwin. Though it tastes quite bland, the curious biological development of the barramundi is anything but conventional. While the mature male spawns around age 3, the same creature shifts gears from male to female at age 6 or 7. The female barramundi, having undergone a complete sex transformation, can carry millions of eggs and can grow over a meter long. Just food for thought to accompany your next beer-battered barra burger.

the opposite side of Gilruth Ave. Wheelchair accessible.) The **East Point Reserve** occupies the peninsula to the north of Mindil and Vestey's Beach, and draws city-loathers with a coastline, picnic areas, and predator-free swimming in Lake Alexander. Wallabies are often spotted, especially in the evening *(Access from East Point Rd. A 45min. bike ride from city. No bus service.)* Walking trails, picnic areas, and views of Darwin Harbour lie in wait at **Charles Darwin National Park.** *(Bennett St. eastbound becomes Tiger Brennan Dr. Follow this for 5km to the park entrance. ☎ 8947 2305. Open daily 7am-7pm.)*

CROCODYLUS PARK. This research and education center holds lions, rheas, iguanas, and other assorted critters in addition to the featured reptiles. Sure, you might encounter crocs in the wild, but they probably won't let you hold them and pose for a picture. *(Take Local bus #5, then walk 10min. ☎ 8947 2510. Open daily 9am-5pm. Feedings and tours 10am, noon, and 2pm. $22, concessions $18, ages 4-15 $11. Shuttle available from city at ☎ 8981 3300. $35, families $90; prices include park entry.)*

OTHER MUSEUMS AND EXHIBITS. At the **East Point Military Museum,** photos and a video display the decimation caused by the Japanese bombing on Darwin Harbour in 1942. *(East Point Rd. at East Point Reserve. It's a 7min. drive or 45min. bike ride from downtown. ☎ 8981 9702. Open daily 9:30am-5pm. $10, seniors $8, children $5, families $28.)* The **Australian Aviation Heritage Centre's** collection of old aircraft is crowned by an old American B-52 bomber. *(10km from Darwin on the Stuart Hwy., served by bus #8. ☎ 8947 2145. Open daily 9am-5pm. $11, students $7.50, children $6, families $28.)* To learn more about Darwin's reef system, visit **Indo Pacific Marine.** A pool with a fascinating self-sustained ecosystem (no feeding, no filters) is the main attraction here. *(On Stokes Hill Wharf. ☎ 8999 6573. Open in the Dry daily 10am-5pm; in the Wet M-Sa 9am-1pm, Su 10am-5pm. $16, concessions $14, under 14 $6, families $38. Free talks every 30min.)*

◤ ACTIVITIES

Scuba diving allows certified divers to explore sunken vessels in the harbor. While Darwin's waters teem with box jellyfish during the Wet, divers are usually safe farther from shore. **Cullen Bay Dive** offers guidance, gear, or certification. (☎ 8981 3049. $35 per dive, $75 with gear; certification approx. $450.) Back on land, **biking** is a convenient way to explore Darwin. A 45min. bike path extends from Darwin City to East Point Reserve (see p. 246).

Darwin also has a choice of gravity-defying adventures. At **The Rock,** on Doctors Gully Rd. next to Aquascene, climbing connoisseurs can tackle a variety of wall climbs in the old tanker. (☎ 8941 0747. Unlimited-length sessions $11; harness rental $3; boot rental free. Open Tu noon-6pm, W noon-9pm, Th-F 10am-9pm, Sa-Su 10am-6pm.) Go **skydiving** from 10,000 ft. with **Pete's Parachuting.** (☎ 1800 641 114. Tandem $299). **Parasailing** with **Odyssey Adventures** provides breathtaking aerial views for breathtaking prices. Sunset flights run from June to September; book ahead. (☎ 0418 891 998. Single $75; tandem $60 per person.)

♫ ▣ ENTERTAINMENT AND FESTIVALS

You can quickly blow your bus fare at the underwhelming 24hr. **MGM Grand Casino** (☎ 1800 891 118). For something original, the infinitely more interesting ▨**Deckchair Cinema** shows offbeat, artsy films (many foreign) under the stars in a sunken amphitheater. Heading away from Darwin Harbour on Bennett St., turn right on McMinn and left on Frances Bay Dr.; the cinema is 100m down on the right. Walking takes 20min., but go in groups or call the shuttle. (☎ 8981 0700. Open in the Dry only. W-Su 7:30pm, additional shows F-Sa around 9:30pm. $11, concessions $9.)

The **Darwin Entertainment Centre,** 93 Mitchell St., between Peel and Daly St., has an imposing coral facade. Call the box office for same-day 50% discounts and free shows. (☎8981 1222. Open M-F 10am-5:30pm.) **Brown's Mart,** 12 Smith St. (☎8981 5522), near Bennett St., hosts productions in one of Darwin's oldest buildings. The **Botanic Gardens Amphitheater** has open-air theater in the midst of the lush gardens.

Darwin celebrates the Dry with a number of festivals. The **Darwin Beer Can Regatta,** held off Mindil Beach in early August, is decidedly not dry. Teams of devout beer-chuggers use their empties to make vessels and race them across the harbor. The **Darwin Cup Carnival** begins in July and ends with Cup Day in August (along with the Territory's Picnic Day). On the second Sunday in June (June 8, 2003), the Greek population of Darwin stages the **Glenti Festival,** a musical and culinary event, on the Esplanade. Ask the tourist office for an **Australian Football League (AFL)** schedule. When the Dry draws near its close in mid-August, Darwin goes for broke with the 17-day **Festival of Darwin** and then awaits the rain.

◼ NIGHTLIFE

Darwin late-night booze scene, alive every night of the week, extends all over the city center, catering primarily to backpackers and tourists looking to party hearty. Pubs and clubs advertise heavily with posters and brochures, hoping to grab the attention of good-looking, scantily-clad backpackers. City law requires all clubs to have a cover, but most charge only a few dollars. Many pubs have clubs attached with separate entrances; others simply start charging a cover around midnight. If you're willing to start your night early, you can dodge the fee at these locales.

▨ **Lost Arc,** 89 Mitchell St. (☎8942 3300). The most reliable party in town is found with the *beautiful* crowd at this funky joint. Extraordinary people-watching from the plush sidewalk couches. Tu-Th and Su live music. Open M-Th and Su 4pm-4am, F-Sa 4pm-2am. Next door, **Discovery** breaks it down on weekends with theme nights ranging from retro to dance. Cover $6-8. Open F-Sa 9pm-4am.

Throb, 64 Smith St. (☎8942 3435). Escape the top 20 blues and break it down at one of Darwin's hippest clubs. This gay and lesbian nightclub is not as raunchy as its name might suggest; the crowd is stylish and chill. Funky pool tables, friendly staff, and by far the best music in town. Sa drag shows at midnight. Cover $5. Open Th-Sa 10pm-4am.

Lizards Outdoor Bar and Grill (☎8981 6511), at the corner of Mitchell and Daly St. This spacious outdoor beer garden, adorned with lush palm trees, features all the fun of a pub in a more clean-cut setting. Best nighttime ambiance in town. Half-pints from $2.50. Th-Su live music, F Latin night. Open M-F 3pm-2am, Sa-Su 11am-2am.

The Victoria Hotel, 27 Smith St. Mall (☎8981 4011). The lines out the door welcome you to the most sexually charged outback-meets-blitzed-backpacker scene. **Settlers** pub downstairs serves beer in a rustic atmosphere. Live music nightly. Open M-F 10am-4am, Sa 11am-4am, Su 4pm-4am. Upstairs, **Banjo's** pool tables draw backpackers early in the night, then the music starts and people dance on everything from tables to the bar. Cover $6 after midnight. Open M-F 4pm-4am, Sa-Su 7pm-4am.

Nirvana (☎8981 2025), on Smith St. near Peary St. Technically not a bar, this upscale Southeast Asian restaurant hosts quality musical entertainment for the price of a drink and some munchies. You must eat to stay and drink one of their delicious concoctions; try a frozen Japanese Slipper for $9. Prices are on the high-side, so don't leave your appetite at home. Tu open jam session. Th-Sa jazz. Open Tu-Sa 9am-2am.

Shenannigans, 69 Mitchell St. (☎8981 2100). Your standard loud and happy Irish pub, always packed with boisterous and primarily male merry-makers. Occasional live music draws locals into the normally entirely backpackers crowd. M karaoke. Tu trivia night. Happy Hour F 4:30-6:30pm. Open M-Sa 10am-2am, Su noon-2am.

Squires, 3 Edmund St. (☎ 8981 9761), off Smith St. behind Woolworth's. Away from the backpacking hordes, locals know the place to go for a no-frills beer and a game of pool. Free BBQ W-F 5-7pm. Th $6 jugs. F $3 schooners. Happy Hour M-F 12:30-1:30pm and 5-6pm. Open M-Sa 11am-4am, Su 5pm-4am. Next door is **Time,** Darwin's original dance club. Cover $6. Open F-Sa 10pm-4am.

🏊 OFF THE COAST: THE TIWI ISLANDS

In the Timor Sea, 80km north of Darwin, are the Tiwi Islands, **Melville** and **Bathurst.** Melville is Australia's second-biggest island, ranking behind only Tasmania. Together, the Tiwis represent 8000km² of Aboriginal-owned tropics. The main attractions are remoteness, contemporary Aboriginal communities, and relaxing beaches. The only way to see the islands is through **Tiwi Tours.** (☎ 8924 1115. Daytrip $298, children $268; 2-day camping leaving Tu and Th $564/$493.)

ARNHEM HIGHWAY: THE TOP END WETLANDS

Intersecting the Stuart Hwy. 33km southeast of Darwin, the **Arnhem Highway** glides for 120km through the **Adelaide** and **Mary River Wetlands** before hitting **Kakadu National Park.** During the Dry, these wetlands are a lush sanctuary for birds and crocs; during the Wet, much of the area floods. The **Fogg Dam Conservation Reserve,** 25km east of the junction of the Stuart and Arnhem Hwy. and 10km north on an access road, is a breathtaking spot to view the winged inhabitants of the area. No binoculars are needed: cormorants, herons, storks, egrets, and ibises fill the air with song. The **Window on the Wetlands Visitor Centre** is another 4km east on the Arnhem Hwy., on one of the three hills that represent the Turtle Dreaming for the Limilngan-Wulna people. (☎ 8988 8188. Open daily 7:30am-7:30pm.)

KAKADU NATIONAL PARK

This World Heritage site is awesome in its size and in its wonders. When the Aboriginal spirit *Warramurrungundji* set out on her daunting task to create much of the Kakadu region, she had an immense vision. At 19,804km², Australia's largest national park contains six distinct ecosystems, four river systems, abundant wildlife, and dozens of Aboriginal outstations and sacred sites where Aboriginal lifestyle and ceremony are still vibrantly practiced and protected. If you came to the Territory to see an untainted piece of Australia, Kakadu is the place.

From the burnt-cinnamon earth of the Dry to the raging waterfalls of the Wet, the ever-changing Kakadu presents a surreal cross between the tropics and the desert. Quiet in the eastern stone cliffs and noisy with birds in the wetlands and low-lying woodlands, Kakadu's music is equally dichotomous. The grassy savanna woodlands, filled with eucalyptus trees, comprise 60% of the park and support a variety of wildlife. Monsoon forests spot the park, and hills and ridges undulate throughout the southern region, giving way to the rugged stone country that juts out of the park's eastern border. Floodplains and billabongs surround Kakadu's four river systems and present a serene expanse of silver and green, while tidal flats and coast in the north offer some of the most diverse flora and fauna.

Intimately intertwined with this awe-inspiring landscape is the living legacy of the Aboriginal community that resides in Kakadu. Aboriginal people have inhabited this land for an estimated 50,000 years and have left the treasure of the world's largest, and possibly oldest, collection of rock art upon its stone escarpments. Today's Aboriginal population in Kakadu has dwindled from the original European estimate of 2000 to a mere 300. The number of clans has likewise decreased from 20 to 12, and of the dozen languages once spoken here, only three remain active. The language of *Gagudju*, spoken here a century ago, lives on in the park's name.

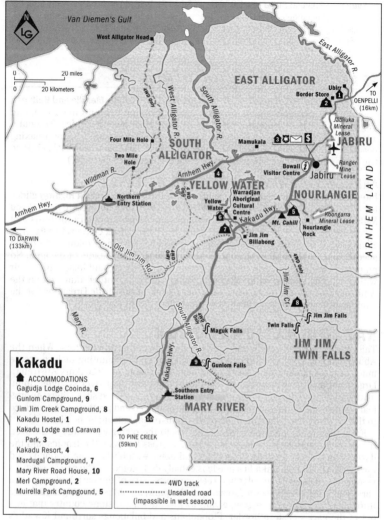

NORTHERN TERRITORY

Kakadu map including:

Van Diemen's Gulf

West Alligator Head

East Alligator R.

EAST ALLIGATOR

Ubirr

Border Store

TO OENPELLI (16km)

Jabiluka Mineral Lease

0 20 miles
0 20 kilometres

4WD Only

West Alligator R.

South Alligator R.

Four Mile Hole

Mamukala

JABIRU

SOUTH ALLIGATOR

Two Mile Hole

Wildman R.

Arnhem Hwy.

Bowali Visitor Centre

Jabiru

Ranger Mine Lease

ARNHEM LAND

Northern Entry Station

YELLOW WATER

Warradjan Aboriginal Cultural Centre

NOURLANGIE

Koongarra Mineral Lease

Arnhem Hwy.

TO DARWIN (133km)

4WD Only

Yellow Water

Kakadu Hwy.

Mt. Cahill

Nourlangie Rock

Old Jim Jim Rd.

Jim Jim Billabong

4WD Only

Mary R.

South Alligator Hwy.

4WD Only

Jim Jim Cr.

Jim Jim Falls

Twin Falls

Maguk Falls

Kakadu Hwy.

JIM JIM/ TWIN FALLS

Gunlom Falls

Southern Entry Station

MARY RIVER

TO PINE CREEK (59km)

Kakadu

🏠 ACCOMMODATIONS
Gagudja Lodge Cooinda, **6**
Gunlom Campground, **9**
Jim Jim Creek Campground, **8**
Kakadu Hostel, **1**
Kakadu Lodge and Caravan Park, **3**
Kakadu Resort, **4**
Mardugal Campground, **7**
Mary River Road House, **10**
Merl Campground, **2**
Muirella Park Campgound, **5**

-------- 4WD track
··········· Unsealed road (impassible in wet season)

Aboriginal people are active in the management and conservation of the park, and about 30% of Kakadu's employees are of Aboriginal descent. Half of Kakadu is still owned by its traditional Aboriginal owners, who leased their land to the Australian National Parks and Wildlife Service in 1978. Cultural sensitivity is a primary goal throughout the park, and the most sacred Aboriginal Dreaming sights remain off-limits to visitors.

ORIENTATION

Kakadu National Park is roughly rectangular. The two entries into the park are the **Arnhem Hwy.** in the north, which runs east-west, and the **Kakadu Hwy.** in the south,

KAKADU AT A GLANCE

AREA: 19,804km².

FEATURES: Stone country, floodplains of the Alligator River System, township of Jaribu, Jim Jim and Twin Falls.

HIGHLIGHTS: Galleries of Aboriginal rock art, walks through grasslands and to sunset lookout points, riverboat cruises, 4WD treks to waterfalls and plunge pools.

INFO: www.ea.gov.au/parks/kakadu

GATEWAYS: Darwin (see p. 239), Pine Creek (see p. 264).

CAMPING: Ranging from free bushcamping to commercial campgrounds (see p. 253).

FEES: $16.25 park entrance fee. Fees are required for Yellow Water River Cruise, Guluyambi East Alligator Cruise, and day tours of Jim Jim and Twin Falls.

which runs northeast-southwest. These two fully paved roads converge in the park's northeastern interior near the township of **Jabiru** (JAB-ber-roo). They remain open year-round, except during the most severe floods in the Wet.

Kakadu is divided into seven regions. The **South Alligator Region** is east of Kakadu's north gate, 120km east of the junction between the Arnhem and Stuart Hwy. It is marked by the flood plains that sprawl around the mighty South Alligator River and includes the Kakadu Resort, 77km from the park entrance. After another 39km, the Arnhem Hwy. enters the **East Alligator Region** and arrives at Ubirr Rd., the 36km turn-off to **Ubirr**, a rock art site and lookout. The Kakadu Hostel and Border Store are near Ubirr.

The junction of the Arnhem and Kakadu Hwy. is about 1km past Ubirr Rd. in the **Jabiru Region.** Just 2km from this junction, tidy **Jabiru** (pop. 2000) is the primary town in Kakadu, with the Kakadu Lodge and Caravan Park, post office, and a grocery store. The **Bowali Visitor Centre** is 5km from Jabiru on the Kakadu Hwy.

The remaining four regions are accessed from the Kakadu Hwy. The turn-off for the **Nourlangie Region** is 21km from Jabiru; a 12km paved road leads to Nourlangie Rock. The turn-off for the **Jim Jim/Twin Falls Region** is 20km farther on the Kakadu Hwy. This 4WD-only road (impassable in the Wet) runs 60km to the Jim Jim Falls camping area and 10km more to Twin Falls. The **Yellow Water Region** is much easier to reach (just 9km farther down the highway). The Warradjan Aboriginal Cultural Centre and Gadgudju Cooinda Lodge are in the Yellow Water area. The south gate of Kakadu is 99km farther on the Kakadu Hwy. through the **Mary River Region,** and **Pine Creek** is another 59km farther. Several reader-friendly maps, like the *Kakadu National Park Visitor Guide and Map* booklet, come with park entry permits.

▆ TRANSPORTATION

Armed with the *Kakadu National Park Visitor Guide and Map*, the most ideal way to do Kakadu is in your own car. A 4WD is by far the most convenient, allow-

BURN, BABY, BURN! During the Dry, the horizon frequently billows with the purple-gray smoke of bush fires. Don't panic: Aborigines have been using controlled bush burning for thousands of years for hunting, communication, ceremony, and horticulture. Under Aboriginal guidance, Kakadu National Park continues to use bush fires for fire management. Burning is done in small patches during the Wet and early Dry season in order to prevent the build-up of thick undergrowth which could provide fuel for Dry season fires. Some bush fires are still caused naturally by lightning late in the Dry, and these are the most dangerous. Seeing a bush fire up close is an eerie experience, especially at night. Bright orange tongues of flame devour the bases of trees and plants, generating a thick, organic odor and a distinct crackling sound.

NORTHERN TERRITORY

ing for a more personal and off-the-beaten-path experience. Renting a 4WD, however, is expensive, and rental companies might not even allow access to certain sights even if the roads are open; check with them before you book. A 2WD will get you to the top tourist destinations in the Dry, except Jim Jim and Twin Falls.

Flights: The Jabiru Airport (☎8979 2411), 6½km east of Jabiru on the Arnhem Hwy., is the base for aerial tours of Kakadu. **Kakadu Air** offers bird's-eye **scenic flights** of Kakadu ($85 per 30min., $135 per hr.). Flights during the Wet are popular since many roads close. Courtesy shuttles run between the airport and Jabiru.

Car Rental: Territory Rent-a-Car (☎0418 858 601) has a desk in the Gagudja Croc Hotel on Flinders St., Jabiru. Small sedans from $94 per day with 100km limit. **4WD unavailable.** Many people rent cars out of Darwin (see p. 239).

◤ TOURS

Daytours from Darwin with **McCafferty's/Greyhound** can be expanded to three or more days. Conductors double as knowledgeable, witty tour guides, although the visit compresses the sights without exploring the park's more rugged, remote gems. You have the option of connecting with tours of the rivers and Jim Jim/Twin Falls. (☎13 14 99 or 13 20 30. $90, not including park entry fee.)

Plenty of **tour companies** offer packages, and almost all 4WD operations work out of Darwin. Some rely on lodge accommodations and others camp under the stars, but all encourage more than two to three days in the park. **Wilderness 4WD Adventures** specializes in tours with biology-savvy guides geared toward fit nature lovers. (☎1800 808 288. 3-5 day $425-645.) **Northern Territories Adventure Tours** also offers 4WD safaris. (☎1800 654 604. Camping 2-5 days $320-675; 3-day "safari in style" $775, includes indoor accommodation.) **Gondwana Adventure Tours and Expeditions** gets kudos for super-cheap prices. (☎1800 242 177. 3-day $375, 4-day $440.) All these tours involve a lot of hiking and hot sun. **AAT Kings** offers slightly less rugged tours of Kakadu in a coach. (☎8941 3844. 1-3 day $147-495.)

WHEN TO GO. Locals say they have a hard time describing Wet Kakadu to Dry season visitors, and vice versa.

The Dry, from April to October, is the most convenient and comfortable season to visit for most travelers. Dry highs average 30°C (86°F), lows 17°C (59°F), and the humidity is low. It can get cold at night; travelers should carry an extra layer and repellent to ward off commando mosquitoes. During the Dry, almost all roads are open except for a few unpaved ones early in the season. Check at the Bowali Visitor Centre for road openings (see **Practical Information,** p. 252). Most camping, accommodations, and attractions operate in the Dry.

The Wet dramatically alters the landscape of Kakadu with its monsoon rains and floods. Locals insist that the Wet is the most beautiful time of the year, as the land teems with foliage and flowers. Still, the humidity, heat—35°C (95°F) highs and 25°C (77°F) lows—and bugs make the park harder to enjoy. The famous falls, particularly Jim Jim and Twin, are at their most powerful but can only be seen from the air. One plus of the Wet—boat cruises are up and running, as the Ubirr drive becomes a river (see **East Alligator** sights, p. 255).

▐ PRACTICAL INFORMATION

Tourist Information: The **Bowali Visitor Centre** (☎8938 1120; www.ea.gov.au/parks/kakadu), 2km west of Jabiru on the Kakadu Hwy., is an excellent source of info. During the Dry, rangers give free daily talks and guided walks. Open daily 8am-5pm. Wheelchair accessible. Reach the **Park Manager** at P.O. Box 71, Jabiru NT 0886.

Travel Agency: Jabiru Tourist Centre (☎8979 2839), Jabiru Plaza. Open M-F 9:30am-5pm, Sa-Su 9:30am-12:30pm and 3:30-4:30pm. Tours can also be booked from hotels.

Ranger Stations: Ranger stations can relay information to the police and clinic from more remote areas, but the stations are only open to the public sporadically (daily 8am-4pm, but rangers are often called away). **South Alligator Ranger Station** (☎8979 0194), 40km west of Bowali Centre near Aurora Kakadu Village. **East Alligator Ranger Station** (☎8979 2291), 36km north of Bowali Centre on the Ubirr Rd. **Jim Jim Ranger Station** (☎8979 2038), down a 2½km road that turns off the Kakadu Hwy., 45km south of Bowali. **Mary River Ranger Station** (☎8975 4578), at the south entry station.

Auto Services: Diesel and unleaded **fuel stations** are at the Aurora Kakadu Village, Jabiru, Cooinda, the Border Store near Ubirr, and the Mary River Roadhouse at the south entrance. **Jabiru's Mobil Station** (☎8979 2001) has **auto repair.** Open daily 7am-8pm.

Potable Water: At Bowali, Jabiru, Cooinda, and Aurora Kakadu Village. *Rangers recommend boiling water from any other source, including the campgrounds listed below.*

Banks: Westpac Bank (☎8979 2432), at Jabiru Plaza, has currency exchange and a 24hr. **ATM.** Open M-Th 9:30am-4pm, F 9:30am-5pm. Cooinda Lodge has **EFTPOS** only.

Police: Jabiru Police, 10 Tasman Crescent (**Emergency** ☎000 or 8979 2122), across the street from Jabiru Plaza at the end of Flinders St.

Swimming: You'll need a cool dip here to wash away the dust and soothe the mozzie bites. The safest places to swim in Kakadu are the lodge pools and the mighty Olympic size **Jabiru Pool.** (☎8979 2127. Open daily 9am-7pm. $2.)

Internet Access: Library (☎8979 2097), at Jabiru Plaza. Open Tu-W 10am-4pm, Th noon-6pm, F 10am-4pm, Sa 10am-2pm. $3 per 15min.

Post Office: (☎8979 2727), at Jabiru Plaza, inside 2 Rivers News Agency. Open M-F 9am-5pm, Sa 9am-noon. **Postal Code:** 0886.

ACCOMMODATIONS, CAMPING, AND FOOD

Commercial accommodations in Kakadu are not ideal for the budget traveler. Options are limited, motel rooms are expensive, and budget dorms leave much to be desired. Advance reservations are strongly recommended in the Dry. Camping is one of the cheapest ways to enjoy the outdoors in Kakadu. There are four large first-come first-served campgrounds spread throughout the park, and also has free camping areas, in all regions, for those who want to rough it. Check the *Visitor Guide* for locations. These areas offer only the most basic facilities (outhouses) or none at all, but are generally uncrowded (Jim Jim and Twin Falls being the exceptions). Travelers should bring plenty of water. Kakadu is known for game in the bush, not on the plate. Dining options, and groceries outside Jabiru, are sparse and expensive; bringing food is recommended. Accommodations and food options are listed within each respective regional section below.

SIGHTS AND HIKES

Kakadu offers a variety of well-established sights for nature lovers and history buffs. Walks and hikes range in difficulty levels to suit all visitors. The main sights are viewed from short, relatively tame walking trails; a few are wheelchair accessible. The climbs to the lookout points at Ubirr and Nourlangie are steeper. A number of excellent, longer walks reward the fit and adventurous who choose to venture farther out into the bush.

HIKING SAFETY TIPS Self-sufficiency is the key to a safe adventure in Kakadu, as help is often hours away.

Bring: Lots of **water** (at least 1L per hour of walking), insect repellent, sunscreen, and sturdy shoes.

Beware: These areas are full of **snakes** and **spiders;** long trousers and thick socks will help protect against bites. **Salties** are also common, so never swim or wade in water sources and stay away from the water's edge.

Call: There are **emergency call boxes** at the carparks of some of the more remote hikes, such as Jim Jim.

All sights and walks are open during the Dry; many are subject to closure during the Wet. The park brochure is a good supplement to descriptions and directions; *Kakadu By Foot* ($3.30), in the Bowali Visitor Centre, gives detailed descriptions of the walks. For experienced hikers, unmarked and **overnight bushwalks** are the most genuine way to see Kakadu without the crowds. These routes generally follow the creek lines and gorges along the escarpment. Routes and campsites on unmarked walks must be approved. For overnight camping permits and route plan approval, contact the Bowali Visitor Centre (see **Practical Information,** p. 252). Permits are free but require one week for processing.

⚑ KAKADU: A REGION BY REGION GUIDE

REGION	MAJOR SIGHTS	ACCOMMODATION	SERVICES
East Alligator	Ubirr, Guluyambi river cruise	Kakadu Resort	Food and fuel at Kakadu Resort
Jabiru	Bowali Visitor Centre, Iligadjarr Walk	Kakadu Lodge and Caravan Park	Food and fuel in Jabiru
Jim Jim/Twin Falls	Jim Jim/Twin Falls	none	none
Mary River	Gunlom	none	Food and fuel at Mary River Road House
Nourlangie	Nourlangie	none	none
South Alligator	Mamukala wetlands	Kakadu Resort	Food and fuel at Kakadu Resort
Yellow River	Gunlom Warradjan Aboriginal Cultural Centre, Yellow Water cruise	Gagudju Cooinda Lodge	Food and fuel at Cooinda

SOUTH ALLIGATOR REGION

ACCOMMODATIONS. Just past the Northern Entry Station, a 4WD-only road extends north into the park. For 80km, it bumps its way to **Van Diemen's Gulf** (no swimming; the sea here is full of the usual culprits). Along this road are two free secluded camping spots, **Two Mile Hole ❶** and **Four Mile Hole ❶,** 8km and 38km from the Arnhem Hwy., respectively. They lack any facilities but offer peaceful camping along the Wildman River. Be prepared, however, for clouds of mozzies. For those not ready to head right into the bush, **Kakadu Resort ❶** (☎ 8979 0166), 73km into the park, offers powered and unpowered sites ($7.50 per person) and twin and double hotel rooms ($195), as well as a swimming pool.

SUPPLIES. Food, fuel, petrol, and beer can all be found at the Kakadu Resort.

CLOSEST RANGER STATION. South Alligator Ranger Station (☎ 8979 0194) is near Aurora Kakadu Village.

HIKES AND SIGHTS. Mamukala Wetlands is a floodplain and birdwatching area off the Arnhem Hwy., 8km east of the South Alligator River crossing and 1km down an access road. A 100m wheelchair accessible path leads to a lookout where the patient can observe snowy egrets and Jabiru storks. In late August and September, the plain comes to life as 25,000 *bamurru* (magpie geese) descend. The bird center has a great display explaining the seasonal cycle of wetlands in Kakadu.

JABIRU REGION

ACCOMMODATIONS. Free camping without facilities can be found on the Kakadu Hwy. at **Malabanjbanjdju ❶** and **Burdulba ❶,** both around 16km south of the junction of the Arnhem and Kakadu Hwy. Both sights are nondescript but give lovely views of Burdulba Billabong. As usual, flies and mozzies can be unbearable at times. **🏕Kakadu Lodge and Caravan Park ❶** is friendly, well-kept, and brimming with comforts such as A/C, linen, towels, a pool, laundry, and bistro. Frequent activities such as free pancake breakfasts and ranger slide shows add to this already excellent caravan park. (☎ 8979 2422. Reception daily 7:30am-7:30pm. Sites $10 per person, powered for 2 $25, all sites have access to amenities; lodge rooms $121; 5-person ensuite cabins with kitchen $199.)

SUPPLIES. The supermarket in **Jabiru Plaza** (open M-F 9am-5:30pm, Sa 9am-3pm, Su 10am-2pm) has a wide selection, and the **Jabiru Cafe ❶,** also in the plaza, has tasty hot dishes for around $6. (Open M-F 7:30am-5pm.)

CLOSEST RANGER STATION. Bowali Visitor Centre. (Open daily 8am-5pm.)

HIKES AND SIGHTS. The Bowali Visitor Centre is a good place to start a tour of the park, but most sights here are man-made. A captivating eight-screen slideshow displays the stunning visual beauty of the park. The **Iligadjarr Walk** (3.8km; 2hr.), leaving from the Malabanjbanjdju or Burdulba camping areas, wanders through a grassy floodplain. Open terrain offers great views of the wetlands. Far to the east, past the airport, the **Ranger Uranium Mine** is the most active mine in Kakadu. (☎ 1800 089 113. Ground tours depart daily from Jabiru Airport 10:30am. 1½hr. $20, children $10. Reservations essential.)

EAST ALLIGATOR REGION

ACCOMMODATIONS. Standard-fee camping 4km from Ubirr can be found at the shady **Merl Campground ❶.** It's spacious and relatively uncrowded, with good reason—ferocious swarms of mozzies make it inhospitable in the Dry. The **Kakadu Hostel ❷,** 3km south of Ubirr, attracts its share of visitors with low prices, A/C, and an above ground pool, but its well-worn appearance, thin walls, and lack of locks on the dorms detract from the overall experience. (☎ 8979 2232. All beds $25.)

SUPPLIES. While Jabiru and its wealth of supplies are a mere 5km away, the **Border Store,** 3km south of Ubirr, has expensive groceries and fuel. Its also pricey but very popular BBQ featuring barra, buffalo, and croc burgers (all $8), can inject some much-craved protein into your otherwise all-Vegemite camping diet.

CLOSEST RANGER STATION. The **East Alligator Ranger Station** (☎ 8979 2291) is 36km north of Bowali Visitor Centre on Ubirr Rd.

HIKES AND SIGHTS. The gem of this region is **Ubirr,** a collection of sandstone outliers on which Aboriginal ancestors created rock art thousands of years ago. A **wheelchair accessible circuit** (1km; 30 min.) passes significant sights such as the Namarrgarn Sisters, which tells the story of the appearance of crocodiles, and the Main Gallery, which displays several different layers of rock art. A steep, rocky

IN RECENT NEWS

RECONCILIATION

Started in 1991 by an act of Parliament, the **Council for Reconciliation** is a body of 25 Australians, 14 indigenous and 11 non-indigenous, whose broad goals are to promote understanding of indigenous culture and help overcome inequities in the treatment of Aborigines and Torres Straight Islanders. Its mission was a 10-year one, set to be complete by 2001, but the huge nature of its task means that it more *began* the conversation on reconciliation than concluded it.

The programs it put in place attempted to use sports teams, cultural and artistic clubs, community service organizations, and other community bodies to, in the words of their mission statement, create a "united Australia" with "justice and equity for all." On some level, the positive effects of their work can readily be seen: the celebration of the achievements of athletes of Aboriginal descent, the explosion in interest in Aboriginal art and dance, the improved network of community centers that address the needs and concerns of Aboriginal communities, and an increase in the participation of Aborigines in managing both the state parks that occupy their traditional land and the tourism businesses that use them.

For those who work, live, and travel in Australia, though, these are mere side notes, stories in the newspaper or on the nightly news, or exceptions to rule. The social and economic divide between the Aboriginal community and the wider Australian community is still very much apparent, and,

climb (250m; 15min.) leads to the top of Ubirr, with a spectacular view of the distant stone escarpment and the emerald floodplains. Sunsets on top of Ubirr are magical, but be prepared to share the experience with chattering tourists. (Open daily Apr.-Nov. 8:30am-sunset, Dec.-Mar. 2pm-sunset.) Four free art site talks are given daily during the Dry; check at Bowali for the schedule.

The ▨**Guluyambi River Cruise** is Kakadu's best boat tour. While the sunbathing saltics on the banks of the East Alligator might try to steal the show, it is the wonderful Aboriginal-guided demonstration of local culture, bush tucker, and hunting tools that is most memorable. The boats are smaller than those of the Yellow River Cruise, and patrons view the shores of Arnhem Land without a permit. The tour runs from the upstream boat ramp. (☎ 1800 089 113. 1¾hr. Departs daily May-Nov. 9, 11am, 1, and 3pm; call ahead Dec-Apr. $30, children $15. Book ahead at the Border Stores for a seat.) The highly recommended **Bardedjilidji Sandstone Walk** (2½km; 40min.) covers much of the same territory on land through weathered sandstone pillars, arches, and caves. From the base of the formations, tree roots extending 20m down the jagged cliffs to the ground are visible. The trailhead is near the upstream boat ramp. **Manngarre Monsoon Rainforest Walk** (1½km; 30min.) brings hikers into one of Kakadu's lush rainforests on a flat and easy trail to a viewing platform. Beautiful and tropical, the walk features occasional croc sightings along the East Alligator River and a few Aboriginal cultural sights.

NOURLANGIE REGION

ACCOMMODATIONS. The only camping option in Nourlangie is the quiet **Muirella Park Campground ❶**, down a 6km gravel track from the Kakadu Hwy. The turn-off is 30km from Jabiru.

SUPPLIES. There are **no supplies** of any kind in the Nourlangie Region.

CLOSEST RANGER STATION. Bowali Visitor Centre. (Open daily 8am-5pm.)

HIKES AND SIGHTS. The principal draw of this part of the park is **Nourlangie** itself, a huge rock outlier used as a shelter and art studio by earlier Aborigines. A wheelchair accessible walking track (1½km; 1hr.) passes the Main Gallery and ascends to a tame lookout. Many mystical images are painted on the walls of Nourlangie, including *Nabulwinj-bulwinj*, a dangerous spirit who eats females after striking them with a yam. The **Anbangbang rock shelter,** formed by a gargantuan boulder leaning perilously over a narrow walkway, steals the show from the artwork. The farthest point on the loop is **Gunwarrde-hwarrde Lookout,** a craggy climb with a view of the distant escarpment, where Aborigines believe Lightning Man *Namarrgon* lives. Three art site talks are given daily in the Dry for free.

While these shorter hikes certainly draw tourists by the bus load, the true gem of the region is the **🖼Barrk Sandstone Bushwalk** (12km, 4-5hr.), one of the longest and most dramatic established walks in the park. It is challenging in parts and certainly only for the fit and sure-footed but, as with most things in life, the greatest rewards only come with a bit of hard work. Branching off from the lookout walk, it heads up straight up Nourlangie's steep sides, offering views vastly superior to any of the lookouts. Snaking across the relatively flat top of Nourlangie, it passes through complex sandstone formations that have the eerie feeling of a lost city. After exposing hikers to the rarely seen and highly beautiful environment that resides only on the top of Kakadu's table-like rock formations. A quick descent takes you to a lengthy level path that travels around Nourlangie back to meet up with the gallery loop. While less exciting than the trek over Nourlangie itself, this totally isolated portion allows visitors to be alone with the sights and sounds of Kakadu's diverse flora and fauna. Along the way you'll pass the **Nanguluwur rock art gallery.** Barrk has steep and technical sections, and sturdy footwear and at least 3L of water per person is essential. Use extreme care on the ascent when clambering over boulders and be forewarned that the trail is difficult to follow at times. Move slowly and keep your eyes peeled for the orange trail markers.

Some of the shorter secondary walks in the Nourlangie Region allow appreciation of the main site from a distance. The **Nawurlandja Lookout** (600m; 20min.) and **Mirrai Lookout** (1.8km; 30min.) are short, steep climbs with good photo-ops. **Anbangbang Billabong** (2½km; 30min.) is an easy and popular walk circling the water with delicate lilies and jagged cliffs (accessible only in the Dry).

JIM JIM/TWIN FALLS REGION

ACCOMMODATIONS. The **Muirella campground ❶** is just before the turn-off. The **Mardugal campground ❶** is 8km past the turn-off and south of Cooinda. Free camping with toilets is available at the **Jim Jim Creek Campground ❶.**

SUPPLIES. There are **no supplies** on this 4WD track or near the falls.

with exceptions, equity is not the day-to-day reality.

Part of the difficulty in understanding why reconciliation still feels a long way off is that the very concept of a "united Australia" means different things to the multitude of communities in the country. The world of sports, a central element to the life and culture of most Australians, is one area where this difference is most apparent. With the help of organizations like the Council for Reconciliation, attempts have been made to use sport as a cultural unifier, giving Aboriginal and non-Aboriginal people a common ground on which to relate and interact, thus breaking down misconceptions and establishing channels of communication and cultural exchange. But despite some success in the area of professional sports, making positive use of the highly active local sports network in Australia has proved more difficult. The integration of community sports teams and leagues was one of the Council's goals, yet sports leagues within Aboriginal communities have resisted all attempts to integrate teams or, at least, to compete against integrated teams. For Aboriginal people, sport is not only recreation, it is a cultural event. Integrated teams and the standards of play imposed by participating against outside teams favor recreation over the cultural side of the competition. For Aboriginal communities, a "united Australia" is one in which respect, not common experience, serves as the unifier. Yet, without this kind of integration, the communities remain separated, true communication is rare, and the future of reconciliation remains uncertain.

CLOSEST RANGER STATION. Jim Jim Ranger Station (☎8979 2038), down a 2½km road that turns off the Kakadu Hwy., 10km south of the Jim Jim/Twin Falls turn-off. A **ranger call box** is attached to the toilet facilities at the Jim Jim Falls carpark.

HIKES AND SIGHTS. The opening day of the 4WD-only access road in the Dry, eagerly awaited by tourists and tour guides alike, is frustratingly uncertain. **Jim Jim Falls,** 60km up a tough road, cascades 150m down into a deep, clear green pool. Shy Jim Jim is not visible for much of the year; in the Wet, the falls rush with roaring intensity. However, the same rain that causes the awesome spectacle also prevents road access to it; the only way to see the falls during the Wet is by air. There is a **lookout** 200m from the carpark. A boulder-ridden **walk** (1km; 25min.) leads to the plunge pool, which remains quite cold for much of the Dry due to lack of direct sunlight. For the most capable hikers, the stunning **Barrk Marlam walk** (3km; 4hr.) branches off the path to Jim Jim. It's a rugged one-way, straight up and across the escarpment, with expansive views of the gorge from the top.

Over the river from the camping area (you must have a decent 4WD, and a snorkel is recommended, for this crossing) and 10km through the woods is ◙**Twin Falls.** They are spectacular—far and away the most amazing sight to visit in the park. After an easy 400m walk, you come to a sandy beach great for swimming. The next step to reaching Twin Falls is a 500m swim up the river, dwarfed on both sides by sheer walls of rock. As birds fly overhead, the lush tropical vegetation that lines the sandy shores sways in the breeze, and the sound of your paddling echoes around this rocky cathedral, you'll swear you've found Kakadu's most heavenly place—at least until you reach Twin Falls. The double falls cascade over natural sandstone steps. With a large sandy beach, cool water, roaring falls, and the endless natural beauty that surrounds you, you'll swear you're in paradise.

Both Jim Jim and Twin Falls are home to **freshies,** which tend to leave people alone, although an occasional **saltie** makes its way into the pools. The park takes all possible precautions to keep salties out, and risk is very low. Still, **swim at your own risk.** For those who lack a 4WD, tours to Jim Jim and Twin Falls depart daily from Jabiru and Cooinda. Try **Katch Kakadu Tours** (☎8979 3315; $127, children $99), **Lord's Kakadu** (☎8979 2970; $125, children $100, YHA discount $5), or **Kakadu Gorge and Waterfall Tours** (☎8979 0111; $130, children $110).

YELLOW WATER REGION

ACCOMMODATIONS. The best place to stay is the peaceful, though occasionally bug-infested **Mardugal Campground ❶,** 2km south of the Cooinda turn-off on the Kakadu Hwy. For standard camping fees collected by a ranger in the evening, you get shower and toilet facilities and some of the best stargazing in the park. The **Gagudju Lodge Coodinga (YHA) ❶,** down a 4½km turn-off in the Yellow Water region, has pricey motel rooms and a muddy, overcrowded campground, as well as budget rooms. The condition of the shared bath, fridge, laundry, and coin-operated BBQ, along with its less than friendly staff, makes a common question in the guest book how exactly the Lodge justifies its prices. (☎8979 0145. Sites $11 per person, powered for 2 $28; budget singles $31; budget doubles $70; motel rooms $270.)

SUPPLIES. Petrol and basic groceries can be purchased at a premium at the **Gagudju Lodge Cooinda.** The lodge also has expensive but filling buffet meals (dinner $14) three times per day. (Open daily 6:30am-7pm.)

CLOSEST RANGER STATION. Jim Jim Ranger Station (☎8979 2038), down a 2½km turn off from the Kakadu Hwy., 45km south of Bowali.

HIKES AND SIGHTS. Yellow Water, part of Jim Jim Creek, is the most popular billabong in Kakadu—not to swim in, but to cruise past meters-long crocodiles sunning themselves on the banks or floating ominously on the surface of the water. On the **Yellow Water Walk** (1½km; 30min.), Jabiru storks, pied geese, and ducks pretend not to notice the clanking noise of the metal walkway. There's also a **wheelchair accessible** platform for viewing the billabong. Still, the most popular way to do Yellow Water is on a **Yellow Water cruise**, where knowledgeable if unenthusiastic guides point out the variety of birds and the occasional croc. The sunrise cruise is the most breathtaking, but exploring Yellow Water by boat is worthwhile any time of day because of the wildlife that can by seen in the wetlands environment, which is difficult to truly explore on foot. (☎1800 553 888. Book at the Gagudju Lodge Cooinda. In the Dry: 1½hr. and 2hr. tours each depart 3 per day; 1½hr. $33, 2hr. $38. In the Wet: 1½hr. tours, 6 per day, depart 7am-5pm; $33.)

Also enlightening is the ▨**Warradjan Aboriginal Cultural Centre**, 1km from the Cooinda Lodge, which shows visitors Kakadu's Aboriginal history. The exhibit is refreshing and places into context much of the disconnected Aboriginal trivia given at the cultural stops on the walking trails. Built in the shape of a *warradjan* (turtle), the center contains fantastic displays of Aboriginal culture, ranging from tools and rock art to biographies of significant local figures. (☎8979 0051. Open daily Sept.-June 9am-5pm, July-Aug. 7:30am-6pm. Free.)

MARY RIVER REGION

ACCOMMODATIONS. The relatively mozzie-free and well maintained **Gunlom Campground ❶**, 11km from the southern entrance of the park and 37km down a gravel road, has showers, toilets, and a generator zone; standard fees apply. The **Wirnwirnmila Mary River Road House ❶** is 11 km south of the park's southern entry. While the facilities leave much to be desired, it does have plenty of options. (☎8975 4564. Reception daily 7:30am-11pm. Sites $6.50 per person, powered for 2 $17; bunks $15; budget singles $30, doubles $40; hotel rooms $90.) Those looking for nicer facilities should head 59km south to Pine Creek (see p. 264).

CLOSEST RANGER STATION. Mary River Ranger Station (☎8975 4578), at the southern entry station.

HIKES AND SIGHTS. This is the land where the rivers begin. In the headwaters of the South Alligator River, a series of falls called **Gunlom** flow rapidly from December to May, but cease almost completely in the Dry. A **wheelchair accessible** footbridge leads to the plunge pool, and a steep walk (1km; 30min.) travels to the top of the falls and a series of enchanting smaller pools and a lovely view of the region. Gunlom is the only escarpment cascade that conventional 2WD vehicles can reach in the Dry via Gunlom Rd., a stone's throw from Kakadu's southern entry gate.

The secondary sights in the region are more challenging for both your car and your legs. **Maguk**, or **Barramundi Falls**, is a smaller cascade; the 4WD turn-off is 32km north of the Gunlom turn-off on the Kakadu Hwy. It flows during both seasons and is reached via a 12km road and then a rocky hike (2km; 1hr.) through monsoon forest. The **Yurmikmik Walking Tracks** pass Wet-season waterfalls. The trailhead is 21km down Gunlom Rd. off the Kakadu Hwy. There are three different circular day tracks (2km, 45min.; 5km, 2hr.; 7½km, 4hr.) and two longer tracks that require overnight permits (see **Practical Information**, p. 260). The 11km walk features a series of waterfalls and the 13½km walk features plunge pools during the Wet. Both of these longer walks are difficult, unmarked, and require good navigation and preparation. Near the Yurmikmik walks is **Jarrangbarnmi**, one of the *djang andjamun* areas that bring catastrophic consequences if entered. This series of pools on **Koolpin Creek** is home to *Bula* and *Bolung*, two Creation Ancestors. Visitor numbers are restricted, and no one can enter the area without a permit and entry key organized by the southern entry station (☎8975 4859).

NORTHERN TERRITORY

ARNHEM LAND

Take the expansive wilderness, serenity, and the cultural spirit found in Kakadu, multiply it by ten, and you still won't be able to do justice to Arnhem Land's grandeur. Sprawling across the entire northeastern region of the Top End, and several times the size of Kakadu, this Aboriginal homeland was established in 1931. It remains largely uninhabited, save for four or five small settlements and about 100 Aboriginal outstations. The area's inland borders are cut square, but the endless coastline takes an untamed, jagged path from the **Cobourg Peninsula** in the west (location of **Gurig National Park**) to the **Gove Peninsula** in the east. Arnhem Land also includes the Groote and Elcho islands off-shore. The natural and cultural treasures here are incredible, but be aware that while there are Aborigines who welcome tourism and its revenues, there are also those who would prefer to see their lands free from the swarms of outsiders.

⚑ PRACTICAL INFORMATION. Venturing into Arnhem Land is a serious matter. There are very few roads (those that do exist are erratically navigable only in the Dry), and there are virtually no signs or services. Moreover, Arnhem Land is off-limits by law to non-Aborigines, so a permit is required to enter.

Permits for entering Arnhem Land vary depending on where you want to go. The **Northern Land Council** in Jabiru issues permits for three locations close to Kakadu. (☎8979 2410. Open M-F 8am-4:30pm.) A permit for **Injalak** ($13.20 per person) can be issued on the spot but might take up to an hour to process. Permits for **Sandy Creek** and **Wunyu Beach** ($88 per person) take longer to process; apply in advance. To venture to the secluded beaches and wildlife of **Gurig National Park** on the Cooburg Peninsula, contact the Parks and Wildlife Commission of the Northern Territory. (☎8979 0244. $211 per vehicle with 5 adults for 7 nights.) For permits to other sections of Arnhem Land, contact Darwin's Northern Land Council (☎8920 5100 or 1800 645 299; fax 8445 2633.)

The road into Arnhem Land from Ubirr crosses a tidal river **(Cahills Crossing).** Check with the Northern Land Council about tidal information before driving or you might find your car tipped over in the saltie-ridden East Alligator River. Driving into Arnhem Land, and especially beyond Injalak, should not be taken lightly; it's wise to go with at least one other person. Bring a shovel, a kangaroo jack, two spare tires, a rope, and plenty of water.

◫ ♫ SIGHTS AND ACTIVITIES. The **Injalak Arts & Crafts Association** (IN-yaluk) is in Oenpelli (Gunbalanya), a short 16km dirt-road drive from Ubirr. The association has artists crafting pandanus baskets, limited edition bark and paper paintings, screen printed textiles, and didgeridoos. The works are distributed to art galleries around the world, but visitors can purchase pieces on-site at prices far, far below those charged for the same work in both Kakadu and Darwin. (☎8979 0190. Open M-F 8am-5pm, Sa 8am-noon.) Injalak also sponsors **⊠Aboriginal-guided tours** through a local rock art gallery whose breadth and isolation put Ubirr and Nourlangie to shame—there are no crowds or roped-off sections here. (2hr. tours $90; max. 6 people. Book ahead.) There are 12 distinct galleries on the rocks, and in addition to the usual images of fish and dancing Mimi spirits, they tell some of the lesser known myths and stories of the Arnhemland region. A series of galleries, viewed in order, warns of dangerous spirits that live in trees, entering the bodies of those who pass by and making them act violent and irrational.

Even remoter than Injalak are Sandy Creek and Wunyu Beach. **Sandy Creek,** on Arnhem's north shore, is popular for excellent barramundi, salmon, and tuna fishing. Ideally, anglers should have a boat, though people do fish from the shore. The drive to Sandy Creek (3hr.) is 4WD only. Also on the northern shore is **Wunyu**

Beach, a long, virtually untouched, and often windy beach that is ideal for relaxing and strolling. Sunbathers and would-be swimmers beware—both Wunyu Beach's and Sandy Creek's water is teeming with **salties.** The drive to Wunyu takes at least 2½hr. on a 4WD road. Neither Sandy Creek nor Wunyu Beach have facilities, but people do camp at their own risk. Campers must bring their own water, food, and shelter. Stopping on the road to Injalak, Sandy Creek, and Wunyu is prohibited.

◘ **TOURS.** For those seeking experienced guides and drivers, tours might be the best way to reach Arnhem Land. Multi-day tours with flights from Darwin run several thousands of dollars; 4WD daytrips from Kakadu are cheaper. Departing from Jabiru and Cooinda are **Outback NT Touring** (☎1800 089 113; $170, children $130) and **Lord's Kakadu and Arnhemland Safaris.** (☎8979 2422. $175, children $110.)

LITCHFIELD NATIONAL PARK

Although shadowed in size and popularity by Kakadu, Litchfield National Park, established in 1986, has natural wonders second to none. Its spring-fed falls and close proximity to Darwin make it a popular daytrip, as its widespread paved access renders the nearby sights more accessible (and therefore more crowded) than its big sibling. Litchfield is a great park for those with less outdoor experience. Staying for more than the day and visiting with a 4WD allows you to explore the more remote waterfalls, chiseled gorges, rock formations, and bush land plateaus that give Litchfield its unique charm.

LITCHFIELD AT A GLANCE	
AREA: 1460km².	**GATEWAYS:** Batchelor, Darwin (p. 239).
CLIMATE: Monsoonal, with distinct Wet (Nov.-Apr.) and Dry (May-Oct.) seasons.	**CAMPING:** Buley Rockhole, Florence Falls, Surprise Creek Falls, Tjaynera (Sandy Creek) Falls (4WD only), Wangi Falls, and Walker Creek.
FEATURES: The Tabletop Range, Reynolds River.	
HIGHLIGHTS: Waterfall after spectacular waterfall, the rigorous 4WD trek to the Lost City and beyond.	**FEES:** Entry free.

NORTHERN TERRITORY

◪ **TRANSPORTATION AND ORIENTATION.** Tours from Darwin to Litchfield abound; some also stop at Kakadu. The cheapest option is a **McCafferty's/Greyhound** bus daytrip that hits all of the sites accessible by sealed roads. (☎8941 5872. $75.) **Darwin Day Tours** runs a similar tour. (☎8924 1124. $104, children $75; lunch included.)

The park is 100km southwest of Darwin. The main entrance (paved access) is reached from the Stuart Hwy. through the township of **Batchelor,** which has food and camping. The Stuart Hwy. turn-off is 90km south of Darwin. From there it is 10km to Batchelor and another 18km to the park entrance. The **Litchfield Park Road** winds its way east through the park, connecting all the sights, including **Florence Falls** (42km from Batchelor) and **Wangi Falls** (68km from Batchelor). Beyond Wangi, the road continues north and provides an unsealed route back to Darwin (115km). Other sights are along a **4WD track** that starts just after Greenant Creek and stretches south along the Reynolds River, passing the Blyth Homestead ruins, Tjaynera Falls, and Surprise Creek. Don't be fooled by maps of the park: the 4WD track connecting the Lost City to the Reynolds River track past the Blyth Homestead ruins is long since closed and overgrown. Litchfield Park Rd. is usually open to all vehicles; the 4WD tracks close in the Wet.

ⓘ PRACTICAL INFORMATION. There is no ranger station, but information is available through the **Parks and Wildlife Commission of the Northern Territory** (☎ 8999 5511) in Darwin, and detailed maps are available for free at the Batchelor Store. Park entry is free. Call ☎ 8976 0282 for **road conditions,** especially during the Wet. The nearest **post office** is in Batchelor. (☎ 8976 0020. Open M-F 9am-5pm, Sa 9am-noon.) **Petrol** is available next door at the Batchelor Store.

ⓘ CAMPING AND ACCOMMODATIONS. Spending a night in Litchfield is highly recommended, if only for the superb stargazing. **Camping ❶** in the park generally costs $6.60 per person for basic unpowered sites with showers and toilets. (Children $3.30, families $15.40.) Payment is made upon entering the campsites at unmanned drop boxes. The **Wangi Falls ❶** campground fills up early in the day and can be uncomfortably crowded; more serene options lie near **Florence Falls ❶** and **Buley Rockhole ❶.** Visitors with a 4WD have extra choices at Florence Falls and **Tjaynera (Sandy Creek) Falls ❶.** Barebones facilities (namely, toilets) exist at the beautiful **Surprise Creek Falls ❶** and pristine **Walker Creek ❶** for a reduced fee. ($3.30 per person, children $1.65, families $7.70.) Be prepared for the inevitable attack of ravenous packs of mosquitos. Caravan camping is allowed only at Wangi Falls and Surprise Creek, and generators are not permitted anywhere in the park.

The better options for caravans (mostly for their lack of mozzies and flies) lie outside the park. **Litchfield Tourist & Van Park ❶** is 4km from the park border, on the way to Batchelor and fishing on the banks of the Finnis River. (☎ 8976 0070. Sites $7, powered for 2 $16.50, families $25; overnight vans for 4 $45; cabins for 2 $55.) Just a bit farther down the road is the family-run **Banyan Tree Caravan Park ❶.** (☎ 8976 0030. Sites $6, powered for 2 $17.) The well-manicured **Jungle Drum Bungalows ❷,** next door to the Butterfly Farm in Batchelor, have Balinese decor and a relaxing atmosphere. (☎ 8976 0555. Dorms $25; cabin singles $68, doubles $92.)

ⓘ FOOD. There is a food kiosk at **Wangi Falls.** (Open daily 9am-5pm.) In Batchelor, the **Butterfly Cafe Restaurant ❶** has hearty home-cooked meals; check out the **Bird and Butterfly Sanctuary** on the premises. (☎ 8976 0199. Cafe open daily 8:30am-4pm and 6-11pm. Sanctuary open daily 9am-4pm. $6, children $3.) Basic **groceries,** as well as LP fuel for stoves, are available at the **Batchelor Store.** (☎ 8976 0045. Open M-F 7am-7pm, Sa-Su 7:30am-7pm.)

ⓘ SIGHTS AND SHORT WALKS. Impressive waterfalls at Litchfield are among the main attractions.

WANGI (WONG-GYE). Crossing streams produce two dramatic falls that plunge into a large, clear pool. Relatively safe swimming and good snorkeling, a kiosk serving meat pies, and all of suburban Darwin dragging eskies behind them combine to make Wangi more of a public beach. Don't just follow the herd into the water, though; be sure to check for closure signs around the swimming area because both freshies and salties are known to get into plunge pool. Swim at your own risk. The walking trail (45min. return) to the top of the falls is nondescript.

FLORENCE FALLS. The carpark is near the lookout point above the falls; to reach the plunge pool at the bottom, take the staircase or the scenic 15min. walk that meanders along with the creek. A short walk (3.2km) through lush monsoon forest connects Florence Falls with **Buley Rockhole,** featuring a number of soothing swimming spots, but Buley can also be reached by car.

TOLMER FALLS. Only a short distance southwest from Florence Falls on the main road, there is another steep fall plunging from a sandstone gorge. Swimming is not allowed due to the gentle ecosystem that is home to ghost bats, but a commanding

DIDGERIDOO 101 So, you want to buy a "didge." According to traditional folklore of the Yolngu Aborigines of northern Australia, the didgeridoo has been around since the beginning of time, though rock paintings tell scientists that they have existed for the past 20,000-50,000 years. The didgeridoo itself is made from a eucalyptus tree naturally hollowed out by termites. Once cut, the bark is shaved from the outside and the mouthpiece is dipped in bee's wax. In the Aboriginal tradition, painted didges are only played in formal ceremonies honoring birth, marriage, or death, but their beauty and higher prices make them ubiquitous in tourist shops. Most stores allow wandering shoppers to have a go at their selection of didgeridoos, and many will package and send them home. Be forewarned, however, that just because something is labeled a didgeridoo and looks like a didgeridoo doesn't mean it is one. If you want an actual musical instrument and not an overpriced and brightly painted piece of wood, buy only from Aboriginal communities, legitimate Aboriginal art stores, or specialized didgeridoo dealers (see **Coco's Place**, p. 245). Also remember that the didgeridoo is an instrument of northern Aborigines, so the farther south you go, the more likely it is you're buying something manufactured for sale to uninformed tourists.

view awaits from the lookout deck. The **Tolmer Creek Walk** (1.2km) takes visitors from the carpark to the lookout platform along the creek and past a natural stone arch; the lookout can also be reached via a cement pathway, only a few hundred km long, from the carpark.

MAGNETIC TERMITE MOUNDS. Officially on Litchfield Park Rd. about 20km from Batchelor, these black mounds range from 50 to 100 years old and are aligned so that their broad backs face east-to-west, in order to soak in the softer sunlight of the morning and evening. Visitors may only view this small collection of mounds from a distance. Just 3km past the Tjaynera falls turn-off, the track passes through field upon field of literally thousands of these mounds, some as large as 7 ft. tall. It is a breathtaking and eerie place with these black slabs, perfectly aligned, stretching off into the hazy distance. (See **Termite Be Giants**, p. 663.)

THE LOST CITY. If you have a 4WD, you can take the 10½km down an access road 40km past the park entrance. Visitors can wander among the haunting natural arrangement of towers of sandstone blocks. Early morning is especially spellbinding, with the structures shrouded in hazy mist and the place all to yourself.

TJAYNERA FALLS (SANDY CREEK FALLS). About 7km off Litchfield Park Rd. on a 4WD-track, Tjaynera is a mild trail (1.7km) matching Wangi's beauty on a smaller scale without the crowds. Continue 20km farther on the track to **Surprise Creek Falls.** Actually a cluster of several falls, Surprise Creek gives those who drive from Litchfield Park Rd. (1hr.) a taste of everything Litchfield has to offer: a large sandy swimming hole, a series of plunge pools, and relaxing waterfall massages under the spray. The fearless can try the high jump from the second pool into the first. The falls, typically deserted, make one of the best sunset spots in the Top End.

STUART HIGHWAY: DARWIN TO KATHERINE

The Stuart Hwy. connects Darwin to Adelaide, SA, drawing a divide in the middle of the continent across red, dry desert terrain. The first stretch from Darwin to Katherine is 314km long and contains a number of pleasant stops along the way.

Only 25km south of Darwin is the turn-off for **Howard Springs Nature Park.** Once used as a WWII rest and recreation military camp but now popular among local civilians, the springs offer swimming (with barramundi and turtles) and a 30min. nature hike. (☎ 8983 1001. Open daily 8am-8pm. Free.) About 10km farther south on the Stuart Hwy. is the turn-off for **Cox Peninsula Rd.**, which leads 11km west to **Territory Wildlife Park.** A cross between a large zoo and *Jurassic Park*, the park encompasses 400 hectares of various habitats and is a top-notch Top End experience. Visitors can enjoy direct contact with all sorts of marsupials, an enclosed tunnel aquarium, the Birds of Prey presentation, a reptile pavilion, a house for nocturnal critters, and plenty of emus. (☎ 8988 7200. Open daily 8:30am-6pm, last admission 4pm. $20, concessions $10, families $42.) **Darwin Day Tours** runs a half-day tour to the park. (☎ 8924 1124. Run daily 7:30am-1:30pm. $47, concessions $43, children $42; includes entrance fee.) After animal gazing, relax the muscles 1km down the road at **Berry Springs Nature Park,** which has picnic spots and lukewarm soaking grounds. (Open daily 8am-6:30pm. Free.)

Eighty kilometers south of Darwin and 7km down an access road lies **Lake Bennett Resort ❶,** an upscale lodge next to a stunning lake. The accommodations are expensive, but all activities are open to day visitors. Swim, canoe ($15 per hr., $40 per day), fish, or play golf before watching the sunset. Guest rooms include fridge, A/C, and TV, with shared bath and kitchen facilities. The staff will meet bus travelers at the Stuart Hwy. (☎ 8976 0960. Sites $10 per person; caravan sites $20, powered $25; dorms $25; twins $170; triples $195. NOMADS.) The turn-off for **Batchelor** and **Litchfield National Park** (see p. 261) is 6km south of the resort.

Between the fuel stops at Adelaide River and Hayes Creek, and 200km from Darwin, **Tjuwaliyn (Douglas) Hot Springs** is a worthwhile stop. The last 7km of the access road to the springs is gravel but tame enough for all cars in the Dry. Be forewarned that, at certain spots, the springs live up to their "hot" name; cooler currents are downstream. **Camping ❶** is available ($3.50, children $1, families $8). **Pine Creek** is the final stop on the route, only 9km from Katherine.

PINE CREEK   ☎ 08

The tiny town of Pine Creek (pop. 650), at the junction of the Stuart and Kakadu Hwy., provides a convenient base for nearby Kakadu. On the main street (named Main Tce.), the **Diggers Rest Motel ❺** has well-kept ensuite cabins with kitchen, TV, and A/C, and doubles as a **tourist center.** (☎ 8976 1442. Reception daily 8am-8pm. Singles $69; doubles $79; rooms for 3-5 people $85-89. MC/V.) Next door is **Ah Toys,** the general store that doubles as a **bus depot.** (☎ 8976 1202. Open M-F 9am-6pm, Sa 9am-12:30pm.) **Greyhound/McCafferty's** runs to Darwin (3hr., 3 per day, $41) and Katherine (1hr., 3 per day, $18). Around the corner on Moule St., the **post office** doubles as a **bank.** (☎ 8976 1220. Open M-F 9am-noon and 1-5pm.) The adjacent **Mayse's Cafe ❶** serves good meals for $6-9. (☎ 8976 1241. Open daily 7am-8pm.) A sluggish **Internet** connection is at the **public library** ($5.50 per hr.). The casual and congenial **Kakadu Gateway Caravan Park ❶** has a range of accommodationse, as well as BBQ, kitchen, TV room, and free laundry. (☎ 8976 1166. Sites can be booked at Ah Toys, or at the reception off Buchanan St. after 3:30pm. Sites $10; ensuite powered sites $22; singles $40; budget doubles $42; doubles $57; twins $67; family rooms $72; swag room with no beds $8 per person.)

KATHERINE   ☎ 08

The only stoplight along the 1500km of the Stuart Hwy. between Darwin and Alice Springs is found in the rough-and-tumble town of Katherine (pop. 11,000). With a history of destructive floods (the most recent in 1998) and subsequent rejuvenation, Katherine remains edgy. Noisy, often drunken, conflict along the main street is not unusual (especially at night). Tourism is the primary industry here, staffed by both the Aboriginal Jawoyn (JOW-win) and Dagoman inhabitants and the white population. While it can be a refreshing blast of civilization after the wilderness of the Kimberley or the outback down south, Katherine is more of a stopover for those on their way to Nitmiluk, Kakadu, Darwin, or Alice Springs.

⚡ 🖪 ORIENTATION AND TRANSPORTATION

Katherine marks the intersection of three main roads. The **Stuart Hwy.** becomes **Katherine Tce.** in town; most shops and services are here. The **Victoria Hwy.** leaves from the northern side of town, past the hot springs and heading eventually to the Kimberley. Finally, **Giles St.** heads east from the middle of town, reaching **Nitmiluk National Park** (29km). The Transit Centre is on the southern end of Katherine Tce., near **Lindsay St.**

Greyhound/McCafferty's buses (☎1800 089 103) stop at the **Transit Centre** on Katherine Tce. and run to: Darwin (4hr., 4 per day, $52); Alice Springs (15hr., 2 per day, $179); Broome (19hr., 1 per day, $226); and Townsville (29½hr., 1 per day, $290). Local car rental agencies are **Territory Rent-a-Car,** 6 Katherine Tce. (☎8971 3183), in the Transit Centre; **Hertz,** 392 Katherine Tce (☎8971 1111), which has some 4WDs; and **Delta** (☎13 13 90), at Knotts Crossing Resort.

🔢 PRACTICAL INFORMATION

Tourist Office: Katherine Region Tourist Association (☎8972 2650), on the corner of Lindsay St. and Katherine Tce., across from the Transit Centre. Open Apr.-Oct. M-F 8:30am-6pm, Sa-Su 10am-3pm; Nov.-Mar. M-F 9am-5pm, Sa-Su 10am-3pm.

Bank: Several **banks** and 24hr. **ATMs** are on Katherine Tce. (All banks open M-Th 9:30am-4pm and F 9:30am-5pm.)

Work Opportunities: Working at hostels in exchange for accommodations is popular in Katherine, but call ahead. **Employment National,** 17 First St. (☎1300 720 126), produces a *Harvest Workers Guide* and can connect with local mango farms during picking season (Sept.-Nov.). Most work is piece-rate.

Police: (☎8972 0111; emergency ☎000), 2½km south of town on the Stuart Hwy.

Internet: Didj Shop Internet Cafe (☎8972 2485), on Giles St. a block west of Katherine Tce. $8 per hr. Also has Aboriginal art. Open Apr.-Oct. M-F 10am-10pm, Sa 11am-7pm, Su 10am-3pm; Nov.-Mar. M-F 10am-7pm, Sa 11am-7pm, Su 10am-3pm.

Post Office: on the corner of Katherine Tce. and Giles St. Open M-F 9am-5pm. **Postal Code:** 0850.

🏠 ACCOMMODATIONS

🛏**Kookaburra Backpackers** (☎8971 0257; kookaburra@nt-tech.com.au), on the corner of Lindsay and 3rd St. Ideal layout, sparkling clean bathrooms shared between 4-8 guests, refrigerator, outdoor picnic table, Internet, and fully-stocked kitchenette. Caring owners offer free transport to and from Transit Centre (3 blocks), pool, and organized BBQs. Laundry $3. Key deposit $10. Runs 3-day camping tour through Kakadu from Katherine to Darwin ($370, includes meals and camping equipment). Reception daily 7:30am-2:30pm and 4:30-7:30pm. Book ahead in the Dry. Dorms $16; twins with TV and fridge $44; light but tasty brekkie included. ISIC/NOMADS/VIP/YHA. MC/V. ❷

Palm Court Backpackers (☎8972 2722 or 1800 626 722), on the corner of 3rd and Giles St. Comfortable, mellow rooms with A/C and toilet. Kitchen, pool, BBQ, and Internet ($2 per 20min.). Free pickup and drop-off. Some workers' accommodations. Laundry $3. Key deposit $10. Bikes $10 per day. Reception daily 6:30am-2pm and 4-6pm. Dorms $16; twins and doubles $46. NOMADS/VIP/YHA. AmEx/MC/V. ❷

Paraway Motel (☎8972 2644; paraway@nt-tech.com.au), on the corner of O'Shea Tce. and 1st St. The nicest of Katherine's many motels, with spotless and wheelchair accessible rooms, pool, spa, laundry, and the town's only security carpark. Reception daily 7am-10pm. Singles from $84; doubles from $94. AmEx/MC/V. ❺

Camping is available along the Victoria Hwy. The **Red Gum Caravan Park** ❶ (☎8972 2239) is 1km from town (a 10min. walk), and has laundry, pool, and BBQ. (Sites $9, for 2 $18, powered for 2 $23; cabins $65, for more than 2 $80.) The **Riverview Caravan Park and Motel** ❷ (☎8972 1011), at the hot springs, has a pool, spa, laundry, and BBQ. (Sites for 2 $16, powered $21; singles $20; doubles and twins $30; budget cabins for 2 $50.)

⬛ FOOD

A giant Woolworth's **supermarket** is across from the Transit Centre, on Katherine Tce. (☎8972 3055. Open daily 7am-10pm.) For those about to head bush, visit **Town and Country Butchery**, on Katherine Tce. across from the junction with the Victoria Hwy. They have the best selection of meats in town, from croc to kangaroo, and they'll Cryovac it for you on the spot so it will last weeks with only refrigeration–no need to freeze. (☎8971 0353. Open daily 7am-6pm.)

Bucking Bull Burger Bar (☎8972 1734), Shop 1 on Katherine Tce. You know a place is good when all the locals have a tab there. Mouthwatering burgers from beef to barra. Great mango smoothies $3.50. Breakfast specials start at $6. Open daily 5am-5pm. ❶

Tommo's Bakery, 14 2nd St. (☎8971 1155), on the corner of Giles St. This large, humble bakery is the place to grab a sandwich (from $3), pastry ($2), or iced coffee ($2). Open M-F 5am-5pm, Sa 5am-1pm. ❶

Paraway Buchanan's Restaurant (☎8972 2644), at the Paraway Motel. While the fancy main dishes like lamb curried prawn can be a bit pricey ($18-22), Buchanan's actually holds the town's best hidden deal. Their themed Thursday night all-you-can eat buffets, ranging from seafood to Chinese, are culinary feasts. Each has a different price, but they start at just $12.50 for pizza and pasta night. Open daily 6:30-9:30pm. ❸

⬛ SIGHTS AND ACTIVITIES

Two kilometers along the Victoria Hwy. from Katherine Tce., **hot springs** bubble along the Katherine River. Popular with tourists of all ages, the springs have swimming, toilets, and wheelchair access along Croker St. Anyone looking to learn more about didgeridoos, their history, their construction, or how to play one, should head to **Coco's Place,** 21 1st St. (☎8971 2889), across from the cinema. Expect to pay more for Coco's expert lessons and precision made didgeridoos. Make your own didgeridoo (and keep it) with **Whoop Whoop** overnight trips. (☎8972 2941. Depart F-Sa. $220.) From May to October, evening **river cruises** provide wildlife spotting and lively dinner around a campfire. **Far Out Adventures** cruises the Katherine River and has BBQ-style meals with BYO. (☎8972 2552. $45, includes pickup.) **Travel North** runs a **crocodile night** along the Johnstone River that includes wine and stew. (☎1800 089 103. Nightly 6:30pm. $42; with pickup $52.)

NITMILUK NATIONAL PARK (KATHERINE GORGE)

Nitmiluk National Park provides water and land activities in a setting as dramatic and striking as its cousins, Kakadu and Litchfield, though on a smaller scale. Composed of a sandstone plateau sliced by rivers and tributaries, Nitmiluk is popular with tourists who have come to admire the rocky cliffs rising from the river, the thick vegetation of the monsoon forest, and the 168 species of birds.

Since 1989, the park has been owned by the local Jawoyn Aborigines, who leased its management for 99 years to the Northern Territory government. Aboriginal livelihood remains a significant presence in the park, and the 450 known galleries of rock art dispersed throughout the region are physical reminders. The name "Nitmiluk" is part of a Jawoyn Dreaming story in which *Nabilil* the dragon names the gorge after hearing the song of the cicada. The death of Nabilil sent water gushing forth to create the Katherine River. Most of the Aboriginal sights in Nitmiluk are not accessible to the public. Those that are, such as the rock art galleries on the Jawoyn loop and the sacred amphitheater on the Jatbula trail, give a flavor of what the vast wilderness around Katherine Gorge is hiding.

NITMILUK AT A GLANCE

AREA: 292,008 hectares.	**GATEWAYS:** Katherine (p. 264).
FEATURES: Katherine River and 13 gorges, Edith Falls, 17 Mile Creek.	**CAMPING:** Permanent campgrounds near the Visitor Centre and at Edith Falls, and registered overnight bush camping.
HIGHLIGHTS: Canoeing down the river, hiking up cliffs and through shady gorges.	**FEES:** Entry free.

ORIENTATION AND PRACTICAL INFORMATION

The 13 gorges on the Katherine River form the centerpiece of Nitmiluk. The primary base to the gorges is the **Nitmiluk Visitor Centre,** at the end of the sealed Gorge Rd. 30km east of Katherine; the Southern Walks and water activities are found here. The second entrance to the park is 40km north of Katherine on the Stuart Hwy., where a 20km access road leads to Edith Falls, a campground, and a few short hikes. The long Jatbula Trail extends from the Tourist Centre to Edith Falls.

> **WHEN TO GO. Climate** is most comfortable for visitors from May-Sept., after the seasonal storms and before the humidity. In the Wet months, sections of the Katherine River flood and make some activities unavailable. However, locals praise the stunning greenery of the Wet before the foliage turns a dreary brown.

Buses: Travel North (☎ 1800 089 103) runs buses from all accommodations in Katherine to the Visitor Centre. 25min., 4 per day, $18 return. Book ahead.

Tourist Info: Nitmiluk Visitor Centre (☎ 8972 1886) provides hiking information and camping permits. A tourist desk in the gift shop takes care of canoe rental, helicopter tours and boat cruises, and reception for the campground. There is also an exhibit on the Jawoyn Aborigines and natural history of the park, as well as a **bistro ❶** (☎ 8972 3150) that serves burgers ($6-7) and Thai chicken salad ($10). Center and shop open daily 7am-7pm. Bistro open daily 8am-8:30pm; Happy Hour 5-6:30pm. Contact the **Parks and Wildlife Commission** in Katherine for more info on Katherine Gorge. (☎ 8972 1886; fax 8971 0702. P.O. Box 344, Katherine NT 0851.)

Tours: Nitmiluk Tours offers **helicopter flights**. 3 gorges $55, 8 gorges $82.50, 13 gorges $137.50. Book at the Visitor Centre. (☎ 8972 1253.)

CAMPING

A shady, but often crowded **caravan park ❶** is available near the Visitors Center, with toilets, showers, laundry, phones, and BBQ facilities. The highlight of a night

NORTHERN TERRITORY

here is the invasion of agile wallabies in search of food at dusk—be sure to clean up after yourself. Register at the Visitors Center. (Sites $8 per person, powered $12.) A second **campground ❶** next to Edith Falls allows tents and caravans, and has showers, BBQ, a food kiosk, and a picnic area, but no powered sites. Plenty of pools and waterfalls cool the grounds. The lower pool, a short walk from the carpark, is a crystal-clear plunge pool with a waterfall. (Sites $5 per person.)

Overnight camping ❶ in the depths of the park is permitted; register at the Visitors Center. ($3.30 per person per night; $50 deposit, $20 if only going as far as Crystal Falls from the Center.) Campsites with toilets and (usually) a water source are along the Jatbula Trail and at the 4th, 5th, and 8th gorges in the Southern Walks area. Fires are permitted along the Jatbula but not in Southern Walks.

◐ NITMILUK BY WATER

From May to September, quiet waters allow for canoeing, boating, and walking. **Nitmiluk Tours** (☎ 8972 1253) does all rentals for water activities, which can be booked at most accommodations in Katherine or at the Visitors Center.

CANOEING. Surging up the Katherine River in single and double person Canadian-style canoes, a cross between a canoe and kayak, is the most popular activity in the park. Paddling on the cooler water is more comfortable than hiking in the year-round sizzling temperature. It's a good idea to find a partner, since paddling is only half the battle of the gorge tour—dragging the canoe across rocky portages is the other. No more than 75 canoes are permitted in the gorge; book ahead. (*Single canoes half-day $30, full-day $41, overnight $82; doubles $44/$61/$122. Half and full-day canoes require $20 cash deposit. Overnight canoes require $3.50 permit and $60 cash deposit.*)

SWIMMING. Taking a dip is another popular activity, but keep in mind that you may be sharing the bath with freshies and power boats, so be careful. Many people like to swim near the boathouse and at the plunge pools at the end of some hikes.

CRUISES. Zoom along the gorges in flat, shaded motor vessels; at the end of each gorge, passengers transfer to a new boat on the next gorge. Be warned: the crowded arrangement makes it hard to enjoy the natural solitude of the area, and the hustling tours destroy any chance of moving at one's own pace. (*Departs from the boat jetty; 2hr.; 4 per day in the Dry; $34, children $13.50.*) Daily "adventure" and "safari" tours combine boating and hiking. (*Departs 9am. 4hr. $49; 8hr. $85.*)

◐ NITMILUK BY LAND

Walking tracks in the park fall into all difficulty levels and range from 2.5km to 66km. The abundant flora, fauna, and rocky outcroppings provide a different view from canoeing, but it is often 10°C hotter on the trail than it is near the water, and the sun can be brutal. The Southern Walks are usually open during the Wet; the Jatbula Trail is not. **For all overnight walks, register with the rangers before setting out.** Semi-detailed topographic maps are $7.50 at the Visitor Centre. Smaller trail maps are available for free.

SOUTHERN WALKS. The main trail of the Southern Walks starts at the Visitor Centre and parallels the gorge at a 1.5km separation. Each individual side trail branches off and heads directly for the gorge. Much of the main trail hiking is through unremarkable but peaceful surroundings; it is the scenery on the short side trails (described below) that provides the vistas of the gorges.

Lookout Loop. (3.7km return, 2hr., moderate.) This steep but well-maintained climb up the side of the gorge offers excellent views of the river and **Seventeen Mile Valley.** After the climb it widens to an easy and smooth walk. Signs along the way detail the park's mythological and geological history. A wonderful warm-up for longer walks.

Windolf Walk. (8.4km, 3½hr., moderate.) The first of the gorge turn-offs and one of the Park's best trails. Following a dry river bed, it comes abruptly to a split, one part leading to a large plunge pool, the other to **Pat's Lookout**. To get to the **Aboriginal rock art** marked on the trail map, go to the right of Pat's, down a narrow, rocky and very steep trail to the water's edge in the gorge. The truly brave can stash their stuff among the rocks and swim to the sandy landing on the far side; follow the canyon wall to the right until you reach the art. The sure footed can follow the bank up the river to the end of the first gorge; if the water is low enough, use extreme caution and cross the natural rock bridge. With slippery rocks and raging water underneath, this can be a harrowing experience. Once across, follow the footpaths to the galleries. (See **Aboriginal Art,** p. 257.)

Butterfly Gorge Walk. (12km, 4½hr., difficult.) A good overview of the region, with woodlands and rock formations giving way to a dense, tranquil monsoon forest in a side gorge. The last few hundred meters take you into a seemingly fantastical world, with dense clouds of butterflies swarming through the trees. After a short, fairly strenuous traverse down the cliff face, the walk ends at a deep swimming spot.

Lily Ponds Trail. (20km, 6½hr., difficult.) Similar to its shorter cousins, Lily Ponds is not the most rewarding of trails. It covers even longer distances and more treacherous terrain, including some very uneven and rocky stretches. The trail ends at a sheltered pool in the third gorge, most often vacant because few day hikers make it this far.

Eighth Gorge and Jawoyn Valley. (30-40km, overnight, very difficult.) The longest of the Southern Walks, Eighth and Jawoyn take too long for a day hike but offer very reasonable distances for an overnight hike, with a return by the middle of the second day. They cover the hardest terrain of the park, however, and should not be attempted without supplies to last between 2 and 3 days. The Jawoyn Valley loop holds a special reward—a series of rock art galleries—for those who brave the distances, though they are not as well preserved or ornate as the galleries near the end of Windolf Walk.

At the opposite end of the Jatbula Trail (below), two short walks leave from the Edith Falls carpark. The **Sweetwater Pool** walk (9km, 4hr., moderate) leads to a waterhole and good camping. The **Leliyn Trail** (5.2km, 3hr., easy) leads to the smaller but equally amazing upper pools.

JATBULA TRAIL. The popular Jatbula Trail is a 66km, five-day, one-way-only sojourn between Nitmiluk Centre and Edith Falls. There are eight 1-4 day segments between the center and Edith Falls, through rainforest pockets, an Aboriginal amphitheater, and waterfalls. The only day walk portion of the Jatbula Trail is the Northern Rockhole walk (16km, 4hr., moderate), which leaves the Tourist Centre, winds through a valley, and ends at a rock face and waterhole.

◉ ABORIGINAL ART

Among the best preserved Aboriginal features are the rock art galleries in the first gorge. Some portions are at least 10,000 years old. Each gallery has layered images, each generation's painting adding to the scene painted by their forbearers. Visitors are welcome to visit and photograph the art, but touching it is strictly forbidden. The lack of a written history among the Jawoyn means interpretation of the work relies on an understanding of the Dreamtime. The descriptions below might help clarify the images for those unfamiliar with Jawoyn symbolism.

West Gallery: Faded to a light red shadow, the original work here can now only been seen as splotches of color. Little is known about the meaning or history of this gallery.

NORTHERN TERRITORY

Central Gallery: Depicting a hunt or ritual, this gallery contains three inverted men on the left, followed by a *Bornorrong*, or brolga bird, being speared by two figures. The meaning of the upside down men is unclear, although some have suggested that their position conveys sleeping, ceremony preparation, initiation, or death. In any case, modern Jawoyn people consider them figures who should not be discussed, so visitors should refrain from commenting on them. The figures are known to be human because they have the correct number of fingers and toes. (Viewers are left to their own devices to discern why they are thought to be male.) Just right of the hunters are six circles; some believe these are *Gortberr*, or bush potatoes, while others argue they are crocodile eggs, depicted as a means of instructing youths on the hunt.

East Gallery: The East Gallery is believed to be the oldest and contains the most layered images. The central male figure, large and powerful, has seven digits on his hands and feet and thus is not human. On the left is a human figure in a headdress; on the right is a *Djugerre*, a female black wallaroo with a joey clearly visible in her pouch. They hold a stick in front of the central figure, off of which dangle black flying foxes. At the figure's feet lie the hazy remains of a large mammal, perhaps a species now extinct. In the background a crowd of humans approach or stand in awe.

DOWN THE TRACK

Heading south down the Stuart Hwy. from Darwin, the lush vegetation and cinnamon earth of the Top End give way to grasses, shrubs, and a deep, barren red that stretches for miles, broken only by occasional rock formations.

VICTORIA HIGHWAY: KATHERINE TO KUNUNURRA

From downtown Katherine, the "Vic" careens westward 512km to Kununurra, WA (see p. 724). There isn't much in between, save two service areas and some stunning scenery. Two hundred kilometers west of Katherine, the **Victoria River Roadhouse ❶** has petrol, a restaurant, and quiet campsites with breathtaking views of the nearby escarpment. (☎ 8975 0744. Sites for 2 $7.50, powered $20, extra person $10; doubles $70; motel rooms from $95.) A few Victoria River **cruises** leave from the Roadhouse (Daily 9am and 4pm. Boat cruise 1½hr., $35. Fishing cruise 2½hr., $50.) The highway passes through **Gregory National Park** (Timber Creek Ranger Station ☎ 8975 0888). The Territory's second-largest national park (after Kakadu) features 2WD-accessible bushwalks and lookouts over Victoria River Gorge, as well as rugged 4WD tracks through the isolated surroundings. **Timber Creek,** a rowdy roadside town, is another 90km west of Victoria River. The **Wayside Inn ❷** has a small restaurant and accommodations. (☎ 8975 0722. Sites $5.80 per person, powered $7; budget singles $48.40; ensuite $87.80; singles $57.50.) River cruises can be booked next door at **Max's Victoria River Boat Tours** (☎ 8975 0850. $55 per 3½hr.). At the 468km mark, **Keep River National Park** is home to Aboriginal rock art sites and a few bushwalks. Camping is permitted at two sites (15 and 28km down a gravel road). Finally, about 480km west of Katherine (but less than 40km from Kununurra) is the border crossing into WA. There are strict quarantines against fruits, veggies, honey, and plant material. Also be aware that Western Australia clocks are 1½hr. behind the Territory's.

STUART HIGHWAY: KATHERINE TO TENNANT CREEK

There are 672 long kilometers between Katherine and Tennant Creek. Those driving the trek should take the proper precautions (see **Transportation,** p. 236).

Twenty-seven kilometers south of Katherine is the 200km turn-off to an unsung gem, **Cutta Cutta Caves Nature Park** (☎ 8972 1940). Meaning "starry starry," the name refers to the delicate calcite crystals that grow within the dark, temperate passages. The cave extends 720m through an underground labyrinth of limestone columns and jagged ceilings, although visitors can only venture through the first 250m (the depths get too cold and reach 99% humidity). **Tours,** the only way to see the cave, are led by fun, knowledgeable guides, and proceed through five chambers. (1hr. Depart daily 9, 10, 11am, 1, 2, and 3pm, except during floods in the Wet. $10.) "Cultural Adventures" are offered at the Aboriginal-owned and -operated tours of **Manyallaluk,** 100km southeast of Katherine (50km on the Stuart Hwy., and a 50km access road. ☎ 8975 4727 or 1800 644 727. Operates Mar.-Dec. On-site 1-day tours $99, children $61. From Katherine 1-day tours $132/$72, 2-day $450/$200.) Another 106km south on the Stuart Hwy. is the township of **Mataranka,** renowned for **Elsey National Park** and the thermal pool near Mataranka Homestead.

TENNANT CREEK   ☎ 08

The dusty outback town of Tennant Creek (pop. 35,000) is the self-proclaimed "Golden Heart" of the NT. Located 988km south of Darwin on the Stuart Hwy., the town is a rugged blip amid an expanse of bush. Australia's last great gold rush in the 1930s, which drew fortune-seekers to the region, put Tennant Creek on the map. Even with a $4 billion output of gold since the 1960s, no one seems to stay for long, but the **Devil's Marbles** (see p. 272), mining history, and the regional artistic flavor of the Warumungu Aborigines all make the pause more engaging.

◼ TRANSPORTATION

Buses: The **Transit Centre** (☎ 8962 1070) is on Paterson St., near the intersection with Stuart St., at the north end of town. Open M-F 7am-6pm and 9:30-11pm, Sa 8am-1pm, later when buses arrive late. **McCafferty's/Greyhound buses** run to: Alice Springs (5-6hr., 2 per day, $101); Darwin (13hr., 2 per day, $130); Katherine (8-9hr., 2 per day, $83); Mt. Isa (7½hr., 1 per day, $97); Townsville (20hr., 1 per day, $193).

Bicycle Rental: Bridgestone Tyre, 52b Paterson St. (☎ 8962 2361), on the corner of Davidson St. Half-day $5, full-day $10. Open M-F 8am-5pm.

◼ ◼ ORIENTATION AND PRACTICAL INFORMATION

The Stuart Hwy., called **Paterson St.** in town, runs from north to south. Intersecting Paterson are, from the north, **Stuart St.** (not to be confused with the Stuart Hwy.) and **Davidson St.,** then **Peko Rd.** from the east, which becomes **Windley St.** west of Paterson. **Memorial Dr.** comes in from the west.

Tourist Office: Tennant Creek Regional Tourist Association (☎ 8962 3388), 1½km up Peko Rd. Provides info and tours. Open May-Aug. daily 9am-5pm; Sept.-Apr. M-F 9am-5pm, Sa 9am-noon.

Currency Exchange: ANZ Bank (☎ 13 13 14), on Paterson St. between Davidson and Stuart St. **Westpac Bank** (☎ 8962 2801), at the corner of Paterson St. and Peko Rd. Both open M-Th 9:30am-4pm, F 9:30am-5pm, with 24hr. **ATMs.**

Police: (☎ 8962 4444), on Paterson St. near Windley St.

Internet Access: At the **public library** (☎ 8962 2401) on Peko Rd. $2.20 per 30min. Open M-F 10am-6pm, Sa 10am-noon. Also at **Switch** (☎ 8962 3124), on Paterson St. just north of the Transit Centre. $2 per 20min. Open M-F 8:30am-5pm, Sa 9am-1pm.

Post Office: (☎ 8962 2196), at the corner of Paterson St. and Memorial Dr. Open M-F 9am-5pm. **Postal Code:** 0861.

ACCOMMODATIONS

■ **Outback Caravan Park** (☎8962 2459), 300m from Paterson on Peko Rd. Shady sites, manicured grass, and fantastic swimming pool. Kitchen, BBQ, laundry, and friendly staff. Sites $8, powered for 2 $20; deluxe ensuite cabins $55-$68. ❷

Tourist's Rest Hostel (☎8962 2719), on Leichardt St. Walk south on Paterson and turn right on Windley St. Friendly and spacious, with an aviary and funny lawn decor. Kitchen, pool, TV, and laundry. Daytrips to Devil's Marbles $55, including 1-night's stay $67. Reception 24hr. Dorms $17, ISIC $16, VIP/YHA $15; twins and doubles $39/$37/$35. NOMADS/VIP/YHA. ❷

Safari Backpackers YHA, 12 Davidson St. (☎8962 2207), west of Paterson St. Small, clean, and comfortable. Shared bath, kitchen, laundry, and lounge. Reception daily 7am-9pm across the street. Dorms $16; twins and doubles $38. YHA discount $2. ❷

FOOD

Paterson St. is lined with takeaway snack bars and restaurants. **Rocky's ❷,** next door to the Transit Centre, provides tasty takeaway-only pizza in a no-frills setting. (☎8962 2049. Open daily 4-11pm. Large pizzas $10-18.) **Top of Town Cafe ❶,** just north of the Transit Centre, has veggie burgers and a sandwich bar, all around $5.50. (☎8962 1311. Open M-F 8am-6pm, Sa-Su 8am-2pm.) **Margo Miles Steakhouse ❸,** across the street from the Transit Centre, has fancy Italian dishes and, of course, plenty of steak for around $18. (☎8962 1311. Open daily 6-9pm, also M-F noon-2pm.) **Mr. Perry's Ice Cream ❶,** on Patterson St. south of Memorial Dr., actually has good Chinese takeaway. (☎8962 2995. Open M-Sa 8am-5:30pm, Su 10am-3pm.) Adjacent is the **Tennant Food Barn,** which offers cheap **groceries.** (☎8962 2296. Open M-W and F-Sa 8:30am-6pm, Th 8:30am-6:30pm, Su 9am-6pm.)

STUART HIGHWAY: TENNANT CREEK TO ALICE SPRINGS

Geologists say it was water erosion. Aborigines credit the Rainbow Serpent. Whatever the cause, the rock formations known as the ■**Devil's Marbles** are beautiful and baffling. Just off the Stuart Hwy., 80km from Tennant Creek, the giant 7m-thick granite boulders balance precariously on one another. Two tours run from Tennant Creek and include a BBQ back in town. **Devil's Marbles Tours,** led by witty and well-informed guides, emphasizes geological and cultural appreciation. (☎0418 891 711. Departs daily 10:30am; $55. Sunrise tours depart M and F 5am; $65.) **Garyo's** is more action-packed, staging numerous photo-ops. (☎8962 2024. Daily tour 11am-5pm. $55.) **Camping ❶** at the Marbles is basic. (Pit toilets, BBQ, no water. $3.30, children $1.65.) The closest town to Devil's Marbles is **Wauchope,** 9km south, which has petrol, food, and **accommodations ❶.** (☎8964 1963. Sites $5, powered $15; motel singles $30; ensuite doubles $70.) Small towns farther along the highway have roadhouses that provide basic services including petrol, food, and accommodations: **Wycliffe Well** (☎8964 1966), rumored to receive frequent UFO visits and have the largest beer selection in all of Australia; **Barrow Creek** (☎8956 9753); **Ti Tree** (☎8956 9741); and **Aileron** (☎8956 9703).

THE RED CENTRE

The dry, desolate Outback at the center of Australia takes its name from the color of the oxidized dust that stretches to the edge of the horizon. To many travelers and Australians, the Red Centre represents the essence of the continent, where flat land perpetually bakes under a scalding sun. Out of this stark landscape, at the geographic center of the continent, rises Uluru (Ayers Rock), a celebrated symbol of the land down under and the largest rock in the world.

Alice Springs is the Outback's unofficial capital and the gateway to the desert beyond. The region's natural wonders include the MacDonnell Ranges, Watarrka (Kings Canyon), Uluru, and Kata Tjuta, all of which do their best to disrupt the rusted monotony of central Australia. These monuments have magnetic appeal, and tourists are attracted like little iron filings, prepared to brave endless distances and remote disasters to experience the "real" Outback.

ALICE SPRINGS   ☎ 08

The only city of any size for a long, long way in any direction and inhabited by only 27,000 itself, Alice Springs is a desert outpost next to the dry Todd River. The sandstone hills of the MacDonnell Ranges loom large over every street corner, constant reminders that this is indeed the Outback. Wilderness dominates here, and the town's lights can't hold a candle to the sparkling night sky of desert country.

Many travelers use Alice to explore the Red Centre, but the city works hard to be independently attractive. It's a relatively young town, only growing rapidly after 1929 when the *Old Ghan* Railway to Adelaide was completed. Today, the reality of the strict divide between Aborigines and the white population is alarmingly strident; nowhere else in Australia is the racial tension so palpable. As white life beats

NORTHERN TERRITORY

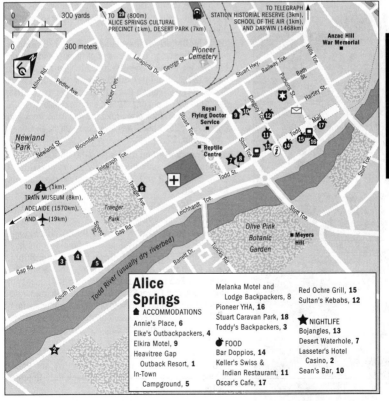

Alice Springs

♠ ACCOMMODATIONS
Annie's Place, **6**
Elke's Outbackpackers, **4**
Elkira Motel, **9**
Heavitree Gap
  Outback Resort, **1**
In-Town
  Campground, **5**
Melanka Motel and
  Lodge Backpackers, **8**
Pioneer YHA, **16**
Stuart Caravan Park, **18**
Toddy's Backpackers, **3**

🍴 FOOD
Bar Doppios, **14**
Keller's Swiss &
  Indian Restaurant, **11**
Oscar's Cafe, **17**
Red Ochre Grill, **15**
Sultan's Kebabs, **12**

★ NIGHTLIFE
Bojangles, **13**
Desert Waterhole, **7**
Lasseter's Hotel
  Casino, **2**
Sean's Bar, **10**

IN RECENT NEWS

TERRITORY BY TRAIN

There are a few questions weighing on every Territorian's mind. What is the economic future of the NT? What can be done about the dangerous fleets of road trains barreling down the highways? Where will people find employment in the wake of decreased mining and seasonal tourism? All of these questions are being addressed through one project: The **AustralAsia Railway.** This 1400km-long railway will at last connect Darwin and the NT's other major towns to Alice Springs, in turn connecting them to the rest of the south and the east coast through existing rail lines. This line is a massive economic investment, with 2km of track laid daily.

In the short run, the railway means big bucks. The construction, to be completed in 2006, has brought nearly 1000 jobs and $400 million in industry contracts. In the long run, the rail will completely transform the nature of Australian trade. Without the railway, the farms and industry of Australia's East Coast choose between exporting slowly at low cost—via southern ports for a long trip around the continent to Asia or the Americas—and quickly at high cost by rail to Alice Springs, then by inefficient road trains up to Darwin. The rail, providing a more efficient route, will render road trains obsolete and turn Darwin into a powerful trade center.

Rail fever is spreading. Lines connecting Katherine to Broome and even to Perth are under consideration, and NT residents are hopeful that passenger service will be introduced to support the region's growing tourism industry.

on about the concrete streets of Alice, Aborigines gather in small circles from dawn until dusk along the Todd River or Todd Street Mall. The scene in Alice is a reminder of Australia's harsh past and current struggle.

▛ TRANSPORTATION

Airplanes: Alice Springs Airport (☎ 8951 1211), 20km south of the city on the Stuart Hwy. Provides domestic service, tourist info, currency exchange, and car rental agencies. **Qantas** (☎ 13 13 13) flies to: Adelaide (2hr., 2 per day, $400); Brisbane (4½hr., 2 per day, $700); Cairns (3½hr., 1 per day, $530); Darwin (2hr., 3 per day, $400); Melbourne (3hr., 2-4 per day, $550); Perth (3½hr., 2 per day, $510); Sydney (3½hr., 2 per day, $550); and Yulara (45min., 3 per day, $250).

Trains: Alice Railway Station is a 20min. walk from central Alice. From George St., take a left on Larapinta Dr., which turns into the Stuart Hwy. and runs into Alice. The *Ghan* runs to: Adelaide (20hr., Tu and F, $225); Melbourne (33hr., Tu, $320); and Sydney (46hr., F, $343). The tourist office and Traveland make reservations, or call ☎ 13 21 47.

Buses: McCafferty's/Greyhound (☎ 8952 7888) **buses** run from the station at the corner of Gregory and Railway Tce. Service to: Adelaide (19-20hr., 1-2 per day, $168); Cairns (33hr., 1 per day, $343); Darwin (18-20hr., 2 per day, $184) via Tennant Creek (5-6hr., 2 per day, $101); Sydney (45hr., 1 per day, $289); and Townsville (28hr., 1 per day, $294). They also provide: 2-day Ayers Rock and Olgas tour ($250); and 3-day Ayers Rock, Olgas, and King's Canyon tour ($279).

Public Transportation: ASBus (☎ 8950 0500), the public bus system, runs infrequently to the outskirts of town. Runs M-F 8 or 9am-6pm, Sa only in the morning. $1.40-2.40.

Taxis: Alice Springs Taxis (☎ 8952 1877) queue on Gregory Tce. just east of Todd Mall.

Car Rental: Territory-Thrifty (☎ 8952 9999), on the corner of Hartley St. and Stott Tce., has cars from $85 per day, 4WD from $115 per day. Open daily 8am-5:30pm. **Hertz,** 76 Hartley St. (☎ 8952 2644), near Stott Tce., rents from $65 per day. **Britz** (☎ 8952 8814), corner of Stuart Hwy. and Power St., is the best deal in town, renting 4WD and campervans with unlimited kilometers from $100 per day, and 2WD starting at $62 (no surcharge for under 25). Open daily 8am-5pm. Local rental companies include: **Advance,** 9 Railway Tce. (☎ 8953 3700); **Boomerang Rental** (☎ 8955 5171); **Maui** (☎ 8952 8049), on the corner of Stuart Hwy. and Power St., with 4WD and campervans; **Outback Auto Rentals,** 78 Todd St. (☎ 8953 5333).

Roadside Assistance: AANT (24hr. ☎8952 1087).

Road Conditions: 24hr. ☎1800 246 199.

Bike Rental: Pioneer YHA (☎8952 8855), $10 per half-day, $16.50 per day.

ORIENTATION

The Stuart Hwy. runs through Alice on its way from Darwin (1486km) to Adelaide (1570km). The **MacDonnell Ranges** form a natural border at the southern side of town, and the break between the east-west ranges, called **Heavitree Gap**, allows both the Stuart Hwy. and the **Todd River** to pass through. Downtown, the major north-south streets are (from west to east) the Stuart Hwy., Railway Tce., Bath St., Hartley St., Todd St., and Leichhardt Tce.; the major east-west streets are (from north to south) Wills Tce., Parsons St., Gregory Tce., Stott Tce., and Stuart Tce. The true commercial center of town is **Todd Mall,** a pedestrian-only stretch of Todd St. between Wills and Gregory Tce.; the two indoor malls are **Alice Plaza** (Todd Mall at Parsons St.) and **Yeperenye Plaza** (Hartley St. north of Gregory Tce.).

PRACTICAL INFORMATION

Tourist Office: Central Australian Tourism Industry Association (☎8952 5800 or 1800 645 199; www.centralaustraliatourism.com), on Gregory Tce. at the end of Todd Mall. Books transportation, tours, and accommodations, sells road and Larapinta Trail maps, and has National Park info. Grab their free excellent city map. Open M-F 8:30am-5:30pm, Sa-Su 9am-4pm.

Budget Travel: Flight Centre (☎8953 4081), on Todd Mall, guarantees the lowest airfares. Open M-F 9am-5:30pm, Sa 9:30am-12:30pm. **Travelworld** (☎8952 7186), on Todd Mall. Open M-F 8:30am-5pm, Sa 9am-noon.

Tours: Mention the word "tour" in any establishment in Alice and you'll have more brochures thrown at you than you could carry with a road train. Booking far in advance is rarely necessary, so have a look around when you get to Alice. Hostel-run tours often include accommodation. **McCafferty's/Greyhound** (☎8952 7888) buses to major Red Centre sights.

Currency Exchange: National Australia (☎8952 1611) and **ANZ** (☎8952 1144) are in Todd Mall, along with **ATMs.** Both open M-Th 9:30am-4pm, F 9:30am-5pm.

Work Opportunities: Alice has a year-round labor shortage that borders on crisis. Those with office or computer skills can get placement through **Work Zone** (☎8952 4300; www.workzone.org), on the corner of Gregory Tce. and Bath St., next to Video EZY.

Library: (☎8950 0555), next to the tourist office. Open M-Tu and Th 10am-6pm, W and F 10am-5pm, Sa 9am-1pm, Su 1-5pm.

Book Exchange: Book Worm 76 Todd St. (☎8952 5843), in the Colocag Plaza. Open M-F 9:30am-5pm, Sa 9:30am-1pm.

SIGNS OF THE TIMES
You may notice that many restaurants throughout the Territory have signs outside demanding "No Thongs. No Singlets. Neat and Clean Dress," or something similar. In Alice Springs, the more subtle read simply "Dress Regulations Apply," but some signs go so far as urging those not following these strictures to "Bugger Off." Many see this as simply an attempt to take the edge off the outback harshness, similar to an American maxim "No Shirt, No Shoes, No Service." But others see in it a thinly-veiled racism, an effort to keep Aborigines, who are perceived as dressing much more shabbily, out of establishments. Shop owners will denigratingly point to a competitor who, with no dress regulations, "has *that* kind of crowd."

THE HIDDEN DEAL

ANNIE'S PLACE

They say you can't please all the people all of the time...well clearly *they* haven't been to Annie's Place. Hidden among the forest of hostels on the streets of Alice Springs, this unassuming backpackers represents the best hidden deal in Alice .

The hostel itself holds some of the cheapest beds in town, despite the fact that its rooms are immaculate and the facilities are second to none. The fun and charming staff, including the incomparable owner/operator, Mulga, make this relaxed place a home-away-from-home for weary travelers.

Annie's **International Cafe** serves up delicious, hot dinners—both meat and veggie—for only $5 for Annie's guests and $7.50 for non-guests. The cafe is always bumping, and especially when there's some sport on the telly, it's got some of the best atmosphere this side of Darwin.

Annie's full-day **Town Tour** is as hysterically funny as it is informative and comprehensive, ·hitting all the major and most of the minor sites. At only $10 per person, it's cheaper than renting a bike, and it includes dinner in the International Cafe. Their 3-day **Ayers Rock, Olgas, and King's Canyon tour** does all three of these tourism meccas in style for only $325, including park entry—far less than the price of one night at any of Yulara's hotels. Call ahead to arrange 5- or 10-day tours from Darwin or Adelaide. *(4 Traegger Ave. ☎ 1800 359 089; www.anniesplace.com. Internet $6 per hr., $3 per hr. until 5pm. Reception daily 5:30am-8pm. 4- or 6-bed dorms $16; doubles $55. MC/V.)*

Emergency: ☎ 000. **Crisis Line** ☎ 1800 019 116.

Police: (☎ 8951 8888), on Parsons St., at the corner of Bath St.

Internet Access: The best deal in town is **Todd Internet** connection. $3 for the first 30min., then charged per minute at $6 per hr. Open daily 9:30am-late.

Post Office: GPO (☎ 8952 1020), on Hartley St. south of Parsons St. Open M-F 8:15am-5pm. **Postal Code:** 0870.

ACCOMMODATIONS & CAMPING

The hostels of Alice are concentrated on or near Todd St. and Gap Rd. All listings have A/C, a pool, and $2 laundry; all recommend booking in advance; most have bike hire from $12-15 per day; and *everybody* will be happy to book tours.

Elke's Outbackpackers, 39 Gap Rd. (☎ 1800 633 354), at Baedem St., 1km south of Todd Mall. Elke's compensates for its distance from town by providing several free shuttles daily. A motel converted into a popular hostel. Each ensuite dorm room has own kitchenette, TV, and balcony. Reception daily 5am-8:30pm. 8-bed dorms $18; twins and doubles $50; motel rooms $75; free breakfast. VIP/YHA discount $2. MC/V. ❷

Pioneer YHA (☎ 8952 8855), on the corner of Parsons and Leichardt St., 1 block off Todd Mall. The most central location in town. What was originally a deckchair cinema is now a comfortable yet impersonal hostel. Large 24hr. free safe and storage. Internet $6 per hr. Key deposit $20. Reception daily 7:30am-8:30pm. 6- to 16-bed dorms $23; 4-bed dorms $26. YHA discount $3.50. Wheelchair accessible. MC/V. ❷

Elkira Motel, 65 Bath St. (☎ 8952 1222), at the corner of Stott Tce. Well-maintained with a bathroom, TV, and A/C in every room, this centrally located motel lives up to its motto of "hospitality in the Outback." Pool, BBQ, and $12 buffet M-F. Reception 7am-8pm. Budget rooms $77-88; standard $95-105; deluxe $105-130. Wheelchair accesible. MC/V. ❺

Toddy's Backpackers, 41 Gap Rd. (☎ 8952 1322), next to Elke's. Courtesy bus meets most flights and buses. Reception daily 6am-8:30pm. Dorms $12-18; singles, doubles, and twins with sink and fridge $44-58; budget motel rooms $44; ensuite motel doubles with TV and fridge $58; free breakfast. NOMADS. MC/V. ❶

Melanka Motel, 94 Todd St. (☎ 8952 2233). This mirror-image to Melanka Backpackers is better-kept and fancier. Large bathrooms, fridge, TV, free coffee, A/C, and heat. Reception daily 7am-9pm. Singles $83; twins and doubles $88; family rooms $99. MC/V. ❺

The closest **camping** option to town is at the aptly-named **In-Town Campground ❶**, on the corner of Breadon and Todd St., near Elke's. Grassy and caravan-free, it is spacious and friendly. (☎8952 6687. Sites $8.) The **Stuart Caravan Park ❶** is 2km west of town on Larapinth Dr. (☎8952 2547. Reception daily 8am-8pm. Sites $10, powered $18.) At **Heavitree Gap Outback Resort ❷**, you will find a motel, bistro, and grazing wallabies. Take the Stuart Hwy. for 3km and make a left on Palm Circuit. (☎8950 4444. Reception daily 7am-9pm. Sites for 2 $18, powered $20.)

🍴 FOOD

If you've got the money to spare, there are a handful of overpriced outdoor cafes on Todd Mall near Gregory Tce. that serve edible grub. Otherwise, **International Travellers Cafe**, in Annie's Place (see **Hidden Deal,** p. 276), has excellent $7.50 dinners ($5 for guests), while **Toddy's** has all-you-can-gorge carnivorous mediocrity for $8.50 nightly at 7pm. Coles 24hr. **supermarket** is on Bath St. at Gregory Tce.

■ **Bar Doppios** (☎8952 6525), on Fan Arcade, at the Gregory Tce. end of Todd Mall. The town's most happening and hippest coffee shop serves extraordinary food at a good price. Australian with a twist, Middle Eastern, and Southeast Asian fare (mains $9-10). Don't miss their exceptional breakfasts served until 11am. Vegetarian and lactose-intolerant friendly. BYO. Open M-Th and Sa 7:30am-5pm, F 7:30am-10pm. ❶

Oscar's Cafe (☎8953 0930), on Todd Mall. For those with a little more cash to spare and in desperate need of a culinary feast, head to north end of the Todd Mall. Swank, sophisticated, and proud of it, Oscar's serves zesty Italian meals in a spacious, well-lit room. The freshly made pasta and succulent meats will leave your mouth watering for another visit. Mains $18-24. Open daily 9am-10pm. MC/V. ❹

Keller's Swiss and Indian Restaurant (☎8952 3188), on Gregory Tce. east of Hartley St. Switzerland and India are exact opposites in geography, climate, political temperament, and cuisine, making for a titillating combo. *And* the food vegetarian-friendly. Spaetzle with mushroom-gruyere cream sauce $15 or vegetable curry $16. Open daily 5:30pm-late. ❸

Sultan's Kebabs, 52 Hartley St. (☎8953 3322). With the feel of a Middle Eastern fun house, Sultan's is Turkish and delightful. Kebabs (with veggie options) from $6. Pizzas from $8. Sweet, sweet sutlac $4. Belly dancers F-Sa 8pm. Open M-Sa 11am-late, Su 5pm-late. ❶

Red Ochre Grill (☎8952 9614), on Todd Mall near Parsons St. Sample what a top-notch chef can do with regional ingredients. Aboriginal artwork and didgeridoo music round out the atmosphere for a memorable but pricey meal. The Wallaby Mignon ($27) and smoked chicken with sun-dried tomatoes and pasta ($19) are delicious. Open daily 6:30am-10:30pm. ❹

📷 SIGHTS

Many sights are near Todd Mall, but more distant sights is difficult without a vehicle. The **Alice Wanderer** shuttle service circles past the major sights in the Alice area. (☎8952 2211 or 1800 669 111. Runs 9am-4pm, departing from the southern end of Todd Mall. All-day ticket $25.) **Annie's Place** (see **The Hidden Deal,** p. 276) runs a funny full-day tour that hits most of the major sights and includes dinner ($10).

CITY CENTER

ANZAC HILL. The best place to view a postcard sunset is atop Anzac Hill, which offers a panorama of the MacDonnell Ranges that seems out of place for a city backdrop. *(Walk to Wills Tce. between Bath and Hartley St.; a metal arch marks the start* *of the easy 10min. "Lions Walk" from the base to the obelisk at the top. Vehicle access is around the corner on the Stuart Hwy.)*

REPTILE CENTRE. Wallet-friendly and truly hands-on fun is yours at this home to snakes, lizards and a saltie. Come, let a python slither on you. *(9 Stuart Tce., on the corner of Bath St. ☎8952 8900. Open daily 9:30am-5pm. Feedings 11am, 1, and 3pm. $7, children $4.)*

ABORIGINAL ARTS AND CULTURE CENTRE. Owned and operated by the Arrernte, the Centre holds the "Didgeridoo University," where you can graduate with a one-hour degree in Didgeridoo Playing—cap and gown extra. There's also a museum and tiny art gallery. *(86 Todd St. ☎8952 3408; www.aboriginalart.com.au. Open M-F 9am-6pm, Sa-Su 8am-4pm. Free; cultural tours $5; Didgeridoo Degree $11.)*

OLIVE PINK BOTANICAL GARDEN. The desert scrub is hardly a "garden," but it's not a bad place for a picnic. Skip the walking trails and plant displays and head for the excellent lookout over the city. *(On the opposite bank of the Todd River, 2km from Todd Mall, is Tuncks Rd.; the garden is down on the left. ☎8952 2154. Garden open daily 10am-6pm. Visitors Center open daily 10am-4pm. Admission by donation.)*

NATIONAL PIONEER WOMEN'S HALL OF FAME. In this frontier land of masculine bravado, this is a refreshing site that provides biographical sketches of over a hundred pioneer women. *(In the Old Courthouse on Parson St. at the corner of Hartley St. ☎8952 9006; www.pioneerwomen.com.au. Open Feb. to mid-Dec. daily 10am-5pm. $2.20.)*

OUTSIDE THE CITY CENTER

DESERT PARK. "No, the desert is not a desolate wasteland but a vibrant habitat, full of life!" is the recurring theme here. To prove it to you, they've got kangaroos, emus, and a nocturnal house. The not-to-be-missed **Birds of Prey** show is one of the only attractions in Alice guaranteed to evoke audible "oohs" and "ahhs." *(8km west of town on Larapinta Dr. Desert Park transfers runs a shuttle every 1½hr. 7:30am-6pm from most accommodations to the park. Call for pickup ☎8952 4667. $30, concessions $20; includes admission. Park ☎8951 8788. Open daily 7:30am-6pm. Birds of Prey show 10am and 3:30pm. $18, children $9.)*

FRONTIER CAMEL FARM. Alice Springs considers itself the camel capital of Australia, and the Camel Farm keeps the dream alive with camel rides. *(4km beyond where Palm Circuit crosses a traffic circle and emerges as the Ross Hwy. ☎8953 0444; www.cameltours.com.au. Open daily 9am-5pm. 1½hr. rides daily 10:30am-noon; Apr.-Oct. also 1-2:30pm. $6, children $3, families $12.)*

TRAIN MUSEUM AND TRANSPORT HALL OF FAME. The *Old Ghan* Train and Museum and the adjacent Road Transport Hall of Fame may be 10km from the city but are still two of Alice's definitive sights. *(Accessible by Norris Bell Ave. off the Stuart Hwy. Train Museum ☎8955 5047. $5.50, concessions $4.50. Hall of Fame ☎8952 7161. $5/ $2.50. Both open daily 9am-5pm.)*

🎵 🎬 ENTERTAINMENT AND NIGHTLIFE

The *Alice Spring News* (90¢) has a "Dive Into Live" section listing upcoming events. The 500-seat **Araluen Centre,** on Larapinta Dr., presents artsy, independent flicks every Sunday, as well as live theater and concerts. *(☎8951 1122. Box office open daily 10am-5pm. $11, concessions $8.80.)* The popular **Sounds of Starlight Theatre** is in the Todd St. Mall a few doors down from Parsons St. Led by one fine didgeridoo player, the performance has a natural beauty that unfortunately gets

THE WORLD'S LARGEST CLASSROOM It's Monday morning, and 140 children ages 4-13 are thousands of kilometers apart, yet singing the national anthem together. The **School of the Air** is central Australia's answer to educating isolated families spread out on remote cattle stations, roadhouses, and Aboriginal lands. The program, stationed in a dozen outback towns, links children with each other and their Alice-based teachers via short-wave radio for three to four hours each week. The network covers 1.3 million square kilometers of land and has been dubbed "the largest classroom in the world." *(Coming from Alice, before the turn-off to the Reserve, a sign on the Stuart Hwy. points down Head St. ☎ 8951 6834. Open M-Sa 8:30am-4:30pm, Su 1:30-4:30pm. $3.50, concessions $2.50.)*

swept away by the overbearing synthesizer and cheap lighting tricks. (☎ 8952 0826. 1½hr. shows Apr.-Nov. Tu and F-Sa 7:30pm. $18, YHA $15.30.) For those with more cash, **Red Centre Dreaming** offers a combination traditional three-course NT dinner with an Aboriginal cultural display including an extensive performance by an Aboriginal dance troupe. (☎ 1800 089 616. Open daily 7pm-10pm. $85, children $49; includes pickup and drop-off from any accommodation.)

Toasty taverns (and very tame dance clubs) are the staple of afterhours Alice. It all starts and ends at ■**Bojangles**, 80 Todd St., south of Gregory Tce., which is everything you could ask for in a saloon: a honky-tonk piano in the corner and a generous helping of outback cowboys...well, at least tourists pretending to be cowboys. Be forewarned, however, that your late-night antics will be broadcast to the world over Bojangles' many webcams scattered throughout the bar; check it out at www.boslivesaloon.com.au. (☎ 8952 2873. Open daily 11:30am-3am. Live music daily. Blues Jam Su 1pm-late.) A few doors down at the Melanka Lodge, the dance floor of the **Desert Waterhole** typically draws the young backpackers. (☎ 8952 7131. Happy Hour 5-7pm, $7.50 jugs. M, W, F, and Su live music 8pm. Open daily 5pm-late.) **Sean's Bar**, 51 Bath St., is frequented mostly by locals and is your best bet for a pint ($6.50) of Guinness. (☎ 8952 1858. Open daily 6pm-late. Live music F-Sa 8pm, open jam session Su.) Across the Todd River and a $10 cab ride from town is **Lasseter's Hotel Casino,** the setting of the climax of *Priscilla, Queen of the Desert.* (☎ 8950 7777. Open Su-Th 10am-3am, F-Sa 10am-4am.)

◨ FESTIVALS AND EVENTS

Heritage Week (April 19-26, 2003) features historical reenactments and displays; the theme for 2003 is water. Around the same time, a month-long horse racing festival, the lavish **Alice Springs Cup Carnival** (April 19-May 5, 2003) entertains at the Pioneer Race Park and culminates with the **Bangtail Muster** parade (May 5, 2003). On the Queen's Birthday Weekend, the plucky cars and motorcycles of the **Finke Desert Race** (June 6-9, 2003) traverse 240km of roadless dusty desert from Alice to the town of Finke in the south. The first Saturday in July hosts the more traditional, agriculture-focused **Alice Springs Show** (July 4-5, 2003). The not-so-traditional **Camel Cup Carnival** race (July 12, 2003; www.camelcup.com.au), including a Miss Camel Cup Competition, is held the following weekend. The **Alice Springs Rodeo** (August 16, 2003) and the **Harts Range Annual Races** (August 2-4, 2003) are both held in August. The definitive Alice Springs festival is the **Henley-on-Todd Regatta** (September 20, 2003; www.henleyontodd.com.au). A good-natured mockery of the dry river, the race is in bottomless "boats" propelled Flintstones-style—by foot. The **Corkwood Festival** (November 23, 2003) is a folk event featuring craft booths during the day and energetic bush dancing at night.

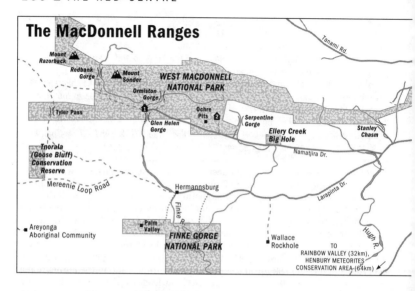

THE MACDONNELL RANGES

To the north of the Uluru-Kata Tjuta and Watarrka area, immediately outside Alice Springs, lie central Australia's mountains. The MacDonnell Ranges roll west to east across the horizon, creating pockets of geological formations and wildlife that break the desert surrounding. From a distance, the green shrub that covers its ridges appears a soft blanket of grass, but up close, Australia's rusty orange earth and rock, prickly ground-cover, and glowing white-ghost gums keep the range rugged. The MacDonnells' pastel colors have inspired painters and photographers, and numerous walking tracks cajole visitors to take a closer look.

THE MACDONNELLS AT A GLANCE

LENGTH: 460km.

FEATURES: West MacDonnell Nat'l Park along Namatjira Dr., Finke Gorge Nat'l Park off Larapinta Dr., several nature parks to the east, and Alice Springs (at Heavitree Gap) in the middle.

GATEWAYS: Alice Springs (see p. 273).

HIGHLIGHTS: Camping, walking, swimming, and stunning scenery.

CAMPING: Throughout; they are described under each sight listing.

FEES: A small fee is charged only at Stanley Chasm (p. 282) and the Hermannsburg Historical Precinct (p. 282).

WEST MACDONNELLS

■ **ORIENTATION.** The gorges and waterholes of the West MacDonnells shelter vestiges of the bygone rainforest era and the 4WD enthusiasts who know that this is where the good stuff is. **Larapinta Dr.** heads out of Alice past the tame beginnings of the West MacDonnells, and **Namatjira Dr.** veers off into deeper territory. A fulfilling loop can be made by continuing on Larapinta Dr., which passes by **Finke Gorge National Park** and connects with the western end of Namatjira Dr. via **Tylers Pass.** If you're willing to brave rough, unsealed roads, hop on board.

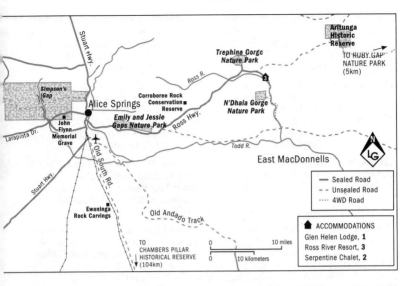

🔰 **TOURS. AAT Kings Tours** does a Larapinta-Namatjira loop in two days by bus. (☎ 8952 1700. www.aatkings.com. Departs daily 7:30am. $170, children $136.) **Centre Highlights** makes a 4WD trek to some West MacDonnell highlights including Finke River and Palm Valley. (☎ 1800 659 574. Departs M, W, and F 7:30am. $105.)

🔰 **HIKING.** For experienced hikers, the best way to see the West MacDonnells and commune with the outback is the **Larapinta Trail,** an enormous hiking trail that starts at the Telegraph Station in Alice and extends 220km west to Mt. Razorback. The trail connects the main attractions and is usually hiked in two- to four-day pieces from one gorge to another. Before attempting the long hikes, seek info from the Park and Wildlife Commission in Alice. (☎ 8951 8211; fax 8951 8258; P.O. Box 1046, Alice Springs NT 0871.) Voluntary registration is a good idea; the $50 deposit is refundable as long as the Parks and Wildlife Commission (☎ 1300 650 730) doesn't end up sending out a search and rescue mission for you. Pick up the flyer *Bushwalks* from the Tourist Office in Alice for a list of hikes.

🔰 **SIGHTS.** West MacDonnells sights lie along two 4WD routes heading out from Alice Springs. The distance from Alice is listed after the name of each site.

LARAPINTA DRIVE

JOHN FLYNN MEMORIAL GRAVE. *7km.* Here lies the local hero who created the bush's "mantle of safety," the minister who brought the Royal Flying Doctor Service to the outback. Because of the sentiment that his gravestone should be something uniquely symbolic of the outback, it was originally adorned with a massive boulder taken from the Devil's Marbles (see p. 272), near Tennant Creek—but the stone became the center of a 20-year battle between the caretaker of Flynn's grave and Aborigines, who regard the Devil's Marbles as sacred and felt they had been disturbed. At last, in 1999, a stone from the East MacDonnells was substituted and the Devil's Marbles stone was returned to its sacred locale.

SIMPSON'S GAP. *18km.* Down an 8km paved turn-off, Simpson's Gap offers some nice hikes and views of jagged red rocks. The **Cassia Hill Walk** is an easy 1.8km (30min.) climb to a lookout. The gap is only a short distance from the carpark down the 20min. **Gap Walk.** The gap swarms with black-footed wallabees; stay on the marked paths and off the rocky slopes. *(Open daily 5am-8pm. Free.)*

STANLEY CHASM. *50km.* Down a 30min. mostly flat path, crowds gather to ogle the glowing orange walls when the sun shines directly into this 80m-high fissure at midday. Aside from this spectacle, the chasm is rather unimpressive, but if you are willing to wade through a waterhole and scramble up the rocky slide at the far end, you can enjoy a deserted second chasm and an overhead view of the first. *(☎8956 7440. Open daily 8am-6pm. $6, concessions $5. Food and drinks available.)*

HERMANNSBURG HISTORICAL PRECINCT. *126km.* Old homes from the early Lutheran mission are here, along with a gallery saluting Aboriginal artist Albert Namatjira. The service station sells the **Mereenie Tour Pass** for the 4WD track to Kings Canyon (see p. 285), and **petrol** and **groceries.** *(☎8956 7402. Open daily Mar.-Nov. 9am-4pm, Dec.-Feb. 10am-4pm. $4.50, children $3. Gallery $3.50.)*

■ **FINKE GORGE NATIONAL PARK.** *146km.* This 460km² park contains the Finke River, reputedly the oldest river on the planet; some stretches date back 350 million years. The park's main attraction is **Palm Valley,** home to the rare Red Cabbage Palm. The unique pockets of plant life, combined with the ancient riverbed, create a timeless air in which bird-watching is effortless. Two worthwhile walks are: the **Mpulungkinya Walk** (5km; 2hr.), which traverses the thickest growth of palms; and the **Arankaia Walk** (2km; 1hr.), which turns back halfway and climbs the valley rim. Keep to the trail when on these walks to avoid further damage to the delicate palm seedlings. Near the full-facilities **campground** ❶ (16km into the park), the **Kalaranga Lookout** (1½km; 45min.) quickly surmounts some steep crags to bring 360° vistas of the park. *(The park is accessed through the 21km 4WD-only road that follows the path of the mostly dry Finke River, off Larapinta Dr. Sites $6.60, children $3.30, families $15.40.)*

NAMATJIRA DRIVE

ELLERY CREEK BIG HOLE. *96km.* Down a 2km rough access road (2WD accesible), and a 100m wheelchair accesible path, is the 18m-deep pool in a creek through a mountain. In the summer, it makes for a very cool dip, but is far too cold for swimming during most of the winter. The nearby **Dolemite Walk** (3km; 1hr.) traverses lush forest through spinifex. **Camping** ❶ with basic facilities including wood BBQ. Caravans permitted. *(Sites $3.30, children $1.65, families $7.70.)*

SERPENTINE GORGE. *102km.* An easy walk along a service road (1hr.) leads to a slim and seductive gorge with little to recommend it except the distinct lack of tourists. The true highlight of Serpentine is the ■**lookout walk,** a short, steep climb starting need the near gorge and ascending to one of the most picturesque overlooks in the entire West MacDonnells.

SERPENTINE CHALET. *108km.* While the ruins of the Chalet are unremarkable, the **bushcamping** ❶ here is not. Isolated down a rough 3km access road, the campsites lack facilities but offer a peaceful resting place and some of the best stargazing in the Red Centre. *(There are 9 campsites, 4 of which can reached with a 2WD.)*

OCHRE PITS. *108km.* Three hundred meters of wheelchair accessible path leads to a platform overlooking the pits, complete with informative signs. From there, it's possible to walk along the riverbed to study the technicolor banded rock walls.

ORMISTON GORGE. *130km.* Welcome to the MacDonnells happy meal. The spellbinding gorge was named by Peter Warburton, who thought the area looked a lot like his own Glen Ormiston back in Scotland. He was right, except for the gorge's dry vegetation, sand dunes, and steep orange cliffs. Somewhat overrun with tour buses, the gorge offers a variety of hikes. A 10min. walk leads to some of the gorge's pools (some 14m deep); head instead for the excellent longer hikes. The **Ghost Gun Walk** (1hr.) climbs the side of the gorge for an impressive lookout, then ends at the far end of the gorge, allowing a wander back to the carpark. Late afternoon is the best, when the orange walls are well-lit and rock wallabies come out to play. The **Pound Walk** (7km; 3-4hr.) is more peaceful, offering some great vistas of the surrounding hills before approaching the gorge from the back. **Camping ❶** available with showers. Caravans permitted. *(Sites $6.60, children $3.30, families $15.40.)*

GLEN HELEN GORGE. *132km.* The **Glen Helen Lodge ❶**, with **petrol**, snacks, and accommodations, is the only draw here. The nondescript gorge itself is only a 10min. walk from the parking lot. *(☎8956 7489. Sites $9, powered for 2 $22; dorms from $19, with linens $29. Helicopter flights of the region $35-$180. Call ahead, as the entire lodge is often booked by large tour groups.)*

REDBANK GORGE. *156km.* The narrow slit through the mountains shades a series of pools too chilly for swimming. 2 **campgrounds ❶** with basic facilities. *($3.30, children $1.65, families $7.70.)*

GOSSE BLUFF. *187km.* You can view the site of the ancient crater up close from the 11km 4WD track, or take in the whole picture from the **West MacDonnell Lookout,** a turn-off near the north end of Tyler Pass.

EAST MACDONNELLS

■ ⬛ ORIENTATION AND TOURS. Just beyond **Heavitree Gap** south of Alice, **Palm Circuit** branches off the Stuart Hwy. and heads east. After a few kilometers, it becomes the **Ross Hwy.** and plunges into the East MacDonnells. The Ross Hwy. narrows to a single lane at times, and the area is filled with wandering **wild camels** which frequently travel down the center of the road. The East Macs are less thrilling geologically than their western counterparts, but they are also less crowded and see fewer tours. Two tours offer daytrips to the area from Alice: **Discovery Ecotours** (☎1800 803 174; 6hr.; departs 6am; $92) and **Emu Run** (☎8953 7057; 9½hr.; departs 8am; $99). All **camping ❶** in this area costs: $3.30, children $2, families $8.

⬛ SIGHTS. The distance from Alice is listed after the name of each sight.

EMILY AND JESSIE GAPS. *10km.* These gaps, both immediately off the Ross Hwy., are important sites in the Aboriginal dreaming. Emily Gap, or *Anthwerrke* in the language of the local Arrernte people, is a part of the three caterpillars storyline. Into the gorge 150m there is a gallery of Aboriginal rock paintings marking the spot where *Intwailuka*, an ancestral hero, cooked and ate caterpillars on his Dreamtime journey. The paintings are vertical lines of alternating colors representing *Ntyarrke, Utnerrengatye,* and *Yeperenye,* caterpillar beings of great significance. Pools of very cold water often obstruct the path into the gap and to the gallery. If the water appears low enough, leave your shoes behind and cross in the center of the pool where the water is shallowest.

CORROBOREE ROCK CONSERVATION RESERVE. *42km.* This rock formation, broad on one side and thin on the other, sticks up like a piece of a collapsed wall in the middle of an empty valley. It is an Eastern Arrernte sacred site that is still used today in ceremonies. A very easy 15min. loop traces the base of the rock. It is asked that you not climb the rock or disturb the flora and fauna around it.

NORTHERN TERRITORY

TREPHINA GORGE NATURE PARK. *65km.* After an 8km partly paved access road, you reach the carpark for the **main campground ❶**. The Trephina Gorge Walk (2km, 1hr.), follows along the gorge rim and at times the sandy riverbed. The Panorama walk (3km, 1hr.) is a loop with an excellent lookout over the whole park. At the John Hayes Rockhole, 4km down a 4WD only track, there is **more camping ❶** and the Chain Ponds walk (4km, 1½hr.), a sojourn past a great lookout on the rim and through a picture-perfect series of pools. The **Hayes Trephina Bluff walk** is a six-hour one-way hike that highlights both regions of the park. Both sites have pit toilets and BBQs.

ROSS RIVER RESORT. *85km.* This laid-back **country inn ❶** caters to an older crowd looking for a more peaceful "outback experience." Check out their collection of historic visitor books, or take a leisurely bushwalk. The highlight of a stay here is their whip cracking and boomerang lesson, complete with tea and damper. (☎ 8956 9711. *Lessons daily 10:30am; $7. Sites $10 per person, powered $15; 2-bed tents $22; 4-bed bunkhouse rooms $22 per person, with linens $33; single and double hotel rooms $125.*)

N'DHALA GORGE. *85km.* A walking track (1½km; 1hr.) leads into a gorge and past a few of an estimated 6000 Aboriginal rock carvings, some of which are 10,000 years old. While respect for local Aboriginal culture mandates that only a small portion of these petroglyphs be accessed, it gives a taste of the variety of images guarded by the park's rough terrain. **Camping ❶** (without water) is available. *(8km south of the Ross River Resort on a 4WD only track, then down a 4km access road.)*

RUBY GAP NATURE PARK. *154km.* A left fork before the Homestead traverses 36km of unsealed road to the **Arltunga Historic Reserve,** the remains of central Australia's first official town. Several short gold mines are open for your spelunking pleasure. 4WD vehicles can push on 39km to the remote **Ruby Gap Nature Park,** with rugged scenery that includes a stunning gorge and excellent **bush camping ❶** (no water). The road is rough; register with the ranger station at Arltunga. Ruby Gap was the site of the first mining rush in central Australia in 1886. What was believed to be precious ruby stones turned out to be relatively worthless garnets, bringing a swift and sudden death to the "ruby boom."

THE SIMPSON DESERT   ☎ 08

South of Alice, the Stuart Hwy. passes Heavitree Gap and Palm Circuit. Past the Stuart's turn toward the south, on the road to the airport, the unsealed and isolated **Old South Rd.** veers right toward the **Simpson Desert.** Stock up on supplies before heading down it. Charles Sturt first explored this part of the Simpson in 1845, so bent on conquering the outback that many of his men died from complications related to the desert's harsh conditions. All **camping ❶** in the area costs: $3.30, children $1.65, families $1.75. Several tours go to the Desert from Alice Springs. **Emu Run** does an afternoon tour of Rainbow Valley, complete with bush BBQ dinner. (☎ 8953 7057; www.emurun.com.au. $89.)

The first worthwhile spot is the **Ewaninga Rock Carvings,** 39km south of Alice. The weathered marking, or petroglyphs, which predate the Egyptian pyramids, are a sacred site for Aborigines. They are symbols of the *Altyerre* (al-CHA-ra), the laws of the Arrernte culture. The most striking part of the pleasant 600m stroll past the carvings is the interpretive signs by the site's traditional owners explaining the carvings' meanings. Another highlight is the expansive dried **mudflats.**

The Aboriginal community of **Maryvale Station,** 62km more along the Old South Rd., marks the 4WD-only turn to **Chambers Pillar Historical Reserve** (4hr. one-way). This sandstone formation was a landmark for early travelers and their carved initials (a practice now subject to high fines). The trek is more hardcore than stupendous, but sunsets at the rock are masterpieces of color. (No water or facilities.)

Rainbow Valley is a jagged, U-shaped ridge standing in the desert like a Hollywood backdrop 22km east of the Stuart Hwy. on a sandy unmarked 4WD track (97km from Alice). The valley is most famous for its winter sunsets, when the red-orange-yellow-bleach white formation is illuminated at the ideal angle. (Toilets and BBQ, but no water.) Another 51km down the Stuart, the unsealed **Ernest Giles Rd.** veers west toward Watarrka; 11km past the turn-off and 4km north on an access road lie the **Henbury Meteorite Craters.** This circular ridge of mountains is the remnant of a 4000-year-old meteorite impact site. Basic **camping ❶** and a self-guided walk (20min.) are available. The Museum of Central Australia's (see p. 273) meteorite exhibit in Alice makes this site much more meaningful. Heading farther south, all that lies along the Stuart Hwy. until Coober Pedy, SA, are overpriced roadhouses rising from endless miles of spiky spinifex shrub.

WATARRKA NATIONAL PARK (KINGS CANYON)

The increasingly popular Watarrka National Park contains the tourist mecca of Kings Canyon, cutting deep, sunburned grooves in a section of the George Gill Mtns. The canyon's concave walls shelter waterholes sustaining tropical greenery. Erosion is visible across the canyon, especially in the domes atop both sides of the precipice. The weathered humps act as staircases to the views atop. Scattered on the canyon roof, the domes create a maze dubbed the **Lost City.**

TRANSPORTATION. There are three different ways to drive to Kings Canyon from Alice Springs. First, the fully-paved route—the **Stuart Hwy.**—runs 202km south to the roadhouse settlement of **Erldunda ❷,** at its junction with the Lasseter Hwy. Travelers changing buses here may end up spending the night. (☎ 8956 0984. Sites for 2 $16, powered $21; motel singles $72; doubles $86.) From the junction, take the Lasseter Hwy. west 110km and turn right on Luritja Rd., which goes north 163km to the Kings Canyon park entrance. Second, vehicles with 4WD can take a "shortcut" along **Ernest Giles Rd.,** a 100km stretch of unpaved road that begins 132km south of Alice off the Stuart Hwy. The road is rough and can take four hours, so the Stuart Hwy. may be faster. Ernest Giles meets Luritja Rd. 100km south of the park entrance. Check local road conditions before attempting this road. Third, it's also possible to reach Kings Canyon from Alice Springs via **Hermannsburg** in the West MacDonnells. Take Larapinta Dr. to the scenic but corrugated 4WD-only **Mereenie Loop Rd.** (200km), which passes through Aboriginal land. There are no accommodations or camping allowed on the Mereenie, so plan to do the drive within one day. A $2.20 pass is required and can be obtained in Hermannsburg at Larapinta Service Station, Glen Helen Lodge, or Kings Canyon Resort, or at the Visitors Center in Alice. Most **tours** to Kings Canyon are included in Uluru-Kata Tjuta multi-day packages coming out of Alice Springs. **Emu Run** runs 12hr. day tours from Alice. (☎ 8953 7057. $150, children $75.)

ACCOMMODATIONS AND FOOD. The **Kings Canyon Resort ❸,** 7km up the road from the canyon turn-off, is the beginning and the end of civilization in Watarrka. The resort has the **Desert Oaks Cafe** (open 11am-2pm), and a **grocery store** in the **fuel station** (open daily 7am-7pm). **Outback BBQ ❸** (open daily 6-9pm) offers pizzas from $17 and steaks from $29. Rooms at the resort have A/C, heat, TV, fridge, shared bath, and kitchen. Comfortable, grassy campsites have flush toilets, showers, and a pool. (☎ 8956 7442; reskcr@austarnet.com.au. Reception daily 6:30am-9:30pm. Book ahead. Sites for 2 $26, powered $29; 4-bed dorms $43, YHA $38; twins $100; quads $168.) Excellent and less touristy camping is available at the well-maintained **Kings Creek Station ❶,** just outside the park's eastern entrance. It's a more low-key outpost with a friendly staff, and you just can't beat the prices at **Camel Safaris,** which start at $5 for a five-minute ride. (☎ 8956 7474; www.kingscreekstation.com.au. Sites $11.20, children $6, families $34.40; powered extra $3; cabin singles $48, includes breakfast.) **No camping** is allowed in the National Park.

🅗 HIKING. The park has three well-marked paths. An easy walk (2.6km; 1hr.) follows **Kings Creek** along the bottom of the canyon. Ending at pleasant shaded viewing platform, it provides great views up the sheer canyon walls. It is not possible to get as far as the tropical growth at the canyon's north end because it is a sacred site to local Aborigines. The premier walk in Watarrka is by far the challenging **🅗Kings Canyon Walk** (6km; 3hr.), scaling the rocky, steep slope around the top of the canyon to provide a complete view of the canyon and surrounding country. Along the eastern edge, you wander through the **Lost City,** a sandstone formation with an eerily man-made quality to it. The view is astounding; on a clear day, you can see Uluru, but don't lose yourself in the scenery—all of the edges are rail-less, so *extreme care* should be taken while hiking. Be sure to take the 300m side trail to the canyon's north edge which gives sweeping views of the canyon. The other side track (20min.) that descends into the **Garden of Eden,** a waterhole shaded by palm trees, is less worthwhile. Those looking for a steeper climb and gentler descent should follow the King's Creek walk and take the Canyon Walk turn-off on your left. For the reverse, start at the trailhead just beyond the info hut by the car park. There's an outhouse and an info display at the parking lot, but no other facilities. The long canyon walk has three emergency call boxes.

The wheelchair-accessible **Kathleen Springs Walk** (2.6km; 1½hr.) winds gently through sandstone valleys to a rockhole sacred to local Aborigines. The access road is 20km south of the Canyon turn-off. The **Sunset Viewing** picnic area with water, toilets, and BBQ, is 1km before the main parking lot but is not as good as the resort's **Sunset Viewing Boardwalk,** with views of the George Gill Range.

YULARA (AYERS ROCK RESORT)

☎ 08

They say you can't squeeze blood from stone...but apparently you *can* squeeze money. Ayers Rock Resort (the municipal name of Yulara applies only because there is a small employee housing district) is a series of hotels and shops stretched along a side road just outside the national park. Capitalizing on Uluru's draw, this Disney World of the Outback forms a sterile and insanely expensive bubble ideal for those who think visiting natural wonders should involve 5-star room service. Prepare to shell out handsomely to stay (and eat) 19km from

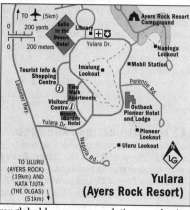

the great monolith; the resort has a stranglehold on accommodations, and prices skyrocket every year. If you have piles of disposable income and truly want to forget you're in the Outback, this place is ideal. If not, grit your teeth and keep your eyes on the distant rocks to remind yourself why you're here.

E TRANSPORTATION. Connellan Airport lies 5km north of town. **Airnorth** and **Qantas** (☎13 13 13) fly to: Adelaide ($675); Alice Springs ($250); Brisbane ($700); Cairns ($600); Darwin ($600); Melbourne ($700); Perth ($625); and Sydney ($597). A free airport shuttle run by AAT Kings meets all flights and picks up from all accommodations. **McCafferty's/Greyhound** (☎13 14 99 or 13 20 30) **buses** depart for Alice Springs daily from the Outback Pioneer Hotel (6hr., 12:30pm, $85). Ayers Rock Resort runs a free village shuttle around the resort loop. (Every 15min., daily 10:30am-12:30am.) **Territory Rent-a-Car** (☎8956 2030), **Hertz** (☎8956 2244), and **Avis** (☎8956 2266) have offices at the airport or at the **Tourist Info Centre** (☎8957 7324). Most backpackers come to Yulara on camping tours out of Alice Springs, which can be combined with various stops to other sites (see **Tours**, p. 275).

A handful of walks around town lead to six different lookout points, all with impressive views. The fit can reach the rocks through pedal power with a bicycle (from $20 per day) from Ayers Rock Campground. Otherwise, to get to Uluru and Kata Tjuta from the resort, you'll need a vehicle. **Uluru Express** (☎8956 2152) offers the most flexible transportation to Uluru ($30, children $15) and Kata Tjuta ($45, children $25). **Anangu Tours** is owned by Aborigines who can share some insider knowledge; book through the Cultural Centre. (☎8956 2123. 2hr. tours $52, children $27, families $158.) **McCafferty's/Greyhound** does a sunset run to Uluru (4hr., departs 3pm, $62) and Kata Tjuta (5½hr., departs 6am, $40); book ahead. If you've got the dough and desire, you can also get there on a **Harley-Davidson motorcycle**. (☎8955 5288. Passenger tours from $65; 5hr. self-drive from $335; deposit $2000.)

7 PRACTICAL INFORMATION. The **Tourist Info Centre,** in the shopping center, has general info, weather conditions, and tour agencies. (☎8957 7324. Internet 30¢ per min. Open daily 7:30am-8:30pm; service desks maintain shorter, variable hours.) The **Visitors Center,** with a grand set of stairs rising from the road near the entrance to the village, has a gift shop and museum of desert animals as well as a detailed history of Uluru. (☎8957 7377. Open daily 8:30am-8pm.) **Petrol** is available at the Mobil station. (☎8956 2229. Open daily 7am-9pm.) The **library** has the cheapest **Internet** access. (☎8956 2351. Open M-F 10:30am-1:15pm and 2-5pm, Sa-Su 1-4pm. $10 per hr.) Other services include: **police** (☎8956 2166); **ANZ bank** with 24hr. **ATM** in the shopping center (open M-Th 9:30am-4pm, F 9:30am-5pm); and a **post office.** (☎8956 2288. Open M-F 9am-6pm, Sa-Su 10am-2pm.) **Postal Code:** 0872.

F ACCOMMODATIONS. For all lodge reservations, call ☎1300 139 889. The **Outback Pioneer Lodge ❸,** on Yulara Dr., has a rather impersonal YHA hostel with barracks-type dorms. Don't get it confused with the hotel portion of the resort, or you might end up booking a more expensive room. (☎8957 7639. Free storage. Reception daily 1-3pm. 20-bed dorms with no locks $32, YHA $29; 4-bed $40/$37.) The **Resort Campground ❶** corners the market on camping, since it is not allowed elsewhere in the park. Campers have access to a pool, kitchen, laundry, hot showers, and BBQ. (☎8956 2055. Sites $12.10, children $5.50, families $35; powered for 2 $29/$5.50/$39.) The next option at Yulara is from $375 for twins and doubles at the **Outback Pioneer Hotel ❺** or cabins at the Campground. Cheap but less conveniently located camping is available 100km east of Yulara at **Curtin Springs ❶.** (☎8956 2906. Powered sites $11, showers $1; rooms from $45.)

⬛ FOOD. Most food in the area is overpriced. The **Outback Pioneer Hotel** has a run-of-the-mill **snack bar ❶** with $7 burgers. Their nightly BBQ with live entertainment (6-9pm) ranges from burgers to emu sausages ($14-24). It's also the only place to buy takeaway **liquor**. (Open daily 11:30am-9pm.)

ULURU-KATA TJUTA NATIONAL PARK

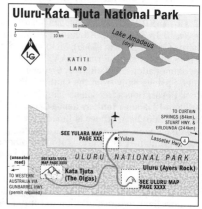

Uluru-Kata Tjuta National Park

Out of the flat, scrub-brush landscape of the Red Centre, Uluru (Ayers Rock) and Kata Tjuta (the Olgas) hulk like hibernating animals. These gigantic rock formations, with smooth ridges and pocket-like caves, break not only the horizon but also the banks of tourists who gather for a once-in-a-lifetime glimpse of "sunset at Uluru." It is no secret that this is the premier sight of central Australia. As the largest rock in the world, fiery-orange Uluru warrants the hype. Nearby Kata Tjuta, a cluster of rounded hump-like mini-Ulurus, are less touristed but no less humbling.

These natural wonders have been revered by the local Anangu Aborigines as a sacred site of the Dreaming for over 22,000 years. Since Uluru's European discovery in 1872 by Ernest Giles, the area has become a tourist mecca. A sense of indigenous loss off-set by industry gain is still present. Today, the park is managed jointly by the National Park Service and Anangu residents. With its natural splendor, cultural significance, and contemporary balancing-act between indigenous livelihood and visitor demands, Uluru-Kata Tjuta just might be the symbol of the Outback. But the hard-earned solitude that lends the Outback its true flavor is missing in this highly-marketed area. Still, Uluru and Kata Tjuta are so stunning that a visit is worthwhile, even for travelers bent on keeping to the backroads.

The typical Uluru tourist routine includes little more than a hurried climb and a few sunset or sunrise snapshots of the rock. While Uluru might be considered "The Rock," a trip to the area is not complete without learning about the meaning of Uluru to the Aborigines who have called the Red Centre their home for 60,000 years. Take a walk around the base of the rock, where indigenous paintings can be found, take a peek at the informative Cultural Centre, and *definitely* explore the skyscraping Olgas—you have not visited Yulara if you miss these sights.

ULURU AND KATA TJUTA AT A GLANCE	
AREA: 1325km²	**HIGHLIGHTS:** The colors of Uluru at sunset and sundown, the Valley of the Winds, walks through Kata Tjuta.
ULURU: 348m in height, 3.1km in length, 1.9km in width, 9.4km around.	
KATA TJUTA: Mt. Olga, its tallest peak, is 546m.	**CAMPING:** No camping is allowed within the National Park. There is a commercial campground at Yulara.
GATEWAYS: Alice Springs and Yulara.	**FEES:** 3-day entry pass $16.25.

TRANSPORTATION. By road, take the Stuart Hwy. to **Erldunda**, 202km south of Alice Springs and 483km north of Coober Pedy, then drive 264km west on the

Lasseter Hwy. Long before Uluru, you'll see **Mt. Connor,** a mesa in the distance. Often mistaken for Ayers Rock, it has its own viewing area right off the highway.

▓ PRACTICAL INFORMATION. The Uluru-Kata Tjuta National Park **entrance station** (☎ 8956 2252) lies 5km past the Yulara resort village, where all visitors must purchase a three-day pass ($16.25). Uluru is 14km ahead, and 4km farther is the turn-off to Kata Tjuta (42km). These roads are all paved. (Park open daily hour-before-sunrise to hour-after-sunset: approx. Dec.-Feb. 5am-9pm; Mar. 5:30am-8:30pm; Apr. 6am-8pm; May 6am-7:30pm; June-July 6:30am-7:30pm; Aug. 6am-7:30pm; Sept. 5:30am-7:30pm; Oct. 5am-8pm; Nov. 5am-8:30pm.) **No camping** is permitted within the park. There are toilet facilities at the Cultural Centre, at the main carpark at Uluru, and at the sunset-viewing area at Kata Tjuta. Picnic facilities are at the Cultural Centre and the Kata Tjuta sunset-viewing area. As in the rest of the Red Centre, the **bush flies** can be unbearable from December to April. Bring mesh netting to cover your face. In case of **emergency,** radio alarms throughout the park can contact a ranger; or call ☎ 8956 3138 (daily 7am-5:30pm).

The **Uluru-Kata Tjuta Cultural Centre,** 1km before Uluru, is an informative effort by the Anangu to enlighten tourists about the rock's history. (☎ 8956 3138. Open daily Nov.-Mar. 7am-6pm; Apr.-Oct. 7am-5:30pm.) Free displays explain the mythical origins of the rock. The center, built with all-natural materials in Aboriginal style, contains an information desk, a snack bar, the **Maruka Arts and Crafts** shop (☎ 8956 2558; open daily 8:30am-5:30pm), and ceramics at the **Walkat-jara Art Centre.** (☎ 8956 2537. Open M-F 9am-5:30pm, Sa-Su 9:30am-2pm.)

Uluru (Ayers Rock)

ULURU (AYERS ROCK)

The Uluru-hype is big, and Uluru is even bigger. The rock is actually only the exposed tip of a giant slab that extends down 5-6km. Eons of geological activity have tilted and eroded once-horizontal sedimentary layers into vertical grooves on the surface of the rock. Up close, meter-long grooves become gorges, and the smooth walls reveal a rough exterior. The strategically situated **sunset-viewing area,** 5km from the rock, is the place to hear the nightly oohs and aahs of awestruck travelers, punctuated by the clicking shutters and useless flashes of hundreds of cameras. The road continues on a **paved loop** around the rock. The **main carpark** and toilets are to the left. A **sunrise-viewing area** is on the opposite side of the rock.

Visit the **Cultural Centre** before heading to the rocks to learn about issues surrounding visiting and especially climbing these natural wonders. Stay on the marked paths and do not approach or touch cultural sights marked off with railings. Also, understand that exploring Uluru will put you in contact with sights meant only for men or women. Members of the opposite gender should avoid looking intently at these sights. Above all, recognize and always keep in mind that you are in a place of great spiritual significance for the Anangu people.

▧ THE CLIMB UP. The Anangu prefer that people not climb because of the spiritual significance the rock represents as the Mala Dreaming track. The Cultural Centre will give you a better understanding of Anangu motivations before you

NORTHERN TERRITORY

decide one way or the other (see **To Climb or Not to Climb,** p. 292). Aside from respecting cultural traditions, realize that it is a difficult hike (a full 2-3hr.), even for the young and able-bodied (notice the plaques at the base that memorialize those who have died—33 total deaths in the past 20 years). Visitors should avoid climbing in the middle of the day or if they have medical conditions or loosely attached accessories—many of the deaths have resulted from individuals chasing after blowing hats or cameras. Due to the high level of risk, the climb is closed on excessively warm or windy days. A fixed chain helps with the lengthy and brutal initial uphill, the steepest part of the climb. Past the chain, including the section that extends beyond the portion visible from the ground, the path, marked by white blazes, meanders along the top of the rock for over 1km. The trail is rugged and requires the scaling of near vertical sections at times 2m tall. The climb absolutely requires rugged footwear with ankle support and at least 2-3 liters of water. The summit rewards hearty mountaineers with an unparalleled panorama of the Red Centre's expanse, broken by Kata Tjuta and Mt. Connor. At the cairn that marks the end of the trail, you can see over the rock's top plateau, an alien landscape of red waves dotted with defiant plant growth. On descending, use extreme care, as any loss of balance could result in a fatal fall. Sliding down in a sitting position over the coarse rock is not recommended; grasp the chain firmly and take small steps, or walk carefully backwards, pulling on the chain for support.

■ **HIKES AROUND THE BOTTOM.** There are several far less adventurous, less dangerous hikes around the base of Uluru. Grab *An Insight into Uluru* ($1), available at the Cultural Centre, for an expanded self-guided tour of these walks.

Circuit Walk. (9.4km; 3.4hr.) This ambitious walk traces around the base of the rock. The flat and relatively easy terrain is broken up only by informative signs along the way. Combined with the pleasure of seeing the rock from all angles, the signs and the solitude give some sense of completeness to an exploration of Uluru.

Mala Walk. (2km; 45min.) Part of the circuit walk, Mala leads from the main parking lot past magnificent walls and a "stone wave" to **Kantju Gorge,** which holds a waterhole of great significance to the Anangu. The trail is flat and wheelchair accessible, and there are a few caves at the base of Uluru. There is a free ranger-guided **Mala Walk** offering a look at Uluru from an Aboriginal perspective; meet the ranger at the Mala Walk sign at the base of Uluru. (1½hr. Daily Oct.-Apr. 8am; May-Sept. 10am. Free.)

Mutitjulu Walk. (1km; 30min.) Served by a smaller parking lot to the right of the loop entrance, Mutitjulu leads to a waterhole that is home to *Wanampi,* an ancestral watersnake. Flat and wheelchair accessible, this track is lined with signs that give information about *Kuniya Tjukurpa,* the woma python.

KATA TJUTA (THE OLGAS)

Perhaps more beautiful than the Rock are the 36 domes scattered over an area several times the size of Uluru. Kata Tjuta (Anangu for "many heads") is the second conspicuous rock formation in the area, and Uluru might just be a ploy to keep tourists away from this less-touted treasure.

The 44km road to Kata Tjuta leaves the main road 4km after the park entrance. The **Dune Viewing Area,** 25km down the road, is at the end of a wheelchair accessible walk (300m), allowing relaxing, all-encompassing views of Kata Tjuta. The **sunset-viewing area** (toilets available) is near the starting points for the two walks.

Olga Gorge walk. (2.6km; 45min.) An easy path that heads straight between a pair of the most daunting domes. The dome on the right is **Mt. Olga** (546m), the highest peak in the range. The lookout at the end is often crowded and the view is no more spectacular than the view from the numerous bridges on the walk.

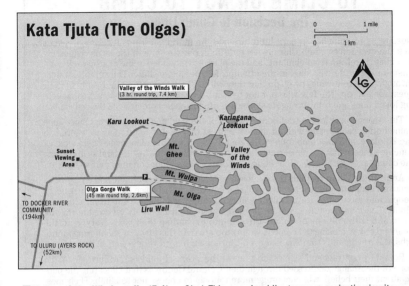

Kata Tjuta (The Olgas)

Valley of the Winds Walk
(3 hr. round trip, 7.4 km)

Karu Lookout

Karingana Lookout

Sunset Viewing Area

Mt. Ghee

Valley of the Winds

P

Mt. Wulpa

Olga Gorge Walk
(45 min round trip, 2.6km)

Mt. Olga

TO DOCKER RIVER COMMUNITY (194km)

Liru Wall

TO ULURU (AYERS ROCK) (52km)

0 — 1 mile
0 — 1 km

■ **Valley of the Winds walk.** (7.4km; 3hr.) This amazing hike traces a majestic circuit through the outer wall of **domes** and into the inner sanctuary. A short and at times steep hike leads to the first of 2 lookouts, offering vistas of the lush valleys running between the humps. After the lookout, the trail splits, going both north and south in a loop. To the south, you head through a narrow gap, emerging at a long set of natural steps. At the top of these steps is the walk's highlight, the **Karingana lookout.** A sweeping view into the gorge, this view is one of the best and least crowded. From there, the trail traces along the base of a dome, bordered on one side by textured stone and on the other by the endless expanse of desert, eventually circling back to the first lookout.

TO CLIMB OR NOT TO CLIMB
The Decision to Climb Uluru

Despite its prominence in park literature and the moral questions it raises, it seems that the decision to climb Uluru is not a difficult one. In spite of the signs requesting that visitors refrain from climbing, and the plaques embedded in the nearby rock commemorating those who died in the attempt, few people hesitate. They climb straight through, eyes following the chain that they will pull against and strain beside in their quest for the top. The few who opt not to climb sit calmly on nearby benches, watching loved ones and total strangers shrink out of existence as they scale the red giant.

The Anangu people, the traditional owners of the land and its caretakers since time immemorial, calmly, and without malice, request that visitors do not climb. Uluru is a sacred place, and the climb follows the route of the ancestral Mala men. There exists a genuine sadness that the dangerous climb is open to the public. As the land's caretakers, the community sees the death or injury of a climber as a failure on their part as hosts.

And yet the climb remains open, closed only when weather conditions conspire to make an accident almost certain. An agreement in the land lease between the Anangu people and Environment Australia means that the Anangu people can never close the climb. Too many people come to the Red Centre focused solely on conquering the rock, and with millions of dollars thrown into expanding the resort every year, the financial risk in closing the climb is simply too great. In this place of slumbering monoliths, the true giant is tourism, and even Uluru itself lies powerless before it.

Bound by contract and helpless to prevent the storm of tourists up Uluru's side, the hope of the Anangu, expressed through their Cultural Centre, is that educating the public about their beliefs will encourage more tourists to choose not to climb. Their message is reinforced by the park-wide effort to make clear that climbing the rock isn't the only option. The Cultural Centre's gift shop sells "I walked around Uluru" and "I didn't climb Uluru" bumper stickers to counter the resort's "I climbed Uluru" merchandise.

While the endless stream of tiny dots disappearing onto Uluru's top make clear that this message hasn't yet achieved widespread acceptance, there is a sense that the processes of cross-cultural exchange is taking place. The Cultural Centre houses a book of letters from visitors to the park who sent back bits of rock, or even sand, that they had previously removed from Uluru, along with notes proclaiming, "I'm sorry, I didn't know…I didn't understand, but now I do…put this back where it belongs."

Although it is easy to blame visitors for cultural insensitivity, they aren't going up the rock as an affront to the Anangu—the challenge of the climb makes such casual carelessness unlikely. From teenagers to pensioners, visitors climb with eyes locked on the top, looking for something. Even objectors admit that the climb is a hearty challenge. For some, it is a mental and physical challenge. For others, walking on the coarse red stone and entering the temple of its crevices are spiritual experiences.

Every tourist that ventures into harsh central Australia is looking for something, looking for the "real" Outback. But after weeks of wandering through land labeled by locals, tour companies, and maps as "The Outback," you are left with the unsettling feeling there is no such thing. A quick glance at a pastoral map of the Northern Territory reveals that all that open expanse, that endless, wild, and rugged land, is actually privately owned cattle farms, most of it sectioned off by barbed wire and "Keep Out" signs.

At the top of Uluru, however, that doubt can be put to rest. Standing atop the beating heart of the Outback, you can at last find the emotion that vibrates in tune with the "real" Outback. The whole of the Australian sky, and the red sand it watches over, pours down onto that one place and puts a kind of capstone on the experience of exploring Australia. In the end, the decision of whether to climb rests with the individual. In the valley between cultural sensitivity and tourism dollars, between the search for knowledge and the quest for understanding, rests the open gateway to the climb.

Nick Horbaczewski is a Researcher-Writer for Let's Go: Australia 2003.

QUEENSLAND

If the continent's natural attractions could be condensed into one state, the result would look something like Queensland, Australia's deliciously layered natural paradise. Queensland changes, east to west, from reef islands to sandy shores, from hinterland rainforest to glowing red Outback. At the base of this fantasyland sits the capital city of Brisbane, a diverse and manageable urban break from the surf and sun, located on the southeastern border of the state. Traveling north, Queensland's coast crawls with backpackers year-round; with the same faces popping up in every town, the journey often feels like a never-ending party. The downside for those on this heavily-touristed route is that real Aussie culture can be masked by the young crowd that floods its shores. Moving from one hot-spot to another can be mind-numbing as you wade through a neverending swamp of brochures, billboards, and tourist packages.

The enjoyment of a Queensland visit will multiply the more you step off this beaten track. Those willing to temporarily trade sandals for hiking boots can explore the rainforest-drenched far north and the jewel-bedecked Outback, where history, like tourism, proceeds at a koala's pace. Inland, you'll encounter charming country towns, pockets of thriving Aboriginal culture, and plenty of history—all without a hint of the rampant tourism of the coast. Across the entire state, opportunities abound for workers seeking to make money and camaraderie as part of the flourishing fruit-picking subculture. In Queensland, appreciating Oz at its extremes can be as simple as driving toward Cape Tribulation and watching the rainforest melt into the pounding surf.

QUEENSLAND HIGHLIGHTS

GREAT BARRIER REEF. Dive this natural wonder and frolic among shimmering schools of fish. (p. 296)

FRASER ISLAND. Fulfill your deepest, darkest 4WD fantasies on the island's massive sand dunes. (p. 352)

TOWN OF 1770. Rent a "tinny" or body board on 1770's prime (and largely untouristed) beaches. (p. 360)

EUNGELLA NATIONAL PARK. Hike through lush rainforest and misty valleys filled with giant ferns. (p. 373)

CAPE TRIBULATION. Drive the rough 'n' tumble Bloomfield Track or camp on a secluded rainforest beach. (p. 420)

▐ TRANSPORTATION

The Queensland coast as far north as Cairns, along with the far north and its interior, is comprehensively serviced by public transportation. Don't underestimate the distances involved; even within the state, many people choose to fly if they want to get from Brisbane to Cairns quickly. If you've got the time for a leisurely trip, though, taking a bus up the coast allows you to stop at innumerable spots along the way. The major bus lines is **McCafferty's/Greyhound** (☎ 13 20 30 or ☎ 13 14 99), and the train line is **Queensland Rail** (☎ 13 22 32). If you have a few friends to chip in for costs or if you're traveling with a family, **renting a car**

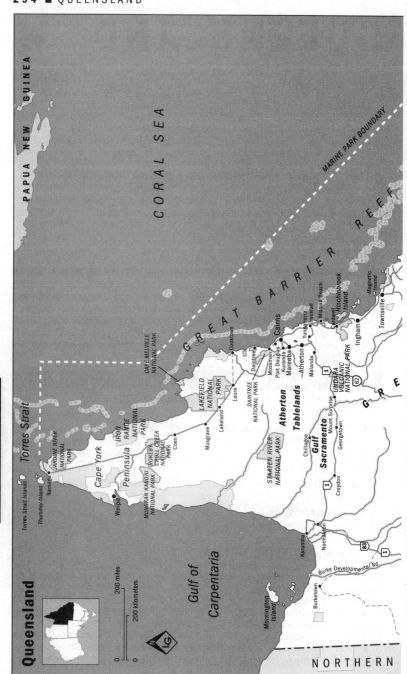

QUEENSLAND

PAPUA NEW GUINEA

CORAL SEA

MARINE PARK BOUNDARY

GREAT BARRIER REEF

Torres Strait

CAPE MELVILLE
NATIONAL PARK

Cooktown

Daintree
Mossman
Port Douglas   Cairns
Kuranda
Mareeba   Atherton
Yungaburra
Malanda   Mission Beach
Tully
Cardwell   Hinchinbrook
Ingham   Island
Magnetic
Island
Townsville

Torres Strait Islands
Thursday Island

Bamaga

JARDINE RIVER
NATIONAL
PARK

IRON
RANGE
NATIONAL
PARK

Cape York
Peninsula

Weipa

MUNGKAN KANDJU
NATIONAL PARK

ROKEBY–
CROLL CREEK
NATIONAL
PARK

Coen

Musgrave

Lakeland

Laura

LAKEFIELD
NATIONAL
PARK

DAINTREE
NATIONAL PARK

Atherton
Tablelands

STAATEN RIVER
NATIONAL PARK

UNDARA
VOLCANIC
NATIONAL PARK

G R E

Chillagoe

Mount Surprise

Gulf
Sacramento

Georgetown

Croydon

Normanton

Karumba

Gulf of
Carpentaria

Mornington
Island

Burketown

Burke Developmental Rd

NORTHERN

Queensland

200 miles
200 kilometers
0
0

LG

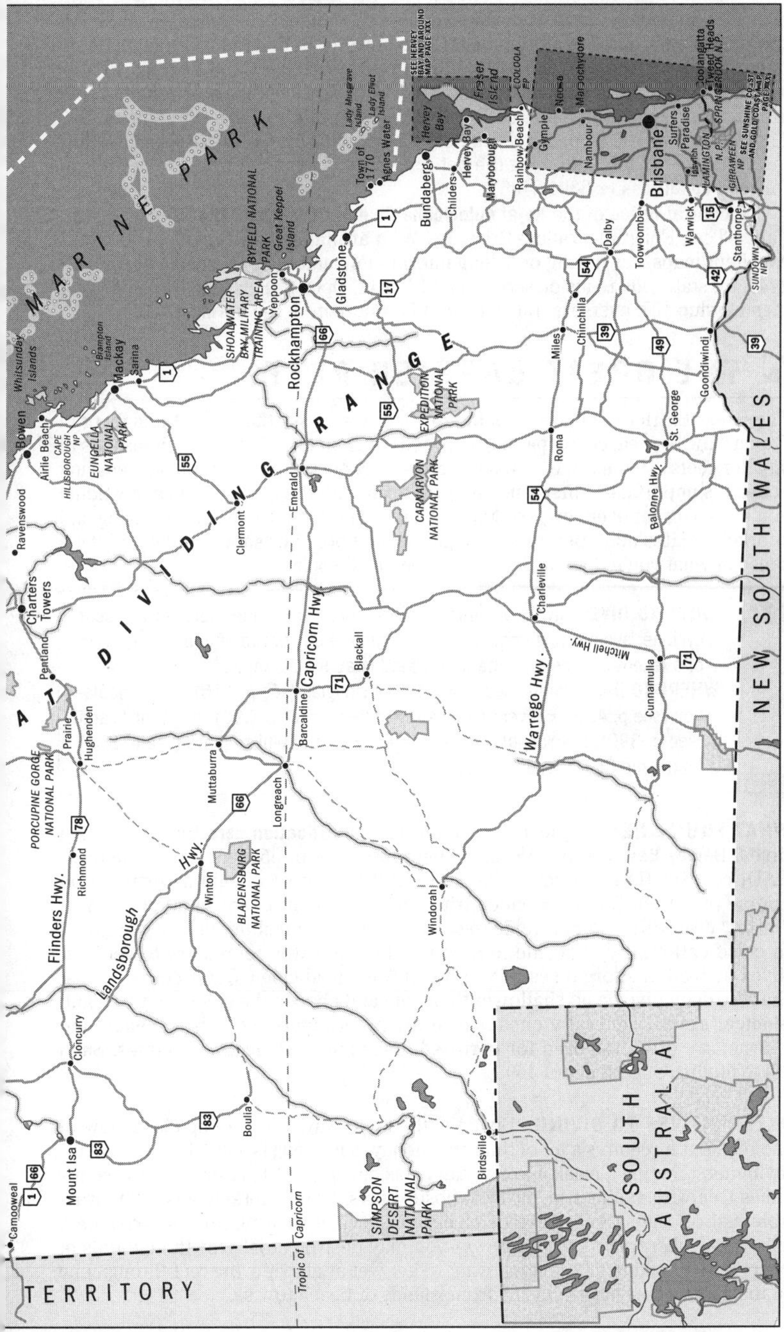
MARINE PARK
GREAT DIVIDING RANGE
NEW SOUTH WALES
SOUTH AUSTRALIA
TERRITORY
Tropic of Capricorn
Whitsunday Islands
Bowen
Airlie Beach
CAPE HILLSBOROUGH NP
EUNGELLA NATIONAL PARK
Brampton Island
Mackay
Sarina
SHOALWATER BAY MILITARY TRAINING AREA
BYFIELD NATIONAL PARK
Great Keppel Island
Yeppoon
Rockhampton
Gladstone
Town of 1770
Agnes Water
Lady Musgrave Island
Lady Elliot Island
Bundaberg
Childers
Hervey Bay
Maryborough
Fraser Island
SEE HERVEY BAY AND AROUND MAP PAGE XX
COOLOOLA NP
Rainbow Beach
Gympie
Noosa
Maroochydore
Nambour
Brisbane
Surfers Paradise
Ipswich
LAMINGTON N.P.
GIRRAWEEN NP
Coolangatta
Tweed Heads
SPRINGBROOK N.P.
SEE SUNSHINE COAST AND GOLD COAST MAP, PAGE XXX
Toowoomba
Warwick
Stanthorpe
SUNDOWN NP
Dalby
Chinchilla
Miles
Goondiwindi
St. George
Roma
EXPEDITION NATIONAL PARK
CARNARVON NATIONAL PARK
Emerald
Clermont
Ravenswood
Charters Towers
Pentland
Prairie
Hughenden
PORCUPINE GORGE NATIONAL PARK
Flinders Hwy.
Richmond
Landsborough Hwy.
Winton
BLADENSBURG NATIONAL PARK
Muttaburra
Longreach
Barcaldine
Capricorn Hwy.
Blackall
Charleville
Mitchell Hwy.
Warrego Hwy.
Cunnamulla
Balonne Hwy.
Windorah
Cloncurry
Mount Isa
Camooweal
Boulia
Birdsville
SIMPSON DESERT NATIONAL PARK
1
15
17
39
42
49
54
55
66
71
78
83

QUEENSLAND

provides the most convenience and freedom to wander off the beaten track. All the major car rental establishments are here, plus dozens of cheaper local ones. To tackle the area from Cooktown north through Cape York as well as some of the desert roads, you'll need **4WD.** This is pricey; it's also tough to find an automatic transmission 4WD (try **Allcar Rentals** in Port Douglas, ☎ 4099 4123). Roads in the tropics are especially harrowing, and often impassible, during and immediately following the **wet season** (Nov.-Apr.). It's best to call ahead for **road conditions** (☎ 3361 2406).

The central office of the **Royal Automobile Club of Queensland (RACQ)** is at 300 St. Paul's Tce., Fortitude Valley, Brisbane. With affiliations worldwide, RACQ has excellent maps, car buying or selling information, and technical services. (☎ 3361 2444, for statewide roadside service call 13 11 11. Open M-F 8:30am-5:30pm. 1-year membership $67, overseas transfer free.) For more info, see **Driving**, p. 33.

◪ THE GREAT BARRIER REEF

The Great Barrier Reef stretches for 2300km from just offshore of Bundaberg to Papua New Guinea, encompassing hundreds of islands and cays and thousands of smaller reefs. This marine wonderland is easily accessible from the Queensland coast. It's important to first familiarize yourself with the types of reef and wildlife you'll see (for an overview, see **Marine Life**, p. 11). *Let's Go* describes diving and snorkeling sites and operators throughout the book, but shop around and get a sense of what you're looking for before you decide on a dive.

> **WHEN TO DIVE:** July to December., November spawntime, north of a recent cyclone; avoid diving from January to March, a day or two after a storm, south of a recent cyclone, or if the wind speed is above 20 knots.
> **WHERE TO DIVE:** Cairns (see p. 400), Port Douglas (see p. 416), Cape Tribulation (see p. 420), Beaver Cay (in Mission Beach; see p. 396), Magnetic Island (see p. 390), *S.S.Yongala* wreck (see p. 388), the Whitsundays (see p. 380) from Airlie Beach (see p. 375).

WHAT YOU'LL NEED. Queensland requires a **certification card** for all certified dives. **Hervey Bay** (see p. 348) and **Bundaberg** (see p. 357) have the cheapest PADI certification courses in the state. But before you begin a certification course or set out for an extended trip, you might want to try an **introductory** or **"resort" dive** with a trained guide to see what diving's all about before you invest in certification. If you decide to do a PADI open water course, try to get boat dives instead of shore dives. If you do an Advanced Open Water course, insist that the deep dive be no shallower than 30m and choose the electives you want. **Medical exams,** generally cheapest in diving hotspots like Airlie Beach and Cairns, are often required for certified dives and certification courses. Such "dive medicals" cost about $60.

ALTERNATIVES TO DIVING. Diving is the ideal way to get an up-close view of the reef, but it requires a lot of time and money. **Snorkeling** is a good alternative for swimmers; renting a mask and fins can be as cheap as $10 per day. Gear is sometimes free with sailing trips or even hostel stays. Good snorkeling is often available just off the shore of islands or beaches. When wearing fins, *be extremely aware of where you are flapping*—you may destroy coral growth hundreds of years in the making. If you don't want to get wet at all, view the reef through one of the **glass-bottom boats** cruising from islands or beach tow ns.

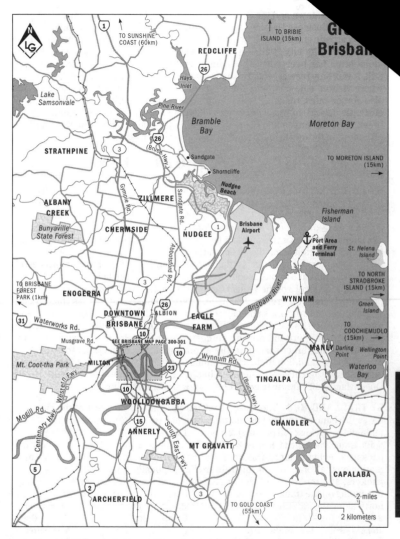

BRISBANE ☎ 07

Commonly unexplored (and unappreciated) by those on the coastal pilgrimage, **Brisbane** (pop. 1,600,000) spreads around its central river with a wide spectrum of interests and attractions. Contrasting riverside to hillside, parkland to high-rise, alterna-chic to yuppie, and classy to seedy, Brisbane today is neither glamorous nor industrial, but instead practical, clean, and full of youthful energy.

The Brisbane River lends an easygoing grace to the city through which it winds. River transportation is simple and pleasant—hulking ferries and slim kayaks glide

ι the South Bank Parklands, between investment banks in
ιstrict and cafes in the trendy West End. The mild climate
ς eager to shed winter jumpers and rev up the city's cultural
is always a good bet for temporary employment, though
. somewhat dampened by the recent economic downturn.
ιtly that Brisbane earned a reputation as a tourist destination.
not only the serene waterfront and peaceful parklands, but
ιcking nightclubs, and live local music. Despite its energy and
owever, Brisbane's daytime attractions can be limited. For a
stle and bustle of city life, the nearby islands of Moreton Bay
offer alma.____ ιdeveloped sand, surf, and seaside hospitality.

◩ INTERCITY TRANSPORTATION

BY PLANE. Brisbane International Airport, 17km (25min.) northwest of the city, has
luggage storage ($4-10 per day) and is served by 23 airlines, including **Qantas,** 247
Adelaide St. (☎3238 2700 or 13 13 13; open M-F 8:30am-5pm, Sa 9am-1pm) and **Virgin Blue** (☎13 67 89; open daily 5am-10pm), a domestic budget airline. The **Travellers Information Service** is located on level 2 of the international terminal, 3km from
the domestic terminal via the $3 **Coachtrans** bus. (☎3406 3190. Open from the first
flight in the morning until the last flight of the night.) The **Roma Street Transit Centre**
in town has info and books accommodations on level 3 (see below).

SkyTrans, on level 3 of the Transit Centre, runs a daily **shuttle bus** between the airport and Transit Centre. (☎3860 6999. Every 30min. 8am-9pm; last bus to city
11:10pm. $9, return $15, same-day return $12, children $5.) A trip to one of the
major hotels costs $11, return $17, and is cheaper for multiple people. A **taxi**
between the airport and downtown costs about $27. Privately owned, **Airtrain**
recently began direct service to the airport, making connections to both Brisbane's Queensland Rail in the city (25min., every 15-30min., $9) and Surfers Paradise (2hr.; 2 per hr.; $21, includes bus transfers). Timetable available from
Queensland Rail's **Transinfo** (☎13 12 30; www.transinfo.qld.gov.au).

BY TRAIN AND BUS. The **Roma Street Transit Centre,** 500m west of the city center, is Brisbane's intercity bus and train terminal. (☎3236 2020. Open daily 4:30am-midnight.). Lockers ($5 per day) are on level 1 and 3; showers are on level 2.

By train, **Queensland Rail** (☎3235 2222; bookings ☎13 22 32; reservations for
packages, including air and accommodations ☎1800 627 655) has offices at Central
Station on the corner of Ann and Edward St., diagonally opposite the Palace Backpackers, and on level 1 of the Transit Centre. Travel times vary considerably
depending on the train. The snazzy new **Tilt Train** is the fastest way to travel; it runs
north along the coast from Brisbane to Rockhampton (book ahead). Trains run to:
Bundaberg (4¼-7½hr., 2-3 per day, $56.10); **Cairns** (32hr., 4 per week, $176); **Gladstone** (6-9¾hr., 1-3 per day, $78.10); **Mackay** (18hr., 6 per week, $130); **Maryborough West** (3½-6¼hr.; 2 per day; $48.40, with connecting bus to **Hervey Bay** $54); **Proserpine** (19½hr., 6 per week, $135.30); **Rockhampton** (7-11½hr., 1-3 per day, $88); **Sydney**
(16hr., 2 per day, $110); and **Townsville** (24hr., 6 per week, $153). Students with ID
and children under 16 travel for half-price.

For long travel itineraries, Queensland Rail's **Sunshine Rail Pass** is good for a
given number of travel days within a six-month span on any Queensland service
and unlimited travel on **Citytrain,** the intracity network. Passes available at the
Queensland Rail booth at Roma Street Transit Centre or Central Station. (14-day
$292, 21-day $338, 30-day $424; students and children half-price. Book ahead.)
There are many other passes available to overseas travelers.

By bus, **McCafferty's/Greyhound** (☎13 14 99) covers destinations along the east coast and offers 10% discounts for ISIC/VIP/YHA and 20% for seniors and children. Adults receive 5% discounts on return fares. **Premier Coach Service** (☎13 34 10) grants 15% discounts for all concessions. **Kirklands Coaches** (☎1300 367 077), with service to the Gold Coast and Byron Bay, gives 25% discounts to YHA holders and seniors and 50% discounts to children. **Suncoast Pacific** (☎3236 1901) also services the Queensland coast and offers ISIC/YHA/VIP holders 20% discounts, seniors 10% discounts, and children 30% discounts. See table, p. 302.

■ ORIENTATION

The Brisbane River meanders through the city, creating easily identifiable landmarks. The river is breached by the **Victoria Bridge,** which connects the city to South Bank. The **Transit Centre** is located on Roma St.; a left turn out of the building and a five-minute walk southeast down Roma crosses **Turbot St.** and leads to the corner of **Albert** and **Ann St.** and the grassy **King George Square** (a front lawn for the grand **City Hall**). **Adelaide St.** forms the far side of the square. One block farther, the **Queen St. Mall** runs parallel; it's a popular pedestrian thoroughfare lined with shops and cafes and the center of Brisbane proper. Underneath the mall and the adjoining **Myer Centre** shopping complex is the **Queen St. Bus Station.**

If you know the British Royal family, you'll have no problem memorizing the streets of the city; continuing south from Queen St., the parallel east-west streets are **Elizabeth, Charlotte, Mary, Margaret, and Alice St.;** Alice borders the **Botanic Gardens.** Intersecting these streets north-south, from the river, are the major streets **William, George, Albert, Edward, and Creek St.**

Brisbane's neighborhoods radiate out from the city center. A right turn out of Roma St. (the commonly used term for the Transit Centre) leads to **Petrie Terrace** and **Paddington,** both most easily reached by passing under the railway bridge and taking the first left up the hill. North of Boundary St. is **Spring Hill,** bordered to the west by **Victoria Park** and a 15-minute walk from the Queen St. Mall up steep Edward St. A 15-minute walk down Ann St., the nightclub-heavy **Fortitude Valley** offers an alternative scene but contains some slightly seedy areas. Fortitude Valley is also home to the small but authentic **Chinatown,** which has served as the film location for several Jackie Chan flicks. Down Brunswick St., at the intersection with Hardcourt St., begins **New Farm,** with its free art galleries and cafes. South of the river, the Victoria Bridge footpath turns into Melbourne St. and heads into **South Brisbane,** crossing Boundary St. six blocks later in the heart of the **West End.** **South Bank** is to the east of the southern end of the bridge; farther along the riverside, **Kangaroo Point** forms a peninsula into the River.

Fortitude Valley and the **West End** can be unsafe, especially at night. Use caution if walking after dark. *Let's Go* recommends hitting the nightlife in groups.

■ LOCAL TRANSPORTATION

BY TRAIN. Citytrain, (Transinfo ☎13 12 30; www.transinfo.qld.gov.au), Queensland Rail's intracity train network, has three major stations and numerous stops throughout the city. The main transit center is at **Roma St.; Central Station** is at Ann and Edward St.; the final station is at **Brunswick St.** One-zone journeys in the city cost $1.80, three zones $3.80. One-day unlimited travel is $8.60, three zones $21.60. (Trains run every 15-30min. M-Th 5am-11:30pm, F 5am-2am, Sa 6am-1am, Su 6am-11pm; times are variable for different destinations. All return trips are free Sa-Su; return is 30% off M-F after 9am. Students and backpackers half-price.)

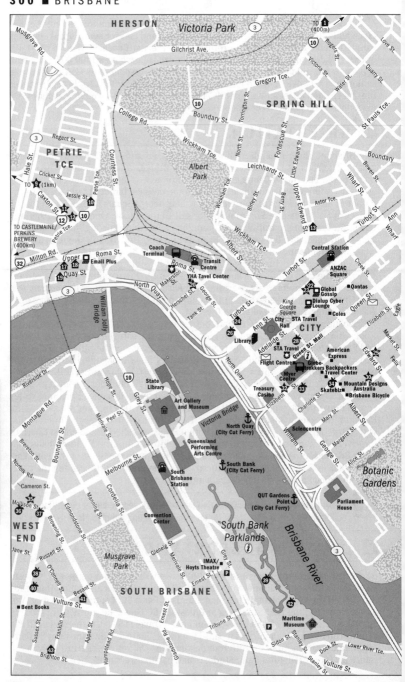

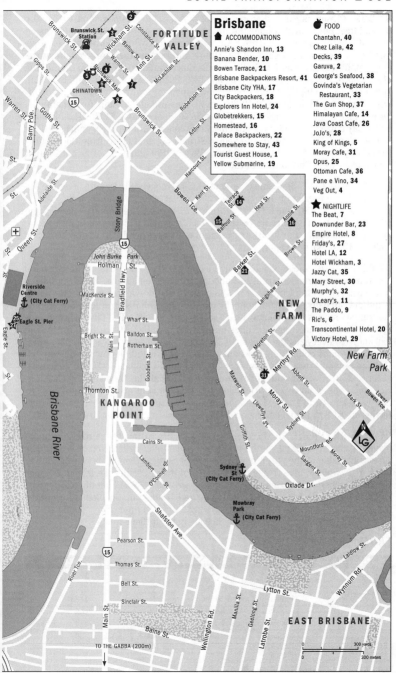

Brisbane

🏠 ACCOMMODATIONS

Annie's Shandon Inn, 13
Banana Bender, 10
Bowen Terrace, 21
Brisbane Backpackers Resort, 41
Brisbane City YHA, 17
City Backpackers, 18
Explorers Inn Hotel, 24
Globetrekkers, 15
Homestead, 16
Palace Backpackers, 22
Somewhere to Stay, 43
Tourist Guest House, 1
Yellow Submarine, 19

🍎 FOOD

Chantahn, 40
Chez Laila, 42
Decks, 39
Garuva, 2
George's Seafood, 38
Govinda's Vegetarian
  Restaurant, 33
The Gun Shop, 37
Himalayan Cafe, 14
Java Coast Cafe, 26
JoJo's, 28
King of Kings, 5
Moray Cafe, 31
Opus, 25
Ottoman Cafe, 36
Pane e Vino, 34
Veg Out, 4

★ NIGHTLIFE

The Beat, 7
Downunder Bar, 23
Empire Hotel, 8
Friday's, 27
Hotel LA, 12
Hotel Wickham, 3
Jazzy Cat, 35
Mary Street, 30
Murphy's, 32
O'Leary's, 11
The Paddo, 9
Ric's, 6
Transcontinental Hotel, 20
Victory Hotel, 29

QUEENSLAND

BY BUS. Citybus is the "all-stops" major service. Most buses depart from the **Queen Street Bus Station,** a huge terminal beneath the Myer Center and the Queen St. Mall. Platforms are named after Australian animals, while central city stops are numbered. Schedules organized by suburb and bus number are availabe at the very helpful **Queen Street Bus Station Info Centre,** located on the ground floor of the Myer Centre. (Open M-Th 8:30am-5:30pm, F 8:30am-8pm, Sa 9am-4pm, Su 10am-4pm.) Most bus stops also post times and a map for that particular route; otherwise contact Transinfo (☎ 13 12 30; www.transinfo.qld.gov.au) for timetables. Fares range from $1.80 to $3.80 (day pass $8.40, concessions $4.20). The blue and white **City Circle bus** #333 runs a frequent city center circuit (M-F), convenient for sight-seeing (90¢). The white and yellow striped **Cityxpress** runs from the suburbs to the city approximately every 30min. Buses #190 and #191 offer convenient routes from West End to New Farm.

BY CAR AND TAXI. ShoeString Car Rentals, 360 Nudgee Rd., Hendra, near the airport, rents from $29 per day. (☎3268 3334. Open M-Sa 7:30am-5pm, Su 7:30am-2pm.) **Integra,** 398 St. Paul's Tce., Fortitude Valley, also rents from $29 per day and offers pickup from the airport. (☎ 1800 067 414. Open M-F 7:30am-5:30pm, Sa 8am-4pm, Su 8am-3pm.) For a **taxi,** try **Yellow Cab Company** (☎ 13 19 24) or **Black and White** (☎ 13 10 08); both operate 24hr.

BY FERRY. Brisbane's excellent ferry system makes good use of the Brisbane River, providing practical transport and cheap sightseeing tours. The sleek **CityCat** runs upstream to the University of Queensland and downstream to Bretts Wharf (CityCats run daily every 20-30min., 5:50am-10:30pm; blue sign at ferry stops). The central city stop is North Quay, near the Treasury Casino. The **City Ferry** operates around the city center and includes more stops than the CityCat (city ferries run daily at least every 20-30min. 6am-10:30pm; red sign at ferry stops). The **Crossriver** runs four routes connecting Brisbane's two banks, including downtown from the Holman St. and Edward St. stops (daily every 15min. 5:30am-10:30pm; green sign at ferry stop). The convenient **day rover pass** allows all-day travel on CityCats, ferries, and council buses ($8.40). Schedules are posted at every dock and stop, or call Transinfo (☎ 13 12 30; www.transinfo.qld.gov.au) for timetables. Fares for all ferries are $1.80-3.80 depending on distance; Aussie students get 50% discounts.

BY BIKE OR IN-LINE SKATES. In Brisbane City alone there are 350km of cycling paths. The City Council publishes a pamphlet called *Brisbane Bicycle Maps,* available at the City Council Customer Service Centre, 69 Ann St., lower level. You can also bike to sights like Mt. Coot-tha or Stradbroke Island. **Brisbane Bicycle,** 87 Albert St., carries a range of bikes. (☎3229 2433. $12 per hr., $25 per day. Open M-Th 8:30am-5:30pm, F 8:30am-8pm, Sa 8:30am-5pm, Su 10am-4pm.) **Skatebiz,** 101 Albert St., rents in-line skates. (☎3220 0157. $11 per 2hr., $27.50 per day. Open M-Th 9am-5:30pm, F 9am-9pm, Sa 9am-4pm, Su 10am-4pm.)

FROM BRISBANE TO:

DESTINATION	COMPANY	DURATION	PER DAY	PRICE
Adelaide	McCafferty's	40hr.	1	$232
Airlie Beach	McCafferty's	18¼hr.	5	$144
	Premier	18¼hr.	1	$123
Bundaberg	McCafferty's	6-7½hr.	4	$58
	Premier	6-7¾hr.	1	$43
Byron Bay	Kirkland's	3½hr.	4 M-F, 2 Sa-Su	$29
	McCafferty's	3½hr.	7	$35
	Premier	3½hr.	3	$31

QUEENSLAND

DESTINATION	COMPANY	DURATION	PER DAY	PRICE
Cairns	McCafferty's	25-30hr.	7	$192
	Premier	25-30hr.	1	$175
Coolangatta/Tweed Heads	Kirkland's	2¼hr.	4 M-F, 2 Sa-Su	$14.50
	McCafferty's	2¼hr.	7	$17
	Premier	2¼hr.	3	$14
Hervey Bay	McCafferty's	6hr.	8	$43
	Premier	5hr.	1	$32
Lismore	Kirkland's	4½hr.	4 M-F, 2 Sa-Su	$33
	McCafferty's	5½hr.	1	$39
	Premier	4½hr.	1	$34
Mackay	McCafferty's	15-16hr.	6	$127
	Premier	15-16hr.	1	$109
Maroochydore	McCafferty's	2hr.	4	$18
	Premier	2hr.	1	$18
	Suncoast	2hr	8 Su-F, 6 Sa	$22.50
Melbourne	McCafferty's	24hr.	1	$182
Mission Beach	McCafferty's	26hr.	4	$187
	Premier	26hr.	1	$168
Mooloolooba	Premier	2-3hr.	1	$18
	Suncoast	2hr.	8 Su-F, 6 Sa	$22.50
Noosa	McCafferty's	2-3hr.	5	$21
	Premier	2-3hr.	1	$18
	Suncoast	2-3hr.	7 Su-F, 5 Sa	$26
Rockhampton	McCafferty's	12hr.	6	$83
	Premier	10-14hr.	1	$76
Surfers Paradise	Kirkland's	1¼-1½hr.	4 M-F, 2 Sa-Su	$14.50
	McCafferty's	1¼-1½hr.	7	$17
	Premier	1¼-1½hr.	3	$14
Sydney	McCafferty's	16-19hr.	6	$93
	Premier	16-19hr.	3	$84
Toowoomba	McCafferty's	2hr.	14	$21

⚡ PRACTICAL INFORMATION

TOURIST AND FINANCIAL SERVICES

Tourist Office: The very busy **Brisbane Marketing Information Booth** (☎3006 6290) is in the middle of the Queen St. Mall, providing info only on companies that are part of its association. Open M-Th 9am-5:30pm, F 9am-8pm, Sa 9am-5pm, Su 9:30am-4:30am. The *Brisbane Visitors'* guide is available at most tourist booths. The **Information Centre** (☎3236 2020), on the 3rd Fl. of the Transit Centre, provides information on accommodations and attractions. Open M-F 7:30am-5:30pm, Sa-Su 8am-4pm.

Budget Travel Offices: Flight Centre (☎3229 9550 or 13 16 00) has 11 offices in the city and a guarantee to beat any quoted current price. Myer Centre office, in front of Coles, open M-Th 9am-5:30pm, F 9am-8pm, Sa 9am-4pm, Su 10:30am-4pm. **STA Travel,** 111 and 57 Adelaide St. (☎13 17 76). Both offices open M-F 9am-5:30pm; 111 Adelaide open Sa 9am-3pm, 57 Adelaide open Sa 10am-4pm. **Backpackers Travel Centre,** 138 Albert St. (☎3221 2225). Open M-F 9am-6pm, Sa 10am-4pm. **YHA Travel Centre,** 154 Roma St. (☎3236 1680), across from the Transit Centre. Open M-Tu and Th-F 8:30am-5pm, W 9am-5pm, Sa 9am-3pm.

Consulate: British Consul, L26, 1 Eagle St. (☎3223 3200).

Banks: Banks on Boundary St. in South Brisbane, Brunswick St. in the Valley, and Queen St. in the city. Most are open M-Th 9:30am-4pm, F 9:30am-5pm. Typically $5 charge for traveler's checks and cash exchange. **ATMs** are located throughout the city. **Ameri-**

IN RECENT NEWS

THE POTTY ROBBERY

In Aussie terms, it's the loo, the toilet, the dunny. For the backpacker, often without a room (or toilet) of her own, it's a small space of privacy in a very public world. That's why we Americans refer to it as a restroom. However, in a Brisbane bathroom, deep in the heart of the city on the Queen Street Mall, I rested a moment too long—and was done in by the dunny.

I was sitting with my head in my hands when a slight rustling sound caused me to raise my eyes to the bathroom door, just in time to see my bag—with wallet, pens, tape recorder, and (heaven forbid) my field copy of *Let's Go: Australia 2002* with notes—lifted up and over the top. Horrified, I scrambled to my feet (yelling inarticulate threats), tripped over my pants (nearly falling head first and forgetting to do the pants up until much later), and rushed out the dunny door. By this time, the thief was nowhere in sight, and I became convinced that he or she was still in the bathroom. I then proceeded to beat down the locked door of another stall, only to realize that its occupant was not my potty robber, but an elderly and very frightened woman. The thief was gone, melted into the anonymous late-day crowds of the city.

My potty robber has taught me a few things. One, keep your wallet close to you, even if it's in the zippered pocket in the pants around your ankles. Two, a bag snatching can happen anywhere, even within the deceptive quiet of the dunny. And three, a dunny is not a home. You should do your business there, and then continue on your way. **—Abby Schlatter**

can Express, 131 Elizabeth St. (☎3229 2729), is open M-F 9am-5pm, Sa 9am-noon.

Work Opportunities: Work and Travel Centre (☎3236 4899; www.backpackersaustralia.com.au) has a desk on level 3 of the Transit Centre. $15 registration fee. Open M-F 8am-8pm, Sa-Su 9am-6pm

LOCAL SERVICES

Backpacking and Camping Equipment: Equipment stores line Albert St. between Elizabeth and Mary St. **Globetrekker,** 142 Albert St. (☎3221 4476). Open M-F 9am-6pm, Sa 9am-4:30pm, Su 10:30am-4:30pm. **Mountain Designs Australia,** 105 Albert St. (☎3221 6756). Open M-Th 9am-5:30pm, F 9am-8pm, Sa 9am-5pm, Su 10:30am-4:30pm. YHA and student discounts.

Bookstores: The Queen St. Mall area has many bookstores. **Bent Books,** 205a Boundary St. (☎3846 5004), in the West End, has a broad collection of secondhand books available to purchase or trade. Open in summer Su-Th 10:30am-6pm, F-Sa 10:30am-9pm; in winter daily 10:30am-6pm.

Library: The **State Library** (☎3840 7666), in South Bank, part of the Cultural Centre. Open M-Th 10am-8pm, F-Su 10am-5pm. Call ☎3840 7785 to book free 1hr. **Internet** access. The **John Oxley Library** (☎3840 7880), on level 4, is devoted to Queensland research and history and holds historical exhibitions. Open Su-F 10am-5pm. Both libraries are reference only. The **Central City Library** (☎3403 4166), on the corner of Ann and George St. in the City Plaza, allows book borrowing and free **Internet** access; book ahead. Open M-F 9am-6pm, Sa-Su 10am-3pm.

Public Markets: Brunswick Markets, on Brunswick St. Mall, Fortitude Valley, is a hippie scene of second-hand items, clothes, and toys. Open Sa 9am-2pm. **Riverside Markets,** along the riverfront on Eagle St. between the Riverside Complex and Eagle St. Pier. Open Su 8am-4pm. For fresh produce, **Farmers' Markets** take place the 2nd and 4th Saturday of every month (8am-2pm) at the Powerhouse Museum in New Farm. The **South Bank Markets** (see **South Bank Parklands,** p. 309) run weekends.

Used Cars: Cheap but Good Cars, 41 McLachlan St., Fortitude Valley (☎3252 7322), with cars from $1000-3000. Open M-Sa 8am-6pm.

Emergency: ☎000. **Police:** ☎3364 6464.

Crisis Lines: Statewide Sexual Assault Helpline ☎1800 010 120. **Suicide Prevention Medical Specialist** ☎1300 360 980.

Pharmacy: Queen St. Mall Day and Night Pharmacy, 141 Queen St. (☎3221 4585), on the mall. Open M-F 7am-9pm, Sa 8am-9pm, Su 8:30am-5:30pm.

Hospital: Travellers Medical Service, Level 1, 245 Albert St. (☎3211 3611). Open M-F 7:30am-7pm, Sa 8:30am-5pm, Su 9:30am-4pm. **Brisbane Sexual Health Clinic,** Level 1, 270 Roma St. (☎3227 8666), offers **free testing.** Open M-Tu and F 9am-5pm, W 8am-noon, Th 10am-5pm; 7:30pm-late by appointment only.

Internet: State Library and **Central City Library** (see above). The several Internet cafes on Adelaide St., between Albert and Edward St., are convenient but access is much cheaper in the Valley. **Dialup Cyber Lounge,** 126 Adelaide St. (☎3211 9095). $4.40 per hr. Open M-Sa 9am-7:30pm, Su 10am-6pm. The pricey **Global Gossip,** 288 Edward St. (☎3229 4033), next to Backpackers Palace, offers fax and copy services in addition to Internet. $6 per hr. Open daily 8am-midnight. **Email Plus,** 328 Upper Roma St. (☎3236 0433). $4 per hr., $1 per 10min. Open daily 9am-late.

Post Office: GPO, 261 Queen St. (☎3405 1434; Poste Restante ☎3405 1448). Half a block from the end of the mall. Open M-F 7am-6pm. Poste Restante open 9am-5pm. For weekend mail, try Wintergarden Center Level 2 (☎3405 1380). Open M-Th 8:30am-5:30pm, F 8:30am-7pm, Sa 9am-4pm. **Postal Code:** 4000 (city); 4001 (GPO).

MEDIA AND PUBLICATIONS
Newspaper: *The Courier-Mail* ($1), or pick up a free *Quest* community paper.
Nightlife: *Time Off, Scene* and *Rave* magazines (free). For info on gay and lesbian nightlife, check out *qp.*
Radio: Rock, Triple M 104.5FM, B105FM, or Triple J 107.7FM; News, 936AM; Tourist Info, 88FM.

ACCOMMODATIONS

Accommodations cluster in four main areas of the city: the pricey and convenient city center; South Brisbane and West End, near the riverside parklands, Cultural Centre, and Boundary St.; Fortitude Valley and New Farm, with cafes, galleries, festivals, and a funky night pulse; and the Petrie Terrace area, less aesthetically pleasing but close to the Transit Centre and Caxton St. party scene. Most of the accommodations listed have pickup and drop-off. Unless otherwise noted, checkout is 10am and key deposit $10. Linen and cutlery are usually free with a deposit.

CITY CENTER
Palace Backpackers, 308 Edward St. (☎3211 2433 or 1800 676 340), on the corner of Ann St. Filling in peak times to its 350-person capacity, this 7-level building is a backpacker landmark. Near-nightly after-hour parties make for noisy halls. 3-story veranda, big kitchen, rockin' backpackers pub (see **Nightlife,** p. 312), Internet, roofdeck, and cafe. Job club. Laundry. Reception 24hr. 5- to 9-bed dorms $20, weekly $126; 3-4 bed dorms $23/$147; twins $26/$168; singles $36/$238; doubles $48/$308. EFTPOS. VIP. AmEx/MC/V. ❷

Explorers Inn Hotel, 63 Turbot St. (☎3211 3488 or 1800 623 288), near the corner of George St. Pleasant budget hotel with an affordable restaurant (meals $11). Compact rooms have bath and TV. Internet. Laundry. No smoking. Reception M-F 6:30am-10:30pm, Sa-Su 7am-10pm; late-night check-ins with advance notice. Singles, doubles, and twins $75; triples $86; quads $97. EFTPOS. AmEx/MC/V. ❺

Annie's Shandon Inn, 405 Upper Edward St., Spring Hill (☎3831 8684). Like Grandma's house, with family snapshots, cozy beds, and pastels. The perfect retreat after too many impersonal hostel dorms. Cold breakfast included. Kitchenette. Laundry. Reception daily 7am-9pm; late-night check-in with advance notice. Check-out 9am. Singles $48, ensuite $58; twins and doubles $58/$68; extra person $10. EFTPOS. AmEx/MC/V. ❹

FORTITUDE VALLEY AND NEW FARM

■ **Globetrekkers,** 35 Balfour St., New Farm (☎3358 1251; www.globetrekkers.net), between Brunswick St. and Bowen Tce. Friendly, small 1890s house with beautiful hardwood floors and furniture. Pool. Unlimited Internet $2. Laundry. Women's dorm. Park your campervan in back and enjoy access to the facilities for $10 per person. Dorms $17, weekly $98; singles $33, ensuite $38; twins and doubles $40/$44; family rooms $50. Reception 9am-9pm. Book ahead. ISIC/NOMADS/VIP/YHA. Cash only. ❷

Bowen Terrace, 365 Bowen Tce., New Farm (☎3254 0458), on the corner of Barker St. Warm colonial house with a mellow, hippie feel. Bedrooms vary; ask for the lovely double with the bathtub and fireplace. Lounge, small kitchen, and large deck; doubles have TV and fridge. Singles $30; twins $40; doubles $44, ensuite $50. Cash only. ❸

Homestead, 57 Annie St., New Farm (☎/fax 3254 1609 or 1800 658 344). Giant murals and rooms with names like "Romeo and Juliet" (the honeymoon suite) and "Blue Mountains" (for nature lovers). Social atmosphere on a quiet street; extremely popular among backpackers. Su BBQ and soccer match. Free bus to airport, Transit Centre, and city. Internet, laundry, TV lounge, kitchen, garden, free hostel outings, and free bike use. Reception daily 7am-7pm. Dorms $16, weekly $80; singles $35/$225; twins and doubles $42/$230. EFTPOS. VIP/YHA. AmEx/MC/V. ❷

Tourist Guest House, 555 Gregory Tce., Fortitude Valley (☎3252 4171 or 1800 800 589; tourist_guest_house@yahoo.com.au), a long trek from the city. Colonial style B&B with front porch; rooms have TV, sink, and fridge. A pleasant setting for families and couples. Dorms $20; singles $45, ensuite $55; twins and doubles $55/$65; triples $65/$80. ❷

PETRIE TERRACE

Yellow Submarine, 66 Quay St. (☎3211 3424). Painted bright yellow inside and out, this little house has a lot of character and community despite slightly tired rooms. Ken or Duncan cooks at least one free dinner a week. Outdoor TV lounge and a new pool. Laundry and kitchen. Courtesy van. Shared bath. No smoking. Book ahead. Reception daily 7am-10pm. 6-bed dorms $19, weekly $105; 3-bed dorms $21/$115; doubles and twins $46. Cash only. ❷

City Backpackers, 380 Upper Roma St. (☎3211 3221 or 1800 062 572). Big, orange building 400m from the Transit Centre. A larger hostel, with a social atmosphere and personable staff. Rooms are clean and comfortable; some are completely renovated. Enormous kitchen, rooftop dining with city views, Internet, laundry, and advanced security system. Courtesy bus. The Irish pub, **The Fiddler's Elbow,** has live music Tu and Sa. 4-, 6-, or 8-bed dorms $17-21; singles $42; twins and doubles $50. VIP/YHA. MC/V. ❷

Banana Bender, 118 Petrie Tce. (☎3367 1157), on the corner of Jessie St. One of the city's original small hostels, with a quiet, relaxed feel. Eating area with city view, Internet, laundry, kitchen, and TV lounge. Reception 7am-10pm. 4-bed dorms $20; 3-bed dorms $21; twins and doubles $23. VIP. Cash only. ❷

Brisbane City YHA, 392 Upper Roma St. (☎3236 1004). Private, clean, and low-key, with a friendly staff. Perfect for couples or friends, not for socialites. Kitchen, cafe, and reading loft. Lockers, laundry, and Internet. 6-bed dorms $19; 3-bed dorms $24; twins and doubles $52-56, ensuite $72. EFTPOS. YHA discount $3.50. MC/V. ❷

SOUTH BRISBANE

Somewhere to Stay, 45 Brighton Rd. (☎3844 6093 or 1800 812 398; reception@somewheretostay.com.au), entrance on Franklin St. A small, homey hostel. Large rooms with bath; some have city views. Swimming pool, big kitchen, tourist office, and free bus to city. Laundry. Internet $5 per hr. Reception 7am-10pm. Check-out 9:30am. 4-bed dorms $15-21, weekly from $90; singles $25-30, weekly from $150; doubles $39-58, weekly from $234. Wheelchair accessible. AmEx/MC/V. NOMADS/VIP/YHA. ❷

Brisbane Backpackers Resort, 110 Vulture St. (☎3844 9956 or 1800 626 452), near the corner of Boundary St. Rooms feel sterile and impersonal, but amenities are worth it. Rooms have bath, TV, fridge, and lockers; some have balconies. Free bus and refund on airport transfers. Tennis court, swimming pool, spa, game room, laundry, Internet, travel desk, bar, and cafe (brekkie $4-5; dinner $5). Reception 24hr. Check-out 9:30am. 8-bed dorms $16, weekly $96; 6-bed dorms $19/$114; 4-bed dorms $20/$120; singles, twins, and doubles $52/$325. EFTPOS. ISIC/VIP/YHA. AmEx/MC/V. ❷

◳ FOOD

The West End specializes in ethnic food and small sidewalk cafes, particularly along Boundary St. and Hardgrave Rd. Chinatown in Fortitude Valley has cheap Asian food, while trendier New Farm and the city center have more expensive eateries and coffee shops. Coles Express **supermarket** is in the Queen St. Mall, between Albert and George St. (Open M-F 8am-9pm, Sa 8am-5:30pm, Su 9am-6pm.) For ice cream, try ▧**Cold Rock,** with locations around Brisbane.

CITY CENTER

▧ **Java Coast Cafe,** 340 George St. (☎3211 3040), near the corner of Ann St. The jungle-like courtyard dining area is an inner-city sanctuary. Our top pick among the city's hundreds of coffee shops. Open M-F 7:30am-4:30pm. ❶

Govinda's Vegetarian Restaurant, upstairs at 99 Elizabeth St. (☎3210 0255). Hare Krishna owners only serve 1 meal per day (except F)—a $7 all-you-can-eat extravaganza. The weekday cafeteria-style setting lacks atmosphere, but the Su $3 feast includes higher quality meals, as well as chanting and dancing. Open M-Sa 11:30am-2:30pm, also F 5:30-8:30pm, Su 5-7pm. ❶

Pane e Vino (☎3220 0044), at the corner of Charlotte and Albert St. As its name suggests, this hip coffee bar serves great pane (try the cheese and pesto bread, $5) and a large selection of wine. Open daily 7am-late. ❶

Opus (☎3229 9915), Eagle Street Pier, along the river. Brisbane's upper crust and business class enjoy a meal along the waterfront. Kangaroo fillet with beet and spinach $20. Open M-F 7am-midnight, Su 7am-4pm. EFTPOS. AmEx/MC/V. ❸

JoJo's (☎3221 2113), on the corner of Queen St. Mall and Albert St. Perched between the chaotic mall and majestic skyscrapers, JoJo's attracts travelers, students, and yuppie businessmen to its grille, Thai, and Italian counters. Dishes cooked to order for $10-27. Daily specials. Open M-Th 9:30am-11pm, F 9:30am-midnight, Sa 11am-midnight, Su 11:30am-10pm. ❹

WEST END AND SOUTH BANK

▧ **George's Seafood,** 150 Boundary St. (☎3844 4100). A tiny seafood shop that will grill, batter, or crumb any fresh fillet for $1 extra. Unbeatable deal: crumbed cod and chips $4.50. Open M-F 9:30am-7:30pm, Sa 8:30am-7:30pm, Su 10:30am-7:30pm. ❶

▧ **Ottoman Cafe,** 37 Mollison St. (☎3846 3555), a block west of the Boundary St. corner. The amazing Turkish cuisine, authentic decorations, and genuine service make for one of the best dining experiences in Brisbane. Be sure to come on Sundays, when all meals are $11. Open W-Su 5pm-late, also F noon-3pm. EFTPOS. AmEx/MC/V. ❸

The Gun Shop, 53 Mollison St. (☎3844 2241), at the corner of Boundary St. A gun shop for 60 years, the corner cafe now hits the bulls-eye with trendy, backpacker-friendly fare. Open W-Su 7am-midnight. EFTPOS accepted. AmEx/MC/V. ❷

Chantahn, 150 Boundary St. (☎3844 8808). This small cafe offers Greek dishes and bargain vegetarian options. Try the chunky chickpea casserole or stir-fry veggies with ginger and chile ($5). Early bird dinner under $10 until 7pm. Belly dancing and plate smashing F-Sa nights. BYO. Open daily 8am-2pm and 5pm-late. ❷

Chez Laila (☎3846 3402), in South Bank Parklands on the boardwalk. A Lebanese restaurant where "people eat to live longer." Outdoor deck overlooking the river and city skyline. The best Lebanese falafel for miles ($15). Open daily 8am-late. ❷

Decks (☎3846 4036), in South Bank Parklands, off Tribune St. Delicious fresh seafood, steak, and a well-stocked all-you-can-eat salad bar. Open daily 11:30am-late. ❷

NEW FARM

🍴 **Himalayan Cafe,** 640-642 Brunswick St. (☎3358 4015). Tibetan and Nepalese delicacies in a warm atmosphere. The back room seats patrons on cushions; a great setting, though service is slow. Diced goat, lightly spiced, cooked with pumpkin and potato $14. Veggie options. Open Tu-Su 5:30-10:30pm. EFTPOS. AmEx/MC/V. ❷

🍴 **Moray Cafe** (☎3254 1342), on the corner of Moray and Merthyr Rd. Quiet location near the river. Attitude without pretense. Hip, popular half-outdoor cafe with bright colors and art, good music, and international, veggie-friendly fare. Best Caesar salad in Queensland, hands-down ($14). Licensed. Open daily 8:30am-late; kitchen closes 10pm. ❸

FORTITUDE VALLEY

🍴 **Garuva,** 324 Wickham St. (☎3216 0124), on the corner of Constancen St. Seductive and intimate. Sit on a cushioned rug as a white curtain is drawn around your table to ensure the utmost privacy. For more daring diners, the throw pillows and candlelight of the cocktail bar appear the prelude to a late-night orgy. Meals from 7 nations; sweet potato and bean curry to shark, all around $14. Book ahead. Open daily 6pm-late. EFTPOS. AmEx/MC/V. ❷

Veg Out, 320 Brunswick St. (☎3852 2668), on the mall. Mix and match veggie and vegan meals. Licensed. Open M-Th 8am-6pm, F-Sa 8am-10pm, Su 10am-5pm. Cash only. ❷

King of Kings Seafood Restaurant, 175 Wickham St., 2nd level (☎3852 1889), halfway between Brunswick St. and Chinatown. Waiters bring trolleys filled with tasty yum cha dishes (around $15 per head). Yum cha open M-F 9:30am-3pm, Sa-Su 8:30am-3pm; also open daily 5:30-midnight for a la carte dinner. EFTPOS. AmEx/MC/V. ❷

🔅 SIGHTS

CITY TOURS. City Sights is a 1½hr. bus tour of cultural and historical attractions. Jump on and off the circuit bus and get unlimited access on public bus and ferry networks. Buy tickets on the bus, from any customer service center, or at most tourist offices. (*Tours leave from City Hall, at the corner of Albert and Adelaide St. Call Transinfo ☎13 12 30 for timetables. Daily every 45min. 9:06am-3:51pm. $20, concessions $15.*) For a tour of the Brisbane River, the large **River Queen** paddlewheel boat departs daily from the Eagle St. Pier, with commentary on passing sights and live accordion music. (*☎3221 1300. 1½hr. tea cruise $24, with lunch buffet $38, seafood buffet $58. 2½-3hr. buffet dinner cruise $52-68. Departs in summer daily 12:15pm and 7:30pm; in winter Tu-Su only. Book ahead.*) **Tours and Detours** (*☎1300 300 242*) offers city and river trips, including a half-day highlight tour (*$44, concessions $40, children $28*), an afternoon float to Lone Pine Koala Sanctuary and Mt. Coot-tha (*$48, concessions $46, children $30*), or a night tour of Brisbane (*$40, concessions $38, children $26*).

CASTLEMAINE/PERKINS BREWERY. XXXX, which proudly proclaims itself as "Queensland's beer," is brewed five minutes from Caxton St. on Milton Rd., adjacent to the Milton train stop. The 45min. walking tour ends with you, an hour, and four tall ones. Meet at the Castlemaine Sports Club, at the crest of Heussler Tce behind the brewery. (☎3361 7597. Tours M-W and sometimes Th 11am, 1:30, and 4pm; occasionally W 6:30pm. $8.50, W 6:30pm with BBQ $18.50. Book ahead.)

CARLTON BREWHOUSE. Thirty minutes south of Brisbane are the brewers of VB, Foster's, and Carlton. The tour may be slightly dry, but the four beers at the end sure aren't. (In Yatala. ☎3826 5858. No public transportation to the brewery; brewery buses leave Tu and Th 11am. Tours M-F 10am, noon, and 2pm. $10, concessions $7.50, children $5. Transport from Brisbane, tour, light lunch, and 4 drinks $30. Book ahead.)

CITY HALL. Opened in 1930, it earned the epithet "Million Pound Town Hall" for its outrageous building cost. The recently restored **clock tower,** a landmark of the city skyline, is 92m high and has an **observation deck.** Inside, the **Brisbane City Gallery** hosts three rotating exhibits; one display is usually by a local artist. (☎3403 8888. Deck open M-F 10am-3pm, Sa 10am-2:30pm. Gallery open daily 10am-5pm. Free.)

QUEENSLAND CULTURAL CENTRE. On the south side of the Victoria Bridge, the Centre coordinates many of Brisbane's artistic venues, including the art gallery, museum, performing arts complex (see p. 311), state library (see p. 304), and theater company. The **Queensland Art Gallery** has over 10,000 works, primarily Australian, Aboriginal, and contemporary Asian. (☎3840 7303. Open M-F 10am-5pm, Sa-Su 9am-5pm. 3 free guided tours daily. Free; special exhibitions $8-15.) The **Queensland Museum** displays dinosaur skeletons, whale models, and live samples of the largest species of cockroach. (☎3840 7640 or 3840 7633; www.qmuseum.qld.gov.au. Open daily 9:30am-5pm. Free; special exhibitions $10-15.)

PARKS AND GARDENS

SOUTH BANK PARKLANDS. Built on the former site of the 1988 World Expo, South Bank offers views of the river, a tree-lined and cafe-dotted boardwalk, and weekly markets. The **man-made lagoon,** surrounded by a real sand beach, fills with sun-seekers during both summer and winter months. (Lifeguard on duty 9am-5pm.) The Parklands also contains a **Maritime Museum,** with wrecks and models. (At the old South Brisbane Dry Dock, south end of the parklands. ☎3844 5361. Open daily 9:30am-4:30pm; last entry 3:45pm. $5.50, concessions $4.40, children $2.80, families $13.80.) On weekends, the park's central thoroughfares are lined with a **crafts village,** featuring crafts, jewelry, psychics, clothing, and massages. (Open F 5-10pm by lantern-light, Sa 11am-5pm, Su 9am-5pm.) The Parklands also organizes free events, including car shows, fireworks, and weightlifting championships. Obtain an event calendar and map of the park from the the **Visitor Information Centre,** in the center of the park at the Stanley St. Plaza. (Accessible by foot, by bus to South Bank or Cultural Centre stops, by CityTrain to South Brisbane station, or by ferry to terminal stop at South Bank. Info Centre ☎3867 2051; www.south-bank.net.au. Open Su-Th and Sa 9am-6pm, F 9am-9pm. Although there are no official gates, the Parklands are "open" 5am-midnight.)

BOTANIC GARDENS. Stroll among palm groves, camellia gardens, and lily ponds. If you search hard, you can see large lizards strolling the ground as well. (A 10min. walk from the city center on Albert St., at the intersection with Alice St. ☎3403 0666. Open 24hr. Free tours depart the rotunda near the Albert St. entrance M-Sa 11am and 1pm.)

MT. COOT-THA. Queensland's premier subtropical garden, the park includes a Japanese Garden, botanical library, tropical dome, and plenty of picnicking green. It also houses Queensland's first **Planetarium.** (☎3403 2578. 45min. programs W-F

3:30pm and 7:30pm; Sa 1:30, 3:30, and 7:30pm; Su 1:30 and 3:30pm. $10, concessions $8.50, children $6, families $28; free exhibit in the foyer.) Hop back on bus #471 to reach the **Mount Coot-tha Summit**, with a view of greater Brisbane that's spectacular at night. The casual **Kuta Cafe ❷** (meals under $12) and the fancier **Mount Coot-tha Summit Restaurant ❺** (mains $25) both have panoramic views. *(Kuta Cafe ☎ 3368 2117; Summit Restaurant ☎ 3369 9922. Kuta open Su-Th 7am-11pm, F-Sa 7am-midnight; Summit open M-Sa 11:30am-midnight, Su 8-10:30am.)* To walk back to the gardens, take the **JC Slaughter Falls track** (2km) from the summit, with an optional **Aboriginal Art loop.** At the bottom of the trail, exit the carpark to the right, and follow the busy main road for ten minutes to the garden entrance. *(7km from the city center. From Town Hall, stop 44, bus #471 takes 20min. to the gardens and 25min. to the summit; 1 per hr. Last bus to city leaves gardens M-F 4:10pm, Sa-Su 5:10pm. Gardens ☎ 3403 2531. Tours M-Sa 11am and 1pm from the info center. Open daily Apr.-Aug. 8am-5pm; Sept.-Mar. 8am-5:30pm. Vehicle access weekdays until 4pm; closed on weekends.)*

BRISBANE FOREST PARK. Picnic, camp, birdwatch, cycle, ride horses, and hike on over 29,000 hectares of The Gap, but only if you have a car to take you there. The park headquarters offers bushwalking maps and contains the **Walkabout Creek Wildlife Centre,** a small sanctuary for wallabies, native birds, and various water creatures. *(60 Mt. Nebo Rd. The #385 bus from Albert St. will get you to park headquarters, but bushwalking trails and camping areas are accessible by private transport only. Rob's Rainfoest Day Tours (see p. 311) brings daytrips M. ☎ 3300 4855. Open M-F 8:30am-4:30pm, Sa-Su 9am-4:30pm. $3.50, concessions $2.50.)*

WILDLIFE

AUSTRALIA ZOO. The crocs get fed every day at in the summer at noon and 1:30pm—a spectacle you won't forget, especially if Crocodile Hunter Steve Irwin is there. Cuddle a python, ogle the world's ten most venomous snake species, feed a kangaroo, and patiently follow the world's oldest Galapagos tortoise. *(In Beerwah, 75km north of Brisbane. Catch the "Crocodile Train" from the Transit Centre; call ahead to arrange free bus from Beerwah station to the zoo. ☎ 5494 1134; www.crocodilehunter.com. $21, concessions $18, children $13, families $59. Open daily 8:30am-4pm.)*

ALMA PARK ZOO. The hands-on zoo has walkthrough kangaroo and deer enclosures, koalas, monkeys, and water buffalo, and allows feeding of some of the friendlier animals. Twenty acres of tropical gardens with BBQs make it an ideal picnic spot. *(Alma Rd., Dakabin. 30min. north of Brisbane on Bruce Hwy., at the Boundary Rd. exit. Take the 9:02am Caboolture train to Dakabin, or take a later train and snag a taxi at the Dakabin station. ☎ 3204 6566; www.almaparkzoo.com.au. Open daily 9am-5pm. Pet koalas daily noon and 2:30pm. $20, concessions and children $10.)*

LONE PINE KOALA SANCTUARY. Pet and hold one of over 130 koalas at the world's largest koala sanctuary. Emus, Tasmanian devils, raucous laughing kookaburras, and lots of hand-feedable 'roos try to raise the average activity level. Check out the wall of fame in the restaurant, where numerous entertainers have been photographed with one of the Pine's koalas. *(Take bus #430 from the Koala platform in the Myer Centre (1 per hr.), or take the Wildlife Cruise 19km upstream on the Brisbane River. Cruise ☎ 3221 0300 or 0412 749 426. Departs North Quay at 10am; free pickup from city accommodations. Return $25, concessions $20, children $15. Sanctuary ☎ 3378 1366. Open daily 8am-5pm. $15, students $13, children $10, families $38.)*

AUSTRALIAN WOOLSHED. Although sheep are the focus, clever sheep dogs steal the show. Help out by feeding the baby farmyard animals or milking the cows, but keep your distance from the freshwater crocs. *(Samford Rd., Ferny Hills. 800m from the Ferny Grove railway station, 30min. north of Brisbane. ☎ 3872 1100; www.auswoolshed.com.au. Open daily 8:30am-4:30pm. $16.50, concessions $12, children $11.)*

QUEENSLAND

⚑ ACTIVITIES

ROCK CLIMBING AND SKYDIVING. Join **Outdoor Pursuit** at Kangaroo Cliffs, past South Bank, for **rock climbing** or **abseiling** every other Sunday at 8:30am. They also journey outside of the city for canyoning trips. *(☎ 3391 8776. $39, canyoning $95. Book ahead.)* If you need practice, try **indoor climbing** with **Rock Sports.** *(224 Barry Pde., Fortitude Valley. ☎ 3216 0492. Open M-F 10am-9:30pm, Sa-Su 10am-6pm. $20 for unlimited climbing.)* A little higher up, **Brisbane Skydiving Centre** will show you the city at 200km per hour from 12,500 ft. *(☎ 1800 061 555. $230; free pickup.)* Or, enjoy a more leisurely flight on a hot air balloon ride over the city with **Fly Me to the Moon.** *(☎ 3423 0400. Weekdays $228, weekends $248. Both include five-star breakfast and pickup.)*

WATER ACTIVITIES. Brisbane has many waterways that are perfect for **canoeing.** Written guides to the popular **Oxley Creek** and **Boondall Wetlands** are available from libraries or the City Council Customer Services counter, in the City Plaza, on the corner of Ann and George St. For rentals, try **Goodtime Surf and Sail.** *(29 Ipswich Rd., Woolloongabba. ☎ 3391 8588. Open M-F 8:30am-5:30pm, Sa 8:30am-4pm, Su 10am-3pm. Canoes from $28 per day; kayaks from $20. Deposit $55.)* **ProDive** goes to the area's reefs and wrecks. *(☎ 3368 3766. Open M-F 9am-6pm, Sa-Su 9am-5pm. Daytrip 2 dives $125, gear $49; pickup included.)*

BUSHWALKING. **Rob's Rainforest Explorer Day Tours** takes you through Mt. Glorious and Samford Valley in Brisbane Forest Park (see p. 310) on Mondays, Glasshouse Mountains and Kondalilla Falls (see p. 347) on Tuesdays and Thursdays, the Green Mountains of Lamington National Park (see p. 330) on Wednesdays and Fridays, or Springbrook National Park (see p. 332) on Saturdays. *(☎ 3357 7061 or 0409 496 607. $55; includes pickup and transport.)*

♫ ENTERTAINMENT AND FESTIVALS

Brisbane hosts seemingly continuous festivals, as well as diverse theatrical, artistic, and musical performances. Call the **Queensland Cultural Centre** (☎ 3840 7444) for a current schedule and info on discounts.

QUEENSLAND PERFORMING ARTS CENTRE (QPAC). The Centre, just across Victoria Bridge in South Bank, is composed of four theaters: the **Concert Hall** hosts symphony and chamber orchestras; the 2000-seat **Lyric Theatre** sponsors drama, musicals, ballet, and opera; the 850-seat **Optus Playhouse** shows dramatic performances; and the 315-seat **Cremorne Theatre** stages smaller, more intimate productions. *(☎ 13 62 46. Tours from the ticket sales foyer M-F noon. $5. Book ahead.)*

OTHER FINE ARTS. The **Queensland Conservatorium** *(☎ 3875 6264)* presents university-affiliated and professional concerts. **Opera Queensland** *(☎ 3875 3030)* produces three operas and one choral concert annually. For contemporary Australian theater, **La Boîte,** 57 Hale St., Petrie Tce. *(☎ 3010 2600)*, on the corner of Sexton St., offers six plays per year. The **Queensland Ballet** *(☎ 3846 5266)*, the oldest professional dance group in Australia, performs an annual program of contemporary classical works and audience favorites. The **Queensland Theatre Company** offers eight shows annually. *(☎ 3010 7600. $20-45.)* For tickets to all above theaters, call **Qtix** *(☎ 13 62 46)*. The **Powerhouse Centre for Live Arts,** 119 Lamington St., adjacent to New Farm Park, is an alternative arts venue, housing performances, dining, and galleries. *(☎ 3358 8600; www.brisbanepowerhouse.org. Box office open M-F 9am-5pm, Sa noon-close.)*

MUSIC, MOOLA, MOVIES. Escape the mainstream with Thursday evening jazz at **Jazzy Cat,** 56 Mollison St. *(☎ 3846 2544; www.jazzycat.com.au. Th jazz 7:30pm-late. Open*

QUEENSLAND

daily 9am-late.) **The Bombshelter,** 200 Main St., Kangaroo Point *(☎3391 2266),* features Saturday Irish jam sessions *(1:30-5pm)* and Sunday afternoon jazz *(3-7pm).* The former state treasury building continues to extort money—but now for "fun"—in the enormous **Treasury Casino.** This Brisbane landmark contains five restaurants, seven bars, over 100 gaming tables, and more than 1000 gaming machines. *(At the junction of Queen, Elizabeth, and George St. ☎3306 8888. Open 24hr.)* For movies, try **Hoyts Theatre** *(☎3027 9999)* for mainstream films or the **IMAX** *(☎3844 4222),* both in South Bank. *(Corner of Grey and Ernest St. Hoyts $13, students $10, children $9; Tu all films $8.80. IMAX shows Su-Th every hr. 10am-9pm, F-Sa every hr. 10am-10pm. $14.50, students $11.30, children $9.50.)* Alternative films play at **DENDY.** *(346 George St. ☎3211 3244; www.dendy.com.au. Open daily 11am-9:30pm. $13, students $10, children $8; M all films $8.)*

SPORTS. The **Entertainment Centre,** on Melaleuca Dr. in Boondall, is Brisbane's largest indoor complex for sports, concerts, and events. *(By Citytrain, take the Shorncliffe line to Boondall Station; 30min., departs at least every 30min. ☎3265 8111, tickets ☎13 19 31 or 3403 6700.)* The **"Gabba"** is Queensland's major **cricket** and **football** stadium, home of the AFL's Brisbane Lions. *(At Vulture and Stanley St., Woolloongabba. Take the bus to the station on the corner of Main and Stanley St. ($2.60) or the train to Vulture St. ☎3435 2222, cricket 3292 3100, footy 3335 1777. Buy tickets from Ticketmaster ☎13 61 22.)*

FESTIVALS. The **Brisbane River Festival** *(☎3846 7444)* celebrates spring the first week of September with fireworks, concerts, and river feasts on the William Jolly Bridge. The **Brisbane International Film Festival** *(☎3007 3007; www.biff.com.au)* is held annually in mid-July; the festival features alternative and retrospective film releases. The **Valley Fiesta** *(☎3252 5999; www.valleyfiesta.com),* also in mid-July, heats up the Valley with street festivals, local bands, and dance performances. On the first weekend of July, the **Jazz and Blues Festival** *(☎1300 655 885; www.jazzandbluesfestival.com.au)* showcases a number of jazz artists at Kangaroo Point for a $20 entry. Most exciting of all, the **Australia Day Cockroach Races** will be run on January 26, 2003, at the Storybridge Hotel, 196 Main St., Kangaroo Point *(☎3391 2266).* Buy your own racing roach, or root from the sidelines.

▨ NIGHTLIFE

Brisbane nights roll by in sweaty nightclubs, noisy pubs, and smoky jazz lounges. Fortitude Valley is home to Brisbane's most exciting nighttime scene, with alternative bars and dance clubs, live music, and several gay establishments. Weekends are huge and weeknights sparse on Caxton St. in Petrie Tce., with a decidedly more mainstream set. The city center is a big draw for backpackers, with its many Irish pubs, drink specials, and rocking Thursday nights.

Be glad you don't have to keep track of the myriad live performances in Brisbane—the Wednesday or Saturday editions of the *Courier-Mail,* as well as free entertainment guides such as *Rave, Time Off, Scene,* and *qp* (a guide to gay and lesbian entertainment and clubs), take care of this task. They are all at the record store, **Rocking Horse,** 101 Adelaide St., and many local nightclubs.

CITY CENTER AND RIVERSIDE

▨ **Mary Street,** 138 Mary St. *(☎3221 1511).* User-friendly but packed. Squeeze your way past a young crowd to the nightclub, grunge stage, pool room, acoustic den, or beer garden. Live music nightly. Cover $7, students $5. Open Th-Sa 5pm-5am.

Victory Hotel, 127 Edward St. *(☎3221 0444),* on the corner of Charlotte St. This classic Aussie pub, with a beer garden, heaps of bars, and a nightclub, might be the busiest in all Queensland. W-Su live bands. Th jug specials. Happy Hour W-Su 7-9pm. Open M-Tu 10am-10pm, W 10am-1am, Th-Sa 10am-3am, Su 11am-3am.

Murphy's, 175 George St. (☎3221 4377), on the corner of Elizabeth St. A crowd of all ages packs this Irish pub. Live cover bands and solo artists nightly. Happy Hour F 5-7pm. Some upstairs accommodations. Open M-W 11am-midnight, Th-Sa 11am-late.

Downunder Bar (☎3211 9277), under the Palace Backpackers. Like it or not, it's Brizzy's backpacker central. Have your hostel key or student card ready (only backpackers and students are welcome) and your international mojo working. Dinner from $9. Food served noon-2pm and 6-9pm. Open M-F noon-3am, Sa-Su 5pm-3am.

Friday's, 123 Eagle St., Riverside Centre (☎3832 2122). A young crowd gets classy at this giant riverfront hangout. The maze of rooms offers eclectic entertainment—dance music, modern tunes, and live music. Th-Sa live bands; Th university night $1.50 drinks 8pm-midnight. $8 cover. Open Su-M 10:30am-late, Tu-Sa 10am-5am.

FORTITUDE VALLEY

■ **Empire Hotel,** 339 Brunswick St. (☎3852 1216), at the corner of Ann St. The true one-stop party venue in town. Downstairs, the **Corner Bar** and **Press Club** cater to a more casual crowd. (Corner Bar open Su-Th 11am-midnight, F-Sa 11am-2am; Press Club open M-Th 5pm-1am, F-Sa 5pm-5am. No cover for either.) The upstairs nightclub, consisting of the **Middle Bar** and **Moon Bar,** satisfies a late-nighter of any breed. To the right, comfy couches and alternative tunes; to the left, fresh and funky chemical beats. Cover $7. Open F-Sa 9pm-5am.

Ric's, 321 Brunswick St. Mall (☎3854 1772). Acoustically and electronically eclectic: this hip hangout is always packed, with outdoor seating, live music, and an upstairs break beat and hip-hop bar. Sa-Su live acts. Open daily 10am-late; upstairs dance club F-Sa nights only.

The Beat, 677 Ann St. (☎3852 2661). Other clubs come and go, but the Beat goes on, turning 24 this year. 5 rooms, 3 beer gardens, and a gay and lesbian crowd. The techno beat is straightforward; the scene is anything but. Th $1 drinks until midnight. Shows daily 11:30pm and 1:30am. Cover M-F $6, Sa-Su $8. Open daily 8pm-5am.

Hotel Wickham, 308 Wickham St. (☎3852 1301). A gay and lesbian pub that becomes an outrageous dance party on weekend nights. Costumes, cabarets—here, anything goes. Shows Tu-Su. Open Su-M 10am-midnight, Tu-Th 10am-3am, F-Sa 10am-5am.

PETRIE TERRACE

The Paddo, 186 Given Tce. (☎3369 0044). Restaurant **Fibber McGees** has fantastic deals. M $6 steaks; Tu $7 jugs; F live bands. The **Saloon Bar** next door has live cover music M-Su and tons of specials. Don't worry if you forgot your cowboy hat; they've got several to spare. Open Su-Th noon-2am, F-Sa noon-3am.

Hotel LA, 68 Petrie Tce. (☎3368 2560), on the corner of Caxton St. Upscale, with plenty of social climbers, but the only place with a weekday crowd. Tu and Th 2-for-1 on drinks and meals 6-10pm. Open daily 7am-5am.

Transcontinental Hotel, 482 George St. (☎3236 1366). The hopping Trans has drink specials Su-M and Th-F. Upstairs nightclub. Smart casual dress. Open daily 9am-4am.

O'Leary's, 25 Caxton St. (☎3368 1933). This sleek Irish pub offers a log fire for the winter and a beer garden for the summer. Live music M and Th-Su. Open M-Th 5pm-midnight, F-Sa 5pm-2am, Su 2pm-midnight.

MORETON BAY AND ISLANDS

With the Gold Coast to the south and the Sunshine Coast to the north, one would expect Moreton Bay to be filled with travelers. Instead, Brisbane's inland location draws journeyers *away* from one of Queensland's most spectacular areas. Don't

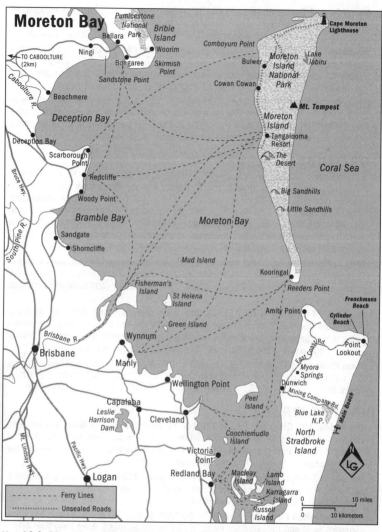

Moreton Bay

Pumicestone National Park
Bribie Island
Bellara
Bongaree
Ningi
Bongaree
Sandstone Point
Woorim
Skirmish Point
Comboyuro Point
Bulwer
Cowan Cowan
Cape Moreton Lighthouse
Moreton Island National Park
Lake Jabiru
Mt. Tempest
Moreton Island
Tangalooma Resort
The Desert
Big Sandhills
Little Sandhills
Coral Sea

TO CABOOLTURE (2km)

Caboolture R.

Beachmere

Deception Bay

Deception Bay

Bruce Hwy.

Scarborough Point
Redcliffe
Woody Point

Bramble Bay

South Pine R.

Sandgate
Shorncliffe

Moreton Bay

Mud Island

Kooringal
Reeders Point
Amity Point
Frenchmans Beach
Cylinder Beach
Point Lookout

Fisherman's Island
St Helena Island
Green Island

Brisbane R.
Wynnum
Brisbane
Manly
Wellington Point

East Coast Rd.

Myora Springs
Dunwich
Mining Company Rd.
Blue Lake N.P.
North Stradbroke Island

Main Beach

Capalaba
Leslie Harrison Dam
Cleveland
Peel Island
Coochiemudlo Island

Mt. Lindsay Hwy.

Pacific Hwy.

Victoria Point
Redland Bay
Logan
Macleay Island
Lamb Island
Karragarra Island
Russell Island

N

Ferry Lines
Unsealed Roads

0   10 miles
0   10 kilometers

QUEENSLAND

let this happen to you. At Manly, at the mouth of the Brisbane River, a comfortable culture thrives in perpetual slow-motion. Across the bay, North Stradbroke Island offers diving, surfing, whale watching, and swimming, while Moreton Island invites adventure travel. Although this area lacks pre-packaged fun, the natural beauty of Moreton Bay is worth self-motivating.

MANLY   ☎ 07

At the friendly harborside village of Manly, there seem to be more boats than people. A quick trip from Brisbane and near most ferry services, the town serves as the perfect accommodations base for exploring the nearby islands, as well as a quiet space to return to after a day spent fishing, sailing, or scuba diving. Lazy Wednesday afternoons bring sailing races, in which visitors can participate at no cost. The main street leads to a jam-packed small boat harbor.

⊟🛇 TRANSPORTATION AND PRACTICAL INFORMATION. From Brisbane, take Citytrain to the Manly stop on the Cleveland line (35-40min. from Roma St., daily at least every 30min., $2.60). With your back to the train station, take the 2nd left-hand turn at the "Boat Harbor" sign to reach **Cambridge Parade,** the main thoroughfare. Cambridge Pde. heads towards the harbor and the **Esplanade,** which runs along the water. The **Tourist Information Centre,** 43A Cambridge Pde., is across from the Manly Hotel. (☎3348 3524. Open daily 10am-3pm.) There is **Internet** at **Manly Video,** 11 Cambridge Pde. (☎3396 0554. $6 per hr. Open daily 10am-9pm.) There is **no bank** in town, but the Shopping Centre, on the corner of Cambridge Pde. and the Esplanade, has an **ATM.** The **post office,** 222 Stratton Tce., also in the Shopping Centre, changes American Express traveler's checks. (☎3396 2735. Open M-F 9am-5pm, Sa 9am-noon.) **Postal Code:** 4179.

🛏🍴 ACCOMMODATIONS AND FOOD. 🛇Moreton Bay Lodge ❷, 45 Cambridge Pde., is a quiet, friendly spot, with spacious rooms, kitchen, TV lounge, and helpful owners. (☎3396 3020. Airport and train pickup. Key deposit $20. Dorms $19, weekly $120; singles $35, ensuite $40; doubles $50/$60; triples $66/$76. VIP.) A neat symmetry divides the hostel from the casual but lovely **Bay Window Cafe and Bar ❸,** where hostel guests get a 10% discount (Food served daily noon-9pm. $2 pots and live music Th nights. AmEx/MC/V.) **Manly Hotel ❹,** 54 Cambridge Pde., is a newly remodeled favorite of businessmen. The hotel has several bars and a **restaurant ❸** that serves three meals daily. (☎3249 5999. Th and Sa karaoke, F-Su live music. Restaurant open daily 7am-9pm; bars open M-Sa 10am-late, Su 11am-late. Singles $39-77; doubles $50-88.) A **grocery store** is in the Shopping Centre (☎3396 1980. Open M-Sa 7am-7:30pm, Su 7am-7pm.)

◩🛶 SIGHTS AND ACTIVITIES. A brisk 20min. walk along the Esplanade from the harbor leads to the center of a nearby town, **Wynnum by the Bay.** Along the way, you'll pass a huge **tidal pool** perfect for a dip. Parks with changing rooms and BBQs run along the Esplanade. From Wynnum, continue walking another 30min., past the end of the harborwalk and through the soccer and cricket fields, to the **Wynnum Mangrove Boardwalk,** a 500m walk guided by informative signs. The mangroves grow in dense concentration, and their roots protrude like small periscopes from the muck, allowing the trees to breathe.

For a more sedate ride, **Manly Eco Cruises** offers family-oriented daytrips and 50min. weekend tours around Moreton Bay from Manly. (☎3396 9400. Daytrips M-F 9am-3pm. Daytrips $89, concessions $75; 50min. tours $15, concessions $13. Book ahead.) For free sailing, show up at the **Royal Queensland Yacht Squadron (RQ)** for the friendly 🛇WAGS (Wednesday Afternoon Gentleman's Sailing) races. Yacht owners are always looking for temporary crew; if you are a beginner, they may teach you. The winning boat gets a bottle of rum. (☎3396 8666. A 10min. walk right down the Esplanade from Cambridge Pde. W noon. Women welcome.)

NORTH STRADBROKE ISLAND ☎07

A fierce cyclone in 1896 cleanly split the land mass once called Stradbroke Island (20km south of Brisbane). While South Stradbroke (see p. 329) has remained relatively uninhabited, its northern neighbor, separated by a 200m channel, is now home to 2700 people. With miles of sandy white surf beaches, famous blue inland lakes, and excellent dive sites, "Straddie" is an ideal step off the beaten path.

QUEENSLAND

☐ TRANSPORTATION. Despite its isolation, North Stradbroke can be reached by a few hops on public transportation from Brisbane. Take **Citytrain** to Cleveland (1hr., usually every 30min., $3.70). From Cleveland, the courtesy bus **"Bessie"** runs from the train station to meet the **Stradbroke Flyer** ferry, which departs for One Mile Jetty in Dunwich. (☎3286 1964. 30min.; every 1½hr. 6:30am-6:30pm; return $12, students $9.) Alternately, buses run from the train station (90¢) to **Stradbroke Ferries Water Taxi** service. (☎3286 2666. 30min.; 10-12 per day, approx. 6am-6pm; return $12, students $10.) Take their vehicular ferry only if you have a car. (1hr., 10-15 per day 5:30am-6:30pm. Return $84 for the car and all its passengers.) **Islands Transport** runs a vehicular ferry to Stradbroke from Redland Bay. (☎3829 0008. $84 per car.) The **North Stradbroke Island Bus Service** runs between Point Lookout, Amity, and Dunwich. (☎3409 7151. 14 per day, less frequently to Amity; M-Su 7:15am-7pm; return $9.) A **taxi** from Dunwich to Point Lookout costs a hefty $30, but it can can be convenient for getting around Point Lookout. (**Stradbroke Island Yellow Cabs** ☎13 19 24). Several companies in Cleveland provide **rental cars** to the island, but 4WD rental is available only in Brisbane.

■☑ ORIENTATION AND PRACTICAL INFORMATION. North Stradbroke Island has three distinct townships: residential **Dunwich,** the ferry drop-off point; **Amity Point,** north of Dunwich, with calm beaches and great fishing; and **Point Lookout,** 22km northeast of Dunwich, with most of the area's accommodations and tourist attractions. **East Coast Road** is the main road connecting Dunwich and Point Lookout; its name changes to **Mooloomba Road** in Point Lookout. The middle of the island consists of lakes, swamps, national park land, and habitat reserves, while sand mines occupy a significant portion of the northern and southern ends.

The **tourist office** books tours and campground sites; it's the yellow building on Junner St., at the base of the Dunwich football green. (☎3409 9555. Open M-F 8:30am-5pm, Sa-Su 8:30am-3pm.) Although there's **no bank** on the island, there is an **ATM** in the Dunwich bottle shop, at the intersection of Junner and Ballow St. Other services include: **police** (☎3409 9020), across from the tourist office in Dunwich; and **Stradbroke Island Medical Centre** (☎3409 8660), at Meegera Pl., off Endeavor St., Point Lookout. (Open M 8:30am-noon and 2-6pm, Tu-F 8:30am-1pm and 2-5pm, Sa 9-11am, Su 10-11am.) The **post offices** in Dunwich and Point Lookout also provide some banking services: **Dunwich Post** is located at 3 Welsby St. (☎3409 9010; open M-F 8am-5pm, Sa 8am-11am) and **Point Lookout Post** is at Meegera Pl., off Endeavor St. (☎3409 8210. Open M-F 9am-5pm.) **Postal Code:** 4183.

☐ ACCOMMODATIONS. Two hostels and a caravan park in Point Lookout, as well as seven **campsites**—two in Dunwich, two in Amity, and three in Point Lookout—comprise the island's budget accommodation. **Camping ❶** is also permitted on all of Flinders Beach and on Main Beach, at least 10km from the causeway. (Shore camping permit $3.90; sites $6.20 per person per night, powered $9.80. Prices higher during school holidays.) Make bookings through the tourist office.

The Straddie Hostel ❷, soon to be **Point Lookout Beach House,** 76 Mooloomba Rd., is halfway between the Guesthouse and the end of Point Lookout, on the left just past Endeavor Rd. The eco-friendly hostel has a relaxed atmosphere, helpful owners, and a funky common room where guests gather. Six-bed dorms have bath and kitchen. (☎3409 8679; snapper@itxpress.com. Free use of snorkeling gear, fishing rods, and boogie boards. Reception 9am-11pm. Dorms $17, weekly $98; doubles $40/$245. Cash only.) **Stradbroke Island Guesthouse ❷,** on the left of the entrance to Point Lookout and close to Home Beach, has $8 transportation from Brisbane on request (in summer M, W, and F; in winter M and F) and an attached dive center. Rooms are sparse but clean. (☎3409 8888. Reception in summer 7am-late; in winter 8am-4pm. Key deposit $10. Dorms $22; doubles $50. VIP/YHA.) **Straddbroke Island Tourist Park ❶**, in Point Lookout on the right, has new cabins and campsites as well as a pool and BBQ area. (☎3409 8127; ladbrooke@ecn.net.au. Reception M-Sa 8am 5pm, Su 8am-2pm. Prices rise considerably during peak. Sites for 2 $13.20, powered $18; cabins for 2 $55, ensuite $57.20; ensuite cabins for 4 $70.40.)

❐ FOOD. Most restaurants are in Point Lookout, along Mooloomba Rd. On the left at the top of the hill towards Point Lookout, still on the outskirts of town, **Straddie Hotel Pub ❷** has a brasserie with mains for around $15 and specials for less. With outdoor pool tables, a bar, and a great view of the beach, it's the local hangout and gets packed on weekends. (☎3409 8188. Food served daily 7:30-9:30am, noon-2pm, and 6-8pm. AmEx/MC/V.) **La Focaccia ❸**, at Meegera Pl. off Endeavor St., serves $15 pasta in an open-air setting. (☎3409 8778. Open daily 9am-9pm. MC/V.) For **groceries,** try Bob's 727 Foodmarket, Meegera Pl., Point Lookout. (☎3409 8271. Open 7am-9pm.) Food on the island is not cheap, so bringing your own is a good idea.

◙ ☑ SIGHTS AND ACTIVITIES. The island is known for its **scuba diving** and amazing marine animal life. **Stradbroke Island Scuba Center,** below the Guesthouse, has 15 dive sites and daily trips. (☎3409 8888. Single dive $85; double $120; 4-day PADI $350; snorkeling $50, including boat trip and gear.) **Stradbroke Island Tours** (☎3409 8051) will show you the island highlights by 4WD in half a day for only $30. **Straddie Adventures** offers popular adventure tours. (☎3409 8414 or 0417 741 963; www.straddieadventures.com.au. Sandboarding 2-4pm $25; sea kayaking and snorkeling 9:30am-12:30pm $35; half-day 4WD tour $55. VIP.)

The easiest and cheapest thing to do on North Stradbroke Island is to walk—miles of unspoiled beaches and seemingly unexplored bush can keep a spirited traveler busy for days. Heading toward the end of Point Lookout on the left is a "Beach Access" sign for **Frenchman's Beach,** a convenient starting point for any beach walk and a popular surfing spot. Across the bakery on the Point lies the entrance to the **◙Gorge Walk,** a 15min. stroll past rocky headlands and gorges, white sand beaches, and blue waters. This walk is famous for **whale-watching** from June to November and dolphins, turtles, and manta rays year-round. The Gorge Walk also passes the **Blowhole,** where crashing waves are channeled up a narrow gorge and transformed into fountains of spray. The swimming **lagoon,** 4½km down Main Beach, is a lovely day hike or picnic spot. **Main Beach** stretches 32km, drawing **surfers** with some of Queensland's best waves during early summer's northerly winds. **Cylinder Beach,** which runs in front of the Stradbroke Hotel, is more swimmer- and family-oriented, but good breaks can be found. **Deadman's Beach,** just before the Point, is a popular snorkeling spot.

On hot summer days, **Myora Springs,** 4km along East Coast Rd. from Dunwich toward Point Lookout, is a refreshing place to cool off. The aptly named **Blue Lake** is a lovely freshwater spot that's part of **Blue Lake National Park.** Drive 8km along Tazi Rd. from Dunwich and follow the signs (regular cars must stop 2.7km away and walk the rest, while 4WD vehicles can drive almost all the way, following a sand track). To tour the beaches with your own 4WD, purchase an access permit from the tourist office or at most campsites ($10.30 for 48hr., $15.40 per week).

MORETON ISLAND ☎07

Remarkably untouristed, Moreton is a haven for the adventurous. Just 35km from Brisbane, visitors can snorkel among shipwrecks, hike or toboggan down sand dunes, spot whales and dolphins, or just take in the sun on 40km of unbroken beach. Hiking trails weave among the dunes and to the top of **Mt. Tempest,** the

QUEENSLAND

world's highest sand mountain. **The Desert** and the **Big Sandhills** are popular sand-boarding spots; wash the grit from your eyes in the **Blue Lagoon**, a clear, freshwater lake with abundant wildlife. Around the northern headland is a walking track that leads to the **Cape Moreton lighthouse** and a panoramic view of the bay, with great opportunities for whale watching from June to November. On the eastern coast-line, **Ocean Beach** stretches the length of the island, while the view from the west-ern side is broken by the **Tangalooma Wrecks,** 14 old dredges sunk 1964-1984.

Five designated **campsites ●** with toilets and showers are located on Moreton ($4), and free camping is allowed on the majority of the island. Pick up a map and pay camp and 4WD fees at the ferry site on the mainland. Tom at **Moreton Bay Escapes** (see below) rents out **beach house units ●** with kitchen that sleep six ($175). Although the majority of the island is designated a national park, three small townships and the massive **Tangalooma Resort** are located on the western side; fuel, food, and basic supplies are available at **Bulwer.**

The best way to get around the island is by 4WD; either rent on the mainland or take a tour with **Moreton Bay Escapes** (☎ 1300 559 355; www.gibrenexpedi-tions.com.au), which offers excellent adventure-oriented trips to the island. The one-day tour from Manly includes sand tobogganning and sailing to the island on *Solo*, a famous Australia racing yacht, but two- to three-day tours are best to get a feel for the island. (Daytrip $95, by moonlight $70; 2-day 4WD with snorkeling, sandboarding, hiking, and fishing $189; 3-day scuba $289; 3-day sail and 4WD $389. Ask about 20% discounts.) Alternatively, **Moreton Island Ferries** leave from Fisher-man's Island for Moreton; to get there, take Citytrain from Brisbane to Wynnum and hire a taxi, or snag a ride from the Manly hostel owner. (☎ 3895 1000. 2hr.; 1 per day M and W-F, 2 per day Sa-Su; $10. Vehicle transport also available.) **Dolphin Wild Island Cruises** also sends a power catamaran from the mainland for a daytrip full of wrecks, dolphins, and sand tobogganing. (☎ 5497 5628. Tours 10:30am-4pm. $89, children $44.) Charter the 10-person **Moreton Island Taxi Service** 4WD, or join them for a full-day tour of the island's highlights. (☎ 3408 2661. Tours M and F-Su; $160.) **Get Wet Sports,** located at the Tangalooma Resort, rents out kayaks and din-ghies and offers guided snorkeling and diving. (☎ 3410 6927. Single kayaks $9 per hr., doubles $12; dinghies $18 per hr.; 1½hr. snorkeling at the wrecks $20, children $16; 3hr. intro dives $70, experienced divers $48.)

OTHER ISLANDS IN MORETON BAY

Moreton Bay is dotted with more than 300 islands perfect for daytripping. Cheap accommodation other than camping is sparse, but a day is plenty to sample the islands' offerings: pristine beaches, snorkeling, and an occasional whale sighting.

COOCHIEMUDLO ISLAND. A popular getaway for locals, Coochiemudlo entices visitors with walkable beaches, restaurants, and occasional crafts markets featur-ing local artists. **Coochiemudlo Island Ferry Service** runs a vehicular ferry from Victo-ria Point Jetty. (☎ 3820 7227. 12 per day. Return $33, pedestrians $2.) **Bay Islands Taxi Service** also services Coochie from Victoria Point (☎ 3409 1145. Every 30min.; M-F 5am-11pm, Sa-Su 6am-11pm; $2.40, children $1.20.) The **Coochie Bus Service** offers a 30min. tour of the island. (☎ 0427 113 686. $5.50, children $2.50.)

BRIBIE ISLAND. At the northern end of Moreton Bay, Bribie is the only island accessible by car. From Brisbane, go 45km north to Caboolture then 19km east. Or take Citytrain from Brisbane to Caboolture, where a bus service runs to Bribie. The **tourist office** is just over the bridge from the mainland. (☎ 3408 9026. Open M-F 9am-4pm, Sa 9am-noon, Su 9:30am-1pm.) Bribie is separated from the mainland by **Pumicestone Passage,** a marine park teeming with mangroves, sea cows, turtles, dolphins, and over 350 species of birds. Vehicles allow easy access to great fishing on the mainland side of the channel and surfing on the eastern side.

ST. HELENA ISLAND. In its glory days, St. Helena was the first prison in Queensland and the only commercially viable prison in the world. Today, St. Helena limits onshore visitors in order to preserve its National Parkgrounds. The only way to visit the island is by the **Cat-o'-Nine-Tails** vessel, which offers day and night tours to the island in which actors role-play St. Helena's colorful past. Cruises run from **Manly.** (☎ 3396 3994. $65, concessions $55, children $35. Night tours $75, children $39. Evening "ghost tour" is not primarily for children. Book ahead.)

GOLD COAST

Gorgeous beaches, thumping nightclubs, excellent theme parks, and plenty of accommodations make the Gold Coast Australia's premier holiday destination. The region's permanent population of 390,000 triples to 1.2 million every summer as Australian and foreign tourists flock to the sun, sand, and parties. The term "Gold Coast" has several possible origins: tourist officials say it's for the stretches of golden sand beaches, but cynics point to high rises and the tacky tinsel glitter of Surfers Paradise. Around Surfers, natural attractions abound—to the south, excellent point breaks have created some of the world's best surfing beaches and to the north, South Stradbroke Island offers a peaceful escape from the bustling coast. A trip to the "Green behind the Gold," the less-touristed but rewarding Gold Coast Hinterland, will complement time spent on the sometimes hectic coast.

Sunshine Coast & Gold Coast

COOLANGATTA & TWEED HEADS ☎07

The name Surfers Paradise might be taken, but the outstanding point breaks off the twin towns Coolangatta, QLD, and Tweed Heads, NSW, have created some of the best surfing in Australia, if not the world. With three surfing beaches and a huge variety of conditions on any given day, this area is the true Shangri-La of surfing. Summer brings a young crowd of surfers and backpackers, as well as families on holiday and retired couples, but any way you cut it, the atmosphere is always relaxed. With less neon, fewer skyscrapers, and better breaks and beaches, Coolie and Tweed Heads is the perfect place for a break from the up-tempo Gold Coast. As locals like to say, they're

QUEENSLAND

close enough to Surfers and far enough away. The Tweed-Coolangatta border is only really marked by discrepancies in daylight savings time, most notably at New Year's Eve, when eager partygoers and champagne lovers run across the street and ring in the new year twice.

▐ TRANSPORTATION

Buses: Coach Trans (☎3215 5000 or ☎13 12 30) runs to **Brisbane** (2¼hr., about every 30min., 6:29am-6:48pm, $14) and **Surfers Paradise** (1hr., every 15-60min., 24hr., $4.35). Buses leave from the corner of Griffith and Dixon St. **McCafferty's/Greyhound** (☎5536 5177 or 13 14 99) stops in town on their way to Brisbane (2hr., 8 per day, $17) and Sydney (15hr., 4 per day, $93). **Suncoast Pacific's** (☎5531 6000) runs to Noosa (5hr., daily 2:45pm, $35) via Maroochy (4hr., $35). **Kirklands** (☎5536 1063) runs 2-4 buses per day to Brisbane (2hr., $15) and Byron Bay (1½hr., $17.50). **Surfside buslines** (☎3215 5000 or 13 12 30) runs the best **public transportation** within the Gold Coast. Routes 1 and 1A run from Kingscliff, NSW up to Paradise Point, including, of course, a stop at Surfers Paradise (45min., every 10-60min., 24hr., $4); a 1-day unlimited pass is $10, or buy sector tickets. Connections will get you to Gold Coast theme parks; buy your admission ticket from the driver and the bus ride is free.

Taxi: Tweed Heads Taxis (☎5536 1144), 24hr.

Car Rental: Tweed Auto Rentals, 21 Appel St., Kirra (☎5536 8000 or 1800 819 051). Rentals from $22, $150 per week.

▟ ▐ ORIENTATION AND PRACTICAL INFORMATION

Entering the twin towns from the Pacific Highway, head east on **Marine Palisade,** which runs parallel to the beach and through **Kirra, Coolangatta,** and **Tweed Heads. Griffith Street,** the main drag of Coolangatta, runs parallel to Marine Pde. one block farther from the coast. At the **Twin Towns Service Club,** Griffith meets **Wharf Street** from the south, the main thoroughfare of Tweed Heads; **Boundary Street** branches northeast from the same intersection, dividing the peninsula into QLD and NSW. At the end of the peninsula is the infamous **Point Danger,** whose cliffs were responsible for Captain Cook's shipwreck. It is now marked by the world's first laser lighthouse and a 270° view of the ocean.

Tourist Office: Tweed Heads Tourist Office, 39 Wharf St. (☎5536 4244 or 1800 674 414), toward the Tweed Mall from the corner of Bay and Wharf St. Their free *Tweed-Coolangatta Visitors Guide* is indispensable. Open M-F 9am-5pm. **Gold Coast Tourism Bureau** (☎5536 7765), at the corner of Griffith and Warner St. Open M-F 8am-5pm, Sa 8am-4pm, Su 9am-1pm.

Banks: Find 24hr. **ATMs** at **National Bank,** 84-88 Griffith St., at the corner of Warner St., and at **Commonwealth Bank** in the Tweed Mall. Both open M-Th 9:30am-4pm, F 9:30am-5pm.

Bookstore: Second Hand Book Shop, 133 Griffith St., near the intersection with Warner. Open M-Sa 8:30am-5:30pm, Su 9am-5:30pm.

Pharmacy: Medicine Shoppe Pharmacy, 32 Griffith St. (☎5536 1013), across from Pipedreams. Open M-F 8am-5pm, Sa 8am-1pm; during holidays Su 9am-1pm.

Internet Access: PB's Oz Internet Cafe, 152 Griffith St. (☎5599 4536), offers a quick connection for $4 per 30min. Open daily 8:30am-7pm. **Coolangatta Internet Cafe** (☎5599 2001) is in the complex on the corner of Griffith and Warner St., bottom level. Open M-Sa 9am-7pm, Su noon-4pm. $4 per 30min.

Post Office: 2 Griffith St., at McLean St. Open M-F 8:30am-5pm. **Postal Code:** 2485.

ACCOMMODATIONS

There are plenty of beds here, but true budget accommodation is limited; book in advance during the high season.

Sunset Strip Budget Resort, 199 Boundary St. (☎5599 5517; www.sunsetstrip.com.au). Close to town and the best breaks, the Sunset Strip has excellent facilities, including an enormous kitchen and pool, as well as recreation and lounge areas. Guests of all ages intermingle happily. Large, yet cozy and personal. Key deposit $10. Reception 7am-11pm. Singles $35; twins, doubles, and triples $25 per person; quads $22.50 per person; rates lower for multiple night stays. AmEx/MC/V. ❸

Coolangatta YHA, 230 Coolangatta Rd., Billinga (☎5536 7644), near the airport, 3km north of Coolie; look for the huge murals. Features kitchen, laundry, game room, BBQ, TV lounge, pool, Internet access ($2 per 20min.), bikes with surfboard racks, daily drop off and pickup at the town center, and the best waves. Courtesy pickup from bus stop with advance notice. Breakfast included. Lockers. Dorms $20, $130 per week including 5 dinners; singles $35; doubles $44. YHA discount $3. ❷

Kirra Beach Hotel (☎5536 3311), on the corner of Miles St. and Marine Pde. It may be around Kirra Point from Coolangatta, but its clean, bright rooms (with private bath and TV) are a stone's throw from some of the world's most perfect barrel waves. Singles $33; doubles $44-55. ❸

Kirra Beach Tourist Park, on Charlotte St., Kirra (☎5581 7744). Once you hit Kirra, turn right onto Coolangatta Rd.; Charlotte St. is the first on the right. Great facilities: laundry, pool, TV room, and jungle gym for the kids. Linen $7. Office open 7am-7pm. Rooms with shared bath $35 for up to 3 people, peak $45; tent and van sites for 2 $20/$26; powered $20/$28; spacious cabin for 4 $65/$110. ❸

FOOD

Restaurants of every kind and clientele thrive on Griffith St. Coles **supermarket** is in Tweeds Mall on Wharf St. and there is a 24hr. **convenience store** on Griffith St.

Little Malaya Restaurant, 52 Marine Pde., Kirra (☎5536 2690), has a tasty menu, including many vegetarian options for $10.50. Open noon-2pm and 5:30-10pm. AmEx/DC/MC/V. ❷

Rainbow Bay Surf Club, 2 Snapper Rocks (☎5536 6390), has an incredible view of Rainbow Bay and the surfers below. Family-oriented and packed in summer, they serve lunch ($5.50-$13), dinner ($12-$16), and drinks. Open 11:30am-2pm, 5:30-8pm. ❸

Portuguese Hot Chicks, 91 Griffith St. (☎5536 6597), near Warner St., has late-night chicken burgers ($4.50) and chips. No promise of hot, Portuguese women. Open M-W 10am-9pm, Th-F 10am-late, Sa 8am-late, Su 8am-9pm. ❶

Sunshine Thai, 157 Griffith St. (☎5599 4442), serves a mean curry ($15) in an elegant setting. Open W-M 5:30-10pm. ❷

NIGHTLIFE

Though the waves are hot, local nightlife leaves a little to be desired. For endless clubs and pubs, head to **Surfers,** nightlife hub of the Gold Coast, just a quick bus away on Surfside buslines (see **Transportation,** p. 320).

Twin Towns Service Club (☎5536 2277), at Griffith and Wharf St. This gigantic space-ship-like club caters to an older crowd, with tons of slot machines, cheap food, and booze in 6 different restaurants, live entertainment, and free M night movies.

QUEENSLAND

Calypso Tavern, 97 Griffith St. (☎5599 2677), features a video wall, plush seating, younger crowd, and live music on Su. Open daily 10am-midnight.

Balcony Beach Club, on Marine Pde., has a chic nightclub feel. Open W-Sa 10pm-3am. Downstairs, the **Coolangatta Hotel** has live music Th-Su, with karaoke Su afternoons and cover bands the rest of the week. Open M-Th and Sa-Su 9am-midnight, F 9am-1am.

Tenpin (☎5536 1606), across from the Tweed Mall, combines disco and bowling in a medley of flying pins, driving beats, and stylish shoes at **Cosmic Rock 'n' Bowl.** Open F-Sa 8:30pm-late.

🦎 🐦 SIGHTS AND ACTIVITIES

Coolangatta-Tweed Heads' greatest attractions are the beaches that line its perimeter. The family-oriented **Rainbow Bay** and **Coolangatta Beach,** off of Marine Pde., have the safest swimming on the Gold Coast. **Flagstaff** and **Duranbah Beaches** lie on the southeast side of the peninsula; the latter is famous among surfers for its fast waves. The three point breaks, **Kirra, Snapper Rocks,** and **Greenmount,** are some of the best in the world.

The walkway that begins to the left of Point Danger, facing the ocean, and continues to Greenmount Beach is beautiful with lush greenery on one side, and sand and sea on the other. You'll trip over kangaroos, emus, and exotic birds at the **Currumbin Wildlife Sanctuary,** 7km north off the Pacific Hwy. on Tomewin St., a Surfside bus stop. Help feed the lorikeets (daily 8am and 4pm); be sure to duck to avoid their diving beaks. (☎5534 1266. Open daily 8am-5pm.) For another pretty view, follow signs for the **lookout** on Razorback, via Wharf and Florence St., to view Mt. Warning (on your right as you enter the lookout clearing) amidst the subtropical greenery of QLD and NSW.

Tweed Endeavor Cruises leads terrific river and rainforest cruises on a 150-person double-decker vessel. (☎5536 8800. 1½hr. cruise W and Su $24, children $12. 4½hr. with BBQ lunch M, W, and F-Su $49. 4½hr. with seafood lunch Tu and Th $58/54.)

> **MIND THE FLAGS.** Swimmers and surfers should obey all posted warnings. **Red flags** mean the water is unsafe; **yellow flags** ask that visitors exercise extreme caution. **Red and yellow flags** mean swimming is safe between the flags. **Green flags** are put up when the water is safe within flagged areas.

Surfers are welcoming and surf shops are on every corner. **Kirra Surf Club,** located where Coolangatta Rd. meets Musgrave St., is an area landmark. You can find board rentals at **Pipedreams** on Griffith St., in the Showcase Shopping Center. (☎5599 1164. Boards half-day $20, full-day $30. Open M-Sa 9am-5pm, Su 10am-3pm.) For a surfing lesson with plenty of one-on-one feedback, call the personable Dennis at **Walkin' on Water.** He'll provide all equipment and get you standing in no time. (☎5534 1886; www.walkinonwater.com. Lessons from $35.)

During the annual **Wintersun Festival** (first week in June), Australia's biggest rock and roll event, the twin cities celebrate Elvis and the rocking fifties and sixties.

SURFERS PARADISE   ☎07

Though Adam and Eve might have packed up and left, today's partygoers pluck the proverbial apple of this Eden night after long, dance-filled night. Narrow urban strips, packed with storefronts, cafes, and other amusements, hug miles of gorgeous beachside. Though towering hotels shade the very beaches that caused their creation, Surfers Paradise is on nearly every backpacker's itinerary. Why? They come for the thundering nightlife and post-pub street stumbling that follows.

Surfers Paradise

⌂ ACCOMMODATIONS
Acquarius, **2**
Cheers, **6**
Gold Coast International
   Backpackers Resort, **10**
Islander Backpackers
   Resort, **20**
Silver Sands Motel, **9**
Sleeping Inn Surfers, **7**
Surf 'n' Sun, **5**
Surfers Paradise
   Backpackers, **11**
Trekkers, **1**

🍴 FOOD
Al Fresco, **8**
Hard Rock Cafe, **17**
Peter's Fish Market, **3**
Seaway Cafe, **4**

★ NIGHTLIFE
Cocktails and Dreams/
   The Party, **13**
The Drink, **15**
M.P., **12**
Melba's, **14**
O'Malley's, **19**
Rose and Crown, **18**
Sugar Shack, **16**

When they wake up, all is calm, the beach is just as beautiful as the day before, and life is good. Then—repeat. Don't be put off, though, by the party atmosphere—Surfers also serves as a convenient base for nearby theme parks, the lush Hinterland, and unspoiled South Stradbroke Island.

▗ TRANSPORTATION

Buses: The **Transit Centre** is at the corner of Beach Rd. and Ferny Ave., 1 block west of Paradise Centre. (Open daily 7am-10pm.) **McCafferty's/Greyhound** (☎ 13 14 99) offers service to: Brisbane (1½-2hr., 7 per day 4:35am-10pm, $17); Byron Bay (2hr., 7 per day 8am-9:15pm, $27); Cairns (30hr., 6 per day 4:30am-8pm, $209); and Sydney (14-15hr., 5 per day, 8am-9:15pm, $93). **Premier Motor Service** (☎ 13 34 10) and **Kirklands** (☎ 1300 367 077; best for Byron Bay and NSW coast) offer similar service with slightly cheaper fares. Lockers are available 6am-8:30pm (12hr. $4-8).

Local Buses: Surfside (☎ 5571 6555 or 13 12 30), the local 24hr. bus company, runs to roadside stops along the **Gold Coast Highway**, as well as the **Pacific Fair Mall** (Bus 1, $2.20 one way), the **theme parks** (Bus 1x or 1a, $2.20-$4.35), and **Southport** (Bus 1, 1a, 3, or 10; $2.20). Buses pick up along the Gold Coast Hwy. and Ferney Ave.; grab a schedule at the Surfside information center, at Cavill and Ferny Ave., near the river. **Gold Coast Tourist Shuttle** (☎ 5574 5111) offers transport to all theme parks with pickup and drop off from local accommodation and unlimited travel on Surfside's service (1-day Gold pass $15, concessions $8; 1-week $60/$30).

Taxis: Regent Taxis (☎ 5588 1234 or 13 10 08). For those not in a hurry, **peddle cabs** are often found on the corner of Cavill Ave. and Gold Coast Hwy.

Car Rental: Kanga Car and Moped Hire, 3024 Gold Coast Hwy. (☎ 5527 6088 or ☎ 1800 671 361), offers the cheapest car rental on the coast (starting at $19

QUEENSLAND

per day); rental available to drivers under 25. Open daily 8am-5pm. **Thrifty** (☎5538 6511), on the corner of Enderley Ave. and Gold Coast Hwy., rents from $42.90.

ORIENTATION

Maps of Surfers are long and thin, reflecting the fact that all the action is squeezed into a strip many kilometers long and just a few blocks wide between the ocean and the **Nerang River.** Three main avenues run parallel to the shore: the **Esplanade,** which skirts the beach; the southbound **Gold Coast Hwy.,** a block over; and **Ferney Ave.,** the northbound Gold Coast Hwy., one more block inland. Surfers centers on **Cavill Mall,** a pedestrian street lined with restaurants, cafes, bars, souvenir shops, and the Paradise Centre. Cavill Mall runs perpendicular to the Esplanade, which continues north past **Main Beach** to the **Marina** and the **Spit,** the end of the peninsula just past Seaworld. **Southport** is located along the Gold Coast Hwy., past Main Beach and 3km northwest of the city center. To the south is **Broadbeach,** home of the enormous Conrad Hotel Jupiter Casino and the monolithic **Pacific Fair Mall.**

PRACTICAL INFORMATION

Tourist Offices: Gold Coast Tourism Bureau (☎5538 4419) is the main tourist office, in a kiosk on Cavill Mall. Open M-F 8:30am-5:30pm, Sa 9am-5pm, Su 9am-3:30pm. The **Backpackers Information Centre** (☎5592 2911 or 1800 359 830), in the transit center, offers information and arranges transport to the hostels in their association. Open daily 8am-5:30pm. After hours, info and a direct phone to hostels are still available.

Banks: Westpac, on the corner of Cavill Ave. and Gold Coast Hwy., has a 24hr. **ATM,** as does **Commonwealth Bank,** right next door on the highway. Both banks open M-Th 9:30am-4pm, F 9:30am-5pm. ATMs are also located in most shopping centers.

Market: A Woolworth's **supermarket** is located in the basement of the Paradise Centre. Open M-F 8am-9pm, Sa 8:30am-5:30pm, Su 9am-6pm.

Police: 68 Ferny Ave. (☎5570 7888), opposite the Cypress Ave. carpark. There's also a substation (☎5583 9733) on the corner of Cavill Mall and the Esplanade.

Medical Services: Gold Coast General Hospital, 108 Nerang St., Southport (☎5571 8211). **Gold Coast Medical Transport** (☎13 12 33). **Day Night Surgery** (☎5592 2299), in the Piazza Mall on the Gold Coast Hwy., for non-emergency care. Open daily 7am-10pm.

Internet Access: Email Centre, 51 Orchid Ave. (☎5538 7500). $5 per hr. Open daily in summer 8:30am-midnight, in winter 9am-11pm. **Mercari Imaging** (☎5538 4937), on the Gold Coast Hwy. between Cavill and Elkhorn Ave., offers a cheap, fast connection ($3.30 per hour). Open daily 9am-8pm. Most hostels also have Internet access.

Post Office: Main branch inside the Paradise Centre, on Cavill Mall. Open M-F 9am-5:30pm, Sa 9am-12:30pm. **Postal Code:** 4217.

ACCOMMODATIONS

In Surfers, hostel staff assume the role of camp counselors, each night leading the troops to cheap meals and pre-packaged fun. Nightclubs provide hostels with plenty of freebies, so any traveler with party intentions should opt for hostel accommodations to avoid high cover charges. For a more restful stay, seek quieter digs at independent or highway hostels; of the listings below, all belong to the party-hard Backpackers Association except Gold Coast International, Silver Sands Motel, and the Islander. Summer and Easter are peak seasons—book ahead and expect prices around $5 higher than current listings. Unless listed otherwise, hostels have free pickup, 10am check-out, $10 key deposit, laundry, and TV rooms.

Trekkers, 22 White St., Southport (☎5591 5616 or 1800 100 004), 3km north of city center; call for free pick-up. 15min. from beach. Guests feel they are a part of this comfortable, social hostel. Spotless rooms, some with private bath; lots of character and TV in all doubles. Free courtesy bus. Saltwater pool, free board and bike use. W BBQ night. Reception daily 7am-8pm. Dorms $21; doubles $50. ISIC/VIP/YHA $20/48. ❷

Sleeping Inn Surfers, 26 Peninsular Dr. (☎5592 4455 or 1800 817 832; www.sleepinginn.com.au), a 10min. walk from the Transit Centre across Ferny Ave. Self-contained units with kitchen and living room are perfect for groups. Mellow atmosphere. Hot tub, pool, Internet, and game room. Reception daily 7am-10pm (11pm in summer), with late night check-in bell. Dorms $21; apartments from $110, for up to 6 people. EFTPOS. ISIC/VIP/YHA/NOMADS/student discount $1. AmEx/MC/V. ❷

Surfers Paradise Backpackers Resort, 2837 Gold Coast Hwy. (☎5592 4677 or 1800 282 800; www.surfersparadisebackpackers.com.au), a 15min. walk south along the highway to the corner of Wharf Rd. and 150m from the beach. Free courtesy bus. Spotless, happy, and family-run, "The Resort" also has outstanding facilities: big kitchen bar, tennis court, pool, free laundry, and dorms with private bath. Free board use. Bicycle rental $5. Sauna ($4 per 45 min.). Internet $1.50 per 15min. Reception daily 7:30am-7pm. Dorms $23; nicer units $27 per person. VIP/YHA discount $2. MC/V. ❷

Gold Coast International Backpackers Resort, 28 Hamilton Ave. (☎5592 5888 or 1800 801 230; www.goldcoastbackpackers.com.au), a 5min. walk north from Cavill Ave. and 2min. from the beach. More modern and less party-oriented than many of its competitors, the Gold Coast International has the feel of a luxury motel, with an impressive reception area and guests keeping more to themselves. Free drink upon arrival with presentation of *Let's Go* book. Bright, small dorms with balcony, TV, and private bath. Bar and beer garden, game room, free board use, Internet, kitchen, and carpark. Key deposit $20. Reception daily 7:30am-10pm. Dorms $20; singles $50; twins and doubles $25 per person. MC/V. ❷

Aquarius, 44 Queen St., Southport (☎5527 1300 or 1800 229 955). Call for courtesy bus or, from Surfers, follow the Gold Coast Hwy. over the bridge and take your first left. Clean rooms, glow worm trips, Internet, pool, spa, and garden. Reception daily 7:30am-10pm. Dorms $18; doubles $44. ISIC/VIP/YHA. ❷

Surf 'n' Sun, 3323 Gold Coast Hwy. (☎5592 2363 or 1800 678 194), on the corner of Ocean Ave., close to beach. Famous for its party atmosphere, though dorms are straight out of the seventies. Private bathrooms, courtesy bus, pool, and Internet. Reception 7-10:30pm. Dorms $25, weekly $126; doubles $55. VIP discount available. ❸

Islander Backpackers Resort, 6 Beach Rd. (☎5538 8000 or 1800 074 393), right next door to the transit station. Rooms are average, but have the best location in town and include use of the swank hotel amenities next door. Bath, TV, balcony, and lockers in rooms. Key deposit $25. Reception 24hr. Pool, hot tub, sauna, squash, tennis, Internet cafe, game room, and sports bar. 4-bed dorms $18; 6-bed dorms $12, but these go quickly. Singles and doubles $50. EFTPOS. NOMADS discount $1. AmEx/MC/V. ❶

British Arms YHA, 70 Sea World Dr. (☎5571 1776 or 1800 680 268; www.britisharms.com.au), on the way to the Spit and close to Main Beach. Though rooms and amenities are basic, a great pub and work for stay opportunities appeal to many backpackers. Reception 8am-9pm. Dorms $22; doubles $51. VIP/YHA discount $1. ❷

Cheers, 8 Pine Ave. (☎5531 6539 or 1800 636 539), just off Ferny Ave. The largest hostel in Surfers. Rooms are no-frill and impersonal, but the bar and beer garden are the best among the hostels. Pool, hot tub, free Internet, $6 BBQ, lockers. Reception daily 8am-10:30pm. Dorms $22. VIP/YHA discount $1. ❷

Silver Sands Motel, 2985 Gold Coast Hwy. (☎5538 6041), at the corner of Markwell Ave. Perfect for couples or small groups seeking more privacy and less partying than offered by the hostels. Modern, beach house rooms have A/C, kitchenette, private bath, and TV. Pool and BBQ. Only 11 rooms; book ahead. Reception 7am-7pm. Doubles $55, $99 during peak season. $25 per head for groups of 3 or 4. AmEx/MC/V. ❸

◘ FOOD

Inexpensive bistros, 24hr. cafes, fast food joints, and Asian restaurants cluster around Cavill Mall. Tedder Ave. near Main Beach is lined with bistros, bakeries, classy cafes, and Ferraris.

Al Fresco, 2991 Gold Coast Hwy. (☎5538 0395), just past Hamilton Ave. This mom 'n' pop Italian eatery will have you smiling the minute you walk in the door and win you over with their excellent pasta ($13.50-$19.50), friendly service, and complimentary creme de cacao. Open daily 5:30pm-late. ❸

Peter's Fish Market, 120 Sea World Dr. (☎5591 7747), toward the Spit. Opt for the best fish 'n' chips in town ($5.50), or try your luck cooking their fresh raw seafood. Open M-F 9am-8pm, Sa-Su 8am-8pm. ❶

Seaway Cafe (☎5591 6970) has snacks to satisfy those who trek to the end of the Spit. Open daily 7:30am-5pm. ❶

Hard Rock Cafe (☎5539 9377), on the corner of Cavill Ave. and Gold Coast Hwy. All glitzy places need one. Open daily 11:30am-late. ❹

Anglers Arms, 50 Queen St., Southport (☎5532 1677). Often the kickoff spot for the Southport hostels' club crawls, the restaurant and bar start the night right with cheap pub food, pool tables, and the ever-present pokies. Open daily 10am-late. ❶

◪ BEACHES, SURFING, AND WATER SPORTS

White sand beaches stretch unbroken 25km from the quiet **Main Beach** on the Spit peninsula all the way south to Coolangatta's Snapper Rocks. Surfers Paradise is a bit of a misnomer, however. The outstanding beach breaks are great for beginners, but the best surfing is to the south. Surfing conditions vary considerably, especially as sand shifts to alter the breaks; local surfers sometimes drive up and down the coast looking for the best waves. Since weather conditions significantly alter an area's quality and danger level, beginners and experienced surfers alike should ask around before hitting the beach. For more detailed info, hang ten to www.coastal-watch.com or listen to 90.9 Sea FM's surf reports. Pay attention to the flags, which designate areas patrolled by Surf Life Savers (red flags indicate danger; half red and half yellow flags indiate that the beach is patrolled and relatively safe to swim).

The most popular beach among boardless beachgoers is **Surfers North.** Near the end of Staghorn Ave. and just north of Surfers Paradise, it's the most central hangout off the Paradise Centre Mall and the recipient of blaring music from the local

WHAT A WHOPPER Throughout Australia, the yellow and red signs for the fast food joint "Hungry Jack's" provoke a mental double-take. Haven't I seen that logo before? Once inside, the mystery deepens. Whoppers? Chicken tenders? My god, they've ripped off Burger King! Hey, Sherlock, it *isn't* a BK imposter. Burger King is well aware of Hungry Jack's—it's theirs. Before Burger King expanded to Oz, some enterprising fellow went to the Australian patent office and got the rights to the name "Burger King," thinking the big boys in the States would pay him off to use the name in Australia. The fast food intelligentsia was not duped, however. Simply changing the name to Hungry Jack's, Burger King set up shop in Australia with the same logo, food, and promotions. And don't even think about it, McDonald's is already here...

radio station during the summer. Farther south is **Broadbeach,** then **Kurrawa,** near the Pacific Fair Shopping Center. **Burleigh Heads** has a popular surfing area, though it can be mobbed and often has dangerous breaks. Recently, surfing has become popular at **South Stradbroke Island,** as well. The beaches there are unpatrolled, however, so use common sense and bring a friend who knows the waters.

For equipment, try the **Surfers Beach Clubhouse** kiosk on the beach end of Cavill Mall. (☎5526 7077. Longboards $15 per hr., $25 per 3hr., $40 per day. Wet suits $5 with a board. Short boards or body boards $10 per hr., $20 per 3hr., $30 per day.) Bag storage free with rental, otherwise $5. Their surf school will get you standing for $45, or $35 for students or backpackers. (Open in summer 8am-5pm; in winter 9am-5pm.) **Gold Coast Kayaking** runs excellent sea kayaking tours from the Spit to South Stradbroke Island, where you snorkel, have tea or brekkie, and go for a bushwalk to the surf beach. (☎0419 7332 02. 3hr. trips 6:30am and 2:30pm. $35, including pickup and drop-off.)

Although their family-oriented (and very affordable) houseboat tour of the Broadwater can get a bit long, **Seabreeze Sports** spices it up with parasailing and waverunner excursions from their boat. (☎5527 1099. Open daily 9am-1pm. Houseboat cruise $22, with parasailing $57, with waverunner $45.)

◎ SIGHTS AND ACTIVITIES

Infinity, (☎5538 2988; www.infinitygc.com.au), at the corner of Ferny and Elkhorn Ave., is a must for groups of all ages. The first of its kind in the world, the attraction's lights and optical illusions create a futuristic maze through 12 different fantasy worlds. Become a wandering microchip in the Electron Maze before jiggling and jiving in the Wobbly. (30min. Open 10am-10pm. $18.90; students $15.90; children $10.90; families $48.90.) For more traditional art, visit the **Gold Coast Arts Centre,** 135 Bundall Rd. (☎5581 6567), 3km from the city center. Puruse the art gallery before catching a show at the 1200-seat theater. (Open M-F 10am-5pm, Sa-Su 11am-5pm. Free.) The **Gold Coast Marathon** (☎5564 8733; www.goldcoastmarathon.com.au) will stream down the coast the first week of July 2003. Mid-October means the Honda Indy 300 (www.indy.com.au), a four-day extravaganza of races highlighted by the Indy event, which follows a track around Surfers and down the Esplanade. Crowds pack the streets and hang out of highrises to see airshows and fireworks. Accommodations are booked months in advance. Avoid Surfers during **Schoolies** (mid-November to mid-December), when the beach is mobbed by teens on summer break. Events include free beach dance parties, concerts, and cinemas.

◤ THEME PARKS AND THRILL RIDES

Packed with domestic tourists and kids on candy highs, Surfers' theme parks are distinctive only for their setting: the town spawns roller coasters as frequently as shopping centers. Tickets to all parks can be bought at slightly reduced prices from the tourist info booth on Cavill Mall. Surfside, Coachtrans, and Gold Coast Tourist Shuttle provide **transportation** to all parks; Surfside offers $3 return transport to the park with purchase of a theme park ticket from the driver. Wet 'N' Wild, Dreamworld, and Movie World are all 20min. north on the Pacific Hwy.; Seaworld is north on Seaworld Dr., on the Spit.

DREAMWORLD. The much trumpeted "Tower of Terror" is the tallest and fastest ride in the world, rocketing from 0 to 160km per hour in only seven seconds. *(☎5588 1111 or 1800 073 300; www.dreamworld.com.au. Open daily 9:30am-5pm. $54, concessions and ages 4-13 $35.)*

PARKING IN PARADISE Everyone knows that there is nothing more irritating than returning to your car to find that the village parking patrol has ticketed you for mistakenly misjudging the two hours that the meter allotted you. No need to fear in Surfers, though: for over 35 years, beautiful betties decked in nothing more than a golden bikini have traveled the streets of Surfers placing coins in meters on the verge of expiring. If you return to your car and find a card from the Meter Maids, know that they've saved you from paying a parking fine. Check them out in the mini Meter Maid Museum, upstairs in the Paradise Center.

WET 'N' WILD. On hot summer days, the whitewater flumes of this water park will cool you down; in the winter, the slides and pools are heated. (☎5573 2255; www.wetnwild.com.au. Open daily 10am-4pm. $33, children and concessions $21.)

SEAWORLD. Lots of fish, dolphins, sharks, seals, some sad-looking pigeons, a few rides, and a hilarious sea lion show are all on display. A new polar bear exhibit brings the Arctic to Oz. (☎5588 2205; www.seaworld.com.au. Open daily 10am-5pm. $54, children and concessions $35. Swimming with dolphins $110, children $45. Arrive early in the morning to reserve.)

MOVIE WORLD. This Warner Brothers park features a new Harry Potter simulation, as well as the 6min. *Wild Wild West* ride, which climaxes in a 70kph, 20m drop into water. (A 25min. drive north of Surfers, on the Pacific Hwy. ☎5573 8485; www.movieworld.com.au. Open daily 9:30am-5:30pm. $52, concessions $33; $48/$32 at info booth.)

OTHER SPILLS AND CHILLS. Several forms of **bungy jumping** and **virtual reality** rides share a small plot on the corner of the Gold Coast Hwy. and Palm Ave. (Most open daily 10am-10pm. Virtual reality $7; bungy $30-$75.) The highlight is the **Sling Shot**, a two-person compartment that propels occupants 80m up at a speed of 160km per hour. (☎5570 2700. $30.)

♫ 🎭 ENTERTAINMENT AND NIGHTLIFE

Aside from partying and drinking, the main nighttime activity in Surfers seems to be getting the best deals on partying and drinking. Most of the hostels provide free passes and cheap meal tickets for several clubs on a given night. The majority of hot spots are on Orchid Ave., known as the "Avenue," and are open until 5am; it seems that people don't get tired in Paradise. **Bring your passport**, as some clubs won't accept other forms of ID. The Gold Coast Backpackers Association organizes events every night; highlights are Tuesday "70s night" and the infamous **club crawl**. (☎1800 359 830. W and Sa 9:30pm. $16 tickets from participating hostels include entry to clubs, a free drink at the three clubs, a photo, and a t-shirt.) High rollers try their luck at **Conrad Jupiters Casino**. (☎5592 1133, box office ☎1800 074 144. Open 24hr.) For details on nightly events go to www.emugigs.com.

- ▨ **Melba's**, 46 Cavill Ave. (☎5538 7411). A restaurant turned classy nightclub by dark, Melba's avoids Orchid Ave.'s meat-market feel. Grooves to mainstream and techno. Happy Hour 4-10pm in the upstairs nightclub, 4-8pm in the downstairs restaurant/bar. Cover in club $8, includes free drink. Restaurant open daily 8am-3am; club W-Th 8pm-5am, F 5pm-5am, Sa-Su 7pm-5am.

- ▨ **Cocktails and Dreams** (☎5592 1955), The Mark, Orchid Ave. Cruise to this constantly packed club, popular with backpackers and more. Organizes events with the hostels, such as Tu 70s night, W and Sa Club Crawl. Downstairs, **The Party** plays an alternative songlist. Cover $5-7. Open F-Sa 8pm-5am, Su-Th 9pm-5am.

Rose and Crown (☎5531 5425), Raptis Plaza on Cavill Ave. Popular with many crowds. Dance and Top-40 play in one room, while talented live bands perform in the other (W and F). Drink specials and prizes (Th and Su). Cover $3-6. Open Tu-W 8pm-3am, Th-Sa 8pm-5am, Su 8pm-2am.

Sugar Shack, 20 Orchid Ave. (☎5538 7600). Fun, casual dance hall that grooves to varied classic hits. Live music Su-M and Th. Cover $3-5. Open daily 11:30am-5am.

The Drink, 4 Orchid Ave. (☎5570 6155). Grind it all night long at Surfers' ultimate dance club. Cover after 10pm $5-10. Open Tu-Su 8pm-5am.

O'Malley's, 1 Cavill Ave. (☎5570 4075). Packed pub with balcony view over the Mall and The Esplanade. Live pop rock music every night. Open Su-Th noon-midnight, F-Sa noon-2am.

M.P., or the **Meeting Place** (☎5526 2337), Forum Arcade. Connects 26 Orchid Ave. to 3171 Gold Coast Hwy. Surfers' only gay and lesbian club, though males predominate. Su $5 cover for free beer and hot dogs, Happy Hour until 8pm, and 3 shows. Open Tu-Th 9pm-late, F-Sa 9pm-5am, Su 5pm-late.

▶ DAYTRIP FROM SURFERS: SOUTH STRADBROKE

Separated from the Spit by a thin channel, South Straddie is one of Surfers' hidden gems. Largely undeveloped and home to friendly free-roaming wallabies, the long, narrow island (22km by 3km) is lined by quiet river beaches on the west side and empty surf beaches and dunes on the east. **Surf Beach,** on the ocean side, is patrolled by lifesavers. The main activity center is the **South Stradbroke Island Resort ❺,** with pools, spas, sauna, watersports, tennis courts, restaurants, and a virtual monopoly on affordable non-camping accommodation. Individual cabins have TV and fridge. (☎5577 3311 or 1800 074 125. $99.)

The island also offers camping options with toilets, showers, and BBQ. **Tippler's camping area ❶** is just 300m from the resort. (☎5577 2849.) **Ferries** run from Gate C of the Runaway Bay Marina, 247 Bayview St., off the Gold Coast Hwy. past Southport. One-way bus fare from Surfers Paradise transit center to Runaway Bay is $3.20, but free for those staying at the resort. (☎5577 3311. 20min.; depart Runaway daily 7am and 10:30am, return 2:30pm and 5pm; return $25, free Su lunch.) The island's other campgrounds are more private and difficult to reach. **Water taxis** (☎04 1875 9789) also leave from Gate C of the Runaway Bay to motor guests to **Currigee ❶** (☎5577 3932; $30 one-way taxi for up to 4 people) and **The Bedrooms ❶** campgrounds (☎5577 2849; $80 one-way. Sites for 2 $12, peak $13.)

GOLD COAST HINTERLAND ☎07

Unbelievably, within an hour or so from the bustling coast, you can bushwalk through subtropical rainforest, enjoy spectacular views, and stroll through laidback towns. The Hinterland makes for a perfect escape from the glitz of the coast; a little exploration will undoubtedly complete your visit to the region.

Travel by car offers the most flexible and wallet-friendly means to see the Hinterland. An easy one-day drive south along **Pacific Highway 1** from the Gold Coast starts at **Nerang,** passes the **Natural Bridge,** descends into the valley, ascends to **Springbrook,** and finally returns to the Coast via **Mudgeeraba** and **Currumbin.** Along the way, you will see turn-offs for Lamington National Park, Mt. Tamborine, Springbrook National Park, and Mt. Cougal National Park. The parks are close enough to one another that two or more can be combined into a multi-day trip. For more info, contact Queensland National Parks (☎13 13 04; www.qld.gov.au).

THE LOCAL STORY

TIM THE YOWIE MAN

I was in Springbrook National Park when I saw it: the footprint of a Yowie—the Australian bigfoot. The track was immense, with deep indentations revealing the hulking size of the monster. I shivered, even though I was viewing the footprint from the safe confines of a small mountain cafe, where it was on display.

So started my interest in yowies, and my affair with Tim the Yowie Man.

Tim the Yowie Man has been searching out yowies since 1994, when he spotted a huge, ape-like creature while doing thesis research in the Snowy Mountains of New South Wales. After the first yowie, he became intrigued by other mysteries of the natural world, officially changing his name to TYM (Tim the Yowie Man) and calling himself a "cryptonaturalist," or one who studies strange animals and other mysterious phenomena. Tim has made a career out of his hobby, traveling worldwide to sleuth out mysterious events, writing a book on his travels, and appearing on local and national television to report his findings. Aside from yowie baiting, he's also explored the Hawaiian lava tubes in search of a beast rumored to live there, braved the depths of murky Scottish waters in search of the Loch Ness Monster, and—perhaps his most daring feat—exposed the secret Australian location of the American TV series *Survivor II* (and airdropped candybars to the contestants). At the age of 28, he's better-traveled than the vast majority of people will ever be, having visited

Alternatively, buses and tours can get you almost anywhere in the Hinterland. **Mountain Coach Company** has a bus tour to Mt. Tamborine and O'Reilly's Park in Lamington National Park from Coolangatta, Burleigh, and Surfers. (☎5524 4249. $42, children $22, families $117; includes pickup and dropoff.) **Scenic Hinterland Day Tours** picks up from Gold Coast resorts and offers a trip to Springbrook and the Natural Bridge, including Purlingbrook Falls, a thousand-year-old forest. (☎5531 5536. $38, concessions $35, under 12 $26, families $115.) **All State Scenic Tours** accesses O'Reilly's Park in Lamington from transit center in Brisbane. (☎3003 0700. Departs Su-F 9:30am, returns 5:45pm. $44 return, ages 4-16 $33.) Some hostels offer tours to Lamington National Park or to see the glowworms at the Natural Bridge.

LAMINGTON NATIONAL PARK

The 200km² of Lamington National Park are split into two accessible sections: **Green Mountains/ O'Reilly's** and **Binna Burra.** The park's 160km of well-trod paths lead to spectacular waterfalls, clear springs, subtropical rainforests, and the NSW border ridge, with magnificent views of Mt. Warning's ancient volcanic crater. Trails appeal to both day-trippers and more serious bushwalkers, ranging in length from 1 to over 20km.

GREEN MOUNTAINS. Green Mountains (and within it, the privately owned **O'Reilly's Park**) can only be reached via Nerang and Canungua along a switch-back road, off the Pacific Hwy. (70km). The **Visitors Center,** on your right as you enter the park, books on-site camping and issues **bush camping ❶** permits. (☎5544 0634. Open M and W-Th 9-11am and 1-3:30pm; Tu and F 1-3:30pm. Register in advance for bush camping ☎13 13 04. $4.) **O'Reilly's ❺,** a rainforest guesthouse in O'Reilly's Park, charges high rates for their location. (☎5544 0644. Singles start at $125; doubles $200.) Take a 15-minute walk among the clouds on the **Tree Top circuit,** a bridge suspended from the heights of some impressive booyong trees. From O'Reilly's, the popular **Toolona Creek circuit** (17km, 5-6hr. return) will take you past numerous waterfalls and stands of native Antarctic beech trees on its way to stunning panoramas. The tracks to **Morans Falls** (4.6km, 1½hr., return) and **Python Rock** (3.4km, 1hr. return) start about 800m downhill from the information center; if you're only at the park for half a day, these routes are your best option. The Morans Falls trail descends deep into the rainforest before opening onto views of the Morans waterfall and gorge and the Albert River.

BINNA BURRA. To get to **Binna Burra,** follow the signs for Beechmont and Binna Burra from Nerang (37km). The **Visitors Center** books **camping ❶** and provides maps of the different hiking circuits. (☎5533 3584. Open Sa-Su 9am-3:30pm, occasionally M-F. Register for a bush camping permit through the Green Mountains park service ☎13 13 04. $4.) The **Binna Burra Mountain Lodge ❶,** on your right 1km past the Visitors Center, offers camping, B&B, and a daily bus service to the coast. (☎5533 3622. Sites $10, powered $13.50; 2-bed safari tents $40, 4-bed $60; B&B from $115 per person. Bus $44 return, children $22.) Your best bet for seeing a koala is along the **Caves circuit** (5km, 1½hr. return), which starts from the information center and winds past sweeping views of Darlington Range and Kweebani Cave. **Ship's Stern circuit** (19km return) passes stands of giant gum and cedar trees as it descends into the Kurraragin Valley; beyond the Lower Ballunjui Falls, eucalypt forests and wildflowers dominate.

TAMBORINE MOUNTAIN

Actually a 600m-high plateau, Tamborine Mountain contains nine small national parks of subtropical rainforest. Short walking tracks reveal countless waterfalls, native wildlife, clear-air vistas, and an attractive town, all just a short drive from the coast. To get to the park, exit **Pacific Hwy. 1** at Oxenford and follow the steep, twisting **Oxenford-Tamborine Rd.;** use low gear. Near the highway exit, check out the **Russel Hinze Park,** a swamp and island refuge for various water birds. Approaching the plateau, the road changes its name to MacDonnell Rd. without warning. Turn right onto Long Rd., right at the roundabout, and left at Geissmann Dr. to reach the **Tamborine Mountain Visitors Center** in Doughty Park, which provides maps and information. (☎5545 3200. Open daily 10:30am-3:30pm.)

Amid the park's greenery lies the town of **Mt. Tamborine,** offering Devonshire tea houses, B&Bs, and pottery shops. It's just an hour's drive from Brisbane and 35 minutes from the Gold Coast, so expect a constant flow of visitors. Pricey beds and limited hiking circuits make Tamborine ideal for a daytrip rather than a prolonged stay. If you do wish to stay the night, several religious centers on Keswick Rd. rent out cheap rooms to backpackers. Try the **OMF International Campsite ❶** (☎5545 3398), with $10 singles and a large kitchen and common room.

Within the park, six easy walking tracks are open to visitors. At times, their natural splendor is dimmed by traffic noises and intruding residential areas. The **Joalah circuit** (2.3km, 1hr.) offers subtropical rainforest and the picture-perfect Curtis Falls, but no vistas.

numerous countries and every single Australian town in his quest for the strange and mysterious.

Recently, I was able to talk to Tim on the phone about his adventures. When I spoke to him, he had just returned from the Australian outback, where he'd been investigating a sighting of *min min* lights (which look something like headlights, but are spotted only in remote areas and appear to follow people). In our conversation, Tim revealed himself to be both optimistic and realistic about his work, with a good dose of Australian humor to balance it all out.

"A lot of what I do, I don't find anything," Tim admitted to me when I asked about the results of the *min min* search. Still, that doesn't stop him from trying, which is more than half the fun. One doesn't have to actually find a yowie to have a great time hiking around and searching for one, he told me. He started hunting for answers, explaining, "I was intrigued—I wanted to solve mysteries." Although Tim does not constrain his sleuthing to his home continent, he told me that Australia keeps more mysteries than most. Because the large island contains tracts of unexplored land and very diverse creatures, there is a higher likelihood that undiscovered creatures exist here.

—**Abby Schlatter**

The **Witches Falls track** (2.7km, 50min.) runs along the western side of the plateau. Although the path offers views of the Dividing Range, there is more backyard than rainforest at the beginning. During the Dry, the raging falls turn into a leaky faucet. **The Knoll trail** (3km) follows Sandy Creek through dense rainforest before opening onto Cameron Falls. Head north on Tamborine Mountain Rd. and follow signs to reach **Cedar Creek Falls,** a stellar hike (4km) in the Cedar Creek National Park.

SPRINGBROOK NATIONAL PARK

As the northernmost remnant of Mt. Warning's explosive past, Springbrook plateau dominates the skyscape west of the Gold Coast. Covering over 2900 hectares of land, the national park consists of three accessible sections: **Springbrook Plateau,** the **Natural Bridge,** and **Mt. Cougal.** Springbrook's most noteworthy attractions include its striking rock formations and waterfalls, well-developed trail system, and fledgling ecotourism projects.

SPRINGBROOK PLATEAU. From the Pacific Hwy., head west on Springbrook Rd. (29km); the park can also be accessed via the Nerang-Murwillumbah Rd. and Springbrook-Nerang Rd. (18km). Follow signs to the unattended **Visitors Center** in the old schoolhouse for maps of the park's walks, lookouts, and camping and picnic areas. (Ranger ☎5533 5147.) **Camping ❶** is available at the Gwongorella picnic area ($4; book in advance through the number above.) Farther south on Springbrook Rd., Canyon Lookout leads to the Twin Falls Circuit (4km) and the popular day-long Warrie Circuit (17km). Both tracks lead through rock wedge caves and behind, around, and under many waterfalls. On a clear day at the **Best of All Lookout,** at the southern end of Springbrook Rd., you'll see Coolangatta and Byron Bay along the coast.

The first accommodation on the mountain to catch the sun, **Springbrook Mountain Lodge YHA ❸,** 317 Repeater Station Rd., is a small hostel near the Best of All Lookout that is perfect for a weekend getaway. (☎5533 5366. Book ahead. Roundtrip bus from Gold Coast $20 with advance notice. Rooms $33 per person, YHA discount $4; self-contained family cabin $88, weekend $132. AmEx/MC/V.)

At the **Forest of Dreams,** pottery guru Errol Barnes showcases over 10,000 glowworms in his noctarium (☎5533 5195; www.glowworms.com.au. On Lyrebird Ridge Rd. Tours daily every 30min., 11am-4pm, $8, children $5.) Glowing bodies of the celestial sort can be seen at **Springbrook Homestead,** the only public **observatory** in Southeast Queensland. (☎5533 5200. On Springbrook Rd., just before the turnoff for Purlingbrook Falls. Suggested donation. Call ahead.).

NATURAL BRIDGE. The Natural Bridge is located on the Nerang-Murwillumbah Rd., 30km from Nerang, or 43km via the Springbrook-Mudgeeraba Rd. Springbrook's most popular sight is on a 1km track, 3km north of the NSW border. The land arch developed as a cavern under a forceful waterfall; eventually, the water broke through the ceiling of the cave to create the arch. At night, the cavern comes alive with bats and glowworms. (Ranger ☎5533 5147.)

IT'S A BIRD! NO... Throughout the Hinterland one can find a rare Australian species known as the lyrebird. Capable of copying up to twenty different sounds that they hear in their environment, the lyrebird originally imitated sounds of other birds and animals. Now, as testament to their invaded habitat, the birds are known to mimic chainsaws, rewinding cameras, and car horns—proof that you can teach an old bird new tricks.

MT. COUGAL NATIONAL PARK. Signs from the Pacific Hwy. between Burleigh Heads (just south of Surfers) and Coolangatta lead to Mt. Cougal via **Currumbin Creek Road** (18km). A rugged part of Springbrook National Park, Mt. Cougal offers several views of Currumbin Creek as it plummets down a **natural water slide** and pools in deep holes. (20min. return. ☎5576 0217.) On your way to Mt. Cougal, don't miss the **Currumbin Rock Pool,** a deep freshwater pool with short cliff dives and smaller pools for lounging (12km from Currumbin). Only very daring folks attempt the slides and jumps at the rock pools; **use caution** and common sense at all of these risky attractions, and obey posted warnings.

SOUTHERN AND DARLING DOWNS

West of the Great Dividing Range lie the hills and valleys of the Southern Downs and the towns of Toowoomba, Warwick, and Stanthorpe. Toowoomba's carefully crafted greenery is only beginning to draw tourists, but the rich agriculture, rustic beauty, and small-town feeling of Stanthorpe and Warwick draw backpackers for seasonal work. Stanthorpe is also the center of Queensland's only wine region, the Granite Belt. For those coming to the Downs with time to spare, Giraween and Sundown National Parks please visitors with their wildflower displays (Sept.-Mar.), rock outcroppings, and spectacular views.

TOOWOOMBA   ☎07

With over 150 parks and gardens, many connected by bike and walking paths, Toowoomba (pop. 90,000) has outgrown its name, which is derived from an Aboriginal word meaning "swamp." Using "Garden City" as a more appropriate alias, Toowoomba consists of a formidable commercial center that fades into a seemingly endless suburbia, backed by breathtaking views of the Dividing Range.

When driving into town from Brisbane on the **Warrego Highway,** turn right at signs for **Margaret Street,** the town's main drag. It runs west through town, crossing the main north-south streets **Lindsey, Hume, Neil, Ruthven,** and **West** downtown. Ruthven St. S. turns into the **New England Highway** to Warwick and Stanthorpe.

McCafferty's (☎4690 9888) **buses** leave from 28-30 Neil St., running to: Brisbane (2hr.; Su-F 13 per day, Sa 11 per day; $21, round-trip $38); Melbourne (22hr., daily 5:20pm, $182); and Sydney (15hr., daily 8:50pm, $88). For northern destinations, connect in Brisbane. Head southeast on Kitchner St. off of Margaret St. and then turn left on James St. to get to the **Toowoomba Visitor Information Centre,** 86 James St. (☎4639 3797 or 1800 331 155; www.toowoomba.qld.gov.au. Open daily 9am-5pm.) The **City Information Centre,** 476 Ruthven St., is more centrally located and offers **Internet** but has less convenient hours. (☎4638 7555. Tourist desk M-F 10am-1pm and 2-4pm; Internet Tu-F 10am-5pm, Sa 10am-2pm. $4.40 per 30min., students $2.20 per 30min.) **Banks** and **ATMs** are easy to find, especially on Ruthven St. The **library** is half a block south of Margaret St. at 27 Victoria St. (☎4688 6670. Open M-Th 9:30am-9pm, F 9:30am-6pm, Sa 9:30am-4pm, Su noon-4pm.) **Postal Code:** 4350.

The family-owned B&B **Self Healing Centre ❷,** 331 Margaret St., provides all the comforts of home, including breakfast, kitchen access, free laundry and Internet, and friendly clutter. Its eclectic walls feature religious decorations. (☎4639 3611 or 1347 6055. Key deposit $10. Dorms and singles $20; doubles $40.) For inexpensive lodgings close to town and the bus station, the **pubs ❷** around Russell and Ruthven St. are the way to go.

Most of Toowoomba's restaurants, bars, and cafes are on Margaret St., also (appropriately) known as "Eats Street." **The Spotted Cow ❷,** at the corner of Campbell and Ruthven St., puts customers in the "moo'd" with raucous rugby union

PIES IN THE BACK OF YOUR HEAD Australia's common magpie birds are known to attack humans that venture anywhere near their nests during the spring breeding season. Many Aussies have felt the sting of a swooping beak while riding their bicycles or taking a stroll in the park. Magpies don't attack, however, when you are looking at them. To avoid having your eyes pecked out, some cautious natives suggest wearing an ice cream container on your head with eyes painted on the back. You decide which is more humiliating—to be attacked by a bird or to wear an ice cream container on your head.

showings, quality pub food, and one-man cover bands on Friday and Saturday nights. (☎4639 3264. Open Su-Th 11am-late, F-Sa 11am-3am.)

The Garden City is home to **Ju Raku En,** Australia's most traditional and largest **Japanese Garden,** located on the University of Southern Queensland campus. The expansive **Queen's Park Gardens,** on Margaret St. between Lindsay and Hume St., are another floral highlight, and **Laurel Bank Park,** one block south of Margaret St. on West St., features a scented garden for the visually impaired. All parks are free and open daily dawn to dusk; they're best visited when at full bloom during the spring and summer. (Sept.-Mar.) The **Carnival of Flowers** (☎4632 4877; www.carnivalofflowers.com.au) is Toowoomba's biggest draw. Held for a week each September (Sept. 19-27, 2003), the carnival features a parade, flower shows, and the exhibition of prize-winning private gardens.

STANTHORPE   ☎07

As the commercial center of the Granite Belt, Stanthorpe (pop. 5000) offers a pleasant escape from the city. A crisp winter climate and location in the heart of Queensland's best wine country make it a prime vacation spot for many Brisbane residents, while abundant fruit-picking opportunities attract hordes of backpackers during the summer months. The town is an ideal base for visiting renowned local wineries and exploring the granite formations and wildflowers of surrounding national parks (Girraween, Sundown, Boonoo Boonoo, and Bald Rock).

🛈 PRACTICAL INFORMATION

Coming in from Warwick off the New England Hwy., Stanthorpe's main street, **High Street,** turns into **Maryland Street** as it bends south in the center of town and then **Wallangarra Road** as it exits town. The **bus station,** at the corner of Maryland and Folkestone St. (☎4681 1434), is inside the Mobil petrol station. **Crisps** and **McCafferty's** each send two **buses** per day to: Brisbane (3½hr. and 5hr., respectively; $36/43); Toowoomba (2hr., $29/37); and Warwick (45min., $17/31). To reach the **tourist office,** 28 Leslie Pde., turn left off Wallangarra Rd. just past the bridge at Quart Pot Creek. (☎4681 2057. Open daily 9am-5pm.) **Banks** and 24hr. **ATMs** line Maryland St. on the left after it turns south.

🛏 ACCOMMODATIONS

Several hostels in and around Stanthorpe help backpackers find picking jobs and drive them to and from work. *Be discriminating in your choice of hostel, however, as several area establishments have been known to take advantage of backpackers doing seasonal work by withholding passports and pay.* The hostels listed below are recommended by the tourist office as honest businesses. Although town pub hotels do not offer placement services, their central locations,

WORK IN STANTHORPE. From September to May each year, the ripened fruit and vegetable fields of the Granite Belt demand **picking,** and thousands of backpackers rush to Stanthorpe to fill the need. September marks the start of the stonefruit harvest (plums, cherries, peaches); December through May is largely tomato and vegetable picking; apples run from February through May. Minimum wage is currently $11.88 per hr., but the amount of cash you make is largely up to you. Some picking jobs are more rigorous than others, with longer hours and higher wages.

low prices, and private rooms attract workers and travelers alike. Numerous cottages around Stanthorpe pamper city folk seeking high-class weekend getaways among the wineries.

Backpackers of Queensland, 80 High St. (☎4681 0999), on the right as you enter town. Backpackers rave about this new hostel, which offers seasonal job placement and transportation, in addition to excellent facilities and nightly dinners ($5). Co-ed dorms house 5 per room; each has its own bath. Lockers, laundry, and Internet access. Key deposit $20. Check-in by 7:30pm or call ahead. Transportation provided to and from bus station. Reservations advised Jan.-Mar. Dorms $20, weekly $125. Wheelchair accessible. AmEx/MC/V. ❷

Country Style Tourist Accommodation Park (☎4683 4358), in Glen Aplin, 9km south of Stanthorpe on the New England Hwy. Don't let the distance deter you; the owner drives backpackers to and from work and the bus station. Job placement. Each dorm includes kitchen, bath, and TV. Internet access. Key deposit $10. 4-bed dorms $18, weekly $120; caravans $75 per week; tentsites $45 per week. AmEx/MC/V. ❷

Central Hotel, 140 High St. (☎4681 2044), on the right as High St. bends south into Maryland St. Offering the cheapest weekly rates in town, Central Hotel's clean, pleasant rooms (some with balcony) are hard to pass up. Kitchen. Singles, doubles, and dorms $25 per person, weekly $80. ❷

Hotel Stanthorpe, 43 High St. (☎4681 2099). Single and twin rooms become a backpacker's haven during harvest. Shared bath. Rooms $18, weekly $85. AmEx/MC/V. ❷

Country Club Hotel, 26 Maryland St. (☎4681 4888). Bargain singles and doubles, if you can handle the noise from the pub and gaming room downstairs. Singles $20, ensuite $35; doubles $35/50. ❷

FOOD

Coffee and lunch shops are mostly located along the main road, but a budget traveler might find them a bit expensive. A Woolworth's **supermarket** is on the corner of High and Lock St. (Open M-F 8am-9pm, Sa 8am-5pm.) There is a corner **grocery,** on the right at the southward bend of Maryland St. (Open daily 8am-7pm.)

Il Cavallino, 130 High St. (☎4681 1556). An Italian trattoria with exquisite dishes, its higher prices ($13-24) are made worthwhile by the leap in quality and atmosphere. Open Tu-Su 5pm-late. ❸

Boulevard Court Restaurant, 68 Maryland St. (☎4681 2828). Chinese dishes feature fresh veggies and meats in sauces blended from local produce. Try the boneless chicken in peach or plum sauce ($12) or a vegetarian option ($5-11). Open daily 11:30am-2pm and 5-9:30pm. AmEx/MC/V. ❶

Regal Cafe, 159 High St. (☎4681 1365). Quick, cheap meals for either sit-down or takeaway. The no-frills fried fish ($3) and the whole Italian-style chicken ($7) are a great bargain. Open M-Sa 8am-7:30pm. ❶

QUEENSLAND

Anna's Restaurant (☎4681 1265; www.annas.com.au), on the corner of Wallangarra Rd. and O'Mara Tce. The perfect reward after a long week's work. Locals praise the weekend Italian buffets (F $23, Sa $28; book ahead) as some of the best food in town. Open M-Sa 6-8:30pm. ❺

⚡ WINERIES

Over thirty famous Granite Belt wineries line either side of the New England Hwy. just south (and a little north) of Stanthorpe. Most offer free wine tasting and some give tours. Unfortunately, the wineries cannot be reached by public transportation or by foot. Tours provide for a jolly day and a late-afternoon nap. The tourist office lists all the local winery tours, but **The Grape Escape** is one of the best. (☎4681 4761; www.grapeescape.com.au. Tours daily 10am-4pm. $60, including pickup, drop off, and lunch. Book ahead.) **Filippo's** offers daily half- and full-day tours. (☎4683 5126. $35, with lunch $45; full-day $51, including lunch.) If you're driving (and wishing you weren't), the way to the wineries is well-marked; most are close to the highway and very accessible by car. **Ballandean Estate Wines** is Queensland's oldest family operated-winery. Each May, it sponsors the **Opera in the Vineyard** festival, a black-tie wine-and-dine opera extravaganza. (☎4684 1226. Open daily 8:30am-5pm. Free tours 11am, 1, and 3pm.) **Golden Grove Estate** (☎4684 1291), just across the road from Ballandean, is a smaller winery with Italian lunches and free wine tasting. Both wineries are 20km south of town off the New England Hwy.; turn right at the Ballandean winery sign after passing the big green dinosaur on your left.

👁 SIGHTS

For a view of the town and more, walk (30min.) or drive (10min.) up to the **scenic lookout** on Mt. Marlay. Follow the street signs up Lock St., across the road from Woolworth's. The 1872 discovery of tin in **Quart Pot Creek** marked the beginning of years of mining around Stanthorpe. Today, amateurs can try fossicking (digging for gems or panning for gold); a license is required, and the **Blue Topaz Caravan Park,** 7km south of Stanthorpe in Severnlea, can supply them. (☎4683 5279. $5.10, families $7.20.) Strike gold at **Thanes Creek Fossicking Area** (☎3237 1435), 40km west of Warwick on Cunningham Hwy.

Stanthorpe has several major festivals: the largest is the **Apple and Grape Harvest Festival,** an extravaganza with a gala ball, rodeo, wine fiesta, and museum exhibition. (☎4681 4111; www.appleandgrape.org. Held even-numbered years at Easter; not held in 2003.) The **Granite Belt Spring Wine Festival** (☎4683 5100; www.springwinefest.com.au), celebrating the start of spring and the release of the new vintage, is held annually at the wineries during the first three weekends in October.

NEAR STANTHORPE: NATIONAL PARKS
In addition to the parks listed below, two New South Wales national parks, **Bald Rock** and **Boonoo Boonoo,** are accessible from Stanthorpe. None of the parks can be reached by public transportation; you need a car to see their splendor.

GIRRAWEEN NATIONAL PARK. Girraween is a popular destination for bushwalkers, birdwatchers, campers, and picnickers. Massive granite boulders, which seem precariously balanced on top of each other, are interspersed among eucalypt trees teeming with lyre birds and home to Queensland's only common wombat population. A 1½-hour return hike takes you to the granite ▨**Pyramid Rock,** which offers a panoramic view of the famous **Balancing Rock** and **Bald Rock,** Australia's second largest rock, situated just across the border in NSW. Be sure to wear hiking boots to scale the smooth boulders. For a more mellow track, complete the **Granite**

QUEENSLAND

Arch loop (25min. return) on your way to Pyramid Rock. The **Castle Rock trail** (1½hr. return) is a moderate climb with a steep final ascent that yields an impressive 360° view. In the spring, **wildflowers** sprout from the bases of rocks; hence the park's name, Girraween, which means "place of flowers" in Aboriginal languages. To get to Girraween, drive 26km south on the New England Hwy.; turn left at the sign, then drive 9km on a sealed road. The **Visitors Center** (☎ 4684 5157), on your left as you enter the park, is usually open seven days a week; the rangers daringly post the day's hours on an erasable board. Nearby, there are picnic, swimming, and rock-climbing areas. Camping is available in designated areas with hot showers, toilets, and BBQ. ($4 per person, families $16. Register in advance ☎ 13 13 04.)

SUNDOWN NATIONAL PARK. Sundown offers rugged bush, chiseled gorges, high peaks, and panoramic views, as well as swimming, fishing, and canoeing in a relatively undeveloped area. The 16,000-hectare park has different geology than neighboring parks, with sedimentary and metamorphic rocks combining to produce sharp ridges. The **Severn River** cuts the park in two. As there are no graded walking tracks, areas of interest can be reached by following the river and side creeks. Bring a compass and a park map (available at park headquarters and the tourist office), as trails are poorly defined and often difficult to follow. The **Permanent Waterhole** is a large waterhole on a major bend in the river, a 20min. hike upstream along the west bank. The **Split-Rock** and **Double Falls** are well worth the three- to four- hour return hike up **McAllisters Creek.** Cross the river east into the creek, being careful not to get sidetracked by the old 4WD track. The friendly ranger Peter and his wife Lynette man the **Camp Headquarters,** on the southwestern edge of the park. Call in advance (☎ 02 6737 5235) to check road conditions and to notify them of your arrival. Camping is accessible by 2WD vehicles and hikers on the western side of the river, near camp headquarters. All sites have pit toilets, fireplaces, and BBQ. ($4 per person, families $16.) To get to Sundown, drive west on Texas Rd. from Stanthorpe and turn left at the signs for Glenlyon (75km). Continue on this road until you reach the dirt road marked by a Sundown National Park sign. You'll reach the park entrance after 4km on the rough dirt track. At the entrance, take the left fork of the track and follow it to the camp headquarters. While the Bruxner Hwy. does lead to Sundown as well, it is much less convenient. Sundown is also accessible strictly by 4WD from the east via the marked turn-off in Ballandean.

SUNSHINE AND FRASER COASTS

And the beach just keeps on coming. See surf and sun, bikes and boards, surfers and sophisticates—or see no one at all. With beaches just as beautiful as those of the Gold Coast, minus the neon and touristy droves, the Sunshine Coast is a slightly warmer vacation-land: here, the sun shines an average of 300 days each year. Quiet beaches and national parks stretch for miles, with resort towns like Noosa Heads rising suddenly from the sand. Fraser Island, the largest island in Queensland's coastal waters, consists of sand, rainforest, and 4WD tracks. Its legendary dunes and freshwater lakes are frequented by a parade of package tours and independent travelers. Both north and south of Noosa, fruit-picking is popular, and a bevy of workers' hostels have sprung up to meet the demand.

MAROOCHY   ☎ 07

Maroochy (pop. 30,000) refers to the area of coast encompassing the towns of **Maroochydore, Alexandra Headlands,** and **Mooloolaba** (north to south). Die-hard surfers fill the beaches, and their stereotypically laid-back attitudes permeate the region. As the urban center, Maroochydore is oriented towards small industry and located at the mouth of the Maroochy River. About 1km southeast, Alexandra Heads is best known for its great surfing waves. Another 2km south, esplanades line Mooloolaba's safe family beach, packed with nightclubs and an aquarium. Maroochy is a popular base for fruit-picking work, with lychee and ginger season from February to March, strawberries from June to October, and tomatoes from November to February. Fruit-picking pays around $12 per hour, and most hostels assist in the job search.

TRANSPORTATION. Suncoast Pacific, Premier, and **McCafferty's/Greyhound** all stop at the Suncoast Pacific terminal in the Scotlyn Fair Shopping Centre on First Ave., off Aerodrome Rd., Maroochydore. **McCafferty's/Greyhound** (☎13 14 99) runs to: Airlie Beach (16hr., 1 per day, $138); Brisbane (2hr., 4 per day, $18); Cairns (26hr., 1 per day, $188); Hervey Bay (3¾-4¼hr., 4 per day, $29); Mackay (14½hr., 1 per day, $124); Noosa (30min., 3-4 per day, $12); and Rockhampton (10hr., 1 per day, $81). **Premier** (☎13 34 10) runs daily to similar destinations at considerably cheaper prices. **Suncoast Pacific** (☎5449 9966) goes to Brisbane (2hr., 8 per day, $23) and the Gold Coast (3hr., 1 per day, $35). The blue **Sunshine Coast Sunbus** (☎13 12 30 or 5450 7888) connects the three towns with hail-and-ride service. Service #1 and #1A run from the Sunshine Plaza down Cotton Tree Pde. and from the Alexandra Headlands to the Mooloolaba Esplanade (M-F every 30min., Sa-Su 1 per hr. to Noosa; $7.50). Service #2 departs from the Sunshine Plaza for Nambour.

ORIENTATION AND PRACTICAL INFORMATION. Aerodrome Rd. is the main commercial strip in Maroochydore. **Alexandra Pde.** runs from the end of Cotton Tree Pde., past Alexandra Headlands, all the way to Mooloolaba, turning into **Mooloolaba Esplanade** near the eastern end. The Wharf, home to the aquarium and many restaurants and shops, is on the right off Parkyn Pde., which is a quick left off the Mooloolaba Esplanade after it bends around by the Surf Club.

The **tourist office** (☎5479 1566) is on Sixth Ave. just off Aerodrome Rd. (Open M-F 9am-5pm, Sa-Su 9am-4pm.) A smaller **info centre** is in Mooloolaba, at the corner of First Ave. and Brisbane Rd. (☎5478 2233. Open daily 9am-5pm.) There are **banks** and 24hr. **ATMs** at the intersection of Horton Pde. and Ocean St., Maroochydore. **Police** (☎5475 2444) are on Cornmeal Pde., and a **7 Day Medical Centre** (☎5443 2122; open M-Sa 8am-8pm, Su 8am-6pm) and **pharmacy** (☎5443 6033) are at 150 Horton Pde. Other services include: **taxi** (24hr. ☎13 10 08; about $10 from Maroochydore to Mooloolaba); **Internet** at **Mooloolaba Embroidery and Internet,** 23 Brisbane Rd., at the corner of Hancock St. (☎5444 0985; $5 per hr; open M-F 9am-6pm, Sa 10am-5pm); and **post offices** at 22 King St., Cotton Tree; 1/32 Brisbane Rd., Mooloolaba; and 10 Ocean St., Maroochydore. (☎13 13 18. All open M-F 9am-5pm.) **Postal Code:** 4557 (Mooloolaba), 4558 (Maroochydore, Cotton Tree).

ACCOMMODATIONS. Most hostels in Maroochy arrange fruit-picking work. **Maroochydore YHA Backpackers** ❷, 24 Schirrmann Dr., is a hike from the center of town, but the friendliness and freebies will blow you away: nightly ice cream, bikes, canoes, boogie boards, and surf boards. Call for free pickup. (☎5443 3151. Trips to the hinterland $10. Large kitchen and common areas, pool, and table tennis. Laundry $2. Reception daily 7:45am-1pm and 5-7pm. Dorms $18; singles $35; twins and doubles $42.) **Palace Backpackers at Mooloolaba** ❷, 75 Brisbane Rd., sports a colorful modern building near the nightlife. The great pool and common area are perfect for partying. Bunk dorms have kitchens on each level. Ensuite dorms with TV and spacious doubles are in a separate, motel-like building. (☎5444 3399 or 1800 020 120. Bike and board hire $5. Reception 7am-10pm. Dorms $21, ensuite $24; ensuite doubles $52. VIP.) **Suncoast Backpackers Lodge ❷**, 50 Parker St., parallel to Aerodrome Dr., Maroochydore, is small, friendly, and clean, with a common space, kitchen, pool table, and continuous tunes. They are also the most serious about fruit picking. (☎5443 7544. Courtesy pickup and drop-off in Mooloolaba. Reception daily 8:30am-1pm and 5-8pm. Dorms $18, weekly $108; twins and doubles $40/$120. VIP.) Maroochy Shire Council operates **caravan parks ❶** in Cotton Tree (☎5443 1253 or 1800 461 253); on Alexander Pde. (☎5443 7917 or 1800 461 917); in Maroochydore (☎5443 1167 or 1800 461 167); and in Mooloolaba (☎5444 1201 or 1800 441 201).

FOOD AND NIGHTLIFE. Maroochy has many good Thai restaurants, but the best is **Som Tam Thai ❷**, on the corner of Fifth Ave. and Aerodrome Rd. (☎5479 1700. Open daily 5-9:30pm. Mains around $14.) **Krishna's Cafe ❶**, Shop 2/7 First Ave., Maroochydore, has all-you-can-eat vegetarian meals. (Lunch $7, dinner $8. Open M-F 11:30am-2:30pm, also F and Su 5:30-8pm. Cash only.) Pick out a pot and paint it at **Hard Clay Cafe ❶**, Shop 2/20 Brisbane Rd., Mooloolaba. It also has great breakfast and gourmet sandwiches for under $5. (☎5444 2144. Open M-Sa 8:30am-5pm.) **Mandolin Seafoods ❶**, 174 Alexander Pde., has cheap, fresh seafood cooked to order. (☎5451 0811. Fish 'n' chips $6. Open M-Th 11am-7:30pm, F-Su 11am-8pm.) Coles **supermarket** is in Sunshine Plaza, off Horton Pde. (☎5443 4633. Open M-F 8am-9pm, Sa 8am-5:30pm, Su 10:30am-4pm.)

Mooloolaba comes alive after dark. **Friday's on the Wharf ❷**, on the River Esp. at Parkyn Pde., is modern, but the weatherboard sheds from the bar retain some of that old coastal Queensland character. (☎5444 8383. Tu Uni night. Restaurant open daily noon-3pm and T-Su 5:30-9pm; nightclub open 9pm-late Tu, F-Sa.) The walls of **O'Malley's ❷**, on Venning St. in the Mooloolaba Outrigger building, seem to sing: "Come ant dance wyt me in Irlaunde." With no less than 17 beers on tap, you'll be dancing in no time. The bistro serves $10-20 Irish fare. (☎5452 6344. Open noon-2pm and 6-8pm. Bar open 10am-late. Live music M-W and F-Sa; DJ Th; karaoke Sa.) At the **Alex Surf Club ❸**, 167 Alexandra Pde. (☎5443 6677), on the beach, you can watch the surfers ride the waves with a cold one in your hand. (Food served daily 6-8pm. Open M-Tu and Th 10am-10pm, W and Su 8am-10pm, F-Sa 10am-midnight. Live music F-Sa. Mains around $20.)

ACTIVITIES. Being in Maroochy means spending time near the water. **Maroochydore Beach** offers good breaks for shortboard riders, while **Alexandra Headlands** can have rips, large swells, and big crowds. **Mooloolaba Beach** is the safest beach for swimming. **Bad Company**, 6-8 Aerodrome Rd., Maroochydore, rents out boards across the street from a good strip of beach. (☎5443 2457. Open M-F 9am-5pm, Sa-Su 8:30am-5pm. Short boards and body boards half-day $15, full-day $20; longboards $25.) If you'd rather ride the pavement, **Skate Biz**, 150 Alexandra Pde., offers in-line skates, bikes, and skateboards. (☎5443 6111. Open daily 9am-5pm. All rentals $12.50 for 2hr., overnight $20.) **Underwater World**, on the Wharf, has a beautiful display of sea creatures; it's the largest oceanarium in the Southern Hemisphere. Kiss a seal (11am, 1, and 3:30pm; $15) or glide through a clear aquarium on a moving walkway, while sharks and giant rays swim inches overhead. (☎5444 8488; www.underwaterworld.com.au. Open daily 9am-6pm; last entry 5pm. $22, students $16, children $13.) Take a dive with the sharks with **Scuba World**. (☎5444 8595. 30min. Certified divers $95, tank and wetsuit only $83. Noncertified, including scuba lesson and aquarium admission $125; double dive on the Sunshine Coast reefs, including equipment $135.) Crew in sailing races at the **Mooloolaba Yacht Club** (☎5444 1355 or 5444 1217), near the end of Parkyn Pde., at noon Wednesday and Sunday. Spots aren't guaranteed, but sign up for the "funsail" and bring a six-pack for the skipper.

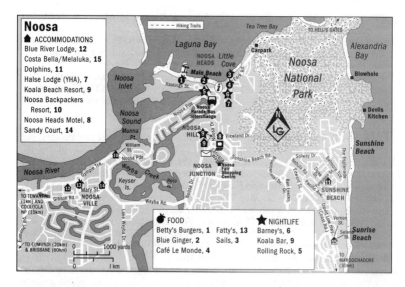

Noosa

♠ ACCOMMODATIONS
Blue River Lodge, **12**
Costa Bella/Melaluka, **15**
Dolphins, **11**
Halse Lodge (YHA), **7**
Koala Beach Resort, **9**
Noosa Backpackers
    Resort, **10**
Noosa Heads Motel, **8**
Sandy Court, **14**

♣ FOOD
Betty's Burgers, **1**   Fatty's, **13**
Blue Ginger, **2**   Sails, **3**
Café Le Monde, **4**

★ NIGHTLIFE
Barney's, **6**
Koala Bar, **9**
Rolling Rock, **5**

NOOSA
☎ 07

Upperclass couples, pensioners, Australian families, and backpackers all come to Noosa in roughly equal numbers to enjoy the gorgeous beaches (Main Beach is great for surfing newcomers), glitzy shopping areas, outdoor dining, and lush greenery. Some criticize Noosa for catering to upscale vacationers with carefully crafted trendiness, but the area manages to draw backpackers in droves anyway, with high quality and fairly accommodating prices for the budget traveler. The cultures intermingle without friction during the day but tend to stick to their own at night. Weary, hungover backpackers may find welcome relief here from the foam and tinsel of the Gold Coast, with activities to suit every whim and rustic inland towns just around the corner. Cooloola National Park, just north of Noosa, is a wilderness ripe for 4WD-ing, hiking, canoeing, and camping.

◧ TRANSPORTATION

Buses: Noosa has no bus terminal; coaches pick up and drop off at **Noosa Parade Bus Interchange. McCafferty's/Greyhound** (☎ 13 14 99) runs to: Airlie Beach (15hr., 2 per day, $137); Brisbane (3hr., 5 per day, $21); Cairns (25hr., 2 per day, $186); Hervey Bay (2¼-3½hr., 5 per day, $25); Mackay (13hr., 2 per day, $123); Maroochydore (30min., 4 per day, $9); and Rockhampton (8½-9½hr., 2 per day, $79). **Premier** (☎ 13 34 10) runs one service per day to the same destinations, at significantly cheaper prices. **Suncoast Pacific** (☎ 5449 9966) goes to: Brisbane (2hr., 7-10 per day, $26); Gold Coast (3hr., 1 per day, $35); Hervey Bay (4hr., 1 per day, $23.50); and Tin Can Bay and Rainbow Beach (2hr., 1 per day, $18).

Public Transportation: Sunshine Coast Sunbus (☎ 13 12 30 or 5450 7888) leaves from the bus interchange and offers frequent hail-and-ride service around Noosa. Service #1 to Maroochydore, Mooloolaba, and Caloundra. Service #10 to Noosa Junction, Noosa Heads, Noosaville, Tewantin, Sunshine Beach, and Sunrise Beach. Service #12 to Eumundi and Cooroy. Fares are around $2.40 for one point in Noosa to another; buses run approximately 7am-7pm, later on weekends.

QUEENSLAND

Taxis: Suncoast Cabs (☎13 10 08) provides 24hr. service.

Car Rental: Thrifty (☎13 61 39) offers cars from $39 per day, as well as pricey 4WDs for Fraser Island, with an esky free of charge. **Europcar,** 13 Noosa Dr. (☎5447 3777), rents from $49 per day. **Noosa Sunrover Rentals** (☎5449 7833) delivers 4WDs to your Noosa accommodation.

Bike Rental: Koala Bike Hire (☎5474 2733) delivers to your accommodation. Bikes $17 for 24hr.; tandems $34 each for 24hr. Open M-Sa 7am-4:30pm, Su 7am-3pm.

ORIENTATION

The Noosa area can be a bit confusing to navigate because its distinguishing features all have remarkably similar names. The three main communities are: Noosa Heads, Noosa Junction, and Noosaville; Noosa National Park is also a prime attraction. These areas are connected by Noosa Drive and Noosa Parade, and are located along the Noosa River, which runs into Noosa Sound and Noosa Inlet. **Noosa Heads** is the main tourist area, and activity revolves around the sidewalk-chic **Hastings St.,** one block north of the **Noosa Parade Bus Interchange.** Many trendy shops, restaurants, upscale hotels, and Main Beach line the street; the entrance to **Noosa National Park** is at its eastern end.

A 15min. stroll south on Noosa Dr. leads to the heart of **Noosa Junction,** Noosa's business center. The **post office, supermarket,** and a string of **banks** are all within five minutes of each other. **Noosaville** is 3km southwest of Noosa Heads, a 30min. walk down Noosa Pde. Its main street, **Gympie Tce.,** is filled with international restaurants, motels, and boat hires. The **Sunshine Beach** area is 3km east of Noosa Junction, but the beachfront accommodation there must be reached by car or by bus, since the walk along the busy David Low Way takes at least 30min. from Noosa Junction. Both Sunshine Beach and nearby **Sunrise Beach** (just try to tell them apart) are popular spots, but the total 40km stretch of sand leaves ample room for sunbathers to spread out.

PRACTICAL INFORMATION

Tourist Office: Tourism Noosa Information Centre (☎5447 4988; www.tourism-noosa.com.au), at the T intersection of Noosa Dr. and Hastings St., is the only official tourism bureau in the city. It's too swamped to be of much assistance, but *Noosa: The Guide* is a good introduction to the town. Open daily 9am-5pm.

Currency Exchange: Banks and 24hr. **ATMs** are on Hastings St., Noosa Heads; Sunshine Beach Rd., Noosa Junction; and Gympie Tce., Noosaville. Open M-Th 9:30am-4pm, F 9:30am-5pm.

Bookstore: Noosa Book Shop (☎5447 3066), in the Suntop Plaza, Noosa Junction. Buys, sells, and exchanges used books. Open M-F 9am-5:30pm, Sa-Su 9am-5pm.

Police: (☎5447 5888), on Langura Court, Noosa Junction (24hr.); also at the corner of Hastings St. and Noosa Dr., Noosa Heads.

Medical Services: Noosa Hospital, 111 Goodchap St., Noosaville (24hr. ☎5455 9200).

Internet Access: Travel Bugs, 9 Sunshine Beach Rd., Noosa Junction (☎5474 8530 or 1800 666 720), offers bookings and job listings. $3 per hr. Open daily 8am-9pm. **Surf Energy Noosa,** 77 Noosa Dr. (☎5474 8208), near the corner of Sunshine Beach Rd., has quick, cheap access. $4 per hr., backpackers $3 per hr. Open daily 8am-9pm.

Post Office: 91-93 Noosa Rd., Noosa Junction (☎13 13 18). Open M-F 9am-5pm, Sa 9am-12:30pm. **Postal Code:** 4567.

ACCOMMODATIONS

Lodging in Noosa comes in three general categories: hostels, motels or hotels, and "holiday units" which are sometimes private homes. Intense competition for budget travelers makes for low hostel prices and perks such as cheap meals, courtesy shuttle service, surfboards, and on-site bars. With Noosa's increasing popularity, there aren't always enough budget beds to go around, and during Christmas and school holiday, rates can double; be sure to book ahead. The best location is in Noosa Heads, near the beach and all the action. Motel and hotel rooms on Hastings St., however, can top $200; they are much cheaper without a beachfront view. Families may find it more economical to rent units or homes; **Accom Noosa** (☎5447 3444 or 1800 072 078; www.accomnoosa.com.au) can help find affordable, longer-stay lodging. Although camping is not allowed in Noosa National Park, it is possible in **Cooloola National Park** (see p. 345).

NOOSA HEADS

🏠 **Halse Lodge (YHA),** 2 Halse Ln. (☎5447 3377 or 1800 242 567), up the hill across Noosa Dr. from the Noosa Pde. bus interchange. This picturesque colonial home, with its stately veranda and large common areas, attracts a mellow, friendly crowd. Close to the beach and Hastings St. A small bar is festive until the 11pm common space lockdown (midnight F-Sa). Laundry $3. Reception daily 7am-8pm. Dorms $22, YHA $20; twins and doubles $50/$46. MC/V. ❷

Koala Beach Resort, 44 Noosa Dr. (☎5447 3355 or 1800 357 457; www.koala-back-packers.com). A 10min. walk from the bus interchange; take a right onto Noosa Dr. and follow it over the hill. Popular with a young, hard-partying crowd. Sparse 5-bed ensuite dorms, courtesy bus, laundry, pool, volleyball court, tiny basement kitchen, and outdoor eating area. Internet $1 per 15min. Reception daily 7:30am-8pm. Dorms $20; walk-through twins and doubles $45. VIP. ❷

Noosa Heads Motel, 2 Viewland Dr. (☎5449 2873), on the corner of Noosa Dr., just up the hill from the Noosa Junction rotary. Just minutes away from the action, but a beautiful jungle-like lot makes it feel hidden in the wilderness. Perfect for families and couples; lovely self-contained units become better as the price gets dearer. Reception 9am-6pm. Downstairs units $70; upstairs units $80; best units $90; extra person $10, max. 4. AmEx/MC/V. ❺

SUNSHINE BEACH AND SUNRISE BEACH

Although these hostels are removed from the Noosa action (30min. walk from the Junction), they are close to the beach. By car, they're off the David Low Hwy.; or, take the #10 Sunbus.

Costa Bella/Melaluka, 7 Selene St. (☎5447 3663 or 1800 003 663; www.mela-luka.com.au). Take the highway to Sunrise Beach; turn left at Vernon St. and make 2 quick rights down the hill. It may lack a communal hostel atmosphere, but you'll have to pick your jaw off the floor after seeing the new, spacious, self-contained Costa Bella units with ocean views and patios. 2 pools, BBQ, and Internet. Laundry in each unit. Free pickup. Reception daily 9am-6:30pm. Older units $40; twins and doubles $46. Costa Bella units shared by 2 couples; $55 per couple, entire unit $110. ❹

Dolphins Beach House, 14 Duke St. (☎5447 2100 or 1800 454 456; www.dolphins-beachresort.com). Energy and friendliness make this a choice Noosa spot, close to the Sunshine Beach shops and shore. Self-contained units are perfect for big groups. Don't get tangled up in the web of hammocks next to the fun outdoor common area. Internet, table tennis, and bike hire ($10). Reception 8am-9pm. Group share beds $18; twins $45; doubles $50. AmEx/MC/V. ❷

NOOSAVILLE

Most of the travelers who stay in this quieter part of town prefer the serenity of the Noosa River to the beaches, which are a 30min. walk away. Mid-range resorts and residences line the streets.

Blue River Lodge, 181 Gympie Tce. (☎5449 7564), directly across from the River and near Noosaville's shops and cafes. Spotless self-contained doubles have 2 bedrooms; one remains locked unless you pay $10 per extra person. Laundry. Units $65. 7th night free. ❺

Noosa Backpackers Resort, 7-13 Williams St. (☎5449 8151 or 1800 626 673). Located on a side street 2min. from the river, 25min. from Main Beach. Happening Global Cafe makes up for distance from the center of town. Courtesy van, game room, swimming pool, and Internet. Reception daily 8am-9pm. 4-6 bed dorms $20; doubles and twins $45, ensuite $55. VIP. ❷

Sandy Court, 30 James St. (☎5449 7225). A half-hostel complex 2min. from the river. Units are motel rooms with bunks, which translates into spacious kitchens, TV lounges, and bathrooms. Parking, laundry, and Internet ($6 per hr.). Free pickup. Check-out 9:30am. Reception 8am-6pm. Dorms $20; doubles $45; motel doubles $65. ❷

▐ FOOD

With over 140 restaurants in Noosa, more than 30 of which are on Hastings St., you can be sure to find some great and reasonably priced food. For oodles of options, head to Noosa Hill and Junction; Hastings St., Noosa Heads; and Gympie Tce., Noosaville. The surf clubs are a great place for a cheap meal or a sunset beer; try **Noosa Heads Surf Life Saving Club,** 69 Hastings St. (☎5447 2355. Open Su-Th 11am-10pm, F-Sa 10am-midnight.) Backpackers, however, tend to eat at the hostels, many of which offer meals for $8 or less. **Betty's Burgers,** a local landmark, serves legendary cheap ($1.80) burgers from their new "burger bus;" follow your nose to the end of Hastings St., away from the national park, turn right at the roundabout, and head toward the beach to the caravan. (Open daily 8am-4pm). Coles **supermarket** is off Sunshine Beach Rd. on Lanyana Way, in the Noosa Fair Shopping Centre, Noosa Junction. (☎5447 4000. Open M-F 8am-9pm, Sa 8am-5:30pm, Su 9am-6pm.)

Café Le Monde, 52 Hastings St., Noosa Heads (☎5449 2366). A local favorite and gathering place for surfer celebs. The express lunch baguettes are great (foot-long $8.50; available 11am-5pm). Live music 4-5 nights a week. Open daily 6:30am-late. ❶

Fatty's, 4 Thomas St., Noosaville (☎5474 4399). Stuff your face with pizza ($16-19) and pasta ($15-17) while watching wipeouts on the big screen. Fat Hour (5-6:30pm) is fatter than your average Happy Hour. Su night live music. Open Tu-Su 5pm-late. ❸

Sails (☎5447 4235), on the corner of Hastings St. and Park Rd., past the info centre, on the beach. Candlelight, sexy music, and succulent seafood ($16-31) will sail you away. Tables set for 2, with the sound of waves in the background. Open daily 8am-10pm. AmEx/MC/V. ❹

Blue Ginger, 30 Hastings St., Noosa Heads (☎5447 3211). Bright and classy; serves gourmet Thai food (mains $13-25). BYO. Open daily 5-9:30pm. ❸

◐ ▐ SIGHTS AND ACTIVITIES

NOOSA NATIONAL PARK. Just 1.4km from the city center, Noosa National Park is a 454-hectare area of tropical vegetation, coastal walking paths, and rare wildlife. With 1.5 million visitors each year, the park bills itself as one of the three most visited parks in Australia. A short walk through the woods from the Noosa informa-

THE LOCAL STORY

SURF'S UP!

Merrick Davis was the 1989 World Pro/ Am Surfing Champion and now teaches lessons at Learn to Surf (see p. 344). Interview August 2, 2002.

Q: You said that you've surfed in 150 different countries. Where is your favorite place to surf?
A: Well, your best place is always going to be home. Hawaii is a great place for professionals, but for beginners, there's some great places in Australia, like the east coast of Australia, Queensland, for example, the Gold Coast, Byron Bay, and Noosa. Noosa's great for people who are just learning because it's a sand bottom, the waves are real gentle, and they break nice and evenly, so you can concentrate on learning to surf rather than getting smashed by the waves.
Q: Do you have any recommendations or special techniques that you teach beginning surfers, or is that secret for the lesson?
A: The secret is just to relax and enjoy yourself and don't try too hard.
Q: What's it like catching a perfect wave?
A: The bigger they are, and the more perfect they are, actually, the more comfortable you become. It's hard to explain, but the sound disappears, and everything goes into slow motion. And if you spend every day in the water surfing and the surf gets bigger and bigger on a daily basis, you can find yourself surfing big waves in no time. If you're in Australia, definitely everyone should try to learn to surf.

tion booth on Hastings St. will land you at the entrance. The park is ideal for walking or jogging, and koalas perch in the trees; they are most often spotted at Tea Tree Bay and the foreshore area, and daily koala sightings are posted at the ranger station. The ranger station, at the entrance to the park, provides maps of five interconnected paths, ranging from 1 to 4.2km. (☎5447 3243. Open daily 9am-3pm.) Due to recent criminal activity, the rangers urge walkers to *never walk alone and stay on frequented paths.* Visitors should take special care around the Alexandria Bay area.

The coastal track, which offers elevated views of the ocean and ends at exhilarating **Hell's Gates,** offers many places to **surf** if you walk in your board; **Tea Tree Bay** and **Granite Bay** are popular among boogie boarders. A beautiful stretch of **beach,** on the eastern side of the park at **Alexandria Bay,** is accessible primarily from **Sunshine Beach.** Water and toilets are available, but camping is prohibited. **Little Cove,** hidden between Hastings St. and the national park, is a charming, secluded beach.

SURFING. With warm water temperatures and a strong surfing community, the Sunshine Coast is a great place to surf. The best season is November to March, as the waves in winter tend to be fickle. Noosa is a wave mecca of five right-hand points, with the bonus of a beautiful backdrop. **First Point** is great for longboarders, while **Little Cove** suits beginners. Some of the best waves can be found at **National Park** and **Tea Tree,** where waves break over granite into long lines and barrel sections. Unfortunately, this is not a secret—in good conditions, both can get extremely crowded. To avoid the crowds, try **Double Island Point** to the north in Cooloola, but beware of strong rips and make sure to bring a friend. On the other side of Noosa National Park, try **Sunshine Beach;** conditions are erratic, but with so much surf, there's almost always a good break somewhere.

Learn to Surf, with lessons taught by world champion Merrick Davis (see **The Local Story,** p. 344), guarantees you'll be standing by the end of one lesson. (☎0418 787 577. Book ahead. $35 per 2hr.) For boards, try **Noosa Longboards,** Shop 4/64 Hastings St., Noosa Head, or 187 Gympie Tce., Noosaville. (☎5474 2828; body boards $15 per 4hr., $20 per day; shortboards $20/$30; longboards $30/$45; open M-F 9:30am-5:30pm, Sa 9:30am-5pm, Su 10am-5pm.); or **Impact Surf,** Shop 1-7 Sunshine Beach Rd., Noosa Junction. (☎5474 9198. Surfboards $15 for 4hr., $25 per day. Open M-F 9:30am-5:30pm, Sa 9:30am-5pm, Su 10am-5pm.) Many of the hostels also hire out boards.

OTHER ACTIVITIES. Kitesurf lets you try out your water wings as kite and surfboard join forces in an exhilarating new sport. (☎5455 6677 or 0412 175 217; www.kite-surf.com.au. 2hr. lesson $95.) **Clip Clop Horse Treks** lets you trot through lakes and bush around Lake Weyba for a day. (☎5449 1254. $165.) **Aussie Sea Kayak Company** runs sea kayaking tours in the waterways around the Sunshine Coast. (☎5477 5335. Daily 2hr. sunset tour with champagne $40, half-day $60; Tu and F-Sa full-day with lunch $105.) Tandem skydive over the coast with **Sunshine Skydivers,** the cheapest operator on the east coast. (☎0500 522 533. 12,000 ft. $240, backpackers $225; 14,000 ft. $290/$275.) To see the Glasshouse Mountains at close range, try rockclimbing and abseiling with **Adventures Sunshine Coast.** (☎5444 8824 or 0409 630 880. Full-day rock-climbing or abseiling $99, children $60; half-day abseiling $69, children $45.)

🎵 🎭 ENTERTAINMENT AND NIGHTLIFE

With its unpretentious surfing mood and prime location, **Barney's,** on Noosa Dr. near Hastings St., is the perfect spot for a late afternoon beer. Get a jug for $8.50—you won't mind taking your time. (☎5447 4544. Happy Hour 4-6pm. Open 10am-late.) **The Koala Bar,** 44 Noosa Dr. (☎5447 3355), in the hostel, overflows with drunken, sun-kissed backpackers. Pool tables, Happy Hour 4:30-7pm, DJ, and nightly specials spice up the evening, which ends abruptly at the stroke of midnight. Wednesday night live bands are extremely popular; Monday theme night closed to non-guests. After Koala's closes, backpackers and trendsetters alike flock to **Rolling Rock,** Upper Level, Bay Village on Hastings St., the only nightclub serving a drop past midnight. Th guest DJs rock the house, while their New York Bar enjoys a quieter scene. (☎5447 2255. Cover M $6; Tu free; W and Su $5; Th-Sa $7. M $3 drinks. Open Su-Tu and F-Sa 8pm-3am, W 9pm-3am, but door closes at 1:30am. Cash only.)

COOLOOLA NATIONAL PARK   ☎07

Extending 50km north of Noosa up to Rainbow Beach is the sandy, white coast and 56,600 hectares of **Cooloola National Park.** Together with Fraser Island, Cooloola forms the **Great Sandy Region,** the largest sand mass in the world. With 20 hiking tracks (ranging in length from several hundred meters to 46.2km) and navigable lakes and waterways, Cooloola beckons both experienced bushwalkers and Sunday strollers. On the eastern side of the park, the beaches are generally uncrowded, but during summer months and holidays, there's a thick blanket of tents and picnickers on the sands.

🚌 TRANSPORTATION. 2WD vehicles can access Elanda Park via the Tewantin-Boreen Rd. or Rainbow Beach via the Bruce Hwy. to Rainbow Beach Rd. (turn-off at Gympie), but the rest of the access points to the park are 4WD only. The two-minute **Noosa Northshore Ferry** (☎5447 1321) transports vehicles from Moorindil St. in **Tewantin** to the northern shore of the Noosa River ($4.50 per vehicle). **Camping permits** are available from the info center on Moorindal St. (☎5449 7792. Camping $4 per person.) From the northern shore, 4WD vehicles can cut across to the beach, the park's primary vehicular thoroughfare. **Rainbow 4WD Hire,** 9 Karoonda Crescent, Rainbow Beach (☎5486 3555), rents 4WDs from $110 per day; price depends upon vehicle size and duration of rental. **Cooloola Cruises and Safaris** picks up in Noosa for a full-day Everglades BBQ cruise. They also offer a two-in-one safari that includes a tour of Cooloola beach. (☎5449 9177 or 1800 657 666. Operates M and W-F. Everglades $79, children $45; 2-in-1 $129/$85.) **Polleys Coaches** travels to Tin Can Bay ($10) and Rainbow Beach ($13) from **Gympie.** (☎5482 9455. Departs M-F 6am and 1:30pm.) **Suncoast Pacific** also runs a daily service to Rainbow Beach from Noosa. (☎5449 9966. 2hr. Daily 9am. $18, concessions $15.)

7 PRACTICAL INFORMATION. Cooloola National Park stretches 50km along the coast from Noosa in the south to Rainbow Beach in the north; the length of the beach can be driven in half a day. Information and **maps** are available from **Cooloola Shire Council**, 242 Mary St., Gympie (☎5482 1911; open M-F 8:30am-4:30pm); **Rainbow Beach Tourist Information Centre**, 8 Rainbow Beach Rd., Rainbow Beach (☎5486 3227; open daily 7am-6pm, longer in summer); **Queensland Parks and Wildlife Service** in Rainbow Beach (☎5486 3160; open daily 7am-4pm); and **Noosa National Park** ranger station (☎5447 3243; open daily 9am-3pm).

F ACCOMMODATIONS. Hidden in the bush but only 20min. from Noosa, **Gagaju ❶** is a stress-free escape on the border of Cooloola National Park and Noosa River. It's as eco-friendly, welcoming, and in touch with nature as a place could be. Dorm accommodation is in 10- to 14-bed bush bunkhouses—it's like camp but much better. (☎5474 3522 or 1300 302 271. Free pickup from Noosa. Running water and laundry. Sites $10 per person; dorms $17. Canoe trips: half-day $22, full-day $32, 3-day $97.) **The Rocks Backpackers Resort ❷**, 3 Spectrum St., Rainbow Beach, is a new, purpose-built hostel that organizes cheap Fraser 4WD trips for groups. Dorms have sink and fridge; some have bath. (☎5486 3711. Dorms $18; doubles $38, ensuite $48.) To go to Fraser with a hostel group from Rainbow Beach, try **Dingo's ❶**, 1 Rainbow Beach Rd., near the beach. Loads of backpackers enjoy hammocks, 8-10 bed dorms, free pickup from Noosa, table tennis, swimming pool, Internet, laundry, and bike and board hire. (☎1800 111 126. Ensuite dorms $15; 3-day 2-night Fraser trip with 2 nights Rainbow Beach accommodation $140.) **Camping ❶** is permitted at 14 sites in the park; some sites are accessible only via walking track or canoe. (Permits $4 per person, some payable at self-registration stations but others must be booked in advance; check with QPWS.)

N SIGHTS. The Cooloola National Park forests hold many natural wonders: rainforests growing from pure sand, winding waterways shaded by mangroves, and characteristic Aussie critters like kangaroos and ground parrots. Even the plants are unusual: endangered *boroniakeysii* (pink-flowered shrubs) mingle with thin, stubborn stalks of blackbutt, and melaluka "tea trees" dye the river a deep black. One of the best ways to enjoy the park is to **canoe** or motor up the **Noosa River**, around **Lake Cootharaba**, Queensland's largest natural lake, and among the **Everglades**, where the dark water creates mirror images of the dense riverbanks lined with sedges. As in any wilderness area, keep **safety** in mind and watch out for the wildlife. Sharks in the river system occasionally approach the shore and swim alongside sting rays, catfish, and jellyfish in the ocean. Use caution when swimming in inland lakes.

The beach in Cooloola is famous for its natural beauty. Extending from Rainbow Beach to Double Island Point are the 200m-high cliffs of the **Coloured Sands.** When the weathering of iron-rich minerals in the dune soils formed the cliffs, they became stained in a complex range of hues; rain intensifies the colors. Aboriginal legend speaks of Rainbow, a representative of the gods who was killed in an attempt to save a beautiful maiden: as he crashed to the ground, his colors permeated the sand. **Carlo Sandblow,** near Rainbow Beach, has great views on both sides. Captain Cook named **Double Island Point** in 1770, when he believed the point was actually islands. The **lighthouse** at the point offers 360° views of the coastline.

SUNSHINE COAST HINTERLAND

Just inland of the Sunshine Coast lies a veritable smorgasbord of tourist delights: stunning national parks, roadside crafts markets, and kitschy tourist traps. Most of the hinterland is inaccessible via public transportation and is best experienced by car. Several tour operators also offer trips to the region, but most involve more driving than hiking. **Storeyline Tours** offers several options, including a driving tour of Montville, the Blackall Range, and the Glasshouse Mountains, or a morning trip to the Eumundi Markets. (☎ 5474 1500. Montville-Glasshouse M half-day $36, concessions $34, children $18; full day $52/$48/$26. Markets W and Sa $12, children $7.) **Noosa Hinterland Tours** hits the same regions and also offers a trip to the Ginger Factory and Big Pineapple. (☎ 5474 3366. Montville-Glasshouse full-day daily $50, children $20; markets $12/$9; Ginger Factory and Big Pineapple $32/$15.) **Off Beat Rainforest Tours** accesses exclusive rainforest on eco-guided walks in Conondale National Park. (☎ 5473 5135. $125, children $80; includes gourmet lunch.)

POMONA. Pomona, north of Eumundi and off the Bruce Hwy., is home to the **Majestic Theatre,** the oldest silent movie theater in Australia and the only fully operating silent theater in the world. (☎ 5485 2330. Wine, movie, and supper Th 8:30pm; $10, children $8. Annual movie festival 1st weekend in Sept.)

EUMUNDI MARKETS. Some hostels in Noosa provide shuttle service ($10) to the famous **Eumundi Markets,** with nearly 300 stalls of everything from sweets to sheets and soaps to boats. Get there early for the good stuff. Wednesday markets are primarily fruits and veggies. (20min. south of Noosa Heads, off the Bruce Hwy; the blue Sunbus runs here. For more info, contact the Eumundi Historical Association ☎ 5442 8581 Open W 7am-1pm, Sa 6:30am-1:30pm.)

YANDINA. In the town of Yandina, just south of Eumundi, the **Ginger Factory,** 50 Pioneer Rd., churns out ginger for the zest on your sushi and the bite in your ale. The factory is the largest ginger processing plant in the Southern Hemisphere. If that doesn't impress you, neither will the factory, though the huge vats of multi-colored ginger in different stages are worth a free peek. (☎ 5446 7096. Open daily 9am-5pm. Free.) Across the street is **Nutworks,** with free multi-flavored macadamia nut tastings. Just off the Bruce Hwy. on the Nambour connection, a huge pineapple marks the entrance to the **Big Pineapple Plantation,** a working fruit and macadamia nut farm. Take the train around the farm ($5.50, children $4) and see pineapple shows. (From Maroochydore, take bus #1a to Nambour. ☎ 5442 1333. Open daily 9am-5pm. Free.)

MONTVILLE AND BLACKALL RANGE. The sheer Blackall Range escarpment rises from the plains to cradle green pastures and rainforests, sprinkled with the old country villages of Mapleton, Flaxton, Montville, and Maleny. Once known for its hippie appeal, Montville now thrives on several blocks of antiques, galleries, crafts, teahouses, and a cuckoo clock shop. (From Noosa, follow the Bruce Hwy. south to Nambour and then turn toward the Blackall Range via Mapleton. The info center is on Main St., Montville. ☎ 5478 5544. Open daily 10am-4pm.)

KONDALILLA AND MAPLETON FALLS. Kondalilla and Mapleton Falls National Parks, both off the road north of Montville, have pleasant trails and picnic areas. The 80m Kondalilla Falls (Aboriginal for "rushing water") are especially gorgeous. Although the **Picnic Creek walk** (1.2km) will technically get you to the lookout and

QUEENSLAND

A RUNNING BET In a Pomona pub in 1957, a bet was made that no one could run up Mt. Cooroora (439m) in less than an hour. In just 40 minutes, Bruce Samuels won himself 40 pounds. The challenge has since become an annual race to be crowned King of the Mountain. The record stands at under 25 minutes to climb this extremely steep 1½km path with its loose stones, slippery spots, and caution signs. Most run the race in about 2hr. and then proceed immediately to the pub.

rock pool, the best views of the rushing waters are sprinkled along the **Kondalilla Falls circuit track** (2.7km) that begins at the lookout. The **Wompoo circuit** (1.3km), at Mapleton Falls, just past Mapleton on the Obi Obi Rd., winds through rainforest to an excellent lookout, though the carpark lookout gives a better view of the falls. (Ranger ☎ 5494 3983. Station open M-F 7:30am-4pm.)

GLASS HOUSE MOUNTAINS. The Glass House Mountains rise abruptly from the rolling farmlands south of Landsborough. According to Aboriginal legend, this group of 13 volcanic plugs represents the father *Tibrogargan*, the pregnant mother *Beerwah*, and their many children. The distinct landscape was formed by gradual weathering since the last volcanic activity 20 million years ago. Walking access is limited to **Mt. Ngungun**, the **Glass House Mountains lookout**, and the lookouts at **Mt. Tibrogargan** and **Mt. Beerwah**, but experienced climbers can continue past the lookouts to the summits. (Ranger ☎ 5494 3983. Signs are posted off the Bruce Hwy. No camping allowed within the park.)

HERVEY BAY   ☎ 07

For many travelers, Hervey Bay (HAR-vee; pop. 43,000) is little more than a pause before heading to Fraser Island. Since most backpackers stay here for a few nights while in transit to Fraser, it makes for one of the craziest party atmospheres on the coast. Bordered by 40km of beach, the bay harbors other forms of life besides the adventure-seekers and dingoes on Fraser. From late July to early November, humpback whales populate the waters, bringing with them a slew of whale-watching vessels and camera-wielding tourists.

▮ TRANSPORTATION

Trains: A shuttle bus links Hervey Bay to **Maryborough Coach Terminal**, on Lennox St., Maryborough (bus leaves 40min. before trains depart Maryborough). The **Tilt Train** (☎ 13 22 32) runs from Maryborough to: Brisbane (4½hr., 1-4 per day, $54); Bundaberg (1hr., 1-2 per day, $25.30); and Rockhampton (4¾hr., 1-2 per day, $64). Concessions half-price.

Buses: Bay Central Coach Terminal, Bay Central Shopping Center, Pialba (☎ 4124 4000). Open M-F 6am-5:30pm, Sa 6am-1pm. **McCafferty's/Greyhound** (☎ 13 14 99 or 13 20 30) and **Premier** (☎ 13 34 10) run to: Airlie Beach (13hr.; 5 per day; Premier $91, McCafferty's $129); Brisbane (5-6hr., 9 per day, $32/$43); Bundaberg (2hr., 4 per day, $12/$26); Cairns (23hr., 6 per day, $167/$177); Mackay (11hr., 6 per day, $97/$113); Maroochydore (4hr., 4 per day, $21/$29); Noosa (3½hr., 5 per day, $19/$25); and Rockhampton (6-6½hr., 6 per day, $43/$72). Premier only runs one service per day.

Taxi: Hervey Bay Taxi (☎ 13 10 08). 24hr.

Bicycle Hire: Rayz Pushbike Hire (☎ 0417 644 814) offers free delivery and pickup. $14 per day; tandems $28. Open daily 7am-5pm.

▰ ▱ ORIENTATION AND PRACTICAL INFORMATION

Hervey Bay is actually a clump of suburbs facing north toward the Bay. Named from west to east, the suburbs are: **Port Vernon, Pialba, Scarness, Torquay,** and **Urangan.** Most action occurs along **The Esplanade** at the water's edge, where takeaway shops and tour booking agencies seem to repeat endlessly. The harbor extends

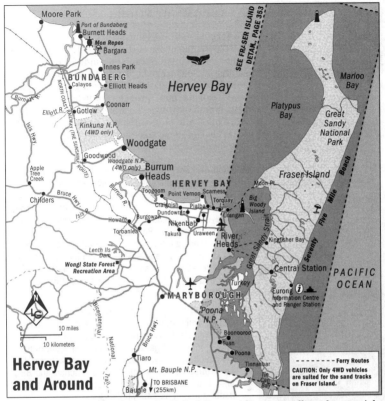

Hervey Bay
and Around

CAUTION: Only 4WD vehicles
are suited for the sand tracks
on Fraser Island.

- - - - - - Ferry Routes

down The Esplanade and around to Pulgul St., providing an excellent place to pick up cheap seafood fresh from the trawlers.

Tourist Office: There are countless booking agents on The Esplanade. The only accredited tourism bureau is the **Hervey Bay Visitor Information Centre** (☎4124 2912 or 1800 811 728), inconveniently located on the Hervey Bay-Maryborough Rd., at the corner of Urrauueen. Open daily 9am-5pm.

Currency Exchange: Banks and 24hr. **ATMs** are located at the bus terminal and on The Esplanade, in Torquay. **National Bank,** 415 The Esplanade (☎13 22 65), has an **ATM.** Open M-Th 9:30am-4pm, F 9:30am-5pm.

Police: (emergency ☎000; 24hr. ☎4128 5333), corner of Queens and Torquay Rd.

Camping Gear: Torquay Disposals and Camping, 424 The Esplanade (☎4125 6511). Open M-F 8:30am-5pm, Sa 8:30am-4pm, Su 8:30am-noon.

Internet Access: Available in many booking offices and at **Bluebird Rentals,** 346 The Esplanade, Scarness (☎4124 2289). 5¢ per min. or $3 per hr. Open M-Sa 8:30am-late, Su 9:30am-late.

Post Office: 414 The Esplanade, Torquay (☎4125 1101). Open M-F 8am-5:30pm. The office at **Bay Central Shopping Centre** (☎4125 9126), across from bus terminal in Pialba, has Sa hours. Open M-F 8:30am-5pm, Sa 8:30-11:30am. **Postal Code:** 4655.

THE LOCAL STORY

JAWSOME!

Sherrie Auld and Greg Wolff are employees at Hervey Bay's Neptune Reefworld, which offers 30min. shark swims. Researcher shark swim and interview July 29, 2002.

Q: They all have their teeth?

A: There are about 12 all together, and yes, they all have their teeth.

Q: Have these sharks all had their breakfast?

A: Ah, well, you'll be getting in there shortly, so...

Q: [Nervous chuckle.] What's to ensure that they don't eat the visitors?

A: Well, nothing really, I guess. They are wild animals, and they are meat eaters; however, they are timid. We've had nearly 1200 people do this so far and not one person's been bitten yet, so...that's the only insurance I can give you.

Q: You said there was a larger shark behind the ledge there that I can't see. Can you just tell me a little bit more about him, so I know what to expect?

A: That's a Wobbegong shark. She's about 1.8m and quite wide. The only reason we ask you not to touch the Wobbegong shark is not that they're an aggressive shark, but that they're actually a very flexible shark and do have the ability to turn around and bite their own tail. So if you're grabbing around the tail and she doesn't want it, *snap!*

Q: Do you have any other advice for me while I'm in there?

A: Just basically relax and don't scare them. They're pretty scary things.

Q: Okay, excellent. Let's do it.

ACCOMMODATIONS

Hostel courtesy buses line up like pigs at a trough to meet incoming buses at the Bay Central Coach Terminal. Many hostels run self-guided Fraser 4WD safaris; while you can book a safari that is not based at your accommodation, you often get free nights when booking tours through certain hostels. Off the beaten path, however, several smaller hostels offer more personal, pleasant stays. Hostels listed have 10am checkout and free pickup and drop-off unless stated otherwise.

Colonial Backpackers YHA (☎4125 1844 or 1800 818 280), on the corner of Pulgul and Boat Harbour Dr., Urangan. Excellent setting, but removed from the center of town. Rustic and sprawling, with pool, spa, volleyball, basketball, tennis, licensed restaurant, and picturesque pond. Perfect for families, couples, and those needing a break from the crowded hostel scene. Reliable Fraser safaris $130. Laundry. Key deposit $10. Reception 6:45am-9:30pm. Dorms $19-21; twins and doubles $46-54; log cabins for 2 $66-76; villas $78-88. AmEx/MC/V. ❷

The Woolshed, 181 Torquay Rd., Scarness (☎4124 0677), 5min. from the beach and shops. This unique smaller hostel has a jungle-like setting featuring waterfalls, ponds, and gardens. Chickens and ducks have the run of the backyard, and rooms have character. Co-ed bathrooms with great showers. Kitchen and BBQ area. Laundry. Reception daily 7am-7pm. Dorms $17; doubles and twins $40. MC/V. ❷

Friendly Hostel, 182 Torquay Rd., Scarness (☎4124 4107). The owners are indeed friendly, if a bit firm; feels like Grandma's house. Partiers need not apply. The place seems more like a B&B without the second B: cable TV, games, and books, fully supplied kitchen, and no bunks. Pickup on request. Laundry. Reception 8am-10pm. 3-bed dorms $19; twins $44. Cash only. ❷

Koalas, 408 The Esplanade (☎4125 3601; www.koala-backpackers.com). Party hostel across from the beach. Cheap meals and bar that bumps till late. Beware add-ons like linen hire $1.50 and heaps of deposits, from cutlery to blankets. Key deposit $10. Reception 7am-7pm. Fraser safari $125. Dorms $18, ensuite $20; doubles and twins $45/$55. VIP. MC/V. ❷

Fraser Roving (NOMADS), 412 The Esplanade (☎4125 3879). The new hostel in town. Although a bit institutional, cheap rates, a friendly staff, and a well-stocked bar predict this will be the hot new party hostel on the block.

Pool and Internet. Key deposit $10. Reception 24hr. 5- to 9-bed dorms $15; 4-bed $18, ensuite $20; doubles $40/$45. AmEx/MC/V. ❶

Smuggler's Rest, 369 The Esplanade, Scarness (☎4128 2122 or 1800 502 115). Although the building needs some work, personable owners offer the most affordable Fraser package, with no hidden costs. Free Sony Playstation, first-run videos $3. Self-contained units with a dorm room and twin or double. Reception daily 6:30am-10pm. Dorms $16; twins and doubles $38. NOMADS/VIP/YHA. MC/V. ❷

🔲 🥄 FOOD AND NIGHTLIFE

Hervey Bay has the usual spread of fast-food and chippers, along with a handful of prohibitively expensive restaurants. Hostel eats are quite good and cheap. For **groceries,** try **Express,** 414 The Esplanade (☎4125 2477; open 24hr.) or **Woolworth's,** on the corner of Torquay Rd. and Taylor St., Pialba. (☎4128 3158. Open M-F 8am-9pm, Sa 8am-5:30pm.) The best party bets are the bars at the larger hostels, especially Beaches, Fraser Escapes, and Koalas (see **Accommodations,** p. 350). **Dolly's,** 406 The Esplanade, is a local bar with live music, pool tables, and $6 jugs from 9-10pm. (☎4125 5633. Open Su-F 9pm-3am, Sa 5pm-3am. Courtesy bus available.)

The Black Dog Cafe, 381 The Esplanade (☎4124 3177). Trendy eatery serves sushi rolls ($5-6) and outstanding teriyaki burgers ($8). YHA/VIP discount 10%. Open daily 5:30pm-late, also Th-Su 10:30am-2:30pm; kitchen closes at 9:30pm. Licensed. AmEx/MC/V. ❶

Prince of Whales, 383 The Esplanade, Torquay (☎4124 2466). Continue whale-watching off the boat at this traditional English pub, complete with dark wood, fireplaces, and giant British flags. Excellent service. Jolly good chicken pies ($15). Open daily 4pm-late; food served until 9pm. MC/V. ❷

China World, 402 The Esplanade, (☎4125 1233), on the corner of Tavistock St. $5 lunch, $11 all-you-can-eat dinner buffet. Open daily 5:30-9pm, also M-F 11am-2pm. AmEx/MC/V. ❷

🥄 ACTIVITIES

WHALE-WATCHING. Weighing up to 40 tons—the equivalent of 11 elephants or 600 people—the humpback whale stops in Hervey Bay on its southern migration after giving birth in the warmer waters up north. The whales assemble in Platypus Bay, 50km from Urangan Harbour, where sightings are undeniably dramatic. Whale-watching is big business from late July to November. Twelve boats in Hervey Bay form the whale-watching fleet: most offer guaranteed whale sightings during the season or your next trip is free. The flagship vessel is the **Spirit of Hervey Bay,** built for whale-watching and underwater viewing, with a whale-listening hydrophone. (☎4125 5131 or 1800 642 544. Departs Great Sandy Straits Marina 8:30am and 1:30pm for a half-day cruise. $77, children $44.) **Quick Cat** offers a half-day, small-boat experience. (☎1800 671 977. Departs Great Sandy Straits Marina daily 8am and 1pm. $68, students $55, children $45.) If the whale season's past and you're still itching for marine mammals, try **Whale Song,** a wheelchair-accessible vessel that looks for dolphins in the off-season. (☎1800 689 610. Half-day seasonal whale-watching daily 7:30am and 1pm. $72, children $40. Dolphin-watching 9am-2:30pm. $60, children $30.)

Every year, the return of the humpback whales is celebrated with the **Blessing of the Fleet,** first weekend in August. The **Whales, Sails, and Fishing Tales Festival,** in November, features an ▨**Electric Light Parade,** with glowing floats. (☎4125 4166.)

QUEENSLAND

DIVING. ▨**Divers Mecca** may be the best place on the coast to do a PADI Open Water certification course. This course is one of the cheapest in Australia and includes four boat dives, not shore dives. *(401 The Esplanade. ☎4124 7886 or 1800 351 626. Courtesy pickups. Open daily 9am-5pm; courses begin M and Th. Intro dive $110; PADI certification $169; advanced open water $242.)*

OTHER ACTIVITIES. Torquay Beach Hire offers beach activities and a 10% discount with presentation of *Let's Go. (Across from 415 The Esplanade, on Torquay Beach. ☎4125 5528. Open daily 7am-dusk. Waterskiing $25 for 10min., canoes $15 per hr., windsurfing $18 per hr., big banana $9 per hr., catamaran $30 per hr.)* Thrill seekers can swim with the sharks at **Neptune's Reefworld** (see **The Local Story,** p. 350), Although the aquarium is sub-par, the sharks look much more ferocious once you jump in the tank with them. *(☎4128 9828. Open daily 9:30am-4:30pm. Free pickup and drop-off. Aquarium $14. Shark swim $40; includes aquarium entry.)* **Skydive Hervey Bay** includes a scenic flight over Fraser Island. *(☎4124 8248. 10,000 ft. $219; 12,000 ft. $264; 14,000 ft. $308.)* **Humpback Camel Safari** offers two-hour rides twice per day. *(Toogoom, 15min. from Hervey Bay. ☎4128 0055; call ahead. Pickup available. $44.)*

FRASER ISLAND ☎07

Fraser Island, the world's largest sand island and a World Heritage-listed national park, attracts 350,000 visitors each year. Backpackers up and down the coast can't stop talking about the island—an untrammeled wilderness scarred only by a 4WD track. It's a must-stop on the trek up (or down) the coast. An idyllic destination for bushwalkers, fishermen, and 4WDers, Fraser is manageable for less experienced outdoorsmen as well. Although a sand island, much of Fraser lies beneath a dense rainforest cover, punctuated by over 200 freshwater lakes. The winds perpetually resculpt the island's topography, but its unique natural beauty is a constant.

▐ TRANSPORTATION

BY BOAT

Most backpackers leave for Fraser from Hervey Bay, but Rainbow Beach, 1½hr. north of Noosa, is also becoming a popular departure point. If you're renting a 4WD, consider leaving from Rainbow Beach, as ferry costs are much lower.

Fraser Island Vehicular Ferry Services runs ferries from several locations (return fare for Fraser Venture, Fraser Dawn, and Kingfisher: $16.50; vehicles $82, passengers $5.50)

Fraser Venture (☎4125 4444), the most convenient for independent 4WDers; leads to the best tracks. From Riverheads to Wanggoolba Creek. 30min.; daily 9, 10:15am, and 3:30pm; Sa also 7am. Returns daily 9:30am, 2:30, and 4pm.

Fraser Dawn (☎4125 4444), from Urangan Boat Harbor to Moon Point. 60min.; daily 8:30am and 3:30pm. Returns daily 9:30am and 4:30pm.

Kingfisher (☎4125 5511), from Riverheads to Kingfisher. 45min.; daily 7:15, 11am, and 2:30pm. Returns daily 8:30am, 1:30, and 4pm.

Rainbow Venture (☎5486 3154), the southernmost access point to Fraser. From Inskip Point near Rainbow Beach (see **Cooloola National Park,** p. 345) to Hook Point. 15min.; continuously 7am-4:30pm. Vehicles $20, includes passengers; walk-ons free.

BY PLANE

Air Fraser Island (☎4125 3600) offers one-way or same-day trips ($50) and an over-night trip, including 4WD hire, return flight, and camping equipment ($190). They also offer a scenic flight over Fraser (30min., $165).

Fraser Island

Ferry Routes
CAUTION: Only 4WD vehicles
are suited for the sand tracks
on Fraser Island.

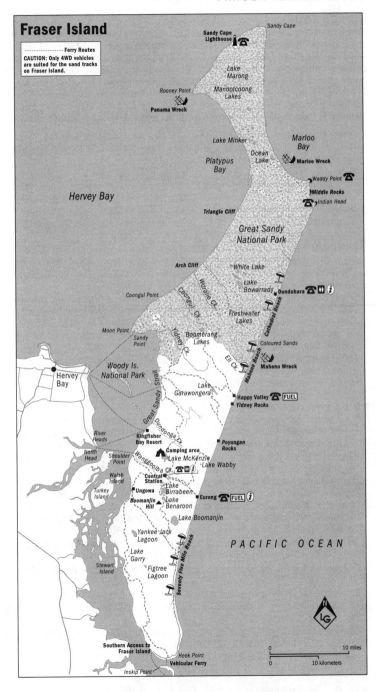

Sandy Cape

Sandy Cape
Lighthouse

Lake
Marong

Manoolcoong
Lakes

Rooney Point

Panama Wreck

Lake Minker

Marloo
Bay

Ocean
Lake

Marloo Wreck

Platypus
Bay

Waddy Point

Middle Rocks

Indian Head

Hervey Bay

Triangle Cliff

Great Sandy
National Park

Arch Cliff

White Lake

Lake
Bowarrady

Dundubara

Coongul Point

Coongul Ck.

Woralie Ck.

Freshwater
Lakes

Cathedral Beach

Moon Point

Boomerang
Lakes

Sandy
Point

Yidney Ck.

Coloured Sands

Eli Ck.

Maheno Beach

Maheno Wreck

Woody Is.
National Park

Lake
Garawongera

Happy Valley

FUEL

Great Sandy Strait

Yidney Rocks

Dundonga Ck.

River
Heads

Kingfisher
Bay Resort

Camping area

Poyungan
Rocks

North
Head

Shoulder
Point

Wanggoolba Ck.

Lake McKenzie

Lake Wabby

Walsh
Island

Central
Station

Lake
Birrabeen

Eurong

FUEL

Turkey
Island

Ungowa

Boomanjin
Hill

Lake
Benaroon

Lake Boomanjin

Yankee Jack
Lagoon

PACIFIC OCEAN

Stewart
Island

Lake
Garry

Figtree
Lagoon

Seventy Five Mile Beach

Southern Access to
Fraser Island

Hook Point

Vehicular Ferry

Inskip Point

N

0   10 miles

0   10 kilometers

QUEENSLAND

GUIDED TOURS

Tours provide a structured, safe, and hassle-free way to see the island, though you'll have to forgo the freedom and excitement of a personal 4WD and outdoor camping. Many buses seat 30-40 people, all of whom shuffle in and out at each stop before continuing on to the next lake. Be sure to inquire about group size before booking your tour; the smaller the group, the more personalized the experience. Tour options are plentiful, but forget daytrips—you'll need at least two days to see the island. Prices are higher than the hostel self-guided specials, but once you've factored in food, permits, and petrol, tours become somewhat comparable in cost.

Fraser Experience Tours (☎ 1800 606 422). Personal, fun, and informative tours with max. 14 in a group. 2-day departs M-W $179. 3-day departs F $285, with Tin Can Bay and Rainbow Beach or cultural option $295.

Trailblazer Tours (☎ 5474 1235 or 1800 626 673). Operates a 3-day tour through Noosa Backpackers Resort. This is the best guided safari package available for a younger crowd, mixing guiding and camping, including Cooloola National Park's Coloured Sands. Departs Noosa M, W, and Sa 8:30am; $245.

Sand Island Safaris (☎ 1800 246 911). More expensive outfit, running comprehensive 3-day tours with max. 16 people. Departs Tu-W and F-Sa; $290.

Kingfisher Bay Wilderness Adventure Tours (☎ 4120 3333 or 1800 072 555; www.kingfisherbay.com). The most expensive but very well-run, with accommodation at the spacious Wilderness Lodge. 4WD bus holds up to 40. 2-day overnight $230; 3-day overnight $297; quad and twin share extra. VIP/YHA discounts.

Fraser Island Top Tours (☎ 4125 3933 or 1800 063 933; www.fraserislandco.com.au). Offers accommodation in the Wilderness Retreat, Happy Valley. Day-tour $88, children $50. Wilderness Safari leaves Tu, Th, and Sa; Northern Adventure leaves Su-M, W, and F; both 2-day tours $179/$125. 3-day safari with stay at Cathedral Beach Resort departs Tu and F $315/$245.

Fraser Venture Tours (☎ 4125 4444 or 1800 249 122). Attracts a younger set to their daytrips and 2-3 day safaris. Quad-share accommodation at Eurong Beach Resort. Day-tour $86; 2-day safari $175; 3-day safari $230-290.

🛈 PRACTICAL INFORMATION

Tourist Office: For information, contact the **Hervey Bay Visitor Information Centre** (p. 348) or **Maryborough Fraser Island Visitor Information Centre** (☎ 4121 4111).

Permits: If you're going over in a car, you'll need a **vehicle permit** ($31; valid for 1 month; includes map and island details). **Camping permits** ($4 per person) are good for all campgrounds except the privately run Cathedral Beach Resort and Dilli Village, both on the east shore. With the permit comes a packet identifying allowed camping areas; some have 9pm noise curfews. Both permits are available from the Riverheads Store, the Rainbow Beach Dept. of Environment, and **Marina Kiosk**, on Buccaneer Ave., Urangan, at the harbor (☎ 4128 9800; open daily 6am-6:30pm).

General supplies: Stock up at Eurong Beach Resort, Fraser Island Retreat at Happy Valley, Kingfisher Bay Resort, Cathedral Beach Resort, or Orchid Beach.

Telephones: Central Station, Dundubara, Waddy Point, Indian Head, Yidney Rocks, and the resorts.

Showers: Cold showers are available at all campgrounds except Lake Allom. Coin-operated hot showers are available at Central Station, Waddy Point, and Dundubara. (50¢ for 3min.; 50¢-pieces only.)

Emergency: ☎ 000. Limited medical assistance also available at ranger stations and the Kingfisher Bay Resort (☎ 4120 3333 or 1800 872 555).

Tow Truck: ☎ 4127 9188 (Eurong) or 4127 9167 (Yidney Rocks).

ACCOMMODATIONS

Accommodation is included in the guided tour packages, but if you are arranging your trip independently, there are heaps of options. **Camping ❶** is by far the cheapest and most convenient island accommodation, enabling visitors to see different parts of the island without returning to one location each night. There are seven main QPWS camping areas, and camping is also allowed on designated beaches, including most of **Eastern Beach** (sites $4 per person; see **Practical Information,** above). **Cathedral Beach Resort and Camping Park ❶** has camping sites. (☎4127 9177. Sites for 2 $27, extra person $5.) **Eurong Beach Resort ❹** offers several budget options, as well as more expensive motel units. (☎4127 9122; www.fraser-is.com. Twins $88, weekly for 4 $500; cottages or 2-bedroom apartments for 4 $100; ocean view rooms for 2 $100; extra person $6.) **Fraser Island Retreat ❹** (☎4127 9144) has individual lodges for two ($110) to five ($150). The upscale **Kingfisher Bay Resort ❺** (☎1800 072 555) is well-hidden in the bush on the western side of the island, offering four-person self-contained cabins for $275.

ACTIVITIES

INLAND. With unbelievably clear waters and white sandy bottoms, Fraser's freshwater lakes are one of its biggest draws. **Lake McKenzie** is the most popular, with two white sand beaches for bathers, shady pine trees, and water in various shades of perfect blue. **Lake Wabby** is at the eastern base of the steep **Hammerstone Sandblow,** which gradually encroaches on this perched lake. Some visitors enjoy sliding down into the lake, but the trip is fast (the drier the sand, the faster) and you hit the water hard—a bad combo for your spine. Walking across the dune feels like crossing a vast desert; in fact, Fraser and nearby **Cooloola National Park** (p. 345) combined have more sand than the Sahara. The southernmost lake, **Boomanjin,** is, like many others, lined with fallen leaves from the overhanging swamp paperbarks and tea trees, which give it tea-colored water that softens the skin and hair. It's the largest lake on Fraser and the largest perched lake in the world. There are also a number of freshwater creeks good for swimming and wading, especially **Eli Creek,** accessible from Eastern Beach. **Wanggoolba Creek** is a silent beauty, muffled by its sandy bottom; the only babbling you'll hear is from other tourists at Central Station or conversations between the eel and catfish inhabitants.

THE EASTERN BEACH. There is a *lot* of beach on Fraser Island, and most of it looks the same, bordered by raging surf and low-lying trees announcing the tentative start of island vegetation. Eastern Beach is perfect for 4WDing, but be careful (see **Driving on Fraser,** p. 356). The drive from Hook Point north to Indian Head takes around 1¾hr. *Do not swim in the ocean,* as tiger sharks and riptides are real dangers. Heading north from Eurong, patches of rocks decorate the beach, with short bypasses at **Poyungan Rocks** and **Yidney Rocks** and a longer route around the **Indian Head** promontory, where one can spot dolphins, sharks, ospreys, and whales (late July to early Nov. on calm days). Almost at the top of passable beachland, a collection of shallow tide pools on **Middle Rocks** called the **Champagne Pools** make prime swimming holes at low tide. Be careful at the pools, as the rocks are slippery and incoming waves can cause serious injury by crashing over the rocks that dam the pools. Other attractions along the beach are **Rainbow Gorge,** the **Pinnacles,** and the **Cathedrals,** all impressive demonstrations of **Coloured Sands** (giant sand formations of countless shades), and the **Maheno shipwreck,** the remains of a massive cruise liner that washed ashore in a storm in the early part of the century.

QUEENSLAND

D-I-N-G-O ... And Dingo was his name-O. Don't confuse these wild creatures with any farmer's dog; keep your distance, and never pet or feed dingoes. The 160 dingoes that roam Fraser Island are some of the purest breed around; they have rarely interbred with domesticated dogs. By feeding the dingoes, however, visitors to Fraser have made them more aggressive and less fearful of humans. Now, dingoes routinely steal food from campsites and occasionally threaten unwary city slickers. If you do happen upon a dingo, *don't run.* Instead, cross your arms over your chest and walk slowly backward, always maintaining eye contact with the dog.

HIKING. Hiking tracks riddle the interior of Fraser, connecting to some lakes that are inaccessible by 4WD. Walking is often cheaper and more rewarding than 4WDing and is the only safe way to access **Western Beach**, a soft white silica paradise. Consider trying a smaller chunk of the island near Central Station (ranger station ☎4127 9191; open daily 10am-noon) like **Lake McKenzie** and **Lake Wabby** before attempting a more ambitious itinerary off the beaten track. If hiking really interests you, contact Phil at **Mango Hostel,** 110 Torquay Rd. (☎4124 2832), in Hervey Bay, for information about setting up itineraries.

⬛ DRIVING ON FRASER

Driving on Fraser is only possible in a 4WD vehicle or a well-equipped motorcycle. Speed limits are established on the island: 80km per hr. on the Eastern Beach and 35km per hr. on inland roads, though 20km per hr. is recommended. **Don't rush—** you can't. The one-laned roads are pure, soft sand; getting stuck is not out of the ordinary (have shovels handy). Allow at least 30 minutes to travel 10km on inland roads. The beaches themselves are registered national highways—all normal traffic rules apply, and the roads are even patrolled by Breathalyzer and speedgun-wielding policemen. Larger vehicles will occasionally stay on the right, however; in any case, always use your blinker. On the beach, drive only on hard, wet sand, and don't try to cross washouts that are above knee deep. Beware the tides; don't drive two hours within high tide.

BEACH DRIVING: THE FACTS. Although beach driving can be a lot of fun, reckless driving can lead to disaster. The most serious danger is **creek cuts** in the beach; test the depth of a creek before attempting to cross. *Don't cross if the water is higher than your knees;* instead, wait for the tide to go down. Hitting washouts at high speed risks the vehicle rolling; it also can break the springs, leading to expensive repair costs. Also, *don't drive at night,* when it is difficult to see and other drivers are more likely to be drunk and foolhardy. Location is important, as well; you're tempting fate by driving on the eastern beaches south of Dilli Village and Ungowa, north of the Ngkala Rocks, around Hook Point, or on the Western Beach.

SELF-DRIVE WITH HOSTELS. Extremely popular among backpackers, these three-day and two-night unguided group 4WD tours bring back stories, dirty clothes, and lots of sand. Unlike in guided tours, guests camp out at night. Hostel self-drive safaris usually cost about $125-130, plus the hidden costs of petrol (about $5-10 per person), insurance (around $15-20), and food and booze ($15-20 per person). Packages include 4WD hire, ferry passes, camping permits, access fees, camping equipment, and full preparatory briefing. Usually, the hostel hosts an afternoon meeting on the day before departure, a 4WD briefing the morning of, and a pre-departure supermarket run. To drive, you must be over 21, but anyone can ride. Bear in mind that the entire group assumes responsibility for vehicle damage, regardless of fault, so it's best to keep an eye on whoever is driving.

When choosing a hostel with which to book your Fraser tour, consider group size (try for a group of 9 rather than 11), vehicle safety, and extra costs. The type of partying you'll get with a group is usually related to the aura at the particular hostel: YHA attracts quieter groups and families, while Beaches, Koalas and Fraser Escapes party hard. **Smuggler's Rest** currently offers the best safari deal, with only eight per group, 4WDs with trunks for luggage storage (as opposed to unsafe roof racks), and insurance included in the $130 cost. Some hostels, including Fraser Escapes, Beaches, and Dingoes, topload their vehicles, making them less stable. The common alternative to roof racks, however, is also undesirable; Koalas loads luggage in the back of vehicles, leaving little room for passengers.

RENT YOUR OWN 4WD. For folks who want the thrill of hurtling down a beach independently, several companies rent 4WDs at comparable costs: 4-seater $130-140; 5-6 seater $150-160, 8-11 seater $160-170. **Aussie Trax** (see below), with new vehicles that are more expensive than standard 4WDs, also offers older model Land Rover ex-military vehicles (multi-day $120; seats 6). Hire companies lend out camping kits for $10-14 per person per day. Some good operators include: **Bay 4WD Centre,** 54 Boat Harbour Dr. (☎4128 2981); **Aussie Trax,** 56 Boat Harbour Dr. (☎4124 4433 or 1800 062 275); and **Safari,** 102 Boat Harbour Dr. (☎4124 4244 or 1800 689 819). All of these companies pick up locally. It's worth asking whether a rental agency belongs to the **Fraser Coast 4WD Hire Association,** the local watchdog. Some hostels, including The Woolshed in Hervey Bay and The Rocks Backpackers in Rainbow Beach, can also arrange cheap 4WD hire for groups.

 HOSTEL FIRE. Located 53km south of Bundaberg, **Childers** struggles to come to terms with the tragic **Palace Backpackers fire** that killed 15 international backpackers in June 2000. Though investigators suspected that arson was the cause of the fire, the tragedy has drawn attention to the need for official guidelines—especially strict fire regulations—over the hostel industry.

BUNDABERG ☎07

Bundaberg (pop. 42,000) is not high on the list of Australia's choice idling spots; most visitors get coffee at the bus terminal, stretch their legs, and hop back on board. However, it is the backpacker locus for vegetable-picking and a great, cheap place to learn to dive. In the fields, backpackers seeking to beef up bank accounts mix with seasoned life-long workers. At the end of the day, it's all about kicking the dirt off your work boots, occasionally splurging on Bundaberg's famous rum, and saving energy for another day in the fields. Some last a day; others, months. Despite Bundy's dearth of activities—or perhaps because of it—the survivors enjoy some of the purest camaraderie on the coast.

▐ TRANSPORTATION

Trains: Queensland Rail (☎13 22 32) is at the corner of Bourbong and McLean St. Ticket office open M-F 4-5am and 7:45am-5pm, Sa-Su 8:45am-1pm and 2-4:15pm. **Tilt Trains** depart for Brisbane (1-2 per day, $56.10); Mackay (1-3 per day, $88); Maryborough (1-2 per day, $20); and Rockhampton (1-3 per day, $51), with bus connections to Hervey Bay ($25.30). Children and students with ISIC 50% discount.

Buses: The Coach Terminal (☎ 4152 9700) is at 66 Targo St., between Crofton and Electra St. To get to town from the station, turn right and pass the roundabout and McDonald's to Bourbong St. **McCafferty's/Greyhound** (☎ 13 14 99 or 13 20 30) and **Premier** (☎ 13 34 10; cheaper, but only one service usually in the middle of the night) run to: Airlie Beach (11hr.; 4 per day; Premier $79, McCafferty's $116); Brisbane (7-7½hr., 5 per day, $43/$58); Cairns (19-20hr., 5 per day, $143/$155); Hervey Bay (1¾hr., 5 per day, $12/$26); Mackay (8½hr., 5 per day, $66/$98); Maroochydore (5½hr., 2 per day, $31/$52); Noosa (5hr., 2 per day, $30/$48); and Rockhampton (4-4¾hr., 5 per day, $32/$56).

Local Bus Transport: Duffy's City Buses (☎ 4151 4226) travel around town and to the Bundy Rum distillery. Buses daily 7:15am-5pm. **Stewart & Sons** (☎ 4153 2646) leaves M-F from the IGA on Woongarra St. for Innes Park (3 per day, $4.40), Elliott Heads (3 per day, $4.60), and Moore Park (2 per day, $4.60).

Taxi: Bundy Cabs (☎ 4151 2345 or 13 10 08). 24hr.

PRACTICAL INFORMATION

Most of Bundy's action takes place on **Bourbong St.**, which runs parallel to and one block south of the **Burnett River.** Crossing Bourbong from west to east are **McLean,** with the rail station, **Maryborough, Barolin,** and **Targo St.**, with the bus station and several restaurants.

Tourist Office: Bundaberg City Visitors Center, 186 Bourbong St. (☎ 4153 9289). Open M-F 8:30am-4:45pm, Sa-Su 10am-1pm. **Bundaberg Regional Visitors Center,** 271 Bourbong St. (☎ 4153 8888; www.bundabergregion.info). Open daily 9am-5pm.

Currency Exchange: ATMs line Bourbong St. between Targo and Maryborough St.

Bookstore: Boomerang Book Exchange, 26 Targo St. (☎ 4151 3812), buys and sells used books. Open M-F 8:30am-5pm, Sa 8:30am-noon.

Police: 256-258 Bourbong St. (☎ 4153 9111), in the city center. 24hr.

Internet: The Cosy Corner, on Barolin St. at the corner of Bourbong, opposite the post office. $4 per hr. Open M-Th 7am-8pm, F 7am-7:30pm, Sa 8am-5pm, Su 11am-5pm.

Post Office: 157B Bourbong St. (☎ 4131 4451), on the corner of Barolin St. Open M-F 9am-5pm and Sa 8:30am-noon. **Postal Code:** 4670.

WORKING IN BUNDY. Experienced workers will tell you that the first few days are the most difficult. If you can bear three or four days of a sore back, though, picking work can be rewarding, especially to the wallet. The wage is generally $10 per hr. after taxes. For speedy pickers, **contract work** is even more lucrative, as you're paid by the bushel. Usually, you'll need to pay for a week's accommodation at a hostel before they'll find work for you. During most of the year, work can be found within a day or so; lulls occur during transitions from one crop to another (generally late Jan.-Feb. and a week or two in Sept.-Aug.). At the site, the farm will teach you what to do—anyone (with proper work authorization, see p. 66) can do it. The one requirement is determination and stamina: the Sunshine Coast is littered with failed fruit pickers who leave Bundy after one rough day in the field. The job involves a fair amount of luck with weather, farmers, personality, and what you're picking; generally, snowpeas and avocados are good and chilies are bad, although preferences vary from person to person. Most workers stay 3-4 weeks, seeking to beef up their bank accounts.

ACCOMMODATIONS

The better hostels in town help find jobs (usually within a day of beginning your search), provide free transport to and from work, have strict alcohol and drug policies, and are equipped with walk-in fridges. Although the hostels listed below are known as reputable businesses, other hostels in town have been known to take advantage of backpackers by withholding their pay and passports. When choosing a hostel, *ask around first* to appraise its character. For those on a looser budget, or just in town for the night, motels are down Bourbong St.; the farther from town, the cheaper. Those not working should consider the backpackers outside of town.

Bundaberg Backpackers and Travellers Lodge, 2 Crofton St. (☎4152 2080), across from the bus terminal at the corner of Targo. The Hilton of hostels, this no-nonsense, air-conditioned haven is the picker's and 'packer's pick of the litter, although non-workers complain about the lack of social atmosphere. Free pickup at train station. Laundry, incredibly sterile TV room. Key deposit $20. Reception daily 7-11am and 2-7pm. Dorms $21, weekly $120. VIP/YHA. MC/V. EFTPOS. ●

Workers and Diving Hostel, 64 Barolin St (☎4151 6097). From the bus station call for a ride, or walk across the street, down Crofton St., and take a left onto Barolin St. (10min.). More social than many of the working hostels in town and still serious about their picking, but 15min. from town. TV lounge, small kitchen; 2-6 person dorms could use a bit of work. Reception daily 8:30am-noon and 3:30-7:30pm. Dorms $18, weekly $110; self-contained units $119/$805. NOMADS. MC/V. EFTPOS. ●

OUTSIDE TOWN

Iluka Forest Retreat, 127 Logan Rd., Innes Park (☎4159 3230 or 1800 657 005; www.coralcoast.org), on the oceanfront, 15km from Bundy. For those not working, another great budget option is close by, hidden in the bush between fields of sugar cane and the Woongarra Marine Park's reef. Spread out cabins make for few people and lots of wildlife. Great for couples. Free snorkel gear and pickup in Bundaberg. Shared amenities and kitchen; linen provided. Reception 7am-7pm. Dorms, doubles, and family rooms all $20 per person. MC/V. ●

Kelly's Beach Resort (YHA), 6 Trevor's Rd., Bargara (☎4154 7200 or 1800 246 141; www.kellysbeachresort.com.au), on the beach. Self-contained villas, pool, tennis court, sauna, eco-tours, 24hr. laundry, pickup from Bundaberg for guests staying multiple nights. Key deposit $10. Dorms $23, members $20; doubles $56/$48.30. 7th night free. AmEx/MC/V. EFTPOS. ●

FOOD

Bundaberg has a few good spots to fill up your tummy and absorb all that rum. Save money by cooking your own with groceries from **Coles** (☎4152 5222; open M-Sa 8am-9pm) and **Woolworth's** (☎4153 1055; open M-F 8am-9pm, Sa 8am-5pm), both in the Hinkler Place Shopping Centre, on the corner of Maryborough and George St. **The Grand Hotel ❶,** 89 Bourbong St. (☎4151 2441), on the corner of Targo, is the most popular joint in town for cheap meals and beers. (Lunch and dinner specials $3-6. Open Su-W 10am-10pm, Th-Su 10am-late; food served daily 11:30am-2pm and 6-8pm.) Relax after a long days work with pizza ($10-19) and pasta ($12-15) from **Numero Uno ❷,** 167A Bourbong St. (☎4151 3666. Open M-F 11:30am-2pm and 5pm-late, Sa-Su 5pm-late. AmEx/MC/V. EFTPOS.) **Zulu's ❸,** 61 Targo St., at the Queenslander Hotel, has a backyard eating area, meals around $15, and $8 jugs of beer. (☎4152 4691. Open daily 10am-2am; food served 11:30am-2pm and 5:30-8:30pm.)

IN RECENT NEWS

PHALLIC THEATRICS

Calling all gentlemen: it's time to drop your pants and sharpen your "dick tricks," as genital origami artists Simon Morley and David Friend term their impressive self-manipulation abilities. The Melbourne-born producers of **"Puppetry of the Penis"** have wowed international audiences with genital gesticulations since their 1997 debut, selling out at numerous comedy festivals and staging shows for big-name stars like U2's Bono, Hugh Grant, and Kylie Minogue. As dumbfounded audience members watch on the big screen close-up, the two artists fashion their genitalia into various shapes, including animal forms and such favorites as "The Eiffel Tower" and "The Loch Ness Monster." Morley first became interested in genital origami when his younger brother demonstrated to him "The Hamburger," an original trick in which the genitals are manipulated into the shape of a patty on a bun. The success of the show has been so great that Morley and Friend are now seeking new recruits to host additional shows; aspiring performers should check **www.puppetryofthepenis.com** for audition details. The puppetry pioneers claim to be equal opportunity employers, accepting applications from both circumcised and uncircumcised hopefuls. Women, however, appear to be out of luck.

SIGHTS AND ACTIVITIES

Diving in Bundaberg is rock-bottom cheap. **Salty's**, 208 Bourbong St., offers an excellent four-day PADI course in an on-site heated saltwater pool, with shore dives to the Coral Coast's volcanic rock reef. (☎4151 6422 or 1800 625 476; www.saltys.net. Open M-Sa 8am-5pm, Su 1-5pm. 4-day classes start M and Th $169. 2 boat dives on the artificial reef $100; 2 shore dives $45; 2 reef dives $215.) **Bundaberg Aqua Scuba**, 66 Targo St. (☎4153 5761), next to the bus terminal, offers two shore dives for $45, two artificial reef dives for $85, and a $169 PADI open water course that includes four shore dives; they also organize cheap accommodation for those in courses. Call both places to organize dive trips to Lady Musgrave or Lady Elliot Islands.

Love it or hate it, Bundy **Rum** is Australia's best-selling spirit. **Distillery tours** are popular but somewhat dull—much is on video and only one drink comes with the price. Duffy's buses, routes #4 (to Bargara, 4 per day) and #5 (to Burnett Heads, 3 per day) stop near the distillery. (☎4131 2900; www.bundabergrum.com.au. Tours every hr. M-F 10am-3pm, Sa-Su 10am-2pm. $7.70, concessions $5.50.)

Celebrating the start of the turtle nesting season, the week-long **Coral Coast Turtle Festival**, in November, features a carnival, shows, markets and parades. **Mon Repos** hosts the largest loggerhead turtle rookery in the South Pacific. During the season, night access to the beach is limited to guided tour groups. (15km from the city center; head east on Bargara Beach Rd. and follow signs to the rookery. ☎4159 1652. Open daily 7pm-2am, Nov.-Mar. 1hr. tours $5, children $2.50

TOWN OF 1770 AND AGNES WATER ☎07

Named for the year of Captain James Cook's second Australia landing, the area's natural beauty remains unmarred by two centuries of sleepy village life. Now, however, 1770 has been discovered a second time: backpackers on the coastal pilgramage have begun to visit the town, drawn by its unspoiled beaches and two national parks. Although the mention of 1770 and Agnes Water still draws a blank for many tourists, it's a magical spot, and it's going to be big.

▣ TRANSPORTATION. McCafferty's/Greyhound (☎13 14 99 or 13 20 30) runs to Fingerboard Rd., 20km from Agnes Water. **Buses** arrive from: Brisbane (9hr., $68); Bundaberg (1½hr., $33); Hervey (3hr., $34); Mackay (6hr., $92); and Rockhampton (3hr., $45). Northbound bus arrives at Fingerboard Rd.

8:35pm, southbound bus 6:50am. Bus transfers to Agnes Water cost $17. Alternatively, **Cool Bananas** (☎ 1800 227 660) offers free pickup from Bundaberg Mondays and Fridays at 3pm and picks up four times per day at Fingerboard Rd.

⚡ ⓘ **ORIENTATION AND PRACTICAL INFORMATION.** Agnes Water is located 123km north of Bundaberg. The town center lies at the intersection of **Round Hill Rd.**, the main access route into town, **Springs Rd.**, which runs south along the shoreline, and **Captain Cook Dr.**, which rambles 6km north to the town of 1770. Most residences and attractions are located in 1770, while basic supplies and accommodations can be found in Agnes Water.

Though privately owned, the **Discovery Centre,** in Endeavor Plaza, Agnes Water, offers friendly advice on all tours and accommodations in town. (☎ 4974 7002; www.discover1770.info. Open M-Tu, Th, and Sa 7am-6pm; W and F 9am-5pm.) The Westpac in Endeavor Plaza does not exchange currency, but there is an **ATM** in the Endeavor Plaza IGA. Other services include: **police** (☎ 4974 9708), in Agnes Water on Springs Rd.; **Internet** at Yok Attack, in Endeavor Plaza (☎ 4974 7454; open daily 9:30am-9pm; $6 per hr.); and **post office** in Agnes Water Shopping Centre. (Open M-F 9am-1pm and 1:30-5:30pm.) **Postal Code:** 4677.

🏠 ⓒ **ACCOMMODATIONS AND FOOD.** 🏕Cool Bananas ❷, on Springs Rd., Agnes Water, is hands-down the friendliest new hostel on the coast, with campfires, free eco-tours, and courtesy pickup and drop-off in Bundaberg or at Fingerboard Rd. Perks include excellent nightly dinner and dessert and free Monday night BBQ. (☎ 1800 227 660. Bikes $8 per day. Internet $4.50 per hr. Reception 7am-11pm; book in advance. Dorms in summer $22, in winter $18. YHA/VIP. MC/V.) **Backpackers 1770 ❷,** Captain Cook Dr., Agnes Water, is quiet and clean, with a great kitchen and spacious ensuite dorms. (☎ 4974 9849 or 1800 121 770. Reception 8am-9pm. 4-bed dorms $18; doubles $40. Cash only.) Alternatively, four caravan parks are located around 1770. **Captain Cook Holiday Village ❶,** on Captain Cook Dr. between 1770 and Agnes Water, has six acres of land and an excellent restaurant. (☎ 4974 9142. Reception 8am-8pm. Sites for 2 $15, powered $17; self-contained cabins $44, ensuite $66. AmEx/MC/V.)

Yok Attack ❷, Endeavor Plaza, serves Thai mains for $10-17. (☎ 4974 7454. Open daily 9:30am-9pm. MC/V.) For cheaper eats, try the pleasant **Palm's Cafe ❶,** at the Petrol station, where burgers are still $4, pizzas start at $3.30, and a coffee is only $1.65. (☎ 4974 9166. Open daily 6am-9pm.) Crash the local pub scene at **1770 Foods and Liquors ❶,** past the Marina on Captain Cook Dr. (☎ 4974 9183. Open daily 10am-late; food served daily 10am-3pm, also W-Su 6-8pm.) **Groceries** can be purchased at the **IGA,** in Endeavor Plaza (☎ 4974 7991; open daily 6:45am-6pm), or at the **Food Store** in Agnes Water Shopping Centre. (☎ 4974 9911. Open daily 6:30am-6:30pm.)

📷 ⓖ **SIGHTS AND ACTIVITIES.** Located on the northernmost surf beach and surrounded by two national parks, 1770 is an unspoiled paradise. Around the rocky headland, a **walking track** leads to panoramic views of blue water and crashing waves. Six kilometers of lonely beach separate the 1770 headland from the short, unmarked trails around Agnes Water, which begin behind the museum on Springs Rd. and lead to **Workman's Beach,** great for surfing and body boarding, as well as several lookout points. Past the picnic area, vehicular access changes to 4WD only; the track continues into **Deepwater National Park.**

To discover the depths of Deepwater, a land-locked series of lagoons, **1770 Adventure Tours** offers canoe tours. (☎ 4974 7068. Pickup and drop-off available. Tours Tu, Th, and Sa 8:30am-2pm. $49.) **LARCS,** enormous ex-military boats with wheels (now painted an innocent pink), rumble through Eurimbula Creek into **Eurimbula National Park.** (☎ 4974 9422 or 1800 177 011. Sunset cruise daily $22; day tours $88.)

QUEENSLAND

For a less conspicuous voyage through area waters, rent your own **"tinny,"** a powered aluminum boat. The cheapest rentals are at **1770 Camping Grounds,** on Captain Cook Dr., at the beach. (☎4974 9286. Day hire $70, half-day $45, $20 per hr.) **Bikes** are available at **Agnes Cycle and Sport,** in Endeavor Plaza. (☎4974 7550. Open M-F 9am-5pm, Sa 9am-1pm. $20 per day, $18 with copy of *Let's Go*.)

1770 is also the best access point for **Lady Musgrave Island,** a coral cay and lagoon on the Great Barrier Reef. **Lady Musgrave Cruises,** at the Visitors Center in Endeavor Plaza, runs pontoon boats to the island. (☎1800 072 110. Day tour includes snorkeling, reefwalking, and glass-bottom boat viewing. Tu-Su. $128, children $64. 2 dives at Lady Musgrave $149.)

CAPRICORN COAST

Straddling the Tropic of Capricorn and stretching from the Fraser Coast to the Whitsundays, this length of coastal tropics consists of one paradise after another. The Bruce Hwy. worms its way north through sugar cane fields and along the shore where some oceanside towns and island getaways have become backpacker havens. Other towns, such as Mackay, still grimace at the sight of sandals and an unwashed t-shirt but lie in proximity to isolated treasures like Eungella National Park. Just a short ferry ride from the mainland, Great Keppel Island beckons travelers from the dusty streets of Rockhampton with seventeen quiet beaches and a small pathway in lieu of a road.

ROCKHAMPTON   ☎07

Australia's self-proclaimed "beef capital," Rockhampton is ruled by the human minority (pop. 60,000), while the cattle majority (pop. 2,500,000) bide their time for revolt. Straddling the Tropic of Capricorn, this Great Barrier Beef is a gateway to Great Keppel Island and the small seaside town of Yeppoon, though there's not much to do in Rocky itself. Historical buildings loom over chain stores and shops on the town's meticulously plotted grid of streets. For the most part, Rockhampton is a serious, conservative town, with its share of hair salons and saddle shops. However, a few interesting cultural activities stir the country dust, providing a day's worth of entertainment.

▐ TRANSPORTATION

Train Station: 320 Murray St. (☎4932 0234), at the end of the road. From the city center, go south (away from the river) on any street, then turn left on Murray St. Lockers available. Trains travel north and south along the coast; the high-speed **Tilt Train** goes to Brisbane (7hr.; daily 7:40am; $88, students and children $44). Taxis into town $7.

Buses: McCafferty's/Greyhound (☎4927 2844). Terminal is behind KFC on Linnet St., off Queen Elizabeth Dr., which becomes Fitzroy St. on the other side of the bridge. Lockers $6-11 for 24hr. **Premier** (☎13 34 10) picks up from the Mobil station, 91 George St., between Fitzroy and Archer St. Premier is cheaper but only sends one bus south (12:15pm) and one north (3:20pm). Both have service to: Airlie Beach (6½hr.; 6 per day; Premier $48, McCafferty's $98); Brisbane (12hr., 7 per day, $76/$83); Bundaberg (4hr., 5 per day, $32/$56); Cairns (17hr., 7 per day, $118/$128); Hervey Bay (6hr., 6 per day, $43/$72); Mackay (4hr., 7 per day, $33/$52); and Maroochydore via Noosa (10hr., 4 per day, $64/$81). For info on transport to Great Keppel Island, see p. 366.

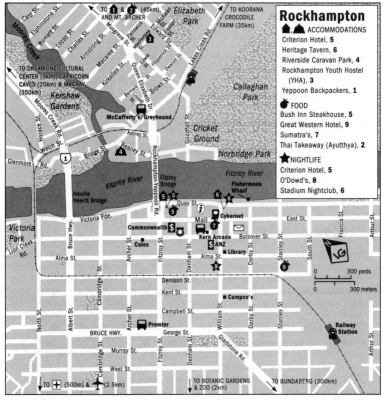

Rockhampton

▲, ▲ ACCOMMODATIONS
Criterion Hotel, **5**
Heritage Tavern, **6**
Riverside Caravan Park, **4**
Rockhampton Youth Hostel
(YHA), **3**
Yeppoon Backpackers, **1**

🍴 FOOD
Bush Inn Steakhouse, **5**
Great Western Hotel, **9**
Sumatra's, **7**
Thai Takeaway (Ayutthya), **2**

★ NIGHTLIFE
Criterion Hotel, **5**
O'Dowd's, **8**
Stadium Nightclub, **6**

Public Bus: The blue **Capricorn Sunbus** (☎ 4936 1002) leaves from Kern Arcade, on Bolsover St. between Denham and William St., and covers most corners of the city M-F 6:30am-5:45pm, Sa 8am-noon. Route maps posted at most stops and are available from the tourist office. Fares from $2-4. Student, children, and pensioner discounts.

Taxi: Rocky Cabs (☎ 13 10 08), or at the corner of Denham St. and the mall. 24hr.

Car Rental: Thrifty, 43 Fitzroy St. (☎ 4927 8755). Open daily 7am-6pm. **Europcar,** 106 George St. (☎ 4922 0044 or 13 13 90). Open M-F 7:30am-5:30pm, Sa 8am-1pm, Su 8am-11am.

✴ ⁊ ORIENTATION AND PRACTICAL INFORMATION

On the south side of the Fitzroy River, the city has a flawless grid design, with most of the action near the river's edge along Quay St. East St. runs parallel one street south from Quay and houses a pedestrian mall between Fitzroy and Denham St. On the north side of the Fitzroy Bridge, Fitzroy St. changes to Queen Elizabeth Dr. and continues on toward Yeppoon.

Tourist Office: Rockhampton Tourist Information Centre, 208 Quay St. (☎ 4922 5339), provides maps and the comprehensive *Rovin' Round Rocky Region.* Open M-F 8:30am-4:30pm, Sa-Su 9am-4pm.

QUEENSLAND

Currency Exchange: Banks and 24hr. **ATMs** are on the East St. pedestrian mall. **Commonwealth Bank,** 74 East St. (☎4922 1733), in the mall, and **ANZ,** 214 Bolsover St. (☎4931 7764), on the corner of William St., are both open M-Th 9:30am-4pm, F 9:30am-5pm.

Camping Equipment: Campco's, 121 William St. (☎4922 2366), on the corner of Kent St. Open M-F 8:30am-5pm, Sa 8:30am-1pm.

Library: 69 William St. (☎4936 8265), on the corner of Alma St. Free **Internet** terminals; book ahead for a 30min. session. Open M-Tu, and F 9:15am-5:30pm, W 1-8pm, Th 9:15am-8pm, Sa 9:15am-4:30pm.

Market: The **Arcade Car Park Markets**, in Kern Arcade on Bolsover St., has crafts and a few veggie stalls. Open Su 8am-12:30pm.

Police: (☎4932 1500), on Bolsover St. between Denham and Fitzroy St. Open 24hr.

Internet Access: Free at the **library,** or connect at **Cybernet,** 12 William St. (☎4927 3633), for $5 per hr. Open M-F 10am-6pm.

Post Office: 150 East St. (☎13 13 18), between William and Derby St. Open M-F 8:30am-5:30pm. **Postal Code:** 4700.

ACCOMMODATIONS

Yeppoon Backpackers, 30 Queen St., Yeppoon (☎4939 8080 or 1800 636 828). A great gateway to explore Great Keppel and a beachside treasure in itself. Pickup from Rockhampton (daily 6pm), or take Young's bus from Rockhampton (6 per day, $7.30). One night in Yeppoon, one on Great Keppel, and all ferry and other transport fees $69. Hostel also runs trips to Cooberrie, Koorana, Fire Rocks (4WD), and "Serenade" boat trips. Pool, spa, kitchen, Internet, laundry, and big TV room. Reception 7:30am-8:30pm. 4-bed dorms $20; doubles $40. VIP/YHA. AmEx/MC/V. EFTPOS. ❷

Rockhampton Youth Hostel (YHA), 60 MacFarlane St. (☎4927 5288). From the bus terminal, turn left on Queen Elizabeth Dr., walk 5min., and cross Musgrave St. Rocky's one youth hostel has a friendly but quiet crowd. Kitchen, laundry, TV room. Free pickup. Packages include 1 night in Rocky, 2 on Great Keppel, return ferry ticket, and shuttle; $98, YHA $93. Key deposit $10. Reception 7-11:30am and 3:30-9:30pm. Dorms $21, YHA $17; twins and doubles $50/$42; Olympic cabins $30/$26 per person. ❷

Criterion Hotel, 150 Quay St. (☎4922 1225), just south of the Fitzroy bridge on the river. Grand and picturesque, with plenty of pictures displaying the building's colorful past. Two bars and a restaurant. Basic rooms have showers and A/C but no toilet; pricier rooms have toilets and TV, and some have fireplaces and balconies. Reception 7am-midnight. Singles $30-50; twins $46-55; doubles $40-55; triples $56-65. AmEx/MC/V. EFTPOS. ❸

Heritage Tavern (☎4927 6996), on the corner of William and Quay St. A heritage-listed hotel, the tavern has a great kitchen and common room for guests; perfect for backpackers. Laundry. Basic singles $25; doubles and twins $35. Singles with A/C, TV, fridge, and balcony $30; doubles and twins $40; quads $60. AmEx/MC/V. EFTPOS. ❸

Riverside Caravan Park, 2 Reaney St. (☎4922 3779), along the river. Park is basic but centrally located. BBQ and laundry facilities. Reception 7am-8pm. Sites $7 per person, powered for 2 $17. Self-contained cabins $42. MC/V. EFTPOS. ❶

FOOD

Beef: it's what's for dinner in Rocky. Buy your own at Coles **supermarket,** in the City Centre Plaza at Fitzroy and Bolsover St. (open M-F 8am-9pm, Sa 8am-5:30pm), and cook it on the free BBQs along the river. Competition among the pub hotels keeps lunches cheap.

Great Western Hotel, 39 Stanley St. (☎4922 1862). The best steakhouse in town, with a rodeo arena out back. The Rocky Rump melts in your mouth for $18. W practice rodeo rides 7:30pm; every second F bull rides. Weekly events include rodeos, meat-cutting, and indoor campdrafts. Cover $8-10 for rodeos; no cover W nights. Open Su-Th 11am-midnight, F-Sa 11am-3am. Food served daily noon-2pm and 6-9pm; no Su lunch. ❸

Sumatra's (☎4921 4900), on the corner of East and William St. A nice change from the steakhouse scene, Sumatra's offers trendy seating on the mall and some veggie options. $5 lunch specials. Open M-Sa 10am-late. AmEx/MC/V. EFTPOS. ❶

Bush Inn Steakhouse, 150 Quay St. (☎4922 1225), in the Criterion Hotel. Recommended by locals as a great place to chew some of Rocky's finest ($14-24). Food served daily noon-2pm and 6-9pm. MC/V. EFTPOS. ❸

Thai Takeaway (Ayutthya), 24 Anzac Pde., Yeppoon (☎4939 3920), on the town's main drag. Recommended by locals, the family-owned eatery attracts patrons from miles around. Open daily 6-9:30pm. MC/V. ❷

🔴 🎭 SIGHTS AND ACTIVITIES

BOTANIC GARDENS AND ZOO. No need to choose; here you can sample native and exotic flora and fauna in one stroke. The zoo has an enormous geodesic dome aviary, chimpanzees, and the usual line-up of Aussie animals. *(15min. ride from the city on Sunbus route #4A; departs from the arcade carpark at least every hr. M-F 7:15am-5:50pm, Sa every hr. 8:15am-12:15pm. $1.90 one-way. ☎4922 1654. Feedings 3-3:15pm. Zoo open daily 8am-4:30pm; gardens open daily 6am-6pm. Both free.)* The **Kershaw Gardens,** stretching 1km along the Bruce Hwy. between Dowling and High St., recreate a natural Australian bush environment. *(Open daily 7am-6pm.)*

DREAMTIME CULTURAL CENTRE. The Centre provides a humble but elegant portrayal of the indigenous peoples of Central Queensland and the Torres Strait Islands. It is set in a park with a meandering trail highlighting different medicinal plants of the area. Learn to throw a boomerang and hear a didgeridoo demonstration at the end of the tour. *(5min. north of Rockhampton by car, on the corner of Yeppoon Rd. and the Bruce Hwy. Sunbus #10 runs from Rocky. ☎4936 1655. Open M-F 10am-3:30pm. 1½hr. tours are best for seeing the park; 10:30am and 1pm; $12.75.)*

CAVING. The **Capricorn Caves** are ancient limestone caves that feature the **cathedral,** with incredible natural acoustics and a natural light spectacle during summer solstice (early Dec. to mid-Jan.). There are both one hour and day tours of the caves. Included in the price is an opportunity to take a self-guided tour through a "dry rainforest." The caverns also host **Wild Caving Adventure Tours,** three hours of rock-climbing, being sardined in 12cm wide tunnels, and squeezing through Fat Man's Misery. *(23km from Rockhampton. ☎4934 2883. Open daily 9am-4pm. Admission and basic 1hr. tour $14, children $7; with transport from Rockhampton $33/$16; day tour with lunch and transport $64/$32; adventure tour $60, book at least 24hr. ahead.)*

ROCKHAMPTON HERITAGE VILLAGE. Experience Rockhampton from white settlement in 1854 through the 1950s in the Heritage Village, an active township that recreates original homes and buildings from that era. Wander the town on your own, or book ahead for a guided tour that includes rides in a horse-drawn carriage and demonstrations of blacksmithing and woodcutting. *(On Boundary Rd., off the Bruce Hwy. #10 Sunbus from Rocky. ☎4936 1026. Open M-F 9am-3pm, Sa-Su 10am-4pm.)*

QUEENSLAND

HIKING. Looming 604m over Rockhampton, **Mt. Archer** offers amazing views of the city and surrounding countryside. Drive 5km from the base to the summit and walk several different tracks at the top. Hardy hikers can trek back to the base on the walking track (11km; 4-5hr.), but you'll need a friend to retrieve you at the bottom, as the walk into town is a long one. Pick up a brochure at the tourist office for more information. *(By car, head northeast towards the summit on Musgrave St. to Moores Creek Rd. and then to German St.)*

FARM STAY. Myella Farm Stay ❺ offers an all-inclusive farmstay with horse and motorbike riding, 4WD tours, cow milking, and, of course, campfires. *(125km southwest of Rockhampton. ☎ 4998 1290. 3-days, 2-nights $240; includes buffet meals, all activities, and return transport from Rocky.)* **Kroombit Cattle Station ❺** offers a farmstay near the Kroombit Tops Rainforest and National Park, 35km from Biloela. Choose between horseback riding ($35-75 per person), 4WD tours of the park ($20-105), and cattle station activities. *(Free pickup from the McCafferty's stop at Biloela. ☎ 4992 2186; www.kroombit.com.au. Ensuite cabin singles $62, doubles $72. Powered and unpowered sites also available.)*

CARNARVON GORGE NATIONAL PARK. This rugged national park is rich with Aboriginal rock art, deep pools, and soaring sandstone cliffs. The gorges, however, are the main attraction. Cool temperatures make March through November the best time to visit, but be aware that night temperatures fall below freezing. National park camping is only available during Australian school holidays. *(500km southwest of Rockhampton and Gladstone on Bruce Hwy. For more info, pick up a map in the tourist office or contact the ranger ☎ 4984 4505.)* **Takarakka ❶,** 4km from the park, has sites and cabins. *(☎ 4984 4535. Sites $8, powered for 2 $22; cabins from $65.)* The luxurious **Wilderness Lodge ❺** *(☎ 4984 4503),* 3km from the park, offers self-contained units starting at $170.

🄴 🄳 NIGHTLIFE AND ENTERTAINMENT

Rocky's nightlife isn't plentiful, but at least it's easy to find: the pub hotels that you stay in are the pub hotels that you eat and party in. The sports-themed **Stadium Nightclub,** on the corner of Quay and William St. in the Heritage Tavern, has 20 TVs to ensure that you won't miss a moment of the action. It also bumps with Top-40 dancing late into the night. *(☎ 4927 6996. Open W-Su 8pm-5am. Cover F-Sa after 11pm $5.)* The **Criterion Hotel,** 150 Quay St., stands as an early meeting place and has three bars and live music Thursday through Saturday. *(☎ 4922 1225. Open M-W 10am-midnight, Th 10am-1am, F-Sa 10am-3am, Su 11am-midnight.)* For a pint of Guinness ($6.20), live rock music (Th-Sa nights), and some Irish grub (mains $16-23), good laddies and lassies hit **O'Dowd's,** 100 Williams St. Every second Friday night, join the Guinness club and drink as much as you can for $25. *(☎ 4927 0344. Open M-Sa 8am-2am, Su 8am-midnight.)*

GREAT KEPPEL ISLAND ☎ 07

The most developed of the largely untouched Keppel Island Group, Great Keppel is surrounded by unbelievably clear waters, 17 beaches with fine snorkeling right off-shore, and a brilliant night sky streaked by shooting stars. Spectacular coral reefs nearby make Keppel a favorite of divers as well. While budget accommodations abound, the island's posh resort doesn't mind the odd backpacker crashing its nightlife or taking its catamaran out for a lazy afternoon. For many visitors, it's enough to curl up on any of the beaches and seize a taste of paradise.

QUEENSLAND

TRANSPORTATION

Before arranging your own transport to Great Keppel Island, consider the **packages** offered by some of the hostels (see **Accommodations**, p. 367). If you choose independent transport, to get to the island you will need a ferry (30min. from Rosslyn Bay) and to get to the ferry you will need a bus (40min. from Rockhampton).

Young's Coaches (Route #20) runs to both ferries from the Kern Arcade, on Bolsover St. between Denham and William St., Rockhampton. (☎4922 3813. M-F 11 per day, Sa-Su 6 per day; $7.50 one-way.) **Rothery's Coaches** also leaves from Kern Arcade but only meets the Tourist Services Ferry. (☎4922 4320. Daily 8, 10:30am, and 1:30pm; $16.50 return, students $13.50, children $8.25.) **Freedom Fast Cats Ferry** leaves from Keppel Bay Marina, Rosslyn Bay. (☎4933 6244. 9am, noon, and 3pm. $31 return, students $25, children $16.) They also run various day cruises starting at $49. **Keppel Tourist Services** runs a ferry to the island from the Great Keppel Island Transit Centre, Rosslyn Bay. (☎4933 6744 or 1800 356 744. Daily 7:30, 9:15, 11:30am, and 3:30pm. $30 return, concessions $22, children $15.)

For drivers, free but unsecured parking is available outside the ferry terminals. Safer is **Great Keppel Island Security Car Park** (☎4933 6670), on the Scenic Hwy. just before the turn-off for Rosslyn Bay, which offers a courtesy bus to the harbor ($6.50 per day, covered $8).

The ferries let passengers out on Fisherman's Beach, the island's main beach. Parallel to the beach is the island's main (and only) drag, the **Yellow Brick Road** (we are in Oz, but the road's dark brown), a pathway that runs the entire commercial strip of Great Keppel, a five-minute stroll. The **Contiki Resort** (☎4939 5044) has Telstra payphones and an **Internet Cafe.** (Open daily 10am-5pm. Min. 2½hr. $10.) There is **no bank** on the island, but many establishments accept credit cards.

ACCOMMODATIONS

When considering accommodations, look at the big picture—many accommodations on the island offer packages that include bus and ferry transfers and rooms on the mainland, easing the price and trouble of arranging transfers yourself. Camping is not allowed on Great Keppel but is increasingly possible on nearby Keppel Group islands. For package information, try **Yeppoon Backpackers** or **Rockhampton YHA** (see **Accommodations**, p. 364).

Great Keppel Island Holiday Village (☎4939 8655 or 1800 180 235; www.gkiholidayvillage.com.au). A friendly, relaxed throw-back to the way the island used to be. Co-ed dorm rooms are average, but stay includes free use of snorkel gear and 4WD drop-offs in the middle of the island every other day for hikers. Also organizes motorized canoe trips ($20) and camping packages on nearby Middle Island $30. Kitchen and BBQ, laundry. Check-out 9am. Reception daily 8:30am-6:30pm. Dorms $24; tents with a wooden double bed $50. Cabins for 2 with shower $90, each extra person up to 4 $15. AmEx/MC/V. EFTPOS. ❷

Great Keppel Island Village YHA (☎4933 6744), affiliated with the Rockhampton YHA. A huge new kitchen and common room, as well as bright, pleasant cabins, make for a clean, well-run stay; perfect for families. A path-connected, plant-surrounded smattering of "safari tents" sits cozily out back. Reception daily 7am-1pm and 3-5pm; check-in at ferry. Dorms $21.10, twins and doubles $47. ❷

Keppel Haven (☎4933 6744 or 1800 356 744). Army-style "safari tents" make a tent village, while bunkhouses and cabins provide more comfortable, expensive stays. The **Haven Bar** is one of two bars on the island (open daily 10am-9:30pm). Very few showers and toilets in tent village. Watch out for hidden costs in village, as well, like linen $6 (doubles $12), plus a $20 deposit. Pay BBQ. Key deposit $10. Amazingly, laundry is free. Checkout 9am. Reception daily 7:30am-5pm. Book through Keppel Tourist Services. Tents 3- or 4-share $18; singles $28; twins and doubles $40. Bunkhouses with linen doubles $80; quads $100. Self-contained cabins for 2 $120. ❷

🔒 🍴 FOOD AND NIGHTLIFE

With a grand total of 11 establishments on the island, Great Keppel has what might be generously termed limited offerings. Food is expensive; stock up prior to departure at **Woody's Supermarket,** 18 James St., Yeppoon. (Open daily 6am-9pm.) **Island Pizza ❸** serves tasty but pricey pizza. (☎ 4939 4699. Open Sa-Su 12:30-2pm, Tu-Su 6-9pm. Cash only.) Have a splash in the water and then a splash in the cup at **Splash Bar,** in the Contiki Resort. (☎ 4939 5044. Live music Su noon-4pm and M 9pm-1am. Open daily noon-midnight, until 2am when nightclub is closed. Nightclub open Tu and Th 11pm-late, F-Sa 9pm-late.)

🔒 ACTIVITIES

Seventeen beaches define the perimeter of Keppel, while all of "civilization" is within an eight-minute stroll. The calm surf is perfect for swimming and snorkeling. **Monkey Beach,** a mere 30min. jaunt south of the hostels, has the best and most accessible **snorkeling; Clam Bay,** on the island's south side, also has a great coral reef for snorkeling. **Long Beach,** a 35min. walk past the airstrip, exists in splendid isolation (1.8km one-way). Inland walks begin on the main track that leads from Contiki's watersports area. Hike to ▨**Mt. Wyndham** for unparalleled views of your paradise (2½hr., 7km return). Other walks go to the **Old Homestead** (5.6km return) and the **lighthouse** (15.4km return). Trail junctures on inland tracks are not well posted, so keep your eyes peeled and bring a map. The *Souvenir Chart of Great Keppel Island* map is helpful for bush walks (50¢ at the Keppel Tourist Services ferry terminal on the mainland or $2 on the island).

The **Beach Shed** (☎ 4925 0624), at Keppel Haven, has jet skis ($30 per 10min.), jet ski tours (1hr. including snorkeling $50), snorkel gear ($10 per day), and kayaks ($10 per hr. Open daily 8:30am-4pm.) The **Keppel Island Dive Centre** (☎ 4939 5022), up the beach, offers dive trips for the certified ($77, with own gear $55) and the uninitiated ($99); tag along and snorkel for $33. **Prodive,** at the Resort, offers similar rates and dives. (Open daily 8:30am-4:30pm.)

To traverse the water with a bit of speed or sport, visit the fellas at the Resort's **watersports area,** just before the resort. They offer everything from high-speed banana rides ($12) to catamaran/windsurfer hire ($15 per hr.) to waterskiing ($25 for 10min.) to parasailing ($60. Open daily 9:30am-4:30pm.)

At the back of the resort, near reception, **Caps Central** makes bookings for non-guests and posts a list of daily activities. (☎ 4939 5044. Open daily 8am-6pm.) For adventure seekers, activities include **Tandem Skydive,** with beach landings. (From $362; the higher the drop, the higher the price.) Also at Caps, the catamaran **Euphoria** runs a three-hour sail and snorkel trip as well as a sunset cruise (both $45). For a slower pace, hop on a dromedary and enjoy **camel riding** on the beach ($40 per 30min. or $60 for 1hr. sunset ride).

NEAR GREAT KEPPEL ISLAND: THE KEPPEL GROUP

The isolated and largely deserted islands in the Keppel Group invite exploration by adventuresome travelers. Coconut-infested **Pumpkin Island** offers beautiful vegetation, coral, and white beaches. A maximum of 28 people on the island choose from the five **cabins ❷** for up to six people; bring your own linen and food. (☎4939 4413 or 4939 2431. Cabins $154.) The island also has toilets, showers, BBQ, drinking water, and plenty of deserted beaches. For transport, call **Freedom Fast Cats** (☎4933 6244) or a water-taxi (☎4933 6133). These are not cheap (ferry $175 for 2, taxi $260-300 return on a boat that can carry 6-10.) **Middle Island, Humpy Island,** and **North Keppel** also offer camping. Permits are available at the QPWS in Rosslyn Bay, adjacent to the Tourist Services office.

WHITSUNDAY COAST

Stretching from Mackay to the small town of Bowen, right above Airlie Beach, the well-deserved claim-to-fame of this coastal stretch is the Whitsunday Islands. Any passerby must experience the islands by spending a few relaxing days sailing on the clear waters, exploring the world underneath the water, and visiting secluded patches of land made of nothing but white sand amidst those waters. Accessed by Airlie Beach, near Proserpine, the Whitsundays characterize this tropical stretch, which draws a crowd but still manages to make every visitor feel the solitude of outback Queensland.

MACKAY   ☎07

Emerging out of miles and miles of sugar cane, Mackay (mick-EYE; pop. 70,000) serves as a convenient gateway to the rainforested national parks inland and the isolated islands offshore, allowing intrepid travelers to explore these wildly contrasting areas of natural beauty. Both within an hour's drive from the city, Eungella and Cape Hillsborough National Parks offer great hiking tracks and distinctive wildlife. While controlled cane fires glow on the night horizon, the moderate heat of the city's nightlife makes it a reasonable spot to spend an evening before striking out into the wilderness.

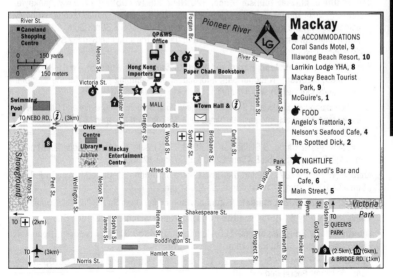

Mackay

▲ ACCOMMODATIONS
Coral Sands Motel, **9**
Illawong Beach Resort, **10**
Larrikin Lodge YHA, **8**
Mackay Beach Tourist
  Park, **9**
McGuire's, **1**

❖ FOOD
Angelo's Trattoria, **3**
Nelson's Seafood Cafe, **4**
The Spotted Dick, **2**

★ NIGHTLIFE
Doors, Gordi's Bar and
  Cafe, **6**
Main Street, **5**

☞ TRANSPORTATION

Trains: The **train station** (☎ 4952 7418) is about 5km south of town on Connors Rd. There is no public transport from the station, but a taxi costs about $10 and some hostels offer free pickup. Purchase tickets at the station (open M-F 9am-4:30pm) or in town at any travel agency. Lockers $2.

Buses: Mackay Bus Terminal, 45 River St. (☎ 4944 2144), is between Gregory and Wood St. **Premier** and **McCafferty's/Greyhound buses** run to: Airlie Beach (1¾-2hr.; Premier 1 per day, McCafferty's/Greyhound 6 per day; Premier $19, McCafferty's $34); Brisbane (14hr., 1/7 per day, $109/$127); Bundaberg (8¼-9¾hr., 1/3 per day, $66/$98); Cairns (9½-12hr., 1/7 per day, $95/$102); Hervey Bay (10¾hr., 1/6 per day, $77/$113); Maroochydore via Noosa (12hr., 1/3 per day, $97/$124); and Rockhampton (4¼hr., 1/7 per day, $33/$52). Student and YHA discounts.

Taxis: Mackay Taxi (24hr. ☎ 13 10 08).

Car Rental: Europcar, 6 Endeavor St. (☎ 4957 5606 or 1300 131 390), starts at $39 per day and offers courtesy pickup. **Avis** (☎ 13 63 33 or 4951 1266) is located at the airport. **Thrifty** (☎ 4942 8755 or 1800 818 050), at the corner of Bruce Hwy. and Sands Rd., offers courtesy pickup from airport.

◀▦ ⚆ ORIENTATION AND PRACTICAL INFORMATION

Mackay's city center is oriented on the southern bank of the Pioneer River. **River St.** runs along the waterfront, and the town's main drag, **Victoria St.**, is the next parallel street to the south. Nightlife and restaurants line **Sydney** and **Wood St.**, which are perpendicular to Victoria St. The **Bruce Hwy.** comes into the west side of town and exits to **Gordon St.**, parallel to and just south of Victoria St. As the Bruce Hwy. enters town and curves to the south, it changes to **Nebo Rd.** and leads to accommodations and the tourist office. The coastline forms Mackay's eastern border.

Tourist Office: Mackay Tourism Office, 320 Nebo Rd. (☎ 4952 2677; www.mackayregion.com), 3km southwest of the city center. Very helpful, although they recommend only businesses that are members of their organization. Open M-F 8:30am-5pm, Sa-Su 9am-4pm. A small **Information Booth** is located in the old Town Hall on Sydney St. Open M-F 8:30am-5pm, Sa 8:30am-1pm.

Parks Office: Queensland Parks and Wildlife Service, 2 Wood St. (☎ 4944 7800; www.epa.qld.gov.au). National park info, maps, and camping permits for the Cumberland Islands ($4 per person per night). Open M-F 8:30am-5pm.

Currency Exchange: Banks and 24hr. **ATMs** line Victoria St. between Gregory and Brisbane St. All offer traveler's check and cash exchange for a $5-7 fee and are open M-Th 9:30am-4pm, F 9:30am-5pm.

Bookstore: Paper Chain, 8 Sydney St. (☎ 4953 1331), sells and buys secondhand books. Open M-F 8:45am-5pm, Sa 8:45am-12:30pm, Su 9am-12:30pm.

Library: (☎ 4957 1787), behind the Civic Centre on Gordon St. Open M, W, and F 9am-5pm, Tu 10am-6pm, Th 10am-8pm, Sa 9am-3pm.

Market: Victoria Street Markets feature arts and crafts. Open Su 8:30am-12:30pm.

Police: 57 Sydney St. (24hr. ☎ 4968 3444), between Victoria and Gordon St.

Internet: Hong Kong Importers, 128 Victoria St. (☎ 4953 3188). $5 per hr. Open M-F 8:45am-5:15pm, Sa-Su 9am-1pm.

Post Office: 69 Sydney St. (☎ 13 13 18), between Victoria and Gordon St. Open M-F 8am-5:30pm. **Postal Code:** 4740.

ACCOMMODATIONS

Although hostels are scarce, budget motels line Nebo Rd. on the way into town. For cheap accommodation in the city center, your best bet is in one of the pub hotels. Alternatively, several caravan parks lie on the outskirts of town.

Larrikin Lodge YHA, 32 Peel St. (☎4951 3728; larrikin@mackay.net.au), a 10min. walk from the city center. Small kitchen/TV area breeds a friendly atmosphere at Mackay's only true hostel. 10-person dorms remain unlocked at all times, so learn to trust or grab a locker. Day tours to Eungella National Park $68. Laundry $2. Reception daily 7-10am and 4:30-9pm. Dorms $20, YHA $16.50; twins $41; family rooms $57. Cash only. ❷

McGuire's, 17 Wood St. (☎4957 7464). Cheapest beds, beer, and lunch in town. Rooms are clean but dreary; bathrooms are somewhat shabby. 4-bed dorm is best. Reception 7:30am-midnight. Dorms $15, 2 nights $20; singles $25, weekly $100-125; twins and doubles $40/$160. MC/V. EFTPOS. ❶

Mackay Beach Tourist Park, 8 Petrie St., Illawong Beach (☎4957 4021 or 1800 645 111), 3km south of the city center, with the beach as a backyard. Great amenities, including pool, camp kitchen, small gym, games room, and wandering peacocks. Reception daily 7am-7pm. Sites for 2 $15.40, powered $21; cabins for 2 $48, ensuite $59; "camp-o-tels" with 2 beds and a table $22. MC/V. EFTPOS. ❶

Coral Sands Motel, 44 Macalister St. (☎4951 1244), between Victoria and Gordon St. Convenient location, large grass courtyard, and quality restaurant complement clean rooms with TV, phone, A/C, and fridge. Laundry and carpark. Reception daily 6am-8:30pm. Check-in 24hr. Doubles $60-70; units with double and single bed $74-83; prices slightly higher in peak season. ❺

Illawong Beach Resort, 77 Illawong Dr. (☎4957 8427 or 1800 656 944; www.illawong-beach.com.au), 6km south of the city center on the beachfront. For a more upscale stay; offers spacious, motel-style self-contained villas with 2 bedrooms, A/C, and TV. Pool, lake, tennis courts, and licensed restaurant. Buffet breakfast included. Reception 7am-6pm. Doubles with garden view $110, ocean view $115, $99 standby special; extra person $16. AmEx/MC/V. EFTPOS. ❺

FOOD AND NIGHTLIFE

One of the most popular restaurants in town, **Angelo's Trattoria** ❸, 29 Sydney St., serves the in-crowd excellent pasta ($14-18) and other Mediterranean fare for around $20-25. (☎4953 5111. Open daily noon-2pm and 6pm-late. AmEx/MC/V.) Cheap fresh seafood to fillet at home or eat-in makes **Nelson's Seafood Cafe** ❶, 171 Victoria St., a favorite of locals and travelers alike, with $5 fish and chips. (☎4953 5453. Open Su-Th 10am-7:30pm, F-Sa 10am-8pm. MC/V.) **The Spotted Dick** ❷, 2 Sydney St., is one of Mackay's better eateries, with wacky decor and crazy cuisine. Meals run $9-19, and wood-fired pizzas are $11. (☎4957 2368. W karaoke; Th-Sa house band. Happy Hour M-F 4:30-6:30pm. Open M-Sa 11am-late, Su 11am-8pm. Kitchen open daily noon-2pm and 6-9pm. AmEx/MC/V.) A Woolworth's **supermarket** is in the Caneland Shopping Centre, off Victoria St. in the northwestern part of the city. (☎4951 2288. Open M-F 8am-9pm, Sa 8am-5pm.)

Mackay's mantra: raise cane in the fields, raise Cain in the pubs. **Main Street,** on the corner of Victoria and Gregory St., is the biggest club in town. DJ-hosted party madness rages around pool tables and two bars. (☎4957 7737. F-Sa cover $5. $2.50 basic spirits 10pm-midnight. Open W-Su 10pm-3am.) Break on through to the other side at **Doors,** 85 Victoria St., where drink specials, a big screen with not-so-subliminal messages like "take home someone ugly tonite," and a great dance pit make for a sweaty night of drunken fun. Downstairs, the more casual set at **Gordi's Bar**

QUEENSLAND

and Cafe spills out onto the street. (☎4951 2611. Doors open Tu-Sa 8pm-3am; cover F-Sa $4. Gordi's open daily 10am-3am; live entertainment nightly.) A crowd of all ages cruises to **McGuire's,** 17 Wood St., for their cheap jugs of Toohey's New ($6) and live entertainment Wednesday through Sunday. (☎4957 7464. Open M-W 9am-1am, Th-Sa 9am-2am, Su 10am-midnight.)

SIGHTS AND ACTIVITIES

While most of Mackay's attractions lie in its surroundings, the town manages a few sights of interest. Pick up the free guide, *A Heritage Walk in Mackay*, from the tourist office to guide you to the historical and cultural hotspots. Don't miss **Queen's Park,** on Goldsmith St. just north of Victoria Park, where the lovely **Orchid Gardens** overflow with delightful flowers. The **Mackay Entertainment Centre,** next door to the library on Gordon St., is your one-stop spot for drama, comedy, and concerts. (☎4957 1777 or ☎1800 646 574. Open M-F 9am-5pm, Sa 10am-1pm; also 1½hr. before shows.) The Centre also hosts the **Mackay Festival of Arts** (www.festivalmackay.org.au) in July, a two-week celebration with concerts, fashion parades, and comedy shows. **Farleigh Sugar Mill** offers two-hour tours during the sugar-crushing season that break down the history of the sugar industry. (No public transport; take the Bruce Hwy. 9km north from the city towards Proserpine, then turn right at Childlow St. ☎4963 2700. Tours June-Nov. M-F 1pm. $15, children $8, families $35.) **Pro Dive Mackay,** 44 Evans Ave., leads diving and snorkeling trips around Keswick Island. (☎4951 1150. Diving $149; PADI course with 2 pool dives and 2 days on the boat $415; snorkeling $139, children $114.)

NEAR MACKAY: BRAMPTON AND CARLISLE ISLANDS

Like Heron Island to the south, Brampton Island is not easily accessible to daytrippers, campers, or anyone unwilling to shell out $146 per person to stay a night at the island resort. Eleven kilometers of National Park **walking tracks** over dunes, past rocky headlands, and through eucalypt forests await those who make the journey. Although only resort accommodation is available on Brampton, nearby Carlisle Island has a **camping ❶** area with toilet, BBQ, and lots of shady trees, but no walking trails. Pick up a trail map and arrange camping permits through the Parks office in Mackay ($4 per person per night). If the guests-only boat transfer to **Brampton Island Resort ❺** (☎4951 4499) is not full, you may be able to grab a spot ($54 return) and arrange a $10 return boat transfer to Carlisle. At low tide, Carlisle is accessible from Brampton via a sand bridge.

BRUCE HIGHWAY: MACKAY TO AIRLIE

MACKAY TO EUNGELLA

The road to Eungella heads out from the south side of Mackay. From Nebo Rd., turn right onto the Peak Downs Hwy. just past the tourist office and follow it until you reach a junction with Eungella Rd. The road leads through the endless sugarcane fields of Pioneer Valley, sometimes ablaze at sunset when unchanging winds make the best time for controlled burning.

After passing the town of Marian on Eungella Rd., the **Illawong Sanctuary** is 4km past **Mirani,** 44km from Mackay. Hand feed the 'roos and ogle at the peculiar ice cream-eating emu. (☎4959 1777. Open daily 9:30am-5pm. $12, children $6; daytrip from Mackay including city tour, sapphire fossicking, and hot meal $50; homestay with dinner and breakfast $45.) Farther along Eungella Rd., in **Pinnacle,** is **The Pin-**

nacle Hotel ❶, where stopping for Wendy's famous ✎homemade pies is a must. (☎4958 5207. Pie $3.50; pie and pot special $5; large dinners with great vegetables $9-11. Open daily 9am-11pm.)

EUNGELLA NATIONAL PARK

Eighty kilometers west of Mackay on Eungella Rd. is the 52,000-hectare **Eungella National Park,** a range of steep rainforest-covered slopes and deep misty valleys. At Eungella, the "land where clouds lie low over the mountains," ten walking trails lead to spectacular hilltop and creekside views. The mountains—natural barriers between this park and other swaths of rainforest in Queensland—trap clouds, causing high precipitation. Red cedars, palms, and giant ferns coat many slopes, and platypi splash in the water at the ravines' bottoms. Over the years, Eungella has seen dramatic changes of focus—it has been prospected for gold, planted with sugar cane, logged, grazed for dairying, and, in 1941, declared a National Park.

Walking tracks are in two sections of the park: the **Finch Hatton Gorge** and **Eungella/Broken River.** Trail maps are at the QPWS office in Mackay or the Ranger Station at Broken River. Although no public transportation runs to Eungella, the park is easily reached via car or the **Flying Kangaroo,** a private bus service between the bus terminal in Mackay and, in succession, Finch Hatton, Eungella township, and Broken River. (☎1300 130 277. Departs Mackay daily 7:45am; departs for the return to Mackay daily from Broken River 2:15pm, from Eungella 2:30pm. $20 one-way.) For an organized tour of the park, **Jungle Johno's Bush, Beach, and Beyond Tours** is led by farmer-*cum*-tour-guide Wayne, who is deeply knowledgeable in topics from horticulture to folklore. He'll take you to Finch Hatton Gorge and Broken River. (☎4959 1822 or 4951 3728. $75, bookings through the Larrikin Lodge $68.) Col Adamson's **Reeforest Adventure Tours** takes daytrips to Eungella and Cape Hillsborough. (☎4953 1000. $85; pensioners, VIP, and YHA $80; children $53.)

FINCH HATTON GORGE. After the Pinnacle Hotel is a well-marked turn-off to beautiful **Finch Hatton Gorge** (10km from Eungella Rd.), distinct from the other accessible regions of the park by its low elevation. Contact the ranger (☎4958 4552) for the latest on trail conditions, as the narrow road dips through several creeks that are often too full to cross after heavy rains. On the dirt road to Finch Hatton Gorge is the idyllic ✎**Platypus Bush Camp ❶**, with rustic open-air huts and sites that afford great views and sounds of the adjacent creek area, with platypi, fireflies, and fruit bats. The camp features an open-air kitchen, a rainforest-walled shower, a creekside hot tub built out of rock, and an amazing cast of characters, human and otherwise. Call Wazza to arrange a pickup. (☎4958 3204. Sites $7.50 per person; dorm bunks $20; doubles $60. Bring your own food.)

Finch Hatton's one hiking track leaves from the picnic area at the end of Gorge Rd. The trail to **Wheel of Fire Falls** (4.2km; 1hr.) follows rapids as they cascade down the rocky riverbed; the last kilometer is a steep climb up stairs. The side track to **Araluen Falls** (400m) leads from the main trail to a zig-zag waterfall that pours into a deep pool. Aboriginal legend blesses nude bathers in the pool with healthy children; you might argue "frozen children," however, once you feel the icy mountain water. In either case, get there early on a summer morn to take a proud paddle for progeny. Heed warning signs and take care on slippery rocks. To see the rainforest from above, make a booking with **Forest Flying** (☎4958 3359; www.forestflying.com), which suspends visitors from a self-propelling treetop cable. (Pickup from Gorge accommodation or kiosk. 2-3hr. depending on group size. $45, children $30.) The folks at Forest Flying also run a mango farm, where there is work availability for WWOOFers (see **Volunteering,** p. 4).

EUNGELLA AND BROKEN RIVER. Continuing on Eungella Rd. 20km past the turnoff for Finch Hatton Gorge is **Eungella township** (pop. 10). Be careful on the road to Eungella, as it climbs 800m in 3km; take the turns slowly. At the top of the hill in Eungella township is the 🏠**Eungella Chalet ❸**, which overlooks the vast Pioneer Valley, where clouds settle into green mountains; sunrises are otherworldly. The licensed restaurant serves breakfast (7-9am), lunch (noon-2pm; $6-13), and dinner (6-8:30pm; $10-25). Bike hire costs $12 per half-day. (☎4958 4509. Singles $38, backpackers on weekdays $28; twins $50/$44; doubles $50; motel suites $72; 1-bedroom cabin $88; 2-bedroom cabin for 5 $109. MC/V. EFTPOS.) Just past the chalet on the right is **The Hideaway Cafe ❶**, with yet another amazing view and great apple strudel ($3.50). The international menu features vegetarian options and gourmet burgers for $6-8. (☎4958 4533. Open daily 8am-4pm.) **Kelly's Coach House and Gallery ❷**, across from the chalet, has cozy dining around the woodstove and chatty hosts. (☎4958 4518. Breakfast 7:30-10am, lunch 11:30am, dinner 6:30pm.)

Nine walking trails depart from trailheads between the Chalet and Broken River; ambitious day-hikers can follow one after another to the river and beyond, but be wary of the long walk back along the highway. Behind the Chalet, the 1½km **Pine Grove Circuit** forks at 700m into the excellent **Cedar Grove Track** (3km, 30min.), which winds past stately red cedars to a roadside picnic area and short lookout track. Two hundred meters down the road from the picnic area is the Palm Grove trailhead (1.8km), which gives you the option of continuing on to Broken River via the **Clarke Range Track** (6½km, 1¾hr.) Five kilometers on Eungella Rd. from the Chalet, you'll cross **Broken River**, with an excellent 🏠**platypus-viewing platform**, a picnic area, a **campground ❶** with toilets and hot showers ($4 per person), and a ranger station. (☎4958 4552. Open M-F 8:30am-5pm). Several additional trails lead from Broken River.

CAPE HILLSBOROUGH NATIONAL PARK

A finger of land jutting from the coastline north of Mackay, Cape Hillsborough National Park contrasts sandy beaches with rugged pine- and eucalypt-covered hills. Rocky outcrops protrude through the tropical rainforest, where kangaroos, lizards, and scrub turkeys roam. Although not as impressive as Eungella, the 816 hectare park makes for a good daytrip from Mackay. Take the Bruce Hwy. 20km northwest from the city to the righthand turnoff for Seaforth Rd.; turn right after another 20km on Seaforth Rd. to reach the Cape. The road to the Cape ends at the **Cape Hillsborough Tourist Resort ❶**, with beachfront access and a pool, BBQ, restaurant, and general store that sells **petrol**. (☎4959 0152; www.capehillsborough-resort.com.au. Reception daily 8am-6pm. Sites $11, powered $16.50; beach huts $66; motel rooms $77. Prices increase during holidays; book ahead. AmEx/MC/V. EFTPOS.) Adjacent to Cape Hillsborough is one of the best northern beaches, **Smalley's Beach,** on a short unsealed road to Bali Bay. Its **campsite ❶** has toilets, water, and the beach as its front yard, but no showers ($4 per person; self-register at the campsite). Another camping option in the area is the **Haliday Hide-away ❶**, a budget caravan park at Haliday Bay. Follow the signs off the Cape Hillsborough road. (☎4959 0367. Sites $10, powered $12; budget cabins in summer $30, in winter $25; self-contained cabins from $35. Cash only.)

Five short walking trails are concentrated on the eastern tip of the Cape. For more info on tracks, pick up a map at the parks office in Mackay, or peruse maps posted at the resort or the seldom-staffed ranger station (☎4959 0410) in the picnic area at the end of the cape. The **Diversity Boardwalk** (1.2km), at the park's entrance, is an aptly named jaunt through many species of mangroves, an area of open woodland with grasstrees and an Aboriginal midden heap (a massive pile of shells). After an initial steep ascent, the **Andrews Point Track** (2.6km one-way; 45min.) follows the ridge around the point, offering five spectacular lookouts and sea breezes. Return via the same track or along the beach, provided the tide is out. At low tide, the rocky beaches of **Wedge Island** become accessible to intrepid explorers, but there are no official tracks on the island. The **Beachcomber Cove Track** (1.6km) provides great views from the ridge before ending at the cove.

AIRLIE BEACH ☎07

Airlie (AIR-lee) was nothing but mudflats until a developer's proposal was turned down by the Shire Council in nearby Bowen (see p. 380) and he moved his project to the oceanside. Equipped with truckloads of Bowen sand, he put the "Beach" in Airlie. The spot was an upscale tourist destination until a pilot strike in the 1980s stalled Queensland's tourism for a year and a half. In a bid for survival, the resorts became budget, and backpackers flocked to them. The variety of activities offered on the nearby waters of the Whitsunday Islands and the Great Barrier Reef has turned the town into the biggest backpacker draw between Brisbane and Cairns. Airlie turns into a raucous party almost every night of the week, with many of the hostels thriving on young people's energy. But when the morning comes, a calm resurfaces as most people set sail to the beckoning islands and outer reefs.

▛ TRANSPORTATION

Trains: The rail station is in Proserpine. **Whitsunday Transit** (24hr. ☎4946 1800) picks up arriving train passengers and runs down Shute Harbour Rd., stopping in the center of Airlie and at some accommodations; timetables available all over town.

Buses: Travel offices and most hostel desks book transport. **McCafferty's/Greyhound** (☎13 14 99) drops off at the end of the Esplanade; accommodations offer courtesy pickups, but most hostels are in walking distance. Prices are listed as non-discounted, but ISIC/VIP/YHA will save you up to $15 on some tickets. **Buses** run daily to: Bowen (1¼hr., 5 per day, $26); Brisbane (18hr., 6 per day, $145); Bundaberg (12hr., 3 per day, $116); Cairns (10hr., 5 per day, $79); Gladstone (9hr., 5 per day, $102); Hervey Bay (13hr., 4 per day, $130); Mackay (2hr., 6 per day, $35); Maroochydore (16hr., 3 per day, $130); Mission Beach (8hr., 3 per day, $83); Noosa (15hr., 3 per day, $137); Rockhampton (7hr., 6 per day, $70); and Townsville (4hr., 5 per day, $50).

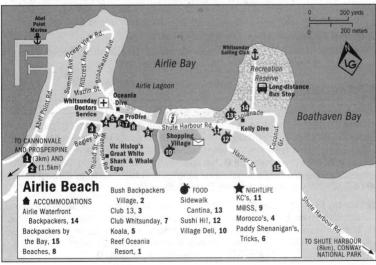

Local Transportation: Whitsunday Transit (☎ 4946 1800) runs between Cannonvale and Shute Harbour at least every 30min. daily 6am-6:40pm, stopping in front of Oceania Dive. 10-trip ticket $19. Airlie Beach to Shute Harbour $4.10. Night service Th-Sa 7-11pm. **Whitsunday Taxi** (☎ 13 10 08) serves the whole area.

■ ⓘ ORIENTATION AND PRACTICAL INFORMATION

The turn-off for Airlie Beach is at Proserpine, off the Bruce Hwy.; the road passes through Cannonvale and on to Airlie Beach (26km). The main road becomes **Shute Harbour Rd.**, running parallel to the water as it nears Airlie; it has most of the town's accommodations and restaurants. At the northern end of town is **Abel Point Marina**, and at the southern end of the town proper, the road veers left to the **Esplanade** or continues straight towards Shute Harbour (8km). Picnic tables and BBQs line the **Beach Walk** parallel to Shute Harbour Rd. Sunbathers laze on the newly created beach or on the grass around **Airlie Lagoon**, which also has a public pool.

Tourist Office: City Tourist Bureau, 348 Shute Harbour Rd. (☎ 4946 6673). Also serves as the Whitsunday Regional Tourist Bureau.

Budget Travel Office: One on every street corner. Some of the hostel tour bookings offer free rooms if you book sailing trips with them. **Where? What? How? Whitsunday,** Shop 1, 283 Shute Harbour Rd. (☎ 4946 5255). Reputable tour office that also books bus reservations. Open daily 7:30am-6pm.

Parks Office: National and Marine Parks Authority (☎ 4946 7022), on the corner of Mandalay St. and Shute Harbour Rd., 2km out of town toward Shute Harbour. Info on camping and national parks. Open M-F 9am-5pm, Sa 9am-1pm.

Currency Exchange: Commonwealth Bank (☎ 4946 7433) charges a flat $10 fee for traveler's checks and foreign exchange. Open M-Th 9:30am-4pm, F 9:30am-5pm. There's an **ATM** there, as well as at **ANZ Bank,** next to the post office.

Police: (☎ 4946 6445).

Medical Services: Whitsunday Medical Centre, 400 Shute Harbour Rd. (24hr. ☎ 4946 6275). Open M-F 7:30am-5:30pm, Sa 9am-1pm. Dive medicals $35. **Whitsunday Doctors Service** (☎ 4946 6241), on the corner of Shute Harbour Rd. and Broadwater Ave. Open M-F 8am-6pm, Sa 11am-1pm, Su 10am-noon. Dive medicals $35.

Internet Access: Everywhere. Expect to pay $4 per hr.

Post Office: (☎ 4946 6515), in the shopping plaza next to McDonald's on Shute Harbour Rd. Open M-F 9am-5pm, Sa 9am-11am. **Postal Code:** 4802.

▌ ACCOMMODATIONS

Airlie's cornucopia of budget establishments can barely keep pace with backpacker demand, so book ahead. Check into deals if booking tours through your hostel; some offer free night stays. Check-out is 10am and key deposit $10, and all major credit cards are accepted, unless otherwise indicated. The nearby Whitsunday Islands offer cheap **camping ❶,** but space is limited (see p. 380). One of the nicest—and only—camping options close to town is at **Island Gateway Caravan Resort ❶** (☎ 4946 6228), 1km past town on Shute Harbour Rd.

Club 13, 13 Begley St. (☎ 4946 7376 or 1800 633 945). Take a right before Morocco's and it's atop the hill to the right; only 100m from the waterfront. You'll feel like you've entered backpacker heaven, with private kitchens and balconies for each "club" of rooms overlooking the harbour. Cooked-to-order breakfast. Reception 7am-9pm. Ensuite dorms $20; doubles $50-55, some with spa. VIP/YHA. ❷

QUEENSLAND

Airlie Waterfront Backpackers (☎ 1800 089 000), on the Esplanade. Very clean, quiet atmosphere. Separate (but shared) female and male kitchens, TVs, and bathrooms. Free pizza voucher for Legends and 10min. Internet. Reception 7am-8:30pm. Dorms $20; 3- and 4-bed $25 per person. ❷

Club Whitsunday (☎4948 1511 or 1800 678 755), on Shute Harbour Rd. A friendly hostel where you don't have to compromise location for comfort. 4-bed dorm rooms with walk-through shared bathrooms. Fan, A/C, and TV. Free hot breakfast (cook your own eggs and bacon), cereal, and toast daily 7-10am. Free luggage storage. Kitchen and laundry. Internet $4 per hr. Reception 7am-8pm. Dorms $18; doubles $47. ❷

Bush Village Backpackers Resort, 2 St. Martins Rd., Cannonvale (☎4946 6177 or 1800 809 256), 1½km out of town. The ultimate in cleanliness and goodwill. Cabins with kitchens and modern bath line a driveway that leads to the pool, porch, TV lounge, and videos. Continental breakfast included. Free shuttle to town 6:30am-11:30pm. Reception daily 7am-7pm. Dorms $22, members $20; doubles $42/$49. ❷

Backpackers by the Bay, 12 Hermitage Dr. (☎/fax 4946 7267 or 1800 646 994), 650m from town toward Shute Harbour. 4-bed bunk-style rooms, chill atmosphere, and amenities galore. BBQ, laundry, pool, game room, Internet, free nightly activities, and a sweet view of the bay. Free pickup and bus to town. Happy Hour daily 5:30-6:30pm (beers $2.50). Reception 7am-7:30pm. Dorms $20; twins and doubles $48. VIP/YHA. ❷

Beaches, 356-62 Shute Harbour Rd. (☎4946 6244 or 1800 636 630; www.beaches.com.au). One of the central party spots (bar opens daily at noon). Dorms in former motel rooms with balcony, kitchenette, bath, TV, and fan. Secured parking, laundry, game room, spacious kitchen, and Internet. Free night with overnight tour or dive course booking. Reception daily 7am-8pm. Dorms $15-20; doubles and twins $50. VIP. ❶

Reef Oceania Resort, a.k.a. **Reef O's,** 147 Shute Harbour Rd., Cannonvale (☎4946 6137 or 1800 800 795; info@reeforesort.com), 3km from town. Prices are low, but the rooms aren't always the cleanest. Pool, volleyball court, free afternoon movies and popcorn, ping-pong, BBQ, bistro, live music nightly, free breakfast, and bar. Free pickup from bus stop, and free hourly bus service to and from town. Reception 24hr. Bunkhouse beds from $6; tropical cabins $13, with A/C $17; doubles $55. ❶

Koala (☎4946 6001 or 1800 800 421; whitwand@whitsunday.net.au), on Shute Harbour Rd. This edition of the famed chain pulls in a varied crowd with their various room options. 4-bed huts have a small kitchen, bath, and satellite TV. Pool, volleyball court, laundry, and Internet. Meal discounts next door at Morocco's. The only campsite in town. Reception daily 7am-8:30pm. Sites $10, extra person $5; dorms $16-18; twins and doubles $46-50; quads $80. VIP. ❶

FOOD

With the exception of a few cafes, practically all of Airlie's restaurants double as bars and clubs after 9pm. If you stay around, you'll undoubtedly be treated to entertainment—you can see and partake in everything from live music to scandalous foam parties. Look for discount flyers around town for drink and meal deals (Beaches, Magnums, and Morocco's are the hotspots). For simple nourishment, there is a **supermarket** right in the middle of town. (Open daily 8:30am-6:30pm.)

Village Deli (☎4964 1121), across from the post office in the Whitsunday Village. Any time of day, you can find some of the most delicious delicacies accompanied by some trendy tunes. Serves uniquely concocted sandwiches ($7), amazing breakfasts and dangerous desserts ($5.50 cake and coffee daily). After 6pm, the tapas bar concocts a largely vegetarian menu, with some meat options. Open daily 8am-9:30pm. ❶

QUEENSLAND

▓ **Sushi Hi!,** 390 Shute Harbour Rd. (☎4948 0400). The only place for raw fish in town, their massive seafood rolls will fill your belly without emptying your pocket ($6.45 for half rolls). Marinated beef, chicken, or fish sandwiches are $7 per foot. Healthy smoothies ($4-6) will keep you buff for the beach. Open daily 10am-9pm. ❶

Sidewalk Cantina (☎4946 6425), on the Esplanade. If you can fight the crowds, take a break inside or on the sidewalk and enjoy some tasty Mexican fare or traditional breakfast options. Mains $18-25. Open M and Th-Su 6pm-late. ❹

Beaches, 356-62 Shute Harbour Rd. (☎4946 6244). An ever jam-packed backpacker mecca. Dinner at long picnic tables. Mains $8-15. Get a free drink if you grab a coupon on the street and show up by about 5pm. Party games start daily around 9:30pm and are followed by dancing until midnight. ❷

◉ NIGHTLIFE

M@ss, 366 Shute Harbour Rd. (☎4946 6266), part of Magnums' metropolis. Nights here get sticky, soapy, noisy, and naked. Live music outside daily 5pm; rowdy games and debauchery follows. Open Su-Th until late, F-Sa until morning.

Morocco's (☎4946 6446), next to Koala on Shute Harbour Rd. Slightly upscale decor with some outdoor tables and a huge TV screen inside. Games and prizes given away daily. Meals for $10-17, but you can usually pick up a $4 discount on the street. Open daily 7-10am and 4:30pm-2am.

Paddy Shenanigan's (☎4946 5055), near Beaches on Shute Harbour Rd. A popular place with Airlie dwellers and a great place to start the night off in style. Dance floor and good music. Open daily 5pm-2am.

KC's (☎4946 6320), on Shute Harbour Rd., on the right before the turn-off for the Esplanade. If you're looking for a big piece of steak and some great live music (check out Babe Ruth M-Tu 9pm), this is the place. A truly relaxing and intimate pub environment. Open daily until late.

Tricks, 352 Shute Harbour Rd. (☎4946 6465), upstairs from Paddy's. Almost always manages to whip up a lively dance party. No cover. Open daily until 5am.

◉ ◈ SIGHTS AND ACTIVITIES

The best things to do in Airlie Beach are visit the Whitsunday Islands (see p. 380) and dive the Great Barrier Reef (see p. 296), but there is no shortage of other activities in the area. Those listed below are affordable and cut away a bit from the mainstream backpacker options.

BY LAND. Conway National Park is a few kilometers east of Airlie Beach. A self-guided **walk** lasts just over an hour and passes wrinkled fig trees, mucky mangrove swamps, and a few rare bottle trees. On the way, stop at the **QPWS** for a detailed leaflet. (QPWS ☎4746 7022. Open M-F 8am-5pm, Sa 9am-1pm.) **Fawlty Tours** has a daily rainforest excursion that features a look at **Cedar Creek Falls.** (☎4948 0999. $42.) For a little bit more of an adrenaline rush, try plowing through the bush on a four-wheeler with **Whitsunday Quad Bike.** (☎0418 745 444. Departs daily; half-day $100.) If you have a car, go to any local tourist office and ask for some **self-drive** suggestions, as the area has several other swimming holes and scenic picnic areas.

BY SEA. Reel it in with **M.V. Jillian;** troll for mackerel, cobia, and tuna, and then enjoy lunch on board. (☎4948 0999. Daytrips depart Abel Point 8:30am; return around 5:30pm. $99.) A more relaxing fishing excursion is aboard the **M.V. Moruya,** a local favorite. (☎4946 6665. Departs daily at 9am from Shute Harbour and returns around 5pm.

Daytrip $90, with YHA or Uni ID $75.) If you're looking for a longer fishing trip to the outer reef in pursuit of the lions of the fishing world, the beautiful **Marlin Blue** has a very experienced captain. Come eye-to-eye with sea turtles and glide underneath the shadows of sea eagles as you explore the islands under your own steam. *(☎ 4946 5044. 1-day trip $275.)* One of the newest trends that is catching on in Airlie is sea kayaking. Join **Kayak Adventures Down Under** for a half-, full-, 2-, or 3-day trip around the islands. Sails offer a bit of help on windy days, and dormitory accommodation is available if you don't want to camp. *(☎ 4946 7172 or 1800 635 334; www.kayakadventures.com.au. Half-day $55, full-day $85, overnight from $240.)* **Ocean Rafting** offers daytrips on a raft that tops 65km per hour. Trips include a chance to dive and tan on the beach, as well as either visit Aboriginal caves or take rainforest walks. *(☎ 4946 6848; www.oceanrafting.com. $66, children $39; lunch $10 extra.)*

BY AIR. Cruise 300 ft. above Airlie with **Whitsunday Parasail.** Afterwards, you can enjoy the resort pool free of charge. *(On the jetty near Coral Sea Resort. ☎ 4948 0000. $49. Jet ski hire $35 for 15min.)* **Tandem Skydiving** will drop with you from the sky from 8000 ft. *(At the Whitsunday Airport, towards Shute Harbour. ☎ 4946 9115. $249.)*

HERE THERE BE "MONSTERS". Hand-feed kangaroos, ducks, and emus—and watch the handlers carefully feed the crocs—at **Barefoot Bushmans Wildlife Park.** The area also features pythons, cassowaries, koalas, and a giant waterslide. *(Lot 2, Shute Harbour Rd., Cannonvale. ☎ 4946 1480. Open daily 9am-4:30pm. $20, children $10, families $55.)* One of Australia's most bizarre sights, **Vic Hislop's Great White Shark & Whale Expo** is a shrine to the owner's unflagging efforts to document—with clippings, photos, and movies—the "dangers of sharks," as well as his efforts to battle against these "monsters." A great white shark he caught sits frozen in a block of ice for your viewing pleasure. *(13 Waterson Rd. ☎ 4946 6928. Open daily 9am-6pm. $15.)*

🉐 DIVING

The scuba scene is hot in the Whitsunday area. Dolphins, whales (in the winter months), turtles, manta rays, and even small reef sharks prowl these waters. The most popular site for overnight trips are on the outer reefs that lie just beyond the major island groups, including the **Bait, Hardy,** and **Hook Reefs.** Occasionally, boats will venture to the Black or Elizabeth Reefs. **Mantaray Bay** is the best spot nearby, even just for great snorkeling. Reasonable prices can be found year-round. All trips incur an extra $5 per day Reef Tax. Be wary of companies that offer very low prices for dive courses; ask where you dive, how many dives you get, and what food, accommodation, and equipment will be available to you.

Reef Jet (☎ 4946 5366; www.reefjet.com.au). This fast boat takes you and 40 other passengers to Bait Reef, a good location for both beginners and advanced divers. The trip departs Abel Marina at 8:30am, returning 4:30pm; $110, children $70; 2 certified dives $45 extra; intro dives $55 extra.

FantaSea Cruises (☎ 4946 5111). Their *Reefworld* catamaran whisks you to the **Reefworld Pontoon** with its underwater observatory. Departs Shute Harbour and Hamilton Island daily. $141, concessions $116, children $71, families $320; includes courtesy bus, lunch, and snorkeling.

Kelly Dive, 1 The Esplanade (☎ 4946 6122 or 1800 063 454; www.kellydive.com.au). 3-day, 3-night trips on either a sailing catamaran or dive boat. Small groups of 20 or 21 people. The *M.V. Sea Reef* departs M and Th 6:30pm and includes 10 dives; $490, doubles $10 extra per person. The *Pacific Star* catamaran departs W and Sa and includes 6 dives; shared cabins $450, private cabins $495.

Oceania Dive, 257 Shute Harbour Rd. (☎4946 6032; www.oceaniadive.com.au). The new 27m boat *Oceania*, the premier dive boat in Airlie Beach, departs Tu and F for a 3-day, 3-night trip to Continental Shelf. The boat carries 30 passengers. Advanced courses available. Up to 10 certified dives $500; 5-day course $535.

Pro Dive, 344 Shute Harbour Rd. (☎4948 1888 or 1800 075 035; www.prodivewhitsundays.com). 4-day course with 2 daytrips to the reef $385; 5-day open-water course $499; all-inclusive 3-day, 3-night trip on *Ocean Pro* $477 certified, snorkelers $355; PADI 6-day courses $685 with advanced certification.

BOWEN   ☎07

One of Queensland's best kept secrets, Bowen lies just 40min. north of Airlie on the Bruce Hwy. Its gorgeous beaches make the town a strong alternative to Bundaberg (see p. 357) as a place to make some cash. Several hostels will arrange $10.45 per hour (pre-tax) **jobs** at local farms during picking season (May-Nov.). Bowen is a stop on every McCafferty's/Greyhound bus. **Bowen Tourism** is at 42 Williams St. (☎4786 4494. Open daily 9am-5pm.)

Horseshoe Bay is the town's biggest attraction. To get there, follow Soldiers Rd. out of town, take a right onto Horseshoe Bay Rd., and follow it to the end. Although it is sometimes crowded by a large elderly population, the small inlet is the perfect place to spend an afternoon. **Murray Bay** is a less frequented and beautiful beach. Turn right off Horseshoe Bay Rd. onto unsealed Murray Bay Rd. The road ends about a 10min. walk from the beach. Soldiers Rd. meets **Queens Bay** directly in the middle. At the far right tip of Queens Bay is **Grays Bay,** with calm water and good **fishing. Bowen Bus Service** runs to the beaches from the library on the corner of Herbert and William St. (☎4786 4414. M-F 3 per day, Sa 2 per day. $2.)

Trinity's ❶ is a hostel out of the center of town, on the corner of Soldiers and Horseshoe Bay Rd. It offers a bus to town, laundry, and Internet. They help set backpackers up with fruit-picking work. (☎4786 4199. $12, weekly $72.) For those not working, the **Horseshoe Bay Resort ❷** is a terrific option with brand-new campsites. (☎4786 2564. Sites for 2 $20, powered $22; on-site vans $28; cabins $43, with A/C and TV $45; motel-style units $60, beachfront $75.)

WHITSUNDAY ISLANDS

Seventy-four islands make up the Whitsunday group, some small enough to walk across in a few minutes, and others lush with waterfalls, long hiking trails, pristine beaches, coral reefs, and even 5-star resorts. The thousands of visitors who flock to this majestic area often come to sail or to see the deservedly famous Whitehaven Beach. Whitsunday Island, home to Whitehaven, is the largest and most appealing to campers and hikers. Other backpacker favorites include Hook Island, with its choice snorkeling spots and Aboriginal cave painting; Daydream Island; Long Island; and the Molle Island Group, of which South Molle is the best. At the posh resorts on Hayman, Hamilton, and Lindeman Islands, many guests arrive by private helicopter or plane, but the islands can make decent daytrips even for those who are strapped for cash.

▐▀ TRANSPORTATION

Choosing which island—or how many—to go to can seem quite overwhelming, especially when you want to see it all. The best way to really experience the island group is by sailing (see p. 383), but it is possible to take ferries to the different islands and spend a day. Hamilton Island is very popular for daytrippers because it has a small metropolis up and running; overnights can be quite pricey. See the different island sections below to help decide your itinerary.

Blues Ferries, a.k.a. **FantaSea** (☎4946 5111). Departing Shute Harbour, one of the only companies to run direct transfers to the islands. Schedules are available at almost any booking office or hostel. 3-8 ferries leave the harbor daily to: Long Island ($25 return); South Molle ($22 return); Hamilton ($42 return). A **Discover Pass** will get you to all 3 in 1 day ($52).

Island Camping Connections (☎4946 5255). Drops campers off at many of the islands' camping spots, and has camping and snorkel equipment for hire. Min. of 2 campers $45-150 person. A multiple-island daytrip is an option, though you'll spend more time on the 100-person boat than you will on the islands.

Whitsunday Island Adventure Cruises (☎4946 5255). Whisks you about the islands, stopping at Whitehaven, South Molle Resort, and Hook Island Resort. A good way to get out on the water and do some snorkeling if you're pressed for time. Departs daily 9am, returns 5:30pm. $69, students $63, children $35; lunch $10.

Whitsunday All Over (☎4946 9499). Ferries passengers to Daydream Island, Long Island, or South Molle; they also have inter-island ferries. Long Island $32 return, South Molle $32; daytrip to both islands as well as Daydream Island with lunch $49.)

Reef Express (☎4946 4447). Runs daily from Abel Point Marina to Hook and Whitsunday Islands in a glass-bottom boat. $76.

Air Whitsunday Seaplanes (☎4946 9111). Flies over the islands. 3hr. reef sight-seeing and snorkeling $245; 6hr. snorkeling at the reef $295, dive $375; 1hr. reef and Whitehaven $175. Flight to Hayman Island to spend entire day $175.

Helireef (☎4946 9102). Runs scenic flights to the reef and beyond. From Hamilton $219; from Airlie $190; 30min. flight from Airlie $199.

THE ISLANDS

The island group is rich with cheap camping options; there are 21 campsites on 17 different islands. Before embarking, you must get a permit from **QPWS** at the **Marine Parks Authority,** on the corner of Shute Harbor and Mandalay Rd., Airlie Beach. (☎4946 7022. Open M-F 9am-5pm, Sa 9am-1pm. Permits $3.85 per night.) Walk-in applications are welcome, but book ahead for smaller campgrounds.

WHITSUNDAY ISLAND. The principal draw of the Whitsunday Islands is the famed ■Whitehaven Beach, a 6km-long slip of white along the western part of the beach. Sand as pure as talcum powder swirls from one edge of the island to the other; at low tide you can practically walk across the inlet. Across the inlet is the longer portion of Whitehaven, where most day-tour companies moor and sail trips stop for sunbathing and swimming. Make sure you get to the **lookout;** from Tongue Bay, it's an easy 650m walk. Be aware: some tour companies will only take you to the portion of the beach that lies across the bay, but Whitehaven might seem a wasted trip unless you see it from above, so ask ahead and make sure the tour includes the lookout. The **campsite ❶** at Whitehaven Beach recently re-opened, and it has toilets, picnic tables, and shelter (peak-season limit 60 people, off-peak limit 24). On the other side of the island is **Cid Harbour,** a common mooring site for the 2-night boat trips. Cid Harbor houses three **campgrounds.** The largest is **Dungong Beach ❶** (limit 36 people), which has toilets, drinking water, sheltered picnic areas, and a walking track (1km; 40min.) that leads to the second campground, **Sawmill Beach ❶** (limit 24 people). The same amenities are provided here. Bring a water supply if you're camping farther south at **Joe's Beach ❶** (limit 12 people). All campsites cost $3.85 per night. There is excellent **snorkeling** in the shallow waters not far from Joe's Beach.

HOOK ISLAND. The beaches on Hook have beautiful stretches of coral just off-shore, literally a stone's throw from **Chalkies Beach** and **Blue Pearl Bay.** (*Let's Go* does not recommend literally throwing stones at beautiful stretches of coral.) On the south side of the island lies **Nara Inlet,** a popular spot for overnight boat trips. About 20min. up the grueling path is a cave shelter used by the sea-faring Ngalandji Aborigines, bordered on both sides by middens (piles of shells). The rare paintings inside date back to 1000 BC and may have given rise to the popular Australian myth that a boatload of exiled Egyptians washed ashore ages ago and left hieroglyphic-like traces in various corners of Queensland. Although the story is unsubstantiated, it is true that at least one glyph in the cave is a good match for "king" in Hieroglyphic Luwian, spoken in ancient Troy.

Maureens Cove (limit 36 people), on Hook's northern coast, is a popular anchorage and has **camping** ❶. Also on the island is **Steen's Beach campground** ❶ (limit 12 people), a good sea-kayaking site. **Hook Island Wilderness Resort** ❶, just east of Matilda Bay, is a bargain resort with a range of activities from snorkeling (1-day $10) to fish and goanna feeding. Remember to bring a towel, kitchen utensils and sleeping bag or blanket. (☎ 4946 9380. Transfers $36. Camping $15 per person, 2 nights $25, children $7.50; hut-style dorms $24; ensuite beach-front cabin for up to 6 $119. Credit cards accepted.) There is an underwater reef observatory (one of the oldest in the world) at the end of the jetty ($8); check with the resort for opening hours.

SOUTH MOLLE ISLAND. South Molle is a national park and offers some of the best **bushwalking** in Queensland. The trek (6km return; 1½hr.) from the resort to 🔳**Spion Kop,** an enormous rock precipice, is a must. Adventurous hikers scramble up the rocks for an absolutely astounding 360° view of the Whitsundays. **Sandy Beach** (limit 36 people) has over 15km of hiking trails. The trip to the island's resort is 5km through the grasslands. Another 1km will take you to Balancing Rock. Many two-night sailing excursions moor offshore, and guests come ashore to bushwalk or use the pool at the **South Molle Island Resort** ❺, located in Bauer Bay. (☎ 4946 9433 or 1800 075 080. Meals and nightly entertainment included. 3-bed rooms $125 per person; 2-bed $138-186 per person. Cheaper standby rates are often available.) The island's water activities facility has waterskiing ($35), catamarans ($10 per 30min.), and jet skiing ($50 per 15min.) plus a long list of other activities. (Open daily 8:30am-4:30pm.) The resort also runs a diving trip to Hardy Reef, departing daily at 8:30am on **Reefjet** and returning at 5:30pm. (☎ 4946 9433. $165, families $368. Min. 3 people.) The easiest and cheapest way to enjoy the resort is to buy an all-inclusive package (room, all meals, and all non-motorized water sports). All island walks are accessible from the resort, and reception can give you a map with descriptions of the different choices.

HAMILTON ISLAND. The mini-metropolis of the Whitsundays, the **Hamilton Island Resort** ❻ has high-rise hotels and a main drag replete with **ATM, general store,** and 14 different restaurants. Golf buggies whisk well-heeled guests from beach-front to marina in minutes—surprisingly, they are the only form of transport on the island. (☎ 4946 9999. Transfer included. Twin or double ensuite bungalows $104; 5-star Beach Club rooms $150 per person.) The pricey activities on the island will leave you breathless and spent. **Jono's Beach Hire,** at the resort, rents catamarans ($30 per hr.), windsurfers ($20 per hr.), and snorkel gear ($12). Soar across a valley on the **Wire Flyer,** a hang glider attached to a 325m-long cable. Follow the signs posted around the island to find it. (☎ 4946 8780. $35, children $25.) **FantaSea** will take you for the day. (☎ 4946 5111. $55 with lunch, children $27.50.)

LONG ISLAND. Only a short journey from Airlie Beach, Long Island has one campground at **Sandy Bay** ❶ (limit 12) and a budget resort called **Club Crocodile** ❺.

The resort's special gives three nights in a twin-share room, all meals, use of the pool and spa, and bushwalking. Its launch departs regularly from Shute Harbour. (☎ 4946 9400 or 1800 075 125. Transfers $32 on **Blue Ferries.** Garden-room singles $209; doubles $398. Listed special: garden rooms $513 per person, children $55.)

DAYDREAM ISLAND. Part of the Molle group, the resort here is the island. Formerly West Molle island, the original resort owners realized that the name Daydream Island Resort was so much more attractive. The resort re-opened under new management in September 2001, and is now known as **Novotel Daydream Island Resort ❺,** a truly lavish 296-room hotel with a luxurious spa. A brand-new outdoor cinema plays new releases nightly. Rooms as high as $500 per night.

OTHER ISLANDS. Hayman Island is known as one of Australia's premier resorts; unless you have $500 for a night's stay, you're not going to visit for more than a day. **Camping ❶** remains one of the most rewarding ways to see the islands. On **North Molle Island** lies the mammoth Cockatoo Beach Campground (limit 48 people), fully equipped with facilities and seasonal water supply. Other fully equipped campsites include **Gloucester Island's** Bona Bay (limit 36 people), Northern Spit (limit 24 people, no water) on **Henning Island,** the small-secluded sites (limit 12 people) at **Thomas Island,** and **Armit Island** (limit 12 people). Basic grounds with simple bushcamping sites and a 12-person limit are Shute Harbour (views of Shute Harbour are actually concealed by **Repair Island**) on **Tancred Island,** Burning Point and Neck Bay on **Shaw Island, Saddleback Island,** Western Beach on **South Repulse Island,** and the four-person sites on **Olden Island, Planton Island,** and **Denmon Island.**

Finally, Boat Port (limit 12 people) on **Lindeman Island,** owned by ClubMed, has great walks. The **Mount Odefield walk** (3.6km) goes from the Airstrip Hut to the summit. The **Loop walk** (6.3km) begins in the same spot but runs along the headlands to the northern beaches. The easiest track goes to **Coconut Beach** (5.2km).

🔲 SAILING THE ISLANDS

Going to the Whitsundays without sailing the islands is like going to Paris without seeing the Eiffel Tower. A sailing safari is one of the most popular activities in Queensland. Some hostels offer a free night's stay if you book tours with them; while this may save you money, it might not be the best experience. Make sure you get the full details on the boat, its capacity, and its history. Go to several agents and gather information before making a reservation. Ask how much time is actually spent on the safari. Many boats offer "three-day, two-night" trips that leave at midday and come back only 48hr. later. When the options are overwhelming, try asking a few more questions. How many passengers does the boat take? Is it primarily a dive boat with a generator that will be running all night filling the tanks (and keeping you awake)? How much sailing is done (weather permitting)? Is snorkel gear included? Do you want to sleep at sea or on one of the island resorts? Even take a late-afternoon stroll (around 4 or 5pm) down to Abel Point Marina to take a look at some of the boats and talk to some of the skippers.

There are four classes of boats at play: the uninspiring **motor-powered**—this includes boats that have sails but nonetheless motor everywhere; the stately **tall-ships,** with rigging of yesteryear and the elegance of age; the **cruising yachts,** which offer more comfort and with smaller numbers may give you the most sailing time; and the proper **racing yachts,** called **maxis,** which are usually well past their racing prime, generally more expensive, and popular with partiers. Travel agents may try to push the maxis (which give higher commissions), with a valid case that these boats will get you to locations faster and thereby give you more time in each place. Then again, the powerboats will get you there even faster, so choose the balance of sail-time versus location-time that suits you best. During the low seasons (Oct.-Nov. and Feb.-Mar.), when discounts can be found, all sailing trips are usually booked solid a few days ahead of time; unless you **book ahead,** your boat may be decided for you or you may miss out altogether. Finally, keep in mind that it can get chilly and wet out on the waves. Boats usually provide waterproof weather jackets, but quick-dry shorts are also a good idea.

We list a few reliable companies below, along with some sample trips, but you are strongly advised to use these as a starting point for researching the options on your own—it will be well worth it, considering that there are many, many sails around the islands that can accommodate a wide variety of tastes and budgets.

🔲 **Southern Cross** (☎4946 4999 or 1800 675 790). *Siska*, 80 ft., offers the most comfort. *Southern Cross,* a former America's Cup finalist, holds 14 guests. *Boomerang* takes 20 guests and is said by some to be one of the best. (Each 3 days, 2 nights; $383). *Solway Lass*, a gorgeous 127 ft. built in 1902, holds 32 guests. (3 days, 3 nights; twins/doubles $399, 4-bed $379. 6 days and 6 nights; $739/$689.)

Prosail (☎4946 5433). Most Prosail 3-day, 2-night trips offer an additional day on *On the Edge* for 50% off. Package deals: 2 days of sailing $155; cruise family rate $213. 3-day trips on 1 of 4 maxis, including the *Matador,* the world's largest maxi, $470-$520. 3-day, 2-night trips on cruising yachts take 12 guests and 2 crew; $470.

Aussie Adventure Sailing (www.aussiesailing.com.au). With a wide range of sailboats, from maxis to the tallships, they service a diverse group of customers. The *Ron of Argyll* fits 12 people for a 2-day, 2-night trip (Depart M, Th, Sa; $385). *Dream Catcher* takes 10 people for the same amount of time and the same price (departs Su, W, and F 2pm). *SV Whitehaven*, a tallship, allows for beach camping (3-day, 2-night trip depart Tu, Th, and Su 1pm; $385).

Queensland Yacht Charters (☎1800 075 013 hires fully equipped boats for those wishing to go it alone; sailing boats include fuel, power boats don't. Not including the hefty $770-1100 bond, rates range from $366 per night for yachts, and $325 per night for power boats, which, when divided amongst a group, often beats the cost of a cruise.

NORTH COAST OF QUEENSLAND

As the Queensland coast stretches farther north, the sandy beaches stretch alongside some of the world's oldest tropical rainforests. To the west of the tropics, the earth becomes dry and the dirt turns red; much of this land sits on former volcanic shelves, its terrain rising high above sea level. Tall green fields, smoking mills, and Bundaberg rum all stand testament to the region's greatest agricultural asset: sugar cane. Off the shores of sunny Townsville, the area's economic and residential center, Magnetic Island offers solitude and koalas in the wild. Between the island and Mission Beach, white beaches glow next to crystalline water, and the Great Barrier Reef expands across the Coral Sea, beckoning travelers and locals alike. The inland territory hides swaths of rainforest populated by birds, bugs, and bouncing 'roos, and between it all, the civilization that clings to the coast wrests its existence from the unrelenting wild.

TOWNSVILLE   ☎07

Townsville is a forest of greenery from which the red rock of Castle Hill rises up to tower over the topaz blue of the Coral Sea. Discover what other tourists and backpackers have blundered past on their pilgrimages north: Townsville is so much

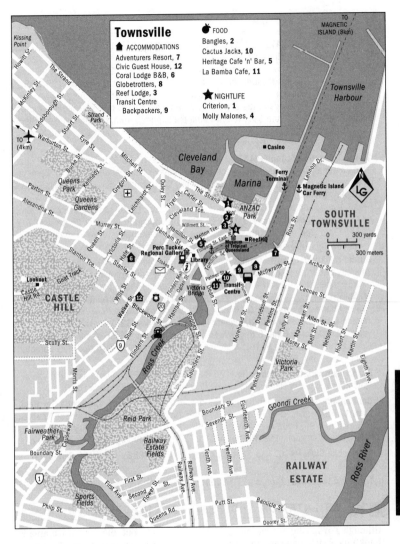

Townsville

🏠 ACCOMMODATIONS
Adventurers Resort, **7**
Civic Guest House, **12**
Coral Lodge B&B, **6**
Globetrotters, **8**
Reef Lodge, **3**
Transit Centre
  Backpackers, **9**

🍎 FOOD
Bangles, **2**
Cactus Jacks, **10**
Heritage Cafe 'n' Bar, **5**
La Bamba Cafe, **11**

★ NIGHTLIFE
Criterion, **1**
Molly Malones, **4**

more than northern Queensland's unofficial capital. It is a laid-back city of beaches, cafes, and palm-lined promenades. After a cyclone hit the shores to the north in 2000, the city has rebuilt and reinvented **The Strand,** 2.2km of beachfront park chock full of cafes, hotels, and bars. The rewards of diving the world-renowned wreck of the *S.S. Yongala* or koala-spotting on Magnetic Island make venturing out of the city well worth the effort. Travelers return from treasure-seeking expeditions to a city with a sophisticated nightlife dominated by good wine and loads of live music venues.

▮ TRANSPORTATION

Flights: The **airport** (☎4727 3211) is west of town. **Qantas** (☎4753 3311), at the Dimmey's entrance in Flinders Mall, flies direct to: Brisbane (1¾hr., 4 per day, $253); Cairns (1hr., 6 per day, $229); and Mackay (1hr., 3 per day, $253). Some of the best deals can be found through former Ansett partner **Flight West** (☎4725 3855; www.flightwest.com.au). An **airport shuttle bus** (☎4775 5544) runs to town daily 5:30am-9pm. Bookings to the airport must be made 30min. before scheduled pickup time. One-way $7, return $11. To drive from the airport to town, take John Melton Black Dr., which becomes Bundock St. Bear right onto Warburton St. and again onto Eyre St. From Eyre St., go left on Denham St. to the town center.

Trains: The **train station** (☎4772 8288, reservations 13 22 32; www.qr.com.au) is at the corner of Flinders and Blackwood St. The *Inlander* train departs W and Su 6pm for: Charters Towers (3hr., $21); Cloncurry (16hr., $85); Hughenden (8hr., $49); Mt. Isa (20½hr., $104); and Richmond (10¾hr., $61). The *Spirit of the Tropics* leaves W and Su 4:10pm heading to: Brisbane (24hr., $153); Bowen (5½hr., $142); Mackay (7½hr., $130); and Rockhampton (13hr., $88). The **Queensland Rail Travel Centre** (☎4772 8358) is to the right of the station. Open M 7:15am-5pm, Tu and F 6am-5pm, W 7:15am-6pm, Th 8:30am-5pm, Sa 1-4:30pm, Su 7:15-10:45am.

Buses: The **Transit Centre** is on the corner of Palmer and Plume St., a 5min. walk from the city center. Open daily 6am-8:30pm. **McCafferty's/Greyhound** (☎13 14 99 or 13 20 30; open daily 5:30am-11pm) runs to: Airlie Beach (4hr., 6 per day, $49); Brisbane (20hr., 6 per day, $166); Cairns (4hr., 6 per day, $51); Cardwell (2¼hr., 6 per day, $33); Charters Towers (2hr., 2 per day, $27); Cloncurry (10hr., 2 per day, $107); Hughenden (4hr., 2 per day, $53); Ingham (1½hr., 6 per day, $26); Innisfail (4¼hr., 6 per day, $47); Mackay (5hr., 6 per day, $67); Mission Beach (3½hr., 4 per day, $47); Mt. Isa (12hr., 2 per day, $119); Richmond (5hr., 2 per day, $68); and Rockhampton (9hr., 6 per day, $103).

Public Transportation: **Sunbus** (☎4725 8482; www.sunbus.com.au) has its main terminus in the center of Flinders Mall. Most tickets $3-4. 24hr. bus passes $10.

Car Rental: Local outfits don't allow cars beyond Charters Towers. **Townsville Car Rentals,** 12 Palmer St. (☎4772 1093). $44 per day, limit 100km. **Independent Rentals,** 25 Yeatman St., Hyde Park (☎4721 4766). $44 per day, 150km. Bigger companies allow unlimited kilometers. **Thrifty** (☎13 13 90), at the airport, rents from $49 per day.

Automobile Club: RACQ, 635 Sturt St. (24hr. ☎4721 4888). Open M-F 8am-5pm, Sa 8am-noon.

Taxis: **Taxi Townsville** (24hr. ☎4772 1555).

▮ ▮ ORIENTATION AND PRACTICAL INFORMATION

Although Townsville is a large city with a complex layout, the downtown area is thankfully easy to navigate. Buses pull into the Transit Centre on **Palmer St.,** which is also where most hostels are located. From Palmer St., it's only a ten-minute walk over the **Victoria Bridge** to the open-air **Flinders Mall;** use the Holiday Inn as a guiding point. The beach and many nice restaurants are set along **The Strand,** a street that runs along the ocean for several kilometers. Most of the cross streets to Flinders will take you to The Strand; the easiest way is to walk east down Flinders, towards ReefHQ, and turn left. **Castle Hill** looms in the city's background and is accessible both by road and by a relatively steep walking trail; take Gregory St. from The Strand, or Stanley St. from town.

Tourist office: Visitors Center (☎4721 3660), the big circular kiosk in the Flinders Mall. Open M-F 9am-5pm, Sa-Su 9am-1pm. **Reef and National Park Information Centre,** Shop 12, Flinders Mall (☎4721 2399), opposite Hoges Cafe, has all your answers on marine life. Open M-F 9am-5pm, Sa-Su 10am-4pm.

Currency Exchange: Bank of Queensland, 16 Stokes St. (☎4772 1799), up from Flinders Mall on the left, often has the best rates. $7 commission. Open M-Th 9:30am-4pm, F 9:30am-5pm. **ATMs** are in Flinders Mall for both Cirrus and Plus transactions.

Police: (☎4759 9777), on the corner of Stanley and Sturt St.

Hospital: General Hospital, (☎4781 9211), on Eyre St. There's also a **doctor's office** across from the Holiday Inn, on the corner of Flinders and Stokes St. (☎4724 0026). Open M-F 8am-5:30pm, Sa 8am-noon.

Internet Access: Internet Den, 265 Flinders Mall (☎4721 4500), next to McDonald's. $6 per hr. Open daily 8am-10pm. Free at the **library** across the mall. Book ahead. Open M-F 9:30am-5pm, Sa-Su 9am-noon.

Post Office: General Post Office (☎4760 2021), in Post Office Plaza, on Sturt St. between Stanley and Stokes St. Open M-Sa 8:30am-5:30pm, Su 9am-12:30pm. Poste Restante open M-F 9:30am-4:30pm. **Postal Code:** 4810.

▚ ACCOMMODATIONS

Townsville is not a backpacker town, which can be nice in some respects. There are a few nice places to stay in town, but don't expect the treatment you've enjoyed along the rest of the coast.

Civic Guest House, 262 Walker St. (☎4771 5381 or 1800 646 619; www.backpackersinn.com). Hands-down the best hostel in town with free F night BBQs and well-made beds. Free courtesy bus. Internet $5 per hr. Kitchen, laundry, and TV lounge. Reception 8am-8pm. 4- and 6-bed dorms $19; singles $38; doubles $42. Ensuites available. VIP. Credit cards accepted. ❷

Globetrotters, 45 Palmer St. (☎4771 3242; globe@ultra.net.au), just east of the Transit Centre. Laundry, pool, BBQ, TV, tropical garden. Reception daily 6:30am-6:30pm. Dorms $18; twins $42, with A/C $44; ensuite triples $60. VIP. ❷

Transit Centre Backpackers (☎4721 2322 or 1800 628 836; www.tcbackpacker.com.au). Surprisingly quiet for its location in the bus terminal and exceptionally clean for its size. Free storage. Laundry, bar, kitchen (cutlery $5 deposit), and huge spa on the balcony. Reception daily 5:30am-11pm. Dorms $17; twins and doubles $40; ensuite family rooms $65. VIP. Credit cards accepted. ❷

Adventurers Resort, 79 Palmer St. (☎4721 1522 or 1800 211 522). One of the biggest backpacker spots in town; feels more like an apartment building than a hostel. Huge, clean bathrooms, kitchen, large common areas, and secure parking. Linen deposit $5. Reception daily 8am-9pm. Dorms $16; singles $29; doubles $38. YHA. ❷

Reef Lodge, 4 Wickham St. (☎4721 1112), off Flinders St. E. More low-key than some other places in town. Double and twin rooms have fridges. Free pickup from Transit Centre. Laundry, BBQ, and kitchen. Reception daily 8am-10pm. Dorms $14; doubles $36; motel rooms $49. ❶

Coral Lodge B&B, 32 Hale St. (☎4771 5512 or 1800 614 613). From Flinders Mall, follow Stokes St. for 4 blocks, turn left on Hale St., and it's on the left. One of only 2 B&Bs in town, this one is clean, friendly, and comfortable. All rooms have A/C, TV, and fridge. Singles $50, self-contained $65; twins and doubles $60/$75. ❹

QUEENSLAND

IN RECENT NEWS

PUT YOUR BUTT OUT

With the dangers of second-hand smoke, or "passive smoking," on the mind of many Australian politicians and citizens, the Queensland government made decisive steps toward lowering the state smoking rate. On May 31, 2002, a series of tough new anti-smoking laws went into effect, in an attempt to turn the tide of this ever-growing health problem. In addition to new prohibitions on tobacco advertising, particularly the kind targeted at younger consumers, and increasing already hefty fines on those who supply tobacco products to minors, lawmakers placed prohibitions on smoking in enclosed public spaces. Smokers are now responsible for putting out their cigarettes before heading indoors to most public places. Owners of restaurants, bars, and pubs must create separate smoking and non-smoking areas; they also have the option of deeming their entire establishment smoke-free.

In general, the public seems to be happy with the new changes. The lead singer of a band reportedly refused to play a venue in Cairns unless the event was completely non-smoking, and smoke-free establishments are actually becoming rather trendy. While smokers now find themselves having to forgo their habit in many public establishments, these new laws do not apply to private homes, vehicles, and some casino areas. And with the region's glorious weather and the preponderance of great parks and sidewalk cafes, there remain plenty of nice places for smokers to light up.

🍴 FOOD

Most of the city's restaurants are along The Strand, Flinders St. E., and on Palmer St., across the river. Flinders Mall hosts the **Cotters Market,** with fruit, vegetables, and crafts Sunday 8:30am-2pm. Woolworth's **supermarket,** 126-150 Sturt St., is between Stanley and Stoke St. (Open M-F 8am-9pm, Sa 8am-5:30pm, Su 9am-6pm.)

🍴 **La Bamba Cafe,** 3B Palmer St. (☎4771 6322), near the corner of Dean St. Bright, colorful walls filled with local art. A popular Southbank breakfast spot. Parisian croissants $4.50. Sandwich baguettes $8. Open daily 8am-2pm; also M-Sa 6pm-late. ❶

Zolli's, 113 Flinders St. (☎4721 2222). Listen to Italian music, imbibe red wine, and dine on truly authentic Sicilian cuisine. Splendid mussel pasta $9, pizza $6-16. Open daily 5pm-late. ❷

Cactus Jacks, 21 Palmer St. (☎4721 1478). Wash down some spicy, sizzling Mexican fajitas ($18) with one of the widest selections of imported beers in town, from Negro Modelo to Moosehead. Open daily from 2pm-late. MC/V. ❸

Heritage Cafe 'n' Bar, 137 Flinders St. East (☎4771 2799). A bohemian coffeehouse with delicious pasta dishes for $10-14. Greek salad $13. Th bucket of prawns and a XXXX beer or glass of wine for $10. Open M-Th 4pm-late, F-Su 5pm-late. ❷

Bangles, 6 Wickham St. (☎4771 6710). Some of the cheapest, most authentic food in town. Enjoy Indian cuisine, like chicken masala or various curries, from $6. Open daily 10am-10pm; sometimes breaks between lunch and dinner around 2:30-6pm. ❶

🤿 DIVING

Kelso Reef, Townsville's most exceptional spot on the Great Barrier Reef, is home to over 400 kinds of coral and schools of tropical fish. **John Brewer, Loadstone, the Slashers,** and **Keeper Reefs** are also close to shore. These sites on the outer reef are fairly well-preserved, but call ahead to dive companies because high winds can obscure visibility. Townsville's best dive site isn't on the reef—in 1911, the ■**S. S. Yongala** went down in the tropical waters off the coast of Townsville. The still-intact shipwreck is considered one of the world's best wreck sites and one of Australia's best dives, but it requires advanced certification or a professional guide.

Adrenalin Dive, 121 Flinders St. (☎4771 6527 or 1800 242 600). A small operation that offers the only daytrip to the Yongala wreck. The boat is nothing more than functional, but the company offers some of the best guided dives in Northern Queensland, along with daytrips to the reef. Yongala trip with gear $179. Reef trips from $130.

ProDive, Reef HQ Complex Flinders St. (☎4721 1760), offers a 5-day open water course including dives to the Yongala ($585) and a 3-day, 3-night cruise to the Yongala aboard the *Pacific Adventure* $485. Open daily 9am-5pm.

Sunferries (☎4771 3855), at the ferry terminal on Flinders St. Takes daytrips to John Brewer Reef. Departs daily 9am, returns 5:20pm. $109, students $84, children $54. 2 certified dives additional $60; discover dive $60. Ask about student concessions.

Diving Dreams, 252 Walker St. (☎4721 2500). Offers dives on the reef, the Palm Islands, and Yongala. Live-aboard 5-day course $550; Island Getaway 5-day course $475; 4-day course $425. Certified live-aboard to Yongala, 3 days, $495.

🔘 SIGHTS

Although Townsville isn't known for its sights, it has about as many interesting museums and worthwhile attractions as any other city in the North. Each first Friday of the month, from May to December, the Strand **Night Markets** display food, crafts, rides, and entertainment (from 5-9:30pm).

REEFHQ. The center was re-opened July 2002, after a huge upgrade and renovation. It features the world's first indoor coral reef—a 2.5 million liter aquarium that scientists have rigged to work like a reef in the ocean. Tours and shows occur almost every hour, including a visit to the sea turtle research facility. *(2-68 Flinders St. ☎4750 0800. Open daily 9am-5pm. $19.50, children $9.50, families $49.)*

MUSEUM OF TROPICAL QUEENSLAND. If you can't get to the Yongala, visit the next best thing: the relics of the *HMS Pandora*, displayed in this flashy new museum, complete with interactive cannon-firing. The museum is great for kids. *(78-102 Flinders St., next to the ReefHQ complex. ☎4726 0606. Open daily 9am-5pm. $9, concessions $6.50, children $5, families $24.)*

BILLABONG SANCTUARY. Several daily presentations allow you to get up-close and personal with wombats, pythons, baby crocs, and more. *(17km south of Townsville. ☎4478 8344; www.billabongsanctuary.com.au. Open daily 8am-5pm. Coach service available. $20, students and seniors $15, children $10, families $47.)*

🔘 ACTIVITIES

Sometimes Townsville can feel simply like a stopover for travelers, but there are plenty of activities to keep you busy during your stay. ◾**Castle Hill** has some challenging **walking paths** that lead to spectacular views of Townsville; the best time to go is around sunset. Bring water and sturdy hiking boots, as the paths can be steep, slippery, and long. **Right Training,** 53 Cheyne St., Pimlico (☎4725 4571), offers a three-hour abseiling and rock climbing combo for $87 on an outdoor cliff. They also have full-day training courses with certification ($175) or a beginner afternoon climb ($55). Pickup can be arranged. **Coral Sea Skydivers,** 14 Plume St., leads tandem jumps daily as well as two- and five-day certification courses for solo jumps. (☎4772 4889; www.coral seaskydivers.com.au. Book ahead. Tandem $240-340.) **White Water Rafting: Raging Thunder Adventures** takes the rapids on Tuesdays, Thursdays, and Sundays. (☎1800 079 977; www.ragingthunder.com.au. Departs 5:25am, returns 6:45pm. $145.)

NIGHTLIFE

Remedy, a free monthly publication, will lead you to all the hottest shows and bars in town. ☒**Molly Malones,** on the corner of Flinders St. E and Wickham St., has live music nightly and Irish jam sessions on Sundays. They also have a great restaurant with mains around $15 and burgers for $10. (☎4771 3428. Open daily 10am-late. No cover.) The locals like to get down at **Club Millennium,** 450 Flinders St. West. With live music, jam sessions, DJs, karaoke, and hardcore rave music, they cover it all. (☎4772 4488. Cover $10-15.) **Mad Cow,** 129 Flinders St. E., features less drinking, live music downstairs Sunday, and no strict dress code. More tavern than nightclub, three pool tables contribute to the somewhat calm atmosphere. (☎4771 5727. W "Cowioki" nights. No cover. Open M-Th 8pm-3am, F-Su 8pm-5am.) A favorite hangout for young locals is **The Criterion,** on the corner of Wickham St. and The Strand, an old hotel pub that turns nightclub. Its sideshow beer garden, the Starter Bar, has your run-of-the-mill wet T-shirt contests and live music. (☎4721 5777. Open Tu-W 5pm-3am, Th-Sa 5pm-5am, Su 2pm-5am.) The newest hot-spot in town is at **The Brewery,** on the corner of Denham and Flinders St. This is the prime place to see and be seen, as Dubliner and multi-award-winning brewer Brendan Flanagan is busy making your delicious home-brewed beers. A full dinner menu also pleases the crowds. (☎4724 0333. No cover. Open daily 11am-late.) Test your connoisseur skills at **Portraits Wine Bar,** 151 Flinders St. E, where wine-tasting occurs the first Tuesday of every month ($8). There are complimentary cheese platters from 5pm on Fridays. (☎4771 3335. Open M-Sa.)

MAGNETIC ISLAND ☎07

When Townsville natives need a vacation, they don't have to go very far; Magnetic Island is only a short ferry ride away. The island's beaches are wide and inviting, and its pockets of eucalypts are dotted with the largest concentration of wild koalas in Australia. The island's only inhabited area is a mere 20km of eastern coast—most of the island is made up of national park. On less crowded beaches, accessible by several walking tracks, people bathe in the buff. During the winter, the forests on the boulder-ridden hills glow at night from the seasonal fires, making the island appear volcanic. Understandably, backpackers flock here in huge numbers to relax, snorkel, and dive. But even in peak season, with the Australian school holiday crowd mixed in, there seems to be plenty of room to stretch out.

TRANSPORTATION

The only public transportation to Magnetic Island is with **Sunferries Magnetic Island,** 168-192 Flinders St. E (☎4771 3855). **Ferries** leave from Flinders St. (30min.; M-F 9 per day, Sa-Su 7 per day; $16 return) and the Breakwater terminal on Sir Leslie Thieses Dr. by The Strand (20min.; M-F 12 per day, Sa-Su 9 per day; $16 return). The only way to get vehicles across the water is on Capricorn Barge Company's **Magnetic Island Car Ferry,** located down Palmer St. You, your car, and up to five friends can chug to the island for $115 return. (☎4772 5422. 1hr.; M-F 6 per day, Sa 3 per day, Su 4 per day. Book ahead.)

There are less than 20km of sealed roads on the island, and the bus system does a fine job of covering all of them. **Magnetic Island Buses** (☎4778 5130) run roughly every 50min.; stops are marked by blue signs. Tickets are sold on the bus ($2-5), and a one-day unlimited pass ($11) is available from the bus driver. Buses operate M-Th 5:25am-8:50pm, F-Sa 5:25am-11:50pm, and Su 6:50am-8:50pm. **Magnetic Island Taxis** (☎13 10 08) charges about $18 to cross the island.

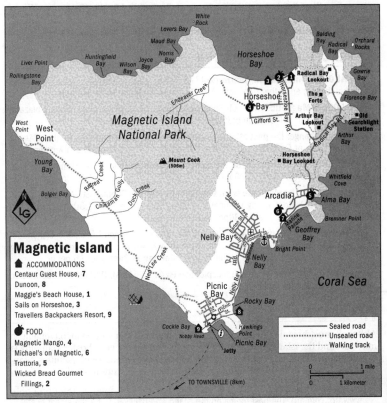

Magnetic Island

🏠 ACCOMMODATIONS
Centaur Guest House, 7
Dunoon, 8
Maggie's Beach House, 1
Sails on Horseshoe, 3
Travellers Backpackers Resort, 9

🍴 FOOD
Magnetic Mango, 4
Michael's on Magnetic, 6
Trattoria, 5
Wicked Bread Gourmet
  Fillings, 2

——————— Sealed road
·············· Unsealed road
- - - - - - - Walking track

0   1 mile
0   1 kilometer

TO TOWNSVILLE (8km)

Renting a "moke" (an open-air, golf-cart-like rig) is extremely popular. **Moke Magnetic,** in the Picnic Bay Mall, rents to 21 and over; rentals includes 60km and petrol costs ($65 per 24hr., under 25 $68). With not much ground to cover, it turns out to be a rather inexpensive and fun jaunt. (☎ 4778 5377. Open daily 8am-5pm. $100 deposit or credit card imprint.) **Tropical Topless Car Rentals,** in Picnic Bay, has small open-roofed cars with unlimited kilometers. (☎ 4758 1111. $60 per day.) Scooters can also be rented in Picnic Bay from **Road Runner Scooter Hire.** (☎ 4778 5222. Under 21 welcome. Open daily 9am-5pm. $28 per day, $38 per 24hr. $100 deposit.)

🔲 ORIENTATION

The island is roughly triangular in shape, and all accommodations, restaurants, and activities are spread out along the east coast. As of October/November 2002, the main port on the island will be in **Nelly Bay.** Plans to build a new resort will follow completion of the marina. From Picnic Bay, the sealed road only runs east, first passing Nelly Bay, which also has the island's main supermarket. Continuing north, **Arcadia,** a 15-minute bus ride from the ferry, has a beautiful beach; two areas to relax are **Geoffrey** and **Alma Bays. Horseshoe Bay,** a 30-minute bus ride from the ferry, is the island's northernmost populated area and includes the watersports center. From Picnic Bay you can also head west on an unpaved road (no mokes allowed) to **West Point,** a popular sunset spot. **Radical** and **Balding Bays,** near Horseshoe Bay, are only accessible by foot or 4WD; the walks are short and rewarding. **Florence** and **Arthur Bays** sit just a bit south and are closer to the main road.

▐ PRACTICAL INFORMATION

Tourist Office: Information Centre (☎4778 5155), next to jetty in Picnic Bay. Books flights, buses, and other transport. Open M-F 8am-4:30pm, Sa-Su 8am-1pm.

Travel Office: Magnetic Travel, 55 Sooning St. (☎4778 5343), in the shopping plaza at Nelly Bay. Open M-F 8:30am-5:30pm.

Currency Exchange: The **post office** is the local agent for Commonwealth Bank. **ATMs** are in Picnic Bay, at **Express** Food Store in Horseshoe Bay, and at **Arkie's** in Arcadia.

Police: (24hr. ☎4778 5270), on the corner of Granite and Picnic St., Picnic Bay. Open M 8:30am-noon, W and F 8:30am-2pm.

Medical Center: The **Magnetic Island Medical Centre,** 68 Sooning St., Nelly Bay (24hr. ☎4778 5614), does diving medical exams for $60. Open M-F 11:30am-5:30pm, Sa 9:30am-1:30pm, Su 11am-1:30pm.

Internet Access: Courtyard Mall Cyber Cafe, Shop 2 Courtyard Mall, The Esplanade, Picnic Bay (☎4778 5407). $6 per hr. Open daily 8:30am-5:30pm. Terminals are also available in most hostels and at the **Tourist Information Centre** for $5 per hr.

Post Office: Picnic Bay Arcade, The Esplanade (☎4778 5118). Open M-F 8:30am-5pm, Sa 9-11am. **Postal Code:** 4819.

▐ ACCOMMODATIONS

Although most hostels offer regular courtesy buses, it can still be inconvenient to move around the island. Consider location when choosing your hostel. Camping is prohibited in the national park, but some hostels have campground facilities. Standard key deposit is $5-10, and all accommodations accept credit cards.

Centaur Guest House, 27 Marine Pde., Alma Bay (☎4778 5668 or 1800 655 680; www.bpf.com.au). The best rooms on the island and believed to be the oldest hostel in Australia. Free activities include wine-and-cheese night (Sa) and pancake and ice cream night (Th). Internet $5 per hr. After hours check-in available. Reception daily 7am-8pm. Dorms $18; singles $35; twins and doubles $42. 5th night free. ❷

Maggie's Beach House, 1 Pacific Dr., Horseshoe Bay (☎4778 5144 or 1800 001 544; www.maggiesbeachhouse.com.au), at the end of the beach road. Gecko's, its posh grill, offers pricey meals but creates the party atmosphere for Horseshoe Bay with a nightly Happy Hour 5-6pm. Cafe, laundry, and Internet. Reception daily 8am-8pm. Dorms $21; doubles $75. VIP. ❷

Sails on Horseshoe, 13-15 Pacific Dr. (☎4778 5117), 300m from Maggie's, on the bay. The newest of the luxury apartments on the island, they make a great place for large groups. 1- and 2-bedroom suites with kitchen, spa, and TV. Reception daily 7am-8pm. 1-room $160, 2-room $210; both sleep several people. ❺

Dunoon (☎4778 5161), on the corner of The Esplanade and Granite St., Picnic Bay. A good deal for groups—sparkling beachfront cottages with kitchen, bath, dining area, and TV. Laundry, pool, BBQ, and children's area. Book ahead. Reception daily 7:30am-5:30pm. Cottage for 2 $110, extra adult $18.50, extra child $7.50. ❷

Travellers Backpackers Resort, 1 The Esplanade, Picnic Bay (☎4778 5166 or 1800 000 290; travellers@ultra.net.au), right in front of the pier. Nightly activities keep visitors going at this motel-turned-giant hostel. Complete with 4 bars and Magnetic's only public nightclub. Kitchen, pool, Internet, and giant resident croc Rin Tin Tin. Reception daily 7:30am-midnight. Ensuite dorms $12-20; twins and doubles $49. VIP/YHA. ❶

FOOD AND NIGHTLIFE

Magnetic Island is known for relaxation, not gourmet cuisine. However, in recent months, the island has begun to change its former image; great restaurants have sprung up and development continues. For the basics, go to the Magnetic Island **Supermarket**, 55 Sooning St., Nelly Bay, the largest on the island. (Open M-F 8:30am-7pm, Sa 8:30am-5:30pm, Su 9am-2pm.) If you want to go out for drinks, the crowds tend to huddle in Arcadia and at Horseshoe Bay.

Trattoria (☎4778 5757), on Alma Bay. Walk past Arkie's towards Alma Bay, and follow the signs to the terrace. Their Mediterranean-inspired menu is the most eclectic and delectable on the island. Try their amazing dips ($9), huge salads ($12), or the pumpkin and garbanzo bake ($17). BYO. Open W-Su 11am-3pm and 6-10pm. ❷

Possum's Cafe, 55 Sooning St., Nelly Bay (☎4778 5409). In addition to great sandwiches ($3-4) and seafood boxes ($9), they also have all-day breakfast ($6-11). Open M-Th 8am-5pm, F-Sa 8am-7pm, Su 8am-3pm. ❶

Wicked Bread Gourmet Fillings (☎4778 5786), next to Maggie's on Pacific Dr. Enjoy a croissant or danish straight from the oven every morning with a cup of coffee. They also sell gourmet cheeses with fresh loaves of bread and feature a large selection of sandwiches from $6.50. Open daily 8am-5pm. ❶

Feedja Cafe (☎4778 5833), on the Esplanade, Picnic Bay. Specializing in fresh, locally grown produce, they dish up some flavorful creations. Focaccias with all the fillings $6.50. Enjoy breakfast and read the paper on the bay. Open daily 8am-late. ❶

Michael's On Magnetic, 5 Bright Ave., Arcadia (☎4778 5645). Recently added Thai lunch takeaway menu. Pastas $8-15, mains $16-23. Coffees $3. Open M-Tu and Th-F 11:30am-2:30pm and 6pm-late, Sa-Su 8:30am-2pm. ❸

Magnetic Mango (☎4778 5018), at the end of Apjohn St., Horseshoe Bay. This sprawling mango plantation, run by friendly owners and local celebrities Rina and Gary, serves fresh mango juice and smoothies for $3, mango cake $6, and sandwiches $6-11. Any purchase from the kitchen gives you free access to the plantation—complete with goats, gold mine, and mini-golf course. BYO. Open M-W and F-Su 10am-9pm. ❶

DIVING

Magnetic Island offers some of the most inexpensive dive opportunities in all of Queensland. A plethora of small wrecks and reefs provide endless exploration. Dive courses, given right off-shore, are very popular. Be sure to inquire about how many dives are included in your course.

Pleasure Dives, 10 Marine Pde., Arcadia (☎4778 5788 or 1800 797 797). Incredible deals on PADI certification classes from the shore (3-day course $199). Also offers 4-day courses with one day on the outer reef ($299), as well as intro dives ($65) and certified dives ($39). Advanced courses to the Yongala wreck $369, to the reef $299. Open daily 8:30am-5pm.

Reef and Island Tours (☎4778 5155; www.reefislandtours.com.au), in the tourist office at Picnic Bay. The largest company with the most expensive trips. Outer reef snorkeling daytrip $132 to Kelso Reef. 2 intro dives $105 extra; 2 certified dives $60 extra.

QUEENSLAND

ACTIVITIES

TOURS. Indulge the child within and careen around Magnetic Island with ☒**Tropi-cana Tours,** 2/26 Picnic St. Pile into a 10-seat Jeep Wrangler, cruise to loud music, feed lorikeets, see beaches, and finish with a plastic cup of wine at sunset. (☎ 4758 1800; www.tropicanatours.com.au. 4hr. afternoon trip $83; milder morning version $50; the Big Kahuna full-day tour with lunch $125.)

GREAT OUTDOORS. The Magnetic Island National Park has several fabulous walking tracks. The popular **Forts Walk** (4km; 1½hr.) virtually guarantees koala spotting. It's best to go 4-6pm, when the critters are just waking up and, in the winter, you can finish by watching the sunset atop the biggest fort. Another option is to take the island path (8km; 3hr.) that leads from Picnic Bay through wetlands and mangroves to **West Point.** Make sure you bring water and sturdy shoes. For a list of the other walks on the island, go to the tourist office, ask the bus drivers, or grab a map at Maggie's. From Horseshoe Bay, two great and short walks lead to **Balding Bay** and **Radical Bay.** At dusk, dozens of rock wallabies come for a hand-fed snack to **Geoffrey Bay,** in Arcadia. **Bluey's Horseshoe Ranch,** 38 Gifford St., Horseshoe Bay, will take you riding bareback along the sand beach of Horseshoe Bay. (☎ 4778 5109. 2hr. $55; half-day $80.)

WATER ACTIVITIES. Magnetic Island Sea Kayaks, 93 Horseshoe Bay Rd., Horseshoe Bay, departs daily 8:15am and returns about noon. (☎ 4778 5424. $45; includes a light tropical breakfast.) Of course, you can always forego quiet contemplation and circumnavigate the island on a roaring jet-ski with **Adrenalin Jet Ski Tours.** (☎ 4778 5533. Half-day tour departs Horseshoe Bay 10am, returns 1pm; $119.)

OTHER ACTIVITIES. At **Magnetic Island Mini Golf,** 27 Sooning St., Nelly Bay., 18 holes of putt-putt can be followed by pool, ping pong, air hockey, and more. (☎ 4758 1066. Open Su-F 9am-5pm, Sa 9am-late. Golf $4.50, children $3. Ask about package deals with other amusements.) **The Magnetic Island Country Club,** Hurst St., Picnic Bay., popular with Townsville and island residents, has a 9-hole course and a licensed bar and restaurant. (Open daily from 8am. $11, 18 holes $16.) Visit koalas, wombats, emus, and talking cockatoos at the **Koala Park Oasis,** Pacific Dr., Horseshoe Bay. (☎ 4778 5260. Open daily 9am-5pm. $10, children $4.)

CARDWELL   ☎ 07

A small village between Mission Beach and Townsville, Cardwell brushes up against an appealing beach, perfect for admiring but not for a dip—salties from the bordering mangrove forests frequent the beach and boat launch. In the middle of several large farming communities, Cardwell is an ideal stop for work. National parks and Wet Tropics Heritage Areas surround Cardwell, providing opportunities for great camping and hiking as well.

    Cardwell Air Charters, 131 Bruce Hwy. (☎ 4066 8468), runs scenic flights over **Hinchinbrook Island** (40min. $80) and the **Undara Lava Tubes** (half-day $215), as well as a special 45min. flight over **Herbert River Gorge,** location of *Survivor II* ($95). Just 4km north of Cardwell is the entrance to **Edmund Kennedy National Park,** which lies right on the coast, its protected mangroves lining the sand. Caravans are not recommended in the park, as the roads are quite rough year-round and can flood during the Wet; no camping is permitted. The towering **Wallaman Falls,** Australia's largest single-drop waterfall, most impressive during the Wet, roars in nearby **Ingham** (53km south). For some safe and scenic swimming nearby, try **Five-Mile Swimming Hole,** a local favorite 8km south of town off the Bruce Hwy.

Most of the establishments in town are along Cardwell's patch of the Bruce Hwy., locally known as **Victoria St.** The "transit centre" is basically a swath of bitumen in the center of town called Brasenose St. **McCafferty's/Greyhound** (☎ 13 14 99 or 13 20 30) **buses** run to Townsville (2hr., 7 per day, $32) and Cairns (3¼hr., 7 per day, $26).

The YHA-affiliated **Hinchinbrook Hostel and Kookaburra Holiday Park ❷**, 175 Victoria St., is by far the best hostel in town. Friendly and immaculate, it offers free pickup from the bus stop (800m away), free bikes, free sporting and fishing equipment, kitchen, saltwater pool, and Internet. Camping gear is available for hire. (☎ 4066 8648; www.hinchinbrookholiday.com.au. Reception daily 8am-6pm. Sites for 2 $16.50; dorms $18; singles $35; doubles $40; motel doubles $61; villas for 1-4 $88.) For those seeking employment, the managers of **Cardwell Backpackers Hostel ❷**, 178 Bowen St., behind Muddie's restaurant, arrange **fruit-picking jobs** ($10-13 per hr.) for guests and bus them to work for $3. Privacy here is sacrificed in favor of a communal atmosphere; guests sleep in a 12-bed dorm enclosed by a partition. (☎ 4066 8014. Kitchen, TV room, and laundry. Dorms $15.40; cubicles $16.50; doubles $35.20.) ▧**Annie's Kitchen ❶**, 107 Victoria St., makes a mean burger for $4-6 and a huge milkshake for $3.50. (☎ 4066 8818. Open daily 6am-8pm.) The 5-Star **supermarket,** 198 Victoria St., offers a decent selection. (Open daily 6am-8pm.)

AROUND CARDWELL AND INGHAM

The area between and west of Cardwell and Ingham (53km south) has some of the most astounding rainforest and national parks, filled with endangered wildlife and massive waterfalls. **Lumholtz National Park** (51km west of Ingham), one of the world's oldest rainforests, is home to several species of endangered plants and animals, as well as the amethystine python, Australia's largest. **Camping ❶** permits can be obtained by self-registration ($3.85 per person).

Another great waterfall, **Jourama Falls,** is located in **Paluma Range National Park** (24km south of Ingham). Look out for freshwater tortoises, goannas, and Ulysses butterflies. Another 20km south, the **Mt. Spec** section of the park attracts visitors with clear streams that run through the summit's green canopies. Camping is available at Big Crystal Creek, but you will need a key from the Townsville (☎ 4722 5211) or Ingham (☎ 4777 3112) QPWS before leaving. Access can be difficult in the Wet. Just 22km south of Cardwell is a turn-off for the fantastic **Murray Falls,** which can make for a nice daytrip. Camping is permitted here.

HINCHINBROOK ISLAND   ☎ 07

Across the Hinchinbrook Channel, just 4km from Cardwell, is Hinchinbrook Island and the unspoiled wilderness of its national park, where granite peaks loom above mangrove swamps. Australia's largest island national park features snorkeling, the endangered manatee-like dugong, and great hiking opportunities. The famous **Thorsborne Trail** (32km; 3-7 days) is the most popular hike on the island, though the number of people allowed on the trail at one time is capped at 40; the park's many shorter walks are also worthwhile. Book at least two to three months in advance, and allow 12 months for specific dates during peak summer months.

Hinchinbrook Island Ferries, 131 Bruce Hwy., offers day-tours of the island, including walks to some of its pristine beaches. One-way tickets are useful if you have a camping permit and want to walk the length of the island. (☎ 4066 8270 or 1800 777 021. $59, day-tour or return $85. Transfers available from Mission Beach and Cardwell.) **Hinchinbrook Wilderness Safaris** will pick you up at George Point and bring you back to Lucinda, south of Cardwell. (☎ 4777 8307. $45.) **Hinchinbrook Marine Cove** (☎ 4777 8377) offers transfers from Townsville and day-tours for $89-99. Spot one of Australia's most elusive creatures with **Dugong Watching** tours; they also

QUEENSLAND

rent boats. (☎ 4066 8555. Departs daily 9:30am, returns 3:30pm. $70, children $40. Boat hire $240 per day.)

Daytrips to the island don't require bookings, but overnight camping trips don't happen spontaneously. Get a permit in advance and read up on various trail options to piece together a trip (camping permits $4 per night). QPWS recommends getting a six-month permit to avoid disappointment. Facilities at the campsite include picnic tables, gas BBQ, water, and toilet. If you don't mind spending the money, the **Hinchinbrook Resort ◉** prides itself on being the ultimate eco-friendly destination, allowing only 50 guests at one time. (☎ 4066 8270 or 1800 777 021; www.hinchinbrookresort.com.au. Treehouse from $337 per person, children $199; beach cabins $150. Rates include all meals and activities.) The folks at the QPWS, located at the **Rainforest and Reef Centre,** 14 Victoria St., Cardwell, on the north side of town near the jetty, are eager to help. They have a free informational walk that details the science behind the rainforest and its inhabitants. (☎ 4066 8115. Open daily 8am-4:30pm.)

MISSION BEACH   ☎ 07

Transformed virtually overnight into a major backpacker destination, this nearly continuous stretch of beach deserves all its hype. Only one and a half hours from Cairns, the town enjoys heavy traveler traffic while remaining peaceful enough for those seeking rest during their coastal trek. Mission Beach is simply beautiful and perfect for sunbathing. The untouched corals and sand cays off the reefs off Mission Beach make it one of the best diving spots on the Great Barrier Reef. On land, the high concentration of cassowaries make for thrilling local rainforest walks.

▐ TRANSPORTATION

McCafferty's/Greyhound buses stop in Mission Beach several times per day. Both run to Cairns (2¼hr., 4 per day, $17) and Townsville (3¼hr., 4 per day, $46). Once you arrive in town, a hostel courtesy bus will take you to your accommodation. You can also use these buses during your stay, but at night you'll need the **Mission Beach Bus Service** (☎ 4068 7400), which runs about once per hour 9am-10pm except Monday and Tuesday, when service stops at 5:50pm ($1.50 per section, day-ticket $10). **Island Coast Travel,** in the Homestead Centre at Mission Beach, is a bus and rail ticket agent. (☎ 4068 7187. Open M-F 9am-5pm, Sa 9am-noon.)

▐ ▐ ORIENTATION AND PRACTICAL INFORMATION

The region known as Mission Beach is actually a group of four communities lining a 14km-stretch of waterfront property. From north to south, these towns are: **Bigil Bay, Mission Beach, Wongaling Beach,** and **South Mission Beach.** The main streets are **Porter's Promenade,** which runs through Mission Beach proper, and **Cassowary Drive,** which runs through Wongaling. A popular landmark is the frighteningly large cassowary statue set in the center of Wongaling Beach. Just off the coast are the **Family Islands,** including the day-trip destination **Dunk Island.**

You'll find the area tourist office in the **Wet Tropics Information Centre,** on Porter's Promenade on the northern edge of town. (☎ 4068 7099. Open M-Sa 9am-5pm, Su 9am-4pm.) Next door, the **Community for Coastal and Cassowary Conservation** stocks a wealth of books on the region. (☎ 4068 7197. Open daily 10am-5pm.)

Services include: the **police** (☎ 4068 8422), 500m past the large cassowary at the corner of Webb Rd. and Cassowary Dr. in Wongaling Beach; **Beverley's,** Shop 15, Hub Shopping Centre, where foreign currency and traveler's checks can be exchanged for no fee (☎ 4068 7365; open daily 9am-5pm); **ATMs** at the **supermarket** in Mission Beach and the Mission Beach Resort; **Internet** at **Traveljunkies,** next to the grocery store in Wongaling (☎4068 8699; open M-Sa 9am-6pm, Su 4-6pm), and at **Cybernet Club,** on the corner of Porter's and Campbell St. (☎4068 7789; open daily 9:30am-6pm); and the **post office,** on Porter's Promenade, which doubles as a Commonwealth Bank. **Postal Code:** 4852.

ACCOMMODATIONS

All hostels offer free pickup at the bus station and courtesy buses to Mission Beach at least four times daily, accept credit cards, and book tours. If you're camping or have a caravan, try **Hideaway Holiday Village ❶,** on Porter's Promenade, or across the street at the Mission Beach **camping ❶** grounds; they're both clean, easy to find, and inexpensive (from $6 per person).

- **The Sanctuary** (☎4088 6064 or 1800 777 012; www.sanctuaryatmission.com), on Holt Rd., Bingil Bay. The most remote accommodation in Mission Beach is also its best. A beautiful hardwood treehouse overlooking the ocean has 14 rooms set in the rainforest, where the only thing between you and the resident cassowaries is the screen protecting you from the mozzies. Cafe serves superb dinners ($14-17). Internet, yoga classes, massages ($55), kitchen, pool, and 18 hectares of rainforest to explore. Twins $23; doubles $55; deluxe cabin singles $105, doubles $120. ❷

- **Scotty's Mission Beach House,** 167 Reid Rd. (☎4068 8676; scottys@znet.net.au), at the end of Webb St., off Cassowary Dr. Free evening drinks and a pool that permits topless bathing definitely make Scotty's a fun place. Attached Scotty's Bar and Restaurant (meals under $12) will please the partygoer. Laundry, TV room with comfy chairs, kitchen, and Internet. Reception daily 7:30am-7pm. 16-bed dorms $18; 4-bed ensuite dorms $21; twins and doubles $35, ensuite $45. VIP. ❷

- **Mission Beach Backpackers Lodge,** 28 Wongaling Beach Rd. (☎4068 8317; mblodge@znet.net.au). From Cassowary Dr., turn onto Wongaling Beach Rd. at the enormous cassowary; the hostel is on your left. A 2-story house with spacious rooms, pool, laundry, and Internet. Reception daily 8am-12:30pm and 1:30-8pm. Dorms $18; twins $37; doubles $39-48. VIP. ❷

- **The Treehouse** (☎4068 7137), on Bingil Bay Rd., Bingil Bay. A YHA-affiliate perched on a hill, not a tree. BBQ, pool, laundry, tiny grocery store, and comfy reading space. Community spirit is encouraged by communal showers (private ones exist) and rooms clustered around common area where music (guests' choice) plays until 11pm. Linen provided. F night all-you-can-eat BBQ $12. Reception 6:30am-8:30pm. Sites $12 per person; dorms $19; twins and doubles $46. ❶

FOOD

Most restaurants are concentrated at the village green along Porter's Promenade. For **supermarkets,** try Foodmarket, on Porter's Promenade, or Foodstore, in Wongaling Beach, next to the big cassowary. (Both open daily 8am-7pm.)

- **Toba,** 37 Porter's Promenade (☎4068 7852), at the Village Green. Authentic furniture and homegrown herbs. Serves a variety of Southeast Asian cuisine including Indonesian fried noodles and Vietnamese and Japanese specialties. Chiang Mai salad $11. Mains $16-25. Open M and W-Su 6pm-late. ❹

- **Coconutz** (☎4068 7397), next to the Village Green on Porter's Promenade. One of the few licensed bars in Mission Beach, it serves up delicious meals as well. Make your own curry or *laksa* combination of meats, noodles, and sauces. Mains $14-20. Happy Hour daily 5:30-6:30pm (beers $3). AmEx/MC/V. ❸

QUEENSLAND

Piccolo Paradise (☎ 4068 7008), on David St. in the Village Green. This popular cafe offers sandwiches on fresh baguettes, pasta, pizza, and a selection of espresso and juices ($3.30). Licensed bar after 6pm. Open daily 8am-9:30pm. ❶

🔘 🗾 SIGHTS AND ACTIVITIES

DIVING. Mission Beach is a unique spot on the reef, where coral drop-offs create long walls of underwater gardens. **Mission Beach Dive Charters** is the only PADI dive center in town. It arranges scuba courses and trips to the *Lady Bowen*, a 105-year-old shipwreck discovered in 1997. The center also makes outer reef daytrips, which include two dives with a maximum of 12 people. (☎ 4068 7277 or 1800 700 112. 4-day open water certification $395; shipwreck and outer reef $136; gear hire $30 extra. Day-trip with intro dive $180.) **QuickCat** also makes trips to the reef, both directly and via Dunk Island. (☎ 4068 7289 or 1800 654 242. Transport $140, reef direct Su and W $80; 2 certified dives $85, 1 intro dive $80.)

HIKING. Several beautiful **walking tracks** are in the area. *Walking Tracks in the Mission Beach Area*, a 25¢ pamphlet available at hostels and the info center, describes several walks in the **Licuala State Forest.** The **Rainforest Circuit Walk** (1.3km; 30min.) is a jaunt under the canopy of Licuala Fan Palms. Start at the carpark of the Tully-Mission Beach Rd. **Licuala Walking Track** (7.8km; 3hr.) stretches north through coastal lowland rainforest to the El Arish-Mission Beach Rd. The **Cutten Brothers Walk** (1½km; 30min.) snakes through mangroves between Alexander Dr. and Clump Point jetty. For longer walks, the **Bicton Hill Track** (4km; starts 3km past the Wet Tropics Info Centre) and the **Kennedy Track** (7km; 4hr.) feature mangrove views, beach, and of course, loads of rainforest.

OTHER ACTIVITIES. Jump the Beach offers tandem skydiving several times per day. (☎ 1800 638 005. Jumps from 8000 ft. $235.)

🎿 DAYTRIP FROM MISSION BEACH: DUNK ISLAND

The **Family Islands,** just off-shore and perhaps the best and shortest excursion from Mission Beach, could be the perfect backdrop for a beach party or evening luau. Dunk Island, a.k.a. the "father island," lies just off-shore: its Aboriginal name is *Coonanglebah*, meaning "Island of Peace and Plenty." Dunk Island became famous through E.J. Banfield's *Confessions of a Beachcomber*, an account of his life on the island from 1897 to 1923. The largest of the islands' nuclear grouping, **Papa Dunk** is the only day-tripper destination. Nearby **Bedarra,** also known as "the mother," is uninhabited, save for a hoity-toity resort. The "twins" are close together and slightly farther out. The smaller land masses at the fringe of the group are the brothers, sisters, and the triplets.

There are three boats that service Dunk Island. Those looking to maximize time on the island should opt for the **Dunk Island Express Water Taxi,** on Banfield Pde., near Scotty's on Wongaling Beach. (☎ 4068 8310. 10min., 5 per day, $22 return.) For lollygaggers wishing to prolong their cruise over to the island, check out **Dunk Island Ferry & Cruises,** which departs from Clump Point Jetty, 1km north of the village green (also departs from Kurrimine Beach). They offer snorkeling (included on all trips), boom netting, and a snack on the longer Bedarra cruise. (☎ 4068 7211. 30-45min; departs daily 8:45am and 10:30am; $21 return, under 10 free. Bedarra cruise $35, under 14 free.) **Quick Cat** also services the island for $19.50 return. (☎ 4068 7289. Departs daily 9:30am, returns 4:45pm.) **Coral Sea Kayaking** has daytrips to Dunk including small brekkie, lunch, environmental interpretation, and snorkeling gear. (☎ 4068 9154. $89; shorter morning and afternoon trips $55.)

The **Dunk Island Resort** ❺ (☎4068 8199) monopolizes all island activities. If the room rates ($170 per person and up) seem prohibitive, don't despair. Just steps from the jetty are some of the best-equipped **campsites** ❶ in North Queensland (permits $3.85 per person per night), with hot showers and unparalleled stretches of beach. This isn't a well-kept secret, however—book about a week in advance during the high season. Day-trippers can purchase the **Resort Experience Pass** at the Watersports shed ($27), which entitles visitors to use of the resort facilities and a meal at BBs, or at EJ's in the resort. **Dunk Island Watersports** (☎4068 8199) issues **camping permits** and rents a slew of water toys: paddle skis ($15 per hr.), sailboards ($20 per hr.), snorkel gear ($15 per hr.), and catamarans ($25 per hr.). The only place to eat on the island, besides the resort's fancy restaurant, is **BB's on the Beach** ❶, next door to Watersports, which serves great burgers ($8.50) as well as salads and yummy snack dishes (☎4068 8199; open daily 11am-7pm). Still, it's cheaper to bring your own. The main attractions on Dunk, aside from the postcard beaches, are the **walking tracks**. The local favorite is the walk circumscribing most of the island (10km; 2-3hr.), which combines Dunk history with diverse landscapes and a trip to the island's highest point. An easier option is the coastal hike (1km; 15min.) up to **Muggy Muggy Beach** from the dock. Not only does Muggy Muggy hide itself in a pocket of 360 million year-old rocks, but it has some of the best snorkeling on the island. **Mount Kootaloo Lookout** (2hr.), the highest point on the island, can offer some of the best views and a good workout. Walking around the whole island can take about three hours and is only recommended for those who are fit enough for a difficult walk; carry water and wear sturdy shoes.

NEAR MISSION BEACH

PARONELLA PARK

Just a little west of nowhere between Cairns and Mission Beach hides the Moorish castle of ▨**Paronella Park** (☎4065 3225). In the 1930s, when Spaniard José Paronella built the main thoroughfare of Paronella, crowds could enjoy its surrounds. In the 1960s, this enchanting parkway diverted from what is now the Bruce Hwy., slipping from tourist itineraries. Winner of Queensland's highest tourism award in 2001, the park has been discovered by the entertainment industry and has served as the backdrop for three movies, eight TV shows, a music video, and an international magazine photo shoot. Enthusiastic park guides give tours of the grounds and then leave you to explore on your own.

Though almost almost inaccessible via public transportation, it is not hard to find a day-tour from Cairns. If you are driving, look for signs along the Bruce Hwy. for Paronella Park (the South Johnstone exit is the fastest); from the Tablelands, follow the signs to South Johnstone and you'll see the sign for the park. If you're not tying the knot or gawking at the handmade architecture, take some time to stroll down Kauri Ave. or feed the fish and eels in the teeming waterfall pool in the ruins of the castle's grand staircase. A **caravan park** ❶ blends into its surroundings. Caravan park guests get 24hr. access to the grounds, including a guided night walk. (Sites $14, powered $16.)

KURRIMINE BEACH

A short drive north of Mission Beach off the Bruce Hwy., Kurrimine Beach is one of the coast's most untouched stretches of sand. This place remains such a secret that you can walk down its miles of coastline watching out only for the hundreds of starfish that rest along the shore. For a few days in July, the tides are just right to reach King Reef by foot. Ask at the local **Hub Cafe** for a tide chart and the best time to visit. Queenslanders are also drawn to this area for its great fishing and relaxing setting. The north end of the beach has a **caravan park ❷**, and the **Kurrimine Beach Holiday Park ❹** is located at the end of Jacob's Rd. (☎4065 6166. Camping $24, powered $26; cabins from $50, ensuite from $61. Book ahead.)

INNISFAIL
☎07

North of Mission Beach and enroute to Cairns is the town of Innisfail. Offering few tourist attractions, the Johnstone River and beautiful beaches make it a pleasant pit stop. Those who stay are drawn to its year-round demand for fruit-pickers.

Just north of Innisfail, the road to the **Atherton Tablelands** (see p. 412) branches inland toward **Millaa Millaa.** The **railway station** is off the Bruce Hwy. west of town, and the **bus stop** is on Edith St. **McCafferty's/Greyhound buses** run daily to Cairns (1¼hr., 7 per day, $16) and Townsville (3½hr., 7 per day, $47). The **Information Centre,** at the corner of Bruce Hwy. and Lannercost St., books tours. (☎4061 7422. Open M-F 9am-5pm, Sa-Su 10am-3pm.) **The Codge Lodge ❷,** 63 Rankin St., near the corner of Grace St., is billed as a sport-fishing resort, but non-fishing types need not shy away. Convenient to the town center, the lodge is hands-down the best budget accommodation in town, providing a kitchen and pool. (☎4061 8055. Reception 24hr. Book ahead during the Dry. Dorms $20; singles $22; doubles $44.)

FAR NORTH QUEENSLAND

The northeast corner of the continent, from Cairns north into Australia's last great frontier, is nothing short of heaven for rugged backpackers and outdoor adventurers. The Great Barrier Reef snakes close to shore here, luring divers with boat trips and visits to the spectacular underwater haven. Vast swaths of tropical rainforest press up close to the Coral Sea by the green-covered mountains of the Great Dividing Range. The rich variety of wildlife and untouched landscape prove that the Far North's greatest attraction is its natural beauty.

Cairns now caters to travelers with city comforts, but the more remote parts of this land remain untamed wilderness. The Captain Cook Hwy. leads modern-day trailblazers north into the rainforest, which becomes incredibly dense around Cape Tribulation. Wilder yet is the Cape York peninsula, starting beyond Cooktown and stretching to the Torres Strait, which separates the Gulf of Carpentaria from the Coral Sea and Australia from Papua New Guinea. The most formidable of Australian roads dares travelers to make the harrowing journey to the tip.

 FRUIT PICKING. A lot of backpackers come to this region not only for its amazing travel destinations, but also to fund future adventures. Northern Queensland is the best place for picking fruit in Australia simply because some fruit or another is always in season, so finding a job is easy. The crops change from week to week—maybe watermelons one month and pineapples the next. Picking fruit is rugged work, somewhat monotonous, and buggy and hot. The pay for picking in Queensland ranges from $11-15 an hour, and some places will offer you accommodation. *Be aware that working without a visa, while it may have been popular in the past, is now very illegal.* Employers, and you, can be charged up to $10,000 for picking fruit illegally.

CAIRNS
☎07

The last sizeable city at the corner of the great tropical outback, Cairns (prounounced "cans") is both the northern terminus of the backpacker route and the premier gateway to snorkeling and scuba diving on the Great Barrier Reef. Neon

TO FLECKER BOTANIC GARDENS (4km), TANKS ART CENTER (4km), ROYAL FLYING DOCTOR VISITORS CENTER (6km), TRINITY BEACH, MOUNT WHITFIELD ENVIRONMENTAL PARK, AND ✈ (4km)

Cairns

🛏 ACCOMMODATIONS
Cairns Girls Hostel, **3**
Caravella's 77, **2**
Dreamtime, **19**
Gecko's Backpackers, **20**
Global Palace, **8**

Inn Cairns, **13**
Mid-City Luxury Suites, **18**
Travellers Oasis, **21**
Tropic Days, **22**
YHA on the Esplanade, **1**

🍴 FOOD
Coffee Cafe, **11**
Perotta's at the Gallery, **7**
Piranha's, **12**
Rattle and Hum, **4**
Verdi's, **14**
The Victory, **10**

⭐ NIGHTLIFE
Johno's Blues Bar, **5**
P.J. O'Brien's, **9**
Shenannigan's, **17**
The Sports Bar, **16**
Tropos, **15**
The Woolshed, **6**

Pacific Ocean

Cairns Harbour

Undersea World Aquarium

Cairns Base Hospital

signs and tourist attractions bombard travelers with colors rivaled only by the flamboyant creatures of the underwater world off-shore. While tidal mudflats preclude traditional beach activities, bars, nightclubs, and cafes provide plenty of diversions for travelers between forays off the coast. The atmosphere of Cairns is friendly, laid-back, and very touristy. More of a big town than a small city, backpackers use Cairns as a home base for launching skydiving trips, scuba vacations, bungy jumps, and white-water adventures, resting in town just long enough to book their next adventure or recover from their latest night out.

▐ TRANSPORTATION

INTERCITY TRANSPORTATION

Flights: The **airport** (☎ 4052 9744) is 6km north of Cairns on Captain Cook Hwy. Follow the signs. Prices and frequency of flights have been changing constantly since Sept. 11, 2001 (check www.qantas.com.au for recent updates). Prices listed are one-way fares. **Qantas** (☎ 13 13 13) has daily flights to: Adelaide (5-8hr., 5-7 per day, $297); Brisbane (2hr., 11per day, $165); Canberra (5hr., 10-13 per day, $318); Darwin (2-5hr., 6 per day, $291); Hobart (6-10hr., 6-7 per day, $362); Melbourne (5hr., 9 per day, $253); Perth (5-10hr., 6-9 per day, $425); and Sydney (3hr., 7-8 per day, $226). Smaller **Flight West Airlines** (☎ 13 23 92) has domestic flights and also flies to Papua

QUEENSLAND

FROM THE ROAD

SIZE DOES MATTER

A lot of people back home ask me why I keep coming to Australia. What is it about Australia? As a young child growing up in Boston, the country intrigued me simply because it was the farthest distance on a map from my front door. It's funny now to me, because it once again is a matter of size and distance that makes me cherish this place. My favorite moments up in the north of Queensland have been ones of perspective. Traveling makes one realize that common saying that this really is such a small world. Several times I have walked into a new dorm room and met someone that I shared a room with at a prior location. I have sat up late at night and talked to people from the other side of the world who have been to the same places, read the same books, had the same passions, or even studied at the same university as I have. Travelers all have such "small world" tales. But Australia's landscape throws all of these feelings out the window. For anyone who has stirred off the main roads in the far north, you know what it's like to feel totally alone, and totally miniscule. After seeing gorges that expand farther than I could imagine, or driving down stretches of red-dirt roads that appear to go on for miles into the horizon, I have felt nature's magnitude. That's why I love Australia—for the perspective it can give you. Traveling here makes you feel connected to the dozens of people you can talk to in a day, and then it can strip it away the instant you step foot in its vastness, in its untouched places, and in its sheer size. —Gretchen Puttkamer

New Guinea. Most hostels run a free shuttle bus airport pick-up service; just call from the terminal. However, to get back to the airport, you'll have to book ahead and pay $7 for **Airport Shuttle** (☎4048 8355). Buses also run to town from just outside the terminal ($4.50). 24hr. **taxis** to town run about $13.

Trains: The train station is wedged between Bunda St. and the Cairns Central shopping mall. From The Esplanade, walk west on Spence St. It's on the right, or straight through to the back of Cairns Central. Lockers $2 per day. **Travel Centre Office** (☎4036 9341, 24hr. bookings 13 22 32) sells tickets. YHA discount 10% for long-distance trips. Open M 7:30am-5pm, W 9am-5pm, F 9:30am-5pm, Sa 7:30am-noon. The **East Coast Discover Pass** offers unlimited travel for up to 6 months and covers rail from Cairns to Brisbane ($205), to Sydney ($293), and to Melbourne ($374). See also **By Train,** p. 43. Trains run to Brisbane (31-32hr.; M-Tu, Th, and Sa 8:35am; $176). The scenic railway to Kuranda departs Su-F 8:30am and 9:30am, Sa 8:30am. (☎4031 3636 for bookings. $31, return $44; student, pensioner, and family discounts available.)

Buses: The bus station is at Trinity Wharf, on Wharf St. Open daily 6:15am-1am. Leave luggage in lockers ($6-11 per day) or with Coral Coaches ($2 per item; open daily 5:30am-6:30pm). **Coral Coaches** (☎4031 7577) goes to: Cape Tribulation (4hr., 2 per day, $37); Cooktown (Inland: 5½hr., W and F-Sa 1 per day, $58; Coastal: 8hr.; June-Oct. Tu, Th, and Sa; $64); Karumba (11½hr., M and W-Th 1 per day, $150); Port Douglas (1¼hr., 8 per day, $22). **McCafferty's/Greyhound** (☎13 20 30) has 10% ISIC/VIP/YHA discounts and runs to: Airlie Beach (11hr.; 6 per day; $75); Brisbane (28hr.; 5 per day; $173); Cardwell (3hr., 5 per day, $25); Ingham (3½hr., 5 per day, $33); Innisfail (1¼hr., 5 per day, $16); Mission Beach (2¼hr., 2 per day, $16); Rockhampton (15hr., 6 per day, $115); and Townsville (6hr., 5 per day, $47). **Premier Bus Service** (☎4031 6495 or 13 34 10) usually has less-expensive rates and VIP/YHA discounts, though they have less frequent departure times.

Ferries: Quicksilver (☎4087 2100) departs from The Pier at the Floreat Jetty to Port Douglas (1½hr.; 1 per day; $24, return $36).

LOCAL TRANSPORTATION

Buses: Sunbus (☎4057 7411; www.sunbus.com.au) on Lake St. in City Place. Fares $1-6; unlimited day pass $9.40, families $21; central Cairns only pass $5. Buses go south into Cairns' suburbs and as far north as Palm Cove but not to the airport.

Taxis: Black and White (24hr. ☎13 10 08 or 4051 5333).

Car Rental: The bigger outfits in Cairns charge those under 21 a surcharge, making rentals pricey. Most of the independent outfits have no age restrictions; make sure to research your options carefully. **National,** 135 Abbott St., has weekly rates starting at $45 per day, 4WD $145 per day (☎4051 4600 or 1800 350 636; open M F 7:30am 6pm, Sa-Su 8am-5pm); **Avis,** 135 Lake St. (☎4051 5911), rents weekly starting at $49 per day, 4WD $160 per day; **A1 Car Rentals,** 141 Lake St., has weekly rates from $39 and a great selection of higher-end vehicles (☎4031 4284; open daily 7:30am-6pm); **Leisure Car Rentals,** 314 Sheridan St. (☎4051 8988), is a bit far from the city center but has free pick-up and less expensive rentals, starting at $45 per day. **Travellers AutoBarn,** 123-125 Bunda St., rents campervans with unlimited kilometers, both local or one-way, from $65 per day. (☎4041 3722 or 1800 674 374. Open M-F 9am-5pm, Sa 9am-1pm.)

Automobile Club: Royal Automobile Club of Queensland (RACQ), 138 McLeod St. (24hr. ☎4051 6543). Open daily 8am-5:15pm.

Bike Rental: SkyDive Cairns, 59 Sheridan (☎4031 5466). A great way to get around the long, flat streets of Cairns. $15 per day; credit card needed for imprint.

ORIENTATION

Cairns is framed by rainforested hills in the west, a harbor in the east, and mangrove swamps in the north and south. In this modern city, the streets are straight and intersect at right angles, so navigation is easy. **The Esplanade,** with its many hostels and eateries, runs along the waterfront. At the street's southern end is **The Pier,** which supports the pricey Pier Marketplace. Farther south, the Esplanade becomes **Wharf St.** and runs past the **Trinity Wharf** and the **Transit Centre.**

Shields St. runs perpendicular to The Esplanade, crossing **Abbott St.** into **City Place,** a pedestrian mall with an open-air concert space. From this intersection, **Lake St.** runs parallel to the Esplanade. Continuing away from the water, Shields St. also intersects **Grafton St.** and **Sheridan St.** (called Cook Hwy. north of the city). The **Cairns Railway Station** is on **McLeod St.** in front of Cairns Central, the city's largest mall. Address numbers start low at the southeastern end of the Esplanade; cross street address numbers start low at the Esplanade end.

PRACTICAL INFORMATION

TOURIST AND FINANCIAL SERVICES

Tourist Offices: Traveller's Contact Point Cairns, 119 Abbott St. (☎4041 4677; cairns@travellers.com.au). Services include mail forwarding and job listings. **Internet** $1.50 per 30min., $2.50 per hr. Open daily 7:30am-midnight. **Tropical Tourism North Queensland,** 51 Esplanade (☎4051 3588), near the Pier, between Spence and Shields St., is the biggest agency in town. Open daily 8:30am-6:30pm. The **Visitors Info Bureau,** on the Esplanade, between Aplin and Florence St., is open 24hr. and has tons of information on accommodations, tours, bike hire, and the city itself.

National Parks Office: Queensland Parks and Wildlife Service (QPWS), 10 McLeod St. (☎4046 6600; fax 4046 6604). The *Australian Guide to National Parks* is helpful but pricey. Open M-F 8:30am-4:30pm.

Budget Travel: Flight Centre, 24 Spence St. (☎4052 1077, 24hr. info 1300 307 735), guarantees to beat any quoted price. Open M-F 8:45am-5pm, Sa 9am-noon. **STA Travel** has two local branches: 9 Shields St. (☎4031 4199; open M-F 9am-6pm, Sa 10am-2pm) and shop 39 in Cairns Central Shopping Centre (☎4031 8398; open M-W and F 9am-5:30pm, Th 9am-7pm, Sa 9am-3pm).

Currency Exchange: The best rates are found at **Caravella's 77** hostel, 77 Esplanade (☎4051 2159; see p. 404). The **American Express Office,** 79-87 Abbott St., 2nd fl. (☎4031 0353), at Orchid Plaza, changes US travelers checks free of charge, but has an $8 minimum charge for currency exchange under AUS$800, 2% commission thereafter. Open M-F 8:30am-5pm, Sa 9am-noon. **Thomas Cook,** 59-63 Esplanade (☎4041 1000), exchanges currency for a $7 flat fee. Open daily 9am-8pm. Another branch at 71-73 Esplanade is open daily until 11pm. Most banks have **ATMs.**

Library: Cairns City Public Library, 151 Abbott St. (☎4044 3720). Open M 10am-6pm, Tu-F 10am-7pm, Sa 10am-4pm. **Internet** $3 per hr.

Ticket Agencies: TicketLink in the **Cairns Civic Theatre,** at the corner of Florence and Sheridan St. (☎4031 9555). Call for ticket prices and show listings.

MEDIA AND PUBLICATIONS
Newspapers: *Cairns Post* (88¢).
Nightlife: *Barfly* (free), available in hostels, stores, and restaurants.
Radio: Rock, Hot 103.5FM; news, 846AM.

EMERGENCY AND COMMUNICATIONS

Police: (☎4030 7000, emergency ☎000), on Sheridan St., between Spence and Hartley St. Open 24hr.

Crisis Lines: Alcohol and Drug Information (☎1800 177 833). **Lifeline** (☎13 11 14).

Pharmacy: Chemmart Pharmacy, Shop 10, 85 Esplanade (☎4051 9011). Open daily 9am-10pm. Gives advice to travelers continuing to Asia.

Hospital: Cairns Base Hospital (☎4050 6250), on Esplanade at the opposite end of the Pier. 24hr. emergency department. More centrally located is the 24hr. **Medical Centre** (☎4052 1119), on the corner of Florence and Grafton St.

Internet Access: Internet access is everywhere in Cairns. **Mago Internet,** on Alpin St. between the Esplanade and Abbott St., has the cheapest rates. **Internet Outpost,** on the corner of Shields and Abbott St., is good for anyone traveling throughout Australia and New Zealand, with its frequent buyer card and discounts. **Cairns City Public Library** (see above) and **Traveller's Contact Point Cairns** (see above) both charge $3 per hr.

Post Office: Cairns General Post Office (GPO), 13 Grafton St. (☎4031 4303), on the corner of Hartley St. Open M-F 8:30am-5pm. **Postal Code:** 4870.

ACCOMMODATIONS

Though geographically small, Cairns is studded with dozens of budget hostels and is second only to Sydney as a backpacker destination. Most hostels are clustered along the Esplanade, but many others are located in the center of town near Cairns Central. Most have a pool, a large kitchen, and coin-operated laundry facilities, and most offer free airport pick-up, lower rates, and free or discounted meals at a local bar. Choose carefully, as some hostels are a bit louder and less relaxing than others. Travelers who visit during the Dry can also play in inter-hostel soccer games. Many hostels offer discounts in the Wet (roughly Oct.-May). Cairns also provides opportunities to splurge for worn-out backpackers looking to regroup.

CENTRAL CAIRNS

Caravella's 77, 77 Esplanade (☎4051 2159; www.caravella.com.au), between Aplin and Shields St., 10min. from the bus station. Internet access, movies, and pool table. Tour bookings. Key deposit $10. About half of the rooms have baths and A/C; ask about them when you book. Flash your *Let's Go* and ask about a $5 discount on your 1st night's stay. Dorms $20; twins and doubles $43. VIP. ❷

YHA on the Esplanade, 93 Esplanade (☎4031 1919; esplanade@yhaqld.org), near the corner of Aplin St., extremely close to nightclubs and cheap restaurants. A no-frills place to crash. Laundry, kitchen, TV, storage, linens, and Internet. Reception 7am-10pm. Dorms $20; twins and doubles $44-46. ❷

Cairns Girls Hostel, 147 Lake St. (☎4051 2767), between Florence and Aplin St. This clean, quiet **women-only hostel** has provided a safe haven for over 30 years. No noise after 9pm, but no curfew. 3 kitchens, 3 bathrooms, 2 lounges, and TV. Reception 7am-9:30pm. Rates on a sliding scale: $16 for the 1st night, $13 by the 4th; weekly $90. ❷

Global Palace (☎4031 7921 or 1800 819 024), corner of Lake and Shields St. The feel of a reality TV show. Rooftop pool, a cinema-screen TV, kitchen with balcony dining, pool tables, tour booking and Internet. Key and cutlery deposit both $20. 3-4 bed dorms with new mattresses (no bunks) $23; doubles and twins $50. VIP. ❷

Mid-City Luxury Suites, 6 McLeod St. (☎4051 5050), right behind Cairns Central. A great stomping ground to rest and regroup. Rooms include living area, fully equipped kitchen, washer and dryer, bathroom, cable TV, Internet lines, and separate bedrooms. Rooms start at $115-140. ❺

Inn Cairns, 71 Lake St. (☎4041 2350). A boutique hotel, providing holiday apartments complete with washer, dryer, kitchen, spa, community BBQ, and pool. Prices start at $120 and go up in the high season. ❺

JUST OUTSIDE THE CITY CENTER

🏅 **Dreamtime,** 4 Terminus St. (☎4031 6753), just off Bunda St., behind Cairns Central and around the corner from Gecko's. Daily shuttles to Pier and bus station. With only 27 beds and 3-4 bed dorms, proprietors Steve and Kathy create a cozy and sociable atmosphere by disallowing TV and greeting guests with fresh towels and good cheer. Pool, BBQ, kitchen. Book ahead. Reception 7:30am-noon and 4-8pm. Dorms $20; twins and doubles (some with fridge) $45. ❷

Tropic Days, 26-28 Bunting St., (☎4041 1521; www.tropicdays.com.au), behind the Showgrounds, north off Scott St.; a 20min. walk west from downtown. Well-traveled owners Gabriel and Kathy have made a home away from home for backpackers, complete with jungle-themed paintings, a neatly tended tropical garden, and a sparkling pool. M BBQ. Free shuttle to city center. Bike hire and TV lounge. Sites $11; 3-bed dorms $18; doubles $42. ❶

Travellers Oasis, 8 Scott St. (☎4052 1377; travoasis@travoasis.com.au). One of the bigger operations on this side of town, with 3 main houses around a courtyard, garden, and pool. Management chose not to buy a TV; they'd rather have guests talking to each other. Coffee and tea included. Sa night BBQ. Reception 7am-noon and 4-8pm. 3- and 4-bed dorms $18; singles $30; twins and doubles $40. ❷

Gecko's Backpackers, 187 Bunda St. (☎4031 1344 or 1800 011 344). Clean, bright rooms, all with comfortable mattresses. Friendly, helpful staff make this small backpackers seem like a second home. Internet $2 per 20min. Reception 7am-noon and 4-8pm. 3- or 4-bed dorms $18; singles $25; doubles $40. ❷

🍴 FOOD

Cairns bubbles with good eats, from all-night kebab and pizza stalls on the Esplanade to upscale restaurants specializing in seafood. Shields St. is known by the locals as "eat street"—wander around and do some menu shopping. Many restaurants offer up to 40% discounts if you are seated before a certain time, normally

7pm. Most of the hostels in town hand out meal vouchers to one of the local watering holes, though cooking is often the most economical dinner option. For basic **groceries,** try Woolworth's, on Abbott St. between Shields and Spence St. (☎4051 2015; open M-F 8am-9pm, Sa 8am-5:30pm, Su 9am-6pm), or Bi-lo Mega Fresh and Coles, in Cairns Central (open M-F 8am-9pm, Sa 8am-5:30pm, Su 9am-6pm).

> **Coffee Cafe,** 87 Lake St. (☎4041 1899). Offers scones, jam, and a pot o' tea for $6 within earshot of the open-air concert hall. Also serves up great lunches ($4-10), dinners ($10 and up), and gourmet dessert. Open M-Sa 7am-9pm, Su 8am-9pm. ❷

> **Piranha's,** 64 Shields St. (☎4051 9459). New to Cairns, this Mexican grill and bar caters to nacho-craving backpackers. Complimentary drinks with meal order during Happy Hour (daily 5-6pm). Open M-Sa for lunch (under $10) and dinner (under $17), Su for dinner only. ❸

> **Verdi's,** 66 Shields St. (☎4052 1010). A fancy-looking Italian restaurant that serves up huge pastas ($15 and up) and fresh salads ($9-13)—expect ample leftovers. Open M-F from noon, Sa-Su from 6pm. ❸

> **Rattle and Hum** (☎4031 3011), on the Esplanade. A very popular spot, where locals and travelers alike enjoy woodfired pizzas ($12-15) in the open air or a drink at the festive bar. Open daily 11:30am-midnight. ❷

> **Perrotta's at the Gallery** (☎4031 5899), corner of Abbot and Shields St., next to the Cairns Art Gallery. A mod-looking cafe with delectable meals; stop in for a pre-gallery brekkie ($4-10) or post-painting dinner ($20-25). Open daily 8:30am-10pm. ❹

> **The Victory,** 62 Shields St. (☎4051 1883). A trendy, intimate dinner setting where tablecloths double as crayon canvases, Victory is one of the few places in Cairns with fine cuisine at a reasonable price. Soup ($7) is delicious, and mains ($12-20) are artfully presented in gigantic portions. F Live music. Open daily 11:30am-late. ❸

⊙ SIGHTS

▨**TANKS ART CENTRE.** The center consists of a trio of WWII diesel tanks transformed into a massive art exhibition space. The best local art is on display here, with each show lasting three weeks. The last Sunday of every month from June to November, Tanks hosts **Market Day,** a free bazaar with live music and plenty of pottery, crafts, and herbs for sale. (*46 Collins Ave. Accessible from Sunbus #1B. ☎4032 2349. Open daily 11am-4pm. $2.*)

FLECKER BOTANIC GARDENS. Right next to Tanks, you can see a Gondwanan (evolutionary flora track) garden, a meandering boardwalk, fern and orchid houses, and a trail that crosses fresh and saltwater lakes. (*Take Sunbus #1B from City Place ($2.30), or drive north on Sheridan St. and take a left onto Collins Ave. ☎4044 3398. Guided walks M-F 1pm. Open M-F 7:30am-5:30pm, Sa-Su 8:30am-5:30pm. Free.*)

MOUNT WHITFIELD ENVIRONMENTAL PARK. The park is the last bit of rainforest in the Cairns area. The park's shorter Red Arrow circuit takes about one hour, while the more rugged Blue Arrow circuit is a five hour return trek up and around Mt. Whitfield. Don't stay after dark—finding a cab or a bus back into Cairns might be difficult. (*Wedged between the Tanks Art Centre and the Botanic Gardens on Collins Ave.*)

PETER LIK GALLERY. You've probably already bought at least 10 of his postcards—now see his pictures in life-size form. Recognized today as one of Australia's best photographers, Lik's popular prints of Australian wildlife are showcased in this modern gallery. (*4 Shields St. ☎4031 8177. Open daily 9am-10pm. Free.*)

KURANDA. The **Skyrail**, a gondola-like cableway, coasts for 7½km above and through the rainforest to this popular mountain town. At the top, a boardwalk snakes through the trees; detailed information on the area is given one stop below. See p. 413 for more on Kuranda. *(Trains leave regularly from the station. If you are driving, go north on the Cook Hwy. and follow the signs. ☎4038 1555; www.skyrail.com.au. 1½hr. $32, children $16. Transfers cost extra.)*

UNDERSEA WORLD AQUARIUM. Houses a small but captivating presentation of the reef's brilliantly colored sea life. Make sure you have time for the shark feedings at 10am, noon, 1:30pm, and 3pm; book ahead and you can even dive with the sharks for 30min.—after you sign the insurance waiver, of course. *(In the Pier Marketplace, near the wharves. ☎4041 1777. Open daily 8am-8pm. $12.50, children $7, families $30, 20% discount for students and pensioners. Shark diving 3:30-8pm. $85.)*

⚡ OUTDOOR ACTIVITIES

Cairns largely owes its tourist town status to its warm winters and proximity to the Great Barrier Reef. At night, travelers stay in town and drink at local pubs, but during the day they're often found outside the city limits, enjoying ghastly thrills, bumps, and spills for reasonable prices. Activities can often be booked from hostels and most companies offer free pickup and drop-off.

▨ CYCLING. Ride with **Bandicoot Bicycle Tours** for an amazing day of cycling, wildlife-spotting, swimming, and relaxation in the tablelands above Cairns. Enjoy rides (3-7km) between trips to waterfalls, giant fig trees, and swimming holes. If you're tired, just catch a lift with the support vehicle. Lunch, morning and afternoon tea are included and feature a vegetarian-friendly BBQ and tropical fruit. *(☎4055 0155; www.bandicootbikes.com. Trips M, W, and F depart 8am, return 6:30pm. $98.)*

BUNGY JUMPING. **AJ Hackett** is a wild New Zealander—ask him about bungy jumping the Eiffel Tower (and then getting arrested for it) or sign up for one of his (legal) Australian jumps. Night bungy on request. *(☎4057 7188 or 1800 622 888; bungy@austarnet.com.au. Open daily 9am-5:30pm. $109.)*

FISHING. Cast for your own bait and then tow the line with **Fishing The Tropics.** They run their 6m boat in the Cairns estuary and the Daintree River. *(☎4034 1500. Half-day $75, full-day $140.)* **VIP Fishing & Game Boat Services** offers similar packages, along with others that feature fly and shark fishing, or hunting the black marlin from June to December. *(☎4031 4355. Half-day $75, full-day $140; marlin trip from $550.)*

HORSEBACK RIDING. Get on horseback in the outback at **Springmount Station**, a family-owned and operated working farm where kangaroos blaze across the plains teeming with birds, and your trusty steed splashes across rocky brooks. Hearty tea and damper and BBQ lunch will keep you nourished. *(☎4093 4493; springmountainstation.com. Half-day $88, full-day $110.)* If, like many guests, you don't want to leave, try a 2-day farmstay ($220) or camp under the Southern Cross *(departs Tu, $242).*

HOT-AIR BALLOONING. Ever wanted to ride beneath a big balloon shaped like a koala? Or how about getting married in one? Here's your chance. **Hot Air Cairns** will take you up, up, and away. Packages with skyrail, rafting, and others available. *(☎4039 2900; www.hotair.com.au. Departs 5am, returns 10am. Packages from $165; includes transfers, breakfast, and other amenities.)*

PARASAILING AND SKYDIVING. What goes up must come down, and these companies let you plummet in style. Parasail 300ft. above Trinity Inlet with **North Queensland WaterSports.** Jet skiing and bumper tubing are also available. *(☎4045*

QUEENSLAND

2735. $50, tandem $90.) Jump tandem with an instructor from 8000ft., or learn to jump solo, with **Skydive Cairns.** *(59 Sheridan St. ☎ 4031 5466. $235, upgrades $48 per 2000 ft.)* For the only beach landing around, try **Skydive Mission Beach;** ask about combined rafting and kayaking packages. *(☎ 1800 638 005. $235, includes transport.)*

WHITEWATER RAFTING. Three companies offer basically the same deal—a wild day of rafting tame enough for beginners. **R 'n' R Rafting,** not for "rest and relaxation," has several options including multi-day and family packages. The longer your trip, the rougher your rapids. *(☎ 4051 7777. Half-day $83, full-day $145; 2-day helicopter in, raft out $630.)* Or, check out **Raging Thunder Adventures** *(24hr. reservations ☎ 4030 7990. Half-day $83, full-day $145).* **Foaming Fury** *(☎ 4031 3460)* has half-day rides *($81)* and full-day rides that include rainforest walks *($125).*

BEACH. Cairns doesn't really have a beach—it has a mudflat. However, the nearby **Trinity Beach** has nice white sand and plenty of private cove areas that keep it from feeling inundated with sunbathers. A bit farther north, **Palm Cove** is a beautiful beach lined with cafes and upscale resorts, offering respite from the burgeoning Cairns nightlife. *(Sunbus #1, 1A, 1B and 2X run to beaches from the depot in City Place. M-F every 30min., Sa-Su every hr.)*

◉ DIVING AND SNORKELING

The most popular way to see Cairns is through goggles (snorkel goggles, that is—though beer goggles come a close second). Every day, rain or shine, thousands of tourists and locals suit up with masks, fins, and snorkels to slide beneath the ocean surface and glimpse the Great Barrier Reef. ◙**Reef Teach,** 14 Spence St., has a two hour lecture by Paddy Colwell, a marine biologist who doubles as a comic. In his own passionate and entertaining way, Colwell teaches about the history of the reef, its biodiversity, and how to avoid harming the reef and yourself. Reef Teach is great even for advanced divers. (☎/fax 4031 7794; www.reefteach.com.au. Lectures M-Sa 6:15pm. $13; includes tea, coffee, and snack.)

As the main gateway to the reef, Cairns is studded with an overwhelming number of dive shops and snorkeling outfits. Knowing which one to choose can be tricky and even a little daunting when you're bombarded with brochures and booking agents. Think about some questions in advance: how long do you want to dive—a day-trip or a multi-day trip? How big a boat do you want? For personal dive instruction and a group atmosphere, smaller boats may be the way to go. Finally, are you going with other divers or with friends who may prefer other water activities? Unless you're all diving, you won't want a dive trip—maybe instead a cruise with diving options such as **Passions of Paradise.** The only place in the area that does snorkel-only sails is Wavelength, in Port Douglas (see p. 416).

In order to dive in Australia, you need an open-water certification, a driver's license for the water. The only way to get this certification is to spend about 4 days and at least $350 in scuba school, where you learn about scuba equipment and diving techniques. To enroll in dive classes, you need two passport-sized photos and a medical certificate from a doctor (they will do a check-up for an additional fee).

Introductory dives offer a taste of scuba diving *without* scuba school. For those not planning to dive more than once, intro dives might be the way to go—you get an idea of what's down there without paying an arm and a leg (provided there aren't any sharks involved). Beware: some companies tack on payments as the day on the reef extends; ask questions, such as how long the actual underwater experience will be, before signing on. If your first taste of the undersea world leaves you hankering for more, many companies offer a second dive for an additional fee.

DIVING DAYTRIPS

Noah's Ark Too (☎4050 0677), located in The Pier. The motto at Noah's: "There are no rules." Relax on a boat that takes up to 28 people, sip a beer, have a laugh, and take the plunge on one of the 10 outer reef destinations chosen on the day of the trip. Departs daily 8:45am, returns 5pm. Certified dives $50, intro dives including a free 10-min. lesson underwater $80; additional dives $30.

The Falla, located in the Pier (☎4031 3488; www.fallacruises.com). A swanky, restored pearl lugger boat (a.k.a. sailboat) is chartered by a small crew, accommodating a maximum of 35 passengers. The divemasters will take novices out for a day on Upolo Reef. Departs daily 9am, returns about 6pm. Base price $60, children $35, families $190; includes lunch. First intro dive $50, second $30. First certified dive $40, second $20.

Passions of Paradise (☎4050 0676), offers full day cruises to Paradise Reef and Upolo Cay. This boat has a young, vibrant spirit; spontaneous conga dancing is not an unknown occurrence on the deck. Face-painting and chocolate cake keep the youngsters happy even at the end of the day. The high-speed catamaran can take between 60 and 70 passengers on the 10hr. trip. Departs 8am. Base price for snorkeling, lunch, and transport $70. Intro dive or 2 certified dives additional $55.

MULTI-DAY TRIPS AND SCUBA SCHOOLS

Pro-Dive (☎4031 5255; www.prodive-cairns.com.au), on the corner of Abbott and Shields St. Their most popular trip is the 5-day learn-to-dive course. Although the price tag may seem hefty at $650, it includes all diving, equipment, 2-nights accommodation, and 5 additional dives. If you're on a tight budget, they also offer a 3 day learn-to-dive trip on Fitzroy Island Dive for $325. This trip includes housing on the island and the camaraderie that comes with having 9-person classes. Open daily 8:30am-9pm.

Cairns Dive Centre, 121 Abbott St. (☎4051 0294 or 24hr. 1800 642 591; www.cairns-dive.com.au). Generally the least expensive to the outer reef, with a "floating hotel" catamaran for its flagship and a smaller boat for daytrips. 5-day live-aboard, learn to dive course $550; 4-day budget course $297. Open daily 7:30am-5pm.

Tusa Dive (☎4031 1248; www.tusadive.com), at the corner of Shields St. and the Esplanade. The first 2 days of their 4-day PADI courses ($572) are run in the classroom by ProDive instructors, but the 2 daytrips to the outer reef are on the speedy new Tusa boats which hold a maximum of 28 passengers. A diver's dive company, Tusa is more expensive than others but is ideal for those who want to get to the outer reef with experts and without the live-aboard experience. 2-day Nitrox certification courses $435. Open daily 7:30am-9:30pm.

Down Under Dive, 287 Draper St. (24 hr. ☎4052 8300; www.downunderdive.com.au). A 2-masted clipper ship with a hot tub takes 2-day (or longer) trips, starting at $210 for snorkelers and $290 for certified divers. The company also offers diver training for those on a budget. A 4-day course starts at $280 for 2 days of pool training and 2 days on Hastings and Saxon Reefs. Open daily 7am-5pm.

🎵 NIGHTLIFE

Despite its widespread and well-deserved reputation as a haven for backpackers, the Cairns nightclub scene is still a few paces behind that of other cities. Still, when you put a bunch of young people in one place at one time, most of whom are fresh off the adrenaline rush of their dive (scuba or sky), the excitement is bound to be explosive. Get your hand stamped before 10pm and the venues are all free. Hostels usually give out a free meal voucher for one of the clubs to draw in the young crowds. For the latest word on the street, political topics, and music gigs, pick up a copy of *Barfly* (free), found all around town.

Ultimate Party is a Cairns pub crawl—basically, a giant mixer for twenty-something tourists—held every Saturday night. Pay $45 for entry into five bars and clubs, a shot in each one, two all-you-can eat meals, entertainment, transport, a photo, and a t-shirt. At the end of the night, if you're able, pick up a book of vouchers for tattoos, adventure trips, and, of course, more alcohol. Sign up at the Tropical Arcade on the corner of Shields St. and Abbott St., or call ☎4041 0332.

The Woolshed, 24 Shields St. (☎4031 6304 for free shuttle bus until 9:30pm). A rowdy all-night party for travelers. Backpackers come here to dance on the tables, drink beer, and enter the M night Mr. and Ms. Backpacker contests. Practically every hostel in town offers meal vouchers ($4 off) for this place. M and W Happy Hour 9:30-11:30pm. $6 pitchers, $3 basics. Cover Su-Th $5, F $6, Sa free before 10pm. Open nightly 6-9:30pm for meals, club open until 5am. Downstairs is the **Bassment,** which plays dance music Th-Sa until 5am. Free until midnight.

Shenannigan's (☎4051 2490), on the corner of Sheridan and Spence St. With all justification, they boast the best beer garden in Cairns; watch the latest sports matches on the 2 large screens, or listen to live music inside 4 nights a week. They also serve up huge meals. M jugs $6 until 1am, Tu Quiz night, F DJ night. Open daily 11am-late.

P.J. O'Brien's (☎4031 5333), in City Place, at the corner of Shields and Lake St., always finds a reason to celebrate. With tables made from beer barrels, authentic Irish memorabilia, and quotes from Yeats in the murals, this place almost looks like an Emerald Isle museum. Pints of Guinness ($5.50) and tasty food (meals $12-18) make P.J.'s the next biggest hot spot in town. Live bands 6 nights a week, Happy Hour F 5-9pm ($4 Guinness). Neat dress required.

Tropos (☎4031 2530), on the corner of Lake and Spence St. The club plays techno, and the dance floor is a stage where the groovers perfect their thang. This is everyone's last stop before bed at the end of the night. You can't miss it—the whirling spotlight can be seen across the street. W retro night. Neat dress required. Cover $5.50, free before midnight. Open daily until 5am.

The Sports Bar, 33 Spence St. (☎4041 2503), is rapidly rising in popularity with its vouchers for $1, heavily discounted meals, and 5-finger Tu. With billiards and multiple TV sets broadcasting all sports all the time, you can stay and enjoy your dinner, or your pint, without missing the big game. Open M-F 11am-5am, Sa-Su 6pm-5am.

Johno's Blues Bar (☎4051 8770), at the corner of Abbott and Aplin St. Red-hot jazz, cool blues, and a dash of rock 'n' roll plays 7 days a week in this rough-around-the-edges club. Th Johno and his Blues Band get the people out on the dance floor, especially after $5 jugs from 6-9pm. The crowd is a mix of backpackers and locals vying for daily prizes, like $100 bar tabs. Free entry most nights.

nu-trix, 53 Spence St. (☎4051 8223), between Grafton and McLeod St. Hard to miss its rainbow-colored marquis. A gay bar and dance club with no dress code. Shows F and Sa nights; cover $5. Open Su and W-Th 9:30pm-late, F-Sa 9:30pm-5am.

📭 DAYTRIPS FROM CAIRNS

TJAPUKAI. Just north of Cairns and off the Cook Hwy. in neighboring **Smithfield** is the national coup of Aboriginal cultural parks: **Tjapukai.** Pronounced "JAB-a-guy," this is the most wholly rewarding, intelligently presented, and culturally fair presentation of Aboriginal myths, customs, and history in all of Queensland. It has been showered with all kinds of awards, including the 1999 Gold Award from the Pacific Asia Travel Association for the best cultural attraction in the world. Give this experience at least half a day. Learn how to throw boomerangs and spears, see a cultural dance show, view a film on Aboriginal history, and more. (☎4042 9999; www.tjapukai.com.au. Open daily 9am-5pm. $28, children $14. Transfers to and from Cairns and the Northern Beaches $17 round-trip.)

ZOOS. Farther along the Cook Hwy. heading north, a pair of roadside attractions offer diversion from the coastal trek. An outback experience for the family 40km north of Cairns, **Hartley's Creek Crocodile Farm** has hundreds of crocs, as well as kangaroos, koalas and cassowaries. Keepers taunt a croc until it eats a hand-fed chicken in the heart-pounding "crocodile attack show" at 3pm. (*☎ 4055 3576; www.hartleyscreek.com. Open daily 8:30am-5pm. $18, children $9, families $45.)* Transportation and tours are available from Cairns on **Hartley's Express** (*☎ 4038 2992)* for $35 (includes admission to the farm), and from Port Douglas on **Coral Coaches** (*☎ 4098 2808)* for $40. The larger **Wild World: The Tropical Zoo,** near Palm Cove on the Cook Hwy., 20min. north of Cairns, lets you get up close and personal with kangaroos and wallabies. There's a comprehensive reptile house, koalas, and public crocodile feedings. (*☎ 4055 3669. Open daily 8:30am-5pm. $24, children $12.)*

CRYSTAL CASCADES. Only 30km from Cairns' center, this freshwater swimming and diving hole can fill up a few hours to make a lazy day more exciting, and it's free. Locals frequent the spot for diving, but be careful. There is also a short hiking trail. (*Drive north along Sheridan St., turn left on Aeroglen, and head Redlynch and follow the signs.)*

NEAR CAIRNS

GREEN ISLAND

Diminutive Green Island (technically a coral cay; see p. 11) barely pushes above the water's surface; its perimeter can be walked in 15min. Though dominated by the luxury resort in the island's center, a short boardwalk through the rainforest and a beach path provide access to nature. The more adventurous can forge their own trail through the dense rainforest, but if you walk long enough, chances are you'll end up back at the resort. Though Green Island is not a budget destination by any means, it's inexpensive to take a ferry over and check out the scene.

The cheapest and quickest way to the island is with **Great Adventures,** which offers a 45min. ferry. Extras include diving (intro dive or 2 certified dives $99), and a choice of snorkel equipment or a ride in a dinky glass-bottom boat for $11 each. (*☎ 4044 9944 or 1800 079 080. Departs Cairns daily 8:30, 10:30am, and 1pm; departs Green Island noon, 2:30, and 4:30pm. $46, day-packages $96; children $23; families $115.)* If you plan on doing any snorkeling or diving, **Big Cat Green Island Reef Cruises** is a better deal, offering a day on the island and either the glass-bottom boat tour or snorkeling gear. (*☎ 4051 0444. Departs Cairns 9am. $54, children $30, families $144.)* The sailboat **Ocean Free** specializes in trips to the island. Travelers aboard the schooner get the chance to dive and do hands-on sailing. (*☎ 4041 1118. Open daily 9am-5:30pm. Departs Cairns daily 9am. $75, children $55. Intro dive $60, for 2 $90; certified dive $45/$60.)*

The real highlight of Green Island is ▣**Marineland Melanesia,** a combination gallery, aquarium, and croc farm 250m northeast of the resort left of the jetty. Come at 10:30am or 1:45pm to watch a live feeding of Cassius, the world's largest crocodile in captivity. You can also hold yearling crocodiles or tour the primitive art collection. (*☎ 4051 4032. Open daily 9:30am-4:15pm. $9.50, children $4.50.)* Just off the end of the jetty is the **Marine Observatory,** from which you can observe bits of the coral reef from 1½m below the surface ($3). The resort has a nice pool surrounded by a couple of boutiques and small cafes (open daily 9:20am-4pm), and the **dive shop** rents snorkeling gear ($11 per day, guided snorkeling trips $15). Instructors outfit day-trippers and take them on an intro dive ($94, certified $66). **Michaelmas Cay,** just north of the island on the outer reef, has good diving and is the site of a natural bird sanctuary. Unfortunately, accommodation at the **Green Island Resort ❺** (*☎ 4031 3300)* runs about $455 per person.

FITZROY ISLAND

Fitzroy Island is much larger than Green Island and is generally a better choice for the budget traveler. There are affordable beds, though most people only go for a day. As a budget alternative to Green Island, its coral beaches and lush rainforest are still pristine—only noise pollution disrupts the tropical scenery. **Sunlover Cruises** does the trip to the island or a combination of the island and Moore Reef. (☎ 4050 1333. Both cruises depart 9:30am, return 5pm. Fitzroy only $36, combo $14; children $18/$7, families $90/$36.) If a cruise sounds too easy, try traveling to Fitzroy Island via **sea kayak** with **Raging Thunder Adventures,** which now owns the resort on the island. A high-speed catamaran takes you most of the way, followed by three hours of reef kayaking, snorkeling, and lunch. An overnight package includes bunk accommodations at the Fitzroy Island Resort and two days of kayaking. (☎ 4030 7907. Day-trip $110; overnight $135.) You can also get to the island via the *Fitzroy Island Flyer*, which leaves from Cairns and the island. (3 times daily. $36, children $18, family $90.) Once there, you can rent kayaks ($10 per day), fishing lines ($20), sailing catamarans ($20 per hr.), and aqua bikes ($10 per hr.). **Raging Thunder Adventures ❸** is seeking to transform the resort into a backpacker's getaway, with shared accommodations and party nights F-Sa. (☎ 4051 9588, 24hr. reservation 1800 079 080. Shared bunks $31; private bunks for 1-3 people $116, 4 people $124; beach doubles $58 per person; beach cabins $250 per family.) The resort has a **pool bar** which serves meals ($5-15) daily 9am-5pm. The **Raging Thunder Beach Bar ❸** serves dinner 6-8:30pm ($12-22). The **Flare Grill ❷** serves continental ($10) and cooked ($10-12) breakfast daily 8-10am.

The resort's **dive shop** offers introductory diving and snorkel gear at bargain rates. (Intro dive $65, certified $50; snorkel gear $12. Open daily 9:30am-4pm.) Snorkel and dive trips leave at 10:30am, 12:30pm, and 2:30pm. The walk to the **lighthouse** (5km return) starts at a clearing adjacent to the **Reefarm**, a prawn breeding farm 1km north of the resort. There are a couple good 500m walks through the rainforest on the northern end of the island as well. Just past the restaurant, the **Secret Garden track** cuts west into the island, while **Nudey Beach track** continues along the coast. The Secret Garden track is easy and has informative nature placards. The Nudey Beach track, a bit more challenging, is made of huge stone slabs leading to boulders at the shore and the occasional nude beach.

ATHERTON TABLELANDS

Although much of northern Queensland is picturesque, nothing quite compares to the Atherton Tablelands. Rolling hills meet unspoiled rainforest, the perfect venue for spotting wildlife and rushing waterfalls. The many tourists who visit Cairns often make the mistake of missing out on a trip to the Tablelands. Those who do take a break from the coastal confusion and spend some unharried days here can find it to be a most rewarding decision. Traveling northeast on the Kennedy Hwy., you'll find the farming village of **Mareeba** and touristy **Kuranda** (p. 413). The southern route via the Gilles Hwy. passes through the residential township of **Atherton,** charming **Yungaburra,** and **Malanda** (p. 415). Bring a sweater in the winter; at an elevation of 1000m, you'll soon forget you're in the tropics.

The mountainous lakeside roads give drivers both a mild challenge and rewarding panoramas. Although driving provides the fullest experience, the Tablelands are accessible without a car. **White Car Coaches,** 8 McCowaghie St., Atherton (☎ 4091 1855), services specials from Cairns to the Tablelands ($22), with stops in Kuranda, Mareeba, Herberton, and Ravenshoe. The **Skyrail Rainforest Cableway,** a 7½km gondola, lifts you up above the rainforest canopy into Kuranda village. A 1½hr. round-trip originates in Carovonica Lakes, 10 minutes northwest of Cairns. (☎ 4041 0007 or 4038 1555. $32, children $16. Open daily 8am-5pm.) The **Kuranda**

Scenic Railway runs an antique train ride from downtown Cairns to Kuranda. Chock full of camera-toting tourists, this bumpy journey comes with relentless, inflection-free commentary. (☎4031 3636. From Cairns Su-F 8:30am and 9:30am, Sa 8:30am; to Cairns Su-F 2pm and 3:30pm, Sa 3:30pm. $31, return $44; discounts for students, children, and seniors.)

KURANDA ☎07

Many travelers get no farther than this mountain town, the gateway to the Tablelands. Its river cruises, street performers, and famous markets draw sightseers from Cairns, though when the town shuts down after the last train leaves in the afternoon, the intrepid traveler is left to wander its historical streets without the crowds. In the morning, the hustle and bustle begins again when the **original markets** (open W-Su) and **Heritage Markets** (open daily 8:30am-3pm) transform the cozy village into a bazaar of arts, crafts, and clothing. In the character of a low-key town, nearly all of Kuranda's shops and restaurants close at 3pm.

Kuranda Backpacker's Hostel ❷ (a.k.a. "Mrs. Miller's"), 6 Arara St., is across the street to the left of the train station on the corner of Arara and Barang St. With its cast iron beds and pressed metal ceilings, you'll feel like you're taking a trip back in time. In the mornings, the proprietor feeds over 50 rainbow lorikeets. Amenities include a kitchen, pool, bike rental, tropical garden, laundry, and free pickup from Cairns. (☎4093 7355. Reception 8am-6pm. Dorms $18; twins and doubles $40.) **Kuranda Bottom Pub Hotel ❹**, on the corner of Coondoo and Arara St. just across the street from Skyrail, sports a garden bar restaurant, a pool, and tidy rooms with bath, fridge and TV. (☎4093 7206. Key deposit $5. Reception M-Sa 10am-10pm, Su 10am-4pm. Singles $44; doubles $55; extra adult $11, extra child $5.50.)

Locals love **Frog's ❶**, 11 Coondoo St., with its spacious porch stretching out back, unless you want to eat out front and watch the shoppers on the main drag. (☎4093 7405. Sandwiches $8; gourmet pizzas $12 and up. Open daily 9:30am-4pm.) Many places serve Devonshire tea, but only the ⬛**Honey House ❷**, at the entrance to the original **Kuranda Markets**, makes its sweets right on the premises. A hive of bees in the store produces Kuranda honey, and the accompanying pumpkin scones are made fresh and from scratch. (☎4093 7261. Open daily 8am-5pm.)

On the drive from Cairns, the road winds steeply through plush rainforest. Right off the Kennedy Hwy., the award-winning **Rainforestation Nature Park** offers everything from Aboriginal tours and walks to a wildlife park. Hop on the amphibious Army Duck, which crosses both land and water to get a real taste of the region's environment. Shuttles leave daily from Kuranda village. (☎4093 9033. Aboriginal culture tours $18, children $9; duck tours $14/$7; wildlife park $10/$6; package available for all attractions.)

One of the most amazing attractions in Kuranda, **Barron Gorge National Park** is a natural wonder. By car, follow the signs from the village's center; the gorge is about 2½km from town. A good walk is also signposted from the center of town—the Kuranda Scenic Railway stops here and allows travelers to hop out for a quick view. A short boardwalk takes those on foot right through the dense rainforest to an incredible lookout above Barron Falls, one of the largest waterfalls in the Tablelands.

MAREEBA AND ATHERTON ☎07

If you mention Mareeba or Atherton to locals in the Tablelands, they might just tell you to pass on through to your next destination. While the towns might lack the quaintness of Yungaburra or the scenic views of Kuranda, they illustrate the true rhythm of life in the Tropical Tablelands. Both towns claim to have "the best weather in the Tablelands," with over 300 days of sunshine a year. A short stop in

Atherton will reveal much about the region's history, and the town of Mareeba has begun to garner attention for its burgeoning industries—90% of Australia's coffee is produced here, as well as the world's only mango wine.

The Coffee Works, 136 Mason St., Mareeba, lures visitors with its aromatic home brews and coffee-tasting tours. Learn about the process and history of coffee-making in Australia. (☎4092 4101 or 1800 355 526. Open daily 9am-4pm. Tours $5.50, includes free tasting of 12 coffees.) A short drive away, the **Golden Pride Winery,** on Bilwon Rd., is the world's only mango wine-producing factory and farm. Drive in and ring the bell for a free taste of their divine dry, medium, and sweet wines. (☎4093 2524. Open daily 9am-10pm. Bottles from $22.) Another great attraction in town is **Granite Gorge,** where locals come to swim and feed rock wallabies or hike the rocky walking trails. **Camping ❶** is permitted ($3 per person).

Atherton, located atop an extinct volcano, is a great base for Lake Tinaroo and other Tableland destinations. There is an **info center** (☎4091 1131) at the **Atherton Snack Bar ❶,** 104 Main St., which has budget meals and homemade cakes. An excellent place to stay, **Blue Gum B&B ❺,** 36 Twelfth Ave. (☎4091 5149), looks over the green hills of the Tablelands and has transfers from Cairns. For budget accommodation, try the **Atherton Travellers Lodge ❷,** 37 Alive St. (☎4091 3552. Dorms $16; doubles $38.) To indulge your sweet tooth, drive down the Gillies Hwy. until you see the sign for **Shaylee's strawberry farm** (☎4091 2962), which sells strawberries straight off the vine, homemade ice creams, and fresh jams (from $3.50).

LAKE TINAROO AND DANBULLA FOREST

Saturated with crater lakes and sprinkled with waterfalls, the volcanic soil of the central Tablelands sprouts bizarre forest along the shores of the **Tinaroo, Barrine,** and **Eacham Lakes.** Unsealed **Danbulla Forest Dr.** circles Lake Tinaroo. The free *Danbulla State Forest* visitor's guide, available from the **QPWS Forest Management,** 83 Main St., Atherton (☎4091 1844), lists sights along the 40min. loop. Contact the **QPWS Eacham District Office** (☎4095 3768) at Lake Eacham for information on walking paths around the lakes. The paved 31km **Lake Circuit Track** around Lake Eacham in **Crater National Park** has muskrat-kangaroos and giant iguanas.

Coming from the gateway town of **Tolga,** off Hwy. 1, a barren road runs through vast farmland before reaching the forested area of Lake Tinaroo. At the entrance to the lake is the **Lake Tinaroo Holiday Park ❶,** which has a kiosk, fuel, and games room. (☎4095 8232. Sites $15, powered $20; cabins $48; holiday unites from $60.) From the entrance to the Danbulla State Forest, the road passes five campsites along the way: Platypus Rock (5.7k), Downfall Creek (9k), Kauri Creek (11.2k), School Point (18.8k), and Fong on Bay (19.2k). **Camping ❶** is a great way to observe the lake and just relax (sites $3.85 per person; toilets available). Note: there is no camping in any of the national parks, only the state forest areas.

YUNGABURRA   ☎07

Tiny Yungaburra (pop. 400) is at the heart of the Tablelands, with Lake Tinaroo and the Danbulla State Forest to the north, waterfalls to the south, Lakes Eacham and Barrine to the southeast, and the volcanic hills of the **Seven Sisters** to the west. The town is handsome, untouched by commercial tourism, yet warm to visitors. Yungaburra hosts the biggest **markets** in the north on the fourth Saturday of each month from 7am to noon. Homemade crafts, fresh produce, and even goats can be bartered at these authentic events. From Cairns, take the Gillies Hwy. 60km west.

Just off the west side of Yungaburra is the **Curtain Fig Tree,** a monstrous strangler fig forming an eerie curtain in the middle of the rainforest. Pick your gaping jaw off the ground and check out the 50m tall, 500 year-old **Cathedral Fig Tree** on the east stretch of Dunbulla Forest Dr. The best place to spot a **platypus** is at the Atherton Shire Council Pumping Station. From Yungaburra, head past the bridge and turn right onto Picnic Crossing Rd. (the road sign is actually 10m ahead of the turnoff). Follow the second right-hand turn. You'll find a concrete picnic table and platypus families near the bend in the river. There is another platypus-viewing spot on the Gillies Hwy. at the **Peterson Creek** crossing, right before town.

Yungaburra's hostel, **On the Wallaby ●**, is superb. The common area feels like a mountain hut with rustic furnishings and a wood-burning stove. The bathrooms and showers are sided with stone and wood, and the bunk rooms are clean and fresh. Enjoy BBQ ($8), kitchen, garden, and laundry. Guests can join tour activities (canoeing, biking, or making your own didgeridoo) on an individual basis. Platypus spotting trips are free. (☎4095 2031. Bike hire half-day $10, full-day $15. Reception 8am-1pm and 4-8pm. Sites for 1 $10, for 2 $15; dorms $20; twins and doubles $45. Cairns transfers $20.) One kilometer south of Lake Eacham is the **Lake Eacham Caravan Park ●**, with showers, laundry, and a small general store. The price includes admission to a garden and petting zoo, where several species of birds can be spotted. (☎4095 3730. Reception 7am-7pm. Sites for 2 $13, powered $16; cabins $54.) **Curtain Fig Motel ●**, 16 Gillies Hwy., in the center of town, has sparkling rooms. (☎4095 3168. Reception 7:30am-8:30pm. Doubles $77, extra person $11.)

The **Gem Gallery and Coffee Shop ●**, 44 Eacham Rd., serves breakfast for under $2. They also have inexpensive opals and free opal-cutting and gold-working demonstrations. (☎4095 3455. Open daily 8am-late.) Next door, **Flynn's ●** has bigger meals and **Internet**. (Open daily for breakfast 7:30-11:30am, lunch until 2:30pm, and dinner until 9pm.) **Yungaburra Market,** on Eacham St. is the local **supermarket**. (☎4095 2177. Open daily 6:30am-7pm.)

MALANDA   ☎07

Only a short distance from Yungaburra, friendly and hospitable **Malanda** was founded in 1911 and grew around its timber industry. Nowadays, residents guard the remaining rainforest, magnificent waterfalls, and rare tree kangaroos. About 25km south of Malanda and beyond Millaa Millaa, the **waterfall circuit** leads past a series of spectacular swimming holes. From the north, a sign points to the falls. Catch the loop from the south by looking for the "Tourist Drive" sign. **Millaa Millaa Falls** is the perfect waterfall: a straight, even curtain with rocks at the bottom and a bit of green on either side. **Zillie Falls** starts off as a sedate creek at the top of the falls. A rocky, slippery-when-wet path through the adjacent rainforest leads to the roaring drop where the cascading **Ellinjaa Falls** spark their liquid fireworks. The last waterfall on the circuit in **Mungalli Falls,** which passes the must-see **Mungalli Creek Dairy.** Owned and operated by the Watson family, this traditional dairy farm serves as fresh as the law allows. (☎4097 2232. Free cheese tastings. Open daily 10am-4pm.) For more information about the falls surrounding Malanda, the **Malanda Falls Visitor Centre** is just past **Malanda Falls** on the way out of town towards Atherton. (☎4096 6957. Open 10am-4pm daily. Tours $2.)

The best place to stay right near the falls is **Travellers Rest ●**, on Millaa Millaa Rd., just past Malanda. This recently renovated country house's biggest draw are the Saturday Night Murder Mysteries. Make a reservation for 8-12 people (about six months in advance), and owners Tracy and Mike will give you characters and stories to prepare for your stay. Visitors enjoy a night of role-playing and mystery, along with dinner and breakfast. (☎4096 6077. Double with breakfast $50. Murder Mystery $60 per person.) The **Peeramon Hotel ●**, on Peeramon Rd., is in (surprise) **Peeramon** between Yungaburra and Malanda. From Atherton, take the first paved road on the right after leaving Yungaburra; from Cairns it's the first paved left after the Lake Eacham exit off the Gillies Hwy. A lady's **ghost**, victim of a double-murder in the hotel, still floats about the place: a photo above the piano captures her, midair and luminescent in a group picture on the front steps. (☎4096 5873. Singles in

QUEENSLAND

the hotel or in the dongers out back $20; doubles $40.) The little-known **Platypus Forest Lodge** ❹, 12 Topaz Rd., 6km east of the town center off Lake Barrine Rd., is a stellar B&B perfect for nature buffs. The owners run an immaculate lodge complete with sauna, hot tub, canoes, wood-burning stove, and loads of hospitality. Out back, platypi, turtles, possums, and tree kangaroos inhabit a swath of rainforest. (☎/fax 4096 5926. Singles $45; doubles $55.) At night, check out Australia's oldest movie theater, the **Majestic Theatre,** at Eachem Pl. For showtimes, call the 24hr. information line at ☎4096 5726, or go to www.majestictheatre.com.au. ($8, children and pensioners $5.)

PORT DOUGLAS ☎07

A sleepy enclave bordered by rainforest, Port Douglas might be nothing more than a collection of quiet vacation homes if it weren't for its burgeoning tourism industry. The Dry brings throngs of nature-lovers, marine enthusiasts, and short-term workers. Snorkel and scuba trips take travelers out to the pristine outer reaches of the Great Barrier Reef and up the coast to the rainforests of Daintree National Park. Others forgo these excursions to simply soak up the rays on Four Mile Beach.

⌨ TRANSPORTATION

Buses: Coral Coaches (☎4099 5351), at the Marina Mirage, runs daily to: the **airport** (1¼hr., 11 per day, $25); **Cairns** (1½hr.; 11 per day; $22, same day return $39, open return $39.50); **Daintree Ferry** ($20, return $36); **Mossman** (30min.; 12 per day; $8, return $14). Buses also run to **Cooktown** via the coast road (during the Dry Tu, Th, and Sa 1 per day; $52) and via the inland road. (W, F, and Su 1 per day; $58.) They also have a local shuttle. **Sun Palm Coaches** (☎4099 4992) runs between the **Rainforest Habitat** and town, stopping at the major resorts and hostels on the way. ($3.50 one-way, $5 return.)

Ferries: Quicksilver (☎4099 5050) leaves Port Douglas for **Cairns** from the Marina Mirage daily at 5:15pm. (1½hr., $24.)

Taxis: Port Douglas Taxis, 45 Warner St. (☎4099 5345). 24hr.

Car Rental: Crocodile Car Rentals, #2 50 Macrossan St. (☎4099 5555), specializes in **4WD** (from $120 per day). Age restrictions apply. **Allcar Rentals,** 21 Warner St. (☎4099 4123), rents cheapos for $60 per day (less if a week or longer rental), 4WD from $95 a day for those 21+. Both rental agencies offer **automatic 4WD**.

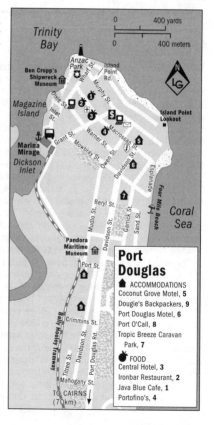

Port Douglas

⌂ ACCOMMODATIONS
Coconut Grove Motel, **5**
Dougie's Backpackers, **9**
Port Douglas Motel, **6**
Port O'Call, **8**
Tropic Breeze Caravan Park, **7**

🍴 FOOD
Central Hotel, **3**
Ironbar Restaurant, **2**
Java Blue Cafe, **1**
Portofino's, **4**

QUEENSLAND

Bike Rental: Port Douglas Bike Hire (☎4099 5799), corner of Wharf and Warner St. Half-day $10, full-day $14, weekly $59. All bikes are mountain bikes and rental includes locks and helmets. Child and tandem bikes available. Open daily 9am-5pm.

Road Report: Royal Automobile Club of Queensland (☎4033 6711; www.racq.com.au) gives all road conditions and closings.

🔷🔷 ORIENTATION AND PRACTICAL INFORMATION

Port Douglas Rd. branches right off of Hwy. 1 (Captain Cook Hwy.) 70km north of Cairns and turns into **Davidson St.** near the end of the Port Douglas peninsula. The streets along the peninsula's edges lead to **Four Mile Beach** (on the Esplanade) to the east and to **Marina Mirage** (on Wharf St.) to the west. The town's main drag, **Macrossan Street,** connects these two streets and hosts most of Port Douglas' shops and restaurants.

Tourist Office: BTS Tours, 49 Macrossan St. (☎ 4099 5665), has all your necessary tours and information, as well as same-day film processing.

Banks: All banks open M-Th 9:30am-4pm, F 9:30am-5pm. **ANZ,** 36 Macrossan St. (☎13 13 14), exchanges currency for a $5 commission and has an **ATM.** No fee for cashing AmEx Traveler's Checks. If heading north, keep in mind that ATMs may be few and far between and cash-outs rarely take foreign bank cards.

Police: (24hr. ☎4099 5220), at Macrossan and Wharf St. Open M-Th 8am-2:30pm.

Medical Services: Port Village Medical Centre, Shop 17 in Port Village Centre on Macrossan St. (24hr. ☎4099 5043). Office open M-F 8am-6pm, Sa-Su 9am-noon. The nearest **hospital** (☎4098 2444) is in Mossman, on Hospital St.

Internet: Mega Byte Internet Cafe, 48 Macrossan St. (☎4099 5568). $6 per hr. Open daily 9am-10pm. **Sheridan's** (☎4099 5770), on the corner of Wharf St. and Warner St., offers the same prices and is usually less crowded.

Post Office: 5 Owen St. (☎4099 5210). On the corner of Macrossan and Owen St., up the hill. Open M-F 9am-5pm, Sa 9am-noon. **Postal Code:** 4871.

🔷 ACCOMMODATIONS

If you've been on the road a while and feel like splurging, Port Douglas might be the place, as expensive options abound. For those on a budget, walk down **Davidson St.** or the **Esplanade** to find a more affordable option.

Port O'Call Lodge (YHA), 7 Craven Close (☎4099 5422 or 1800 892 800). Take a left off Port Douglas Rd. onto Port St. as you come into town. This incredibly comfortable, motel-like hostel has laundry, a pool, kitchen, bike rental, and Internet. Free shuttle bus to Cairns (departs M, W, and Sa 8:30am; call for a 10am lift north from Cairns). The popular bistro serves large, tasty meals daily (mains $8-11; open 6-9pm) and swings during Happy Hour (5pm-7pm). Free lockers. Reception 7:30am-7:30pm. Check-out 9:30am. 4-bed dorm with bath $21, YHA $19.50; deluxe motel rooms $45, during the Dry $95. VIP, NOMADS. ❷

Dougie's Backpackers, 111 Davidson St. (☎4099 6200 or 1800 996 200; www.dougies.com.au). Known as the party hostel around town, equipped with games, hammocks, and a bar (open 4pm-midnight). Sip champagne and watch for crocs on their free steam train (every Su). Laundry, Internet, kitchen, TV, pool, and bike rental ($1 per hour). 15min. walk from town center. Free bus to Cairns M, W, and Sa 8:30am; free pick up in Cairns at 10:30am same days. Dorms $21; doubles $60. Sites for 1 $12, for 2 $20; $70 per week for 1. NOMADS/VIP/YHA. ❷

Tropic Breeze Van Park, 24 Davidson St. (☎4099 5299 or 4099 5235). A mere 100m from the beach and right behind an IGA supermarket and petrol station. Reception 8am-7pm. Sites for 2 $17.50, powered $21, extra person $5; cabins for 2 next door at the **Village** $63.50. ❷

Coconut Grove Motel, 58 Macrossan St. (☎4099 5124). Well-maintained rooms, sits nestled in the trees and offers a break from the backpacking scene. Restaurant, laundry, kitchen, BBQ area, TV, and 2 pools. Reception 8am-7pm. 6-bed dorms with bath $20; motel rooms with TV, A/C, and fridge from $80; doubles $90. AmEx/MC/V. ❷

Port Douglas Motel, 9 Davidson St. (☎4099 5248). If you've got a few friends to share the cost, this place is a find, just a 2min. walk to the beach. All rooms impeccably clean and equipped with kitchenettes, bathrooms, TV, A/C, and covered carpark. Prices range from $80-100 depending on the number of people. ❺

🔾 🔒 FOOD AND ENTERTAINMENT

If you know what you want to eat, chances are **Macrossan St.** will have it. Some of the new trendier restaurants setting up fort in Port Douglas might ask an arm, a leg, *and* your credit card for portion sizes that pale in comparison to some of the less expensive outfits. For meals overlooking the water, head to Marina Mirage, where several restaurants line the peaceful harbor.

🍴 **Ironbar Restaurant,** 5 Macrossan St. (☎4099 4776), is a family-friendly restaurant catering to the resort crowd. The main attraction is the cane toad races, headed by local entrepreneur Clancy, every Tu, Th, and Su at 8pm ($3, children free) and 9:15pm (adults only). Choose your own finely dressed amphibian; the winner (human, not toad) gets a free drink. The kitchen offers huge kangaroo burgers, skewered croc, and barbecued prawns for $4-27. Open M-F 11am-2am, Sa-Su 8am-2am. AmEx/MC/V. ❸

Portofino's, 31 Macrossan St. (4099 5458). While expensive Mediterranean and pasta dishes entice the hungry traveller, the extensive and affordable gourmet pizza list truly delivers ($11.50-15). Enjoy one of their several wine options out front on the terrace or out back in the romantic courtyard. Open daily for dinner. AmEx/MC/V. ❷

Central Hotel, 9 Macrossan St. (☎4099 5271), in the center of town, is primarily a local bar with live, local bands Tu-F nights. The bar also broadcasts all national sporting events and runs a local jackpot every Monday night. Stubbies $4. Open daily until midnight. ❶

Java Blue Cafe, (☎4098 5814), corner of Wharf and Macrossan St. Where Bill Clinton eats when he's in Port Douglas. Enjoy huge salads ($7-10), a full breakfast ($15), good veggie options, or a sandwich on one of several types of fresh bread. Open daily 8am-5pm. ❷

Mango Jam, 24 Macrossan St. (☎4099 4611), with its lively terrace and good portions, is a great lunch option. Be sure to try their famous mango daiquiris or munch on one of their lesser-known but equally noteworthy pizzas. Lunch special $11.50; meals $14-26. Open daily noon-2am. AmEx/MC/V. ❸

Coles Supermarket, in Port Village Shopping Centre on Macrossan St. between Wharf and Grant St. Open M-F 8am-9pm, Sa 8am-5:30pm, Su 9am-6pm.

👁 🔾 SIGHTS AND ACTIVITIES

The Rainforest Habitat, on Port Douglas Rd. coming into town, has eight acres, three enclosures, and over 1000 animals without cages or any discernible fear of people. Mingle with the cockatoos and parrots, tickle a fruit bat's tummy, or scratch a wallaroo behind the ears. Early risers can also enjoy "Breakfast with the Birds," a full buffet (with champagne) in the aviary. (8-11am. $38, children $19; includes entry fee.) There is also a restaurant and souvenir shop on premises. (☎4099 3235; www.rainforesthabitat.com.au. Open daily 8am-5:30pm; last entry 4:30pm. $24, children $12. 10% student discount. Wheelchair accessible.)

At the east end of Macrossan St., **Four Mile Beach** is almost always quiet. This gorgeous stretch attracts an array of locals, topless backpackers, and swanky resort-types. For safety reasons, swim between the flags. (Lifeguard on duty M-Sa 9:30am-5pm.)

Extra Action Watersports (☎4099 3175 or 0412 346 303) is just north of Marina Mirage. Steve, the owner and self-defined "action man," can set you up with any number of heart-stopping adventures. **Parasailing** adventures last 20 minutes. (Solo $120, couple $85 each; 2hr. family packages $275.)

Visitors can **snorkel** independently or with several private outfits, most of which depart from Marina Mirage. **Sailaway-Low Isles,** 23 Macrossan St., fits snorkeling, riding in a glass-bottom boat, and "boom netting" into one day, but does not go out to the outer reef. (☎4099 5799; www.reefandrainforest.com.au. Departs daily 8:45am. 7hr. $105, children $60, families $285. Call for booking.) **Wavelength,** just north of the Marina Mirage, also offers daily snorkeling-only trips. Two boats depart daily at 8:30am for eight-hour ventures to the outer reef with a marine biologist on board. (☎4099 5031. $130, children $90.)

◤ SCUBA DIVING

Port Douglas is an excellent destination for **scuba divers.** Portions of the Great Barrier Reef lie just off Four Mile Beach and offer a plethora of marine life. When selecting a dive or snorkel shop, ask plenty of questions. Knowing boat capacity, dive difficulty, and site destinations ahead of time is important.

Quicksilver Diver (☎4087 2100; www.quicksilver-cruises.com), in the Marina Mirage. The biggest operation in town, Quicksilver picks up divers at Cairns before continuing up to Port Douglas. Ride a high-speed catamaran to the outer reef and spend the day on a pontoon enjoying submersible rides, snorkeling, and lunch buffet. All equipment included. Catamaran departs daily 10am. $156, children $80.50. Special snorkeling tours with a marine biologist, additional $33. Introductory dive, additional $113; certified dive additional $71. Quicksilver also offers a 4-day PADI course. (☎4099 5050; www.quicksilverdive.com.au. $510.)

Poseidon Outer Reef Cruises, 34 Macrossan St. (☎4099 4772; www.poseidon-cruises.com.au). This 1-boat operation offers dive courses in conjunction with Discover Dive at **The Links Health Club** (☎4099 5544; www.discoverdive.com.au), a five-star, PADI dive center specializing in small group training. The $570 4-day open water course departs M and W, and PADI referrals run $225 per day. Advanced, Rescue, and Divemaster courses are also available. A brand new boat takes groups of 50 to the reef daily. Departs 8:30am and returns 4pm. Open daily 9am-6pm.

Haba Dive, (☎4099 5254), in the Marina Mirage. Offers 2 dives on each daily trip. Groups of 40 depart 8:30am with free pickup and lunch. Intro dives $190, additional dive $35; certified dives $170, with equipment $200. Snorkeling $130, children $75.

◪ DAYTRIP FROM PORT DOUGLAS: MOSSMAN GORGE

For those looking to escape the nonstop activity of Port Douglas life, Mossman Gorge provides unrivaled peace and quiet. Part of the **Daintree National Park,** the gorge has several hiking paths originating from the visitors' parking lot (follow signs). The shorter paths to the Mossman River and swimming holes are easy, but the 2.4km circuit track in the thick of the rainforest is slightly more challenging.

Q
U
E
E
N
S
L
A
N
D

Be prepared to hop over small creeks (and an occasional small lizard) during the Wet. On any of the trails you'll feel engulfed by the magnificent green canopy.

Coral Coaches runs to **Mossman** (30min.; 10 per day; $8, return $14). Some hostels also provide a few daily shuttles, though you might get stranded for longer than you desired until the next shuttle returns. If **driving**, take Hwy. 1 north from the junction to Port Douglas for about 20km. Follow the brown signs for Mossman Gorge and turn left across from the Mossman State High School. Drive about 4km to Kuku Yalanji and 1km more to the carpark at the gorge.

If you want to learn the secrets of the rainforest, spend time with an Aboriginal guide from **Kuku-Yalanji Dreamtime Walks,** on the road to the gorge. The tour covers traditional medicines and bush tucker, and includes tea and damper. The Aboriginal-owned operation also has a Visitors Center and shop. (☎4098 2595. Open M-F 9am-4pm. Tours M-F 10am, noon, and 2pm. $16.50, children $8.25. Bookings essential. Mini-bus pick-up service for 10am walk from Port Douglas and Mossman $41, children $20; includes walking fee.)

DAINTREE   ☎07

Daintree is an excellent gateway to the rougher frontier land of the north. Kingfishers, kookaburras, and friendly faces abound in this tiny forest village (pop. 120). The town's main economic assets are the estuarine crocodiles (or salties) that live in the Daintree River; boatloads of camera-toting croc-seekers pass through the village daily. Daintree Township is about 6km north of the turn-off for the Daintree Ferry on the Cook Hwy. Beware that this portion of the road can flood; call 4033 6711 or one of the local restaurants for road conditions.

If you're not visiting on an all-inclusive tour package from Port Douglas or Cairns, you can book a river tour at the **Daintree General Store** (☎4098 6416) which also serves as the town watering hole and **post office.** Most river excursions are similar, varying primarily in length (from 1-2½hr.). Prices range from $17 to $30; children travel for less. Check out **Daintree Electric Boat Cruises** (☎1800 686 103) or **Daintree River and Reef Cruise Centre** (☎4098 6115). **Daintree Wildlife Safaris** (☎4098 6125) also cruise for crocs on Geko Dundee's personal access only portion of the Daintree. **Chris Dahlberg** runs excellent morning bird-spotting tours from the Daintree jetty. (☎4098 7997. 2hr. $35. Bookings essential.)

The ◨**Red Mill House** ❹ is reason enough to visit Daintree. A TV room, swimming pool, and BBQ are just some of the extras that convince many guests to stay longer than they originally planned. Daily breakfast is made of fruit from the tropical garden in the backyard. The older part of the house has one single ($60), one double ($70), and one triple ($99) with bathroom facilities and a spa. The newer section offers four queen-size rooms with bath for $88. (☎/fax 4098 6233; www.redmill-house.com.au. MC/V.)

CAPE TRIBULATION   ☎07

About 15km north of the Daintree River, 'Cape Trib' is in the heart of **Daintree National Park** and is more of a landmark than a township. When locals talk about it, they're usually referring to a large general area served by Cape Tribulation Rd., which runs north past Cow Bay, Alexandra Bay, Thornton Peak, and the Cape. Travelers continuing up the coast from Daintree will use the **Daintree Ferry,** which shuttles across the river from 6am-midnight. (Walk-on passengers $1, cars $8.) The fantastic Cape Tribulation Rd. from Daintree to Cape Trib is anything but what its name would suggest. The rainforest crashes down onto the ocean surf, and every inch of forest is teeming with wildlife. Conservationists and capitalists are locked in a heated struggle over the future of these forests: while the former vie to prevent the Cape from obtaining electricity, tourist-minded businesses see modernization as the way to open the wilderness to travelers.

▐▄ TRANSPORTATION AND PRACTICAL INFORMATION. If driving, bear right after the ferry; this sealed road first passes the **Alexandra Range Lookout,** on the right. Just a few kilometers farther is the **Environmental Centre,** and the turn off for **Cow Bay,** on Buchanan Creek Rd. A half-hour drive farther north on Cape Tribulation Rd. passes **Cooper Creek** and finally the area known as **Cape Tribulation.** A 4WD-only road then continues on to **Cooktown** (see p. 424).

The distances between locales make getting around somewhat difficult without a car. However, the two main hostels provide shuttles to various sights and offer a number of adventures on their own premises. **Coral Coaches** stops in **Cow Bay.** (Cairns ☎ 4031 7577, Port Douglas ☎ 4099 5351. Departs Cairns 11am; Port Douglas 8:00am, 5pm. $30.) There is no official information center in Cape Tribulation. The **Queensland Parks and Wildlife Service (QPWS) ranger station** has public info, but the hours are extremely limited. (☎ 4098 0052. Open M-F 9:30-11:30am.) Two other sources of info are the Daintree Rainforest Environmental Centre and the Bat House (see **Sights and Activities,** p. 418). **Rainforest Village,** a few kilometers before Cooper Creek, sells groceries and petrol, and has a phone and a post box. (☎ 4098 9015. Open 7am-7pm.) The "last fuel" sign is slightly misleading; fuel is only a short distance away in Cape Tribulation (see **Wujal Wujal,** p. 423).

▐ ACCOMMODATIONS. Hostels here reflect the active beach and rainforest atmosphere that is Cape Trib. The last two accommodations listed below are located on the way to Cape Tribulation from Daintree.

Crocodylus Village (☎ 4098 9166; crocodylus@austarnet.com.au), on Buchanan Creek Rd., east off Cape Tribulation Rd. Take a right after the Daintree Environmental Centre if heading north from Daintree Ferry. Coral Coaches (☎ 4098 2600) runs there from Cairns for $32. This hostel is a backpacker oasis organically entwined with the rainforest, with several open-air cabins scattered around a large wooden patio. Laundry, pool, horseback riding, sunrise paddle trek in a hybrid kayak/canoe, and guided bushwalks. Complimentary bus to the beach four times a day. Reception 7:30am-11:15pm. Book ahead. Cabin rooms $20, YHA $18; ensuite cabin for 2 $65, each extra person $10, ages 5-15 $5, children under 5 free. ❷

PK's Jungle Village (☎ 4098 0400). More appropriately called "PK's Jungle Party," this hostel is about 400m past the "Welcome to Cape Tribulation" sign. " The nightly entertainment pales in comparison to the weekly theme parties, usually 4-keggers. If you miss the first daily Happy Hour, don't worry—there's another. Volleyball, horseback riding, guided bushwalking, and bike rental (half-day $12, full day $20). Laundry, kitchen, bar, and pool. Reception 7:30am-7pm. Check-out 9:30am. Dorms $24; doubles $65; triples $82; quads $104. VIP. ❷

Cape Trib Beach House (☎ 4098 0030). A rainforest camping ground converted into a rainforest cabin resort and only accessible by a partially sealed road. Relax on their pristine beach with forest dragons and butterflies. Laundry, bar, restaurant, pool, Internet. 4 and 6-bed dorms $25-32; family-style cabins for 4 with A/C $89-99; beachfront cabins with queen beds $109. ❸

Coconut Beach Rainforest Resort (☎ 4098 0033 or 1800 816 595), just past Cooper Creek. For those looking to splurge, this resort features the finest of facilities set right on the beach. Rooms from $280. ❺

Lync Haven, (☎ 4098 9155). Wildlife sanctuary by day, accommodation by night, Lync Haven is a hostel, eatery, and petting zoo all in one. Dorms $20, ensuite $30; self-contained units from $149-165; powered sites $5. ❷

Daintree Manor, 27 Forest Creek Rd. (☎/fax 4090 7041). Just north of the river, the Manor offers breathtaking views, 24hr. power, beautiful handmade furniture, and a TV lounge with good reception. Rooms from $99, breakfast included. ❺

QUEENSLAND

Camping is at **Rainforest Village ❶** (☎4098 9015), a few kilometers before Cooper's Creek (sites $18, powered $20), or at **Noah's Beach Camping ❶**, just after Thornton Beach, on the right. At Noah's, fill out a camping permit ($3.85 per person, families $15.40) and put it in the box provided.

🍴 **FOOD. Fan Palm Cafe and Boardwalk ❷**, on Cape Tribulation Rd., right after the Ice Cream factory, is a new restaurant catering to the backpacker set. They use all fresh fruits and vegetables and cater to vegetarians. (☎4098 9119. Open in the Dry W-Su 10am-midnight, in the Wet Th-Su 10am-5pm. Mains $10-15, entrees $8-14. Lunch menu $5-14.) **Lync Haven ❷** is perhaps the most amusing eating establishment with its wildlife sanctuary full of orphaned 'roos to pet and feed. Options include burgers ($5-7) and sandwiches ($4) plus a veggie-friendly dinner menu (everything under $12). They also have a wide range of accommodations. (See above. ☎4098 9155.) **The Waterhole Cafe ❶**, on Bailey's Creek Rd., specializes in Indonesian cuisine (meals $8.50), although they do serve burgers (including veggie) and all-day breakfast. The cafe shakes down with live music on the weekends.

📷 🎒 **SIGHTS AND ACTIVITIES.** All attractions on Cape Tribulation involve the wet tropics. **The Daintree Rainforest Environmental Centre,** just before Cow Bay off Cape Tribulation Rd., is a popular stop-off. The center is informative and unique, with a 23m canopy tower that allows visitors to view the rainforest from above the trees. The ticket price includes a guided walk on the rainforest boardwalk (40min.), wet tropic movies, and access to a reference library. (☎/fax 4098 9171. Open daily 8:30am-5pm. $11, children $5.50, families $27.50; $8.80 for those lodging in the area.) A free walk around **Jindalba**, just 450m up the road from the Centre, has picnic facilities, bathroom, and sign-posted walks. The **Bathouse**, opposite PK's on the west side of the highway, is a less extensive source of forest info, but the all-volunteer staff will be happy to take your picture with their giant flying fox, Rex. (☎4098 0063; www.austrop.org.au. $2 donation.) Just down the road from the Bathouse is 🏠**Dubuji**, a visitor area with a spectacular 1.2km boardwalk through a variety of coastal forests and mangroves, a must for all visitors. Farther south is the **Marrdja** boardwalk through old growth rainforest and eerily beautiful mangrove forest, home to many species of birds, including the threatened cassowary.

Cape Tribulation Wilderness Cruises explores the mangroves of Cooper Creek in search of crocodiles. (☎4098 9052. Daily departure times vary. 1hr. $19. Bookings essential.) **Rum Runner** is one of the several tours based out of Cairns that runs daily trips to the reef off the Cape. (☎4098 9249 or 0500 509 249. Free bus to beach from all Daintree/Cape Trib resorts, snorkeling equipment included. Introductory dives $114; min. age 12.)

Tropical Sea Kayaks (☎4098 9166) offer a popular two-day, one-night trip to **Snapper Island** for $179 (available at the Crocodylus Village). This excursion features reef walking, snorkeling, and beach camping, including all equipment, as well as fully prepared meals. **Wundu Trail Rides,** between Lync Haven and the Rainforest Village, leads horseback tours of the coral coast. Long pants and covered shoes are recommended for this excursion through the Daintree Tea Plantation. (☎4098 9176. Departs twice daily. 3hr. guided rides $55, 10% discount for groups of seven or more; min. age 10.)

ROUTES TO COOKTOWN

There are two routes from Cape Tribulation to Cooktown—one inland, one coastal. The Bloomfield Track is the coastal route, which beats through 150km of bush as it swerves and dips, hugging the sides of precipitously steep mountains. When it's in bad condition, the Bloomfield Track is impassable. In "good" condition, the road is about as much fun as can legally be had in a 4WD. Views of the rainforest and the coastline are amazing, and fording the rivers can be exciting. The trek takes about five hours, with lots of veering, jagging, bumping, straying, and dancing—whatever is necessary—to avoid large potholes and fallen trees. Call ahead for road conditions and bring lots of cash, as most places don't take credit. If you'd rather not be the one clutching the steering wheel, **Coral Coaches** (☎4098 2600) departs from Port Douglas three times a week.

The inland route to Cooktown is not as exciting in terms of four-wheel driving as the coastal track, but it's mostly paved. The amazing landscape will leave your jaw agape as you wind through thick rainforest and over mountainous terrain and green hills. The Brahma cattle that roam the road on certain sections, especially in the late afternoon, can pose a threat to drivers; nevertheless, kangaroos and wallabies reign as the top roadside decoration. Better road conditions allow drivers to focus less on the next pothole and more on the fantastic views.

BLOOMFIELD TRACK. Hold on to your hats! The track, while attempted by locals in 2WD, is a playground for those who want an intense 4WD experience. From Cape Tribulation, the road turns to dirt. A little over an hour later is **Wujal Wujal**, a tiny Aboriginal community with a **convenience store** and a basic **service station.** (☎4060 8101. Store open M-Th 8am-4:30pm, F 8am-noon; service station open M-Th 8am-4:30pm, F 8am-11:30am.) Off the road, **Bloomfield Falls** are a terrific place to relax after the hard ride, but watch out for those feisty crocs.

Between Wujal Wujal and Cooktown, the mountains pull back from the coast as you drive on a dirt road through the dry savannah. North of the bridge to Wujal Wujal, the road is much less treacherous. Along the way, there are occasional general stores and small-town hotels. An **IGA Express,** in Ayton, has basic groceries and supplies as well as a phone and toilets around the corner. (Open M-F 8:30am-5:30pm, Sa-Su 8:30am-4pm.) **Bloomfield Cabins and Camping ❷** serves lunch and dinner ($5-15) and has rooms for 2 from $49. (☎4060 8207; www.bloomfieldscab-ins.com.) The final one and a half hour stretch of road before Cooktown leads to the **Lion's Den Hotel ❷,** where records of countless wayfarers are scrawled over the walls inside. (☎4060 3911. Open daily 8am-late. Beer $3.50, pub grub $12 per plate. Campsites with showers $5 per person. **Pay phone** in front.)

INLAND ROUTE. There are a handful of interesting stop-offs on this route through the farm and grasslands of the Far North. The prettiest, **Mount Molloy,** is a 10min. drive (27km) southwest of Mossman on Peninsula Developmental Rd. The **Mount Molloy National Hotel ❷** is a large, aged building built in 1901. The rooms are a bit dusty, but homey, with comfy beds and a pub downstairs. (☎4094 1133. Reception at pub 10am-midnight. Meals $9-15, specials $6. Singles $25; doubles $40.) A **picnic area** with hiking info and public restrooms is 500m from the hotel.

Mount Carbine sits 28km north of Mt. Malloy. Once a prosperous mining town, it now consists of three roadside buildings. The **Mount Carbine Roadhouse ❶** has petrol, food, backpacker lodging, and Brahma bulls outside. (☎4094 3043. Meals $5-7, milkshakes $3. Open daily 7am-7pm. Singles $15; doubles $25; extra person $5. EFTPOS accepted. V.)

Continuing north, the road begins to literally cut through the hills, with walls of stone outcroppings flanking the pavement. The **Palmer River Roadhouse ❶,** 110km north of Mt. Molloy, is decorated with various murals tracing the area's mining history and offers standard Far North pub fare. (☎4060 2020. Open daily 7am-10pm. Sites $5.50; powered caravan sites $12.50. No credit cards; EFTPOS.) Farther north (145km from Mt. Molloy), the bitumen gives way to a gravelly, snaky descent through the hills with beautiful views of the landscape.

THE LOCAL STORY

COOKTOWN ADVENTURES

Linda Rowe wrote Paradise Found: A Cape York Adventure *about her experiences as owner of Cooktown's Croc Shop and her love for the region. Interview June 21, 2002.*

Q: So did you just camp out there for eight or nine years?

A: I lived in a tent for 5 years, but then I got pretty upmarket and got a caravan. I just lived right on the side of the Wenlock River. And then for the shop, there was a little tarp on the roof. People would kind of come down, drive through the river, pull up at the shop. Some people would camp for the night, or else just drive to the top of the river bank and just carry on.

Q: How did you originally get up there—just with a 4WD?

A: Yeah, just driving around Australia, and thought, I'll go up there. It was fun. One thing that everybody's fascinated by are the crocodiles. One time these poor bikers came through and asked where they could sleep the night because they were in swags. By midnight, I heard this guy screaming and raced up there to see what was going on. This huge 8m python just came down out of the tree and there's dinner. Luckily for him, it started swallowing from the elbow—he couldn't open his jaws wide enough for his head so he spat him out. All his mates are saying, "Look, you had a nightmare." Then I had a look at his arm and it was all instantly black and blue and there's sort of blood all up his arms. People worry about crocodiles and they don't realize that there are man-eating pythons up there as well.

COOKTOWN ☎ 07

In the winter, the south wind sweeps through Cooktown's dusty streets, bringing with it the travelers who have abandoned the monotony of packaged tours and pre-paid holidays. Many find themselves staying longer than they planned, captivated by the life in a town where the bars close when the last patron leaves and shoes are an infrequent sight. Though Europeans arrived here in 1770 when Captain Cook's ship, the *Endeavor*, was grounded on the Great Barrier Reef, Cooktown's residents do not want to see much more change or development take place. The discovery of gold a century later at nearby Palmer's field turned the sleepy town into a port metropolis with over 30,000 residents. When the gold ran out, almost everyone picked up their stakes and sojourned to the southern goldfields. The tenacity of the 1600 who remain today has created a history-rich, eccentric community, full of small-town friendliness.

▐ TRANSPORTATION

Buses: Coral Coaches (☎ 4098 2600) has service between Cooktown and Cairns. Endeavour Farms Trading Post is the local ticketing agent. To Cairns by inland route (5hr.; W, F, and Su 2:30pm; $68) via Lakeland (1¼hr.), Cape Tribulation (4¼hr.), Cow Bay (4¾hr.), Kuranda (4¾hr.), Mareeba (4¼hr.), Mossman (6hr.), Mt. Carbine (3¼hr.), Mt. Molloy (3½hr.), and Port Douglas (6½hr.); or by coastal route (7½hr.; Tu, Th, and Sa 3pm; $64) via Lion's Den (30min.).

Car Rental: The aptly named **Cooktown Car Hire** (☎ 4069 5007) is one of the only options this far north. It has **4WD** starting at $99.

Taxis: Cooktown Taxis (☎ 4069 5387). Service from 6:30am to when the pubs close.

Automobile Club: RACQ, Cape York Tyres (☎ 4069 5233), at the corner of Charlotte and Furneaux St. 24hr. towing. Open M-F 7am-7pm, Sa-Su 7:30am-6pm.

Service: AMPOL Station (☎ 4069 5354), at the corner of Hope and Howard St., has groceries. Open 24hr. EFTPOS. AmEx.

▐✦ ▐ PRACTICAL INFORMATION

Cooktown Development Rd. becomes **Hope St.** as it runs north toward **Grassy Hill.** Two blocks to the west, **Charlotte St.** holds most of Cooktown's shops and services. It's crossed by several streets, including Boundary, Howard, Hogg, and Walker St. Heading east on Walker St. leads to the Botanic Gardens and Finch Bay. At the northern-most end of town, Charlotte St. runs along the water, curves eastward, and becomes **Webber Esplanade** but is not a through road.

Tourist Office: The Croc Shop (☎ 4069 5880), on Charlotte St. next to Anzac Park. Visit local legend Linda Rowe (see **The Local Story,** p. 424) for tips on trekking to the top. Open M-F 8:30am-5:30pm, Sa 8:30am-noon.

Banks: Westpac (☎ 4069 6960), on Charlotte St., between Green and Furneaux St., has an **ATM** but no currency exchange. Open M-F 9am-4:30pm.

Police: (☎ 4069 5320), across from the wharf on Charlotte St. Staffed M-F 8am-4pm; after hours, use intercom at the office door.

Medical Center: Cooktown Hospital (☎ 4069 5433), on the corner of Ida St. and the Cooktown Developmental Rd., on the way out of town heading south.

Internet: Cooktown Computer Stuff (☎ 4069 6010), on Charlotte at Green St. Open M-Su 9am-5pm $6 per hr., min. $2 charge.

Post Office: (☎ 4069 5347), on Charlotte St., across from the Sovereign Hotel. Open M-F 9am-5pm. **Postal Code:** 4871.

📷🛏 ACCOMMODATIONS AND FOOD

Pam's Place (☎ 4069 5166), at the corner of Charlotte and Boundary St., is the back-packer hub of Cooktown. Perks include large kitchen, linens, laundry, bar, pool table, swimming pool, garden, and morning shuttles to the bus station and airport. Key deposit $10. Bike hire. Sites $8; dorms $19; singles $36; doubles $46. EFTPOS $1 per transaction. YHA. MC/V 3.5% surcharge. ❶

Seagren's Inn, 12 Charlotte St. (☎ 4069 5357). An historic building dating back to 1880, with a restaurant and accommodations. 6-bed dorms $20; doubles and family rooms $55-95. ❷

Hillcrest Bed and Breakfast (☎ 4069 5305; www.cooktowninfo.com), at the base of Grassy Hill on Hope St., is a pleasant B&B with a sunny garden, veranda, pool, and res-taurant. Laundry. Doubles $50, extra person $5-10; 3 motel units with TV, A/C, and bath $65. Continental breakfast 7am-9am $7. MC/V. ❸

Alamanda Inn (☎/fax 4069 5203), across from the Ampol station on the corner of Hope and Howard St., offers tidy guest house rooms amidst beds of flowers. All rooms have A/C, fridge, TV, and sink. Singles $40; doubles $55; family units $75. MC/V. ❸

Cooktown Caravan Park (☎ 4069 5536; www.cooktowncaravanpark.com), on Hope St., at the end of Developmental Rd., is one of the nicest places to camp in Cooktown, fea-turing perhaps the best showers in all of Australia. Owners John and Mary Noonan will enthusiastically reveal the area's must-see spots. Sites $16, powered $19. ❷

Groceries can be purchased at the **IGA Supermarket,** on the corner of Hogg and Helen St. (☎ 4069 5633. Open M-W and Sa 8am-6pm, Th-F 8am-7pm, Su 10am-3pm.)

👁 SIGHTS

JAMES COOK HISTORICAL MUSEUM. The crown jewel of a town obsessed with the landing of Captain Cook, this former Catholic convent, built in 1889, has been expanded and renovated to house relics from Captain Cook's voyage, including the anchor and cannon he jettisoned here. A recent addition to the building is the Endeavour Gallery, which exhibits Cook's famous ship. *(On Helen St. at Furneaux St. ☎ 4069 5386. Open daily 9:30am-4pm. $7, discounts for children.)*

COOKTOWN CEMETERY. This cemetery, with its highly segregated plots divided into sections for white, Aboriginal, and Jewish residents, is the subject of many legends. The Chinese Shrine lies at the farthest left-hand corner of the cemetery, where 30,000 slaves and their possessions were buried. Fact sheets about the cemetery can be found at any local accommodation. (*On McIvor River-Cooktown Rd.*)

OTHER SIGHTS. Twenty years ago, the city brought the **Botanic Gardens,** off Walker St., back to life after they were left to decay following the gold rush. The locals swim at **Finch Bay,** reached by following Walker St. to its end. The walking path leading to the bay branches into the trail to secluded **Cherry Tree Bay.** The trail from Cherry Tree Bay to the lookout is not well-marked at the beach, and its challenging vertical inclines are unsuitable for small children. Along the road to the lighthouse, on **Grassy Hill,** is an excellent lookout; from the lighthouse you can see the ocean and reef. During the Queen's Birthday weekend in June (June 6-10, 2003), the **Cooktown Discovery Festival** features truck-pulling and pie-eating competitions, reenactments of Captain Cook's landing, and other entertainments.

CAPE YORK   ☎ 07

The Cape consists of rugged, intense landscape and narrow mountain roads, a journey that's both a challenge and a risk. There are three ways to see Cape York: by reading about it in a book, by traveling with a professional guide, or by going with your friends—if y'all have a 4WD, some wilderness experience, and a thirst for adventure. This trek is not for the faint-hearted, and it would make for a less than ideal holiday weekend. (While spectacular, the area is also isolated from many basic services, and, depending on road conditions, the trip up and back may take up to 2 weeks.) But those who do make an attempt, or who drive even part of the southern route, are rewarded with gorgeous sunsets, lush savannahs, packs of wild hogs, inquisitive kangaroos, silver-crested cockatoos, and much more. Cape York is nature in its pristine form, for better and for worse.

THE BASE OF THE CAPE

Even if you haven't the time, the money, or the stamina for the full journey up the Cape, you can get an exciting sample of wilderness within a reasonable distance of Cooktown. A good two- to three-day trip runs 62km north of Lakeland along **Peninsula Developmental Rd.** to the famed Aboriginal rock art at Split Rock, the outpost town of Laura, the truckstop at Musgrave (2hr. north, entrance to the **Lakefield National Park**), and then east along the rugged **Lakefield Rd.** and **Battle Camp Track** to complete the circuit. Many people take this road in 2WD, though during the Wet, 4WD might be necessary. If you travel on Battle Camp Rd., you'll ford at least three rivers and graze large potholes, making even short distances longer to cross.

Just like the roads, Cape York natives are tough as nails. There's close to nothing in these towns, so don't go looking for the Holiday Inn. **Laura** (pop. 100) has the **Quickan Hotel ❸.** (☎4060 3255. Open daily 10am-midnight; breakfast 7-8am, lunch 11:30am-1:30pm, dinner 7-8pm. Meals from $11. Sites $5, powered $8; beds $28, with all meals $58.) Limited supplies are available next to the pub at **The Ampol Station Laura.** (☎4060 3238. Open daily 7:30am-6pm.) The **Ang-gnarra Visitors Center,** across from the Laura Cafe, has a practically treeless **Caravan Park ❶** with a pool, laundry, and not quite sparkling bathrooms. (☎4060 3214. $5, powered $6.) Laura's one must-see sight—and it is amazing—is **Split Rock,** a series of ancient Aboriginal art sites. (15min. self-guided walk $5; 3hr. walk $10.) Bring a hat, sunscreen, hiking shoes, and water. The **Ang-gnarra Aboriginal Corporation** (☎4060 3200) offers tours.

An hour southwest of Laura (50km, 4WD only), the Aboriginal-run **Jowalbinna Bush Camp ❶** also offers tours. (☎4060 3236. Sites $11 per person per night; cabins

$69; permanent tents $80. Half-day tour of rock art sites $80, full-day $115; meals included.) Call the **Adventure Company ❷** (☎4051 4777) to book cabins, meals, and tours. (Breakfast $11, lunch $14, dinner $25.) The first pit stop north of Laura on Peninsula Developmental Rd. is 75km away, in Lakefield National Park. It's the **Hann River Road House ❶,** run by Bushy and his sister Sue. Pitch your tent here and fill up on gas or a tasty burger. (☎4060 3242. Sites $6; caravans $10; rooms $18.)

LAKEFIELD NATIONAL PARK

This region of mango-lined floodland features forests, plains, lagoons, and rivers and is Queensland's second largest national park. From October to December, the average temperature in the park is near 36°C (97°F), and thunderstorms are common; in the Wet (Dec.-Apr.) the park is completely inaccessible.

Musgrave, on the Peninsula Development Rd. and 138km north of Laura, is the perfect juncture for exploring the park. The tiny town includes the **Musgrave Roadhouse** (☎4060 3229; open daily 7:30am-10pm), **Musgrave Roadhouse Pub,** and **Musgrave Roadhouse Lodge ❶.** (Sites $5; singles $30; doubles $48.) In good conditions, the 4WD-only drive from Musgrave to Lakefield Ranger Station takes about three hours; Cooktown to New Laura Ranger Station via Battle Camp Rd. (4WD only) takes three hours; Cairns to Laura takes five hours.

To strike the heart of the park, travel back toward Cooktown along the **Battle Camp Track,** named after a battle between miners and Aborigines during the gold rush; though, drivers might attest it should be named after their own battle with the elements. During the Wet, the track is submerged in water, but in the Dry, Lakefield is transformed into a bird sanctuary extravaganza. Crocodiles, feral pigs, and wallaroos are also commonly spotted critters—keep that in mind as you drive through its three rivers. After entering the Battle Camp Track, north of Musgrave, travel east along the clearly-marked track past Lowlake. Bring some emergency supplies and be prepared for a long trip. It could take you seven hours or more to drive that route. Also be aware that locals avoid the route, so you may be alone for quite a while if something goes wrong.

Camping ❶ in these areas is by permit only ($3.85); these can be obtained through self-registration at any of the three stations (assuming spaces are available). The **ranger station** is located in the middle of the park, 112km from Musgrave. Registration for Kalpowar, Seven Mile, Melaleuca, Hanushs, and Midway sites can be obtained here. There are also boards with information on current road conditons, from both the rangers and from anyone who is passing through and has been on the roads. (☎/fax 4060 3271. Open daily 9am-5pm.) Camping in the southern half of the park requires a permit from the New Laura Ranger Station, while the Lakefield base requires a northern camping permit. There are also stations at Lakefield, Bizant, and at Hann Crossing. *Never camp as close as 50m to any water, as the entire park is infested with estuarine crocodiles.* If you want to catch a glimpse of the crocs, shine a powerful light at the water during the night, keeping a good distance away from the water's edge, and you will see their red eyes glaring just underneath the surface.

COEN   ☎07

North of Musgrave, Peninsula Developmental Rd. swerves up and down. Its frequent dips are often filled with small creeks, which can swell to rivers during the Wet. After 109km, the road reaches **Coen** (pop. 300 on a busy day). There's not much to do here; most visitors just stop in on their way to the top to fill up on petrol and provisions. Make sure that you have enough cash on hand, as many places in town do not accept credit cards.

Most services are found on Regent St. The **Ambrust General Store** offers groceries, petrol, pay phone, and camping. (☎4060 1134. Store open daily 7:30am-6pm.)

Many establishments here close or operate minimally during the Wet. The **QPWS** office (www.epa.qld.gov.au) has info packets on nearby parks and campgrounds.

🏠**Homestead Guest House ❸**, filled with gold rush memorabilia, is a bit of a time capsule. (☎ 4060 1157. Laundry and kitchen. Reception 7am-9pm. Singles $40.15; twins and family rooms $29.15 per person. No credit cards.) The pub and social center of Coen is the **Exchange Hotel ❸**, with beer, pool table, and pay phone. (☎ 4060 1133. Reception 10am-10pm. Hotel singles $39, doubles $50. Self-contained motel singles $52, doubles $72.)

NORTH OF COEN

Another 65km north along Peninsula Developmental Rd., a track of red earth and white sand filled with dips (read: miniature rivers cutting through the road) at every turn, leads to the **Archer River Roadhouse ❶**. This place is a nexus of travelers venturing to and from the Tip and is a welcome reminder that, yes, life exists somewhere along these lonesome roads. The kitchen serves the usual fare of beer, burgers (including the famous Archer Burger), and full meals ($16). Three-bed units and one double are modern, clean, and well-maintained. A suitable campground is also available. (☎/fax 4060 3266. Reception 7am-10pm. Sites $6 per person; singles $40; doubles $60.) Parts of the nearby **Archer River** dries up in the Dry. Camping is popular from June to September. Northeast of the Archer River, **Iron Range National Park** (128km to the Ranger Station) is the largest area of tropical lowland rainforest in Australia, filled with cuscus, parrots, butterflies, and the northern native cat. Access to the park is very difficult, in both the Wet and Dry seasons; be both well-equipped and experienced if you plan to visit. Those who take on the challenge will be rewarded with perfect solitude and great fishing.

Beyond the Archer River, Peninsula Developmental Rd. bears west to the bauxite-mining town of **Weipa,** where those not into fishing or bauxite ore will probably be bored to pieces. Many who do make the trek go for the jobs; for those with a work visa and a willingness to brave the elements, the journey might be worth it. From Weipa, **Telegraph Rd.** forks off to the north toward **Jardine River National Park** and the town of **Bamaga** at the very tip of the Cape. This section of the trip, while long and often strenuous, is often the most rewarding.

THE TREK TO THE TIP

If you've ventured past Coen, you are probably heading to the Tip. Travel from Coen onwards should be well-planned; make sure you have enough water, fuel, food, and time. Visiting the Cape is a battle, whether it's against crocs, river crossings, or the long, bumpy roads. Still, the victory is oh-so-sweet. North of the Archer River, the Cape's jungle becomes wilder, its heat hotter, its tracks rougher, and its wet season wetter. The trip all the way to the Torres Strait, which separates Australia from Papua New Guinea, is only for the hardest-of-the-hardcore, born-for-the-bush traveler. And what's to do there? Walk a kilometer from the northernmost campground, stick your toe in the water, write your name in the sand, turn around, and head back to civilization. Unless you own a car, you can't get to the northernmost point without spending some hard cash on a 4WD. **Britz,** 411 Sheridan St., Cairns, has a four-day minimum for 4WDs or campers going to the top of the peninsula. If you're deciding whether or not to pay for full-coverage insurance (see **Insurance at a Glance,** p.77), just take a look at the pictures of some of the vehicles who have attempted the Tip. (☎ 1800 331 454. In the Dry, 4WD from $194 per day, campers from $231, not including insurance. Open daily 8am-4:30pm.)

Aside from renting a 4WD, **tour packages** are often the only option. Departing from Cairns, retired bombardiers air-drop mail over the Cape on **Cape York Air;** pilots will let passengers accompany them on their daily runs. (☎ 4035 9399. $236-472. Tu and Sa tours to the Cape $670.) If you can scramble up as far as the Jardine

River, **John Charlton's Cape York Boat Adventure** can show you the rest for a very reasonable fare. (☎ 4069 3302. Full-day trips start at $125; self-drive $475.) **Billy Tea Bush Safaris,** an award-winning company, combines 4WD, flying, and boating in their trips to Cape York from Cairns. (☎ 4032 0077. Trips from $2100.)

CENTRAL AND WESTERN QUEENSLAND

Queensland's interior is unforgiving—water is scarce and constant threats, such as locusts, have hardened farmers. There are no "cowboys" here. The correct title for a greenhorn is "jackaroo" (see **The Local Story,** p. 224)—or "jilleroo," as the gender may be. From the third year, a worker comes to be called a "stationhand," and, from this point on, to refer to him or her as a "jackaroo" or "jilleroo" is a strike against his or her pride. While outback towns can be unkind or indifferent to outsiders, the people here maintain an ethic of trust. A peculiar sort of fierce friendliness often serves to convey their intense pride in the isolated lands they inhabit. Folks look you in the eye, and if they don't like what they see, you'll know it.

Queensland's vast interior is traversed by a few highways, unsealed in patches. Generally in better shape than north-south roads, there are several east-west routes: the **Warrego Hwy. (54)** goes west from Brisbane eventually reaching the Mitchell Hwy.; the **Capricorn** and **Landsborough Hwy. (66),** from Rockhampton to the Gemfields, Barcaldine, and Mt. Isa; the **Flinders Hwy. (78),** from Townsville through Charters Towers and Hughenden to Mt. Isa; and the **Gulf Development Rd. (1),** including part of the **Kennedy Hwy.,** from the Atherton Tablelands outside Cairns through the Gulf Savannah to Normanton. Connecting them all, the so-called **Matilda Hwy.,** the major north-south road, actually encompasses fragments of the Mitchell, Landsborough, and Capricorn Hwy. and the Burke Developmental Rd.

CAPRICORN AND LANDSBOROUGH HWY.

The road west from Rockhampton cuts a diagonal through Queensland's Gemfields. **Route 66** is called the **Capricorn Hwy.** until its junction with the Matilda Hwy. in Barcaldine when it becomes the **Landsborough Hwy.,** which passes through Longreach and Winton and meets the Flinders Hwy. two hours east of Mt. Isa.

GEMFIELDS

Wanna be a millionaire? You might try digging in the dirt in Queensland's Gemfields. Fossicking in this area draws thousands of tourists each year. The income is hardly steady, but it can be lucrative. An unemployed couple recently uncovered a gem worth a million dollars, and a 14-year-old matched that a few years back.

The folks at **Namoi Hills Cattle Station ❷** will take you to the Gemfields for a day of sapphire satisfaction guaranteed. If you don't find a jewelry-quality sapphire, they'll refund your money ($155). The ranch itself alternates between being a quiet cattle station and a typical backpacker's bonanza replete with drinking, tabledancing and other such bonding activities. This transformation takes place every other day when the Oz Experience buses pull into camp. (☎ 4935 9277. Make-your-own didgeridoo day $160. Beds $18; including dinner, continental breakfast, and a tour featuring didgeridoo playing, whip cracking, and boomerang throwing $40.)

Affluent **Emerald** (pop. 10,000), where no emerald has ever been found, is a major agricultural center for grain, cotton, and Mandarin oranges. A convenient stop on **McCafferty's/Greyhound** (☎ 4982 2755) route to Mt. Isa, the town is a stepping-off point for the Gemfields. Stop at the **Central Highlands Visitor Information Centre,** in the center of town on Clermont St., before venturing into the Gemfields.

During the second week of August, the Gemfields come to Emerald for the annual **Gemfest.** (☎ 4982 4142. Open M-Sa 9am-5pm, Su 10am-2pm.) The new **Central Inn ❸,** 90 Clermont St., has clean rooms with TV. (☎ 4982 0800. Breakfast included. Singles $39; doubles $49.) There's a Coles **supermarket** on the corner of Clermont and Opal St. in the Market Plaza. (☎ 4982 3622. Open M-F 8am-9pm, Sa 8am-5pm.) The **Emerald Public Library,** 44 Borilla St., has free **Internet.** (☎ 4982 8347. Open M noon-5:30pm, Tu and Th 10am-5:30pm, W 10am-8pm, F 10am-5pm, Sa 9am-noon.)

Forty kilometers west of Emerald, **Anakie** lies in the prime fossicking region. This village holds the last **petrol** station for 125km, and **The Big Sapphire Info Centre,** 1 Anakie Rd. (☎ 4985 4525. Open daily 8am-6pm.) If you need some reviving, you can buy tea and cake here for $3. Most tourists drive 10-18km farther north to **Sapphire** or **Rubyvale,** where you can stop along the road to sort through pre-dug buckets of dirt ($5.50 per bucket). The **Rubyvale Caravan Park ❶,** on Main St. has a small heated pool. (☎ 4985 4118. Reception 7am-8pm. Sites $11, powered $16; cabins for 2 $45. Credit cards accepted.) Along the Capricorn Hwy., you'll pass through **Barcaldine** (bar-CALLED-in), at the junction with the Longreach Hwy. McCafferty's **buses** stop at the **BP station** on the corner of Oak and Box St. (☎ 4651 1333. Open daily 6:30am-9pm.) The **Artesian Hotel ❶,** 85 Oak St., has mostly iron-bar four-poster beds. (☎ 4651 1691. Reception 10am-noon. Singles $10; double $20; family rooms $20.) There is an IGA **supermarket** at 179 Oak St. (☎ 4651 2207. Open M-F 8am-6pm, Sa 8am-1pm.)

LONGREACH   ☎ 07

The micropolis of Longreach (pop. 4500) is the largest town in the Central West. With its own Pastoral College and School of Distance Education, Longreach acts as the public service and educational center for the area. Visitors might forget they're in the Outback when they walk down **Eagle St.,** crowded with cafes, shops, and plenty of pubs and jukeboxes to keep the town hopping.

The town's biggest attraction is not actually in town: the **Australian Stockman's Hall of Fame and Outback Heritage Centre** is a massive multimedia museum off the Landsborough Hwy. (☎ 4658 2166; www.outbackheritage.com.au. Open daily 9am-5pm. $20, ages 8-16 $9.50, under 8 free.)

McCafferty's/Greyhound buses depart from **Longreach Outback Travel,** 115A Eagle St., (☎ 4658 1776; open M-F 8:30am-5pm, Sa 8:30am-noon and 3:30-4:30pm, Su 10:30-11:15am and 3:30-4:30pm), with service to Brisbane (daily at 4:10pm; $102, concessions $82) and Rockhampton (2 per week, $65). The **Information Centre** is at Qantas Park on Eagle St. (☎ 4658 3555; www.longreach.qld.gov.au. Open M-F 9am-5pm, Sa-Su 9am-1pm.) Free **Internet** is at the **library,** 96 Eagle St. (☎ 4658 4104. Open Tu and Th 9:30am-1pm, W and F 12:30-5pm, Sa 9am-noon.)

The cheapest place to stay is the **Royal Hotel ❶,** 111 Eagle St., but keep in mind that the pub downstairs hosts a disco 9pm-2am every Friday and Saturday. (☎ 4658 2118. Reception Su-Th 10am-11pm, F-Sa 10am-2am. Dorms $11; singles $22; self-contained single units $55; doubles $66.) The **Longreach Caravan Park ❶,** 180 Ibis St. at the corner of Owl St., is a bit quieter. (☎ 4658 1770. Reception daily 7am-10:30pm. Sites $14.30, powered for 2 $16.50; self-contained cabins for 2 $50, with shared toilets $28.) The IGA Cornett **supermarket** is on the corner of Eagle and Swan St. (☎ 4658 1260. Open M-W 8am-6:30pm, Th-F 8am-8pm, Sa 8am-4pm.)

THE FLINDERS HIGHWAY

A long, lonely route, Flinders Highway is primarily a straight shot from Townsville to Mt. Isa, though it passes through quite a few small outback towns along the way. Ravenswood and Charters Towers are only a daytrip away from the coast, yet remote enough to offer a taste of the outback. As you head farther west, towns

THERE'S SOMETHING ABOUT MATILDA Win-
ton and Kynuna duke it out over the matter of *Waltzing Matilda*. Winton's North Gregory Hotel was the site of Banjo Paterson's first performance of Australia's unofficial national anthem, but truckstop Kynuna (163km northwest) is much closer to the actual billabong in the song, and *they've* got the original music score. Kynuna may be the real deal, but Winton's the site of the brand-new **Waltzing Matilda Centre,** 50 Elderslie St. With statues, holograms, and an underwater "ghost," it is probably the only center in the world dedicated to one song. (☎4657 1466; www.matildacentre.com.au. Open daily 8:30am-5pm. $14. Cafe open daily 9am-4pm.) In Kynuna, Richard Magoffin, a one-man crusade against Winton's historical inaccuracies, performs his own history of *Waltzing Matilda* at his **Swagman Hall of Fame.** (☎4746 8401. Book ahead. Open daily 8am-10pm. Show daily 7:30pm; $15. Donation required.)

only get smaller, marked only by a lower speed limit, general store, and petrol pump. Most traffic heads straight to Mt. Isa, the largest city in the world in area and a true mining outpost that serves as a gateway to the Northern Territory.

CHARTERS TOWERS   ☎07

South of the Atherton Tablelands, the land dries out and old outback towns begin to punctuate a barren landscape. Once nicknamed "The World" for its cosmopolitan flair, Charters Towers, 1½hr. (128km) west of Townsville, was the hub of Queensland, but only traces of its glory days remain in the enthusiastic residents who call this town home.

📧🛂 TRANSPORTATION AND PRACTICAL INFORMATION. The Queensland Rail Station (☎13 22 32) is on Enterprise Rd. on the east side of town. **Trains** go to Townsville (3hr., Tu and Sa 10:02am, $21) and Mt. Isa (17hr., Su and W 9:03pm, $98). **McCafferty's/Greyhound** and **Douglas buses** depart from the corner of Gill and Church St. to Townsville. (1¾hr., daily, $22.) Book tickets at **Traveland,** 13 Gill St. (☎4787 2622. Open M-F 8am-5pm, Sa 9am-noon.)

The center of Charters Towers is created by the simple T-intersection of **Mosman** and **Gill St.,** known as the **Historic City Centre.** Government offices and "The World" theater run along Mosman St., while most shops, restaurants, and banks descend down Gill St. The **Information Centre,** 74 Mosman St., is at the top of Gill St., to the left of City Hall. (☎4752 0314; www.charterstowers.qld.gov.au. Open daily 9am-5pm.) There are several **banks** with **ATMs** strung along Gill St. The **RACQ** (☎4787 2000) agent is at Gold City Wreckers, 21 Dundee Ln. The **library** is in the Old Bank, 34 Gill St. (☎4752 0338. Open M, W, and F 10am-1pm and 1:45-4:45pm; Tu and Th 1:45-4:45pm; Sa 9:30am-noon.) **Internet** is at Charters Towers Computers (open M-F 9am-4pm and Sa 9am-noon; $6 per hr.) and at the library ($5 per hr.).

🏠🍴 ACCOMMODATIONS, FOOD, AND NIGHTLIFE. The York Street Bed and Breakfast ❸, 58 York St., is a friendly place to stay but a 15min. walk from the center of town. (☎4787 1028. Lodge rooms with continental breakfast $25; rooms in house with cooked breakfast $60-70.) For something cheaper, try the **Waverly Hotel ❷** at the end of Mosman St. (☎4787 2591. Singles $22; twins $33.) **Charters Towers Caravan Park ❶,** 37 Mount Leyshon Rd., is a 20-minute walk south of town. (☎/fax 4787 7944 or 1800 357 944. Linen available. Reception 7am-7pm. BBQ Tu and Th nights. Sites for 2 $11, powered $17; ensuite caravans with A/C $29; cabins $48.)

A few of the hotels around town serve counter meals (from $5). For over 24 different dishes, go to the **Golden Mine Restaurant's ❶** smorgasbord, 64 Mosman St. (☎4787 7609. Open for lunch M-F noon-2pm, for dinner daily 5-9:30pm. Lunch $7, dinner $9.) Woolworth's, on Gill St., has **groceries**. (☎4787 3411. Open M-F 8am-9pm, Sa 8am-5pm.) Nightlife in Charters Towers is confined to **Pegasus Night Club,** 33 Gill St., in the White Horse Tavern, which plays a techno/retro mix. (☎4787 1064. Open F-Sa 10pm-3am.) All other fun goes down at the various hotels around town, with good old-fashioned beer drinking and pokies.

◩ **SIGHTS AND ACTIVITIES.** The big attraction in town is the largest **gold-producing mine** in all of Queensland. Tours are booked through the tourist office (W $13). **Gold Nugget Scenic Tours** runs a 2½hr. sight-seeing tour around town, departing the tourist office M-F at 9:30am. (☎4787 4115. $22, concessions $20.) **Geoff's City and Bush Safari** will keep you laughing and informed. (☎4787 2118. Departs daily 9:30am and 1pm. $20, children $10.) See the entire city and its sights in a 90min. **walking tour.** (☎4787 2374. Departs from Stock Exchange M-F 10am. $8.) The **Zara Clarke Museum,** at the corner of Gill and Mary St., has an authoritative display of Charters Towers memorabilia including an old fire wagon and an iron lung. (Open daily 10am-3pm. $4.40.) Two cattle stations nearby hire backpackers for a couple of weeks and offer "City Slicker" holiday packages: **Bluff Downs ❷** is a rough-and-ready real working cattle station—mud, blood, and billabongs included. This one is for those seeking the authentic Outback. (☎4770 4084. Sites for 2 $18, powered $20; dorms $20, with meals $55. No credit cards.) **Plain Creek ❸** probably better suits the tenderfoot. (☎4983 5228. Camp and caravan sites $17; full board, including bed, meals, and all activities $165.)

FROM PENTLAND TO RICHMOND

PENTLAND. About halfway between Charters Towers and Hughendon (120km from Charters and 148km from Townsville), Pentland (pop. 300), is a good place to stay if the sun is setting and the 'roos are on the road. There is a **general store** with **post office** (☎4788 1130; open M-F 9am-7pm, Sa 10am-noon, Su 5-7pm), a **Shell Service Station** (☎4788 1254; open M-F 7am-7pm, Sa-Su 7am-6pm), and a couple cheap places to stay. The **Pentland Caravan Park ❶** has sites, a swimming pool, and a convenience store. (☎4788 1148. Sites $11; powered caravan sites $13.20; singles $28; doubles $39; cabins $60.) The **Pentland Hotel ❹** serves food, and their spotless rooms have TV, fridge, and bath. (☎4788 1106. Singles $50; twins and doubles $60.)

HUGHENDEN. Hughenden (HYU-enden) marks the eastern edge of Queensland's marine dinosaur territory: stop into the **Visitor Information Centre,** 37 Gray St., to see the **Muttaburrasaurus skeleton** they've got standing in the back. Memorabilia from the gold-mining days has also been donated by local families and is on display. (☎4741 1021. Open daily 9am-5pm. $2.) Budget accommodation in Hughenden is limited to the ambitiously-named **Grand Hotel ❶,** 25 Gray St. (☎4741 1588; dorms $12; singles $15; twins and doubles $35), and the **Allan Terry Caravan Park ❶.** The caravan site is neatly kept, with swimming pool, laundry, and kitchen. (☎4741 1190. Reception M-F 6am-9pm. Sites for 2 $10, powered $14; cabins $60.) Across the street, new and immaculate rooms are a bit more expensive at **Wright's Motel ❹,** 20 Gray St. They also have a fully-licensed restaurant available for room service. (☎4741 1677. Singles $42; doubles $50.) Once in Hughenden, you're only 113km from the next outback outpost—Richmond. **Porcupine Gorge,** a pretty natural valley, is 63km north of town. **Adventure Wildlife and Bush Treks** runs from the caravan park and has full-day trips to the Gorge ($45, with food $65) and camping trips to the White Mountains and Mt. Emu Goldfields ($50 with your own vehicle). If you brave the mountains on your own, make sure to get the **required registration** at the **NPWS office** in town (☎4741 1113) or in Charters Towers (☎4787 3388).

RICHMOND. West of Hughenden along the Flinders Hwy., Richmond packs an impressive paleological punch. **Kronosaurus Korner,** 93 Goldrin St., is both the regional **Visitor Information Centre** and the **Richmond Marine Fossil Museum,** housing the bones of local Cretaceous creatures. (☎4741 3429. Open daily 8:30am-4:45pm. $9.) Heading towards Mt. Isa on the Flinders Hwy., you'll see the **BP Roadhouse,** which has a big menu, petrol, showers, and toilets. (☎4741 3316. Open daily 6am-9pm.) **Internet** is at the **library,** 78 Goldring St. across from the Visitors Center. The brand-new **Moon Rock Cafe ❶,** in the Visitors Center, cooks up a few more veggie-friendly options than the typical roadhouse ($3-4). The **Richmond Caravan Park ❶,** on your way into town from Hughendon before the Visitors Center, is of exceptional value, with newly refurnished facilities that have A/C, shared bathrooms, and kitchen. (☎4741 3772. Key deposit $10. Sites $11, powered $14; twin-share bunk house $17 per person; cabins $50.) The **Mud Hut Motel ❹,** 72 Goldring St., has pub rooms with A/C and TV, as well as dorms in the back. (☎/fax 4741 3223. Singles $44; doubles $60; dongas $20-25.) There is a BuyRite **supermarket** on Goldring St. (Open M-F 7:30am-5pm, Sa 7:30am-12:30pm, Su 7:30am-noon.)

MOUNT ISA ☎07

Years ago, when the subject of Mount Isa came up, backpackers' conversations sobered up and casual laughter dwindled. This was the city where hitchhikers on their way to the Northern Territory broke down and bought a bus ticket. With the improvement of roads, travelers can now make this long, and sometime bleak, trip without too many hassles. Besides the thousands of roadkill, not many obstacles prohibit people from making this popular—or simply necessary—trek. The motel is king, and two- and three-trailer road trains crowd the roadhouses on the outskirts of town. While here, take the time to see why so many loyal residents, who vowed only to stay a year, have settled in the Outback for life. Before heading on, take a deep breath, try not to choke, and get ready to cross the desert.

▉ **TRANSPORTATION.** The **train station** (☎4744 1203) is on Station St.; go over the Leichhardy Bridge and take a right onto Rose St. (Open M and F 11:15am-6pm, T-Th 8am-3:30pm.) The *Inlander* train departs 6pm Monday and Friday to: Charters Towers (16hr.); Hughenden (11¼hr.); Richmond (9¼hr.); Townsville (19hr.) via Cloncurry (3½hr.). **McCafferty's/Greyhound,** 27-29 Barkly Hwy., is at Campbell's Tours and Travel; from town, take Grace St. west over the river until it ends and the terminal is on your right. (☎4743 2006. Open M-F 6am-7:45pm, Sa 6-9:30am and 5:30-7:45pm.) **Buses** run to: Alice Springs ($203); Brisbane ($143); Cairns ($161); Charters Towers ($106); Darwin ($232); Richmond ($56); Rockhampton ($211); and Townsville ($113). Call **United Cab** 24hr. ☎13 10 08. **RACQ** is at 13 Simpson St. (☎4743 2542, after hours 0417 714 162.)

▉▉ **ORIENTATION AND PRACTICAL INFORMATION.** The city center is a manageable four-by-four grid, bounded by **Isa St.** to the north, **West St.** to the west, **Mary St.** to the south, and **Simpson St.** to the east. The **Barkly Hwy.** enters from Northern Territory and runs parallel to the **Leichhardt River** until the **Leichhardt Bridge** turns left over the water into the city center, becoming **Grace St.** From Cloncurry in the east, the Flinders Hwy. becomes **Marian St.**

Harvey World Travel, 27-29 Barkly Hwy., next to the McCafferty's/Greyhound terminal, is a budget travel office. (☎4743 2006. Open M-F 8am-5:30pm, Sa 9am-1pm.) The **Riversleigh Fossils Centre,** 19 Marian St., books mine tours ($20 for a surface tour, $60 to go underground; advance bookings *essential*), heritage city tours ($25.30), and several other area attractions, including four-day safaris to **Lawn Hill** ($495). (☎4749 1555. Open M-F 8:30am-4:30pm, Sa-Su 9am-2pm. Fossil Display $9, children $5, pensioners $6, families $24.) Other services include: **Commonwealth Bank,** 23 Miles St. (☎4743 5033; open M-Th 9:30am-4pm, F 9:30am-5pm); **police,** 7 Isa St., at the corner of Miles St. (☎4743 1111; open 24hr.); **Internet** at the **library,** 23 West St. (☎4744 4256; $2 per hr.; open M-Th 10am-6pm, F 10am-5pm); **post office** on the corner of Camooweal and Isa St. (☎4743 2454; open M-F 8:30am-5pm) and also in Mt. Isa Square opposite K-Mart Place. (☎13 13 18. Open M-F 8:45am-5:15pm, Sa 9am-11:45am.) **Postal Code:** 4825.

ⅱ█ ACCOMMODATIONS AND FOOD. The **Artisans Block and Sleeper ❷,** 62 Marian St., feels like home after the long roadtrip. Enjoy a cozy atmosphere and the new renovations in the back, including a crafts center, BBQ, wok, and beds underneath the stars. (☎0412 962 069. Dorms $22; singles $55; doubles with brekkie $61.) **Traveller's Haven ❷,** at the corner of Pamela and Spence St., is another budget option, with free pickup, a nice pool, and a feeling of camaraderie. (☎4743 0313. Linen $2. Key deposit $5. Reception daily 6:30am-1pm and 5-7pm. Dorms $17; singles $30; twins and doubles $40. VIP. MC/V. EFTPOS.) You'll get the best value for money at the newly renovated **Central Point Motel ❸,** 6 Marian St., which is also the most centrally located accommodation listed. (☎4743 0666. Saltwater pool. TV, A/C, bath, and kitchenette in room. Singles $66; doubles $75. AmEx. EFTPOS.) **Boyd's Hotel ❸,** 16-20 West St., near the corner of Marion St., is one of the cheapest hotels in Mt. Isa. The serviceable rooms have A/C and sinks. (☎4743 3000. Rooms $30, recommended ensuite $37.) **Mt. Isa Van Park ❶,** 112 Marian St., is clean and well tended with lots of long-term residents. (☎4743 3252. Reception daily 7:30am-6:30pm. Sites $14, powered $17; brand-new ensuite self-contained cabins for 2 with TV, A/C, and kitchen $55, extra adult $5.50, extra child $2.50.)

The **Buffalo Club ❶,** on the corner of Grace and Simpson St., offers a $9.50 all-you-can-eat lunch buffet. Look decent: collared shirt yay, sandals nay. (☎4743 2365. Open daily 8am-2am.) The **Irish Club ❶,** on the corner of Buckley and 19th Ave., has several bars, many food options, and lots of pokies. (☎4743 2577, courtesy bus 0411 427 256. Open daily 8am-3am.) Coles **supermarket** is in K-Mart Centre, on Marian St. (☎4743 6007. Open M-Sa 8am-9pm.)

◪ SIGHTS. Mt. Isa's excitement lies mostly underground, where most of its workforce toils in 12hr. shifts. Take a four-hour **Underground Mine Tour** into the belly of the beast. Put on the suit and hat and enter the winding maze of tunnels. Book through the Riversleigh Centre as far ahead as possible. (☎4749 1555. M-F 2 per day. $60.) The center also books surface mine tours ($20) as well as Aboriginal tours ($55) of the area. Australia's biggest **rodeo** comes to Mt. Isa in August, along with the world's greatest rodeo legends. **Lake Moondarra** is just 15min. west on the Barkly Hwy.; **Lake Julius** is another 90km farther and a great fishing spot. At night, view the lit-up desert from the town's **lookout** on Shacketon St., off Marian St.

THE GULF SAVANNAH

The area between the Atherton Tablelands and the Gulf of Carpentaria along the **Gulf Developmental Rd.,** the Gulf region revels in remoteness. This is the outback's Outback. The Gulf's attractions include historic "nowhere-to-nowhere" trains, gorges, and lava tubes. The Gulf can be an escapist fantasy or a city slicker's nightmare. The sea can be reached by Karumba Point Rd. off the Gulf Developmental Rd., 4km before **Karumba** (pop. 600) and 72km northwest of **Normanton.**

The Dry (Apr.-Oct.) is the time to visit, though even then the road conditions can be bad. Road reports are issued by the **Gulf Savannah Tourism,** 74 Abbott St., in Cairns (☎4051 4658; open M-F 8:30am-5pm), as well as in local info centers and RACQs. The most common route through the region is the **Gulf Developmental Rd.,** linking Cairns to Normanton, where it joins the desolate north-south **Burke Developmental Rd.** These are primarily single-lane, cattle-strewn, kangaroo-enticing sealed roads. Conventional vehicles are fine on most roads during the Dry, but caravans should avoid unsealed roads. If you want to brave the Wet, 4WD is essential. Never drive the Ootann Rd. connecting Mt. Surprise and Chillagoe or anywhere along the Mt. Isa-Riversleigh-Lawn Hill National Park route without 4WD.

The eastern Gulf's most awesome attraction is a 40min. drive from Mt. Surprise. The **Undara Volcano** erupted 190,000 years ago, creating 69 **lava tubes** in the middle of dense rainforest, with caverns averaging 10m high and 15m wide. **Undara Experience** visits nine of them. Follow their motto and "enjoy a tube with some friends." (☎4097 1411. 2hr. tour daily 8, 10:30am, 1, and 3:30pm $33; half-day tours daily 8:30am and 1pm $63.) Camp ❶ at Undara ($5 per person) or stay in the **tent village** ❷ ($18 per person; linen $6), Wilderness Lodge ❸ ($24), or Lava Lodge ❺ ($75).

Just 90km west of Undara, visit the other result of these formerly volcanic grounds—the **Tallaroo Hot Springs** ❶. Take a tour through the bubbling and boiling springs and swim in the naturally fed pool—just don't jump in the springs, as they can reach 70°C (158°F. $8.80, children $5.50. Sites $5.30, children $4.40.)

SOUTH
AUSTRALIA

Prophets of the Australian backpacking scene are known to wander the deserts of the land, telling all who listen: "There is only one South Australia, and Adelaide is its capital." Amazingly, this message has been heeded by a relatively small number of pilgrims. Most travelers bypass the chosen land and race from Melbourne to Uluru via requisite stopovers in Adelaide and Coober Pedy. But for those who take the time to learn and love this state, with its fly-specked and harsh but beautiful Outback north, the lovely coasts of the Eyre and Fleurieu Peninsulas, and Adelaide, the world's biggest country town, a new truth about the east coast will become evident: the best thing about Queensland's touristy beaches is the road toward South Australia.

Highway 87, which connects Coober Pedy with Port Augusta to the south and Alice Springs to the north, will remind the most forgetful of city slickers where exactly humanity stands on the scale of things: the stars up above join together in the glowing white choir of the Milky Way, and the harshest, driest, most sun-scorched country this side of the SA-WA border will either capture your heart and imagination or send you scrambling for the next bus to someplace wetter. The ancient Flinders Ranges, a portfolio of spectacular sculpting by five billion years of geological processes, is generally known more for wildlife than for nightlife (if one discounts all the nocturnal animals roaming the bush), but in nearby Parachilna, the backpacker gods handed down one hell of a good time.

Here, in the driest state on the driest continent on earth, the population chants this mantra: save water, drink wine. While Coopers' line of beers is the homebrew, a good chunk of the state's economy rests on the fine vintages produced throughout the state: the Barossa and Clare valleys east-northeast of Adelaide, the McLaren Vale and Fleurieu Peninsula region to the south of the capital, and the Coonawarra region all provide a more refined way to get bloody pissed.

South Australia's long coastline offers everything: sheltered bays for swimming; surfing beaches exposed to the great Southern Ocean where the waves roll in, high and mighty; large populations of seals, sea lions, and steel-blue fairy penguins; on-site locations from the filming of *Jaws;* great fishing from any angle; and a breezy respite from the oft-raging inferno further inland.

⌐ TRANSPORTATION

If you don't have a car, the best way to see South Australia is by bus. **McCafferty's/ Greyhound** (☎ 13 14 99 or 13 20 30) runs between Adelaide and Melbourne, Sydney, Alice Springs, and Perth, stopping over at a few destinations in between. **Premier Stateliner** (☎ 8415 5555) services smaller towns throughout South Australia. Three major train lines run through South Australia: the **Overland** to Melbourne, the *Indian Pacific* to Perth, and the legendary *Ghan* to Alice Springs. For more train information, see **By Train**, p. 440.

Major **car rental** companies with branches in SA include **Hertz** (☎ 13 30 39), **Avis** (☎ 13 63 33), and **Thrifty** (☎ 1300 367 277). Local outfits, often with lower prices, are

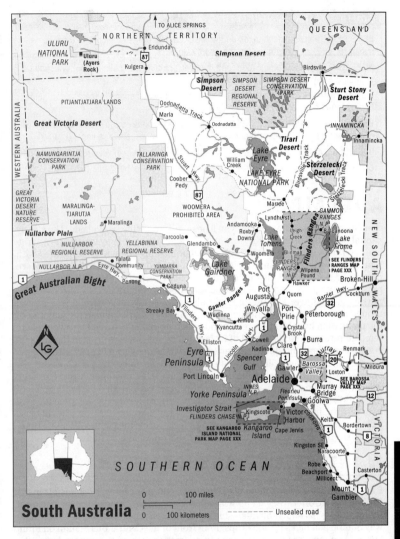

South Australia

listed throughout this chapter. A conventional vehicle is fine for wine and beach country, but 4WD is strongly recommended for forays into the outback. Another good option, often more practical for those traveling alone or going to more remote places, is to book a **tour.** Many choose the jump-on, jump-off flexibility of backpacker buses like the youthful **Oz Experience** (☎ 1300 30 00 28) or the twenty-something favorite, **Wayward Bus** (☎ 8232 6646); plenty of local organizations also run excellent trips. Most hostels give tour advice and book for guests, often at a discount. Still, the greatest way to see the state is to buy a used car or 4WD and sell it when leaving the country—this provides the ultimate in freedom and flexibility.

SOUTH AUSTRALIA HIGHLIGHTS

EYRE PENINSULA. Find yourself on the deserted, cliff-fringed beaches of the Eyre Peninsula (p. 496) or lose yourself in the nearby Outback. (p. 491)

ADELAIDE. Relax and enjoy good food, festivals, culture, and calm in South Australia's capital, the city of churches. (p. 438)

FLINDERS RANGES. Gain a new perspective on time and space in the ancient, gently folding mountains of the Flinders Ranges. (p. 483)

KANGAROO ISLAND. Sleep under the tranquil Australian stars in the company of echidnas, fur seals, goannas, kangaroos, koalas, wallabies, and sea lions. (p. 459)

BAROSSA VALLEY. Enjoy the fruits of South Australia's premier wine region. (p. 467)

COOBER PEDY. Chill out in the underground hostels of Coober Pedy. (p. 492)

ADELAIDE ☎ 08

"Quality of life" is a catch-phrase you'll hear and read often in Adelaide. The stately capital of South Australia, *Tandanya*, the place of the red kangaroo to the Aboriginal Kaurna people, is a surprisingly cosmopolitan big country town, infused with a progressive attitude and a determination to enjoy life. South Australians are proud of Adelaide, and visitors will find themselves smitten by its parklands and museums, its proximity to beaches and wineries, and its devotion to nightlife, music, and culture. The first completely planned city in Australia is centered around a one-mile-square grid, separated from the suburbs, where the majority of the population lives by vast green parklands. The city is pervaded by a youth-centered culture while still mindful of its heritage; residents take pride in the graceful colonial buildings and flourishing arts scene while enjoying a big-city lifestyle.

Life's finer pleasures are far less expensive in Adelaide than in its east coast counterparts. With more restaurants per capita than any other Australian city, Adelaide can satisfy any palate at any budget and wash it all down with some of the world's best wines. The city's cultural attractions, headed by the Adelaide Festival of Arts, include a symphony, small experimental theaters, and world-class galleries and museums. For those seeking a faster pace, the nightclubs along Hindley St., the pubs in the city center, and the cafes on Rundle St. fit the bill.

✖ INTERCITY TRANSPORTATION

BY PLANE. The **Adelaide Airport** is 7km west of the city center. Most hostels in the city or Glenelg offer free pickup with advance booking. Failing that, the cheapest way is the **Skylink Airport Shuttle,** which runs to both the airport and Keswick Railway Station and picks up and drops off in front of the Central Bus Station on Franklin St. You must pre-book by phone to go from the city to the airport, but at the airport you can catch the bus at the domestic terminal directly in front of the currency exchange, or to the left as you exit the international terminal. (☎8332 0528; bookings 7am-10pm. Daily, every 30min., 5am-9pm; $7, return $12.) For two or more people, a **taxi** will end up being cheaper and more convenient than the Skylink bus. **Taxis** to the city run $11-15.

International travelers can get huge discounts on domestic one-way fares. **Regional Express (Rex)** (☎13 17 13; www.regionalexpress.com.au), formed from the merging of Kendell and Hazelton Airlines in August, 2002, is the biggest local carrier, with flights to 35 South Australian cities, including Coober Pedy, Kangaroo Island, Mt. Gambier,

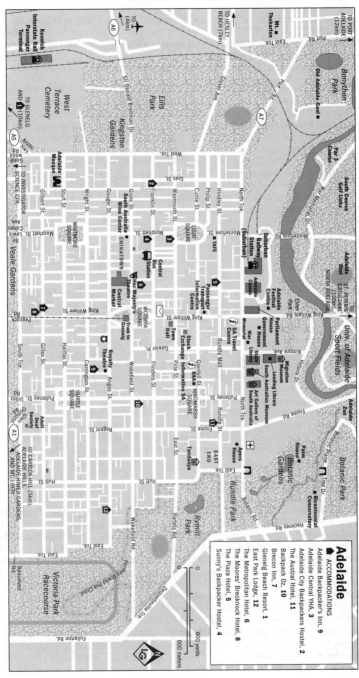

SOUTH AUSTRALIA

Adelaide

ACCOMMODATIONS

Adelaide Backpacker's Inn, 9
Adelaide Central YHA, 3
Adelaide City Backpackers Hostel, 2
The Austral Hotel, 11
Backpack Oz, 10
Brecon Inn, 7
Glenelg Beach Resort, 1
East Park Lodge, 12
The Metropolitan Hotel, 6
The Moores' Brecknock Hotel, 8
The Plaza Hotel, 5
Sunny's Backpacker Hostel, 4

TO PORT ADELAIDE (12km)
Keswick Interstate Rail Passenger Terminal
TO GLENELG AND (10km)
TO INVESTIGATOR SCIENCE CTR
TO HENLEY BEACH (7km)
TO ADELAIDE (4km)
Bonython Park
Old Adelaide Gaol
Mt. Thebarton
West Terrace Cemetery
Ellis Park
Kingston Gardens
Bonwood Rd
Anzac Hwy
Yeale Gardens
Sir Donald Bradman Dr.
West Tce.
Glover Ave.
Port Rd.
East Tce.
South Course Golf Links
Par 3 Course
Adelaide Oval
NORTH ADELAIDE
War Memorial Dr.
Montefiore Rd.
ST PETER'S CATHEDRAL (100m)
Univ. of Adelaide
Adelaide Sport Fields
Univ. of Adelaide Sport Fields
Adelaide Mosque
Gilbert St.
Sturt St.
Wright St.
Gouger St.
Morphett St.
Gilles St.
Halifax St.
Carrington St.
Pulteney St.
Regent St.
Gray St.
Hindley St.
Currie St.
Philip St.
Waymouth St.
Grote St.
Franklin St.
North Tce.
South Australia Wine Center
CHINATOWN
Central Bus Station
Passenger Transport Information Centre
TAFE
LIGHT SQUARE
Suburban Railway Station
Adelaide Festival Centre
Adelaide Casino
Parliament House
Government House
War Memorial
SA Travel Centre
State Library
Migration Museum
South Australian Museum
Art Gallery of South Australia
Elder Park
Kintore Ave.
Victoria Dr.
Adelaide Zoo
Pain House
Bicentennial Conservatory
Botanic Park
Botanic Gardens
Botanic Rd.
Hackney Rd.
Frome Rd.
Tree Rd.
Central Market
Her Majesty's
Theatre
VICTORIA SQUARE
Town Hall
Tram to Glenelg
Royalty Theatre
King William St.
Gawler Pl.
Stock Exchange
Information SA
Pirie St.
Flinders St.
Grenfell St.
Rundle Mall
Rundle St.
RAA
HINDMARSH SQUARE
East St.
Frome St.
Pulteney St.
North Tce.
Ayers House
EAST END
Tandanya
HURTLE SQUARE
Angas St.
Wakefield St.
Hutt St.
Bartels Rd.
Rundle Park
Rymill Park
Adult Deaf Society
Glen Osmond Rd.
TO GARRICK HILL (3km), ADELAIDE HILLS, AND MT. LOFTY.
TO ADELAIDE HIMEJI GARDENS, AND MT. LOFTY.
East Tce.
South Tce.
East Tce.
Wakefield Rd.
Flemington Grand Prix Circuit
Victoria Park Racecourse
Fullarton Rd.
Beaumont Rd.
Dequetteville Tce.

0   600 yards
0   600 meters

A6
A7
A5
A1

and Port Lincoln. Prices have varied widely since the merger. **Airlines of South Australia (ASA; ☎8682 5688** or **1800 018 234)** services Port Lincoln and Port Augusta. **O'Conner** services Mt. Gambier and Mildura. **Emu Airways (☎8234 3711** or **1800 182 343)** services Kangaroo Island ($206). **Virgin Blue (☎13 67 89)** and **Qantas (☎13 13 13)** also offer competitive fares, and local backpackers travel agencies can often get you discounts.

BY TRAIN. Student prices for train travel have begun to rival those for bus travel, and it can be a good option for those who put comfort first (imagine spending 34 hours on a bus). All interstate and long-distance country trains use the **Keswick Interstate Rail Passenger Terminal (☎13 21 47)**, which is just off the southwest corner of the central city grid, about 1km west of West Tce. The **Skylink Airport Shuttle** stops at Keswick and drops off at the central bus station and several points downtown. (☎8332 0528. Daily every 30min. 5am-9pm; $3.50, return $6. Book ahead.) **Taxis** from the city run about $6. The Keswick terminal has parking. Only suburban commuter trains use the **Adelaide Railway Station (☎8218 2277)**, on North Tce.

The **Australian Rail Travel Centre**, 18-20 Grenfell St., lets you buy tickets downtown. (☎8231 4366. Open M-F 8:30am-5:30pm, Sa 9am-1pm.) The **Overland** runs to Melbourne (12-13½hr.; departs M, Th-F, and Su 9am; $57, students $40, children $33). The *Ghan* runs to Alice Springs (19hr., departs M and Th 3pm, $197/$99/$89). The *Indian Pacific* runs to Perth (39hr., departs Tu and F 6pm, $283/$142/$128). The *Indian Pacific* and *Ghan* run to Sydney (24-25hr.; departs W and Su 7:45am, Sa 10am; $176/$88/$79). All three trains offer a 10% YHA discount.

BY BUS. Adelaide has two central bus stations on Franklin St. **McCafferty's/Greyhound (☎13 14 99** or **13 20 30)** has a station at 101 Franklin St., while **V/Line, Firefly,** and **Premier Stateliner** pull into 111 Franklin St. National bus companies provide regular service to and from Adelaide at fares that generally beat rail and air travel, but savings come at the price of comfort. **McCafferty's/Greyhound** runs to: Alice Springs (20hr., 1 per day, $177); Brisbane (29hr., every other day, $232); Darwin (34hr., 1 per day, $371); Melbourne (10hr., 2 per day, $59); Perth (34hr., 1 per day, $264); Sydney (22hr., 1 per day, $127); and Yulara/Ayers Rock (20hr., 1 per day, $147). A new, budget-minded carrier, **Firefly Express (☎8231 1488** or **1800 631 134)** runs to Melbourne (10-11hr.; departs daily 7:30am and 8:30pm; $45), where you can connect to Sydney (Adelaide to Sydney $95). **V/Line (☎8231 7260)** runs a daily coach/rail combination to Melbourne via Bendigo (12hr.; $58, students and children $29). Within South Australia, **Premier Stateliner (☎8415 5555)** is the main carrier, serving over 200 destinations state-wide. The free *State Guide*, available at the tourist office and many hostels, is indispensable for planning area travel.

☀ ORIENTATION

Downtown Adelaide is a mere square mile, bordered by North, East, South, and West Terraces. The city is bisected north to south by **King William St.;** streets running east to west change names when crossing King William St. **Victoria Square** lies at the center of the city grid, while **Light Square** in the northwest quadrant and **Hindmarsh Square** in the northeast quadrant are also important landmarks. **Rundle St.,** home to chic sidewalk cafes, top-notch eateries, and vibrant nightlife, runs from East Tce. west to Pulteney St. in the city's northeast quadrant (known as the **East End**), while the pedestrian-only **Rundle Mall,** the city's main shopping area, extends west to King William St. from the intersection of Rundle and Pulteney St.

Keswick, which includes the railway station, is about 2km southwest of the central grid, and the beach suburb of **Glenelg** is 12km southwest of the CBD via the Anzac Hwy. (A5) or the Glenelg Tram. **North Adelaide,** a smaller grid centered on the trendy bistros and shopping of upscale **O'Connell St.,** sits a couple kilometers north of the CBD in the middle of the parklands that extend north from the banks of the River Torrens. Northwest of the CBD, on the Port River, is the suburb of **Port Adelaide.** The **Adelaide Hills,** including Cleland Conservation Park and Mt. Lofty lookout, are east of the city. Although Adelaide is relatively peaceful, *the parklands are unsafe at night,* especially near the **River Torrens** and in the southwest corner of the city. **Hindley St.** also demands extra caution at night.

⊏ LOCAL TRANSPORTATION

BY PUBLIC TRANSPORTATION. Adelaide is serviced by a web of public buses and trains that make up an integrated public transport system called the **Adelaide Metro,** which also runs two free bus services around the city: **Beeline** and **City Loop.** These yellow buses are easily identified and wheelchair accessible. Beeline runs in the city center, from the railway station on North Tce. to Victoria Sq. and back. (Every 5min. M-Th 7:40am-6pm, every 5min. F 7:40am-9pm; every 15min. Sa 8:30am-5:20pm.) City Loop, true to its name, runs both directions around a loop that covers the north half of the city, including stops at North, East, and West Tce. as well as most major tourist attractions, Central Market, and near the bus station. (Every 15min. M-Th 8:30am-6pm and F 8:30am-9pm, every 30min. Sa 8:30am-5pm.)

To roam farther, there are bus and train routes that comprise TransAdelaide's suburban system. The **Passenger Transport Information Centre,** at the corner of King William and Currie St., has route schedules and an info line. (☎8210 1000. Open M-Sa 8am-6pm, Su 10:30am-5:30pm.) **Single tickets** are good on any service (return included) for two hours and can be purchased from drivers and vending machines. (Single trip M-F 9am-3pm $1.90; all other times $3). Daytrip tickets ($5.70) allow one day of unlimited travel on any service and can be purchased when boarding buses or trams, but must be bought beforehand for trains. An option for those staying longer is the **multitrip ticket,** which must be purchased prior to boarding (10 trips $20, off-peak $11).

The best way to get to **Glenelg** and the beach is by the trams ($3; M-F 9am-3pm $1.90) which run every 15-20min. from Victoria Sq. to Moseley Sq. (30min.; M-F 6am-midnight, Sa 7:30am-midnight, Su 8:50am-midnight.) It's much cheaper to explore on your own, but for a guided tour of the area, **Adelaide Explorer** does a city-to-Glenelg hop-on, hop-off three-hour tour. Pick up the small bus anywhere on the route or join at 38 King William St. (☎8231 7172. Daily 9, 10:30am, noon, 1:30, and 3pm. $30 per day, ages 6-14 $15, families $70; 2nd day $7.) **CitySightseeing Adelaide** (☎8261 0588) offers a hop-on, hop-off tour on London-style red double-decker buses and comes by each stop on its route every 30min. ($25, children $12.50; backpackers $20 if booked through hostel. Tickets can be purchased onboard.)

BY CAR. Hertz, 233 Morphett St. (☎13 30 39); **Budget** (☎13 27 27 or 8223 1400), on the corner of North Tce. and Frome St.; **Avis,** 136 North Tce. (☎8410 5727); and **Europcar,** 142 North Tce. (☎13 13 90; the cheapest of the big boys, from $50 per day, with no one-way fees), have counters at the airport and in town. **Thrifty** (☎8211 8788 or 1300 367 227) is affiliated with **Caudell's Explorer Self-Drive,** 296 Hindley St. (☎8410 5552), which offers 2WD from $50 and 4WD from $69-100 per day. The best outfit for 4WD rentals is **Complete Ute and 4WD Hire,** in the suburb of Findon, with free drop-off and pickup anywhere in the city. (☎8244 5333. 4WD with 200km from $99, prices negotiable for longer rentals. Min. age 21.) **Bush Bashers,** 175 Hart St., Glanville, also has 4WD hire. (☎8242 3033. 4WD with 200km from $120, with unlimited km $140. Min. age 25.)

Those under 25 can get cheaper rates from smaller agencies. These companies are scattered around the suburbs, but most pick up and drop off in town.

SOUTH AUSTRALIA

The Adelaide-based **Smile Rent-a-Car,** 163 Richmond Rd., has no surcharge for drivers under 25, unlimited kilometers, and friendly service. (☎8234 0655 or 1800 624 424. From $35-45; insurance $10 per day.) **No Frills Car Rental,** 235 Waymouth St., has no age limit and hires cars from $33 per day. (☎8212 8333 or 1800 999 978. $10 flat-rate insurance required.) **Excel Rent-a-Car,** on Richmond Rd. about 1km east of the airport, can arrange one-way rentals for no extra cost. (☎8324 1666. New cars from $38 per day.) **Koala Car Rentals** (☎8352 7299), on Sir Donald Bradman Dr., has cars from $31 per day.

For campervans or motorhomes, **Britz,** 376 Burbridge Rd. (☎8234 4701 or 1800 331 454), in Brooklyn Park, has two- to six-berth vans (from $126 per day) and one-way rental with unlimited kilometers. Ask about **relocation deals,** where you pay as little as $1 per day plus petrol costs to take a car or camper from Adelaide to another city in a set amount of time (3 days for the 10hr. drive to Melbourne). **Skippy Camper Rentals,** 1505 South Rd., Darlington (☎8296 2999), has regular campervan rentals (min. 5 days, one-way available) as well as some used campervans and 4WDs for sale with buy-back options.

BY TAXI. Cabs are easy to find, and a 15min. ride is usually around $12. **Des's** (☎13 10 08), **Diamond** (☎13 24 48), **Yellow** (☎13 22 27), and **Access Cabs** (☎1300 360 940; wheelchair accessible) all provide service.

BY BICYCLE. Adelaide is just big enough to frustrate walkers yet small enough to be easily biked. Ambitious bikers can also easily tackle outlying areas. Many city streets have designated cycling lanes. The **Linear Park Bike and Walking Track** (40km) runs along the River Torrens from the ocean to the Adelaide Hills. **Flinders Camping** (☎8223 1913), 187 Rundle St., is the best place to rent a bike. (Open M-Th 9am-5:30pm, F 9am-9pm, Sa 9am-5pm, Su 11am-4:30pm. First day $15, extra day $10.) Other rental options include **Elder Park Mountain Bike Hire,** behind the Festival Centre on the south bank of the Torrens. (☎8223 6271 or 0400 596 065; open M-F 9:15am-5pm, Sa-Su 9:15am-6pm; $20 per day, family rates available) and some hostels (see **Accommodations,** p. 443).

⚡ PRACTICAL INFORMATION

TOURIST AND FINANCIAL SERVICES

Tourist Office: South Australian Travel Centre, 18 King William St. (☎1300 655 276; www.southaustralia.com), is the city's main info center. Open M-F 8:30am-5pm, Sa-Su 9am-2pm. **Glenelg Tourist Information Centre,** Foreshore (by the jetty), Glenelg (☎8294 5833). Open M-F 9am-5pm, Sa-Su 10am-4pm. **Information SA,** 77 Grenfell St. (☎8204 1900), has Internet and information. Open M-F 9am-5pm.

National Parks Information: Dept. for Environment, Heritage, and Aboriginal Affairs Information Centre, 77 Grenfell St. (☎8204 1910; fax 8204 1919). Open M-F 9am-5pm. The **RAA Headquarters,** 41 Hindmarsh Sq. (☎8202 4600), has info and maps.

Travel Agencies: YHA Travel, 135 Waymouth St. (☎8414 3000). Open M-F 9am-6pm, Sa-Su 10am-1pm. The **Backpackers' Travel Centre,** 117 Waymouth St. (☎8212 8188). Open M-F 9am-6pm, Sa 10am-4pm. **STA Travel** is at 235 Rundle St. (☎8223 2426; open M-F 9:30am-5:30pm, Sa 10am-3pm) and 38a Hindley St. (☎8211 6600; open M-Th 9:30am-5pm, F 9:30am-6:30pm, Sa 11am-4pm). The **Wayward Bus Central Office,** 119 Waymouth St. (☎8410 8833), is open daily 9am-5pm.

Work Opportunities: Centrelink, 55 Currie St. (☎13 10 21) or 156-158 Jetty Rd., Glenelg (☎8306 9099). Open M-F 8:30am-4:30pm. *Advertiser* has classifieds on W and Sa. Most hostels also have info or message boards that list seasonal employment.

Consulates: U.K. Consulate, on Grenfell St. (☎8212 7280).

Currency Exchange: Almost any time, if you're dressed nicely, at **Adelaide Casino,** at North Tce. and Railway Tce., in the same building as the train station. Passport or driver's license required. Open Su-Th 10am-4am, F-Sa 10am-6am. **American Express,** Shop 32, Rundle Mall (☎9271 8255). Open M-F 9am-5pm, Sa 9am-noon. **Thomas Cook,** 4 Rundle Mall (☎8231 6977). Open M-Th 9am-5pm, F 9am-7pm, Sa 10am-4pm, Su 10am-2pm.

LOCAL SERVICES

Bookstores: Borders Books, 97 Rundle Mall (☎8223 3333; open daily 9am-9pm), has one of the best selections of books in the city.

Library: State Library of South Australia (☎8207 7248), on North Tce. at the corner of Kintore Ave. Book ahead, by phone or in person, for free 30min. **Internet,** or wait for free 15min. slots.

Ticket Agency: Most cultural and sporting events (especially football matches) are booked through **BASS** (☎13 12 46; www.bass.sa.net.au; open M-Sa 9am-8pm; $2.75 service charge per ticket), at a booth at the Visitors Center on King William St. **VenueTix** (☎8223 7788) is the place to go for cricket and basketball tickets.

RAA: State Headquarters, 41 Hindmarsh Sq. (touring info ☎8202 4600 or 13 11 11). Open M-F 8:30am-5pm, Sa 9am-noon.

MEDIA AND PUBLICATIONS

Newspapers: *The Advertiser* ($1).

Nightlife: "The Guide" in the Thursday *Advertiser*. *Rip it Up* and *db* on the nightlife and alternative club scene (free). For gay nightlife, try *Blaze* or *Gay Times* (free).

Radio: Rock, 104.7FM; Pop, 107.1FM and 102.3FM; News, ABC 831AM; Tourist Info, 88.1FM.

EMERGENCY AND COMMUNICATIONS

Emergency: ☎000.

Pharmacy: Midnight Pharmacy, 11 West Tce. (☎8231 6333). Open M-Sa 7am-midnight, Su 9am-midnight.

Medical Assistance: Royal Adelaide Hospital (☎8222 4000), on North Tce.

Internet Access: See **libraries** (p. 443). There's also free email at the **Enigma Leisure Lounge and Bar** (see p. 451) if you buy a beer or coffee. Most hostels have kiosks.

Post Office: General Post Office, 141 King William St. (☎8216 2222), at the corner of King William and Franklin St. Open M-F 8am-6pm, Sa 8:30am-noon. Poste Restante can be picked up M-F 7am-5:30pm, Su 9am-1pm. **Postal Code:** 5000.

⚓ ACCOMMODATIONS

Unless otherwise noted, all listed hostels have 24hr. access, kitchen, laundry, free linen, $10 key deposit, 10am check-out, free luggage storage, and tour and bus booking facilities. All take Mastercard and Visa, though some have minimum charge requirements. Adelaide hostels are rarely full in winter, but book a day or two ahead in summer and a week ahead during festivals. Those looking to escape the city should consider staying in the beach suburb of Glenelg (see p. 451) or in the Adelaide Hills to the east of town (see p. 452).

SOUTH AUSTRALIA

HOSTELS

🏨 **Adelaide Central YHA,** 135 Waymouth St. (☎8414 3010). The most popular backpackers in town despite the sometimes sterile, cavernous atmosphere. The 250-bed complex has A/C and clean rooms with individual reading lights. Friendly staff, kitchen, TV, pool tables, and smoking room. Close to the best pubs. Internet $1 per 10min. Bike hire $10 per day. No lockout, no curfew. Check-out 9:30am. Dorms $22; doubles $55, ensuite $70. YHA discount $3.50. ❷

🏨 **Glenelg Beach Resort,** 1 Moseley St., Glenelg (☎8376 0007 or 1800 066 422), 1 block from the shore. 20min. tram from Victoria Sq. This award-winning complex offers a full range of rooms. Licensed, with a lively bar, pool tables, small karaoke stage (W and F-Sa nights), common area with videos, and game room. Quiet time after 10pm, but downstairs in the bar, theme nights range from beach party to the "bar Olympics." Clean rooms are high-ceilinged. Bike hire half-day $10, full-day $15. Free wine tours Th, Adelaide tours Tu. Free pickup and drop-off. Internet $1 per 15min. Dorms in summer $20-22, in winter $18-20; singles $55; doubles $66; family rooms $110. VIP. ❷

🏨 **Brecon Inn,** 11 Gilbert St. (☎8211 8985 or 0418 896 931). This quiet hostel is a little removed from the action but modern, clean, and well-designed, with a friendly staff, daily *Simpsons* viewings, and access to live-in manager Adam's extensive DVD collection. Laundry, employment info, TV/DVD lounge, free local calls, lockers, comfy beds, Internet access ($1 per 15min.), and, best of all, 10% off at the pub next door. 6-bed dorms $19; 4-bed $22; singles $35; doubles $50. NOMADS. Wheelchair accessible. ❷

🏨 **Adelaide City Backpackers Hostel,** 239 Franklin St. (☎8212 2668), a few blocks east of the bus station. Put chandeliers, carpet, stained glass, and 50 beds into a historic restored home, and call it a hostel. Homey and welcoming, this place feels more like an upscale B&B than a budget hostel. A/C or fans; free pickup from bus, train, and plane; free brekkie, dessert, and Su BBQ. Inexpensive bar and a courtyard. Dorms $20; twins and doubles $52; family rooms available. ISIC/VIP/YHA. ❷

🏨 **Backpack Oz,** 144 Wakefield St. (☎8223 3551 or 1800 633 307), on the corner of Pulteney St. The closest backpackers to Rundle St., this intimate 50-bed hostel facilitates meeting people, a process furthered by the sociable staff. The building was a pub 120 years ago and guests can still buy a $3 beer whenever the office is open. Rooms have A/C and sweets on the pillows. Free pickup, employment info, TV/video lounge, and tour bookings. Free breakfast and free W night dinner. Internet $4 per hr. Reception 6am-10pm. Dorms $19; singles $45; twins and doubles $48. 7th night free. ❷

East Park Lodge, 341 Angas St. (☎8223 1228; eastpark@dove.com.au). A 20min. walk from Rundle St. Diverse clientele enjoys airy, newly renovated rooms in this quirky old 3-story building. Fantastic view of Adelaide Hills and the city. Only pool in town, pool table, TV lounge, kitchen, free breakfast, free dinner Tu and Th, and a multilingual staff. Make your own didgeridoo for $80. Bike hire (half-day $12, full-day $17) and limited car and motorbike hire (half-day $30). Free pickup. Reception 7am-8pm. Check-out 9:30am. 4-bed dorms $20; singles $54; twins and doubles $55. VIP. ❷

Adelaide Backpacker's Inn, 112 Carrington St. (☎8223 6635 or 1800 247 725; abackinn@tne.net.au), a 10min. walk from Victoria Sq, with 2 buildings opposite each other. Free nightly apple-pie-and-ice-cream desserts that are never rationed (4000 pies baked yearly), free rice, and $4 all-you-can-eat breakfasts (with everything from fry-ups to fruit) make this a popular stop for malnourished backpackers. Free bikes and videos give them something to do once they've recharged. Free pickup and drop-off. Internet $1 per 15min. Great Su night BBQ $5. Reception 6am-8pm. Dorms $20; singles $38; twins and doubles $52. 7th night free. ❷

Sunny's Backpacker Hostel, 139 Franklin St. (☎8231 2430 or 1800 225 725), next to the bus station. Small, friendly hostel with 48 beds in crowded bunk rooms, clean communal bathrooms, and an outdoor patio. Female dorm has separate bath. Pool table and TV lounge. Internet $1 per 15min. Free pancake breakfast 8-9am. Reception M-F 6am-9pm, Sa-Su 6am-12:30pm and 5-8pm. Dorms $20; twins $50. VIP/YHA. ❷

HOTELS

The Moores' Brecknock Hotel, 401 King William St. (☎8231 5467). The Moores welcome you to comfy, clean rooms with fluffy doonas in a quiet part of town. Added bonus is the laid-back, authentic atmosphere in the Irish pub downstairs. A/C, shared bath, and free breakfast. Singles $45; doubles $65; extra person $15. ❹

The Austral Hotel, 205 Rundle St. (☎8223 4660). Spacious rooms are not as adorned as the pub downstairs, but once you've experienced the convenience, you won't want to stay anywhere else. The downstairs pub gets loud on weekends. Slightly more expensive than a hostel, but you get privacy, a fantastic location in the swankiest part of town, and lot of fun. Key deposit $10. Singles $35; twins and doubles $55; quads $80. ❸

The Plaza Hotel, 85 Hindley St. (☎8231 6371). Good location and a slightly classier atmosphere than its pub-hotel brethren. Recently renovated and centered around a courtyard. Clean ensuite rooms have TV, fridge, and fan. Singles $50; doubles $60. ❹

The Metropolitan Hotel, 46 Grote St. (☎8231 5471), across from the Central Market. For those who feel more at home near pubs and pokies, standard pub life in Adelaide doesn't come any cheaper. The pub was built in 1873; rooms are clean and functional, and the location is good. Singles $30; doubles $50. ❸

▣ FOOD

Gouger St., in the city center near Victoria Sq., offers a wide range of good, inexpensive ethnic cuisine. **Rundle St.**, in the northeast section of the city, caters to the young hipster set, as students forgo lectures in nearby Adelaide University in favor of strong cups of espresso. Clusters of restaurants can also be found on the upscale **Hutt St.** in southeast Adelaide and North Adelaide's equally upscale **O'Connell St.** The flashy but cheap **Hindley St.**, across King William St. from **Rundle St.**, is the best spot for 24hr. eats. **Jetty Rd.**, in the beachside suburb of Glenelg, also bursts with cafes and ice cream shops. **Supermarkets** dot the city, particularly on Rundle Mall, Hindley St, and Victoria Sq. Coles, next to Central Market on Grote St., is very close to Victoria Sq. (Open M-Th midnight-6pm, F midnight-9pm, Sa midnight-5pm, Su 11am-5pm.)

For a real Aussie experience, late-night snackers have visited the **"Pie Carts,"** outside the Adelaide Train Station on North Tce., since 1915. The infamous pie floater ($4)—an Aussie meat pie swimming in a thick pea soup and topped with tomato sauce—is a South Australian original and potentially habit forming.

GOUGER STREET

Gouger St. (GOO-jer), a popular spot for sidewalk dining, houses the ▨**Central Market,** a gourmand's fantasy, with free samples to boot. (Open Tu and Th 7am-5:30pm, F 7am-9pm, and Sa 7am-3pm.) The area of Gouger St. around the market comprises Adelaide's Chinatown. Open throughout the weekdays, most Gouger St. restaurants close for lunch on weekends.

▨ **Noodles,** 119 Gouger St. (☎8231 8177). Serves exactly that: noodles in every shape, form, and color for just $7.20. Comes with generous servings of chicken, beef, seafood, or veggies for a few dollars more. BYO. Open M 5:30pm-late, Tu-F 11:30am-3pm and 5:30pm-late, Sa-Su 5:30pm-late. ❶

Gaucho's, 91 Gouger St. (☎8231 2299). Outstanding Argentinian food in a setting best for those trying to impress their companion. Try the chili-laced oysters *del diabolo* ($12.50) or any of the other fancy mains (average about $18). Open M-F 11:30am-2pm and 5:30-10:30pm, Sa-Su 5:30-10:30pm. ❸

S O U T H   A U S T R A L I A

Cafe Fusilli, 68-72 Gouger St. (☎8221 6884). Masquerading as a standard Italian cafe by night, by day, Fusilli is a budget traveler's dream. Huge bowls of homemade spaghetti with melt-in-your-mouth garlic bread are the daily lunch special and cost just $6.50 from 11:30am-4pm ($12 for dinner). Open daily 9am-10pm. ❷

Matsuri, 167 Gouger St. (☎8231 3494). Meaning "festival" in Japanese, Adelaide's best sushi restaurant features a rock garden and a shoes-off rule. 6-piece packs $3-10. Noodle dishes $9-15. Open M, W-Th, and Sa-Su 5:30pm-late; F noon-2pm and 5:30pm-late. ❷

RUNDLE STREET

Rundle St., one block south of North Tce., flows east from Rundle Mall and offers something to suit every palate and pocketbook. It is *the* place to be in Adelaide, day or night, and offers an incredible range of options.

▨ **Amalfi,** 29 Frome St. (☎8223 1948), between Rundle St. and North Tce. This popular and usually packed "Pizzeria Ristorante" sneaks onto upscale gourmet dining lists with relatively budget prices. Come early to avoid waiting for a table. Pasta dishes $13-18. Meat mains $14-19. For many locals, it's all about the pizza (small $10-12, large $17-20). Finish it off with divine tiramisu. Open M-Th 11:30am-3pm and 5:30-11pm, F 11:30am-3pm and 5:30pm-midnight, Sa 5:30pm-midnight. ❷

▨ **Lemongrass,** 289 Rundle St. (☎8223 6627). This popular and pleasant restaurant is said to have the best Thai food in town. The creative menu includes Aussie twists on Thai standards (kangaroo pad thai, croc curry) and quality daily lunch specials for $6.50. Mains range from $10-18, while appetizers start at about $5 (spring rolls 3 for $6.50). Open M-F 11:30am-3pm and daily 5pm-late. ❷

Red Dust Cafe and Restaurant, 231 Rundle St. (☎8223 1033). Large portions of standard and innovative Aussie fare, good value, and that long-time staple of Rundle St. life: outdoor tables on the sidewalk. $7-10 meal specials, usually incorporating kangaroo, emu, or some other distinctly Aussie meat, along with salads, burgers, and sandwiches ($5-12). Open daily 11am-10pm or later. ❶

Al Fresco, 260 Rundle St. (☎8223 4589). This people-watching landmark serves a tempting range of Italian cakes, focaccia, dynamite coffee, and the best gelato in the city (small $2.75). They also have sandwiches, salads, pasta dishes ($6-12), and a full breakfast menu ($5-8). Pick up a light meal in minutes or linger over a latte for hours. Open daily 6:30am-late. ❶

Cibo Espresso, 218 Rundle St. (☎8232 9199), on the corner of Rundle and Frome St., is the best caffeine jolt in the city, starting at $2.50 and masquerading in a multitude of fine disguises. Fresh-baked pastries, tasty sandwiches, and panini. Pulses with caffeine-seekers until late. Open M-Th 7am-11pm, F-Sa 7am-1am, Su 8:30am-5pm. ❶

Vego and Love'n It!, 240 Rundle St. (☎8223 7411), hidden up a set of stairs on the first floor. Large portions of deliciously concocted vegan and vegetarian meals ($7-10) make this an extremely popular daytime eating spot. Funky bohemian atmosphere only adds to the experience. Tofu ice cream $1.50. Juices $2. Open M-F 10am-5pm. ❶

THE BEST OF THE REST

The rest of the city is a melange of cafes, pubs, and posh restaurants. Many downtown pubs offer cheap meals.

▨ **The Gilbert Place Pancake House** (☎8211 7912), off King William St., between Currie and Hindley St. In a city that shuts down early, a sign reading "this door will never close" is a welcome sight for hungry eyes. Fanciful $7-9 pancake creations (Jamaican banana, Bavarian apple) and Tu all-you-can-eat specials ($5). Also oversized sundaes ($7) and all manner of standard breakfast fare ($5-10). Open 24hr. ❶

Quiet Waters BYO, 75 Hindley St. (☎8231 3637). Large range of vegetarian dishes for those disgruntled with an overwhelmingly meat-eating state. Mains from $7. Open daily noon-2pm and 5:30-9pm. ❶

Lizard Lounge, 172a Hutt St. (☎8237 0210). This small cafe and its exciting menu are a mouthful of the utmost fun. Coffee, tea, and hot chocolate are not cheap ($4-6) but you're paying for atmosphere. Liqueur coffees ($6.50) are killer. Light snacks and mind-boggling desserts ($6-9) add to the revelry. Open M-Sa 7pm-late. ❷

◎ SIGHTS

It's easy to spend a day indulging cultural cravings without tiring your legs or opening your wallet. Adelaide's sights and museums are all located along (or just off) North Tce., the city's cultural boulevard, and nearly all of them are free.

▨ SOUTH AUSTRALIAN MUSEUM. This gracious building is the brilliant center-piece of the North Tce. cultural district. It holds huge whale skeletons, native Aus-tralian animal displays, rocks and minerals, and even an Egyptian mummy, along with a fascinating collection of artifacts (tools, weapons, clothing, photos) from the early days of European interaction with native Pacific Islanders. The real high-light of the museum is the **Australian Aboriginal Cultures Gallery,** which has the larg-est collection of Aboriginal artifacts in the world. *(Next to the State Library, on North Tce.* ☎*8207 7500, tour info 8293 5666. Open daily 10am-5pm. Museum tours M-Tu and Th-F 11am; W 11am and 2pm; Sa-Su 11am, 2, and 3pm. Free. Gallery tours daily 11:30am, 12:30, and 1:30pm. $10, concessions $7. Wheelchair accessible.)*

▨ ART GALLERY OF SOUTH AUSTRALIA. This gallery showcases Australian, Asian, and European prints, paintings, sculpture, decorative arts, and Southeast Asian ceramics. The collection of Australian art is especially impressive. There is a charge for the eclectic temporary exhibitions in the basement. *(North Tce. near Pulteney St.* ☎*8207 7000, info desk 8207 7075; www.artgallery.sa.gov.au. Open daily 10am-5pm. Free. 1hr. tours M-F 11am and 2pm, Sa-Su 11am and 3pm. Free. Wheelchair accessible.)*

▨ TANDANYA—NATIONAL ABORIGINAL CULTURAL INSTITUTE. The first major Aboriginal multi-arts complex in Australia hosts continually rotating exhibitions of indigenous artwork from around the country. Focusing on both contemporary and traditional expressions of Aboriginal culture, it is nothing short of fascinating. *(253 Grenfell St., at the corner of East Tce. on the City Loop bus route.* ☎*8224 3200; www.tan-danya.com.au. Open daily 10am-5pm. $4, concessions $3. Book ahead for guided tours and talks. Didgeridoo performances M-Th and Sa-Su noon; Torres Strait Islander dance F noon.)*

MIGRATION MUSEUM. Combining history and oral tradition to explain patterns of immigration and exclusion that have shaped South Australian society, the museum's graphic stories and photographs make for an excellent, if sobering, visit. The museum, housed in the former buildings of Adelaide's Destitute Asylum, is particularly relevant now, as immigration policy has become one of the nation's most hotly contested political issues. *(82 Kintore Ave., off North Tce., behind the state library.* ☎*8207 7580. Open M-F 10am-5pm, Sa-Su 1-5pm. Free, $2 donation suggested.)*

ADELAIDE BOTANIC GARDENS. Acres of landscaped grounds surround heritage buildings, a small lake with black swans, and meandering walkways. The lush and peaceful grounds contain the **Australian Arboretum** and the **Yarrabee Art Gallery.** The **Bicentennial Conservatory,** the largest glasshouse in the Southern Hemisphere, and its neighboring rose gardens, are the only sections with an entrance fee. Inside the conservatory, the computer-controlled atmosphere simulates a tropical rainforest, complete with misty rain. *(On North Tce.* ☎*8222 9311. Gardens open M-F 8am-sunset, Sa-*

Su 9am-sunset. Conservatory open daily 10am-4pm; $3.30, concessions $1.65. Free garden tours leave from restaurant-kiosk M-Tu, F, and Su 10:30am.)

ADELAIDE ZOO. Now home to more than 1300 animals, the century-old zoo still has some Victorian buildings. The Southeast Asian rainforest, the sea lions, and the children's feeding area zoo are some of the most popular exhibits. *(On Frome Rd., less than 2km north of the city and a 15min. walk from North Tce. through the Botanic Gardens or down Frome Rd. Take bus #272 or 273 from Grenfell St. Popeye boats from the Festival Centre also run to and from the zoo in summer. ☎8267 3255. Open daily 9:30am-5pm. $14.50, concessions $11.50, children $8. Guided tours daily 11am and 2pm.)*

ADELAIDE GAOL. Forty-nine prisoners were executed here before its closure in 1988, but the displays focus on the plight of female inmates and the daily activities of a prisoner—namely, smoking. *(18 Gaol Rd., Thebarton. A moderate walk northeast of the city or 5min. ride to Stop 1 on bus #151, 153, 286, or 287 from North Tce. ☎8231 4062. Open M-F 11am-4pm. $8, concessions $5.50, children $4.50. Guided tours Su 11am-3:30pm.)*

HAIGH'S CHOCOLATES VISITORS CENTRE. Australia's oldest chocolate maker, Haigh's has been churning since 1915. It is also known as the original creator of the hugely popular chocolate **Easter Bilby,** an effort to displace the tyrannical Easter Bunny. (The bilby, a type of bandicoot, is a native endangered species; the rabbit is an introduced pest.) Free tastings and complimentary tea and coffee make this a nice place for a daytime caffeine booster. *(154 Greenhill Rd., 1 block south of South Tce. and just east of Pulteney Rd. ☎8271 3770. Open M-F 8:30am-5:30pm, Sa 9am-5pm. Free guided tours with tastings M-Sa 1 and 2pm. Book ahead.)*

ⓐ ACTIVITIES

Outdoor goods stores abound on Rundle St., most of which can point you towards the city's best purveyors of outdoor activities.

MOUNTAIN BIKING. Rolling On Mountain Bike Tours has guided tours around Adelaide, its forests and vineyards, and the Barossa Valley, ranging from one day to two weeks in length. It's a good choice even for those without much riding experience—trails are fairly flat and there's a backup vehicle if you get tired. (☎8358 2401. Day-tours from $79-99, 2-week "Wine and Wildlife" tour $1400; many options in between. Bike hire. Also see **By Bicycle,** p. 442.)

SNOW AND ICE. At **Mt. Thebarton,** 23 East Tce., Thebarton, you can ski, snowboard, sled, or skate year-round on South Australia's only real "Permasnow." Okay, it's all indoors and the ski run is actually a 150m bunny hill, but where else can you ski for $9? Take bus #151, 153, 286, or 287 to stop 2 from North Tce. (5min.), or walk 15 minutes from the northwest of the city. (☎8352 7977. "Fridge nights" F-Sa with DJs and lights. Open M noon-4pm, Tu and Th 10am-4pm, W and F 10am-4pm and 7:30-10pm, Sa-Su 12:30-4pm and 7:30-10pm. Skiing or boarding $9 per hr.; equipment $5.50-10. Skating $8.50; skates $2.25.)

EARTH AND SKY. Rock Solid Adventure offers abseiling, rock climbing, and a two-night caving trip to Naracoorte Conservation Park. (☎8322 8975. Abseiling and rock-climbing $64 per 4hr, $71 per 5hr.; spelunking $210.) **SA Skydiving** is pleased to assist in your free-fall fantasies. They also offer a full-day solo jump course. (☎8272 7888. Tandem $285, solo $385; video $66.)

SURF, SCUBA, AND SWIM. Surf Break Surf Classes offers lessons with pro-surfer Rebecca Osborne. (☎0210 8166 or 8327 2369. From $20 per hr.) **Red Sun Safaris** provides day-long outings that combine a Victor Harbor surf lesson and a McLaren

Vale winery tour. (☎ 0838 8456 or 8276 3620; $69, including transfers, lunch, and all equipment.) **Glenelg Scuba Diving** runs daily boat dives to Adelaide's wrecks and reefs and a four-day PADI certification class. (☎ 8294 7744. Dives from $66; equipment hire available. 4-5 day PADI class $295-345.) The **Adelaide Aquatic Centre,** on Jeffcott Rd., North Adelaide, is a huge indoor complex with a 50m pool, a diving and water polo area, and aqua-aerobics classes. Walk 30min. from North Tce. up King William St.; or take bus #231, 233, 235, or 237 from Victoria Sq. or from stop Z3 in front of the Festival Centre on King William St. (☎ 8344 4411. Pools open in summer daily 5am-10pm; in winter M-Sa 5am-10pm, Su 7am-8pm. Gym open M-F 6am-10pm, Sa 6am-6pm, Su 9am-5pm. Pool $5, concessions $3.50; gym $9/$6.)

BEACH IT UP. Don't miss the beach suburb of **Glenelg**, with its lovely swimming beach and cafe culture. Inline skates can be hired at the main Glenelg beach on summer weekends, and there's often free outdoor entertainment. During the summer, the smooth sand of Glenelg's **Holdfast Bay** is also a great spot to try your hand at beach volleyball or parasailing. (☎ 1119 1653; from $45.)

SPECTATOR SPORTS. Australian Rules Football (mostly Sa) is played in the suburb of West Lakes (Adelaide Crows) and in Port Adelaide (Port Power). **Cricket** (Oct.-Mar.) is played at the **Adelaide Oval**, north of the city along King William Rd. There is a 2½-hour tour of the Oval that focuses on "Cricket's Greatest Batsman," the late Sir Donald Bradman. (☎ 8300 3800. Tours Tu and Th 10am; Su 2pm, except on match days. $5. Museum open Tu and Th 10am-1pm. $2. Tickets and schedules available at BASS ☎ 13 12 46 or VenueTix ☎ 8223 7788.)

▣ ENTERTAINMENT

A two-minute walk north on King William St. from its intersection with North Tce. at Parliament House will bring you to the huge, white **Adelaide Festival Centre** (☎ 8216 8600). Situated on the Torrens River, this is the focus of Adelaide's formal cultural life. Pick up a calendar of events from inside the Festival Centre complex, access the schedule online at www.southaustralia.com, or call BASS (☎ 13 12 46), the ticketing company that handles all events at the Centre. The **State Opera of South Australia** (☎ 8226 4790; www.saopera.sa.gov.au), the **Adelaide Symphony Orchestra** (☎ 8343 4111), and the **State Theatre Company of South Australia** (☎ 8231 5151; www.statetheatre.sa.com.au) all perform at the Festival Centre; it's also the place for big-name traveling musicals and theater performances. **Elder Hall,** on North Tce., part of the University of Adelaide, has concerts as well as some chamber performances by the Adelaide Symphony. (☎ 8303 5925. Lunch concerts F 1:10-2pm; $2.) Some of the best music around town is found in Adelaide's vibrant bars, clubs, and pubs (see **Nightlife**, p. 450), where local bands strut their stuff.

Adelaide's most accessible **alternative cinemas,** both on Rundle St., are the **Palace Eastend** (☎ 8232 3434) and **NOVA** (☎ 8223 6333). **Mercury Cinema,** 13 Morphett St., just off Hindley St., has super-artsy fare. (☎ 8410 0979; www.mrc.org.au. $10-13.) Tuesday night is usually discount night at movie theaters across Australia. Mid-December through mid-February brings **Cinema in the Botanic Gardens,** outdoor showings of popular and classic movies. (Tickets at gate or through BASS ☎ 13 12 46. $13, concessions $10, children $8.50.)

◼ FESTIVALS

Adelaide has dubbed itself the "Festival City": check *The Guide, dB,* or *Rip it Up* for listings. ▨**WOMADelaide,** an enormously successful **WO**rld **M**usic **A**rt and **D**ance festival, will celebrate its 10th anniversary February 21-23, 2003. **Arts**

Project Australia runs the three-day show in Botanic Park, with dozens of acts from dozens of countries and workshops on six stages, while a "global village" sells international food and crafts. All walks of life come to enjoy this can't-miss festival. If you're planning on visiting Adelaide at this time, make sure to book lodging well in advance. (☎8271 9905. Weekend tickets $115, students and concessions $95; daily ticket prices from $45.) **Feast** (late Oct. to mid-Nov.) is Adelaide's annual lesbian and gay festival, with three weeks of masquerades, parties, and concerts (☎8231 2155).

A biennial event next occurring February 17 to March 14, 2004, the **Adelaide Festival of Arts** (☎8216 4444; www.adelaidefestival.org.au) is considered one of the world's best arts festivals. Overlapping with the Adelaide Festival, the **Adelaide Fringe Festival** (☎8100 2000) features artists out of the mainstream, and is considered by many Adelaide residents to be the true hallmark of their city's identity: progressive, entertaining, and resolutely doing its own thing.

▣ NIGHTLIFE

The **East End,** which, very roughly, includes Rundle St. east of the mall, Pulteney St., and Pirie St., is the center of Adelaide's "pretty" scene and teems with University students and twenty-something professionals on the weekends. Bouncers here and at most of the city's dance clubs are very mindful of **dress code.** This usually means no sneakers, no T-shirts, no tank-tops, no flip-flops, and no hats, but can also be extended to include no jeans. The cafe scene dominates this area, as uni students and others drink schooners and smoke on the sidewalk. **Hindley St.** in the **West End** is home to many X-rated venues as well as numerous fly-by-night dance clubs. Rundle Mall itself, next to Hindley St., is quiet at night except for the columns of semi-inebriated partygoers marching from the pubs of Rundle St. to the clubs of Hindley St. and Light Sq. (or vice versa). The **Light Square** area is encircled by popular clubs. For more nightlife info, see **Media and Publications,** p. 443.

PUBS

▣ **Grace Emily,** 232 Waymouth St. (☎8231 5500). The chillest bar in Adelaide, for the moment, is not on Rundle or Hindley but here on Waymouth St. Decor is 1950s viewed through a kaleidoscope, with a squatting Buddha surveying the laid-back scene from the mantle above the bar. Live music 4-5 nights per week, Open daily 4pm-late.

Austral, 205 Rundle St. (☎8223 4660). Known affectionately by locals as the "Nostril," this bar draws a young crowd. Live bands in the beer garden F-Sa, DJs Su-Th. If nothing's happening here, there's probably nothing happening in town. Open daily until late.

Charlie's Bar, 233 Victoria Sq. (☎8217 2000), in the Hilton Hotel. Surprising as it may seem, this bar in the Hilton, abutting the lobby's posh piano bar, hosts popular "Backpacker Nights" on Tu and Th. Upon presentation of a voucher (available at most hostels and travel agencies), backpackers receive a free curry with rice, a free beer, and are charged Happy Hour drink prices all night (beers $1). Open 4pm-very late.

P.J. O'Brien's, 14 East Tce. (☎8232 5111). Adelaide's resident Irish pub, P.J.'s vast interior is packed weekend nights with a young-20s crowd. Mix of backpackers and Adelaide natives. Near Rundle St., in Adelaide's nexus of nightlife. Strict on the dress code F-Sa (no sneakers), more lax during the week. Open Su-Th noon-late, F-Sa noon-4am.

The Stag Hotel, 299 Rundle St. (☎8223 2934), on the corner of East Tce. The bumping dance floor upstairs connects to a wraparound balcony for talking with that person you were just grinding with, or perhaps snogging them a bit (the latter seems to be the more popular option). That notwithstanding, this is a pretty classy place and attracts 20-somethings looking to let loose. Open daily 3pm-3am.

Edinburgh Castle, 233 Currie St. (☎8410 1211). Owned by a gay couple with a mainly gay male clientele. Open M-Th 11am-midnight, F-Sa 11am-1am, Su 2pm-midnight.

NIGHTCLUBS

Church, on Synagogue Pl., just off Rundle St. (☎8223 4233). Occupying a former Synagogue, this is a heavyweight in the Adelaide club scene, attracting the young, sleek Rundle St. crowd. Techno downstairs, hip-hop upstairs. "Greed," an 80s-themed party, runs F 9pm-1am. Cover $8-10, entry often free before midnight (look for the spotlight).

Supermild, 182 Hindley St. (☎8212 9699). Smart, laid-back atmosphere that usually lives up to its name. Live music on Su. Good DJs and an intimate, relaxed feel make this a popular late-night place. Open Su-Th 9pm-late, F-Sa 9pm-5am.

Garage, 69 Light Sq. (☎8212 6969). Promises one thing: to groove all year long. If this place isn't packed and beautiful, you're in the wrong place. Dress nicely or the Goliaths at the door will become angry. Cover $8. Open F and Su 10pm-late, Sa 10pm-8am.

Enigma Leisure Lounge and Bar, 173 Hindley St. (☎8212 2313). Hip, intimate multi-functional hangout is a cafe by day and a bar/club by night. Downstairs, purple-lit leather couches and free Internet terminals in addition to the usual pool table and dart board. Upstairs at the club, W is drag night and Th is reggae. Cover for club $6-8. Open M-Tu 11:30am-5pm, W-Th 11:30am-5pm and 8pm-late, F 11:30am-late, Sa 8pm-late.

Cargo Club, 213 Hindley St. (☎8231 2327). A strong holdout from recycled Top-40 tunes, live music ranges from jazz to African and draws a crowd that can't decide whether it is trendy or alternative. DJs F-Sa. Cover around $8. Doors open 10pm, but the party usually doesn't get going until at least 1am and doesn't stop until 5 or 6am.

Heaven II, 7 West Tce. (☎8211 8533). This bright purple building at the corner of North and West Tce. offers a hedonistic mix of alcohol, dance music, lycra, and nubile 20-somethings. Features DJs, local bands, and internationally renowned acts. Once a month Heaven floods with soap suds during the foam party. Cover usually $7-10. There's almost always a line F-Sa and St. Heaven's gates open 8-10pm W-Su.

The Planet, 77 Pirie St. (☎8359 2797). If you've come to the Land Down Under looking for tainted love or karma chameleons, go to "Hit Factory," this club's popular Friday tribute to the 80s. W is "Planet Disco," complete with '70s outfits, and Sa means house music and tightly packed, writhing young bodies. Cover $6-10.

▶ DAYTRIPS FROM ADELAIDE

PORT ADELAIDE. Port Adelaide features an historic port and lighthouse, a unique market, several antiques shops and art galleries, self-guided walking tours of landmark buildings, and several museums. The **Visitors Center** (☎8447 4788; open daily 9am-5pm), on Commercial Rd. at the corner of Vincent St., has information and maps. The **Lighthouse,** on the wharf in front of the market, which gives a great view of the area. (Open M-F 10am-noon, Su 10am-5pm. $1.) **Fisherman's Wharf** (☎8341 2040), Lighthouse Sq., on Commercial Rd., is the place to be Sundays 8am-5pm, selling everything from CDs to seafood to used books. Several companies operate **river cruises** (1¾hr.) on the Port Adelaide River that offer occasional dolphin sightings. (Departs daily at midday. $2.50-6. Book at wharf-side kiosks.) To reach Port Adelaide, take bus #151 or 153 from North Tce. opposite Parliament house, and get off at stop #40 (about 30min.). The Outer Harbor railway line links the port and the North Tce. railway station (20min., M-F every 30min. 9am-midnight).

SOUTHERN BEACHES. Closest to Adelaide, **Christies Beach** has a park and many small shops along Beach Rd. For snorkelers or divers, the **Port Noarlunga Aquatic Reserve** is a shallow reef accessible from the end of the jetty. South again,

IN RECENT NEWS

POPULATION DECLINE

In 2001, Australia's population reached 19,387,000 with a rate of increase of just 1.2%, low even by the standards of other developed nations. By comparison, the U.S. is roughly the same size in terms of landmass but has more than 14 times that number of people. Population experts predict that the population growth rate will continue to decline over the next 30-50 years and that preventing a decline in population will probably require between 60,000 and 80,000 immigrants per year until at least 2050. While some politicians argue that incentives are necessary to stimulate population growth, others point out that a declining rate might not be so bad. The gradual aging of the population that is predicted to continue is a result of a low fertility rate coupled with high life expectancy, both of which are indicators of good health care, educational systems, and women's status. A lower population density creates fewer stresses on the environment and results in less suburban sprawl, release of greenhouse gases, and landfill creation. Critics of the existing rates, however, say that a higher population could produce more goods and wealth and could allow Australia to gain power in the global economy. They advocate "baby bonuses" and paid maternity leave as ways to promote higher fertility rates without relying on massive immigration increases. The country has not yet reached a consensus on this controversial and complex issue, and public debate will no doubt continue for many years to come.

Seaford has a walking and biking track along the cliffs. At the swimming beach **Moana,** cars can park by the water. **Maslin Beach,** directly west of McLaren Vale, was Australia's first "unclad" beach and still hosts the **Nude Olympics** each January. Farthest south, **Aldinga Beach** is convenient to Willunga. Take the Noarlunga line **train** from Adelaide Railway Station (North Tce.) to Noarlunga. Transfer to bus #741 at the Noarlunga Interchange for Maslin, Christies, or Moana Beach. For Port Noarlunga, take bus #741, 742, or 745. Full-day ticket $5.60 for both train and bus or $2.90 for each.

NEAR ADELAIDE: ADELAIDE HILLS

The Adelaide Hills area has become renowned for conservation efforts, such as those in Warrawong Sanctuary, and for its beguiling drives that weave through tree-covered rolling hills. Huge expanses of national park surround Mt. Lofty, broken up by wineries, orchards, conservation lands, and picturesque hamlets.

Despite their seclusion, the various points of interest in the Hills are easy to get to. Much of the Adelaide Hills is a 15-40min. drive east from the Adelaide city center, along Hwy. A1 (known as Glen Osmond Rd. and leaving from the CBD grid's southeast corner). The Hills are accessible by the Adelaide Metro system ($3). Call the **info line** (☎8210 1000) for route info and timetables. Most buses are considered part of the Adelaide system and charge the same fares (see p. 441). Bus #163 and 163F, leaving from Grenfell St. (stop G2), are the two main routes to the Hills; #165, 165F, 166, 166F, 840, and 843 will also get you there. Most of the routes follow Hwy. 1 through Stirling and Aldgate (stop #49) before cruising down Main St. in Hahndorf (stop #55, about 45min. from the CBD. To get to Mt. Lofty or Cleland, the best way is to take #163, 165, or 166 from Grenfell St. to the town of **Crafers,** 14km southeast of the city, where you can change to bus #823 to Cleland/Mt. Lofty; the connection can be difficult to make, so check bus schedules beforehand. **Gray Line** runs a "taste of the Adelaide Hills" **tour** on Tu and Sa 9:30am-5:30pm and a briefer afternoon "highlights" tour that leaves daily at 1pm and returns at 5:30pm. (☎8374 1270 or 1800 634 724. $75 full-day, $45 half-day.) The **Adelaide Hills Visitors Center** is at 41 Main St., Hahndorf. (☎8388 1185 or 1800 353 323; www.visitadelaidehills.com. Internet access $2 per 20min. Open M-F 9am-5pm, Sa-Su 10am-4pm.)

MOUNT LOFTY SUMMIT AND CLELAND PARK. The biggest attraction in the Adelaide Hills is Mt. Lofty, visited by 500,000 people annually and part of Cleland Conservation Park. Take the South Eastern Fwy. out of the city, exit at Crafers, and follow the signs (20-25min.). The ⊠**Mt. Lofty Summit** has spectacular views of the city, the coast and, on a clear day, even Kangaroo Island. The complex at the summit includes a **cafe** and an **Info Centre** with extensive info about hikes in the surrounding Cleland Conservation Park. There is a hiking trail connecting the summit with Cleland and other trails that go around the summit. (☎8370 1054. Open daily 9am-5pm.) On the road leading to the summit, south of Mt. Lofty, the **Mt. Lofty Botanic Gardens** are a great place for a picnic or a leisurely stroll. (☎8228 2311. Open M-F 9am-4pm, Sa-Su 10am-5pm.) The limited-access **Mt. Lofty YHA ❶**, 20km from Adelaide, is an easy choice for an overnight in the Adelaide Hills. (Book through Adelaide Central YHA/YHA Travel ☎8414 3000; pick up keys from Mt. Lofty Summit Info Centre. Dorms $16.50, entire cabin $140.) The **Cleland Conservation Park** (☎8339 2444) is a wildlife sanctuary that allows visitors to roam freely amongst the (tame) wildlife; pet the fuzzy koalas at the **Wildlife Park.** (Open daily 9:30am-5pm. $9.50, children $5.50.) **Aboriginal Cultural Guided Tours** are given on Yurridla Trail. (☎8339 2769. W and Su 11am and 1:30pm. $3.)

ALDGATE. Aldgate is a good base for exploring the Hills, as it is also close to Warrawong Sanctuary and easily accessible. Buses #163, 163F, and 165 run here from Adelaide (20-30min.). ⊠**Geoff and Hazel's ❹**, 19 Kingsland Rd., is a three-bedroom, eco-friendly hotel, the perfect antidote to crowded hostels, featuring a balcony, cozy lounge room and kitchen, log fire, hammocks, free breakfast, veggie garden, and friendly chickens. From Adelaide, turn right on Kingsland Rd. at the town's main intersection and walk 100m up the hill. (☎8339 8360. Internet $2 per hr. Breakfast and linen included. Book ahead. Singles and twins $50.)

WARRAWONG SANCTUARY. The Adelaide Hills area has recently become famous for its conservation efforts, thanks largely the ⊠**Warrawong Sanctuary,** on Stock Rd. in Mylor. Over 15 years ago, John Wamsley decided to build an elaborate "vermin-proof fence" to keep out cats, foxes, and other feral animals introduced to the Australian continent by European immigrants. Now all manner of native Australian species, some virtually extinct elsewhere, flourish here: bettongs, wallabies, rainbow parrots, short-nosed bandicoots, and innumerable native bird species all call this place home. By car, get off the Highway at Stirling and follow the signs for Warrawong. (☎8370 9197. Admission only by guided walks at dusk or dawn, 5:45pm or 6:30am; $22, children $17.50. Wetlands walks daily 11am and 3pm; $15. Book ahead. Cabins and restaurant. Overnight accommodation packages include 2 meals, 2 tours, and lodging; $150, children $70; weekend $225/$95.)

⊠**HAHNDORF.** Originally settled by German Lutherans in 1839, the most touristed village in Adelaide Hills looks like something from a German fairy tale. Most businesses in town are on Main St., including the area's **Visitors Center,** several **ATMs,** some restaurants and shops, and the **post office**, 73 Main St. In an area fast becoming known for its wines, **Hillstowe Wines,** 101 Main St., offers a tasting opportunity at its cellar door on the west end of Main St; be sure to try the shiraz. (☎8388 1400. Open daily 10am-5pm.) The **Beerenberg Strawberry Farm,** on the eastern edge of town, allows visitors to pick strawberries daily during the strawberry season, from October to May. (☎8388 7272. Entry $1, strawberries $6 per kg.) **Accommodations ❺** around town consist mostly of motels and B&Bs, starting at about $85.

SOUTH AUSTRALIA

FLEURIEU PENINSULA

The Fleurieu Peninsula (FLOOR-ee-oh) stretches southeast from Adelaide, encompassing the luscious vineyards of McLaren Vale, miles of coastline, and several charming seaside towns. The region's proximity to Adelaide has made it a popular weekend getaway, but there are affordable accommodations to be found and the Fleurieu's popularity rarely translates into crowding. Beautiful drives weave through quiet hills covered with sheep or vineyards and lead to tranquil beaches and jaw-dropping views.

TRANSPORTATION. Premier Stateliner runs between Adelaide and Goolwa, through the towns of: McLaren Vale; Willunga; Victor Harbor; Port Elliot; and Middleton. (☎8415 5555. M-F 5 per day, Sa 2 per day, Su 1 per day.) Buses to Cape Jervis, departure point for the Kangaroo Island ferry, are handled by **Sealink** (see **Kangaroo Island: Transportation,** p. 459).

TOURS OF THE FLEURIEU. Enjoy Adelaide operates a popular tour from Adelaide, with stops at two wineries in McLaren Vale, a train ride, and an evening Granite Island Little Penguin tour. (☎8332 1401. M, Th, and Sa-Su 2:30pm. $55, children $36.) **Camel Winery Tours,** based at the Camel Farm between Kangarilla and McLaren Flat, offers a one-day winery safari on camelback with up to seven winery visits and lunch included. (☎8383 0488. Starts at 10:30am. $80.) **Just Cruisin Chauffeur Car** provides the opportunity to tour the peninsula in a 1962 Cadillac, highlighting wineries, nature, galleries, and the region's history. The company also offers 4WD tours of the peninsula. (☎8383 0529. From $170 per day.) The ◙**Glenelg Beach Resort** (see p. 444) has fun tours from Adelaide to McLaren Vale.

MCLAREN VALE   ☎08

Just 45 minutes (37km) south of Adelaide, the idyllic, sleepy set of vineyards near the small town of McLaren Vale (pop. 2000) sit in the grassy inland knolls of the Fleurieu Peninsula. The McLaren Vale wine region, which centers around the town of McLaren Vale and nearby Willunga and McLaren Flat, has nearly 70 vineyards, most of which process world-class wines and operate cellar-door sales and tastings. While its proximity to Adelaide has meant the proliferation of pseudo-trendy cafes and B&Bs in recent years, there's still enough charm in the Vale to make it a worthwhile stop. The area also boasts the outstanding stretch of beaches surrounding the small town of Aldinga, just west of McLaren Vale.

Premier Stateliner (☎8415 5555) comes through town from the Adelaide central **bus station** (1hr.; M-F 4 per day, Sa 2 per day, Su 1 per day; $6). The best way to get to McLaren Vale is with a group of friends, a car, and a *designated driver*. The police take drink driving seriously; it is not uncommon to find Random Breath Testing Units (known as Breathos) on main roads to and from wine regions. To get to McLaren, drive out of Adelaide on **Main South Rd.** Follow Hwy. A13 off of Main South Rd. on to Victor Harbor Rd., and bear left onto Main Rd., McLaren Vale's main drag. The **McLaren Vale and Fleurieu Visitor Centre,** on the left, offers a map of the wineries and handles B&B bookings. (☎8323 9944.Open M-F 9am-5pm, Sa-Su 10am-5pm.) The road from the Visitors Center south to **Willunga** has wineries at every turn. **McLaren Flat,** on Kangarilla Rd., 3km east of McLaren Vale is, not surprisingly, also surrounded by wineries. Main Rd. in McLaren Vale has a **supermarket,** a **post office, ATMs,** and a number of cafes.

The majority of accommodations are old-world B&Bs (book through the Visitors Center), but most travelers make the area a daytrip from Adelaide. In **Willunga,** down Willunga or Victor Harbor Rd. from McLaren Vale, the **Willunga Hotel ❸,** on High St., offers clean, classic pub-hotel rooms and generous counter **meals ❷** from $10. (☎8556

2135. Breakfast included. $30.) Of the peninsula's many caravan parks, the **McLaren Vale Lakeside Caravan Park ❶**, on Field St., is most conveniently located for wine-tasting trips. (☎ 8323 9255. Sites $15, powered $18; vans with bath from $40; cabins from $58.) The **supermarket**, at the corner of Main Rd. and Kangarilla Rd., is open daily 9am-9pm.

NEAR MCLAREN VALE

WINERIES. McLaren Vale is the best-known wine area in South Australia after the Barossa Valley. The majority of the nearly 70 vineyards and wineries in the region, 45 of which offer cellar-door tastings and sales, are small and family-owned; notable exceptions include **Hardy's, Andrew Garret, Middlebrook,** and **Seaview.** Most cellar doors are open from 10am to 4:30 or 5pm daily; the Visitors Center has maps and a complete list of hours for all vineyards. For more information on vineyard touring, see p. 471.

    Wirra Wirra Vineyards (☎ 8323 8414), on McMurtrie Rd., follow signs from Willunga Rd. Once you've tasted the "Church Block Red," you won't want to leave. Open M-Sa 10am-5pm, Su 11am-5pm.

    Dennis of McLaren Vale (☎ 8323 8665), on Kangarilla Rd. Anyone who considers herself or himself a discerning and well-educated drinker would be remiss to leave the Vale without sampling Dennis's version of the oldest alcoholic beverage in recorded history, hot spiced mead. Made from fermented honey and scented with cloves, it is warmed before serving to bring out the aromas. It is also reputed to be a legendary aphrodisiac. Open M-F 10am-5pm, Sa-Su noon-5pm.

    Hamilton Fine Wines (☎ 8523 8211), on Main Rd. One of the biggest producers in the McLaren region. The airy cellar door is on the road toward Willunga. Open M-F 10am-5pm, Sa-Su 11am-5pm.

    Marienberg Wines, 2 Chalk Hill Rd. (☎ 8323 9666), just 100m from the info center. Founded in 1966 by Ursula Pridham, Australia's first female winemaker. Open daily 10am-5pm.

    Hardy's Tintara (☎ 8323 9185), on Main Rd. The largest winery in the area. Reds, whites, sparkling wines, ports, and brandy are all made here, and its location in the heart of town makes it one of the area's most popular stops. Open daily 10am-4:30pm.

BEACHES. Just a few kilometers west of McLaren Vale, the beaches near Aldinga are among the finest you'll find on the Fleurieu. A beautiful and popular stretch of beaches line Aldinga Bay and include, from the south, **Sellick's Beach, Silver Sands Beach, Aldinga Beach, Port Willunga,** and **Maslin's Beach.** There is car access to the beach at Sellick's and Aldinga, and you can drive on the sand from one end to the other even in a 2WD, although you should be careful to stay out of the deep sand ($4.50 per car for beach access). **Maslin's Beach,** 5km north of Aldinga, is perhaps the best stretch. There is history here, as well: it was the first official "unclad bathing" beach in Australia, and, by the looks of it, those first pioneering nudists have stayed. There is still a one-day "nude Olympics" each year in January. The nude portion starts 500m south of the carpark, so fully clad bathers can also enjoy this spectacular expanse of sand encircled by limestone cliffs.

    Area accommodation is mainly found in **caravan parks,** with the **Beach Woods Eco Tourist Park ❶**, atop the cliffs at the south end of Maslin Beach, reigning as the best of the bunch, with easy beach access. (☎ 8556 6113. Sites $12, powered $17; budget rooms $15.40 per person; on-site 2-person vans $35; 2-person cabins from $55). In Aldinga, the **Aldinga Bay Holiday Village ❺** (☎ 8556 5019) has good deals for larger groups, with four-person cabins from $70 and budget cabins for up to twelve people for $120. Aldinga has a **general store** with groceries, a post office, and petrol.

VICTOR HARBOR
☎ 08

Sheltered from the Southern Ocean by the sands of Encounter Bay, Victor Harbor (pop. 4600) has been popular with Adelaide weekenders since it was used as the summer residence of South Australia's colonial governors. It is safe to say that the town is fully on the tourist-beaten path, with the little penguins of Granite Island, along with the Clydesdale-powered tram that takes tourists there, proving a reliable draw. Mid-week, however, finds the quiet seaside town half-asleep and as peaceful as one could hope. Victor Harbor is now both an almost painfully romantic seaside spot and a decent base for surfing in Encounter Bay. Aside from that, the town also boasts a summer temperature as much as 10°C cooler than steamy Adelaide and whales swimming by the shore from May to October.

[**TRANSPORTATION. Premier Stateliner buses** (☎ 8415 5555) run from Adelaide to Stuart St. in Victor Harbor (1½-2hr.; M-F 5 per day, Sa 2 per day, Su 1 per day; $14.), continuing to Port Elliot, Middleton, and Goolwa. Buy tickets at **Travelworld** (☎ 8552 1200), in the Harbor Mall on Ocean St. To get to Kangaroo Island, book a **Sealink** bus to Cape Jervis and buy ferry tickets at the **Sealink Bookings Office** in the same building as the Visitors Center at the start of the Granite Island Causeway. (☎ 1800 088 552. 2 per day to Cape Jervis; $11. Book ahead. Open daily 9am-5pm.) Other services include: **taxis** (☎ 8552 2622); **RAA** (☎ 13 11 11 or 0427 527 033); and **Victor Rent-a-Car,** 66 Ocean St. (☎ 8552 1033; 25+; from $66 per day).

▚ ⁊ **ORIENTATION AND PRACTICAL INFORMATION.** Victor Harbor is 85km south of Adelaide on the Main South Rd. Flinders Pde. runs along the ocean beneath the shade of massive fir trees; the main commercial drag, Ocean St., runs a block behind, becoming Hindmarsh St. Victoria St. is the main street on the western side of the city and leads to the highway toward Cape Jervis. The **Tourist Information Centre,** near the causeway to Granite Island, is at the foot of Flinders Pde. (☎ 8552 5738 or 8552 7000. Open daily 9am-5pm.) Other services include: **ATMs** on Ocean St.; **police,** on Torrens St. (☎ 8552 2088); **library,** 10 Coral St., just off Ocean St., with free **Internet** (☎ 8552 3009; open Tu-Th 10am-5:30pm, F 10am-6pm, Sa 10am-1pm); and a **post office,** 54 Ocean St. (M-F 9am-5pm). **Postal Code:** 5211.

▛⟟ **ACCOMMODATIONS AND FOOD.** The **Anchorage ❷,** on the corner of Coral St. and Flinders Pde., offers waterfront lodging at budget prices, along with a restaurant and ship-shaped cafe/bar with live music on the weekends. (☎ 8552 5970; victor@anchorage.mtx.net. Key deposit $10. 4- to 6-bed dorms $17; hotel singles $40; doubles with continental breakfast $65-70.) The 100-year-old **Grosvener Junction Hotel ❷,** 40 Ocean St., has simple, pleasant rooms and a balcony with great views. (☎ 8552 1011. TV lounge and fridge, but no kitchen. Continental breakfast included. Backpackers $25; singles $30; doubles $60.) **Victor Harbor Beach Front Caravan Park ❷,** 114 Victoria St., is on the west side of the city, before the second roundabout on the road toward Cape Jervis. (☎ 8552 1111. Key deposit $10. Book ahead in summer. Sites for 2 $16, powered $18, beachfront $24; cabins from $50.)

For a sit-down meal, the **Anchorage Bar and Restaurant ❶,** on Flinders Pde., has mains from about $10. (☎ 8552 5970. Breakfasts and lunches from $6. Open daily 8am-late). The **Original Victor Harbor Fish Shop ❶,** 20 Ocean St., offers fish 'n' chips ($7-13) and burgers for $6-9. (☎ 8552 1273. Open Su-Th 9am-7:30pm, F-Sa 9am-8:30pm.) Woolworth's **supermarket** is in the Victor Central Mall on Torrens St. (Open daily 7am-10pm.)

◙ ◪ **SIGHTS AND ACTIVITIES.** Little penguins win top billing on **Granite Island,** although the island is also home to a **walking trail** (45min. loop), a cafe, and a brilliant **lookout** with views back to the town and over expansive **Encounter Bay.** Entry is free if you take the ten-minute stroll across the causeway, but you can also cross on a Clydesdale-drawn tram. (Tram runs daily every hr. 10am-4pm; extended hours during holidays. $6 return, children $3.50.) The **little penguins** can only be seen at dusk; access to the island is limited to those on the guided penguin tour to insure penguin safety. The **Penguin Interpretive Centre** is open 30min. before the guided penguin walks, which start on the island side of the bridge. (☎8552 7555. $10, concessions $9, children $7. Daily in winter 5:30pm, in summer 9pm.)

The neighboring towns of Port Elliot, Middleton, and Goolwa (see below) are accessible by a **coastal drive,** the **Encounter Bikeway,** and the Goolwa to Victor Harbor **Cockle Train.** The bikeway follows the coastline for 24km between Goolwa and Victor and is popular with bikers, in-line skaters, and even pedestrians tackling shorter sections. Rent a bike at **Victor Harbor Cycle and Skate,** on Victoria St. (☎8552 1417; half-day $14, full-day $20) and in Goolwa at the Goolwa Caravan Park at Laffin Pt. on the eastern edge of town (☎8555 2737; half-day $15, full-day $20). The Cockle Train follows the route of Australia's first steel railway, laid between Goolwa and Victor in 1854. The train now takes 30min., with trips nearly every day during January, April, and July but just once a week in the off season. Check with the information centers in Goolwa or Victor to see when it's running (one-way $14, return $20; children $11/$7).

Near the causeway entrance, the **South Australian Whale Centre,** 2 Railway Tce., traces Victor's evolution from whaling to whale watching. (☎8552 5644. Open daily 11am-4:30pm; $5, children $2.50.) For the latest **whale-sighting** info, call the center's hotline (☎1900 931 223; 75¢ per min.). **Urimbirra Wildlife Park,** 5km from Victor Harbor up the road toward Adelaide, has koalas, wetland birds, and dingoes. (☎8554 6554. Open daily 9am-6pm. Koalas at 11am, 2, and 4pm; croc feeding 1:30pm. $8.)

Try your hand at **parasailing** through **Odyssey Adventures,** on the Victor Harbor-Granite Island causeway. (☎0418 891 998; $65, $55 each for groups of 6 or more; operates Nov. to Apr.; book ahead.)

PORT ELLIOT AND MIDDLETON   ☎08

While vacation homes are beginning to make the Victor-to-Goolwa stretch one long entity, Port Elliot has retained a perfect beach-town feel. The Fleurieu Hwy. passes along the north side of town, assuming the name North Tce., while The Strand, the town's other significant street, heads south from North Tce. opposite the Royal Family Hotel. A small IGA **supermarket** (open daily 8am-7pm) is next to the hotel on North Tce., and The Strand is lined with an assortment of antiques and second-hand shops. ▨**Arnella by the Sea (YHA) ❷,** 28 North Tce., occupies the oldest building in the town, with beautiful early-Australian style rooms, spacious kitchen, and leafy back patio. The owners also arrange bike hire and tours. (☎8554 3611 or 1800 066 297; narnu@bigpond.com. Reception daily 8am-noon and 2-8pm. 3-bed dorms $22, YHA $20; singles $33/$30; twins and doubles $55/$50; family rooms $66/$60.) The **Royal Family Hotel ❸,** just west of the Arnella on North Tce., offers standard pub accommodation and the only bar in town (☎8554 2219; singles $30, doubles $40). Just west is the **Port Elliot Caravan and Tourist Park ❷** (☎8554 2134; sites $16, powered $20; cabins from $55), fronting beautiful (and appropriately shaped) **Horseshoe Bay,** the town's main beach. Signs lead there from North Tce. and a walking trail to a lookout over the bay departs from the beach's west end. To the west of town, **Boomer Beach** is less protected than Horseshoe Bay and its bigger waves make it a popular surf spot.

Middleton, just 5km east of Port Elliot, consists of little more than a petrol station, a general store, and a caravan park, but is reputed to have the best **surfing** on the Fleurieu at its spectacular beach.

SOUTH AUSTRALIA

GOOLWA   ☎08

Goolwa's has the peaceful airs of both a river town and a seaside hamlet. Its proximity to Adelaide has made it a popular weekend and vacation spot, with prices escalating accordingly. At the northern end of **Coorong National Park** (see p. 476), it is an ideal jumping-off point for waterborne adventures.

The town's main street is the road from Adelaide, which becomes Cadell St. in town and leads to the waterfront before making a westward turn and becoming Victor Harbor Rd., passing through Middleton and Port Elliot en route to Victor. The **Signal Point Interpretive Centre**, at the end of Cadell St., on the waterfront, books local tours and boat excursions. (☎8555 3488. Open daily 9am-5pm.) The **police** can be reached at ☎8555 2018. **ATMs**, the **post office**, and restaurants can all be found on Cadell St., as can the **library** (☎8555 2030; open M-F 10am-5pm, Sa 9:30am-12:30pm; **Internet** free). The Foodland **supermarket** is on the Victor Harbor Rd. in the Goolwa Village Shopping Centre (open M-Sa 8am-7pm, Su 9am-6pm).

The **PS Murray River Queen ❷**, a floating motel permanently docked at the Goolwa wharf, has unbeatable views and surprisingly comfortable accommodation, though budget travelers will have to settle for below-deck accommodation with a small porthole for a window. (☎8555 1733. Budget singles $20; doubles $38; upper-deck staterooms $130.) Camping and cabins are available at the **Goolwa Caravan Park ❶**, on Noble Ave. at the far eastern end of town, where you can also rent bikes or canoes. (☎8555 2737. Bike hire $15 per half-day, $20 per full-day; canoes $10 per hr. Sites $15, powered $18; cabins for 2 from $53.)

The █**Signal Point (River Murray) Interpretive Centre**, on the Wharf in Goolwa, provides a fascinating education in the role of the Murray River in the life and economy of South Australia, along with remarkable exhibits on Aboriginal culture and storytelling in the region. (☎8555 3488. $5.50, concessions $4.40, children $2.75. Open daily 9am-5pm; last entrance 4pm.) The recently completed **bridge** to **Hindmarsh Island**, across the Murray River from Goolwa, has opened up the island to real-estate developers, to the anger of many locals. But it also enables the visitor to drive right out to the Murray's mouth and see the **pelicans** that feed there regularly. Other lookout points on the island feature birds and the massive **barrages** built in the 1930s to separate fresh river water from seawater.

The **Encounter Bikeway** and **Cockle Train** link Goolwa to Victor Harbor (see p. 456 for both). **Boat** excursions into the northern reaches of **Coorong National Park** or out to the Murray's mouth are popular, as well, with several tours operating from Goolwa's wharf (see p. 476). The free █**Wellington Ferry**, at the small hamlet of Wellington, crosses the Murray River, taking about eight cars across on each pass (open 24hr.). **Jet skis** can be hired at **Goolwa Jet Ski Hire** (☎8555 2573) and **canoes** and **bikes** are available from the Goolwa Caravan Park.

CAPE JERVIS   ☎08

Approaching Cape Jervis, the Southern Ocean stretches endlessly into the distance, broken only by occasional views of Kangaroo Island, as the road descends, seeming to disappear into the water ahead of you. Cape Jervis serves mostly as the jumping-off point for the **Kangaroo Island ferry.** Most simply shoot through en route to or from the ferry without stopping to appreciate the quiet solitude or the unique █**Cape Jervis Station ❶**, an amalgam of accommodation and activities options to suit any budget or taste, once solely a sheep station. Options range from the decked-out train car called the *Orient Express* (doubles $70) to the backpacker set-up in the cottage-like Shearers' Quarters ($20 per person). The Sealink bus picks up and drops off at the gate, and guests are entitled to free ferry transfers. (☎8598 0288. Sites $14, powered $17; dorms $20; singles from $50; doubles from $65, both with breakfast.) The rest of the "town" consists of the **pub/gas station/general store** complex between the Station and the Ferry. There is a **Sealink** office at the ferry dock, but book well in advance.

The **Deep Creek Conservation Park ❶**, 13km from Cape Jervis on the road to Victor Harbor, contains 4500 hectares of coastal bushland and features sea-coast views of the Backstairs Passage and Kangaroo Island, as well as bush-walking and relative solitude. **Blowhole Beach,** a steep 3km from Cobbler Hill picnic area, and **Deep Creek Cover,** 6.4km from Tapanappa Campground, are spectacular walks that cross the Heysen Trail. The **Park Headquarters** (☎8598 0263), by the entrance to the park, is usually unstaffed but is well-stocked with maps and info, and is one of several points to self-register for day passes ($5 per car) and camping permits. ($15 per night for the Stringybark area, near the ranger station, the only one with toilets and showers, or $6 per night for any of the 3 more remote, and beautiful, bushcamping sites.)

KANGAROO ISLAND ☎08

Queensland shows off the Great Barrier Reef, Victoria flaunts the Great Ocean Rd., the Northern Territory struts Kakadu, and South Australia retorts with Kanga-roo Island (KI). It's expensive to get there and around, but the island's abundant wildlife and impressive array of activities and attractions make it a worthwhile destination. KI (pop. 4100) was home to the first European settlement in South Australia in 1836 but was abandoned for Adelaide four years later when timber and freshwater supplies at Kingscote proved insufficient. Early islanders repre-sented a healthy mix of sealers, whalers, and escaped convicts, but today the most suspect elements of the sparsely-populated island are the hordes of tourists who launch their daily assaults via the ferry from Cape Jervis and flights from Adelaide.

The island has 21 national and local conservation parks, including the magnifi-cent Flinders Chase National Park. All of these offer good opportunities to see kangaroos, koalas, wallabies, goannas, and even echidnas; to stroll among a col-ony of Australian sea lions; to watch New Zealand fur seals wave-surf; and to climb over and through awesome geological formations.

▐ TRANSPORTATION

GETTING THERE

BY FERRY AND COACH. As **Kangaroo Island Sealink** has the monopoly on trans-port to Cape Jervis and the island, prices are steep and discounts are hard to come by. Student concession fares apply only to those 18 and under, and those bringing cars still have to pay for passenger tickets. **Ferries** take about an hour to cross the Backstairs Passage between Cape Jervis and Penneshaw and depart four times daily, with additional sailings during peak times. (Bookings are mandatory; call ☎13 13 01 or 8202 8688 daily 7:30am-10pm. $64 return, children $32; cars $138 return.) Sealink offers connecting **coach** service between Adelaide and the Cape Jervis ferry dock from Adelaide's central bus station, 101 Franklin St. (Book ahead. 2 hr.; 2 per day; one-way $16, return including ferry $96.) One Sealink coach per day in each direction also connects Cape Jervis to the Fleurieu towns of Victor Harbor and Goolwa. (Book ahead. Goolwa to Cape Jervis 7am, Cape Jervis to Goolwa 8:30pm. 1½hr. $11 one-way.)

BY AIR. Two airlines depart from Adelaide's airport, each two to four times per day, and land at **Kingscote Airport,** 13km from the town of Kingscote at Cygnet River. **Regional Express (Rex)** occasionally has good deals on airfares, especially

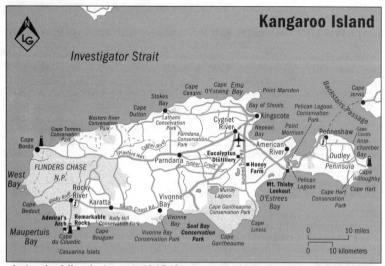

during the fall and winter. (☎ 13 17 13; www.regionalexpress.com.au) **Emu Airlines** is not as earthbound as its flightless namesake and the Adelaide to Kingscote run is its only regular route. (☎ 8234 3711 or 1800 182 353. From $93 one-way with a 2-week advance purchase.) The **airport shuttle** service that runs to Kingscote must be pre-booked. (☎ 8553 2390. $12 per person.)

GETTING AROUND

There is **no public transportation** on the island, so bring a car over on the ferry (return $138) or rent one ($80-120 per day) if you don't want to be on a tour ($160-250, usually including coach, ferry, and accommodation). Those silly enough to plan on walking, riding a bike, or hitching around the island will have to content themselves with the island's eastern towns: main attractions are 75-100km from Penneshaw and Kingscote, and passing motorists can be few and far between.

The limited **Sealink coach service** runs between Kingscote and the ferry terminal in Penneshaw (1hr.) stopping in American River (30min.) on the way, but if that's all you see of the island, it won't be worth the ferry ticket price. Book ahead for Sealink coaches that leave Kingscote (7am and 5:30pm). Two per day leave Penneshaw (10am and 7pm) and arrive in Kingscote ($11) via American River ($8).

> Those **driving** should be alert and control their speed at all times and especially at dusk: animals do not respect the rules of the road and are easily confused by headlights.

BY CAR. Most of the primary tourist thoroughfares are paved and unsealed roads leading to major sights are generally in good condition, so a 4WD is helpful but not necessary. Rental companies offer free shuttles between the airport and Kingscote as well as a ferry pick-up option. **Budget** has offices in Penneshaw next to the Sealink office and in Kingscote at 57a Dauncey St. They rent to those over 21, though you must be at least 25 to rent a 4WD. (☎ 8553 3133 or 0408 815 737. From $76 per day for a small car to $153 per day for a 4WD.) You must be over 25 to rent from Hertz-affiliate **Kangaroo Island Rental Cars,** on the corner of Franklin St. and Telegraph Rd., Kingscote, which also arranges competitive fly-drive packages.

(☎8553 2390 or 1800 088 296. Full-day with 200km for manual $83, for 4WD $138.) **Penneshaw Car Rentals** rents small, late model cars with A/C and caters to those over 21. (☎8593 0023 or 1800 686 620. Half-day with 100km $65, full-day with 240km $90; upgrade to unlimited km for $20 extra.)

TOURS. Most tours are led by friendly, knowledgeable guides and hit the "must-see" sights. One-day tours can be grueling, with most lasting 10-12 hours. Tours that allow at least one night on the island are a much better way to go. Several companies run good two- and three-day tours departing from Adelaide.

CampWild Adventures (☎1800 444 321) offers a 3-day 4WD camping trip that hits all the big sights at a relaxed pace. Fun activities include sandboarding, ATV rides, and sleeping under the stars. Departs in summer daily; in winter Tu, Th, and Sa. $350, ISIC/ YHA $320. Price includes pickup in Adelaide, private ferry with dolphin watching, meals, accommodation, and park entrance. Max. 10 people.

Wayward Bus (☎8410 8833) runs a popular 2-day tour from Adelaide's Central Bus Terminal. Their fun tour covers all the big sights, running along the south coast the 1st day and covering Flinders Chase and the north coast the 2nd day. Departs M, W-Th, and Sa 6:30am; additional departures Oct.-Apr. $310. Price includes all transport (including ferry), meals, park entry fees, and accommodation at the KI Wilderness Resort.

Adventure Tours Australia (☎1300 654 604) offers a good 2-day tour, along with a 3-day 4WD tour that hits more remote areas. Slightly older than 20-something crowd. 2-day leaves M, W, and Sa 7am; $315. 3-day departs M, Th, and Sa 7am; $410.

Sealink (☎13 13 01) covers the big sights from Adelaide, Cape Jervis, or Victor Harbor. Standby-rates are 15% off and must be booked a day ahead; availability is limited in peak season. Departs Adelaide 6:45am, returns 10:30pm. From Adelaide $179, flight $341; from Cape Jervis $149; from Victor Harbor $171; from Penneshaw $99.

Gray Line Adelaide Sightseeing (☎1300 838 687) runs a day-tour similar to Sealink. Hotel pickup available. Departs daily 6:45am. Return to Adelaide from $180.

Kangaroo Island Ferry Connections (☎8553 1233 or 1800 018 484) offers a day tour with pickup and drop off in Penneshaw that covers all the big sights and includes morning tea, lunch, and a backpacker-friendly price. $85; with flight to the island and ferry/ coach back to Adelaide the same day $236.

BY BIKE, CAMEL, AND OTHER MEANS. Penneshaw Youth Hostel and **Kangaroo Island Central Backpackers,** in Kingscote, both hire bikes (full-day around $20). **Bob's Bikes,** 1 Commercial St., Kingscote, rents single and tandem bikes. (☎8553 2349. $6.50 per hr., $16.50 per day; tandems $9/$27.50). Be warned, however, that you're not going to see much of anything by bike—the island is simply too big. For an aerial view of the island's sights, sign up for a breathtaking flight with **Kangaroo Island Wilderness Flights** in Parndana. (☎8559 4254. $65 per person per 30min., $120 per hr.) **KI Outdoor Action** offers day or evening ATV tours. (☎8559 4296. Surfboards, kayaks, and snorkelling gear also available for rent.) Finally, if you've always wanted to camp out with a camel, try **Kangaroo Island Camel Safaris.** They offer all-inclusive trips for two or more nights on Dudley Peninsula. (☎8553 1147. From $85 per person per night. Call in advance.)

■■ 🔏 ORIENTATION AND PRACTICAL INFORMATION

Kangaroo Island's 4500km² make it Australia's third-largest island after Tasmania and Melville in the NT. The ferry lands in Penneshaw, on the northern shore of Dudley Peninsula, at the **east end** of the island. From there, most visitors follow Hog Bay Rd. towards American River and Kingscote, both to the west of Penneshaw. The inland Playford Hwy. heads west from Kingscote through the middle of the island before ending at Cape Borda at the island's northwestern tip. The South Coast Rd. diverges from the Playford Hwy. 15km west of Kingscote and swings through the **south coast,** leading to the main entrance to Flinders Chase National Park, which covers most of KI's **west end,** as well as a junction with the West End Hwy., which runs north through Flinders Chase into the Playford Hwy. The Playford Hwy., South Coast Rd., and West End Hwy. are all sealed roads, but access roads to many sights along the way are unsealed. The unsealed North Coast Rd. is accessible via the Playford Hwy. and leads to the **north coast's** tranquil beaches.

The **Gateway Visitors Information Centre** is just outside Penneshaw, on the road toward Kingscote (☎8553 1185. Open M-F 9am-5pm, Sa-Su 10am-4pm.) Aside from Kingscote and Penneshaw, **petrol stations** and **general stores** can be found at: American River, Vivonne Bay, the KI Wilderness Resort, Island Beach, and Parndana. Many of these stores have limited selections, so stock up on the mainland or in Penneshaw or Kingscote before heading out. The **Island Parks Pass** allows unlimited access to Seal Bay, Kelly Hill Caves, Flinders Chase, and the Cape Borda and Cape Willoughby lighthouse tours. (Valid for 1 year. Available at any of the locations and the visitors center. $30, children $22, families $80.) Penguin tours, adventure caving, and camping in Flinders Chase are not covered by the pass.

> **! WILDFIRE!** Kangaroo Island, like many of South Australia's rural areas, treats the threat of wildfire seriously. **Fire Ban Season** lasts from the start of December to the end of April, the driest months of the year. During this time, there are a series of restrictions on camping fires: the fire must be contained in a BBQ, cooker, or fireplace, and cannot be bigger than one square meter in area. You must stay with the fire while it is lit. On particularly dry days the Country Fire Service might call for a **Total Fire Ban,** in which case only gas or electric stoves or BBQs can be used and many walking trails are closed. Never toss cigarettes or matches from cars. For more info, call the CFS hotline (☎1300 362 361).

THE EAST END

PENNESHAW   ☎08

Penneshaw (pop. 250) is the primary ferry arrival point from Cape Jervis on the mainland. A quick stroll up North Tce. from the ferry jetty leads to the pub, **petrol station,** and a few small restaurants; Nat Turner St. connects North Tce. to the **post office** (open M-F 9am-5pm, Sa 9-11am) and to Middle Tce. The **Kangaroo Island Gateway Visitors Centre,** 1km down the road toward Kingscote from Penneshaw's ferry terminus, serves as the island's info center, providing maps, camping permits, and tour info. (☎8553 1185. Open M-F 9am-5pm, Sa-Su 10am-4pm.)

Penneshaw's main attraction, besides the ferry, is its **little penguins.** Each night after sunset, the 30cm penguins waddle back to their burrows along the coastline. The **Penguin Interpretive Centre** is just east of the ferry dock, off Middle Tce. The lighted wooden boardwalk is closed after dusk, making guided tours the only way to really see the penguins. (☎8553 1103. Tours including penguin center admission daily at 8:30pm and 9:30pm; in winter 7:30pm and 8:30pm. $6, concessions $4.50.)

Kangaroo Island YHA ❷, 33 Middle Tce., offers roomy, colorful six-bed rooms with stove, refrigerator, and bath, as well as motel-style doubles and triples. (☎8553 1233. Reception M-F 9am-5pm, Sa-Su 9am-12pm. Dorms $23; twins and doubles $73; triples $86. YHA $19/$60/$68.) **Penneshaw Youth Hostel ❷,** 43 North Tce., has simple accommodations, with kitchen, TV lounge, and a small courtyard. (☎8553 1284. Reception 7:45am-7:30pm. 8-bed dorms $19; singles $35; twins and doubles $44.) The hostel also

SOUTH AUSTRALIA

runs diving tours, including a half-day resort course ($83), a three-day PADI certification course ($310), and personalized longer tours. Both hostels have cheap restaurants attached. The IGA Welcome-Mart, on Middle Tce., has **groceries.** (Open M-F 8:30am-6pm, Sa-Su 8:30am-4pm.)

KINGSCOTE   ☎ 08

Kingscote (pop. 1500), KI's largest town, can be a welcome stop for civilization-starved visitors returning from the western end of the island. The Esplanade runs along the water and becomes Kingscote Tce. and then Chapman Tce. moving south. Most of the shops and services are one block in from the beach on **Dauncey St.** which is intersected by Telegraph Rd., Commercial St., Murray St., and Drew St. Services include: **tourist info** at the **Kingscote Gift Shop,** 78 Dauncey St. (☎8553 2165; open daily 8:30am-6pm; camping permits and Island Parks Pass available); the **Sealink** office, next to the Newsagent on Dauncey St. (☎13 13 01; open M-F 9am-5pm, Sa 9am-noon); an **ATM** at Bank SA, on Dauncey St.; **police** (☎8553 2018); **RAA** (☎8553 2162); the island's only **hospital** (☎8553 4200; call 000 for an ambulance); free **Internet** at the **library,** 41 Dauncey St., opposite Bank SA (☎8553 4516; open M 1-5pm, Tu-Sa 9:30am-5pm); and a **post office** on Dauncey St. (☎8553 2122. Open M-F 9am-5pm, Sa 9am-noon.) **Postal Code:** 5223.

At dusk, the rocky coast on the north side of town awakens with penguin activity. Guided tours of the **penguin burrows** depart twice nightly from the Ozone Hotel, at the corner of Chapman Tce. and Commercial St. (☎8553 2381. Tours in summer 9pm and 9:40pm; in winter 7:30pm and 8:30pm. Arrive 30min. early. $7, children $5.50, families $20.) **Pelicans** take center stage at the jetty at their 5pm feedings. Check times at the **KI Marine Centre,** on the wharf. (☎8553 3112. $2 donation.)

The **Queenscliffe Hotel ❺,** on Dauncey St., offers ensuite pub rooms in the heart of town with TV, fridge, and coffee-maker at inflated prices. (☎8553 2254. Singles $60; doubles $70; in winter $50/$60.) **Ellson's Seaview ❹,** on Chapman Tce. on the south side of town, has large rooms in the guest house that share a clean bathroom and are cheaper than those in the main motel. Ask for a sea view. (☎8553 2030. TV, fridge, tea and coffee included. Reception 8am-8:30pm. Singles $58; twins and doubles $70, extra person $10; ensuite motel singles from $115, doubles from $125.) The **Kangaroo Island Central Guesthouse and Hostel ❷,** 19 Murray St., four blocks from the coast, offers spartan but clean quarters and the cheapest beds in town. (☎8553 2711 or 0428 123 129. Reception M-F next door at the second-hand shop. Dorms $20; twins and doubles $45; family room for 4 $65.)

Roger's Deli and Cafe ❶, 76 Dauncey St., offers pies and hamburgers for $2-5 as well as Asian cuisine for $10-15. (☎8553 2053. Open Su-Th 8am-6pm, F-Sa 8am-9pm.) **Blue Gum Cafe ❶,** across from Roger's, serves pancakes with ice cream and maple syrup ($6) and sandwiches ($4-7) in a cheery setting. (☎8553 2089. Open M-F 7:30am-5:30pm, Sa 7:30am-12:30pm.) A Foodland **supermarket** is on the corner of Commercial and Osmond St. (open M-F 9am-5:30pm, Sa 9am-12:30pm) and an IGA supermarket is on Dauncey St. (Open M-F 9am-5:30pm, Sa 9am-noon.)

THE SOUTH COAST

Many of KI's most noteworthy (and touristed) sights line the south coast and are accessible via the recently paved South Coast Rd., which will also take you to Flinders Chase. The midday hours tend to see heavy day-tour traffic.

■ **SEAL BAY CONSERVATION PARK.** Arguably Kangaroo Island's finest natural attraction, Seal Bay Conservation Park allows visitors to stroll through one of the few remaining colonies of **Australian sea lions.** A hike along the boardwalk brings you within viewing of the sea lions, but to get onto the beach, guided **tours** (45min.)

are the only option. Despite heavy tourist traffic, standing ten feet from an 800-pound bull is a memorable experience. Pricier **sunset tours** reveal what happens in a seal colony when the sun goes down. *(60km along the South Coast Rd. from Kingscote; allow 45min. to drive. ☎8559 4207. Tours depart Feb.-Nov. every 30-45min. daily 9am-4:15pm; Dec.-Jan. 9am-7pm. Tour and boardwalk access $10, concessions $7, families $25. Boardwalk only $6.70/$5.20/$19. Sunset tours Dec.-Jan. only $20/$12/$50.)*

LITTLE SAHARA. A short drive west of Seal Bay, Little Sahara's surprisingly large dunes are here for the climbing. A 20min. walk leads to the top of a high sand ridge, where you'll realize your folly if you thought you were going to walk to the beach from here: it's very, very far away. You'll also have great views of the surrounding dunes and a fun tumble back down toward your car. In the summer, try to avoid midday—this is the Sahara, after all. *(From Seal Bay, turn left when you get back to South Coast Rd. After about 5km, take the first road left. The road into the carpark is about a 5min. drive from the main road, but the last stretch is rough; use extra caution.)*

VIVONNE BAY. Vivonne Bay, just west of Seal Bay and Little Sahara on the South Coast Rd., hosts one of the few petrol stations and general stores on the western part of the island. (Open daily 8am-8pm.) It also hosts a stunning curve of sandy **beach** that is home to the island's lobster fleet and is ideal for picnics and popular with surfers. The beach was recently voted one of the cleanest in Australia. Swimming at Vivonne Bay should only be attempted near the boat jetty or in the mouth of the Harriet River, as the rest of the beach has a strong undertow. Vivonne Bay also houses the **Kangaroo Island Outdoor Education Field Study Centre,** which organizes lessons on local wildlife. *(From the general store, it is 3km down an unsealed road to the beach. Outdoor Ed. Centre is just off the South Coast Rd., behind the store. ☎8559 4232. Classes from 2 days to 3 weeks; accommodation provided. Call ahead.)*

KELLY HILL. The **Kelly Hill Caves,** on South Coast Rd. about halfway between Vivonne Bay and the Flinders Chase Visitors Center, are the main attraction of **Kelly Hill Conservation Park.** The largest cave area is accessible on a 40min. guided tour. **Adventure Caving tours** require advance booking and cover some of the smaller, more delicate caves. There is a picnic area near the carpark, as well as several walking trails that wind through the surrounding bushland. *(25km west of Vivonne Bay and 20km east of Flinders Chase. ☎8559 7231. Tours daily Feb.-Nov. 10, 11am, noon, 1:30, 2:30, 3:30pm. Additional tours available Dec.-Jan. at 12:45 and 4:30pm. $7, concessions $5.50, families $20. Adventure tours daily 2pm; book ahead. $23-34, concessions $14-19, families $59-87.)*

HANSON BAY SANCTUARY. This privately owned wildlife sanctuary, 10km west of Kelly Caves and 4km west of the turnoff for Hanson Bay, has become one of the island's prime koala-viewing spots. Many of the koalas here were brought from the area around the Rocky River Visitors Center in Flinders Chase when the population there grew too large. Though usually asleep, koalas can be spotted by patient visitors in the eucalypts along the entrance road. *($2 adults, children free.)*

SURFING. Kangaroo Island also provides ample opportunities to hit the **surf.** Visit the Kangaroo Island Gateway Visitors Center in Penneshaw for the *Surfing Guide,* which details the breaks along the south coast at **Hanson Bay, Vivonne Bay, D'Estrees Bay,** and **Pennington Bay.** The most convenient of these are Vivonne and Pennington Bays, both accessible via sealed roads and both good for all levels of surfers, though the big waves and rocky breaks at Hanson and D'Estrees make them suitable for advanced surfers only. Contact the info center for weather conditions. Full-length wetsuits are the rule, as the water is cool year-round.

THE WEST END

The West End of the island is where the wild things are. You will find few shops and restaurants out here, so bring some food along. The serene and secluded ▨**Flinders Chase Farm ❶** is the perfect place to stargaze and rest up before or after the sights and trails of Flinders Chase. On a 2000-acre sheep and cattle farm just 15min. north of the park entrance on the West End Hwy., the friendly owners offer self-contained cabins and spotless dorms with full kitchen, BBQ, and bathrooms. (☎8559 7223; chillers@kin.net.au. Linen provided. Dorms $15; cabins for 1 or 2 $50.) The **Western KI Caravan Park ❶** is 4km east of the Flinders Chase entrance on the South Coast Rd. (☎8559 7201; beckwith@kin.net.au. Sites $15, powered $18; tent hire from $20; cabins for 2 from $80.) The **KI Wilderness Resort ❸**, on South Coast Rd. just before the entrance to Flinders Chase, offers all manner of accommodation, from dorms to a luxury suite with private spa. (☎8559 7275. No backpacker kitchen. 4-bed dorms $35; ensuite doubles $80; luxury motel $120 single, $160 double; spa suite $300.) The Resort also has **petrol** and a **general store**, as well as a **pub ❶** (takeaway burgers and sandwiches served noon-3pm, from $5; dinner served 6-8pm, counter meals from $10), a relatively upscale **restaurant ❹** (mains from $15 to $35), and **Internet** access (coin-operated, $2 per 15min.)

FLINDERS CHASE NATIONAL PARK

Occupying the western end of the island, the rocks and animals of Flinders Chase are the jewel in KI's crown. Here you'll find wildlife, hiking, campsites, and some of the island's top attractions. Just over 100km from Kingscote, the newly rebuilt **Visitors Center** is at Rocky River, along the South Coast Rd., and has information, maps, and limited supplies, and also sells day-passes and camping permits. (☎8559 7235; fax 8559 7268. Open daily 9am-5pm. One-day park entry $6, children $3.50, families $15.50.) The most popular sights are clustered 15-20km south of Rocky River along a sealed road. The more remote sections of the park are accessible only via unsealed roads but can usually be reached by a 2WD.

The **Remarkable Rocks,** precariously perched on a 75m coastal clifftop, are huge hunks of granite sculpted into bizarre shapes by 750 million years of ice, wind, water, and lichens. Be careful on this rocky playground, as climbing up is inevitably easier than coming down. Five kilometers west of Remarkable Rocks, **Cape du Couedic** houses a red-capped sandstone lighthouse and a couple of short clifftop hikes. Just south of the lighthouse, a footpath winds to the edge of Cape du Couedic and then to the limestone cave of **Admiral's Arch.** A few thousand New Zealand **fur seals** call this area home and can be seen sunning themselves on the rocks and playing in the surf.

Flinders Chase National Park has **four camping sites ❶**, all non-powered with toilet facilities. The **Rocky River site,** near the Visitors Center, offers convenience and the only showers, but the sites are in a dirt clearing. Nine cheaper sites are 13km into the park at **Snake Lagoon,** where wildlife is much more plentiful. The two other sites are in the less frequented northern section of the park. The campground at **West Bay,** 20km west of Rocky River along an unsealed road, is beautifully remote and just 200m from the beach at the island's westernmost point. The campground at **Harvey's Return** is on the north coast. Permits are available for all sites at Rocky River Visitors Center. (☎8559 7235. Book ahead. Caravans allowed only at Rocky River and Snake Lagoon. Rocky River site $15; all other sites $6. Day fees must be paid in addition.) You can also rent a rustic **cabin ❷** at one of Flinders Chase's three lighthouse stations. (Book ahead ☎8859 7235. Linen $11.50 per person. $15-38 per person, children $6.50. Min. charge: Cape du Couedic $112.50, Cape Borda $50.40, and Cape Willoughby $75.)

Numerous short **hikes** and excellent two- to seven-day coastline treks are available for bushwalkers in Flinders Chase, and a drive to the western shore leads to some of the less touristed areas of the Park. Hikers should pick up the *Walking Trails in Kangaroo Island Parks* brochure from any Visitors Center. The **Breakneck River Trail** (6km; 2hr.) is a fairly easy, almost entirely flat, well-marked hike through a progression of plant communities, ending at a small beach with huge waves. Look for echidnas and rare, glossy, black cockatoos. The trailhead is on West Bay Rd., 13km from the Visitors Center. The **Snake Lagoon Hike** (3.3km; 1½hr.) is shorter with more interesting terrain, but also more demanding. The trailhead, with toilets and campsites, is at Snake Lagoon on West Bay Rd., 9km from the Visitors Center. The most popular wildlife-spotting trail is the **Black Swamp Walk,** a 4km (2hr.) loop that departs from the Visitors Center and runs through areas frequented by koalas, platypuses, kangaroos, wallabies, echidnas, and goannas. Those interested in undertaking a longer trek must inform the rangers at the Visitors Center of their plans. The truly ambitious can try the five- to seven-day trek from Hanson Bay to Cape Borda or shorter sections in between.

THE NORTH COAST

Thanks largely to the fact that it is accessed only by unsealed roads and bypassed by most tours, the north coast is still a tranquil place. Most of the roads are in very good condition, though, and can be handles by a 2WD. The remote lighthouse at **Cape Borda,** on the island's northwest tip, is open for tours (☎8559 3257. 5 daily 11am-3pm. $6.70, children $5.20.) Nearby **Scott's Cove** allows views east to the towering cliffs at Cape Torrens and Cape Forbin. There is camping at the **Harvey's Return ❶** site, one of the Flinders Chase campgrounds. **⊠Western River Cove,** at the mouth of the Western River, holds perhaps the prettiest and most secluded of all the north coast's beaches. The turnoff is on the Playford Hwy., 8km east of its junction with the West End Hwy, and the unsealed road leads to a carpark next to the river; a short stroll (5min.) across a footbridge and along the river brings you to the beach. The sandy cove, enclosed on either side by towering cliffs, is ideal for swimming, and there are toilet and BBQ facilities, with camping allowed by permit (available at Gateway Information Centre). **Snelling Beach,** about 15km east of Western River Cove, is a larger beach, with a long sweep of empty sand and gentle waves suited to swimming. From the west, the descent down Constitution Hill offers stunning views of the beach framed by surrounding cliffs and hills. From Snelling, North Coast Rd. continues 15km east to **Stokes Bay,** the one northern beach where several tours stop. From the carpark at the rocky cove, a short walk through a boulder field leads to a white sand beach surrounded by cliffs and a safe swimming area as well as protection from windy days that make more exposed beaches less welcoming. There are picnic areas, toilets, a snack-bar, and campsites. Northern beach waves are notoriously inconsistent, but Stokes is your best bet for surfing. Eighteen kilometers northwest of Kingscote along a sealed road is the 4km-long beach at **Emu Bay,** a wide expanse with vehicle access and safe swimming that tends to receive more tourist traffic.

CENTRAL WINE REGIONS

Nowhere is wine more a part of South Australian life than 70km northeast of Adelaide, in the famous Barossa Valley. Grapes from the Barossa and its more rural neighbor, the Eden Valley, produce some of Australia's best wines. The Clare Valley, 45min. north of Barossa and a contender in the same game, is filled with smaller, more specialized wineries. Some of the vines in the area date back to the

1840s, when the first German settlers planted their cuttings from Europe and prayed they would thrive. More than 150 years later, there's no doubt those prayers have been answered many times over. For the budget traveler, wine tasting has the dual benefit of being both a free buzz and a justifiably cultural and educational endeavor. Though you may arrive a wine novice, the ample opportunities afforded to compare wines and chat with winemakers ensures that you will leave a more erudite drinker. For other major Australian wine regions, see McLaren Vale (p. 454), Hunter Valley (p. 145), Rutherglen (p. 641), and Yarra (p. 587).

BAROSSA VALLEY   ☎ 08

Perhaps Australia's most well-known wine region, the Barossa Valley lives up to its reputation, with wines to suit all palates and budgets and a culture that places high value on wine, food, and hospitality. Most of Australia's largest wine companies are based here, along with plenty of renowned family operations. Though the vineyards are a fine sight in any season, those visiting during the vintage, from mid-February to late April or early May, will get to see them laden with fruit. They might even be able to taste-test the different types of grapes, see them being harvested or pressed, or land themselves a picking job in the process.

▐ TRANSPORTATION

A car affords the greatest flexibility, a tour leaves the details and driving to others, and a bicycle makes for an enjoyable day if the weather is fine; even your own two feet can bring a day of good tasting. Renting a car in Adelaide is strongly recommended for those bent on doing a serious wine tour, as many wineries are out of the way. Follow Scenic Rte. 4 for a breathtaking drive as it makes a large loop through the region, passing the main towns and the bulk of the wineries. Driving parties always should keep a **designated driver** absolutely alcohol-free. Barossa Valley's police are diligent and unforgiving when it comes to *drink driving*.

Buses: Barossa Adelaide Passenger Service (☎8564 3022; after hours 8564 0325) runs to and from Adelaide (1-3 each way per day) stopping at: Angaston ($14); Nuriootpa ($13); and Tanunda ($12). Children and seniors half-price. No reservation required, and pickups at various hotels in the Barossa can be arranged.

Train: The **Barossa Wine Train** (☎8212 7888) runs restored 1950s passenger trains from Adelaide's central rail terminal on North Tce. to Tanunda, leaving in the morning and returning the same afternoon. (Departs Tu, Th, and Sa-Su. $70 return.). They also run tours (see below).

Taxi: Barossa Valley Taxi (☎ 1800 BV TAXI or 8563 3600), Tanunda. Book early. About $13 from Nuriootpa to Tanunda. 24hr. service.

Automobile Clubs: Royal Automobile Association in Gawler (☎8522 2478), Tanunda (☎8563 2123), and Williamstown (☎8524 6268).

Bike Rental: Mountain bikes at **Barossa Bunkhaus Traveller's Hostel** (☎8562 2260), Nuriootpa ($10, $14, or $18 per day; $2 less for guests), or **Tanunda Caravan and Tourist Park** (☎8563 2784. $6 per hr., $10 per half-day, $15 per day.)

◼✳ ▐ ORIENTATION AND PRACTICAL INFORMATION

The Barossa Valley's wineries and small hamlets are centered around a triangle made up of three main towns: bustling Tanunda and the quieter towns of Nuriootpa and Angaston. Approaching from Adelaide via **Gawler,** the **Barossa Valley Hwy.** passes through **Lyndoch** (pop. 1000) and **Rowland Flat** before entering the main

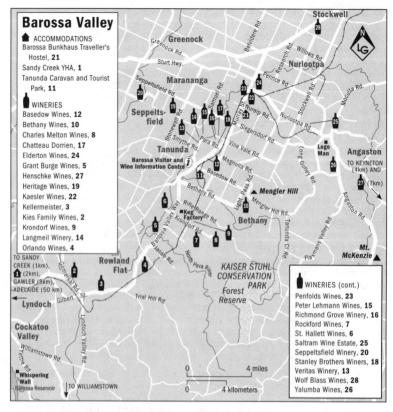

Barossa Valley

ACCOMMODATIONS
Barossa Bunkhaus Traveller's
   Hostel, **21**
Sandy Creek YHA, **1**
Tanunda Caravan and Tourist
   Park, **11**

WINERIES
Basedow Wines, **12**
Bethany Wines, **10**
Charles Melton Wines, **8**
Chatteau Dorrien, **17**
Elderton Wines, **24**
Grant Burge Wines, **5**
Henschke Wines, **27**
Heritage Wines, **19**
Kaesler Wines, **22**
Kellermeister, **3**
Kies Family Wines, **2**
Krondorf Wines, **9**
Langmeil Winery, **14**
Orlando Wines, **4**

WINERIES (cont.)
Penfolds Wines, **23**
Peter Lehmann Wines, **15**
Richmond Grove Winery, **16**
Rockford Wines, **7**
St. Hallett Wines, **6**
Saltram Wine Estate, **25**
Seppeltsfield Winery, **20**
Stanley Brothers Winers, **18**
Veritas Winery, **13**
Wolf Blass Wines, **28**
Yalumba Wines, **26**

town of **Tanunda** (pop. 4000), 70km northeast of Adelaide. There, the highway's name changes to **Murray St.** as it continues on to **Nuriootpa** (noor-ee-OOT-pah; pop. 3500), called "Nuri" by the locals. From there, **Nuriootpa Rd.** leads east to **Angaston** (pop. 2700). If you bypass Gawler and take the **Sturt Hwy. (A20)** from Adelaide, the road (B19) enters the Barossa from the north at Nuriootpa.

The **Barossa Visitors Center,** 66-68 Murray St., Tanunda, handles bookings for the nearly 90 B&Bs in the area and provides maps. (☎ 1300 852 982 or 8563 0600; www.barossa-region.org. Open M-F 9am-5pm, Sa-Su 10am-4pm.) The banks in the valley all have **ATMs.** The **post office** on Murray St. in Tanunda is next to the Visitors Center. (Open M-F 9am-5pm.) The Nuriootpa Library, on Murray St. on the south edge of town, has free **Internet** access (☎ 8562 1107; open M-W and F 9am-5pm, Th 9am-6pm, Sa 9am-noon), as does the Tanunda **Library,** also on Murray St., across from the Visitors Center. (☎ 8563 2729. Open M-F 9am-5pm, Sa 9am-noon.)

ACCOMMODATIONS

Lodging in Tanunda tends to be more expensive than in Nuriootpa or Angaston. That said, there are plenty of affordable places to stay in the area, and for those looking for something a little more upscale, there are nearly 90 B&Bs in the region. For the cheapest pub accommodation, head to Angaston.

SOUTH AUSTRALIA

▨ **Barossa Bunkhaus Traveller's Hostel** (☎8562 2260), on Nuraip Rd. just south of Nuriootpa. SA's first hostel opened 19 years ago and is still run with the same warm welcome. Intimate, impeccably clean, and set in a vineyard, you can practically reach out and touch the grapes from your bedroom window. The Adelaide bus (see **Transportation**, p. 467) drops off and picks up on request. TV, fireplace, kitchen, pool, and bike hire. Book ahead in peak season. 12 beds. Dorms $15; 4-person cottage for 2 $50, extra person $15. ❶

Barossa Brauhaus Hotel, 41 Murray St., Angaston (☎8564 2014). The best deal of the area's generally pricey pub-hotels, the Brauhaus offers clean, high-ceilinged rooms with free continental breakfast. Singles $30; doubles $55. ❸

Tanunda Hotel, 51 Murray St., Tanunda (☎8563 2165), within easy walking distance of shops and restaurants. Its bar is also a popular spot on the weekends. Clean singles with shared facilities $50; doubles $60. Ensuite singles $60; doubles $70. ❹

Tanunda Caravan and Tourist Park (☎8563 2784), just south of Tanunda on Barossa Valley Way. Convenient location. BBQ, kiosk, and laundry. Sites $14, powered $18; basic on-site vans for 2 from $35; cabins for 2 $45-85. ❶

Sandy Creek YHA, in Sandy Creek Conservation Park, 2km from Lyndoch. This limited-access hostel has 16 beds in a restored stone farmhouse. Book ahead with the YHA Travel Centre, 135 Waymouth St., Adelaide (☎8414 3000). $17, under 18 $12. ❷

▊ FOOD

The Barossa is not just about wine—food is also a high priority, though the area's high quality food also tends to be pricey. The main streets of Tanunda, Nuriootpa, and Angaston are littered with yuppie joints from casual luncheries to elegant dinner spots. Don't be put off by the atmosphere; weekly and daily specials abound, and bakeries and tea-rooms often offer a taste of the region's food at good prices. Many of the wineries have lunch rooms or **bistros,** notably St. Hallett (see p. 472). **Bakeries** have shelves full of traditional German breads, cakes, and pastries, as well as heartier meals and sandwiches. All three towns have **supermarkets**

Vintner's Grill (☎8564 2488), on Nuriootpa Rd. between Nuri and Angaston. One of the best of the upmarket bunch, Vintner's blends modern Australian with traditional Barossan to come up with dishes like pan-fried quail ($19) and spiced kangaroo steak ($22), always accompanied by an appropriate wine. Lunches around $15. Open daily. ❸

Angas Park Hotel (☎8562 1050), on Murray St. in Nuriootpa. A local favorite with quality dinners starting around $10. Open daily noon-2pm and 6-8pm. ❷

Angaston Hotel, 59 Murray St., Angaston (☎8564 2428). Daily lunch specials from $6; dinners starting at $8. Open daily noon-2pm and 6-8pm. ❶

Schaedel Haus, 47 Murray St., Nuriootpa (☎8562 4394). For something lighter and non-alcoholic, Schaedel Haus is the best of the area's tea rooms, with $2 teas and light sandwiches from $4. Open Tu-Sa 9am-4:30pm. ❶

La Buona Vita, 89 Murray St., Tanunda (☎8563 2527). A consistent budget option, with $10 pizzas and $8-10 light meals. Open daily noon-late. ❶

Shangri-La, 51 Barossa Valley Way, Nuriootpa (☎8562 3559). Thai meals start at $8. Open M and W-Su 5:30-8:30pm, W-F also 11:30am-2:30pm. ❶.

▊ WINERIES OF THE BAROSSA VALLEY

The complete tour of the more than 50 wineries that offer cellar door tastings requires Bacchanalian spirit, Herculean effort, and Gargantuan ability to hold your liquor. Tanunda's tourist office has a full list. Most people "only" visit four to six in

SOUTH AUSTRALIA

THE BIG SPLURGE

WINE ON THE MOVE

If you've got some cash to burn, check out these splurge options, guaranteed to provide a moving, even uplifting, perspective on South Australia's beloved wine region.

The **Barossa Wine Train** offers upmarket day and overnight tours that connect with train service, enabling visitors to go from train to coach to winery without breaking a sweat. (☎8212 7888. Ultimate Day Tour $139 per person, overnight packages from $325 per person.) Remember: the train can chug, but a wine drinker must *sip.*

Prefer to get high instead? A number of more exotic aerial tours have sprung up recently as well. **Barossa Helicopters** bills its trips as a "photographer's utopia." (☎8524 4209. From $396 per 30min. for up to 4 passengers; no drinking.) **Barossa Balloon Adventures** offers a one-hour flight with "memories that will last a lifetime." (☎8389 3195. $231 per person, children $165; includes champagne breakfast.) **Air Tours South Australia** (☎0419 806 262) can take you from the coast to the Barossa to the outback, starting from $250 per person.

Whoever said wine and adventure travel had to be mutually exclusive?

 Some **traveling tips:** don't be tempted to buy a wine because it's won an award. The efficient tourism industry has created enough competitions that virtually every winery has been recognized for some "outstanding" achievement. Find your own taste. Many a so-called expert's sobriquet is mere snobbery. Let your own palate be your guide. Finally, narrow roads, high-speed traffic, and random police search points and breathalyzers don't mix well with wine. Be smart: choose a designated driver, or hop on an inexpensive, informative day tour.

a day, and that is plenty for a nice buzz—each winery has free tastings, with no obligation to purchase. Most cellar doors are welcoming, with yuppies and backpackers mingling peaceably, using fine wine as a social lubricant. The **vintage,** when grapes are harvested, lasts from late February into April or early May. Vintage time is when you can see and taste all the different varieties of grapes and see the harvest and pressing occur. It is also the time to find **picking jobs.** (Check at cellar doors, or try calling the SA Student and Youth Council Job Prospects line at ☎8552 7455.) Most wineries in Barossa are open daily from 10am to 4 or 5pm.

WHETTING THE PALATE. If you don't understand what all the fuss over wine is about (and even if you do), start your Barossa visit with an hour at **The Barossa Wine Centre,** 66-68 Murray St., Tanunda, in the same building as the tourist office. The exhibits make the craft of wine-making and the etiquette of wine-tasting accessible to novices. (☎8563 0600. Open daily 10am-4pm. $2.50.) For safety and liability reasons, wineries have discontinued tours of production facilities, although if you show up at any of the smaller wineries during vintage, you're sure to catch a glimpse of grapes being pressed and barrels filled. Two wineries offer tours of their vineyards and buildings, focusing on the wine-making process and traditional methods: **Seppelt Winery** on Tourist Rte. 4 in Seppeltsfield (☎8568 6212; tours M-F 11am, 1, 2, and 3pm, Sa-Su 11:30am, 1:30 and 2:30pm; $7, children $5) and **Yaldara,** Gomersal Rd., Lyndoch. (☎8524 0225. Tours daily 10:15am, 1:30, 2:30, 3:30pm. $5.) **Wolf Blass Wines,** 97 Sturt Hwy., on the north side of Nuriootpa, also has a small but informative wine heritage museum near its tasting rooms. (☎8568 7311. Open M-F 9:15am-5pm, Sa-Su 10am-5pm. Free.)

STUMBLING AROUND. If you're exploring on foot, four wineries just north of Tanunda are connected by

A QUICK WINE PRIMER Wine tasting, like anything else, has its own vocabulary. Australia's, and the Barossa's, most famous red grape varieties are **Shiraz** (often called Syrah outside Australia) and **Cabernet Sauvignon. Riesling, Semillon Blanc,** and **Sauvignon Blanc** are Barossa's best-known whites. Sparkling wines are simply the ones with bubbles. (Champagne is the most famous kind of sparkling wine, but only sparkling wine produced in the Champagne region of France has earned the right to be called champagne.) Fortified wines are sweeter wines with added alcohol, often called dessert wines in North America and liqueur wines in Europe. **Port, sherry,** and **vermouth** are some of the most well-known fortifieds. Dry is the opposite of sweet. Crisp means the wine has an acidity, roughly the opposite of smooth or soft. In general, taste white before red, dry before sweet, and sparkling before fortified. Bouquet, a word usually used to describe older wines, is the same thing as aroma, used with younger wines. You needn't use any of these words, though; the important question is whether or not you like what you're tasting. Cheers!

the **Para Road Wine Path** (foot or cycle only) through the vineyards. On the left side of Barossa Valley Way as you head north out of Tanunda, you'll find the first, the small **Stanley Brothers Winery,** with a picnic area and pottery and jams for sale at the cellar door. (☎ 8563 3375. Open M-F 9:30am-5pm, Sa-Su 11am-5pm.) Not far away on Para Rd., **Richmond Grove Winery,** on the banks of the small Para River, specializes in Rieslings and has picnic areas among the gum trees. (☎ 8563 7303. Open M-F 10am-5pm, Sa-Su 10:30am-4:30pm.) Down Para Rd. and down the Wine Path, **Peter Lehmann Wines** buys grapes from about 200 growers and crushes more than 10,000 tons of grapes every year. (☎ 8563 2500. Open M-F 9:30am-5pm, Sa-Su 10:30am-4:30pm.) The last winery on the wine trail, **Langmeil Winery,** at the corner of Para and Langmeil Rd., has a good tasting range in a cellar door dating from the 1840s. (☎ 8563 2595. Open daily 11am-4:30pm.) Though not part of the Wine Path, the **Chatteau Dorrien,** at the corner of Seppeltsfield Rd. and Barossa Valley Way, is about 1km north of the Stanley Bros. Winery and features specialty honey mead wines. (☎ 8562 2850. Open daily 10am-5pm.)

TAKIN' THE TOUR BUS. Most Barossa tours are full-day round-trip outings departing daily from Adelaide in small buses (about 20 people). Each tour visits a different group of wineries, so if you have your heart set on tasting a specific wine, it pays to check around. **Groovy Grape Getaways** is the most popular backpackers tour to the Barossa. (☎ 1800 661 177 or 8395 4422. $65.) If you're more serious about wine, or less than thrilled about spending a day drinking with 22-year-olds, **Prime Mini Tours** runs a small tour. (☎ 8293 4900. $59 per person. Free pickup.) Another popular tour is run by **Enjoy Adelaide** and includes lunch, all the usual stops, and four wineries. (☎ 8332 1401. $50, children $34.) If you're staying in the Barossa, **Valley Tours** has a full-day winery and sights tour. (☎ 8563 3587. $47 including lunch, pickup and return to Barossa Valley accommodations. Full-day without lunch $39; half-day $28.)

RIDING SHOTGUN WITH THE DESIGNATED DRIVER. For those not confined to walking distance, the options seem endless. While you're more likely to see familiar wines at the bigger producers, the small wineries offer a more intimate setting and a better chance to learn about wines from the people who actually make them.

🖾 **Rockford Wines** (☎ 8563 2720), on Krondorf Rd. east of Tanunda. Not to be missed, this small winery emphasizes the winemaking history and traditional methods of the Barossa. It is housed in stone cottages that enclose a courtyard where grapes are pressed with traditional barrel-presses. The premium here is on craftsmanship and quality, not quantity; wines here are so good that they have to limit the number of bottles people are allowed to buy. Open M-Sa 11am-5pm.

■ **St. Hallett Wines** (☎8563 7070), on St. Hallett Rd., just south of Tanunda. Since 1944, St. Hallett has made every drop of their wine exclusively from Barossa or Eden Valley fruit. Premium red table wines are the specialty; try the flagship Old Block Shiraz. Open M-Sa 7:45am-4:30pm, Su 10am-4:30pm.

■ **Bethany Wines** (☎8563 2086), on Bethany Rd., just east of Tanunda. In a former quarry high above the rest of the valley, with a panoramic vista and lovely picnic areas, the Schrapel family and friendly cellar door staff will make you feel right at home while you sample their acclaimed Shiraz and Riesling. Try the surprisingly delightful sparkling Pinot Noir and sweet White Port. At vintage time, watch as grapes are dumped into the clifftop gravity-fed crusher that sends the juice to holding tanks below. Open M-Sa 10am-5pm, Su 1-5pm.

Saltram Wine Estate (☎8564 3355), on the Nuriootpa-Angaston Rd., just outside Angaston. Smooth, fruity, and fabulously decadent, Saltram's Semillon is the stuff from which dreams are made. This winery has been working on their reds, whites, and ports since 1859 and recently opened the popular **Salters Bistro** on-site. Open M-F 9am-5pm, Sa-Su 10am-5pm. Bistro open daily 11:30am-3pm, also F-Sa for dinner.

Orlando Wines (☎8521 3140), at Rowland Flat. Some 250,000 people each year pay respects at this cellar door, home to one of the area's largest and oldest wineries. Tracing its roots back to 1847, the winery has built a reputation around its **Jacob's Creek** label, Australia's largest wine export brand that last year shipped 5.4 million cases to 53 different countries. Open M-F 10am-5pm, Sa-Su 10am-4pm.

Henschke Wines (☎8564 8223), on the main road in Keyneton. Don't be put off by this winery being out of the way; it's one of the most highly regarded by the locals. Open M-F 9am-4:30pm, Sa 9am-noon.

🔵 🎵 SIGHTS AND ENTERTAINMENT

Designated drivers, take heart: not every attraction in the Barossa requires drinking. **Mengler Hill Lookout,** on Mengler Hill Rd. east of Tanunda, near Bethany on Tourist Rte. 4, is definitely worth a stop to see the rows of vines stretching in every direction. The road linking Williamstown and Sandy Creek passes **Barossa Reservoir,** with its famous curved **Whispering Wall,** where murmured confidences can be heard meters away. Though it's hard to imagine South Australia before wine, the **Kaiser Stuhl Conservation Park,** 2km southeast of Tanunda, demonstrates what the Barossa looked like before the vines and has two well-marked walking paths.

As if you needed an excuse to drink, festivals abound. Foremost among these is the biannual **Barossa Vintage Festival** (April 21-27, 2003), a celebration of all things viticultural, including the long-lost barefoot stomping of grapes. The **Barossa Jazz Weekend** occurs annually in August (August 16-17, 2003) and adheres to a surefire recipe for festival success: wine, food, and good tunes. Every October, the **Barossa International Music Festival** (☎8564 2577) celebrates the arrival of spring with music to suit any taste and, of course, a wine for every palate.

CLARE   ☎08

Between Adelaide and the South Australian Outback, Clare (pop. 4000) and its neighbor, Burra, constitute the final outposts of civilization before the Flinders Ranges. The Clare Valley, running north from Auburn up to Clare along the Main North Rd., hosts some 30-odd vineyards in a group that's more compact and exclusive than those of their southern cousin the Barossa Valley. The higher altitude gives a respite from some of the lowland heat associated with the Yorke Peninsula, allowing soaring pine and fur trees to point skyward over the golden-brown terrain—golden-brown, that is, except for those lush carpets of vineyard green.

◪ TRANSPORTATION. Driving from Adelaide (136km south of Clare), take Main North Rd. through Elizabeth and onto the Gawler bypass, then turn left at the exit to Tarlee. Main North Rd. runs through the town and passes most of the wineries before reaching Clare. On the road from Auburn to Clare, signs pointing to "Historic Mintaro" lead to a spectacular 12km drive. **Mid North Passenger Service** runs one bus Su-F from Adelaide, leaving from the Foodland Plaza carpark. (☎ 8823 2375. $19.30.) Once in Clare you can rent bikes to cycle along the beautiful **Riesling Trail** or take private bus tours of the Valley (see p. 473).

🚲 PRACTICAL INFORMATION. In Clare itself, Old North Rd. runs one block east of Main North Rd., the highway on which visitors enter from Auburn. At the north end of town, Farrell Flat Rd. heads east through the hills towards Burra. The **Clare Valley Tourist Information Centre**, 229 Main North Rd., in the town hall, has maps and the *Clare Valley Secrets* booklet. (☎ 8842 2131. Open M-Sa 9am-5pm, Su 10am-4pm.) Services include a **police station** (☎ 8842 2711) and free **Internet** at the **Clare Library**, 33 Old North Rd., one block east of the post office. (☎ 8842 3817. Open Tu, W, and F 10am-6pm, Th 10am-8pm, Sa 10am-noon.) All the banks along Main North Rd. in town have **ATMs**. The **post office**, 253 Main North Rd., is open M-F 9am-5pm. **Postal Code:** 5453.

◪ ACCOMMODATIONS. The historic **Clare Hotel ❷**, 244 Main North Rd., dates from 1848 and has both clean, standard pub rooms and ensuite motel rooms. (☎ 8842 2816. Pub rooms with shared bath $22 per person; ensuite motel singles with TV $50; ensuite doubles $55.) The award-winning **Clare Caravan Park ❶**, 3km south of town on Main North Rd., has a lake, pool, and laundry, and is well-positioned for winery tours. (☎ 8842 2724. Reception 8am-7pm. Sites $14 per person, powered $18; self-contained cabins for 2 $43-49; on-site vans from $32.) Those looking for a unique experience may want to try at the elegant Georgian mansion at **Martindale Hall ❺**, east of Mintaro, about 20min. from Clare by car (see p. 474).

◪ FOOD. **Price's Traditional Bakery ❶**, 269 Main North Rd., north of the post office, has been churning out pies, pastries, and sausage rolls for over a century; try the $1.50 honey log with fresh cream or a sandwich from $3. (☎ 8842 2473. Open M-F 8am-5pm, Sa 9am-1:30pm.) The staff of the friendly **Chaff Mill Country Kitchen ❸**, 308 Main North Rd., cooks breakfast, lunch ($6-16), and dinner ($16-22) of the steak and pasta persuasion. (☎ 8842 3055. Open M and W-Su 10am-9pm. Closed M lunch.) The **Clare Hotel ❶**, 244 Main North Rd. (☎ 8842 2816), reigns in the counter meal battle, offering $7 daily lunch specials. Clare has two **supermarkets:** the Foodland, 47 Old North Rd. (open M-Sa 8am-7pm, Su 9am-7pm) and the IGA, across from the post office on Main North Rd. (Open daily 8am-8pm.)

◪ WINERIES OF CLARE VALLEY. The Clare Valley is the northernmost wine production area in South Australia, cooler than the much larger Barossa Valley. Nearly 40 wineries operate here, though not all have cellar doors. If a winery has tastings, however, the folks at the Clare tourist office know; pick up a guide to the valley before you set out. The granddaddy of Clare wines is the famous **Riesling,** though nearly every other grape and wine variety has now gained a foothold. An old railway line, parallel to Main North Rd., has been converted into the 27km scenic **Riesling Trail.** The trail runs between Clare and Auburn and is suitable for walking and biking (one-way 2hr. by bike). Convenient car parks in Clare, Sevenhill, Watervale, and Auburn allow for walkers to take shorter journeys. The trail passes farms and vineyards, as well a few wineries, including Sevenhill Cellars. Bikes can

SOUTH AUSTRALIA

be hired in Clare from **Clare Valley Cycle Hire,** 32 Victoria Rd., in a private house opposite the elementary school. (☎8842 2782 or 0418 802 077. Half-day $16.50, full day $22.) The tourist office also has info on many mini-bus and private tours, including **Clare Valley Experiences** (☎8843 4169) and **Clare Valley Tours** (☎0418 832 812); these tend to be comprehensive but pricey (from $60 half-day, $95 full-day).

■ **Sevenhill Cellars** (☎8843 4222), on College Rd., Sevenhill, 6km south of Clare. The Jesuit brothers of St. Aloysius Church started the wine craze in the Clare Valley, opening Sevenhill, Australia's only religious winery, in 1851. In the 150 years since, the tradition has continued. Though Sevenhill initially produced sacramental wines, today an impressive range of fine reds, whites, and fortified wines comprise 75% of their output. Open M-F 9am-4:30pm, Sa 10am-4pm.

Taylors Wines (☎8849 2008), on Taylors Rd. just north of Auburn, 25km south of Clare. The largest winery in the Clare Valley, and the largest estate on one site in Australia, housed in an enormous castle-lookalike. All wines are made from grapes grown on the estate, and all are bottled here. Family-owned, they've won many awards with their cool whites and hearty reds. Open M-F 9am-5pm, Sa 10am-5pm, Su 10am-4pm.

Leasingham Wines, 7 Dominic St., Clare (☎8842 2785). A perennial medal-winner and venerable Clare institution. The appeal is rounded out by a lovely setting, friendly service, and small wine-making museum. Riesling was developed here, but the winery is now pushing ahead with reds. Open M-F 8:30am-5pm, Sa-Su 10am-4pm.

NEAR CLARE: MINTARO

The tiny speck of civilization that is "Historic Mintaro" is little more than a picturesque collection of ancient stone buildings hosting a winery, several cafes, B&Bs and antique shops, and also a secret: the stunning ■**Martindale Hall ❺,** an elegant Georgian mansion rising up out of the surrounding farmland like a bizarre mirage 3km east of Mintaro. Now an upscale B&B and museum, the mansion was built in 1879 for sheep baron Edmund Bowman and is now open for self-guided tours that bring to life the gracious lifestyle of a country gentleman, replete with an enormous billiards table and a Hemingway-esque display of guns and hunting trophies. Most rooms retain period furniture, and the hosts even offer a *Clue*-like murder mystery night called "Incident at Martindale." The mansion was featured in the film *Picnic at Hanging Rock.* (☎8843 9088. Open M-F 11am-4pm, Sa-Su noon-4pm. $5.50, concessions $3.80, children $1.10. B&B Su-F $95 per person; Sa group bookings only.) **Mintaro Wines,** on Leashingham Rd., is a small family winery with excellent reds. (☎8843 9046. Open daily 9am-5pm.) One of the best parts of any side-trip to Mintaro is the 12km drive out there, which winds through rolling hills covered with tall trees and vineyards. Head south from Clare on Main North Rd. toward Auburn and take the road marked "Historic Mintaro." From the Clare-Burra Rd., follow the signs reading "Martindale Hall" to the south.

BURRA ☎08

While Burra (pop. 2100) has molded its tourism industry around the area's historically prolific mines, the quiet atmosphere and calm surrounds are also a compelling reason to visit. The historic mining town, 40km (30min.) northeast of Clare on the main route to Sydney via Broken Hill, plays up its copper roots. Burra is content to move at a slower pace than its nearby neighbor Clare, and the resulting tranquility, combined with historical and very comfortable accommodation, might convince you to make Burra your base for exploring the wineries of the Clare.

■✶▸ **ORIENTATION AND PRACTICAL INFORMATION.** The town is centered around a creek. The highway leads to **Market Square,** at the intersection of Market and Commercial St. The **Visitors Center,** 2 Market Sq., books mining and Clare Valley winery tours and has copies of the helpful *Burra and Beyond*. (☎ 8892 2154. Open daily 9am-5pm. Most tours half-day $28-35.) The Bank SA on Market Square has an **ATM**. There is free **Internet** access at the **library**, in the school at the end of Bridge Tce., north of the creek. (Open M, W, and F 9am-5pm; Tu and Th 9am-8pm.) The **post office** is on Market Sq., next to the IGA supermarket. **Postal Code:** 5417.

📷🏠 ACCOMMODATIONS AND FOOD. In the 1840s, when many miners lived in mud dugouts along the banks of Burra Creek, the South Australian Mining Association built the 📷**Paxton Square Cottages ❺**, on Kingston St., just over the small bridge visible from Market Sq., on the east side of town. The 32 restored two- to four-room cottages have stone floors, kitchens, fireplaces, and bath. (☎ 8892 2622. Doubles $65, each extra person $12.) The 154-year-old **Burra Hotel ❷** is in the town center on Market Sq. and offers basic pub rooms with an exceptional balcony overlooking the square. (☎ 8892 2389. Singles $25; doubles $40.) Locals say that the **Burra Hotel ❶** has the best meals, with lunch specials from $6 and dinners from $8. (☎ 8892 2389. Open daily noon-2pm and 6-8pm.) Market Square has an IGA **supermarket.** (Open M-F 8:45am-5:30pm, Sa 8:45-11:30am, Su 10am-2pm.)

📷 SIGHTS. If you have a car and want to see the town's mining history, buy the **Burra Passport** at the tourist office, which includes all details for a self-guided driving tour of the area. (Base passport $11, concessions $9; entrance to all 4 area museums $20/$18.) The best part of the Passport is the key, which you can use to get into eight locked sights, including the old **Redruth Gaol** (the first South Australian jail built outside of Adelaide and used in the movie *Breaker Morant* in 1979), the spooky **Unicorn Brewery Cellars**, the old **Burra Smelting Works, Hampton Village** (archaeological remains of an old township), and miners' **dugouts.**

The **Burra Mine**, known as the **Monster Mine**, was the world's largest copper mine in the 1870s and saved the state from bankruptcy. **Morphett's Enginehouse Museum,** on the site of Burra Mine, details the mechanical aspects of the mine and the pumps that brought 15 million liters of water out of the ground each day. (Open M, W, and F 11am-1pm; Sa-Su 11am-2pm. $4.50, concessions $3.50.) The **Bon Accord Mining Museum** focuses on the social history of the mines by telling the stories of individual miners. (Open Tu-Th 1-3pm, Sa-Su 1-4pm. $3.50.)

For those tired of copper, **Mongolata Gold Mine,** 23km east of Burra, offers a guided tour of the old government battery and of the mine underground. (☎ 8892 2233 or 0428 922 573. $10, children $5. Call ahead.) **Burra Trail Rides,** Basin Farm, 3km northeast of Burra off the road to Morgan, has horse rides starting at $15 per hour and stock driving rides for one to three days, with meals and camping gear supplied. (☎ 8892 2627 or 0427 808 402. All skill levels easily accommodated. Call ahead or book at the Burra Visitors Center.)

THE LIMESTONE COAST REGION

A good name can be a boon to tourism. Realizing this, the southeastern portion of South Australia has joined the battle to coin a catchy and marketable name. This region, which includes both the 200km stretch of coast from the mouth of the Murray River at Goolwa down to the Victorian border and inland cities such as **Mt. Gambier** and **Naracoorte,** has been dubbed the "Limestone Coast." Still, the region has much more going for it than its flashy new name, boasting two national parks, many smaller conservation parks, a number of quiet seaside towns, and a significant amount of—you guessed it—limestone. The coast has also annexed some inland towns and attractions, such as the area's largest city, Mt. Gambier, and one of the area's star attractions, the caves at Naracoorte. From the north, the **Princes**

Hwy. splits from the inland **Dukes Hwy.** at Tailem Bend and hugs the coast for about 200km, passing Coorong National Park and going as far as Southend before turning inland toward Mt. Gambier.

Though it is best seen by car, **Premier Stateliner buses** (☎ 8415 5500) runs through the region daily on the Adelaide to Mt. Gambier run. The inland route runs from Adelaide through Tailem Bend, Penola, and Naracoorte on its way to Mt. Gambier (Sa-Th 1 per day, F 2 per day), while the coastal route starts and ends at the same places, but runs through Tailem Bend, Meningie, Kingston S. E., Robe, Beachport, and Millicent (Sa-Th 1 per day, F 2 per day). The best place to start any Limestone Coast adventure is at one of the helpful information offices that bookend the region: **The Signal Point Interpretative Centre** in Goolwa in the north (☎ 8555 3488; open daily 9am-5pm) and the **Visitors Center** in Millicent in the south (☎ 8733 3205; open M-F 9am-5pm, Sa-Su 9:30am-4:30pm). Both offer the *Limestone Coast Secrets* information booklet and *The Tattler*, the essential publication covering the Coorong and other area parks.

COORONG NATIONAL PARK

The Coorong is an endlessly alluring stretch of white-sand dunes, dry salt lakes, and glittering lagoons. It is a bird habitat of renowned ecological importance, a popular and prodigious fishing area, and a prime spot for outdoor recreation. Birds flying in from as far away as Siberia have made the Coorong a popular summering spot for the aviary set. While primarily made up of wetlands and waterways, the park includes almost 46,000 hectares of sand dunes. The dunes of the Younghusband Peninsula shelter a series of lagoons over 100km long.

Virtually the only way to access the Park's northern reaches is by **boat,** which is best attempted from the town of **Goolwa** (see p. 458), at the mouth of the Murray River on the Fleurieu Peninsula. Several tours highlighting the area's birdlife operate from Goolwa, including **Coorong Cruises.** (☎ 8555 1133. Departs Tu, Th, and Su 9am; returns 5pm. $75, children $45.) **The Spirit of the Coorong** has more ecologically minded tours. Half-day tours depart M and Th at 12pm, while full-day tours depart at 10am on W and Su (☎ 8555 2203 or 1800 442 203. Half-day $57, children $40; full-day $74/$48.) **The Coorong Experience** runs tours for smaller groups, ranging from a half-day to several days and accommodating special interests in bushwalking, photography, or Aboriginal culture. (☎ 8555 2222. Max. 8 people.)

The sealed **Princes Hwy.** skirts much of the Coorong and passes scenic lookouts along the way, as well as a number of campgrounds, historic sites, and walking trails, all detailed in *The Tattler*. Most of the campsites and other attractions are accessible via 2WD on well-maintained dirt roads, but access to the **beach** on the far side of Younghusband Peninsula is via 4WD track or walking only. **Jacks Point,** 24km south of the tip, provides a shelter and binoculars to observe the pelicans nest on islands in the lagoon. Just south of **Salt Creek,** the **Loop Rd.,** a well-maintained unsealed side road, branches off from the Princes Hwy. and traces the shore of the Lagoon for 13km, providing a closer look than the sealed road will afford you. About 5km south of where the Loop Rd. rejoins the Princes Hwy., a marked turn-off for the ⬛42 **Mile Crossing** leads down an unsealed road past ephemeral lakes 3km to a campsite, from where a 4WD track through the dunes leads to the beach. For those without a 4WD, this point provides the most convenient **walking access to the beach,** as a marked trail winds 1.3km through the towering dunes to a magnificent stretch of seashell-covered beach and sweeping views of the Southern Ocean (about 1hr. return; bring water). If you do have a 4WD, a cruise along the beach between the dunes of Younghusband Peninsula and the crashing waves is the best way to see the ocean side of the park. From the 42 Mile Crossing, you can drive north to the **Tea Tree Crossing** or south to the **32 Mile Crossing,** the **Wreck Crossing** (summer only), or the **28 Mile Crossing.**

Campsites ❶ are available at Pranka Point, the 42 Mile Crossing, and along the Loop Rd. and the Old Coorong Rd. The sites at Pranka Point and the 42 Mile Crossing are among the few that have water and toilets. **Permits** ($6 per car per night) are required and can be obtained via self-registration at most sites or at the Signal Point Interpretive Centre in Goolwa (see p. 458), the Parks Office in Meningie (see below), or the Big Lobster in Kingston S. E. (see below). There are also caravan parks in Meningie, Policeman's Point, Salt Creek, and Kingston S. E. and motel rooms at the roadhouses in Policeman's Point and Salt Creek. For a budget snack, dig into the sand at the ocean's edge to find cockles, which can be pried open and eaten raw. Get **petrol** and supplies at the parks gateways (see p. 477)—Meningie in the north or Kingston S. E. in the south—as it is a barren 146km between the two.

SOUTH FROM FLEURIEU PENINSULA: PRINCES HIGHWAY

The road from Tailem Bend south toward Mount Gambier runs along the Coorong, providing excellent access to both the wetlands of the coast and the beaches farther south. **Meningie** is the gateway to Coorong National Park (see p. 476) and is a nice place for a quick swim. The **National Parks and Wildlife Service** has an office at 34 Princes Hwy. (☎8575 1200) where you can pick up *The Tattler*, which covers southeastern coastal parks from Goolwa to the Victoria border. **Kingston, S. E.,** Meningie's southern counterpart, is the more interesting of the Coorong's gateways. The town's most famous resident, **Larry the Lobster,** is a huge metal and fiberglass hulk towering over a snack bar and **information center** (open daily 9am-5pm) on the roadside at the northern edge of town. **Robe,** 41km farther south and surrounded by water on three sides, is a sleepy little beach town with Victorian buildings and good surf. There is **tourist information** and **Internet** at the **Robe Institute and Library,** on Mundy Tce. (☎8768 2465. Open M-F 9am-5pm, Sa-Su 10am-4pm.)

Beachport (pop. 400), 44km south of Robe, is a great place to relax. The **Beachport Visitors Center** is on the western side of town, along Millicent Rd. as you enter. (☎8735 8029. **Internet** $3 per 30min. Open M-F 9am-5pm, Sa-Su 11am-4pm.) It provides maps for the splendid 8km **scenic drive** along the limestone cliffs of the coast and for the short **walking trails** that branch off from the drive. The friendly **Bompas Hotel ❷** faces the water near the jetty in a nicely restored historic building dating from 1876. (☎8735 8128. Backpackers $20; ensuite doubles $80.) Beachport's sister city **Southend** (pop. 296) is the gateway to the oft-neglected **Canunda National Park,** which encompasses 9300 hectares of coastal habitat and nearly 50km of coast between Southend and Cape Banks to the south. The park's main attraction in the Southend region is Cape Buffon, from where the **Cape Buffon Loop** traverses the clifftops and provides some outstanding lookouts (1hr., 2.5km). The longer **Seaview Walk** covers the cliffs to the south of Cape Buffon (2.5hr. return, 6km). The **Bevilaqua Ford site ❶** has both water and toilets. You can get a permit ($6 per car) by self-registering at the site or at the **Parks Office** (☎8735 6053) in Southend, on Rainbow Rocks Rd. as it heads toward the park. The **Visitors Center** in **Millicent** is 20km farther south from Southend. (☎8733 3205. Open M-F 9am-5pm, Sa-Su 9:30am-4:30pm.)

MOUNT GAMBIER   ☎08

Mt. Gambier (pop. 21,000), resting on the side of a volcano, grew around a freshwater-producing cave that still lies at its center. The city's water is now drawn from Blue Lake, a mile-deep lake that sits in the volcano's crater and shimmers with an intense shade of blue through the warmer months of the year. The lake is the city's primary tourist attraction, though during the winter it takes on a decidedly less impressive gray hue. Mt. Gambier's size makes it a good base for exploring the nearby wineries of the Coonawarra region and the caves of Naracoorte.

SOUTH AUSTRALIA

⬛ ⬛ TRANSPORTATION AND PRACTICAL INFORMATION. **V/Line buses** stop at the Shell Blue Lake service station, 100 Commercial St. W, and run to Adelaide daily (☎8725 5037; 6hr., $47) either via the coastal towns of Robe, Beachport, and Kingston or via the inland towns of Naracoorte, Tailem Bend, and Murray Bridge; and Melbourne (7hr.; M-Sa 2 per day, Su 1 per day; $56) via the Victorian cities of Portland, Port Fairy, Warrnambool, and Geelong. Book at the Shell station.

The Princes Hwy. becomes **Jubilee Hwy.** in the city and passes through the downtown area several blocks north of Commercial St. The town's commercial area lies around the intersection of Bay Rd. (Penola Rd. north of Commercial and Commercial St., and extends a few blocks in every direction. The **Visitors Center,** Jubilee Hwy. E., is part of the **Lady Nelson Centre** (see **Sights,** p. 478) and has a huge landlocked ship on its front lawn. (Both centers ☎1800 087 187. Open daily 9am-5pm.) Services include: **Library,** in the Civic Centre, with free **Internet** (☎8721 2540; open M, W, and F 9am-6pm; Tu 9am-5pm; Th 9am-8pm; Sa 9-11:30am); **police,** on Bay Rd. (☎8735 1020); and **post office,** 30 Helen St. (Open M-F 9am-5pm.) **Postal Code:** 5290.

⬛ ACCOMMODATIONS. ⬛**The Jail ❷,** off Margaret St., promises to scare wayward backpackers straight with a short, voluntary prison sentence. This recently converted prison was "decriminalized" in 1995. The friendly owners coordinate a number of activities for their inmates, from monthly jam sessions to regular sandboarding trips to the coast ($25 per person, board and transport provided) to on-demand paintball skirmishes ($30 per person. ☎8723 0032 or 1800 626 844. Internet $2 per 15min. Dinner $10. Dorms $20, doubles $44.) The **Blue Lake Motel ❶** is at 1Kennedy Ave.—turn left off Jubilee Hwy. W, about 1km east of the Lady Nelson Centre. Though removed from the town center, it offers clean ensuite rooms with four bunks each and well-priced motel rooms. (☎8725 5211 or 1800 088 291. Linen $2. Dorms $14; singles $45; doubles $55.) **Blue Lake City Caravan Park ❷,** on Bay Rd. just south of the lake, is a veritable Disneyland of caravan parks. It's spotless, with a pool, tennis and basketball courts, an 18-hole golf course, and outdoor cooking facilities. (☎8725 9856. Sites $18, powered $21; caravans from $63.)

⬛⬛ FOOD AND NIGHTLIFE. The Central Business District is packed with chip shops and takeaway joints, supermarkets and greengrocers. For a quality meal that won't break the bank, **Cafe Belgiorno ❷,** on the corner of Percy and Mitchell St., next to the Oatmill complex, is a local favorite. Its wood-fired pizzas ($9) have been annually voted among Australia's best in a nationwide competition. (☎8725 4455. Open daily 11am-late.) For good burgers and steaks, head to **Baltimore's ❶,** in the Oatmill complex on Percy St. (see below), where all lunches are under $10 and their special "movie meal-deals" will get you a meal and ticket to the theater next door for $17.50. (☎8724 8441. Open Tu-Su 1:30am-10pm.)

Many a drunken stumble has started out at **Flanagan's Irish Pub,** on Ferrers St., just south of Commercial St. E. with live music and a lively singles scene Thursday through Saturday nights (open until 1:30am; pints $5). The **Mount Gambier Hotel,** 2 Commercial St. W., has high ceilings, pool tables, and occasional live music and dancing (open until 3am). **Blueberry's,** next to Baltimore's in the Oatmill complex, draws a younger crowd into its cavernous space, half of which is a dance floor and the other half a pool-hall. (Open until 3am.) **Shadows,** in an old Bank building on Penola Rd., a block north of Commercial St. is the place for the real late night dance party. (Open until 4:30am, but doors shut at 3:30am. Cover $5 F-Sa.)

⬛ SIGHTS. Bay Rd. goes south through town to passing views of **Blue Lake.** The lake itself fills the crater of a volcano that erupted 4000-5000 years ago, and holds nine million gallons of water, which are used as the town's supply. You can only get to the lake's surface by a 45min. tour that goes down to the pumping station in a glass lift. (☎8723 1199. Daily tours every hr. Nov.-Jan. 9am-5pm; Feb.-May 9am-2pm; June-Aug. 9am-noon; Sept.-Oct. 9am-2pm. $5.50, children $2.)

Just south of the Blue Lake, by the entrance to the Blue Lake City Caravan Park, a road marked "Wildlife Reserve" leads up to a network of walking tracks that access Mt. Gambier, the **Devil's Punchbowl,** and the now-dry **Leg of Mutton Lake.** The 2.3km walk to the top of the mountain is best attempted in the morning. Those looking for similar views but a shorter hike can follow the signs to the **Centenary Tower** carpark, from where a 20min. walk leads to the tower and sweeping views of the lakes, the city, and the surrounding landscape all the way to the coast ($2; open when flag is flying from the tower). There is also a boardwalk and wildlife park at **Valley Lake,** just west of Mutton Lake and a 3.6km walking trail around the rim of Blue Lake, accessible from the pumphouse carpark.

While the nearby caves at Naracoorte (see below) get all the attention, there are a couple interesting holes in the ground right in the town center. The **Cave Gardens,** at Bay Rd. and Watson Tce., surround the town's original water source, and are the centerpiece of the town square park, with roses and trickling waterfalls (always open, lit at night, free). The flooded **Engelbrecht Cave,** on Jubilee Hwy. W. between Victoria Tce. and Ehret St., is a popular spot for adequately trained **cave divers.** Two of the cave's chambers are open for viewing. (☎ 8725 5493. Open daily 11am-3pm. Tours on the hour. $5.50, concessions $2.50.)

Just north of the town of Penola, about 20km north of Mt. Gambier on the road to Naracoorte, lies the **Coonawarra wine region,** a small stretch of vineyards that suddenly come out of the arid landscape. Twenty wineries in the region, the oldest dating from 1890, offer cellar-door sales and tastings, with a complete listing in the Food and Wine Guide available at the Lady Nelson Centre.

NARACOORTE   ☎08

Naracoorte's primary draw is the magnificent network of underground caves that lie 12km south of town. the famed Naracoorte Caves have recently been named a World Heritage site for their extensive deposits of 500,000-year-old megafauna fossils, including the oversized **sthenurine kangaroo.** The town was also crowned Australia's tidiest five times during the 1990s. Roughly 125km west of Horsham, VIC, on the Wimmera Hwy., and 100km north of Mt. Gambier along the Riddoch Hwy., Naracoorte is a forgettable place, but the caves deserve a visit.

Almost everything in this small town is on one of two streets, **Ormerod (Commercial)** and **Smith St.,** running parallel on either side of the village green. From the south, the Riddoch Hwy. from Mt. Gambier leads to the village green, becoming **Gordon St. Premier Stateliner buses** on the inland Mt. Gambier to Adelaide route pass through town once a day in each direction, stopping on the south side of the village green (☎8762 2466; 1hr. to Mt. Gambier, 5hr. to Adelaide). Services include: **ATMs** and banks in CBD; **library** with free **Internet,** across from the Naracoorte Hotel (open M 10am-5pm; Tu-W and F 9:30am-5pm; Th 10am-8pm; Sa 8:30am-noon); **police,** 56 Smith St. (☎8762 0466); and **post office,** 23 Ormerod St. (open M-F 9am-5pm). **Postal Code:** 5271.

Naracoorte Backpackers ❷, 4 Jones St., is mostly a workers' hostel but has standard dorm beds for those stopping over as well. Those looking to make a little cash should talk to the friendly owners, who organize crews to work in nearby vineyards. (☎8762 3835, or 0408 823 835. Internet $2 per hr. Dorms $21, YHA $18.) The **Naracoorte Hotel-Motel ❸,** 73 Ormerod St., offers standard hotel rooms with sinks and a nice balcony, as well as motel rooms with TVs and private baths. (☎8762 2400. Singles $27, motel-style $55; doubles $47/$66.) **Bool Lagoon ❷** provides toilets, but no showers, and permits are via on-site self-registration ($15 per

SOUTH AUSTRALIA

car, $7 per motorbike). To camp in the new **campground at the caves ❷**, with toilets, showers, and BBQ area, you'll need to get **permits** at the Conservation Park ticket office in the Wonambi Fossil Centre. (☎8762 2340. Open daily 9am-5pm; $18 per car.) The Foodland **supermarket** is on Ormerod St. (Open M-F 8:30am-8pm, Sa 8:30am-5pm, Su 9:30am-5pm.)

NEAR NARACOORTE: NARACOORTE CAVES

Twelve kilometers south of town is the **Naracoorte Caves Conservation Park,** a well-marked 4km west off the Riddoch Hwy. The **Wonambi Fossil Centre** is next to the carpark, with info on one of only two fossil sites in Australia awarded World Heritage protection. It is also the place to purchase tickets for cave tours and camping permits. (☎8762 2340. Open daily 9am-5pm.) The only self-guided attractions are the fossil center and **Wet Cave,** one of the larger caves and a good introduction to caving. Other caves are accessible via guided tours lasting 30min. to one hour. One of the younger caves in the park, the **Alexandra Cave** features five chambers full of delicate calcite stalagmites, stalactites, straws, and flowstone. **Blanche Cave** lacks these delicate decorations, but has immense columns and windows caused by a partial collapse of the roof. The most famous of the caves, the **Victoria Fossil Cave,** discovered in 1969, contains the remains of nearly 100 different species of Pleistocene fauna from 10,000 to two million years ago. Infrared cameras have been installed in **Bat Cave** to allow tourists to view the 300,000 resident bats without disturbing their breeding grounds. Tours are available daily 9:30am-4pm on various routes. (Tickets from the Wonambi Fossil Centre. 1 tour $9.50, concessions $7.50, children $5.50; 2 tours $16/$13/$10; 3 tours $23/$18/$14; 4 tours for the cave-aholic $28/$22/$17.) The rangers insist you wear **closed-toed shoes.** Bring a sweater as the temperature is a constant 17°C. Caving trips are available for both novices and advanced spelunkers. Book ahead via the Park's office. **Camping ❷** is allowed at an on-site campground and requires a permit, obtainable from the Wonambi Fossil Centre ($18 per carload; $10 per motorcycle).

YORKE PENINSULA

On Yorke, sandy flats punctuate rolling farmland, and sheer cliffs, looming over the hinterland, storm into the sea. The peninsula's extraordinary fertility has made it one of South Australia's leading grain-producing areas. What isn't farmed is covered in scrub forest, and the only unfarmed tracts are in Innes National Park. The peninsula has a vaguely boot-like shape, with its northern cuff defined by its history of copper-mining. After copper went bust in the 1920s, historical tourism, farming and ranching, and fishing—both recreational and industrial—became increasingly important. Visitors should take heed: in the summer a hot northern wind sweeps the peninsula, bringing with it a relentless swarm of flies. Refuge is on hand at beach towns like Wallaroo, but the real highlight of the region is the spectacular Innes National Park, with mind-blowing ocean views, electrifying surfing beaches, and gorgeous camping.

THE COPPER TRIANGLE   ☎08

With Wallaroo's popular beaches at its apex, the northern towns of Kadina, Wallaroo, and Moonta are collectively known as the Copper Triangle (or Coast). This trio of mining towns sprung up as a result of discoveries of large copper deposits in the 1860s. After a worldwide copper glut in the 1920s, the largest mines closed, and the towns now revolve around the seasonal influx of Adelaide weekenders at holidays. All three towns celebrate the Cornish heritage of the Yorke Peninsula during *Kernewek Lowender*, the world's largest Cornish festival (May 17-19, 2003). Wallaroo is on the ocean, Kadina is the largest and most cosmopolitan, and Moonta plays its Cornish and mining heritage to the hilt, though it also has a beach at Moonta Bay just a few miles west of town. Enormous grain silos dominate the shoreline, but the beaches are pleasant and usually uncrowded.

⚒ ORIENTATION AND PRACTICAL INFORMATION. Kadina is 50km northwest of Port Wakefield and Wallaroo is another 9km west of Kadina. Moonta is 17km southwest of Kadina and 16km south of Wallaroo. **Premier Stateliner** runs **buses** from Adelaide via Port Wakefield to all three towns. (☎ 8415 5555. Buses depart from Adelaide M-F 2 per day, Sa-Su 1 per day. $20, concessions $12.)

The **Moonta Station Visitors Center,** on Kadina Rd. in the old railway station, serves the whole Copper Triangle and stocks two helpful tourist guides: the locally produced *Cousin Jack's Guide to the Copper Coast* and the glossier *Yorke Peninsula Secrets.* (☎ 8825 1891. Open daily 10am-5pm.) The newly opened **Kadina Visitors Center,** on Moonta Rd. 2km southwest of town, has info on the whole Peninsula and can also give you both of the regional guides. (☎ 8821 2333. Open M-F 9am-5pm, Sa-Su 10am-4pm.) A 2min. walk from the center of Kadina, the beautiful new **Kadina Community Library,** 1a Doswell Tce., offers free **Internet.** (☎ 8821 0444. Open M 9am-1:30pm, Tu-W and F 9am-5:30pm, Th 9am-8pm, Sa 9:30am-11:30am.) Kadina is proud to host some of the peninsula's only **ATMs,** the area's **RAA** services (☎ 8821 1111 or 0418 859 070), and a **police** station (☎ 8828 1100). There is a **post office** in each of the three towns (all open M-F 9am-5pm).

🍴 ACCOMMODATIONS AND FOOD. Basic pub accommodations are easy to find in all three towns, except during long weekends or school holidays. For freedom from pubs, refuge can be found at the beautiful ▨**Sonbern Lodge Motel ❸,** 18 John Tce., Wallaroo. The relaxing courtyard garden and friendly owners help make any stay here relaxing. (☎ 8823 2291. Singles $28, ensuite $46; doubles $44/63. Most have balcony. Deluxe motel singles $67; doubles $84.) In Kadina, pub rooms and cheap meals (from $5) can be found at the **Wombat Hotel ❷,** 19 Taylor St. (☎ 8821 1108. Singles $25; doubles $40; includes light breakfast.) In Moonta, the **Cornwall Hotel ❷,** 18 Ryan St., opposite the post office, has cheap counter meals. (☎ 8825 2304. Singles $20; doubles $40; most rooms with balcony, some with kitchens. Meal specials from $6.50.) Caravan parks abound on Yorke, and the Copper Coast has its fair share. There is a park on the beach at Moonta Bay and three along Wallaroo's waterfront, the best of the bunch being the **North Beach Caravan Park ❶,** right on the beach. (☎ 8223 2531. Sites $12.50, powered $16.50; self-contained cabins for 2 from $66.)

The entire Yorke Peninsula is famous for its Cornish cuisine, especially the pasty (about $2.50), but only Moonta is bold enough to claim the moniker "Australia's Little Cornwall." **Skinner's Jetty Fish Cafe ❷,** on Jetty Rd., Wallaroo, has fresh seafood and wood-oven pizza (mains $10-24). (☎ 8823 3455. Take-away counter open daily 10am-9pm. Boathouse cafe open daily noon-8:30pm. Dining room open F-Sa 6-9pm and Sa-Su 7:30-10am.) Moonta's impeccably kept **Cornish Kitchen ❶,** 8 Ellen St., serves up Little Cornwall's best pasties ($2.50) and other light meals for $5-7. (☎ 8825 3030. Open daily 10am-3:30pm.) For **groceries,** try the Woolworth's along the Wallaroo Rd. in Kadina (open daily 7am-9pm).

🏖 SIGHTS AND BEACHES. The multi-award-winning ▨**Banking and Currency Museum,** 3 Graves St., in Kadina, is a tribute to tender—money lines everything, from the walls to the doors. (☎ 8821 2906. Open Su-Th 10am-4:30pm; closed June. $4, children $1.) Of the area's beaches, **North Beach** in Wallaroo is the best. The beach is just north of the jetty, with signs directing drivers toward the car-accessible beach entrance. Once on the sweeping beach, you can enjoy a stroll or rent a jet ski ($50 per 30min.), kayak ($10 per hr.), or sailboat ($30 per hr.) from **Wallaroo Watersports** (☎0418 198 397), at the south end of the beach near the caravan park.

■ INNES NATIONAL PARK

Innes National Park, on the southwest tip of the peninsula, is the real attraction of the Yorke. It's primarily known as a fantastic spot for surfing and the Western Whipbird, which was rediscovered in the area in 1965. Visitors may not catch sight of these rather shy creatures (which make a grating "happy-birthday-to-you" call), but they will see the area's stunning sculptured headlands and crashing waves. A daytrip to the park from the Copper Triangle is about a 2hr. drive each way.

The park is virtually inaccessible without a car. The **Yorke Peninsula Passenger Service** (☎1800 625 099) runs **buses** daily from Adelaide to Yorketown for $28.40. However, buses go no farther than **Warooka**, west of Yorketown, and Stenhouse Bay is more than 50km farther, requiring a car for any measure of flexibility in exploring the park. A **day-pass** costs $6 per vehicle or $3.50 per motorcycle (fee waived if camping) and can be purchased from the **Visitors Center** or from any of the self-registration stations near the entrance to the park. The park's main road, 26km long, is sealed and suitable for conventional vehicles. Although the side roads to beaches and overlooks are not sealed, they are accessible with a 2WD. The park can only be entered or exited from Stenhouse Bay, at its far eastern edge.

The **National Park Visitors Center** (☎8854 3200; open M-F 9am-4:30pm, Sa 10am-3:30pm, Su 10:30am-2pm) sells day-passes and camping permits and has guides for walking, driving, fishing, and surfing in the park. The **Innes Park Trading Post,** just inside the park entrance, hosts a **general store** and **petrol station,** can refill scuba tanks, and has info on fishing and surfing. The attached **Rhino Tavern** ❷ has mains from $12. (☎8854 4066. Store open daily 8am-7pm, tavern open daily 11am-late.)

Innes hosting a number of **campsites** ❶ in prime locations. No bookings are required for sites in the park; register at the Visitors Center or at one of the self-registration bays for camping in designated areas. Sites at **Pondalowie Bay** have water and toilets ($15 per vehicle). All other camping areas cost $6 per vehicle. There is also a **caravan park** ❶ in Marion Bay just before the park entrance. Several **lodges** and **huts** are available; contact the Visitors Center for bookings. All the cabins are in **Inneston.** Most of them have been renovated, and some have solar-powered lighting, full kitchens, and flush toilets. The lodges sleep four to ten people and require a minimum booking of two nights, with better deals for larger groups. (Cabins $23-$73 per night. Booking and payment due 2 weeks in advance.) The **Stenhouse Bay Lodge** ❶ is across the road from the Trading Post at the park entrance. (☎8854 4066. $15 per person.)

Nearly everything is accessible via the sealed road that runs through the park.. There are seven well-marked walking trails in the park ranging from 10min. to 3hr. in duration (pick up the *Innes Walking Trails* brochure at the Visitor Centre). Highlights include the layered limestone cliffs and spectacular views at **The Gap,** views of the Althorpe Islands from **Chinamans Hat,** and the sunset views from **West Cape,** which overlooks Pondalowie Bay. Those planning to **surf** should check conditions at the Visitors Center and pick up the *Southern Yorke Peninsula Surfing Guide.* The only beaches in the park safe for **swimming** are Dolphin Beach and Shell Beach, both sheltered by Spencer Gulf at the park's Northwestern edge. For **fishing,** get information at the Trading Post. They're usually biting at Jolley's Beach, Royston Head, and Brown's Beach.

FLINDERS RANGES

With its lack of craggy peaks, you can see that Flinders is ancient country, one of the three oldest mountain formations in the world. The main road (Hwy. 47) drifts between kangaroo-filled flatlands and sagebrush-covered hills. Dirt-tracks (4WD-only) lead through beautiful gorges. Flinders is most popular from April to October, when the nights are chilly and the days sunny. It's hot in summer, but for drivers with A/C or hardcore hikers, it's worth the trip. The Ranges begin at the northern end of the Gulf of St. Vincent and continue 400km into South Australia's northern Outback, ending near Mt. Hopeless.

GUIDED TOURS

Many tours heading from Adelaide to Alice Springs stop at Flinders. **Wallaby Tracks Adventure Tours,** run by the Andu Lodge in Quorn, picks up in Port Augusta or Adelaide and leads tours into central Flinders, including bushcamping and stops at Wilpena Pound, Aboriginal art sites, and Bunyeroo Gorge. (☎ 8648 6655 or 1800 639 933. 2-3 days $199-299.) **Quorn Flinders Ranges Eco-Tours,** 2 Railway Tce. (☎ 8648 6016), offers 4WD tours into **Dutchman Stern Conservation Park** (half-day $44) and northern Flinders tours (5 days). Self-drive tours are also available; inquire at Quorn's **Mill Motel,** 2 Railway Tce. (☎ 8648 6016), or at the Visitors Center.

Adelaide Sightseeing offers the marathon one-day return jaunt to Wilpena Pound. (☎ 8231 4144; $156.) **Wayward Bus,** 237 Hutt St., Adelaide, has an eight-day tour covering the Flinders and Coober Pedy. Travelers bus to Coober Pedy, then travel to the William Creek Pub and back south through the Flinders and the wine valleys. (☎ 8232 6646. $730, including meals and accommodation.) **Outback 'n' Coastal 4WD Adventures** has three-day Flinders camping trips. (☎ 0417 856 712; max. 7; $330.)

PORT AUGUSTA   ☎ 08

Located at the intersection of Hwy. 1, heading west toward the Nullarbor; and Hwy. 87, connecting Adelaide in the south with Coober Pedy and Alice Springs to the north, Port Augusta (pop. 14,800) promotes itself as the "Crossroads of Australia." Travelers who stop here are almost all on their way elsewhere.

The **School of the Air,** 39 Power Crescent, on the east edge of town, is an amazing foray into distance learning that began in 1958 (see **The World's Largest Classroom,** p. 279. ☎ 8642 2077. Tours daily 10am. Donation $2.) Another highlight is the fascinating **Arid Lands Botanic Gardens,** 400m north of town off the Stuart Hwy., which has bushwalking trails with labeled plants. (☎ 8641 1049. Open M-F 9am-5pm, Sa-Su 10am-4pm. Free.) The **Wadlata Outback Centre,** 41 Flinders Tce., has an excellent hands-on display of the stories, culture, and land of the Outback. (☎ 8642 4511. Open M-F 9am-5:30pm, Sa-Su 10am-4pm. $9, concessions $6.)

The **bus station** is opposite the library on Mackay St. The highway becomes **Victoria Pde.** in the city. Most action is on **Commercial Rd.,** with **post office, banks,** and **ATMs.** Services include: **Tourist Information Office,** 41 Flinders Tce., in the Wadlata Outback Centre building (☎ 8641 0793; open M-F 9am-5:30pm, Sa-Su 10am-4pm); **National Parks and Wildlife Service,** 9 Mackay St. (☎ 8548 5300); and the **library,** on the corner of Mackay and Marryatt St., with free **Internet.** (☎ 8641 9151. Open M and F 9am-6pm, Tu-W 9am-8pm, Th 9am-9pm, Sa 10am-1pm, and Su 2-5pm.)

The **Bluefox Lodge ❷,** at the corner of Trent Rd. and Hwy 1, offers free pickup from the bus station, seasonal vegetables, Internet ($2 per 15min.), and a lounge with a pool table and videos. Owners also arrange car and 4WD hire; buy, sell, and rent quality camping gear at very reasonable prices (tent and stove $10 per day; used tents sold for $90) and book Outback tours. (☎ 8641 2960. Dorms $17; doubles

SOUTH AUSTRALIA

and twins $42.) **Port Augusta International Backpackers ❶**, 17 Trent Rd., though not fancy, is ridiculously cheap, with free email, pickup, laundry, bicycle use, and breakfast. (☎8641 1063. Dorms $11.) Coles **supermarket** is on the corner of Jervois and Maryatt St. (☎8641 1700. Open daily 6am-9pm.)

SOUTHERN FLINDERS

MT. REMARKABLE NATIONAL PARK

Near the industrial town of **Port Pirie, Mt. Remarkable National Park** (15,632 hectares) is the pride of the southern Flinders Range. The area is perfect for laid-back bushwalking, camping, and animal watching, not to mention a couple of winding drives that serve as a gentle introduction to the Flinders Ranges. The summit of **Mt. Remarkable** can be approached on a 4hr. return hike from a trail starting 3km north of **Melrose** (24km south of Wilmington), along Main North Rd. The **Alligator Gorge trail** (1.2km; 1hr. return) has the best scenery on the eastern side of the park. Alligator Gorge is accessible at Wilmington, on Main North Rd. between Clare and Port Augusta, or by the cross-park trail (26km; 10hr.) from Mambray Creek.

The **park headquarters** is on the western side of the park at Mambray Creek, 45km north of Port Pirie, directly off Hwy. 1 on a road lined with magnificent eucalypts. There is a pay station with trail maps; a 54-site **campground ❶** with water, toilets, BBQ, and picnic areas; and access to bushwalks through canyons or over ridges. (☎8634 7068. Park fees $6 per vehicle, $14 per vehicle to camp; bushcamping $4.) Bushcamping is prohibited during the fire ban season, from Nov. 1 to Apr. 30. **National Parks and Wildlife** (☎8634 7068), in Port Augusta, has more details.

The hamlet of **Melrose**, on the eastern side of the park 20km south of Wilmington, sits peacefully in the shadow of Mt. Remarkable and makes a good base for hikes in the park. The **Melrose Caravan Park ❶** is a good budget option. (☎8666 2060. Sites $13, powered $16; dorms $15; vans from $39.) **Bluey Blundstone's Blacksmith Shop ❶** has a coffee shop as well as a B&B, all centered on an intimate and flowery courtyard. (☎8666 2173. Open M and W-F 11am-4pm, Sa-Su 10am-5pm.) Despite being the oldest licensed bar in the Flinders, the **North Star Hotel ❹** offers free **Internet** access to all customers. (☎8666 2110. Rooms $45-60.)

CENTRAL FLINDERS

The most famous and accessible attractions of the Flinders, including the vast amphitheater-like Wilpena Pound, are in the central part of the range. Here, Outback novices can be awed by mountains and great open spaces. To reach Quorn, Hawker, Rawnsley Park, or Wilpena Pound via public transport, take **Stateliner** through Port Augusta. (Adelaide ☎8415 5555; Port Augusta ☎8642 5055. Departs Adelaide and Port Augusta W, F, and Su 1 per day; returns Th, F, and Su.) If you have a McCafferty's/Greyhound bus pass, Stateliner fares into the Flinders are half-price. Stateliner services Port Augusta via Hawker and Quorn and Wilpena Pound (Th-F and Su). Connections to Adelaide are available from all three buses. Wilpena Pound marks the end of public transport into the range. Private tours offer the cheapest and most flexible ways to reach the Central Flinders without a car.

QUORN   ☎08

Smack in the middle of the Flinders Ranges, Quorn is the outback town of the movies, both figuratively and literally. Its historical streets and hilly backdrop have appeared in at least nine films, including the WWII epic *Gallipoli*. Nearby attractions such as the stunning **Warren Gorge** and accessible bushwalks like **Dutch-**

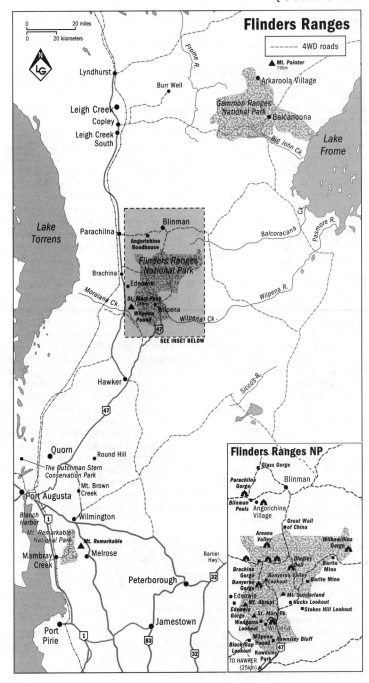

Flinders Ranges

- - - - - 4WD roads

▲ Mt. Painter
790m

Arkaroola Village

Gammon Ranges
National Park

Balcanoona

Big John Ck.

Lake Frome

Frome R.

Lyndhurst

Burr Well

Leigh Creek

Copley

Leigh Creek
South

Balcoracana Ck.

Pasmore R.

Lake Torrens

Parachilna

Blinman

Angorichina
Roadhouse

Flinders Ranges
National Park

Brachina

Edeowie

St. Mary Peak
1165m ▲

Wilpena

Wilpena
Pound

Balcoracana

Wilpena R.

Wilpena Ck.

47

SEE INSET BELOW

Moralana Ck.

Siccus R.

Hawker

47

Quorn

Round Hill

The Dutchman Stern
Conservation Park

Mt. Brown
Creek

Port Augusta

Blanch
Harbor

1

Wilmington

Mt. Remarkable
National Park

▲ Mt. Remarkable

Mambray
Creek

Melrose

Peterborough

Barrier
Hwy

32

Port
Pirie

1

Jamestown

83

32

Flinders Ranges NP

Glass Gorge

Parachilna
Gorge

Blinman

Blinman
Pools

Angorichina
Village

Great Wall
of China

Aroona
Valley

Wilkawillina
Gorge

Dingley
Dell

Brachina
Gorge

Bunyeroo Valley
Lookout

Barite
Mine

Bunyeroo
Gorge

Barite Mine

Edeowie

Mt. Sunderland

Hucks Lookout

Edeowie
Gorge

Mt. Abrupt

Stokes Hill Lookout

St. Mary Pk.

Wangarra
Lookout

Wilpena

Black Gap
Lookout

Wilpena
Pound

Rawnsley Bluff

TO HAWKER
(25km)

Rawnsley
Park

0   20 miles
0   20 kilometers

N

man's Stern and Devil's Peak make this a convenient base for daytrips. The friendly pubs and country hospitality create a relaxing atmosphere for admiring the Flinders' beauty and recharging before heading north.

TRANSPORTATION AND PRACTICAL INFORMATION. Quorn is on Hwy. 47, 40km northeast of Port Augusta and Hwy. 1, and 340km north of Adelaide. **Stateliner** runs from Adelaide to Quorn via Port Augusta. (☎8415 5555. 1 per day Su, W, and F. $46.) The **Quorn Newsagency** is the local ticket agent (☎8648 6042). **Andu Lodge** (☎1800 639 933; see below) offers the cheapest and most flexible travel service; they will pick up or drop off, by arrangement, in Port Augusta, Wilpena Pound, Devil's Peak, and Dutchman's Stern. The volunteer-staffed **Flinders Ranges Visitors Center** is at 3 7th St., between First St. and Railway Tce. (☎/fax 8648 6419. Open M-F 9am-5pm, Sa-Su 9am-4pm.) The only **ATMs** between Port Augusta and Wilpena are in the Transcontinental Hotel and the Austral Hotel, both on Railway Tce. Some service stations will give cash advances through **EFTPOS**. Services include: **police** (☎8648 6060); **Northern Roads Conditions Hotline** (☎1300 361 033); a sparsely-stocked IGA **supermarket** on 7th St., across from the info office (open M-F 8am-6pm, Sa-Su 9am-4:30pm); **Internet** at the **library**, on West Tce. (☎8648 6101; open M 8:30am-4pm, Tu and F 8:30am-6pm, W-Th 8:30am-5pm, Sa 10am-noon); and **post office,** 21 Railway Tce. **Postal Code:** 5433.

ACCOMMODATIONS AND FOOD. 🗺Andu Lodge ❷, 12 First St., is a friendly hostel and an excellent base for a Flinders holiday, with clean rooms, an enormous kitchen, bike hire, and Flinders tours. Short-term staff (min. 2 weeks) are hired in exchange for free accommodation, bike use, breakfasts, and a Flinders trip. (☎8648 6898. Dorms $24; singles $34; twins and doubles $54; YHA discount $4.) The **Quorn Caravan Park ❶**, at the east end of Silo Rd., offers caravan park basics plus some sad-looking caged kangaroos at the entrance. (☎8648 6206. Sites $14, powered $17.50; vans $34; cabins from $56.) There are also unpowered **camping ❶** sites in **Warren Gorge**, a beautiful spot 14km northwest of town off the Arden Vale Rd.; check at the Visitors Center (see **Practical Information,** p. 486).

The **Quandong Cafe and Bakery ❶**, 31 First St., offers home-cooked food in a pleasant little place that doubles as a gallery for local artists. (☎8648 6155. Open Tu 9:30am-3pm, W-Su 9:30am-4pm. Breakfast $8, sandwiches and salads from $5.) The town houses a tasty Thai takeaway (meals $5-9) inside the **Buckaringa Better Buy Market ❶**, an emporium for everything from beach toys (not much use here) to computer joysticks from circa 1989. (☎8648 6381. Open M and W-Sa 9am-7pm.) For sit-down meals, the **Criterion Hotel ❶**, Railway Tce., offers the cheapest specials in town ($6) with all-you-can-eat salad bar (open daily noon-1:45pm and 6-8pm); the other **pubs ❶** around town also offer quality meal specials from about $7.

HIKING. With the base of the hike only 9km from town, Quorn has one of the most rewarding easier hikes in the area: **Devil's Peak** (2hr. return) affords stunning 360° views across the Flinders region. Hikers who climb **Dutchman's Stern,** a bluff 10km north of Quorn, are rewarded with views of **Spencer Gulf.** Two main walks include a ridgetop hike (8.2km; 4hr. return) and a loop walk (10½km; 5hr.). Another 10km north of Dutchman's, the stunning **Warren Gorge** is home to a number of short hikes and scrambles but is best known as a prime spot to view yellow-footed **rock wallabies. Mt. Brown Conservation Park,** 16km south of town on Richmond Valley Rd., contains the usually dry **Waukerie Falls** and **Mt. Brown.** Allow at least seven hours for the roundtrip to the summit and back. (Open Apr.-Nov.)

WILPENA POUND AND FLINDERS RANGES NATIONAL PARK

Wilpena Pound is the stuff of legends. Immortalized in many of Hans Heysen's landscapes, this is some of the best scenery in South Australia. The Pound, a four- to five-hour drive, looks like a huge crater, but is actually a hilly syncline (geological downfold) outlined in jagged quartzite faces. The surrounding national park offers spectacular views, challenging hikes, and a glimpse into Aboriginal and geological history. The unsealed roads running along the outside of the Pound are a 4WD playground: the area includes small stream-crossings and gravelly inclines.

▛▟ TRANSPORTATION AND PRACTICAL INFORMATION. Most of the tours through the Flinders stop by Wilpena Pound. You can also take the **Stateliner bus** (☎8415 5555) to the Pound from Adelaide (7hr.; Su, W, and F 1 per day; $61) or Port Augusta (departs Su, W, and F 1 per day; returns Th, Su, and F 1 per day; $31). In an **emergency,** contact the Visitors Center (see below) or the **Wilpena Pound Resort** (☎8648 0004; open 24hr.) to be connected to emergency services.

The helpful **Wilpena Visitor Centre** is the park's headquarters, offering general park and hiking info, day-passes ($6), camping permits (day and camping passes can also be done via self-registration stations at the park entrances), and bookings for scenic flights, 4WD tours, and horse tours. (☎8648 0048. Open daily 8am-6pm.) There's a **general store** just behind the Centre with a limited supply of camping essentials, slightly pricey **petrol**, an **ATM**, and **Internet** access. (Open daily 8am-6pm. Internet $6 per 30min.)

▛ ACCOMMODATIONS. Camping ❶ is available in the park and can be paid for at the Visitors Center or via self-registration stations (sites $10 per vehicle). A few sites have toilets and water. For a shower, hit the refurbished **Wilpena Campground ❶**, next to the Visitors Center. (Check-in at the Visitors Center. Sites for 2 $16, powered $22, extra person $4.) The **Wilpena Pound Resort ❷** operates a restaurant, bar, campground, and upscale motel a few hundred yards down the road from the Visitors Center. The resort has rooms with A/C. Bar meals are tasty and cheaper ($9-15) than the restaurant ones. (☎8648 0004 or 1800 805 802. Bar and restaurant open daily 6:30-8:30pm. Linen $5. Dorms $22; doubles from $95.)

◪ HIKING. To explore **Wilpena Pound,** you must sweat or spend a bit, since no cars are allowed into the Pound itself. For any walk, advise someone of where you're going and for how long; also make sure to sign the logbook at trailhead info boards. The brochure, *Bushwalking in the Flinders Ranges National Park*, is available at the Visitors Center. Almost all the hikes leave from the Visitors Center and follow the same path for the first 2km. After the trail climbs a bit, it crosses a creek and then leads to **Hill's Homestead,** a cabin with toilets.

A short, steep walk up **Wangarra Hill** behind the homestead leads to the lower (10min.) and upper (20min.) lookouts over the Pound. A shuttle **bus service** from the Visitors Center to the Pound cuts 2km off the trip each way, leaving you about 1km from Hill's Homestead (1.6km from lookout) and making it a 90min. excursion up to Wangarra and back (4-6 buses per day; $4 return). Visitors should leave pets at home: the park is full of fox traps with a chemical produced by Australian plants that is harmless to native animals but lethal to foxes and dogs (see **Poison Risk,** p. 690). A high-intensity scrambling climb for serious hikers, the rocky trail to **St. Mary's Peak** (15km return, 6hr.; longer loop 20km return, 8hr.), will yield the most spectacular views of the Pound.

Many visitors consider the 50km **◪drive** through the park's gorges, with their sheer, colored walls and harsh geological ramparts, more beautiful than the walk into the Pound itself, with the stretch through **Bunyeroo Gorge** and **Brachina**

THE BIG SPLURGE

PRAIRIE HOTEL

Though you may at first think it merely a hallucination of your desert-addled mind, the **Prairie Hotel** in Parachilna is a true outback oasis that offers both budget and luxury accommodation, as well as innovative cuisine that's surely the best for hundreds of miles in any direction. The hotel's rustic elegance is the perfect treat after a day of churning up dust on Outback roads. The hotel itself features the original pub-hotel building, completely renovated, plus a spacious and beautifully modern new wing, as well as a landscaped courtyard and fantastic restaurant. Film crews shooting movies or 4WD commercials (the Flinders provide the perfect terrain for showing off that cornering power) often stay in the luxury section. The friendly folks at the hotel can also book 4WD and Camel tours for you, as well as set you up with accommodations on a working cattle station.

The hotel's scrumptious and multi-award winning **restaurant** does wonderful things with outback meat, offering a delicious emu burger ($15), a meat-lovers pizza ($13), and a feral mixed grill ('roo, camel, emu, goat $24). The scene in the bar can get rambunctious, and it stays open until the crowd decides to leave. (☎8648 4844; info@prairiehotel.com.au. Food served noon-8:30pm. Luxury singles from $120.)

Gorge as its highlight. For those heading north to Parachilna, Leigh Creek, or the Oodnadatta Track, this is the most fun way to get back to the paved Hwy. 47, which you will rejoin 20km south of Parachilna, at the outlet of Brachina Gorge. The turn-off for the gorges is 4km north of the Wilpena junction on the road toward Blinman. These roads require a certain amount of undercarriage clearance but are usually accessible to both 2WD and 4WD. A handful of companies offer **flights** in four- to six-seater planes, including **Air Wilpena.** (☎8648 0004. From $80 per person for 20min., $65 with 3 or more people. Small group and backpacker discounts.) Check at the Visitors Center for prices for some of the numerous **4WD treks** that operate in the area (from $50 per person).

NEAR FLINDERS RANGES NATIONAL PARK

RAWNSLEY PARK STATION. Rawnsley Park Station (☎8648 0008), south of the park off the road between Wilpena and Hawker, is an outdoor activity smorgasbord, offering horseback riding (min. 2 people; $45 per hr.; $55 per 2hr.; half-day $90; full-day $145), scenic flights (min. 2 people; 20min. $75; 45min. $120), 4WD tours (half-day $75; full-day $110 includes lunch), mountain bike hire ($10 per hr., half-day $30, full-day $50), and sheep shearing. The station also has a full range of **accommodations ❷,** including a 48-bed bunkhouse that is often booked out by groups. (Sites $16, powered $22; bunks $18; on-site vans for 2 $45; cabins for 2 $60.) **Internet** access is available at the remote outpost as well. ($2 per 10min.)

PARACHILNA. The best way to get to Parachilna, just north of the park, is to drive the 4WD track out the back of the park via Brachina Gorge, joining Hwy. 83 just south of town. Across the street from the ▧**Prairie Hotel ❺** (see **The Big Splurge,** p. 488) at the **Parachilna Overflow ❷,** backpackers enjoy the sparkling pool, a newly renovated kitchen and bar area with Internet, and rooms with A/C, though the bathrooms are a bit basic. (☎8648 4814. Sites $17.50; dorms $25; cabin singles $30, doubles $50.) For in-town fun, check out the 2.9km-long coal train as it passes by on its trip from the coalfields at Leigh Creek to the power plant at Port Augusta. Watching that beast roll by with an outback sunset as a backdrop will make you appreciate just how far out in the middle of nowhere you really are.

BLINMAN POOLS. The 32km drive from Parachilna to Blinman is an unsealed, rocky road that passes through the spectacular **Parachilna Gorge** and past stunning scenery (4WD preferable; cars with low clearance will have a rough trip). The hostel at **Angorichina ❶**, halfway between Parachilna and Blinman, has a general store with **petrol** and tire repair. (☎ 8648 4842. Store open M-Sa 8:30am-6:30pm, Su 9:30am-6:30pm. Sites for 2 $14, powered $16; dorms $12, linen $5; cabins $30-65.) From the carpark, a hike to the spring-fed ▨**Blinman Pools** (10km return; 4hr.) follows Blinman Creek as it winds its way back towards two separate waterfalls.

NORTHERN FLINDERS

This is where the vastness of the Australian Outback hits home, as the mountains grow ever larger, the gorges ever deeper, and other humans ever scarcer. To cover the couple hundred kilometers between **Flinders Range National Park** and **Gammon Ranges National Park,** drivers can either come up through **Wilpena** (see p. 487) and **Blinman** (see p. 489) or stick to the highway from Hawker and follow the pavement as far as Copley. The stops described here are along that highway, though the dirtroad route to Gammon will show you what the back of beyond is really about.

Travelers looking to head north of Gammon and Arkaroola will most likely require a **Desert Parks Pass.** For info, call the Desert Parks Pass Hotline (☎ 1800 816 078) or talk to the rangers at Balcanoona in Gammon Ranges Park or at the Parks Office in Port Augusta (☎ 8648 5300). The pass costs $80, is good for a full year, and allows unlimited access to the Simpson Desert, Innamincka, Lake Eyre, and Dalhousie areas, among others. It comes with a packet of brochures and great regional maps. Call the **Road Conditions Hotline** (☎ 1300 361 033) before setting out.

LEIGH CREEK   ☎ 08

After Coober Pedy, Leigh Creek is the largest town in the state north of Port Augusta. The town, 22km south of the coalfield, was entirely planned and built by the **Electricity Trust of South Australia (ETSA)** between 1979 and 1984. It consists of gently curving residential streets lined with trees and gravel "lawns," all clustered around a shopping center.

The **Visitors Center** is near the supermarket in the central mall. (☎ 8675 2723. Open M-F 9am-4pm, Sa-Su 10am-2pm.) The landscaped downtown area has a **pub** and a well-stocked **supermarket** (open M-F 9am-5:30pm, Sa 9am-12:30pm). **Internet** is free at the school library. (Open M and W-Th 8:30am-4:30pm, Tu and F 8:30am-4:30pm and 7-9pm, Sa 9am-noon.) **Leigh Creek South Motors** has **petrol,** tires, showers, and toilets. (☎ 8675 2016. Open M-Sa 8am-8pm, Su 9am-8pm. Showers $3.30.) The **Leigh Creek Hotel ❺** in town isn't cheap, but all rooms are ensuite, with TVs, telephones, and fridges. (☎ 8675 2025. Singles $75; doubles $85.) The **Caravan Park ❶** is on the outskirts of town. (Sites $11, powered $17; cabins from $50.) Leigh Creek is near the Oodnadatta Track (see p. 495).

GAMMON RANGES NATIONAL PARK

This is where central Australia gets serious. The 128,228 hectares of the Gammons are more craggy, exotic, stunning, and isolated than the southern Flinders. While there are hiking trails and some short 2WD accessible roads in the Gammons, the park is best explored on unsealed 4WD tracks. Wilderness experience is a must, and you should be sure to bring enough food, water, and emergency supplies to remain self-sufficient during your stay. The ▨**4WD Loop Road** (70km; 4-5hr.) is a great introduction to off-roading and the easiest way to see the park's scenery. Keep an eye out for rare animals, like the yellow-footed

IN RECENT NEWS

WOOMERA PROTESTS

Over Easter weekend of 2002, Australian demonstrators toppled a fence at the Woomera Detention Centre, allowing 33 of the center's hundreds of detained refugees to escape. Within a few weeks, harsh desert conditions took their toll and all of the refugees were rounded up.

Some residents of Woomera see the current protests as the latest of a rabble-rousing, anarchist element of the population rather than a reaction to a legitimate cause. Military testing at the Woomera Protected Area led to protests in the 1960s and 70s, and the current protests seem, in one resident's words, as if "the children of the hippies don't have anything good to do with their lives, so they're just trying to be hippies like their parents." In other words, they're protesting just for protesting's sake.

Despite this sentiment, the escape focused more attention on an already highly-charged debate over the treatment of refugees and asylum-seekers. Though the detention centers are said to be temporary holding areas for those whose visa requests are being processed, what they amount to in reality, according to civil rights advocates, are high-security prisons with inadequate facilities and potentially harmful conditions for children. Visa requests can be a lengthy process, and appeals filed by those denied visas can stretch it out even longer. Protestors and advocates claim that the centers are an unjust criminalization of people whose only crime was attempting to escape oppressive conditions in their homelands.

rock wallaby and the wedge-tailed eagle, as well as more common ones, such as kangaroos, emus, and feral donkeys. Check in at the **NPWS** headquarters in **Balcanoona**, where the rangers have info on bush-camping and bushwalking, along with maps, brochures, and the **Desert Parks Pass** (see p. 489). There are also public **toilets** ($2), rainwater-fed **showers** ($2), and a **pay phone** in Balcanoona. It is important to plan ahead, as the Ranger Station is not always staffed. Less experienced nature-lovers can camp at **Italowie Camp** or **Weetootla Gorge,** both accessible via 2WD and connect with shorter trails (2km-16km) at the park's fringe. **Cabins** are operated by the parks service: the **Balcanoona Shearer's Quarters ❶,** at the ranger station in Balcanoona, can sleep up to 19 people in rustic but comfortable rooms centered on a communal kitchen and lounge. (Dorms $12; no linen.) **Grindell's Hut ❶,** on the 4WD loop and accessible only via 4WD, is a beautiful self-contained cabin in the middle of the park. (Cabin for 8 $75.) **Nudlamutana Hut ❶** is on the park's north side. (Cabin for 4 $53.) For all the huts, make reservations through the Parks Office in Hawker (☎8648 4244) and pick up keys at the Balcanoona office (☎8648 4829). **Lake Frome,** 38km east of Balcanoona (4WD only), features sprawling lake-beds covered in glistening salt. No access is allowed after 3pm, when the area becomes a designated Aboriginal hunting ground.

ARKAROOLA

A 61,000-hectare private conservation park, Arkaroola abuts the northern boundary of Gammon Ranges National Park. The **Arkaroola Wildlife Sanctuary** is an amazing example of land reclamation and showcases stunning terrain. Founders Reg and Griselda Sprigg turned an abused-sheep station overrun with non-native flora and fauna into an almost entirely reclaimed refuge with native plants and animals. The **ridgetop tour** ($66) from the **observatory** is a highlight of the Flinders, a geology lesson on the go as you climb impossibly steep roads and stop periodically to take in the view of the ancient granite mountains. There are several **self-drive 4WD tracks** in the preserve as well as **scenic flights** (from $88 per person). **Arkaroola Village ❶,** a mountain-oasis just 32km north of Balcanoona, has a tourist office, campsites, and a motel. (☎ 1800 676 042 or 8648 4848. Reception open daily 7:30am-6:30pm. Sites $11, powered $17; singles $32; motel singles $60.) There is also a general store, a **petrol** station, and the only **restaurant ❷** for many miles (mains from $12).

DRIVE CAREFULLY. The area off the Stuart Hwy. is not for the casual tourist. With most roads unsealed, a 4WD is essential. Though arid, this area is subject to flash flooding, and is especially dangerous to drive in the summer. Plan your trip with park officials and check road conditions on the **Northern Road Conditions Hotline** (☎ 1300 361 033). Carry plenty of water for long drives (both for drinking and for your car), and take at least 2 spare tires. Check in with officials and notify friends or family before and after your journey. If your car does break down on a remote road, do not panic and or start walking—people die every year when they make this mistake. Stay with the car; it provides shade and can be spotted more easily by search parties.

OUTBACK SOUTH AUSTRALIA

North and west of the Flinders, the Australian Outback surpasses legend and becomes dirt real. Unsealed roads stretch out endlessly, crossing baked earth that your car will tease into a maddening cloud of dust, passing intimidating signs that read "Next gas: 454km" or "Danger: extreme conditions ahead." This is a land of rare oases and abandoned railroad tracks, of the stone ruins of farmhouses and the mythical dog-fence (see **The Great Dog Fence,** p. 496). You'll find immense tracts of parkland, large (and completely dry) lakes, and enough wide open space to lose yourself many times over. Prime tourist season in the Outback is from April to October, with peak season in the winter months, particularly July; summers are hot, with temperatures reaching 45°C (113°F) even in the shade, and swarms of bush flies make their presence felt.

STUART HIGHWAY: ADELAIDE TO COOBER PEDY

As the Stuart Hwy. winds its way north and west toward the opal capital of the world, there is little to see other than the harsh reality of the bright red, arid terrain. It doubles as pasture land, most of which is unfenced, so look out for free-roaming sheep and cattle. In the more remote areas north of Port Augusta, fuel prices will increase the farther you venture into the Outback, so it's a good idea to stop off in **Port Augusta** or **Pimba** before heading on into the baked red unknown.

WOOMERA. Originally designated a "secret" town by the British military, Woomera was created in 1947 as the unofficial capital of the **Woomera Prohibited Area,** a long-range weapons testing area that once covered 270,000km² and is still the largest land-locked military test site in the world. The pre-planned village of Woomera, 7km north of Pimba, sits at the edge of the Area, known affectionately as "the range" by the locals. Joint European and Australian forces created the village, the location of which wasn't revealed on maps until the 1960s, and from 1970 to 1999, the American military was the primary partner in the Joint Defence Facility-Nurrangar, a satellite and missile tracking center. Reassuringly, the base is currently geared more toward satellite launching than bomb testing. With a history like this, it's not surprising that the **Woomera Heritage Centre,** on Dewrang Ave. in the middle of town, professionally details the nuclear bombs, radio astronomy, and families of Woomera's unusual past. (☎ 8673 7042. Open daily 9am-5pm. $3.) The town also has a hotel, a **caravan park ❶,** a big **supermarket,** and a **petrol** station. Woomera has made headlines recently thanks to the Refugee Detention Centre that opened in 1999, shortly after American forces left (see **In Recent News,** p. 490).

SOUTH AUSTRALIA

THE HIDDEN DEAL

FORE!

Budget travelers, take heart: *Let's Go* has found a golf course within your price range. And this is no ordinary course: players never have to worry about replacing divots, they never hit trees, they needn't drive little carts, they never land in the rough, and water hazards are nowhere in sight. Impossible? Nope. Welcome to golf in the Outback, where land is cheap, water precious, and grass nonexistent. The desolate ground may be hard, flat, almost treeless, and bone-dry, but that hasn't stopped Coober Pedy from installing an 18-hole course. There's not a scrap of fairway or tinge of bright green in sight, and so the greens fee is quite literal: $10 gets you a small square of green astroturf. Carry it around and set it down whenever it's time to take a whack at the ball. Regular cars are allowed on the course, though golfers must give right-of-way to cars when the fairway doubles as the road. Smart golfers use fluorescent orange golf balls both for visibility and because bearded dragons on the course mistake the white balls for their own eggs and steal them. Plaid pants remain optional. *(Just west of town on Seventeen Mile Rd. Green hire $10; club hire $10.)*

GLENDAMBO. Glendambo, 250km southeast of Coober Pedy, is the last stop and **petrol** station before the mining town. The BP here runs both the **motel ❺** and the backpacker accommodation and **campsites ❶**. (☎8672 1039 or 8672 1035. Motel sites $14, powered $18, shower $2.50; dorms $16; singles $81; doubles $84; no linen.) About 100km north of Glendambo, the highway doubles as an emergency landing strip for the Royal Flying Doctor Service (see **What's up Doc,** p. 697).

COOBER PEDY ☎ 08

This remote outpost is the most interesting (and popular) stop on the long, dry haul between Alice Springs and Adelaide. The "Opal Capital of the World" draws 150,000 tourists a year, partly because there's nowhere else to stop, and partly because the town is utterly unlike any place else on earth. Over half of the 3500 residents live underground in homes almost invisible from the outside. Homes, churches, shops, and even hostels are carved out of the earth to escape the extreme temperatures, which can reach 50°C (122°F) in the summer and plunge on winter nights. The town owes its name to Aboriginal observation of this abnormal behavior: "coober" means "white man" in a local dialect, while "pedy" means "hole in the ground." Men outnumber women five to one (in the early days, it was 400 to one) and nearly everybody in town has some connection to opals—80% of the world's opal supply is pulled from the ground in the region. Though the local economy is increasingly dependent on mining tourists' wallets, the town retains the unique character of its opal-mining heritage.

TRANSPORTATION. McCafferty's/Greyhound (☎13 14 99 or 13 20 30) makes daily runs to Coober Pedy from Adelaide and Alice Springs. Virtually every tour between Adelaide and Alice stops off in Coober Pedy. The Stuart Hwy., running north-south across the country, goes straight through Coober Pedy. **Budget** (☎8672 5333; 4WD from $99 per day) and **Thrifty** (☎8672 5688; 2WD $99 per day), at the Desert Cave Hotel, rent cars. **Taxis** (☎0408 893 473) are also available.

ORIENTATION AND PRACTICAL INFORMATION. Coober Pedy is 685km (6-8hr.) south of Alice Springs, 730km southeast of Uluru, 538km north of Port Augusta, and 846km (8-10hr.) north of Adelaide. The turn-off from the Stuart Hwy. leads into **Hutchison St.,** the main street and location of virtually every establishment. The helpful **Tourist Information Centre**

(☎8672 5298 or 1800 637 076; open M-F 8:30am-5pm) is at the south end of Hutchison St., across from the bus depot, but most people start at the unofficial tourist office, **Underground Books**, on Post Office Hill Rd. just off Hutchison St., which serves as the booking agent for tours. (☎8672 5558. Open M-Sa 8:30am-5:30pm, Su 10am-4pm.) Other services include: **ATM** at Westpac Bank; **police** (☎8672 5056); **RAA** (☎8672 5230), at Desert Traders; free **Internet** at the school **library,** Paxton Rd. (☎8672 5077; open M-F 8:30am-5pm, Sa-Su 1-5pm); and a **post office** (☎8672 5062) in the miners' store. **Postal Code:** 5723.

DON'T WALK BACKWARD! Outside town boundaries, 1.5 million **abandoned mine shafts** make the danger of carelessly stepping backward and plummeting to your death very real. Signs around town, though co-opted by the tourist industry, are no joke; do not explore opal fields by yourself. Techniques of mining make it difficult to fill in the holes, so they are left open and uncovered.

ACCOMMODATIONS AND FOOD. Radeka's Backpacker's Inn ❷, at Hutchison and Oliver St., is a clean, comfortable maze of underground "caves" 6½m below ground. There are no doors, but the underground rooms are cool in the summertime and infuse your Coober Pedy experience with authenticity. (☎8672 5223. Kitchen, pool table, Internet $2 per 10min., TV room, bus pickup and drop-off, and the cheapest bar in town. Linen $2. Dorms $22; doubles $52. VIP/YHA.) The much smaller **Joe's Backpackers ❷** is across from Radeka's. If the owners, Maria and Joseph Kmet, look familiar, perhaps you saw them in the film *Priscilla, Queen of the Desert.* (☎8672 5163. Dorms $18; singles $40; doubles $52. VIP/ YHA.) **Riba's Underground Camping ❶** is on William Creek Rd., outside of town. Coming from Port Augusta, turn off 4km before Hutchison St. (☎8672 5614. Aboveground sites $6, powered $8; subterranean sites $9.) Visitors interested in **homestays ❹** should call Annie, who runs a traditional B&B in her underground home (☎8672 5541. Singles $55; doubles $75.)

Run by an immigrant Sicilian family, **John's Pizza Bar ❶**, on Hutchison St., serves great pizza for $6-10. (☎8672 5561. Open M-Sa 11:30am-10:30pm, Su 5-10pm.) The **Gemstone Cafe and Bakery ❶** (☎8672 3177; open daily 9am-7pm), on Hutchison St., has burgers and sandwiches, along with Elvis posters and **Internet** access ($4.40 per 30min.). The IGA **supermarket** is on Hutchison St. (Open M-Sa 8:30am-7pm, Su 9am-7pm.)

TOURS AND SIGHTS. Radeka's Desert Breakaways Tours is popular with backpackers. The tour includes many stops around town and the opal fields, a trip out to the Breakaways, and a chance to noodle for your own opals. (☎8672 5223. 4½hr.; $35.) **Joe's Tours,** run by Joe's Backpackers, covers a similar itinerary. (☎8672 5163. 4-5hr. Departs 1pm. $28.) **Riba's Evening Mine Tours** takes guests into a mine for a 1½hr. tour. (☎8672 5614. Daily 7:30pm. $14.) For those who want to see a little more of the Outback, a scenic flight on **Wrightsair** might be the answer. (☎8670 7962. Local flights $45; Lake Eyre flights $135. Book at Underground Books.) **Dave Burge's Lunch at the Lake Day Tour** is a full-day tour that covers 500km, including Lake Eyre, guided by a 35-year Coober Pedy resident. (☎8672 5900. Departs daily 8am. $130, includes lunch and snacks.) For an unforgettable look at the Outback, join the mail carrier on the 12hr. **Mail Run** that covers a triangular route stopping at points of interest along while delivering mail to cattle stations along the route. (☎1800 069 911 or at Underground Books ☎8672 5558. Departs M and Th 9am. $95. Book ahead.)

The town's **underground churches** are usually open to visitors. The oldest of these churches is the **Sts. Peter and Paul Catholic Church.** Another sort of under-

SOUTH AUSTRALIA

ground shrine that might make some women uncomfortable is **Crocodile Harry's Crocodile's Nest,** the home of the legendary womanizer, adventurer, and crocodile-slayer who was the model for the character Crocodile Dundee. About 6km west of town on Seventeen Mile Rd., the walls of Harry's home are covered with underwear, graffiti, and photos of a much younger Harry wrestling crocodiles the size of dinosaurs. ($2 donation requested for entry.) Outside town, **The Breakaways** are a set of flat-topped mesas. The track on **Moon Plain** (70km return; 2hr.), a post-apocalyptic lunar landscape of glinting rocks and the occasional browned piece of vegetation, is fun to explore. You can still see tracks where the *Mad Max III* cars raced, and drive along the road where the drag queen in *Priscilla* rode on the roof. The famous **Dog Fence** is about 15km outside of town (see **The Great Dog Fence,** p. 496). Those looking to sharpen their swing should hit the town **golf course** (see **The Hidden Deal,** p. 492).

◻ **OPAL SHOPPING.** Coober Pedy is glinting with opal pushers and their wares, but not all are quality. Decent opals will give off multiple colors beyond the base color as you turn it in the light. The greater the intensity of these secondary colors, the better the opal. As all men know, size doesn't necessarily matter (one researcher, however, begs to differ—see **From the Road,** p. 370), and smaller opals are often of better quality. When buying, choose an opal store that's particularly well-lit; dim stores may be hiding flaws. Educating yourself a bit about the stones before rushing off to buy is also a good idea. The **Umoona Opal Mine,** on Hutchison St., has informative displays and offers tours of a decommissioned opal mine (☎ 8672 5288. Open daily 8am-7pm. Tours 4 per day. $8, children $4.)

OFF THE STUART HIGHWAY: OODNADATTA TRACK

The ◼**Oodnadatta Track,** one of the most famous outback tracks in Australia, runs 619km from Marree, north of Leigh Creek in the Flinders, through William Creek and Oodnadatta to Marla, 235km north of Coober Pedy on the Stuart Hwy. The track includes the vast salt-beds of **Lake Eyre,** immense stretches of baked red nothing, ruins of ancient farm homes, and the legendary Dog Fence. It mostly follows the route of the *Old Ghan* train line that used to connect Alice Springs with points south; remnants of the *Ghan* abound, including abandoned locomotives in Marree, the track-bed, and a couple of impressive and surprising latticed-steel railway bridges. The unsealed road can be driven (carefully) in a 2WD vehicle, though most do it in a 4WD; ask about road conditions in Marla or Marree before taking off, or call the **Northern Road Conditions Hotline** (☎ 1300 361 063). Regardless of your vehicle, the best advice is to slow down: the faster you go, the higher the likelihood of multiple flat tires. The Marree Hotel offers a handout on the drive.

MARREE. A mostly unsealed 120km northwest of Leigh Creek, **Marree** is the official starting point of both the **Oodnadatta** and **Birdsville Tracks,** with the former heading northwest to the Stuart Hwy. and the latter slicing through the **Sturt Stony Desert** and parts of the **Strzelecki Desert** to the northeast en route to far western Queensland. The town possesses a surfeit of outback charm: locomotives from the *Old Ghan* dominate the town center, children play on the dusty football/cricket grounds (jokingly labeled the MCG in reference to the famous Melbourne Cricket Grounds), where not a single blade of grass is to be found, and the Afghan section of the town cemetery and the reconstructed ruins of a mosque uphold the memory of the Muslim cameleers who were the lifeblood of early Outback settlements.

The **Marree Hotel ❸** is a friendly repository of outback history. (☎ 8675 8344. Dinner from $12. Singles $35; doubles $65.) The **Drover's Rest Tourist Park ❷** is on the south side of town. (☎8675 8371. Sites $16, powered $20; budget cabins from $25 per person; cabins for 2 from $80.) The **Oasis Cafe**, next door to the Hotel, has **internet** access, does tire repair, sells the cheapest **petrol** in town, and stocks maps of the area. (☎8675 8352. Internet $2.50 per 10min. Open daily 7:30am-7pm.) The **Marree General Store**, which doubles as the **post office**. (☎8675 8360. Store open daily 8am-8pm; post office open M-F 9am-4pm.) **Postal Code:** 5733.

LAKE EYRE. **Lake Eyre,** 90km northwest from Marree and Australia's largest salt lake, acts as the drainage for an area approximately the size of Western Europe. The Oodnadatta Track brushes up against the southern edge of **Lake Eyre South,** the smaller of the Lake's two parts, and a brief detour lets you drive right up to its salty edge. The two access roads to the larger **Lake Eyre North** are 4WD only, and depart from Marree (94km to the lake) and from a turn-off on the track 7km south of William Creek (64km to the lake). **Campsites ❶** are available near the lake on both access roads; passes are available at the Marree General Store or at the self-registration stations at the Lake Eyre National Park entrances (day-pass $10; overnight pass $18; free with Desert Parks Pass). The **NPWS info line** (☎1800 816 178) provides lake conditions. Take the weather into account before going, as temperatures up to 50°C (122°F) in the summer can make it unwise and unpleasant to visit.

WILLIAM CREEK. The next watering hole is 204km northwest of Marree at **William Creek** (technically on Anna Creek cattle station, which is the world's largest at nearly half the size of Tasmania), where airplanes can land and taxi right to the town's only substantial building, the 🅆**William Creek Pub ❶.** Covered with signs and bedecked with visitors' bras, boxers, driver's licenses, foreign currency, and various other curiosities, this is the idiosyncratic Outback pub you've been looking for. (☎8670 7880. Linen $5. Sites $3.50; bunks $14; singles $25.) The pub also has **petrol** and tire repair. Drivers can head east to Coober Pedy directly from William Creek (164km east). **Explore the Outback Camel Safari** (☎8670 7846) lets you see the Outback from the back of an ornery camel.

OODNADATTA. **Oodnadatta** is a sad-looking town 203km northwest of William Creek, but it has precious amenities, including **car repair** facilities and the **Pink Roadhouse ❶,** which offers valuable info on the area, **petrol,** groceries, and emergency supplies. Check road and weather conditions with Pink's or with the **police** (☎8670 7805). The roadhouse also has a **post office** and accommodations. (☎1800 802 074 or 8670 7822. Open daily 8am-6pm. Sites for 2 $14.50, powered $20; ensuite cabins for 2 $80; hotel-style doubles $45; backpackers "shack" $10 per person.) They can also arrange car repairs and vehicle recovery (☎1800 802 074). From here, you can either continue northwest on the track to its end at Marla (210km) or head southwest to Coober Pedy (195km). Oodna is also a good base for the **Rocks Track** (4WD only), a rough road that heads north to the beautiful, swimmable oasis at **Dalhousie Springs** (190km north) and the expansive **Simpson Desert,** both popular destinations (**Desert Parks Pass** required for both; see p. 489).

MARLA. **Marla,** where the Oodnadatta Track rejoins the known world, is an overgrown highway rest area that sits approximately halfway between Adelaide and Alice Springs. The **Traveller's Rest Roadhouse ❸** has **petrol** (open 24hr.), a bar, a restaurant, a small **supermarket,** and accommodations (☎8670 7001. Budget cabin singles $30, doubles $40; motel singles $70, doubles $75). For those heading north towards Uluru and Alice, get petrol here: your next petrol station will be **Kulgera,** 180km north just over the Northern Territory border..

THE GREAT DOG FENCE Meryl Streep's woeful cries of "the dingo ate my baby" would have been cut short if only she had lived south of the longest fence in the world. Stretching for 5600km from Queensland through the northwest corner of New South Wales and over to Penong, SA at the start of the Nullabor Plain, the Great Dog Fence delineates "dingo country," keeping the wild dogs firmly in the north. The fence, completed in 1940, is mostly 6-foot-high wire matting but around bigger cities is electrified. "Sheep country," to the south, is separated from "cattle country," to the north. Though more than twice as long as the Great Wall of China, each part of the fence is regularly maintained by full-time dog fencers dotted along the route. Occasionally, though, the dingoes break through, panicked cries of "the fence is down" ring through the local towns, and soon mangled sheep carcasses dot the landscape.

EYRE PENINSULA

Most international tourists this far west in South Australia are bound for or coming from Western Australia. The tourist folks on the Eyre know this, and they market the peninsula as "Australia's Best Detour" and merely suggest travelers add 295km to their itineraries and pop down for a breath of fresh Eyre. In the driest state on the driest continent on earth, the Eyre Peninsula provides a welcome belt of coves with pounding, fish-filled surf—all removed from the urban bustle

▐ TRANSPORTATION

Premier Stateliner (Adelaide ☎8415 5555, Ceduna ☎ 8625 2279, Port Lincoln ☎8682 1734, Whyalla ☎8645 9911) is the only public **bus** carrier on the Eyre with frequent service, though Greyhound stops in Ceduna on the way to Perth. Stateliner runs between Adelaide and Whyalla (M-Th and Sa-Su 5 per day, F 6 per day; $40). Buses also leave Adelaide bound for Port Lincoln, stopping in towns along the eastern coast (depart Adelaide M-F 2 per day, Su 1 per day; depart Port Lincoln daily 2 per day). Stateliner runs an overnight bus from Adelaide to Ceduna via Streaky Bay (depart Adelaide Su-F 1 per day; depart Ceduna daily 1 per day).

By car, traversing the Eyre Peninsula means diverging from the inland Hwy.1 (Eyre Hwy.), which runs 468km straight across the top of the peninsula from Whyalla to Ceduna. The highlights of the Eyre are found on a triangular, coastal route via the Lincoln Hwy. and Flinders Hwy. (Alt. Hwy. 1), which takes 763km to connect the same two towns.

WHYALLA   ☎08

Aboriginal for "place of the water," Whyalla is mainly a fishing town, offering little to the passing tourist beyond basic amenities and choice fishing spots. The **Whyalla Tourist Centre** is on the east side of the Lincoln Hwy., next to the enormous ship that houses the Maritime Museum. (☎8645 7900. Open M-F 9am-5pm, Sa 9am-4pm, Su 10am-4pm.) The **Westland Shopping Centre,** on the corner of McDouall Stuart Ave. and Nicholson Ave., has two **supermarkets** and a food court. **ATMs** abound on Forsyth St. in the city center. The **library,** in the Civic Centre on Patterson St., just off Darling Tce., has **Internet.** (☎8645 7891. Open Tu-W and F 10am-6pm, Th 10am-8pm, Sa 9am-noon.) The friendly **Hotel Spencer ❸,** on the corner of Forsyth St. and Darling Tce., has spotless ensuite rooms with TV, fridge, and A/C. (☎8645 8411. Singles $28-$33; doubles $44.) The **Whyalla Foreshore Caravan Park ❶,** on Broadbent Tce., is 2km from the post office and close to the beach. (☎8645 7474. Sites $12, powered $16; on-site vans for 2 $28; cabins for 2 $44-53.)

ALTERNATE HIGHWAY 1: WHYALLA TO PORT LINCOLN

As Alt. Hwy. 1 speeds along the west coast, the road hosts a few dots of civilization tucked away in seaside breaks from the monotonously rolling plains. The quiet, friendly towns of **Cowell, Arno Bay, Port Neill,** and **Tumby Bay** are good places to stop and rest. All four have **pub hotels ❸** (singles around $30; twins and doubles $40), **caravan parks ❶,** small supermarkets, **petrol stations,** and post offices. **Cowell,** 111km south of Whyalla, offers one of the safest and best fishing areas in South Australia at its **Franklin Harbour,** as well as a thriving oyster industry and the nation's only commercial jade mining. Tourist information is available at the **Town Council Office** on Main St., fronting the jetty. The **Franklin Harbor Hotel ❸,** 1 Main St., has clean rooms and a balcony overlooking the harbor. (☎8629 2015. Singles $30; doubles $45. Continental breakfast included.) The **Commercial Hotel ❸,** 24 Main St., offers similar accommodations. (☎8629 2181. Singles $28; doubles $44.) The tiny fishing town of **Tumby Bay,** 50km north, offers the only backpacker option in the region: the **Seabreeze Hotel ❶,** with dorms and pokies. (☎8688 2362. Dorms $15; singles $20, ensuite $40; doubles $30/$50. NOMADS.)

PORT LINCOLN   ☎08

At the southern tip of the Eyre Peninsula, breezy and busy Port Lincoln (pop. 13,000) lords over **Boston Bay,** a natural harbor more than three times the size of Sydney Harbour and the second-largest in the world. Port Lincoln was to be the state capital, but inadequate fresh water destined today's politicians for Adelaide instead—in place of parliaments, Port Lincoln is graced with public toilets called the "Loo-vre." The town has done just fine, building itself into Australia's premier aquaculture center as well as the exporter of the largest tonnage of commercial fish in the country. Port Lincoln is a frequent a stopover en route to nearby parks and the more remote attractions of the Eyre Peninsula.

▐▆ TRANSPORTATION. Premier Stateliner buses depart from their booking office, across from the Pier Hotel on Lewis St., a half-block south of Tasman Tce. (☎8682 1288; open M-F 8am-6:45pm, Sa 8:30-11:30am) and run to Adelaide via Port Augusta. (Su-F 2 per day, Sa 1 per day. $50 to Port Augusta, $72 to Adelaide. Book ahead.) For a **taxi,** call ☎13 10 08.

▆▐ ORIENTATION AND PRACTICAL INFORMATION. The shores of Boston Bay line the town's northern edge. Nearly everything of interest is within easy walking distance of **Tasman Tce.,** the main drag that runs along the water, becoming London St. at the east end of town. Tasman Tce. hosts most of the town's major hotels, pubs, cafes, and tourist shops. A few blocks inland, **Liverpool St.** runs parallel to Tasman, providing shopping, a small movie theater, and restaurants before it heads north at the western edge of town and becomes the Lincoln Hwy. to Tumby Bay and Whyalla. **Mortlock Tce.** is the town's main north-south thoroughfare, heading south from the middle of Tasman Tce. and forking at the southern edge of town, with one branch heading toward Coffin Bay and Elliston to the west and the other towards Lincoln National Park and Whaler's Way to the south.

The **Visitors Center,** 3 Adelaide Pl., offers local info as well as permits for nearby parks. (☎8683 3544. Open daily 9am-5pm.) **ATMs** are at Tasman Tce. and Liverpool St. The **library,** in the Spencer Institute of TAFE building, just off Tasman Tce., has free one-hour **Internet** sessions. (☎8688 3622. Open M-Tu and Th-F 8:30am-5pm, W 8:30am-8pm, Su 1-5pm.) Other services include **police** (☎8688 3020) and a **post office** at 68 Tasman Tce. (Open M-F 9am-5pm.) **Postal Code:** 5606.

SOUTH AUSTRALIA

▐▍▐▐ ACCOMMODATIONS AND FOOD. The Pier Hotel ❷ (☎ 8682 1322), at the center of Tasman Tce., offers adequate rooms, some with bay views and most with minimal frills, and the stumble-home convenience of having the raucous epicenter of Port Lincoln nightlife downstairs. (Singles $25, ensuite with TV $35; doubles $30/$45. Live music Th-Sa until late.) Though not quite as central, the **Hotel Boston ❷**, on King St. near the silos at Tasman's west end, is comfortably away from the bustle of Tasman Tce. and features slightly nicer rooms than the Pier. (☎ 8683 1211. Singles $25, ensuite with TV $35; doubles $35/$50.) The recently renovated **Grand Tasman Hotel ❹** (☎ 8682 2133), on the corner of Bligh St. and Tasman Tce., has sparkling ensuite rooms with TVs. (Singles $50; doubles $65. Breakfast included.) **Kirton Point Caravan Park ❶**, at the end of London St. (Tasman Tce.), has a waterfront setting 3km from the town center. (☎ 8682 2537. Sites $9 per person; cabins from $27.) The **Cafe del Giorno ❷**, 80 Tasman Tce., offers light Italian meals for $8-12. (☎ 8683 0577. Open daily 9am-10pm.) Many **pubs ❶** offer dinner specials from $6. Coles **supermarket** is on Liverpool St. (Open M-Sa 6am-6pm.)

◩ ◲ SIGHTS AND ENTERTAINMENT. Port Lincoln is home to the one-of-a-kind **Tunarama Festival,** a four-day extravaganza of fireworks, sand castles, and seafood held annually on the Australia Day long weekend in late January. The festival also features live music, a rodeo, and a highly competitive tuna-tossing contest. (☎ 1800 629 911. Festival Jan. 24-27, 2003.) The **Mediterraneo Festival,** held annually over the Easter long weekend, focuses on the fresh seafood and fine wines of the region, with cooking expositions and live music.

For a truly unique experience, take the popular tour of the **Port Lincoln Seahorse Farm,** 5 Mallee Crescent, Australia's only sea horse breeding facility. (☎ 8683 4866, bookings 8683 3544. Tours 30min., daily 3pm. Book through Visitors Center. $5, children $4.) The **Parnkalla Walking Trail** (14km) follows the shoreline from the historic Boston House, several kilometers north of the city, to Murray's Point Preserve on Murray's Point south of town. The trail offers a number of impressive views of Boston Bay; a guide detailing the numerous historical and scenic stops along the way is available at the Visitors Center. At the **Glen-Forest Animal Park,** 15km northwest of Port Lincoln, you can get up close to dingoes, kangaroos, wombats, and camels. (☎ 8684 5053. Open daily 10am-5pm. $9, children $7; minigolf $6.) Six kilometers north of Port Lincoln on Lincoln Hwy., **Boston Bay Wines** turns out first-rate whites and reds. (☎ 8684 3600. Open Sa-Su 11:30am-4:30pm.)

FLINDERS HIGHWAY: PORT LINCOLN TO CEDUNA

COFFIN BAY

A mere 47km from Lincoln toward Ceduna, you'll find the lazy town of **Coffin Bay,** gateway to the magnificent **Coffin Bay National Park,** 17km west of the main highway. This peninsular park is a remote beach heaven; surfers, picnickers, and pelicans coexist peacefully among the dunes, estuaries, and bays. 2WD vehicles can access **Yangie Bay** (15km from the entrance), **Almonta Beach** (16km from entrance), and **Point Avoid** (18km from entrance), while 4WD vehicles can drive onto **Gunyah Beach** via a road through the dunes, and can also reach the more remote areas of the park, such as **Black Springs** (28km from entrance), **Sensation Beach** (50km), and **Point Sir Isaac,** the westernmost point in the park (55km). **Bushcamping ❶** is allowed only at designated sites, all of which have toilets and limited rainwater supply. Camping permits and maps are available at the park entrance. (Entry $6 per car; camping $6 per car.) Tourist info is available from **Beachcomber Agencies** on the Esplanade. (☎ 8685 4057. Open daily in summer 8am-7:30pm; in winter 8am-6:30pm.) **National Parks and Wildlife Service** (☎ 8688 3111), in Port Lincoln, has further info, as does the Port Lincoln Visitors Center.

The **Coffin Bay Caravan Park ❶** is on the Esplanade in Coffin Bay. (☎ 8685 4170. Sites $14, powered $18; on-site vans for 2 from $28; cabins for 2 from $40, extra person $7.) The **Coffin Bay Hotel/Motel ❺**, just south of town on the road toward the park, is a bit pricey, but it's the only hotel option in town, hosting one of the town's only **ATMs**. (☎ 8685 4111. Singles $65; doubles $75.)

The 🏠**Mount Dutton Bay Woolshed ❶** is 52km northwest of Port Lincoln and 22km southeast of a tiny town called **Coulta**. The historic building, with backpacker accommodations in the back and a museum in the front, is right on a beautiful waterfront. As many as 1200 sheep were once kept here; today, the building houses up to 36 backpackers. (From Alt. Rte. 1, via either Farm Beach Rd. from the east or Brookaburra Rd. from the west. ☎/fax 8685 4031. Museum open M-Sa 10am-5pm; $3. Sites $12; dorms $17.)

CEDUNA

At the far west corner of the triangular Eyre circuit, the Flinders Hwy. (Alt. Hwy. 1) meets up with the more direct and dull Hwy. 1 (Eyre Hwy.), rolling into the town of Ceduna, civilization's last watering hole before the arid westward trek across the Nullarbor Plain toward Perth. The **ATMs** in town are the last ones for 1300km heading west, although **EFTPOS** services are available at most roadhouses along the way. Ceduna provides the basic beds, beans, and booze, plus a few relaxing beaches. **Decres Bay,** 12km from town in the **Wittelbee Conservation Park,** is a good swimming beach; a little farther on is **Laura Bay,** with more of the same. Finding Decres Bay Rd., which departs from the south side of town, from the town center will most likely require a map, available at the tourist office—the office also provides permits to camp in Laura Bay or Decres Bay. **Ceduna Gateway Visitors Centre,** 58 Poynton St., is laden with info on fishing and outback tours; it is also your best source of info on the Nullarbor crossing (be sure to pick up a copy of *The Nullarbor: Australia's Great Road Journey*). It also has **Internet** access and booking for buses. (☎ 8625 2780. Open M-F 9am-5:30pm, Sa-Su 10am-4pm. Internet $5 per 30min.) The **police** are at ☎ 8626 2020. For a **taxi**, call ☎ 2825 3791.

Ceduna Greenacres Backpackers ❷, 12 Kuhlmann St., on the right fork as you come into town from the east, is marked with a red sign, partly hidden by trees. It has muraled concrete walls, metal bunks in small rooms, an airy courtyard, and a free home-cooked dinner and continental breakfast. Friendly owner Vaughn often hosts field trips to go crabbing or fishing, or to the spectacular (and not widely known) natural rock pool at the 🏠**Point Brown Swimming Hole**—location divulged on a need-to-know basis only. (☎/fax 8625 3811 or 0427 811 241. Dorms $16.50.) The best caravan park in the area is the **Shelly Beach Caravan Park ❶**, 3km east of town on the Decres Bay Rd., right on a beautiful beach, which has reasonable backpacker accommodations as well. (☎ 8625 2012. Sites $15, powered $17; cabins from $55; backpacker cabins $25 per person.) The well-stocked Foodland **supermarket** is on the corner of Kuhlmann and Poynton St. (☎ 8625 3212. Open M-W and Sa 8am-6pm, Th-F 8am-7pm, Su 9am-4pm.) **Bill's Chicken Shop ❶**, on Poynton St., serves the town's best fried chicken, fresh fish and chips ($8), and deli sides. (☎ 8625 2880. Open daily 9am-9pm.)

HIGHWAY 1: CEDUNA TO PORT AUGUSTA

For those coming from the Nullarbor, the scrub-covered stretch of Hwy. 1 running from Ceduna to Port Augusta will seem like a tropical rainforest. It's not an interesting drive, punctuated only by several nearly identical tiny towns, each marked by enormous grain silos along the railroad tracks and a few dusty streets behind them. If **Wirrulla** (92km from Ceduna), **Poochera** (140km), **Minnipa** (170km), **Wudinna** (209km), and **Kimba** (310km) were lumped together to form a mega-town in the Northern Eyre peninsula, it would still only have one horse in

SOUTH AUSTRALIA

it. Most of the towns mentioned above have **petrol,** a small **supermarket** or general store, and accommodation. People driving straight through at 110km per hour (or substantially above, though *Let's Go* does not recommend such behavior) should be able to make the trip in 4½hr. There are petrol stations every 100km or so across this stretch of road, though competitive prices make it cheaper to fill up in Port Augusta or Ceduna before setting out. Accommodations on this stretch of road are limited to a few down-at-heel pokie hotels. Wudinna has an **Internet** cafe on the west side of town in the **Wudinna Telecentre.** (Open M-F 9am-5pm. $5 per 30min.) Kimba's **Cafe @54 ❶,** on the town's main street, also has Internet ($2.75 per 30min.), along with cappuccinos ($2), sandwiches ($5), and burgers. (☎ 8627 2822. Open M-F 10am-5pm.)

At one of two area tourist information joints in **Kimba,** a strange creature looms in front. Cemented on top of its little hill, the ■**Big Galah,** a huge, pink bird, motionlessly celebrates the halfway point across Australia and keeps a watchful eye on all the traversers of the Eyre Hwy. The tourist center (☎ 8627 2766) is open daily 8am-5pm, although the Big Galah never sleeps.

CROSSING THE NULLARBOR

Explorer Edward John Eyre minced no words describing the Nullarbor Plain, calling it "a hideous anomaly, a blot on the face of Nature, the sort of place one gets into in bad dreams." The place is shunned by the Aborigines as the waterless home of *Dijarra,* an immense legendary serpent. Welcome to the Nullarbor—a treeless plain that could contain England, the Netherlands, Belgium, and Switzerland, with 7000km^2 to spare. **McCafferty's/Greyhound** (☎ 12 20 30) bus drivers make this grueling desert haul to Perth from Ceduna (23hr., $264) or Adelaide (36hr., $264).

The Eyre Hwy. is smooth, black bitumen all the way, finally completed in 1976 after construction began during World War II. The **Ninety Mile Straight** (147km) from **Caiguna, WA** to **Balladonia, WA** is the longest straight stretch of highway in the country. The road is traveled fairly heavily compared with the empty roads up north; it's rarely more than 100km between roadhouses with fuel, but repair facilities are few and far between. This is a road train route, so all drivers should brace for the turbulence from passing 25m trucks. Bring along bottled water, warm clothing, and blankets. Drivers should make sure their cars are equipped with a jack, spares, coolant, and oil, and should have a mechanic check their vehicle. The **RAA** (☎ 13 11 11) has more info. Each of the **roadhouses** along the way has **EFTPOS** and major credit card facilities, almost all have a caravan park and camping sites, and most have cheap accommodations. **Yalata Medical Service** (☎ 8625 6237) is the best bet for medical service on the Nullarbor. **Police** are located at Penong (☎ 8625 1006) and **Ceduna** (☎ 8628 7020); the Penong police can refer you to medical services as well. There are **quarantine checkpoints** at Norseman for westbound travelers and Ceduna for eastbound travelers. For details of roadhouses and scenic detours, pick up the free brochure, *The Nullarbor: Australia's Great Road Journey,* at the tourist office in Ceduna if coming from the east or at the Norseman tourist office if coming from the west. You can also purchase the glossy and photo-filled *Exploring the Eyre Highway: Across the Nullarbor* for $8 at either Visitors Center. **Commemorative crossing certificates** (now *there's* something for the mantle) are free at either office after completing the journey.

Nullarbor Traveller is a backpacker-oriented camping trip that runs from Perth to Adelaide. Travelers snorkel, whale watch, explore caves, and camp under the stars. For those with the cash and the time, this is the way to cross in style. (☎ 8364 0407. 9-day Adelaide to Perth $945; 7-day Perth to Adelaide $735.)

EYRE HIGHWAY: CEDUNA TO BORDER VILLAGE

After leaving Ceduna on the long road west, hundreds of windmills and wheat silos signal the approach of **Penong**, 73km west of Ceduna, and its **hotel ❸**. (☎8625 1050. Singles $35; doubles $45.) At **Cactus Beach,** 21km south of Penong along a well-maintained gravel road, you can watch territorial, top-notch surfers maneuver along **Castles, Cactus,** and **Caves,** the names of the famous breaks at one of Australia's best surfing beaches. Beginners enjoy the sandy bottom at **Shelly Beach,** east of Point Sinclair. Down the main road, 78km west of Penong, backpacker accommodation is available at the all-encompassing **Nundroo Hotel Motel Inn ❶**. (☎8625 6120. Reception open 7am-10pm. Rooms $14.50 per person.)

Yalata Roadhouse ❶, 51km west of **Nundroo,** is a decent camping spot. (☎8625 6986. Open daily in summer 7am-10pm; in winter 8am-8pm. Sites $5 per person, powered $10.) A permit is required to enter the township of **Yalata** itself, home to an Anangu Aboriginal community (pop. 500), 200km north of Hwy. 1. The **Head of Bight,** 78km west of Yalata, has stunning views of blue ocean, with sand dunes to the right and sheer cliffs to the left. Between May and October, the view gets even better, when 60 to 100 **southern right whales** breed, calve, and nurse here before returning to sub-Antarctic waters for the summer. Whale watching permits ($8) are required and available from Yalata Roadhouse or the **White Well Ranger Station** on the road south to Head of Bight from mid-July to October. (☎8625 6201. Call ahead for hours.) By the time you reach the fuel stop at **Nullarbor,** 94km west of Yalata, you're officially on the treeless plain. There's accommodation at the **Nullarbor Hotel Motel ❷**. (☎8625 6271. Reception 7am-11pm. Singles $20; doubles $30.)

Gorgeous coastal lookouts line the Nullarbor, just a few hundred meters off the main road. The **Bunda Cliffs** (50km) plummet 90m straight down into the Southern Ocean. The cliffs start at Twin Rocks at Head of Bight and extend 200km to just east of Border Village. There's cheap accommodation at **Border Village ❷,** 188km west of Nullarbor, as well as a huge fiberglass kangaroo named Rooey II. (☎9039 3474. Singles $21; doubles $41.) This is also the **agricultural roadblock** before entering WA (it's at Ceduna if you're going east), where any fruit, vegetables, honey, and plant material will be confiscated to stop the spread of the fruit fly. Check with the **agriculture department** for a list of restricted items. (In WA ☎9311 5333, in SA 8269 4500.) As you enter Western Australia, it's 193km from Border Village to **Norseman** (☎9039 1010; open 24hr.; see p. 697), the official end of the Nullarbor Plain.

SOUTH AUSTRALIA

TASMANIA

Hot, desolate, barren Australia seemed to be a perfect solution for the British Empire's 18th-century prison-overflow problem. Parliament members happily sent their rabble across the oceans, washed their hands, and went to tea. But as offenses continued, penal officials in New South Wales decided to ship the troublemakers away once again. Australia was already at the end of the earth, but the isle of Van Diemen's Land was at the end of Australia. Banishment to the seemingly wild little island, now known as Tasmania, was the worst punishment available, reserved for the most heartless of criminals.

Silly Poms. What was thought to be an inhospitable, weatherbeaten rock was in fact the lushest corner of the continent. Still, the penal settlements in the gorgeous areas near Hobart and Strahan were indeed brutal, and the native Aboriginal populations were decimated by the new colony through invasion and outright genocide. Over the years, Tasmania has turned from blood red to leafy green. An upsurge of conservation efforts, centralized social policies, and liberal activism mark today's political scene. The struggle against the proposed Franklin-Gordon dam in the early 1980s foreshadowed Tassie's involvement in the Australian conservation movement. Though Tasmania has historically had a politically and socially conservative government, their Green party has been represented in the state's governing coalition twice in the past decade.

Only 3% of the visitors to Australia make it down under Down Under, but Tassie is well worth the time and money spent getting there. A third of the state is under government conservation, mostly under the name Tasmanian Wilderness World Heritage Area, which includes one of the last great temperate rainforests on the globe. Bushwalkers from around the planet come to Tasmania's mountainous interior to explore the Overland Track, one of the premier hiking trails in the Southern Hemisphere. The uninhabited west coast bears the brunt of the Southern Ocean's fury, but the storms rarely push past the mountains, so the east coast and midlands are pleasant year-round. Tiny holiday villages filled with prosperous fishing fleets and vacationing families speckle the shore. In the southeast, the capital city of Hobart, Australia's second-oldest city, welcomes yachts from Sydney every December in a glorious and internationally famous turnout. Rolling farmland stretches north from Hobart to Launceston, Tasmania's second city and northern hub. But perhaps most spectacular about this magical island is its amazing natural diversity, its uncanny ability to house so many different species and environments in such a small space. In fact, some of Tassie's best known species can be found only within its borders, such as the slow-growing Huon pine, which can live for millennia, and the Tasmanian devil, a mysterious, scavenging marsupial. Many travelers try to see the island in just a few days, but once they lose themselves in the wilderness and history of Australia's secret stowaway, they might never get enough of Tasmania.

TRANSPORTATION

Tasmania has three principal gateways: Hobart (by air), Devonport (by *Spirit of Tasmania* overnight ferry or air), and Launceston (by air or to its George Town port by *DevilCat* ferry). The state then divides comfortably into south, northwest, and northeast zones as the respective domains of the gateway cities. Getting around on a budget is a bit of a challenge. There is no rail network, and the main

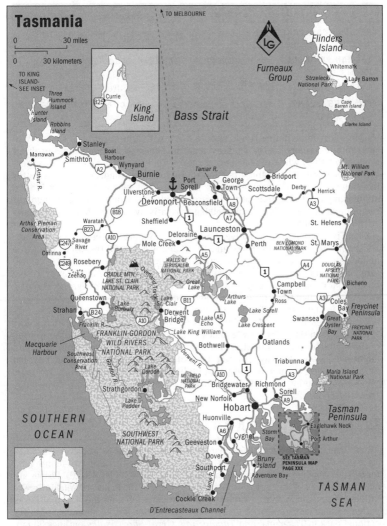

Tasmania

0   30 miles

0   30 kilometers

TO KING
ISLAND-
SEE INSET

TO MELBOURNE

Bass Strait

Furneaux
Group

Flinders
Island

Whitemark

Strzelecki
National Park

Lady Barron

Cape
Barren Island

Clarke Island

Three
Hummock
Island

King
Island

B25

Currie

Hunter
Island

Robbins
Island

Marrawah

Smithton

Stanley

Boat
Harbour

Wynyard

A2

Burnie

Ulverstone

Devonport

Port
Sorell

Tamar R.

Beaconsfield

George
Town

Bridport

Scottsdale

Derby

Herrick

Mt. William
National Park

A3

St. Helens

Arthur R.

Arthur Pieman
Conservation
Area

Waratah

B18

B23

Sheffield

A10

Mole Creek

Deloraine

1

Launceston

1

A8

A7

Perth

BEN LOMOND
NATIONAL PARK

St. Marys

247

Savage
River

Corinna

249

Rosebery

Zeehan

WALLS OF
JERUSALEM
NATIONAL PARK

A5

Great
Lake

DOUGLAS
APSLEY
NATIONAL
PARK

A4

St. Marys

Bicheno

Queenstown

Strahan

B24

CRADLE MTN.-
LAKE ST. CLAIR
NATIONAL PARK

Lake
Burbury

Overland Track

A10

Lake
St. Clair

Derwent
Bridge

B11

Arthurs
Lake

Campbell
Town

Ross

Lake Sorell

1

A3

Coles
Bay

Swansea

Freycinet
Peninsula

Great
Oyster
Bay

FREYCINET
NATIONAL
PARK

Macquarie
Harbour

Franklin R.

FRANKLIN-GORDON
WILD RIVERS
NATIONAL PARK

Southwest
Conservation
Area

Gordon R.

Lake
Gordon

Lake King William

Lake
Echo

A5

Lake Crescent

Bothwell

Oatlands

Maria Island
National Park

Strathgordon

Lake
Pedder

MT. FIELD
NATIONAL
PARK

Derwent R.

A10

Bridgewater

1

Richmond

Triabunna

A3

New Norfolk

Sorell

A9

Hobart

SOUTHERN
OCEAN

Huonville

A6

SOUTHWEST
NATIONAL PARK

Geeveston

Cygnet

Storm
Bay

Bruny
Island

SEE TASMAN
PENINSULA MAP
PAGE XXX

Tasman
Peninsula

Eaglehawk Neck

Port Arthur

Dover

Southport

Adventure Bay

Cockle Creek

D'Entrecasteaux Channel

TASMAN
SEA

N

LG

bus lines—**Redline** and **TWT's TassieLink**—are expensive, limited, and infrequent. TassieLink offers **Explorer Passes,** which are worth the investment when using their buses as a touring service (valid 7 days within any 10-day period $160, 21 days within 30-days $260). On the bright side, many hostel managers offer reasonably priced shuttles and tours on a call-and-request basis. Seek local recommendations and information boards. *Note: Both Tassielink and Redline expected to raise prices when Let's Go: Australia 2003 went to print. For the most accurate prices, pick up a timetable or contact the companies directly.*

Renting a **car** here is more popular than on the mainland. The gateway cities have small companies offering cheaper, older cars. Visitors unaccustomed to

TASMANIA

TASMANIA HIGHLIGHTS

SALAMANCA MARKET. Score a bargain and enjoy street performances in Hobart's eclectic shopping district. (p. 511)

TASMAN PENINSULA. Tour the ruins of convict-built buildings at Tasmania's biggest tourist attraction. (p. 513)

OVERLAND TRACK. Get into the bush on the world-famous Overland Track. (p. 524)

FLINDERS ISLAND. Camp in utter remoteness or scope the other 54 Furneaux Islands from the peaks of Strzelecki National Park. (p. 540)

Tassie's narrow, winding roads should drive with added caution. Check with the rental company on their policy regarding unsealed roads; some prohibit them altogether, while others increase the liability excess. 4WD vehicles, necessary for winter travel and a portion of Tassie's backroads, come with better insurance policies on unsealed roads. Be aware that speed cameras are hidden along many roads and that petrol is rare outside of towns or cities. Though not recommended by *Let's Go*, **hitchhiking** is relatively popular but often means sticking to the main roads.

Biking is a satisfying alternative, especially on the more accessible east coast. *Bicycling Tasmania*, by Terry and Beedham, is a helpful resource. The three major gateway cities have rental outfits catering to cycle touring, but gear will rarely be found outside of these major outfitters. If you're planning on extensive bushwalking, pick up a copy of *100 Walks in Tasmania*, by Tyrone Thomas, which has detailed track descriptions and excellent maps.

Tours also make seeing Tassie easy and enjoyable, allowing travel to places otherwise inaccessible. The **Adventure Tours** (☎ 1300 654 604; 3-day $335-355, 7-day $705) and **Down Under Tours** (☎ 1800 064 726; 5-day $415, 7-day $595) offer touring options which include bookings for accommodation and everything that you might need along the way. The tours are often frequented by a younger crowd more interested in the pub and post-pub life than in real sightseeing. **Taz Tours** offers similar options starting from Devonport (☎ 0408 261 705; 4-day $549, 6-day Overland Track $995).

◣ NATIONAL PARKS

All of Tasmania's national parks charge an entrance fee. A 24hr. pass costs $3.30 (vehicles $9.90). For those planning to visit many parks, there's a two-month pass for $13.20 (vehicles $33) or an annual pass for $19.80 (vehicles $46.20). Passes are available at most of the park entrances, or from any of the **Parks and Wildlife Service** offices. Parks and Wildlife prints two helpful pamphlets on the National Parks within Tasmania: *Tasmania: A Visitor's Guide* has a brief summary of every national park in Tasmania, and *Tasmania's Great Short Walks* outlines 30 fantastic walks most under one hour (both free). They also publish a handy booklet to reduce your environmental impact called the *Essential Bushwalking Guide & Trip Planner* (free). For more information, contact the head office in Hobart, 134 Macquarie St. (☎ 6233 6191), or visit their website at www.parks.tas.gov.au.

Gear, including stove, tent, sleeping bag, and sleeping mats, can be rented only in the three large cities of Tasmania: **Hobart, Launceston,** and **Devonport.** Most require that the gear be returned, but some have deals with Redline Coaches to return the gear for a fee, though the bond may not be refunded. The Service Tasmania offices in these cities have a list of all stores who rent gear.

Hobart

🛏 ACCOMMODATIONS
Adelphi Court YHA, **1**
Central City
  Backpackers, **8**
Narrara Backpackers, **14**
Montgomery's YHA, **5**
Pickled Frog
  Backpackers, **7**
Transit Centre
  Backpackers, **10**
🍴 FOOD
Ball & Chain Grill, **12**
Drifters Internet Cafe, **13**
Little Bali, **9**
Mures Fish Centre, **6**
Retro Cafe, **11**
A Taste of Asia, **3**
Trattoria Casablanca, **2**

HOBART

☎ 03

Perhaps the most cosmopolitan city on Tasmania, this capital city rests at the mouth of the Derwent River, at the foot of Mt. Wellington, shielded from the great Southern Ocean by a scatter of islands and breakwaters. Hobart (pop. 195,500), Australia's second-oldest city, was originally a penal colony; the city was established in part by a booming mining industry. Despite its success, Hobart somehow escaped the need to become large or complex. Extremely laid-back, it remains largely defined by its combination of strong-willed environmental activists and its artists and boutiques, with nearly everyone content to enjoy a slower pace of life than those on the mainland. Almost all of Tassie's visitors make at least a short stop here, getting one last dose of urban life before heading into the great beyond.

✈ INTERCITY TRANSPORTATION

Plan ahead—air and road are the only ways in and out of Hobart, and buses run infrequently. Many visitors travel by hitchhiking, although *Let's Go* does not recommend hitchhiking.

TASMANIA

BY PLANE. Hobart Airport is 18km east of Hobart on Hwy. A3. International flights must make connections on the mainland. **Qantas** (☎ 13 13 13) flies to Melbourne at least ten times per day ($85-230) and Sydney at least three times per day ($158-320). International travelers can get better deals; bring your passport and international ticket. **Redline Airporter Bus** shuttles between the airport and lodgings. (☎ 1938 2240. $8.80, return $16.)

BY BUS. Timetables for Redline and TWT's TassieLink services can be picked up from Hobart's main **bus depot,** 199 Collins St.

Redline Coaches (☎ 1300 360 000, line open daily 6am-9pm) runs buses to: Bicheno (4¾hr., M-F 1 per day, $36.10) via Launceston; Coles Bay turn-off (4½hr., M-F 1 per day, $35); Devonport (4½-5hr., 2 per day, $38.10); Launceston (2½hr., 3 per day, $22.40) via Oatlands (1¼hr., 3 per day, $12.50); St. Helens (3½-7hr., Su-F 1 per day, $35.20); St. Marys via Launceston (3-6½hr., Su-F 1 per day, $34); Swansea (4hr., M-F 1 per day, $30.30). Student and VIP/YHA discount 20%.

TassieLink (☎ 1300 300 520) runs buses to: Bicheno (3hr.; W, F, and Su, in summer also M, 1 per day; $24.20); Coles Bay turn-off (2¾hr.; W, F, and Su, in summer also M, 1 per day; $24); Lake St. Clair (3½-4hr.; Tu and Th, in summer also F and Su 1 per day; $36); Queenstown (5hr.; Tu, Th-F, and Su 1 per day; $45); St. Helens (4¾hr.; F and Su 1 per day; $32.20); and Strahan (6-8hr.; Tu, Th-F, and Su 1 per day; $52). In summer (Dec. −1-Apr. 16) daily service (usually W) and destinations increase: Cockle Creek (3½hr.; M, W, and F 1 per day; $52); Lune River (2½hr.; M, W, and F 1 per day; $23); Mt. Field National Park (1½hr., M-Sa 1-2 per day, $24); Scotts Peak (3¼hr.; Tu, Th, and Sa 1 per day; $58.10); Southwest hiking trails (Timbs Track, Mt. Anne, Red Tape) (2-3hr.; Tu, Th, and Sa 1 per day; $55).

Hobart Coaches, 21 Murray St. (☎ 6233 4232), runs to Cygnet (1hr.; M-F 9am, 3:10pm, and 5:15pm; $8) and Kettering (45min., M-F 2 per day, $8).

◢ ORIENTATION

Most tourist attractions and services are compacted into the downtown area west of the wharves of Sullivan's Cove. South of the Cove and packed with antique shops and cottages, **Battery Point** is one of the oldest sections of the city. The northern border of Battery Point is defined by **Salamanca Place,** a row of old Georgian warehouses that have been renovated as shops and restaurants. **Franklin Wharf,** adjacent to Salamanca Place, is the departure point for numerous harbor cruises. Hobart is backed by the **Wellington Range,** which affords fine views from the imposing **Mt. Wellington,** dominant on the western skyline, and the smaller **Mt. Nelson** to the south. The city proper can be easily navigated on foot, while public buses run to the outer reaches of the suburbs.

Beyond the **Queen's Domain** north of downtown, the **Tasman Bridge** spans the Derwent River. There, the Tasman Hwy. (A3) heads east and connects to A9 and the Tasman Peninsula. **Brooker Ave.** leads north up the Derwent Valley, becoming Hwy. 1 to Launceston, and connecting to A10 toward points west. **Davey St.** leaves downtown as A6, heading southward toward the Huon Valley and Bruny Island.

▛ LOCAL TRANSPORTATION

Buses: Metro **city buses** run through Hobart and the suburbs. (☎ 13 22 01. Daily 6am-midnight. Purchase tickets on-board. $1.30-3 depending on number of sections traveled.) "Day Rover" tickets ($3.40) allow unlimited travel all day after 9am. **The Metro Shop,** 9 Elizabeth St., in a corner of the Post Office, has a complete timetable for 50¢. Open M-F 8:30am-5:15pm.

Taxis: City Cabs (24hr. ☎ 13 10 08). City to airport $35-40.

Ferries and Cruises: The best deal around is **Captain Fell's Historic Ferries**, whose dinner cruise departs from Franklin Wharf. (☎ 6223 5893. 2½hr. Daily 6pm. $23-25.) **Roche O'May Ferries** sails from Brooke St. Pier to the Wrest Point Casino. (☎ 6223 1914. Daily 10:30am, noon, 1:30pm, 3pm. $13.) The **Lady Nelson**, whose tour departs from Elizabeth St. Pier, gives less commercial river cruises of a more historical nature. (☎ 6234 3348. 1½hr. In summer Sa-Su 11am, 1pm, 3pm; in winter Sa-Su noon and 2pm. $6.)

Tours: Day tours organized by **Tigerline** (☎ 1300 653 633) or **Experience Tasmania** (☎ 6234 3336) are good if you're short on time. Both offer pickup and an array of combination tours to the highlights of the Hobart region. Book through the tourist office (☎ 6230 8233), with a hostel reception, or direct with the company. 2hr. to full-day tours $22-105; min. 4 passengers.

Car Rental: Car rental agencies are everywhere in Hobart. Off-season rates run as low as $17 per day. Listed companies rent to ages 21-24. **Autorent Hertz,** 122 Harrington St. (☎ 6237 1111), rents top-end cars from $40-50 per day. For a YHA discount, call ☎ 13 30 39 and quote Discount Program number 317961. **Thrifty,** 11-17 Argyle St. (☎ 6234 1341, airport 6248 5678), rents from $46. **Range** and **RentABug,** 136 Harrington St. and 105 Murray St. (☎ 6231 0678), from $28, including minibuses and campervans. **Selective Car Rentals,** 47 Bathurst St. (☎ 6234 3311 or 1800 300 102), from $25.

Automobile Club: RACT (☎ 6232 6300, 24hr. roadside help 13 11 11, insurance queries 13 27 22), corner of Murray and Patrick St. Open M-F 8am-5:30pm, Sa 8am-1pm.

Bikes: Derwent Bike Hire (☎ 6268 6161), just past the Cenotaph on the cycleway at the Regatta Ground, hires road and mountain bikes, tandems, and inline skates from $7 per hr., $100 per week, and $200 per month. Open Sept.-Dec. and Feb.-May Sa-Su 10am-5pm, Jan. daily 10am-5pm; closed June-Aug.

◤ PRACTICAL INFORMATION

TOURIST AND FINANCIAL SERVICES

Tourist Office: Hobart Tasmanian Travel and Information Centre, 20 Davey St. (☎ 6230 8233), at Elizabeth St., books accommodations and cars ($2.20 fee), as well as tours and walks (free). Open in summer M-F 8:30am-6pm, Sa-Su 9am-6pm; in winter M-Sa 8:30am-5:30pm, Su 9am-5pm.

Budget Travel Office: YHA's Tasmanian Headquarters, 28 Criterion St., 2nd fl. (☎ 6234 9617). Travel insurance, passport photos, tickets, and travel advice, in addition to YHA memberships and hostel bookings. Open M-F 9am-5pm.

Currency Exchange: Mobs of banks, most with **ATMs,** crowd in and around Elizabeth St. Mall. Most banks have a $5-10 fee. **Thomas Cook,** 40 Murray St. (☎ 6234 2699), charges $7 or 2% of traveler's checks. Open M-F 9am-5pm.

Tasmanian Parks and Wildlife Service: Service Tasmania, 134 Macquarie St. (☎ 6233 6191), in the Service Tasmania Bldg. Open M-F 8:15am-5:30pm.

Forestry Tasmania: 79 Melville St. (☎ 6233 8203). Open M-F 8:30am-5:30pm.

LOCAL SERVICES

Bookstores: ◪ **Fullers Bookshop,** 140 Collins St. (☎ 6224 2488). Classy selection and wonderful upstairs cafe. Open M-F 9am-5:30pm, Sa 9am-4pm, Su 10am-4pm. **Hobart Bookshop,** 22 Salamanca Sq. (☎ 6223 1803), has richly stocked shelves of new and second-hand books. Open M-F 9am-6pm, Sa-Su 10am-5pm.

TASMANIA

Library: 91 Murray St. (☎6233 7529), at Bathurst St. Reference library open Feb.-Nov. M-Tu 9:30am-6pm, W-F 9:30am-9pm, Sa 9:30am-2:30pm; Dec.-Jan. M-Th 9:30am-6pm, F 9:30am-9pm, Sa 9:30am-12:30pm. **Internet** $1, plus $6 per 30min.

Market: Salamanca Market at Salamanca Pl. Open Sa 8am-3pm. See **Sights**, p. 510.

Outdoor Equipment: Gear stores cluster along Elizabeth St. near Liverpool St. These are the only places to rent gear outside of Launceston and Devonport. **Jolly Swagman's Camping World,** 107 Elizabeth St. sells gear and rents tents ($50 per week, $300 bond), stoves ($25/$100), packs ($30/$200), and sleeping mats ($5/$15). Open M-F 9am-6pm, Sa 9am-3:30pm. Service Tasmania has a list of all options to rent gear.

Fishing Equipment: Get info and fishing tackle (starting at $25 per day) at **Bridges Bros.,** 142 Elizabeth St. (☎6234 3791). Open M-Th 9am-5:30pm, F 9am-6pm, Sa 9am-1pm. *Angling Code for Inland Fisheries,* available at the tourist office, outlines all regulations.

MEDIA AND PUBLICATIONS
Newspaper: *The Mercury.*
Entertainment: *The Mercury* includes *Gig Guide* on Thursday and *EG* on Friday.
Radio: Rock, Triple J 92.9FM; News, ABC 729AM; Tourist Info, 88FM.

EMERGENCY AND COMMUNICATIONS

Emergency: ☎000.

Police: 37-43 Liverpool St. (☎6230 2111). **Lost and found** (☎6230 2277).

Hospital: Royal Hobart Hospital, 48 Liverpool St. (☎6222 8308).

Pharmacy: Corby's Everyday Pharmacy, 170 Macquarie St. (☎6223 3044). Open daily 8am-10pm, holidays 8am-10pm.

Hotlines: Crisis Watchline (24hr. ☎13 11 14). **AIDS Hotline** (☎1800 005 900). Staffed M-F 9am-5pm. **Alcohol and Drugs Hotline** (24hr. ☎1800 811 994).

Internet and Fax: Service Tasmania, 134 Macquarie St. (☎1300 135 513). Open M-F 8:15am-5:30pm. Has 6 **free terminals.** 30min. limit. Also try **Drifters Internet Cafe** (see p. 510) and the **library** (see **Local Services,** above).

Post Office: 9 Elizabeth St. (☎6236 3577; fax 6234 9387), at Macquarie St. It was from this post office that Roald Amundsen sent a telegram announcing he'd reached the South Pole. Open M-F 8am-5:45pm. **Postal Code:** 7000.

♆ ACCOMMODATIONS

Book well ahead during the December summer festival.

Narrara Backpackers, 88 Goulburn St. (☎6231 3191). Turn left off Harrington St. This 3-story house offers spotless accommodation with a cozy atmosphert. Off-street parking. Laundry. Free Internet. Bike hire. Reception daily 8am-10pm. Dorms $17; twins and doubles $44. ❷

The Pickled Frog Backpackers, 281 Liverpool St. (☎6234 7977). The red front directly behind the Transit Centre is the newest addition to town. With clean rooms, a warm atmosphere, and free breakfast, it's hard to beat. Off-street parking. Large dining area and free bike and pack storage. Internet $2 per hr. Dorms from $17. YHA/VIP and student card discounts. ❷

Central City Backpackers VIP, 138 Collins St. (☎6224 2404 or 1800 811 507), on the 2nd floor through the Imperial Arcade. A large hostel with a kitchen, common areas, and a great location. Downstairs lounge has pool table, TV, and a bar (stubbies $3-4; open Nov.-Apr. nightly 6pm-late). Sleepsheet $1, full linens $2. Laundry. Internet $2 per 10min. Key deposit $5. Reception daily 8am-9pm. 6-bed dorms $18; 4-bed dorms $20; singles $34; twins and doubles $44. Cash or traveler's checks only. ❷

Transit Centre Backpackers, 199 Collins St. (☎/fax 6231 2400), above the bus terminal. Bright, spacious common area. Friendly proprietors live on-site. Fireplace, heaters, extra doonas for the winter chill, TV, kitchen, laundry, pool table. Free storage. No alcohol permitted on premises; coffee and tea included. Reception daily 8am-11pm. Dorms from $17. ❷

Adelphi Court YHA, 17 Stoke St., New Town (☎6228 4829). Take a Metro bus from Argyle St. to stop 8A opposite the hostel, or a bus from Elizabeth St. to stop 13. Adelphi is the pricey mothership of the Tasmania YHA fleet. Large common area with booking office, grocery kiosk, wash basins in rooms, laundry. Continental breakfast $4.50. Key deposit $10. Reception Dec. 16-Mar.14 daily 7:30-10:30am and 4-9pm, Mar. 15-Dec. 15 8-10am and 4-7pm. Dorms $24, YHA $20; singles $5!/$47; twins $58/$54. ❷

Montgomery's YHA and **Montgomery's Private Hotel,** 9 Argyle St. (☎6231 2600). Located downtown. Clean kitchen, common room with TV. Laundry. All rooms have phones; hotel rooms have towels, color TVs, and refrigerators. Storage, tour bookings. Reception daily 8am-9pm; after-hours go to the pub or phone next door. Dorms $23 per night, YHA $16-20; hotel twins and doubles $65-89; family rooms $105-119. ❷

▎ FOOD

Hobart showcases a dizzying array of international cuisine: restaurants downtown serve meals from every pocket of Asia, while the pubs and grills of Salamanca Place serve lunch and dinner once brekkie is finished at the cafes. The best part of town for dining is Elizabeth St. in North Hobart, where a cluster of decent restaurants represent a great variety of cuisines—from Turkish to Mexican to Vietnamese. For a taste of traditional local fare, the ultimate Tassie tucker is abalone or salmon with a Cascade beer. **Purity,** 69 King St., Sandy Bay (☎6211 6611) or 189 Campbell St., North Hobart (☎6234 8077), is an inexpensive **supermarket.** (Both open M-W and Sa 8am-6pm, Th-F 8am-9pm.) Get organic and bulk foods at **Eumarrah Wholefoods,** 45 Goulburn St., at the corner of Barrack St. (☎6234 3229. Open M-W 9am-6pm, Th-F 9am-7pm, Sa 9am-3pm.) The Saturday **Salamanca Market** has deals on produce, sauces, spreads, honey, and cheese. (Open Sa 8am-3pm.)

Retro Cafe, 33 Salamanca Pl. (☎6223 3073), on the corner of Montpelier Retreat. Regulars enjoy fine food and excellent coffee. There's great people-watching at the Salamanca Market on Sa. It can be hard to get a seat, but their all-day brekkie bagel ($11) is worth the scramble. Open M-Sa 8am-6pm, Su 8:30am-6pm. Cash only. ❷

Trattoria Casablanca, 213 Elizabeth St. (☎6234 9900). Recently renovated, this classy Italian restaurant has black-and-white photos from its namesake movie on the walls. Pastas in 15 varieties ($11-16) and pizzas ($9-22). Open Su-M 5:15-10pm, W-Th 5:15-11pm, F-Sa 5:15pm-late. ❷

Mures Fish Centre (☎6231 2121), Victoria Dock. A complete seafood complex. The sea-level **Bistro** serves up the town's best fish'n'chips ($8). Separate, licensed beverage counter. Open daily 11am-9pm. The **Upper Deck** has fine dining lunches (noon-2:30pm) and winter dinner specials (6-10pm; both from $15). To starboard, **Orizuru** (☎6231 1790) makes fresh sushi (lunches $13-14; entrees $7-12; mains $17-26). Open M-Sa noon-2:30pm and 6-9:30pm. **Polar Parlour** has ice cream and desserts. Open daily 8am-9pm. ❸

A Taste of Asia, 358 Elizabeth St., North Hobart (☎6236 9191). A favorite with locals. Quirky Asian-inspired cuisine, from sushi to stir-fry. The large takeaway plates ($11) are a great deal. Open M-Th noon-8pm, F noon-9pm, Sa 4:30-9pm. ❷

Drifters Internet Cafe, Shop 9, 33 Salamanca Pl., The Galleria (☎6224 6286). Good homemade soups ($5), foccacias ($6-7), and cappuccino ($2.50). Even better are the 'zines, great music, and Internet access ($2 per 10min., $9 per hr.). Open M-Sa 10am-6pm, Su 11am-6pm. ❶

Ball and Chain Grill, 87 Salamanca Pl. (☎6223 2655). Wood tables filled with plates of char-grilled meats. Although slightly pricey (steaks $10-30), all mains come with a fantastic all-you-can-eat salad bar. Open noon-3pm and 6pm-late. ❹

Little Bali, 84a Harrington St. (☎6234 3426). Tiny orange dining room bright with wicker lampshades and flying animals. Good, quick Indonesian meals (small $6, large $8.20; 50¢ table surcharge). Open M-F 11:30am-3pm and 5-9pm, Sa-Su 5-9pm. ❶

Machine Laundry/Cafe, 12 Salamanca Sq. (☎6224 9922), behind Salamanca Pl.; enter through Kennedy Ln. or Wooby's Ln. A funky new approach to laundry combines Italian fare ($6-12), breakfast until 3pm ($8-11), and desserts ($7) with washing machines (wash and dry $5 each). Open daily 8am-6pm. ❷

◉ SIGHTS

Hobart is brimming with interesting convict history. The excellent free brochures *Hobart's Historic Places, Sullivan's Cove Walk,* and *Women's History Walk,* available from the tourist office, are a great place to start.

DOWNTOWN

TASMANIAN MUSEUM AND ART GALLERY. Fine displays explore Tasmania's early convict history, unique ecology, and artistic heritage. The colonial-era art section is strong, while the mega-fauna models include a 10-foot kangaroo. *(40 Macquarie St., near the corner of Argyle St. ☎6211 4177. Open daily 10am-5pm. Guided tours leave from the bookstore W-Su 2:30pm; tours can also be arranged. Free.)*

PENITENTIARY CHAPEL AND CRIMINAL COURTS. One of the oldest, best-preserved buildings in Tasmania. Inside are the courtrooms and gallows of the grim 1830s. *(6 Brisbane St. Enter on Campbell St. ☎6231 0911. Tours M-F 10, 11:30am, 1, and 2:30pm. $7.70, concessions $5.50. Ghost tours ☎0417 361 392. Daily 8pm. Book ahead. $7.)*

MARITIME MUSEUM. This facility highlights Tassie maritime heritage, with a focus on local shipping and whaling. Accounts of more recent catastrophic shipwrecks make for some riveting reading. *(16 Argyle St., in the Carnegie Building on the corner of Davey St. ☎6234 1427. Open daily 10am-5pm. $6.60.)*

CYCLEWAY. Along the western bank of the Derwent River is a bicycle path with views of Mt. Wellington, the Regatta Grounds, the Tasman Bridge, Government House, the Queen's Domain, the Royal Botanical Gardens, and the shipyards in Hobart. *(Brochure with maps available from tourist office for $3.85.)*

OTHER SIGHTS DOWNTOWN. At Sullivan's Cove, the **Elizabeth, Brooke,** and **Murray St. Piers** harbor most of Hobart's large vessels. Look for the Antarctic Research Expedition's giant orange icebreaker, *Aurora Australis,* sometimes docked at Macquarie Wharf on the Cove's north side. **Constitution** and **Victoria Docks** are teeming with popular fishmongers and marine restaurants. Several companies run **harbor cruises** from this area (see **Ferries and Cruises,** p. 506).

THE MOUNTAINS

MT. WELLINGTON. Several kilometers west of Hobart, Mt. Wellington (1270m) is a must-see. The top is extremely windy, cold, and often snowy. On a clear day, you can see the peaks of half the state, all clearly marked on signs in the observation shelter. The summit is also home to a huge telecommunications tower that can become crowded with vehicle visitors, but surrounding walking tracks are spectacular. The road to the top occasionally closes due to snow and ice. **Fern Tree**, on the lower foothills of the mountain, is a lovely picnic area with walking tracks up the slope. *(Take the #48 or 49 Fern Tree bus to stop 27, at the base of the mountain. Getting to the top without a car may involve shelling out some dough for a narrated van trip up the road. Mt. Wellington Shuttle Bus Service $25 return. Bookings ☎ 0417 341 804 (min. 2 people). Experience Tasmania (☎ 6234 3336) tours $35, concessions $32. Observation shelter open daily 8am-6pm. For track details, get the Mt. Wellington Walk Map ($4) from the tourist office.)*

MT. NELSON. South of central Hobart, the mountain offers views of Hobart and the Derwent estuary. A signal station at the top, part of the chain that connected Port Arthur to the capital, also has a restaurant. *(Take the #57 or 58 Mt. Nelson bus to its terminus. Road to the top open daily 9am-9pm. Restaurant open daily 9:30am-4:30pm.)*

SALAMANCA PLACE AND BATTERY POINT

SALAMANCA PLACE. This row of beautiful Georgian warehouses contains trendy galleries, restaurants, and the shops of the much-celebrated Salamanca Market. Busy all day, the outdoor market offers a wonderfully chaotic diversity of crafts, produce, performers, and good times. *(Open Sa 8am-3pm.)*

ANTARCTIC ADVENTURE. This pleasant discovery center-*cum*-amusement park combines facts and fun, offering 20min. planetarium shows of the Southern Hemisphere's starry sky. The most popular exhibit, the Blizzard, simulates downhill speed skiing. *(2 Salamanca Sq. ☎ 6220 8220 or 1800 350 028. Open daily 10am-5pm. Planetarium show daily every hour 11am-4pm, subject to change. $22.50, concessions $17.50, under 14 $11.25, families $40.)*

BATTERY POINT. Adjacent to Salamanca Place is the lovely historic neighborhood of Battery Point, where many of Hobart's convict-era buildings have been preserved. The Battery Point National Trust leads tours through the village, or you can do a self-guided tour by referring to walking brochures available from the tourist office. *(Tours depart Franklin Sq. Wishing Well Sa 9:30am. 2½hr. $10, children $2.50.)*

PRINCES PARK. On the edge of Battery Point, just behind the Esplanade, this green space on a hill offers views of blue, blue water through the trees. The park was once the site of Mulgrave Battery, Battery Point's oldest building, once a signal station relaying messages as far away as Port Arthur.

NORTH AND SOUTH

⊠ CADBURY CHOCOLATE FACTORY. One of Hobart's most popular attractions, Cadbury provides tours showing all stages of the chocolate process, with free tastings every step of the way. *(☎ 6249 0333 or 1800 627 367. In Claremont, north of Hobart and the Derwent River. Take the Claremont service #37, 38, or 39 to the factory. Tours M-F 9, 10, 10:30, 11am, noon, 12:30, and 1:30pm. 1hr. Advanced booking required. $12.50, concessions $9, children $6.50.)*

⊠ CASCADE BREWERY. This is the place for those who prefer death by beer rather than chocolate. Built in 1832 by Mr. Degraves, who drew up the plans while in prison for debt default, it's the oldest brewery in Australia, producing 800 stubbies per minute. *(131 Cascade Rd. Take the Claremont service #43, 44, 46, or 49 to stop 17. ☎ 6221 8300. Tours M-F 9:30am and 1pm. 2hr. Bookings essential. $11, concessions $7.50, children $4.50. Free beer at the end.)*

⊠ BONORONG WILDLIFE PARK. See, hear, pet, and feed the beasts that roam the island's wilderness. Orphaned and injured Tasmanian devils, koalas, quolls, wombats, and birds live in enclosures, while 'roos bounce, emus chuckle, and pea-cocks strut their stuff. Every visitor gets a bag of kangaroo feed; make sure to catch the devil feeding at 11:30am or 2pm. *(North of Hobart in Brighton. Metro bus X1 from Hobart to Glenorchy Interchange connects with #125 or 126 to Brighton, 1½hr. From Brighton, it's a 30min. walk. By car, it's a 25min. drive north on Hwy.1; follow the signs in Brighton.* ☎ *6268 1184. Open daily 9am-5pm. $10, children $5.)*

HISTORIC FEMALE FACTORY AND ISLAND PRODUCE TASMANIA FUDGE FACTORY. Once the Hobart jail and a factory for women and children in the 1820s, the site is now home to building ruins, memorial gardens, and fine confectioners. The poignant tours split their time between the historic site ("lest we forget") and today's small, handmade production of fudge and truffles. Did someone say non-sequitur? *(*☎ *6223 3233. 16 Degraves St., South Hobart, near Cascade Brewery. Take bus #43, 44, 46, 47, or 49 from Franklin Sq. to stop 16, cross onto McRobies Rd., and walk right onto Degraves St. Shop and gardens open M-F 8am-4pm. Tours M-F 10:30am. 1¼hr. $6.60, conces-sions $5.50, children $3.30, families $16.50. Free samples. Book a day ahead.)*

ROYAL TASMANIAN BOTANICAL GARDENS. With 13 hectares and 6000 species, this is the largest public collection of Tasmanian plants in the world and the larg-est collection of conifers in the Southern Hemisphere. Founded in 1818, they are also the second oldest gardens in Australia. The wildly popular Al Fresco Theatre runs an outdoor play in January and "Shakespeare in the Garden" in February. *(North of the city, near the Tasman Bridge. Take any bus, including the MetroCity Explorer, headed to the eastern shore to stop 4 before the bridge; or take the X3-G express to Bridgewater, which stops at the main gate. Or walk 25min. from the city to Queen's Domain past Government House.* ☎ *6234 6299. Open daily Oct.-Mar. 8am-6:30pm, Apr. 8am-5:30pm, May-Aug. 8am-5pm, Sept. 8am-5:30pm. Free. Outdoor Theatre $22, concessions $11.)*

🎭 ENTERTAINMENT

Check out the entertainment listings in the *EG* insert of Friday's *Mercury* newspa-per. The arthouse cinema is the **State,** 375 Elizabeth St., in North Hobart, with indie films in glamorous facilities. (☎ 6234 6318. $11, W $7, concessions $7.50.) The **Theatre Royal,** 29 Campbell St., the oldest theater in Australia, produces reliably good shows. (☎ 6233 2299. Box office open M-F 9am-5pm, Sa 9:30am-1pm. $22-42.) The more experimental **Peacock Theatre,** 77 Salamanca Pl., is in the Salamanca Arts Centre. (☎ 6234 8414. $4-15.) The **Tasmanian Symphony Orchestra,** 1 Davey St., in the Federation Concert Hall at the Hotel Grand Chancellor, is over 50 years old but still holds performances every few weeks. (☎ 6235 3633 or 1800 001 190. Box office open M-F 9:30am-4:30pm, Sa concert days, and all concert nights. $35-49, conces-sions $20.) The **Wrest Point Hotel,** 410 Sandy Bay Rd., at Nelson Rd., is the oldest casino in Australia. The emphasis is on pokies, but there are real gaming tables upstairs. Many of the bars also have live bands or DJs. (☎ 6225 0112. Tables open Su-Th 2pm-2am, F-Sa 2pm-4am; machines open Su-Th 1pm-2am, F-Sa 1pm-4am.)

🌙 NIGHTLIFE

Hobart is often mocked for its lukewarm nightlife. While this isn't the place to find a world-class club scene, there are definitely places to party. Once again, Sala-manca Place draws the masses.

The New Sydney Hotel, 87 Bathurst St. (☎ 6234 4516). An extremely popular Irish pub where margaritas (a dubious Irish tradition) are the most popular beverage ($10). Tu-Su live music, mainly cover bands. Cover Sa $3. Open M noon-10pm, Tu noon-midnight, W-F 11:30am-midnight, Sa 1pm-midnight, Su 4-9pm.

Syrup and **Round Midnight,** 39 Salamanca Pl. (☎6223 2491). Above and next to Knopwoods Pub, it's packed late nights on weekends. **Syrup,** on the 1st floor, is a mellow lounge-bar with appetizers and live DJs that morphs into a club at midnight. **Round Midnight,** on the 2nd floor, hosts live bands and guest DJs. F-Sa cover $4-7. Both open in summer 6pm to wee hours; in winter W 9pm-2am, F 9pm-4am, Sa 9pm-7am or later.

Club Surreal, 86 Sandy Bay Rd. (☎6223 3655), at the corner of St. George's, upstairs from St. Ives Hotel. Surreal Saturday nights are jam-packed with an 18+ crowd wanting to get their dance on. Huge video screens, TVs on the floor, and techno and disco dance floors connected with a slippery slide. Open W 9pm-3am, F-Sa 10:30pm-4:30am. Cover W $4, F-Sa $8.

THE SOUTH

Anchored by its capital city of Hobart, Australia's southern end thrives with humble communities and outdoor wonders. Ninety minutes east, the Tasman Peninsula and Port Arthur stand testament to Tassie's colonial history. To the west, the entrance to the vast Southwest National Park welcomes visitors to the Tasmanian Wilderness World Heritage Area. In between, amid the hop vines of the Derwent Valley and the apple orchards of the D'Entrecasteaux Channel, are the homes of people who know they've found the good life. Wandering through groves of Huon pines or trekking with camels along Bruny's beaches, you're bound to agree.

TASMAN PENINSULA AND PORT ARTHUR ☎03

The narrow **Eaglehawk Neck** isthmus connects the Tasman Peninsula to the rest of Tasmania. Tourist buses now funnel through the very place where guard dogs once ravaged would-be escaped convicts. Initially known as the "Black Line," military units once dumped Aborigines and repeat offenders over the peninsula's steep cliffs and narrow neck into rumored shark-infested waters. From 1830 to 1877, 12,000 convicts were shipped to **Port Arthur** for offenses ranging from petty thievery and "skulking without permission" to murder. The ruins of the many convict-built sandstone buildings are Tasmania's most popular tourist attraction, drawing 250,000 visitors annually. If Port Arthur's commercialism is too much, escape the crowds in the surrounding wilderness. The Tasman coastline, now a National Park, is particularly astounding; well-beaten walkways and open tracks provide some of the most phenomenal views in Tassie.

▐ TRANSPORTATION. There is no real Port Arthur town, just services to the site. **TassieLink** (☎1300 300 520) is the only **bus** company servicing the tourist attraction, departing the depot in Hobart M-F 4pm for the YHA and Port Arthur Motor Inn. (2¼hr. Book at the YHA. Buses depart Port Arthur M-F 6am, holidays 7am, Sa 1pm. $15.)

A one-hour drive north, the **Sorell** is the main stop en route to the Suncoast (via the A3). **Redline** (☎1300 360 000) **buses** run to Hobart. (50min.; M-F 5-8 per day, Sa 2 per day; $4.) **TassieLink** runs up the East Coast (W, F, and Su morning; also M morning in summer) to: Bicheno (2½hr., $18.40); Coles Bay (2½hr., $17.40); St. Helens (3¾hr., F and Su, $29); Swansea (2hr., $14); and Triabunna (1hr., $8.40).

▐ PRACTICAL INFORMATION. By the Eaglehawk Neck Historic Site on the A9, the **Officers Mess** has basic **groceries** and takeaways. (☎6250 3722. Open in summer daily 8am-8pm; in winter Su-Th 9am-6:30pm, F-Sa 9am-7:30pm.) There is a **Visitors Center** in the Port Arthur Historic Centre. (☎6251 2371. Open

TASMANIA

The Tasman Peninsula

🛏 ACCOMMODATIONS
Eaglehawk Neck
    Backpackers, **1**
Port Arthur Garden Point
    Caravan Park, **3**
Seaview Lodge
    Host Farm, **2**
YHA, **4**

8:30am-8pm.) In Sorell, the **Westpac bank**, with 24hr. **ATM**, is at 36 Cole St. at the junction of A3 and A9. (Open M-Th 9:30am-4pm, F 9:30am-5pm.) There is **Internet** ($3 per 15min., $8 per hr.) at The Arts and Crafts building on Andersons Rd., off A6. They also rent bikes ($8 per hr., $20 per day), canoes ($16 per hr., $65 per day), kayaks ($10 per hr., $45 per day) and some gear. (☎6250 3103. Open daily 7am-7pm.) There's a **post office** at 19 Gordon St., Sorell. (☎6265 2579. Open M-F 9am-5pm.) **Postal code:** 7172.

🛏 **ACCOMMODATIONS.** The **Seaview Lodge Host Farm ❷,** 732 Nubeena Back Rd., Koonya, has a fairy-tale hilltop location, overlooking 90 acres of land. **Tassie Experience & Eco Tours** runs out of the farm. Driving from A9 in Taranna, follow B37 9km to Nubeena Back Rd., and then head 1½km up to the farm. TassieLink drops passengers off in Koonya 30min. before arriving in Port Arthur; free pickup is available from Koonya or Port Arthur. (☎6250 2766. Linens $5. Laundry $2. Bike hire $15. Dorms $16; twins and doubles $35-40.) The **Port Arthur YHA ❷,** on Champ St., the first left past the entrance to the historic site, sits mere meters from the ruins and houses a resident ghost named Alice. (☎6250 2311. Reception daily 8:30am-10am and 5-10pm. Dorms $24, YHA $18.) The **Port Arthur Garden Point Caravan Park ❶,** is left off A9, 1km before the historic site. (☎6250 2340. Dorms $15; sites for 2 $16, powered $18; cabins $65-85.)

SIGHTS. The prison, lunatic asylum, hospital, and church of **Port Arthur Historic Site** are a visible reminder of Australia's convict heritage. The downstairs museum area attempts to bring this heritage alive, allowing visitors to pick a convict and follow his history. The short **walking tours** of the grounds and the free **boat tours** provide further insight into convict life. A 20min. harbor cruise past the **Isle of the Dead,** the colony's cemetery, and **Point Puer,** the convict boys' colony, is included in the price of admission; book at the visitor complex. Cruises that actually land on the Isle of the Dead cost an extra $6.60. The overwhelmingly popular **Historic Ghost Tour** runs nightly, offering spooky stories, creepy shadows, and a bit of history. Admission tickets and Ghost Tour tickets can be purchased from the YHA or the visitor complex front desk. (☎ 1800 659 101. Open daily 8:30am-8pm, but most buildings close at 5pm; allow 4hr. to explore. Admission $20, concessions $16, children $9; after 4:30pm $9. Ghost Tour 90min., times vary, $14.)

PORT ARTHUR SHOOTINGS. On Sunday, April 28, 1996, a gunman killed 35 people in Port Arthur historic site and township. The shock to Tasmania and Australia still lingers; the violence triggered gun law reform. Information on the murders is available in any Tasmanian bookstore and in a free booklet of the court transcription available at the visitors' desk. Be considerate of the Port Arthur community by not asking staff and shopkeepers about the incident.

AROUND THE TASMAN PENINSULA

Much of the Peninsula's coastline makes up **Tasman National Park,** which is lined by cliff-top **hiking trails.** Peter and Shirley Storey's handy *Tasman Tracks*, available at tourist shops on the peninsula, details about 50 walks and has good maps. The **Tasman National Park Tours** offers a variety of tours from Port Arthur to the Cliffs and Coves tour. (☎ 6250 3157. 2-3hr. First person $88, second $44, third $33, children $22.) Another new way to view the spectacular cliffs of the park is with **Port Arthur Cruises** on the **Tasman Island Wilderness Cruise.** This two-hour cruise views the highest sea cliffs in Australia and is the only way to get close to Tasman Island. (☎ 6231 2655. Book 24hr. in advance. Departs 8:15am on demand. $49.)

One of the region's most intriguing sights is the **Tessellated Pavement,** located just before Eaglehawk Neck. This natural platform of sedimentary rock has grooves and splits across its surface, etched by the salt crystals left behind as sea water evaporates. The crystals dry up in the tiny cracks of the rock and then expand, cutting open the rock and giving it the appearance of tile. The carpark is 500m up Pirates Bay Dr., an easy 15min. return walk to the beach.

Continuing on A9 just past Eaglehawk Neck is C338, which leads to the **Devils Kitchen** and **Tasman Arch** carparks. Both cliffside sights are easy 10-15min. return walks. Continue along the moderate gravel track to **Patersons Arch** (15min.) and **Waterfall Bay** (45min.), where it links up with the steep **Tasman Trail** (1¼hr.) to the falls and **Waterfall Bluff.** (1½hr.) Walking from Devils Kitchen to **Fortescue Bay** can be a breathtaking 6-8hr. or overnight walk. Basic **camping ❶** is available with drinking water, showers, and toilets. (Sites $5.50. Park fees apply.) The Fortescue **ranger** (☎ 6250 2433) has details. To get to Waterfall Bay by car, take the first right off C338 and follow 4km to the cul-de-sac; for Fortescue Bay, follow a 12km signposted, unsealed road east off A9, south of the B37 Taranna junction.

From Fortescue Bay, the Tasman Trail leads to **Cape Hauy.** (4hr.) Starting with a deep descent from the campground, this very difficult trek passes by the spectacular **Monument,** featuring the dolorite spires of **The Candlestick, The Needle,** and **The Lanterns,** popular among ambitious rock climbers. The three-day return trip to **Cape Pillar** is something to write home about. **Camping ❶** is available at **Lime Bay.**

T A S M A N I A

(Pit toilets, water. $3.) Check with the park office for updates and summer ranger activities. **Parks and Wildlife** (☎ 6250 3497) is on A9 before the Rescue Centre.

The **Tasmanian Devil Park Wildlife Rescue Centre**, in Taranna, houses devils, 'roos, and wallabies, all feedable and touchable—well, except the devils. They also have the only free flight show on Tasmania and devil feedings daily at 10am, 11am, and 1:30pm. (☎ 6250 3230. Open daily 9am-5pm. $15, children $7.50, families $40; subject to change.)

D'ENTRECASTEAUX CHANNEL

The channels, islands, and caves south of Hobart were first charted by Frenchman Bruni d'Entrecasteaux in 1792, more than a decade before the first English settlement in the area. The valley's cool climate and fertile soil, nourished by the Huon River, make the area perfect for growing berries, pears, and apples. The town of Cygnet provides services to the area, and antique shops and vineyards pepper the pastoral land between the river and the D'Entrecasteaux Channel. Bruny Island offers a tranquil escape into the wild, and a stop can be made in Geeveston before launching into the southwest. While the area is pleasantly tucked away from the tourist hubbub, seclusion has a price: there is nary an ATM or petrol station to be found, so plan ahead. The widely circulated *Southern Tasmania's Waterways and Wilderness* is a useful navigational aid for the region.

CYGNET AND THE HUON VALLEY ☎ 03

Near the mouth of the Nicholls Rivulet on Port Cygnet and 60km southwest of Hobart, the friendly, artsy community of Cygnet hosts seasonal fruit pickers and year-round travelers en route to the Huon Valley. Several testaments to the region's booming fruit trade lie on A6 to Huonville from Hobart. **Doran's Jam Factory** has been churning out fruit preserves since 1834. Their spiced apple butter is the local favorite; savor it with scones in their tea room. (☎ 6266 4377. Open daily 10am-4pm. Free self-guided tours and samplings.) Down the road, **The Huon Apple and Heritage Museum,** in Grove, is filled with apple industry paraphernalia. The 90-year-old peeling machine is the core of the exhibit; visitors are invited to eat the finished products. A whopping 500 varieties of apples are on display from March to June. (☎ 6266 4345. Open daily Sept.-May 9am-5pm, June and Aug. 10am-4pm. $4.) This region of Tasmania is locally known for its cool-climate wines, many of which are available at the **Hartzview Vineyard and Wine Centre,** 10km east of Cygnet near Gardners Bay (via B68 and C626; keep an eye out for the grape sign). In addition to its own pinot noir and fruit wines, Hartzview provides products from the area's smaller vineyards. (☎ 6295 1623. Open daily 9am-5pm. Tastings $2, refunded on purchase.)

Hobart Coaches leaves from 21 Murray St. in Hobart for the Cygnet carpark. (☎ 6233. 1hr., M-F 5:15pm, $8.) The ◪**Balfes Hill Huon Valley YHA & Backpackers** ❸, 4 Sandhill Rd., Cradoc, 4½km north of Cygnet, caters to eager workers willing to pick berries or prune orchards November to May. The hostel managers will help find employment and provide transportation ($10 per week or $1 per trip). The new building has comfortable bunks, clean bathrooms, a kitchen, a video lounge, ping-pong, billiards, laundry, and a phone. Call ahead for pickup from the bus stop. (☎ 6295 1551. Twins $39, ensuite $43. YHA discount $3.) For a more rustic experience, **Talune Host Farm** ❺, at the intersection of B68 and C627, offers self-contained cabins for families. (☎ 6295 1775; wombat@talune.com.au. Call ahead. Prices vary.) Three **pubs** along Mary St., and the ◪**Red Velvet Lounge** ❶, 87 Mary St., provide the only options for eating out; the Lounge is part art gallery, part wholefoods store, and part cafe. (☎ 6295 0466. Pizza with heaping portions of salad and macaroni salad $10. Open daily 9am-6pm.) Of the three **supermarkets,** Value-Plus, on Mary St., is open longest. (Open daily 7:30am-9pm.)

BRUNY ISLAND   ☎ 03

Bruny was the first bit of land Abel Tasman glimpsed when he stumbled on Tasmania in 1642. Later, Captain Cook and his understudy Captain Bligh (of *Mutiny on Board H.M.S. Bounty* fame) both visited the island and believed it to be part of the mainland—they were proven wrong when d'Entrecasteaux sailed through the channel in 1792. Bruny once bustled with a great whaling industry, but timber and agriculture reign today. North Bruny is home to 1000-year-old frayed-looking trees called "blackboys," while South Bruny houses most of the island's 500 locals and tourists. The island captivates its visitors—families and adventurers alike—with dramatic coastal scenery, remnants of an exploratory past, and plenty of space to bushwalk, bike, paddle, and swim.

▐▄ TRANSPORTATION. Ferries (☎6273 6725) run roughly every hour between Kettering and Bruny. (15min.; M-Sa 6:50am-6:30pm, F 6:50am-7:30pm, Su 8am-6:30pm; return fare for cars $21-26, motorcycles $11-15, bicycles $5, pedestrians free. Cash only.) **Hobart Coaches** leaves 21 Murray St. in Hobart for the ferry terminal. (☎6234 4077. 45min., M-F 4 per day, $6.) The island itself has **no public transportation;** visitors without a car are left relatively immobile.

▐ PRACTICAL INFORMATION. The **Visitors Center** is across the channel in Kettering, by the ferry terminal. (☎6267 4494 or 1800 676 740. Open daily 9am-5pm.) The Adventure Bay General Store, 712 Adventure Bay Rd., has **petrol, EFTPOS,** and **groceries.** (Open daily 7:30am-8pm.) The Bruny Island Online Access Centre, at the Bruny Island District School in Alonnah, has **Internet,** scanning, and fax service. (☎6293 2036. Open Tu 2pm-5:30pm; W 9am-noon, 1-4pm, and 6-9pm; Th 1-4:30pm; F 1-4pm and 6-9pm; Sa 1-4pm. $5 per 30min.) There are **no banks or ATMs** on the island. The **post office,** at the Alonnah General Store, just off B66 in Alonnah, also has **petrol.** (Open daily 7:30am-7pm.) **Postal Code:** 7150.

▐▘▝ ACCOMMODATIONS AND FOOD. The **Adventure Bay Holiday Villages ❶,** at the end of the road in Adventure Bay, are all decorated with bleached whale bones. (☎6293 1270. If after dark, ring bell to the right of door. Coin-op showers. Laundry. Sites for 2 $12, powered $14; on-site vans for 2 $32; cabins for 2 $50.) South Bruny's **Lumeah ❷,** in Adventure Bay, offers spacious doubles, huge common areas, a brick fireplace, laundry, and BBQ. Boat trips (1½hr., $85), camel treks (30min., $18; 2½hr. with tea $65), and massages (1hr., $40) are among Lumeah's offerings. (☎6293 1265; lumeah@tassie.net.au. Linens $2. Closed June-Aug. Rooms $80.) If you are looking to splurge for some fantastic views, phenomenal landscapes, and rooms with personality, stay at one of the **Morella Island Retreats ❺.** (☎6293 1131; retreats@morella-island.com.au. Breakfast $15. Doubles $150-250.) At the start of the Penguin Island and Grass Point tracks, many of the island's protected lands offer free **camping ❶.** Cloudy Bay on the southern part of the island and Jetty Beach near the lighthouse require national park passes. These, along with Neck Beach, on the south end of the isthmus between North and South Bruny, offer sites with pit toilets, no water, and no firewood. Contact the ranger at the **Labillardiere State Reserve** (☎6298 3229) for more info.

The ▨**Hothouse Cafe ❸,** 46 Adventure Bay Rd., 6km north of Adventure Bay, is a sheltered outdoor cafe with fantastic food and a beautiful garden, perfected by a panoramic view of the sea. The cafe's ambience more than makes up for its somewhat limited selection and slightly pricey meals. (☎6293 1131. Open daily in summer 10am-late, in winter 10am-5pm. Gardens and Gumtree maze $3.)

TASMANIA

IN RECENT NEWS

FOXY PEST

The European red fox, introduced by settlers to mainland Australia in the 1850s for sport hunting, is considered the single most devastating threat to Australia's endemic fauna. With few natural predators, the fox has succeeded in reproducing widely, taking advantage of the largely defenseless native wildlife, and wreaking disease-ridden havoc on the poultry and sheep of Australia's agricultural industry.

There is terrified talk around Tasmania that foxes have made their way over from the mainland. Whether their crossing be accidental or otherwise, these stowaways could have a devastating impact on Tasmania's environment, threatening nearly a dozen native species of animals, including many species of small marsupials unique to Tassie. Currently, animals like the wombat, platypus, and quoll thrive due to the island's lack of natural predators. The introduction of an animal as intelligent and adaptive as the fox bodes poorly for these creatures and others, such as the eastern barred bandicoot, the small macropods, white-breasted sea eagle, and even the Tasmanian devil.

Service Tasmania is frantically searching for these animals and asks that anyone who believes to have sighted a fox contact the 24hr. service immediately at ☎ 1300 FOXOUT (1300 369 688). For more information, including an information sheet detailing how to identify the presence of foxes, visit the Parks and Wildlife website (www.dpiwe.tas.gov.au/inter.nsf/WebPages/SJON-52J8U3?open).

SIGHTS AND ACTIVITIES. The ■Bligh Museum, 880 Adventure Bay Rd., contains fascinating old maps, marine photos, and memorabilia relating to the explorers who landed here, including Cook, Bligh, Flinders, and d'Entrecasteaux. (☎ 6293 1117. Open daily 10am-3pm. $4.) The **Bruny Island Charters** offer popular ecotours (1½hr., 3hr., or full-day) of the surrounding waterways, departing from the Adventure Bay Jetty. (☎ 6234 3336. Book in advance. $60-130; standby rate on 3hr. tour after 6:30pm the night before.) The **Cape Bruny Lighthouse,** built by convicts between 1836 and 1838, is 30km southwest of Adventure Bay on an unsealed road. (☎ 6298 3114. Open daily 10am-4pm. Tours by arrangement $10, children $2.) Near the lighthouse, hike down the hills and through the coastal heath and coves of the **Labillardiere Reserve** (complete 7hr.; alternate circuit 1½hr.; moderate), but beware that trails are often poorly marked. From September to February, fairy penguins and muttonbirds roost on the Neck of the island. Parks and Wildlife runs free nightly **tours** from the Neck at dusk during the summer. The island is also a haven for rare white wallabies, diverse birdlife, dolphins, seals, and migrating southern right whales. **Cloudy Bay** has some of the best surf in Tasmania, while **Jetty Beach** offers more sheltered waters suitable for children. Some of the best views of the area can be had from the **Fluted Cape circuit** (3hr.), which starts at the end of the beach on the southeast end of Adventure Bay. Though only moderately challenging, the track includes the tops of some of the highest cliffs in Australia.

FAR SOUTH: GEEVESTON AND GATEWAYS TO WILDERNESS

Winding 25km south from Huonville along the d'Entrecasteaux Channel, A6 meets **Geeveston,** a town teetering on the edge of the southwest wilderness. In the last Ice Age, Aborigines lived in the area's caves, protected today as part of the Tasmanian Wilderness World Heritage Area. **TassieLink buses** (☎ 1300 300 520) run from Hobart to: Cockle Creek (3½hr.; M, W, and F 9am; $52); Dover (2hr.; M-F 3-6 per day; $15); and Geeveston (1¼hr.; M-F 4-6 per day, Sa-Su 1-3 per day; $11.20). For info on **flights** to the area, which run about $100 per person each way, contact **Par-Avion Wilderness Tours** (☎ 6248 5390) at the Cambridge Airport, 20km from Hobart, or **Tasair Wilderness Flights** (☎ 6248 5088).

The **Visitor Information** is in the **Forest and Heritage Centre** on Church St. (☎ 6297 1836. Open daily 9am-5pm. Museum $5. **Internet** $2 per 30min.) Church St. has several **supermarkets** (open Su-Th 8:30am-

6:30pm, F 8:30am-7pm); a few **ATMs,** and a **post office.** (☎6297 1102. Open M-F 9am-5pm, Sa-Su 3-7pm.) **Postal code:** 7116.

The **Geeveston Forest House ❶,** at the end of Church St., has free laundry. (☎6297 1102. Singles and doubles $14. Book at the post office.) The region has many **camping** options, with free sites at the **Tahune Forest Reserve ❶,** 27km west of Geeveston, **Hastings Forest ❶,** 13km west of Dover, and **Cockle Creek ❶,** 25km south of Lune River. All are off of unsealed roads and offer pit toilets and drinking water. Cockle Creek also has a phone.

Even if you're not camping, follow the unsealed **Arve Road Forest Drive** from Geeveston to the Huon River to see native Huon pines, which take 500 years to mature and can live up to 2500 years. The easy **Huon Pines Loop Trail** (20min.) starts at the carpark past the Tahune Forest Reserve campground. Nearby, take the Arve Loop Rd. to the **"Big Tree,"** an 87m, unbelievably wide swamp gum. About 10km northwest of Lune River are the **Hastings Caves,** which house impressive dolomite formations. (☎6298 3209. Tours every hr. in summer 10am-6pm, in winter 11am-4pm. $12, concessions $10; includes entry to the thermal springs.) The Lune River area is also known for fresh and saltwater fishing. The carpark past the free camping area in **Cockle Creek** marks the end of Australia's most southerly road. An easy walk (4hr. return) from the campground goes to South Cape Bay, the closest you can get to **Australia's southernmost tip** and neighboring Antarctica. The campground is also the endpoint of **South Coast Track** (85km). Most people hiking the full track fly into **Melaleuca** and walk back out six to nine days later. Some combine it with the **Port Davey Track,** extending it another five days. The area west of Cockle Creek is part of the **Southwest National Park** (see p. 520). Park passes are available from the Geeveston Forest and Heritage Centre.

DERWENT VALLEY AND THE SOUTHWEST

Largely untouristed, the southwest affords a quiet wilderness experience that nevertheless keeps its visitors in awe. The agricultural Derwent Valley and the wild southwest are divided by the River Derwent, flowing from Lake St. Clair down to Storm Bay. Ridgeline after ridgeline of rocky peaks roll into the southern shores of this quiet Tassie valley. Stretching expansively toward the Southern Ocean, Southwest National Park includes the vast hydroelectric Lake Gordon and Lake Pedder, both the subject of heated environmental debate.

NEW NORFOLK ☎03

A misty valley enfolds the small town of New Norfolk, 25km northwest of Hobart on the Derwent. The climate is perfect for growing hops—regional cultivators harvest up to 45 tons per day. **Oast House,** on the Lyell Hwy. east of town, was once used to dry the harvest; now it's New Norfolk's most hopping tourist attraction, with a museum, gallery, and cafe. (☎6261 1030. Open Sept.-Dec. W-Su 9:30am-5pm, Jan.-May daily 9:30am-5pm. $4.) Eleven kilometers west of New Norfolk, the **Salmon Ponds** and **Museum of Trout Fishing** constitute the oldest trout hatchery in the Southern Hemisphere. (☎6261 1076. Open daily 9am-5pm. $5.)

TassieLink (☎1300 300 520) runs **buses** to: Hobart (40min.; Tu, Th-F, and Su 1 per day; $5.10); Lake St. Clair (2½hr.; Tu and Th 1 per day; $26); and Queenstown (4½hr.; Tu, Th-F, and Su 1 per day; $40). **Hobart Coaches** (☎6233 4232) runs from Hobart to Circle St. in New Norfolk (50min.; M-F 6 per day, Sa 3 per day; $5.10.) The **Derwent Valley Information Centre** is on Circle St. (☎6261 0700. Open daily 10am-4pm.) The **police station,** 14 Bathurst St., has free **Internet** access. (Open M-F 9am-

5pm.) The **Bush Inn Hotel** ❸, 49-51 Montagu St., north on the Lyell Hwy., includes full breakfast. (☎ 6261 2256. Singles $33; twins and doubles $55.) The **New Norfolk Esplanade Caravan Park** ❶, on the riverbank, has coin-op showers and laundry. (☎ 6261 1268. Key deposit $5. Crowded sites for 2 $10, powered $14.) The Woolworth's **supermarket** is on Charles St. (Open M-W and Sa 8am-6pm, Th-F 8am-9pm.)

MT. FIELD NATIONAL PARK

At Mt. Field, Tasmania's first national park and a good hour from Hobart, summer visitors enjoy bushwalks and waterfalls, while winter visitors head for the slopes to downhill and cross-country ski. Bus companies do not service the park or its ski fields during the winter. **TassieLink** (☎ 1300 300 520) runs **buses** December to mid-April to: Hobart (1½hr., M-Sa 1-2 per day, $24); Lake St. Clair via Gretna (3hr.; Tu, Th, and Sa 1 per day; $30); Scott's Peak (1¾hr.; Tu, Th, and Sa mornings; $58.10). Some tour companies lead trips from Hobart: **Bottom Bits Bus** offers well-led, full-day tours during the summer. (☎ 1800 777 103. $69.) **Closer to Nature** offers more expensive full-day tours year-round. (☎ 6288 1477. $100.) Rangers lead free walks, slide shows, and nighttime wildlife-watching trips during the summer. Maps and park passes are available at the entrance station. Continue 100m up the road to the **park shop** (☎ 6288 1526) for more park info, takeaway food, and souvenirs. The **Mt. Field Information Line** (☎ 6288 1319) has a recording on ski and road conditions.

The National Park Office administers three basic six-person **cabins** ❶ near Lake Dobson with mattresses, a wood heater, firewood, and cold water. (☎ 6288 1149. Book ahead. $10 per person.) The park shop also runs a self-register **campground** ❶ near the park entrance with showers, bathrooms, BBQ, and laundry. Its grounds fill with pademelons, and the creek is home to platypuses. (Sites $6 per person, powered $8.50.) Past the park on B61 (Gordon River Rd.), **Mt. Field YHA** ❷ provides basic beds in rooms without locks or lockers. (☎ 6288 1369. Book at pub across the road. Laundry. Linens $1. Dorms $19. YHA discount $3. Cash only.) Food options are scarce; some get groceries in New Norfolk. Twelve kilometers west in Maydena, **Harry's mini-market** closes at 9pm.

The park can be divided into two distinct areas. The lower slopes near the park entrance have picnic and BBQ facilities, a park shop, and easy walks to the tallest flowering plant in the world and a trio of waterfalls. **Russell Falls,** a paved walk (10min.) from the carpark through wet eucalypt forest, has long been a favorite destination. The worthwhile trek along the steep gravel road to **Lake Dobson** (16km) leads through eucalypts, mixed forest, sub-alpine woodland, and alpine mosaic. The upper slopes offer a network of extended bushwalks amid glassy highland lakes. The easy **Pandani Grove Nature Walk** (1hr.) circles Lake Dobson and introduces unusual wildlife, including pineapple grass, bright red scoparia, endemic conifers, pencil King Billy pines, and platypi.

Though snow cover varies, skiers travel up the slope by tow or by making their own tracks in the backcountry. Without 4WD, Lake Dobson Rd. can only be accessed with 2WD and chains; the ski fields are a 40min. walk past the carpark. The ski kiosk rents skis and lift tickets.

SOUTHWEST NATIONAL PARK AND THE GORDON RIVER DAM

Highway B61, better known as **Gordon River Rd.,** continues through Maydena, winding 86km through the rugged mountains of Southwest National Park. The road passes through the settlement of **Strathgordon** (pop. 15), 12km before its abrupt end at the Gordon River Dam (about 1½hr.). **TassieLink** (☎ 1300 300 520) runs summer service between Hobart and Scotts Peak (3¼hr.; Tu, Th, and S 1 per day a; $58.10) via Timbs Track (2hr., $55), Mt. Anne (2¾hr., $55), and Red Tape Track (3hr., $55). The park is largely inaccessible by road, stretching south to Melaleuca and Cockle Creek, between which runs the **South Coast Track.** The construction of the Gordon River Dam system brought condemnation from international environmental activists, who argued that the dams would destroy the region's wild beauty. Regardless, the dams were built, and today the Gordon River Power Station is the largest in Tasmania, producing roughly a third of the state's energy—by itself, the station is capable of powering the entire city of Hobart.

Carved out of the Tasmanian Wilderness World Heritage Area, the unnatural Lakes Gordon and Pedder are captivating. **Hydro's Visitor Centre,** on a ledge above the dam, has brochures on the dam's construction and history. Take 196 steps down to the top of the dam. (☎6280 1134. Open daily Nov.-Apr. 10am-5pm, May-Oct. 11am-3pm.) **Lake Pedder** can be viewed from both the main road and the entirely unsealed **Scotts Peak Rd.** This difficult road forks off the Gordon River Rd. 28km into the park at Frodshams Pass, ending 36km later at the Huon Campground. Just 2½km into Scotts Peak Rd. is the short and sweet **Creepy Crawly Nature Trail** (20min.). Longer walks go from Timbs Track to the **Florentine River** (4hr. easy rainforest walk), the **Eliza Plateau** (6hr.; difficult ridge climb to Mt. Eliza), and Lake Judd (8hr. unmarked track with difficult river crossings). Picnic and campsites at the **Huon Campground ❶** grant easy access to the **Arthur Plains** and **Port Davey** walking tracks. Other sites are at **Edgar Dam ❶,** 8km before the end of Scotts Peak Rd., and **Teds Beach ❶,** east of Strathgordon. Strathgordon's **Lake Pedder Motor Inn ❺** is the only other park accommodation. (☎6280 1166. Singles $60-95; twins and doubles $75-110.) **Trout fishing** is plentiful on Lake Gordon and Lake Pedder from August to April. (License required.) For park info, contact the entrance station (☎6288 2258), or rangers at Mt. Field. (☎6288 1141)

THE WESTERN WILDERNESS

From windy Strahan to the deep glaciers of Lake St. Clair and the slopes of Cradle Mountain, the scenic splendor of Tasmania's west sits amidst highland pine forests. In the wilderness, millennia-old Huon pines share the forest with deciduous beeches that come ablaze in autumn as well as bellied parrots, quolls, devils, wombats, echidnas, 'roos, and wallabies.

As one of the world's great temperate wildernesses, it also is one of its last. Most of the land became protected in 1982 by the UNESCO Tasmanian Wilderness World Heritage Area, though logging and mining still threaten the areas just outside the national park. While the area's well-trammeled trails justifiably attract plenty of visitors, most of the west is entirely unspoiled by human contact; lush rainforest, forbidding crags, windswept moors, and swirling rivers have been left almost as they were when explorers first came to the region. Aborigines native to Tasmania, however, have lived here for over 30,000 years. Today, the cultural sites are being returned to their rightful owners, and life goes on noticeably unchanged.

CRADLE MOUNTAIN ☎03

If you haven't seen a picture of mystic Cradle Mountain rising above quiet Dove Lake, you must not be in Tasmania. Visited by hundreds of thousands of wilderness lovers every year, the mountain is Tassie's most iconic landmark. The area is a complex glacial fabric of creeks and crags that shelter the state's unique jewels: sweet-sapped cider-gum woodlands, rainforests of King Billy and celery-top pine, and carpets of cushion plants. Species long thought to be extinct, such as freshwater crayfish, mountain shrimp, and velvet worms have been found alive and kicking around Cradle Mountain. Naturalist Gustav Weindorfer called Cradle Mountain the place "where there is no time and nothing matters."

📧 TRANSPORTATION. Maxwell's Coach and Taxi Service (☎6492 1431) makes frequent, unscheduled runs between the campground, the Visitors Center ($3), Dove Lake ($9), and offers 24hr. service to the northwest (see **Lake St. Clair**, p. 523; book ahead). **TassieLink** (☎1300 300 520) departs Tu, Th, and Sa from Cradle Mountain Visitors Center and the campground to Devonport (1½hr., $28), Launceston (3½hr., $44), and Strahan (3¾hr., $28).

🛈 PRACTICAL INFORMATION. Cradle Mountain-Lake St. Clair National Park is the northernmost end of the **Tasmanian Wilderness World Heritage Area.** It is a 1½hr. drive south from Devonport on B19 and B14 and then west on C132 to the park entrance. From the west, follow A10 from for 2hr to C132 into the park. There is no direct road through the park. Visitors may most easily reach Lake St. Clair via the Cradle Link Road (C132) and the Muchison and Lyell Highways (A10). Park fees apply ($9.90 daily fee per vehicle; up to 8 people). The **Visitors Center,** just past the park entrance off of C132, features displays with helpful layouts of the walking tracks and a public telephone. (☎6492 1133. Open daily in summer 8am-5:30pm, in winter 8am-5pm.) A 7½km gravel road runs south from the Visitors Center to **Waldheim** and **Dove Lake.**

🛏🍴 ACCOMMODATIONS AND FOOD. In peak season, accommodations fill up fast, so book ahead. On the entrance road, 2km outside the park, the **Cradle Mountain Tourist Park ❶** provides sites, basic Alpine huts (intended for campers when it's raining), bunk rooms, self-contained cabins, and heaps of amenities. There's an unequipped cooking shelter with BBQ and a kitchen for hostelers. (☎6492 1395; cradle@cosycabins.com. Reception daily 8am-8pm. Sites $6-10 per person, powered $10-12; 3-bed Alpine huts $12-16; bunks $17-23; cabins for 2 $70-80. VIP/YHA.) The Visitors Center runs the eight **Waldheim Cabins ❺,** 5½km inside the park. The Overland Track begins right outside at the Ronny Carpark. Heating, basic kitchen, showers, composting toilets, and limited generated power for lighting are provided. (☎6492 1110. Bunk cabins from $70-80 for up to 3; each extra person $10-19; 8 people maximum.) *Bring your own food*—there is no produce at Cradle Mountain. The **Cradle Mountain Lodge General Store,** right outside the park, sells basic supplies at inflated prices and has the only **payphone** with touch-tone service. (Open M-F 9am-5pm, Sa-Su noon-4pm; extended summer hours.) Grab some pancakes at **Moina Tearoom ❶,** at the intersection of Cradle Mountain Rd., only 20min from Cradle Mountain. (☎6492 1318. Open daily 7:30am-5:30pm.)

MARSUPIALS FROM HELL It doesn't spin around faster than you can see it, and it's rarely seen in convict stripes. Still, the Tasmanian devil is a remarkable creature. These marsupials are rarely more than 45cm high and aren't built for speed, being far more adept at climbing than at running. Their jaws are their most striking feature, full of jagged teeth and usually open wide. These powerful chompers can crush bones up to 7½cm in diameter and allow the devil to eat almost anything. Devils are entirely carnivorous, hunting small mammals as well as scavenging carrion. Once common throughout Australia, they were driven off the mainland by dingoes; however, they thrive in Tasmania to the point of being considered a pest in some areas. While devils' attacks on humans are limited to the occasional theft of souls, they do sometimes kill farm animals. They are also extremely noisy, particularly when feeding, and are very irritating when they take up residence under people's houses. Despite their abundance, you won't often see the nocturnal, secretive critters in the wild; your best hope for spotting one is a wildlife park.

✎ HIKING. Cradle Valley is the northern trailhead for the **Overland Track,** Tasmania's most prominent walk, traversing the length of the Cradle Mountain-Lake St. Clair National Park (see **Overland Track,** p. 524). The Cradle Mountain area has a web of tracks. The free park brochure map is of little use for all but the **Dove Lake Circuit** (2hr.), the most popular and environmentally friendly walk—a beautiful, mostly boardwalked lakeside track through old-growth forest. The map for sale at the Visitors Center ($4.20) is good for all other day-hikes. The first stage of the **Overland Track** and its side tracks offer more arduous climbs: the hike up to **Marions Lookout** (1223m) begins along the Dove Lake track, continuing steeply to the summit, and returning via **Wombat Pool** and **Lake Lilla** (2-3hr.); the ascent of **Cradle Mountain** (1545m) is a difficult hike from Waldheim or Dove Lake past Marions Lookout, involving some boulder-climbing toward the summit (6hr.). Registration is advised for any walks longer than two hours. It rains 275 days a year, is cloudless on only 32, and can snow at any time—dress accordingly. Tracks around the Visitors Center and the Cradle Mountain Lodge include a rainforest walk and **Pencil Pine Falls** (10min.). The lodge organizes bike hire (half-day $20, full-day $25; deposit $200) and a number of activities: walking tours (2½-3hr., $20), canoe trips (2½hr., $40), fly fishing (2½hr., $45), horse riding (1hr., $35), and abseiling (3hr., $40).

LAKE ST. CLAIR   ☎03

Half of the headline act of the **Cradle Mountain-Lake St. Clair National Park,** Lake St. Clair is Australia's deepest lake as well as the source of the River Derwent. Its Aboriginal name is *Leeawuleena* ("sleeping water"), appropriate for this serene juxtaposition of mountain, wood, and water. The lake anchors the southern end of the famous **Overland Track** (see p. 524), with Cradle Mountain at its northern terminus. There are also a number of day hikes and a few family-friendly nature trails near the lake.

Lake cruises with commentary run the length of the lake from the Cynthia Bay jetty. (Daily at 9am, 12:30, and 3pm; in winter also 2pm. Echo Point $15, Narcissus Bay $20.) A return cruise is also available (book ahead at the tourist office; 1½hr.; $25, children $20). **Walking tracks** radiate from **Watersmeet,** 20 minutes from Cynthia Bay. The **Platypus Bay Trail** (1½-2hr.) makes an easy, enjoyable loop through the woods to the water. Longer hikes head west to the sub-alpine forests of **Forgotten** and **Shadow Lakes** (3-4hr.) alongside waratah (flowering Nov.-Dec.); over the ridge, you can tackle steep, weather-beaten **Mt. Rufus** (7hr. return). If you take the ferry out in the morning, the lakeside hike to Cynthia Bay from Narcissus Bay amid rainforest, tea-tree, and buttongrass takes 5hr.; it's 3hr. from Echo Point.

TassieLink (☎ 1300 300 520) **buses** depart from the **Derwent Bridge Wilderness Hotel** and the Visitors Center for: Hobart (2¾hr.; in summer daily, in winter Tu, Th-F, and Su; $36); Launceston (direct 3hr.; in summer M, W, F, and Su; $54); Queenstown (1½hr.; Tu, Th-F, and Su, in summer also W; $21.30); Devonport (6hr., $58.40). From Queenstown, further connections are possible to: Cradle Mountain ($42.30); Devonport ($58.40); Launceston (7½hr., Tu and Th, $74)—see **Queenstown,** p. 527. **Maxwell's Coach and Taxi Service** (☎ 6492 1431) operates a small 24hr. charter service in the Cradle Mountain-Lake St. Clair region to: Derwent Bridge (10min., $6); Frenchman's Cap (30min., $15); Hobart (3hr., $65); and Queenstown (1¾hr., $35). The **Visitors Center** at **Cynthia Bay,** at the southern end of the lake, is accessible via a 5km access road that leaves the Lyell Hwy. just west of Derwent Bridge. Register for any extended walks, especially the Overland Track. (☎ 6289 1172. Open daily Feb.-Dec. 8am-5pm; Jan. 8am-7pm.) Next door, **Lakeside St. Clair** is a tourist info center, restaurant, and booking agency. (☎ 6289 1137. Open daily in summer 9am-8pm, in winter 10am-4pm. Fishing gear $15 per day; canoes $30 per 2hr.)

FROM THE ROAD

LIFE IN THE FAST LANE

I finished the fantastic Overland Track in four days. Since I had left my car at Cradle Mountain, upon reaching Lake St. Clair I had no vehicle. Having met a funny Dutch guy along the road, we decided that we would try to get to the carpark by hitching. As luck would have it, not only were we picked up twice to make it all the way to Cradle Mountain that day, but we were picked up by a race car and one of Tasmania's richest men.

I spent the first day off the Track standing by the road juggling stones, tossing the frisbee we'd used as a plate on our hike, and waiting for a car to take pity on us. After nearly two hours, one finally did, and it happened to be a race car. The driver of the car was the general manager of one of the largest car dealerships in Tasmania, and the car had been a pace car for the rally race. Though I had to coach myself not to vomit while sliding around in the back seat, Matt (the Dutch guy) and I got to ride all the way to Queenstown in this leather-interior race car.

After being dropped off at the end of Queenstown, Matt and I decided to attempt to get to Cradle that night. A small and powerful Mercedes stopped in front of us and motioned for us to hop in. The driver of this fantastic car was none other than Roger Smith, one of the richest Tasmanians ever. Matt and I were overwhelmed and shocked at our good luck—to the race-car driver and the multi-millionaire we give great thanks. —**Holly Fling**

Let's Go does not recommend hitchhiking, even with millionaires.

The park has free **camping ❶** sites within the entrance with walking access only and pit toilets. The closest camping is a 10min. walk from Cynthia Bay toward Watersmeet; other sites are located at **Shadow Lake, Echo Point,** and **Narcissus Bay. Lakeside St. Clair ❶** has several accommodations just outside the park entrance with coin-op showers, a pay phone, and a kitchen with a wood-fire stove. (Sites $6 per person, powered for 2 $15; doona $5; electrically-heated backpacker bunks $25.) Opposite the Lake St. Clair access road on the Lyell Hwy. is the barn-sized **Derwent Bridge Wilderness Hotel ❸,** which has **petrol.** Backpacker rooms are in the cramped, modular units detached from the main hotel building. (☎ 6289 1144. Singles and doubles $25.) The hotel serves **meals ❷** at reasonable prices. (Open noon-2pm and 6-8pm.)

> ⚠ **COLD KILLS.** Many people come to Tasmania to hike the endless, untamed wilderness. Make no mistake: Tasmania's wilderness is still wild and can kill you. The greatest hazard in the wilderness is the unruly weather that can shift from zephyr to gale in a heartbeat. Even in the warmer months, carry heavy and waterproof clothing to prevent hypothermia, a lowering of the body's core temperature that can be fatal (it can snow, even blizzard, in summer). Dehydration is also a common cause of hypothermia, so take care to stay hydrated. The way to avoid hypothermia is preparation: plan your trip wisely. Do not attempt bushwalks without the proper equipment and experience. Ask about the expected conditions. Wear wool or fiber pile clothing, including gloves and a hat. Wet cotton, especially denim, is deadly. The Parks and Wildlife Service can advise on gear.

THE OVERLAND TRACK

Connecting **Cradle Mountain** and **Lake St. Clair** through 80km of World Heritage wilderness, the Overland Track is Australia's most famous trail. Every year, approximately 8000 folks attempt the track and most take five to eight days to complete it. Purists contend that the track has become a congested highway, but its grandeur cannot be denied. The ascent of the state's tallest peak, **Mt. Ossa** (1617m), makes a good daytrip. The fickle weather will undoubtedly soak a portion of your journey. See **The Overland Track,** p. 526, for an overview of its various sections.

The heavy traffic is having a disastrous impact on the path's fragile alpine ecosystems, so practicing minimum-impact bushwalking is crucial. Stay on the track, spread out when there is no track, walk on rocks, wear lightweight walking boots, rotate campsites, and use fuel stoves only. The *Essential Bushwalking Guide* is available at the normal brochure kiosks. The track huts fill easily, so hikers must carry **tents.** If you are planning to walk the track, write to request an information kit at the **Parks and Wildlife Service.** (☎ 6492 1133; fax 6492 1120. Cradle Mountain Visitor Center, P.O. Box 20, Sheffield TAS 7306.) The national park permit costs $13.20 and a copy of the *Overland Track Map and Notes* ($10) is essential. The track itself can be undertaken from either Cradle Mountain (see p. 521) or Lake St. Clair (see p. 523); starting from Cradle Mountain gives the slight downhill advantage of heading toward Lake St. Clair and also allows for a ferry trip if necessary.

STRAHAN ☎ 03

The only community of any size on the entire west coast, Strahan is Tasmania's ecotourism capital, serving as a gateway to Franklin-Gordon Wild Rivers National Park and to all the glories of the southwest wilderness, including the World Heritage Area. Little more than a sleepy fishing village for most of the 20th century, Strahan vaulted into prominence when environmental protestors sailed from the town's wharf, situated on Macquarie Harbour, to successfully blockade the construction of dams on the Franklin and lower Gordon Rivers in the early 1980s. Since then, environmentalism is on the rise and tourists come by the boatloads and planeloads to experience the reverberations of a good cause.

⌷ TRANSPORTATION. TassieLink (☎ 1300 300 520) **buses** through Queenstown (45min., $7) to: Devonport (5½-7hr., $37.10); Hobart (5¼-6½hr.; Tu, Th-F, and Su, in summer also W; $45) via Lake St. Clair (4hr., $21.30); Launceston (7hr.; Tu, Th, and Sa; $53) via Cradle Mountain (3½-4½hr.; Tu, Th, and Sa, in summer also M; $60). Intuitively enough, **West Coast Bike Hire** (☎ 6245 0680) rents bikes, and **Strahan and West Coast Taxis** provides taxis (☎ 0417 516 171).

⚑ PRACTICAL INFORMATION. The **Strahan Visitors Center,** on the Esplanade, is run by a theater company. The center also has the cheapest **Internet** in town at $3 per 30min. (☎ 6471 7622. Open daily Nov.-Apr. 10am-7pm; May-Oct. 10am-6pm.) The **Parks and Wildlife Office,** in the historic customs house on the Esplanade, sells passes to national parks. (☎ 6471 7122. Open M-F 9am-5pm.) **Azzas** (see below) has **petrol** and an **ATM** inside. The **police** (☎ 6471 8000) are on Beach St., and the **post office** is at the Customs House (open M-F 9am-5:30pm). **Postal Code:** 7468.

⌂⌂ ACCOMMODATIONS AND FOOD. For a treat, the **Cape Horn ❺** cabins on Frazer St. have a fantastic view of the water and offer a pleasant stay without the outrageous prices that seem to plague the town. (☎ 6471 7169. Continental breakfast $5 per person; fully contained studio $65-85; self-contained cottage $75-105, extra adult $20, extra child $15.) The **Strahan YHA ❷,** 43 Harvey St., has kitchens and a resident platypus. From the Strahan wharf, with your back to the water, go left along the Esplanade; as it goes inland, it becomes Bay St. and then Innes St. Take a right onto Andrew St. and the first right onto Harvey St.; the hostel is right before the hill. (☎ 6471 7255; strahancentral@trump.net.au. Reception daily 4-8pm. Dorms $21.50, members $18; twins $47/$40; doubles $54/$47.) The **Strahan Caravan Tourist Park ❶,** on the corner of Andrew and Innes St. near the hostel, has basic amenities and a tiny kitchen with no utensils or pots. (☎ 6471 7239. Reception daily 8am-7pm. Sites for 2 $15, powered $20; on-site vans for 2 $45; ensuite cabins $65-75.) **Strahan Central ❶** is a posh cafe and crafts store on the corner of Herald St. and the Esplanade. (☎ 6471 7612. Open M-F 9am-5:30pm, Sa-Su 10am-5:30pm. Meals $6.50-13.) The hotels also offer good counter meals. **Azzas,** near the campground, has **groceries.** (Open M-Sa 6:30am-9pm, Su 6:30am-8:30pm.)

TASMANIA

THE OVERLAND TRACK Here is an overview of Oz's most famous trail.

Ronny Creek to Waterfall Valley (10km return; 3-5hr.) The first ascent past Crater Lake is the steepest of the entire hike. A short walk through rainforest brings you to an old abandoned hut, a perfect place for a breather as the trek heads straight up on a rocky walk with large steps up above the lake; this area of the trek is the most difficult, but the top features a breathtaking view from **Marions Lookout.** The track leads to **Kitchen Hut** and then **Cradle Mountain.** The track remains flat before heading down to a plateau next to **Benson Peak** and a cliff with views of the valleys. The trail narrows in the forest before rounding the corner to Waterfall Valley Hut.

Waterfall Valley to Lake Windemere (7¾km return; 1½-2½hr.) This portion lands in a flat, open moor. The track's boardwalk is rotting in many spots and the trail gets rocky as you head towards Lake Windemere. **Barn Bluff** looms behind as you are surrounded by pencil pines. With a slight incline, the path heads to a great view of Windemere after circling **Lake Holmes.** The trail then heads to the lake (no camping allowed). Be careful to stay on the track in this ecologically vulnerable area. After rounding **Lake Windemere,** Windemere Hut is only about 500m on the right.

Lake Windemere to Pelion Hut (16¾km return; 6hr.) The track begins in the marsh area of **Pine Forest Moor** but quickly enters rainforest for a steady climb to Pelion Hut, becoming a rocky road with eerie white and scraggly trees before heading back into the woods. After multiple river crossings, the track plateaus, offering a view of Mt. Oakleigh, Pelion East, and Mt. Ossa at the **Forth Gorge Lookout.** Heading back into the woods, the track slopes upward, emerging after a continuous uphill along the old Innes Track at the **Frog Flats.** The track then returns to a steady climb of the other side of the valley through the woods to the plains and New Pelion Hut. This portion gets little sun and is well worn, so look out for the mud and the track lines.

Pelion Hut to Kia Ora Hut (9km return; 3hr.) The track quickly enters the forest before heading into the eucalypts of the **Douglas Valley.** The moist and dark walk climbs 300m uphill in 4km to reach the **Pelion Gap,** which has a great view. The last bit of the track to Kia Ora is relatively flat and exposed (look out for snakes) in Pinestone Valley with multiple glacier erratics. The track briefly enters forest before arriving at Kia Ora Hut. The Kia Ora Hut is a short walk from a swimming hole and waterfall.

Mount Ossa Summit (3hr. return) This strenuous hike to the summit of Tasmania's tallest mountain cannot be missed. A steep but short forest climb leads to a boardwalk which encircles around the peak to the base of **Mt. Doris,** ascending to a plateau. This portion of the track is hard to see during the ascent and crosses over and up large rocks. The track leads up one final summit to reach the large and level top of Mt. Ossa, offering one of the best views in Australia.

Kia Ora Hut to Windy Ridge Hut (10km. return; 2¾-3¾hr.) The track travels beneath **Castle Crag** before hitting **Du Cane Hut.** The track then enters the sassafras and myrtle forest of **King Billy.** Splitting off from the main track are paths to **D'Alton Falls** and **Ferguson Falls,** along the **Mersey River.** Just 15 minutes ahead, the track for the **Hartnett Falls** splits off to the left. A slight incline of 200m over 2km brings you to the top of the **Du Cane Gap.** After the small summit, the track descends steeply, becoming narrow, muddy, and bumpy.

Windy Ridge Hut to Narcissus Hut (9km return; 3hr.) This flat stretch runs mostly in dark eucalypt forest. Narcissus is nearby when you hear the birds.

Narcissus Hut to Cynthia Bay (17½km return; 5hr.) This easy walk through lush rainforest divides: one path leads to Lake Marion and the other continues onward on the Overland. The Echo Point Hut is nearly halfway from Narcissus, along the edge of Lake St. Clair. The last few hours of the Overland flatten out into lush rainforest.

◆◪ **SIGHTS AND ACTIVITIES.** Sailing into its ninth year and still going strong, the local play *The Ship That Never Was*, humorously explores the last great escape from Sarah Island's penal settlement. (Shows Jan. daily at 5:30 and 8:30pm, Feb.-Dec. 5:30pm. $12, concessions $9.) Also in the Visitors Center is **West Coast Deflections,** an exhibit on Aboriginal and settler life which features artwork and reconstructions of their dwellings ($3.50, concessions $2.50). The track to **Hogarth Falls** (40min. return) a few hundred meters from central Strahan, is rampant with wildlife. Accessed through **People's Park,** the track follows **Botanical Creek,** home to aquatic critters, including the elusive platypus. North of town at the end of Harvey Rd., **Ocean Beach** stretches from Macquarie Head in the south to Trial Harbour over 30km north. The longest beach in Tasmania, its brooding surf and windy dunes *makes swimming unsafe.* In late Sept., thousands of **mutton-birds** descend on the beach after flying 15,000km from their Arctic summer homes and go about laying their one egg of the season. Observe from the wooden platform to reduce erosion. The fantastic **Henty Dunes** rise 30m high just 14km towards Zeehan. The dunes are sacred to the Aborigines, though 4WD tours explore the area and camping and dogs are allowed (though the area has no amenities). Consider going by bike or taxi ($2 one-way) to avoid parking fees.

Strahan is at the northern end of the fully protected Macquarie Harbour, one of Australia's largest natural harbors at 100km^2. The placid, tannin-stained waters become choppy only at **Hell's Gates**—the narrow and dangerous strait where the harbor meets the Southern Ocean. The strait is the smallest in the world leading into a harbor and many ships have been wrecked on surrounding reefs and rocks.

◪**World Heritage Cruises,** on the Esplanade, runs the least expensive trips through the harbor and up the Gordon River (south of Sarah Island), including passage through Hell's Gates and into the tempestuous Southern Ocean, a one-hour guided tour of Sarah Island, and 30min. at Heritage Landing up-river to admire a 2000-year-old Huon pine. (☎6471 7174. Smorgasbord $9. 5½hr.; departs daily 9am; $55, children $25; YHA discount 10%.) **Gordon River Cruises** offer similar trips with posher seating and dining arrangements. (☎1800 628 286; $55-118, lunch buffet $12 on lower decks). **West Coast Yacht Charters,** on the Esplanade, offers sailing trips to **Sir John Falls, Heritage Landing,** and other sites. (☎6471 7422. 1 night $140; 2 nights $360.) The **Wild Rivers Jet** gives a faster and more violent tour of the King River. (☎6471 7174. $48.) **Wilderness Air** has pricey seaplane flights to Sir John Falls that venture far beyond cruise-accessible territory. (☎6471 7280. 1½hr., $132.) **World Heritage Scenic Flights** (☎6471 7718) tours surrounding heritage areas and Cradle Mountain by plane or helicopter ($110-180). **Strahan Adventures** (☎6471 7776) offers kayak tours to hunt for platypi (3hr., $80) or history tours around the harbor for $50. **4-Wheelers** offers guided 4-wheeler adventure tours on the Henty Sand Dunes (☎0419 508 175; $35) and **Devilish Adventures Sandboarding** rents sandboards and toboggans (☎0419 646 738; $20 per hr.).

QUEENSTOWN

☎03

In 1883, Mick and Bill McDonough, also known, for mysterious reasons, as the Cooney Brothers, discovered a large outcropping of copper; initially thinking they'd struck iron, they termed it the Iron Blow. Now the story gets somewhat complicated. The **Mount Lyell Gold Mining Company** formed in 1888, searching not for iron or copper but rather for gold. But only two ounces of the precious metal were discovered in every ton of rock, so the Company redirected its efforts toward copper in 1891, by which time millions of pounds of copper had already slipped away. The smelter they built to process the copper ore wreaked environmental havoc. Nearly every large tree in the surrounding hills was felled to feed the smelter, while the young growth was killed by the thick yellow sulphur haze

TASMANIA

released during the pyritic processing; additionally, the newly exposed topsoil was washed into the Queen River by heavy rainfall. The town (pop. 2200 and falling) currently resembles a lunar wasteland in the midst of dense vegetation.

The **Mt. Lyell Mine** still chugs along, with tours exploring the working areas. All tours leave from the office at 1 Driffield St. Daily surface tours visit the old open-cut mines, the working copper mine, and other sites. (☎ 6471 2388. Book ahead. 1hr. Daily Sept.-May 9:15am and 4:30pm, June-Oct. 9:15am and 4pm. $15, children $7. Underground tours 2½hr., $55.) The old Iron Blow open-cut mine, just off the Lyell Hwy. near **Gomanston,** offers views of surrounding barren hills and of the water-filled crater. The **ABT Wilderness Railway Restoration Project,** a restored railway will, once completed, leave from Queenstown Station on Driffield St. and go to Strahan. Call ☎ 6471 1700 for completion details and current destinations.

The thin road to Queenstown snakes above steep ravines (allow 45min. to Strahan). **TassieLink** (☎ 1300 300 520) runs to: Hobart (4¾hr.; Tu, Th-F, and Su, in summer also W; $45) via Lake St. Clair (2hr., $36); Launceston (5-6hr.; Tu, Th, and Sa, in summer also M; $53) via Cradle Mt. (2½hr., $21) and Devonport (4-5hr., $37.10); and Strahan (45min.; Tu, Th-F, and Su; $7). The **Mt. Lyell Mine Office** is the town information center. (☎ 6471 2388. Open daily in summer 8am-5pm, in winter 10am-4pm.) **Parks and Wildlife** (☎ 6471 2511) is represented by **Centrelink/Service Tasmania,** 34 Orr St., next to the post office. (☎ 1300 135 513. Open M-F 9am-5pm. Free Internet.) The **post office** (open M-F 9am-5pm) is at 32 Orr St. **Postal Code:** 7467.

The **Empire Hotel ❷,** 2 Orr St., retains some of the former glory of its heyday as a miners' pub. (☎ 6471 1699. Meals $10-20. Singles $25; twins and doubles $40, with bath $50.) **Queenstown Cabin and Tourist Park ❶,** 17 Grafton St., is across the river, 2km from town center. (☎ 6471 1332. Sites $9, for two $18; powered $10/$20; backpacker beds $20/$27; on-site caravans $40/$8; self-contained cabins for 2 $65.)

FRANKLIN-GORDON WILD RIVERS NATIONAL PARK

After the completion of the Gordon River Dam project in the early 1970s, Hydro Tasmania proposed a new dam along the lower Gordon, just below its intersection with the Franklin. This proposal set off years of river blockades and over 1200 civilian arrests. Conservationists of the early 1980s were successful in scuttling the scheme, and the National Park became part of the new **Tasmanian Wilderness World Heritage Area.** On its way from Strahan to Hobart, the **Lyell Hwy.** (A10) runs between Queenstown and the Derwent Bridge through the park, which is otherwise roadless for kilometers to the north and south. To use any of the Park's facilities, purchase a National Parks Pass ($3.30 per person, $10 per vehicle per day up to 8 people), and *Wild Way,* which lists points of interest along the Lyell Hwy.

Three walks in particular stand out. The 10min. **Nelson Falls Nature Trail,** hidden in wet rainforest 25km east of Queenstown, leads to a lovely cataract. ▓**Donaghys Hill Lookout** (40min. return), 50km east of Queenstown, should not be missed. The track holds mind-blowing views of the Franklin River Valley and **Frenchman's Cap,** its principal peak (1443m, 3- to 5-day return hike to the top). The **Franklin River Nature Trail,** 60km east of Queenstown, is a well-maintained 20min. circuit through rainforest. Between Queenstown and Nelson Falls, **Lake Burbury ❶** has swimming, boating, trout fishing, and camping surrounded by mountains. (No showers or laundry. Sites $5.) Between Nelson Falls and Donaghys Hill, the **Collingwood River** also has free basic **camping ❶** with fireplaces and picnic facilities. Roadside lookouts at **Surprise Valley** and **King William Saddle** (67km and 70km east of Queenstown, respectively) offer views of the eastern side of the wilderness area. The saddle marks a major divide of Tasmania, with the dry plains and highlands to the east; to the west, an annual rainfall of 2.5m flows into the Franklin-Gordon rivers, through wet rainforest, and out to Macquarie Harbour.

THE NORTHWEST

The ferry brings most Tasmanian visitors to the Northwest first, and after time on the Overland Track and the Franklin River, many have a hard time leaving. World Heritage wilderness is the big draw in the Northwest, punctuated by seaports on the northwest coast and mining towns on the western highways. As an Aboriginal homeland, a fierce wilderness, an ecotourism jackpot, a mining mother lode, and a land of colonial convict myth-memory, the Northwest sees the currents that dominate Tasmania's identity play out their drama in the starkest relief.

DEVONPORT   ☎ 03

It might come as a shock that so many people arrive in Tasmania through Devonport (pop. 25,000); its grim waterfront on the Mersey River, dominated by a cluster of huge gray silos, seems hardly inviting. Though most visitors primarily use Devonport as a gateway to Tassie, a pleasant afternoon can be spent north of town walking around the point to explore the Aboriginal museum and its rock carvings.

▐⟌ TRANSPORTATION

The **airport** is 6km east of the city center on the Bass Hwy. **Regional Express** (☎ 13 17 13) and Qantas-affiliated **Southern** (☎ 13 13 13) operate flights to Melbourne. (1hr., 4 per day, $125-250.) Though a couple of buses serve the airport, times vary and service is generally inconsistent. **Taxis Combined** is a pricier but more reliable alternative. (☎ 6424 1431. One way to town $17-20.) The **ferry** *Spirit of Tasmania* departs from Melbourne. Breakfast, dinner, and accommodation are provided. (☎ 13 20 10 or book ahead at Visitor Centre. 13-14½hr.; M 7:30pm, W and F 6pm; return Tu and Th 6pm, Sa 4pm; $124-158, cars $40-55, bikes $21-27.) The **Mersey River Ferry "Torquay"** transports from east Devonport back to the city center. With your back to the Spirit of Tasmania terminal, turn left at the road and head down the first street to reach the water; the shuttle ferry wharf is straight ahead. (Runs M-Sa on demand; $1.70, children and students $1.20, bikes 50¢.)

Redline Coaches, 9 Edward St. (☎ 1300 360 000; open daily 6am-9pm), runs daily buses to: Hobart (4½-5hr., 2 per day, $38.10); Launceston (1½hr., 2-5 per day, $15.70); Stanley (2-2½hr., 1-2 per day, $18); Wynward (1½hr., 1-2 per day, $11.40) via Burnie (1hr., 2-6 per day, $8). **TassieLink** (☎ 1300 300 520) buses leave the Visitors Center to: Cradle Mountain Visitors Center (1½hr., in summer 1 per day, $28); Strahan (6hr., $44.10) via Queenstown (5hr.; Tu, Th, and Sa, in summer also M; $37.10). Major car rental companies have counters at the airport and ferry terminals, including **Hertz** (☎ 6424 1013; open daily 8am-6pm; also at 26 Oldaker St.) and **Thrifty,** across from the ferry. (☎ 6427 9119. Open daily 6:30am-7pm. $42-69 per day; age 21-24 $15 per day surcharge.) Smaller firms are often cheaper; try **Advance**, at the airport and 11 Esplanade (☎ 6427 0888; open daily 9am-5pm) or **RentABug,** 5 Murray St. (☎ 6427 9034. Open M-F 8:30am-5:30pm, Sa 8:30am-noon.)

▐⟌ ORIENTATION

The port of Devonport is the mouth of the **Mersey River,** with the ferry terminal on its eastern bank. Devonport is bounded to the west by the **Don River** and to the south by the **Bass Highway** (Hwy. 1), which includes the only bridge across the Mersey. The city center lies on the western bank, with **Formby Street** at the river's edge and the **Rooke Street Mall** one block inland, both intersected by **Best Street** and **Stewart Street** running away from the river; most of the essentials lie within a block of these four streets. North of this square, Formby St. leads to **Mersey Bluff** and **Bluff Beach** at the western head of the river. The Bass Hwy. heads west to Burnie (46km) and southeast to Launceston (97km) and Hobart (300km). B14 leads through Spreyton and Sheffield to **Cradle Mountain** (1½hr.).

⚑ PRACTICAL INFORMATION

Tasmanian Travel and Visitor Information Centre, 92 Formby Rd., around the corner from McDonald's, books accommodations and transport. (☎6424 8176. Open daily 9am-5pm; Travel Centre only M-F.) ☒**The Backpackers' Barn,** 10-12 Edward St., has all the info you need about bushwalking and the Overland Track. The building also offers a restroom with book exchange, showers, and a bulletin board for announcements. The Barn will even ship boxes of superfluous gear to Hobart for $7.50 each. (☎6424 3628. Open M-F 9am-6pm, Sa 9am-noon. Gear can be sent back by Redline Coaches for a fee. Lockers $1 per day, $5 per week, with optional free backpack storage for 1 day. Tents $8 per day, $40 for Overland Track; sleeping bags $5; packs $25; cook set $5; stove $25. **Store 44,** next to the post office on Stewart St., has the cheapest **Internet.** ($4 per hr. Open M-F 7am-5:30pm, Sa 7am-2pm.)

⚑ ACCOMMODATIONS

Formby Road Hostel, 16 Formby Rd. (☎6423 6563), 500m south of the city center. This brick Victorian house features roomy common spaces, a clean kitchen, and excellent company. Linens $3. Laundry. Free bike use. Reception open whenever necessary. Dorms $14; doubles $35. Cash only. ❶

Tasman House Backpackers, 169 Steele St. (☎6423 2335). Take Mersey Link bus #20 from Rooke St. to stop 173, across from the hostel. From Formby Rd. on the river, go west along Steele St., past the sign and around the block to reach the entrance—left on Lovett St. and a quick left on Tasman St. Lacks a homey feel, but the rooms are clean and the kitchen often has free veggies and fresh bread. Free city center pickup; $3 ferry shuttle. Free storage. Laundry. Internet $5 per hr. Reception daily 8am-10pm. Dorms $12; twins $14; doubles $30, ensuite $38. VIP. **Tasman Bush Tours** operates out of the house, with day-trips from $53 and 6-day Overland Track trips from $690. ❶

Molly Malone's Irish Pub, 34 Best St. (☎6424 1898), is the only hostel remotely near the city center. Rooms have sinks, heat, and live music from the downstairs pub on weekends. No laundry or parking. Key deposit $10. 4-night max. stay. Check-in at the pub. Dorms $14; doubles $50. ❶

Mersey Bluff Caravan Park, Bluff Rd., on Mersey Bluff beach (☎6424 8655). Reception 8am-noon, 1pm-6pm, 7pm-9:30pm. Sites $7 per person, powered for 2 $16.50; on-site caravans $44; cabins $55. ❶

◗◖ FOOD AND ENTERTAINMENT

The **Rooke Street Mall** overflows with standard chippers and fast food. The tastiest, most original meal in town may be found at ☒**Café Natur** ❶, next to the Backpackers Barn on Edward St. Grab a veggie burger ($5.50) and a fresh fruit smoothie for lunch. (☎6424 1917. Open M-F 9:30am-4:30pm, Sa 9:30am-2pm.) **The Cheesecake Shop** ❶ bakes fantastic cakes daily and offers the **Movie Deal:** $12 buys you a drink, a piece of cake, and a movie ticket at the cinema next door. (Open M 10am-7pm,; Tu-Th, Su 10am-9:30pm; F-Sa 10am-10pm.) Renusha's Indian Restaurant ❷, 153 Rooke St., near the corner of Oldaker St., will spice up your diet. (☎6424 2293. Open M-Th 5:30-9:30pm, F-Sa 5:30-11pm, Su 5:30-8:30pm. Takeaway $11-14; eat-in $15-19 with $15 minimum charge.) Coles **supermarket** is on Formby Rd. and Best

St. (Open M-W and Sa 8am-6pm, Th-F 8am-9pm.) **Spurs Saloon,** 18-22 King St., has a country-western theme, video games, and pool tables that attract a young crowd. (☎6424 7851. F-Sa live music. Open W-F 4pm-1:30am, Sa 5pm-1:30am.) **Warehouse,** next to Spurs, is actually a dance club. (Cover $5-6. Open F-Sa 10:30pm-3am.)

⊙ SIGHTS

Tiagarra Aboriginal Cultural Centre and Museum, a 30min. walk from the city center to Mersey Bluff near the lighthouse, explores 40,000 years of Tasmanian Aboriginal history. (☎6424 8250. Open daily 9am-5pm. $3.30, children and students $2.20.) A 15min. walk around the bluffs leads to controversial **rock engravings**—a few have been stolen, and some skeptics say wind and rain are the true artisans. From the lighthouse, the shimmering, blue Bass Strait and surrounding red-orange cliffs are gorgeous. A pleasant bicycling and walking path leads all the way to the point from the city and rounds the edge towards the back beach.

NEAR DEVONPORT

The **Leven Canyon Reserve,** about 60km southwest of the city near Nietta, has a lookout with stunning views of Leven Gorge. To get there, take the Bass Hwy. west, then B15 south to Nietta, then C128 to the Canyon. A bit to the north of the canyon off C125, the **Gunns Plains Caves** feature underground wonders as well as a creek with platypi and freshwater crayfish. (☎6429 1335. Tours daily on the hour 10am-4pm. $9, children $4.)

  Narawntapu National Park, formerly known as Asbestos Range, is a small coastal heathland reserve 40km east of Devonport. With ample fishing and swimming opportunities at Bakers Beach, the park is also popular for its walking tracks and abundant wildlife. The park is accessible by car only via three gravel roads. From Devonport take C740, which heads north from B71 between Devonport and Exeter. Register to camp at **Springlawn,** just past the park entrance. Sites have flush toilets, BBQ, tables, water, and a public telephone. (☎6428 6277. Park fees apply.) Two more scenic **camping ❶** areas are 3km farther down the road on the beach near **Griffiths Point** and **Bakers Point,** and have pit toilets, fireplaces, tables, and water. (Firewood included. Sites $4, families $10.) The easy **Springlawn Nature Walk** (45min.) passes through scrub and lagoons past wallabies and pademelons (their smaller relatives). The moderate track continues up to **Archers Knob,** revealing a view of the surrounding hills and coastline. (2hr. return.)

DELORAINE AND SURROUNDS   ☎03

In the foothills of the Great Western Tiers, huddled in the agricultural Meander Valley between Devonport and Launceston, Deloraine functions as a perfect base for exploring the World Heritage wilderness to the southwest.

◨🔃 TRANSPORTATION AND PRACTICAL INFORMATION. Redline buses (☎1300 360 000) run out of Cashworks, 29 W Church St. (☎6362 2143), with daily service to: Burnie (1¾hr., $16); Devonport (1½hr., $11); and Launceston (45min., $8). **Deloraine Visitor Information Center,** 98 Emu Bay Rd., doubles as the folk museum. (☎6362 3471. Open M-F 9:30am-4pm, Sa 1-3:30pm, Su 2-4pm. Museum $2.) Services include: **ANZ** with **ATM** on the corner of Emu Bay Rd. (open M-Th 9:30am-4pm, F 9:30am-5pm); **police** (☎6362 4004), on Westbury Pl.; a **pharmacy** at 62-64 Emu Bay Rd. (open M-F 8:45am-5:30pm, Sa 9am-noon); **Online Access Centre,** behind the library at 2 Emu Bay Rd., with **Internet** (☎6362 3537; open M 10am-5pm, Tu and Th 10am-4pm, W and F 10am-7pm, Su 1-4pm; $3 up to 30min., $5 per hr.); **post office** at 10 Emu Bay Rd. (☎6362 2156. Open M-F 9am-5pm.) **Postal Code:** 7304.

ACCOMMODATIONS AND FOOD. The **Deloraine Highview Lodge YHA** ❷, 8 Blake St., is the best hostel around, with views of Quamby Bluff and the Great Western Tiers, comfy bunks, and proprietors who can arrange tours. Go up Emu Bay Rd., turn right on Beefeater St., then left on Blake St. (☎ 6362 2996. Reception M, W, and F 10am-noon and 5-10pm; Tu, Th, and Sa-Su 8-10am and 5-10pm. Dorms $19.50, YHA $16.) The **Apex Caravan Park** ❶, on West Pde., parallel to Emu Bay Rd. off the roundabout, has river sites and showers for $4 per person. (☎ 6362 2345. Sites for 2 $12, powered $15. V/MC.) For lunch, stop in at **Deloraine Deli** ❷, 36 Emu Bay Rd., and grab some homemade lasagna for $11. (☎ 6362 2127. Open M-F 9am-5pm, Sa 9am-2:30pm.) The Woolworth **supermarket** is at 58 Emu Bay Rd. (Open M-W and Sa 8am-6pm, Th-F 8am-9pm.)

PARKS. A 1½hr. drive southwest from Deloraine will take you to an awe-inspiring section of the **Walls of Jerusalem National Park.** A hike (8hr. return) to the top of Mt. Jerusalem gives an amazing 360° view. Less trafficked than Cradle Mountain, the park contains the same craggy bluffs, vales, and ridges, with lakes and stretches of green moss. The mostly duckboarded track begins from a carpark with a pit toilet off the Mersey Forest Rd. (C171). The first hour is a steep walk to the park's border and down into the Walls. From there, it's relatively level except for inclines through the gates of the Walls. A compass, a $9 park map, and over-night equipment are required, even for dayhikes, due to the highly variable weather. The Walls are not to be taken lightly; rangers recommend it only to expe-rienced hikers. (☎ 6363 5182. Call ahead. Park fees apply.)

About 35km west of Deloraine off B12, **Mole Creek Karst National Park** (☎ 6363 5182), is home to two spectacular caves. The enormous **Marakoopa Cave** features a glowworm chamber, while **King Solomon's Cave** is much smaller with fewer steps and more colorful formations. Temperatures in the caves can be a chilling 9° Cel-sius. Park fees do not apply, but NPWS runs tours for a fee. ($8.80, both caves $14; children $4.40; families $22.)

About 25km south of Deloraine on A5 and then C513 awaits the fantastic **Liffey Forest Reserve.** If your car can handle the steep, potholed dirt road, it is well worth the visit, as it is less frequented by tourists and houses some of the lushest forests in Tasmania. Hike out to the great **Liffey Falls** (45min. return) on the well main-tained track and viewing blocks.

THE NORTHWEST COAST: ALONG THE A2

West of Devonport, Bass Hwy. 1 and A2 Hwy. trace the northern coast of Tasma-nia. Bass Hwy. passes through Ulverstone and Burnie before reaching the junction where A2 continues northwest and A10 branches south toward Queenstown, Zee-han, and Strahan. From Burnie, A2 continues past Wynyard (18km) and Rocky Cape National Park (30km) to Smithton (74km) and nearby Stanley (66km).

BURNIE. The area's major transport hub is Burnie, a declining paper mill town. **Redline,** 117 Wilson St. (☎ 1300 360 000), connects Burnie to: Boat Harbour (30min., M-F 1-2 per day, $5); Deloraine (1½hr., 2-6per day, $16); Devonport (45min., 2-6 per day, $8.40); Launceston (2¼hr., 2-5 per day, $21.10); Stanley (1½hr., 1-2 per day M-F, $12); Wynyard (20min., M-F 1-2 per day, $3). The **Tasmanian Travel and Informa-tion Centre** is in the Civic Centre complex. (☎ 6434 6111. Open M-F 9am-5pm, Sa 10am-1pm.) An **ANZ Bank** with an **ATM** is on the corner of Wilson and Cattley St. (Open M-Th 9:30am-4pm, F 9:30am-5pm.) The only budget accommodation is the **Treasure Island Caravan Park** ❶, 253 Bass Hwy., 4km away in Cooee, with an indoor pool. (☎ 6431 1925. Sites $10, powered $12; dorms with kitchen $14; caravans $35; cabins $55.) Burnie's most savory sight is the ☒**Lactos Cheese factory,** on Old Sur-rey Rd. (☎ 6431 2566. Open for free tastings M-F 9am-5pm, Sa-Su 10am-4pm.)

ROCKY CAPE NATIONAL PARK. Rocky Cape National Park (☎6458 1100) features a mountainous coastline, rare flora, and **Aboriginal cave sites.** The two ends of the park are accessible by separate access roads. The 9km eastern access road turns off A2 12km west of Wynyard and leads to walking tracks and **Sisters Beach.** The 4km western access road, 18km further down A2, ends at a lighthouse and great views of Table Cape and the Nut. Aboriginal caves can be accessed from both entrances via short walking tracks; the **Coastal Route** track traverses the length of the park (11km; 3hr.). There is no Visitors Center, but the shops near both entrances stock park brochures. The small park is geared toward day use; the low-growing vegetation is still recovering from a severe bushfire and offers little protection from the sun during extended walks. The **Nut,** a huge volcanic plateau about 20km northeast of Rocky Cape in nearby **Stanley,** makes a good daytrip. Take a steep but short (10-15min.) plod up to the top of the Nut and then a leisurely walk (45min.) around. A **chairlift** goes up (open in summer daily 9:30am-5:30pm, in winter 10am-4pm; $6 return, children $4), and the **Nut buggy tour** carts people around the top ($5; closed in winter).

THE NORTHEAST

Tasmania's northeast is blessed with a sunny disposition. Folks here grow up listening to Melbourne radio, drinking Boag's beer, and disdaining the political antics of the South. The pleasant coastline is dotted by quiet fishing and port towns that make suitable summer holiday spots for families with young children. Both sides of the Tamar (TAY-mer) River are home to vineyards and fruit farms.

LAUNCESTON   ☎03

Built where the North and South Esk rivers join to form the Tamar, Launceston (LON-seh-ston; pop 90,000) is Tasmania's second-largest city and Australia's third-oldest, founded in 1805. The intense historic rivalry between Hobart and Launceston manifests itself most clearly in beer loyalty: Boag's is the ale of choice in the north, Cascade in the south. Though this university town continues to grow, steeple-tops still rise above the town's many red and green roofs, vigilantly guarding Launceston's character, vitality, and old-world Victorian charm.

◤ TRANSPORTATION

Flights: Launceston Airport, south of Launceston on Hwy. 1 to B41. **VirginBlue** flies daily to Melbourne ($89, return $178). **Tasmanian Shuttle Bus Services,** 101 George St., provides airport **shuttles** that meet flights and will pickup from accommodations but only run 9am-6pm. (☎6331 2009. $10.)

Buses: The **Redline Coaches** terminal is at 18 Charles St. (☎6336 1444; reservations 1300 360 000 daily 6am-9pm; www.tasredline.com). Their buses run to: Bicheno (2¾hr., M-F 1 per day, $25); Burnie (2½-3hr., 2-5 per day, $21.10); Deloraine (45min., 2-5 per day, $8); Devonport (1½hr., 2-5 per day, $15.70); George Town (45min.; M-F 2-3 per day; $8.20, $10 from Melbourne ferry); Hobart (2½hr., 2-7 per day, $22.40); Oatlands (1¼hr., 2-7 per day, $16.30); St. Helens (2¾hr., Su-F 1 per day, $22.10); and St. Mary's (2hr., Su-F 1 per day, $18). **TassieLink** buses (☎1300 300 520) leave from Gateway Travel Centre to: Cradle Mountain (3½hr., in summer 1 per day, $44); Lake St. Clair (3hr.; Tu and Th, in summer also F and Su; $74); Strahan (8hr.; Tu, Th-F, and Su; $60) via Queenstown (7hr.; Tu, Th-F, and Su, $53).

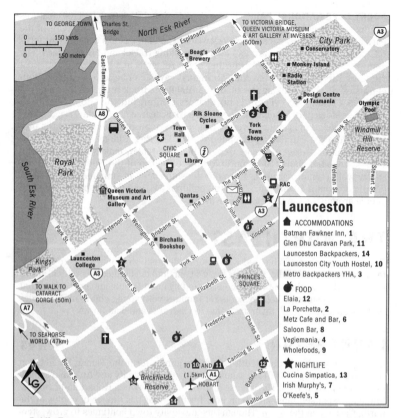

Launceston

ACCOMMODATIONS
Batman Fawkner Inn, **1**
Glen Dhu Caravan Park, **11**
Launceston Backpackers, **14**
Launceston City Youth Hostel, **10**
Metro Backpackers YHA, **3**

FOOD
Elaia, **12**
La Porchetta, **2**
Metz Cafe and Bar, **6**
Saloon Bar, **8**
Vegiemania, **4**
Wholefoods, **9**

NIGHTLIFE
Cucina Simpatica, **13**
Irish Murphy's, **7**
O'Keefe's, **5**

Public Transportation: Metro (☎ 13 22 01) buses run daily 7am-7pm. Fares $1-3. The bright orange **City Go Round bus** (☎ 6336 3133) hits all major tourist destinations including the museums, brewery, and the gorge. 24hr. $6, concessions $3, families $15; buy on board.

Taxis: Taxi Combined (☎ 6331 5555 or 13 10 08). Fare to airport $20-30.

Car Rental: Budget (☎ 6391 8566), at the airport, from $40 per day. Ages 21-24 $18 surcharge. **Economy,** 27 William St. (☎ 6334 3299), from $31, rents to ages 17+.

Automobile Club: RAC Tasmania (☎ 6335 5633, 24hr. 13 11 11), at the corner of York and George St. Open M-F 8:45am-5pm.

Bike Rental: Launceston City Youth Hostel, 36 Thistle St. W, (☎ 6344 9779), starts at $10 per day and but usually rents on a weekly basis with all the gear for long trips. **Rik Sloane Cycles,** 10-14 Paterson St. (☎ 6331 9414), rents 21-speeds for $22 per day, $92.40 per week. Open M-F 9am-5:30pm, Sa 9am-2pm.

ORIENTATION AND PRACTICAL INFORMATION

The town is best explored by foot, since most attractions are within four blocks of the **Brisbane St. Mall** and all the streets are one-way. The city center is bounded on the north by the **North Esk River** and on the west by the **South Esk,** which flows

TASMANIA

through the Cataract Gorge. From here, A8 runs north to George Town; Hwy. 1 heads south to Hobart through the Midlands and west to Deloraine and Devonport; A3 snakes east to St. Helens and the east coast.

Tourist Office: Gateway Tasmania Travel Centre (☎6331 4844, bookings 6331 3679; www.gatewaytas.com.au), on the corner of St. John and Paterson St. 1hr. walking tours from the center M-F 9:45am, $11. Open M-F 9am-5pm, Sa 9am-3pm, Su 9am-noon.

Currency Exchange: Commonwealth Bank, 97 Brisbane St. (☎6337 4432). Open M-Th 9:30am-4pm, F 9:30am-5pm. The mall has several **ATMs.**

Hiking Equipment: Allgoods, 71-79 York St. (☎6331 3644), at St. John St. Huge, inexpensive, and comprehensive, including army surplus and maps. Basic equipment hire at their **Tent City** annex, 60 Elizabeth St. Open M-F 9am-5:30pm, Sa 9am-4pm. For quality equipment at good rates and excellent advice and instruction on all things outdoors in Tasmania, head to ▨ **Launceston City Youth Hostel,** 36 Thistle St. W (☎6344 9779; tasequiphire@email.com). Experienced manager Doug Snare will be happy to help you prepare for your journey and outfit you right down to your socks. Tents from $20 per week, boots from $20 per week, stoves from $7 per week.

Bookstore: Birchalls, 118-120 Brisbane St. (☎6331 3011). Australia's oldest bookshop. Open M-F 8:30am-6pm, Sa 8:30am-5pm, Su 10am-4pm. **All Booked Up,** 81 Brisbane St. (☎6334 7066). Excellent selection, especially of literature and Australiana. Open M-F 8:45am-5:30pm, Sa 9am-4pm, Su 11am-3pm.

Library: 1 Civic Sq. (☎6336 2625). Open M-Th 9:30am-6pm, F 9:30am-8pm, Sa 9:30am-12:30pm. **Internet** $2.50 per 15min. (see below).

Police: (☎6336 3701), on Cimitiere St. Enter through Civic Square.

Internet: Service Tasmania (☎1300 366 773), in Henty House, Civic Sq., has 3 free terminals. Open M-F 8:15am-4:45pm. **Cyber King,** 113 George St. (☎0417 393 540). $5 per 30min., students $4; student Happy Hour M-F 3-6pm $3 per 30min. Open M-F 9am-8pm, Sa 9am-6pm, Su 10am-6pm. Also, see **Library,** above.

Post Office: 107 Brisbane St. (☎6331 9477). Open M-F 9am-5:30pm, Sa 9:30am-1pm. **Postal Code:** 7250.

⌐ ACCOMMODATIONS

▨ **Metro Backpackers YHA,** 16 Brisbane St. (☎6334 4505 or 0401 666 436; www.backpackersmetro.com.au). Swanky addition to the hostel scene in the town center. Wall-to-wall carpeting, comfy lounge with satellite TV, large kitchen and balcony with BBQ, off-street parking, and laundry. Info center twice as good as the official one. Ask manager Mark about his flags. Internet $2 per 10min. Linen $3. Bike rental $15 per day. Reception daily 7:30am-10pm. Dorms in summer $23, YHA $20; in winter $19/$16. Themed doubles and twins in summer $55/$50; in winter $45/$40; family rooms in summer $85/$80; in winter $75/70. ❷

Launceston Backpackers, 103 Canning St. (☎6334 2327; www.launcestonbackpackers.com.au), across from Brickfields Reserve, off Bathurst St., a 7min. walk from the city center. Large kitchen, free long-term storage, and laundry. Internet $2 per 10min. Key deposit in summer $10. Female-only dorms on request. Reception daily 8-11am and 1-10pm. 4- to 6-bed dorms $17; twins $37; doubles $39. VIP discount $1. ❷

Batman Fawkner Inn, 35 Cameron St. (☎6331 7222), next to La Porchetta. If you don't need cooking facilities, hop on over to the Inn to get a clean bed, duvet, towel, ensuite, and a TV all to your own. Complimentary tea and coffee in each room. Singles $25; twins $60; doubles $70; extra bed $10. ❷

Launceston City Youth Hostel, 36 Thistle St. W (☎/fax 6344 9779), opposite the Coats Patons building at Glen Dhu St. Turn right onto Howick from Wellington St., then left onto Glen Dhu St.; or take Metro #24 from Allgoods to stop 8; 15min. walk to town. Large, spacious building with clean beds. Coin-op shower (10¢), free linens, security lockers, and midnight quiet time. No co-ed dorms. Bike and hiking equipment rental. Dorms $15, 3 nights $39; singles $20; family rooms $40. VIP/YHA discount $2. ❶

Glen Dhu Treasure Island Caravan Park, 94 Glen Dhu St. (☎6344 2600), 2km from downtown. Follow directions to City Youth Hostel. Lots of noise from neighboring Hwy. 1. BBQ, showers, laundry, outdoor campers' kitchen with kettle, hot plate, and toaster-oven. Reception daily 8:30am-7pm. Sites for 2 $16, powered $18; caravans $40; cabins $65. MC/V. ❷

🍴 FOOD

Coles **supermarket** is at 198 Charles St. (☎6334 5744. Open M-W and Sa 8am-6pm, Th-F 8am-9pm.) Organic **Wholefoods Launceston** is at 54 Frederick St. (☎6331 7682. Open M-F 10am-6pm, Sa 9am-5pm, Su 11am-5pm.)

La Porchetta, 35 Cameron St. (☎6331 7464). The cheapest good Italian eats in town. No pizza over $11. Eat at the relaxed eatery take it away. Open daily 11:30am-9pm. ❶

Elaia, 238-240 Charles St. (☎6331 3307), 2 blocks south of Princes Sq. Mediterranean decor and classy food. Great focaccia ($10.40). Busy F-Sa for dinner. Mains $11-20. Open M-Sa 9am-late, Su 10am-5pm. ❸

Vegiemania, 64 George St. (☎6331 2535). Tasmania's first vegetarian and vegan restaurant. Omelettes $9, curry from $12. $6 lunch special. Open M-F noon-2pm and 5-10pm, Sa 5-10pm, Su 5-9pm. ❶

The Metz Cafe and Bar, 119 St. John St. (☎6331 7277), on the corner of York St. Upscale pizza pub and wine bar attract a mixed crowd of young business folk, couples, students, and travelers. Pizzas $14-18. Open daily 8am-midnight. ❸

Saloon Bar, 191 Charles St. (☎6331 7355), in Hotel Tasmania. It's hard to find more for your money than at this western teeny-bopper hangout. Heaping plates of roast or mixed veggies for $5. Burgers $7, Porterhouse steak $12. W and Sa live music; cover $3. Kitchen open daily noon-9pm; bar open Su-Tu noon-midnight, W-Sa noon-3am. ❶

👁 SIGHTS

The most spectacular sight in Launceston is the handiwork of the South Esk River—the **Cataract Gorge Reserve.** A 20min. walk from Paterson St. toward Kings Bridge, it's not exactly pristine wilderness; the First Basin of the gorge has been popular since the town's settlement and now hosts peacocks, an exotic tree garden, a restaurant, and a free swimming pool. Walking tracks run on either side of the river from King's Bridge; the one on the north side is easy, while the one on the south climbs to the gorge's rim for excellent views of the cataracts. *It is not advisable to walk around in this area after dark.* The **Band Rotunda,** on the First Basin's north side (cross the Basin on the swinging Alexandra Suspension Bridge), and the **Duck Reach Power Station,** at the far end of the gorge, provide info on the gorge. (☎6337 1288. Rotunda open M-F 9am-4pm, Sa-Su 9am-4:30pm. Power station open daily dawn-dusk.)

The **Queen Victoria Museum and Art Gallery** is split between the exhibits at **Royal Park** and at **Inveresk.** Royal Park, on the corner of Cameron and Wellington St., houses an impressive local and natural history display focusing on Tasmania's wildlife. The upstairs gallery offers a brief but sweet peek of Tasmanian sculpture, paintings, ceramics, and textile art. The Planetarium is part of the complex. The **Inveresk Museum** (cross the river on Tamar St.) houses a Tasmanian art gallery, exhibits on immigration to Tasmania, artifacts from the Pacific, and a fantastic display of ⬛**Aboriginal shell necklaces.** Be sure to check out the Maireener shells and the rice shells. (☎6323 3777. Open daily 10am-5pm. Both museums $10. Planetarium shows Tu-F 3pm, Sa 2 and 3pm. $3.30, children $2.20, families $7.70. No children under 5.)

Launceston is blessed with an abundant supply of parks all around town. The **City Park,** at Tamar and Brisbane St., harbors a war memorial, botanical conservatory, and an enclosure teeming with **Japanese macaque monkeys.** (Open Mar.-Sept. M-F 8:30am-4:30pm, Sa-Su 9am-4:30pm; Oct.-Mar. M-F 8:30am-5:30pm, Sa-Su 9am-5:30pm.)

For sightseeing from an aerial perspective, **Cable Hang Gliding,** in the Trevallyn State Recreation Area, sails above the Trevallyn Dam Quarry beyond the Gorge's Second Basin and the Duck Reach Power Station. (☎0419 311 198. Open Dec.-Apr. daily 10am-5pm; May-Nov. Sa-Su 10am-4pm. $10.) The less dramatic **chairlift** runs across the First Basin. (☎6331 8367. Open Sept.-May daily 9am-4:30pm; June-Aug. Sa-Su 9am-4:30pm. $6.60, children $4.40.)

⬛ ACTIVITIES

A great way to enjoy the city and its fantastic surroundings is on a tour. ⬛**Devil's Playground Ecotours** (☎6458 2020; www.devilsplayground.com.au) offers day tours, with excellent guides, lunch, and all entry fees included. Among the most popular tours are Cradle Mountain (W and Su, $80) and Waterfalls, Caves, and Wildlife (F, $80). For wild adventures, try **Tasmanian Expeditions,** 110 George St. (☎6334 3477 or 1800 030 230. Half-day rock climbing/abseiling $75; 2-day cycling and canoeing $352; 3-day Cradle Mountain and Freycinet National Parks $473.) Finally, spend a day with informative guide Lee on **Tasmanian Wilderness Tours** (☎0418 520 391 or 6394 3212; www.tigerwilderness.com.au) either touring the wine region of the northeast on the Wine and Waterfall Tour (half-day $48, concessions $43, under 16 $20) or exploring Cradle Mountain at the Marakoopa Glow Worm Cave and other stops along the way (full-day $95, concessions $80, under 16 $40).

For more pampered relaxation, the **Aquarius Roman Baths,** 127-133 George St., has an indoor frigidarium (cold bath), tepidarium (warm bath), caldarium (hot bath), and rubarium (heat lamps) in the style of ancient Rome—unfortunately, there are no vomitoriums. (☎6331 2255. Open M-F 8:30am-9pm, Sa-Su 9am-6pm. $20, doubles $33.) For an illuminating overview of the beer-brewing process followed by free samples, take the **Boag's Brewery** tour, 21 Shields St. (☎6331 9311. Open M-Th 2:30pm. Tours 1-1½hr. Free.)

⬛**Seahorse World,** 47km north of Launceston on A7 at Beauty Point, harvests the little creatures for the pet trade, but has several tanks full of the beautiful animals, including varieties like the weedy seadragon. Take the free one-hour tour of the facility that describes the harvesting process, shows the baby seahorses, and finishes with an informative film on the strange animals. (☎6383 4111; www.seahorse.world.com.au. $15, concessions $12, under 16 $8, families $35. Open daily 9:30am-4:30pm; last tour 3:30pm.)

🎵 ENTERTAINMENT

Many downtown pubs have live music on weekends; the best and most popular is **Irish Murphy's,** 211 Brisbane St., two blocks from the mall. (☎6331 4440. Happy Hour F and Su 4-6pm and 9:30-10pm, M-Tu and Sa 9-10pm, W-Th 9:30-10pm. W-Su live music. Cover F-Sa $3. Open Su-W noon-2pm, Th-Sa noon-2am.) Have a pint of Guinness on tap at **O'Keefe's ❶,** on the corner of York and George St. If you just can't make it home, they have dorms upstairs for $15 a bed. (☎6331 4015. Live music W-M 10pm-2:30am. Open daily 11am-3am.) The hip **Cucina Simpatica,** 57 Frederick St., by the Brickfields Reserve, hosts live jazz on Sunday afternoons. (☎6334 3177. Open daily 10am-10pm.)

⚑ DAYTRIPS FROM LAUNCESTON: GEORGE TOWN

North along A8 (50km), on the east side of the cove where the Tamar River meets the Bass Strait, lies George Town. Once considered the capital of the north, George Town now acts more as an historical center and Launceston's port. It does, however, lay claim to the title of the oldest *town* in Australia and the third oldest settlement. Now, mellow and quiet, it affords visitors serene views across the river and—if you're lucky—glimpses of glorious pink sunsets over the western hills.

The town's seafaring history has been preserved in the **Pilot Station & Maritime Museum** in **Low Head,** 5km north of the town. Established in 1805, this convict-built estate is the oldest continuously operating facility of its kind in Australia, with displays on artifacts like beer bottles salvaged from shipwrecks. (☎6382 1143. Open daily 8am-8pm. $3.) The road ends at the **Low Head Lighthouse,** with great views of the peninsula and the *DevilCat.* (☎6382 1211. Gate to the lighthouse locked at 6pm.) **Fairy penguins** and seals use some of the beaches around George Town and Low Head as nesting places during the spring. **Fairy Penguin Twilight Tours** leads nightly tours one hour before sunset. (☎0418 361 860. No tours May-June. $10, children $6.) **Seal & Sea Adventure Tours** offers seal-watching tours of the Hebe Reef and Tenth Island. (☎6382 3452 or 0419 357 028. 3-4hr.; 3 or more people $94 each with $200 min. charge; families $280.)

Riverline buses (☎6382 1484) leave from Pinos Hardware, 21 Elizabeth St.; the Shell Station, 32-36 Main Rd.; the ferry terminal to Launceston (45min.; M-F 2-3 per day; $8.20, $10 from *DevilCat*) and on to Hobart (2½hr., $27). The **Visitors Center** is on the road entering town from the south. (☎6382 1700. Internet $2 per 30min. Open daily Aug.-Sept. 10am-2pm; Oct.-July 9am-5pm.) The **Online Access Centre,** next to the **library,** in Regent Sq., also has **Internet.** (☎6382 1356. Open M-F 9am-1am, Sa-Su noon-1am. $5 per 30min.) **Banks,** the **police station** (☎6382 4040), and the **post office** (open M-F 9am-5pm) cluster on Macquarie St. **Postal Code:** 7253.

George Town itself doesn't warrant more than a day's visit, but if you visit the delightful ⚑**Traveller's Lodge (YHA) ❶,** 4 Elizabeth St., you will definitely spend the night. Turn left at the third roundabout. The super-cozy lodge doubles as the Heritage Cable Cottage with the oldest tree in George Town in the backyard. (☎6382 3261. Sites $10; bunks $22, YHA $18; doubles $50.) There's a **supermarket** at 8 Bathurst St. (Open M-W and Sa 8am-6pm, Th-F 8am-9pm.)

THE A3 EAST: LAUNCESTON TO THE SUNCOAST

MT. VICTORIA FOREST RESERVE. The Reserve is 45 minutes past Scottsdale. From A3, follow signs south to Ringarooma and continue 15km on mostly unsealed roads to the carpark. The strikingly thin single-drop **Ralph Falls,** reckoned to be the tallest in Tassie, is a ten-minute walk from the carpark, and Cashs Gorge lies 30 minutes beyond. The waterfall also happens to be the site of ⚑**Norm's Lookout,** which provides a fantastic view of the gorge below. The tough hike up Mt. Victoria passes a melange of ecosystems and a panorama of the whole Northeast, from Ben Lomond to Flinders Island.

DERBY. Derby is a historic tin-mining town. The quirky **tourist centre/butcher shop** (☎6354 2364; open daily 5am-5pm) and the **painted fish rock** are on the north side of A3 heading east, past the second bridge. Derby's big draw is the ⚑**Tin Mine Centre,** which boasts a tea room, museum, reconstructed mining village, and the opportunity to pan for miniscule gemstones. (☎6354 2262. Open daily Sept.-May 9am-5pm; June-Aug. 10am-4pm. $4.50, children $2.50, families $12.)

CLOSER TO ST. HELENS. Blue Lake is in South Mt. Cameron on B82 as you approach **Gladstone** and **Mt. William National Park,** about 12km northeast off A3. An inadvertent product of mining, Blue Lake's unearthly shade of aquamarine is due to the mineral composition of the soil. The **Weldborough Pass Scenic Reserve,** just beyond Weldborough, offers a rainforest walk guided by "Grandma Myrtle" right by the highway. The 15min. circuit weaves beneath huge tree-ferns and myrtle beeches. About 30min. west of St. Helens, in the middle of a pasture in Pyengana just off A3, **Pub in the Paddock—St. Columba Falls Hotel ❸** recalls a time before pubs had to be Irish, Western, or have pokies to attract customers. Slops, the beer-drinking pig, draws droves of fans. (☎6373 6121. Open daily 11am-late. Meals served noon-2pm and 6-8pm. Singles $25; doubles $35.) Nearby, the 90m cascading **St. Columba Falls** unleashes 42,000L per minute. Drive ten minutes beyond the pub on an unsealed road ending at a carpark, then walk ten minutes to the falls.

BRIDPORT   ☎03

Bridport lies along the sheltered beach of **Anderson's Bay** at the mouth of the **Brid River.** With few sights, Bridport lends itself to relaxing on the beach and enjoying the estuary: there are birds to spot, oysters to dig up, and beach cricket to play.

📟🔀 TRANSPORTATION AND PRACTICAL INFORMATION. The **Redline** (☎1300 360 000) **bus** from Launceston to Scottsdale (1¼hr.; M-F 2 per day, Su 1 per day except Jan.; $10.60) connects with **Stan's Coach Service** to Bridport. (☎6356 1662. 30min., M-F 2 per day, $3.) Everything in town is on Main St., including the **Bridport 2000 Plus Visitor Centre** (☎6356 0280; open M-Sa 10am-4pm, Su 10am-1pm) and the **Service Tasmania,** which has free **Internet.** (☎1300 135 513. Open M-F 9am-5pm.) Bridport has **no bank,** but there is an **ATM** at the Bridport Ex-Service and Community Club. (Open M-Tu 11am-12:30pm and 3:30-8pm, W-Th 11am-12:30pm and 3-10pm, F-Sa 11am-11pm, Su 11am-7pm.) Tubby's **supermarket** has **EFTPOS** and a **post office** desk. (☎6356 1282. Open daily 7am-7pm; post office open M-F 9am-5pm.) **Postal code:** 7262.

🏠🍴 ACCOMMODATIONS AND FOOD. The 🛏**Bridport Seaside Lodge YHA ❷,** 47 Main St., is a budget traveler's dream. There's a large kitchen, tidy rooms, free canoes, tea and coffee, and a veranda with views of the estuary beach. (☎6356 1585. Free canoe use. Dorms $19; doubles $46-51; twins $46-29; YHA discount $3.) **Bridport Caravan Park ❶,** on Bentley St., has close-quarter wooded sites along the beach. (☎6356 1227. Sites $11, powered $15, extra person $5.) Bridport has the standard takeaway joints, but the real find for cheap and tasty eats is **Springfield Fisheries ❶,** the fish slaughterhouse, on Main St. just before crossing the bridge into Bridport. Survive the spectacle of bloody fish guts to buy hot smoked frozen vacuum-sealed trout. (☎6356 0556. Open F 8am-4pm. $8 per kg.)

📷 SIGHTS. A 30min. shoreline stroll north from the Main St. bridge past the old pier takes you to the **Mermaids Pool** swimming hole. Extend the walk past **wildflowers** in the spring by heading down Main St., turning right just past Walter St., and looping back around along the coast (2½hr.). Another walk to **East Sandy Point** (1½hr. return) grants great views and leads to huge dunes. To get to the start of the track, follow Main St., which turns into Sandy Points Rd., and park at the gateway where the road becomes a rough 4WD track.

By car, the 77km drive from Launceston to Bridport passes the **vineyards** and **farms** of the **Tamar Valley:** take A8 to B81 near Rocherlea, and then B83 to B82 in Pipers River. Be sure to pick up a copy of the *Northern Tasmania Wine Route* to assist in your navigation and choices. The **Delamere Vineyard,** 4238 Bridport Rd., is

TASMANIA

open for tastings. (Tastings daily 10am-5pm. Free, but $2 if off a bus.) About 2km off B82 is **Pipers Brook Vineyard,** 1216 Pipers Brook Rd., which offers daily tours. (Open daily 10am-5pm; tastings $3. Tours Dec.-Mar. daily 11am and 2pm.) The **Bridestowe Estate Lavender Farm,** off B81, 52km from Launceston, has lavender products and an informative video on the harvesting of the acres of lavender growing in their fields. It cannot be missed December through January, when the flowers are in bloom. (☎6352 8182. Open Nov.-Apr. daily 9am-5pm; May and Sept.-Oct. M-F 10am-4pm; June-Aug. by appointment. Free except for Dec.-Jan.)

MT. WILLIAM NATIONAL PARK

More of a hill than a mountain, Mt. William overlooks a quiet stretch of coast in the sunny northeast corner, east of Bridport. The gentle 180m peak has views of the **Furneaux Islands** (see below), which once provided a bridge between Tassie and the mainland. The major reason to visit Mt. William is to safari among marsupials. Wallabies are everywhere, and echidnas pop up in the daytime. At dusk, chest-high Forester kangaroos are in motion, as well as smaller pademelons, wombats, and chazzwazzers. After dark—with a good flashlight—spot brushtail possums, spotted-tail quolls, and Tasmanian devils. Eagle-eyed visitors might even glimpse the rare New Holland mouse.

Mt. William is a relatively isolated national park with no facilities. Bringing **drinking water** is essential; head to Gladstone for food or petrol. In an emergency, call the **ranger** (☎6357 2108) at the north entrance. No buses run to the park, but **Terry's Bus Service** (☎6357 2193) meets **Redline** coaches in Derby and goes to Gladstone (1½hr., M-F 12:30pm, $2), about 20km southwest of the park entrance. From St. Helens, the drive takes about 1½hr. The gravel access roads are a bumpy ride even at slow speeds. The turn-off is signposted from Gladstone, and the popular north entrance is by the hamlet of **Poole;** the south entrance is by **Ansons Bay.** Both ends of the park offer ample free coastal **camping** ❶ (only at designated sights), hiking, and beach walks. Park fees apply. The northern access road leads to **Forester Kangaroo Dr.,** past the turn-off for **Stumpy's Bay** and its camping areas, and on to the trailhead for the **Mt. William walk** (1hr.; moderate).

FLINDERS ISLAND   ☎03

The largest of the Furneaux Group islands (pop. 800), approximately 60km northeast of Tasmania, Flinders Island is exceedingly remote, unpopulated, and blessed with a preponderance of natural beauty. It caters to the enterprising, adventuresome outdoor enthusiast though getting to the island can be challenging. **Island Airlines** runs flights out of Launceston. (☎1800 645 875. 40min.; 1-4 per day; $270 return, $400 return to Melbourne.) **Sinclair Air Charter** will take up to 5 passengers from Bridport. (☎6359 3641. $280 one-way min. charge.) **Southern Shipping** can carry up to 12 passengers on their **cargo freight** from Bridport to Lady Barron. (☎6356 1753. From 8hr. up to 37hr. M evening; returns Tu, arriving Bridport W. $77 return, children $44. Book 1 month in advance and bring food.) The island's **Information Centre,** 7 Lagood Rd., in Whitemark, has everything you would want to know about the island. Pick up a *Critter Spotters Guide,* a *Walking Guide to Flinders Island,* and any and all info about accommodations and rental cars. (☎6359 2380. Open M-F 9am-5pm.) Even though Flinders is a Tasmanian municipality, rental companies generally forbid long ferry vehicle transport. **Bowman & Lees Car Hire** (☎6359 2388), **Flinders Island Car Rentals** (☎6359 2168), **Flinders Island Transport Services** (☎6359 2010), and **Flinders Island Lodge Furneaux Car Rentals** (☎6359 3521) rent cars on the island; most accommodations do as well. No bike hire is available on the island. Whitemark also has all basic amenities, including: **Walkers Supermarket,** which has **petrol** (☎6359 2010; open M-F 9am-5:30, Sa 9am-noon); a Westpac **bank** (open M-Th 11am-2:30pm, F 11am-2:30pm and 4-5pm); **Inter-**

net at Service Tasmania (open M-F 10am-4pm); and a **post office** (open M-F 9am-5pm). **Postal Code:** 7255.

The island has fantastic **camping,** usually along the beaches; otherwise, budget stays are hard to come by. **Flinders Island Cabin Park ❶,** 1 Bluff Rd., near the airport, has numerous accommodations and hires cars for $55 per day. (☎6359 2188. Sites $5, powered $7; cabins for 4 with outside amenities: $45 for 2, extra person $10; family cabins $65 for 2, extra person $10.) **Interstate Hotel ❷,** in Whitemark, has basic rooms, modern rooms, and ensuites. (☎6359 2114. Singles $21-46, with brekkie $30-55; twins and doubles $37-66/$55-84.) For a real treat, the island is fully supplied with B&Bs and farmstays; check www.flindersislandonline.com.au, which is constantly updated. For a real treat, **Flinder Island Local Food Hampers** (☎6359 2219) delivers gourmet picnics.

At 756m, Mt. Strzelecki in **Strzelecki National Park** (☎6359 2217) is the highest point on the island, from which you can see the other 54 Furneaux Islands, and, if you're lucky, Wilsons Promontory in Victoria. This moderately challenging walk (3km; 5hr.) traverses fern gullies and craggy outcrops. Be sure to bring plenty of water as many of the track is exposed to sun and wear sturdy shoes, as the track goes over large rocks. Park fees apply. Test your luck by digging for **Topaz diamonds** in Killiecrankie. Rent a shovel and bucket ($4) and a treasure map ($4) from the **general store.** (☎6359 8560. Open daily 9am-5pm.) The store also rents cars ($66 per day) and runs sealwatching tours ($55 per person).

THE SUNCOAST

Tasmania's east coast is the island's softer side, where the weather and even the people are milder. With its mountainous interior, this side of Tassie is sheltered from the storms that pound the west. Agriculture and holiday tourism when summer travelers come for fishing, swimming, and loafing in the sun—sustain the towns. The drive along the coast can ease the weariest traveler.

SAINT HELENS   ☎03

St. Helens, off A3 just south of Mt. William National Park (see p. 540), is the largest and northernmost of the east coast vacation villages. Getting the treasures some 15km northeast of town requires a car and the ability to handle weaving gravel roads. **Humbug Point,** via Binalong Bay Rd., offers great walks and views, while **St. Helens Point,** via St. Helens Point Rd., has free camping with pit toilets, decent fishing, and good surf at **Beerbarrel Beach.** North of Humbug Point, the **Bay of Fires Coastal Reserve,** named for the red rocks that Capt. Tobias Furneaux mistook for fire, has long beaches and basic campsites. The access road ends at the privately owned **Gardens** and **Margery's Corner. Leda Falls** (1½hr. drive) is open to the public at Cerise Brook on Medea Cove Rd.

Redline (☎6376 1182) **buses** sell tickets at the newsagency at Quail and Cecilia St. and run to: Hobart (4-5hr., Su-F 1 per day, $37); Launceston (2½hr., Su-F 1 per day Su-F, $22.10); and St. Mary's (40min., Su-F 1 per day, $5). **TassieLink** (☎1300 300 520) runs to: Hobart (4½hr., F and Su 1 per day, $35.20) via Bicheno (1hr., $9.50), the highway turn-off for Coles Bay (1¼hr., $11), and Swansea (1¾hr., $13.20). The **St. Helens Travel Centre,** 20 Cecilia St., makes TassieLink bookings. (☎6376 1533. Open M-F 9am-5pm, Sa 9am-noon.) **St. Helens History Room,** 59 Cecilia St., offers local history and **tourist information.** (☎6376 1744. Open M-F 9am-5pm, Sa 9am-2pm; history room $2.) A 24hr. **ATM** is available at **Trust Bank,** 18 Cecilia St. **Service Tasmania,** 23 Quail St., has 30min. free **Internet.** (☎6376 2431. Open M-F 8:30am-4:30pm.) The **post office** is at 46 Cecilia St. (☎6376 5350. Open M-F 9am-5pm.) **Postal Code:** 7216.

The **St. Helens YHA ❷**, 5 Cameron St., off Quail St., has all you might need in a 1970s-fabulous setting. (☎6376 1661. Reception daily 8-10am and 5-10pm. Dorms $20, YHA $16; doubles $40/$36.) The standard **St. Helens Caravan Park ❶** is 1½km from the town center on Penelope St., just off the Tasman Hwy. on the southeast side of the bridge. (☎6376 1290. Sites for 2 $12-17, powered $17-22, ensuite $25-28; on-site caravans $30-40; cabins $39-80.) The ■**Wok Stop ❶**, 57a Cecilia St., hasdishes in all spices and sizes. (☎6376 2665. Open M-Sa 11:30am-8:30pm, Su noon-8pm.) The ValuePlus **supermarket** is at 33 Cecilia St. (☎6376 1117. Open daily 7:30am-8pm.)

South of the Scamander Township on A3 between St. Helen's and Coles Bay awaits a fantastic little stop for lunch, the ■**Eureka Farm ❷**. Full of fresh fruit and homemade ice cream, the small cafe within the farm serves an excellent, if short, menu. Meals range $8-12 and include fresh salmon and focaccias. (☎6372 5500. Open Nov.-May sunrise to sunset. Cash only.)

BICHENO
☎03

The spectacular 75km drive south from St. Helens along A3 traces the coastline's sand dunes and granite peaks to the small town of Bicheno (BEE-shen-oh; pop. 750). With its rocky seashore, a neighborly community, and proximity to postcard penguins and national parks (Freycinet and Douglas-Apsley), Bicheno is an enchanting town you won't want to leave. It's hard to avoid beach activities while enjoying the 3km coastal track that begins at the bottom of Weily Ave., left off Burgess St. The walk leads past the blowhole, the marine reef around Governor Island, and numerous nooks for swimming, snorkeling, and diving.

Redline buses leave from the Four-Square Store on Burgess St. (open M-Sa 8am-6:30pm, Su 8am-6pm) and run to the Coles Bay turn-off (10min., M-F 1 per day, $5), continuing to Swansea (35min., $8), with connections to Hobart (5hr., $36.10) and Launceston (2¾hr., 1 per day Su-F, $22). **TassieLink** (☎1300 300 520) runs **buses** to: the Coles Bay turn-off (5min.; W, F, Su 1 per day; $2.30); Hobart (3hr.; W, F, Su 1 per day; $24.20); Launceston (2½hr.; W, F, Su 1 per day; $23); St. Helens (1hr., F and Su 1 per day, $9.50); Swansea (40min.; W, F, and Su 1 per day; $5.10); and Triabunna (1½hr.; W, F, and Su 1 per day; $11). **Bicheno Coach Service** (☎6257 0293) runs to Coles Bay (40min., M-Sa 1-4 per day, $8) and **Freycinet National Park** (50min., $8), making Redline and TassieLink connections from the Coles Bay turn-off. The **Tourist Information Centre** (☎6375 1333) is the surf shop in the town center. It books nightly **penguin-spotting** tours year-round (1hr.; $15, children $7), glass-bottom boat tours (45min., $15), and 4WD tours (2½hr., $35), and sells surf gear and boogie boards. The **Online Access Centre** is on Burgess St. near the Primary School. (☎6375 1892. Open M-W and F 9am-noon and 2-5pm, Th 9am-noon and 6-9pm, Sa 10am-noon. $5 per 30min.) The Value-Plus **supermarket** (open daily 7:30am-6pm) and the **post office** (with limited **banking;** ☎6375 1244; open M-F 9am-12:30pm and 1-5pm), are in the area of the A3 elbow in the town center. **Postal Code:** 7215.

For a fantastic view of the ocean, all the amenities of home, and the opportunity to pick your own fresh fruits and vegetables, stop in at the ■**Bicheno Berrie Retreat ❺**, about 4km outside of town heading north on A3. Each unit has its own washer and dryer, VCR and videos, books, and free continental breakfast. The view from the balcony of Unit 1 (sleeps 6) cannot be beat. (☎6375 1481. Singles $60; units for 2 $105, extra person $25.) The **Bicheno Hostel ❶**, 11 Morrison St., lies off A3 behind a little white church near the post office. Guests get 10% off penguin tours, comfortable bunks, coastal views from the kitchen, and access to a free washer. (☎6375 1651. Dorms $15.) Both **pubs** in town have counter meals.

DOUGLAS-APSLEY NATIONAL PARK

Douglas-Apsley lacks the poster appeal of a mountain or rainforest, but it's the last significant dry eucalypt forest in Tasmania. Its elevation to national park status in 1989 marked the greening of Tassie politics. No roads lead through the park.

The **Apsley waterhole** is a deep pool in the middle of the slow Apsley River, 10min. from the southern carpark. A loop to the **Apsley River Gorge** (3hr.) follows a track from the north side of the waterhole uphill and back down into the gorge, returning on an undefined track downstream along the river. The return trip includes moderate climbing, rock scrambling, and river crossings, so only attempt it when the river is low and the rocks are dry. A **lookout** on the upper banks of the right-side of the river marks the waterhole (15min. return). The three-day **Leeaberra Track,** running from north to south to prevent the spread of root-rot fungus, goes the length of the park. It requires experience, a map, and a compass. Signs along the **lookout walk** introduce the park's tree species, such as the blue gum, black wattle, and native cherry—springtime brings beautiful wildflowers. An unusual number of creatures lurk in the park, such as the endangered Tasmanian bettong and southern grayling fish.

The popular southern end of the park (Apsley River), is a 15min. drive from **Bicheno,** the nearest service center—the park has no telephones or drinking water. The obscure southern access road leaves A3 5km north of Bicheno, heading west along 7km of gravel road. The northern access road from St. Marys, mostly along the **MG logging road,** is even harder to find. There is no bus service to the park, but the **Bicheno Coach Service** can charter a **minibus** from Bicheno. (☎6257 0293. To southern entrance: 2 people $30 return, $15 each extra person; northern entrance: 1-4 people $50 return, 5-12 people $100 return.) Free **campsites ❶** with pit toilets are near the carparks, and others are 50m from the Apsley waterhole. The nearest **rangers** (☎6375 1236) are in Bicheno. Park fees apply.

COLES BAY   ☎03

The tiny township of Coles Bay is the service center for **Freycinet National Park.** Its sunny shelter in the lap of **Great Oyster Bay** satisfies many summer vacationers, while its remote location (27km south on C302 off A3 between Bicheno and Swansea) ensures elevated prices. **TassieLink** (☎1300 300 520) and **Redline** (☎1300 360 000) **buses** run as close as the turn-off for Coles Bay on A3 south to Hobart (3-5hr., Su-F 1 per day, $24-35) and north to Launceston (2½hr., Su-F 1 per day, $22); from the turn-off, take **Bicheno Coaches** (☎6257 0293) to town (30min.; M-Sa 1-3 per day; $6.30, return $12) or the park (40min., $7.50, return $14). **Freycinet Rentals,** 5 Garnet Ave. (☎6257 0320), rents Canadian canoes ($60 per day), dinghies ($25 per hr.), and 16 ft. runabouts ($80-140). They also rent camping gear and other essentials for the area, like flippers and goggles. The **supermarket,** on Garnet Ave., offers limited **banking** and **petrol** and houses the **Visitors Center, a coffee shop,** and the **post office.** (☎6257 0383. Open M-Th 9:30am-4pm, F 9:30am-5pm.) There is **Internet** at the Freycinet Cafe and Bakery on the Esplanade behind the YHA. (☎6257 0272. $6 per hr. Open daily in summer 8am-9pm; in winter 8am-5pm.)

The **YHA-affiliated Iluka Holiday Centre ❷** is at the western end of the Esplanade. The interior may be sparsely decorated, but it's just a hop, skip, and jump away from the beach. (☎6257 0115 or 1800 786 512; iluka@trump.net.au. Reception daily 8am-6pm. Sites $16, powered $20; dorms $22, YHA $19; twins and doubles $44-51; on-site vans for 2 $50.) **Freycinet Backpackers ❷** is part of the **Coles Bay Caravan Park ❶,** 3km north of town off the Coles Bay main road, or an easy 30min. walk round Muir's Beach. They offer a great kitchen, free laundry, and a return bus voucher to walking tracks. (☎6257 0100. Book 3 months ahead during peak summer season and holidays. Linen $4.50. Reception daily 8am-9pm. Sites for 2 $13.20, powered $15.40; twins $16.50 per person 1st night, $13.50 each extra night, 7th night free.)

Tours out of Coles Bay range from sea charters to kayak tours to scenic flights. **Freycinet Sea Charters** have two- to six-hour tours all along the coast. (☎6257 0355. Departs 10am and 3pm, or by arrangement.) **Freycinet Air** does scenic flights over the National Park and Wineglass Bay. (☎6375 1694. From $75 for 2.) **Freycinet Adventures** does day tours with sea kayaking ($45-130), abseiling ($80), 4-wheel motorbiking ($55-80), or renting kayaks and moutain bikes. (☎6257 0500; info@freycinetadventures.com). **All4Adventures** (☎0438 509 022) also does 4WD tours of the park from $55 per person.

FREYCINET NATIONAL PARK

Just a three-hour drive from Hobart or Launceston, Freycinet National Park (FRAY-sin-nay) is home to red-granite **Hazards** and photogenic **Wineglass Bay**.

Bicheno Coaches stops in Coles Bay en route to the park's tracks. (☎6257 0293. Departs M-Sa morning, Su and return service by bookings only. $8.80, return $16.) They also offer service between Coles Bay, the Coles Bay turn-off (30min., $6.30) and Bicheno (40min., $7.50); at the turn-off, you can connect with TassieLink and Redline services to other destinations (see **Coles Bay**, p. 543). An hour walk away, Coles Bay is the service center for Freycinet, but for information on the park, stop at the **visitors kiosk**, near the park entrance. Register and pay at the kiosk; park fees apply. (☎6357 0107. Hours vary. Entrance $10 per car plus up to 8 passengers, $3.50 per person or additional passenger.) **Campsites ❶** with wood, water, and basic toilets are available. (Sites $5, powered $6.)

At an outdoor theatre past the kiosk, rangers offer free programs, including nocturnal walks and primers on Aboriginal land use. (Dec.-Jan. 3 per day.) A few kilometers down, just past the Freycinet Lodge, there's a turn-off on an unsealed road for Sleepy Bay (1.8km) and ■**Cape Tourville Lighthouse** (6.4km). It's an easy 20min. return walk to the Bay, which offers good swimming and snorkeling; the Lighthouse provides amazing views of the coast. Honeymoon Bay, popular for snorkeling, and Richardson's Beach, popular for swimming, are also on the main road. All major walking tracks begin at the carpark at the end of the road; a moderate 33km hike around the whole peninsula takes two to three days. Be sure to bring your own fresh water on day hikes. The **Wineglass Bay Lookout walk** (1-2hr.) is a classic choice: the fairly steep trail climbs up through the red-granite Hazards and opens onto a fabulous view of the bay and Freycinet peninsular mountains. The four- to five-hour loop by Wineglass Bay and Hazards Beach (11km.) is a pleasant alternative, though you might want to bring some bug spray, as the flies can get nasty. Though the **Mt. Amos track** (3hr.) is taxing, it has spectacular views. The white sands of Friendly Beaches can be accessed via the 4½km unsealed Friendly Beaches Rd., 18km north of Coles Bay. Free **campsites ❶** are available at **Isaacs Point** (with pit toilets) and **Ridge Camp;** neither has fresh water.

TRIABUNNA ☎03

On **Prosser Bay,** 50km southwest of Swansea and 87km northeast of Hobart, Triabunna (try-a-BUN-na; pop. 1200) is a tiny town where you can stock up on food before heading to Maria Island. **TassieLink** (☎0030 0520) runs to: Hobart (1½hr.; W, F, and Su 1 per day; $14); Sorell (1hr.; W, F, and Su 1 per day; $8.40); St. Helens (2½hr., F and Su 1 per day, $20.40); and Swansea (45min.; W, F, and Su 1 per day; $6). They also connect to the **Eastcoaster Island Ferry** in Orford. (5min.) The **Tourist Information Centre,** at the Esplanade, has **Internet.** (☎6257 4090. Open daily 10am-4pm. $2 per 5min.) When managers Don and Fran renovated the 12-acre ■**Udda Backpackers (YHA) ❷,** 12 Spencer St., they also incorporated hospitality and home-baked cookies. The solitude and comfort of this small, personal hostel may convince you to extend your stay. Follow Vicary St. toward the fire station, turn left

DEADLY SPEARS Aborigines crossed over to Tasmania from mainland Australia during the last Ice Age 30,000 years ago. When the ice caps melted, the isthmus connecting Tasmania to the continent flooded with water, isolating the colonists. For 30 millennia, Tasmanian Aboriginal culture thrived. Tasmanians pursued a semi-nomadic existence, following seasonal food supplies within a well-established home range. Fire was used to drive game out of the bush onto the spears of waiting hunters, and the periodic burning of vegetation shaped the terrain. Although stones were used as tools, the Aborigines used no stone-tipped weapons or implements. Instead, spears were fashioned entirely from wood, hardened in fire and sharpened with stone tools. The result was a highly effective weapon that could be thrown with deadly force at a range of 60m. Analysis has revealed that these ancient Aboriginal spears had a weight distribution and aerodynamics similar to today's javelins.

after the bridge onto a gravel road, and then left onto Spencer St.; signs point the way. (☎ 6257 3439. Free Maria Island ferry pickup. Dorms $16; twins and doubles $36.) **Triabunna Caravan Park** ❶ is at 6 Vicary St. (☎ 6257 3575. Sites $12, powered $14; on-site vans for 2 $30.) Value-Plus **supermarket** is at Charles and Vicary St. (Open daily 8am-6pm.)

MARIA ISLAND NATIONAL PARK

Maria (muh-RYE-uh, as in Mariah Carey) Island has housed penal colonies, cement industries, whalers, and farmers. Today, the island national park is almost devoid of civilization, preserved for its historical and biological significance. The ruins of a settlement at **Darlington**—along with the area's abundant wildlife, natural beauty, and isolation—are the island's main attraction. Brochures about the park are available at the tourist office in Triabunna; the ferry has detailed descriptions of walking tracks. Walks wander through the **Darlington Township** ruins (1½hr.), over the textured sandstone of the **Painted Cliffs** (2hr., best at low tide, check schedule at Visitors Center), and to the rock-scramble up **Bishop and Clerk.** (4hr.)

To reach Maria, the **Eastcoaster Express catamaran** departs Eastcoaster Resort, 5km from both Triabunna and Orford. (☎ 6257 1589. 30min. Late-Dec. to Apr. 9am, 10:30am, 1, and 3:30pm. Daytrip $19, overnight $22; bikes and kayaks $3.) Take the turn for Louisville Pt./Maria Island Ferry off A3. To get beyond the Darlington ferry wharf, walk or bring a mountain bike. On the island itself, there are no shops or facilities save a **Visitors Center,** with maps and brochures, and a **ranger station** (☎ 6257 1420) with a telephone. The **Old Darlington Prison** ❶ has been resurrected into six-bed units, each with a table, chairs, and fireplace. (Book ahead with ranger. Shared toilets, sinks, and hot showers. Beds $8, children $4, families $22.) The island has three **campsites** ❶: **Darlington,** with ample grassy space (sites $4.40, families $15); **French's Farm,** 11km south down the main gravel road, with an empty weatherproof farmhouse, pit toilet, and rainwater tanks; and **Encampment Cove,** 3km down a side road near French's Farm, with a small bunkhouse and pit toilet..

CENTRAL EAST

From Launceston to Hobart, the convict-built Heritage Hwy. runs through the agricultural midlands, one of Tasmania's few reasonably flat areas. Central Tassie has little of the sweeping scenic grandeur characteristic of the rest of the island, offering instead a landscape of colonial sandstone architecture amidst golden fields.

TASMANIA

BEN LOMOND NATIONAL PARK

Tasmania's premier **ski resort** and largest Alpine area, **Ben Lomond National Park** (☎6336 5312), is about 50km southeast of Launceston. The lifts are nothing to brag about, the slopes (1300m at peak) are easier than those on the mainland, and there's a lot less snow. Regardless, if you're in Tassie and you want to ski, this is the place to go. During the summer, regular park fees apply; during the winter, entry costs $12 per car. To reach the park, follow A3 3km east out of Launceston, then take Blessington Rd. (C401) 40km to Ben Lomond Rd. and the park entrance. From here, a steep 18km unsealed access road leads up to the ski village; rent chains at the base ($15, fitting $5). **TassieLink** runs a **charter service** from Launceston. (☎1300 300 520. 12-seater $400.) **Ski rental** costs $40 per day. (☎6372 2574. Snowboards $50, with equipment $80; deposit $100. Lift tickets $20-30, students $10-15; beginner packages from $75.) Plateau walks are suitable in spring and summer for wildflower photo-ops and views from **Jacobs Ladder Lookout**. The **Creek Inn** ❷, at the top of the access road, plays host all year. (☎6372 2444. Dorms $20.) There is free **camping** ❶ with drinking water, 1km outside the park entrance.

VICTORIA

Victoria may be mainland Australia's smallest state, but it's blessed with far more than its share of fantastic cultural, natural, and historical attractions. Its environment runs the gamut from the dry and empty western plains of the Mallee to the inviting wineries along the fertile banks of the Murray River, from the ski resorts of the Victorian Alps to the forested parks of the Gippsland coast. Nowhere else in Australia is so much ecological diversity only a daytrip away. The capital of the state and the cultural center of the nation, sleek and sophisticated Melbourne overflows with eclectic ethnic neighborhoods, seaside strips, and student haunts. With acres of verdant gardens, countless artspaces, and a vibrant never-tiring atmosphere, it's no wonder that many Aussies claim that the best-kept secret about Australia is Melbourne.

Victoria's most distinctive attractions are found on the coast. West of Melbourne, the breathtaking Great Ocean Road winds its way along the roaring ocean. Hand-cut between 1919 and 1931 from the limestone cliffs, the road passes surfing beaches, coastal getaways, temperate rainforests, and geological wonders, including the Twelve Apostles rock formations, which poke precariously from the sea like jagged fingers. East of the capital, the coastline unfolds past Phillip Island's penguin colony and the beach resorts on Mornington Peninsula, heading into Gippsland. Here, crashing waves collide with granite outcroppings to form the sandy beaches at the edge of majestic Wilsons Promontory National Park. East Gippsland's beaches slowly give way to stony, sandy bird-filled tidal estuaries.

Most of Victoria's interior is remarkable less for its natural grandeur than for its historical significance. The mountainous exceptions are the ranges of the Grampians National Park, whose mammoth beauty evokes awe to humbled onlookers. North of the Grampians, the river-wrought lands of the Wimmera and the scraggly plains of the Mallee don't overwhelm at first sight, but the subtleties of the bush have their own delicate, small-scale beauty. Victoria's historical heart beats to the drum of the mid-19th century gold rush, which flooded central Victoria with seekers of reward. When the ore waned, a host of dusty country towns were left in its wake, today preserved in tourist-oriented nostalgia—the Goldfields and the Murray River towns in north and Central Victoria live fondly in a fascinating past of mangled miners and rugged riverboats. In his wanderings throughout the Hume Corridor, legendary bushranger Ned Kelly had a plan to stick it to the man. Today, this area is a fertile land of small-scale wineries cast pale by Australia's ski mecca, the High Country. The 20th century has brought extensive agricultural and commercial development, including several massive hydroelectric public works projects that continue to impact the state's ecosystems. Still, Victoria's physical beauty remains, tempered by a refined sensibility and cosmopolitan flair that add a touch of class and culture to Australia's down-to-earth grit.

▣ TRANSPORTATION

Getting around Victoria is a breeze, thanks to the very complete, super-efficient system of intrastate trains and buses of **V/Line** (☎ 13 61 96; www.vlinepassenger.com.au), which runs an information center at its main terminal in Melbourne's Spencer Street Station. V/Line has a few interstate options, but more complete national service is offered by the conglomerate **McCafferty's/Greyhound** (☎ 13 14 99 or 13 20 30; www.mccaffertys.com.au or www.greyhound.com.au). Renting a car

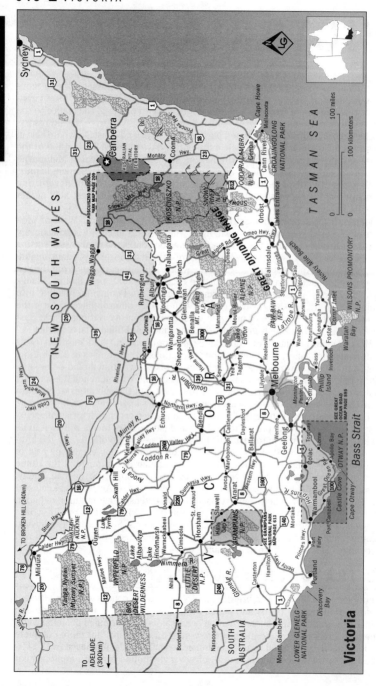

Victoria

allows considerably more freedom, and Victoria's highway system is the most extensive and easily navigable in the country. To cut down on occasionally prohibitive rental costs, check ride-share boards at any hostel. The **Royal Automobile Club of Victoria (RACV),** 360 Bourke St., between William and Queen St., Melbourne (☎ 13 19 55 or 9703 6363; emergency roadside assistance ☎ 13 11 11; www.racv.com.au), has great maps and sells short-term traveler's insurance. Members of automobile clubs in other countries may already have reciprocal membership. To join in Victoria, the basic RACV Roadside Care package (including 4 free service calls per year and limited free towing) costs $50, plus a $30 first-time-joiner's fee for those over 21. For more info on car insurance, see **Insurance at a Glance,** p. 47.

VICTORIA HIGHLIGHTS

TWELVE APOSTLES. Play unabashed tourist at the spectacular Twelve Apostles rock formations in the Port Campbell National Park. (p. 602)

THE LEDGE. Abseil 60m down The Ledge in Grampians National Park. (p. 616)

RUTHERGLEN WINERIES. Pamper your palate with free tastings at Rutherglen Wineries. (p. 641)

TAGGERTY. Experience a living phenomenon at a self-run, eco-friendly farm. (p. 636)

WILSONS PROM. Experience this UNESCO Biosphere Reserve's diversity of terrain on the Sealers Cove dayhike. (p. 648)

SCENIC DRIVE. Take in the magnificent sights with a two-day scenic drive around Snowy River National Park. (P. 659)

MELBOURNE   ☎ 03

Melburnians themselves are likely to tell you that there are countless reasons why this metropolis deserves the oft-touted designation as the planet's most liveable city. It's also a great place to visit. Even as the capital of Victoria and Australia's second-largest city, Melbourne gets a bad rap as a travel destination because it lacks a singular icon like Sydney's Opera House or the Northern Territory's Uluru (Ayers Rock). But rather than capitalizing on any single attraction, the city blends cosmopolitan sights, sounds, artistry, and an energy that is likely to catch any lingering visitor. If you resist falling prey to the "a city is just a city" mentality, you will easily fall under Melbourne's spell and relish in all it has to offer. Both ultramodern skyscrapers and ornate neogothic edifices line its wide streets, and the rumble of the green-and-gold trams accompany the roar of thousands of sport fanatics at the Melbourne Cricket Grounds (MCG). You might spend one hour window-shopping at Southbank's chic boutiques, and the next comparing fruit amid the bustling clamor of the Queen Victoria Market, or strolling through an expansive city garden. Students enjoying late-night caffeine sessions in smoky Fitzroy cafes coexist with clubhoppers raging until 6am in South Yarra and Prahran. Sprawling over 6200 square kilometers and home to over three million denizens, Melbourne needs to be savored, not just seen.

It all began rather inauspiciously in 1825, when John Batman sailed a skiff up the Yarra, got stuck on a sandbank, then justified his blunder by claiming that he had found the "place for a village." Then named Batmania (Gotham City was already taken), the diminutive burg underwent a phenomenal growth spurt at the onset of the Victorian Gold Rush three decades later. "Marvelous Melbourne" celebrated its coming-of-age in 1880 by hosting the World Exhibition, which attracted over a million people. When the Victorian economy crashed in the 1890s following a series of bank failures, Melbourne's infrastructure collapsed, and its fetid open

VICTORIA

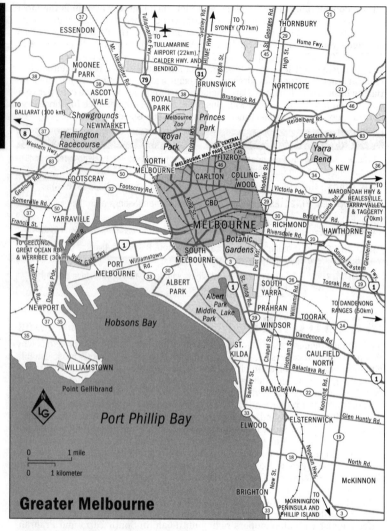

Greater Melbourne

sewers earned it the nickname "Marvelous Smellbourne." By the early part of the 19th century, though, things other than the sewage were up and running again, and Melbourne posed a legitimate challenge to Sydney for the honor of being named Australia's capital. While the Canberra compromise ultimately deprived both metropolises of this status, Melbourne was more than happy to serve as temporary home to the government until the Parliament House was completed. The city's 20th-century apex was the 1956 Olympic Games, which brought Melbourne's love for sport to an international audience.

The subsequent years have seen even more population growth and an increasingly international flavor; most of the recent immigrants hail from China, Southeast Asia, Italy, and Greece (Melbourne has the world's third-largest Greek population after Athens and Thessaloniki). Today, Melbourne's various neighborhoods—the frenetic Central City, alterna-funky Fitzroy, Italianate Carlton, mellow St. Kilda, chic South Yarra, and more—invite exploration and lie within minutes of each other via tram. The weather is temperate (though beware of frequent rainstorms); most of the time, it's great for beach-going or walking along the Yarra at night. With picturesque waterfronts, numerous parks, famous sporting events, and a world-class cultural scene, Melbourne coaxes visitors to relax and enjoy all the attractions of a large city with less of the tourist hype.

MELBOURNE HIGHLIGHTS

AUSSIE RULES. Catch a game of Aussie Rules Football, Melbourne's sports obsession, at the historic Melbourne Cricket Ground. (p. 573)

QUEEN VICTORIA MARKET. Get great bargains in the Queen Victoria Market. (p. 574)

BOTANIC GARDENS. Forget you're in the city in 36 acres of urban parkland. (p. 576)

MOOMBA FESTIVAL. Partake in the unbridled pandemonium of Moomba. (p. 580)

METRO. All you wanna do is *dance* at this five-level sweatfest, the largest club in the Southern Hemisphere. (p. 585)

◼ INTERCITY TRANSPORTATION

BY PLANE. Boomerang-shaped **Tullamarine International Airport** is 25km northwest of Melbourne (30min. by car) and has three terminals. The international terminal houses several outfits and sits in the middle of the two domestic terminals, Qantas and Virgin Blue (formerly the now-defunct Ansett terminal). Visit www.melair.com.au for extensive information on all airport services. **Skybus** (☎ 9335 2811) provides ground transport to Melbourne's Spencer St. Station in the city center. ($12, return $21; every 20min. in either direction during the day and evening, every 30-60min. overnight). **Taxis** to the city center cost roughly $35 and take about 25 minutes. **Car rental** companies are clustered to the left, when exiting from the international arrival terminal (see **By Car**, p. 558).

International terminal: Houses 25 airlines and all international arrivals and departures. **Qantas international** (☎ 13 12 11) operates on the first floor. **Travelers Information** (☎ 9297 1805), directly in front of arriving international passengers as they exit, books same-day accommodations, provides maps and brochures, and has a backpacker bulletin board. **Lockers** ($6-9 per day) are on either end of the international terminal.

Domestic terminals: Qantas (☎ 13 13 13; www.qantas.com.au) heads the left terminal and **Virgin Blue** (☎ 13 67 89; www.virginblue.com.au) heads the right. Each flies to all Australian capitals at least once daily, and they have similar fares.

BY BUS AND TRAIN. Spencer Street Station, at the intersection of Spencer and Bourke St., is the main intercity **bus** and **train station.** (☎ 9619 2340. Open daily 6am-10pm.) **V/Line** (☎ 13 61 96; www.vlinepassenger.com.au) offers unlimited travel passes within Victoria for seven days ($75) to overseas tourists only. **Countrylink** (☎ 13 22 32; www.countrylink.nsw.gov.au) covers multiple-day passes to destinations in NSW as well as to Melbourne and Brisbane (see **Local Transportation**, p. 556). **Great Southern** (☎ 13 21 47; www.gsr.com.au) has destinations across Australia. The **Melbourne Transit Centre,** 58 Franklin St. (☎ 9639 0634; open daily 6am-10:30pm), near Elizabeth St., is the hub of **McCafferty's/Greyhound** (☎ 13 14 99 or 13 20 30; www.mccaffertys.com.au or www.greyhound.com.au). They are listed in the chart below (see p. 555) as **McCafferty's.**

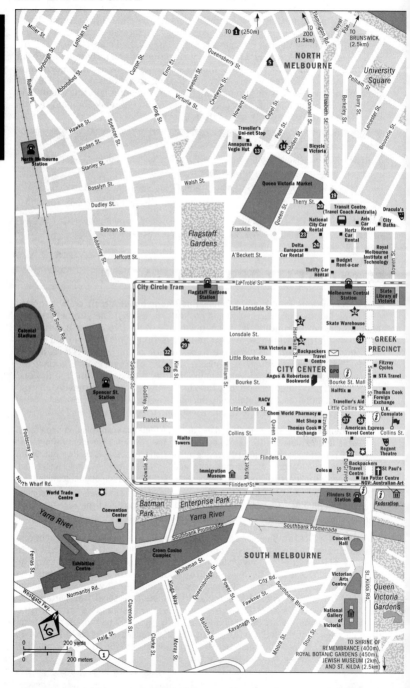

VICTORIA

Central Melbourne

⌂ ACCOMMODATIONS
Chapman Gardens YHA Hostel, **1**
The Friendly Backpacker, **33**
The Greenhouse Backpacker, **39**
Hotel Bakpak, **23**
Hotel Lindrum, **40**
Hotel Y, **20**
The Melbourne Connection, **32**
The Nunnery, **17**
Queensbury Hill YHA, **5**
Stork Hotel, **19**
Toad Hall, **24**

🍎 FOOD
Boba Pearl Bubble Tea
   Restaurant, **16**
Cafée Baloo, **28**
Crossways Food For Life, **38**
Fast Eddy's Cafe, **35**
Guernica, **21**
Hopetoun Tea Rooms, **37**
Jimmy Watson's Wine Bar, **3**
Krome Kafe, **31**
La Porchetta, **14**
Mario's, **11**
Nyala, **25**
Retro Café, **4**
Robert Burns Hotel, **10**
Tiamo, **2**
Teayara Cafe and Gallery
   Restaurant, **29**
Thresherman's
   Bakehouse Café, **6**
Toto's, **15**
Vegie Bar, **8**
Veg Out Time (positive
   eating), **7**
White Lotus, **13**

★ NIGHTLIFE
Bar Open, **9**
Club UK, **34**
Labour in Vain, **18**
Metro, **36**
Mi Casa es tu Casa, **22**
Pugg Mahones, **27**
Rue Bebelons, **26**
Scubar, **30**

✈ ORIENTATION

The heart of one of the world's largest urban sprawls, Melbourne's lively, dense core comprises a geometrically precise city center surrounded by a slew of distinctive suburbs. The city center alone could take up the whole of an abbreviated visit, but the surrounding neighborhoods are where the true spirit of Melbourne lives. For those keen to conquer the entire polis, the irreplaceable *Melway* guide has detailed street directories of Melbourne and surrounds; pick it up in any bookstore (around $40), or photocopy the desired pages from the library.

CITY CENTER. The city center, also known as the Central Business District (CBD), is composed of a well-arranged rectangular grid of streets bordered by **Spencer St.** to the west, **La Trobe St.** to the north, **Spring St.** to the east, and **Flinders St.** (which borders the Yarra River) to the south. Five major streets run east to west: La Trobe (the northernmost), Lonsdale, Bourke, Collins, and Flinders. To the north of all but La Trobe are "little" streets—roads named after their southern superior (for example, Little Collins St. is just north of Collins St., and Flinders Ln. is just north of Flinders St.). Nine streets cross this grid running north to south: Spencer (the westernmost), King, William, Queen, Elizabeth, Swanston, Russell, Exhibition, and Spring. **Spencer St.** runs by the primary bus and train depot, bridges the Yarra River to South Melbourne, and carries trams #12, 75, 95, 96, and 109. Directly in the middle, **Elizabeth St.** carries major northbound tram lines (#19, 57, 59, and 68). One block east, **Swanston St.** also has north-south trams (#1, 3, 5, 6, 8, 16, 22, 25, 64, 67, and 72). On the east end, **Spring St.** borders Parliament and the Treasury and Carlton Gardens.

The eastern half of the city contains most restaurants and sights. **Bourke St. Mall** (a pedestrian stretch of Bourke St. between Elizabeth and Swanston St., traversed by trams #86, 95, and 96) swarms with people every day; the giant screen "alt.tv" at Bourke and Swanston St. marks the heart of the city. Both **Hardware Ln.** (running north-south between Lonsdale and Bourke St.) and **DeGraves St.** (running north-south between Collins and Flinders St.) are alley-like pedestrian walks that contain shops, restaurants, and cafes with outdoor seating. The area just north of the city center bordered by La Trobe, Queen, Elizabeth, and Victoria St. borders Queen Victoria Market and is a hive of budget accommodations, while East Melbourne contains **Fitzroy Gardens** (p. 572) and Victoria's sporting shrine, the **Melbourne Cricket Ground.** (p. 573. Take tram #48, 70, or 75 from Flinders St.)

NORTH MELBOURNE. North Melbourne is a pleasant mix of bungalows, flats, refurbished residences, and neighborhood shops and eateries, all easily reachable from the city center. Forming its eastern edge, **Elizabeth St.** heads north from the city center and passes the **Queen Victoria Market** with its abundant, inexpensive food stocks and wares; travel west along Victoria St. (traversed by tram #57) to find loads of cool budget eateries. William St. heads north from the city center past **Flagstaff Gardens** and becomes **Peel St.** Peel and Elizabeth St. intersect near the University of Melbourne, where Elizabeth continues northwest under the name **Flemington Rd.** (along which trams #55 and 59 continue) to the **Melbourne Zoo** (p. 574). At this intersection, Peel St. becomes **Royal Pde.** (tram #19), which borders the University and becomes **Sydney Rd.** to the northern suburb of Brunswick.

CARLTON. Melbourne's unofficial "Little Italy," Carlton begins at **Nicholson St.** and extends west past the Carlton Gardens, to the **University of Melbourne.** On **Lygon St.**, its primary thoroughfare, upmarket Italian bistros, somewhat cheaper *gelaterias* and *pasticcerias*, and a smattering of ethnic and eclectic foods cater to a crowd of old Mediterranean types and college students. Public transportation does not go along Lygon St. in Carlton. To get there, either take a tram up Swanston St. (#1, 3, 5, 6, 8, 16, 22, 25, 64, 67, or 72) and then walk east along Queensberry or Faraday St., or take #96 from Bourke St. up Nicholson St. and walk west along Faraday St.

BUSES AND TRAINS FROM MELBOURNE TO:

DESTINATION	COMPANY	DURATION	TIMES	PRICE
Adelaide	McCafferty's	9-10hr.	3 per day	$54
	V/Line	10½hr.	1 per day	$57
Albury	V/Line	3½hr.	4-6 per day	$42.90
Alice Springs	McCafferty's	28hr.	1 per day	$214
	Great Southern	36hr.	1 per week	$292
Ararat	V/Line	3hr.	3-5 per day	$29.70
Ballarat	V/Line	1½hr.	7-12 per day	$15.20
Bendigo	V/Line	2hr.	5-11per day	$22.90
Bright	V/Line	4½hr.	1 per day	$42.90
Brisbane	McCafferty's	27hr.	3 per day	$156
	Countrylink	35hr.	1 per day	$177.10
Brisbane (via Sydney)	McCafferty's	30hr.	4 per day	$144
Cairns	McCafferty's	56hr.	2 per day	$329
	Countrylink	70hr.	4 per week	$339.90
Canberra	V/Line	8½hr.	1 per day	$55
	McCafferty's	8hr.	2 per day	$56
Castlemaine	V/Line	1½hr.	5-11 per day	$16.70
Darwin	McCafferty's	50hr.	1 per day	$389
Echuca	V/Line	3½-4hr.	2-9 per day	$29.70
Geelong	V/Line	1hr.	11-26 per day	$9.50
Mildura	V/Line	9½hr.	1 per week	$59.20
Perth	McCafferty's	42½hr.	1 per day	$280
	Great Southern	60hr.	2 per week	$340
Sydney	McCafferty's	11-15hr.	4 per day	$59
	Countrylink	11hr.	2 per day	$110
Yulara (Ayers Rock)	McCafferty's	25hr.	1 per day	$285

FITZROY. Fitzroy, Melbourne's bohemian district, is a shopping mecca for those looking for cutting-edge new or used clothing, music or books, or some of the best cafe and restaurant societies. While it's packed with style and populated with "ferals" (Australians' term for the nose-ring crowd), Fitzroy is blessedly low on attitude, and its establishments house a healthy mix of freaks, families, and everyone in between. Tram #11 runs the length of **Brunswick St.,** the main artery of Fitzroy. **Smith St.** makes the boundary between Fitzroy and its eastern neighbor, **Collingwood,** and is home to a number of fine eateries and factory outlet stores. Just east of Smith are a handful of **gay bars** (and a fair number of straight ones too). The blocks of **Johnston St.** between Brunswick and Nicholson St. in Fitzroy form the smallish Latin Quarter, with stores, restaurants, tapas bars, and dance clubs.

SOUTH MELBOURNE. The Yarra divides Melbourne into the more working-class suburbs of the north and the fancier ones to the south. South Melbourne, west of St. Kilda Rd. and stretching south from the West Gate Freeway to **Albert Park,** is an exception. More blue-collar than adjacent communities, this neighborhood has some quality restaurants and nightspots along its main drag, **Cecil St.** It's also a quick walk to the park, the **Royal Botanic Gardens** (p. 576), the city center, or the **beach** at Port Phillip Bay. Take tram #96 or 12 from Spencer St.

West of South Melbourne along Port Phillip Bay are three of Melbourne's quietest, most posh suburbs. **Station Pier** marks the division between Port Melbourne, the more commercial side of the area, and the more urbane Albert Park, an upscale residential neighborhood with stately seaside bungalows; ferries to **Tasmania** depart from Station Pier at the terminus of tram #109.

SOUTH YARRA AND PRAHRAN. South Yarra and Prahran (per-RAN) span the area enclosed by the Yarra to the north, St. Kilda Rd. to the west, Dandenong Rd. to the south, and William St. to the east. The focus of Melbourne's gay community, **Commercial Rd.** runs east-west, separating South Yarra from its southern neighbor Prahran. The district's main street is **Chapel St.;** the section of the boulevard that lies in South Yarra is the commercial incarnation of the fancy suburbs south of the river. On sunny Sundays, the beautiful people come here to shop for Prada and Versace and then snipe about the catty salesgirls while sitting in sleek, pricey sidewalk bistros. Don't let the snots rub off on you; good deals abound in Melbourne. Seek out Chapel St. where it gets a little more down-to-earth south of Commercial Rd. in Prahran, closer in spirit to St. Kilda. **Greville St.** branches west from Chapel and is a den for second-hand clothing, record stores, and bizarre restaurants. Trams #78 and 79 run slowly along Chapel St. By tram from Flinders St. Station, #8 travels below the Botanic Gardens, then along Toorak Rd. to its intersection with Chapel St., while #5 and 64 head south along St. Kilda Rd., and then go east along Dandenong Rd. to Chapel. The quickest way to get to there from the central city, though, is to hop a **Sandringham Line** train from Flinders St. Station to South Yarra, Prahran, or Windsor Stations—each lies only a few blocks west of Chapel St.

ST. KILDA. Though it's a bit removed to the southeast of the city center (and officially in the city of **Port Phillip,** see p. 588), St. Kilda is a budget hotspot with cheap accommodations and popular eateries. Trams #12 and 96 bring people to St. Kilda from Spencer St. Station, while #16 runs from Flinders St. Station. Tram #16 travels along **St. Kilda Rd.** and passes Melbourne's two largest green spaces, the **Royal Botanic Gardens** via **Albert Park.** At **St. Kilda Junction,** St. Kilda Rd. and Fitzroy St. intersect; from here, Fitzroy curves south towards the waterfront, becoming the Esplanade. **Barkly St.** runs south from the junction on the other side, completing a triangle with Fitzroy St. and the Esplanade. The junction of Fitzroy and Barkly St. is **Grey St.,** and is the focus of St. Kilda's budget accommodations. The last street that branches south from Fitzroy St. before it turns into the Esplanade is **Acland St.,** the southern end of which is one of Melbourne's many excellent cafe districts, distinguished by its old-time cake shops.

⌐ LOCAL TRANSPORTATION

PUBLIC TRANSPORTATION. Melbourne's superb public transportation system, the **Met,** comprises light-rail trains, buses, and trams. (☎ 13 16 38; www.victrip.com.au. Open daily 7am-9pm for inquiries.) **Tram** routes criss-cross the metropolitan area and are the most useful for navigating the city and its proximate outskirts. On weekdays, they run every 3-12min., nights and weekends every 20min. or longer; services operate M-Sa 5am-midnight, Su 8am-11pm. You don't actually have to show your pass to ride trams, but if an inspector decides to make a spot check and you're without a valid ticket, expect a $100 fine.

For those honest riders, the entire network comprises three Met zones, though you'll stay in Zone 1 unless you travel out to a distant suburb. Tickets are sold at stations, on board trams and buses (coins only), and at the **Met Shop,** 103 Elizabeth St., near Collins St. (Open M-F 8:30am-4:55pm, Sa 9am-1pm.) **Tickets** within Zone 1 can be used on any of the three types of transportation, and are valid for unlimited

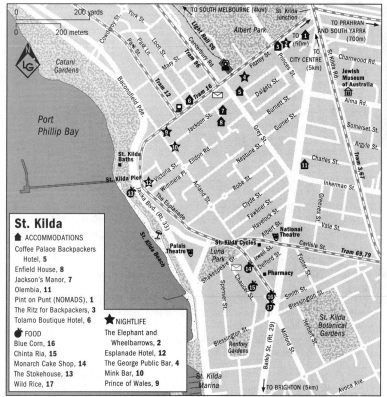

St. Kilda

🏠 ACCOMMODATIONS

Coffee Palace Backpackers
  Hotel, **5**
Enfield House, **8**
Jackson's Manor, **7**
Olembia, **11**
Pint on Punt (NOMADS), **1**
The Ritz for Backpackers, **3**
Tolarno Boutique Hotel, **6**

🍎 FOOD
Blue Corn, **16**
Chinta Ria, **15**
Monarch Cake Shop, **14**
The Stokehouse, **13**
Wild Rice, **17**

⭐ NIGHTLIFE
The Elephant and
  Wheelbarrows, **2**
Esplanade Hotel, **12**
The George Public Bar, **4**
Mink Bar, **10**
Prince of Wales, **9**

travel for a two hours ($2.60), a day ($5.10), a week ($22.20), a month ($83.30), or a year ($897). **Concession** rates are roughly half-price; you qualify if you are under 15 years old or have a valid Australian university ID (ISIC cards or international university IDs not accepted) or pensioner card. Only two-hour tickets can be purchased from coin-operated machines on board trams and buses. If you're going to be in town for a while, the long-term passes save a lot of time, money, and hassle; buy them at a station machine or ticket counter. If you purchase your ticket anywhere but on a tram itself, you must validate it by putting it in any of the electronic green boxes on the tram; you can be fined for not doing this even if you have a ticket. These instances are rare, but the government is privatizing the Met; commercial interests may be more rigorous than government laxness. For more info and route maps, grab the free *Met Fares and Travel Guide* from any station.

The burgundy-and-gold **City Circle Tram** circumnavigates the **Central Business District (CBD)**, provides running commentary on the city's sights and history, and is **free** (every 10min.; Su-W 10am-6pm, Th-Sa 10am-9:30pm). The bus and **light-rail train** systems are mostly for commuters going to residential areas or distant suburbs, and you can't board without a valid Metcard. There are train stops at **Melbourne Central, Flagstaff Gardens, Parliament,** and **Spencer St.,** though the main rail hub is the beautiful banana-colored **Flinders St. Station** at the southern foot of Swanston St., identifiable by its big clock.

BY CAR. The usual national car-rental chains mostly have offices in the Melbourne city center and at the airport, but it's cheaper to rent in the city, as the airport offices generally include a 9% airport tax. They tend to rent only to people over age 25, though some accept renters aged 21-24 with a **surcharge.** Prices for all fluctuate frequently due to seasons and specials. National agencies include:

Atlas (☎ 9663 6233, airport 9335 1945; www.atlasrent.com.au). In Melbourne Transit Centre, 58 Flinders St., or at the airport. Open M-F 7:30am-6pm, Sa-Su 7:30am-2:30pm. From $68 per day, $11 surcharge.

Avis, 20-24 Franklin St. (☎ 9663 6366, airport 9338 1800). Open M-Th 7:30am-6:30pm, F 7:30am-7pm, Sa-Su 8am-5pm. From $60, $25 surcharge.

Budget, 398 Elizabeth St. (☎ 13 27 27 or 9203 4846, airport 9241 6366), on the corner of A'Beckett St. Open M-Th 8am-6:30pm, F 8am-7pm, Sa-Su 8am-5pm. From $55, $16.50 surcharge.

Delta Europcar, 101 A'Beckett St. (☎ 13 10 45 or 9600 9025; www.deltaeuropcar.com.au). Open M-F 7:30am-6pm, Sa-Su 8am-5pm. From $40, $12 surcharge.

National Car Rental (☎ 9348 9449), on the corner of Franklin and Elizabeth St.: same rates as **Delta,** its owner. Open M-Th 7:30am-6pm, F 7:30am-6:30pm, Sa 8am-5pm.

Hertz, 97 Franklin St. (☎ 9663 6244, airport 9338 4044). Open M-Th 7:30am-6pm, F 7:30am-7pm, Sa 7:30am-5pm, Su 8am-5pm. From $56, $15 surcharge.

Thrifty, 390 Elizabeth St. (☎ 8661 6000, airport 1300 367 227). Open M-Th 7:30am-6pm, F 7:30am-6:30pm, Sa-Su 8am-5pm. From $65, $15 surcharge.

Backpacker Car Rental, 103 Railway Ave., Werribee (☎ 9731 0700). Charges $138 per week for the Melbourne metro area, but provides a better all-Victoria rate at $193 per week, which includes unlimited kilometers, insurance, and RACV roadside assistance; drivers must be at least 23 years old.

The **Royal Automobile Association of Victoria** (**RACV;** ☎ 13 13 29), on the corner of Little Collins and Queen St., with a second location at 360 Bourke St. (☎ 13 19 55), is a comprehensive driving resource with good maps for sale. Members receive emergency roadside assistance. Backpackers commonly join forces and buy or rent a used car. A good but out-of-the-way option for long-term rental is **Car Connection** near Castlemaine, 120km northwest of Melbourne. They offer a station wagon for up to six months for $1950 plus a $750 insurance charge and full camping equipment for two for $250. Being a bit out of town, they also provide free pickup from Melbourne airport or any city hostel as well as free first-night lodging in Castlemaine. (☎ 5473 4469; www.carconnection.com.au. Open M-F 9am-5pm.)

There are also tons of **bargain agencies** that are only half-joking about the quality of their cars. **Rent-a-Bomb** (☎ 13 15 53; www.rentabomb.com.au) has eleven offices in the Melbourne area; their main office is at 149 Clarendon St. (☎ 9696 3939). The deals can run as cheap as $12 per day; still, weigh the savings against the potential costs of breaking down in the middle of nowhere. For information on driving in Australia, see **On The Road,** p. 48.

BY TAXI. If you're out after the Met stops running at midnight, you'll have to take a taxi. Cabs can be hailed at any time of day on the street. All companies have a $2.80 base charge plus $1.31 per km. There's a $1 surcharge when you arrange cab pickup by phone and if you ride between midnight and 6am. The misnamed **Silver Top** (☎ 13 10 08) and **Black Cabs** (☎ 13 22 27) are both yellow.

BY BICYCLE. An extensive **bike trail** runs along the Yarra, and others loop through Albert Park and Middle Park, along the Port Phillip beaches, and around North Melbourne's gardens. Southern Melbourne's flat bayside roads make for low-impact, scenic cycling. **St. Kilda Cycles,** 11 Carlisle St., has good rates. (☎9534 3074. Open M-F 9am-6pm, Sa 9am-5pm, Su 10am-4pm. $15 per half-day, $20 per day.) Or try **Fitzroy Cycles Bike Hire,** 224 Swanston St. (☎9639 3511. Open M-F 9am-6pm, Sa 9:30am-5pm. $9 per hr., $35 per day.) Rates include helmets and locks. Many hostels rent bikes for little or no charge. **Bicycle Victoria (BV),** 19 O'Connell St. (☎9328 3000 or 1800 639 634; www.bv.com.au), provides insurance for members (yearly membership $63, concessions $57, families $78-88) and free info for nonmembers on rules of the road and bike-related events.

🔁 PRACTICAL INFORMATION

TOURIST AND FINANCIAL SERVICES

Tourist Offices: Melbourne Visitor Information Centre, (☎9658 9658 or 13 28 42; www.melbourne.vic.gov.au), in Melbourne Town Hall, on the corner of Little Collins and Swanston St. Brochures, maps, and bookings for Melbourne and Victoria. Open M-F 9am-6pm, Sa-Su 9am-5pm. In 2002, the new Visitors Center, formally known as **I Melbourne** (☎9658 9658), opened in Federation Square, across from Flinders St. Station at the corner of Flinders St. and St. Kilda Rd. The sprawling new center offers Internet and email, transport and entertainment ticket sales, ATM, the **Best of Victoria** (☎9663 0800) accommodations and tour booking service, and the **Melbourne Greeter Service,** which gives free 2-4hr. tours of the city tailored to your personal interests. Tours offered in 25 languages. Arrange by filling out a brief application at least 3 working days in advance (book online at www.melbourne.vic.gov.au). There are also info booths at **Bourke St. Mall** and **Flinders St. Station.** Both open M-F 9am-5pm, Sa 10am-4pm, Su 11am-4pm.

Disabled and Elderly Travelers Information: Travellers Aid, 169 Swanston St., 2nd Fl. (☎9654 2600), has a tearoom with old-fashioned fittings along with great services. Open M-F 8am-5pm. Also at Spencer St. Station (☎9670 2873). Open M-F 7:30am-7:30pm, Sa-Su 7:30am-11:30am. Will meet and assist elderly and disabled travelers on trains and buses M-F 7:30am-7:30pm, Sa-Su 7:30am-11:30am. Arrange ahead.

Gay and Lesbian Information: The ALSO Foundation, 35 Cato St., Prahran (☎9510 5569; www.also.org.au). Gay and lesbian helpline (☎9510 5488 or 1800 631 493).

Outdoors Information: Natural Resources and Environment (NRE), 8 Nicholson St., on the corner of Victoria Pde., East Melbourne (☎9637 8325, hotline 13 61 86; www.nre.vic.gov.au). Maps and info on licenses. Open M-F 8:30am-5:30pm. Also call **Parks Victoria** (☎13 19 63; www.parks.vic.gov.au) for all state and national park info.

Budget Travel: YHA Victoria, 83-85 Hardware Ln. (☎9670 9611; www.yha.com.au). Provides a full listing of YHA hostels and a booking service. YHA member international booking surcharge $5, domestic surcharge $2 after first 2 bookings. Non-YHA member domestic surcharge $2, no non-member international booking. Attached budget travel agency. Open M-F 9am-5:30pm, Sa 10am-1pm. **STA Travel's Victorian Headquarters,** 260 Hoddle St., off Johnston St. in Fitzroy, and *all* over Melbourne and its surrounds, including 208 Swanston St. (☎9639 0599). Open M-F 9am-6pm, Sa 10am-4pm. **Backpackers World,** 167 Franklin St. (☎9329 1990), in Hotel Bakpak. Open M-F 8am-9pm, Sa-Su 9am-8pm. Also at 35 Elizabeth St. (☎9620 2300). Open M-F 9am-6pm, Sa 11am-5pm. **Backpackers Travel Centre,** Shop 1, 250 Flinders St. (☎9654 8477; www.backpackerstravel.net.au). Open M-F 9am-6pm, Sa 10am-4pm. Also at 377 Little Bourke St. (☎9642 1811). Open M-F 9am-5:30pm, Sa 10am-3pm.

Consulates: Canada, Level 1, 123 Camberwell Rd., East Hawthorne (☎9811 9999). Open M-F 8:30am-5:15pm. **Great Britain,** Level 17, 90 Collins St. (☎9650 4155). Open M-F 9am-4:30pm. **United States,** Level 6, 553 St. Kilda Rd. (☎9526 5900). Open M-F 8:30am-noon and 1-4:30pm.

Currency Exchange: 109 Collins St. (☎9654 2768). Open daily 8am-8:40pm. All banks exchange money during regular operating hours. Open M-Th 9:30am-4pm, F 9:30am-5pm. **American Express** (see below) exchanges all traveler's checks free of commission. **Thomas Cook Foreign Exchange,** 261 Bourke St. (☎9654 4222), near Swanston St., has a $7 commission on checks and cash. Open M-F 9am-5pm, Sa 9am-2pm, Su 11am-3pm. Several banks have offices at the airport. 24hr. ATM outlets adorn the city.

American Express Travel Services, 233 Collins St. (☎9633 6318). Buys all traveler's checks (no charge); min. $8 or 2% fee on cash exchanges. Poste Restante for AmEx card or traveler's check holders. Wire transfers. Open M-F 9am-5pm, Sa 9am-noon.

LOCAL SERVICES

Bookstores: Angus & Robertson Bookworld (☎9670 8861; www.angusrobertson.com.au), on the corner of Elizabeth and Bourke St., is huge and has frequent blowout sales. Open M-Th 9am-6pm, F 9am-8pm, Sa 9am-6pm, Su 10am-5pm.

Library: State Library of Victoria, 328 Swanston St. (☎9669 9888), on the corner of La Trobe St. Open M-Th 10am-9pm, F-Su 10am-6pm.

Ticket Agencies: Ticketek (☎13 28 49 or 1800 062 849; www.ticketek.com.au), and **Ticketmaster** (☎13 61 00; www.ticketmaster7.com.au) for sports, performances, and other events. Handling fee for phone booking. Both open daily 9am-9pm. **Halftix,** a booth on Bourke St. Mall opposite Myer Department Store, sells half-price tickets on performance day (Su performances sold Sa); often sells out by 2pm. Cash only; no phone orders. Open M 10am-2pm, Tu-Th 11am-6pm, F 11am-6:30pm, Sa 10am-2pm.

Employment Assistance: Most *Let's Go* accommodations listed have employment bulletin boards; some help find temp jobs free of charge. **WorldWide Workers** (☎9328 8560), in the lobby of **Hotel Bakpak** (see **Accommodations,** p. 561), charges $40 to join but provides free Internet access, discounted beer and travel, and access to top jobs. Open M-F 1-5pm. Melbourne's biggest daily paper, *The Age*, has classifieds on Sa and can be accessed online at www.theage.com.au or picked up for free at the Melbourne Museum.

EMERGENCY AND COMMUNICATIONS

MEDIA AND PUBLICATIONS

Newspapers: The main newspapers are *The Age* ($1.10) and *The Herald Sun* (99¢) for local coverage and *The Australian* ($1.10) for national news.

Nightlife: *InPress* and *Beat* (www.beat.com.au), released on Wednesday (free). For gay news and nightlife, check out *MCV* (by subscription, but found in most gay establishments) and *B.News* (free, released every other Th).

Entertainment: *Age*'s Entertainment Guide and *Herald Sun*'s Gig Guide, found in Friday's paper.

Radio: Alternative, Triple R 102.7FM; Rock, Triple J 107.5FM and Triple M 105.1FM; News, 1026AM; Tourist Info, 88FM.

Emergency: ☎000.

Police: 637 Flinders St. (☎9247 6666) and 226 Flinders Ln. (☎9650 7077).

Crisis Lines: Victims Referral and Assistance Hotline (☎9603 9797). **Centre Against Sexual Assault** (☎9344 2210). **Lifeline Counseling Service** (☎13 11 14). **Poison Information Service** (☎13 11 26). **Coast Guard Search and Rescue** (☎9598 7003). **Alcohol and Drug Counselling** (☎9416 1818).

Helpful numbers: Directory assistance ☎12 23, international ☎12 25; collect calls ☎1800 REVERSE (1800 738 3773); translation and interpretation ☎13 14 50.

Pharmacy: Many along Elizabeth St., including **ChemWorld** (☎9670 9370), on the corner of Elizabeth and Little Collins St. Open M-W 7:30am-6pm, Th 7:30am-6:30pm, F 7:30am-8pm, Sa 9am-5pm, Su 11am-5pm.

Hospital: St. Vincent's Public Hospital, 41 Victoria Pde., Fitzroy (☎9288 2211). Take any tram east along Bourke St to stop #9. **Royal Melbourne Hospital,** on Grattan St., Parkville (☎9342 7000). Take tram #19 from Elizabeth St. to stop #16.

Internet Access: There are 8 free terminals at the **State Library** (see p. 560); sign up in advance for 30min. sessions. The library's email terminals are for Australian citizens and residents only (including foreigners with a work visa or Australian student ID). In the city itself, prices tend to hover around 11-15¢ per minute. A major exception is **Traveller's Uni-Net Stop,** 211 Victoria St. (☎9326 4418), 1 block west of Vic Market, offering 8¢ per min. or $4.40 per hr. Open daily 9am-midnight. Another good deal is **Backpacker's World,** 167 Franklin St. (☎9329 1990), in Hotel Bakpak. $6 per hr.; prepaid Happy Hours $3.50 per hr. Open M-F 8am-9pm, Sa-Su 9am-8pm. St. Kilda's backpacker trades keep competitive pricing of about 7¢ per minute; multitudes of Internet shops line Fitzroy St.

Post Office: GPO (☎9203 3076), on the corner of Elizabeth and Bourke St. Mall. Fax and Poste Restante services. Open M-F 8:15am-5:30pm, Sa 10am-1pm. **Postal Code:** 3000 (CBD). The **Melbourne Airport** has a post office with full fax, photocopy, and Poste Restante services. ☎9338 3865. Open M-F 9am-5pm, Sa-Su 10am-4pm. **Postal Code:** 3045.

GETTIN' IT ONLINE IN MELBOURNE

www.visitvictoria.com Comprehensive government web site with tons of info on food, nightlife, accommodations, and events in Melbourne and all of Victoria. Events searchable by type, town, and date.

http://melbourne.citysearch.com.au An eating and drinking guide, up-to-date entertainment listings, and a comprehensive business directory.

www.mdg.com.au A selection of the best restaurants in Melbourne, searchable by location and cuisine, with online reservation placement.

⚑ ACCOMMODATIONS

Melbourne's tourist industry supports numerous budget accommodations to host its backpacker population. The two biggest hostel hives are **St. Kilda** and the area just **north of the city center** enclosed by La Trobe, Queen, Elizabeth, and Victoria St. The YHA-affiliated hostels in **North Melbourne** tend to be quieter and more sedate, popular with at least as many school groups and elderly travelers as 20-something backpackers, while the accommodations in the **city center** are as boisterous as they are conveniently located. **South Yarra** and **Prahran** lie farther afield but are preferred by those who enjoy the proximity to these districts' shopping and nightlife. The St. Kilda options generally make up for what they lack in cleanliness with an unquenchable thirst to party.

Availability drops during the **high season** (roughly Nov.-Feb.) and most accommodations raise their prices a tad ($2-4). The more popular hostels tend to be booked solid during these periods (and are also in demand during school holidays June-Aug.), so be sure to book far in advance. During summer holiday, you can usually find accommodation at universities. **Melbourne University** (Ormond College ☎9344 1121) offers B&B accommodations January and February and again in July. (Students $50 per night, non-students $55; longer than 5 days $45/$50; dinner $10.) **Monash University** (Halls of Residence ☎9905 6200) provides singles with shared bath for $30 per night from December to late January; these are not just for students. **Chisholm College** caters toward backpackers, be they students or not. (☎9479 2875. Singles $18.50, weekly $119; doubles $28/$180; available Nov. 24 to early Feb.) Take bus #350 (45min.) or #250 (1hr.) from Flinders St. Station.

Unless noted otherwise, all accommodations have a common room with TV, hall baths, 24hr. access, luggage storage, a guest kitchen, laundry machines ($2-3 wash, $1-2 dry), free linens, and no chore requirements. An increasingly popular form of deposit is an international passport in lieu of cash. You can generally get your passport back for the evening should you need it for ID purposes (many bars and clubs do not take student IDs or drivers' licenses).

CITY CENTER

■ **The Greenhouse Backpacker,** 228 Flinders Ln. (☎9639 6400; www.ron.com.au). Near Swanston St. Reception is on the 6th Fl. Most rooms have 4 beds with spring mattresses. Large lockers, sparkling bathrooms, cable TV, communal dining room, industrial-size kitchen, and roof garden. Helpful staff offer regional tours, job advice, and travel services. Pub crawl every Th night in coordination with The Friendly (see below). Free Internet 30min. per day. Coffee, tea, and first-morning brekkie included. Dorms $23, weekly $147 when booked 1 week in advance; singles $45; doubles $60. Wheelchair accessible. ❷

The Melbourne Connection, 205 King St. (☎9642 4464; www.melbourneconnection.com). Take the free city tram to Spencer and Lt. Bourke St. and walk one block up Lt. Bourke to King St. A small, clean, and friendly hostel, with standard dorm accommodations, nicer twins and singles, and very nice doubles overlooking a busy street. Ask for a room on the first (above street, "ground" level) floor. Internet $3.50 per hr. Tour bookings desk. Reception 8am-noon and 5:30-8:30pm. 12-bed dorms $20, weekly $115; 6-bed $22/$130; 4-bed $23/$140; 3-bed $24/$150; singles $45/$280; doubles $58/$350. Wheelchair accessible. Credit cards 5% service charge. ❷

The Friendly Backpacker, 197 King St. (☎9670 1111 or 1800 671 115; friendlybpacker@optusnet.com.au), 1 block east of Spencer St. Station at the corner of Little Bourke St. Not the mega-hostel like its brother the Greenhouse, but smaller and friendlier. Hallway lounges on each of 4 floors encourage interaction; cable TV and TV/VCR with movie collection encourage loafing. Weekly in-house and on-the-town activities. Heat and A/C, free Internet 30min. per day, coffee and tea, and first-morning brekkie included. Key deposit $10. Book 1 week in advance Oct.-May. Free pickup from bus station, Tassie ferry, and around town. Dorms Oct.-Mar. $23, weekly $147; Apr.-Sept. $21/$133. Wheelchair accessible. ❷

Hotel Lindrum, 26 Flinders St. (☎9668 1111; www.hotellindrum.com.au). Throughout Melbourne, you'll find small, snazzy, and pricey hotels called "boutique." If this kind of establishment is your ticket, then baby, you won't know whether you've come to the Hotel Lindrum or your own private Mecca. Big old beds, antique furniture, a bar, and lots of hardwood. All rooms have A/C and heat, direct telephone and fax lines, dataports, TV, CD players, and a whole lot of style. A breakfast to linger over is included in the price. Hardly standard Standard suites in summer $300, F-Su $215, in winter $210; superior suites $315/$230/$225; deluxe suites with great views of the city $330/$290/$254; junior suites large enough for 3 $345/$260/$225. ❺

JUST NORTH OF THE CITY CENTER

Walk uphill on Elizabeth St. past La Trobe St. or take tram #19, 55, 57, or 59 to some of the nicest budget accommodations in town.

■ **Hotel Bakpak,** 167 Franklin St. (☎9329 7525 or 1800 645 200; www.bakpak.com/franklin/index), between Elizabeth and Queen St. This cavernous 6-level facility can sleep up to 650 and has established itself as a pulsing, party-hearty nerve center for

Melbourne's backpacker scene. Bathrooms can be a mystifying trek from far-away rooms, and paper-thin walls may compromise privacy (or sleep), but no one beats Bakpak's cornucopia of amenities, including a budget travel agency, free airport pickup, free entry to local gym, employment service, basement "Roo Bar," cafe, Internet $6 per hr., small movie theater, and unique "Cabana style" showers. Roo Bar parties with daily Happy Hours that offer amazingly cheap drinks pave the way to friendship for many travelers. No smoking. Breakfast included. 10- to 16-bed barrack $18; smaller dorms $20-22; singles $55; twins and doubles $60. VIP. ❷

■ **Stork Hotel,** 504 Elizabeth St. (☎9663 6237; www.storkhotel.com), at the corner of Therry St., adjacent to the QVM. Brimming with character, this historic building is an entertaining, and dare we say, educational, home-away-from-home. All rooms have gorgeous antique bedsteads and their own informative themes; ask for the Great Ocean Road room, the Foster's Lager room, or, yes, even the Ned Kelly room, a lonely-hearts' single with a little extra presence (see **Old Melbourne Gaol,** p. 574). Ground-floor pub attracts a quirky mix of locals and travelers and hosts live music featuring area artists nightly (no cover) and occasional plays. Sunny cafe attached makes cheap meals with fresh market produce. Towel and soap included. 5-bed dorms $25; singles $48; twins and doubles $58. ❷

Hotel Y, 489 Elizabeth St. (☎9329 5188 or 1800 249 124; www.travel-ys.com), between Therry and Franklin St., less than a block from the Transit Center. The Y has the feel of a luxury hotel with stellar ensuite rooms, snazzy lobby, and the sleek Cafe Y. Internet $2 per 30min. Coffee, tea, TV, phone, soap, and shampoo in every room. The roof garden and hallway picture-windows offer high-rise views of the city below. Check-in 1pm. Budget singles $80, deluxe with A/C $99; twins and doubles $93/$120; triples $109/$131. YMCA/YWCA 10% discount. Book several weeks ahead; credit card to confirm booking. ❺

Toad Hall, 441 Elizabeth St. (☎9600 9010; www.toadhall-hotel.com.au), between A'Beckett and Franklin St. A classier, more reserved place, several cuts above the frenetic backpacker scene, Toad Hall combines the intimacy of a B&B with the conveniences and attentive staff of a large inn. Airy kitchen, plant-filled patio, quiet reading room, and basement den with cable TV, VCR, and stereo. Shared bathrooms; larger dorms have bath. Cushy quilt included. Laundry facilities and off-street parking. Heat in private rooms and larger dorms. Key deposit $20. Reception daily 7am-10pm. Dorms in summer $25, in winter $20; singles, twins, and doubles $60; ensuite $90. Bookings advised. VIP/YHA. MC/V. ❷

NORTH MELBOURNE

Residential North Melbourne is quieter and more relaxed than the city center. Though its accommodations are quite a hike from downtown, it's accessible by tram #57 and 59 from Elizabeth St. and tram #55 from William St.

■ **Chapman Gardens YHA Hostel,** 76 Chapman St. (☎9328 3595; chapman@yhavic.org.au). Take tram #57 north to stop 18 and turn right onto Chapman St.; the hostel is on the left. Small but cozy rooms in a quiet, residential neighborhood, with a gazebo out back. As a newly-designated eco-hostel, the C-Gardens uses solar heating, recycles everything from clothing to food waste, and raises their own worms to fertilize the backyard herb gardens. Free parking, bike hire, and passes to the City Baths. Breakfast $5. Luggage storage $2. Key deposit $10. Reception daily 7:30am-12:30pm and 2-10pm. 3-, 4-, and 5-bed dorms $24, YHA $21; dorm twins $26/$22; singles $44/$40; doubles $54/$50. May-Nov. 7th night free. Book ahead. ❷

Queensberry Hill YHA, 78 Howard St. (☎9329 8599; queensberryhill@yhavic.org.au). Take tram #55 north from William St. to stop 11 on Queensberry St., then go 2 blocks west to Howard St. Fairly institutional but unquestionably functional, this YHA is a 348-

room congregation of services beyond simple shelter from the storm. Free parking and bike hire, passes to city baths, rooftop patio with BBQ, licensed bistro, travel agency, huge kitchen, and pool tables. Internet $4 per hr. Currency exchange $2. 2-week max. stay. Dorms $26, YHA $22; singles $59/$55; ensuite doubles $75-86/$65-78; family rooms $89/$85; apartments $115. Book ahead in summer. Wheelchair accessible. ❸

FITZROY

■ **The Nunnery,** 116 Nicholson St. (☎9419 8637 or 1800 032 635; www.bakpak.com/nunnery). Stop 13 on tram #96, at the northeast corner of Carlton Gardens. Housed in the former convent of the Daughters of Mercy, this heavenly hostel has dorms with high ceilings, halls that are snazzily decorated with an incongruous mix of religious paraphernalia and New Age psychedelia, a breezy wooden deck with BBQ, rooms with balconies overlooking the Gardens, and unbeatable proximity to the "bohemian" pleasures of Brunswick St. The attached "guest house" (122 King St.) is considerably quieter, with upscale "boutique" rooms featuring classy wicker furniture and fireplaces. Towel and soap included. Wine, cheese, and weekly raffle F night, fluffy pancakes Su brekkie. Internet $2 per 30min. Key deposit $20 or passport. Check-out 9:30am. Reception 8am-8pm. 10-12 bed dorms $20; 6-8 bed $22, weekly $144; 4-bed $25/$165; 3-bed $27; singles $50/$315; bunk twins $55-60/$380; twins and doubles $60-70/$450; triples $85/$560. Boutique doubles $85, family rooms $90. VIP. ❷

MIDDLE PARK

Middle Park Hotel, 102 Canterbury Rd. (☎9690 1882; www.middleparkhotel.com). Across from the Middle Park stop on trams #95 and 96. 1km from St. Kilda, less than 400m from the beach. Quality budget accommodation in a restored 1890s building with high ceilings, clean rooms, spacious hallway showers, and lastly, what we all secretly crave in a hostel, a microbrewery. Watch your beer be born on the spot. Pub food $3-12; attached **Shebah** serves pricier dishes M-Sa noon-3pm and 6-9pm. Job placement assistance. No heating, though thick doonas are provided. Towel and M-F breakfast included. Key deposit $10. Reception M-F 7:30am-5pm, Sa 9am-1pm; arrange ahead for after-hours or Su check-in. 4-to 6-bed dorms $17, weekly $98; singles $25/$195; doubles $50/$250. ❷

SOUTH YARRA AND PRAHRAN

■ **Chapel St. Backpackers (NOMADS),** 22 Chapel St., Prahran (☎9533 6855; www.csbackpackers.com.au), just north of Dandenong Rd. across from Windsor train station, on tram routes #78 and 79. One of the best places in town, just a stumble from both Melbourne's best nightlife and St. Kilda. Staff is super-friendly and guests are social, often teaming up to hit the local hotspots. Dorms and doubles all have refreshingly clean bathrooms. Heat and A/C. Breakfast included. Internet $6 per hr. Key deposit $20. Check-out 10:30am. 6-bed dorms $20, weekly $133; 4-bed $23/$154; twins $50/$322; doubles $70/$483. Prices rise slightly in the summer. ❷

Claremont B&B (NOMADS), 189 Toorak Rd., South Yarra (☎9826 8000 or 1300 301 630; www.hotelclaremont.com), 1 block east of the South Yarra train station, on tram route #8. The only budget stay in one of the poshest sections of Melbourne. A beautifully refurbished 1886 building, it retains much of its Victorian charm while still providing all the modern amenities. Clean, bright rooms with hardwood floors, wrought-iron beds, heaters, ceiling fans, and TVs. Small but spotless hall baths. Breakfast and towels included. Internet $6 per hr. Singles $58; doubles and twins $68; additional person $15; peak season $10 surcharge. Reservations essential. ❹

Lord's Lodge, 204 Punt Rd., Prahran (☎9510 5658). Take tram #3, 5, 6, 16, 64, or 67 south on St. Kilda Rd to stop 26 and walk east 2 blocks along Moubray St. A bit removed from St. Kilda but a short walk to Chapel St., several tram stops, Albert Park,

THE HOUSE OF BAD TASTE If you drive down Canterbury Rd. from St. Kilda toward the city center, be prepared for a double-take. Along the right side of the road, amidst scores of standard modern homes, there stands a monstrous creation: a house with a completely flat front covered in shiny laser-blue paneling. If your eyes aren't too sore, take a closer look. Yep, that's Pamela Anderson's face imprinted across the entire two-floor facade. You gotta wonder if the neighbors enjoy watching the owner drive his car out of the busty blonde's mouth every morning. Ouch.

and Commercial Rd. This reasonably clean dig attracts seasoned travelers of all types. All rooms have heaters, lockers, and fridges, except for the one tiny single dubbed the "dog's box." 3 surprisingly elegant private bungalows out back have TVs, mini-fridges, and cute black-and-white tiled floors. Coffee and tea included. Cheap Internet and fax. Reception M-Sa 8:30-11:30am and 5-6pm, Su 8:30-11:30am. 4- to 8-bed dorms $18, weekly $115; dog's box $25; doubles and bungalows $45, in summer $55. ❷

The Hatton Hotel, 65 Park St. (☎9868 4800; www.hatton.com.au). A petite "boutique," with just 20 rooms, a silver spoon's throw from the Botanic Gardens. Flowery scents waft into elegantly appointed (and super-clean) chambers, where much care is given to color-coordination and preservation of the building's 19th century eccentricities. All rooms ensuite, with A/C and heat, kitchenette with sink, microwave, fridge, TV, king- or queen-sized bed, hair dryer, and iron and board. Standard doubles and twins $175; "superior" $195; 1 very special double with antique Asian furniture $275. ❺

ST. KILDA

St. Kilda is **backpacker heaven,** with dirt-cheap and often unkempt, grungy hostels—but hey, you get what you pay for. The hostels, centered around Grey St., largely mirror the precinct's fun-loving, gritty flavor. Though removed from the city center, it's easily accessible by tram (stop 133 on lines #16 and 96). The beach, restaurants, and lively nightlife of St. Kilda are in easy reach. If you're coming in March, book way ahead to avoid the hassle of the Grand Prix crowd (see p. 580).

Olembia, 96 Barkly St. (☎9537 1412; www.olembia.com.au), tucked behind a small canopy near the intersection with Grey St. You'll never believe you're in a hostel. Gorgeous living room with sofas and fireplace, glass doors, and a loving feline named Alexander the Great. Ornate, high-ceilinged heated rooms with comfy mattresses are impeccably clean as are the bathrooms. Sincere and friendly staff will point you to all the best places in town. Was home ever this good? Free parking. Bike hire $12 per day. 1 week max. stay. Key deposit $10. Reception 7am-1pm and 5-8pm. 3- to 4-bed dorms $24; singles $46; twins and doubles with box-springs $70. Book ahead in summer. ❷

Jackson's Manor, 53 Jackson St. (☎9534 1877; www.jacksonsmanor.com.au). The one-time home of a rich English architect, this little yellow Edwardian gem attracts a quieter crowd. Well heated and impeccably clean throughout, with comfortable rooms and a spacious living area featuring plants, stained glass windows, and a large oriental rug. Amenities include a furnished kitchen and ping pong and foosball room. Internet $4 per hr. Job and travel assistance. The proximity of the other Grey St. backpackers without all the grunge. Free parking. 6-to 10-bed $19, weekly $128; 4-bed $24/$150; singles $58/$380; twins and doubles $60/$380. $12-14 discount for weekly stays. ❷

Pint on Punt (NOMADS), 42 Punt Rd. (☎9510 4273 or 1800 737 378; admin@pinton-punt.com.au), just north of St. Kilda Junction, on the corner of Peel St. Take tram #3, 5, 16, 64, or 67 from Flinders St. Station. New and clean, the Pint has large rooms with new mattresses. Free continental breakfast, and 30% discount offered on pub meals downstairs. Open mic W nights and live music Th-Su, but rooms generally stay quiet. Free pickup from city or airport; arrange ahead. Internet $1 per 15min. Key deposit

$10. Check-in at reception 7am-noon or at the bar until 1am. Bar open M-Sa noon-1am, Su noon-11pm. 4- to 6-bed dorms $17-22; singles $35; twins and doubles $45. 7th night free. NOMADS/VIP/YHA. ❷

Enfield House, 2 Enfield St. (☎1800 302 121; infoenfield@bakpakgroup.com). Take tram #16 or 96 to stop 30 by Fitzroy and Grey St. Walk half a block down Grey St., turn right on Jackson St., then left onto Enfield St. Another B&B-stylish gem. Same owners as **Hotel Bakpak** downtown, but much more mellow. Front living room hosts M movie nights on a funky old-time projector. Circus-colored heated rooms and shared bathrooms are clean. Job assistance. Free continental breakfast M-F, pancakes Sa-Su. Reception M-F 8am-8pm, Sa-Su 8am-1pm and 5-8pm. 4-to 8-bed dorms $19-20; singles $40; twins and doubles $50; triples $62. 7th night free. Prices rise $2-3 in summer; book ahead. VIP. ❷

Coffee Palace Backpackers Hotel, 24 Grey St. (☎9534 5283 or 1800 654 098; www.backpackerscentre.com), 1 block off Fitzroy St. Really popular, but only with those who enjoy a party atmosphere. Plenty of amenities, including travel and employment services, a games room, and free pickup from bus station or airport. Hallway walls are notable for their impressive artwork but not for their soundproofing. Morning pancakes included. Internet $5 per 80min. Key deposit passport. 6-bed dorms $18; 4-bed $19, ensuite $22; twins and doubles $44. Pay 2 nights stay in full on arrival in winter and receive 3 free nights. Prices rise in summer. VIP. ❷

The Ritz for Backpackers, 169 Fitzroy St. (☎9525 3501 or 1800 670 364). Tram #16 lets off at stop 132 out front. Just above the **Elephant and Wheelbarrow** (see p. 585), the Ritz is friendly, active, and absolutely mad in summertime. Group activities inspire close bonds between staff and guests. Rooms are fairly sparse, but the 10-bed apartment suite upstairs has a couch, kitchen, and large windows with a view of Albert Park. Heaters available in winter; deposit for doona. Free morning pancakes. Key deposit passport or license. Check-out 9:30am. Internet $5 per hr. Reception 6am-10pm. Limited positions available to work in exchange for accommodation. Dorms $18-20; twins and doubles $44-48; apartment suite $20 per person. Prices rise in summer. VIP. ❷

Tolarno Boutique Hotel, 42 Fitzroy St. (☎9534 0200 or 1800 620 363; www.hotleto-larno.com.au). An upscale paradise of just 31 rooms, with bar/restaurant downstairs and fine attention to detail everywhere. Built in 1884 to be the mayor's mansion, the building underwent additions and renovations in the 1930s and '60s and emerged with an amalgam of styles: from Deco to rococo to retro, it's (as its owners say) "glowing inside and out." Suites $115-275, all with TV, heat, queen-sized bed, and coffee maker; balconies, kitchenettes, and Japanese baths available. Twin-shares for up to 3 $150. ❺

▣ FOOD

Of the Australian cities known for great food, Melbourne has perhaps the most diversity, taking its cuisine from its multicultural makeup. Explore steamy China-town holes-in-the-wall, Fitzroy *café couture*, Carlton's Italian cuisine, South Yarra's sidewalk bistros, or St. Kilda's mix of backpacker-targeted and upscale eateries. Interesting hybrids arise, with Chinese restaurants serving french fries, sushi, and cappuccino. The city's restaurants constitute a scene in and of themselves; on most nights, Melburnians pack into their favorite eateries until closing time (which is often whenever the proprietors feel like shutting the doors). Enjoy.

CITY CENTER

Amid the fast-paced urban jungle of Melbourne's CBD lurk what seem like a million fantastic eateries, hidden away in labyrinthine corridors or diminutive crannies between high-rise buildings. Many are Asian, representing Chinese, Japanese, Indian, Nepalese, Sri Lankan, Malaysian, Indonesian, and Vietnamese flavors.

Neon-pulsing **Chinatown** fills the stretch of Little Bourke St., hemmed in by colorful red gates between Swanston and Exhibition St. Blink and you'll miss the **Greek Precinct**, on Lonsdale St. between Swanston and Russell St. It's only a half dozen or so pricey Hellenic restaurants and taverns, but serves god-like baklava. Many of the coolest cafes, most with a European air, call the CBD home as well; they often lurk in narrow brick pathways (such as the **Block Arcade**, between Collins and Little Collins St.) that snake through the city. For those do-it-yourself folks, a Coles 24-hr. **supermarket** hides amidst the bustle of Elizabeth St. just north of Flinders St. Above all, the city center rewards the adventurous gourmet; wander around with only your nose and palate as a guide and you're sure to find a culinary treasure.

Cafée Baloo, 260 Russell St. (☎9663 3226), between Little Lonsdale and Lonsdale St. Mixes South Asian fare with pasta and sandwiches in an environs that attains just the right balance of darkly trendy and friendly. Bowls of produce displayed out front go into heaping portions of tasty curry and pasta with or without meat, all around $6-10. 50¢ table charge per person; no alcohol. Open M-F noon-10pm, Sa-Su 4-10pm. ❶

Hopetoun Tea Rooms (☎9650 2777), in the Block Arcade off Elizabeth St., ground level. Enjoy very fine teas (from $5) in super-posh, evergreen surrounds. A nice spot to alight in the afternoon: your betters will be impressed by your good taste in tea room. Also serves light fare under $20. Open M-Th 9am-5pm, F 9am-6pm, Sa 10am-3pm. ❷

Teayara Cafe and Gallery Restaurant, 230 King St. (☎9600 2777), between Little Bourke and Lonsdale St. Opened in May 2001, this classy dive offers quality pastas ($6), 3-course lunch boxes ($15-25), coffee and cake specials ($4), and a gradual integration of Indonesian fare. Upstairs seating amongst authentic Indonesian paintings, masks, and furniture provides a romantic and exotic setting. Fully licensed and BYO. Open M-Sa 7am-late. ❶

Krome Kafe, 273 Swanston St. (☎9663 8199). Dark, little, and laid-back, the Krome is all style. Breakfast is served all day, and there's an extensive cocktail selection. Live entertainment F night. Open Su-Th 8am-11pm, F-Sa 8am-1am. MC/V. ❷

Fast Eddy's Cafe, 32 Bourke St. (☎9662 3551). A favorite of the late-night crowd for its 24hr. greasy breakfast and burgers. ❶

NORTH MELBOURNE

The Queen Victoria Market (QVM; see p. 574) serves as the focal point of culinary North Melbourne. In fact, much of the city congregates here, where you can get all the fresh ingredients you need to cook up a fabulous and inexpensive dinner. The surrounding area is home to some fine eateries as well. From the city, take any tram north on William or Elizabeth St.

La Porchetta, 302-308 Victoria St. (☎9326 9884), across from the QVM. "The Pizza Institution." Hundreds of tantalizing wood-fired pizzas (small $4.80, medium $6.10, large $7.20), in styles from Margarita to Mexican, all of excellent quality at unbeatable prices. Takeaway available. Fully licensed and BYO wine only. Open M-Th 11am-midnight, F-Sa 11am-1am. ❶

The White Lotus, 185 Victoria St. (☎9326 6040). 1 block west of QVM. Entirely vegan menu at this glowing white resto attempts to guide the "way to heaven," following the Buddhist tenets of Tien Tao. All meals prepared without meat, animal products, or even onions and garlic. Carnivores will be placated—nay, amazed—by the excellent imitation meat dishes, like mock abalone made from soy and wheat gluten or the spicy Mongolian "beef." Meals $8-14. Dine-in or takeaway. BYO. Open daily 5:30-11pm, also Th-F noon-2:30pm. ❷

Vic Marketplace (☎9320 5822), in the QVM. The covered arcade has excellent budget fare, mostly made from fresh goods sold next door. **Vic Fish** serves a $6.50 fish 'n' chips

THE HIDDEN DEAL

CROSSWAYS FOOD FOR LIFE

Satisfy your spirit and your stomach at this literal hole-in-the-wall Melbourne eatery. Imagine a place where people from every walk of life—backpackers, businessmen, and even nomadic wanderers—converge to consume mass quantities of carbs and good karma. At Crossways, fantastic food is the great equalizer of the classes; all can partake in these generous offerings. The all-you-can-eat vegetarian lunch specials change daily and include rice, vegetable, dessert, and choice of lassi for a mere $5.50 ($3.80 concessions). Sit and soak up the positive vibes of the contented masses, or ponder the mysteries of the universe with your table's own copies of "On the way to Krishna" and the "Introduction to the Bhagavad-gita." By your fifth plateful of veggie goodness, you'll feel that everpresent weight lift from your shoulders; *Let's Go* guarantees you'll leave shiny and happy, with a whole new perspective on life. Crossways's narrow doors are difficult to spot, but the periodic Hare Krishna chanters outside help point the way to both food and enlightenment. *(123 Swanston St., across from Town Hall. ☎ 9650 2939. Open M-Sa 11:30am-2:30pm.)*

lunch packet. **Afghan** purveys Middle Eastern breads, kabobs, falafel, and dips ($4-7). The **Consciousness Cafe** has healthy salads and sandwiches ($4-6). Hours vary, but market usually open Tu and Th 6am-2pm, F 6am-6pm, Sa 6am-3pm, Su 9am-4pm. ❶

aioli, 229 Victoria St. (☎9328 1090), 2 blocks west of QVM. Bright green and red walls and a garden out back only enhance the phatitude of this classy, healthy culinary establishment. A variety of wraps run $6, while the uniquely blended "aioli cleanser" drink goes for $3.50. Open Tu-Sa 7:30am-4:30pm, Su 10am-3pm. ❶

CARLTON

The best known street in Carlton is **Lygon St.,** where tons of chic Italian pizzerias, cafes, and gelaterias combat budget but tasty Thai and Vietnamese joints along the five-block stretch between Queensberry St. to the south and Elgin St. to the north. The eclectic nature of the area decidedly draws in a diverse crowd; and despite its attendant student traffic from the nearby University of Melbourne, most of the Italian eateries remain out of the budget traveler's range. There are, however, a fair number of affordable non-Italian places, and a few cafes where you can find cheap dishes. Hawkers outside all the major restaurants after nightfall ensure that not too much exploration is necessary to find a fine eatery.

▨ **Threshermans Bakehouse Café,** 221 Faraday St. (☎9349 2319). Long communal tables and brick floors transport you to a farm in the south of France and set you up for the best dining value in Carlton: $6 for a large plate of Asian stir-fry, $3.80 for a foccacia pizza, $5 for soup and bread. With all the money you've saved on dinner, head over to the other counter for a delicious cannoli ($2.50) or an enormous slice of cake ($4.20). Fresh, creative fruit juices ($3.70) are squeezed before your very eyes. After 4pm, day-old pastries are just $1. Internet $2 per 20min. Open daily 6am-11pm; hot food served 11am-11pm. ❶

▨ **Jimmy Watson's Wine Bar,** 333 Lygon St. (☎9347 3985). With over 300 wines to choose from and courses on wine appreciation, Jimmy's, one of the oldest wine bars in Melbourne (since 1962), caters to an older local crowd for the most part. But your more discerning Uni-ites can definitely be found at the bar. Traditional restaurant serves meals that run from $40. Open M 10am-6pm, Tu-Sa 10:30am-10:30pm. ❺

Tiamo, 303 Lygon St. (☎9347 5759). Dark and flavorful, this pasta palace dishes out a range of Italian fare of the same quality as its pricier neighbors across the way. Its next-door sequel, **Tiamo2** (☎9347 0911), serves a more sophisticated selection in a lighter, classier setting. Cooked-to-perfection pasta $10-12, creamy tiramisu $6, breakfast until noon $4-11. Licensed and BYO. Tiamo open M-Sa 7am-11pm, Su 8am-10pm; Tiamo2 open M-Sa 9:30am-10:30pm. ❷

Toto's, 101 Lygon St. (☎9437 1630). Big and busy, Toto's serves a range of meals (from pasta to sirloin to fish-of-the-day), but their pizza's the real sensation. 3 sizes and about a dozen combinations, all hot, chewy, and flavorful ($7-11). Breakfasts $3.40-4.50; all-you-can-eat lunch $10. Licensed and BYO wine. Open daily 8am-11pm. V. ❶

Boba Pearl Bubble Tea Restaurant, 122 Lygon St. (☎9663 0498). Serves excellent Chinese noodles and more ($7-9), but the real story here is the 62 varieties of tea and tea-related frozen drinks ($3.50, 50¢ for extra jelly cubes) available. Put some lychee, peppermint, taro, or red bean into your day. Open daily 11am-late. ❶

FITZROY AND COLLINGWOOD

The heart of Melbourne's bohemian scene and cafe society lies in Fitzroy, along **Brunswick St.** between Gertrude and Princes St. Particularly on sunny weekend days, hippies, post-hippies, ferals, and freaks of every ilk frequent the countless artsy coffeehouses and eateries. As always, though, much mainstream and wanna-be chic intermingles with their opposites in an attempt to feel cutting edge. The area gets progressively posher as you go south along Brunswick, closer to the city. The stretch of Johnston St. just west of Brunswick St. is Melbourne's Latin Quarter, with Latin dance clubs, Iberian grocers, and several great—but pricey—tapas bars. There are also dining options galore along **Smith St.** in Collingwood.

▨ **Nyala,** 113 Brunswick St. (☎9419 9128). The best of East Africa, with some Gambia and Morocco thrown in for kicks. Nyala is all about flavor; meat and vegetable mains ($11-15) retain their natural savory goodness while enhanced by special combinations of season and spice. If you're strapped for cash, try one of the tasty dips, served with the delightfully satisfying thin Mahloul bread ($5.50). You'll have room for one of their rich desserts ($4-6) and still be able to reach the $10 per person min. (only on F-Sa nights). Open Tu-Su 6-10:30pm, also W-Su 11:30am-3pm. ❷

Guernica, 257 Brunswick St. (☎9416 0969). Award-winning nouveau-Aussie cuisine doesn't come cheap, and this place (with $30 mains) is no exception. Great fusion and seafood wins you over. Open daily 6-10:30pm, also Su-F noon-3pm. ❺

Vegie Bar, 380 Brunswick St. (☎9417 6935). A converted warehouse where Fitzroy's large meat-averse population gathers to chow guilt-free, single-g "vegie" meals. They promise "food for the body and soul" and serve it up in heaping portions. Mains all under $9.30. Quiet during the day, but evenings draw a crowd. Loads of vegan and wheat-free options. Fully licensed and BYO wine only. Open daily 11am-10pm. ❶

Veg Out Time (positive eating), 406 Brunswick St. (☎9416 4077). Also at 63a Fitzroy St., St. Kilda (☎9534 0077). If there's a shortage of seating at Vegie Bar, try slightly more basic and more brightly lit Veg Out for its cheap Indian and Thai delights ($6-9). Vegetables are indeed the last vessels of good in this evil world. Open daily 4-10pm. ❶

Mario's, 303 Brunswick St. (☎9417 3343). This cafe is hard to spot—a small neon sign bears its name—but it sports some of the best breakfast buys in town ($7-10), served all day. Those who spurn the first meal of the day can grab $9-17 pasta dishes or just pop in for a gourmet dessert ($5-7). Fully licensed. Open daily 7am-midnight. ❷

Retro Café, 413 Brunswick St. (☎9419 1299; www.retro.net.au), on the corner of Westgarth St. If you think the bright yellow facade on the building is cool, check out the waterfall and TV-turned-aquarium inside. Meals run the gamut in both price and cuisine, from Mediterranean stuffed grape leaves ($6) to the age-old Aussie kangaroo with roasted root veggies ($19). 2-course menu $28 per person; 3-course $33. Live music every Th 8:30pm, cover $5. Open daily 7am-late; breakfast served until 6pm. Bar open M-Sa until 1am, Su until 11pm. ❹

Robert Burns Hotel, 376 Smith St. (☎9417 2233). Just north of Johnston St. Behind the non-Iberian name hides great value Spanish fare. Eat in the large, simple restaurant, or for a cheaper meal, sit in the bright front bar. Beyond the standard tortilla, the Robbie Burns serves a range of steaks $12-24. Seafood galore from $10. Paella $15 per person, 2-person min. Tapas served from 2:30pm in the bar. Nightly live music. Bar open M-Sa 11am-midnight; kitchen open M-Sa noon-2:30pm and 6-10pm. MC/V. ❸

SOUTH YARRA AND PRAHRAN

Preened, pricey South Yarra aggressively markets itself as the place to see and be seen, and its mod-Oz bistros with sidewalk seating see their share of black-clad fashion mavens after a day of shopping on Chapel St. There are some excellent budget options though, particularly south of Commercial St. in more down-to-earth Prahran. The ubiquitous coffee bars are a wallet-friendly way to sample the scene (cappuccino around $2.50). Check out the Prahran Market, on Commercial Rd. at Izett St., for cheap, fresh produce, meat, and ethnic foodstuffs.

■ **Borsch Vodka and Tears,** 173 Chapel St. (☎9530 2694). A divine, warm little den of many (60, to be precise) vodkas ($5-6 per shot), dumplings, sausages, and of course that cool beet-y soup, borscht (soup $6.50, mains $14-19). The Spirytus is 80-proof and good for whatever ails ya—you bring the tears. Open daily 10am-1am. ❸

■ **Gurkha's Brasserie,** 190-192 Chapel St. (☎9510 3325; www.gurkhas.com.au). Delicious Nepalese cuisine comes at a reasonable price in an ornate restaurant bedecked with lanterns and peaceful South Asian music. It might take you a while to figure out what to order, but a good bet is the *Dal Bhat Masu*, which comes with your choice of meat curry (the goat is wonderfully tender), soup, and rice or bread for only $14. Mains $11-19. Licensed and BYO wine ($1 corkage per person). Open daily 5:30-10:30pm. ❷

Jamon Sushi, 205 Greville St. (☎9510 2928). Around the corner from the bustle of Chapel St., this place is not cheap, but the sushi is absolutely divine. After two bites of the sushi and roll combo platter, the $30+ you just forked over will be but a distant memory. Sushi or sashimi platters $18-27; sushi and nori roll lunch boxes $15-22. Fully licensed. Open daily 6:30pm-late. ❺

Gelato Bar, Shop 3, 534 Chapel St. (☎9824 0099). Offering some of the cheapest meals in South Yarra, this new and colorful cafe is a good break from shopping or people-watching. Deli-style focaccia sandwiches, filled pastries, and calzones ($6); homemade gelati indulgence ($3-6). For a substantial snack, try one of their enormous seasoned breadsticks, served hot ($1). Open daily 8am-late. ❶

ST. KILDA

With all the hipness of South Yarra and Chapel St. but far less pretentiousness, St. Kilda offers diverse and exciting menus in quality affordable eateries interspersed with many decidedly non-budget options. The result is a delightful mix of value and vogue. You can't go wrong with the holes-in-the-wall or fancier bistros on Fitzroy St.; the Barkly St. end of Acland St.—legendary among locals for its divine cake shops—also has a menagerie of great cuisine of all ethnic stripes. Coles 24hr. **supermarket** is in the Acland Court shopping center near Barkly St.

■ **Chinta Ria,** 94 Acland St. (☎9525 4666). The point of "soul" in a local Malaysian restaurant triangle (its sister fares are home to the "jazz," 9/176 Commercial Rd., Prahran; and "blues," 6 Acland St., St. Kilda). New York chic but still contemplative, Ria matches its delectable $15-19 mains with comparable quality. Fried rice and noodle selections $8-12. The changing dessert menu is sweet and sinful ($7-10). Open daily noon-2:30pm; also M-Sa 6-10:30pm. MC/V. ❸

Monarch Cake Shop, 103 Acland St. (☎9534 2972). The oldest cake shop on Acland St.'s cake-shop row (est. 1934 in Carlton, moved to St. Kilda late-1930s) and still the best. Their famous plum cake is the most popular seller ($3 slice), but the chocolate *kugelhopf* is near bliss ($13-14). Open daily from 7-9am to 10pm. ❶

Wild Rice, 211 Barkly St. (☎9534 2849). Also at 159 Chapel St., South Yarra. Enter this dark store front to find an imaginative universe of vegan delicacies. Meals are based on the principle of "macrobiotics": basically, they use only seasonal produce in order to "balance the body's energy." Rice, veggie, and noodle mains $10-14, but pakhoras and tofu pockets fall under $7. Lush garden courtyard out back. Deluxe veggie brekkie served Su 9am-3pm. Open daily noon-10pm. ❷

Blue Corn, 205 Barkly St. (☎9534 5996). Very fresh Mexican fare at excellent prices. Try the array of dips with blue corn bread (guacamole, salsa, black turtle bean dip, and olive chipotle$10) or the lime and swordfish taco ($12). Open M-Su 6-10pm. ❷

The Stokehouse, 30 Jacka Blvd. (☎9525 5555), near the St. Kilda Baths. With decks for observation of the sea in fine weather and a downstairs bar for shelter in the foul. Pricier contemporary Australian fare and grill items (from $25) in the restaurant; pizza and fish 'n' chips in the bar. Bar-cafe open M-Sa 11am-late, Sa-Su 10am-late; restaurant and bar open daily noon-midnight. ❺

◎ SIGHTS

CITY CENTER

▨ **RIALTO TOWERS.** Rising 253m above the city, the Rialto Towers is the tallest office building in the Southern Hemisphere. The 55th floor observation deck provides spectacular 360° views of the city and surrounds. The assuredly addictive "Zoom City" live-action video cameras allow you to zoom in and see people crossing the street all the way across town. **Rialtovision Theatre** plays a 20-minute film, *Melbourne, the Living City* that highlights tourist spots with cheesy music and dramatic, wide-angle shots. *(525 Collins St., 1 block east of Spencer St. Station, between King and William St. ☎9629 8222; www.melbournedeck.com.au. Open Su-Th 10am-10pm, F-Sa 10am-11pm. Film every 30min. Film and deck $11, concessions $8, children $6, families $30.)* To those without the deep pockets, **Hotel Sofitel,** at the opposite end of Collins St., at the intersection with Exhibition St., offers a similar view, free of charge. Take the elevator to the 35th floor bathroom, lean out the window with care, and stare into the abyss of the Melbourne skyline.

▨ **IMMIGRATION MUSEUM.** Chronicling the 200 years of Australian immigration, the museum combines collected artifacts with a moving soundtrack, much of which is triggered by visitors' footsteps in the gallery. A mock ship in the main room shows typical living quarters aboard ocean-going ships from the 1840s to the 1950s. Recent efforts have also begun to explore the Aboriginal experience as a struggle to maintain a sense of continuity among a foreign culture. Ground-floor resource center contains links to immigrant ship listings as well as a genealogy database. *(400 Flinders St.; in the Old Customs House on the corner of William St. A City Circle Tram stop. ☎9927 2700. Open daily 10am-5pm. $7, concession and YHA $5.50, children $3.50, families $18; resource center free. Wheelchair accessible. AmEx/DC/MC/V.)*

ST. PAUL'S CATHEDRAL. The Anglican cathedral, completed in 1891, impresses not in its scale but in the intricacy of its detail. The beautifully stenciled pipes of the 19th-century Lewis organ are easy to miss; look up to the right of the altar. Evening song services echo throughout the hallowed hall Monday through Friday 5:10pm and Su 6pm. *(Presides over the corner of Flinders and Swanston St., diagonal to Flinders St. Station. Enter on Swanston St. Open daily 7am-6pm. Free.)*

STATE LIBRARY OF VICTORIA. A great space to read or work, with a variety of international newspapers, the State Library is worth a visit if just for the interior design. The whole place is undergoing a $200 million renovation (completion date set for 2004) that will most notably reinstate glass to the roof of the Domed Reading Room, a spectacular octagonal space soaring 35m high. An eastern section, formerly the home of the Museum of Victoria (see p. 560), holds a fraction of the permanent collection of the **National Gallery of Victoria** (p. 575) while the gallery undergoes renovations. *(At La Trobe and Swanston St. ☎9669 9888; www.slv.vic.gov.au. Free tours M-F and every other Sa 2pm. Open M-Th 10am-9pm, F-Su 10am-6pm.)*

CHINATOWN. The pagoda gates at the corner of Swanston and Little Bourke St. indicate your arrival at a two-block stretch of Asian restaurants, groceries, and bars that was first settled by Chinese immigrants in the 1870s. A block and a half east, the back-alley **Chinese Museum** houses *Dai Loong* (Great Dragon), the **biggest imperial dragon in the world** (not the longest, which is in Bendigo VIC) and a staple of Melbourne's Moomba festival (see p. 580) that is so huge it has to be wound around two entire floors. The third floor provides a brief but honest look at ethnic discrimination as well as some great photographs of influential Chinese community members in the early 20th century. *(22 Cohen Pl. ☎9662 2888. $6.50, concessions $4.50. Open daily 10am-4:30pm. Wheelchair accessible.)*

PARLIAMENT OF VICTORIA AND OLD TREASURY. Victoria's parliament is a stout, pillared 19th-century edifice every bit as stolid and imposing as a seat of government should be. Free tours detail the workings of the Victorian government and the architectural intricacies of the parliament chambers. *(on Spring St. north of Bourke St. A City Circle Tram stop. ☎9651 8568; www.parliament.vic.gov.au. Tours when Parliament is not in session 10, 11am, noon, 2, 3, and 3:45pm. No self-guided tours.)* Designed in Italian Palazzo style by a 19-year-old prodigy, the **Old Treasury Building** contains a museum chronicling Melbourne's past, including some great stories about the idiosyncrasies of the city's first years. The gold vaults in the basement were built to prevent a crime wave that plagued the Treasury during the Victorian Gold Rush; they now house a multimedia exhibit detailing daily life and events of Melbourne's gold-rush era. *(On Spring St., at Collins St. ☎9651 2233; www.oldtreasurymuseum.org.au. Open M-F 9am-5pm, Sa-Su 10am-4pm. $5, concessions $3, seniors $4, families $13.)*

FITZROY GARDENS. These gardens, originally planted in 1848 and laid out in the shape of the Union Jack, bloom year round. On the south end is Cook's Cottage, a small stone home constructed by Captain James Cook's family in England in 1755 and moved to Melbourne in 1934 to celebrate the city's centennial. Cook never actually reached the site and may not even have spent time in this house, but the information room has a concise but complete history of his voyages. Next door, the colorfully stocked Conservatory greenhouse has seasonal plants and flowers. Weekends in December through January often bring concerts and other summer events to the gardens. *(Gardens bordered by Lansdowne, Albert, and Clarendon St. and Wellington Pde. Tram #48 or 75 from Flinders St. Free garden tour W 11am, starting from the conservatory. Cook's Cottage: ☎9419 4677. $3.30, concessions $2.20. Conservatory: ☎9419 4118. Free tour W 12:30pm. Both open daily 9am-5pm. For more info, visit www.fitzroygardens.com.)*

ST. PATRICK'S CATHEDRAL. A beautiful product of Gothic revival, St. Patrick's comes replete with grotesque gargoyles, stained glass, and a magnificent altar. Among the traditional Catholic relics you'll also find an Aboriginal message stick and stone inlay, installed as a welcoming gesture to Aboriginal Catholics and a reconciliation for past wrongs against their people. ◪The cathedral is most spectacular by night, when its 106m spires are illuminated by floodlights. *(West of the Fitzroy Garden's northwest corner on Cathedral Pl. ☎9662 2332. Open 7:30am-6pm. Free guided tour*

M-F 10am-noon. No tourists during mass M-Sa 7-7:30am and 1-1:20pm, Sa 8-8:30am, Su 7am-12:30pm and 6-7:30pm.)

YARRA PARK AND THE MELBOURNE CRICKET GROUND (MCG). First established in 1853 and expanded in 1956 for the Olympics and again in 1992 to seat 92,000, the MCG functions as the sanctum sanctorum of Melbourne's robust sporting life. It houses Australian Rules Football (AFL) every weekend in winter, including the Grand Final the last Saturday in September. There are also, of course, cricket contests (Oct.-Apr.), highlighted by test matches between Australia and South Africa, England, New Zealand, Pakistan, and the West Indies. The north side of the MCG contains the **Australian Gallery of Sport and Olympic Museum,** further celebrating Australia's love for sport. The venue houses the **Australian Cricket Hall of Fame** (which requires some understanding to appreciate), an AFL exhibition, a new feature on extreme sports, and the **Olympic Museum,** with a focus on Australian achievements and the 1956 Melbourne games. The best way to see the stadium and gallery is by a guided tour from the northern entrance, which offers unique insight into the MCG's history, allowing you to step inside the player's changing rooms, the **Melbourne Cricket Club Museum,** and onto the hallowed turf itself. Entertaining guides make the one-hour tour worth the price even if you don't have the slightest idea what the hell a wicket, over, or googlie are. *(Take the Met to Jolimont. ☎ 9657 8888; www.mcg.org.au. Tours led by former presidents of the club run on all non-event days on the hour, and often every 30min., 10am-3pm. $18, concessions $13, families $44. Admission includes tour and access to galleries with audiocassette guide.)* AFL games are also a must, allowing you to experience firsthand an essential aspect of Melburnian culture. To achieve, or at least mimic, authenticity, order a meat pie and beer, choose a favorite team, and blow out your vocal chords along with the passionate crowd. Make sure to stay for the winning team's song played after the game. *(All in Yarra Park, southeast of Fitzroy Gardens across Wellington Pde. Accessible via trams #48, 70, and 75. Tickets $15-22, concessions about half-price; prices vary by entrance gate, so search around.)*

MELBOURNE PARK (NATIONAL TENNIS CENTRE). To the west across the railroad tracks from the MCG and Yarra Park sits the ultramodern tennis facility, **Melbourne Park.** The entire complex, composed of the domed Rod Laver Arena, the new and sleek Vodafone Arena, and the numerous outer courts, hosts the **Australian Open** Grand Slam event every January. You can wander around and see the trophies and center court for free or take a 40min. guided tour. Though you can't follow in their footsteps on the center court, the outer courts give proximity to greatness for a $16-24 hourly playing fee. During the Open, a $20 **ground pass** will get you into every court except center; go during the first week and you'll see all the big-names beating up on the freshmen in the outer courts. *(Take tram #70 from Flinders St. Open M-F 9am-5pm. Tours $5, concession $2.50. Australian Open tickets ☎ 9286 1600. To hire a court, book at ☎ 9286 1244.)*

NORTH OF THE CITY CENTER

CARLTON GARDENS AND MELBOURNE MUSEUM. Spanning three city blocks, the verdant gardens, criss-crossed with pathways and spectacular fountains, offer peaceful repose and potential possum sightings (just check around the trash cans in the evening). Standing within the gardens is the grandiose **Royal Exhibition Building,** which was home to Australia's first parliament and now sometimes hosts major expositions, temporary exhibits, and, more often, rug and furniture blowout sales. Behind the Exhibition Building stands the multimillion dollar **Melbourne Museum,** a new, stunning facility that contains a range of science-related galleries, including an IMAX theatre (see **Film,** p. 579), a rainforest, an Aboriginal center, a children's museum, and a mind and body gallery. *(Bordered by Victoria, Rathdowne, Carlton, and Nicholson St. On the city circle tram, or take tram 96. Museum ☎ 8341 7777; www.melbourne.museum.vic.gov.au. $15, concessions $11, ages 3-16 $8, families $35. Museum and IMAX showing $20/$12/$15/$55. Open daily 10am-5pm. Free after 4:30pm. Public tours of Royal Exhibition Building daily 2pm; $5, with museum admission $3. Wheelchair accessible.)*

■ **OLD MELBOURNE GAOL.** This stalwart prison was completed in 1845 and housed a total of 50,000 prisoners in its 84 years. The main structure has three levels of cells linked by iron catwalks. The tiny cells each house small displays about everything from the history and specifications of the jail to fascinating stories about **Ned Kelly's gang,** though the creepiest displays feature the stories and death masks of the most notorious criminals executed here. Kelly, Australia's most infamous bushranger, was hanged in the jail in 1880, and a scruffy wax likeness approaches his fate on the original trap door and scaffold. Downstairs is the suit of armor that Kelly—or one of his cohorts—wore in the gang's final shoot-out with police. Wonderfully spooky evening tours led by professional actors provide a chillingly vivid sense of its horrible past. Or, satiate your thirst for armor with a Ned Kelly magnet-set or a Ned Kelly soda in the gift shop on your way out, and be thankful you've escaped—no criminal ever did. *(On Russell St. just north of La Trobe. ☎ 9663 7228; click on "properties" at www.nattrust.com.au. $15, concessions $10, children $8, families $40. Night tours W and F-Su 7:30pm. $19, children $11, families $46. Bookings essential for night tours; call Ticketmaster ☎ 13 61 00. Open daily 9:30am-4:30pm.)*

QUEEN VICTORIA MARKET. The modernizing development that brought the rest of Melbourne into the 21st century and, some would say, into the Mall of America, somehow passed over the QV Market, perhaps because it was already, by definition, devoted to shopping. It remains an old-fashioned, open-air market, abuzz with hundreds of vendors hawking their wares to the thousands of Melburnians who pack in for excellent bargains on produce, dairy products, and meat. Saturdays and Sundays see the market at its frenetic best. Don't be afraid to bargain with vendors; good deals can turn into amazing ones after noon, when sellers are anxious to empty their stock. Walking tours explore the market's history and cultural importance and include plenty to eat. From late November to early March, the market is also open at night (6-10pm), when the focus turns multicultural. *(On Victoria St. between Queen and Peel St. Open Tu and Th 6am-2pm, F 6am-6pm, Sa 6am-3pm, Su 9am-4pm. ☎ 9320 5822; www.qvm.com.au. Tours depart from 69 Victoria St., near Elizabeth St. Food tour Tu and Th-Sa 10am: $22. History tour 10:30am: $17. Book ahead ☎ 9320 5935.)*

MELBOURNE ZOO. Many sections of this world-class, 1862-established zoo are expertly recreated native habitats that allow visitors to view animals much as they live in the wild. The African Rainforest—with pygmy hippos, arboreal monkeys, and gorillas—is first-rate, with a new and elaborate Asian elephant exhibit. Of course, you won't want to miss the Aussie fauna, which include echidnas, wombats, goannas, emus, flying squirrels, and red kangaroos with whom visitors can play—if the 'roos feel like it, that is. *(On Elliott Rd., north of the University of Melbourne. M-Sa take tram #55 from William St. to the Zoo stop; Su take tram #68 from Elizabeth St. ☎ 9285 9300; www.zoo.org.au. Free tours for the elderly and disabled M-F 10am-3pm, Sa-Su 10am-4pm. Open Mar.-Dec. daily 9am-5pm; Jan. M-W 9am-5pm, Th-Su 9am-9:30pm; Feb. M-Th 9am-5pm, F-Su 9am-9:30pm. $15.30, concessions $11.40, ages 4-15 $7.60, families $41.40.)*

SOUTH OF THE YARRA RIVER

SOUTHBANK. The riverside walk that begins across Clarendon St., Southbank, has an upmarket shopping and sidewalk-dining scene. It's most crowded on sunny Sundays, when an odd mix of skater kids, toned health nuts, and the Armani-clad

VICTORIA

gather here to relax, show off, and conspicuously consume. The area extends along the Yarra for two very long city blocks. While you could easily squander your entire budget here within a day, you can window-shop, people-watch, and get some great views of Flinders St. Station and the city skyline for free. There are also a slew of expensive but enjoyable river ferry rides as well as really cool fountains, wacky sculptures, and endlessly-imaginative sidewalk chalk drawings.

■ SHRINE OF REMEMBRANCE. A wide walkway lined with tall, conical Butan cypresses leads to this imposing temple, with columns and a ziggurat roof, that commemorates fallen soldiers from WWI. Crowning the central space are a stepped skylight and the **stone of remembrance,** which bears the inscription "Greater Love Hath No Man." The skylight is designed so that at 11am on November 11 (the moment of the WWI armistice), a ray of sunlight shines onto the word "Love" on the stone. Don't worry about missing this impressive solar-architectural feat; the effect is simulated a bit anti-climactically every 30min. with artificial light, after which volunteer guides give excellent talks about the site's significance. Lining the outer corridor are books listing names of the Australian heroes who perished in WWI. Ascend to the shrine's balcony for spectacular views of the Melbourne skyline and the neighboring suburbs. Or, venture down into the crypt and view the colorful division flags and memorial statues. Outside, veterans of subsequent wars are honored with a memorial that includes the **perpetual flame,** burning continuously since Queen Elizabeth II lit it in 1954. *(On St. Kilda Rd. www.shrine.org.au. Open daily 10am-5pm. $2 donation requested.)*

VICTORIAN ARTS CENTRE. This enormous complex is the central star of Melbourne's performing arts galaxy. The 162m white-and-gold latticed spire of the **Theatres Building** is a landmark in itself, and inside there's more room for performance than most cities can handle. home to the **Melbourne Theatre Company, Opera Australia,** and the **Australian Ballet,** this eight-level facility holds three theaters (see Performing Arts, p. 578) that combined can seat over 3000. The Theatres Building also serves the visual arts, as its private **Performing Arts Museum** sets up regular, often free exhibits of performing arts-related clothing, pictures, and memorabilia in the building's foyers. Next door is the 2600-seat **Melbourne Concert Hall,** which hosts the renowned **Melbourne Symphony** and the **Australian Chamber Orchestra**; its chic **EQ Cafebar** (☎ 9645 0644) is a bit pricey but offers award-winning meals and great views of the Yarra. Finally, the third tier of the Victorian Arts conglomerate, the **Sidney Myer Music Bowl,** is across St. Kilda Rd. in King's Domain Park. After extensive renovations, the bowl will be the largest capacity outdoor amphitheater in the Southern Hemisphere, sheltering numerous free and not-so-free summer concerts. Its "Carols by Candlelight," in the weeks before Christmas, draws Victorians by the sleighloads. Sunday the Centre plays host to a free arts & crafts market from 10am-5pm. *(100 St. Kilda Rd., at the east end of Southbank, just across the river from Flinders St. Station. ☎ 9281 8000; www.vicartscentre.com.au. Open M-F 7am-late, Sa 9am-late, Su 10am-after the last show. Free. Guided tours leave from Arts Center shop, Level 6, Theatres Building M-Sa noon and 2:30pm. $10, concessions $7.50. Special Su 12:15pm backstage tour $13.50.)*

NATIONAL GALLERY OF VICTORIA. This massive gallery had to adopt the confusing post-phrase "of Victoria" when the Australian National Gallery was built in Canberra. Still considered to house the finest collection in the Southern Hemisphere, the NGV is undergoing a $136 million renovation with an announced completion date of mid-2003. In the meantime, a surprisingly large 1% of the collection can be viewed in the postmodern facilities of the **Ian Potter Centre NGV: Australian Art** in the new Federation Square building at Swanston and Flinders St. This new center, a strikingly original huddle of prisms of glass and steel, has three levels of Aboriginal, colonial, and contemporary Australian art. Most of the major international pieces, however, will be in Victorian regional museums, or maybe even in your hometown abroad, until the distant grand reopening. *(180 St. Kilda Rd. and Federation Sq. ☎ 9208 0222; www.ngv.vic.gov.au. Gallery open daily 10am-5pm. Free guided tours M and W-F 11am, 1, and 2pm; Tu 1 and 2pm; Sa 2pm; Su 11am and 2pm. Admission to permanent collection free. Wheelchair accessible.)*

KING'S DOMAIN AND ROYAL BOTANIC GARDENS. Over 50,000 plants fill the 36 acres stretching along St. Kilda Rd. east to the Yarra and south to Domain Rd. The gardens first opened in 1846, and the extensive array of mature species reflects 150 years of care and development. Stately palms unique to Melbourne share the soil with twisting oaks, rainforest plants, possums, wallabies, and a pavilion of roses. A number of walking tracks highlight endemic flora. There's also a steamy **rainforest glasshouse** and lake where you can have tea and feed the ducks and geese. *(Open daily 10am-4:30pm.)* Special events, such as outdoor film screenings, take place on summer evenings (see **Cinema,** p. 578). The **Aboriginal Heritage Walk** explores the use of plant-life by local Aboriginal groups in ceremony, symbol, and food. *(Th 11am and alternate Su 10:30am. $15.40, concessions $11, ages 12-16 $6.60. Book ahead.)* Near the entrance closest to the Shrine of Remembrance are the **Visitors Center** and the **observatory.** The Visitors Center houses an upscale cafe, the Terrace Tearooms and Conference Center, and a garden shop. *(Open M-F 9am-5pm, Sa-Su 10am-5:30pm.)* The observatory includes an original 1874 telescope only accessible by day tours, which give a close-up look at the 'scopes; night tours allow visitors to use the instruments with the help of qualified astronomers. *(Tours W 2pm. $6.60, concession $4.40. Night tour Tu 7:30pm; $15.40, concessions $11, families $37.40. Book ahead.)* The small cottage by Gate F is the **La Trobe Cottage,** home of Victoria's first lieutenant governor, Charles Joseph La Trobe. *(Open M, W, and Sa-Su 11am-4pm. $2.20.)* Tours leave from the cottage to **Government House,** the Victorian Governor's official residence. *(4 Parliament Pl. ☎ 9654 4711; www.rbgmelb.org.au. Tours $11, concessions $9, children $5.50. Book ahead. Gardens ☎ 9252 2300. Open daily Nov.-Mar. 7:30am-8:30pm; Apr.-Oct. 7:30am-5:30pm. Free. Tours of the garden depart the Visitors Center Su-F 11am and 2pm. $4, concessions $2. Wheelchair accessible.)*

MELBOURNE AQUARIUM. Focusing on species of the Southern Ocean, this high-class facility offers a unique look at Australia's lesser-known wildlife. It's three levels of fishtastic fun, from an open-air billabong to a 2.2 million liter "Oceanarium," featuring a glass tunnel that allows visitors to walk beneath roaming sharks and giant rays. Don't miss the car-turned-aquarium wittily dubbed "A fish called Honda." *(On King St. at the corner of Queenswarf Rd., across from the Crown Casino. ☎ 9923 5999; www.melbourneaquarium.com.au. Open daily Jan. 9:30am-9pm, Feb.-Dec. 9:30am-6pm; last admission 1hr. before close. $20, concessions $13, children $10, families $50. MC/V.)*

ST. KILDA

Bayside St. Kilda lies just far enough away from the city to be relaxed, but close enough to maintain a lively vibe during the day; at night, more of the same citywide scene of black-clad bar hoppers appear. St. Kilda has recently undergone a repolish of its former seedy image of drugs and prostitution; although reverberations of the past still linger, a new attitude is coming to life. There aren't a lot of tourist sights *per se*, but the offbeat shops, gorgeous sandy shoreline, and comfortably mixed population of the weird and the ordinary are indeed a sight to behold. St. Kilda Beach is easily accessed by any number of trams (see **Orientation,** p. 554), and swarms with swimmers and sun-worshippers during summer. The **Esplanade,** along the length of the strand, is a great place for in-line skating and jogging. On Sundays, the Esplanade craft market sells art, toys, housewares, and everything else, all impressively handmade by the stall holders.

WHAT'S THAT ON THE SIDEWALK? Part of Melbourne's oft-cited liveability is the attention paid to public art. Deb Halpern's **Ophelia** on Southbank, is the fat-lipped, multi-colored, Y-shaped visage that has become one of the city's most prominent icons. On the pavement in front of Halpern's work, look for the ephemeral chalk drawings of Bev Isaac. North along Swanston St. in front of the State Library of Victoria, a stone cornice with part of the word **"library"** protruding from the pavement draws a crowd for its astounding uniqueness and quirky street artistry. Perhaps the most popular of the sculptures is the group of **three businessmen** cast in bronze standing at the corner of Swanston and Bourke St. Their emaciated frames and wild-eyed expressions inspire amusement in most onlookers, though the work was originally underwritten by the government of Nauru and meant to reflect the greed and spiritual impoverishment of the Australian businessmen who plundered the tiny Polynesian country's natural resources.

LUNA PARK. The entrance gate of this St. Kilda icon is a grotesque, mammoth funhouse face. Venture through its mouth to find classic carnival rides all permanently protected by the historical commission, which is attempting to honor the park's near-century long existence. Built in 1912 by a triad of American entrepreneurs hoping to capitalize on the fame of Coney Island's successful Luna Park (built in 1903), Melbourne's Luna has the largest wooden roller-coaster in the world. Its copy-cat construction set off a similar project, with the same backers, in Sydney in 1935. Sadly, Sydney's Luna is to be torn down in 2003; luckily, Melbourne's should see some new rides by summer of that year. (On the Lower Esplanade. ☎9525 5033; www.lunapark.com.au. Free entry. Unlimited ride tickets $30, ages 4-12 $20; single rides $6.50, ages 4-12 $5, ages 1-3 $3. Open F 7-11pm, Sa 11am-11pm, Su 11am-dusk; public and school holidays M-Th 11am-5pm, F-Sa 11am-11pm, Su 11am-7pm.)

ALBERT PARK. Adjacent to Fitzroy St. on the north lies Albert Park, the southern extension of Melbourne's vast park system, with ample green space, free BBQs, tennis courts, and groups of kids playing footy. The Grand Prix course is here, which you can drive on, abiding by speed limits of course (see **Recreation**, p. 579). The huge interior lake is great for sailing or paddleboating, but no swimming is allowed. (For info, call Parks Victoria ☎13 19 63.)

JEWISH MUSEUM OF AUSTRALIA. The Jewish Museum outlines both the history of the Jewish people as a whole and the 200-year experience of Australia's 90,000 Jews from the time of the First Fleet. A stunning hallway draws a timeline of Jewish history, complete with fascinating and state-of-the-art multimedia displays. The Belief and Ritual Gallery provides a thorough overview of Judaism's basic tenets, including a painfully detailed French woodcut of a circumcision ceremony. There are also rotating displays of art and Judaica, and an extensive reference library and archive, available for use upon request. (26 Alma Rd., east of St. Kilda Rd. by stop 32 on tram #3 or 67. ☎9534 0083; www.jewishmuseum.com.au. Museum open Tu-Th 10am-4pm, Su 11am-5pm. $7, students and children $4, families $16. Present a print-out of the front page of the web site and get a 50% discount on admission. 30-40min. tours of the adjacent synagogue Tu-Th 12:30pm, Su 12:30 and 3pm; free with admission. Wheelchair accessible.

🔳 ENTERTAINMENT

Melbourne prides itself on its style and cultural savvy, and nowhere is this more evident than in its entertainment scene. The range of options can seem overwhelming: there are world-class performances at the Victorian Arts Centre, edgy experimental drama in Carlton and Fitzroy, popular dramas and musicals in opulent theatres, and a panoply of independent and avant-garde cinema. The definitive web site for performance events is www.melbourne.citysearch.com.au.

PERFORMING ARTS

Book for larger shows through **Ticketek** (☎ 13 28 49 or 1800 062 849; www.ticketek.com) or **Ticketmaster7** (☎ 1300 136 166; www.ticketmaster7.com), or try **Halftix** for half-price same-day tickets (see **Ticket Agencies**, p. 560); for smaller productions, call theater companies directly. The hard-to-miss **Victorian Arts Centre**, 100 St. Kilda Rd., sports an Eiffel-like spire right on the Yarra across from Flinders St. Station. It houses five venues: the **State Theatre** for major dramatic, operatic, and dance performances; the **Melbourne Concert Hall**, for symphonies; the **Playhouse**, largely used by the Melbourne Theatre Company for plays; the **George Fairfax Studio,** similar to the Playhouse but smaller; and the **Black Box,** for cutting-edge, low-budget shows targeted at an under-35 audience. (☎ 9281 8000, box office ☎ 1300 136 166; www.vicartscentre.com.au. Tickets range from free to $180; $6.88 transaction fee when not purchased at box office. Box office open M-Sa 9am-9pm.)

La Mama, 205 Faraday St., Carlton (☎ 9347 6948), about halfway up Lygon St. Head east on Faraday; it's very near the intersection, hidden down an alleyway and behind a parking lot. Serving up esoteric Australian drama in a diminutive, black-box space since 1967. M nights see fiction readings, and some Sa nights (when there's no performance) plays are read. Similar cutting-edge work performed at the affiliated **Carlton Courthouse Theatre,** 349 Drummond St., just around the corner in the old courthouse building, across from the police station. Tickets $10-14. Free tea and coffee at performances. Wheelchair accessible.

Last Laugh at the Comedy Club, 380 Lygon St., Level 2, Carlton (☎ 9348 1622), in Lygon Ct. Melbourne's biggest comedy-club scene, with big-name international jokesters. Ticket prices vary depending on the act. Show starts 8:30pm.

National Theatre (☎ 9534 0221; www.nationaltheatre.org.au), on the corner of Barkly and Carlisle St., St. Kilda. Offbeat, cosmopolitan fare, like modern dance, drama, opera, and "world music." Tickets prices depend on the show, but generally fall between $10-60.

Palais Theatre (☎ 9534 0221), on the Esplanade, St. Kilda. Holds the largest chandelier in the Southern Hemisphere. Seats 3000. Tickets $40-60.

Princess' Theatre, 163 Spring St. (☎ 9299 9850). Cheesy, big-budget musicals. 1500-seat venue around since 1885. Tickets $40-80. Book through Ticketek (☎ 13 28 49).

Regent Theatre, 191 Collins St. (☎ 9299 9500), just east of Swanston St. Dazzlingly ornate. Once a popular movie house founded in 1929 and dubbed the "Palace of Dreams"; now hosts big-name touring musicals and international celebrity acts. Seats 2000. Tickets $50-80. 2hr. tours of Regent and Forum every Tu; $18, students $15. Book ahead.

The Forum, 150 Flinders St. (☎ 9299 9700). Looks like a combination of an Arabian palace and Florentine villa, with a few gargoyles thrown in for good measure. Big-budget dance and drama ($50-80), as well as periodic concerts ($20-30) and even occasional movies.

Dracula's, 100 Victoria St. (☎ 9347 3344; www.draculas.com.au), on the corner of Cardigan St. in Carlton. 2hr. cabaret shows with a vampire horror-comedy theme. Show, dinner, and a "ghost train" ride from the entrance to the cocktail bar $40-60.

CINEMA

Melbourne has long been the center of Australia's independent film scene, and there are tons of old theaters throughout the city that screen artsy and experimental fare as well as old cinema classics. The arthouse crowd logs on to www.urbancinefile.com.au, which features flip reviews of the latest stuff. The annual **Melbourne International Film Festival** (see **Festivals**, p. 580) showcases the year's international indie hits, and the **St. Kilda Film Festival** (see **Festivals**) highlights short films of all shapes and sizes. An especially select crew of home-grown flicks can be viewed in late July at the **Melbourne Underground Film Festival,** a slightly ornery and occasionally bizarre showing from local students in Fitzroy. You'll have to have your eyes peeled to catch it; check for posters and pray—there's a reason they call it underground. Plenty of cinemas in the city center show mainstream first-run movies as well. **Movieline** (☎ 13 34 56) has a ticketing service and recorded info on showtimes and locations. At the theater, try a "choc-top," the chocolate-dipped ice-cream cone that's a staple of Melbourne movie-going ($2-3).

■ **Astor Theatre** (☎ 9510 1414; www.astor-theatre.com), on the corner of Chapel St. and Dandenong Rd., St. Kilda. Spectacular Art Deco theater that still bears many of its original furnishings and all of its stately beauty. Mostly repertory and reissues. Seats 1100. Many double features. $11, concessions $10, children $9; book of 10 tickets $80.

Cinema Nova, 380 Lygon St., Carlton (☎ 9349 5201), in Lygon Ct. Indie and foreign fare. Claims the oxymoronic title of "second-largest art-house megaplex in the world." $13, concessions $10.50, children $7.50. Special M $4.50 before 4pm, $7 after.

IMAX, Melbourne Museum, Carlton (☎ 9663 5454; www.imax.com.au), off Rathdowne St. in the Carlton Gardens (see p. 573). Daily screenings of 5 films every hr. $15, concessions $12, children $10, families $42; 3-D shows $1 extra ($4 for families). Su-Th 10am-10pm, F-Sa 10am-11pm. YHA and RACV discount 20%, NOMADS 10%.

Moonlight Cinema (☎ 9428 2203; www.moonlight.com.au), in the Royal Botanic Gardens. From mid-Dec. to early Mar., movies play on the central lawn, with a licensed bar and gourmet catering. Films start at sundown, approximately 8:45pm; tickets can be purchased at the gate from 7:30pm. $13.50, concessions $10.50, children $9.

The Kino, 45 Collins St. (☎ 9650 2100), downstairs in the Collins Place complex. Independent and foreign films. $13.50, concessions $10.50; M special $8.50.

SPORTS AND RECREATION

Melburnians refer to themselves as "sports mad," but it's a good insanity, one that causes fans of footy (Australian Rules Football), cricket, tennis, and horse racing to skip work or school, get decked out in the costumery of their favorite side, and cheer themselves hoarse. Their hallowed haven is the **Melbourne Cricket Ground (MCG),** adjacent to the world-class **Melbourne Park** tennis center (see p. 573). A new ward, **Colonial Stadium,** right behind Spencer St. Station, has begun to share footy-hosting responsibilities with the more venerable MCG and also hosts the majority of local rugby action. The lunacy peaks at various yearly events: the **Australian Open,** a Grand Slam tennis event in late January; the **Grand Prix** Formula-One car-racing extravaganza in March; the **AFL Grand Final** in late September; the **Melbourne Cup,** a "horse race that stops a nation" in early November; and cricket's **Boxing Day Test Match** on Dec. 26 (see **Festivals**, p. 580).

Melbourne's passion for sport is not limited to spectator events. City streets and parks are packed with joggers, skaters, and footy players. The newly refurbished, crushed gravel tan track that circles the Royal Botanic Gardens is best for **running;** stick to the track, as recreational activities are strictly prohibited in the Gardens proper. Other great routes include the pedestrian paths along the Yarra, the Port Phillip/St. Kilda shore, and the Albert Park Lake. All of these wide, flat spaces make for excellent **in-line skating** as well. **City Skate,** Wednesday at 9pm, draws local bladers together at the Victorian Arts Centre near the waterfall; folks convene and break into smaller groups based on preferred city route and skill level. You can rent equipment at the **Skate Warehouse,** 354 Lonsdale St. (☎ 9602 3633.

$7.50 per hr., $12.50 per 3hr., $17.50 per day, $27.50 for F-M. Open M-Th 10am-6pm, F 10am-9pm, Sa 9am-5pm, Su 10am-5pm.)

The **beach** in St. Kilda, accessible by tram #16 and 96, is not Australia's finest, but it'll do for sun and swimming. **Albert Park** (see p. 577) has a lake good for sailing but not for swimming. Just inside its Clarendon St. entrance, **Jolly Roger** rents boats. (☎9690 5862. Sailboats $26-38 per hr.; rowboats $32 per hr.; aquabikes $13 per 15min. Open Tu-Su 8:30am-4:30pm.) The **Melbourne City Baths,** 420 Swanston St., on the corner of Franklin St., offer two pools, sauna, spa, squash courts, and a gym in a restored Neoclassical building. (☎9663 5888. Open M-Th 6am-10pm, F 6am-8:30pm, Sa-Su 8am-6pm. Pool $3.80, 10-ticket pass $34.20; sauna and spa $8.20.)

GAMBLING

The Australian penchant for "having a flutter" (betting) reaches its neon-lit apotheosis at **Melbourne's Crown Casino,** 8 Whiteman St., at the western end of Southbank. A little slice of Las Vegas down under, this $1.6 billion complex houses the most gaming tables of any casino in the world, plus five-star accommodations, luxury shopping, Elvis impersonators, fog-filled, laser-lit jumping fountains, a perennially packed Planet Hollywood, and three **nightclubs:** Heat, Club Odeon, and the Mercury Lounge. The evening pyrotechnic displays out front on the Yarra are not to be missed; every hour, starting at 7pm, you'll think it's some sort of independence day celebration. Independence from gambling? Not likely. Minimum bets are around $5, though the more cautious can start at the less cut-throat "how to play" tables. (☎9292 8888. Open 24hr., and busy just about every one of those hours.)

FESTIVALS

Melburnians create excuses for city-wide street parties any time of the year. Below are the city's major events. For a complete guide, grab a free copy of *Melbourne Events* at any tourist office, or do an events search at www.visitmelbourne.com. All dates listed are for 2003.

Midsumma Gay and Lesbian Festival, *Jan. 12-Feb. 3, 2003* (☎9415 9819; www.midsumma.org.au). 3 weeks of homosexual hijinks all over the city ranging from the erotic (a "Mr. Leather Victoria" contest) to the educational (a Same-Sex Partners Rights workshop), with lots of parades, dance parties, and general pandemonium.

Australian Open, *Jan. 13-26, 2003* (tickets ☎9286 1175; www.ausopen.org). One of the world's elite 4 Grand Slam tennis events, held at Melbourne Park's hard courts.

Foster's Australian Grand Prix, *Mar. 6-9, 2003* (tickets ☎13 16 41; www.grandprix.com.au). Albert Park, St. Kilda. Formula One frenzy holds the city hostage.

Moomba, *Mar. 7-10, 2003* (☎9650 9744; www.melbournemoombafestival.com.au). Named after the Aboriginal word for "party," Moomba is basically a non-stop 4-day city-wide fête amid food, performances, and events.

Melbourne Food and Wine Festival, *Mar. 28-Apr. 12, 2003* (☎9412 4220; www.fmelbfoodwinefest.com.au), on Collins St. A free and delicious way to celebrate Melbourne as Australia's "culinary capital," or just an excuse to get drunk, stuffed, and more drunk.

International Comedy Festival, *Mar. 27-Apr. 20, 2003* (☎1900 937 200; www.comedyfestival.com.au). Huge 3-week international and Aussie laugh-fest, with over 1000 gut-busting performances.

International Flower and Garden Show, *Apr. 2-6, 2003* (☎9639 2333). Royal Exhibition Building and Carlton Gardens, Carlton.

Anzac Day Parade, *Apr. 25, 2003* (☎9650 5050). ANZAC vets in the Commemoration March head down Swanston St. and St. Kilda Rd. to the Shrine of Remembrance.

St. Kilda Film Festival, *late May-early June* (☎9209 6711). Palais Theatre and George Cinemas, St. Kilda. Australia's best short films: documentary, experimental, and comedy.

International Film Festival, *mid-July-early Aug.* (☎9417 2011; www.melbournefilmfestival.com.au). The cream of the international cinematic crop, plus top-level local work.

Royal Melbourne Show, *late Sept.* (☎9281 7420; www.royalshow.com.au). At Ascot Vale. Sideshow alleys, rides, entertainment, animal exhibitions for judging.

Melbourne Fringe Festival, *Sept. 28-Oct.19, 2003* (☎9481 5111; www.melbourne fringe.org.au). Centered around local artists, the festival opens with a parade on Brunswick St., Fitzroy. Performance and parties all across town.

Melbourne Festival, *Oct. 9-25, 2003; Oct. 7-23, 2004* (☎9662 4242; www.melbournefestival.com.au). A 3-week celebration of the arts, attracting world-famous actors, writers, and dancers for over 400 performances, workshops, and parties in 30 different venues.

Skyy Australian Motorcycle Grand Prix, *late Oct.* (☎9258 7100; www.grand prix.com.au). Phillip Island. Fast bikes (instead of fast cars). Going around a track. Fast.

Spring Racing Carnival, *mid Oct.-late Nov.* (☎9258 4666; www.racingvictoria.net.au). Flemington Racecourse. Australia's love for horse racing reaches fever on the pitch.

Chapel St. Festival, *Nov. 3, 2003* (☎9529 6331). 250,000-300,000 people crowd Chapel St from Dandenong to Toorak Rd for entertainment and mayhem.

Melbourne Cup Day, *Nov. 4, 2003.* On the first Tuesday every November, Melburnians, along with the rest of Australia, put life on pause to watch, listen, or talk about the most hyped-up and fashionable horse race in the country. Ladies, gents, and Australia's elite come dressed to impress for a comical and entertaining day at the races.

Melbourne Boxing Day Test Match, *Dec. 26-30, 2002* (☎9653 9999; www.baggygreen.com.au). More than 100,000 cricket fans pack the MCG to root for the boys in green and gold against top cricketers from around the world.

◪ NIGHTLIFE

Melbourne pulses with a world-class nightlife scene. Only a handful of venues play the standard bass-heavy club remixes of familiar mainstream dance hits. Most feature DJs (some with international followings) who spin funky, mind-bending original selections of techno, house and deep house, trance, drum 'n' bass, jungle, garage, and breakbeats—all eminently danceable. Tons of retro nights feature '70s and '80s faves, with crowds in campy period wear. Covers are ubiquitous outside of Fitzroy and range up to $20, but you get your money's worth—few clubs close earlier than 3am; some rage nonstop from Thursday all the way until Sunday night.

There are three main areas for **nightclubs.** Downtown tends to be straighter (as in less gay and more mainstream), though you'll find a little bit of everything. South Yarra and Prahran have the trendiest venues and the best **gay scene** (see **Gay Melbourne,** p. 582). Though most clubs in the area are gay-friendly, predominantly gay places are concentrated along Commercial Rd., with a smattering in Collingwood. Fitzroy and St. Kilda are much more casual, tending toward grungy but good music shows and charging the cheapest covers, if any at all. Melburnians take their nightlife seriously—the more you pay and the trendier the venue, the more attitude you get at the door. Nonetheless, rude treatment comes free of charge at fading venues too. Venues, genres, and cover charges change with bewildering rapidity. To keep up, read the exhaustive weekly listings in *In Press, Hr,* and, to a lesser extent, *Beat,* magazines; all are free and released every Wednesday. For music shows, the best coverage is in The Age's *Entertainment Guide* (*EG*) or the Herald-Sun's *Gig Guide,* in their respective Friday papers.

GAY MELBOURNE. If you've ever watched the TV show *Queer as Folk,* then you'll know that Melbourne is Australia's "second" gay city (after Sydney, of course). Melbourne has a warm and wonderful queer culture, conjuring itself up especially in neighborhoods like Fitzroy, Carlton, Prahan, and St. Kilda, which particularly shine during the **Midsumma Festival,** a celebration of sport and art throughout the city in January and February, and the **Melbourne Queer Film and Video Festival,** which takes place in March. To see and be seen in the city year-round, check out free newspapers *Melbourne Star Observer* and *Brother Sister* for interesting venues. There are lots of good nightlife options, too: **Commercial Rd.** in Prahan is probably Melbourne's most infamous strip, and **Gipps St.,** near Fitzroy, also boasts a lively scene. More info can be culled by browsing www.out.com.au or www.also.org.au, or dialing the **Gay and Lesbian Switchboard Information Service** (☎0055 or 12504), a 24hr. line that gives out info on everything from support groups to nightlife.

There is a blurry but important distinction between bars and pubs in Melbourne. The **bars** tend to be a bit more chill but no less slick than their nightclub cousins; bars don't have covers, though. Drinks are expensive (beer bottles $4-4.50, wine and mixed drinks $4.50-5.50), and wine and spirits are the intoxicants of choice; many bars don't have beer taps at all. Most **pubs,** on the other hand, charge less for drinks (half-pint pots $2.30-2.80, pints $4.50-5, mixed drinks $3.50-4.50), are loud and raucous, and have live entertainment on weekends (cover $3-8), making the distinction between pub and club somewhat blurry as well. Most venues try to lure backpackers with cheap drink specials (pots as low as $1-1.50) and often keep taps flowing until early in the morning or even 24hr.

BARS AND PUBS

CITY CENTER

Rue Bebelons, 237 Little Lonsdale St. (☎9663 1700). There's no sign outside; you have to be in the know. The consummate Melburnian bar, relaxed and lounge-y in a South American, we-are-obsessed-with-the-color-red sort of way. Excellent selection of wines ($3-4) and spirits ($4.50-6) and hokey old posters and European LPs (not for sale; they are affixed to the walls around you, take a look). The deep house music and dim lighting create the ideal atmosphere for a brooding solitary drink or an intimate *tête-à-tête* over a plateful of munchies ($4). Open Tu-F 8am-3am, Sa 11am-3am, Su 2-8pm.

Mi Casa es tu Casa, 213 Franklin St. (☎9329 0785). This giant venue wants nothing more than to smooth your feathers after a long day in the city. An eclectic assortment of local art, plush and purple beading, and an open fire all get filtered through a soundtrack of trip-hop, lounge, and disco. This is not your average CBD place: it's your home away from home. Open M-Sa 11am-3am.

Pugg Mahones, 106-112 Hardware St. (☎9670 6155), between Little Lonsdale and Lonsdale St. The name comes from a variation on the common Irish imperative, "pogue mahone," best translated into English as "kiss my ass." This dive packs in a lively all-ages crowd with live music on weekends. Take the time to study their selection of Irish beers on tap and their decorative farm equipment above the door. M backpacker night; $3.50 pints of the Aussie brews. Guinness $6. No cover, but M lines can extend out the door. Open daily 11am-3am.

FITZROY AND COLLINGWOOD

Rainbow Hotel, 27 St. David St. (☎9419 4193). A dive with some of the best live music in Melbourne. Su after 5pm, you get a stageful of blues and gospel you won't soon forget. Packed with locals of all ages, this pub helps you understand how the Melburnian soul got so oversized. Open daily 3pm-1am.

Labour in Vain, 197 Brunswick St. (☎9417 5955). 5 self-proclaimed beer lovers started this little joint on the site of an 1850s hotel that bore the same name. Today it hops with locals from every walk of life; talk to the barstaff, and they'll direct you to someone with similar interests. Owner Andrew B. proudly displays his 30-year collection of old and rare beer bottles and will gladly expound on the history of brewing in Australia. Bar opens daily anytime between 1:30 and 3:30pm (really, whenever the staff recovers from the previous night) and closes daily 1am.

Bar Open, 317 Brunswick St. (☎9415 9601). Portraits of the Queen Mum on thickly painted red walls oversee the youngish, slightly yuppified crowd in these intimate environs. W-Sa nights local jazz and funk talent; Tu night features weekly showings of short films of the "bizarre" genre. No cover. Open daily noon-2am.

Planet Afrik, 99 Smith St. (9419 2687), near Gertrude St. Energy-filled Reggae and African beats do tend to encourage enthusiastic dancing, but the more mellow denizens of this planet may be found relaxing on the lounge's bar or couches. F is reggae and calypso-driven, Sa brings soca bands from the Congo and elsewhere. Cover Sa $5, on special nights $8. Open Th-Su 6pm-3am.

Night Cat, 141 Johnston St. (☎9417 0880). Sometimes there's substance behind trendiness. The Night Cat is an exception to the rule that if (a) the beautiful people like it, and (b) the beautiful people are willing to wait on a line to get in, it must suck. Night Cat purrs with gorgeous Deco floors and an orange aura. The jazz here may not be super-authentic, but there's something to be said for the general slink of the place. Cover $5. Open Th-Su 8pm-1am.

Perserverance, 196 Brunswick St. (☎9417 2844). The gorgeously fake-distressed front may cause you to mistake this corner pub for a bombed-out bistro somewhere south of the Rhein. A standout on Fitzroy's Brunswick St. for the attention paid to decor, with a huge, gleaming oak bar spanning two rooms and massive candelabras lit up at night. Perseverance takes all kinds—from yuppies to young ne'er-do-well artists to mom 'n' dad—and packs them in to tiptoe-ing room by 10pm on weekends. Courtyard out back, occasional live music and dancing. Open W-F noon-3am, Sa-Su 3pm-3am.

Builder's Arms, 211 Gertrude St. (☎9419 0818), at Gore St., halfway between Brunswick and Smith St. Large and lively bar of all ages and orientations. Sedate back seating area, the sweaty velvet-curtained dance room, and always-crowded front bar. Very gay-friendly; popular Th "Q&A" (Queer and Alternative) night. W live alternative music 9pm-midnight; Th-Sa DJs and disco; Su live blues, roots, and soul. Th-Sa arrive by 9:30pm to avoid lines. Open M-Th 5pm-1am, F-Sa 5pm-1am, Su 3-11pm.

The Tote, 71 Johnston St. (☎9419 5320), at Wellington St., one block east of Smith St. A somewhat seedy front bar gives way to energetic Aussie indie, punk, hardcore, and metal played nightly in the back. Bar area is free but music runs $4-12 if anyone is actually manning the door. Open M-Th noon-1am, F-Sa noon-3am, Su 6-11pm.

The Peel Hotel and Dance Bar (☎9419 4762), on the corner of Peel and Wellington St. An institution in Melbourne's gay nightlife, the Peel is more down-to-earth than its Commercial Rd. counterparts. The club pumps commercial house to an almost exclusively gay-male crowd. The attached pub is more laid-back and straight-friendly, with cheap drinks (pots $1.40-3, spirits $3.50-5.50) and relaxed conversation. Club cover $5-7. Open Th-Su 11:30pm-8am; pub open M-Tu 5pm-3am, W-Sa 5pm-5am, Su 5pm-1am.

Glasshouse Hotel, 51 Gipps St. (☎9419 4748), just down the road, off Wellington St. Historically a gay bar, now Melbourne's only lesbian venue. Its predominantly female crowd varies comfortably in age, dress, and attitude; while some may spend the evening playing pool, others can be found dancing on the bar. Th pool competition; F-Sa retro DJs.

THE LOCAL STORY

HEY MISTER DJ!

If it weren't available anywhere on the planet over the net, Melbourne's **PBS 106.7 FM** might be reason enough to venture within the city limits. Like music? Chances are you are a dyed-in-the-wool hater of the radio, but you don't hate PBS! Broadcasting since 1979 and all volunteer-organized and run, down to the folks who mop the studio floors late at night, PBS plays an insanely luxurious and varied 24-freakin'-hour set every single friggin' day. That's right—all this fantastic blues, soul, funk, r&b, jazz, hip-hop, rock, hardcore, alternative, reggae, dancehall, klezmer, world music, electronica, metal, garage, country, cajun, and bluegrass (and not to mention all that a cappella!) is delivered direct to your radio, *sans hassel* and commercial-free. The station is member-supported ($66 per year, concessions $33; "Friend for Life" $1100), and while travelers may not be among those most inclined to join, expanding the PBS listener base helps to keep the station in existence, thus rescuing it from an eternity spent looping the latest Kylie Minogue anthem. Noteworthy shows include: **The Formula,** a hip-hop compendium F 8:30-10pm; **Burning Bitumen,** an unhealthy dose of stoner, garage, and glam rock Th midnight-2am; and the freshener-upper **Blue Juice** Su 11am-noon, a crisp cocktail of blues, soul, jazz, and ska. Are these guys saving the planet single-handedly or what? PBS broadcasts from 47 Easey St. in Fitzroy (☎8415 1067; www.pbsfm.org.au). Rock.

Su live bands. Cover $3, F-Sa after 11pm $5. Open Th 7pm-1am, F-Sa 7pm-5am, Su 7pm-midnight.

SOUTH YARRA AND PRAHRAN

Bridie O'Reilly's, 462 Chapel St. (☎9827 7788), with an additional location at 62 Little Collins St. (☎9650 0840), in the CBD. Bringing rural Ireland to posh South Yarra, Bridie's is always busy and a guaranteed good luck of the Irish time. Live cover bands every night; Irish folk Su-Th, more contemporary covers F-Sa. A new beer takes the emerald limelight each month, served to well-dressed young patrons for $5.50 a pint (normally $6.80). St. Patrick's Day is Guinness-drinking mayhem, with lines extending several blocks down Chapel St. Did we mention this place is Irish to the max? No cover. Open Su-Th 11am-1am, F-Sa 11am-3am. AmEx/DC/MC/V.

La La Land, 134 Chapel St. (☎9533 8972). A gallery, winebar, and retreat for weary space cadets. Behind the plush red curtains Gidget finds a lounge to rest her weary head. Wine by the glass $6.50-8, bottles from $30. Melting smorgasbord of dip-ables plus pot o' fondue $20. Beers $6-12. Open daily 5pm-late.

The Social, 116 Chapel St. (☎9521 3979). An upscale lounge and eatery catering to the well-dressed and those drooling momentarily upon their hemlines. Find your place in one of the seating arrangements and watch the merry games of ring-around-the-martini and hide-and-go-seek-me-another-Cristal, darling. See, being social can even be fun! Brunch served daily until 6pm ($7-12 mains). Mixed drinks $6-8. The search for the ever-elusive individual who will arouse the most ardor in others without going home with any of them sometimes causes a wait at the door. Open daily 11:30am-late.

Xchange, 119 Commercial Rd. (☎9521 2620). Relaxed gay pub-lounge gets rowdy W-Su after 10:30pm, when regular drag queens take control in the small back "show bar." Come see the famous Lucy, BananaDrama, and the Dynamic Duo. Happy Hour daily 5-7pm. Cover $5 W-Su after 10pm. Free Internet access for patrons. Men only, for the most part. Open Su-Th noon-2am, F-Sa noon-3am. MC/V.

ST. KILDA

🏨 **Esplanade Hotel,** 11 Upper Esplanade (☎9534 0211; www.espy.com.au). Multifaceted seaside hotel known fondly as the "Espy." Down-to-earth Lounge Bar carries 3-4 live music acts every night and live reggae Su afternoons. Beneath is a gritty pub that hosts live country and old blues Sa nights. Upstairs is the ornate Gershwin Room, where crowds flock to bigger-name live music acts Sa (cover $8-10) and comedy acts Tu and

Su (cover $10). Happy Hour with $1.50 pots in pub 3 days a week, 5-7pm. Pub open M-Th 11am-9pm, F-Sa 11am-midnight, Su noon-9pm. Lounge Bar open M-Th noon-midnight, F-Sa noon-1:30am, Su noon-11:30pm; in summer, open daily until 1am.

■ **The George Public Bar,** 125 Fitzroy St. (☎9534 8822). Not to be confused with the **George Melbourne Wine Room** next door that carries over 500 wines ($18-500), the subterranean George Public bar is super-stylish in an understated kind of way, featuring old-fashioned fittings and a tall, room-length zinc bar. Try their "world-famous" chili mayo chips; only $4 for a big basket. Live music Sa 4-7pm and Su 6-9pm; trivia night M 7:30pm. Open Su-Th noon-1am, F-Sa noon-3am.

The Elephant and Wheelbarrow, 169 Fitzroy St. (☎9534 7888). Twin brother of the E&W on the corner of Bourke and Exhibition St., CBD. A very fun "traditional English pub" known mostly for its M "*Neighbors* Night," where cast members of this popular Aussie soap opera mingle with patrons and help with trivia games (cover $27). Live classic rock, oldies, and jazz W-Su nights. No cover. Open daily 10am-3am.

Prince of Wales, 29 Fitzroy St. (☎9536 1177; www.theprince.com.au). Long-standing local haunt divided into two downstairs bars: the corner bar attracts a blue collar, grungy crowd, while the other side is a popular gay bar. M nights are a backpacker haven with $1 pots 8pm-1am. Tu night pool competitions start at 7:30pm; entry $2, winner takes all. Upstairs, 1st F of every month is a "girlbar" for lesbians only. Downstairs bar open M and F-Sa noon-3am, Tu-Th and Su noon-2am.

Mink Bar, 2b Acland St. (☎9536 1199). The elusive red door next to the Prince of Wales. Considered one of Melbourne's best cocktail bars, Mink has enough vodka variations to make you sink like an old Russian sailor. Open daily 6pm-2 or 3am.

NIGHTCLUBS

CITY CENTER

■ **Metro,** 20-30 Bourke St. (☎9663 4288; www.metronightclub.com). Simply unbelievable. The largest club in the Southern Hemisphere, the Metro packs in a younger (18-25), straight crowd on weekends for a major scope-and-scam scene. 9 bars and 5 levels of dance action; the ground floor's the most frenetic, with fog, flashing lights, and a triangular plane of green laser. The 2nd floor has live music and catwalks; the 3rd has an observation deck with plush and private booths: they call it "God's Bar." Marble staircases, brass banisters, and Victorian ceilings spared since the building's theater days form an odd but idiosyncratic juxtaposition with Metro's space-age glitz. Th: "Goo," alternative-grunge; F: "BOOM BOOM BOOM," featuring remixed versions of your soul, funk, and R&B favorites; Sa: "Pop," mainstream dance hits. Call ahead for dress code and arrive before midnight. Cover $5-11. Open Th 9pm-5am, F 10pm-2:30am, Sa 9pm-6am. Accepts major credit cards; ATM inside.

Club UK, 169 Exhibition St. (☎9663 2075). Perhaps more British than Britain itself, Club UK quivers with ubiquitous Union Jacks, strikingly accurate Prince Charles cartoons, and pulsating Brit beats. Popular among uni students and backpackers, this club attracts outrageous dress and a notably young, mixed gay-straight crowd. 3 levels of Pommy madness: subterranean dance-pit, ground-level pub, and balcony. W draws a huge crowd for $2 pints. Cover $2 W after 9pm, $5 Th after 10pm. Open W-Th 4pm-3am, F-Sa 4pm-5am.

Scubar, 389 Lonsdale St. (☎9670 2400). Prototype for the tacky bachelor pad, this smallish downstairs venue is befitted with red velvet walls, big plush pillows, beaded curtains, a ceiling aquarium with tropical fish, and candles galore. Most active Th-Sa, with DJs spinning through the night and occasionally a live band: Th breakbeats, F smoother grooves, Sa techno, and sometimes African-style percussion. Tapas bar serves light food. Cover $5 Th-Sa after 10pm. Open W-F 4pm-5am, Sa 7pm-5am.

SOUTH YARRA & PRAHRAN

▨ Revolver, 1st fl., 229 Chapel St. (☎9521 5985). One of the most happening alternative clubs in the city, with a mixed crowd of uni kids, black-clad clubgoers, and edgy, multiple-pierced, skate-punk dred-heads. Dance area frequented by various alternative bands on weekends; afterwards a DJ takes over for groovy late-night dancing. The calmer mega-lounge has pool, campy table arcade, retro furniture, and mini-chandeliers. Strong Sa afternoon reggae, dub 'n' bass sets. Lines can get long; don't worry, once you're in you can stay the weekend. Thai food available at the in-house restaurant; Sa-Su breakfast from 5am. Cover $5-10 Th-Sa after 9pm. Open M-Th noon-3am, F noon-Su 3am nonstop.

Salt, 14 Claremont St. (☎9827 8333). Lovers of costly minimalism flock to Salt's narrow dance floor, where penetrating bass entices a scantily-clad young crowd to get their groove on. Featured in Madison Avenue's "Who the Hell are You?" music video. W Retro, Th Uni night, F Asian techno. Dress sharply and come early. Cover $7-15. Open W 11pm-5am, Th 10pm-3am, F 11pm-7am, Sa 10pm-7am.

The Market, 143 Commercial Rd. (☎9826 0933). Melbourne's hippest gay club (straight-friendly), The Market's hard-working dance floor changes faces each night. Th alternates between drag and cabaret, while F is a self-titled "Meat Market," featuring beefy brawny male pole dancers. The weekend "straightens" out a bit, with two commercial DJs Sa and a funk-soul-R&B DJ for "Burning" Su. Big circular dance floor is the main scene for grinding, though on busy nights crowds throb all the way to the upstairs balcony. Cover $5 Th, $8 F-Sa, $10 Su after 10pm. Open Th-Su 9pm-late. MC/V.

Diva, 153 Commercial Rd. (☎9824 2800). Small but very popular gay bar (straight-friendly) with tons of themes and drink specials. W "Diva Angels" drag show, Th "Sex, Drugs, and Pop Music," F "Happy Days," Sa "Retro" ('80s and '90s) with our famous lady Lucy (see **Xchange,** p. 584). No cover. Lines after 1am, especially Sa. Open W-Sa 9:30pm-3am. MC/V.

Dome, 19 Commercial Rd. (☎9529 8966). Melbourne's most popular and expensive nightclub is the place to be seen. The main arena is a vast, crowded, sweaty vortex of dance action, where box-dancing glowstick mavens groove to progressive house. Off to the side is "Jane's Bar," where the gay/lesbian crowd generally congregates; drag shows start at 3am. Cover $15. Dress sharply. Open Sa 11pm-9am.

▶ DAYTRIPS FROM MELBOURNE

HEALESVILLE SANCTUARY. An open-air zoo, the Healesville Sanctuary lies in the Yarra Valley, 65km from Melbourne. Its minimum-security and daily "Meet the Keeper" presentations allow visitors to interact with and ask questions about the native creatures; keeper talks start at 11am and occur roughly every 30min. The Sanctuary also has programs on Warundjeri Aborigines and Aboriginal culture. (On Badger Creek Rd. From Melbourne, take the Met's light rail to Lilydale, then take McKenzie's tourist service bus #685. for about 35min. Only 2 buses go directly from the station weekdays at 9:40 and 11:35am. McKenzie's ☎5962 5088. Sanctuary ☎5957 2800; www.zoo.org.au/hs. Open daily 9am-5pm. $16.40, concessions $13.60, ages 4-15 $7.40, families of 6 $46. Free guided tours 10am-3pm; call ahead.)

WERRIBEE PARK AND OPEN RANGE ZOO. For a relaxing daytrip from Melbourne, the mansion at **Werribee Park** is a good bet, with serene sculptured gardens, an imposing billiards room, and an expansive nursery wing. From October to May, 5000 roses bloom in the state-pruned garden. (On K Rd. 30min. west of Melbourne along the Princes Hwy., or take the Weribee line to Weribee, then bus #439. ☎9741 2444 or 13 19 63. Open daily 10am-5pm. $11, concessions $6.60, ages 3-14 $5.20, families $26.70. Wheelchair accessible.) You can go on safari among animals from the grasslands of Australia, Africa, and Asia at Victoria's **Open Range Zoo,** just behind the mansion on K Rd. To explore on your own, take the two 30min. walking trails; a tour of the 200-hectare park takes about three hours. (☎ 9371 9600; www.zoo.org.au. Open daily 9am-5pm; entrance closes at 3:30pm. 50min. safaris daily 10:30am-3:40pm. $16.40, concessions $9.10, ages 3-15 $6.10, families $33.10. Wheelchair accessible.)

ORGAN PIPES NATIONAL PARK. Australia is all about unique geological formations, and the Melbourne area features one of its own: the Organ Pipes National Park. Although the 6m metamorphic landmarks look more like french fries than organ pipes, they're still a good daytrip or stop en route to the central Goldfields. Look for the **Rosette Rock,** which resembles a flowing stone frozen in time (400m past the Organ Pipes). The park is also a laboratory for environmental restoration and has been largely repopulated with native plants and trees since the early 1970s, when weeds concealed the pipes. The park has picnic and BBQ facilities and charges no entrance fee. (Just off the Calder Hwy. (Hwy. 79), 20km northwest of Melbourne. Public transport from Melbourne is slightly tricky: take tram #59 from Elizabeth St. to Essendon Station, then switch to bus #483 to Sunbury. ☎ 9390 1082. Open daily 8am-4:30pm; on weekends and public holidays during daylight savings 8am-6pm. Wheelchair accessible.)

HANGING ROCK RESERVE. The unique rock formations on this bit of crown land were featured in the famous 1975 film (first a novel by Joan Lindsay) *Picnic at Hanging Rock,* in which two young girls and their teacher disappear during the course of a school outing. (Calder Hwy., past Organ Pipes National Park; follow signs and enter at the south gate on South Rock Rd. Or, take V/Line from Spencer St. Station to Wood End and walk or take a cab 7km from the station. ☎ 5427 0295. Open daily 8am-6pm. $8 per car.)

PUFFING BILLY STEAM RAILWAY. The train is a relaxing way to see the interior of northeast Victoria's Dandenong Ranges. The billowing vapor serves momentarily to remind the traveler of simpler times, but quickly dissipates into the verdant netherworld of lush rainforest terrain. Note: you will be sharing this choo-choo with many small children. (40km east of Melbourne on the Burwood Hwy. to Belgrave. Or, take a 70min. Connex Hillside Train (☎ 13 16 38) from Flinders St. Station. ☎ 9754 6800; www.pbr.org.au. Train from Belgrave to Lakeside: 1hr.; 2-5 per day; $24.50, concessions $19.50, children 4-16 $11.50, families $50. From Belgrave to Gembrook: 1¾hr., 1-2 per day, $34.50/ $27.50/$16.50/$70.)

NEAR MELBOURNE

YARRA VALLEY WINERIES

Though not as well-known or as heavily visited as the Hunter Valley, NSW (see p. 145) or the Barossa Valley, SA (see p. 467), the Yarra Valley produces some top-grade wines. Located about 60km from Melbourne, the Yarra's vineyards were started in 1835 with 600 procured vine cuttings from the Hunter Valley. After a depression in the 1890s decimated wine demand, the Yarra basically shut down. Grapes were replanted in the 1960s, and today the Yarra has more than tripled its size from its peak in the 1800s. The Yarra's cool climate makes it ideal for growing Chardonnay, Pinot Noir, and Cabernet Sauvignon grapes; virtually every one of the over 30 wineries produces wines of these varieties. Quality sparkling wines abound, as Chardonnay and Pinot Noir are two of the principal grapes used for the bubbly. Sample also the various Yarra Shirazes, which often have some exciting light and peppery work going on. For more info on touring wineries, see p. 470.

☑ PRACTICAL INFORMATION. Public transportation options to the wineries are limited; Lilydale, 10-20km outside the Yarra, is on the Met train line, but after that there's no way to get to the wineries without hiring a car; remember *Let's Go* does not recommend drinking and driving, and perhaps more importantly, neither do the police. Pick up a free *Wineries of the Yarra Valley* or *Wine Regions of Victoria* at the Melbourne tourist office, or check out www.yarravalleywineries.asn.au. For accommodation information in the area, call ☎5962 2600. There are several tour options from Melbourne, though the best and most affordable is the unimaginatively named **Backpacker Winery Tours** (☎9877 8333; www.backpackerwinerytours.com.au). The $79 tour runs virtually every day and offers pickup and drop-off at major hostels, free tastings at four wineries, and a gourmet lunch overlooking the valley, not to mention knowledgeable commentary and lessons on wine quality and tasting from guides who have worked in the industry themselves.

◪ **WINERIES.** You can't go wrong with any of the options, especially at the normal price of $2 for a taste of their whole selection (tasting fee usually refundable upon purchase). Hours vary, but wineries are generally open daily 10am-5pm. Call and arrange a walkthrough with the winemaker. Here is only a selection of the many establishments in the valley.

Yering Station, 38 Melba Hwy. (☎9730 1107; www.yering.com). 1hr. east of the city. On the site of Yarra's 1st vineyard founded in 1838, Yering's tasting area has a delightful art gallery, and the multi-million dollar complex next door has a top-notch restaurant with a huge glass wall overlooking the Valley. Bottles $13-45. Open M-F 10am-5pm, Sa-Su 10am-6pm; restaurant open daily 10am-6pm.

St. Huberts (☎9739 1118), on St. Huberts Rd. Founded in 1863, this small winery offers a very popular Cabernet. It is also 1 of only 4 Australian wineries to produce the Rhone River Valley Roussane, a unique flavor great for mixing. All its wines are exclusively sold here. Bottles $19-30. Open M-F 9:30am-5pm, Sa-Su 10:30am-5:30pm.

Oakridge Estate, 864 Maroondah Hwy. (☎9739 1920; www.oakridgeestate.com.au). A more modern feel than many of its Yarra neighbors, Oakridge carries several award-winners, including its 1997 Cabernet Sauvignon voted "Best Red Wine in Australia" as well as best cabernet sauvignon in the world for that season. Bottles $18-40. Open daily 10am-5pm; cafe open daily noon-3pm.

Yarra Ridge, 179 Glenview Rd. (☎9730 1022). Even with award-winning wines, these humble winemakers don't boast their success on their labels. They're all about quality, and you'll find it particularly in their Pinot Noir. Bottles $16-45. Open daily 10am-5pm.

Domaine Chandon (☎9739 1110; www.chandon.com.au), "Green Point," on Maroondah Hwy. The most polished spot in the Yarra, with a walk-through exhibit on the process of producing sparkling wine and breathtaking views of the valley from its restaurant. No free tastings—only $5.50 flutes with a free bread, cheese, and chutney plate, or $20-40 bottles to go. Free tour 3pm, or guide yourself with the informative plaques. Open daily 10:30am-4:30pm.

PORT PHILLIP AND WESTERNPORT BAYS

Two strips of land, the Bellarine Peninsula to the west and the Mornington Peninsula to the east, curve south from Melbourne around Port Phillip and Westernport Bays. In 1803, the first Europeans to settle Victoria arrived here, at a site near Sorrento. Though their squalid effort lasted less than a year, by the late 19th century, the area's spectacular views and temperate climate had attracted swarms of summer homes. The area remains largely a wealthy getaway, but just enough budget opportunities exist to allow everyone to enjoy the awesome scenery, sandy beaches, and excellent surfing.

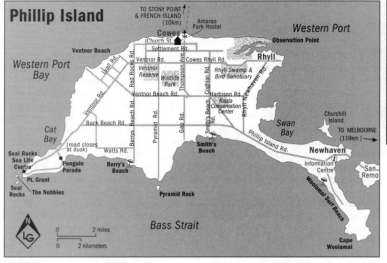

Phillip Island

TO STONY POINT
& FRENCH ISLAND
(10km)
Amaroo
Park Hostel

Western Port

Church St
Settlement Rd.
Cowes
Observation Point

Ventnor Beach

Lyall Rd.

Western Port
Bay

Ventnor Rd.
Cowes Rhyll Rd.
Rhyll

Red Rocks Rd.

Ventnor
Reserve
Thompson Ave.
Wildlife
Park
Rhyll Swamp &
Bird Sanctuary

Coghlan Rd.

Ventnor Rd.

Ventnor Beach Rd.
Harbison Rd.

Koala
Conservation
Center

Ventnor Rd.

Berrys Beach Rd.

Back Beach Rd.

Pyramid Rd.

Gap Rd.

Smith's Beach Rd.

Rhyll Newhaven Rd.

Churchill
Island

Cat
Bay

(road closes
at dusk)
Watts Rd.

Smith's
Beach

Swan
Bay

Phillip Island Rd.

TO MELBOURNE
(119km)

Seal Rocks
Sea Life
Centre

Penguin
Parade

Berry's
Beach

Newhaven

Information
Centre

San
Remo

Pt. Grant

Seal
Rocks
The Nobbies

Pyramid Rock

Woolamai Surf Beach

Bass Strait

N

LG

0   2 miles

0   2 kilometers

Cape
Woolamai

PHILLIP ISLAND   ☎ 03

Phillip Island has become synonymous with the endearing Little Penguins that inhabit its southwest corner. A whopping 3.5 million visitors a year gather to witness these creatures scamper back to their burrows nightly in a "Penguin Parade"—be prepared for a touristy crowd. A plethora of other wildlife abound, including koalas, wombats, seals, and hundreds of species of birds, all easily spotted on nature walks or at wildlife centers. Large breakers crashing against the island's southern shore create a surfers' mecca in summer, and the Grand Prix motorcycle race draws bikers and their fervent followers in early October. Despite the crowds, the rolling hills and vibrant blue Bass Strait waters make Phillip Island a great place to relax for a few days.

⎁ TRANSPORTATION. Phillip Island lies across a narrow strait from **San Remo,** 145km southeast of Melbourne. Numerous backpacker-oriented tours take groups to the island. **Duck Truck Tours,** run by the folks at Amaroo Park Hostel (see below), includes Melbourne transfers, up to three nights at the hostel, a guided tour of the island, meals, and a half-day of bike use. (☎5952 2548. $146, VIP/YHA $115.) By car, Phillip Island is two hours from Melbourne; take the South Eastern Arterial (M1) to the Cranbourne exit to the South Gippsland Hwy. (M420), then turn onto the Bass Hwy. (A420) and finally onto Phillip Island Tourist Rd. (B420) This road becomes Thompson Ave. when it reaches **Cowes,** the island's biggest township. **V/Line buses** serve Cowes from Melbourne (3hr.; May-Nov. 1 per day, Dec.-Apr. F-Su 2 per day; $16). To purchase V/Line tickets in town, head to **Cowes Travel** (☎5952 2744; open M-F 8:30am-5:30pm, Sa 9am-11am) or **Going Places Travel** (☎5952 3700; open M-F 9am-5:30pm), both on Thompson Ave.

⎘ PRACTICAL INFORMATION. Once on Phillip Island, you'll see the **Phillip Island Information Centre** on the right after the bridge. (☎5956 7447; www.phillipisland.net.au. Open daily 9am-5pm.) Buy tickets for the Penguin Parade here to avoid long queues. Other services include: **police** (☎5952 2037); **hospital** (☎5952

VICTORIA

2345); **ATMs** on Thompson Ave.; **Internet** at **Waterfront Computers,** 130 Thompson Ave. (☎5952 3312; $1.50 per 15min.; open M-F 9am-5pm, Sa 10am-1pm); **post office,** 73 Thompson Ave. (Open M-F 9am-5pm.) **Postal Code:** 3922.

⌐⌐ ACCOMMODATIONS AND FOOD. The only budget lodging on Phillip Island is the **Amaroo Park Hostel (YHA) ❶,** 97 Church St., Cowes; head down Thompson Ave. and hang a left on Church St. Though mostly a trailer park, the backpacker accommodations are lovely, with nice wooden furniture, a pool table, a **pub** with cheap drinks, and an outdoor verandah with BBQ. The friendly staff runs tours (including ones to the Penguin Parade) and serves a $7 dinner and a $6 cooked breakfast. (☎5952 2548; amaroo@waterfront.net.au. Internet. Swimming pool. Call to inquire about pickup in Melbourne. Book ahead. Sites $11; dorms $21, YHA $17.50; doubles $52, $45.) If you're looking for a splurge, it doesn't get much better than **Holmwood Guesthouse ❺** on Chapel St. at the corner of Steele St. Relax in the guest lounge with open fire or on the sunny verandah overlooking the garden with your home-cooked breakfast. Each guest room has its own name and character. (☎5952 3082. Guest rooms $150; self-contained units $175.)

For all-day breakfast, head for the **One Stop Shop ❶,** 58 Chapel St. (☎5952 1439. Open daily 7am-8:30pm.) Your best bet for lunch is the **Phillip Island Bakery ❶,** at the corner of Thompson Ave. and Chapel St.; sandwiches and hot pies are under $3. (☎5952 2027. Open M-F 7am-5pm, Sa-Su 7am-4:30pm.) For more upmarket eats, **Café Terrazzo ❷,** 5 Thompson Ave., serves up a range of pasta and wood-fired pizza ($8-15) in a whimsically painted bistro. (☎5952 3773. Open daily 5-9pm, also in summer F-M noon-3pm.) An IGA **supermarket** is at the corner of Thompson and Chapel St. (☎5952 2244. Open M-Sa 7:30am-8pm, Su 8:30am-6pm.)

◪◩ ACTIVITIES AND WILDLIFE. Phillip Island's tourist magnet is the **Little Penguin Parade,** at the Phillip Island Nature Park. Each night, anywhere between a handful and 1000 penguins return to their burrows after lengthy fishing expeditions to rest or tend to their hungry chicks. People await the penguins from a large grandstand along the boardwalk at sunset; after a 30min. to 1hr. wait, the penguins emerge, and their parade lasts nearly an hour. The **Information Centre** provides extensive information about the penguins, including interactive exhibits. (☎5951 2800; www.penguins.org.au. Open daily from 10am-10:30 or 11pm. $14, children $7, families $35. Wheelchair accessible.)

Although the penguins are the main draw, Australia's largest colony of **Australian fur seals** lives just offshore from the **Nobbies** rock formation. A boardwalk approaches the Nobbies, enabling you to take in the beautiful eroded hills and crashing sea. (Open 7:30am-dusk.) The **Seal Rocks Sea Life Centre** displays local marine life, a video of the seals, and a Disney-esque boat ride past animated displays tracing the area's seal hunting and conservation history. Pop $1 in the binoculars on the boardwalk to see the coolest thing this place has to offer—the seals themselves. (☎1300 367 325. Open 10am-dusk. $11, students $8.80, children $5.50, families $30.80.) The **Koala Conservation Centre,** south of Cowes on Phillip Island Rd., is a sanctuary housing 23 koalas in eucalypt canopies. The nocturnal marsupials are most active at feeding time, 1½ hours before dusk. (☎5952 1307. Open daily in summer 10am-7pm; in winter 10am-6pm. $5.60, children $2.60, families $14.) The Bunurong Aborigines originally lived on **Churchill Island,** but it then became one of the first European settlements in Victoria. The scenery at this historic site is enjoyable. (☎5956 7214. $7.70, children $3.70. Open daily 10am-4:30pm.) The Information Centre offers a **Rediscover Nature Ticket,** which covers the Parade, the Koala Centre, and Churchill Island. ($19, children $10, families $46.)

Throughout the year—but particularly in summer—Phillip Island offers great outdoor recreation. Surfers swarm to the island's southern coast, and the Information Centre provides a *Surfing Guide to Phillip Island*. **Island Surfboards,** 147 Thompson Ave. and 65 Smith's Beach Rd., can set you up with a board and excellent instruction. (☎5952 3443. Boards $10 per hr., $30 per day. 2hr. lesson $35.) To fully enjoy the area, take a scenic flight with **Phillip Island Air** (☎5956 7316; $39-99) or view the area by boat on **Bay Connections**. (☎5952 3501. 2hr. cruise $45, students $41, children $30, families $130.) **Cape Woolamai,** on the southeast corner, has the island's highest point, numerous walking trails, and a patrolled beach for swimming between the flags. Bushwalking trails cover the island, ranging from casual to hard; the info center's pamphlet *Discover Phillip Island Nature Park* is a good resource to start planning bushwalks.

SORRENTO ☎03

Though slightly more pricey, Sorrento (pop. 1500) draws handfuls of summer visitors to its history-rich parklands and rocky cliffs for fine surfing and a relaxing getaway. Near the very tip of the Mornington Peninsula, the resort is a pleasant stop along the fantastic drive from Melbourne.

▊▊ TRANSPORTATION AND PRACTICAL INFORMATION. From Melbourne, take a **train** to Frankston (1hr., $6.50), then **bus** #788 to stop 18 (1½hr.; M-F 12 per day, Sa 6 per day, Su 5 per day; $7.30). If you're coming from the Great Ocean Road, you can reach Sorrento via **ferry** from Queenscliff, on the Bellarine Peninsula (1hr;, 5-9 per day; $7, cars $36-38). The **Information Centre** is on St. Aubins Way, on the shore next to the boat launch. (☎5984 5678. Open daily 10am-4pm.) Along **Ocean Beach Road,** Sorrento's main street and a traffic nightmare, you'll find numerous **ATMs**. There is **Internet** at the **Sunny Side Up** next to the water on Point Nepean Rd. (☎5984 4255; open daily 8am-3pm; $1 per 10min.) and a **post office** on 16 Ocean Beach Rd. (Open M-F 9am-5pm.) **Postal Code:** 3943.

▊▊ ACCOMMODATIONS AND FOOD. From the roundabout at the inland end of Ocean Beach Rd., follow the YHA signs up Ossett St. to the **Sorrento Backpackers YHA ❷,** 3 Miranda St. Only five minutes from Back Beach, this backpacker retreat has an outdoor patio with BBQ, kitchen, and Internet ($2 per 15min.). The hostel operators will eagerly lead you to beautiful walking tracks and can secure discounts on everything from horse rides to swims with dolphins. (☎5984 4323. Book 1 week ahead in summer. Dorms $25, YHA $19.)

Ocean Beach Rd. is lined with eateries. **Stringer's Cafe ❶,** 2-8 Ocean Beach Rd., offers made-to-order sandwiches and salads. (☎5984 2010. Meals $3-8. Open daily 8am-5pm.) There's also a **supermarket** next door. (Open Su-F 8:30am-5:30pm, Sa 8:30am-6pm; in summer M-Th 8am-7pm, F-Sa 8am-7:30pm, Su 8am-6pm.) For Danish hot dogs ($4) and amazing ice cream, head for **The Little Mermaid ❶,** 70 Ocean Beach Rd. (Open daily in summer 11am-10pm; in winter Sa-Su 11am-10pm.) **Hotel Sorrento ❷,** 5 Hotham Rd., provides a chance to enjoy a beer ($2.60) while watching the sun set over the bay. (☎5984 2206.)

▊ SIGHTS. The town's main attraction is its gorgeous blue bay at the bottom of Ocean Beach Rd. While the bay is popular for swimming and sailing in summer, take caution: the riptides here change rapidly. For an unforgettable experience, swim with dolphins and seals with **Polperro Dolphin Swims.** (☎5988 8437. 4hr. Sept.-Apr. 2 per day. $70, YHA discount.) The most popular area to hang out and **surf** is **Back Beach,** on the west of the peninsula. You can learn to surf with the **Sorrento Surf School,** on Ocean Beach Rd. (☎5988 6143. 2hr. lesson $30.)

NEAR SORRENTO: MORNINGTON PENINSULA

Mornington Peninsula National Park is divided into different regions of coastline and bush country spanning over 40km across. On the western tip of the peninsula is **Point Nepean,** is 6km of nearly undeveloped land. The best way to see this part of the park is by bus from the **Visitors Center,** at the end of Point Nepean Rd. (☎5984 4276. Open daily 9am-5pm; Dec.-Feb. 9am-dusk. Buses depart daily 9:30am-3pm in summer every 30min.; in winter every hr. $12.40, concessions $7.50; park fees included.) Disembark at the first stop and walk the rest of the way (3½km one-way) to **Fort Nepean,** a military base, and take the bus from there ($10.50).

This fantastic drive along the peninsula is also dotted with a plethora of **vineyards** and picnic stops. The **Dromana Estate Vineyards,** on Harrisons Rd. in Dromana, is open for tastings. (☎5987 3800. Open daily 11am-4pm. Tastings $3.) Pick-your-own fruit farms also abound; check out **Sunny Ridge,** on the corner of Mornington-Flinders and Shands Rd. (☎5989 6273. Open Nov.-Apr. daily 9am-5pm; May-Oct. Sa-Su 10am-4pm. $8 per kg of strawberries.)

QUEENSCLIFF   ☎03

Rustic, relaxing, and maybe even a little romantic, tiny Queenscliff perches peril-ously on the easternmost tip of the **Bellarine Peninsula,** 120km southwest of Mel-bourne, overlooking one of the most dangerous stretches of water on the seven seas. With grand old architecture and a leisurely ambience well suited to beach-sit-ting and twilight strolls, many travelers choose Queenscliff to start, or end, their journey on the Great Ocean Road (see p. 594).

Take the **V/Line train** from Melbourne to Geelong (1hr.; M-F 27 per day, Sa 19 per day, Su 11 per day; $13.20), and then **McHarry's Buslines** (☎5223 2111. 1hr.; M-F 9 per day, Sa 7 per day, Su 4 per day; $6-8). **Ferries** run from the Sorrento Pier, just across the bay (1hr.; 5-9 per day; $7, cars $36-38). The **Visitor Information Centre** is at 55 Hesse St. and has **Internet** for $3 per 30 min. (☎5258 4843. Open daily 9am-5pm.) Services include: ANZ **bank** at 71 Hesse St. (open M-Th 9:30am-4pm, F 9:30am-5pm); **post office,** 47 Hesse St. (☎5258 4219. Open M-F 9am-5pm.) **Postal Code:** 3225.

The jewel in the crown of hosteling, the YHA-affiliated ▣**Queenscliff Inn B&B ❷,** 59 Hesse St., offers an elegant but affordable taste of the town's luxury. A red brick 1906 Edwardian building, the Inn boasts a gorgeous drawing room with an open fire and a convenient kitchen. The delectable breakfast ranges from continental ($6) to full cooked meals for $13.50. (☎5258 3737. Linens $2.50. Dorms $19; singles $30; doubles $46; family rooms $78.) If you can't get a bed here, some of the scuba diving outfits rent out bunkbeds. Try the **Queenscliff Dive Centre ❸,** 37 Learmonth St., opposite Town Hall. (☎5258 1188. Bunks from $30; private rooms from $57.) Queenscliff Dive Centre runs scuba certification classes and conducts snorkeling tours where you can swim with a colony of playful fur seals and dolphins. (☎1800 814 200. Book ahead. 2hr. tour from $40.) The **Marine Discovery Centre** also runs informative events during the summer. (☎5258 3344. Tours $3.50.)

For a light lunch starting at $4 or a $3 milkshake, rub elbows with locals at the **Promenade Cafe ❶,** 1 Symonds St. (☎5258 2911. Open daily 8am-5:30pm; in winter 10am-5pm.) **Mietta's ❷,** 16 Gellibrand St., offers delicious Italian fare, ranging from a delicate tomato bruschetta to a homemade basil ravioli. (☎5258 1066. Open daily 10am-8pm; in winter 10am-3pm. Meals $9.50-12.) There's a **supermarket** at 73 Hesse St. (☎5258 1727. Open M-Th and Sa 9am-6pm, F 9am-7pm, Su 9am-5pm.)

GEELONG   ☎03

The second largest city in Victoria, Geelong (juh-LONG; pop. 175,400) is on the shore at the western end of Port Philip Bay, an hour southwest of Melbourne on the Princes Hwy. (Hwy. 1). Of interest to the traveler primarily as the departure point for buses and trains heading to the **Great Ocean Road** and other points west, Geelong is a pleasant place to stop for a day, as this former hub of the wool trade is in the process of remaking itself with tourists in mind. The revamped waterfront and surprisingly interesting wool museum attest to this visitor-friendly focus.

⊏⊓ TRANSPORTATION AND PRACTICAL INFORMATION. The **V/Line Station** (☎ 13 61 96), on the western edge of the downtown area, remains Geelong's most important building for most travelers. **V/Line** runs **trains** to Melbourne (1hr., daily every hr., $9.50) and Warrnambool (2¼hr., 3 per day, $27). V/Line **buses** depart for the **Great Ocean Road** from the station, making numerous stops before arriving in Apollo Bay (2½ hr.; M-F 4 per day, Sa-Su 2 per day; $20.30). Buses also head to Ballarat (1½hr.; M-Sa 3 per day, Su 2 per day; $11). The Princes Hwy. (Latrobe Tce.) runs north-south along the western edge of town, while Moorabool St. heads south from the waterfront. Its intersections with Malop and Little Malop St. host most of the town's action. The monolithic Market Square mall lies at that intersection and contains the **post office** (M-F 9am-5:30pm, Sa 9am-1pm), a Safeway **supermarket** (open daily 8:30am-6pm), and a **Visitors Center.** (☎ 5222 6126. Open daily 9am-5pm.) Other visitors centers are located in the Wool Museum (☎ 5222 2900; open daily 9am-5pm) and next to the carousel on the waterfront (open daily 10am-4pm). **Banks** with **ATMs** line Moorabool St., and free **Internet** access is available at the Court House Cafe (see below) or at the **public library,** on Little Malop St., on the south side of Johnston Park. (☎ 5222 1212. Open M-F 10am-8pm, Sa 9:30am-noon, Su 2-5pm; book ahead.) **Postal Code:** 3220.

⌐ ACCOMMODATIONS. Though far from the waterfront, **Irish Murphy's ❷,** 30 Aberdeen St., has laundry, kitchen facilities, and a comfortable TV lounge. The pub below features beautiful wood finishing and a friendly staff. To get there from the train station, take a right on Fenwick St., keeping Johnston Park to your left, then make a right on Ryrie St. and follow it for two blocks as it becomes Aberdeen St. (☎ 5221 4335. Pub open M-Th 11am-midnight, F-Sa noon-1am, Su noon-11pm. Bunks $19, linens $3; doubles $48.) Closer to the waterfront, the **Carlton Hotel ❸,** on Malop St. between Gheringhap and Moorabool St., offers decent private rooms with shared baths above a pub with pool tables. (☎ 5229 1954. Singles $39; doubles $59.) Several B&Bs and motels are southwest of the V/Line station on Aberdeen St.

⊏⊐ FOOD. A variety of eating options line Moorabool St. as it approaches the bay, while Little Malop Street hosts slightly more upscale cafes and restaurants. The easygoing **Wharf Shed Cafe ❷,** on East Beach Rd., to the right of where Moorabool St. meets the waterfront, offers a wide-ranging menu (brick oven pizza $10, cajun chicken with couscous $16) and features a lively bar and live music Friday nights. (☎ 5221 6645. Open daily 10am-11pm.) For some backpackers, the all-you-can-eat buffet at **Smorgy's ❷** might be reason enough for a stopover in Geelong. Its location 300m out into the bay, on the end of Cunningham Pier, affords exceptional views. (☎ 5222 6444; all-you-can-eat lunch 11:30am-2:15pm, $11; dinner 5-9:15pm, $16.) At the corner of Gheringhap and Little Malop St., just off the southeast corner of Johnston Park, the **Courthouse Cafe ❶** is a cool spot with outstanding salads ($8), sandwiches ($6), and free **Internet.** (☎ 5229 3470. Open M-F 7am-5pm.)

◙ SIGHTS. Geelong's main tourist attraction is the informative and fascinating **Wool Museum,** housed in a handsome stone building at 26 Moorabol St., a block back from the waterfront. Live weaving demonstrations and interactive displays illustrate the centrality of the wool industry in the history of the region. (☎ 5227 0701. Open daily 9:30am-5pm. $7.30, concessions $6, children $4.) The museum is a short walk from the **waterfront,** an attraction in itself, with a sculpture park, Cunningham Pier, a swimming beach with a kiddie pool, and an 1892 **carousel** living out its days in a glass-enclosed shelter on a pier at the end of Moorabool St. ($3, children $2.) **Johnston Park** is worth a look, with well-kept lawns and an overgrown and ornate gazebo greeting visitors as they emerge from the train station.

GREAT OCEAN ROAD

The Great Ocean Road is one of the world's greatest vehicular experiences and one of Victoria's proudest tourism showpieces. The area traversed by the road is renowned for surfing and scenery, music festivals and national parks, and fishing and hiking. An astoundingly vast array of plant and animal life is visible and easily accessible along the shores. Tossed up by winds that blow unimpeded across thousands of miles from Antarctica, the same Southern Ocean waves that sculpted the coast's unearthly stone pillars and arches were also responsible for the region's hundreds of shipwrecks. This is the stuff that great road-trips are made of.

The Great Ocean Road region encompasses the entire serene and spectacular southwestern coast of Victoria, from Torquay to Portland, though the Road itself is just the 200km stretch that links Torquay to Warrnambool before being absorbed by the Princes Hwy. Heading west, the first part of the Road is called the **Surf Coast.** Stretching from Torquay to Lorne, this area hosts some of the country's best surfing and endless miles of beaches for wandering and swimming. The **Otway Ranges,** on the 73km stretch from Anglesea to Apollo Bay, has a cool, rainy climate that nurtures tree ferns, large pines, breathtaking waterfalls, and a range of fauna, culminating in the **Otway National Park,** just west of Apollo Bay. Rejoining the shoreline on the other side of the park, the aptly named **Shipwreck Coast** features unrelenting winds and unpredictable offshore swells made the region a graveyard for 19th-century vessels but also shaped the famous ◙**Twelve Apostles** rock formations. Moving west, discover whales off **Warrnambool,** mutton birds in **Port Fairy,** seal colonies at **Cape Bridgewater,** towering sand dunes in **Discovery Bay Coastal Park,** and estuary fishing in **Lower Glenelg National Park.**

The best place to start any adventure along the Great Ocean Road is the helpful and informative **Visitors Center** in Torquay, where you can find very good maps and helpful suggestions. If coming from the west, the Visitors Centers in Portland and Warrnambool will outfit you with the same array of maps and guides. The *Great Ocean Road Official Visitors' Guide* is helpful and free, while the glossy magazine *The Great Ocean Road* is a good compendium of postcard-perfect photos but offers little in the way of information. The most useful handouts are the excellent maps, including the *Great Ocean Road Official Touring Map* and several others that offer more detail on specific sections of the road, all available free at the info centers. General tourist info can be found at www.greatoceanroad.org.

▣ TRANSPORTATION ON THE GREAT OCEAN ROAD

PUBLIC TRANSPORT. The most satisfying way to see the Great Ocean Road is by **car.** Public transport along the road is infrequent and inconvenient and probably won't get you everywhere you want to go. **V/Line** (☎ 13 61 96) **trains** from Melbourne will get you as far as Geelong. **Buses** run both ways along the Great Ocean Road between Geelong and Apollo Bay, passing through Torquay, Anglesea, Lorne, and other towns along the way (M-F 4 per day each way, Sa-Su 2 per day). On Fridays year-round and also on Mondays from December to January, one special **"coast link" V/Line bus** runs each way between Apollo Bay and Warrnambool, making stops in Port Campbell and other towns along the way, with brief stops at tourist lookouts

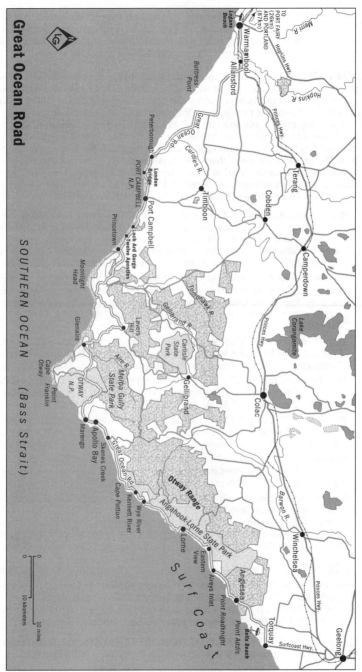

Great Ocean Road

along the Shipwreck Coast; otherwise, it is difficult to progress farther west than Apollo Bay via public buses. **Bicycling** along the highway is becoming increasingly popular, but the narrow, winding road (with no shoulder in most places) and the hilly topography of some sections combine to make it a difficult bike tour

BUS TOURS. Bus tours along the Great Ocean Road offer more flexibility than public transport and are the best way for those without a car to see the area. Tours generally come in two varieties: those that make a loop starting and ending in Melbourne and those that run between Melbourne and Adelaide. Tours returning to Melbourne generally only go as far as Port Campbell before turning north and taking the inland Princes Hwy. back to the city, but they are the best way for those not interested in heading to South Australia to see the Road. For those heading west from Melbourne to Adelaide, there are a number of 3-day tours connecting the cities via the Great Ocean Road at prices rivaling air or rail travel between the two cities. Those short on time can choose to do the trip all at once, while some companies allow those with more time to take as many layovers as they want.

Otway Discovery (☎9654 5432 or 1800 444 432) is the most affordable and flexible of the loop tours. The friendly drivers run along the Road from Melbourne to Port Campbell and then back to Melbourne via the inland route, allowing free hopping on and off. There is no time limit, but you only get to do the loop once and the bus only travels west along the Road, so don't miss anything: you can't go back. Departs daily 7am. $65.

Wildlife Tours (☎9534 8868; www.wildlifetours.com.au) runs a one-day highlight tour of the Great Ocean Road (Melbourne to Port Campbell), as well as structured 3-day return tours that include the Grampians and 3-day Melbourne-to-Adelaide trips. Stopovers may be allowed, provided the next bus has room for you. Highlights $54; return tours $139; Melbourne-Adelaide $159. ISIC/NOMADS/VIP/YHA.

Autopia Tours (☎9326 5536; www.autopiatours.com.au) runs structured 3-day return tours and 3-day Melbourne-Adelaide trips that incorporate the Great Ocean Road and Grampians but don't allow hopping on and off. 3-day $150, Melbourne-Adelaide $160.

Let's Go Bush Tours (☎9662 3969) gives you dinner, breakfast, and accommodation on a 2-day tour. Cool name, but no affiliation. Tours depart W and F-Sa. $99, with meals and accommodation $124.

Wayward Bus (☎08 8410 8833 or 1800 882 823; www.waywardbus.com.au) runs a 3½-day Adelaide trip via the Great Ocean Road and allows up to 6 months of jumping on and off. $310 includes breakfasts, lunches, planned pitstops, and 3 nights' lodging.

Oz Experience (☎1300 300 028; www.ozexperience.com) runs a popular 3-day journey along the Road in both directions between Melbourne and Adelaide, allowing you to hop on and off for up to 6 months. $185, ISIC/YHA $176.

Groovy Grape Getaways (☎1800 661 177; getaways@groovygrape.com.au) runs a popular, quality, backpacker-oriented all-inclusive 3-day trip in either direction between Melbourne and Adelaide, hitting all the main sights and providing all accommodation, meals, park entrance fees, and a knowledgeable guide. $260 per person. Departs Melbourne Tu and F 7am; departs Adelaide Tu and Sa 7am. No hop-on/hop-off allowed.

TORQUAY   ☎03

Wave seekers and beach bums who feel like they've wandered too far from Byron Bay, take heart: there's great surfing in Victoria, and Torquay (tor-KEY), at the eastern end of the Great Ocean Road, is its capital. The first city along the Surfcoast stretch, it is a town suffused with the laid-back vibe of surf culture.

⊟⊠ TRANSPORTATION AND PRACTICAL INFORMATION. V/Line buses (☎13 61 96) leave from outside the Bernell Caravan Park by the Bell's Beach hostel on the Great Ocean Rd. Buses head north to Geelong (45min.; M-F 4 per day, Sa-Su 2 per day; $5) and west on the Great Ocean Road, making numerous stops, including Lorne (1hr., $10), before arriving in Apollo Bay (2hr.; M-F 4 per day, Sa-Su 2 per day; $17.20). **Bellarine Transit** (☎5223 2111) provides buses to Geelong (M-F 8 per day, Sa-Su 3 per day; $5). Most commercial activity takes place along the Surfcoast Hwy. (Geelong Rd.), a continuation of the Great Ocean Rd., or just off the highway on Gilbert St., where there is a well-marked shopping district with **ATMs** and food options. The **Visitors Center,** 120 Surfcoast Hwy., is in the Surfworld Museum in the Surf City Plaza retail center. (☎5261 4219. Open daily 9am-5pm. Internet $7 per hr.) **Rental cars** are available at Bells Beach Backpackers ($35-$50 per day).

⌐⌐ ACCOMMODATIONS AND FOOD. Book in advance for the Easter surfing competition. **Bells Beach Backpackers ❷,** 51-53 Surf Coast Hwy., is a brightly-painted, bungalow-style bunkhouse with a pronounced surfing mood set by posters, magazines, and nearly constant screenings of surf documentaries. Bell's Beach also has immaculate bathrooms, lockers, bikes, Internet ($5 per hr.), and good vibrations. (☎5261 7070 or 1800 819 883. Key and linens deposit $10. Dorms in peak-season $22, off-peak $19; doubles $55/$45. NOMADS.) Close to Bell's Beach but farther from town, **Pointbreak Backpackers ❷,** 185 Addiscott Rd., is about 8km southeast via the Great Ocean Rd. (watch for sign marking turn-off). Tucked away down a quiet road, this 15-bed hostel has a full kitchen, BBQ, laundry facilities, a book exchange, and a courtesy bus to the town center and the beach. (☎5261 5105. Internet $6 per hr. Dorms in summer $20, in winter $17.) **Bernells Caravan Park ❸,** 55 Surfcoast Hwy., next to Bells Beach Backpackers, has a pool, spa, and tennis court. (☎5261 2493. Check-in 1:30-8pm. Powered sites from $25; cabins from $50.) The **Torquay Hotel ❺,** on Bell St., has nice rooms and the only pub in town. (☎5261 6046. Open daily 10am-1am. Doubles from $85.)

Hordes of surfers with the munchies provide a large market for the takeaways and chippers that dominate Torquay's food scene, centered on Gilbert St. and on Bell St. near the beach. The **Bees Knees Cafe ❶,** on the corner of Gilbert and Pearl St. downtown, has tasty sandwiches and burgers ($6) and heavenly fruit smoothies. (☎5261 4074. Open M and W-Su 9am-6pm.) **Spooner's ❶,** 57 Geelong Rd., is a cheap and friendly coffeehouse next door to the complex of surf shops. (☎5261 3887. Open daily 9am-5pm.) There's a Foodworks **supermarket** with a LiquorWorks attached on Gilbert St. (Open daily 7am-10pm.)

◪ SURFING AND BEYOND. Peak **surfing** season is from March to August. The **Torquay Surf Beach** off Bell St., a ten-minute walk from Bells Beach Backpackers, starts a string of surfable beaches that stretches down the coast. The king of them all is **Bells Beach,** where the reef breaks attract top professional surfers for the Easter **Rip Curl Pro Classic.** It's a ten-minute drive from town, although the most scenic way to reach it is via the **Surf Coast Walk,** a trail that begins at the beach at Torquay. The trail, which is great for mountain biking, follows the coast for nearly 35km, passing **Jan Juc,** the second-best surfing site around (also safe for swimmers) and continuing on to Point Addis, Anglesea, and Airey Inlet. For closer swimming beaches, cross the highway from Bells Beach Backpackers and continue straight for ten minutes to Zeally Bay, where **Cozy Corner, Torquay Front Beach,** and **Fisherman's Beach** await. There is also a **nude beach** on that side of town, accessible by walking north along the beach from Fisherman's Beach.

The colossal **Surf City Plaza,** 101 Surfcoast Hwy., hosts dozens of surf retailers selling everything you'll need to look the part, from flip-flops to sunglasses to board shorts to boards. (Most open daily 9am-5pm.) Hang a left before the big buildings to find the bargains at one of several factory outlets, which sell "imperfect" goods at closer to perfect prices. (Most open M-Sa 9am-5pm, Su 11am-5pm.)

At the back of the plaza, **Surfworld** has interactive displays and a hall of fame of Australia's most venerated surfers. (☎5261 4606. Open daily 10am-4pm. $6.50, concessions and NOMADS $4.50.) If you prefer sky to surf, **Skydive Torquay,** at Tiger Moth World Adventure Park 3km north of Torquay, offers tandem jumps from 10,000 ft. above the beautiful Great Ocean coastline. (☎9432 2419 or 0413 863 929; www.skydivingassoc.com.au. $315, 5% credit card fee. Call ahead for pickup.)

FROM TORQUAY TO LORNE

POINT ADDIS. The turn-off to **Point Addis** appears abruptly, about 5km out of Torquay. The point offers outstanding views of Victoria's western coast, serrated by silty clay and gray cliffs. The path at the right side of the carpark leads to a long stretch of empty beach, while a trail to the left 200m before the carpark will take you to the **Pixie Caves,** a small cove beach on the east side of the point with small caves carved out of the sandstone. Between Point Addis and the highway is the beginning of the recently cleared **Koorie Cultural Walk** (2km; 1hr. return) which leads through the **Ironbark Basin Reserve.** Displays along the way elucidate the history of the Koorie Aborigines who once inhabited the area.

ANGLESEA. Most visitors stop just long enough to visit the **beach** at the mouth of the Anglesea River, or the **golf course** on the northwestern edge of town, which has a reputation as a can't-miss place to see kangaroos. Signs lead the way from the Great Ocean Rd. to both the beach and the golf course. Surfing lessons, including loan of boards and wetsuits, can be had at short notice from **Go Ride A Wave** (☎5263 2111), with one lesson at $44 or a four lesson package for $132. The company also operates out of Torquay and Lorne. For immaculate accommodation, try **Anglesea Backpackers ❷,** 40 Noble St. (☎5263 2664. Check-in after 3:30pm. Dorms $22, off-peak $18; ensuite from $50.)

LORNE   ☎03

The relaxing town of Lorne thrives on contradictions: it boasts impressive mountains alongside expansive beaches, hosts grimy backpackers in the shadow of million-dollar vacation homes, and forces trendy shops and bistros to share space with surf shops and chippers. Contrast has not bred conflict, however, and the tourism mastermind who once dubbed Lorne "the place of well-being" was right on the mark. Sandwiched between the temperate rainforests of Angahook-Lorne State Park and a popular beach, Lorne has activities to please anyone.

The Great Ocean Rd. morphs into **Mountjoy Pde.** as it passes through town. **Buses** depart four times daily during the week and twice daily on weekends from the Commonwealth Bank at 68 Mountjoy Pde. to Apollo Bay (1hr., $5.50), Geelong (1½hr., $13), and Melbourne (2½hr., $25). The **Visitors Center,** 144 Mountjoy Pde., a few blocks west of the V/Line stop, has excellent maps and information on activities, hiking, and camping in the area. (☎5289 1152. Open daily 9am-5pm.)

Great Ocean Backpackers (YHA) ❷, on the east side of the Erskine River, is a colony of wooden cabins set amid the trees on the hillside behind the supermarket. Birds of all shapes and colors fly in to share your breakfast on the front porch. The extremely knowledgeable staff give guests a lift to trailheads. (☎5289 1809. Book ahead. Dorms $23, YHA $19; twins and doubles $54/$44.) **Erskine River Backpackers ❷,** 4 Mountjoy Pde., is on the west bank of the river at the bend in the road on the east end of town. Most rooms open onto a leafy courtyard, and the bathrooms feature large and luxurious bathtubs. (☎5289 1496. Dorms $20, deluxe $25; doubles $60) Free **camping ❶** without amenities is available inside the Angahook-Lorne State Park (☎5289 1732), or just behind town (check in at the Tourist Office before setting up). Complete camping facilities are available 10km west of town at the beautiful **Cumberland River Camping Reserve ❷**. (☎5289 1790. Sites $17; cabins from $59.) The Visitors Center has information on the numerous **B&Bs ❼** in the area, most starting around $100 per night. Ridgeway's **supermarket,** 1 Great Ocean Rd., is on the Melbourne side of the river. (Open M-Th and Su 8am-7pm, F 8am-8pm, Sa 7am-8pm.) Get the best fresh fish on the **pier** toward the west end of town. (Open daily 9am-6pm.)

    ◪**Qdos Gallery and Artzbar,** on Allenvale Rd., is one of the finest arts venues in this part of Victoria. The **Qdos Film Society** has free outdoor screenings of classic movies most Friday nights. The **cafe ❸** has fresh food dailyand a constantly changing menu, with mains running $12-20. (☎5289 1989; www.qdosarts.com. Gallery open Nov.-Easter M-Tu and Th-Su 10am-6pm; Easter-Oct. M and F-Su 10am-5pm. Bar open Sa-Su until 1am; live music Sa.)

NEAR LORNE: ANGAHOOK-LORNE STATE PARK

The 22,000 hectare reserve offers over 64km of walking trails in the Lorne area that meander through temperate rainforests and past striking waterfalls. While it is helpful to have a car to access most of the trailheads, several walks take off from the town itself. The best of these is the hike up to **Erskine Falls** (9km; 3hr. one-way), which follows and criss-crosses the Erskine River through the temperate rainforests of the Park and past **Splitter Falls** and **Straw Falls** before arriving at Erskine Falls. These 38m falls are the most famous in the area and have attracted tourists since the trail was constructed in 1890, including a visit by Rudyard Kipling in 1891 that inspired a later poem. A much shorter walk from town will bring you to **Teddy's Lookout,** a high point at the southern edge of town that presents sweeping views of forested mountains abutting wide-open ocean. (30min. walk; go up Bay St. from the Great Ocean Rd. in Lorne and make a left on George St.) The **Allenvale Mill Site,** a 30min. walk from town along Allenvale Rd., is a good jumping off point for a hike to **Phantom Falls** (about 1hr.), where you can either turn around or continue on to the Cora Lynn Carpark, where you can join the **Green Break Track** back to Allenvale Rd. (8km, about 2½hr.)

    The other main trailheads in the area, the **Blanket Leaf Picnic Area** and the **Sheoak Picnic Area,** are best reached with a car, though you can also walk to them. Various simple tracks begin at the **Sheoak Picnic Area,** a one-hour walk or 15min. drive up Allenvale Rd. from Lorne. The walk to **Sheoak Falls** follows a gentle track by the creek and eventually reaches the ocean (1½hr.), while the **Lower Kalimna Falls Walk** (1hr.) leads beneath a waterfall, which can be seen from above on the **Upper Kalimna Falls Walk** (1½hr.). A fairly easy walk (1½hr. return) connects the **Blanket Leaf** carpark to **Cora Lynn Cascades.** Other hikes from Blanket Leaf head to Phantom Falls (3½hr.) and to Allenvale Rd. at the Allenvale Mill Site (4hr.).

    Before heading off on any adventures in the area, a stop at the Lorne **Visitors Center** is a good idea, as they will have the latest information on trail and campsite closures and conditions, as well as maps. There are a number of **free camping sites ❶** in Angahook-Lorne (the biggest is on Hammonds Rd. in Airey's Inlet to the east of Lorne); camping in picnic areas or carparks results in a fine. **Allenvale Mill,** a 200m walk-in from the carpark, has toilets (tents only). The **Wye River Rd.,** a 20min. drive west on the Great Ocean Rd., has 15 sites that are all accessible by car.

APOLLO BAY   ☎03

Apollo Bay sits in an idyllic cove at the base of the most rolling set of hills around. Though the town can seem somewhat subdued when the sun's not out, its placid setting, ample accommodations, and easy access to activities in Otway National Park make it a popular stop along the Great Ocean Road, and its annual music festival is among the biggest in Australia.

TRANSPORTATION AND PRACTICAL INFORMATION. The Great Ocean Rd. is the main street through town, with side streets running north off it. **Buses** leave from the front of the Visitors Center (M-F 4 per day; Sa-Su 2 per day) going to: Geelong (2½hr., $20); Lorne (1hr., $5.40); and Melbourne (3½hr., $28). Buses to Warrnambool (3½hr., $24) and other points west along the Great Ocean Rd. leave Fridays only, except in December and January, when they operate once on Monday as well. The above-average **Tourist Information Centre,** 157 Great Ocean Rd., books accommodations and tours and advises on road closures and campsite availability in the Otways. (☎5237 6529. Open daily 9am-5pm.) The stretch of highway through town also has two 24hr. **ATMs** and an **Internet** cafe.

ACCOMMODATIONS AND FOOD. The small ◙**Surfside Backpackers ❶,** on the corner of the Great Ocean Rd. and Gambier St. at the west end of town, has a record player instead of a TV, as well as ocean and beach views from the lounge and some rooms. Robyn, the owner, is one of the friendliest, most helpful people you're likely to meet. (☎5237 7263 or 1800 357 263. Internet $2 per 10min. Book ahead. Reception daily 8-10pm. Sites $10; dorms $18; doubles $40-55. MC/V.) Farther from the beach is the relaxed **Apollo Bay Backpackers ❷,** 47 Montrose Ave., on a quiet residential street. (☎0419 340 362; backpack@vicnet.net.au. Dorms $17; singles $40; doubles $45.) On Murray St. on the north side of town, the **Bay Pines Motel and Guesthouse** offers basic private rooms in the **guesthouse ❶** and nicer rooms with private baths in the **motel ❹.** (☎5237 6732. Guesthouse singles $15, doubles $30; motel singles $45, doubles $75.) West of Apollo Bay 20km, 7km south of the Great Ocean Rd. on the Cape Otway Rd., **Cape Otway Backpackers ❶,** part of the accommodation menagerie at **Bimbi Park,** sits right on the edge of the Otway Ranges; the beach is a 20min. walk through the national park, and horseback riding can be arranged. (☎5237 9246. Book ahead. Sites from $15; dorms $20).

Bay Leaf Cafe ❷, on the Great Ocean Rd. near Hardy St., serves a great breakfast all day ($5-9) as well as tasty lunches and creative dinners. (☎5237 6470. Mains $6-20. Open daily 8am-9pm.) **The Sandy Feet Cafe ❶,** 139 Great Ocean Rd., is a health-nut's paradise, with veggie burgers ($5.50), salads ($4-6), and crepes galore. (Open daily 9am-5pm.) For the tastiest—and only—kangaroo steaks in town ($19), head to **Wayne's Cray Pot Bistro ❸,** at the south end of town on the Great Ocean Road (☎5237 6240. Open daily noon-9pm.) There are two **supermarkets** on the Great Ocean Rd. as it goes through town, both open M-Sa 8am-8pm and Su 8am-6:30pm.

SIGHTS. While the Otways get all the attention, there are plenty of things to see right around town, starting with the gently curving bay itself, best viewed from either the **Mariner's Lookout** (on Mariner's Lookout Rd.) or the **Crow's Nest** (on Tuxion Rd.). Recreational **fishing** is a popular pastime in Apollo Bay, both from the beach and from chartered fishing boats; book at the Visitors Center. (4hr. tours $60 plus $5 for required fishing permit.) Apollo Bay's most illuminating feature are its **glow worms,** which are actually the larval stage in the life-cycle of a local fly. **Otway Eco-Guides** offers glow worm tours in Otway National Park, as well as tours to see koalas and other wildlife. (☎5237 6529, or inquire at Visitors Center. 1hr. tour from $18.) Those looking for a bit of exercise might want to try a **mountain biking** tour with **Otway Expeditions.** (☎0419 007 586; from $30). Surfers should stop by **Hodgy's Surf Center,** 143 Great Ocean Rd., which offers daily lessons (2hr., $40). The **Apollo Bay Shell Museum,** on Noel St. at the western edge of town, is the quirkiest museum you're likely to find on the Great Ocean Road. (☎5237 6395. Open daily 9:30am-8pm. $2.50.) **Triplet Falls,** a quiet getaway near Laver's Hill (40km west of Apollo Bay on the Great Ocean Rd.), is a three-tiered waterfall reached by taking the Lavers Hill-Beech Forest Rd. from Lavers Hill, turning right onto Phillips Rd., then following signs on unsealed roads. Each year, the town grooves to the folksy sounds of the **Apollo Bay Music Festival** (Mar. 28-30, 2003), which attracts acts from all over Australia and the world and a crowd that consumes every available bed and campsite in town (book ahead for that weekend).

NEAR APOLLO BAY: THE OTWAYS

The Otway Range stretches 60km west of Apollo Bay and encompasses three major parks: **Otway National Park, Otway State Forest,** and **Melba Gully State Park.** Within the cool, temperate rainforest, myrtle beech trees provide shade while tree ferns dominate the eye-level scenery, occasionally animated by wallabies, possums, and gray kangaroos. Waterfalls cascade down steep hillsides to form clear creeks. The walk through Melba Gully is short (30min. return), but promises exposure to a unique, fragile environment and a chance to view the mildly famous and suitably large "Big Tree," a 200-year-old Otway messmate. The turnoff for Melba Gully Rd. is about 5km past Lavers Hill, heading west on the Great Ocean Rd. from Apollo Bay. The **Mait's Rest trail** (45min. loop) is one of the best-known rainforest walks in Victoria, beginning 17km west of Apollo Bay along the Great Ocean Rd. Shortly after Mait's Rest is the turn-off for the **Cape Otway Lightstation.** (☎5237 9240. Open daily 9am-5pm. $8, concessions $5; daily guided tours $11/$5.)

Maps for Otways' well-marked walks are available at the **Apollo Bay Tourist Info Centre** (☎5237 6529). A 4WD can make the pothole-filled tracks much easier to navigate. For camping, check into the vast Bimbi Park (see **Accommodations,** p. 600), or use one of the five **camping ❶** areas in Otway National Park. In summer, pitch at **Blanket Bay;** follow Lighthouse Rd., then watch signs for a left turn. (☎5237 6889. Sites $10.20.) The **Aire River** camping areas are reached from the Great Ocean Rd., another 5km west by way of the Horden Vale turn-off. The Aire River is suitable for swimming, and three walks diverge from the grounds. (☎5237 6889. Sites $10.20.) Both **Parker Hill** and **Point Franklin** have small camping areas with few facilities. (☎5237 6889. Sites $4.20.) **Johanna Beach** has a basic campsite and the best **surfing** in the area, though the beach is not safe for swimming. Take the sealed Johanna Rd. from the Great Ocean Rd. (☎5237 6889. Sites $10.20.)

PORT CAMPBELL   ☎03

Port Campbell was once most notable to mariners: it's the only safe harbor on one of the nastiest yet most picturesque coastlines in the world, the treacherous stretch of the Shipwreck Coast from Apollo Bay (100km east) to Warrnambool (66km west). Today, the sleepy fishing village is best known as the gateway to Port Campbell National Park and the famed Twelve Apostles rock formations. The daytime tourist traffic can be busy, but come sunset Port Campbell is pretty tranquil.

🖅🔃 TRANSPORTATION AND PRACTICAL INFORMATION. The Great Ocean Rd. becomes Lord St. in town and is the center of all the action. **Buses** leave once a week (F, also M Dec.-Jan.) from in front of Ocean House Backpackers and head to Melbourne ($30.40) and Warrnambool ($8.40), stopping at most towns along the way in either direction. The **Visitors Center,** on the corner of Morris and Tregea St., one block south of Lord St., has a wealth of data for all things related to the Great Ocean Road. (☎5598 6089. Open daily 9am-5pm.) The **post office** is in the **Port Campbell General Store,** Lord St., which also has basic **groceries.** (☎5510 6255. Open daily 8am-7pm.) **Postal Code:** 3269.

🞐 ACCOMMODATIONS. Facing the beach on Cairns St., **Ocean House Backpackers ❷** is clean, simple, and friendly, with ocean-views from some rooms. (☎5598 6223; check in at the Camping Park if owner is not there. $25, low-season $20.) The **YHA Hostel ❷**, 18 Tregea St., one block south of Lord St., has a large kitchen and a lounge with a wood stove. (☎/fax 5598 6305. Key deposit $5. Internet $2 per 15min.

Reception 8-10am and 4-9pm. Dorms $21, YHA $17; doubles $40; cabins $58.) The **Port Campbell National Park Cabin and Camping Park ❷**, next to the info center on Morris St., has BBQ, showers, and laundry. (☎5598 6492. Reception 8:30am-9pm. Sites for 2 $16; ensuite cabins from $75, extra adult $11, extra child $5.)

◫⬚ FOOD AND ENTERTAINMENT. The throngs of tourists have attracted a surprising number of pricey restaurants for such a small town, but cheap food can still be had. The best place to get some casual eats is downstairs at the **Koo Aah Shop ❶**, on Lord St., which serves up fish, lentil, and noodle dishes with an Asian influence, as well as beef burgers for $7 and big sandwiches for $5. (☎5598 6408. Open daily 10:30am-late.) The only local **pub** is on the corner of Morris and Lord St., and the attached **Cray Pot Bistro ❷** serves up filling meals for $10-15. (Food served daily 8am-8pm; drinks served weekdays until 11pm, weekends until 1am.)

◎ SIGHTS. The gentle Port Campbell **Discovery Walk** (2½km) begins at the cliff base at the western end of the beach or at the carpark west of the bay. While local surfers paddle out to the breaks off of the points on either side of Port Campbell's small bay, the small beach along Cairns St. is probably a better place to take a dip. **Port Campbell Boat Charters** offers crafts for diving, fishing, or sightseeing expeditions. (☎5598 6411 or ask at the Mobil Service Station; from $40 per person.) Two companies offer **helicopter tours** of the Twelve Apostles: **12 Apostle Helicopters** (☎5598 6161) and **PremiAIR** (☎5598 8266). Both companies take off from helipads behind the parking lot at the Twelve Apostles Visitors Center, and both offer 15min. ($70) and 20min. ($90) tours. You can also see the Apostles in a small plane from **Peterborough Airfield.** (☎5598 5441. 20 min. flight for up to 3 $80.)

NEAR PORT CAMPBELL

TWELVE APOSTLES AND LOCH ARD. The ◪**Twelve Apostles,** 12km east of Port Campbell on the Great Ocean Rd., are the most famous of the rock formations in the area, and for good reason. Once you see them, you'll hardly notice the other people on the lookout point until you begin to wildly snap your own photos and realize that all the best vantage points are already taken, especially if you're there at sunset. The **Interpretive Centre** is open daily 9am-5pm and has ample parking and a walkway under the highway leading to the viewpoints. **Gibson Steps,** about 2km east of the Twelve Apostles, allow a descent and a view from sea level, from which you can better appreciate the enormous scale of these towering monoliths. Another worthwhile stop-off, 3km west of the Twelve Apostles, towards Port Campbell, is **Loch Ard Gorge,** named for the clipper *Loch Ard* that wrecked there in

---

NOT HIS LUCKY DAY In the process of forming the Twelve Apostles, waves curling into the sides of jutting cliffs bored tunnels, which in turn left archways. The archways eventually collapsed, leaving the solitary stacks that still stand. The London Bridge formation displays an intermediate stage of this erosion process. It was once conjoined with a second arch that linked it to the mainland. In 1990 the other arch collapsed, leaving a man and woman stranded. After about an hour a helicopter came by and circled the high and dry pair. As they began to rejoice, they realized that it was a news 'copter seeking an interview. The couple refused to give one, and so the news 'copter just filmed them from a distance and flew off. Later that day, the six o'clock news reported the story. Apparently, the guy had called in sick to work, so when his boss saw him stranded on the London Bridge, he was in big trouble. Even worse was that his *wife* was watching the news at home. Serves the bastard right.

1878, killing 52 passengers. The park around the gorge offers numerous lookout points and short walks venturing to points of interest like **Thunder Cave,** the **Island Archway, Mutton Bird Island,** and the **Blowhole,** a churning and spitting lake of sea water a few hundred feet inland, connected to the ocean by an underground tunnel. Allow an hour or so to walk around and take in the views.

BAY OF ISLANDS AND BAY OF MARTYRS. To the west of Port Campbell, the **Bay of Islands Coastal Park** begins at the little Peterborough and stretches 33km west along the coast. A number of scenic viewpoints allow views of other limestone oddities, from pillars to islands to arches, all shaped by the Southern Ocean and the unrelenting Antarctic winds from 3000km away. Notable features include **The Arch, The Grotto,** and **London Bridge** (less of a bridge than it used to be; see **Not His Lucky Day,** p. 602). The **Bay of Martyrs** and **Bay of Islands** viewpoints (both turn-offs clearly labeled on the Great Ocean Rd.), perhaps the best along this stretch, offer stunning views and walks among smaller limestone formations on the beach.

WARRNAMBOOL   ☎ 03

Warrnambool (pop. 29,600) is just big enough to support a dance-until-3am nightlife scene and a host of amenities not found elsewhere along the coast, yet it still manages to maintain a decidedly small-town feel. It also has beautiful beaches and right whales in residence for half the year. The whales combine with the sand and surf to make Warrnambool a popular holiday destination.

▐ TRANSPORTATION. The **West Coast Railway Station** (☎5561 4277) is on the south end of town, just north of Lake Pertobe on Merri St. **V/Line trains** run to Melbourne (3½hr.; M-F 4 per day, Sa-Su 3 per day; $39) and Geelong (2½hr.; M-F 4 per day, Sa-Su 3 per day; $28). V/Line **buses** run to: Apollo Bay (3hr.; F, also M Dec.-Jan.; $24); Ballarat (2½hr., M-F 1 per day, $20.30); Mount Gambier (2½hr., 1 per day, $30.40); Port Fairy (30min.; M-Sa 2 per day, Su 1 per day; $4.80); and Portland (1½hr.; M-Sa 2 per day, Su 1 per day; $14). In town, **Transit Southwest** runs seven bus routes across the city, with stops at each location roughly on the hour; pick up a timetable from the Visitors Center or buy one at a newsstand for 20¢. (☎5562 1866. $1.20, concessions 75¢.) For a **taxi,** call ☎13 10 08.

▐ ORIENTATION AND PRACTICAL INFORMATION. The Princes Hwy., which becomes **Raglan Pde.** in town, runs along the northern edge of the downtown area. The town's main streets run south from Raglan Pde., with Banyan St., on the east side of downtown, heading down to the bay, the beach, and the breakwater. **Liebig St.,** the town's main drag, heads south from Raglan Pde. at the McDonald's, crossing Lava St., Koroit St., and Timor St. before winding up at Merri St. on the southern edge of downtown. It is lined with most of the restaurants, pubs, **banks,** and **ATMs.** The **Visitors Center,** 600 Raglan Pde., provides free maps of the area. (☎5564 7837. Open daily 9am-5pm.) Services include: **police,** 214 Koroit St. (☎5560 1179); **library,** at the south end of Liebig St., with free **Internet** (☎5562 2258; open M-Th 9:30am-5pm, F 9:30am-8pm, Sa 9:30am-noon); and a **post office,** on Koroit St., between Kepler and Liebig St. (Open M-F 9am-5pm, Sa 9:30am-12:30pm.) **Postal Code:** 3280.

▐ ACCOMMODATIONS. Book ahead November through March. ◾**Warrnambool Beach Backpackers ❷,** 17 Stanley St., offers clean and colorful rooms with close proximity to the beach. Though a little distant from the downtown action, this place has everything a backpacker could want, including Internet ($5 per hr.), a licensed bar, TV with DVD, a pool table, a full kitchen, free use of mountain bikes and canoe, coin laundry, and good meals for $5-7. The back bunkrooms are spacious, clean, and quiet. (☎/fax 5562 4874; johnpearson@hotmail.com. Key deposit $10. Reception 7:30am-10pm. Dorms $20; doubles $50. No credit cards.) The **Stuffed Backpacker ❷**, 52 Kepler St., just south of Koroit St., has clean, simple rooms in a laid-back and friendly environment. Check in with Leo, the friendly owner, in the candy shop next to the cinema. (☎5562 2459. Key deposit $5. Reception 9am-midnight. Dorms $18; singles $25; doubles $45; prices lower in winter.) **Western Backpackers and Motel ❷**, at the corner of Kepler and Timor St., has doubles with spotless shared bathrooms, kitchen, laundry, and TV lounge with wood fireplace. The motel section has ensuite singles and doubles, heat, A/C, fridge, tea and coffee, and TV. (☎5562 2011; thewestern@ansonic.com.au. Singles $18, weekly $99; doubles $33; twins $36. Motel singles $45; doubles $55; twins $59.)

◖◗ ◖◗ FOOD AND NIGHTLIFE. For a sit-down meal, you can't go too wrong in any of the restaurants at the bottom of Liebig St. Brunch is fantastic at hip **Fishtales ❶**, 63-65 Liebig St., which specializes in fish, vegetarian pasta, and Asian food for under $10. (☎5561 2957. Open daily 8am-10pm. AmEx/DC/MC/V.) **Bojangles ❷**, 61 Liebig St., serves inventive wood-fire pizzas for $13-16 (takeaway $10-12) piled high with delicious creative combinations. (☎5562 8751. Open daily 5pm-late.) The 24hr. Coles **supermarket** is on Lava St. between Liebig and Kepler St.

The neighborhood around the bottom of Liebig St. is also where Warrnambool hits the pubs. The funky **◪Liquid Lounge**, 58 Liebig St., is half New York, half Arabian Nights, and fully the best place in town. Sink into the comfy couches and imbibe a few cocktails while nodding your head to whatever the DJ is spinning. Be sure to check out the bathrooms. (Cover $5-10. Beers from $3. Open daily 3pm-1am). The traditional nightlife triumvirate consists of the **Seanchai Irish Pub**, next to the Liquid Lounge, where the Guinness flows like intoxicating water (pints of Guinness $6.40; open until 1am); **The Whaler's Inn,** across from Seanchai, which is a popular post-Seanchai destination (pints $4, cocktails from $5; open until 3am); and **The Gallery Nightclub,** on the corner of Kepler and Timor St., where the die-hard head late-night and dance until the wee hours. (Open until 3am.) For **karaoke,** check out the **Victoria Hotel** on Friday nights (open until 1am), and for tasty Margaritas ($6-10), try **Taco Bill's,** on the corner of Liebig and Timor St. (Open 5pm-1am.)

◙ ◪ SIGHTS AND ACTIVITIES. The most popular thing to do in Warrnambool from May to October is to watch whales. The info center has booklets on the continuously tracked **southern right whales.** Every winter in late May or June, a population of whales stops just off **Logans Beach,** to the east of the Bay, to give birth to their calves. They stay until September or October, when they return to the Antarctic to break their five-month fast. To watch the beasts roll, blow, and breach, tourists gather on viewing platforms built above the beach to protect the delicate dune vegetation. These right whales used to be hunted in large numbers all along the Victorian coastline, but have been protected for several decades. The whales are big, but binoculars are still helpful.

If your visit doesn't coincide with that of the whales, don't despair, the endlessly amusing **◪Flagstaff Hill Maritime Museum,** on Merri St., is fascinating even for those not intrigued by nautical history. The ten-acre museum is an outdoor re-creation of a late 19th-century coastal village. The stunning masthead **Loch Ard peacock,** taken from the wreck of the *Loch Ard* in 1878, is located in the Public Hall. Only two people survived the wreck, but this giant ceramic fowl escaped with only a tiny chip. (☎5564 7841. Open daily 9am-5pm; last entrance 4pm. Lighthouse open 11am-noon and 1-2pm. $12, concessions $9, children $5.)

Boasting ample beach-space and parks, Warrnambool is a great spot for outdoor recreation. The 3.4km **Promenade** lining Warrnambool Bay is popular with cyclists, in-line skaters, and evening strollers. For the best sunset views, head to **Thunder Point,** just west of the Bay, where there is a lookout point and walking trails along the coast and inland along the Merri River. You can also walk from the breakwater at the bay out to **Merri Island** (at low tide), where you might see little penguins. Families will enjoy the new **Adventure Playground,** adjacent to Lake Pertobe. The park, built over 35 hectares of former swampland, features a maze, giant slides, and lots of children screaming in joy. The protected bay has a beautiful, curving **beach.** For top-notch surf lessons at good prices, talk to Tristan at the **Easyrider Surf School.** (☎0418 328 747. Daily 2 hr. group lesson $33; private lesson $55; boards and wetsuits provided.) **Great Ocean Road Trail Rides** offers day or evening horse rides on the beach and nearby trails. (☎5562 8088. 1hr. $28; 2hr. $44.)

NEAR WARRNAMBOOL

TOWER HILL. Between Warrnambool and Port Fairy, the main attraction is the **Tower Hill State Game Reserve,** situated in a volcanic crater, with an entrance clearly marked from the Princes Hwy. It swarms with all sorts of Aussie wildlife, from kangaroos to koalas to emus and many other types of birds. The drive around the crater's rim, accessed via the road to Koroit, offers great views of the Reserve, but to really get a good look at the wildlife, try one of the many walking paths around the reserve. A map of the trails is available at the helpful **Information and Natural History Centre,** which also has toilets, picnic areas, and BBQ facilities nearby. (Park ranger at center M-F 9:30am-4pm.)

CHILDERS COVES. About 35km east of Warrnambool (back towards Port Campbell), the Great Ocean Road swings west and the Childers Cove Road continues straight south, through ranches and farms to this perfectly secluded and beautiful set of coves and beaches. This secluded set of beachy coves consists of **Stanhope Bay, Murnane Bay,** and **Childers Coves,** though they are collectively known as Childers Coves. Nestled among cliffs, they are ideal for swimming, suntanning, and escaping the crowds. To get there, leave the Great Ocean Rd. shortly after Mepunga West and rejoin it just before Nirranda, or vice versa. The turn-off is clearly marked in both directions, and the cove is about 10km off the highway.

PORT FAIRY   ☎03

In 1826, Captain James Wishart sailed the cutter *Fairy* into the mouth of the River Moyne in search of potable water. From the 1850s to the 1880s, Port Fairy was the busiest Australian port outside Sydney, loading ships headed for the Motherland. Activity has slowed considerably since the late 1800s, but Wishart might still be proud of the small, peaceful, and surprisingly cosmopolitan town that remains. In March it hosts one of the country's biggest folk festivals; for the rest of the year, the historic buildings, beautiful beaches, and relaxing vibe are the main attraction.

▐▛▐ TRANSPORTATION AND PRACTICAL INFORMATION. Buses leave from the Tourist Information Centre on Bank St. to Warrnambool (M-F 3 per day, Sa 2 per day, Su 1 per day; $4.80), where trains depart for: Melbourne (M-F 4 per day, Sa-Su 2 per day; $38); Portland (3 per day, $9); and Mount Gambier (M-F 2 per day, Sa-Su 1 per day; $29). Historical details and a walking tour map are available from the **Tourist Information Centre,** on the south end of Bank St. (☎5568 2682. Open daily 9am-5pm.) Services include: **police** (☎5568 1007); **RACV** (☎5568 2700, after hours 5568 1017); **hospital** (☎5568 0100); and a **post office,** 25 Sackville St., which has **Internet.** (Open M-F 9am-5pm. $5 per hr.) **Postal Code:** 3284.

⌂ ☐ ACCOMMODATIONS AND FOOD. In a house built by Port Fairy's first official settler, William Rutledge, the **YHA Hostel ❷**, 8 Cox St., has TV, Internet, a friendly lounge area, and a kitchen. (☎5568 2468. Book ahead for March. Reception daily 8-10am and 5-10pm. Dorms $21, YHA $17; doubles $52/$45.) The **Dublin House ❺**, 57 Bank St., has a garden and doubles of varying elegance. (☎5568 2022. Doubles $80-200.) **Eumarella Backpackers ❷** is 17km west of Port Fairy in Yambuk, 200m south of Hwy. 1. The remote hostel is a converted 19th-century schoolhouse, run by the Peek Whurrong people of the Framlingham Aboriginal Trust. It's next to the Deen Maar, Victoria's first Indigenous Protected Area. (☎5568 4204. Kitchen, laundry, and canoe hire. Dorms $16.50.)

Rebuking the fishing culture, the town has recently become an artists' haven, and has a fledgling artsy cafe scene, particularly on Bank and Sackville St. The sticky date pudding at **Cobb's Port Fairy Bakery ❶**, 25 Bank St., will change your life for the better. (☎5568 1713. Open daily 8am-5pm.) The IGA Everyday on Sackville St. is both **grocery store** and bottle shop. (Open daily 8am-8pm.)

◙ SIGHTS. The main attractions here are the **beach** and **wharf.** The beach is excellent for swimming (lifeguards on duty Sa-Su), and the wharf is a great place to watch the ships come in or get a fresh seafood meal at one of the chippers. Maps of suggested **walking tours** covering the town's historical sights and buildings are available at the Visitors Center. Visits can be arranged to **Lady Julia Percy Island,** 19km out in the Bass Strait, home to seals, fairy penguins, and peregrine falcons. Contact the Visitors Center for information. **Mulloka Cruises** (☎5568 1790), stationed at the harbor, does daily 30min. bay cruises ($10 per person). **Kitehouse,** on the corner of Bank and Grant St., sells any kind of kite or wind sock and rents bicycles. (☎5568 2782. Open daily 10am-5pm.) Almost every bed on the Shipwreck Coast is hired out in March during the **Port Fairy Folk Festival,** held over Australia's Labor Day weekend (Mar. 8-10, 2003). The festival attracts folk, blues, country, and traditional music acts from all over Australia and the world. During the weekend, the streets come alive with music and vendors and the population of the town jumps from 2600 to over 30,000. (☎5568 2227. Order tickets months in advance.)

NEAR PORT FAIRY: MT. ECCLES NATIONAL PARK

Some 20,000 years ago, igneous activity formed **Mt. Eccles,** and the volcanic turbulence continued until about 7000 years ago. Because the volcano is relatively young, many of its topographical features are in excellent condition, not yet muted by time. Filling the three main volcanic craters below the mount, **Lake Surprise** is a beautiful place to walk or swim—although if the volcano decided to erupt again, any swimmers would be quickly boiled alive. Maybe that's the surprise. The park is well known for its koala population; these crabby creatures like to live in the thick manna gum woods near the lake and are most active around dusk. The brush-tailed phasogale—an almost-extinct, tiny marsupial—also calls Mt. Eccles home.

Macarthur, the point of entry to the park, is about 40km north of Port Fairy and 42km south of **Hamilton** on Hwy. C184. Within the park, well-marked walking tracks lead to several relics of the mountain's volcanic past. About 50 years ago, the northwest slope of the mountain was quarried for scoria (a porous volcanic rock that makes up much of the slope and was used in road-making). This destructive land use was put to an end when the area was declared a national park in 1960, but the slowly revegetating scar remains as a reminder of this ugly past. The **Crater Rim Nature Walk** (1hr. return) passes all of the park's topographical features, including lava cave and lava canal, both formed, not surprisingly, by liquid-hot magma. The **Lake Surprise** trail (a 45min. loop) descends from the parking lot into the crater, and follows the lakeshore all the way around. The walk isn't challenging, except for the fairly steep ascent out. For the more adventurous, the **Natural**

VICTORIA

Bridge Walk or the Lava Canal Walk (both 4hr. return) allow a more extended foray into the park's lava fields. The Lava Canal Walk follows the broad, deep lava canal south through a clear forest with little undergrowth for about 1½km, and then gets wild. The trail follows the canal and a stone wall, so it's hard to get lost, but it can be slightly overgrown at times. The Natural Bridge trail leaves from the main parking lot, visits Dry Crater, and ascends Mt. Eccles to an excellent view of the terrain just covered. Rangers can provide **camping** ❷ permits and information about the bushland around the park. (On-site info center, at park entrance, open daily 9am-5pm. 4-person sites Dec.-Jan. $12, Feb.-Nov. $9; self-serve registration. Call ahead during school vacations; ☎5576 1338 or the Parks Victoria info line at ☎13 19 63.)

PORTLAND   ☎03

Maritime history buffs may take pleasure in Portland's storied past, but most travelers focus more on the beds, supermarkets, and roads that make it an ideal jumping off point for the Great South West Walk, Discovery Bay National Park, and Lower Glenelg National Park. This area was once a base for whalers, sealers, and escaped convicts, before the Henty brothers and their sheep enterprise permanently settled it in 1834. While the Henty name lives on in town, adorning everything from a tire dealership to a hair salon to a bottle shop, it is Portland's proximity to beautiful Parks that induces travelers to stop here.

▐▛▌ TRANSPORTATION AND PRACTICAL INFORMATION. V/Line buses depart from the north side of Henty St., just west of Percy St. One heads east through Port Fairy (1hr., $10) to Warrnambool (1½hr.; M-Sa 2 per day, Su 1 per day; $14), where connections can be made to Melbourne. One bus per day heads west to Mount Gambier (1½hr., $13). On Friday morning (Dec.-Jan. also M), a bus runs to Apollo Bay (4hr., $39), Lorne (5hr., $44), and Port Campbell (2½hr., $25). Tickets can be purchased at **Jet-Set Travel,** around the corner from the bus stop at 67 Percy St. (☎5523 3332; M-F 9am-5pm). The two main north-south streets in town are the water-front **Bentinck St.,** with cafes, takeaway joints, and pubs, and **Percy St.,** one block west, which has the majority of the town's commercial activity. The **Henty Hwy.** enters the city from the north and becomes Percy St. downtown. Percy and Bentinck St. are connected in the center of town by, from north to south, **Henty, Julia,** and **Gawler St.** At the southern end of town, Bentinck St. becomes **Cape Nelson Rd.** and heads southwest to Cape Nelson State Park. On Lee Breakwater St., down the hill between Bentinck St. and the bay, in a strange-looking gray building just north of the fishing jetty, is the **Portland Visitors Center.** In the same building, the **Portland Maritime Discovery Centre** has informative displays on the region and its fishing and whaling history, as well as a cafe with nice views of the water. (Both the Visitors Center and the museum are open daily 9am-5pm; museum admission $7.70, $5.50 concession.) More information on the Lower Glenelg and Discovery Bay (as well as useful maps) can be obtained from the **Parks Victoria** office, 8-12 Julia St. (☎13 19 63. Open M-F 9am-4:30pm.) **Internet** access is available at at the **library** on Bentinck St., just south of Gawler St. (☎5523 1497. Open M-Tu and Th-F 10am-5:30pm, Sa 10am-noon. $2 per 30min.; book ahead.) The **post office** is at 108 Percy St. **Postal Code:** 3305.

▐▝▐ ACCOMMODATIONS AND FOOD. Close to the waterfront in town, the **Gordon Hotel** ❷, 63 Bentinck St., provides above-average pub accommodation with a regal balcony and great harbor views. The kitchen is limited but continental breakfast is included. (☎5523 1121. Singles from $23; doubles from $33.) For those willing to venture farther afield, the opportunity to fraternize with sheep and wake up to the sounds of breaking waves awaits at **Bellevue Backpackers ❷**, Sheoke Rd., on the way to Cape Nelson, about 10min. from Portland. (☎5523 4038. Dorms $20.)

The best place to multi-task is **Sully's Wine Bar and Internet Cafe ❶**, 55 Bentinck St., where you can check your email ($6 per hr.), get a quality meal at a good price ($6-14; sandwiches $3.50), and relax with a nice beverage (full bar, despite the name; beers from $3, wine from $4) all at once. (☎5523 5355. Open M-Th 9am-9pm, F-Sa 9am-11pm.) **Port Of Call ❷**, 85 Bentinck St., has good coffee, great views, and a variety of fresh fish options. (☎5523 1335. Open daily 8am-late.) A large Safeway **supermarket** is on Percy St., across from the post office (open daily 7am-10pm).

■ ■ **SIGHTS AND HIKING.** Though this stretch of waters is far safer today than in the 1800s, many ships once became all-too-intimately acquainted with the ocean floor in or near the Portland Harbor. The **Maritime Discovery Center** memorializes some of those ships and celebrates the city's history as a fishing and whaling center. The prize of the display is the reconstructed skeleton of a sperm whale, complete with a bench built under the rib cage. (☎5523 2671. Open daily 9am-5pm. $7.70, concession $5.50). Behind the Maritime Center, a restored 1885 **cable tram** will take you on a waterfront ride to several of Portland's main tourist attractions. (Tickets can be bought onboard or at the Maritime Center. $10, concessions $8.) The free **gardens,** on Cliff St. toward the commercial wharf from Bentinck St., are worth a look, and their dizzying array of plant life is on display all day every day.

The waters off of Portland are popular with both divers and fishermen. For the experienced **diver,** equipment rental and charters are available at the **Dive Shop,** on Townsend St. (☎5523 6392. Open M-F 9am-5:30pm, Sa 10am-4pm. Gear rental from $55; 3-week diving class $390). **Fishing** charters and **harbor cruises** are available from **Southwest Charters.** (☎5523 3202 or 0418 306 714. Prices vary; call ahead.) For a very different kind of tour, check out the **gigantic aluminum smelter** cunningly landscaped to soften the aesthetic blow delivered by metal-processing plants. This "Smelter in the Park" is a great example of environmentally conscious design. (Book through the Visitors Center. 2hr. tours M, W, and F 10am and 1pm. Free.)

Starting and ending at Portland's information center, the looping, 250km **Great South West Walk** rambles along the coast through the Discovery Bay Coastal Park, then doubles back through the Lower Glenelg National Park. The walk traverses a variety of terrains and provides a grand introduction to the wildlands of southwest Victoria. Campsites are provided all along the trail for walkers, and detailed maps are available at the Portland Visitors Center. The trail is clearly marked, occasionally with a black emu badge but more often with red metal arrows and signs pointing you in the right direction. Daytrip-access sections range from 8-20km in length, although shorter sections, the most accessible of which are in Cape Nelson State Park (see p. 608), can be walked as well. Most of those choosing to walk it in its entirety do so in about 12 days. If you want to walk a section and need pick-up or drop-off services, call **Friends of the Great South West Walk.** (☎5523 5262; gbennett@datafast.net.au. Prices for this service vary depending on distances and time of year.) Register with the info center before setting off.

NEAR PORTLAND

CAPE NELSON STATE PARK

Cape Nelson State Park, a 243-hectare reserve, lies just 11km southwest of Portland and plays host to some beautiful bushwalks, impressive coastal cliffs, a prime surf beach, and the **last manned lighthouse** in Victoria. The view from the lighthouse alone is worth a trip out here. (☎5523 5100. Entrance daily 11am-3pm. $7.70, $5.50 concessions.) The best approach to the park is to head south out of

Portland on Bentinck St., which becomes Cape Nelson Rd., and then make a left on Sheoke Rd., heading east. As Sheoke Rd. swings south, it becomes the Scenic Rd., and almost immediately you'll see the parking lot for **Yellow Rock,** the area's top surf spot, where a boardwalk leads down from the cliff tops to the beach and provides several sitting areas to take in the view of the yellowish monolith for which the beach is named. For more info, consult with *Surfs Up in Portland* compiled by the Portland *Observer,* available at the Maritime Center.

The **Great South West Walk** (see p. 608) intersects the park, affording the opportunity to walk short sections of it; one of the best is the **Enchanted Forest** walk (3km return), which winds through groves of short trees twisted into strange shapes by strong winds. The carpark is just off Sheoke Rd., about halfway to the lighthouse. The **Sea Cliff Nature Walk** (a 3km loop) begins at the Sea Cliff parking lot, at the intersection of the Scenic Rd. and Cape Nelson Rd., and includes displays explaining some of the rare plants and animals protected in the park. The **Lighthouse Walk** (6km, marked with blue arrows), which can be started from either the Sea Cliff carpark or the lighthouse, wanders through inland areas and joins with the Great South West Walk east of the lighthouse for spectacular clifftop views of the ocean.

There's no camping in the park itself, but the **lighthouse-keeper's cottage ❺** is perfectly secluded and offers stunning views. (☎5523 5100. Doubles $100, extra person $30; entire house up to 12 persons $360; book ahead.) Another option out this way is the small **Bellevue Backpackers ❷** (see **Accommodations and Food,** p. 607), which sits on the northern edge of the park near Yellow Rock.

DISCOVERY BAY COASTAL PARK

Discovery Bay Coastal Park stretches 55km from Portland to the South Australia border. Connecting the sea to freshwater lakes and swamps are mobile dunes up to 20m high; be sure to stay on the marked walking tracks. **Cape Bridgewater,** at the park's southern end, 18km west of Portland via the Bridgewater Rd. (from town, take Otway St. west until it becomes Bridgewater Rd.), holds a resident **seal colony,** excellent surfing and swimming, and three of the park's most well known attractions: the **Blowholes,** the **Petrified Forest,** and the **Springs.** Limited **tourist info** is available at the kiosk on the beach (open daily 9:30am-5pm). The carpark for the seal walk is just up the hill from the beach, on the left side of the road. From there, an occasionally steep cliff trail leads to a **viewing platform** above a rockshelf on which Australian fur seals like to sun themselves. A less strenuous but longer hike to the seals runs in the opposite direction, following the Great South West Walk from the blowholes carpark to the seal walk carpark, but requires that you find a way back to your car at the blowholes (9km, 3hr.). **Seals By Sea** tours run 45min. cruises from Cape Bridgewater, allowing you to get up close and personal with the seals. (☎5526 7247. $20, concessions $17. Book ahead). The **Cape Bridgewater Holiday Camp ❷** offers great views of the stunning bay and beach as well as a range of options, from backpacker-style bunks to the more refined (and possibly sacrilegious) accommodations offered in the town's original church, dating from 1870. (☎5526 7267. Dorms $18; doubles from $40; church doubles $66, extra persons $10.)

At the end of Bridgewater Rd., on the western side of Cape Bridgewater, is a parking lot with access to the Springs, the Blowholes, and the Petrified Forest. To the left is the **Petrified Forest** (20min.), eerie rock formations in cavities left when trees rotted away. Back toward the carpark, the **Blowholes** are at the foot of the sea cliffs. Virtually indistinguishable from tidal pools, the **Springs** (1hr.) are in fact freshwater springs formed as rainwater seeps through limestone farther inland. From Cape Bridgewater, the Bridgewater Lakes Rd. will lead you back to the Nelson-Portland Rd., passing by the Amos Rd. turnoff, which leads to a nice surf break at **White's Beach** on the northern side of the Cape, and the freshwater **Bridgewater Lakes**, a popular swimming, boating, and picnicking area, on the way. Shortly after Bridgewater Lakes Rd. rejoins the main road, a well-marked turnoff heads into **Mt. Richmond National Park,** where an 8km sealed road will bring you to the summit of Mt. Richmond and views towards the towering dunes of Discovery Bay. Short, clearly marked hikes branch off from the picnic area at the top of the mount, with the **Ocean View Walk** (a 1hr. loop) leading to sweeping views of, well, the ocean. The park and its abundant bird life and wide variety of wildflowers (best seen in spring) are 18km west of Portland on the Portland-Nelson Rd. (C192).

About 40km west of Portland is **Swann Lake,** which hosts the park's most impressive dunes. It's also the first **campsite ❶** you'll encounter heading west from Portland. The 8km unsealed road to the campsite is occasionally steep and a bit bumpy, but perfectly driveable in a regular car. From the carpark, those with 4WD vehicles can drive through the dunes to the beach, while those without will have to walk the 2km to the beach. The dunes at Swann Lake and other places along Discovery Bay are popular venues for sandboarding. Gary, at The Jail Hostel in Mount Gambier (see **Accommodations,** p. 478), runs frequent sandboarding trips, providing boards and transport between Mount Gambier and Swann Lake (☎ 1800 626 844 or 08 8723 0032; $25 per person). Farther up the coast, there is a popular **camping** and picnic area at **Lake Monibeong ❶,** accessed by a rough 8km unsealed road through tall pine forests, and plentiful **surf fishing** at **Nobles Rocks,** 7km from Nelson but accessible only by 4WD. Look for the Quarry Rd. turn-off, shortly after Lake Monibeong Rd.

LOWER GLENELG NATIONAL PARK

Lower Glenelg National Park protects a rich patch of dense forest surrounding the Glenelg River. The best way to see the interior of the park and commune with nature is via canoe. The Glenelg River meanders its way through virtually the entire length of the park and passes a succession of **campsites ❶,** many accessible only to boaters. Three or four days of paddling will bring the waterborne from Dartmoor, on the Princes Hwy., to the mouth of the river at Nelson. Several companies based in Nelson rent canoes ($25-$30 per day) and will drop you off at the starting point on the northeast edge of the park. **Nelson Boat and Canoe Hire** has a variety of canoes and kayaks to choose from and has special group rates (☎ 08 8738 4048; from $25 per day). **Southwest Canoe Service** runs a daytrip that covers the stretch of river just above the Margaret Rose Caves and includes a stop at the caves and pickup and drop-off in Nelson (☎ 08 8725 6844; $27.50 per person). The **Nelson Visitors Centre and Parks Victoria Office,** on Leake St. in Nelson, provides camping permits and can answer questions about river conditions and canoe rental. (☎ 08 8738 4051. Open daily 9am-5pm.)

A 4WD is the next best way to see the park, as several tracks access its interior. Even without a 4WD, **Glenelg Dr.** makes the park accessible to all. The 22km road meanders through dense forest alive with the sounds of birds, passing occasional river views. Be aware that many of the tracks branching off of Glenelg Dr. are in considerably worse condition. To access the road from the east, turn right onto the Nelson-Winnap Rd. shortly after passing the Lake Monibeong turn-off and then make a left onto Glenelg Dr. about 12km after that. From the west, take the North Nelson Rd. north out of Nelson. Glenelg Dr. will appear on your right after a few minutes.

Limestone dominates the topography, and percolating rainwater or underground watercourses have formed many caves. The largest and most spectacular (and the only ones open to the public) are the **Princess Margaret Rose Caves,** 2km east of the South Australia border and about 15km south of the Princes Hwy. (☎ 08 8738 4171. Tours daily 10, 11am, noon, 1:30, 2:30, 3:30, and 4:30pm. $6, concessions $4.50, children $2.50.) This area also features a few nature walks, a large wooded picnic area with BBQ, and limited **camping ❶** facilities. Camping arrangements must be made before 5pm with the ranger at the **Caves Information Center** (sites for 4 people $9.50; on-site cabins $40). From Nelson, the most convenient access to the caves is either by water (see canoe info above and boat info below) or by a 15km unsealed road that heads north from the highway a few kilometers west of Nelson. Those partial to sealed roads will have to drive on west to Mount Gambier and take the Princes Hwy. back east.

The **Glenelg estuary,** the longest in Victoria, is one of the prime **fishing** spots in the region. Boats can be rented in **Nelson,** the nearest settlement to the park, though fishing gear is less easy to attain. See **Nelson Boat and Canoe Hire,** above. **Glenelg River Cruises** runs a variety of cruises upriver to the Caves and beyond as well as cruises in the estuary. (☎ 08 8738 4191. From $15 per person.) Just 7km west of Nelson on the road to Mount Gambier, a turn-off leads to the **Pic-caninnie Ponds Conservation Park.** Here, amidst acres of wetlands that support a number of bird species, lies a deep pond, popular with divers and snorkelers, as visibility can exceed 40m. Permits to snorkel are available at the **Mt. Gambier Dept. of Environment and Natural Resources,** 11 Helen St., Mount Gambier (☎ 8735 1177; $8), though you can see quite a bit just by walking out to the edge of the platform and peering over into the depths.

OUTBACK VICTORIA

Outback Victoria exemplifies the natural diversity that makes Victoria one of the only places in Australia where so many varying ecosystems are within a daytrip away. Composed of several ill-defined, overlapping regions, Outback Victoria encompasses mountains, lakes, swamps, wildlife reserves, rich farmland, and rugged bushland. West of the Goldfields, inland Victoria rises among the rugged peaks of Grampians National Park before gradually settling into an immense plain that stretches west into South Australia and north into New South Wales. The **Wimmera** region draws its name from the river that begins in the Grampians and wanders north past the surprisingly lush Little Desert National Park. Also traditionally included in the Wimmera region are parts of South Australia: the Coonawarra wine region, the Naracoorte cave system, and Mount Gambier (see p. 477). West of Horsham on the Wimmera Hwy., **Mt. Arapiles** draws rock climbers to its 1300 thrilling ascents. North of Little Desert and west of the Sunraysia Hwy., all the way up to Mildura, is the semi-arid expanse of the **Mallee,** named for the *mallee eucalypt,* a hardy water-hoarding tree that thrives in the rugged plains. Agricultural pressure, increasing salinity, and the introduction of alien species like goats, cats, and bees are steadily eroding the once vast areas of mallee scrub. An array of national parks in the region seek to preserve this unique habitat.

GRAMPIANS (GARIWERD) NAT'L PARK

In 1836, Major Mitchell, in command of a British expedition, stumbled upon a range of mountains he designated as the Grampians, after a range in his home country of Scotland. Ensuing hordes of settlers steadily pushed the Koori Aborigines out of their ancestral home of Gariwerd. A visit to the park now promises both the rich history of Aboriginal culture (80% of the Aboriginal rock art sites in Victoria can be found here) as well as breathtaking ranges, abundant wildlife, rare birds, and a springtime carpet of technicolor wildflowers.

VICTORIA

THE GRAMPIANS AT A GLANCE

AREA: 167,000 hectares.	**GATEWAYS:** Halls Gap (east); Horsham (north); Dunkeld (south).
WHERE: The end of the Great Dividing Range. 260km west of Melbourne.	
	CAMPING, HIKING, CLIMBING: 13 sites, 160km of walking track, and a variety of rock climbs.
FEATURES: Koori rock paintings, the Balconies (Jaws of Death), MacKenzie Falls, climbs in the Wonderland Range and Hollow Mountain.	
	FEES: Camping $11 for up to 6 people per car. $5 per additional car.

ORIENTATION AND TRANSPORTATION

The northern approach passes through **Horsham,** at the junction of Western and Henty Hwy., roughly 18km north of the park. From the south, the town of **Dunkeld,** on the Glenelg Hwy., provides access via Mt. Abrupt Rd. From the east, the closest town is **Stawell,** 26km away. The **most convenient point of entry** is on the eastern edge of the park at **Halls Gap.** This is the park's only town (and it's small), but it has the basic amenities and is within walking distance of many of the park's points of interest. When reading about the town's offerings, remember that, unless otherwise noted, everything is bunched together in a small strip on Grampians Rd., also called Dunkeld Rd., which runs from Halls Gap to Dunkeld.

One **V/Line** bus per day leaves across from the newsagent for: Ararat (1hr., $12); Ballarat (2½hr., $25); Melbourne (4½hr., $40); and Stawell (30min., $8). Several companies also run multi-day tours from Melbourne and Adelaide, often incorporating the Great Ocean Road along the way.

WHEN TO GO. While the region's climate is somewhat mild, winter poses a problem for anyone who hates the cold, as nights can get rather chilly. Road conditions in winter might not be as suitable or safe for driving. In the Dry (May-Oct.), waterfalls can be somewhat, well, dry and not as exciting.

PRACTICAL INFORMATION

The **Brambuk National Park and Cultural Centre,** 2½km south of Halls Gap town center on Dunkeld Rd., is the best resource for would-be hikers and bush campers. The engaging displays provide excellent information on the Grampians' flora, fauna, and history. (☎5356 4381. Open daily 9am-5pm. Hiking maps $3.30; donations appreciated.) From outside Halls Gap, **Parks Victoria** (☎13 19 63; www.parks.vic.com.au) is an excellent resource. The Halls Gap **Visitors Center** in the town center has great info and can answer questions about the park. (☎5356 4616 or 1800 065 599. Open daily 9am-5pm.) The **news agent** next door also has plenty of maps as well as an **Internet** kiosk. (Open daily 7am-7pm. $2 per 10min.) The Mobil **petrol** station has camping supplies, basic provisions, and an **ATM.** (☎5356 4206. Open daily 7am-8pm.) The **post office** is hidden in the well-marked bottle shop. (Open M-F 9am-5pm.) **Postal Code:** 3381.

ACCOMMODATIONS AND CAMPING

The quality of the accommodations here is as high as the Grampians themselves.

▧ **Grampians YHA Eco-Hostel** (☎5356 4544; grampians@yhavic.org.au), a 10min. walk north of the town center on Grampians Rd., at the corner of tiny Buckler St. Clean,

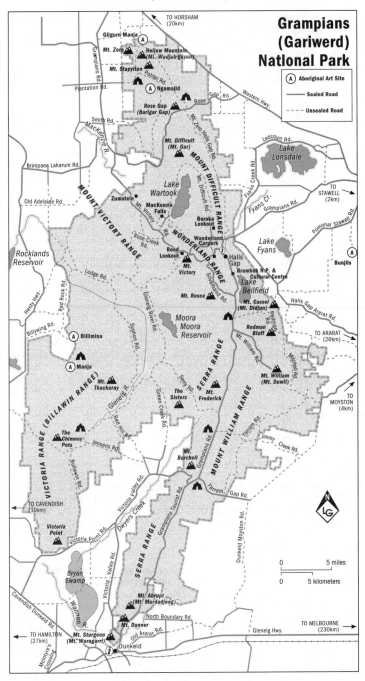

Grampians (Gariwerd) National Park

VICTORIA

Ⓐ Aboriginal Art Site
— Sealed Road
--- Unsealed Road

TO HORSHAM (20km)

Gilgurn Manja Ⓐ
Mt. Zero ▲
Hollow Mountain (MT. Wudjub-guyun)
Mt. Stapylton ▲
Ⓐ Ngamajid
Grampians Rd.
Pohler Rd.
Plantation Rd.
Rose Gap (Barigar Gap) ▲
Rose Gap Rd.
Western Hwy.

Smith Rd.
MacKenzie R.
Mt. Zero Halls Gap Rd.
Mt. Difficult (Mt. Gar) ▲
Ledcourt Rd.
Lake Lonsdale
Brimpaen Laharum Rd.
MOUNT DIFFICULT RANGE

Lake Wartook
Zumstein
MacKenzie Falls
Mt. Difficult Rd.
Frans Creek Rd.
Old Adelaide Rd.
Fyans Cr.
TO STAWELL (2km)
MOUNT VICTORY RANGE
Mt. Victory Rd.
Boroka Lookout
Grampians Rd.
Pomonal Stawell Rd.
Rockand Reservoir
Rose Creek Rd.
Wonderland Carpark
WONDERLAND RANGE
Reed Lookout ▲
Lake Fyans
Red Rock Rd.
Lodge Rd.
Mt. Victory ▲
Silverband Rd.
Halls Gap
ℹ
Brambuk N.P. & Cultural Centre
Ⓐ Bunjils
Henty Hwy.
Glenelg River Rd.
Mt. Rosea ▲
Lake Bellfield
Billywing Rd.
Ⓐ Billimina
Moora Moora Reservoir
Mt. Cassel (Mt. Didjun) ▲
Redman Rd.
Redman Bluff ▲
Halls Gap Ararat Rd.
TO ARARAT (20km)
Siphon Rd.
SERRA RANGE
Mt. William Rd.
Mitchell Rd.
Ⓐ Manja
Mt. Thackeray ▲
Red Hill Rd.
Serra Rd.
The Sisters ▲
Mt. Frederick ▲
Mt. William (Mt. Duwil) ▲
Yarram Rd.
TO MOYSTON (4km)
VICTORIA RANGE (BILLAWIN RANGE)
Glenelg R.
Green Creek Rd.
MOUNT WILLIAM RANGE
Jimmy Creek Rd.
The Chimney Pots ▲
Jensens Rd.
Bullawin Rd.
Grampians Rd.
Mt. Burchell ▲
Yarram Gap Rd.
TO CAVENDISH (10km)
Victoria Valley Rd.
Dwyers Creek
Grampians Tourist Rd.
Dunkeld Moyston Rd.
N
LG
Victoria Point
Victoria Point Rd.
SERRA RANGE
0   5 miles
0   5 kilometers
Bryan Swamp
Wannon R.
Mt. Abrupt (Mt. Murdadjoog) ▲
Cavendish Dunkeld Rd.
Mt. Danner ▲
North Boundary Rd.
Old Ararat Rd.
TO MELBOURNE (230km)
TO HAMILTON (27km)
Mt. Sturgeon (Mt. Wuragarri) ▲
ℹ Dunkeld
Glenelg Hwy.
McIntyre's Crossing

classy, and comfortable, as well as more luxurious, scenic, and sharply decorated than your everyday budget digs. State-of-the-art kitchen, dining area, plush sofas by the fire, TV room with VCR, adventure booking office, and laundry. Internet $2 per 15min. Linens included. Key deposit $10. Reception daily 8-10am and 5-10pm. Busy year-round; book ahead. Heated dorms with lockers $24, under 18 $21; singles $52; twins and doubles $54; family rooms $74. YHA discount Apr.-Dec. $4, Jan.-Mar. $5. MC/V. ❷

Tim's Place (☎5356 4288; www.timsplace.com.au), on Grampians Rd., 500m north of the town center. The most central of the 3 hostels. Easily the smallest, coziest, and most intimate, attracting a diverse group of travelers. Free tea and coffee, unlimited breakfast, and linens. Internet $6 per hr. Mountain bike use and free tickets to the Brambuk Centre Dreaming Theatre (see **Sights**, p. 614). Arrange for pickup in Melbourne or Adelaide that includes a tour of Grampians sights ($70 return; less if in transit to Melbourne or Adelaide). Dorms $20; singles $35; doubles $46. ❷

Brambuk Backpackers (☎5356 4250; www.brambuck.tourvic.com.au), across from the National Park Centre on Dunkeld Rd. Very clean rooms, all with lockers, heaters, and bath. Big kitchen, laundry, BBQ, Internet $2 per 10min. Affiliated with the **Brambuk Cultural Centre;** free tickets to the Dreaming Theatre. Breakfast included. Key deposit $10. Reception 9am-12:30pm and 3:30-7:30pm (in summer 4-8pm). Sites for 1 $10, for 2 $15, includes light breakfast and use of bathrooms; dorms $19; singles $38; doubles $48; ages 10-16 $13, under 10 $8. MC/V. ❶

Halls Gap Caravan Park (☎5356 4251; hgcp@netconnect.com.au), in Halls Gap center. Many walking trails start just behind the campground. Linens $7. Key deposit $20. Sites for 2 $17, holidays $20; powered $21/$23, extra person $5. On-site caravans for 2 $47/$53. Discounts for longer stays. MC/V. ❷

There are 13 major **camping** ❶ areas in the national park, all with toilets and fireplaces and most with water. All sites are first-come first-served; campers must pay $10.70 (up to 6 people or 1 vehicle, additional vehicles $4.70) for permits available at the National Park Centre. Rangers advise stopping at the Centre first for a complete map of the park's campsites and new relevant information. Bush camping is free but is forbidden in the Wonderland Range, the Lake Wartook watershed, and other areas demarcated accordingly on maps. Go to the Park Centre for details.

🍴 FOOD

The cheapest eats are at the **pub** ❶, 3km north of town on Grampians Rd. (meals until 8pm), and at **Ralphy's** ❶, in the center of town. (☎5356 4348. Open daily 8:30am-8:30pm.) **Suzie's Halls Gap Tavern** ❷, toward the Brambuk Centre on Dunkeld Rd., has expensive mains but daily specials. (☎5356 4416. Open daily 8am-10:30pm. Breakfast special 8:30-11am $4; 3-course set menu daily until 7pm $10.) The **Friendly Grocer** next to the newsagent in the town center has terribly unfriendly prices. (Open daily 7am-9pm.) Some food items can be purchased at the Mobil station or at YHA reception; otherwise, buy food before arriving.

👁 SIGHTS AND LOOKOUTS

Before you head into the park, go to the **Brambuk Aboriginal Culture Centre,** behind the National Park Centre 2½km south of Halls Gap, which has small but excellent displays on the culture and history of the **Koori,** southwest Victoria's native people. The **Dreaming Theatre's** 15min. light-and-sound show tells a traditional Koori story. Periodic workshops and evening activities include boomerangs, didgeridoos, and Koori traditional dance. The Centre also offers a **guided rock-art tour.** (☎5356 4452. Open daily 9am-5pm. Entry free. Theatre $4.40, concessions $2.80, families $16.40. 2hr. tours Su-F 10am-noon. $15, concessions $11, children $8; book ahead.)

Unfortunately, most sights are a good distance from Halls Gap and require a car to reach. Many tourists frequent the spots though—hikers report finding rides at the Park Centre or at their accommodations, though *Let's Go* does not recommend hitchhiking. Alternately, **Halls Gap Taxis** (☎ 0429 943 691) offers pickup and drop off at almost anywhere around the park. The **Balconies** (Jaws of Death), the Grampians' predominant icon, lie about 1km up from the Reed Lookout carpark off Mt. Victory Rd. The mostly flat approach (20min.) ends in sweeping panoramas. The Balconies themselves, a pair of parallel slabs of sandstone, jut out over the steep sides of Mt. Victory. Those who brave the steep, slippery path to **MacKenzie Falls,** which begins at the carpark just off Lake Wartook Rd., are rewarded with one of Victoria's most spectacular waterfalls—an 11m wall of crashing water. A new wheelchair accessible approach was recently opened. **Zumstein picnic area,** west of Lake Wartook on Mt. Victory Rd, is extremely popular because it crawls with kangaroos, but you can see herds of hopping 'roos just about everywhere in the park. Five **Aboriginal art sites** are open to the public but are considerably far apart. **Touring Downunder** runs a full-day **Aboriginal Culture and Art Sites Tour** from the Brambuk Centre that includes informational talks, the Dreamtime Theatre, a bush tucker lunch, afternoon tea, and visits to three art sites. (Book through Brambuk ☎ 5356 4452. Tours 9:30am-5:30pm. $69.)

▧ HIKING

Although extremely rugged, the Grampians is very user-friendly; most of its highlights can be reached via relatively easy walking trails, without the need to camp overnight in the bush. It is thus a favorite among families and nature lovers of the less-hardcore variety while at the same time catering to the expert hiker with more difficult tracks. Many walks in the Northern and Southern Ranges are incredibly rewarding but difficult to reach without a car. The **Wonderland Range** adjacent to Halls Gap in the park's eastern end holds a number of the main attractions. **Mt. Victory Rd.,** in particular, is loaded with phenomena to impress even the staunchest urbanite. The indispensable *Northern Walks, Southern Walks,* and *Wonderland Walks* maps (each $3.30) in the Park Centre give details on hiking and driving.

Some Wonderland walks lead to serene waterfalls, curious rock formations, and the occasional hookah-smoking caterpillar. To the south, **Victoria Valley** is carpeted with red gum woodlands and is home to emus and kangaroos. **Manja** and **Billimina,** at the park's western border, contain some of the Grampians' best **Aboriginal art sites.** Experienced hikers might want to tackle some of the steep trails on the Grampians' highest peak, **Mt. William** (1168m), at the park's extreme eastern end; the actual "trail" to the summit is disappointingly fully paved and well-traveled. The Wonderland hikes vary by difficulty and duration (from 30min. to 6hr. to several days). The trails below start near Halls Gap; all distances reflect return trips:

Wonderland Loop. (9.6km; 5hr.) Starts in back of the town center carpark. Cross the suspension bridge and turn left before the Botanical Gardens. Of medium difficulty, this hike traverses many of the most touristed sites, though strenuous detours abound off the track. A perfect family outing, the half-day loop along well-formed tracks leads first to the photogenic **Splitters Falls** and the **Venus Baths,** a series of rock pools popular for swimming in summer. The trail continues through the lush forest along a river to the carpark, then up the spectacular **Grand Canyon** and eventually to the narrow rock tunnel **Silent Street** (not recommended for the claustrophobic). At the awe-inspiring **Pinnacle,** sweeping views of three valleys reward every breathless hiker. The quick descent through stringy-bark forests offers unobstructed ridge-line views when you're not looking down to avoid rocks and tree roots.

VICTORIA

Boronia Peak Trail. (6.6km; 2-3hr.) Starts past the kangaroo fields next to the Brambuk Centre or alternately from the narrow path by the bridge just north of Tim's Place. A little harder than the Wonderland Loop, but shorter. The dense trees add to the tranquil solitude of this much less touristed route without obscuring bird and other fauna watching. The mostly medium-grade terrain ends in a short unmarked rock scramble to the peak. With a large lake to the south, flat bush country to the east, and the jagged Wonderland range to the west, the view is worth the haul to the top.

Boroka Lookout Trail. (12.4km; 4-5hr.) Same starting location as Wonderland Loop; turn right off the trail just before Splitters Falls. The toughest hike from Halls Gap. An unrelentingly steep ascent to this lookout in the **Mt. Difficult Range** rewards with spectacular views of the **Fyans Valley** and the **Mt. William Range,** the rough slopes of which have been aptly named the Elephant's Hide (also viewable from the nearby carpark).

Chatauqua Peak Loop. (5.6km; 2-3hr.) Starts from behind the Recreation Oval on Mt. Victory Rd., 100m from the intersection with Grampians Rd. The hike opens with an up-close view of the tranquil **Clematis Falls,** best seen after rain. The final 400m boulder climb to the peak is long and strenuous, but the views of Halls Gap and the valley are perfect. The less mobile can skip the boulder hop; the main trail continues on through to **Bullaces Glen,** a lush fern gully, and ends in the botanical gardens in Halls Gap.

▲ OTHER ADVENTURES

There are opportunities galore and plenty of companies around to book your next requisite adrenaline rush. All outfits provide free pickup in Halls Gap and often cheaper group rates. The **Adventure Company** (☎5356 4540; www.adventureco.com.au), in the Grampians YHA, offers adventure in every length and level, including canoe trips (2-3hr., $39), 25km downhill bike rides ($49), and a range of full- and half-day rock climbing and abseiling courses ($39-95). One abseil drops you 60m over ▓**The Ledge** (no experience necessary; YHA discount 10%.). The above activities can be booked directly or through the **Grampians Central Booking Office,** in the Halls Gap newsagent. (☎5356 4654; www.grampianstours.com. Open daily 9am-5pm, but desk may be unattended during tours.)

The Booking Office also runs the **Grampians Bushwalking Tours,** which focus on wildlife or visual highlights (4WD nature or highlights tour: $69 per half-day, $99 per day; full-day budget tour $29; 4WD mountain sunset tour $69; discovery bushwalk $49 per half-day, $79 per day; nocturnal spotlight walk $12, families $39). **Grampians Adventure Services,** in Shop 4 of the Stony Creek stores in Halls Gap center, runs a number of activities and tours and also rents mountain bikes. (☎5356 4556; www.grampians.org.au/gas. Open daily 10am-5pm. Climbing and abseiling $35-85; bike tours $30-40, night $30. Bike hire also available.)

LITTLE DESERT NATIONAL PARK

The Little Desert is not, in fact, a desert. So-christened because early settlers found the land ill-suited for farming, the Desert's 132,000 hectares are covered with diverse vegetation and wildlife. In the late 1960s, the government announced that 80,000 hectares of the park would be subdivided and cleared for farmland, sparking one of Australia's first major preservation campaigns, which the environmentalists won. The harsh landscape won't wow you with sweeping vistas or spectacular wonders like the Grampians, but it beckons with subtle beauty: a delicately blooming wildflower here, a rare bird there.

⌗ TRANSPORTATION

The Little Desert is best approached from **Nhill** (pop. 1900), north of the central parkland or from **Dimboola** (pop. 1500), on the Wimmera River to the east. Two **V/ Line** (☎ 13 61 96) **buses** per day Sunday to Friday and one Saturday depart Nhill from the stop opposite Rintoule's Travel Service, with service to: Adelaide (4hr., $50); Ararat (2-4hr., $27); Ballarat (4-5hr., $42); Bendigo (4hr., $34); Dimboola (30min., $5); Horsham (1-2hr., $10); and Melbourne (5½-6½hr., $52). Trips from Dimboola are 30min. shorter and include an additional departure Monday to Saturday. Dimboola's bus station is on the corner of Lochiel and Hindmarsh St.; the bus also stops at the Caltex Roadhouse on the corner of High and Horsham St.

⚡ PRACTICAL INFORMATION

The **ranger station,** on Nursery Rd. in **Wail,** is 5km south of Dimboola on the Western Hwy. (☎ 5389 1204. Open M-F 8am-4:30pm.) **Parks Victoria** (☎ 13 19 63; www.parkweb.vic.gov.au.) and the **Hindmarsh Info Centre** in Nhill, on Goldsworthy Park along Victoria St. (☎ 5391 3086; open daily 9am-5pm) have information on the area. **Rintoule's Travel Service** is at 37 Victoria St. in Nhill. (☎ 5391 1421. Open M-F 9am-5pm.) **Commonwealth Bank,** 14 Victoria St., Nhill, has a 24hr. **ATM.** (☎ 5391 1033. Open M-Th 9:30am-4pm, F 9:30am-5pm.) Dimboola has no ATMs. **Nhill Online Solutions,** 121 Nelson St., has **Internet** access. (☎ 5391 1910. Open M-Tu and Th-F 10am-5pm, W 10am-9pm, Su 2-6pm. $3 per hr., $1.50 min. charge.) The **post offices** are in Nhill, 98 Nelson St. (☎ 5391 1256; open M-F 9am-5pm; **Postal Code:** 3418), and Dimboola, 61 Lloyd St. (☎ 5389 1542; open M-F 9am-5pm; **Postal Code:** 3414).

⌂ ◖ ACCOMMODATIONS AND FOOD

Get the complete experience at **Little Desert Lodge** ❶, set on over 600 acres of bush and owned and operated by Malleefowl expert Whimpey Reichelt and his wife Maureen. Take Nhill-Harrow Rd. 16km south of the Nhill town center; signs point the way. (☎ 5391 5232; littledesertlodge@wimmera.com.au. **Dinners** ❹ when there's a full house ($20-25). Campsites for 2 $12.50, powered $15; bunks with no linens $24; singles with linens $48; twins and doubles $58. Book well ahead. MC/V.) The lodge and aviary are also a nature-lover's mecca (see **Sights and Activities,** p. 618).

The **Farmers Arms Hotel** ❷, 2 Victoria St., in Nhill, is a decent pubstay with clean, basic rooms, a TV lounge with refrigerator, and friendly staff. (☎ 5391 1955. Reception 10am-1am. Singles $20, weekly $100.) In Dimboola, along Horseshoe Bend Rd., 4km from the Dimboola post office, **Little Desert Log Cabins and Cottage** ❺ is right in the bush, a stone's throw from the park entrance, and offers self-contained cabins with the works. (☎ 5389 1122. Doubles from $75. Group discounts. MC/V.)

There are two **camping areas** ❶, one just south of **Kiata,** a hamlet on the Western Hwy. between Nhill and Dimboola, and the other at **Horseshoe Bend** and **Ackle Bend,** south of Dimboola. Both campgrounds have fireplaces, tables, and toilets. The fee covers six people and one vehicle ($11; additional vehicle $5; payable at any ranger station or in the pay receptacles at the campsites). Bush camping is allowed in the western and central blocks only and must be vehicle-based.

Nhill's restaurant pickings are slim. Get **groceries** at the IGA on Victoria St. (Open M-Th 8:30am-6:30pm, F 8:30am-7pm, Sa-8:30am-6pm, Su 9am-6pm.) Most pubs in both Nhill and Dimboola offer lunch and dinner.

CHICKS IN THE OVEN Most birds warm their unborn young with the heat of their bodies. But the endangered **Malleefowl** (*Leipoa ocellata*) have come up with a way to save on babysitting and still get out of the nest. The gray, beautifully patterned, pheasant-like birds use their large feet to build mounds out of dirt, sticks, and tree litter, in which the females deposit their eggs. Each mound takes weeks or months to build; often, mounds over a century old are reused. The sun and the tree-litter's fermentation warm them once completed. Over the next months, dad and mom work the natural incubators until they are nearly a meter high and five wide, controlling the thermostat by changing the sand and litter layers' depths—the temperature of a mound's interior varies by fewer than two degrees over several months. Once hatched, the chicks dig themselves out of their nurseries and are immediately on their own.

👁 🐦 SIGHTS AND ACTIVITIES

Little Desert's unique ecology is best explored on foot, although 4WD drivers can usually use the rough, unpaved roads (often closed in winter) to reach remote corners. An excellent 30min. introductory walk leads to the lookout on **Pomponderoo Hill,** showing off typical Little Desert terrain. Go through the gate marked "Gateway to Little Desert" at Dimboola (not the official park entrance), turn left immediately after crossing the Wimmera River bridge, and go south, following the "National Park" signs; the trailhead is 1km past the actual park entrance. Other **walks** begin at the campground south of Kiata and at Gymbouen Rd., south of Nhill; large map boards at each campground show the trails. The truly hardcore can take on the 84km **Desert Discovery Walk,** a one- to four-day trek across the eastern section of the park that can be tackled in parts or all at once. Detailed brochures on all the walks are available at ranger stations and tourist offices. The well-marked walk is best attempted in spring, when the weather is mild and the wildflowers are in bloom. Overnight campers should register at Wail's Park Office (☎ 5389 1204).

The **Little Desert Lodge** (☎5391 5232) provides direct access to bushwalks, including the Lodge Loop (1hr.) and the Stringybark Loop (45min.). They also run 4WD tours, including a visit to Whimpey's **Malleefowl Sanctuary,** a stretch of protected land that attracts international birdlovers. (See **Chicks in the Oven,** p. 618. Half-day tour $35; full-day $70. Min. 6 persons.) The **Malleefowl Aviary** at the Little Desert Lodge offers a more pampered, up close view. (Open M-Sa 9:30am-4:30pm, Su 1:30-4:30pm, or by appointment. $5.50, children $3.)

Oasis Desert Adventures, at the eastern entrance of the park in Dimboola, offers day tours, flower walks, fishing trips, boomerang and spear throwing, raft and hut building, orienteering, yabbying, canoe hire, and more. Owner Paul Lehmann, a local boy, will tailor activities to your interests. (☎ 0419 394 912; oda@netconnect.com.au. Book ahead. From $15 depending on type and duration of activity.)

GOLDFIELDS

In 1851, the first year of Victorian statehood and just two years after the California gold rush, this most precious of metals was discovered in the unassuming burg of Clunes. A year later, the *London Times* reported that 50,000 diggers had already converged upon Victoria's goldfields. To the chagrin of Victorians, who had taken pride in the fact that free persons had settled in Victoria before convicts had, ex-convicts from Van Diemen's Land (present-day Tasmania) floated over to join the crowds. Gold proved the great equalizer of classes, as convicts hardened by years of manual labor and rugged immigrants from all corners of the world dug ore more efficiently than their effete bourgeois counterparts, and the silk-clad landed gentry soon found themselves having to rub elbows with an unpedigreed nouveau riche. The established classes didn't willingly allow this social shake-up and forced the government to invoke mining taxes and grog prohibition, factors that ultimately led to the brief and bloody Eureka Rebellion of 1854 (see p. 14). The Victorian prospectors eventually extracted more ore than even the Californian '49ers, but by the end of the 19th century, the mines were largely exhausted, and most of the boom towns withered away to ghost towns. A few, such as Ballarat and Bendigo, remain substantial cities, and others, such as Castlemaine and Maldon, have been preserved as historical relics. These remaining cities and townships of the gold-fields region, occupying the central area of western Victoria, afford travelers the opportunity to enjoy the recreated gold-rush spectacles, handful of wineries, and hurly-burly frontier spirit that grew out of this short wave of settlement to so pow-erfully in shape Australia's national character.

BALLARAT ☎ 03

Victoria's second largest inland city (pop. 83,000), Ballarat is the self-appointed capital of the Goldfields and the birthplace of Australian democratic idealism: the site of the Eureka Rebellion. The most important of the boom towns during the gold rush, it clings to its gracious yet boisterous 1850s image. When miners first started working the Ballarat goldfields, the pickings were easy; alluvial gold, weathered from upstream rocks, was visible to the naked eye in the riverbeds. Although the gold is long gone, much of the 19th-century architecture has been preserved, and the city's golden past has been channeled into a bustling tourist trade that centers on **Sovereign Hill**, a replica of an old gold town, replete with townspeople dressed in period attire. Huge, elegant Victorian buildings line the main street, and Ballarat's begonias garner fame among gardeners.

TRANSPORTATION

Trains and Buses: V/Line (☎ 13 61 96) services both buses and trains, depending on destination, from **Ballarat Station,** 202 Lydiard St. N., reached by bus #2 from Curtis St. Service to: Ararat (1¼hr., 6 per day, $12.30); Bendigo (2¼hr., 2 per day, $20); Cas-tlemaine (1½hr., 1 per day, $15.20); Daylesford (40min., 1 per day, $10); Geelong (1¾hr., 3 per day, $11); Maryborough (1hr., 1 per day, $11); and Melbourne (1½hr., 12 per day, $15.20). Frequency varies Sa-Su.

Public Transportation: (☎ 5331 7777), most **bus** routes depart from behind Bridge Mall, on Curtis St. $1.55 ticket valid for 2 hours of unlimited use. Purchase from driver. Helpful transit guide (20¢) from tourist office or on bus. Services typically run every 35min. M-F 7am-6pm; Sa limited schedule. **Ballarat Taxis** (☎ 5331 3355) line up in the city center and run personal tours of Ballarat and nearby wineries.

Car Rental: Avis, 1104 Sturt St. (☎ 5332 8310). $39, limit 200km per day. **Budget,** 106 Market St. (☎ 5331 7788). $55 per 200km.

ORIENTATION AND PRACTICAL INFORMATION

Ballarat straddles the Western Hwy., called **Sturt St.** as it runs through town east to west. The **train station** is a few blocks north of Sturt on **Lydiard St.** From the station, turn left on Lydiard and cross Mair St. to get to Sturt St. At its eastern end, Sturt becomes **Bridge Mall,** a pedestrian mall with shops, restaurants, and supermarkets.

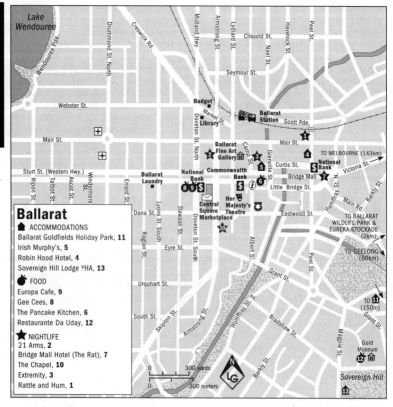

Ballarat

🏠 ACCOMMODATIONS
Ballarat Goldfields Holiday Park, **11**
Irish Murphy's, **5**
Robin Hood Hotel, **4**
Sovereign Hill Lodge YHA, **13**

🍎 FOOD
Europa Cafe, **9**
Gee Cees, **8**
The Pancake Kitchen, **6**
Restaurante Da Uday, **12**

⭐ NIGHTLIFE
21 Arms, **2**
Bridge Mall Hotel (The Rat), **7**
The Chapel, **10**
Extremity, **3**
Rattle and Hum, **1**

Tourist Office: 39 Sturt St. (☎ 5320 5709 or 1800 648 450; www.ballarat.com) From the V/Line station, walk left along Lydiard to Sturt St., turn left, and walk 1 block downhill to the corner of Albert St. Signs point the way. Free maps. Open daily 9am-5pm.

Banks: Banks and **ATMs** line Sturt St.

Laundromat: Ballarat Laundry, 711 Sturt St., near Raglan St. Open daily 6am-10pm.

Police: (☎ 5337 7222), on the corner of Dana and Albert St., behind the tourist center.

Internet Access: Free at the **library,** 178 Doveton St. N (☎ 5331 1211), but you must sign up for borrowing privileges. Book ahead. Open M 1-6pm, Tu-Th 9:30am-6pm, F 9:30am-7pm, Sa 10am-1pm, Su 1:15-4pm. **NetConnect Communications,** 33 Peel St. S (☎ 5332 2140). $5 per 30min. Open M-F 9am-5:30pm.

Post Office: (☎ 5336 5736), in the Central Sq. Marketplace. Fax services. Poste Restante. Open M-F 9am-5pm, Sa 9am-noon. **Postal Code:** 3350.

▶ ACCOMMODATIONS

Ballarat's accommodation market aims mostly at Melburnian families on weekend trips, but there are some budget options. Rooms tend to be in short supply because of the city's popularity with school groups, so book well in advance.

Sovereign Hill Lodge YHA (☎5333 3409; www.sovereignhill.com.au), on Magpie St. at Bourke St. Take bus #9 or #10 from Bridge Mall to Sovereign Hill or walk for about 20min. up a steep hill by following Peel St. south at the eastern end of Bridge Mall; take a left on Grant St. and then right on Magpie St. By car, follow signs to Sovereign Hill, then to the lodge from Geelong Rd., a continuation of Main Rd. The buildings retain an 1850s style but are in excellent condition. Laundry, kitchen, TV lounge, and bar. Heat, but no A/C. Linens included. Courteous staff issues discounted tickets for all Sovereign Hill events. Reception Su-M 7am-10:30pm, Tu-Sa 24hr. book in advance due to hordes of school groups. Dorms $22, YHA $19; singles $27. Limited wheelchair access. ❷

Irish Murphy's, 36 Sturt St. (☎5331 4091; ballarat@irishmurphys.com.au). A popular Aussie pub chain with live music Th-Su nights (F-Sa after 10pm cover $3). Clean, unadorned doubles at the top of the stairs might be a tad loud for the light dozer. Solution: drink downstairs until the bar closes. Communal unisex bathroom. No heat or A/C. Key deposit $5. Check-in after noon. Dorms $16, with linens and doona $19. ❷

Robin Hood Hotel, 33 Peel St. N (☎5331 3348). Fairly basic pub bunk accommodations with good location one block from Bridge Mall. Not quite as clean as Irish Murphy's, but you can spend most your time at the billiards bar and award-winning bistro downstairs. No heat or A/C. Book several days in advance on holidays and weekends. Bunks $25. ❷

Ballarat Goldfields Holiday Park, 108 Clayton St. (☎5332 7888 or 1800 632 237; www.ballaratgoldfields.com.au). Campsites and cabins 300m from Sovereign Hill. Kitchens, recreation rooms, playground, heated pool, and heated communal bathrooms. Internet $2 per 10min. Reception daily 8am-8pm. Book cabins in advance. Sites for 2 $19; powered $21, in summer $22; powered with bath $26/$28; 4- to 6-person ensuite heated cabins with A/C, kitchenette, and color TV from $65. ❶

⌐ FOOD

Sturt St. is lined with fish 'n' chips shops, bakeries, and other takeaway places. The best cafes are up the hill, especially between Dawson and Doveton St. Lake Wendouree provides a serene view for numerous cafes as well. Coles 24hr. **supermarket,** a produce shop, and a bakery are at the far eastern end of Sturt St., behind the Bridge Mall. Several inexpensive eateries sit just east of Sovereign Hill.

The Pancake Kitchen, 2 Grenville St. S (☎5331 6555). This restored 1870s building dishes out pancakes and crepes in assorted fruit or meat incarnations ($8-18). Daily specials and Tu half-priced drinks. Fully licensed or BYO. Open M 10am-10pm, Tu-Th 10am-late, F-Sa 7:30am-late, Su 7:30am-10pm. ❷

Gee Cees, 427 Sturt St. (☎5331 6211). Bright, big, and busy, Gee Cees serves gourmet food in an informal yet stylish setting. Order food (mains $13-22, pastas $11-15, pizzas $10-17) at the counter and drinks at the bar while a youthful waitstaff maintains fast service. Go early on weekends—it's crowded with locals and tourists alike. Food served daily 8am-late; bar open Su-Th until 11pm, F-Sa until midnight. ❷

Restaurante Da Uday, 7 Wainwright St. (☎5331 6655). A quick hop away from Sovereign Hill, this one-room establishment serves Indian, Thai, and Italian cuisines ($7-20). It's not often that you can order tortellini with a side of spring rolls and a mango lassi. They also have a cheaper takeaway menu. Reservations compulsory F-Su. Fully licensed or BYO (wine only). Open daily noon-2pm and 5:30-10:30pm. ❷

Europa Cafe, 411 Sturt St. (☎5331 2486). A mix of Mediterranean fare and New York artistic mood. Chalkboard menu changes weekly—an informality of the youthful staff. Most meals around $10. The large window counter is a great place to try one of their 79 Aussie wines. Fully licensed or BYO. Open Su-W 8:45am-6pm, Th-Sa 8:45am-late. ❶

OUR PROUDEST DEFEAT The story of Ballarat's Eureka Rebellion, Australia's closest brush with civil war, is told *ad nauseum*. During the gold rush, the colonial government in Melbourne set up a system to milk the miners of their spoils. Miners had to pay a license fee whether or not they found gold—and the regular license hunts filled the governor's pockets. The "police" were ex-convicts drafted to "keep order" in the bustling gold towns. A digger found without a license was ordered to pay a fine of £10 or was chained to a log until he could (to keep the arrested man's hands in the cuffs, the police often smashed them with a mallet so they would bruise and swell). When Scottish miner James Scobie was murdered outside the hotel of a government supervisor, the already tense situation boiled over. The miners formed a reform league and shortly set up a stockade on the Eureka Lead. They burned their licenses, swore allegiance to the Southern Cross flag, and defended themselves valiantly—albeit briefly—when government forces attacked the next day. On December 3, 1854, 30 miners were killed and 114 taken prisoner. But the brutality outraged the rest of Australia, and reforms were soon passed abolishing the licenses and giving miners representation and voting rights. All those charged with High Treason were acquitted, and the miners' leader, Peter Lalor, later became Speaker of the House. Ballarat retains a stronghold on its past by billing itself "the birthplace of Australian democracy."

🎵 ENTERTAINMENT

On weekends, the **Bridge Mall** at the east end of Sturt St. fills with pedestrians and street musicians. Numerous hotels and pubs serve as venues for live bands. The **Bridge Mall Hotel,** 92 Bridge Mall (☎5331 3132), fondly known as **The Rat,** encourages up-and-coming musicians and draws university students from the area. Locals report the night scene hops at **Irish Murphy's** (see **Accommodations**) for drink, **Rattle and Hum** (Peel St.) for live music, and **21 Arms** (Armstrong St.), **Extremity** (Camp St.), and **The Chapel** (Dana St.) for dance. The historic **Her Majesty's Theatre,** 13 Lydiard St. (☎5333 5888; www.hermaj.com), presents live drama, with tickets ranging anywhere from $20-40. Call ahead for show information. **Blood on the Southern Cross,** a twice-nightly 80-minute sound and light show under the open night sky at Sovereign Hill, is worth the price. It introduces diggers' lives on Sovereign Hill and recounts the bitter Eureka Rebellion, with a deep-voiced recorded narrator and delightfully melodramatic music. (☎5333 5777. M-Sa, also Su during holiday periods. $30, concessions $24, children $16, families $84. Book ahead.)

👁 SIGHTS

The Ballarat tourism network offers a *Welcome Pass* that includes two-day unlimited entry to Sovereign Hill, the Gold Museum, and the Eureka Stockade and Fine Art Gallery. ($32, concessions $22, children $15, families $82. Purchase from tourist office or at attractions.) Inquire at the Visitors Center about tours of Ballarat's historic areas. The **Ballarat Begonia Festival** (Feb. 28 to Mar. 10, 2003) is an open-air arts and crafts fair. **Royal South Street** music, debate, and performance competitions attract top talent (Aug.-Oct.) Locals recommend walking the tree-lined pathways of Victoria Park, south of Lake Wendouree, or hiking up to the lookout on Black Hill (from Chisholm St., north off Peel St.) for quiet nighttime views.

🏛 SOVEREIGN HILL. While a reconstructed gold town built around a mine won't make you rich, Sovereign Hill will at least give you a taste of the past. Sovereign Hill staff, dressed in period attire, roam about town as miners and townfolk.

Exhibits include gold-pouring, candle-making, smelting, musket-firing, and a 40min. tour of the mine that reveals the harsh conditions of mining life. Pan for gold yourself or ride the horse-drawn carriage through the streets of this outdoor museum. *(Take bus #9 or 10. Signs point the way. ☎ 5331 1944. Open daily 10am-5pm. Combined admission with Gold Museum $25, concessions $18, families $65.)*

GOLD MUSEUM. Declaring that "the story of gold is firmly linked to the story of man," this Sovereign Hill appendage traces the importance of gold across time and cultures. It also houses an expensive collection of gold coins, ornaments, and replicas of the two largest gold nuggets ever found. If you somehow grow tired of gold, the museum also features some interesting but unrelated exhibits, including a section on the Chinese in Australia, an Aboriginal display with an assortment of boomerangs, and the Ballarat Sports Hall of Fame, containing the Sydney 2000 Olympic torch. *(Next to Sovereign Hill, on Bradshaw St. ☎ 5331 1944. Open daily in summer 9:30am-6pm; in winter 9:30am-5:20pm. $6.30, concessions $4, children $3.10.)*

EUREKA STOCKADE. This sleek $4 million multimedia adventure commemorates the Eureka Rebellion on the site of the miners' stockade. The modern complex dons a giant Southern Cross flag in the shape of a sail. If you've already seen **Blood on the Southern Cross** (see **Entertainment,** p. 622), the 1hr. self-guided tour may be a little redundant. *(Eureka St. at Rodier St. Take bus #8. ☎ 5333 1854; www.sovereignhill.com.au/eureka.htm. Open daily 9am-5pm. $8, concessions $6, children $4, families $22.)*

▓BALLARAT WILDLIFE PARK. The park's 14 acres of open bush are home to some of Australia's diverse fauna, including fearsome saltwater crocodiles and Tasmanian devils, and less imposing emus, goannas, wombats, koalas, and free-roaming 'roos that will eat right out of your hand. The weekend crocodile feed is a special thrill. *(On York St. at Fussel St. Take bus #8 or 9 or drive down York St. off Main Rd., midway between Sovereign Hill and Eureka St. ☎ 5333 5933; wildlife@lin.cbl.com.au. Tours 11am. Open daily 9am-5:30pm. $14, students $12, children $8, families $39.)*

▶ DAYTRIPS FROM BALLARAT: WINERIES

Most vineyards in the Ballarat region began production in the 1980s. With cool-climate Chardonnays becoming increasingly popular, the region is regarded as up-and-coming. Pick up the *Wine Regions of Victoria* booklet in local tourist offices. At **Dulcinea Vineyard,** owner Rod Stott says: "I believe in education." He urges visitors to roam his small cellar and vineyard, tasting his delectable blends as he answers questions on the way. Take the Midland Hwy. from Ballarat north 11km toward Creswick. (☎ 5334 6440; dulcinea@cbl.com.au. Open daily 9am-5pm. Bottles $10-18.) **St. Anne's Vineyards,** 22km east of Ballarat and 77km from Melbourne off the Western Hwy., has free tastings in a cool, blue stone cottage. A peppery red Shiraz and a fortified tawny port top the list. (☎ 5368 7209. Open M-Sa 9am-5pm, Su 10am-5pm.)

FROM BALLARAT TO BENDIGO

The Midland Hwy. goes north from Ballarat toward Bendigo, meeting the Calder Hwy. (from Melbourne) at Harcourt, 9km north of Castlemaine.

DAYLESFORD AND HEPBURN SPRINGS. Daylesford is 107km northwest of Melbourne and 45km northeast of Ballarat. Visitors come here to soak in the waters of its neighbor, Hepburn Springs, which contains the largest concentration of curative mineral springs in Australia. Aborigines revered the springs even before European settlement, but many guest cottages and B&Bs have sprung up recently. New Age commercialism has infused these quiet communities with healing crystals, essences, oils, and aromatherapy. While most of the restaurants and services are in Daylesford, the spa complex is in Hepburn Springs, 4km north. Buses run between the towns, but it is a pleasant 40-minute walk if you're up for it. The **Hepburn Regional Park** lets you pump your own mineral water, but take care to avoid falling into abandoned mine shafts (maps at info center).

Most of the area's lovely guest cottages and B&Bs will set you back $80-100 per night. **Continental House ❷**, 9 Lone Pine Ave., described by some of its patrons as a living work of art (and by others as a hippie hideout), is secluded behind an impressively dense 5m tall hedge just a few hundred meters from the spa. Refresh yourself at this strictly vegetarian, strictly relaxed guest house with tranquil common areas, a full kitchen, and basic bunkrooms. Health banquet every Sa night. Prices vary depending on length of stay and, in the case of private rooms, number of people. (☎ 5348 2005. Linens $3. Bunks $25, concessions $18; singles $35/30; doubles $27/23.) The **Hepburn Spa Resort,** in Hepburn Springs, provides the works. Services range from the normal pool and spa (weekdays $9, weekends $11) to massages (45min., $50-55) to flotation tanks (30min., $33-39). Use of spring waters is free. Prices are expected to rise slightly for 2003. (☎ 5348 2034. www.hepburnspa.com.au. Open M-Th 10am-7pm, F 10am-8pm, Sa 9am-10pm, Su 9am-7pm.)

CASTLEMAINE. Sleepy and provincial, this town 120km northwest of Melbourne in the central Goldfields has quiet charm. If you've got money to spare, stay at the **Old Castlemaine Gaol ❹**, on Bowden St., overlooking the town atop the hill to the west of the railroad station. The 1861 jail held felons, lunatics, and juvenile offenders before its 1990 renovation into a well-heated and ventilated B&B. The dungeons, once the site of horrific torture, now house a wine bar and lounge. The Gaol won't take groups smaller than 20 unless a large group is already here, but even if you're not staying, it's worth taking a self-guided tour. (☎ 5470 5311; www.gaol.castlemaine.net.au. Tours $5, children $2.50, families $11. Call ahead. Double bunks $55.) In case the jail thing just doesn't work out, nearby Maldon has the surprisingly nice **Central Service Centre Accommodations ❸**, at the merging of Main and High St. This garage-turned-hotel features heating and A/C, bathroom, TV, fridge, and coffee and tea in every room. (☎ 5475 2216. Reception 8am-5:30pm. Singles $30; doubles and twins $60.) Just 4km east of Castlemaine toward Chewton is the wild and popular **Dingo Farm Australia.** Here you can witness an attempt to keep purebred dingoes from becoming extinct. Although dangerous in the wild, nearly 100 of these canines are domesticated, sheltered, and bred here. (☎ 5470 5711; www.ins.net.au/dingofarm. $8, children $4. Large groups book in advance.)

BENDIGO ☎ 03

Like almost all the Victorian goldfields' towns, Bendigo (pop. 85,000) sprang into existence in the 1850s when scores of miners flooded in, lured by the promise of success. But while many of its neighbors were tossed from prosperity to obscurity by the boom and bust cycle, Bendigo continued to prosper into the 20th century thanks to its seemingly endless supply of gold-rich alluvial quartz. (Though it stopped mining commercially in 1954, Bendigo still holds rank as the second-highest gold producer in the country.) Such abundance lured gold-seekers from across the globe—notably a significant Chinese population—resulting in a period of harsh discrimination. It also brought many gold magnates, who used their early fortunes to turn the fledgling city into a Victorian showcase. Now, the town's early diversity has created a progressive sense of tolerance in a nearly homogenous nation, while the grandiose Gothic buildings and wide thoroughfares with names like Pall Mall ("Pell Mell") imbue Bendigo with a certain Anglophilic nostalgia.

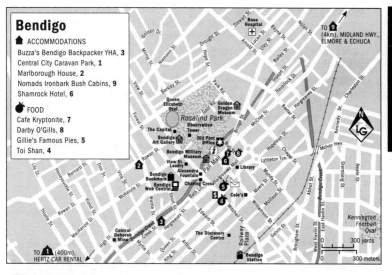

Bendigo

🏠 ACCOMMODATIONS

Buzza's Bendigo Backpacker YHA, **3**
Central City Caravan Park, **1**
Marlborough House, **2**
Nomads Ironbark Bush Cabins, **9**
Shamrock Hotel, **6**

🍴 FOOD

Cafe Kryptonite, **7**
Darby O'Gills, **8**
Gillie's Famous Pies, **5**
Toi Shan, **4**

🔲 TRANSPORTATION

Trains and Buses: Bendigo Station is behind the Discovery Centre at the south end of Mitchell St. **V/Line** (☎ 13 61 96) has **trains** and **buses,** depending on destination, to: Adelaide (8½hr., 1 per day, $57); Ballarat (2hr., 1 per day, $20); Daylesford (1¼hr., 1 per day, $10); Geelong (3¾hr., 1 per day, $33); Maldon (2hr., 2 per day, $7) via Castlemaine (22min., 11 per day, $5); Maryborough (1hr., 3 per day, $13); Mildura (5hr., 4 per day, $52); Melbourne (2hr., 11 per day, $23); and Swan Hill (3½hr., 2-3 per day, $26). Infrequent service Sa-Su. Round trips Tu-Th 30% off.

Public Transportation: Local **buses** depart from the corner of Hargreaves and Mitchell St. **Taxis** line up along Queen St. between Mitchell and Williamson St.

Car Rental: Hertz (☎ 5443 5088), at the corner of High and Thistle St. From $42 for 300km per day. **Budget,** 150-152 High St. (☎ 5442 2766), near the Central Deborah Mine. $55 for 330km per day.

■❄🛈 ORIENTATION AND PRACTICAL INFORMATION

Bendigo is a combination of well-planned streets and winding gold gullies originally packed down by diggers' feet. Most points of interest are near the city center, bounded on the south and east by the railroad tracks and on the north by Rosalind Park. The **Calder Hwy. (Hwy. 79)** from Melbourne runs into the city center, becoming **High St.,** then **Pall Mall** (at **Charing Cross**), then **McCrae St.,** and eventually **Midland Hwy.,** which leads to Elmore and Echuca. The popular pedestrian **Hargreaves Mall** extends one block along Hargreaves between Mitchell and Williamson St.

Tourist Office: 51-67 Pall Mall (☎/fax 5444 4445 or 1800 813 153), in the Victorian post-office building. Mini-museum detailing Bendigo's history. Open daily 9am-5pm.

Currency Exchange: National Bank (☎5443 9399), on the corner of Queen and Mitchell St. Open M-Th 9:30am-4pm, F 9:30am-5pm. 24hr. **ATM.**

Bookstore: Bendigo Bookmark, 29 High St. (☎5441 7866), will buy, sell, and exchange. Open M-F 9:30am-5:30pm, Sa 9:30am-1pm. **Book Now** (☎5443 8587), on Farmers Ln. off Bridge St., carries cheap secondhand books. Open daily 10am-5pm.

Public Library: 251-259 Hargreaves St. (☎5443 5100; www.ncgrl.vic.gov.au). **Internet** access. (Free 15min., $3 per additional 30min.) Open M-F 10am-7pm, Sa 10am-1pm.

Emergency: ☎000. **Police** (☎5440 2510), on Bull St. behind the law courts.

Internet Access: In the public library, see above. **Bendigo Web Central,** 36 High St. (☎5442 6411), has a fast connection and charges $2 per 15min., $3 per 30min., or $5 per hr. Open M-F 9am-9pm, Sa-Su 10am-7pm.

Post Office: (☎13 13 18), on the corner of Hargreaves and Williamson St. Open M-F 9am-5pm, Sa 9:30am-12:30pm. Poste Restante. **Postal Code:** 3550.

🏠 ACCOMMODATIONS

The strip of Calder Hwy./High St. running south of town is loaded with cookie-cutter chain motels. You can find some nicer motels and B&Bs ($50-90) with historical charm along McCrae and Napier St. just northeast of the city center.

🔲 **Nomads Ironbark Bush Cabins** (☎5448 3344; www.bwc.com.au/ironbark), on Watson St. Located 5km from the city center, the Ironbark is out of walking distance, but the owners will pick you up from Bendigo station. A refreshing and pleasant taste of the bush with 6 small, tidy cabins that sleep 5 to 9 people. A recently-built 5-room dorm features cozy 4-bed ensuite rooms. All cabins have heating, bathrooms, refrigerators, and coffee makers. Towels and linens included. BBQ (dinner $12) and bar (beer $2.50) in evenings around the campfire, and a brand-new 75m waterslide to keep you cool in summer. On-site horseback riding $20 per 30min., $28 per hr. Special weekend package deals include horseback riding and meals. All beds $20. ❷

Marlborough House, 115 Wattle St. (☎5441 4142; http://home.primus.com.au/marlboroughhouse), on the corner of Rowan St. A gorgeous B&B that looks a bit like a palace and makes guests feel a bit like royalty. The 130-year-old house overlooks the city and sits just a block from the Sacred Heart Cathedral. Guests are pampered with a courtyard garden, intimate library, and TV room. Sunlit bedrooms are spacious and well-decorated, and all contain queen-sized beds (twins available) and delightful ensuites. Full breakfast included in room price; guests order from the house menu and are served in the dining room. Reception 24hr. Singles from $90; doubles and twins from $145. ❺

Buzza's Bendigo Backpacker YHA, 33 Creek St. (☎/fax 5443 7680; buzza@bendigo.net.au). A comfortable converted house in a quiet residential area close to the center of town. Three individual shower/bathrooms offer some welcomed privacy, while the large dining room and the reading room with open fireplace and TV allow guests to interact at their leisure. Linens and towels included. Laundry $2. Internet $2 per 30min. Free parking. Check-in 8-11am and 5-10pm. Dorms $21, YHA $17; singles $34/$30; doubles $49/$42. Family suite also available. Wheelchair accessible. ❷

Shamrock Hotel (☎5442 0333), on the corner of Pall Mall and Williamson St. A local landmark, the Shamrock offers a range of accommodations. All rooms are nicely furnished and have heat, fridge, minibar, TV, and free tea/coffee. "Traditional Rooms" (comfortable, with shared bath, can fit up to 4) $70; ensuite rooms $95; 2-room suites $180. Reception M-F 7:30am-8:30pm, Sa 7:30am-9:30pm, Su 8am-7:30pm. ❺

Central City Caravan Park, 362 High St. (☎/fax 5443 6937), at Beech St. Take bus #1 from Hargreaves Mall. The CCCP, a former YHA affiliate, is the cheapest place around, offering minimalist hostel accommodation with full kitchen, comrade. Sites for 2 $14; powered $18; dorms $15. Reception daily 9am-10pm. ❶

FOOD

Most popular restaurants are near the tourist office, especially on Bull St. and Pall Mall; Main St. also has several options. Budget-friendly restaurants are all around town. The **Hargreaves Mall** has a food court that bustles during lunch hours. Coles 24hr. **supermarket** is on the corner of Myers and Williamson St.

Cafe Kryptonite, 92 Pall Mall (☎ 5443 9777). Features meals ($8-20) almost as colorful as its interior design, as well as several veggie options and a braggable selection of wine and tea (from $3). Open daily 10am-late. ❷

Darby O'Gills (☎ 5443 4916), on the corner of Bull and Hargreaves St. This pub touts itself as "a touch of the Irish, a taste of the world," but their pub grub outshines their international cuisine. Beautiful stained-glass windows and dark-wood bar. Open M-Sa noon-2:30pm; also M-W 6-9pm, Th-Sa 6-9:30pm. ❷

Gillie's Famous Pies (☎ 5443 4965), on the corner of Hargreaves Mall and Williamson St., features meat pies and sweet cakes ($2-3) either inside or via the "Pie Window." Open M-Th 8:30am-6pm, F 8:30am-7pm, Sa 9am-5pm, Su 10am-4pm. ❶

Toi Shan, 65-67 Mitchell St. (☎ 5443 5811). All-you-can-eat smorgasbord ($9.30-10.30) and convenient self-serve takeaway packs ($4-7). ❶

SIGHTS

CENTRAL DEBORAH MINE. Tours take visitors 61m down the last mine to stop operating commercially in Bendigo. Explanations of mining history and techniques are interactive; volunteer and you may even get to show off your skill with the drill. True thrill-seekers can try the **Underground Adventure Tour,** in which participants don miner's garb and go down extra levels to use real mine equipment for two hours. (76 Violet St. ☎ 5443 8322, group bookings 5443 8255; www.central-deborah.com. Open daily 9am-5pm. Regular tours 6 per day, every 70min. $16.50, concessions $14.50. Underground Adventure: with lunch $53, concessions $48, children $28; with morning/afternoon tea $45/$41/$23. Discounts available for families and groups larger than 10.)

LANDMARKS. Tours, complete with recorded commentary, cover the town using the restored turn-of-the-century tram system (1hr.; $12.90, concessions $11.50, children $7.50, families $37.) Trams run hourly, picking up from the elaborate **Alexandra Fountain** near the tourist office or from the Central Deborah Mine. The late-Victorian feel of Bendigo's architecture is most pronounced along **Pall Mall,** which is littered with more neo-Gothic touches than you can shake a spire at. Most impressive are the **old post office building** (which now houses the Visitors Center) and the adjacent Bendigo Law Courts, both with ornate facades on all four sides. The **Shamrock Hotel,** at the corner of Williamson St. and Pall Mall, began as a roaring entertainment hall in the golden 1850s. **Rosalind Park,** on the site of the old 1850s police barracks north of Alexandra Fountain, is a vast expanse of greenery scattered with winding pathways, trees, and statues—including a fairly unflattering likeness of Queen Victoria. If you brave the 124-step climp up its observation tower, the reward is a view of Bendigo and the surrounding gold country.

GOLDEN DRAGON MUSEUM. This collection provides an overview of both Chinese culture in Australia and its particular impact on Bendigo. Displays offer a look at the Chinese-Australian experience in the place they dubbed "Dai Gum San" (Big Gold Mountain), but do gloss a bit over the racism that Chinese-Australians often faced. The collection's highlight is the fantastically ornate Sun Loong, the longest imperial dragon in the world at just over 100m. (5-9 Bridge St. ☎ 5441 5044. Open daily 9:30am-5pm. $7, concessions $5, children $4, families $20. Garden only $2.20, children 60¢.)

🎵 🎭 ENTERTAINMENT AND NIGHTLIFE

Pubs are everywhere. Most are tame local hangouts that close around midnight, but weekends can be rowdier when tourists funnel into its small watering holes. The main late-night entertainment options are on the few blocks of Pall Mall and Hargreaves from Williamson to Mundy St. The **Old Crown**, 238 Hargreaves St., is a smoky neighborhood haunt filled with families by day and burly locals at night. (☎ 5441 6888. F-Sa karaoke; F live music. Occasional cover $3. Open Th-F until 1-2am, Sa until 3am.) **Darby O'Gills,** on the corner of Bull and Hargreaves St., offers a selection of Irish beers on tap ($3.50 a pot) and live music (W-Sa) starting at 10pm. (No cover. Open until 1-2am.) There's more live music at the **Sundance Saloon,** on Pall Mall and Mundy St., which hosts Melbourne's top cover bands on Thursdays. (☎ 5441 8222. Open Th-Sa 8:30pm-late.) The **Golden Vine,** 135 King St. (☎ 5443 6063), attracts a young local crowd with its chill music and late nights.

MURRAY RIVER

Australia's longest river, the Murray, rambles along the New South Wales-Victoria border for 2600km before meeting the sea in South Australia's Encounter Bay. The river became an essential transportation artery in the late 19th century, its waters supplied by giant freight-toting paddlesteamers. Extensive rail and road networks rendered these boats obsolete by the end of the 1930s, and they have since been reincarnated as tourist attractions. Today the river feeds production of vegetables and fruits (including wine grapes) through a complex irrigation system. It's also a favorite spot for picnicking, water sports, and fishing, drawing travelers for a day or a week of relaxation along the banks of the grand old Murray.

ECHUCA ☎ 03

As the closest point to Melbourne along the Murray, Echuca was once Australia's largest inland port, a clearinghouse for the wool and agricultural products of southern New South Wales. A massive red gum wharf was built to accommodate the paddlesteamers and barges, and a lively array of hotels, brothels, and breweries was built to accommodate the men who sailed them. River traffic declined in the late 1800s, and Echuca's major industry is now an object of nostalgia—many boats have been preserved, and the town now possesses the world's largest flotilla of side-wheel paddlesteamers. Old-time facades dominate its main streets, and a late-19th century feel pervades the town. Despite its exterior, Echuca has the bustle of an entirely modern city, and its tourist industry—though not exactly exciting—avoids the theme-park hokeyness of other historic river towns, making this the best place to immerse yourself in the Murray riverboat culture.

▐ TRANSPORTATION

V/Line buses run from the **Visitors Center** or the Ampole Road House on the Northern Hwy. to: Albury (3-4hr., 1-3 per day, $23-39); Bendigo (1¼hr., 1-3 per day, $7); Melbourne (3½-4hr., 4-6 per day, $31); Mildura (5½hr.; 1 per day M, W, Th, and Sa; $38); Swan Hill (2hr., 1-2 per day, $21). A **steam locomotive** from Melbourne now runs on the last Sunday of every month. The train leaves Melbourne at 8:15am, arrives at the Echuca Station at noon, and then gives its riders four hours to tour Echuca before leaving for Melbourne at 4pm. (☎ 5221 8966. Open M-F 9am-5pm. Economy non-A/C tickets $50, with guided tour $70; children $10/25; concessions $30/50; families $100/148. Book ahead.)

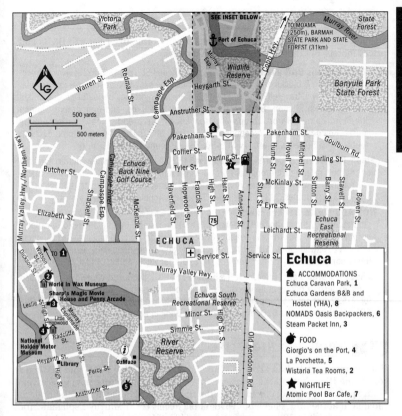

Echuca

♠ ACCOMMODATIONS
Echuca Caravan Park, 1
Echuca Gardens B&B and
    Hostel (YHA), 8
NOMADS Oasis Backpackers, 6
Steam Packet Inn, 3

🍴 FOOD
Giorgio's on the Port, 4
La Porchetta, 5
Wistaria Tea Rooms, 2

★ NIGHTLIFE
Atomic Pool Bar Cafe, 7

✥ 🛈 ORIENTATION AND PRACTICAL INFORMATION

Echuca, from the Aboriginal word meaning "meeting of the waters," lies about 200km north of Melbourne at the intersection of two rivers, the **Campaspe** (north-south) and the **Murray** (east-west), and of two highways, the **Murray Valley Highway** and **Northern Highway.** Echuca's main drags are **Hare** and **High Street,** parallel roads that run north-south from the Murray River to the Murray Valley Hwy. Follow the **Cobb Highway** past the **Visitors Center** across the Murray to Echuca's twin city of **Moama** in New South Wales, notable predominantly for its array of gambling clubs.

The **Visitor Information Centre,** 2 Heygarth St., is on the Echuca side of the Echuca-Moama bridge. (☎5480 7555 or 1800 804 446; www.echucamoama.com. Open daily 9am-5pm.) **ANZ, National,** and **Commonwealth banks** with 24hr. **ATMs** are side by side on Hare St. just south of Anstruther St. (All open M-Th 9:30am-4pm, F 9:30am-5pm.) The **library,** at the corner of Heygarth and High St. catty-corner to McDonald's, offers **Internet** access. (Research free, email $2.50 per 30min. Book ahead at ☎5482 1997. Open M-Tu and Th-F 10am-5:30pm, W noon-8pm, Sa 10am-1pm, Su 2-4pm.) There's a **post office** on the corner of Hare and Anstruther St. (Open M-F 9am-5pm, Sa 9am-noon.) **Postal Code:** 3564.

ACCOMMODATIONS

Echuca's accommodation scene consists mostly of luxury riverside B&Bs and pricey motels, but there are a few budget options.

Echuca Gardens B&B and Hostel (YHA), 103 Mitchell St. (☎5480 6522; www.echuca-gardens.com), 8 blocks east from the city center. The second-oldest hostel in Australia. Think you're well-traveled? The engaging owners are more so. Beautiful gardens filled with fruit trees. Kitchen, BBQ, cozy lounge, open fireplace, and memorable German Shepherd named Baron. Sauna and spa encourage friendly conversation among guests. Key deposit $10. Reception daily 8-10am and 5-10pm. 4-bed dorms $22.50; doubles $45.50, ensuite with TV $68.50. YHA discount $3.50. MC/V. ❷

Steam Packet Inn, 37 Murray Esplanade (☎5482 3411). A worthwhile splurge. Located on the port in one of the original port buildings and decorated in 1860s style. Guests are pampered with ensuite rooms, A/C, refrigerators, electric blankets, and color TV. Singles $71; doubles $93; B&B singles $81; B&B doubles $113. ❺

NOMADS Oasis Backpackers, 410-422 High St. (☎5480 7866; nomads@origin.net.au), on the corner of Pakenham. In town, well-kept. Caters largely to backpackers who come to pick fruits in season. Courtesy bus transports to picking sites. Kitchen, TV lounge, and Internet ($5 per hr.). Room key gets discounts locally. Linens included. Reception 24hr. 3- to 12-bed dorms $18, $108 per week. AmEx/DC/MC/V. ❷

Echuca Caravan Park, Crofton St. (☎5482 2157). Gigantic, but choked with campervans, especially during holidays, due to idyllic location right on Murray. No linens. Sites for 2 $22, off-peak $20; powered $24/$22; 5- or 6-person ensuite cabins $80-98/ $65-78, extra persons $10, extra children $5. Book in advance. MC/V. ❶

FOOD AND NIGHTLIFE

The standard Australian array of chip shops, grub-serving pubs, and fast-food joints line High St., and the Murray Esplanade has some more upmarket riverfront spots. Have large, cheap meals the four licensed clubs across the river in Moama. If at the port, check out **Wistaria Tea Rooms** ❷, 51 Murray Esplanade, for a delicious meal in 19th-century style. (☎5482 4210. Open 8am through lunchtime.) The omnipresent, budget-friendly **La Porchetta** ❶ pizza and pasta chain beckons at 192 Annesley St., attached to the King Pin bowling alley. (☎5480 1130. Open M-Th 11am-9pm, F-Sa 11am-11pm, Su 11am-9:30pm. MC/V.) **Port Precinct Cafe** ❶, 591 High St., serves breakfast all day ($5-11) and inexpensive gourmet burgers ($4-6) by an open fire. Their **Internet cafe** is unfortunately not as cheap. (☎5480 2163. $2 per 12min., $9 per hr. Open daily 8am-5pm or later. AmEx/DC/MC/V.) **River Palace** ❷, 614 High St., offers over 100 Szechuan and Malay dishes. (☎5482 3152. Takeaway daily noon-2:30pm; dine-in from 5pm. AmEx/DC/MC/V.) For a splurge, visit **Giorgio's On the Port** ❸, 527 High St., which is not actually on the port, but serves awesome Italian meals from $15.50 nevertheless. (☎5482 6117. AmEx/DC/MC/V.) There is also a 24hr. Coles **supermarket** on the corner of High and Darling St.

Numerous pubs on High and Hare St. are peopled by friendly locals. The most active are the **Harvest Hotel** at the corner of Hare and Anstruther St., the **Shamrock** on High St. near the port, the **Bridge Hotel** on Murray Esplanade by the port, and the **American Hotel** at Hare and Pakenham St. A younger crowd chills at the **Atomic Pool Bar Cafe,** 207 Darling St., which has free pool all day Sa-Su. (☎5480 2227. Open Tu-Th 5pm-1am, F 5pm-2am, Sa noon-2am, Su noon-11pm. F-Sa cover $5 after 10pm.)

⊙ SIGHTS

Although most of Echuca's sights center around its paddlesteamer history, the small river-town atmosphere provides some great day-strolls whether or not history is your motivation.

HISTORIC PORT. The main attraction in Echuca is its port, consisting of the wharf and several historic buildings. The 1865 red-gum wharf has three levels to accommodate changing river conditions. Blacksmith and woodturning shops sell handmade wares, and a steam display explains the workings of the portentous invention that brought on the Industrial Revolution. (*Historic Port Area, along Murray Esplanade.* ☎ *5482 4248; www.portofechuca.org.au. Open daily 9am-5pm. $10, concessions $8.50, children $6, families $27.50.*)

PORT PRECINCT. The port precinct, which is free for strolling, has several old hotels on display. The **Star Hotel** is equipped with every fraternity brother's dream: a secret underground tunnel that allowed drinkers to escape police raids after the place was de-licensed in 1897; the **Bridge Hotel,** Echuca's first, has a carefully preserved suite and gallery upstairs. At the other end is the old **Customs House,** which exacted tariffs from passing watercraft during Echuca's days as the commercial hub of the Murray. Today, the Customs House building is home to the **Murray Esplanade Cellars,** which exacts a tariff of zero dollars for sampling its excellent wines and spirits. (*2 Leslie St.* ☎ *5482 6058. Open daily 9am-5pm. Free entry.*) An even tastier stop is **Iron House Coopers** (☎ 5480 6955), in the old Freeman's Foundry at 13-17 Murray Esplanade, where you can sample a myriad of intriuging port wines, including Jack Daniels and Jim Beam varieties. (*Open M-Sa 9am-5pm, Su 10am-5pm.*)

PADDLESTEAMERS. Several paddlesteamers still ply the waters off the old port—they're now open to the public for leisurely cruises. The Port Authority runs one-hour cruises on **P.S. Pevensey** or **P.S. Alexander Arbuthnot.** Buy tickets at 52 Murray Esplanade. (☎ *5482 4248. 5 per day. $15.50, concessions $12, children $6. Joint port and cruise: $20/$17/$11, families $49.50.*) A private company runs the paddlesteamers **Pride of the Murray** and **Emmylou;** the *Emmylou* is worth the slightly higher price, and if you really want to splurge, overnight **accommodation** ❺ is available from $180 per person. (*Buy tickets at the Custom House Agents or at 57 Murray Esplanade.* ☎ *5482 5244. Pride of Murray: 1hr.; 6 per day; $13.50, seniors $12, children $6.50, families $38. Emmylou: 5 per day; 1hr.; $16.50, children $9; 1½hr. $20, children $10.*) Beginning in September of 2002, the P.S. Canberra will also offer 1hr. cruises. (*$15, seniors $13.50, children $6.*)

WORLD IN WAX MUSEUM. Although not particularly relevant to the history of the Murray, the wax museum in front of the port could be the most fun place in town. Figures include dignitaries both foreign and domestic, arranged by era and disposition (amusingly, Stalin, Hitler, and Castro share a case with Churchill). Humorously informative notes line the walls. (*630 High St.* ☎ *5482 3630. Open daily 9am-5:30pm. $9, concessions $8, children $4.50. YHA discount $1.*)

SHARP'S MAGIC MOVIE HOUSE AND PENNY ARCADE. Adjacent to the port, this small building houses Australia's largest collection of working penny arcade machines, from strength tests to fortune readers. An array of antique cinematic equipment continuously screens turn-of-the-century newsreels, comedy shorts, and historical documentaries. It's a bit pricey, but kind of cool considering that Australian pennies stopped circulating in 1966. Admission includes five pennies. (☎ *5482 2361. Open daily 9am-5pm. $12, concessions $10, children $8. Tickets valid all day.*)

NATIONAL HOLDEN MOTOR MUSEUM. For car-lovers or those who want a fascinating perspective on an iconic slice of Australiana, the Holden Motor Museum is a must-see. It showcases over 50 years of "Australia's Own" automobile, with over 40 lovingly restored Holden models including the only one of the space-age 1969 experimental "Hurricane." The amusing video retrospective spotlights not only the car, but also Australia's love for Holden ads. *(7-11 Warren St. ☎ 5480 2033. Open daily 9am-5pm. $6, concessions $4.50, children $3, families $14. MC/V.)*

OZMAZE. After living in the past all day, you may want to get lost for awhile. This huge wooden maze is constructed in the form of Australia, Tasmania included, without the 'roos, wombats, and beer. *(On the Echuca side of the Echuca-Moama bridge. ☎ 5480 2220; www.ozmaze.com.au. Maze $7.50, seniors $6, families $26-32.50. Mini golf $6, children and seniors $5.50, families $22-27.50. Open W-M 10am-4pm.)*

■ DAYTRIP FROM ECHUCA: BARMAH FOREST

Just 31km from Echuca on the Cobb Hwy., the **Barmah State Park and State Forest** is the largest red-gum forest in Victoria. The 22,000 hectares are well-endowed with roads and walking tracks, but rain and high water levels render many impassable. The **Dharnya Centre,** on Sand Ridge Rd. near the park entrance, 9km from the Barmah General Store, provides maps and info on road conditions, and presents an engaging display on white treatment of Aborigines. (☎ 5869 3302. Open daily 10:30am-4pm.) **Camping ❶** is free and abundant in the park, and fishing is excellent (fishing licenses required for those 18+). When water levels are high enough, the wetlands can be explored by boat or canoe. **Kingfisher Wetland Cruises** offers 2hr. trips. Purchase tickets from Barmah General Store or from the *Pride of the Murray* stand on the Esplanade in Echuca. (☎ 5480 1839. M, W, Th, and Sa-Su 12:30pm. $18, seniors $16, children $12.) **Gondwana Canoe Hire,** on Moira Lakes Rd. on the way to the park entrance from Barmah, hires canoes. (☎ 5869 3347; www.geocities.com/gondwanahire. $25 per hr., $35 per half-day, $50 per day, $75 per 2 days, $30 per day for 3 or more days.) There is no public transport to the park; **V/Line buses** arrive once per day in Barmah, 10km away. *Let's Go* does not recommend hitchhiking, but kind-hearted locals headed toward the park have been known to lend the occasional ride. You can ask at the youth hostel or check postings there.

SWAN HILL   ☎ 03

Tranquil, rural Swan Hill, located on the Murray River about 340km northwest of Melbourne, is ideal for families, caravaners, and all who value peace over pace. The area is thick with nurseries, craft shops, tea rooms, wineries, and other serene pastimes. This part of the Murray has great fishing, and its relaxing rented-houseboat cruises are especially popular among seniors.

▣ TRANSPORTATION. V/Line trains leave daily for Melbourne (4½hr., $47.90) from the station on Curlewis St., between McCrae and Rutherford St., near the Giant Murray Cod. Bus service is available to: Adelaide (6hr., 1 per day, $46.40); Albury (5½-7hr., 1-2 per day, $39.10); Echuca (1½hr. 1-2 per day, $20.30); Kerang (40 min., 2-3 per day, $6.90); and Mildura (2½hr., 2-3 per day, $32.30).

⊠ PRACTICAL INFORMATION. Swan Hill's civic activity centers on the manicured strip of Campbell St. (Murray Valley Hwy.) between Rutherford and McCallum St. The **Swan Hill Development and Information Centre,** 306 Campbell St., on the corner of Rutherford St., is one block west of the river. (☎ 5032 3033 or 1800 625 373; www.swanhillonline.com. Open daily 9am-5pm.) Heaps of banks with 24hr.

ATMs are on Campbell St., especially near McCallum St. (All banks open M-Th 9:30am-4pm, F 9:30am-5pm.) The **library**, 53-67 Campbell St., offers free **Internet** access for research and email at $1 per hr. (☎5032 2404. Book ahead. Open M 2-5pm, Tu and Th-F 10am-5:30pm, W 10am-5:30pm and 7-8:30pm, Sa 10am-noon.) There's a **post office** on 164 Campbell St. (Open M-F 9am-5pm.) **Postal Code:** 3585.

🛏🍴🎵 ACCOMMODATIONS, FOOD, AND NIGHTLIFE. Budget accommodations are few, as most of Campbell St.'s numerous motels run $40-110 per night. If you're driving, the **Commercial Hotel ❶**, 14km south at Lake Boga, on Marraboor St. off Station St. from the highway, may be your best option. The pub accommodation includes continental breakfast, kitchen, laundry, and electric blankets. (☎5037 2140. Singles $15; doubles $20; families $25. MC/V.) Otherwise, the **Pioneer Settlement ❷**, on Horseshoe Bend, reserves one of its three lodges for backpackers when they're not booked with school groups. There is a kitchen and TV lounge, but only two bedrooms have doors. (☎5036 2410. Linens $5.50. Book ahead. 4- to 6-bed dorms $16.50 first night, each extra night $11, weekly $70. AmEx/DC/MC/V.) The **Riverside Caravan Park ❷**, 1 Monash Dr., on the river adjacent to the Pioneer Settlement, has a pool and spa, BBQ, kitchen, and small grocer. (☎5032 1494. Linens $8. Sites for 2 $20-22, powered $22-26; on-site caravans $45-65; cabins $59-127. Reception daily 8am-8pm. MC/V.) **Cafe Allure ❸**, 147 Campbell St., serves up an eclectic mix of gourmet breakfasts, smoothies, and rich, large focaccias for under $13. Don't be suspicious of the questionably named "Salmonetta" pizzetta. (☎5032 4422. Open M-Tu 9am-4:30pm, W-Su 9am-9pm.) For dinner, both the service and the Italian fare at **Quo Vadis ❷**, 255-259 Campbell St., are superb. (☎5032 4408. Pizza and pasta section open daily 5pm-late; restaurant open daily 6pm-late.)

🎯 SIGHTS. The **Horseshoe Bend Pioneer Settlement**, on Horseshoe Bend, is the oldest outdoor museum in Australia. Heading south on Campbell St., turn left on Gray St. and cross the railroad tracks. A full century (1830-1930) of the history of frontier agricultural settlement is represented by original buildings and olde-tyme equipment. Dressed in old-fashioned clothing, the employees perform uproarious slapstick street theater; paddlesteamers cruise the river along the banks of the settlement, and nighttime brings the **Mallee Heritage Sound and Light Show,** a family-friendly, if slightly hokey, cart-ride through history under the southern stars. (☎5036 2410. Open daily 9am-5pm. $16, children $9, families $41. Mallee Show $10, children $6, families $26. Cruise on the paddlesteamer *Pyap* 1 hr.; 2 per day; $12, concessions $8, children $7, families $31. Joint passes available.) Smaller than the Pioneer Settlement, but almost as engaging, is the **Swan Hill Art Gallery**, housed in a modern mud-brick structure next door. Three rotating galleries showcase local work. There's also a permanent collection of contemporary Australian art, concerts, films, and lectures. Free guided tours are offered every Sunday at 1:30pm. (☎5036 2430. Open Tu-F 10am-5pm, Sa-Su 11am-5pm. Free, donations suggested.)

Swan Hill is also proud of its **fishing.** That pride has resulted in the **Giant Murray Cod.** Towering over its living brethren, it is quite possibly the largest Murray Cod in the world. The statue measures 6m by 11m by 6m, and was originally built as a prop for the movie *Eight Ball.* It now guards the north end of the rail station on Curlewis St. The best fishing holes (mainly cod and carp) are 20 minutes away; ask for updates at the **Natural Resources and Environment** office, 324 Campbell St. (☎5033 1290. Open M-F 9am-5pm.) The NRE also has info on the town's **required fishing license** ($5 for 48hrs., $10 per month, $20 per year in Victoria).

Swan Hill has its share of outlying vineyards. **R.L. Buller and Son** is 14km north on the Murray Valley Hwy. (☎5037 6305. Open M-Sa 9am-5pm, school holidays and long weekends Su 10am-5pm.) **Best's St. Andrews** is to the south near Lake Boga. (☎5037 2154. Open M-F 9am-5pm, Sa 10am-4pm.) Both offer tastings.

MILDURA ☎ 03

With its wide, palm-lined streets and bustling riverside wharf, Mildura is an oasis in dry Mallee country. The cleverly harnessed waters of the Murray support thriving citrus groves and make Mildura one of Australia's most productive fruit-growing areas; as such, it attracts hordes of backpackers seeking itinerant work (the best time of year is Feb.-Mar., but every month except May is good). It's also one of the sunniest parts of Australia, and were it not for the massive irrigation system, the landscape would be as arid as the Outback that stretches to the horizon. Enjoy it while you're here; Mildura is the last bastion of green for a long, long time.

☐ TRANSPORTATION. The train and bus station is on 7th St., across from the northern end of Langtree Ave. **V/Line** runs to: Albury (10hr.; 1 per day Tu-W, F, and Su; $62); Echuca (5hr.; 1 per day Tu-W, F, and Su; $38); and Melbourne (7-9hr., 2-3 per day, $60.60) via Bendigo (5-7hr., $53) and Swan Hill (3-4hr., $32.30). **Countrylink** runs to Sydney (15hr., daily 4am, $110). **Tom Evans** coaches (☎5022 1415) services Broken Hill (3½hr.; M, W, and F 9am; $49).

☐☐ ORIENTATION AND PRACTICAL INFORMATION. Well-planned Mildura is laid out in a grid on the southern bank of the Murray. In the city center, 7th-10th St. run roughly east-west. They're encountered in numerical order, with 7th St. closest to the river. These cross the north-south avenues, from the westernmost Olive Ave. through Pine, Lime, Langtree, Deakin, and Madden Ave. The commercial center, the strip of Langtree Ave. from 7th to 10th St., includes a **pedestrian mall** from 8th to 9th where speakers blare endless elevator jazz.

Tourist Office: Mildura Visitor Information and Booking Centre, 180-190 Deakin Ave., on the corner of 12th St., is housed in the brilliant Alfred Deakin Centre; look for the silver tornado sculpture out front. (☎5021 4424; www.milduratourism.com. Open M-F 9am-5:30pm, Sa-Su 9am-5pm.)

Car Rental: All major companies are in the airport, 8km out of town on the Sturt Hwy., with rentals from $55-70 per day.

Work Opportunities: Ask for the thorough and free *Working Holiday and Backpacker Information Sheet* from the Visitors Center, or check with the **Mildura Harvest Labour Office** on Deakin Ave. near 10th St. (☎5021 1432. Open M-F 9am-5pm.) Work can often be found in the *Sunraysia Daily's* employment section.

Library: In the Visitors Center. Has free **Internet** access. (☎5023 5011; book ahead.)

Police: On Madden Ave. between 8th and 9th St. (☎5023 9555).

Post office: On the corner of 8th and Orange Ave., and in the Langtree Ave. Mall. Open M-F 9am-5pm. **Postal Code:** 3500.

☐ ACCOMMODATIONS. Most of Mildura's budget stays are backpackers designed with the migrant worker in mind. Basic rooms, work placement, and transport to work run about $18 per night ($100-110 per week). ☒**Riverboat Bungalow ❷,** 27 Chaffey Ave., near 7th St. A five-minute walk from the train station, this laid-back hostel is complete with a large aquarium and tropical decor throughout, bedrooms named after paddlesteamers, clean bathrooms, and a lounge area with free pool. Friendly guests bond through evenings by the backyard campfire and weekend canoe trips on the Murray. A second bungalow is now at 206 8th St, offering the same amenities plus swimming pool. (☎5021 5315. Linens and cutlery included. Internet $5 per hr. Dorms $18, weekly $110. VIP.) **NOMADS Mildura International Backpackers ❶,** 5 Cedar Ave., off 11th St., has two full kitchens and two lounge areas. (☎/fax 5021 0133. Dorms $13, weekly $110.) **Riviera Motel ❶,** 157 7th St. (☎5023 3696. Reception from 4pm. 4-bunk ensuites $15, weekly $85.)

▮▮ **FOOD AND NIGHTLIFE.** Mildura's restaurants are surprisingly varied. The **Langtree Avenue Mall,** one block west of Deakin Ave. between 8th and 9th St., has a few cheap takeaways, while the strip of Langtree between 7th and 8th St. is a veritable international bazaar. **Fasta Pasta ❷,** 30 Langtree Ave., serves up delicious gourmet-tasting pastas ($7-13), pizzas ($10-15), and vegetarian options at reasonable prices. (☎5022 0622. Open M-Sa 11:30am-3pm and 5-10pm, Su 11:30am-3pm and 5-9:30pm.) **Siam Palace ❶,** 35 Langtree Ave., serves Chinese and Thai dishes. The steal is the $5 lunch and dinner special, which offers a choice of dishes with steamed rice. (☎5023 7737. Open Su-Th 5:30-10pm, F-Sa noon-2pm and 5:30-late.) A 24hr. Coles **supermarket** is at the corner of 8th St. and Lime Ave. A few nightclubs are at 8th St. and Langtree Ave. The **Sandbar** warms the chilliest of winter nights with its tropical motif. (☎5021 2181. Happy Hour daily 5-8pm; W-Sa live bands 10:30pm. Open Tu noon-midnight, W-Sa noon-3am. Cover $5 F-Sa after 10pm.)

▣ **SIGHTS.** Mildura is the base camp for nearby national parks and the outback. The **Visitors Center** has info and booking all the commercial tours. For nearly 30 years, Tom Evans has been running tours in the Mildura area, bringing his encyclopedic knowledge on his **Junction Tours** (☎5027 4309) to Mungo National Park (see p. 234; W, F, and Su $66); local hotspots (Tu, Th, and Sa; $50-68); or Broken Hill (Su-Tu, 3 days and 2 nights of camping for $462). **Harry Nanya Tours** runs half- and full-day trips focusing on Aboriginal history and the Dreaming. (☎5027 2076 or 1800 630 864; www.harrynanyatours.com.au. Mungo: $60, concessions $52, families $132. Wentworth: 2 per day; half-day $27.50, $22, $66; full-day $55, $52, $132. Canoe tours: 5hr. $55, overnight with camping $155 per night.) A new company, **Jumbunna,** runs trips to Mungo as well as a Mildura nature walk. These tours are guided by an Aboriginal guide and focus on tribal culture and the outback. (☎0412 581 699. Day-tour $64, concessions $60, children $30, families $160.)

The 1881 paddlewheeler **Rothbury** cruises to Trentham Estate winery. (☎5023 2200. 5hr., Th 10:30am, $46, children 5-14 $20. Evening cruise with dinner and live entertainment, 3hr.; Th 7pm, $20; book ahead.) Of the seven local wineries in the immediate area, the most internationally famous is **Lindemans,** on Edey Road in Karadoc. To get there, you'll most likely need a car; drive from Mildura through Red Cliffs, then look for the signs. (☎5051 3285. Open daily 10am-4:30pm.)

HUME CORRIDOR

The Hume Hwy. links Melbourne and Sydney, shuttling visitors 872km through relatively unspectacular scenery. However, those intrepid travelers who venture an hour or two off the Hume are rewarded with beautiful mountain vistas and powdery ski slopes, world-class wineries, the legend of folk hero Ned Kelly come alive in Glenrowan, dusty hamlets, and quietly inviting country towns. Farther west along the Murray Valley Hwy., in Yarrawonga and Cobram, the Murray's sun-drenched banks lend themselves well to fishing, swimming, and snoozing. Across the river, the Hume continues north, winding its way through New South Wales.

MARYSVILLE AND LAKE MOUNTAIN ☎03

A small town only one and a half hours northeast of Melbourne, Marysville is best known as the closest town (22km) to cross-country ski mecca Lake Mountain. **The Mystic Mountains Tourist Information Centre,** on Marysville's main drag, Murchison St., posts Lake Mountain snow reports and road conditions, and provides informa-

FROM THE ROAD

THE DROP BEAR

Kangaroos, emus, and drop bears, oh my! Australia is known for its unique flora and fauna, and nearly every first-time visitor to Australia will crane their heads in eager anticipation of an encounter with one of the country's native animals. Aussies will warn you about the dangers of a kangaroo encounter ('roos can rip your stomach open with their powerful hind feet) or of getting too close to one of the country's deadly snakes. They might also warn you of the drop bear, a carnivorous version of the cuddly koala. But before you start smearing yeast by-products all over your face, read between the lines.

Drop bears are bigger and darker than koalas, with squinty eyes and hearts of evil. They spend their days perched in trees, waiting patiently for a human to walk by. When one does, they drop out the trees, latch onto the human's head, and begin to feed. Many Aussies wear *akubra* hats made of rabbit (it is a well-known Aussie fact that drop bears hate the taste of rabbit). Another Aussie secret is to put Vegemite, that ever-useful yeasty delicacy, behind one's ears—drop bears, like many others, hate the taste of Vegemite.

This fearsome creature is entirely fictional, but they definitely got me on this one.

—Megan Creydt

tion on accommodations. (☎5963 4567; www.mmtourism.com.au. Open daily 9am-5pm.) For local **snow and road conditions,** call ☎5963 3205 or check www.snowreport.vic.gov.au.

While the area's best lodging lies 21km up the road at Taggerty's Australian Bush Settlement (see below), the **Marysville Caravan Park ❷,** on Buxton Rd., is by the Steavenson River at the end of Murchison St. (☎5963 3443. Sites for 2 from $16, powered from $19; caravans from $52; cabins from $47; prices rise in-season. MC/V.) For quick and cheap eats, check out the **Marysville Country Bakery ❶,** on the corner of Murchison St. and Pack Rd. (☎5963 3477. Open daily 7am-6pm. Sandwiches $2-5, pies and pasties $3-4.)

The 31km of regularly groomed cross-country **ski trails** at Lake Mountain are packed in-season (entry fee $20; trail fee $10, children $5). Take the Maroondah Hwy. (Hwy. 34) to Woods Point Rd. (Hwy. 172). **Chains** are required for the drive up Lake Mountain during winter. Back in Marysville, local shops rent skis, skates, toboggans, chains, and outerwear; just about everything is under $30. One of Victoria's highest waterfalls is out in the bush near Marysville: **Steavenson Falls,** 4km down Falls Rd., is illuminated nightly by its own hydroelectric power. A 30min. ascent to the top of a nearby peak gives a great view of the falls and leads to a 40min. trail downhill through the town.

The real highlight of the Marysville is ■**Bruno's Art and Sculpture Garden,** 51 Falls Rd. (hang a right by the bakery off Murchison St.). Inside Bruno's home is an extensive collection of paintings and collages; outside is a lush garden generously adorned with Bruno's sculptures. Often whimsical, the subtle creations are powerfully expressive and show great imagination. (☎5963 3513. Garden open daily 10am-5pm. Gallery open Sa-Su 10am-5pm. Gallery and garden $5, ages 12-16 $2; garden alone $3; under 12 free.)

NEAR MARYSVILLE: TAGGERTY AUSTRALIAN BUSH SETTLEMENT

Taggerty is 104km northeast of Melbourne on the Maroondah Hwy. (Hwy. 34), 4km after Buxton. If you ask, the V/Line **bus** from Melbourne to Eildon will also stop at Taggerty at the 104km marker of the Maroondah Hwy. (daily 3pm, $14). The ■**Taggerty Australian Bush Settlement ❷** (☎5774 7378; www.green.net.au/australian_bush_settlement) provides a splendid stay, whether you plan to spend a night or several months. The 80-acre farm, near the Cathedral Range National Park (on the right off the highway heading from Marysville to Taggerty), simulates an early pioneer village. The host, Bronwyn Rayner, is the embodiment of selfless sacrifice. She has operated Taggerty for more than 20 years, building it into a combination hostel, campsite, working farm, classroom, museum, and youth development facility. Rayner cultivates an organic vegetable garden and cares for a variety of unwanted, misfit, or orphaned animals ranging from sheep and horses to wombats and kangaroos. Guests and visitors can interact with the animals, and the working farm and bush settlement serve as a backdrop for educational programs run for both standard classrooms as well as at-risk kids. Taggerty also houses an extensive collection of 19th-century bush memorabilia, including costumes, carriages, and an 1853 Norwegian slab hut. Bronwyn's latest inspiration is environment-friendly housing, and she hopes to devote a portion of the Settlement property to developing environmentally sustainable buildings and farming.

Lodging comes in four degrees of comfort and privacy: sites ($10 per person); small, rustic cabins ($20); the hostel-like lodge ($20); and the homestead. The cream of the crop, the homestead is the richly decorated recipient of *Home Beautiful*'s 1990 Home of the Year and Design of the Year. A private double room with king-size bed and classic free-standing bath is luxurious ($70); in the next room, the "opium bed" by the fireplace is less private but an interesting experience ($25). Room and board may be available in exchange for work on the farm—call ahead to arrange a meeting. All lodgings come with excellent kitchen and toilet facilities in-room or nearby, and all prices include continental breakfast—and most likely both tea and company from Rayner and those in her care.

MANSFIELD ☎ 03

Mansfield's *raison d'être* is its proximity to Mt. Buller, allowing tourists to stop and rent skis and chains before making the 45km ascent to Victoria's most popular ski resort. The **Mansfield Passenger Terminal** is at 137 High St. **V/Line buses** (☎ 13 61 96) serve Melbourne (3hr., 1-3 per day, $30) and Mt. Buller (1hr., 2-3 per day, $34 round-trip) during ski season. For $104, V/Line will take you round-trip from Melbourne to Mt. Buller; this price includes snow fees. Law requires all vehicles heading to Mt. Buller to carry **snow chains** from the Queen's Birthday weekend (June 6-9, 2003) until the end of the ski season. You can leave them in the trunk, but there are spot checks and hefty fines for not carrying them at all.

The **Mansfield Visitors Centre** is just out of town at 167 Maroondah Hwy. (☎ 5775 1464, bookings 1800 039 049; reservations@mansfield-mtbuller.com.au. Open daily 9am-5pm.) Heading east into town on **High St.**, the town's main drag, you'll find ski rental places and a few **ATMs**. The **library**, at the corner of High and Collopy St., has **Internet;** you must fill out a form, even for one-time use. (☎ 5775 2176. Open Tu 2-8pm, W 9:30am-1pm, Th-F 9:30am-5:30pm, Sa 9:30am-noon. $2 per 30min.) The **post office** is at 90 High St. (☎ 5775 2248. Open M-F 9am-5pm.) **Postal Code:** 3722.

Ski Centre Mansfield, 131 High St. (☎ 5775 2859 or 1800 647 754), and its nearby affiliate, **PJ's Ski Hire,** 149 High St. (☎ 5775 1624), rent chains (full-day $15) and a wide range of ski equipment and clothing. (Open June-Oct. Sa-Th 6am-7pm, F 6am-midnight.) There are similar ski hire joints all along High St. Shopping around is easy, but they all offer comparable deals (full-day skis, boots, and poles $25-30; snowboard and boots $45-50).

The best budget beds in town are at the ⊠**Mansfield Backpackers Inn ❷,** 116 High St., part of the Mansfield Travellers Lodge. The friendly new owners keep the place clean and comfortable, and provide a kitchen, lockers, TV, and a pool table. (☎ 5775 1800; travlodge@cnl.com.au. Book 1-2 weeks ahead. Reception 24hr. Dorms $20-23; singles $54-60; doubles $66-85; families $115-135.) The **Commercial Hotel ❸,** one of the pubs near the intersection of High and Highett St., offers simple lodging with shared bath. (☎ 5775 2046. Singles $30; doubles $50; includes continental breakfast.) For cheap, good eats, try the **Ski Inn Cafe ❶,** 61 High St., which

**IN
RECENT
NEWS**

INSURANCE CRISIS

The litigation and insurance frenzy characteristic of the United States has hit Australia, causing real (and often exaggerated) changes to tourism. In just the past year, insurance rates for activities such as horseback riding and rock climbing have sky-rocketed (one adventure operator reported his rates to be four times higher than those of only a year ago). This has meant that many operators unable to afford such rates are temporarily out of business.

The crisis has affected those outside the adventure tourism arena as well. National Parks tours have had to undergo evaluation and subsequent implementation of new safety restrictions. Likewise, farms and wineries that previously offered guests opportunities to explore their premises or pet animals have also had to discontinue those services.

Some changes seem a bit more panic-based than necessary; many building owners now post signs asking patrons to keep children from playing on or near the buildings for fear of litigation should there be an injury.

With initiatives under way, it seems to some that it will only be a matter of time until this insurance crisis is remedied. Many are skeptical, however, and worry that this crisis signals a more permanent change in the Australian tourism industry. Improvements may be made, and the industry brought back from its crippled condition, but with the constant threat of litigation, it will never fully return to its once easygoing, trust-based nature.

offers tasty chicken breast burgers ($5), a range of fish and chips options, and pastries. (☎ 5775 2175. Open 6am-9pm.) For quality fresh produce, stop by the **Mansfield Fruit Palace,** 68 High St. (☎ 5775 2239. Open M-F 8:30am-6pm, Sa 8am-2pm.) There are two **supermarkets: Foodworks,** 12 Highett St. (☎ 5775 2255), and **IGA,** 47 High St. (☎ 5775 2014). Both are open daily 8am-8pm.

MOUNT BULLER   ☎ 03

Victoria's largest ski resort, Mt. Buller is a three hour drive from Melbourne, with arguably the best terrain in Victoria. Though it's not the Alps or Rockies, it's a mecca for Aussie skiers and snowboarders from mid-June through early October.

⌨ TRANSPORTATION AND PRACTICAL INFORMATION. Along with **V/Line** (see Mansfield), **Mansfield-Mount Buller Bus Lines** (☎ 5775 2606) operates coach service to Mt. Buller from Mansfield. (1hr., 6-8 per day, $34.) **Snowcaper Tours** departs from Melbourne and offers tour packages that include return transport, entrance fees, and a full-day lift ticket. Participants leave Melbourne at 4am and return by 9:30pm. (☎ 5775 2367, reservations 1800 033 023. Mid-week $110, Sa-Su $120.) All buses pull into the **Cow Camp Plaza,** in the center of Mt. Buller village.

If going by car, bring **snow chains** (it's the law) and take Hwy. 164 (Buller Rd.) east to Mt. Buller. (Car admission $20 per day; overnight fee Su-Th $3.30 per night, F-Sa $6.60 per night.) Free parking is on the side of the mountain. To get to the village from the parking lot, visitors without luggage can take a free shuttle; those with luggage must take a taxi ($10). Beware: all these daily charges add up fast. Consider taking the bus, especially if you're staying on the mountain for a while.

The village is the hub of accommodation, food, and ski services. The Cow Camp Plaza houses lockers, restaurants, phones, ATMs, and **Cow Camp Alpine Ski Rentals.** (☎ 5775 6082. Skis, boots, and poles $28; snowboard and boots $40-45.) The **Information Centre,** in a tower opposite the plaza, has maps of the resort and slopes, as well as info on work and long-term accommodations options. (☎ 5777 7600, reservations 1800 039 049; reservations@mansfield-mtbuller.com.au. Open during ski season daily 8:30am-5pm; in summer, visit the post office.) The **lift ticket office** sits across the village center from the info tower. (☎ 5777 6052. Day pass $60, weekend $70.) For the latest **snow conditions,** call the Official Victorian Snow Report (☎ 1902 240 523. 24hr. 55¢ per min.); visit www.vicsnowreport.com.au or www.mtbuller.com; tune into 93.7FM; or check the local ski shop. La Trobe University has **Internet** at the Reception Office, Level 5, on New Summit Rd. (☎5733 7080. $4 per 30min.) The Resort Management Building in the village center has a **post office.** (☎5777 6013. Open daily 8:30am-5pm.) **Postal Code:** 3723.

ACCOMMODATIONS, FOOD, AND NIGHTLIFE. The **Mount Buller YHA Hostel Lodge ❹** is the least expensive lodging on the mountain, and you can literally ski to its front door. The dorms are well-heated. (☎5777 6181. Book at least 3 weeks ahead July-Aug. Ski lockers available. Reception daily 8-10am and 5-10pm. Dorms $55, YHA $50. 20% discount during Winterfest in mid-June.) Next door to the YHA, the **Kooroora Hotel ❺** has more intimate four-person dorms with showers. There is a 15% guest discount for on-site ski hire. (☎5777 6050; kooroora@big-pond.com. Open only during ski season. Reservations require a 50% deposit. 18+ only. Dorms M-Th $70, F-Su $80.)

ABOM ❶, on Summit St., couldn't be further from its full name (Abominable). Despite the menacing polar bear lurking next to the doorway, this European-style resort is the perfect refuge from the cold with affordable bistro fare. (☎5777 6091. Pizza slice $5, toasted sandwich $4.) The **Cow Camp Plaza** houses two upstairs eateries. The **Pancake Parlour and Skiosk ❶** (☎5777 6503) serves up typical short stacks ($6), delicious varieties like Hot Bavarian Apple and Jamaican Banana ($10), and plain fast food (hot dogs $5). Both are open from 8 or 9am until late; hours depend on crowds.

Kooroora's Pub is hands-down the place to go for nightlife; besides a great atmosphere, it's the only place on the mountain regularly open past midnight. Bands (Sa) and DJs (every other night) rage until 3am; its kitchen is open until 10pm. **Mooseheads Bar,** downstairs at the ABOM, caters to a more laid-back, couch-lounging crowd. With the cheapest spirits on the mountain ($5), the Happy Hour from 4-6pm might just be the happiest time to visit. (Open 5pm-2am.)

SKIING. Intermediate runs dominate, but several expert trails are sprinkled on the southern slopes. On the south face, **Fanny's Finish** and **Chute 1, 2, and 3** separate the skiers from the snowbunnies. First-time skiers have plenty of long runs to choose from, as well as numerous lesson packages. The lift capacity is excellent and lift lines are usually not long. Those ready for an aerobic challenge will find 75km of cross-country skiing trails (30km groomed) and an entire mountain, **Mt. Stirling,** set aside for their use. (Resort management ☎0419 514 655; information 5777 6532; ticket office 5777 5625. Open during daylight. No overnight accommodations on the mountain except camping.) The **Information Centre** (next to the carparks) contains information, a public shelter with fireplace, ski and toboggan hire, and food. (Car entry $20; trail $8.80; cross-country ski hire $33; telemark $45.)

MOUNTAIN BIKING AND HIKING. In the summer, a plethora of tracks and lift access to the top make mountain biking is the thing to do at Buller. Lifts operate daily from December 26 to the end of January, then on long weekends until Easter. Cheaper biking without a chairlift is possible, as are free hikes. The **Summit Walk** (1½hr. return, moderate), beginning and ending at the clock tower, rewards hikers with views of the High Country below. Popular with mountain bikers, a longer hike to **Mount Stirling via Corn Hill and Howqua Gap** (5-7hr. return, moderate) offers a grand perspective of Mt. Buller. The info center has maps and details.

WANGARATTA ☎03

Referred to endearingly as "Wang" by locals, Wangaratta (pop. 25,000) is a quiet, river-strewn neighborhood seated conveniently at the junction of the Hume Hwy.

and the Great Alpine Road. Though the town has few tourist attractions, it can be a suitable base for exploring Victoria's alpine country and nearby vineyards.

⌨🖳 TRANSPORTATION AND PRACTICAL INFORMATION. V/Line (☎13 61 96) runs from the station on Norton St. to: Melbourne (2½hr., 3 per day, $33.10); Albury (1hr., 3 per day, $11); Wodonga (1hr., 3 per day, $8.40); Bright (1½hr., 1 or 2 per day, $11); and Rutherglen (30min., 1 per day, $4.80). Countrylink runs to Sydney (9hr., 2 per day, $90.20).

The Hume Hwy. from Melbourne runs into town as Tone Rd., becoming Ryley St., then **Murphy St.** for the stretch through the city center. Murphy intersects Ford, Ely, Reid, and Faithfull St. as it runs northeast. **Ovens St.** runs parallel to and northwest of Murphy St. The **Visitors Center** is on Tone Rd. 1km southwest of the city center. (☎5721 5711 or 1800 801 065. Open daily 9am-5pm.) The **library,** 62 Ovens St., has **Internet.** (☎5721 2366. Book ahead. Open M-Tu and Th-F 9:30am-6pm; W 9:30am-8pm; Su 9am-noon. $2 per 30min. Max. 1hr.) The **post office** is at the intersection of Murphy and Ely St. (Open M-F 9am-5pm.) **Postal Code:** 3677.

🖳🖰 ACCOMMODATIONS AND FOOD. The **Billabong Motel ❸,** 12 Chisholm St., at the end of Reid and a block east from Murphy St., has basic heated rooms with linens and TV. (☎5721 2353. Singles $30, ensuite $35; doubles $40-45.) **Wangaratta Backpackers ❷** is 5km north of town on the Old Hume Hwy., making them difficult to reach without car. (☎5721 2624. Dorms $18, linens included.) Across the Ovens River on Pinkerton, just north of Faithfull St., is **Painters Island Caravan Park ❶.** (☎5721 3380. Reception 8am-8pm. Sites $7.50 per person, powered for 2 $17.60; on-site caravans $33; cabins $44, ensuite $55.)

🖫**Scribbler's Cafe ❶,** 66 Reid St., has cheap deluxe sandwiches ($7-9), veggie options, and cuisine from around the globe. (☎5721 3945. Open daily 8am-5:45pm. Kitchen closes around 5pm. BYO. AmEx/MC/V.) **Vespa's Cafe ❸,** at Reid and Ovens St., has a bar specializing in local wine, a delightfully eclectic menu, and themed event nights once a month. (☎5722 4392. Open Tu-Th 9:30am-10:30pm, F-Sa 9:30am-midnight. Entrees around $10, mains $19. MC/V.) Safeway **supermarket** is on Ovens St. between Reid and Ford St. (open daily 7am-midnight), and Coles 24hr. supermarket is on Tone Rd., south of the city center.

◨ SIGHTS AND WINERIES. The best day trip is 15km southeast via Oxley Flats Rd. at the **Milawa Gourmet Region.** The classy **Brown Brothers Vineyard,** on Snow Rd., could sate a small nation with its five tasting bars. Every course at its Epicurean Centre restaurant includes its own accompanying wine. (☎5720 5500. Open daily 9am-5pm; restaurant open daily 11am-3pm.) Around the corner on Factory Rd., the 🖫**Milawa Cheese Factory** has free samples of gourmet cheeses handmade from the milk of local goats, ewes, and cows. (☎5727 3588. Open daily 9am-5pm.)

Back in Wang, **Kaluna Park** (☎5751 1238) offers ample space for picnic and play just east of Murphy St. Visitors can bike, hike, or ride horses on the **"Murray to the Mountains Rail Trail."** The 94km paved trail follows historical railway lines and passes through Bowser, Beechworth, and Myrtleford all the way to Bright. Wangaratta's renowned **jazz festival** (☎5722 1666 or 1800 803 944; www.wangaratta-jazz.org.au), the first weekend of November, ranks among Australia's best; accommodations can be booked out as early as June.

Just up the Hume Hwy. (Hwy. 31), nearby Glenrowan is where folk hero/notorious bushranger Ned Kelly was finally corralled. Its prime attraction is the $2.5 million animatronic **Ned Kelly's Last Stand,** a corny, cultish narrative presentation—entertaining to kids and at least appreciated by adults. (At the **Glenrowan Tourist Centre.** ☎5766 2367. Daily every 30min. 9:30am-4:30pm. $16, concessions $14, ages

5-15 $10, families $45.) Next door is the **Ned Kelly Memorial Museum and Homestead** (☎5766 2448. $3.50, children $1.)

RUTHERGLEN   ☎02

At the heart of Victoria's most renowned wine region, Rutherglen is an excellent base for touring the surrounding wineries. The Murray Valley Hwy. (Hwy. 16), called Main St. in Rutherglen, runs from Yarrawonga (45km west) through Rutherglen to Albury (50km east). **V/Line buses** leave Rutherglen's BP service station for Melbourne via Wangaratta (3½hr.; M, W, and F 6:35am; $39). Purchase tickets from the news agency on Main St. **Webster** Bus Service shuttles to Albury at 9:30am on weekdays from the BP station west of the city center (☎6033 2459; $7). The **tourist office**, in the Jolimont Cellar building on the corner of Drummond and Main St., is the place to go for a potentially dangerous combination of winery literature and bicycle hire. (☎6032 9166 or 1800 622 871. Open daily 9am-5pm. One-day rental, including helmet, pump, and bottled water $22.) The **post office** is at 83 Main St.

The **Victoria Hotel ❸**, 90 Main St., offers cozy budget rooms with heaters, electric blankets, linens, towels, and breakfast. (☎6032 8610. Singles and twins $30 per person; doubles $55, ensuite $66. Third night free if you stay 2 nights Su-Th. MC/V.) **Rutherglen Caravan Park ❶**, 72 Murray St., has tent space as well as luxurious cabins by the lake. (☎6032 8577; rutherglencvanpark@iprimus.com.au. Sites for 2 $13, powered $16.50; fully-furnished cabins $40-75. Wheelchair accessible. MC/V.)

For a real treat, eat at **Parker Pies ❶** (formerly the Rutherglen Tea Rooms), 86-88 Main St. Their chicken, cheese, ham, and mustard pie was voted best chicken pie in Australia in 2000; the ultra-friendly staff deserves national recognition as well. (☎6032 9605. Pie $5, with large plate of pasta, chips, and potato salad $10.) The IGA **supermarket**, 95 Main St., caters to all your budget needs. (☎6032 9232. Open M-W 7:30am-7pm, Th-F 7:30am-7:30pm, Sa 7:30am-7pm, Su 8:30am-6pm.)

The quiet hamlet of Corowa is just 10km northwest of Rutherglen in NSW and is best noted as a great place for jumping out of planes. **Skydive Corowa**, at the Aerodrome 2km west of town, has many jumps and, for serious beginners, a certification course. Licensed jumpers pay dirt-cheap rates according to altitude. (☎6033 2435 or 1800 446 448. Tandem jump $299; static line full-day training and next-day jump $310; accelerated free-fall full-day training and next-day jump $460; licensed jumpers $60, $30 with your own chute.)

NEAR RUTHERGLEN: THE WINERIES

Rutherglen's temperate climate allows vineyards to keep grapes on their vines longer, favoring full-bodied red wines and fortified varieties like Tokay and Muscat. Choosing from among the excellent local wineries can be quite difficult, especially since they all offer free tastings. For those traveling by car, the *Rutherglen Touring Guide*, available at the **Visitors Center** and most wineries, is an indispensable free map. Or grab a free *Muscat Trail Map* for help navigating by bike. For a campier tour, take a horse-drawn stagecoach from **Poachers Paradise Hotel**, 120 Main St. (☎6032 9502. Daily 10am and 1pm. Three wineries in 2hr. $15 per person, under 7 free. Bookings essential.) **Grapevine Getaways** designs tours based on individual interests and requests. Groups of 20 or more can arrange pick-up from just about anywhere, including Melbourne and Sydney. (☎6032 9224 or 0407 577 241; www.grapevinegetaways.com.au. From $30; bookings essential.) For more information on touring vineyards, see p. 471.

The Rutherglen vineyards sponsor several festivals throughout the year. The most popular is the carnival-like **Rutherglen Winery Walkabout** (on Queen's Birthday weekend) featuring food and entertainment at the estates and a street fair downtown. True connoisseurs would probably prefer to skip the big production and

VICTORIA

instead sample the impressive food and wine combinations during the **Tastes of Rutherglen** (Labor Day weekend in March).

 All Saints Estate (☎ 6033 1922; www.allsaintswine.com.au). Head northwest of Rutherglen via Corowa Rd., then north on All Saints Rd. If you're only going one place, go here. The most polished, tourist-oriented winery-going experience around. Confirms romantic visions of what wineries should look like, with towering elms lining the driveway, a red-brick castle tasting room, and a sculptured rose garden with central fountain. Marked self-guided tour past picture-perfect gardens, huge display casks, and a playground; pick up map from the cellar door. Peek into the **Chinese Dormitory and Gardens** on the grounds for a sense of early laborers' living conditions. Just behind the castle, the **Rutherglen Keg Factory** manufactures kegs and offers a number of kegs and wine racks for show or purchase. Free delivery to Rutherglen for cyclists. Winery open M-Sa 9am-5:30pm, Su 10am-5pm. Restaurant open Su-F 10am-5pm, Sa 10am-7pm; book ahead on weekends. Keg factory open M-Sa 9am-5pm, Su 10am-5pm. AmEx/DC/MC/V.

Cofield Wines (☎ 6033 3798), northwest of Rutherglen on Distillery Rd., just off Corowa Rd. Small and family-run. Signature bubbly, fantastic sparkling shiraz. Enormously popular **Pickled Sisters Cafe** next door. Cellar door open M-Sa 9am-5pm, Su 10am-5pm; cafe open M and W-Su 10am-4pm. AmEx/MC/V.

Chambers Rosewood Winery (☎ 6032 8641). An easy-to-miss building on Barkley St., 1km from the tourist office. Simple, unpretentious, easygoing tasting area gives no hint of the international praise lavished on its rare Tokays and Muscats. Open M-Sa 9am-5pm, Su 11am-5pm. MC/V.

Gehrig Estate (☎ 6026 7296), 22km east of town on the Murray Valley Hwy. Claims to be Victoria's oldest winery. Produces a wide range including excellent shiraz and durif. Open M-Sa 9am-5pm, Su 10am-5pm. AmEx/MC/V.

Fairfield Vineyard (☎ 6032 9381). Head east from Rutherglen on the Murray Valley Hwy. Idyllic old cellar building even better than their selection of wines. Open M-F 10am-4pm, Sa 10am-5pm. AmEx/DC/MC/V.

HIGH COUNTRY

Victoria's High Country, tucked between the Murray River and Gippsland's thick coastal forest, is a contrast to Australian sights like Surfers Paradise or the Red Centre. Ancient forests display dazzling autumn leaves, and rambling valleys nurture spring flowers in colors that only the rare sunset can capture. In winter, Mt. Hotham and Falls Creek offer the continent's best skiing. In summer, abseilers, climbers, and mountain bikers taunt the steep slopes and cliffs of Mt. Buffalo.

CHAIN ME. All vehicles heading into the mountains must carry tire chains from the Queen's Birthday (June 9, 2003) until October 1.

THE OWENS HIGHWAY TO ALPINE ROAD

BEECHWORTH ☎ 03

Beechworth, Victoria's best-preserved gold town, lies off the Owens Hwy. to the northeast. Traces of gold were discovered here in February 1852; miners swarmed to the area. By 1866, over 4.1 million ounces had been found. Today, visitors flock to Beechworth for museums, a "conversation" with Ned Kelly in the courthouse where he stood trial, or a treat from regionally renowned Beechworth Bakery.

The bus stop is on Camp St., just west of Ford St. **V/Line buses** (☎ 13 61 96) run to: Bright (1hr., 1-2 per day, $5); Melbourne (3-4hr., 1-4 per day, $39); and Wangaratta (35min., 1-6 per day, $5.50). **Wangaratta Coachlines** (☎ 5722 1843) runs on weekdays to Albury (1hr., 2 per day, $7.10), making stops in Yackandandah (15min., 2 per day, $3.50), Baranduda (30min., 2 per day, $7.10), and Wodonga (45min., 2 per day, $7.10). The **Visitors Center** (☎ 1300 366 321 or 5728 3233) is in Shire Hall on **Ford Street,** Beechworth's main north-south street.

Beechworth overflows with B&Bs. The info center can help you select an accommodation based on price, theme, or amenities. Centrally located **Tanswells Commercial Hotel ❸,** 30 Ford St., offers basic rooms with shared bath and a common lounge. (☎ 5728 1480. Singles $40; doubles $60.) The **Lake Sambell Caravan Park ❶** lies 1½km outside of town on Jarvis Rd. (☎ 5728 1421. Laundry, BBQ. Sites $15, powered $18; caravans for 4 $35; cabins for 4 $50.)

No one who prizes anything leavened should miss the award-winning ■**Beechworth Bakery ❶,** 27 Camp St. Tasty focaccias ($5-7), loaves (San Francisco sourdough $3.35), and desserts keep the crowds coming back. (☎ 5728 1132. Open daily 6am-7pm.) For a splurge, try **The Bank Restaurant ❺,** 86 Ford St. Situated in the old Bank of Australasia building (built in the 1850s), the dining rooms have 18-foot ceilings and beautiful period decor. Mains like beef wellington with bearnaise potatoes, baby leeks, and tarragon juice ($29) can be complemented by a variety of regional wines. (☎ 5728 2223. Open daily from 6:30pm, Su lunch from noon.)

Inquire at the info center about local **bike rentals** and 1½-hour **walking tours** of historic Beechworth. (Half-day bike rental $19. Tours daily 11am and 2pm; $10, concessions $8, children $5.) Behind the Visitors Center, on Loch St., the **Burke Museum** displays gold-rush era artifacts, the oldest and most comprehensive known collection Southwest Victorian Aboriginal weapons, and stuffed animal and bird specimens including the Thylacine, a now-extinct Tasmanian marsupial wolf. (☎ 5728 1420. Open daily 9am-5pm. $5.50, concessions $3.50, children $3.) At the Beechworth **cemetery,** north of the town center on Cemetery Rd., you'll find the **Chinese Burning Towers** and rows of simple headstones—reminders of the Chinese presence in gold-rush Beechworth. Chinese miners once outnumbered whites five to one, but their tight-packed graves testify to the discrimination they faced. Inside the **Beechworth Historic Court House,** 94 Ford St., the courtroom has been preserved in its 19th-century condition, right down to the dock where bushranger Ned Kelly stood during his trials and the cells in which he and his mother were (at separate times) detained. A soundscape system recreates the trial as you walk through. Watch out at the cells—Ned and his mother aren't too shy to speak to visitors. (☎ 5728 2721. Open daily 9am-5pm. $4, concessions $2.50, families $10.)

MOUNT BUFFALO NATIONAL PARK

Mt. Buffalo rises imposingly alongside the Great Alpine Rd., signaling the site of a rich sub-alpine ecosystem with plenty of outdoor adventure opportunities throughout the year. Founded in 1898, Mt. Buffalo is one of Australia's oldest national parks, and though its craggy walls may intimidate from afar, the gentle, heavily family-oriented ski slopes are mainly for beginner and intermediate skiers.

The **park entrance gate** (☎ 5756 2328) serves as the primary information source on site, though the actual **Parks Victoria Office** is 20km beyond the entry. (☎ 5755 1466 or 24hr. 13 19 63; fax 5755 1802. Open daily 8am-4pm; usually staffed M-F early mornings and late afternoons.) The entrance, 5km north of Bright (see p. 644), is just off the Great Alpine Rd. roundabout by Porepunkah. (Entrance fee $12.50, off-season $9; concessions half-price; guests of mountaintop lodging free.)

The clean, simple lines of the main lounge and bistro at the **Mt. Buffalo Lodge ❶,** 7km along the main road from the **Visitors Center,** overlook the slopes. (Mains $4-

10.) Inside, a ski shop serves both cross-country and downhill skiers. The rates are comparable to those in Bright (downhill package $29; 1½hr. ski lesson, lift pass, and equipment $72). Guests have access to laundry, a games room, a small bouldering wall, and a TV lounge. There is a **family unit ❺** with 16 beds, a kitchen, and shared facilities. (☎5755 1988 or 1800 037 038. Twin lodge units $90 per adult; family unit $750; less in off-season.) Great **campsites ❶** lie beside Lake Catani, 2km beyond the park office. Some are caravan-accessible, and there are toilets, water, hot showers, and a laundry basin. (Open Nov.-Apr. 6-person sites $12-24. Prices vary seasonally; book at the entrance station.)

Lift passes are available for the **Cresta Valley site** adjacent to the Mt. Buffalo Lodge. (Half day $45; 2-day $92; ages 8-15 $34 per day. Lift ticket and lesson package $72, under 16 $55.) In the park, 11km of groomed (and two more ungroomed) cross-country ski trails lie across the road from the Mt. Buffalo Lodge parking lot at Cresta Valley. There's no fee for cross-country skiing; ask for the information sheet at the entrance gate. (On-site rental of cross-country skis and boots $16 per day.) The dramatic mountain road up the flanks of Mt. Buffalo winds through dense eucalypt forests, obscuring whatever surprises lurk around the next hairpin turn. Occasional views of thrilling **waterfalls** plunging over sheer cliffs into deep gorges punctuate the drive. Within the park are some spectacular lookouts as well as numerous walking tracks. The most challenging hike is **The Big Walk** (11.3km; 4-5hr. from Park Entrance to the Gorge Day Visitor Area). It ascends over 1000m in only 9km as it climbs the plateau. The **Eurobin Falls** track (1½km; 45min. return) is much shorter, with a trailhead approximately 2km past the park entrance. Beginning with an amble and ending in a steep clamber, the walk features spectacular views of the falls careening down the bare rock. At the top of the mountain, adjacent to the Mt. Buffalo Chalet, **Bent's Lookout** dazzles with a panoramic sweep across the Buckland Valley. On clear days, **Mount Kosciuzsko** is visible. Driving past the park office toward the Mt. Buffalo Lodge, you'll see numerous marked walking trails. The steep but relatively short **Monolith Track,** across from the park office, leads to a precariously balanced granite monolith and is definitely worth the effort (1.8km; 1hr. circuit).

Mt. Buffalo's warm-weather activities are as popular as its winter ones. Abseilers go over the edge near Bent's Lookout year-round. The **Mount Buffalo Chalet Activities Centre** (☎5755 1500; www.mtbuffalochalet.com.au) runs rock climbing, caving, and rugged mountaineering expeditions. The climbing on the north wall of the Gorge is world-renowned. The site of the 1986 World Championships, Mt. Buffalo's hang-gliding excels. Lake Catani is a small man-made lake perfect for swimming, fishing, and canoeing; its surroundings also provide good bushwalking.

BRIGHT   ☎03

While it's primarily a base for winter skiing at Mt. Hotham, Falls Creek, and Mt. Buffalo, Bright is an apt name for this town of radiant natural beauty and glowing hospitality. Excellent budget accommodations and proximity to snowfields, wineries, and larger cities make Bright a great base for outdoor extravaganzas.

Bright is 79km southeast of Wangaratta along the **Great Alpine Rd.** (renamed **Gavan St.** while in town). The town center lies hidden off the highway behind a roundabout with an Art Deco clock tower. Both **Barnard** and **Anderson St.** link the main drag, **Ireland St.,** with Gavan St. The **Bright Visitor Centre** is at 119 Gavan St. (☎5755 2275 or 1800 500 117; bright@dragnet.com.au. Open daily 8:30am-5pm.) Public transportation in and out of Bright is limited and expensive, so having a car helps. However, **V/Line** (☎13 61 96) serves Melbourne (4½hr., 1-2 per day, $44) and Wangaratta (1½hr., 1-2 per day, $11).

Bright's centrally located backpacker accommodation is the ⬛**Bright Hikers Backpackers Hostel (VIP) ❷**, 4 Ireland St. on the second floor, across from the post office. Guests can borrow a limited selection of snow chains and skiing gear. Kitchen, dorms, and bathrooms are sparklingly clean. (☎5750 1244; hikers@netc.net.au. Linens $3. Suspension mountain bikes $10 per 2hr., $1 per additional hr. Internet $2.50 per 10min. Reception 9am-10pm. Dorms $19, weekly from $105; doubles $37/$245.) The **Bright & Alpine Backpackers ❶**, 106 Coronation Ave., is five minutes outside town; follow the Great Alpine Way east past the info center, turn sharply right onto Hawthorne St. then left onto Coronation St. The backpackers is on the right, just before the small bridge. The facility is filled with nostalgia but does show its age. (☎5755 1154. Kitchen, laundry. Linens $5. Reception 24hr. Sites $8, powered $9; singles $16; doubles $30.)

Gear shops and businesses cater to adrenaline junkies. At the center of town, a handful of ski-hire establishments will outfit you with ski and snowboard equipment, snow chains, and clothing. **Adina Ski Hire**, 15 Ireland St., offers both new and used budget skis for rent. (www.adina.com.au. Open Su-Th and Sa 7am-7pm, F 7am-late. Downhill skis, boots and poles $39 per day, $115 per week; budget $29/$86; snowboard and boots $50/$125. Deposit required. 20% YHA discount.) **Bright Ski Centre**, 22 Ireland St. (☎5755 1093), and **JD's for Skis** (☎5755 1557), on the corner of Burke and Anderson St., offer similar services and hours.

Warm thermal air currents make the valleys surrounding Bright ideal for hanggliding and paragliding—the area was home to the 1986 World Championships. **Alpine Paragliding**, 6 Ireland St., next to Bright Hikers, offers intro flights as well as advanced options and licensing courses. (☎5755 1753. From $130.) **Bright Microlights** (☎5750 1555) offers a 15min. introductory "Bright Flight" ($95). Their 20min. "Mt. Buffalo Flight" takes you over the gorge and then glides back to earth ($125).

The local ranges are perfect for mountain biking during warm, dry weather. **CyclePath Adventures**, 9 Camp St. (☎5750 1442 or 0427 501 442; www.cyclepath.com.au), has customized and fully supported one- to five-day high-country, singletrack, and food and wine gourmet bike tours. **Adventure Guides Australia** (☎5728 1804 or 0419 280 614) conducts full-day abseiling from $120, single and multi-day caving trips from $140, full-day rock climbing from $140, and bushwalking and camping excursions. All but rock-climbing are year-round, though they're all subject to weather and are more sporadic in winter.

MOUNT HOTHAM

With Victoria's highest average snowfall, 13 lifts, and a partnership with nearby Falls Creek (see p. 646), Mount Hotham is Victoria's intermediate and advanced skiing and snowboarding headquarters. Mt. Hotham is considered the hottest place in Victoria for all thrill-seekers, but it is held in especially high regard by **snowboarders.** The slopes are more challenging than in the rest of Australia, with short but steep double black diamonds cutting through the trees in the **"Extreme Skiing Zone."** Beginner skiing is limited, though lessons are available. With a constant stream of uni groups filling club lodges in the ski season, the mountain is a little younger and a little more hip than nearby Falls Creek, though *après*-ski offerings are more or less on par with its rival. In the summer, Hotham is relatively quiet, with nature trails and a few shops and lodgings open for visitors.

From the north, Mt. Hotham is accessible in the winter by a sealed road. Entrance from Omeo to the south is safer and more reliable, but inconvenient for those in Melbourne or Sydney. To get to Mt. Hotham by **bus,** depart from Melbourne's Spencer St. Station (6¼hr., 1 per day, $115 return); Wangaratta Railway Station (3¼hr., 1 per day, $80 return); or Bright's Alpine Hotel (1½hr., 2 per day,

$35 return). There is an extra bus each Friday. Contact **Trekset Tours** (☎9370 9055 or 1800 659 009; www.mthothambus.com.au) to book.

 Info on current road, weather, and slope conditions is available at ski rental shops and local-area accommodations, online at www.hotham.net.au, and at ☎1902 240 523 (all Victorian Resorts) or 1902 240 644 (Mt. Hotham and Falls Creek) for a 50¢ per minute fee.

There's a fee to enter the resort, payable at the tollbooth 1½hr. from Bright on the Great Alpine Rd., though it is waived if you're just driving through without stopping. (Cars 3hr. $12; 1-day and 1-night $23; 2-day and 2-night $46; season pass $250; lift tickets not included.) From mid-October to the Queen's Birthday in June (June 9, 2003), resort admission is free. Drivers heading from Bright can rent mandatory **snow chains** from **Hoy's A-Frame Ski Centre**, on the right just after the school bridge in Harrietville. (☎5759 2658. $27, deposit $50.) These can be returned to the BP **petrol station** in Omeo, on the south side of Mt. Hotham.

The resort is constructed around the Great Alpine Rd., which climbs the mountain. The lodges cluster to the south, with ski lifts and services farther north. Village buses transport folks for free around the resort. The **Visitors Center** (☎5759 3550; www.mthotham.net.au) is on the first floor of the Resort Management building, just above the Corral carpark. Directly across the street, Hotham Central houses the **Snowsports School office** (☎5759 4444), ski rental places (downhill package $27; snowboard and boots $55), a small **grocery store**, and a **lift ticket** office, which sells passes valid both here and at Falls Creek. (Full-day ticket $62-78, children $35-40; lift and lesson packages from $89.) Tickets for round-trip **helicopter rides** to Falls Creek are $96 with a valid lift ticket or $99 without. Trips must be booked in person on the day of travel. The Big D lift hosts night skiing from late June to October. (Open W and Sa 6:30-9:30pm. With lift ticket $6, without $11.)

Lodging on Mt. Hotham is pricey, and Bright's excellent hostels offer an inexpensive alternative. **Mount Hotham Accommodation Service** (☎5759 3636) can sometimes place you in a club lodge cheaply. The **Summit bar ❶**, in the Snowbird Inn, features outstanding views, live bands (Th and Sa), happening crowds, and five-drink jugs for $7.50 from 4:30-6:30pm. (☎5759 3503. Open daily 3:30pm-2am.)

FALLS CREEK ☎03

An hour's drive from Bright along roads with sweeping views of the Victorian Alpine country, **Falls Creek Ski Resort** (☎5758 3733; www.skifallscreek.com.au) takes guests as high as 1842m. **Lift ticket** prices are comparable to other resorts. ($62-78 per day, children $35-41; lifts plus lesson $89-110, students $66-81, children $62-74.) The ample snowfall, both natural and man-made, is a selling point, and the spread of trails means that bad weather conditions from one direction leave good skiing elsewhere on the mountain. Few trails are very long and most are intermediate-level runs. Advanced skiers can expect to spend more chairlift time than snow time. An area of black diamond trails known as **The Maze** and a snowboarding terrain park with a **half-pipe** are opened as snowfall permits. A Kat service transports skiers in heated Kassbohrers up the back-country slopes of **Mt. McKay** (1842m) for thrilling black and double-black diamond bowl runs ($69 with lift pass). Falls's ambiance is more family-oriented than nearby Mt. Hotham's (see p. 645), though their partnership gives multi-day skiers the chance to try both (lift tickets are priced the same and allow access to both resorts).

Driving to the slopes from June to October requires carrying **snow chains** (24hr. rental in Tawonga and Mt. Beauty $18-22) and paying a hefty entrance fee (overnight $30-38; $15 each additional night). It is more practical to stay in Bright and use public transport to reach the resort for the day. **Pyle's Falls Creek Coach Services** (☎5754 4024) runs a ski-season service from Melbourne (6hr., 1-2 per day, $117 return), Albury (3½hr., 1-2 per day, $63 return), and Mt. Beauty (50min., 5-8 per day, $33 return). All prices include entrance fee.

Activity is concentrated at the edges of the village. The **Falls Creek Information Centre** is at the bottom of town, opposite the day parking lot, and has info on lessons, packages, and lodgings. (☎5758 3490; fallsinfo@fallscreek.albury.net.au. Open daily 9am-5pm.) Staying on the mountain lets you sleep longer, party later, and make snow angels outside, but the privilege does not come cheap. A horde of small, independent lodges offers varying styles of accommodation; the folks at **Central Reservations** (☎5758 3733 or 1800 033 079) can direct you.

Quiet stays in the delightfully swanky ▨**Alpha Lodge ❸**, 5 Parallel St., are available year-round. It has an excellent kitchen and roomy commons area. (☎5758 3488; manager@alphaskilodge.com.au. Drying room, laundry, BBQ garden, and sauna. 4-bed dorms $24-91; 2- to 3-bed ensuite dorms $30-103.) The **Frying Pan Inn ❹**, 4 Village Bowl Cir., offers basic, motel-style dorms at the base of the Summit and Eagle chairlifts. The location is excellent. It's also the place to be on weekends, when there are live bands, dance parties, and drink specials to fuel the debauchery. (☎5758 3390. Drying closet, no kitchen. Pub open daily 5pm-late; bistro open daily 8am-8pm. Ensuite dorms $40-75.) **The Man**, 20 Slalom St., is the heart of the nightlife, with food, beer, live bands, multiple bars, pool tables, fusbol, and even Internet access. (☎5758 3362. Open daily noon-late. Internet $5 per 30min.)

An active summer resort as well, Falls Creek has bushwalking, horseback riding, tennis, and water activities from October to June. A smaller number of lodges are open for housing during the summer (call Central Reservations ☎5758 3733 or 1800 033 079 for current openings), but prices are lower. During Victoria school holidays in summer, one lift is opened for mountain biking, conditions permitting. Take the chair up and then bike down the snow-free trails ($15).

GIPPSLAND

Southeast of Melbourne, the Princes Hwy. snakes toward the border of New South Wales, loosely following the contours of the Victoria coast through verdant, rolling wilderness interspersed with extensive lake systems and small towns. Undeveloped and sparsely populated, this belt hosts eco-tourists and inspires frequent struggles among developers, loggers, and environmentalists. National parks pepper the region; highlights include backpacking through Wilsons Promontory and Croajingalong, boating on the Snowy River, and paying homage to the spiritually-charged Den of Nargun in Mitchell River.

FOSTER ☎03

While gold-hungry miners flocked to Foster in search of supplies and a warm bed, most of today's visitors are headed to the park; Foster is just 30km north of the entrance. To drive from Melbourne (170 km), take the South Eastern Arterial (M1) to the South Gippsland Hwy. (M420), following signs first to Phillip Island, then to Korumburra (where the highway becomes A440), and finally to Foster. **V/Line** (☎13 61 96) **buses** run from Melbourne (2¾hr.; M-Su 4:30pm, F 6pm; returns M-Sa 7:49am, Su 3:25pm; $25 one-way), requiring that you spend the night in Foster before shuttling to the Prom with the **Foster-Tidal River Bus Service** (see below). **Tourist information** is inside the Stockyard Gallery at the end of Main St. toward the Prom. (☎5682 1125. Open Th-Su 10am-4pm.) **Parks Victoria** staffs an office in the same building. (☎5682 2133. Open M-F 8am-4:30pm.)

Cozy **Foster Backpackers Hostel ❷**, 17 Pioneer St., is the most affordable option, with shared kitchen and outdoor BBQ. Ask the owners about their **farm hostel ❷**. From the S. Gippsland Hwy., turn right onto Main St., then left on Bridge St.; Pioneer St. is on the right and the hostel on the right side. (☎ 5682 2614. Checkout 10am. Main hostel dorms $20; fully contained doubles $50. Farm hostel $25/$50.) Margaret from the Visitors Center also kindheartedly rents out the **"Rose Cabin" ❸** behind her house. Surrounded by grapefruit groves and blueberry bushes, it includes a solar-powered shower. (☎ 5682 2628. Each person $35, max. 2.) Foodway, on the corner of Main St. and Station Rd., sells **groceries**. (Open M-Sa 7am-7pm, Su 8am-6pm.)

WILSONS PROMONTORY NATIONAL PARK

Despite fame and popularity, with 400,000 visitors a year, **the Prom** is also one of the most unspoiled and diverse natural reserves in the world. Partly preserved as a national park back in 1898 and now a UNESCO World Biosphere Reserve, the Prom is off limits to settlement and most transportation. Jutting out to form the continent's southernmost extreme, tidal flats and marshland meet clusters of heath, towering gum forests, and rich fern gullies. The diverse flora creates habitats for scores of native marsupials, reptiles, birds, insects, and sea creatures.

Now connected to the mainland by parallel sandy ridges, at various points in its history the peninsula was an island, while at another time, these ridges extended south all the way to Tasmania. For more **information** on Wilsons Promontory, call ☎ 1800 350 552, or visit the Parks Victoria website (www.parks.vic.gov.au).

THE PROM AT A GLANCE	
AREA: 490km² of parkland; 83km² of marine parks.	**GATEWAYS:** Foster and Yanakie.
	CAMPING: Must register with the ranger. Fees vary through the park.
FEATURES: A UNESCO World Biosphere; home to Mt. Oberon and Sealers Cove.	
	FEES: $9 per vehicle. Fishing permits are required; all payments and inquiries at Tidal River.
HIGHLIGHTS: Easy to challenging hikes and walk, from day to overnight routes.	

🖪🔢 TRANSPORTATION AND PRACTICAL INFORMATION. From Foster, turn left at the end of Main St. onto the **Foster Promontory Rd.**, which snakes 30km to the park entrance, nearly 10km past Yanakie (entry $9 per car). Without a car, the only transport into the park is by the **Foster-Tidal River Bus Service**, run by Anne at the Foster Backpackers Hostel (see above), delivering passengers from Foster to Tidal River. (☎ 5682 6614. By request. One-way $15 with min. 2 people; entrance fee included.) Some touring companies offer daytrips into the park; try **Duck Truck Tours**, which carts people over from Phillip Island. (☎ 5952 2548. $60. See p. 589.)

From the entrance station, the park's only sealed road, **Wilsons Promontory Rd.**, winds 30km along the Prom's western extremity, providing many opportunities to turn off for picnics and hikes. The road ends at **Tidal River**, a township overshadowed by the park's natural splendor. Many take overnight hikes or daytrips from this area. During its busiest periods, the park runs a **free shuttle bus** between the Norman Bay carpark, at the far end of Tidal River, and the Mt. Oberon carpark. (From Norman Bay every 30min. in summer 8am-7pm; in winter 8am-4:45pm. From Mt. Oberon every 30 min. in summer 8:15am-7:15pm; in winter 8:15am-5pm.)

Visitors who wish to stay overnight, obtain a fishing license, or get weather updates should go to the **Tidal River Information Centre** at the end of the main road. Visitors must **register** bushwalking and camping plans with park officials here. (☎ 5680 9555. Open daily 8am-5pm.) A 24hr. **Blue Box** phone for contacting a ranger

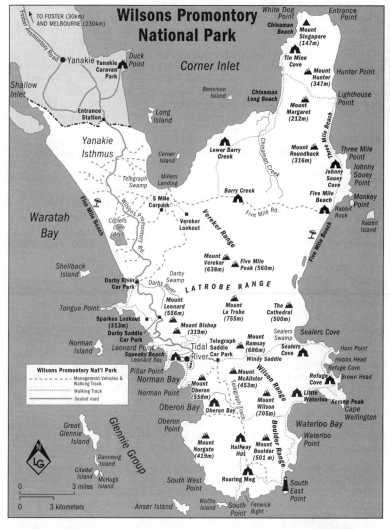

is outside the info center. Tidal River also has a free storage room for superfluous gear, along with the last toilets, pay phones, and food available before the bush. During peak season, Tidal River's amenities include an **open-air cinema,** with a 9:15pm nightly screening of a recent release. Purchase tickets at the cinema 45min. before showtime. ($10, children $7.)

ACCOMMODATIONS AND CAMPING. Finding accommodation in the Prom during the summer months is notoriously difficult, but the park reserves last-minute, first-come **campsites ❷** for non-residents of Victoria at Tidal River (2 nights max. stay; $18.50 peak, off-peak for up to 3 people $15.) For outstation

camping ❶, there's usually no need to book in advance, but you must obtain a permit and pay nightly fees ($5.10, children $2.55). All sites have a one-night maximum stay, except **Roaring Meg** campsite and northern sites (2-night max.). Bouncing site to site must be registered with the info center. Toilets in outstation sites have no toilet paper, and no sites are powered.

Still, getting more than a canvas roof is difficult in summer. Try to reserve three to six months in advance, and even earlier for summer weekends. **Cabins ❺,** all over the park, have bath, kitchen, and living room. (Singles and twins Sept.-early Apr. $136, late Apr.-Aug. $124; bunk-style units from $61.20; 4- to 6-bed huts from $50.). Book through **Tidal River Info Centre** (☎5680 9555; wprom@parks.vic.gov.au).

🗺 **HIKING.** To best experience the Prom, tackle a few bushwalking trails and take a dip in its crystal-clear water. Although most visitors sample the Prom in a day, allow three to five days to really savor it. The Visitors Center's *Discovering the Prom* ($15) details the over-100km of trails that criss-cross the park, and *Down Under at the Prom* ($19) points to dive sites for scuba and snorkeling. One of the most popular swimming beaches is at **Norman Bay,** past Tidal River.

SHORT HIKES. Past the Yanakie entrance to the park, the first left leads to the **Five Mile Track Car Park,** allowing access to the northern reaches traversed mostly by overnight hikers. A short detour along the Five Mile Track leads to the **Miller's Landing Nature Walk.** The easy walk (4km; 1½hr.) leads through banksia woodlands to the dwarf mangroves and mudflats of Corner Inlet. Several short walks (1-2km) depart from Tidal River, including: **Whale Rock** (0.7km; 20-30min.), a loop track winding gradually uphill through tea-tree, banksias, and sheoaks to a delightful view of Mt. Oberon; and **Loo-errn Track** (2km; 1hr.), a boardwalk designed for those with limited mobility leading through swamp paperbark to an overlook. For a slightly longer hike, try **Squeaky Beach Nature Walk** (5km; 1½hr.), which passes through dunes, coastal scrub, and granite outcroppings to Pillar Point. Look for wombats in the scrub, and once on the beach, slide your feet to hear the remarkably uniform white-grained quartz sand squeak. **Lilly Pilly Gully Nature Walk** (4.7km; 2hr.), starting from the Lilly Pilly carpark 2km up the road from Tidal River, follows a slight incline through coastal woodlands of paperback thickets and eucalypt forest into the rainforest. This walk can be extended by leaving from Tidal River (6.7km; 4hr.); the section between Tidal River and Lilly Pilly Gully is wheelchair accessible. About 5km up the main road is a turn-off for the Mt. Oberon carpark, where the **Mount Oberon Nature Walk** begins. The walk (6.8km; 2-3hr.) climbs steadily up to the summit, leading to one of the best sunrise spots in the park.

DAY-HIKES. For more ambitious hikers, three incredible day-hikes cover some of the Prom's most beloved spots. In the park's southern half, **Tongue Point Track** (9.4km; 3-4hr.) starts from Darby Saddle (6.7km north of Tidal River) and proceeds, sometimes steeply, past two sweeping lookouts to a small granite peninsula with a stunning view of the coast. The **Oberon Bay Track** (12.4km; 5hr.) leaves from Tidal River and follows Norman Bay Beach, whose yellow sands mirror the scenic coastline along the western bays to Oberon Bay. In the opposite direction, departing from the Mt. Oberon carpark, the ⚑**Sealers Cove Track** (19km; 5-6hr.) takes you across nearly every environment in the Prom.

OVERNIGHT HIKES. The overnight hikes in the south are absolutely worth the time and extra preparation, as they allow hikers to relish the multitude of terrains and spectacular secluded spots. The less-traveled northern part of Wilson's Prom has a circuit but lacks toilets. The most popular two- to three-day hike sweeps 36km around the eastern coastal areas along well-maintained trails to Sealers Cove (9.6km), Refuge Cove (16.6km), and Waterloo Bay (24km), but to take in the

Prom's full beauty, a four- to five-day hike down to the lighthouse and the south-east point is definitely recommended. Overnight camp areas are near walking tracks; make sure to carry a gas or fuel stove, as fires are not allowed at any time. The following outlines the legs of the southern overnight hike leading to sites.

VICTORIA

Telegraph Saddle Carpark to Sealers Cove. (9.6km, 2½hr.) This track leads through a stretch of stunning rainforest filled with brown stringybark and banksia, then into a Messmate forest of austral mulberry and musk daisy-bush before arriving at Windy Saddle. The forest is darker and the terrain muddier as the trail heads into Sealers Swamp. Keep an eye out for colorful fungi. The track switches to a boardwalk before opening out to the magnificent cove.

Sealers Cove to Refuge Cove. (6.5km; 2hr.) The fantastic coastal views offered by this track may distract you from its slight rolling. The track can get muddy as you head inland, but eventually the coast merges into lush forest. Climbing a few large granite rocks rewards you with a stunning view. The track is poorly marked at this point, so stay on the high side of the first rock; directly ahead, at the top of another large rock, is the pebble track. A short route along the coast heads inland again into stringy bark, then a fern-filled rainforest. A short decline leads you to the beach before heading briefly back into forest, taking you to a campground with water, a flushable toilet, and diving.

From Refuge Cove to Waterloo Bay. (7km; 3-4hr.) The track ascends steeply in some parts through stringy bark woodland, dipping briefly into a small gully before heading up again to reach the Kersops Peak lookout. Leave your pack at the signpost to catch a glimpse of the approaching bay by the detour (0.6km, 10min. return); look out for snakes, as the track has many overhanging plants. Keep your eyes peeled for hump-back whales. The track then heads steeply down to the beach and traces the coast on an extremely narrow track with raised roots and large rocks. After a quick bend around the coast the track inclines before heading back into the forest briefly. The beach, directly in front of the Waterloo Campground, is a fantastic spot for a quick dip.

Waterloo Bay to Lighthouse. (10.9km; 4-5hr.) The longest straight incline on the hike leads above Waterloo Point. This uphill stretch is exposed to the sun, has sword-grass, and is quite rocky—you will no doubt be gasping for air while gaping at the coast. Heading inland, the track opens onto a large faced rock with an amazing view, then passes through a short stretch of cut forest, enters a eucalyptus forest, and heads down into rainforest. The track rolls through fern forests to the branching for the lighthouse. If you can get a bed there (bookings through Tidal River), it's doubly worthwhile to make the incredibly steep trek. Otherwise, leave your pack to make the detour (2km return).

The Lighthouse to Roaring Meg. (3.7km, 1-1½hr.) Though short, this portion of the track is a rollercoaster of ups and downs. The track is mostly in the moist rainforest so be wary of mud and leeches. Turn right when the track empties onto the Telegraph Track (a road) and follow the road 0.7km until it splits to offer the walking track to Roaring Meg (2.3km farther) on your left. Deceptively flat to start with, the track returns to extreme ups followed directly by downs finally ending at the bridge over the creek (the campsite's water supply). The campsite also offers a short hike (7.4km; 2.½hr. return) out to the **southeasternmost point** in mainland Australia.

Roaring Meg to Halfway Hut (via walking track) and Oberon Bay. (3.3km; 1¼hr.) Though the road is shorter, the walking track has better scenery. After a short steep incline, the track remains relatively flat before opening into a short growth forest. A left at Telegraph Track will lead you downhill along the road to the Halfway Hut. This campground has a composting toilet, water, and a small stone hut. The flat track leading to Oberon Beach crosses dry and shaggy forest. Walk along the beach to the right and cross over a small tidal pool to see the track to Tidal River.

Oberon Bay to Tidal River. (6.2km; 1½-2½hr.) Climbing the entire length of the point, the track finally flattens out at the rounding of the peninsula. Head down the beach (do not walk up on the grassy dunes) and inland to the next trailhead to round Norman Point. This final peninsula requires a steady climb but offers fantastic views of Little Oberon Bay and its many islands. Rock steps make the track slightly easier, and as the last point is rounded, Norman Bay comes into view and the track leads steadily down to the sand. For the best views, walk the length of Norman Beach, heading inland at the final fence markings to reach a wooden track leading directly into the campground.

YARRAM ☎03

Yarram's most outstanding feature is its proximity to the **Tarra-Bulga National Park.** A 15km turn-off in Toora, about a third of the way between Foster and Yarram, will lead you to **Agnes Falls,** the highest single-span waterfall in Victoria, dropping 59m into the Agnes River. In the other direction, about 30km east of Yarram, you can access the southern portion of **Ninety Mile Beach,** an unusually long and quite exceptional stretch of white-sanded coastline extending past Lakes Entrance. To reach **Woodside Beach,** popular for **swimming** and **surfing,** follow the S. Gippsland Hwy. to Woodside and turn right onto Woodside Beach Rd.

Yarram is 50km east of Foster on the S. Gippsland Hwy., which becomes Commercial Rd. as it passes through town. The **Harvey World Travel** office on Commerical Rd. sells **V/Line bus** tickets to Melbourne via Foster. (☎5182 6322. 3½hr., departs M-Sa 7am, Su 2:35pm; $30.40. Office open M-F 9am-5pm, Sa 9am-noon.) The **Tourist Information Centre,** in the old Court House at Commercial Rd. and Rodgers St., gives a plethora of info. (☎5182 6553. Open M-F 10am-4pm, Sa-Su hours vary.) The **library,** on Grant St., has **free Internet**. (☎5182 5135. Open M and Th-F 10am-6pm, Tu-W 2-6pm, Sa 10am-noon.) **Banks, ATMs,** and **pharmacies,** and a **post office** (open M-F 9am-5pm) are on the main street. **Postal Code:** 3971.

Budget accommodations in the area are limited. The **Windmill Caravan Park ❶** has clean cabins and basic amenities with a playground and tennis court just 1km south of town on the S. Gippsland Hwy. (☎5182 5570. Sites $10, powered $15; caravans $40; cabins $45, ensuite $50.) If you are willing to spend a few extra bucks, head next door to the **Ship Inn Motel ❸.** (☎5182 5588. Singles $59; doubles $69, deluxe $75.). For food, the **Federal Coffee Palace ❸,** 305 Commercial Rd., is definitely the hippest place in town, with cushioned chairs, books, board games, and $3 lattes. Try their $16 chicken filet with apricots and camembert. (☎5182 6464. Open Tu 11am-5pm, W-Th 10am-10pm, F-Sa 11am-late, Su 9am-4pm.) IGA **supermarket** is in the Yarram Plaza. (☎5182 6033. Open M-F 8am-6pm, Sa 8am-1pm.)

TARRA-BULGA NATIONAL PARK

The Tarra-Bulga National Park, a section of the **Strzelecki Ranges,** features breathtaking rainforests filled with fern trees and lyrebirds. It can be approached from either the **Tarra Valley Road** through the Tarra Valley or the unsealed **Balook Yarram Road** through the Bulga Forest. Not far from **Yarram** (follow the signs), they connect perpendicularly to **Grand Ridge Road,** forming a great loop through the forest. The ascent through the **Tarra Valley,** along a narrow and windy 25km stretch of sealed road, passes through lush fern, eucalypts, and occasional patches of yellow wildflowers. Don't take any unmarked roads without 4WD—conditions vary and the area is rarely patrolled. About 20km up the road lies the superb **Tarra Falls.** Another kilometer up, at the Tarra Valley picnic area, follow the easy **Tarra Valley Rainforest Walk** (1.2km; 30min. return) through the rainforest to **Cyathea Falls.**

At the junction of Grand Ridge Rd. and Balook Yarram Rd. is the **Tarra Bulga Visitor Centre,** with maps and info on day-walks and driving tracks. (☎5196 6166. Open Sa-Su and holidays 10am-4pm.) From here you can follow the **Lyrebird Ridge Track** (2.4km) to the **Ash Track** (1km) to access the **Fern Gully Nature Walk** (500m). This short walk is the site of the **Suspension Bridge,** which stretches high above a breathtaking fern gully that houses birds, wallabies, bats, and bush rats. To reach the

Fern Gully Walk directly, head down Grand Ridge Rd. about 1km past the Visitors Center to the Bulga carpark. The **Forest Track** (4.3 km; 1½hr. return) is a slightly longer but moderate walk through the park, leaving from the Visitors Center.

There is no bush camping in the park, but there are two **caravan parks** inside the forest, along Tarra Valley Rd. Coming into the park from Yarram, the first one you'll hit is the **Nangeela Tourist Park ❶**, 1369 Tarra Valley Rd. (☎5186 1216. Sites for 2 $13, powered $16; cabins for 2 $55, for families $61-79.) About 2km further up the road, the **Tarra Valley Caravan Park ❶**, 1385 Tarra Valley Rd., serves meals ($23) on Friday and Saturday nights. (☎5186 1283. Sites for 2 $13-15; powered $16-18; cabins for 2 from $42-72, extra adult $8.) Both parks have bathrooms, showers, laundry, game room, and a small selection of groceries in the office.

BAIRNSDALE   ☎03

Bairnsdale is a useful place to refuel before venturing into **Mitchell River National Park** or the **Australian Alps.** The town also boasts the magnificent **St. Mary's Church.** Completed in 1937, the church showcases spectacular murals by Italian artist Frank Floreani. (Open daily 9am-5pm; service daily at 9am.)

About 275km east of Melbourne and 35km west of Lakes Entrance, Bairnsdale is accessible by the Princes Hwy. (A1), called **Main Street** in town. Bairnsdale is the starting point of the **Great Alpine Road,** a 300km drive that takes you through the **Australian Alps,** near the **Falls Creek Ski Resort,** to **Wangaratta.** You can also walk in the Alps on the **Australian Alps Walking Track,** which begins in Walhalla (approximately 50km from Bairnsdale) and goes all the way to Mt. Tennent (655km), outside Canberra. This epic bushwalk over many of the area's highest mountains can be completed in ten weeks. For more info, contact **Parks Victoria.** (☎ 13 19 63.)

Bairnsdale has a train station with no trains, but there are plenty of **V/Line buses** on MacLeod St. (☎5152 5592), across from the tourist office and down Pyke St. Buses run to Melbourne (4hr.; M-F 3 per day, Sa-Su 2 per day; $42) via Sale, where you switch to a train (1hr.), and to Lakes Entrance (30min.; M-F 4 per day, Sa-Su 1 per day; $9). **Bairnsdale Visitors Centre,** 240 Main St., between McDonald's and the church, has a knowledgeable staff. (☎5152 3444. Open daily 9am-5pm.) The library around the next block on Service St. has **free Internet.** (Open M 10am-5pm, Tu 10am-1pm, W and F 9am-6pm, Th 9am-7pm, Sa 9:30am-noon.)

The accommodations in Bairnsdale are limited. Try camping in **Mitchell River National Park** (below) or stay at the **Espas Arts Resort** on Raymond Island (below). If you are driving out to Bairnsdale from Yarram, there is a spotlessly clean caravan park about half way in **Stratford Top Tourist Park ❶.** The very friendly owners have tons of information. There is also a kitchen, BBQ area, one dorm for backpackers, and even musical bathrooms. (☎5145 6588. Sites for 2 $15-16, powered $17-18; dorms $18; vans $35-44; cabins $40-58.) Locally, you can try **Mitchell Gardens Holiday Park ❶,** at the eastern end of Main St., where there are clean showers, kitchen, laundry, and a pool. (☎5152 4654. Sites $14, powered $17-22; cabins $40-69, ensuite $51-84; holiday units $66-104.) Safeway **supermarket** is behind McDonald's. (Open M-Th 8am-7pm, F-Sa 8am-8pm, Su 9am-6pm.)

LEGENDS OF THE GUNNAI
For at least 18,000 years, the Gunnai (or Kurnai) Aboriginal people have inhabited Gippsland. To discourage their children from disobeying tribal laws, the Gunnai told them fables. One explains the fallen link between Tasmania and the mainland (at Wilsons Promontory). One day, the story goes, two children at play removed a sacred object from the land and brought it to their mother. The ground crumbled into the sea, breaking up families and drowning many Gunnai. The moral for you: don't remove anything from Australia's national parks.

NEAR BAIRNSDALE

RAYMOND ISLAND. Raymond Island is a great daytrip for wildlife spotting, especially on weekends. **Buses** run from Bairnsdale to nearby Paynesville (30min.; M-F 4-5 per day, Sa 1 per day; $7.25); from there, you can take a 2min. **ferry** to the island. (☎0418 517 959. Ferry runs M-F 7am-10:30pm, Sa 7am-midnight, Su 8am-10:30pm. Cars $5.) The tiny island has a huge population of **wild koalas,** which are most easily spotted off Centre Rd. and the walking tracks that branch off of it toward the south. **Raymond Island Koala Tours** offers biologist-led tours around the island. (☎0409 515 630. Tours W and Su 9 and 11am. $10, children $5, families $25.) For those looking to koala-watch in style, **First Bumper Carriage Co.** provides Clydesdale-drawn carriages. (☎5634 8267. Weekends and holidays 10:30am-2:45pm. 25min. tours $8.50, children $5, families $25.)

Though Raymond Island has no grocery stores, **Ferry Ride to Flowers ❶,** a nursery and tea garden on 1st St., serves excellent fresh food without breaking the bank. (☎5156 0257. Open Th-Su and holidays 10am-4:30pm; in summer 9am-5pm. Sandwiches $2.80-3.20.) The island is dotted with cozy bed and breakfasts, and the **Espas Arts Resort ❸** is a sparkling but pricey facility near the ferry and right on the water. The complex also has a cafe with an equally pricey menu. (☎5156 7275. Call ahead. Cafe open F-Sa 10am-late, Su 10am-5pm. Doubles $80, extra person $10.)

EAGLE POINT. Just south of Bairnsdale, off C604, and right next to Paynesville, Eagle Point is best known for its gigantic **mud silts,** second in size only to ones on the Mississippi River in the United States. The silt jetties stretch out for kilometers, with the Rivermouth Road traveling their length. Aside from a few potholes, the road is suitable for a 2WD. Grab some fishing gear and head out for one of the many prime spots along the jetty. Two caravan parks line the waters in town and offer a quiet night's rest. **Lake King Waterfront Caravan Park ❶** has a games room, pool, laundry, and spots to pop up your tent to catch the sunrise. (☎5156 6387. Sites $13-18.15, powered $17-24.20; onsite caravans $35.20-53; ensuite units $47.30-69.30.) Slightly larger and with permanent residents, **Eagle Point Caravan Park ❶** is the first park entering town on Bay Rd. (☎0409 382 542. Sites $6-8, powered $15-22; ensuite cabins $45-90. $5 key deposit.) Both have petrol.

MITCHELL RIVER NATIONAL PARK

Flowing from the alpine high country down to the Gippsland Lakes, the Mitchell River bisects the 12,200 hectares of rainforest that comprise the park. Canoeing, rafting, and hiking through the **Mitchell River Gorge** are the best ways to see the park's splendors. To reach the park from Bairnsdale (45km), turn right about 3km west of town onto Lindenow Rd., which becomes Dargo Rd.; a number of well-labeled right-hand turns lead from here. Most roads through the park are unsealed and are navigated more safely in a 4WD.

Beside the gorges and high cliffs looming over the river, most daytrippers venture into the park to pay respect to the **Den of Nargun.** Gunnai/Kurnai legend describes Nargun as a giant stone female creature who destroyed intruders by reflecting their spears and abducted children who strayed from camp. The **Den of Nargun Circuit** (1hr.) loops around **Bluff Lookout,** sweeping down to the **Mitchell River** and the Den of Nargun before heading back up to the carpark. Wear appropriate clothes—much of the walk is in chilly rainforest, and many steps are made of rocks, which are slippery when wet. You can sit by the water's edge to absorb this site's mystical energy, but the cave's fragile stalagmites make it **unsafe to enter.**

There are two places to **camp** in the park. **Angusvale ❶** can be reached by turning right off Dargo Rd. onto the unsealed Mitchell Dam Rd. (River water only; pit toilets. Free.) The other, at **Billy Goat Bend ❶,** is accessible only by foot: turn right off Dargo Rd. onto Billy Goat Bend Rd., follow to picnic area, and then hike in about 1km. (Free.) **Bairnsdale Parks Victoria** (☎5152 0400) has more information.

LAKES ENTRANCE ☎03

Lakes Entrance is the unofficial capital of the Gippsland Lakes region, the largest inland waterway in the Southern Hemisphere. With expansive beaches, excellent fishing, and numerous boating opportunities, caravan parks, and mini-golf courses, it comes as no surprise that Lakes Entrance is extremely touristy and very crowded during the summer.

◨◪ TRANSPORTATION AND PRACTICAL INFORMATION. V/Line buses leave near the post office and head to Narooma, NSW (5½hr., 1 per day, $55) and Melbourne (5hr.; M-F 2 per day, Sa-Su 1 per day; $50-65) via Bairnsdale. (30min.; M-F 4 per day, Sa-Su 1 per day; $9.) **McCafferty's/Greyhound** also stops here on its Sydney-Melbourne route. (Daily eastbound 1:15pm, westbound 1am. $55.) For reservations, call **Esplanade Travel,** 309 Esplanade. (☎5155 2404. Open M-F 9am-5pm.)

The Princes Hwy., called the **Esplanade** in town, becomes a waterfront strip lined with largely unimpressive shops. The **Lakes Entrance Visitors Centre,** on the western end of the Esplanade, has plenty of regional information. (☎5155 1966. Open daily 9am-5pm.) Most **banks** and **ATMs** are a few blocks east of the Visitors Center. The **library,** 55 Palmers Rd., up the hill at the east end of town, offers free **Internet** access. (☎5150 9100. Open M-F 8:30am-5pm.) The **post office** is at 287 Esplanade. (☎5155 1809. Open M-F 9am-5pm.) **Postal Code:** 3909.

▟▐ ACCOMMODATIONS AND FOOD. Beach camping is fun but illegal, and the area is frequently patrolled—luckily, reasonably priced alternatives are everywhere. **Riviera Backpackers (YHA) ❷,** 5 Clarkes Rd., off the eastern end of the Esplanade. Ask the bus to stop at the hostel bus stop. This excellent motel-style YHA earns high marks for its clean facilities and has a large lounge with TV, a solar-heated pool, billiards, bike rental ($1 per hr., $5 per day), laundry, kitchen, Internet ($2 per 15min.), and safe storage. (☎5155 2444; riviera@net-tech.com.au. Reception 24hr. Heated dorms, twins, and doubles all $18 per person; weekly $108. Book a few weeks ahead for Dec.-Jan.) **Echo Beach Tourist Park ❷,** 33 Roadknight St., 1 block from the Esplanade, is a 4-star park with kitchen, BBQ, laundry, pool, spa, TV, and billiards. (☎5155 2238. Reception 8am-10pm. Powered sites $19-31; self-contained ensuite cabins $55-120.)

The Esplanade brims with takeaway food shops, and the hotels in town tend to have good bistros in the mid-price range. Get **groceries** at Foodworks, 30-34 Myer St. (☎5155 1354. Open daily 8am-7:30pm.) Or for **bulk foods,** try Lakes Health Bar, 10 Myer St. (Open M-F 8am-5pm, Sa 9am-noon.) **Pinocchio Inn Restaurant ❷,** 569 Esplanade, usually has a special: all-you-can-eat pasta or 2 large pizzas for $22. (☎5155 2565. 10% YHA discount. Open daily 5pm-late; in summer noon-3am.) **◪Riviera Ice Cream Parlour ❶,** opposite the footbridge on the Esplanade, sells an award-winning farm-produced ice cream in 35 flavors and generous portions ($2-5.70). Try the "frog on a log" ($3.70). (☎5155 2972. Open daily 9am-5pm; in summer 9am-11pm.) **Tres Amigos, The Mex ❸,** 521 Esplanade, serves huge portions of mild but tasty Mexican food. A light meal ($4-9) and a side order will fill most bellies, while mains ($15-19) may burst them. (☎5155 2215. Open W-Su 5:30pm-late.)

◩◪ SIGHTS AND ACTIVITIES. The **Jemmys Point Lookout** at the western end of town affords a perfect view of the patchwork Gippsland Lakes. To reach **Ninety Mile Beach,** the town's biggest attraction, cross the footbridge opposite Myer St.

From the snack bar and toilet area, a walking track (1hr.) follows the coast to the man-made boat entrance to the deep, blue waters of the Bass Strait. Most visitors hire boats from one of the jetties along Marine Pde. Try **Victor Hire Boats**, on the north arm of Marine Pde. (☎5155 3988. 8-passenger cabins $25 per hr., each extra hour $15.) A bit further down, **Portside Boat Hire** has more options. (☎5155 3832. 6- to 8-passenger cabins $30 per hr., $55 per 3hr.; 12-passenger BBQ boat $38 per hr. plus fuel; canoes $10 per hr.) Both places are generally open during daylight hours. **Barrier Landing** is the western strip of land created by the entrance. Only accessible by boat, the landing has great fishing and rests by both a lake beach and a **surf beach**. Contact **Mulloway**, on the Marine Pde., for a three-hour **fishing trip**. (☎5155 3304. Trips 9am-noon and 1-4pm. $38.) To find out where to fish, pick up the *East Gippsland Fishing Map* ($8) at the Visitors Center.

The **Wyanga Park Winery**, on Baades Rd., provides for less active entertainment. Drive there by following the signs from Myer St. or take a cruise to the vineyard on *The Corque* for lunch or dinner at **Henry's Cafe**. (☎5155 1508. Open Su-W 9am-5pm; free tastings Th-Sa 9am-8pm. 2-5hr. cruises daily at 11:30am and 3:30pm. $40-60 including tea or meal. Book ahead.) **Lake Tyers Boat Trips**, 10km east of town in Lake Tyers, offers relaxing afternoon cruises on Victoria's largest electric boat. (☎5155 1283. $18.50, children $11.) The **Griffith Sea Shell Museum**, just west of Centrepoint on the Esplanade, is a fantastically bizarre rainy-day stop with shells in an unbelievable number of shapes, colors, and sizes. Don't miss the psychdelic black light coral exhibit. (☎5155 1538. Open daily 9am-5pm. $6, children $2.50.)

BUCHAN ☎03

Loads of people visit the town of Buchan (rhymes with "tuckin'"; pop. 200), 58km north of Lakes Entrance and 50km northeast of Bruthen, either on the Snowy River scenic drive or to tour the spectacular limestone Buchan Caves. Buchan is surrounded by rolling hills at the base of the Snowy River Valley and is a base for some serene bushwalks within Snowy River National Park.

⌐⚂ TRANSPORTATION AND PRACTICAL INFORMATION. No public transport serves Buchan, so most backpackers arrive on touring buses bound for Melbourne or Sydney. Driving from Lakes Entrance, take the Princes Hwy. 23km east to Nowa Nowa, turn left onto C620, then right onto C608, following signs to Buchan. From Orbost or starting the Snowy River National Park Scenic Drive (this takes longer but offers better views), turn left off Princes Hwy. to veer under the overpass, then right at the T stop, and then look for the next right onto Buchan Rd.

Just south of the Buchan Caves, the small town center contains a **general store** with basic food and **tourist information**. (Open M-F 8:30am-5:30pm, Sa 8:30am-12:30pm, Su 9am-1pm; holidays 8:30am-5pm.) The **Parks Victoria office** right before the caves has the most info on camping and the national parks area, as well as tickets for the caves and reservations for the 100 closely-packed campsites in the area. (☎5155 9264. Sites $11.30-15, powered $16-20.) The **Buchan Outreach-Resource Centre**, 6 Davidson St., over the bridge onto Orbost Rd. then right onto Davidson St., has **Internet** access. (☎5155 9294. Open daily 9am-4:30pm. $3 per hr.) The **post office** is across from the general store. (Open M-F 9am-5pm.) **Postal Code:** 3885.

⌐⚃ ACCOMMODATIONS AND FOOD. The ▨**Buchan Lodge ❷**, left after the bridge on Saleyard Rd. just north of the town center, provides outstanding budget accommodation in a beautifully constructed wooden building. The grand main room houses a lounge, dining area, wheelchair facilities, and a well-decked kitchen. (☎5155 9421. Breakfast included; complimentary tea and coffee all day. Bunks $20.) **Willow Cafe ❷**, the muralled house a few doors down from the post office, has tasty meals. (☎ 5155 9387. Open daily 9am through dinner.) Afterward, amble across the street to the **pub** at the **Caves Hotel.** (☎ 5155 9203. Open M-Sa 11am to 10pm-1am, Su noon-8pm.)

◪ ◩ SIGHTS AND HIKING. The 260-hectare **Buchan Caves Reserve,** just past the town center before the bridge, is up to 25 million years old. It reaches depths of over 50m and houses impressive stalactites and stalagmites. The two big caves, **Fairy Cave** and **Royal Cave,** open alternately for guided tours. (1hr. In summer 10, 11:15am, 1, 2:15, 3:30pm; in winter 11am, 1, 3pm. $11.30, children $5.60, families $28.70.) For more of a challenge without all the railings and floodlights, book a group tour of Federal Cave through Buchan Lodge. (Min. 5 people. $15.)

The Buchan Caves Reserve has a few pleasant bushwalks, none longer than 2½hr. The **Spring Creek Walk** (1½hr, 3km) travels the Tea-tree track past limestone and old volcanic rock; leading to Spring Creek Falls and returning by the lower Kannoka Track, you will pass through a fern-filled forest. Keep an eye out for lyrebirds. The Parks Office (above) has more information on other short walks.

SNOWY RIVER NATIONAL PARK

Some of the most extreme wilderness in Australia, the Snowy River National Park surrounds the once mighty Snowy River with jagged hills dressed in green. It was the rugged beauty of this landscape that inspired Banjo Paterson, author of *Waltzing Matilda*, to pen his bush ballad *The Man From Snowy River*, which glorifies those who choose to take on the harshness of bush life among these "pine-clad ridges." Once an underwater landmass, the park stretches across vastly distinct ecosystems, from rainforest to rainshadow. Many rare species call this place home, including the brush-tailed rock wallaby and the tiger quoll. Whether you bushwalk, white-water raft, camp, canoe, or drive the six-hour scenic loop, the Snowy River and its surrounding mountainside prove an impressive wonder

E TRANSPORTATION. The fantastic scenic drive around the park can be made in six hours. The park road is mostly unsealed, becoming increasingly windy and narrow as it heads north. Its suitability for 2WD vehicles depends on the weather, road conditions, and your confidence as a driver. Call **Parks Victoria** in Orbost (☎ 5161 1222) or Buchan (☎ 5155 9264) for up-to-date reports. If you are driving from Buchan, you can take either the **Buchan-Gelantipy Rd.** (C608) through the countryside, or the unsealed **Tulloch Ard Rd.** through the forest, both of which end in Gelantipy. To reach Tulloch Ard Rd., head north out of Buchan and take a right on Orbost Rd. Continue straight on Basin Rd. and turn left onto Tulloch Ard. The Buchan-Gelantipy Rd. leads through **Wulgulmerang,** the last place to get petrol and supplies until you reach Bonang east of the park. Fill up before entering the park, as the stations keep odd hours. About 1km down the road, take the right fork onto Bonang-Gelantipy Rd., which follows a gradual descent past **MacKillop Bridge** and continues east until its intersection with **Bonang Main Rd.** You can either take this all the way to Orbost or turn right onto **Yalmy Rd.** to reach the eastern sections of the park. **Eastour,** out of Orbost, drives people through the Snowy River region. (☎ 5154 2969. 1-day $140. For more info, see **Errinundra National Park,** p. 658.)

⌂ ACCOMMODATIONS. The ▥**Karoonda Park YHA ❷,** 1½hr. from the Princes Hwy. and 40km north of Buchan on the Buchan-Gelantipy Rd. (C608), has a swimming pool, ping-pong, billiards, darts, tennis, bar, wheelchair facilities, and Internet access. An extra few dollars buys you a fantastic evening feast, and after two nights as a paying guest, useful hands can stay longer as farm workers in exchange for room and board. The YHA has many adventure options: overnight rafting trips (seasonal; $110, backpackers $75); overnight horseback trips ($110, backpackers $75); abseiling (intro $10, full 40m $25); and indoor rock climbing ($5). Oz Experience stops here; call ahead for pickup from Lake's Entrance. (☎5155 0220. Dorms $24, YHA $20; with board $39, backpackers $36. Motel singles $26; doubles $52.) About 30km farther north along the dirt track en route to Suggan Buggan and Jindabyne, NSW (see p. 211), is the tranquil mountain retreat of **Candlebark Cottage ❸**, at "Springs" along the Snowy River-Jindabyne Rd. On a hill 1km from the main house, this secluded cottage sleeps eight, with a double bed and six loft bunks. Popular with cyclists and families, the cottage is ideal for bushwalking, trout fishing, or winter expeditions. (☎5155 0263. $30; for 2 $55; each extra person $25.) The most popular **campsites** in the park are **MacKillop Bridge, Raymond Falls,** and **Hicks Campsite.** Raymond Falls and Hicks Campsite can be reached off Yalmy Rd. on dirt tracks suitable for 2WD. All have pit toilets; only MacKillop Bridge has a $9 fee.

ORBOST   ☎03

Orbost, a logging town 60km northeast of Lakes Entrance, serves mostly as a pit-stop on the way to nearby beaches and national parks. The town is the start and finish of the Snowy River National Park Scenic Drive, and two worthy but seldom visited sights lie about an hour away, inaccessible by public transportation. To the north, **Errinundra National Park** is home to Victoria's largest stretch of rainforest. To the south, **Cape Conran** offers beautiful beaches away from the tourist hubbub.

V/Line buses run to Orbost from: Bairnsdale (1½hr., 1-2 per day, $21); Canberra (5hr., 2 per week, $53); Melbourne (5½hr., 1-2 per day, $53.40). Buy tickets at **Orbost Travel Centre,** 86 Nicholson St. (☎5154 1481. Open M-F 9am-5:30pm, Sa 9am-noon.) By car, Orbost is just off the Princes Hwy. via Lochiel or Salisbury St.; both exits intersect with Nicholson St.

The **Snowy River Orbost Visitors Centre,** on Lochiel St. just off the Princes Hwy., has info on East Gippsland's national parks and two outdoor paths that snake through manicured rainforest. (☎5154 2424. Open daily 9am-5pm.) In town, there are **ATMs;** the Business Centre **library,** just off Nicholson on Ruskin St., with free **Internet** (☎5150 9100; open M-F 8:30am-5pm); and a **post office,** on the corner of Nicholson and McLeod St. (Open M-F 9am-5pm.) **Postal Code:** 3888.

The **Orbost Club Hotel ❷,** 63 Nicholson St., is an average budget accommodation with standard Australian-Chinese menu options. (☎5154 1003. Singles $25; doubles $30; twins $35; triples $50.) The **Snowy River Kingfruit Shopping Complex,** 28 Salisbury St., is the best option for food and supplies. (☎5154 1577. Open M-Sa 8:30am-5:30pm.) Foodway, on Nicholson St. opposite the hotel, has **groceries.** (☎5154 1206. Open daily 8am-8pm.)

NEAR ORBOST

ERRINUNDRA NATIONAL PARK

Normally, cool rainforests like the Errinundra are dominated by ancient myrtle beeches, as in the Otway Ranges of southwestern Victoria. Here, however, black olive berry and cinnamon-scented sassafras cover the forest floor, while a wet eucalypt overstory extends through much of Errinundra Plateau. Approach the forest either by the winding **Bonang Rd.** from Snowy River in the north or by Princes Hwy. from the south. About 11km south of Bonang and 54km east of Orbost, these roads intersect with the two ends of Errinundra Rd., which leads into the park. The signs and markers within the park are unbelievably inconsistent—be sure to get a map beforehand and have adequate petrol and enough daylight time to get out. Most of the roads in the park are unsealed, but navigable in a 2WD vehicle on a good day; on a rainy day, call the **Parks Victoria** office in Orbost to

SCENIC DRIVE. Best driven over two days, with a stop in Gelantipy or the campgrounds at MacKillop Bridge, the scenic drive is a great way to experience the area's highlights. Be sure to grab the *Snowy River Country Trail* brochure in Orbost before you head toward Buchan.

1. **BUCHAN TO SELDOM SEEN.** From Buchan along Tulloch Arc Rd., start your journey at Ash Saddle, halfway to Gelantipy. From here, the Betts Creek Track (1-2km; 30min.) begins an easy loop through a magnificent stretch of massive, old-growth mountain ash. Follow the Betts Creek 4WD track and look to your left for a narrow trail leading through a break in the trees. Continuing farther north, the Seldom Seen Track is a left-hand turn 15km north of Gelantipy. Suitable only for 4WD vehicles or walkers, this 7km uphill track leads to the Mt. Seldom Seen Fire Tower.

2. **HANGING ROCK.** Heading into the park, **Bonang-Gelantipy Rd.** offers outstanding views, but the road becomes increasingly windy and narrow, veering perilously close to the edge. Take care: drive extra slowly and prepare to meet oncoming traffic at each turn. The first sight is **Little River Falls**, with a 400m walking track leading to a viewing platform. Back on the main road, a sign for **Alpine National Park** leads left to a steep unsealed road. This road goes to **Hanging Rock**, or World's End, one of the park's best but least known lookouts. To reach Hanging Rock, turn left after the bridge (Milky Creek Track), left at Rocky River Ridge Track, and left again at Hanging Rock Track (5km, 4WD vehicles only). The rock is a 10min. descent, with a view of the countryside.

3. **HIKE IT UP.** Back on the main road, 1km further into the park, lies the 400-million-year-old **Little River Gorge**, the steepest gorge in Victoria (500m). A 400m trail leads down to the gorge from the carpark. **MacKillop Bridge,** spanning the Snowy at the north of the park, is the starting point of the busiest walking track in the park. The **Silver Mine Walking Track** (15½km; 3½-5hr.) passes by old silver mines, offering spectacular views of the river and mountains to the west. Unfortunately, this track is poorly maintained and often difficult to see, especially along the river—a compass and map are necessities. The track starts along the 4WD **Deddick Track,** passes through native pines, rises steadily to some fantastic lookouts, then drops down to a poorly marked walkers-only track. Stick close to the river and eventually you will approach an overnight hiker campsite. The walk ascends again to an amazing lookout before heading back down toward the bridge. For the less ambitious, the **Snowy River Track** (1½km, 30min.), leaving from MacKillop Bridge, is a self-guided nature walk along the Snowy.

4. **THE FINAL LEG.** MacKillop Bridge soars 30m above luxuriously warm and clear waters, though damming for hydroelectricity has cut water flow to less than 5% of its original levels. This is the source of some debate in the vicinity, as community activists rally to "Let the Snowy Flow Again!" Whitewater rafting, canoeing, and kayaking are popular when water levels permit. The scenic drive continues around the park toward Bonang, the only source of petrol near the park after Gelantipy. The road from Goongerah onwards is sealed and slightly less windy, traveling through dense forest before returning you to Orbost.

check for closures. (☎ 5161 1222. Open M-F 8am-5pm.) There are a few operators in Orbost with tours to Errinundra, but they tend to be pricey. **Eastour** leads trips upon request, including an Errinundra 4WD day tour. (☎ 5154 2969. $130.)

To tackle the park on your own, get a map and the *Guide to Walks and Tours* (available at the info center in Orbost) and ask which tracks are in good condition. Most visitors make their first stop at **Errinundra Saddle,** where Errinundra Rd. passes through the plateau. For more of an uphill challenge, climb to the top of **Mt. Ellery,** over 1000m above sea level, for a grand view of the forest (2.5km return). To get there, take Errinundra Rd. to Big River Rd. at the Mt. Morris picnic area, and follow signs to Mt. Ellery. The **Coastal Range track** (25km; 6hr.) is an easy to moderate daytrip along an old 4WD track that showcases the forest's unique features. Farther down the road, you'll hit the **Goonmirk Rocks track** (1km; 30min.), which leads through mountain plum pines, silver wattle, and in springtime, the red flowers of the Gippsland waratah. The most popular place to **camp ❶** near the park is **Ada River,** on the southern section of Errinundra Rd. **Frosty Hollow** is a remote camping area in the park's eastern reaches; take Bonang Rd. to Gap Rd. to Gunmark Rd. to Goonmirk Rocks Rd. to Hensleigh Creek Rd. Both are **free,** with pit toilets and a water source, though there are also other campsites within the park.

CAPE CONRAN

Cape Conran and its Coastal Park are just 35km southeast of Orbost via Marlo. This area offers a solitary and rugged melange of dunes, heath, wetlands, swamps, and woods. From Orbost, go south down Nicholson St. to Marlo-Cape Conran Rd. and follow it to the end. From farther east, turn left off Princes Hwy. onto Cabbage Tree Rd., 30km east of Orbost, and avoid the right fork to Marlo. The road ends at Marlo-Cape Conran Rd.

Coming from Orbost, there are some serene spots on the road past **Marlo.** One of the best is **French's Narrows,** where the Snowy River meets the sea, about 5km east of Marlo. Two thin strips of land divide the murky river's end from its shallow estuary and the breaks of the Bass Strait. Five kilometers farther down the road is **Point Ricardo,** a secluded beach popular for fishing. A short jaunt from the accommodations options is the main East Cape Beach. The two primary walking options both begin at the carpark on the beach at the end of the road, where there is a map. The mainly coastal **Dock Inlet Walk** (28km; 5-6hr.) is for the physically fit and ambitious. The **Cape Conran Nature Trail** goes inland (2.5km; 1hr.) and has a map and information sheet for all the markings along the way. Because of occasional flooding, check with rangers (☎5154 8438) before setting out. The Yeerung River is popular for **fishing** and **swimming.** The best places to swim are Sailors Grave (East Cape Beach) and Salmon Rocks (near West Cape Beach).

If you plan to spend the night on the Cape itself, the only options are the **Parks Victoria cabins ❸** or camping at **Banksia Bluff,** left off Cape Conran Rd. onto Yeerung River Rd., just before East Cape Beach. The eight wooden self-contained cabins, one of which is wheelchair accessible, are comfortable and right next to the beach. Bring sleeping gear, towels, and food, though the Marlo supermarket drops by daily around 11:30am with groceries. (☎5154 8438. Book well in advance. Cabins for 4 $76, peak season $115.) **Campsites ❷,** though more plentiful, are also in demand. (Sites for 4 $14, peak season $18.40.) If they're booked, the **Burbang Caravan Park ❶,** tucked in the forest about 3km back up the road toward Marlo, has its own tennis court. (☎5154 8219. Sites $14-16; vans for 6 $28-45; cabins $55-88.)

CROAJINGOLONG NATIONAL PARK

Tracing Victoria's eastern coastline from the New South Wales border to Sydenham Inlet is phenomenal Croajingolong (crow-a-JING-a-long) National Park. Recognized by UNESCO as a World Biosphere Reserve, it extends nearly 100km and covers 87,500 hectares. Visitors can scamper amid boulders lodged into sandy beaches, frolic in rivers that empty into the ocean, tumble down massive sand dunes, or hike out to the lighthouse. Busy during peak season, the park remains uncrowded the rest of the year.

VICTORIA

▚ ⁊ ORIENTATION AND PRACTICAL INFORMATION

Croajingolong is 450km east of Melbourne and 500km south of Sydney. Gateway towns Cann River and Mallacoota serve as good bases for those unprepared to camp. The Princes Hwy. passes through Cann River and Genoa before crossing the border into New South Wales; a smaller highway winds south to Mallacoota, and the road leading down to Point Hicks and Mueller's Inlet branches off from Cann River. From Cann River, a 45km drive down unsealed roads (the Tamboon Rd. and then left on Pt. Hicks Rd.) leads to the **Thurra** and **Mueller Rivers.** The Tamboon Rd. forks off from Cann River to lead to Point Hicks Rd., ending at a trail to the Point Hicks Lighthouse.

Cann River and Mallacoota both provide services for the park. In Cann River, the **Parks Victoria Information Centre,** on Princes Hwy. near the east end of town, has info on the park's road conditions and area accommodations. (☎5158 6351. Open daily 9am-5pm; in winter M-F 9am-4pm.) Cann also provides a **supermarket** across from the Cann River Hotel (open M-F 8am-6pm, Sa 8am-1pm, Su 9am-1pm) and a stop for **buses** heading to Melbourne (6½hr., 1 per day, $58) or Canberra (4hr., 1 per day M and Th, $47). Mallacoota's services include: a **Parks Victoria Office** on the corner of Buckland and Allan Dr. (☎5158 0219; open M-F 9:30am-noon and 1-3:30pm); a 24hr. **laundromat** at 57 Maurice Ave. (wash $3.40, dry $1 per 8min.); and two **supermarkets** at the top of Maurice Ave. (Both open daily 8:30am-6:30pm.)

⌂ ACCOMMODATIONS

There are four main camping areas within the park, as well as several in the immediate surrounds. The campgrounds at **Thurra** and **Mueller Rivers ❶** are now run by the folks at Point Hicks Lighthouse, so Parks Victoria has no info on availability ($13.50 per night.). Both have fireplaces, pit toilets, and river water; Thurra is more popular because of its private sites and overnight parking. Between Cann River and Genoa is a turn-off for **Wingan Inlet ❶,** another campsite with popular bushwalking, as well as fireplaces, pit toilets, a water source, and fantastic fishing. (Inquire at Parks Office for permit. Sites $12-15.). Fifteen kilometers southwest of Mallacoota, heading out along Betka Rd., the **Shipwreck Creek Campsite ❶** has only 5 sites. (Fireplaces, pit toilets, limited tank water. Sites $9-13.) While there are few bushwalking tracks out of this site, you can head out to the beach for the day (though swimming is not recommended) or start the **Wilderness Coast Walk.** There is also the 600-site **Mallacoota Camp Park ❷,** on Allan Dr. in Mallacoota, with waterfront lookouts by the Howe Range. (☎5158 0300. Sites $15-19, powered $17-25.50.)

Outside the park are several options for those not camping: the **Cann River Hotel ❷,** on the Princes Hwy. toward the west of Cann River, is a standard pubstay. (☎5158 6221. Singles $20; doubles $30.) In Mallacoota, the **Mallacoota Hotel YHA ❷,** 51-55 Maurice Ave., is a motel-style hostel with a bistro and a pub that fills after 9pm. There is a small kitchen with cooking supplies, but no common room or TV. (☎5158 0455. Swimming pool. Bunks $21.50, YHA $18.) If you and some friends prefer to stay in the park, one of the two **cottages ❸** beside the Point Hicks Lighthouse might be worthwhile. (☎5158 4268. Linens $15. Cottages for 8 $220-260.)

◉ ⌖ SIGHTS AND HIKING

A number of day hikes leave from the vicinity of the park's main campgrounds, while the popular **Wilderness Coast Walk** takes at least two days to complete. To minimize impact on the environment, all overnight hikers must receive a permit from the Parks Victoria office in Cann River or Mallacoota before hitting the trail.

Heathland Walk. (2km return, 30min.) This short walk from the Shipwreck Creek Day Visitor Area brims with rare and endangered wildflowers during spring and early summer; keep an eye out for wild orchids. The track affords gorgeous views of Little Rame Head and the Howe Range as it heads to the communal cooking area.

Lighthouse Walk. (5km return, 1½hr.) This easy walk leads to the Point Hicks Lighthouse, built in 1888, with a great beach, perfect for swimming, along the way. Call ☎5158 4268 to arrange vehicle access. Canoes $35 per day. Lighthouse tours M and F-Su 1pm, daily during holidays 1pm. $7, children $4, families $20.

Dunes Walk. (4km, 2hr.) Starts near campsite 14 in Thurra River to lead through tea-tree forest to 150m-high dunes, the hemisphere's second highest. But there are no signposts in the dunes, so you've got to either leave breadcrumbs or return along the river.

Elusive Lake Walk. (6km, 2hr.) Heads from Wingan to the lake through fields of wildflowers. Only about 3km before Genoa, coming from Cann River, is the unsealed 7km road (2hr. return) leading to the base of the Genoa Peak summit. It winds toward the steep climb with two fantastic lookouts over the surrounding mountain ranges. The second lookout, nearly 1km past the larger one, requires a couple hair-raising ladder ascents.

Wilderness Coast Walk. This 70km overnight trek takes you along a beautiful, sandy shoreline, punctuated by grassy outcroppings and massive algae-coated boulders at the water's edge. There are 10 campsites ($5 each) along the walk, starting with Shipwreck Creek and terminating at Bemm River. Though there is no public transportation out there, a local in Mallacoota named **Tony Gray** will transport you for a large fee. (☎5158 0472 or 04 0851 6482.)

NEAR CROAJINGOLONG: GABO ISLAND   ☎03

To really leave the beaten path, go to **Gabo Island,** 14km from Mallacoota. Connected to the mainland until the isthmus eroded away at the turn of the century, Victoria's easternmost isle is made of vibrant red granite. Quarried from the island in a Herculean feat in 1862, the **lighthouse** (Australia's second tallest at 47½m) continues to steer ships clear. Gabo Island also houses the world's largest colony of **little penguins**—over 40,000 adults. The **Light Station ❶** can lodge up to eight people. (For 6 $90, low-season $70; additional persons $10. Book through Mallacoota's Parks Victoria ☎5158 0219.) Transport to the island can be tricky. **Wilderness Coast Ocean Charters** in Mallacoota takes powerboat tours out to the islands on demand. (☎5158 0701.) If you don't want to sea-kayak, the **Mallacoota Air Service** (☎04 0858 0806) flies to the island. **Air Sapphire** (☎6495 3678), **Merimbula Air Services** (☎6495 1074), and **Shortland Air Services,** based in Marlo (☎5154 8265), also bring a minimum number of people to the island on demand.

WESTERN AUSTRALIA

Western Australia is distinct from the rest of the country in many ways, but the most glaring is its overwhelming size. WA covers about a third of Australia, and visitors soon realize that simply getting from place to place will occupy much of their time in this state. Tiny pieces of the map translate into full, draining days of driving or busing on empty roads. The upside of WA's immensity is a collection of landscapes and activities that no other area in Australia can match. Yet, most visitors—like most Australians—don't bother to explore the West, believing that it's just a desolate backwater. Even native Westralians usually only see a fraction of their state. Of WA's 1.8 million people, 1.4 million live in the Perth area, and most of the rest are close to the coast, along the vineyards of the south or the surf-pounded capes of the north. Perth, WA's capital, is a modern city complete with skyscrapers, four universities, and several suburbs. People throughout the state have a friendly, relaxed interest in the hardy tourists that do make it out west, and with good reason: tourism has become one of the state's economic mainstays, and a lot of effort has gone into making WA a tourist-friendly destination.

From quokkas in the south to camels and salties in the north, WA is home to a range of Australian wildlife. The state's interior is covered with miles of bushland, spinifex grass, and sandy plains, and between August and November the land comes alive as carpets of 8000 wildflower species bloom along the coast south from Exmouth into the Great Southern. The Southwest is the domain of old-growth forests. The majestic karri, one of the world's largest trees, reaches heights of 80m, the reason it is subject to the state's thriving wood-chipping industry. In the north, the desert gives way to the rugged tropical vegetation of the Kimberley. A few rough roads carve through the huge expanses of rainforest, around unearthly rock formations, and past waterfalls that cascade into the Indian Ocean.

Because of their isolation, Westralians have developed an independent nature. In 1933, a state referendum revealed a two-to-one preference to separate from the Commonwealth of Australia. Secession never became a political reality, but the self-sufficient spirit remains an undercurrent. While many Westralians depend on heavy industry for their livelihood, a growing number are fighting to protect their state's natural resources. Ecotourism of natural attractions has begun to edge out the fishing and animal husbandry industries. Best of all, West Australia has generally avoided the overdevelopment and tourist saturation that some find so distasteful about the east coast. With that in mind, the time is right to go West.

▐▔ TRANSPORTATION

Because of the distances between attractions and the dearth of long-haul transportation, many travelers—even budget travelers—**buy a car** for long visits (see **Buying and Selling Used Cars**, p. 46). A thriving gray market exists for used cars, 4WDs, and campervans, fueled by message boards and the *West Australian* classifieds. **Used car dealerships** line Beaufort St. in and around Mt. Lawley, north of Northbridge. Before paying, have the car checked by a mechanic. Some car dealers prey on backpackers and don't honor warranties. The **Royal Automobile Club (RAC),** 228 Adelaide Tce., Perth, at the corner of Hill St., offers inspections for members and

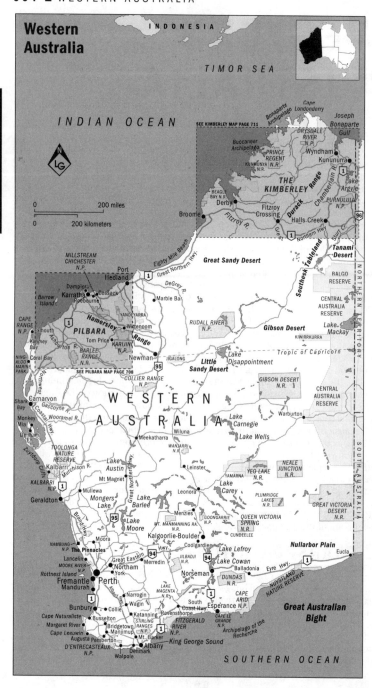

Western Australia

INDONESIA

TIMOR SEA

INDIAN OCEAN

SEE KIMBERLEY MAP PAGE 711

Bonaparte Archipelago

Cape Londonderry

Joseph Bonaparte Gulf

DRYSDALE RIVER N.P.

Buccaneer Archipelago

PRINCE REGENT

KUNUNYA N.R.

Wyndham

Kununurra

THE KIMBERLEY

Durack Range

Chamberlain R.

Great Northern Hwy

Lake Argyle

PURNULULU N.P.

96

BEAGLE BAY N.R.

Derby

Fitzroy Crossing

Halls Creek

Broome

Fitzroy R.

Tanami Desert

Southeast Tableland

Sturt Cr.

Northern Hwy

RALGO RESERVE

MILLSTREAM CHICHESTER N.P.

Eighty Mile Beach

Great Northern Hwy

Great Sandy Desert

NORTHERN TERRITORY

Port Hedland

DeGrey R.

CENTRAL AUSTRALIA RESERVE

Dampier
Karratha
Cossack
Roebourne

Marble Bar

Barrow Island

YANDEYARRA

Wittenoom

RUDALL RIVER N.P.

Gibson Desert

Lake Mackay

CAPE RANGE N.P.

Ashburton R.

Hamersley

PILBARA

Tom Price

KARIJINI N.P.

Range

KIWIRRKURRA

Exmouth

Klehey Bay

Coral Bay

BARLEE RANGE N.R.

Newman

JIGALONG

Little Sandy Desert

Lake Disappointment

Tropic of Capricorn

NING ALOO MARINE PARK

SEE PILBARA MAP PAGE 708

COLLIER RANGE N.P.

GIBSON DESERT N.R.

CENTRAL AUSTRALIA RESERVE

Carnarvon

Gascoyne R.

WESTERN

AUSTRALIA

Lake Carnegie

Warburton

Shark Bay

Wooramel R.

Coastal Hwy

Lake Wells

SOUTH AUSTRALIA

Monkey Mia

Denham

Wiluna

Meekatharra

TOOLONGA NATURE RESERVE

WANJARRI N.R.

NEALE JUNCTION N.R.

Zuytdorp Cliffs

Kalbarri

Murchison R.

Lake Austin

Leinster

YAMARNA N.R.

YEO LAKE N.R.

KALBARRI N.P.

Mt Magnet

Leonora

Lake Carey

PLUMRIDGE LAKES N.R.

GREAT VICTORIA DESERT N.R.

Geraldton

Mullewa

Mongers Lake

Great Northern Hwy

Lake Barlee

Menzies

GOONGARRIE N.P.

QUEEN VICTORIA SPRING N.R.

Moora

Lake Moore

MT. MANMANNING RA. N.R.

Kalgoorlie-Boulder

CUNDEELEE

NAMBUNG N.P.

The Pinnacles

95

Coolgardie

Lake Lefroy

Nullarbor Plain

Eucla

Lancelin

MOORE RIVER N.P.

Great Eastern Hwy

Merredin

JILBADJI N.R.

94

Lake Cowan

Rottnest Island

Northam

York

Balladonia

Eyre Hwy

Fremantle

Perth

Mandurah

Norseman

NUYTSLAND NATURE RESERVE

Narrogin

DUNDAS N.R.

CAPE ARID N.P.

Great Australian Bight

Bunbury

Wagin

LAKE MAGENTA N.R.

Collie

South Coast Hwy

Esperance

Cape Naturaliste

Busselton

Katanning

Ravensthorpe

CAPE LE GRANDE

Margaret River

Bridgetown

STIRLING RANGES N.P.

FITZGERALD RIVER N.P.

Archipelago of the Recherche

Cape Leeuwin

Augusta

Manjimup

Pemberton

Mt. Barker

D'ENTRECASTEAUX N.P.

Albany

King George Sound

Walpole

Denmark

SOUTHERN OCEAN

0 ___ 200 miles

0 ___ 200 kilometers

N LG

WESTERN AUSTRALIA HIGHLIGHTS

ROTTNEST ISLAND. Get up close and personal with quokkas (rat-like wallabies) at the only place they exist on earth. (p. 678)

BIBBULMUN TRACK. Hike the ultimate western adventure on this popular 964km trail. (p. 679)

BUNBURY. Frolic with Flipper in the Southwest's dolphin mecca. (p. 680)

NINGALOO REEF. Swim with whale sharks along 250km of Indian Ocean coral. (p. 704)

CABLE BEACH. The sunset camel rides in Broome never fail to impress. (p. 711)

GIBB RIVER ROAD. Stumble upon a tropical gorge and other surreal wonders along this untouched desert track. (p. 718)

provides roadside assistance. (☎ 13 17 04, roadside assistance ☎ 13 11 11. One-year membership $86.90; inspections from $100.) For more info, see **On the Road,** p. 48.

If you plan to drive through the desert, bring plenty of water, petrol, a spare tire, a beacon, and a fanbelt. A cellular phone is a handy gadget to have along, as well, but make sure it has coverage where you're headed. Winter and early spring are the safest times to drive the Great Northern Hwy. because temperatures are lower and traffic more frequent. Throughout WA, you'll share the highway with **road trains,** massive tractor-trailers. Don't assume their turn signal is an attempt to communicate that it's ok to pass them; several people have been killed making this mistake. *Let's Go* does not recommend hitchhiking, but some people do it. The most reliable way to get a ride is to check hostel message boards.

With the exception of the Kalgoorlie to Perth route, serviced by the *Indian Pacific* and Westrail Prospector trains, and a commuter train from Perth to Bunbury, passenger **rail** service is essentially nonexistent. **South West Coach Lines** and **Westrail** operate **bus** services southwest of Perth. **Integrity** Buslines services towns between Perth and Broome, and **McCafferty's/Greyhound** and EasyRider run buses throughout the state. Try to book at least a day ahead; space may be limited and the bus might not even stop unless the driver knows you're waiting. If you plan on a lot of bus travel, cheaper passes are available. For more info, see **By Bus,** p. 43.

Portions of Western Australia can be toured by **bicycle,** but you must carry significant amounts of water. In northern WA, it's not advisable to bike in the hotter, wetter months. Advise regional police and the **Royal Flying Doctor Service** of your itinerary. The **Ministry of Sport and Recreation** (☎ 9387 9700) has more info.

A bewildering range of guided group **tours** are available around Perth and throughout the state. Tourist officials, travel agents, and hostel managers can help narrow the options. Standard prices for four- to five-day tours through the Southwest—to Monkey Mia, Kalbarri, and the Pinnacles—are around $450.

PERTH ☎ 08

Perth, the city of "no worries," is quickly becoming a city of bustling business and booming tourism. Still, it all seems to work somehow; 19th-century churches look surprisingly comfortable nestled between glass skyscrapers. Proximity to Asia and an increasing role as a tourist gateway to both WA and Australia have given Perth a cosmopolitan population and a bustling feel. Single blocks offer cuisine from every continent, and tours leaving for a thousand destinations are advertised in shop windows everywhere. In such an energetic metropolis, it's easy to forget that Perth is the world's most isolated capital city (Adelaide is a soporific two-day drive away), but a short trip outside the city limits will quickly remind you that the surrounding areas are a different story. Indeed, 90% of the state lives within these few square kilometers. For those less enamoured with the new Perth, nearby historic Fremantle (known as "Freo") is a link to the slower-paced past.

■ INTERCITY TRANSPORTATION

WESTERN AUSTRALIA

BY PLANE. Flights arrive at and depart from Perth Airport, east of the city. The international terminal is 8km away from domestic terminals; keep this in mind if you're planning a connection. **Qantas** (☎ 13 13 13) flies daily to: Adelaide (2¾hr., $223-657); Brisbane (4½hr., $296-850); Cairns (indirect, $429-803); Darwin (3½hr., 247-759); Melbourne (3¼hr., $242-735); and Sydney (4hr., $269-816). For trips within the state, try **Qantas** (www.qantas.com.au) or regional carrier **SkyWest** (www.skywest.com.au). Most major towns in WA are serviced by one or both.

There are a few transport options between the city and airport. **TransPerth buses** #36, 37, and 39 run between the domestic terminal and the city, leaving from the north side of St. George Tce., stop 39 (35min., every 30min, $2.90). An **Airport City Shuttle** (☎ 9475 2999) runs frequently between most city hotels and hostels in Perth and both the domestic ($11) and international ($13) terminals. The **Fremantle Airport Shuttle** goes to both terminals, departing daily from the Fremantle Railway Station regularly until midnight; pickup at Fremantle accommodations is available 24hr. when booked in advance. (☎ 9383 4115. $15.) A **taxi** to the city center costs around $25 from domestic terminals and $25-30 from the international terminal.

BY TRAIN. All eastbound trains depart from the **East Perth Terminal,** on Summer St. off Lord St., a 25min. walk northeast of the city center. **TransPerth trains** transport between the station and the city center every 15min. on weekdays and every 30min. on weekends. **Westrail** (☎ 13 10 53; www.westrail.wa.gov.au) serves Bunbury (2hr., 2 per day, $20) and Kalgoorlie (8hr., 2 per day, $55). The *Indian Pacific* runs east to: Adelaide (43hr., $283); Melbourne (56hr., $340); Sydney (65hr., $459). Students and cardholders are half-price.

BY BUS. Westrail (☎ 13 10 53) runs buses from the East Perth Terminal. The more expensive **McCafferty's/Greyhound** (☎ 13 14 99 or 13 20 30) departs from Perth Station in the city center. **Southwest Coach Lines** (☎ 9324 2333) leaves from the Perth City Bus Port, Mounts Bay Rd. See the table on p. 668.

BY CAR. There are over a hundred rental companies in greater Perth. Some quote dirt-cheap daily rates, but read the fine print—many have 100km driving limits, voiding your insurance if you drive north of a certain limit. As in most industries in Perth, there are often backpacker specials. All companies listed rent to drivers over 20, usually with an extra charge of up to $10 per day for under 25. **Bayswater,** 160 Adelaide Tce. (☎ 9325 1000), or 13 Queen Victoria Ave., Fremantle (☎ 9430 5300), allows trips as far north as Carnarvon or to Port Hedland for an extra $100 total. **Cottesloe Car and Ute Hire,** 2 Servetus St., Swanbourne (☎ 9383 3057), does not allow its cars to go north. **Atlas Rent-a-Car,** 36 Miligan St. (☎ 9481 8866 or 1800 659 999), allows travel to Exmouth. Though costs vary depending on distance and vehicle, rates in the city are reasonable: $35-45 per day ($25 off-season) for 100km per day; weekly rates are cheaper. Though there are sometimes exceptions, **4WD vehicles** are generally the only way to explore unsealed areas; 4WDs start at $100 per day, often with extra charges for unlimited kilometers and drivers under 25. **ATC,** 145-151 Adelaide Tce. (☎ 9325 1833), and **South Perth 4WD Rentals,** 80 Canning Hwy., Victoria Park (☎ 9362 5444; enquire@sp4wd.com.au), rent 4WD. **The Travellers' Club,** 499 Wellington St. (☎ 9226 0660), across from the train station, helps backpackers with rentals. Some hostels have special deals with local companies.

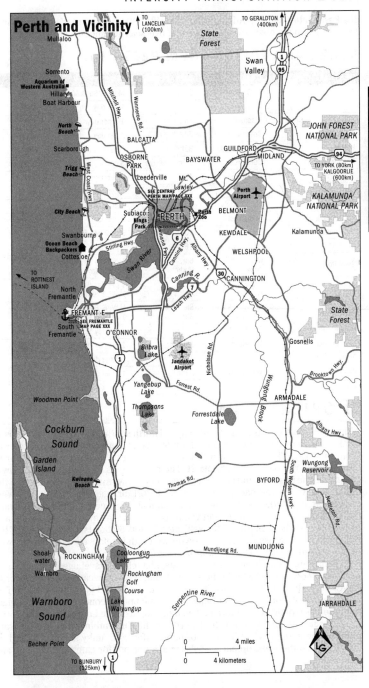

Perth and Vicinity

SEE CENTRAL PERTH MAP PAGE XXX

SEE FREMANTLE MAP PAGE XXX

TO LANCELIN (100km)

TO GERALDTON (400km)

State Forest

Swan Valley

Mullaloo

Sorrento

Aquarium of Western Australia ■

Hillary's Boat Harbour

North Beach

Scarborough

Trigg Beach

City Beach

Swanbourne

Ocean Beach Backpackers

Cottesloe

TO ROTTNEST ISLAND

North Fremantle

FREMANTLE

South Fremantle

O'CONNOR

BALCATTA

OSBORNE PARK

Leederville

Subiaco

Kings Park

Mitchell Hwy.

Wanneroo Rd.

BAYSWATER

GUILDFORD

MIDLAND

Mt. Lawley

Perth Airport

JOHN FOREST NATIONAL PARK

TO YORK (80km) KALGOORLIE (600km)

KALAMUNDA NATIONAL PARK

Kalamunda

PERTH

Perth Zoo

BELMONT

KEWDALE

WELSHPOOL

CANNINGTON

Canning Hwy.

Albany Hwy.

Kwinana Fwy.

Canning Fwy.

Swan River

Stirling Hwy.

West Coast Hwy.

Canning R.

Leach Hwy.

Bilbra Lake

Jandakot Airport

Yangebup Lake

Thompsons Lake

Forest Rd.

Nicholson Rd.

Gosnells

State Forest

Brookton Hwy.

Woodman Point

Cockburn Sound

Garden Island

Kwinana Beach

Forrestdale Lake

ARMADALE

Wungong Brook

Albany Hwy.

Wungong Reservoir

Thomas Rd.

BYFORD

South Western Hwy.

Netterton Rd.

Shoalwater

Warnbro

ROCKINGHAM

Cooloongup Lake

Rockingham Golf Course

Lake Walyungup

Mundijong Rd.

MUNDIJONG

Serpentine River

JARRAHDALE

Warnboro Sound

Becher Point

TO BUNBURY (125km)

0   4 miles

0   4 kilometers

WESTERN AUSTRALIA

The Royal Auto Club, 228 Adelaide Tce. (☎9421 4400), offers roadside assistance (☎ 13 11 11) to members of RAC or several overseas automobile associations.

BUSES AND TRAINS FROM PERTH TO:

DESTINATION	COMPANY	DURATION	TIMES	PRICE
Adelaide	McCafferty's	36hr.	M-W, F, Su 6:30am	$226
Albany (via Bunbury)	Westrail	6-8hr.	1 per day	$38
Albany (via Mt. Barker)	Westrail	6hr.	1-2 per day	$38
Augusta	Southwest	5-5½hr.	2 per day	$30
Broome	McCafferty's	32hr.	1 per day (F, Su 2)	$266
Bunbury	Southwest	2½hr.	3 per day	$19
Busselton	Southwest	4hr.	3 per day	$22
Carnarvon	McCafferty's	12hr.	1 per day (W, F, Su 3)	$103
Darwin	McCafferty's	56hr.	1 per day	$496
Dunsborough	Southwest	4½hr	1 per day	$24
Esperance	Westrail	10hr.	Su-F 2 per day	$58
Exmouth	McCafferty's	16½hr.	1 per day	$200
Geraldton	McCafferty's Westrail	6hr. 6-8hr.	1 per day (W, F, Su 3) 1-2 per day	$37 $40
Kalbarri	McCafferty's Westrail	8hr. 8hr.	1 per day (W, F, Su 2) M, W, F 8:30am	$76 $50
Kalgoorlie	McCafferty's Westrail	8hr. 8hr.	M-W, F, Su 1 per day	$101 $54
Margaret River	Southwest	4½hr.	2 per day	$27
Monkey Mia	McCafferty's	12-14hr.	1 per day (W, F, Su 3)	$134
Pemberton (via Bunbury)	Westrail	5½hr.	1-2 per day Su-Th	$35
Port Hedland	McCafferty's	24hr.	1-2 per day	$186
York	Westrail	1½hr.	1-2 per day Su-F	$11

◪ ORIENTATION

Although Perth's streets are not quite aligned north-south and east-west, it helps to think of them as such, and locals will understand what you mean if you refer to them that way. The east-west avenues run parallel to **Wellington St.** The north-south streets run parallel to **William St.** The railway cuts east-west through town, separating the business and government center of downtown to the south from the cultural, culinary, and backpacker center of Northbridge. Downtown, east-west streets **Hay** and **Murray St.** become pedestrian malls between William and Barrack St. Shopping arcades and overhead walkways connect the malls to each other and to the Perth Railway Station. The **Wellington St. Bus Station** is a block west of the railway station, across William St. Downtown Perth is relatively safe, but not well lit. *It's probably best not to walk alone at night.*

In **Northbridge,** a multitude of restaurants, nightclubs, travel agencies, and budget accommodations cluster in the square bounded by Newcastle St. to the north, James St. to the South, Beaufort St. to the east, and Russel Sq. to the west. A few blocks north of Northbridge on Beaufort St., the up-and-coming **Mt. Lawley** neighborhood has wonderful restaurants and more sophisticated nightlife. In the northwest, **Leederville,** one stop north of Perth on the Currambine line, is a pleasant place to spend the day, with plenty of pubs, cafes, and funky shops centered on Oxford St. To the west, upmarket **Subiaco** is a hotspot for cafes and cuisine, and has weekend market stalls on either side of the Subiaco train stop on the Fremantle line. Great, green **Kings Park** rises just southwest of downtown, overlooking the city and the Swan River. Although technically its own city and 30min. away, **Fremantle (Freo)** is effectively part of greater Perth. While Perth is the central business district, Freo is the laid-back fishing port and hotbed for the arts. **TransPerth** buses and trains run regularly between the two (30min.). The Fremantle train also passes through **Swanbourne** and **Cottesloe,** lively beach suburbs.

▐ LOCAL TRANSPORTATION

Like all cities of a million-plus people, Perth takes up a bit of space. However, downtown and Northbridge are compact and easy to navigate on foot. Most hostels and the tourist agency provide free maps. The free **CAT bus services** whisk passengers around downtown Perth and Fremantle. The **blue CAT** runs a north-south loop from the Swan River to Northbridge; the **red CAT** runs east-west from West Perth to East Perth. The new **Fremantle CAT** runs a skinny loop along the harbor. (☎ 13 62 13. Blue CAT every 7min., weekends every 15min.; M-Th 6:50am-6:20pm, F-Sa 6:50am-1am, Su 10am-5pm. Red CAT every 5min.; M-F 6:50am-6:20pm, Sa-Su 10am-6:15pm. Freo CAT every 10min.; M-F 7:30am-6:30pm, Sa-Su 10am-6:30pm.)

The **TransPerth** network of **buses, trains,** and **ferries** is divided into eight **fare zones** connecting to outlying areas; a two-zone ride costs $2.90 and will get you from the city center to the airport, Fremantle, or the beach. Save your **ticket stub**—it allows transfer between bus, train, and ferry services. Tickets are generally valid for two hours. **All-day passes** ($7.30) and **multi-ride cards** are available at TransPerth Info-Centre machines and newsagents. It's tempting to ride without paying, but $50 penalties await freeloaders who get caught, and there's no shortage of ticket-checking officers on trains. Maps, timetables, and additional info are available by phone (☎ 13 62 13) or at the four TransPerth InfoCentres: Plaza Arcade, Wellington St. Bus Station, City Busport, and the train station.

It's also easy to get around by **taxi;** a ride between the international airport terminal and Northbridge costs between $25 and $30. **Swan Taxi,** 1008 Wellington St. (☎ 13 13 30), or **Black and White Taxi** (☎ 13 13 88) can be hailed around the city, especially along Wellington St. or William St. The tourist office has maps of **bike** routes. The **Bicycle Transportation Alliance,** 2 Delhi St. (☎ 9420 7210), has info, maps, and advice on bike routes. Bikes can be rented at Kings Park or stands around the city.

▐ PRACTICAL INFORMATION

TOURIST AND FINANCIAL SERVICES

Tourist Offices: Perth Visitors Center (☎ 1300 361 351; fax 9481 0190), on the corner of Wellington and Forrest Pl. Open M-Th 8:30am-6pm, F 8:30am-7pm, Sa 8:30am-5pm, Su 10am-5pm; off-season M-Th 8:30am-5:30pm, F 8:30am-6pm, Sa 8:30am-4:30pm, Su 10am-3pm. **Fremantle Tourist Bureau** (☎ 9431 7878), on the corner of High St. and William St., Kings Sq. Open M-F 9am-5pm, Sa 9am-4pm, Su noon-5pm.

Outdoors Info: CALM, 17 Dick Perry Ave. (☎ 9334 0333), near the corner of Hayman Rd. and Kent St., Kensington. Take bus #33 east to stop 19. Open M-F 8am-5pm.

Budget Travel: YHA Western Australia, 236 William St., Northbridge, and Raine Sq. on William St. downtown (☎ 9227 5122; enquiries@yhawa.com.au), arranges YHA discounted travel and sells memberships. **STA Travel,** 100 James St., Northbridge (☎ 9227 7569). Open M-F 9am-5pm, Sa 10am-3pm. Branch at 53 Market St., Fremantle (☎ 9430 5553). Open M-F 9am-5pm, Sa 10am-3pm, Su 11am-3:30pm.

WESTERN AUSTRALIA

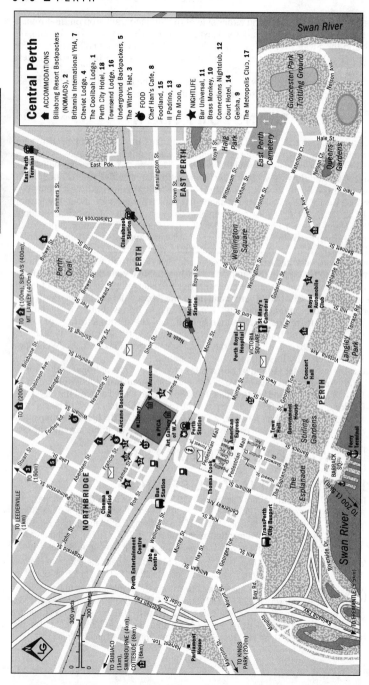

Central Perth

▲ ACCOMMODATIONS
Billabong Resort Backpackers (NOMADS), 2
Britannia International YHA, 7
Cheviot Lodge, 4
The Coolibah Lodge, 1
Perth City Hotel, 18
Townsend Lodge, 16
Underground Backpackers, 5
The Witch's Hat, 3

● FOOD
Chef Han's Cafe, 8
Foodland, 15
Il Padrino, 13
The Moon, 6

★ NIGHTLIFE
Bar Universal, 11
Brass Monkey, 10
Connections Nightclub, 12
Court Hotel, 14
Geisha, 9
The Metropolis Club, 17

Embassies and Consulates: Canada, 267 St. Georges Tce. (☎9322 7930); **Ireland,** 10 Lilika Rd., City Beach (☎9385 8247); **United Kingdom,** 77 St. Georges Tce. (☎9221 5400); **United States,** 16 St. George's Tce. (☎9231 9400).

Currency Exchange: Thomas Cook (☎9481 7900), at the Piccadilly Arcade on Hay St. Open M-F 8:45am-4:45pm, Sa 10am-2pm. **American Express,** 645 Hay St. Mall (☎9221 0777), London Court. Foreign exchange open M-F 9am-5pm, Sa 9am-noon. **ATMs** and **banks** everywhere, especially on William St. in Northbridge and on Hay St. in the mall area between Barrack and William St. Most ATMs accept **Cirrus/Plus.**

Work Opportunities: Most hostels, particularly bigger ones, maintain notice boards with job openings. A great resource, particularly for work in the WA countryside, is **Workstay,** 158 William St., 1st fl. (☎9226 0970). Workstay maintains a network of farms and other horticultural businesses that need temporary labor. They are well-coordinated with area hostels and have a burgeoning network in Perth. They also have a growing network of pubs outside Perth that are looking for barmaids. As of Aug. 2002, a **membership** costs $25 per year and pub work $50 per year, though prices are due to rise. Employment agencies in Perth are generally uninterested in backpackers staying less than a couple of months. **Drake International,** 190 St. George's Tce. (☎13 14 48), recruits long-term employees. **Hays Personnel Services,** 172 St. George's Tce. (☎9322 5198), may be a bit more traveler-friendly. **Adecco,** 37 St. George's Tce. (☎9461 4800), is another option. **Free Spirit,** 18-20 Howard St. (☎9485 0788), off St. Georges Tce. near William St., is a good resource for traveling office workers. A **job center** with a searchable database is on the corner of Wellington and Milligan St., though most of its resources are reserved for Australian residents. (Open 8:30am-4:30pm.)

LOCAL SERVICES

Public Markets: Subiaco, at the Pavilion at the corner of Rokeby and Roberts Rd. Open Th-F 10am-9pm, Sa-Su 10am-5pm. **Fremantle:** 84 South Tce. Open F 9am-9pm, Sa 9am-5pm, Su 10am-5pm.

Library: The **Alexander Library Building** (☎9427 3111), at the north end of the Perth Cultural Centre. **Internet** for research only. Open M-Th 9am-8pm, F 9am-5:30pm, Sa-Su 10am-5:30pm. Wheelchair accessible.

Ticket Agencies: For sporting events, try **Ticketmaster** (☎13 61 00; www.ticketmaster7.com), at Perth Entertainment Centre at Wellington and Miligan St., and in the underground at 713 Hay St. Mall. Open M-F 9am-5:30pm, Sa 9am-1pm. For theatrical and musical events throughout the city, reach **BOCS Tickets,** Perth Concert Hall, 5 St. George's Tce. (☎9484 1133; fax 9221 2241). Open M-F 8:30am-5:30pm.

MEDIA AND PUBLICATIONS
Newspapers: *The West Australian* (88¢).
Backpackerism: *TNT* gives reviews of Australian destinations and info on all things backpacker. *GoWest* has a free classified section for travelers.
Nightlife: *XPress* and *Hype* come out weekly (free). For gay nightlife, try the weekly *Out in Perth* (free). *Women Out West* is a lesbian monthly ($4.50).
Radio: Rock, 96FM and 92.9FM; News, ABC 720AM; Tourist Info, 88FM.

EMERGENCY AND COMMUNICATIONS

Emergency: ☎000.
Police: ☎9222 1111; Fremantle ☎9430 1222.
Hotlines: Sexual Assault (24hr. ☎1800 199 888). **AIDS/STD Line** (☎9429 9944).
Hospital: Royal Perth Hospital (☎9224 2244), on Wellington St. near Lord St.

THE HOBBLIT

Maybe it was the fall I'd taken in Cape Leeuwin-Nauraliste, or the 20km hike through the Stirlings and Porongurups, but by my first night in Perth, my right foot had given out. But the show—or at least the research—must go on, and so the next morning I hobbled to the local pharmacy. After searching the mysterious backrooms, the clerk emerged to report that the pharmacy's arsenal of walkers and walking assistance contrivances had dwindled to a single child's cane, and he suggested I try the senior citizens center. Another ten minutes of cringing brought me, travel-grubby and dishevelled, to the center. The look on the receptionist's face showed that the center was not frequented by limping, haggard twenty-something Americans, and her suspicion was only slightly reduced when I explained my predicament. However, she finally saw fit to get the center's director, if only for security purposes.

The director seemed bewildered at first, but eventually understood. They did have one pair of crutches that had been abandoned by an unknown patron, she said. I could borrow them if I promised to bring them back. We inched our way down the hall to the lost and found room, my twisted steps in a dead heat with a walker-wielding senior. And then, there they were...my blessed chariot, a pair of rickety wooden crutches. I flew back down the hall, to the suspicious glare of the receptionist, who demanded that I give her my *real* name and number, as she apparently had me pegged as a professional crutch thief. I swung out the door, back to work. **—Scott Roy**

Internet Access: Student Uni Travel, 513 Wellington St. (☎9321 8330), offers 15-20min. free email. Open M-F 8am-6pm, Sa 11am-3pm. The going rate in Northbridge is $3 per hr. Fast connections include: **Internet Go Go,** 150 William St., Northbridge (☎9226 3282), at $3 per hr., and **net.CHAT,** shop 14, Wesley Way Arcade, Market St., Freo (☎9433 2011). 10¢ per min., $4 per hr. Open daily 8-11am and 9-11pm.

Post Office: 3 Forrest Pl. (☎9237 5460). Poste Restante M-F only. Open M-F 8am-5:30pm, Sa 9am-12:30pm, Su noon-4pm. **Fremantle GPO,** 13 Market St. (☎9335 1611). Open M-F 8:30am-5pm. **Postal Code:** 6000 (Perth); 6160 (Fremantle).

■ ACCOMMODATIONS

Perth has many luxury hotels and a glut of hostels, with little in between. Hostels downtown and in Northbridge tend to be large and institutional places to party and find out what's happening. North of Northbridge, converted houses afford more privacy and space. Check the classifieds of the *West Australian* for listings of rooms and flats to lease; they can be cheaper than hostels for longer stays. All hostels listed book or help out with tours, will generally pick up, and offer luggage storage, on-site laundry facilities, and kitchens. Call ahead if arriving late.

CITY PROPER

▨ **The Witch's Hat,** 148 Palmerston St., Northbridge (☎9228 4228; witchs_hat@hotmail.com). This beautiful pointed building was built in 1837 by the architect of the Horseshoe Bridge, which takes William St. over the train station. Hardwood floors, grand front hall, and a brick courtyard in a quiet neighborhood just north of Northbridge. Most dorms have 4 or 6 beds. Internet $5 per hr. Dorms $19; twins $49; doubles $54. ❷

▨ **Billabong Resort Backpackers (NOMADS),** 381 Beaufort St. (☎9328 7720). A new, swanky megaplex. An old college dormitory renovated into a state-of-the-art, 180-bed hostel with exercise room, game room, library, and pool. Internet $4 per hr. 4-bed dorms $20, 6-bed $19, 8-bed $18; singles, doubles, and family rooms $55. ❷

Britannia International YHA, 253 William St., Northbridge (☎9328 6121; britannia@yhawa.com.au). A massive place with 10-bed dorms and dining space. Internet $4 per hr. Reception 24hr. Dorms $19; singles $27; doubles $52. YHA. ❷

Townsend Lodge, 240 Adelaide Tce., East Perth (☎9325 4143). A great deal for basic singles. Internet $4 per hr. Singles $33; 3+ nights $22, students $20. ❸

Underground Backpackers, 268 Newcastle St. (☎9228 3755; fax 9228 3744). Enough beds to accommodate an army. 6- to 10- bed dorms with big windows and high ceilings. Bar, pool, and brick basement lounge in a good location. Internet $5 per hr. Dorms $19; 4-bed dorms $21; twins and doubles $55. ❷

Cheviot Lodge, 30 Bulwer St. (☎9227 6817; www.cheviotlodge.com), close to the East Perth train station. This homey, attractive former college residence has lots of desks and furniture, along with partitions or curtains between beds, affording more privacy. Fairly regular art workshops. Free Internet. Dorms $15-17; twins $38; doubles $42. ❷

The Coolibah Lodge, 194 Brisbane St., Northbridge (☎9328 9958). A maze of lounges, dorms, and kitchens in a remodeled colonial home. Will help guests find work in Perth or in the country through Workstay. Mostly 4-bed dorms, two 6-beds. Free pickup. Internet $2 per 20min. Dorms $20; singles $36; doubles $50-52. VIP. ❷

Perth City Hotel, 200 Hay St. (☎9220 7000). Nice motel-style rooms in a basic hotel. One of Perth's cheaper hotels. Doubles $83; triples $94; quads $105. ❺

FREMANTLE

▨ **YHA Backpackers Inn Freo,** 11 Pakenham St. (☎9431 7065; fax 9336 7106). From the train station, turn right onto Phillimore St., then left onto Pakenham. Attractive, spacious renovated warehouse space. Relaxed and normally quiet. Reception 7am-11:30pm; 24hr. check-in available. Dorms $18; singles $30; doubles $44; family rooms $60. NOMADS/VIP/YHA. ❷

▨ **Sundancer Backpackers Resort,** 80 High St. (☎1800 061 144). This brand-new hostel is a restored turn-of-the-century hotel, with one of the most interesting, elegant hostel lobbies around. Fresh futuristic artwork, giant metal fish sculpture, and heated spa. No A/C. 4-, 6-, and 8-bed dorms $17-20; doubles $50, ensuite $70; family rooms $70. ❷

Cheviot Marina Backpackers, 4 Beach St. (☎9344 2055; fax 9433 2066). Turn left down Elder St. from train station (becomes Beach St.). A big, sunny place with a friendly lounge upstairs and discounted drinks at the bar next door. Internet $1 per 20min. Dorms $14; singles $27; twins and doubles $35. VIP/YHA. ❶

Old Firestation Backpackers, 18 Phillimore St. (☎9430 5454; fax 9335 6828), at Henry St. Unlimited Internet, laundry, videos, digital jukebox. Most rooms have TVs. Finds work for guests. Some may not like the security cameras linked to the office. Cheap curries from the connected restaurant. Dorms $17; twins and doubles $44. ❷

His Majesty's Hotels (☎9335 9516), on the corner of Mouat and Phillimore St. Huge, somewhat bare doubles and smaller singles in a historic hotel with a classy bar downstairs. Singles $35; doubles $70, ensuite $110. ❸

◖ FOOD

Perth's cuisine is tremendously varied. Northbridge has a horde of delicious Italian restaurants and noodle houses. Culinary diversity peaks in Mt. Lawley, where a dozen nationalities are represented in two blocks. Subiaco is elegant (and pricey). In Fremantle, sophisticates loll about in cafes on the Cappuccino strip.

Grab meats and produce at **City Fresh Fruit Company,** 375 William St. (open M-Sa 7am-8pm, Su 7am-7pm), or hike to the more comprehensive **Foodland,** 556 Hay St. (open M-Th 8am-6:30pm, F 8am-8pm, Sa 9am-6pm, Su 10:30am-6pm). For cheap, quality imported bulk pasta, cereals, and deli foods, elbow through the crowds into **Kakulas Brothers Wholesale Importers,** 185 William St. (Open M-F 8am-5:30pm, Sa 8am-5pm.) In Fremantle, **Kakulas Sister** emulates her Perth sibs on the corner of Market and Leake St. (open M-F 9am-5:30pm, Sa 9am-5pm, Su noon-5pm).

THE INSIDER'S CITY

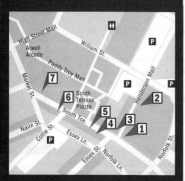

VERY FREO

Fremantle offers a cosmopolitan oasis where you can sip lattes while casting glances over wire-rimmed glasses or digging through stacks of literary treasures. It's a great way to spend an afternoon and is, in local parlance, "very Freo."

1 Browse the famous **Fremantle Markets** for anything and everything you could imagine

2 Find that out-of-print literary gem you've been seeking at **Magpie Books** (☎9335 1131)

3 **The Mill Bakehouse** is a great place to grab a pastry and coffee (☎9430 4252)

4 Look sophisticated while sitting at a sidewalk table with your latte at **Dome** (☎9336 3040)

5 There's always something happening at the **Kulsha Multicultural Centre and Performance Space** (☎9336 4554)

6 Elbow through the crowds for a latte and cake or a cocktail at **Gino's** (☎9336 1461)

7 Peruse the extensive selection at **Elizabeth's Secondhand Bookstore** (☎9433 1310)

A number of pubs and clubs cater specifically to the backpacker set (vegetarian-friendly), enlivening the crowds with free meals and drink specials. The determined can find free food almost every night. M: **The Deen**, 84 Aberdeen St. (☎9227 9361); Tu and Th: **hip-e-club** (☎9227 8899), on Newcastle and Oxford St. in Leederville; W: ▨**The Post Office** (☎9228 0077), on Aberdeen and Parker St.

CITY PROPER

▨ **Il Padrino**, 198 William St. (☎9227 9065). Perth's best pizza ($15-25). Tu dinner half-price pizza and $10 pasta. Open Tu-F 11am-3pm and 5pm-late, Sa 5pm-late. ❹

Chef Han's Cafe, 140 Oxford St., Leederville (☎9328 8122). With a few locations around Perth, Chef Han is the emperor of local budget cuisine. Delicious, fast heaps of vegetarian-friendly noodle and stir-fry for $6-8. Open daily 11am-10pm. ❶

The Moon, 323 William St. (☎9328 7474). A space-age-retro diner filled late at night by the young, black-clad, and trend-setting. Several veggie options. Pasta, seafood, burgers $10-18. Open daily 5pm-late. ❷

Subiaco Hotel (☎9381 3069), on the corner of Hay and Rokeby St. Award-winning nouveau cuisine from risotto to lamb and rabbit in an elegant setting ($17-25). ❹

Siena's, 500 Beaufort St., Mt. Lawley (☎9227 6991), and also 115 Oxford St., Leederville (☎9444 8844). One of countless great restaurants in Mt. Lawley. Delicious cakes, pizzas, and pasta $12-20. Open noon-11pm; sometimes closed in the afternoon. ❸

FREMANTLE

▨ **Cicerello's**, 44 Mews Rd. (☎9335 1991). One of Western Australia's classic fish 'n' chips joints. Hang out with the hundreds of multicolored fish in the 15m fish tank while you munch on their well-fried brethren ($5-10). Open daily 10am-8:30pm. ❶

Hara Cafe, 33 High St. (☎9335 6118). Good, cheap vegetarian meals. Thalis $6-9, teas $3.50 a pot. Open M-Tu 11am-4pm, W-F 11am-9pm, Sa-Su noon-9pm. ❶

Fiorelli, 19C Essex St. (☎9430 6119). Friendly staff and satisfying Italian food ($12-16). All-you-can-eat pizza/pasta special Tu and W nights ($11). Open daily 10am-3:30pm and 5-10pm. ❷

Roma, 9-13 High St. (☎9335 3664). Good Italian food in a relaxing atmosphere ($11-18). Try the ravioli ($8) or spaghetti ($7). Open M-Sa noon-2pm and 5pm-late. ❷

◙ SIGHTS

CITY PROPER

PERTH ZOO. The Australian section has frilled lizards, crocodiles, echidnas, and wallabies, while the African Savannah has lions, meerkats, and rhinos. If you can dodge all the strollers, it's a pretty good time. *(On Labouchere Rd. in South Perth. Take the blue CAT to the jetty and then ferry across the river for $1.10, or take bus #35 from the City Bus Port. 24hr. infoline ☎9474 3551. Open daily 8am-5:30pm. $14, children $7, under 4 free.)*

AQUARIUM OF WESTERN AUSTRALIA. Leafy sea dragons, saltwater crocodiles, and four kinds of sharks make AQWA their home. Walk through a tunnel surrounded by fish and feed animals in a pool. Adults can book ahead to dive with the sharks or swim with the seals for $90. *(North of Perth along the West Coast Hwy. at Hillary's Harbour, off the Hepburn Ave. exit. Take the Joondalup train to Warwick, then the #423 bus to Hillary's. $3. ☎9447 7500. Open May-Nov. daily 10am-5pm; Dec.-Apr. M-Tu and Th-Su 10am-5pm, W 10am-9pm. $20, concessions $16, children $12.50, under 4 free.)*

KINGS PARK. A spectacular view of the Perth and Swan River can be seen from Kings Park, perched atop Mt. Eliza just west of the city. Its **Botanic Gardens,** next to the **War Memorial,** are home to 1700 native species; free walks depart from the karri log opposite the Memorial daily at 10am and 2pm. *(A 20min. walk by foot west from the city center up St. George's Tce., or take the red CAT to stop #25. Free parking. Info center ☎9480 3600. Gardens open daily 9am-4pm.)*

BEACHES. The Perth beach experience is calm and carefree, with numerous clusters of shops and cafes. Families flock to **Cottesloe Beach,** on the Fremantle train line, for swimming and mild surf, while teenage boys wander north to **Swanbourne Beach** to ogle the nude sunbathers. *(Bus #71, 72, or 75 or a 2km walk from the Swanbourne stop on the Fremantle train.)* **City Beach** is a great swimming spot. *(Bus #81, 84, or 85 from the stop in front of Hobnobs on Wellington St.)* **Scarborough** has bigger surfing waves and crowds of twenty-somethings. *(Bus #400 from Wellington St. Station.)* Surfers rip through the tubes at **Trigg Beach,** just north of Scarborough; the waves here can get a bit rough for swimming. *(Joondalup train to Warwick, then bus #423.)*

EARTH, SEA, AND SKY. Captain Cook Cruises has a selection of tours, including cruises to the Zoo to Aboriginal Heritage Tours ($15-80). Rent catamarans and windsurfs on the south bank off Mill Point Rd., opposite the city center. **Malibu City Dive** has diving tours to Rottnest Island (see p. 678), noted for its unique corals and fish, and also offers scuba certification classes. *(126 Barrack St. ☎9225 7555. Rottnest trips including equipment start at $135, without equipment $80.)* **Planet Perth** has several tour options, from a short night tour of a wildlife park with kangaroos, koalas, and Tasmanian devils to trips farther afield to many WA destinations. *(☎9225 6622. Tours start at $40.)* For Pinnacles tours (see **Nambung NP,** p. 699), popular options are **West Coast Explorer** *(☎9418 8835),* **Redback Safaris** *(☎9275 6204),* and **Travelabout Outback Adventures.** *(☎9244 1200. Tours from $90.)* **W.A. Skydiving Academy** offers tandem jumps. *(199 William St., Northbridge. ☎9227 6066 or 1800 245 066. From $220.)*

CULTURAL CENTRE

The Perth Cultural Centre, abutting William St. in Northbridge, packs several good museums and performance centers as well as the city library in a mere city block.

THE ART GALLERY OF WESTERN AUSTRALIA. This gallery has large collections of modern and classical Australian art including some Aboriginal carvings and paintings, and also hosts traveling international exhibits. *(☎9492 6600. Open daily 10am-5pm. Free guided tours Tu-Sa 1pm, F 12:30pm. Free, except for special exhibitions.)*

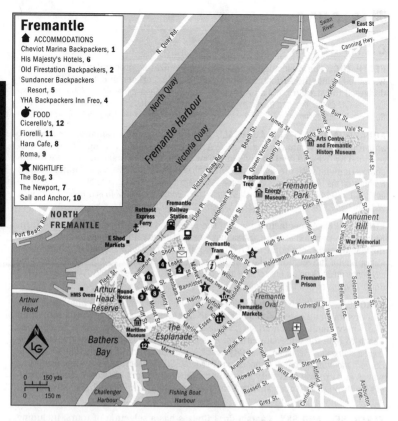

Fremantle

🏠 ACCOMMODATIONS
Cheviot Marina Backpackers, **1**
His Majesty's Hotels, **6**
Old Firestation Backpackers, **2**
Sundancer Backpackers
   Resort, **5**
YHA Backpackers Inn Freo, **4**

🍴 FOOD
Cicerello's, **12**
Fiorelli, **11**
Hara Cafe, **8**
Roma, **9**

⭐ NIGHTLIFE
The Bog, **3**
The Newport, **7**
Sail and Anchor, **10**

PERTH INSTITUTE OF THE CONTEMPORARY ARTS. PICA has contemporary and student art and hosts evening performances. Pick up a booklet of events or call for schedules. (☎9227 6144. Open Tu-Su 11am-7pm. Gallery free, performance prices vary.)

THE WESTERN AUSTRALIAN MUSEUM. The museum has exhibits on WA's natural history and culture. The discovery center has drawers of shells, bugs, old shoes, and anything and everything else. Don't miss the blue whale skeleton and the Aboriginal exhibit. (☎9427 2700. Open daily 9:30am-5pm. Donation requested.)

THE BLUE ROOM. The Blue Room provides an energetic venue for local theatre. Productions are chosen by application and range from classics to experimental pieces by local playwrights. (☎9227 7005; www.blueroom.net.au. Cover charges $10-20.)

FREMANTLE

FREMANTLE PRISON. Get a thorough look at a maximum-security prison without committing a felony. It is striking that the facilities seem so primitive, given that the prison was closed only 12 years ago, following a riot. (☎9430 7177. Tours every 30min.; last tour 5pm. Spooky candlelight tours W and F; book ahead. Open daily 10am-6pm. $14.30, concessions $11, children $7.15, families $48.50.)

FREMANTLE MARKETS. One can find just about anything in the markets, from clothing to a massage. Fresh veggies abound; produce prices hit rock bottom around closing time on Sunday. *(On the corner of South Tce. and Henderson St. Open F 9am-9pm, Sa 9am-5pm, Su 10am-5pm.)*

TOURS. The **Fremantle Trams** *(☎9339 8719)* run several tours of the city. *(Each of 4 1-3hr. tours has different departure times. Depart from in front of Town Hall on High St. $10-15, children $3-5, families $20-30.)* They also run "Ghostly" tram Tours. Visitors settle their nerves with fish 'n' chips, served on board, while they visit graveyards, the old crematorium and the prison, along with less spooky sites like the Arts Centre. *(F 7pm. $35, children $30.)*

▓ NIGHTLIFE

There's no shortage of good pubs, clubs, or cafes with amiable, relaxed crowds. The budget scene in Northbridge rages deep into the night on weekends. Mt. Lawley and Subiaco have more upscale, subdued scenes. Pick up the free weeklies *XPress* and *Hype* at hostels, news agencies, or record stores or visit the website www.perthtribe.com to find out what's on. Covers and dress codes are rare, but jeans may get the occasional scowl and most places require closed-toed shoes.

Perth is reasonably **gay- and lesbian-friendly;** for up-to-date event info, listen to *Sheer Queer*, a gay and lesbian radio program on 92.1FM (Th 11pm-1am) or check out the free *Out in Perth*, a gay and lesbian newspaper. The lesbian publication *WOW* comes out monthly ($4.50). The best resource may be the ▓**Arcane Bookshop,** 212 William St., which is full of info on Perth's gay and arts scenes. (☎9328 5073; arcbooks@highway1.com.au. Open M-W and Sa 10am-6pm, Th-F 10am-9pm, Su noon-5pm.)

NORTHBRIDGE AND CITY PROPER

▓ **The Grosvenor,** 339 Hay St. (☎9325 3799). Perth's premier venue for live music. Various events in spaces ranging from small and intimate to big and loud. Live band Th. Contests showcase mobs of local bands. Su generally more acoustic. Covers around $5. Open daily for dinner, W-Sa until midnight, Su until 10pm.

The Brass Monkey (☎9227 9596), on the corner of James and William St, Northbridge. A big, fun place; serves local microbrews. Pool tables and indoor courtyard. Connected to suave wine bar and brasserie. Open M-Th 11am-midnight, F-Sa 11am-2am, Su noon-10pm.

Bar Universal, 221 William St., Northbridge (☎9227 9596). Live jazz, sake, and a slightly older, sophisticated crowd. Dress code. Open M-Tu 4pm-midnight, W-Th 4pm-1am, F-Sa 4pm-2am, Su 4-10pm.

Connections Nightclub, 81 James St., Northbridge (☎9328 1870). A popular gay-owned club with DJ-spun house and techno beats. Theme nights like "Hawaii night." Shows F and Su. Cover $3-10. Open Tu-W and F 10pm-6am, Sa 9pm-6am, Su 9pm-1am.

The Court Hotel, 50 Beaufort St., Northbridge (☎9328 5292), on the corner of James St. The scene here varies from drag queens and theme nights like "bears' night"—for big hairy men and their fans—to a standard dance pub. In summer, live bands play outside in the beer garden. Open M-Sa 11am-midnight, Su 3-10pm.

Metropolis Club, 146 Roe St. (☎9228 0500). Glitzy, multi-level dance club like its sister location in Freo (see **Fremantle,** below). Cover $5 F after 11pm, Sa after 10pm. Open F 9pm-5am, Sa 9pm-6am.

Geisha, 135a James St. (☎9328 9808). Pulsates with various genres of dance music, sometimes from celebrity guest DJs. Open Th-Su 10pm-late.

The Jazz Room, 677 Beaufort St., Mount Lawley (☎9271 1792). Along with nearby Luxe, one of the centers of the calmer, sophisticated Mt. Lawley scene, with full bar and leather couches. DJs spin downtempo W and F-Sa. No cover. Live bands Th nights; cover $5-10. Open W-Th 9pm-1am, F-Sa 9pm-5am.

The Hip-E Club (☎9227 8899), on the corner of Newcastle and Oxford St., Leederville. Groovy 60s and 70s club, with 80s Su. Free entry until 10 or 11pm. Tu and Th backpacker nights with free BBQ. Open 8pm-1am.

FREMANTLE

The Bog, 189 High St. (☎9336 7751). Away from the South Tce. scene, but there's almost always something going on here. Tu free food and $6 jugs of beer. Open M 6pm-4am, Tu-Sa 6pm-6am, Su 8pm-1am.

Sail and Anchor, 64 South Tce. (☎9335 8433). British pub with a wide variety of intoxicating poisons. More locals, fewer backpackers. Freo is the home of Redback beer; this is a good place to hoist one. Open M-Th 11am-midnight, F-Sa 11am-1am, Su 11am-10pm.

The Newport, 2 South Tce. (☎9335 2428). Pool room, outdoor space, and a dark smoky area. Good place to see local bands. Cover varies. Open M-Th 11am-midnight, F-Sa 11am-1am, Su noon-10pm.

Metropolis Club, 58 South Tce. (☎9228 0500). Glitzy, multi-level dance club. Cover $5 F after 11pm, Sa after 10pm. Open Th 9pm-6am, F 9pm-5am, Sa 9pm-6am.

NEAR PERTH

ROTTNEST ISLAND

Called a "rat's nest" by Dutch explorers who mistook the island's quokkas (wallabies) for giant rats, Rottnest Island is an 11km-long hunk of limestone off the coast near Fremantle (30min. by ferry). The island was settled by farmers in 1830 but became a prison for Aborigines in 1838. Today, the island is a class-A nature reserve where tourists and locals flock to cycle, swim, snorkel, and surf. The quokkas, Rottnest's unofficial mascots, roam about the island unafraid of humans.

TRANSPORTATION. Several companies offer similarly priced **ferry service** to Rottnest from Perth, Fremantle, and Hillary's Harbour. **Oceanic Cruises** (☎9325 1191) departs from Pier 2 of the Barrack St. Jetty (daily 8:45 and 10am; $55, children $16) and from the East St. Jetty or B Shed on Victoria Quay, Fremantle (daily 9:45 and 11:45am; same-day return $40, children $13, extended-stay $5 extra). They offer free pickup from Perth hotels and the Freo train station. **Rottnest Express** has several daily departures from Victoria Quay, Fremantle. (☎9335 6406. Same-day return $40, children $13; extended stay $5 extra.) Both ferries offer $5 VIP/YHA discounts. Courtesy buses depart from the main jetty roughly every hour and head to the accommodations in Geordie Bay, Kingstown, and the airport. The **Bayseeker Bus** is a good way to get around the island (45min. loop around the island; every hr. 8:30am-4:30pm; day-ticket $5.50). The best way to see Rottnest is by bike—the island is only 11km by 4½km—though Rottnest's rolling hills can be tough to navigate. **Rottnest Island Bike Hire** has a wide selection that includes bike buses for family groups. (☎9292 5105. 1-speed $15 per day, 18-speed $20; $25 deposit. Locks and required helmets included. Open daily 8:30am-5pm.)

PRACTICAL INFORMATION, ACCOMMODATIONS, AND FOOD. The **Visitors Center** is 150m to the left of the jetty at Thomsons Bay. (☎9372 9752; fax

9372 9775. Open daily 8am-5pm.) To the right of the jetty is a pedestrian mall with an **ATM,** the **post office,** and the bakery. North of the mall 400m is the **nursing post.** (☎9292 5030. Open daily 8:30am-4:30pm.) The **YHA Kingstown Barracks Youth Hostel** ❷ is in Kingstown, a 20-minute walk or a quick bike ride from the Visitors Center. A free shuttle bus runs from Thompsons Bay every 30min., 8am-9pm. The hostel is inside an old army barracks with simple, spacious rooms. (☎9372 9780; fax 9292 5141. Reception 8am-5:30pm. Dorms $21, YHA $18; family rooms $49/$42.) Though there are meals available in the barracks complex ($7), it's a good idea to bring food. The Thomsons Bay settlement has a pricey general store with **groceries.**

☑ ACTIVITIES. Rottnest's beaches are emptier as you head away from settled areas—go far enough and you may have a cove all to yourself. **Narrow Neck** and **Salmon Bay** offer good **fishing,** and **The Basin, Pinky Beach,** and **Parakeet** are among the many good swimming spots near the settlement. **Little Salmon Bay** and **Parker Point** have good snorkeling, and **Strickland Bay** has good surfing. Whales and dolphins are often seen from the windy cliffs at **West End.** Ask at the Visitors Center for a booklet of "snorkel trails" ($5.50). **Rottnest Malibu Dive** is the only dive shop on the island. (☎9292 5111. Snorkel gear $16.50; 1 dive $60, 2 dives $110.)

SOUTHWEST

The Southwest coast of Australia is experiencing a boom in both tourism and residency. It's not hard to see why—Mother Nature has indeed been kind to the Southwest. The adventurous can surf, spelunk, and bushwalk in the Stirling and Porongup ranges or dive with dolphins in the warm coastal waters. Solace-seekers can sample award-winning local vintages, peruse local art studios, gaze at the springtime wildflowers, watch for whales, or drive down forest-lined roads.

⫟ TRANSPORTATION

The easiest way to see the Southwest is by car; many sights are well off the bus routes, and public transportation in many of the towns is either inadequate or nonexistent. Once you get completely out of Perth, the 3hr. drive south toward Margaret River takes you past shoreline, forests, farms, cattle stations, and the occasional limestone quarry. Several options exist for the auto-less. The **Easy Rider Backpackers** bus offers a three-month pass ($209) that covers bus service between most regional hostels. (☎9226 0307. Dec.-Feb. 6 per week; Sept.-Nov. and Mar.-May 4 per week; June-Aug. 2 per week. 24hr. notice required for pickup.) **Westrail's** (☎13 10 53) 28-day Southern Discovery Pass ($134) allows for travel to most southern and eastern destinations including Albany, Esperance, and Kalgoorlie.

EPIC HIKES. The popular **Bibbulmun track** runs 964km from Kalamunda, outside Perth, to Albany, passing through North Bannister, Dwellingup, Collie, Ballingup, Bridgetown, Manjimup, Pemberton, Northcliffe, Walpole, and Denmark. The trail passes campsites, shelters with bunks, and towns with hostels and B&Bs that pick up hikers from the trails. For more coastal adventures, the **Cape-to-Cape trail** runs 140km between the Naturaliste and Leeuwin lighthouses, passing coastline and karri forests as it winds through Leeuwin-Naturaliste National Park. Either track can be easily divided into sections or even used for short day hikes. Contact any local **Conservation and Land Management (CALM)** office for details (www.calm.wa.gov.au).

FROM PERTH TO BUNBURY

The drive south from Perth to Bunbury features wineries and forests perfect for those who may not make it farther south. There are about 20 wineries, some of which offer tours and wine tastings, along the 100km of Rte. 1 between Perth and **Yalgorup National Park.** The park itself features nature reserves, miles of dunes, stromatolites, and a forest of tuart and jarrah trees with peppermint undergrowth. Drive carefully; kangaroos in the road are frequent, as are emus, wallabies, and several species of trans-hemisphere migrating birds. Two good ways to see the park are at **Clifton Beach** (turnoff onto Clifton Downs Rd. 2km north of the Lake Clifton Tavern) and on the road marked by the Yalgorup National Park sign, just south of the turnoffs for Pinjarra and Warnoona. Here you'll find the **Heathlands self-guided walk** (on the left after you turn into the park) as well as other trails and beautiful clear lakes. There is camping at the **Martin's Tank campsite ❶**, 7km from the turnoff then 2km down an unsealed road. (Pit toilets; no running water. Sites for 2 $10, extra person $5.50.) **Preston Beach Caravan Park ❶**, 3km beyond the turnoff for the campsite, is a good source of park info and accommodations. (☎9739

1111. Caravan sites for 2 $7, powered $21; cabins for 4-6 $60-85; extra person $5.)

Watch for the **wrecked truck** hanging 10m up in a tree on the south-bound site of Rte. 1, reminding passersby that speeding isn't all fun and games. This stretch of highway also offers various scenic detours, the southernmost of which takes you through **Australind** along the beach. In Australind, the 500m boardwalked outcropping into the estuary is a good opportunity for birdwatching.

BUNBURY   ☎08

Two hours (180km) south of Perth, Bunbury (pop. 28,000) is a unique combination of cosmopolitan and sleepy. Over 100 charismatic dolphins have made the shores of Bunbury their home for decades, and recently more and more Westralians have decided to do the same. Though there is no shortage of dolphin-admiring visitors, Bunbury has escaped the tourist deluge that plagues Monkey Mia (see p. 702).

🚍 **TRANSPORTATION.** Heading south by train, downtown Bunbury is 3km from Wollaston, the southern end of WA's **train** network. Present your ticket stub on the bus for a free lift downtown. **South West Coachlines,** in the Old Railway Station at

Carmody Pl. and Haley St. (☎9791 1955; open daily 8am-7pm), runs to Perth (2½hr.; 3 per day; $20.20, students $10.10) and Augusta via Busselton and Margaret River (2½hr.; daily 4:20pm; $32, students $16). Local **buses** circle the city. (Runs M-W and F 7am 6pm, Th 7am-9pm, Sa 7am-1:15pm. $1.80, $2.70 for outlying areas.)

🛈 PRACTICAL INFORMATION. The Old Railway station houses the **Bunbury Visitors Center** (☎9721 7922; open M-Sa 9am-5pm, Su 9:30am-4:30pm), the bus station, and the **Bunbury Internet Cafe.** (☎9791 1254. $4 per hr. Open M-Sa 8am-4:30pm.) Services include: several **banks** along Victoria St.; **police** (☎9791 2422), on the corner of Wittenoom St. at Stephen St.; and a **post office** in the Bunbury Plaza Shopping Centre on Spencer St. just south of downtown. (☎9721 3551. Open M-F 9am-5pm, Sa 9-11am.) **Postal Code:** 6230.

🛏🍴 ACCOMMODATIONS AND FOOD. The ▨**Wander Inn YHA ❷,** 16 Clifton St., near Wittenoom St., has ping-pong and pool tables, BBQ, and clean, brightly colored rooms. The hostel provides snorkel gear, rents bikes and surf boards, and can book dolphin tours, bushwalking, and kayaking. (☎9721 3242. Internet $4 per hr. Dorms $22; singles $33; doubles $53; family rooms $69. VIP/YHA.) For a change of pace, the tranquil **Castlehead Bed and Breakfast ❸,** 44 Elinor Bell Rd., 10km north of town, offers clean, beautiful rooms with estuary views. Take the scenic drive off of Old Coast Rd. in Australind and turn inland onto Elinor Bell Rd. (☎9797 0272. Singles $40, ensuite $50; doubles $65/$75.) The main strip, on Victoria St. between Wellington and Clifton St., has many pricey restaurants. For more frugal options, try **Orka Kabobs and Turkish Bakery ❶,** 57-59 Victoria St. (☎9791 2440), or **V Cafe ❶,** 57 Victoria St., next door. Coles **supermarket** is in the Centrepoint Shopping Center, behind the tourist office. (Open M-W and F 8am-6pm, Th 8am-9pm, Sa 8am-5pm.)

◨ SIGHTS. Dolphins are the main draw for most tourists in Bunbury. The nonprofit **Dolphin Discovery Centre,** on Koombana Dr., has an interesting collection of sealife specimens and interactive exhibits on the biology of the region. (☎9791 3088. Open daily Oct.-Apr. 8am-5pm; May-Sept. 9am-3pm. $2, children $1, families $5.) Dolphin-sighting tours are run by **Naturaliste Charters** from the jetty on Koombana Dr. (☎9755 2276. 1½hr. Daily 11am and 2pm. $27, students $24, children $20. Swim tours $90, students $80.) **Newcomers Land and Sea Charters,** run out of the Lighthouse Beach resort, also offers tours. (☎9721 1311. Call for times and prices.)

Across from the Dolphin Discovery Centre, the **Mangrove Boardwalk** weaves through the southernmost mangrove ecosystem in WA. The **Big Swamp Estuary** on Prince Philip Dr. has over 70 species of birds, and the **Big Swamp Wildlife Park,** also on Prince Philip Dr., has white kangaroos, tawny frogmouths, and many birds. From Ocean Dr., turn onto Hayward St. and look for the sign at the next roundabout. (☎9721 8380. Open daily 10am-5pm. $5, pensioners $4, ages 2-12 $3.) The **Marlston Hill Lookout,** near the oceanside end of Koombana Dr., has a 360° view. There are beautiful beaches along Ocean Dr., including the popular **Back Beach.**

MARGARET RIVER AREA   ☎08

Around Margaret River, dramatic rock and coral formations rise from the pounding surf, vast cave systems weave through the subterranean depths, celebrated vineyards cover the countryside, and artisans of every medium create works of beauty. With so much to do, many will find themselves lingering longer than they planned on the area's westernmost tip.

WESTERN AUSTRALIA

⚑❋⌐ ORIENTATION AND TRANSPORTATION

Margaret River lies 100km south of Bunbury on the **Bussell Hwy.** (Hwy. 10). The scenic **Caves Road** branches from the Bussel Hwy. at **Busselton**, 52km from Bunbury, and winds its way to Margaret River, through wineries and beaches as well as the towns of **Yallingup** and **Dunsborough.** About 45km south of Margaret River, **Augusta** is at the intersection of the Blackwood River and the ocean.

The size of the region and lack of centralized attractions makes transportation a hassle. The best way to get around is by car. **Avis** (☎1800 679 880), **Hertz** (☎9758 8331), and **Budget** (☎9757 2453) all have offices in Margaret River. You can also rent bikes at various places in town. **South West Coachlines** stops at Charles West St., two blocks from the Bussell Hwy., Margaret River, and goes to Perth (4½hr., 2 per day, $25). **Westrail** (☎13 10 53) uses **Harvey World Travel,** 109 Bussell Hwy., as its Margaret River agent. (☎9757 2171. Open M-F 9am-5pm, Sa 9am-noon.)

▮ PRACTICAL INFORMATION

Tourist Offices:

Margaret River Tourist Bureau (☎9757 2911; www.margaretriverwa.com), on the corner of Bussell Hwy. and Tunnbridge St. Has maps, countless fliers, and a wine showroom. Open daily 9am-5pm.

Busselton Tourist Bureau (☎9752 1288), at Peel Tce. and Causeway Rd. Open M-F 8:30am-5pm, Sa 9am-4pm, Su 10am-4pm; May-Sept. same except Su 10am-2pm.

Dunsborough Tourist Bureau (☎9755 3299), in the shopping center on Seymour Blvd., Dunsborough. Books tours.

Caves Park Store (☎/fax 9755 2042), on Yallingup Beach Rd. near Caves Rd. Yallingup info.

CALM, Busselton office, 14 Queen St. (☎9752 1677); Margaret River office (☎9757 2322), on the Bussell Hwy. north of town. National Park hiking and camping info. Open M-F 8am-5pm.

Augusta Tourist Office (☎9758 0166), on Blackwood Ave., the town's main drag. Open M-F 9am-5pm, Sa-Su 9am-1pm.

Work Opportunity: Manpower, 157 Bussell Hwy. (☎9757 3911; www.manpower.com.au), serves as an employment agency for people looking for short-term work Work is easier to find in winter; area is flooded with eager job-seekers in summer.

Police: 42 Willmott Ave. (☎9757 2222), Margaret River.

Internet Access: River Video, 103 Bussell Hwy., Margaret River. $2 per 15min. Open daily 9am-9pm.

Post office: 53 Townview Tce. (☎9757 2250), 1 block up Willmott Ave. from Bussell Hwy., Margaret River. Open M-F 9am-5pm. **Postal Code:** 6285.

⌂⌂ ACCOMMODATIONS AND CAMPING

There are several well-located hostels in the area. For those looking to splurge, contact the Margaret River Tourist Bureau (☎9757 2911) to book at one of the many wonderful B&Bs. Rooms fill up quickly from October to March; be sure to book in advance for summer weekends. From June to August, bargains abound. Contact CALM (see p. 682) about camping in Leeuwin-Naturaliste National Park.

MARGARET RIVER

Margaret River Lodge (☎9757 9532), on Railway Tce., 1½km southwest of the Bussell Hwy. off Wallcliffe Rd. Standard hostel rooms close to wineries. Free pickup from bus station, bike and bodyboard rentals, pool, and organic vegetable garden. Internet $5 per hr. Sites $12; dorms $24-26; doubles $58, ensuite $68. YHA discount $3.50. ❶

Surfpoint Resort (☎9757 1777), on Riedle Dr. south of Prevelley, just north of Gnarabup Beach and within walking distance of the Rivermouth area. Clean and spacious. Bike and boogie board rental, BBQ, Internet $5 per 30min. Book ahead in summer. Dorms $23; doubles $56; ensuite $85; discounts in off-season. ❷

Inne Town Backpackers, 93 Bussell Hwy. (☎9757 3698 or 1800 244 115). The only backpackers, ahem, in town. Clean and friendly. Men's bathroom features painting of bearded XXXX-guzzling (see **Beer Glossary,** p. 700) transvestite mermaid. Book ahead year-round. Laundry. Internet $2 per 20min. Dorms $18; doubles $48. ❷

Matan's Lodge (☎/fax 9757 2936), on Caves Rd., after a right turn-off from Wallcliffe Rd. going away from town. Houses emus, 'roos, and an art gallery. Basic rooms but idyllic common spaces. 3-bed rooms $85; occasional winter backpacker specials $18. ❸

Prevelly Park Beach Resort (☎9757 2374), on the way into Prevelly Park taking Wallcliffe Rd. west out of town. Sites $10-14; basic on-site vans $85. ❶

BUSSELTON, DUNSBOROUGH, AND YALLINGUP

Three Pines Beach YHA, 285 Geographe Bay Rd., Dunsborough (☎9755 3107). Excellent location on the beach. Managers Adrian and Rod are level-headed, knowledgeable, and always a good time. Books tour. Dorms $24, YHA $20; doubles $54/$50. ❷

Busselton Backpackers, 14 Peel Tce., Busselton (☎9754 2763). Basic rooms. Laundry. Dorms $18; doubles $35. ❷

Hideaway Holiday Homes, 24 Elsewood Ave., Yallingup (☎9755 2145). Beware, there's no Elsewood street sign. Big ensuite cabins. Simple, with several bathrooms and a kitchen but no linen. Doubles from $45; 6-bed rooms from $85. ❹

Yallingup Holiday Park (1800 220 002), as you enter Yallingup. Great location near the biggest surf break in the area. Sites for 2 $32, off-season $17, extra person $10; cabins $130/$45, ensuite $160-195/$80-95. ❸

Dunsborough Lakes Caravan Park, 2-48 Commanage Rd. (☎9756 8300), off the Bussell Hwy. just north of Dunsborough. 1-3 bed cabins $85-160. ❺

AUGUSTA

▨ **Baywatch Manor Resort YHA,** 88 Blackwood Ave. (☎9758 1290). Relaxed atmosphere and spacious, well-maintained quarters, where visitors tend to lounge rather than party. Owners arrange tours and whale-watching. Dorms $20; doubles $55, ensuite $65. ❷

Doonbanks Caravan Park, (☎9758 1517; www.netserv.net.au/doonbank), just north of town on Blackwood Ave. Camp kitchen, BBQ. Sites $14, powered $18. ❶

▨▨ FOOD AND NIGHTLIFE

Margaret River's restaurants are good but pricey. Dewson's **supermarket,** next to the tourist office on the Bussell Hwy. in Margaret River, sells **groceries.** Small restaurants line **Dunn Bay Rd.,** which runs through Dunsborough. Many area wineries also have restaurants. In Augusta, there is a **fruit market** and **grocery store** on Blackwood Ave., north of the tourist office.

Goodfellas Cafe Woodfire Pizza, 114 Bussell Hwy. (☎9757 3184). Huge bowls of pasta and exotic pizzas in a candlelit setting. Meals $12-18. Open daily 5:30-9pm. ❸

The Green Room, 113b Bussell Hwy. (☎9757 3644). Locals rave about the burgers ($6-8) and specials. Open daily 11am-6pm, later Th-Sa. ❶

Settler's Tavern, 114 Bussell Hwy. (☎9757 2398). Live bands play this popular booze spot 4 nights per week. Pool tables and big screen TV. 21+. Cover varies. Open M-Th noon-midnight, F 11am-2am, Sa 10am-1am, Su noon-10pm. ❷

◉ SIGHTS

The area boasts over 70 wineries, dozens of art galleries, and numerous farms that offer food tastings, demonstrations, and farmstays. A large number of activities are clustered close enough to Margaret River to make them accessible in a daytrip, but not everything is within walking distance. Those interested in Margaret River's galleries and artisans should check out www.mrartisans.com for information.

WINERIES. Most wineries are clustered in the area bordered by Caves Rd. and Johnson Rd. between Yallingup and Margaret River. For an enjoyable tour, mix older vintners, such as **Cullen,** which are usually more personable, with the many newcomers, such as **Howard Park,** which have gorgeous estates and great views.

Those walking from Margaret River can reach at least two wineries on foot. **Chateau Xanadu** features an award-winning chardonnay and an elegant but welcoming setup. *(Walkers and bikers may use the gravel service road. Take Railway Tce. 3km south to Terry St. Drivers should take the smoother main entrance off Boodijup Rd. ☎9757 3066. Open daily 10am-5pm.)* The **Cape Mentelle** winery was one of the first in the area; it remains a relaxed, friendly place. *(Just off Wallcliffe Rd. south of town. ☎9757 3266. Open daily 10am-4:30pm.)* A longer walk could include the beautiful gardens and wines of **Voyager.** *(☎9757 6354. Open daily 10am-5pm.)* Bikers have the additional option of taking a tour of the production facilities at **Leeuwin Estate Winery.** *(Off Gnarawy Rd. ☎9759 0000. 1hr. tours daily 11am, noon, and 3pm; $8. Open daily 10am-5pm.)*

WINE TOURS. While hiring a car makes area wineries more accessible, it could put a damper on drinking. A popular option for those seeking to drink is a wine tour, which generally costs about $45 for a half-day and $80 for a full-day. The widely acclaimed **Great Wine, Food, Forest Bushtucker Tour** packs in a drive through a karri forest, a gourmet lunch, and six vineyards. *(☎9757 9084. 5hr. tours daily at noon. $50.)* **Taste the South** will cater the tour to your interests. *(☎9756 7958; tastethesouth@netserv.net.au.)* A more economical option is the mini wine tour run by **Margaret River Vintage Wine Tours,** which visits Voyager, Leeuwin, Redgate, and Xanadu for $25. *(☎9757 1008; winetours@swisp.net.au. Tours daily 2:30pm.)* **Cape Naturalist Limousines** *(☎9756 7778)* will customize a tour for up to six people for $95 per hr.

FOOD AND DRINK TASTINGS. The Margaret River area offers a variety of free food and drink tastings to complement its famous wines. **The Candy Cow** *(☎9755 9155)* in Cowaramup, **Margaret River Chocolate Company**

CAN'T DIG TO CHINA, BUT... Want to get away from it all—as far away as possible? A *Washington Post* writer uncovered an interesting bit of trivia. **Cumberland Rock,** one of the myriad rocks in the waters off Cape Leeuwin, is the "antipode" of Washington, D.C., its exact opposite geographical point on the globe.

(☎ 9755 6555), north of Cowaramup, and the **Fudge Factory** (☎ 9758 8881), in Margaret River, satisfy many a sweet tooth. **Fonti Farm,** north of Cowaramup, and nearby **Margaret River Cheese Company** (☎ 1800 687 383) offer cheese and yogurt tastings. Finally, two breweries are open to the public. **Bootleg Brewery,** on Pusey Rd. in Wilyabrup, touts itself as "A beer oasis in a desert of wine." (☎ 9755 6300. Open daily 10am-4:30pm.) **Wicked Ale Brewery,** on Helmsley Rd. in Wilyabrup, has novelty beers, including chocolate, citrus, passionfruit, and ginger. (☎ 9755 2848. Open M and W-Su 10am-5pm.)

OTHER SIGHTS. The 2km-long **Busselton Jetty** is a thin plank jutting way out into the Indian Ocean. It's a good hike to the end of the jetty, and waters below are a popular seasonal diving area. (At the end of Queen St. in Busselton. $2.50, children $1.50; trolley to the end $7.50, children $2.50.) The **Eagles Heritage Raptor Wildlife Centre,** on Boodjidup Rd. near Margaret River, Australia's largest collection of birds of prey, is dedicated to education, rehabilitation of injured birds, and breeding projects. (☎ 9757 2960. Open daily 10am-5pm. Flight displays daily 11am and 1:30pm. $8, seniors $6, children $4, families $20. Wheelchair accessible.) Ten kilometers south of Augusta is **Cape Leeuwin,** Australia's southwesternmost point. A **lighthouse** built in 1895 guards the spot. (Open daily 9am-5pm. Last tour leaves at 4pm. $6, children $3.)

▲ OUTDOOR ACTIVITIES

The beaches and surf along the coast are stunning. **Caves Rd.** south of Margaret is one of the area's most spectacular drives, running through karri forests and past hundreds of hidden caves, seven of which are open to the public. **Biking** is a good way to get around, and there are many rewarding bike trails. **Gull's Petrol Station,** 111 Bussell Hwy., in Margaret River, rents bikes. (☎ 9758 7038. $7 per hr., $15 per half-day, $20 per day, $70 per week. $50 deposit; helmet and waterbottle included.) There are also a number of **walking tracks** and **canoeing** opportunities in the region.

LEEUWIN-NATURALISTE NATIONAL PARK. Spanning much of the coast from Cape Naturaliste to Cape Leeuwin, Leeuwin-Naturaliste National Park encompasses wild forests, untouched beaches with jagged rock formations rising from the water, caves with fossils of extinct megafauna, remote campsites, excellent whale-watching spots, lighthouses, and many walking trails. The CALM offices in Dunsborough and Margaret River service the park. **Canto's Spring ❶** is a basic campsite where thundering waves crash on enormous boulders rising from the sea. From the site, you can walk north along ocean cliffs or south through the majestic Boranup forest. (At the Lake Cave turn-off from Caves Rd. south of Margaret River. Pit toilets. Self-register. Sites $6, children $2.) Whales can be seen from **Cape Naturaliste, Gracetown, Canal Rocks,** and **Injidup Beach.** There are bushwalks all along the coast and near Margaret River. Cape Naturaliste's walks wind past the lighthouse to expanses of sand. Finally, just next to the park, the **Boranup Maze** is a huge shrub labyrinth best visited in summer ($2.50, children $1.50).

CAVES. A network of caves runs through Margaret River, containing fossils of extinct species, as well as evidence of Aboriginal occupation as early as 32,000 years ago. Though the most historically interesting caves are inaccessible to the public, the seven caves that are open are amazing. The two southernmost caves,

⚐**Jewel Cave** (the most magnificent), and **Lake Cave,** are lighted and offer guided tours. **Mammoth,** nearest to Margaret, has tape-guided tours of its lighted caves. (☎9757 5714. Jewel and Lake tours daily every 30min. 9:30am-4:30pm. Mammoth open daily 10am-4pm. Each cave $14.50, children $6, families $40. All 3 $35/$15/$100.) **Moondyne** is unlighted but offers guided flashlight tours. (☎9757 5714. Tours daily 2pm. $20, children $10.) **Calgardup** and **Giands** are less impressive but provide the solace of plunging underground unguided. Giands is the more strenuous of the two. (☎9757 7422. Open daily 9am-5pm; last entry 4:15pm. $10, children $5.) Near Yallingup, **Ngilgi Cave** (☎9755 2152) provides both guided, lighted tours (daily every 30min. 9:30am-3:30pm; $14, children $5, families $38) and guided flashlight "adventure" tours. (Daily 9:30am. 2½-3½hr. $40; 1½-2hr. $20, children $10.)

SURFING. Packs of grommets (young surfers) learn the ropes in the relatively tame surf at **Rivermouth** and **Redgate** near Margaret River; more experienced surfers delight in the breaks off **Surfer's Point,** or head farther north to **Gracetown.** There are tons of other surf spots in the area; stop at **Beach Life Surf Shop,** 117 Bussell Hwy., near the tourist office, for info and advice or to set up a surfing lesson. (☎9757 2888; 24hr. surf report 1900 922 995. $75; group lessons $35 per person.)

Farther north, **Yallingup Beach** was one of the first breaks surfed in WA (in the 1950s). The best time for surfing is October through April, though it gets very crowded, especially in December and January. The two best spots in the Yallingup area are Yallingup Beach itself, right in front of Yallingup's Surf Shop at the bottom of Yallingup Beach Rd., and **Smith's Bay,** just south of Yallingup Beach.

DIVING AND SNORKELING. In Dunsborough, Eagle and Meelup Bays both have great beaches for snorkeling and surfing; turn-offs are well marked on Cape Naturaliste Rd., north of town. **Bay Dive and Adventures,** 26 Dunn Bay Rd. (☎9756 8846), in Dunsborough, offers diving, diving classes, and snorkeling trips. **Cape Dive** (☎9756 8778) is one of a few outfitters that run diving trips to the wreck of the *HMS Swan* off Cape Naturaliste. **Hamelin Bay,** near Augusta, is another good dive and snorkel spot. Indeed, the bay may be beautiful to the point of distraction—the area has seen 11 shipwrecks since 1882. You can scuba or snorkel the four visible wrecks, but you have to swim from shore. Check with someone before diving; the wrecks are old and shift around a bit. Swimming here is sheltered, and fishing in the area is superb. Stingrays often feed below the boat ramp. **Augusta Hardware and Scuba Supplies,** on Blackwood Ave. across from the post office, has diving info and gear. (☎9758 1770. Open M-F 8:30am-5:30pm, Sa 8:30am-4:30pm, Su 9am-1pm.)

OUTDOOR TOURS. Several companies organize half- or full-day adventure tours, most of which can be booked through tourist bureaus. ⚐**Naturaliste Charters** runs **whale-watching** tours that bring sightseers to the Humpback whales off Augusta (see p. 683) in the winter and Dunsborough in the spring. (☎9755 2276. Departs daily from Boat Ramp on Geographe Bay Rd. in Dunsborough. 3hr. $45, children $25, under 4 free.) **Boranup Eco Walks** gives walks through karri and jarrah forests. (☎9757 7576. Day walks 1½-3hr. $10-15, children $5-8; night walks 1½hr. in summer $12, children $6. Book ahead.) **Outdoor Discoveries** runs abseiling outings and other expeditions. (☎0407 084 945. From $65 per person.) **Milesaway Tours** runs canoe tours. (☎1800 818 102. 1-day $75, children $40; 2-day $230.)

GREAT SOUTHERN

Sprawling karri and tingle forests, rugged mountain ranges, and the vast nothingness of the Nullarbor Plain are all part of the beautiful region known as the Great Southern. The South Western Hwy. links the region's many parts and Albany func-

90-TON THREESOME If you take a whale-watching trip in the Southwest, look for groups of Humpback whales traveling in threes. Why three? These mammals, each weighing around 30 tons as adults, are too big for private sexual intercourse. Male sexual organs are too large and unwieldy; they are 14% of the length of their entire body. Thus, an interested couple must get help from another whale for everything to work properly. Perhaps that's what true friends are for.

tions as an urban hub for the sparsely populated southern coast, but by the time you reach Esperance, Perth's cosmopolitanism seems a world away. The agricultural Great Southern is home to a number of respected vineyards, many of which offer complimentary wine-tastings. Tourism has become an economic mainstay, peaking in the spring wildflower season and in the summer, when the beaches around Denmark, Albany, and Esperance are most inviting. Winters in the Great Southern can be chilly, so be sure to bring a warm jacket.

WALPOLE-NORNALUP NATIONAL PARK

Walpole-Nornalup National Park incorporates forests of giant tingle trees, inlets from the ocean, sand dunes, pristine beaches, and the wildlife-rich Frankland River, which affords blissful boating. The **Tree Top Walk,** 13km east of town, is a 600m metal catwalk through the canopy of tingle trees. The views are incredible, but those scared of heights be forewarned—the swaying walkways reach heights of 40m. (☎9840 8200. Open daily 9am-5pm, last admission 4:15pm. $6, children $2.50, families $14.) The **Ancient Empire** boardwalk, a short, pleasant walk, departs from the Tree Top Walk info center and passes through a grove of red tingle trees. **The Giant Tingle Tree** can be reached by a good gravel road 2km east of town and a peaceful 2km jaunt through tingle forests. The **Bibbulmun Track** (see p. 679) runs through town, along the inlet shore, and out past the Giant Tingle Tree. A short but steep hike winds through **wildflowers** up **Mt. Frankland,** 12km from town. The park's beautiful drives include the gravel **Hilltop Road,** which passes the Giant Tingle and Circular Pool, the **Valley of the Giants Road** through towering forests, and the **Knoll Drive,** which passes dunes and dramatic views of the inlets. The inspiring **Mandalay** and **Conspicuous Cliffs** beaches lie roughly 15km east and west of town, respectively, with about 5km of good gravel road to each of them. ($9 per car.)

WALPOLE   ☎08

Tiny, congenial Walpole is nestled in the middle of the national park and makes an excellent home base. **Westrail buses** (☎13 10 53) run once a day to Albany and Bunbury. The volunteer-staffed **Walpole-Nornalup Visitors Centre,** on the highway, is a great source of information on the many nearby natural wonders and can book tours. (☎9840 1111. Open M-F 9am-5pm, Sa-Su 9am-4pm.) There's a **CALM office** nearby. (☎9840 1027. Open M-F 8am-5pm.) Telecentre, on Vista Ave., has **Internet** access. (☎9840 1395. Open Tu-F 9am-5pm. $8 per hr.) Nockolds St. holds a **post office** (☎9840 1048; open M-F 9am-5pm) as well as **groceries** and **camping supplies** at Foodland and the BP gas station. Transportation for the auto-less has always been a problem here; the condition was recently improved by the addition of a **taxi service** at the Tingle All Over YHA. (☎9840 1041. $15 return to Tree Top Walk.)

The staff of **Walpole Backpackers ❷** includes forestry experts who give tours. Rooms are well-maintained. (☎/fax 9840 1244. Laundry and kitchen facilities. Reception 24hr. Dorms $19; twins and doubles $48; family rooms $70.) **Tingle All Over YHA ❸,** on Nockolds St., has a BBQ, kitchen, laundry, and a beautiful chess set with two-foot pieces made from red gum and jarrah woods. (☎9840 1041. Dorms $20; singles $35; twins and doubles $48. YHA discount $1.) The **Rest Point Holiday**

WESTERN AUSTRALIA

PICK ON SOMEONE YOUR OWN SIZE If you are walking along a sandy path and find a very small mound with a few large holes in it, you may be foolishly inclined to knock gently with your foot to see who is home. But stand back, because it's likely the home of the bull ant—or several bull ants, to be more exact. Each ant is over one inch long, extremely aggressive, and has the ability to inflict excruciating pain. When they figure out where you are, they will stand facing you in a fighting stance. If they do manage a sting, the pain is terrible and lasts a week.

Village ❶ is right on the water west of town. (☎ 9840 1032. Boat rental 1hr. $25, 4hr. $45; canoes $10 less. Sites $9 per person; cabins for 2 $55-75, extra person $25.) **Camping** is also available at Mt. Frankland Crystal Springs and other locations. In nearby **Denmark,** you can find volunteer organic farm work through Willing Workers on Organic Farms (WWOOF; see **Volunteering,** p. 69).

STIRLING RANGE AND PORONGURUP NATIONAL PARKS

These two ranges, separated by a mere 30km, have very different histories and geologies. The Porongorups date back over a billion years, making them one of the most ancient volcanic formations on the planet. The Stirlings were formed more recently. Giant eucalypts are found up the sides of the Porongorups, while in the higher Stirling Range the vegetation is hardier scrub. Both offer hiking and, in spring, the bloom of over 1600 species of wildflowers.

 TRANSPORTATION AND PRACTICAL INFORMATION. From Albany, the Porongurups are 30km north on the **Chester Pass Rd.** The Stirling Range is another 30km further along the road. **Porongurup Rd.** is a sealed road running west through the park to Mt. Barker, 15km from the park. **Stirling Range Dr.** is a pretty but corrugated road running west through the Stirlings from Chester Pass.

   Westrail buses (☎ 13 10 53) run to Mt. Barker from Albany or Perth once per day. The helpful Mt. Barker **tourist office,** in the old train station, has information about the parks and the town. (☎9851 1163. Open M-F 9am-5pm, Sa 9am-3pm, Su 10am-3pm.) It is possible to walk from the Porongurup Shop and Tearooms to the Porongup trails. However, the best way to see the parks is by car. Rental is easily arranged in Albany (p. 689). There are **ranger stations** in Stirling Range National Park at Moingup Spring (☎9827 9320) and Bluff Knoll (☎9827 9278). The nearest **hospital** (☎9826 1003) is in Gnowangerup.

 ACCOMMODATIONS AND FOOD. The **Porongurup Shop and Tearooms ❷,** on Porongurup Rd. at the main entrance to Porongurup National Park, has a homey, down-to-earth feel. They offer Internet access ($5 per hr.) and and good food, including vegetables fresh from the garden ($10-15). Upon request, the owners will try to arrange a pickup from Mt. Barker or Albany, making a stay here the best option for the auto-less. (☎9853 1110. Dorms $20.) In the Stirling Range National Park, the **Stirling Range Retreat ❶** is just beyond the turn-off for Bluff Knoll. The owners have slide shows ($3) and guided orchid and bird walks ($15-20) in season. (☎9827 9229. Sites $9 per person; powered for 2 $22, extra person $9; dorms for 2 $38, extra person $19; cabins for 2 $45-125.) In Mt. Barker, **Chill Out Backpackers ❷,** 79 Hassell St., off the start of Porongurup Rd., has good rooms in a beautiful A-frame building. (☎9851 2798. Singles $17; doubles $34.) At the north end of Mt. Barker is the **Mt. Barker Caravan Park ❷.** (☎9851 1691. Singles $17; cabins for 2 from $44.) Food options in town are limited, but there's a roadhouse in the BP. In the Stirling Range, there's a cafe near the Retreat and a restaurant at the winery up the road. Supavalu, on Lowood Rd., sells **groceries.**

⊠ HIKING. There are three major hikes in the Porongurups. The **Tree in the Rock circuit** (6km; 3hr.) originates at the end of Bolganup Rd., clearly marked off Porongurup Rd. After passing a sizeable eucalypt sprouting from a crack in a boulder, the track continues to Hayward Peak for panoramic views of the surrounding country, then along a ridge of Nancy Peak and Morgan's Views. A **side trail** (2hr.) off of the Tree in the Rock circuit wings up the sometimes slippery rock of the Devil's Slide up to a summit of stark rock faces and towering granite. The equally challenging **Castle Rock trail** is a manageable 45min. jaunt to the side of a massive granite boulder perched on the mountaintop. The last 30m include a scramble through a crevice, a short ladder, and a catwalk affording tremendous views.

Within the Stirlings, there are a variety of walks. The most popular is ⊠**Bluff Knoll,** the highest peak in Western Australia at 1094m. The Aboriginal name of *Bullah Meual* ("Great Many Face Hill") reflects its multi-faceted shape. The trail that climbs its sides (3-4hr. return) is smooth, complete with stairs, but it is very steep. The views of the surrounding formations from the top are exhilarating, and the contrast with the flat, vast surrounding farmlands is impressive. **Toolbrunup Peak,** the second-highest in the park, is a challenging 3hr. scramble over rocks of varying sizes that can be slippery when wet. A shorter hike (2½hr. return) with steep spots is **Mount Trio.** From the saddle, you can choose the East or North Peak.

Both parks require a $9 per car entry fee, which is good in both parks for one day. Alternatively, a four-week pass good at all WA national parks, available at the Bluff Knoll Cafe in Porongurup, costs $22.50 per car. All of the trails listed here are accessible by smooth gravel roads shorter than 10km. Other trails in the Stirlings require longer drives along the corrugated Stirling Range Dr.

ALBANY
☎08

Established in 1826, Albany was the first colonial settlement of Western Australia, beating out Perth by a year. From colonial outpost to whaling village to its current prosperity as a regional center, Albany remains proud of its past and confident in its present.

▣ TRANSPORTATION. Westrail buses (☎ 13 10 53) depart from in front of the tourist office to: Bunbury (6hr., 1 per day, $37) via Walpole, Pemberton, Augusta, and Margaret River; Esperance (6hr., M and Th, $43); and Perth (6hr., 1-2 per day, $38). The two hostels in town have a steady stream of travelers sharing rides; hitchhikers usually wait by the "Big Roundabout" on the Albany Hwy, 2km west of the north end of York St., though *Let's Go* does not recommend hitchhiking. **Love's Bus Service** provides city transport for $2 a trip (☎9841 1211; Open M-Sa). Car rental is easily arranged in Albany: try **King Sound Vehicle Hire,** 145 Albany Hwy. (☎9841 8466); **Crossroads Autos,** 42 Sanford Rd. (☎9842 2993); or **Albany Car Rentals,** 386 Albany Hwy. (☎9841 7077). Prices range from $40-50 per day.

▨ PRACTICAL INFORMATION. York St. runs north-south through the center of town. The **tourist office** is in the Old Railway Station, just east of the southern end of York St. near Stirling Tce. (☎9841 1088; fax 9842 1490. Open M-F 8:15am-5:30pm, Sa-Su 9am-5pm.) There is **Internet** and good coffee at **Argyle's Bistro,** 42 Stirling Tce. (☎9842 9696. Open daily 7am-7pm. $4 per 30min.)

▟▢ ACCOMMODATIONS AND FOOD. Albany has no shortage of budget accommodations. The very lively **Albany Backpackers ❷** is on Spencer St., around the corner from Stirling Tce. and one block east of York St. It has elaborately painted rooms with themes ranging from underwater life to the Pinnacles. (☎9842

5255. Internet $5 per hr., first 10min. free. Reception 8am-9pm. Dorms $22.50; doubles $52. ISIC/NOMADS/VIP/YHA.) The **Albany Bayview YHA ❷**, 49 Duke St., two blocks west of York St., is another good option with a nice view of the bay and free movies. Visitors can rent bikes, boogie boards, and fishing gear. (☎/fax 9842 3388. Internet $1 per 10min. Dorms $21; twins and doubles $48; family rooms $66. YHA discount $2.50.) The ▨**Cruize-Inn ❸**, 122 Middleton Rd., is one step up from hostelling, with beautiful, homestyle accommodations complete with kitchen and TV lounge. (☎9842 9599. Singles $33; doubles $55; triples $80.) **Middleton Beach Holiday Park ❷**, at the end of Middleton Rd., is farther from the center of town, but right on the beach. (☎9841 3593. Sites $24, powered $25; off-season $20/$21.)

Dylan's on the Terrace ❷, 82 Stirling Tce., serves sandwiches and burgers for $6-8 and meals for $10-15. (☎9841 8270. Open M-Th 7am-11pm, F-Su 7am-midnight.) SupaValu, on York St. near Stirling Tce. has **groceries.** (Open daily 7am-9pm.)

◨ **SIGHTS.** Albany has the distinction of being home to the world's largest whaling museum. **Whaleworld,** on Frenchman Bay Rd. past the Gap and Blowholes, is on the site of Australia's last whaling station, which closed in 1978. There are blubber vats, a whaling boat, and loads of other paraphernalia. (☎9844 4021. Open daily 9am-5pm. 30min. tours every hr. 10am-4pm. $13, concessions $10, children $5, families $30.) You can see the whales live with **Southern Ocean Charters,** a.k.a. **Big Day Out.** (☎0409 107 180. Departs May-Oct. daily 9:30am. $37.)

Apart from whales, Albany's most impressive sights are in ▨**Torndirrup National Park,** 20km south of town on Frenchman Bay Rd. The **Natural Bridge** is a rock formation that spans 24m above crashing waves. The **Gap** has dramatic waves pounding into a 30m inlet. At the **blowholes,** spray from the coean below shoots out 10m high through a crack, though only in rough weather. *Do not go beyond the blowholes; people have died trying to get a good photo.* Albany also boasts Western Australia's most recent shipwreck, the intentionally submerged **Perth,** a decommissioned navy vessel with the distinction of being the only Royal Australian Navy ship hit by enemy fire in the past 50 years. It serves as an artificial reef for divers. Another recent addition is the **Wind Farm,** east of Frenchman Bay Rd. The **Middleton Bay Scenic Path** runs from **Middleton Beach,** just outside of town, to Emu Point. **West Cape Howe National Park** (about 30km west of Albany) has a treacherous 4WD track through pristine bush and beach. Those in 2WD can head to **Shelley** and **Dunsky** beaches or to **Two Peoples Bay Reserve,** 35km east of town..

FROM ALBANY TO ESPERANCE

As the South Coast Hwy. slices eastward, forests give way to farmland, which, in turn, gives way to arid brush. Massive road trains comprise most of the erratic traffic. Petrol stations appear only every 50 to 75km, many with limited hours, so fuel up in Albany before heading out, especially if traveling on weekends or at night. The temptation to speed is great, but take care; the 500km stretch to Esperance is subject to high crosswinds and winter flooding.

POISON RISK! Signs all over the south of Western Australia warn of the poison risk from fox baits. What's going on? An Australian plant, to which indigenous creatures had grown immune, was observed to kill foreign species with extreme prejudice. Biologists managed to isolate the unique poison, synthesized the toxic chemical in the plant, injected it into pieces of kangaroo meat, and air-dropped them all over the southern wilderness regions of Western Australia to protect native fauna from foxes, an introduced predator. The project has been working well, so if you happen upon a tasty meat morsel along the Bibbulmun Track, *don't eat it.*

As there's no shortage of 'roo-auto collision stories, you might want to stay the night along the way rather than drive in the dark. Most of the small towns between Albany and Esperance have caravan parks and basic motels. **Jerramuhgup Caravan Park ❶** is just over 200km from Albany. (☎ 9835 1174. Sites $9 per person; ensuite cabins $55; family ensuite cabins $75.) The friendly folks at **Ravensthorpe Caravan Park ❶** are another hour east. (☎ 9838 1050. Dorms $11-13; sites for 2 $15.50; cabins for 2 from $30, extra person $5.)

Westrail buses (☎ 9326 2813 or 13 10 53) run between Albany and Esperance via Ravensthorpe (M and Th, $41). The **Ravensthorpe/Hopetoun Tourist Bureau,** on the South Coast Hwy. in Ravensthorpe, publishes a guide to the area; check the tourist offices in Albany or Esperance. (☎ 9838 1277. Open daily when possible; in summer 9am-5pm, in winter 9am-4:30pm.) **EFTPOS** is available at most petrol stations.

FITZGERALD RIVER NATIONAL PARK

Halfway between Albany and Esperance lies the enormous **Fitzgerald River National Park.** Named a "Biosphere Reserve" for the abundance and diversity of its wildlife, the park hosts rare creatures like the **Malleefowl** (see p. 618); the **Chuditch,** a carnivorous marsupial; and the **Dibbler,** a marsupial once thought to be extinct. **Whales** can be seen from the tower at Point Ann, near the western edge of the reserve. The park is also home to thousands of species of plants, including dazzling spring wildflowers from September to November.

Accessing the park can be difficult. All park roads are unsealed, and most are unpleasant or downright impassible by 2WD; caravans shouldn't bother trying. Ocean kayaking along the coast is dangerous and should only be undertaken by experts. This park has two main access points: **Bremer Bay** on the western end and **Hopetoun** on the eastern end; a few unsealed roads run south from the South Coast Hwy. to the park. To get to Bremer Bay from the South Coast Hwy., turn right onto Bremer Bay Rd. about 120km east of Albany, then travel 65km east. Hopetoun is 50km south of Ravensthorpe on Ravensthorpe Hopetoun Rd. Hammersley Rd. cuts through the park from the highway to Hopetoun.

The area features good rock climbing, abseiling, diving, and hiking of all skill levels. The **East Mount Barren Walk** (3hr.), starting about 12km west of the Hopetoun entrance, is of medium difficulty and features great views of the beach; try also the **Horrie and Dorri Walk** (1-2hr.) or the **West Mount Barren Walk** (1-2hr.), or take a three- to five-day walk along the coast from Bremer Bay to Hopetoun. Plan ahead—the park lacks the readily accessible information and spate of tour companies that one finds elsewhere. Bob Wilson of ⊠**Great Southern Adventure Tours** in Bremer Bay (☎ 9837 4067) is an adventure jack-of-all-trades who can design itineraries that include one or many activities from canoeing to bushwalking to abseiling and rock climbing. He also has maps for the as-yet primitive coastal walk.

Passes for the park are available at **CALM** offices in Albany (☎ 9842 4500) or Esperance (☎ 9071 3733) and the tourist bureau in Ravensthorpe. Deposit day passes in an honor box at the entrance ($9 per vehicle). **Four Mile Beach** (just west of Hopetoun) and **Saint Mary Inlet** (at Point Ann) are the easiest **campsites ❶** to access by car (Sites for 2 $10, extra person $5.50, children $2). To reach **Point Ann,** a particularly good whale-watching spot, take Pabelup Dr. from the north or Devils Creek Rd. from the west. Fires are not allowed, but gas BBQs are available for free at Mylies, Point Ann, Quoin Head, and Fitzgerald Inlet. There are no reliable sources of water in the park, so be sure to bring enough. **Mt. Madden, Mt. Short,** and **Mt. Desmond** are not in the park itself but are all near Ravensthorpe and offer excellent views of the area. **Cheynes Beach** in **Waychinicup National Park** is also highly recommended. There are **ranger stations** in the park at East Mt. Barren (☎ 9838 3060) and on Murray Rd. (☎ 9837 1022), toward Bremer Bay.

THE BIG SPLURGE

TAYLOR STREET TEAROOM

Esperance may be a long way from any metropolitan center, but the **Taylor Street Tearoom** will make you feel like you've stumbled into a cosmopolitan paradise. Sit on the deck on a warm summer morning and gaze out over the rippling sea or cozy up to the fireplace on a cool Esperance night.

Your biggest decision may be when to go. In the morning, breakfast beckons with smoked Tasmanian salmon omelettes ($12) or the buffet, featuring everything under the sun. After being pummeled by Southern Ocean waves all morning, get back with the Surfer's Revenge—a fried flake fillet with lettuce, tomato, and tzatziki ($12). Dinner entices with herbed kangaroo with parsnip, baba ghanoush and braised capsisum ($20), or Master Stock Duck, a half-duck poached in aramatic soy stock with Chinese vegetables and sesame seeds ($25). Friday nights feature local musical talent. Any time is a great time for the tastebud-teasing selection of cakes ($4-5), from white chocolate to peaches and cream, and a smooth mocha ($3).

Whatever you choose, the friendly staff and calming decor at the Taylor Street Tearoom will make any traveler feel a bit more at home in the middle of the Southwest outback. (*In Esperance, next to the Taylor St. jetty.* ☎9071 4317.)

ESPERANCE ☎08

Esperance (pop. 13,000) may be rather remote—it's 400km from the nearest stoplight—but it has magnificent surroundings and some of the best beaches and diving in all of Australia. The town's coastline is unsurpassed and nearby **Cape Le Grand National Park** is one of the southwest's true jewels. Summer tourists flock to the area to swim, fish, dive, and explore nearby parks.

⬛ TRANSPORTATION. Westrail buses (☎13 10 53) stop near the tourist office and run to: Albany (6-10hr.; Tu-W and F-Sa 8am; $43); Kalgoorlie (5hr.; W and F 8:35am, Su 2pm; $38); and Perth (10hr., M-Sa 8am, $58). Several **car rental** companies have offices in town: **Stopover** (☎9071 0312), **Budget** (☎9071 2775), and **Avis** (☎9071 3998) have various deals for around $45 to $55 per day. *Let's Go* does not recommend hitchhiking, but hitchhikers head to the north end of Dempster St.

⬛⬛ ORIENTATION AND PRACTICAL INFORMATION. The **South Coast Hwy.** (Monjingup Rd.) intersects Harbour Rd., which runs south into town. The **Esplanade** flanks the bay, and **Dempster St.** snakes along roughly parallel to it. The **tourist office** is near the center of town, on the corner of Dempster and Kemp St. (☎9071 2330; fax 9071 4543. Open Sep.-Apr. M-F 8:45am-5pm, Sa-Su 9am-5pm; May-Aug. M-F 8:45am-4pm, Sa-Su 9am-4pm.) **Internet** access is at **Computer Alley,** 69c Dempster St. (☎9072 1293. Open M-F 9am-5pm, Sa 9am-noon.)

⬛⬛ ACCOMMODATIONS AND FOOD. The **Blue Waters Lodge YHA ❷,** 299 Goldfields Rd., near the intersection of Dempster and Norseman St., is across the street from the ocean. Formerly a Royal Australian Air Force (RAAF) building in Kalgoorlie, it was transported to Esperance, reassembled, and spruced up. The hostel is a pretty 15min. walk to the city center along the harbor bike path. Perks include pool table, Internet ($6 per hr.), and book exchange. (☎/fax 9071 1040. Free bus station pickup and drop off. Dorms $19; singles $26; twins $43; families $58. YHA discount $3.) **Esperance Backpackers ❷,** 14 Emily St., a 20min. walk north of town, runs reasonably priced tours. (☎9071 4724. Internet $4 per 30min. Free pickup from the bus stop. Dorms $10; twins and doubles $48. NOMADS/VIP/YHA.) **NOMADS Shoestring Stays ❷,** 23 Daphne St., also runs tours. (☎9071 3396. Internet, free bike hire, and free pickup and drop-off. Dorms $18; doubles $42. NOMADS/VIP/YHA.) The **Esperance B&B By**

the Sea ❺ is a striking new house with comfortable rooms featuring views of Blue Haven Bay. (☎9071 5640; www.esperancebb.com. Singles $70; doubles $90.) The **Esperance Seafront Caravan Park** ❷ is next to the YHA at the base of Goldfields Rd. (☎9071 1251. Linen $3. Sites for 2 $15.50, powered $18.50, extra person $4; caravans for 2 $51; ensuite holiday units $85.) There is good **camping** ❶ in Cape Le Grand National Park, 60km east of town ($9 per car; sites for 2 $12.50, extra person $5.50), and on **Woody Island** in Esperance Bay (sites from $9). Duncan's SupaValu **supermarket** is at the corner of Andrews and Dempster St. (Open M-W and F 8am-6pm, Th 8am-8pm, Sa 8am-5pm.)

◪ ◪ **SIGHTS AND ACTIVITIES.** Drivers or bikers with strong legs should try the 38km loop along the ◪**Great Ocean Drive**, which snakes along the coast and by the (sometimes) **Pink Lake.** The tourist office has maps and the road is clearly marked. Take care if biking: the road is narrow and curvy, and with such stunning coastal views, drivers may have a hard time keeping their eyes on the road. The drive begins at the southern end of Dempster St. and turns right onto Twilight Beach Rd., passing great beaches, including **Blue Haven** and **Twilight.** The rotary lookout at the beginning of the drive on Wireless Hill is a great place to watch the sunset.

Diving around Esperance is quite good. **Sanko Harvest,** the second-largest **wreck dive** in the world, is popular among experienced divers. **Esperance Diving and Fishing** guides dives and charter fishing trips. (☎9071 5111. Diving from $80. Fishing charters from $145.) **Peak Charles National Park,** an hour and a half north of Esperance along the Coolgardie-Esperance Hwy., has **rock climbing;** inquire at the CALM office, 92 Dempster St. (☎9071 3733. Open M-F 8:30am-4:30pm.) **Mackenzie's Island Cruises,** 71 The Esplanade, runs daily cruises to Woody Island if enough people show up. (☎9071 5757. $53, under 16 $20.) The 4WDing along the beach and among the sand dunes north of town is incredible, but beware of patches of quicksand.

◪ CAPE LE GRAND NATIONAL PARK

Nature has outdone herself at ◪**Cape Le Grand National Park.** Hiking trails of all durations and difficulties pass cavernous granite formations dating back 2.5 billion years, affording breathtaking views of the coast and weaving through an astoundingly diverse array of plants that becomes even more striking in the orchid-filled spring. The reds, oranges, and golds of the rock mingle with the many greens of the plants and the blues of the lichens. Take Goldfields Rd. north to Fisheries Rd., turn right onto Marivale Rd., and right again onto Cape Le Grand Rd.; signs point the way. For transport to the park, ask at Esperance Backpackers or Shoestring Stays about tours (see p. 692).

A 15km coastal track connects the park's five stunning bays. From west to east, these are: Le Grand Beach, Hellfire Bay, Thistle Cove, Lucky Bay, and Rossiter Bay. The bays themselves are wonderful, with white sand, green and blue waters, and very friendly 'roos, but the scenes along the tracks between them are even more impressive. The stretch from **Le Grand Beach to Hellfire** (3hr.) is a hard walk through sandy coastal plains and along the slopes of the lichen-encrusted **Mt. Le Grand.** The track from **Hellfire to Thistle** (2½hr.) is challenging, weaving through low scrub and snowy banksia flowers. The track from **Thistle to Lucky** is the easiest of the four legs but is still a challenge, with heart-stopping views of caves, waves, and stunning granite forms. The moderate hike from **Lucky to Rossiter** features more granite outcrops, where rock-resistant plants cling to windswept dunes. Those attempting the 15km walk should register with the ranger. Another track ascends **Frenchman Peak** to magnificent views of coast and sea. In summer, there is good snorkeling and an occasional dolphin appearance, but beware of riptides.

GOLDFIELDS

Hundreds of kilometers east of Perth and nearly an equal distance north of Esperance, a handful of towns cling to existence in Western Australia's harsh interior. Two things keep these towns from disappearing altogether: water, piped in from the coast, and gold. In 1893, a group of Irish prospectors stumbled onto an area that would become the Golden Mile, the most gold-rich square mile in the world, and the city of Kalgoorlie was born. For the traveler, Kal offers a drastic contrast to the rest of the beach-mad southwest, but it's a long trip to get there and a long trip back, with nothing in between but 'roos and road trains. Unless particularly interested in gold mining, those heading west to Perth from Eyre should consider taking the South Coast Hwy., which allows a much more relaxing and varied trip.

GREAT EASTERN HIGHWAY

Long (600km) and mind-numbing, the drive from Perth to Kalgoorlie along the Great Eastern Highway is good training for a Nullarbor crossing. The traffic in Perth's eastern suburbs can be frustrating, but the tension melts away as you drive through the verdant fields and wildflower-filled forests of the Darling Range. By the time you reach the nowhere towns of Merredin and Southern Cross, the only traffic is swaggering road trains bearing farm equipment and even buildings. This part of the highway is not as well maintained, so fuel up whenever possible.

Merredin (pop. 3700), which contests Kalgoorlie's claim to the world's longest road train (Merredin's is over 600m), is the largest town on the Great Eastern between Coolgardie and Perth. The **tourist office, post office, bank,** and **supermarket** are all within one block of each other on Barrack St., which is just one block north of the highway. The comfortable **Hay Loft Coffee Lounge ❶**, next to the tourist office, is one of several nice places in town.

Coolgardie is a dusty frontier town that serves mainly as a residential satellite for families of Kalgoorlie miners. The main street, Hwy. 94 (Bayley St. in town), houses a **tourist office.** (☎9026 6090. Open daily 9am-5pm.) There are no **ATMs** in town, but most roadhouses have **EFTPOS**, and the post office does banking. The **Caltex Roadhouse ❸**, on Bayley St., rents simple, clean rooms. (☎9026 6049; fax 9026 6756. Singles $40; doubles $51.)

KALGOORLIE-BOULDER   ☎08

The twin towns of Kalgoorlie and Boulder (total pop. 30,500) claim an impressive catalog of odd superlatives—the largest hole in the southern hemisphere, the richest mile of gold mine on the planet, the only brothel in the world open for tours, and Australia's longest roadtrain (though Merriden, to the west, contests this claim). Lined with impressive old Victorian hotels, downtown "Kal" is a surprisingly photogenic place. Today, with the romance of prospecting long gone, mammoth mining interests run the show. It's a dusty, grimy place, where dumptrucks, dynamite, and drills toil away all day long. Still, pay can be high, and workers flood the area's hostels, creating an atmosphere that backpackers may find a bit gritty.

▐▛ TRANSPORTATION

The **airport** is south of Boulder off Gatacre St. **Qantaslink** and **Skywest** offer daily service to Adelaide (Sa-Su) and Perth (1-3 times per day, times and prices vary). The **bus stop** is between the tourist office and the post office on Hannan St. **McCafferty's/Greyhound** (☎13 14 99 or 13 20 30) runs to Perth (8hr.; M, W, and F 10:45am; $102; book at tourist office). From the tourist office, **Goldfields Express** runs to Perth (8hr.; M 10:55am, Tu and Th-Sa 2:45pm, W and F 11pm; $88, YHA $70).

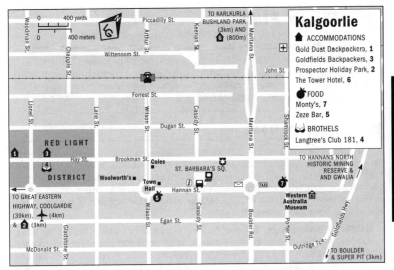

Kalgoorlie

🏠 ACCOMMODATIONS
Gold Dust Backpackers, 1
Goldfields Backpackers, 3
Prospector Holiday Park, 2
The Tower Hotel, 6

🍎 FOOD
Monty's, 7
Zeze Bar, 5

🍸 BROTHELS
Langtree's Club 181, 4

WESTERN AUSTRALIA

⚠️ **WORKING IN KAL.** The main reason people come to Kal is to work, but finding a job in mining is not as easy as one might expect. Many mining companies will only hire employees who have previous experience and pass a drug test. They also require safety training and certification, which takes time and costs money. It can be done, but it isn't a breeze—non-mining jobs may be easier to come by. The service industry offers a fairly good number of jobs, though job openings in this sector reportedly come and go with no particular pattern. **Gold Dust Backpackers** (see p. 696) is a good place to start your search.

Westrail Prospector trains depart from the station on the corner of Forrest and Wilson St. for Perth (8hr., 1-2 per day, $56) and Esperance via Norseman (5hr.; M, W, and F 5pm; $37).

 ## ORIENTATION AND PRACTICAL INFORMATION

The **Great Eastern Hwy.** (Hwy. 94 from Coolgardie) becomes **Hannan St.,** the main drag, running northeast through town. One block northwest is **Hay St.,** the **red light district,** where the town's hostels occupy former brothels. Lionel St., Wilson St., and Boulder Rd. are all major roads running perpendicular to Hannan and Hay St. To reach Boulder from downtown Kalgoorlie, turn right on Boulder Rd. at the north end of Hannan St. and follow it into Lane St.

The **tourist office** is at 250 Hannan St., (☎9021 1966. Open M-F 8:30am-5pm, Sa-Su 9am-5pm.) **Internet** is available at **NetZone,** to the left of the tourist office. (☎9022 8342. Open M-F 10am-7pm, Sa-Su 10am-5pm. $10 per hr.) The **post office** is on Hannan St., south of city center. (Open M-F 8:30am-5pm.) **Postal Code:** 6430.

The police maintain that no areas of Kalgoorlie-Boulder are particularly unsafe, although they do warn to *be careful of deep mining holes* when bushwalking. Much of the city is poorly lit, and it is a good idea to exercise caution after dark. The center of Kal's red-light district, Hay St., with neon-adorned tin shacks advertising sauna and spa services, is home to three working brothels. *Women may not want to walk alone in this area after dark.*

> **PRETTY IN PINK** Why are many lakes in Western Australia pink? The *Dunaliella salina* algae and a bacteria called *Halobacterium cutirubrum* thrive along the salt crusts at the bottom of lakes, living in water with salinity as high as 35% sodium chloride—over 10 times the salinity of seawater. When salinity, temperature, and sunlight are at high levels, the bacteria produce beta carotene to protect themselves, breaking out into natural pink hues. The algae is even farmed in some places to make food coloring or dietary supplements.

ACCOMMODATIONS

At the turn of the 19th century, Kal boasted 93 hotels, more than any other town its size in the world. There are still a heap of nice places to stay in town, though they tend to be pricey. On the other end, most budget accommodations are geared toward long-term workers. This leaves Kal's two backpacker hostels smack in the middle of the red light district. The **caravan parks** on the way out of town toward Coolgardie are a good alternative.

Goldfields Backpackers, 166 Hay St. (☎9091 1482 or 0412 110 001; fax 9091 1484), near the intersection with Lionel St. Dingy place with shared kitchen, laundry, lounge, and swimming pool. There's a notice board for work opportunities. The one cheap place in town more oriented towards travelers than long term workers. Offers transport around the city for a fee. Dorms $18; singles $28; doubles $44. ❷

Gold Dust Backpackers, 192 Hay St. (☎/fax 9091 3737). Clean, with kitchen and nice lounge spaces. Slightly rowdier crowd. Workers and travelers generally housed in separate dorms. The management has good luck finding jobs for guests. Offers transport around the city for a fee. Internet $6 per hr. Dorms $17; singles $30; twins and doubles $45. ISIC/NOMADS/VIP/YHA. ❷

Prospector Holiday Park (☎9021 2524), on the corner of the Great Eastern Hwy. and Ochiltree St. Sites from $13, powered $20; cabins from $58. ❶

The Tower Hotel (☎9021 3211), on the corner of Bourke and Maritana St., northwest of Hannan St. Nice rooms and an in-house movie channel. Doubles from $75; family rooms $116. ❺

FOOD AND NIGHTLIFE

Monty's ❸ (☎9022 8288), at the corner of Hannan and Porter St., is open 24hr. and has $9 pasta on Tuesdays and mains from $17-25. The **Zeze Bar** ❸, at the corner of Hannan and Wilson St., makes excellent woodfire pizzas from $14-20. (☎9021 3046. Open daily noon-2:30pm and 6-9pm.) **Cafes** line Hannan St.; many open early and close late. Kal boasts nearly 30 **pubs;** many cluster at the corner of Hannan and Maritana St. Coles **supermarket** is at the corner of Wilson and Brookman St. (Open M-W and F 8am-6pm, Th 8am-9pm, Sa 8am-5pm.)

SIGHTS

The best place to learn about mining is the extensive ■**Mining Hall of Fame,** located at **Hannans North Historic Mining Reserve,** a right turn off Goldfields Hwy., 2km north of Hannan St., features biographies of mining legends, demonstrations of gold pouring and panning, and a tour of an underground mine. (☎9091 4074. Open daily 9am-4:30pm. $16.50, concessions $12, children $8.50, families up to 6 $42. Without underground tour $10, children $5, families $33.) The **Super Pit,** an immense open-pit working mine, is the largest hole in the Southern Hemisphere. For an added treat, the miners often set off explosions at 1pm. The lookout is just outside town;

head toward Boulder on the Goldfield's Hwy., then turn left at the sign for the pit. (Open daily 6am-7pm, except when closed for blasting. Free.)

The recently-refurbished **Langtree's Club 181,** 181 Hay St., may be the world's only working brothel that offers tours. (☎9026 2181. 18+. Tours daily 11am, 3, and 7pm; also Sa-Su 1pm. $25.) There are a few mining ghost towns north of Kalgoorlie, but in most, not even much rubble remains. The exception is **Gwalia,** a 2hr. drive north on the Goldfields Hwy., adjoined to the settlement of Leonora. Several outfits have **bush tours;** Aboriginal guide Geoff Stokes (☎9093 3745; geoffstokes@bigpond.com) runs day tours ($80) and camping trips ($170 per night) focusing on Aboriginal culture and native plants and animals.

NORSEMAN ☎08

About 100 years ago, "Hardy Norseman" was tethered here overnight as his rider slept. The restless horse pawed at the dusty ground, uncovering a chunk of gold. Prospectors rushed to the area, and the town of Norseman was born. Today, most travelers are on their way elsewhere. For those heading north from Esperance, Norseman is the first encounter with the Goldfields. For those heading east across the desolate Nullarbor Plain, it is the last taste of civilization for over 1000km.

The **tourist office,** on Robert St., one block east on the highway between Sinclair and Richardson St., has information about Norseman and traveling the Eyre Hwy. They also offer free showers, a dream come true for Nullarbor survivors. (☎9039 1071. Open daily 9am-5pm.) The people of Norseman were shocked when ANZ bank recently installed an **ATM.** There is **Internet** at the **Telecentre** on Robert St. (☎9039 0538. Open M-F 9am-4pm. $2.50 per 15min.)

The family-run **Lodge 101 ❷** on Prinsep St. (the Coolgardie-Esperance Hwy.) offers comfortable accommodations. Backpackers can use a small kitchen and an outdoor sheltered lounge area. (☎9039 1541. Dorms $17; singles $28; twins $48.) The town's hotels and motels have restaurants, but there are no great budget options. The SupaValu, 89 Robert St., has **groceries.** (Open M-F 8:30am-6pm, Sa 8:30am-5pm, Su 9:30am-1pm.) The **BP 24-hour Travelstop,** north of town at the exit for the Eyre Hwy., has a diner, convenience store, and **petrol.**

CROSSING THE NULLARBOR

The **Eyre Highway,** running between Norseman and Adelaide across the **Nullarbor Plain** (see p. 500), is a grueling desert haul by car or bus; on a Greyhound **bus,** it's a mind-boggling 26hr. trek ($230, YHA discount 10%). The one noteworthy sight is the pink **Lake McDonald** near Penong. **Ninety Mile Straight,** the longest completely straight stretch of highway in Australia, begins just west of Cocklebiddy. For questions on what is allowed across the border into SA, call the **agriculture department.** (☎9039 3227 in WA, ☎8625 2108 in SA; www.agric.wa.gov.au.) The **tourist office** in Norseman has helpful info and handles bus bookings. When you reach **Ceduna** at the eastern corner of SA's **Eyre Peninsula,** pick up a Nullarbor certificate of completion at the tourist office. (For more info on the Eyre Hwy., see p. 500.)

WHAT'S UP DOC? The Nullarbor spans bewildering expanses of nothingness, punctuated by a few isolated outposts where passersby gas up or take a breather. How do a few hundred residents spread out over these thousands of kilometers cope with emergencies, not to mention basic medical needs? Australia's **Royal Flying Doctor Service** provides vital medical services to 80% of continental Australia from 20 air bases across the country. For 70 years, doctors have flown into remote communities in planes outfitted as medical centers, setting up makeshift clinics in homesteads and carting trauma victims up into the skies. The Flying Doctor has become an Australian icon for overcoming the "tyranny of distance."

BATAVIA COAST AND MIDLANDS

The region just north and east of Perth represents different things for different people. For windsurfers, Lancelin and Geraldton offer world-class gusts. Fishermen reap the bountiful harvest of the Batavia Coast's treacherous waters. Farmers supply wheat from huge tracts of land across the Midlands and graze sheep on coastal areas. For many backpackers, the region is little more than the long, straight, and somewhat monotonous Brand Hwy., running 600km north from Perth to the jagged gorges of Kalbarri and beyond with a stop at the ghostly Pinnacles. But those willing to do some exploring along the way will be treated to a beautiful coastal road with views of the sea, thrilling watersports, a glorious wildflower season (June-Nov.), and pristine coastal dunes.

LANCELIN ☎ 08

Lancelin (pop. 800), 126km north of Perth, is often regarded as the windsurfing capital of Australia. The Aborigines called the area *Wangaree*, meaning "Good Fishing Place," and this small fishing village still thrives upon the ocean's bounty, working the seas from September to June. But Lancelin is equally a place of good winds, and thrillseekers flock here from October through March to ride its air currents. The famed Ledge Point Sailboard Classic is held in the second week in January, but even in the off-season, there's almost always a good breeze.

🖫🖊 TRANSPORTATION AND PRACTICAL INFORMATION. There is no public transportation to Lancelin, but **Coastal Coachlines** runs **buses** from Perth to nearby Regans Ford. (☎9652 1036. 2hr.; departs Perth train station M-F 4:30pm; $14. Book ahead.) Alternatively, the YHA will pick up from Perth for $25. The easiest way to reach Lancelin is by car; from Perth, take Bulwer St. to Charles St., which becomes Hwy. 60 (Wanneroo Rd.). A **4WD vehicle** can drive the beach and along the dunes up the coast to **Cervantes.** Proceed with caution, and check with the **tourist info center,** 102 Gingin Rd., to see if the beach is suitable. (☎9655 1100. Open daily 9am-6pm.) Lancelin has one small shopping strip on Gingin Rd., which includes a surfshop, two bakeries, a **supermarket** (☎9655 1172; open daily 7am-7pm), and a **Telecentre,** 127 Gingin Rd., with **Internet.** (☎9655 2033. Open M-F 9am-3pm. $8 per hr.)

🖬 ACCOMMODATIONS. The sparkling, well-run **🖾YHA Lancelin Lodge ❷,** 10 Hopkins St., has a comfy lounge, free bikes, boogie boards, fishing rods, a lovely kitchen, and a new pool. It's only a short walk to Lancelin's beautiful beach, and the people couldn't be nicer. (☎9655 2020; fax 9655 2021. Internet $6 per hr. Dorms $17; doubles $45; family rooms $60.) The other budget alternative is the **Lancelin Caravan Park ❶,** just down Hopkins St. from the YHA—you can't miss the sign. (☎9655 1056. Sites $9 per person, powered $11; on-site vans $22.)

🖾 ACTIVITIES. **Windsurfing** lessons and equipment are available at **Werner's Hotspot** (☎9655 1553). Another Lancelin attraction is its sand dunes, accessible by car, which extend for miles to the north and east of town. The dunes are a 4WD playground and also a practice area for the Australian **military. Desert Storm Adventures** offers a one-hour veritable rollercoaster ride over the dunes in a schoolbus with monster truck tires and an equally monster stereo. You don't crush any cars, but it's a fun trip all the same.(☎9655 2550. $35, concessions $30, children $25.)

The tourist center and hostels provide maps of several coastal **nature walks** in the area. Lancelin's coral reefs are unusually close to shore, which makes for good snorkeling and diving. The lagoon on the far side of **Lancelin Island,** a bird sanctuary within swimmable distance, is one of the best spots. Very experienced divers enjoy the **Key Biscayne Dive** around an old drilling rig, 19km northwest of Ledge Point. **Lancelin Surf and Dive,** 127 Gingin Rd., rents scuba, snorkeling, sandboarding, and surfing gear. (☎9655 1441. Dive gear $55 per day; sandboards, surfboards, and snorkels $11 for 2hr., $22 per day. Open daily 8am-4pm; later in summer.) Fishing in the area is also good; casual anglers cast right off the jetty.

NAMBUNG NATIONAL PARK: THE PINNACLES

Between Lancelin and Geraldton, the **Pinnacles Desert,** in **Nambung National Park,** is a popular destination for day-tours from Perth. The barren, jagged landscape isn't really a desert at all but an expanse of sand dunes with thousands of wind-eroded limestone pillars up to 4m tall. Dutch sailors sighting the rocks from the sea mistook them for the ruins of an ancient city. The park has a ghost town-like feel, and the forms of the worn rocks are intriguing. The best time to visit is at sunrise, sunset, or under the full light of the moon.

The park is a good 250km north of Perth, near the small town of **Cervantes.** **McCafferty's/Greyhound** (☎13 14 99 or 13 20 30) drops off right in town (2hr., 1 per day, $25). Perth day-tours range from $80-100, though there are cheaper deals in winter. **West Coast Explorers** (☎9418 8835), which arrives at sunset, and **Redback Safari** (☎9275 6204) are popular. In Cervantes, **HappyDay Tours** (☎9652 7244) gives three-hour walking tours ($25) and **Turquoise Coast Enviro Tours** (☎9652 7047) gives driving tours of the Pinnacles ($30). However, it's hard to see many advantages to a guided tour over an independent walk around the Pinnacles—the walk is easy and no 4WD is necessary. Hiring a car and driving with friends is the cheapest and most flexible way to see the park ($9 per vehicle). Allow one hour west from the left turn off the Brand Hwy.

In Cervantes, the Shell station acts as the **tourist bureau** (☎9652 7041; open daily 8am-6pm). **Pinnacles Beach Backpackers ❷,** 91 Seville St., on the corner of Seville and Barcelona St., offers sunny rooms near the beach. (☎9652 7377; fax 9652 7318. Dorms $19; doubles $50, ensuite $60.) **Pinnacles Caravan Park ❷** is at the end of Aragon Rd. on the beach. (☎9652 7060. Powered sites $18; on-site vans from $22.) **Camping ❶** is allowed at Hangover Bay but not in the park itself.

GERALDTON ☎08

Geraldton (pop. 24,000) is the gateway to the beautiful **Abrolhos Islands,** where the diving is superb. Windsurfers eager to test their skill in the strong southerly winds also flock to Geraldton every summer.

◪◪ TRANSPORTATION AND PRACTICAL INFORMATION. From the Brand Hwy., head straight through the rotary up Cathedral Ave. to get to the town center. The town's main drag, **Chapman Rd.,** and the shop-lined **Marine Tce.** both run parallel to the coast and intersect Cathedral Ave. **McCafferty's/Greyhound** (☎13 14 99 or 13 20 30), **Westrail** (☎13 10 53), and **Integrity** (☎1800 226 339) run buses to Perth (6hr., 2-3 per day, $40). McCafferty's runs to Broome ($300) via Carnarvon ($65) and Exmouth ($190). Integrity hits the same destinations for considerably cheaper. The **tourist office** is inside the Bill Sewall Complex at the corner of Bayly St. and Chapman Rd., about 1km north of Cathedral Ave. (☎9921 3999; fax 9964 2445. Open M-F 8:30am-5pm, Sa 9am-4:30pm, Su 9:30am-4:30pm.)

◪◪ ACCOMMODATIONS AND FOOD. The convenient **Batavia Backpackers ❷,** next to the tourist office, has oceanfront balconies and private dorms. (☎9964 3001. Dorms $17; singles $22; twins $35. ISIC/VIP/YHA.) **Geraldton YHA Foreshore Backpackers ❷,** 172 Marine Tce., a block southwest of Cathedral Ave., has a rustic flavor, ample space, and a refreshing lack of bunk beds. (☎9921 3275; fax 9921 3233. Free pickup and drop-off. Internet $7 per hr. Dorms $18; singles $27; twins

THE LOCAL STORY

HAIL TO THE CHEF

Gary Finlay owns Finlay's Fresh Fish BBQ in Kalbarri, WA. Interview July 18, 2002.

Q: Have you seen the fishing industry change much?

A: Yeah, heaps. The fastest, most advanced fishing fleet in the world is along this coast here. Most sophisticated in the world, with technology and electronics. And with that it's lost a lot of its identity. Now it's all dollars driving it whereas before it used to be the satisfaction of being a hunter, a successful hunter, and the lifestyle that went with it. But now there's no lifestyle with it—it's just competitive, hard, aggressive work. Y'know, catch it before the other bloke catches it. And that's sad in a lot of ways.

Q: Do you ever have entertainment around the restaurant?

A: Yeah, if you play some songs or sing, you get some free tucker. We've had this opera singer from Fremantle. He finished his meal and just got up and sang one of the fisherman's operas, "Peter the Fisherman" or something like that. Personally, the sensation was tingly for me. We had entertainers like Flauvia from *Cirque du Soleil*—she did the dance routine. We had belly dancers, Scottish bagpipes, even the champion zither player from America.

Q: I see you've got the piano.

A: The piano's had so much talent on it it's incredible, from 7-year-old kids who just muck around to concert pianists. We had a sign on there: "Piss off. This piano is for pleasure, not pain." Little kids used to muck around with it all the time.

and doubles $42; family rooms for 2 $37, children $5.50. ISIC/NOMADS/VIP/YHA.) The **Belair Caravan Park ❶** is just south of town on Willcack Dr. (☎9921 1997. Sites $14.50, powered $17.50; cabins from $30; chalets from $58.) The **Ocean Centre Hotel ❺**, on the corner of Foreshore Dr. and Cathedral Ave., has nice rooms. (☎9921 7777. Singles $85, ocean view $105.) Woolworth's, on Sanford and Durlacher St., has cheap **groceries.** (Open M-F 8am-6pm, Th 8am-9pm, Sa 8am-5pm.)

◙ ◪ SIGHTS AND ACTIVITIES. Most people come to Geraldton for one reason: **windsurfing.** The best conditions are October to November and March to April, though it is good year-round. Bring your own gear or rent at **Sailwest,** at the Point Moore Lighthouse on Chapman Rd. south of town. (☎9964 1722. Windsurfing gear $90 per day, surfboards $30, lessons $25 per hr. Open M-F 9am until the wind reaches 20 knots, Sa-Su 10am until 20 knots.) The best windsurfing in the area is at **Point Moore,** the windiest spot around. **St. George's Beach** has tamer winds, but also a shallow reef that can be dangerous. Surfers prefer **Greys Beach, Sunset Beach,** and **Back Beach.** The **Abrolhos Islands,** an archipelago comprising over 120 islands, about 60km off of Geraldton, were the site (and cause) of the Batavia wreck. The islands are rich in marine life, making for incredible diving. With a fast boat, **Odyssey Abrolhos** (☎0428 382 505) runs daytrips to the islands, and both the Odyssey and **Eco Abrolhos Tours** (☎9964 7887) offer extended tours (from $200). **Abrolhos Air Services** (☎9923 3151) takes visitors on sightseeing flights from $165.

KALBARRI NATIONAL PARK
Kalbarri National Park encompasses miles of sandstone sculptures, carved by the elements over millions of years. The rugged red-and-white landscape is further enhanced in the late winter and early spring by countless wildflowers.

◪ ◪ ◪ PRACTICAL INFORMATION, ACCOMMODATIONS, AND FOOD. The **tourist bureau** is in nearby Kalbarri, on Grey St. to the left of Woods St. when facing the ocean. (☎9937 1104; fax 9937 1474. Open daily 9am-5pm.) The **Department of Conservation and Land Management (CALM)** office (☎9937 1140) is on the Ajana-Kalbarri Rd., 1km east of town. **Kalbarri Backpackers ❷**, 52 Mortimer St., offers decent rooms, a pool, cozy lounges, BBQ, bike rental ($9 per day), 4WD rental (ages 25+ $77 per day), and free use of snorkel gear and boogie boards. Beware the spiders in the bathrooms, though you won't have to look at their extensive webs when the lights shut off after five minutes. From the tourist bureau, turn right on Grey St., then right on Woods St. (☎9937 1430; fax 9937 1563. Dorms $18; doubles $44. 7th night free.) **Kalbarri Anchorage Caravan Park ❷**, across from the jetty at the north end of Grey St., is in a pretty location with an enclosed kitchen. (☎9937 1181; fax 9937 1806. Sites for 2 $20, on-site vans $40; extra person $5.) **⬛Finlay's Fresh Fish BBQ ❷**, on Magee Crescent, serves up tasty seafood ($10-18; see **The Local Story,** p. 700). To get there from Grey St., turn left at Porter St., right on Walker St., then right onto Magee Crescent. (☎9937 1260. Open Tu-Su 5:30-8:30pm.) Foodland **supermarket** is in the Ampol station on Grey St. (☎9937 1100. Open daily 7am-6pm.)

⬛⬛ SIGHTS AND ACTIVITIES. The park has two main sections: the coastal cliffs and the river gorges. Along the 10km of the coastal road just south of the town of Kalbarri, numerous sideroads lead out to soaring cliffs overhanging the Indian Ocean. The **Natural Bridge** was created by waves that eroded part of a cliff, leaving a rock slab bridging a gap filled with crashing white caps. Nearby, **Island Rock** rises 20m from the surf. Other impressive formations include **Red Bluff Lookout, Eagle Gorge,** and **Rainbow Valley.** Some visitors are disappointed to discover that Pot Alley and Mushroom Rock are just more rocks and ocean. The eye-popping **cliffside hike** (10km one-way; 4hr.) takes in the whole series of cliffs, running from Eagle Gorge to the Natural Bridge. A shuttle drops hikers off at the Natural Bridge daily for the hike back into town. (☎9937 1161. Departs daily 9:30am. $9.)

The river gorges section of the park, carved by the waters of the Murchison River, features top-down views of the gorges and hikes along the jagged ledges of the river bank. **Nature's Window** is a red rock arch that frames a river landscape behind it. It is found near the beginning of the **loop trail** (8km; 4hr.), a challenging but rewarding climb that runs along clifftops, down to the river bed, and then along the river level ledges before climbing up again to the top of the gorge. Keep the river on your right and stay close to water level, even if it seems like you're not on the trail. To experience those gorges inaccessible by road, the intensive 38km **hike** from the Ross Graham lookout farther west past the Hawks Head lookout to the Loop trail runs along the path of the river. Allow four days and hike in groups (CALM recommends parties of five or more). For any overnight hiking, alert **CALM** (☎9937 1140) beforehand. Access to the River Gorges area costs $9 per vehicle. Bring exact change in case no one is on duty. The park's unsealed roads are generally in good 2WD condition, but it's always a good idea to check with CALM.

Tours are plentiful and provide access to otherwise-unreachable areas of the park. **⬛Kalbarri Adventure Tours** has a day-long "Canoe the Gorges" trip stopping at Nature's Window and the Z Bend. The hikes in and out are tough at parts but worth the sweat. (☎9937 1677. M-Tu, Th, and Sa; $60.) **Kalbarri Safari Tours** runs a full-day trek along Z Bend. (☎9937 1011. Tu-W, F, and Su; $60.) **Kalbarri Bush and Wildflower Tours** offers half-day tours to the Z Bend and Nature's Window. (☎9937 1742. $40.) Abseil down the gorges with **Kalbarri Abseil** (☎9937 1618; daily, $60) or **sandboard** 280 ft. down the superbowl with **Kalbarri Safari Tours** (M, Th, and Sa; $60).

THE LITTLE PRINCIPALITY Along the North Coast Hwy.
between Geraldton and Kalbarri, Australia takes a hiatus. **Hut River Province** is a 75km^2 area that claims to be its own principality. This island of royalty was created by Prince Leonard George Casley with a few twists of the law for a few benefits of tax evasion. Visitors of Prince Leonard (a former farmer) and his very own principality can get a special stamp in their passport, Hut River postage stamps, and currency. If you happen to bump into the Prince around town, ask him to show you his realm.

Kalbarri Explorer Ocean Charters has sunset dolphin and whale trips, morning whale-watching trips from August to November, and deep sea fishing on demand. (☎9937 2027. Sunset 2hr.; $44, morning $49. 6hr. fishing., $130.) Plant lovers will appreciate the herbarium and nature trail at the **Kalbarri Wildflower Centre,** on the North West Coastal Hwy., 1km before Kalbarri. (☎9937 1229. Free bus service daily 10am from tourist office. Open June-Nov. daily 9am-5pm; $2. Guided 1hr. walks Aug.-Oct. daily 10am; $6.) **Rainbow Jungle,** on Red Bluff Rd. about 3½km south of town, is a parrot breeding center. (☎9937 1248. Open Tu-Sa 9am-5pm, Su 10am-5pm; last entrance 4pm. $8.50, ages 4-16 $3.50.)

OUTBACK COAST AND GASCOYNE

The Outback Coast is an unfathomable expanse of bushland, broken up only by termite mounds and the occasional befuddled emu crossing the road. Although the distances between towns are daunting, the desolate landscape holds its own sense of wonder. The dazzling ocean that abuts this semi-desert counters its sparseness with a lush flowering of marine life, from the dolphins and dugongs of Shark Bay to the whale sharks and coral of the Ningaloo Marine Park. Winter is peak season, when Perthites park themselves along the sunny coast.

SHARK BAY

Shark Bay, Western Australia's much-touted World Heritage area, was the site of the earliest recorded European landing in Australia. In 1616, Dutch Explorer Dirk Hartog came ashore at Cape Inscription on the island that now bears his name. Today, Shark Bay is known mainly for the dolphins at Monkey Mia, tranquil shell beaches, and the "living fossils" (stromatolites) at Hamelin Pool. The best way to see the area is by car or on a tour; buses are infrequent.

MONKEY MIA. At Monkey Mia, the Indian bottlenose dolphins of Shark Bay swim right up to the shore to be fed by herds of tourists. The dolphins have been visiting Monkey Mia since the time it was nothing but a sheep-farming area, but in the past ten years, the playful creatures have become an international sensation. Some think Monkey Mia provides an unparalleled opportunity to interact with intelligent, sociable animals; others find it a contrived and exploitative show.

One-day access to the site is $6, a family pass costs $12, and four-week passes are $9, although it only takes an hour or two to "do" the Monkey Mia dolphin bit. Generally there are three feedings between 8am and 1pm each day; it's best to get there early in the morning. The reserve is home to an **info center** and the **CALM office,** which has displays, videos, and talks. (☎9948 1366. Open daily 8am-4pm.) **Aristocrat II** (☎9948 1444; open daily 8am-4pm) and **Shotover** (☎9948 1481) offer comparable cruises to see marine life through underwater windows. Summer crowds can spot sharks, turtles, and dugongs (an endangered species of seacow). In winter, however, the only animals spotted are dolphins, which are plentiful near shore. (☎9948 1446. $29-49, children $14-20.)

The **YHA Monkey Mia Dolphin Resort ❶,** right next to the dolphin interaction site, has backpacker beds in cramped, aging campervans, and sites. (☎9948 1320; fax 9948 1034. Sites $9; dorms $18; vans from $38.) Bring food to Monkey Mia; the restaurants and mini-mart food shop (open 7am-6pm) are expensive. The road to Monkey Mia from Denham is well-marked and departs from the western tip of Knight Tce. Those without cars can take the Denham YHA's **shuttle.** (Guests free; others $5. Departs daily 7:45am, returns 4:30pm.)

VEGEMAY, VEGEMITE The infamous Vegemite that pops up all over Australia was not always Vegemite. In an effort to boost sales, Vegemite took a name change as Parwill in 1928—a play off the English Marmite, another splendid spread of yeastiness. When you've got an Australian accent, Marmite sounds like "Ma might," and Parwill sounds like "Pa will," as though whatever confidence Ma lacks, Pa possesses. Nobody got this complicated joke, though, so the spread was quickly renamed Vegemite. For more fascinating Vegenews, check out www.vegemite.com.au.

DENHAM. The westernmost town in Australia is perhaps the best base for exploring Shark Bay. The main street, **Knight Tce.**, runs parallel to the beach. The Greyhound **bus** departs for the Overlander Roadhouse on the North West Costal Hwy. from the Caltex station on Knight Tce. (M, Th, and Sa 5am and 6pm). The area is best seen by car; **Shark Bay Car Hire** (☎9948 1247), on Knight Tce., rents cars. The **tourist bureau,** 71 Knight Tce., a few doors down from the Shell station, is very helpful and has **Internet** access. (☎9948 1253; fax 9948 1065. Internet $5 per 30min. Open daily 9am-5pm.) A few doors down, the **CALM,** 67 Knight Tce., provides information and sells National Park passes. (☎9948 1208. Open M-F 8am-5pm.) The **post office** is on Knight Tce. (Open M-F 8am-4:30pm.) **Postal Code:** 6537.

The facilities at the **YHA Denham Bay Lodge ❷,** on Knight Tce., 100m south of the bus stop, are a real treat—dorms are shared ensuite units with a kitchen. (☎9948 1278; fax 9948 1031. Free bus to Monkey Mia daily 7:45am, returns 4:30pm. Dorms $21; twins and doubles $48. ISIC/VIP/YHA.) The **Denham Seaside Tourist Village ❷,** at the western end of Knights Tce., is another budget option. (☎9948 1242. Sites $17, powered $20, with bath $23; cabins from $45, extra person $7.) Tradewinds **Supermarket** is at the BP Station. (Open daily 7am-7pm.)

OTHER SITES. Hamelin Pool, 100km south of Denham and 34km west of the Overlander Roadhouse, is home to a white shell beach and living **stromatolites,** communities of cyanobacteria that are the oldest known life form on Earth. It is thought that these creatures released the first significant amount of oxygen into the atmosphere, making the earth hospitable to latecomers like ourselves. The colonies aren't that photogenic, but it's at least worth a stop to say thanks. To reach these sights, you need a car or tour. **Shark Bay Coaches** (☎9948 1601) gives tours to the stromatolites and Shell Beach ($45). **Camping** is available at the **Hamelin Pool Caravan Park ❶.** (☎9942 5905. Sites for 2 $12, powered $13; extra person $2.) For **info** on the area, inquire at the tea rooms in the caravan park. (Open daily 8:30am-5:30pm.)

Fifty kilometers north of the turn-off to the Hamelin Pool along the Denham-Hamelin Rd. is the turn-off for **Shell Beach,** a dazzling 60km expanse of tiny white shells up to 15m deep. Bring something to sit on. In the northern reaches of Shark Bay, 4WD tracks lead to **Steep Point** and the tip of **Cape Peron North,** which are great coastal areas for swimming and fishing. **Camping ❶** is available in Peron National Park but only 4WD vehicles can access the sites. (Sites for 2 $10, extra adult $5.50, extra child $2.) There is also free camping with permit at various beaches along the road to Denham. (☎9948 1218. No advance booking; max. 3 days.)

CARNARVON ☎08

Carnarvon (pop. 7000) is a good place to catch your breath between destinations on the west coast, but most people come here looking for work at the 170 local fruit plantations or to see the 30m-high blowholes north of town.

🖪🚻 ORIENTATION AND PRACTICAL INFORMATION. McCafferty's/Greyhound (☎13 14 99 or 13 20 30) runs daily to: Coral Bay ($68), Exmouth ($68), Perth

WESTERN AUSTRALIA

($108), Broome ($254), and Darwin ($509). **Integrity** (☎1800 226 339) goes to Exmouth (M and W 8:30am, $68) via Coral Bay ($60) and Perth (M, W, and F; $108). A big yellow plastic banana welcomes visitors as they head into town along Robinson St. from the North West Coastal Hwy. The center of Carnarvon is **Robinson St.**, between **Babbage Island Rd.** and **Olivia Tce.**, which passes along the water. The **tourist bureau** is at 11 Robinson St., in the Carnarvon Civic Centre at the corner of Stuart St. (☎9941 1146; fax 9941 1149. Open M-F 8:30am-5pm, Sa 9am-noon.)

WORKING IN CARNARVON. There are really only two consistently successful ways to find work in Carnarvon. Those with their own mode of transport can visit the **plantations** that line the north and south sides of the Gascoyne River and inquire about work. Those without transportation are dependent on the **Carnarvon Backpackers**, who find work for guests (the process generally takes 3-5 days) and provide transportation to work sites. They keep a list of guests looking for work and pass out available jobs to those waiting the longest.

ACCOMMODATIONS AND FOOD. Carnarvon Backpackers ❷, 9790 Olivia Tce., south of Robinson St., has small, self-contained units that were built for American scientists on the Apollo and Gemini missions. With a large contingent of working travelers, the management has heaps of info on jobs, though some may find the no-alcohol rule restrictive. There's BBQ, off-street parking, A/C, fans, and canoe use. (☎/fax 9941 1095. Internet $1 per 10min. Dorms $18-20, weekly $114; doubles $47/ $270.) The **Carnarvon Tourist Centre Caravan Park ❷**, 108 Robinson St., is five blocks down Robinson St. from the tourist office. (☎9941 1438. Book ahead in winter. Sites $16, powered $18; clean cabins with TV and A/C for 2 $50, extra person $5.)

Woolworth's, in the shopping center on Robinson St., has cheap **groceries**. (☎9941 2477. Open M-W and F-Su 8am-8pm, Th 8am-9pm.) There is a weekly **produce market** on Robinson St. across from the tourist bureau (Sa 8:30am-noon.)

SIGHTS. Babbage Island Rd. runs along the coast to **Pelican Point** and makes for a pleasant bike ride among mangroves. Along the way, the mile-long jetty has good fishing and crabbing. A drive or bike ride east of town, on the back roads just north of the North West Coastal Hwy., passes many banana and mango **plantations.** Fresh fruit and veggies are plentiful and cheap; ask if you can collect the unsellable fruits lying on the ground. **Carnarvon Bus Charter** visits the plantations as well as the shrimp factory, boat harbor, salt mine, blowholes, jetty, and the OTC—the out-of-use NASA communications center on the outskirts of town. (☎9941 1146. Town tour $28, children $17; saltmine and blowholes $50/$39.) **The Blowholes,** off a 50km dirt road off a turn-off 24km north of town, are natural wave-driven water jets that spurt 30m in choppy weather. Together with the eroded moonscape surrounding them, they make a wondrous site that shouldn't be missed. A lovely beach is 1km south. Carnarvon is a popular base for trips to **Mt. Augustus,** the largest rock in Australia at twice the size of Ayers Rock. The trip is 460km by car on Gascoyne Junction, a 2WD unsealed road that can get rough; check road conditions at the tourist bureau before leaving. **Stockman Safaris** runs treks to the **Kennedy Range** and a sheep station. (☎9941 3116. 1-day $120, 3-day $600.)

CORAL BAY ☎08

Coral Bay is one of two gateways (Exmouth is the other) to the splendid Ningaloo Marine Park. The Ningaloo Reef, over 250km long, starts south of Coral Bay and stretches north around the Northwest Cape and back into Exmouth Gulf. The town itself is a street crowded with a resort, caravan park, and dive shops. The beach is a good for snorkeling and swimming.

Divers flock to Ningaloo in droves, and while they'll find more options in Exmouth, Coral Bay proves a quieter alternative destination. **Ningaloo Reef Dive Centre** (☎9942 5824), in the shopping arcade, offers two-dive trips from $150 and a certification course for $350 (starts Sa). **Power Dive** offers intro dives; an air-hose connects you to the surface and you can go down to 6m. (☎9942 5889. $50.)

The Perth-Exmouth **McCafferty's/Greyhound** (☎13 14 99 or 13 20 30) and **Integrity** (☎1800 226 339) **buses** head to Perth (Su and Th, $200) and Exmouth (M, $60). **The Mermaid's Cave,** in the shopping arcade on the right side of the road as you enter Coral Bay, is a good resource for tourist info and books tours for Coral Bay Adventures. (☎9942 5955. Open M-Sa 9am-1pm and 2-5pm, Su 9am-1pm.) In the People's Park Caravan Village, the **Fins Cafe ❸** is popular for seafood and **Internet.** (Open 7:30am-10pm. $6 per hr.) The shopping center has a small **supermarket** (☎9942 5988; open daily 7:30am-7pm) and Coral Bay News and Gifts, also the local **post office** (☎9942 5995; open M-F 8:30am-5pm). **Postal Code:** 6701.

The monolithic **Ningaloo Club ❷,** opened in late summer 2002, has an amazing pool, spotless kitchens, BBQ, Internet ($5 per hr.), and a stonework patio—the facilities can't be beat. The brightly lit rooms have lockers. Even though it's huge, it fills up fast, so book well in advance. (☎9948 5100; www.ningalooclub.com. 10-bed dorms $18, with A/C $20; 4-bed dorms $20/$22; twins and double $60/$65; ensuite doubles $80/$85. VIP discount $1. MC/V.)

EXMOUTH
☎08

The scuba diving epicenter of the west coast, Exmouth (pop. 3500) is the place to swim with easygoing whale sharks and manta rays. The colorful Ningaloo Reef is complemented on land by the beautiful Cape Range National Park. The main township area is inland and not much to look at, but as a diving and fishing destination, Exmouth can't be beat.

⌨🏠 TRANSPORTATION AND PRACTICAL INFORMATION. Most action takes place around **Maidstone Crescent,** which intersects **Murat Rd.** at both ends. **McCafferty's/Greyhound** (☎13 20 30) **buses** run to Perth (1-2 per day, $220) and Broome (1 per day, $260). **Integrity** (☎1800 226 339) also runs to Perth ($220). The Exmouth Tourist Village provides **car rental.** (☎9949 1101. Ages 21+ from $40 per day; 4WD ages 25+ from $110 per day). The **tourist bureau** is on Murat Rd. (☎9949 1176; fax 9949 1441. Open M-Sa 8:30am-5pm.) The shopping center just off Maidstone houses a **pharmacy** (open M-F 9am-5:30pm, Sa 9am-12:30pm) and a SupaValu **supermarket** (open Th-F 7am-7:30pm, M-W and Sa-Su 7am-7pm). The **hospital** is two blocks west, on Lyon St. near Fyfe St. (☎9949 1011. Dive medicals $60 cash; call ahead.) **Internet** is available at **Blue's Net Cafe,** in the back of the shopping center. (☎9949 1119. $3 per 30min. Open daily 10am-7pm.) **Challenge Bank,** on Learmouth St., is home to Exmouth's only **ATM.** Across the street is the **police station** (☎9949 2444) and the **post office** (open M-F 9am-5pm). **Postal Code:** 6707.

🏠🏕 ACCOMMODATIONS AND CAMPING. Most of the backpacker joints in Exmouth are part of sprawling tourist villages, which have their own dive shops and tours in addition to sites, cabins, or in some cases hotel rooms. Many people stay wherever they're doing their diving course—some places even offer package deals. Competition among Exmouth's tourist parks has led them to offer guests lots of freebies, including free bike use, BBQ, swimming pools, and A/C. **Excape Backpackers ❷,** within the Potshot Resort on Murat Rd., has spacious brand new dorms. Reception is at the resort bar. (☎1800 655 156. Key deposit $10. Dorms $19, with a scuba package $14; twins $55. VIP/YHA. MC/V.) **Winston's Backpackers ❷**, in the Ningaloo Caravan and Holiday Resort on Murat Rd., along with Coral Coast Dive, has tiny rooms in a well-kept building with a kitchen, pool table, and boat hire. (☎9949 2377. Dorms $18.) Although slightly out of the way, the **Sea Breeze Resort ❺**, next to the naval base north of town, offers spotless, classy hotel rooms, as well as kitchens and access to the base's pool and gym. (☎9949 1800. Hotel rooms from $90-130, with frequent special discounts. MC/V.) **Camping ❶** is permitted in designated sites within Cape Range National Park (sites for 2 $10, extra person $5.50; vehicle entry fee not included), but don't camp elsewhere—rangers do patrol. Fires are prohibited and there is no water in the park, so come prepared.

🍴🌙 FOOD AND NIGHTLIFE. The **Rock Cod Cafe ❷**, just after the Ampol station on Maidstone Crescent, has seafood specials, pasta, and burgers for $7-19. (☎9949 1249. Open daily 9:30am-9:30pm.) Behind the shopping center, **Whaler's Restaurant ❸** does delicious gourmet food ($10-20) in an upscale setting. (☎9949 2416. Open daily 8:30am-3pm; also Tu-Su 6:30pm-late.) Another popular choice is the **Golden Orchid Chinese Restaurant ❸**, in the shopping complex, with its $18 all-you-can-eat buffet. (☎9949 1740. Buffet Th 5:30-9pm.)

There are two nightlife options in town. **Grace's Tavern,** on Murat Rd. across from the Exmouth Tourist Village, is a pleasant hangout with indoor and outdoor areas. (Open M-Sa 10am-midnight, Su 10am-10pm.) The **Potshot Resort,** on Murat Rd., has a complex of nightspots with an elegant main bar, the Bamboo Room (called "the bimbo bar" by locals), and the more-crowded Vance's Bar. Friday is the big night, when beer flows until the wee hours. (☎9949 1200. Open M-Th 10am-midnight, F 10am-1:30am, Sa 9:30am-1:30am, Su 10am-10pm.)

NINGALOO MARINE PARK

Most people come to Exmouth and Coral Bay to see the impressive Ningaloo Reef, and the town is full of dive shops catering to all experience levels. Introductory PADI courses are as cheap as they come at $300-330; they take four or five days and include four ocean dives. Arrange a diving medical in advance, or put up $60 in cash at the local clinic (see **Practical Information,** p. 705). Shop around before choosing a dive shop; all have certified instructors, good equipment, and a specified instruction regime, but class size and quality of instruction vary. For veteran divers, there are many great dives in the area, including **Lighthouse Bay, Navy Pier, Muiron Islands,** and the **Hole-in-the-Wall,** on the outside of the reef near the North Mandu campsite.

The cheapest PADI course in town is run by **Coral Coast Dive,** near Winston's Backpackers in the Ningaloo Caravan Resort, with training facilities at the naval base; it has computer-oriented PADI classes with a maximum class size of six. (☎9949 1004. Dives from $90; classes $300.) **Diving Ventures** is a big, Perth-based operation with four-day PADI courses and two reef dives. (☎9949 2300. PADI M and Th, $350; 2 dives $120.) **Village Dive** has resort pier dives and well-organized PADI classes. (☎9949 1101. Pier dive $70; PADI $330.) **Exmouth Dive Centre** (☎9949 1201) has a sleek boat, upper-level classes, and pier and island dives from $150.

Whale shark snorkeling is inordinately expensive (about $275, 1 dive $50 extra) but also a unique experience you won't get any other way. The Ningaloo is one of the few areas in the world where the world's biggest fish visit consistently; they appear most frequently between March and June. A number of the dive shops listed above do whale shark tours. The best surfing is found at **Surfers Beach** at Vlamingh Head, at the northern end of the cape.

CAPE RANGE NATIONAL PARK

The rugged limestone cliffs and long stretches of sandy white beaches of **Cape Range National Park** lie to the west of Exmouth on Yardie Rd., providing a haven for bungarras, emus, and Stuart's desert peas. The solar- and wind-powered **Milyering Visitor Centre,** 52km from Exmouth, hands out maps and info on the parks. (☎9949 2808. Open daily 10am-4pm. Day-pass $9 per car. No water.) The sealed main road into the park leads to the north to the tip of the cape and then south along the west coast of the cape to Yardie Creek, which makes it a relatively long trip. Unsealed roads (Shothole Canyon Rd. and Charles Knife Rd.) run across the cape into the eastern section of the park, but they can be rough going—check with CALM (☎9949 1676) before heading in this way. If you don't have a car, try the Cape's excellent shuttle service, **Ningaloo Reef Bus,** which stops at the lighthouse, Yardie Creek, Turquoise Bay, Reef Retreat, the Milyering Visitor Centre, and Tantabiddi Reef. (☎9949 1776. M-W and F-Su $22 to Turquoise Bay, children $11; includes park entry.)

The park has just a few short walking trails, giving nice ocean views and some quality time with the jagged sandstone, but little else. The best is the **Mandu Mandu Gorge Walk** (3km; 1hr.), which treks along the gorge ridge to a nice lookout, then descends to return through the gorge itself. **Yardie Creek Walk** (1½km; 1½hr.) lets visitors explore a limestone ledge, native to only this small region of WA. The longer **Bajirrajirra Walk** (8km; 5hr.) is not worth the effort, and the **Shothole Canyon Walk** (250m; 15min.) goes up to a great lookout over the entire cape but requires going 17km south of Exmouth to get to the carpark on Minilya-Learmonth Rd.

Swimming and **snorkeling** are very popular along the pristine tropical coast. The ceaseless rip tides caused by the reef can make swimming very dangerous outside of sheltered coves. **Turquoise Bay, Sandy Bar,** and **Mesa Bay** are the best swimming spots, although their fine sands and windy nature means sun-bathing there can be more like a sand-blasting. *Extreme care should be taken in the water,* which houses a number of dangers—everything from coral cuts to painful stingray spine injuries and even lethal cone shell and blue-ringed octopus bites. Before hitting the surf, pick up a **marine safety card** at the Visitors Center. At all times, avoid interacting with wildlife and always wear protective shoes in the water.

For great views, head up to the lighthouse just north of the park's entrance for an expansive 360° overlook. Another kind of viewing pleasure can be found at the clothing-optional **Mauritius Beach,** which has the most wind-sheltered sun-bathing, and, in the early summer months, acts as a sea turtle rookery.

THE PILBARA

The Pilbara is a harsh land. Hundreds of kilometers of arid, undeveloped Outback separate the region's small, industrial towns, bumpy dirt roads weave through its mountainous, mineral-rich interior, and the searing temperatures of summer hold dangers for those who don't come prepared. In many ways a terrestial replica of purgatory, the Pilbara rarely attracts more than a passing glance from those heading to more interesting destinations, with a stop perhaps at Karijini National Park.

Industrial towns dot the long stretches of empty highway, offering basic amenities at regular intervals. **Karratha** is the region's administrative center and home to the largest mall outside of Perth, containing an ATM, pharmacy, and two **supermarkets** (both open until midnight). The mall, police, and hospital are clustered between Warambie and Welcome Rd. off Balmoral Rd., which intersects Dampier Rd. at both the east and west ends of town. The fairly plain **Tourist Bureau** is on Karratha Road 1km south of town and offers one of the town's few **Internet** hookups. (☎9144 4600. $5 per 30min. Open M-F 8am-5:30pm, Sa-Su 8am-3:30pm.) The

WESTERN AUSTRALIA

HOLD YOUR BREATH About 40km west of the Auski Road-house lies the town of Wittenoom, incorporated in 1947 as a home for asbestos miners. Asbestos tailings were used extensively as landfill in town, and the road from Wittenoom through Wittenoom Gorge is actually paved with the stuff. Despite the early warnings of health researchers, asbestos mining continued until 1966. Many residents of Wittenoom have contracted mesothelioma, and government officials still warn against travel to the area. Despite this, a handful of die-hard Wittenoomans continue to hang on. The government ordered the shut-off of water, electricity, and phone service to the 25 or so remaining residents on January 1, 1997. But the holdouts arranged a deal with Telstra for phone service, and a court challenge has kept power and water flowing. Though area tourist bureaus refuse to distribute info about Wittenoom or even to give directions, a handful of still-healthy residents push Wittenoom as a destination, trying to preserve the memory of the town that Western Australia would like to forget.

Karratha Backpackers ❷, 110 Wellard Way, off Searipple Rd., is slowly improving its modest facilities under enthusiastic new managers. (☎9144 4904. Free bus pickup M-F. Dorms $20; spacious doubles and twins $50.)

The North West Coastal Hwy. continues 35km east to Roebourne, a virtual ghost town. You can cool off at **Settler's Beach,** 12km north of Roebourne, one of the few

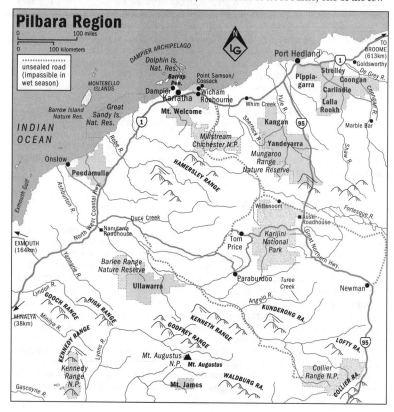

Pilbara Region

safe swimming spots in the area, or just push on 203km to **Port Hedland.** Little more than a port, a huge mountain of salt, and an iron ore plant that operates around the clock, Port Hedland is an industrial town. The shopping center at the south edge of town, on the corner of Wilson St. and Cooke Point Dr., has an Action **Supermarket.** (Open M-W and F 8am-8pm, Th 8am-9pm, Sa-Su 8am-5pm.) At the west tip of the peninsula, Wedge St. holds the **Port Hedland Welcome Centre** (☎9173 1711; Internet $5 per 30min; open M-F 8:30am-5pm, Sa 8:30am-4pm, Su noon-4pm), a 24hr. **ATM,** and the **post office.** (Open M-F 9am-5pm.) **Postal Code:** 6721.

Dingos Oasis Backpackers ❷, on Kingsmill St., has a unisex bunk house and a sprawling ocean view. (☎9173 1000. Dorms $18; twins and doubles $50; A/C extra.) For a cozier feel, try the family-run and well-kept **Harbour Backpackers ❷,** on Edgar St. (☎9173 4455. Free bus pickup. Dorms $16.)

From Port Hedland, the Great Northern Hwy. winds 600km along the coast to **Broome** (see p. 711). Roadhouses can be up to 300km apart, so fuel up whenever you get the chance and take your time, as kangaroos, cows, sheep, and wild camels populate the barren scrubland along the way.

KARIJINI NATIONAL PARK

Once an ancient sea floor, Karijini National Park is now a rugged and magnificent wonderland in the heart of the Pilbara. Within Karijini's domain, sheer gorges slice through the mountains, revealing colorful bands of rock and harboring cool freshwater pools and waterfalls. Homeland to the Banjima, Innawonga, and Kurrama Aboriginal people, the park takes its name from their traditional word for the Hamersley Range. Aboriginal legend has it that the gorges of Karijini were formed by *Thurru,* giant serpents that once snaked through the rocks and now reside within the glistening waters of Karijini. While in recent years the short and very basic walks in the park have started to draw tour buses, the park's true glory is only found deep within the gorges and remain guarded from crowds by challenging and sometimes dangerous passageways.

KARIJINI NATIONAL PARK AT A GLANCE	
AREA: 100,000km²	**HIGHLIGHTS:** Hiking the expansive gorges. Swimming in the rock pools.
FEATURES: Junction Pool, Dales Gorge, Kalmina Gorge, the Hancock and Weano Gorges, and Fortescue Falls.	**CAMPING:** Sites for 2 $10.
GATEWAY: Tom Price.	**FEES:** $9 per vehicle entry fee.

⬛ TRANSPORTATION. It will take a car or a tour to conquer Karijini. The park's northern entrances, through Yampire Gorge and Wittenoom, are closed. Both are contaminated by asbestos, inhalation of which can cause cancer or death (see **Hold Your Breath,** p. 708). The roads beyond its two southern entrances at either end of Karijini Dr. are unsealed but 2WD-accessible during most of the dry, but a 4WD is safer. Check road conditions before heading to the park (☎1800 013 314).

There are several tour groups that go into Karijini, offering very tame looks around, although **Snappy Gum Safaris** has more adventurous options, including a three-day trip that includes a scale of the perilous 25m waterfall in the Weano Gorge area. (☎9185 3141. $350.) **Dingo's Desert Trek Adventure Tours** also covers the area. (☎9173 1000. 3-day tour Tu and Sa, $400.)

⬛ PRACTICAL INFORMATION. Karijini is a big place with fairly scant infrastructure, so come prepared. The one-day park entrance fee is $9 per car. Untreated **water** is available in the park at a turn-off near the Visitors Center and on

Banjima Dr. near the turnoff for Weano gorge (treating recommended), but it's best to carry a lot when you arrive. **Petrol** and supplies are available west of the park in **Tom Price** and at the **Auski Roadhouse** (see below) to the northeast. Maps, updates on road conditions, and weather forecasts can be found at area tourist bureaus as well as at Karijini's **Visitors Centre**, near Fortescue Falls.

The impressive, multi-million-dollar new **Visitors Centre** has exhibits on local flora and fauna, geology, and Aboriginal and colonial history, but little practical information. It also has showers. (☎9189 8121. Showers $2 per 20min. Open daily 9am-4pm.) For more concrete park know-how, ask attendants at park entrances and campsites, or contact the **CALM ranger station** (☎9189 8157, after-hours emergency 9189 8102). There is an **emergency radio** in the Weano gorge day-use area, and the good people of Tom Price provide the nearest medical and rescue services.

■ ■ **ACCOMMODATIONS AND CAMPGROUNDS. Camping ❶** is permitted in the rocky, designated areas near Weano Gorge, Joffre Falls, and Fortescue Falls. (Sites for 2 $10.) For more comfy quarters, head to the **Tom Price Tourist Park ❶** (☎9189 1515; sites $7.70 per person, powered $19.80 per site; 4-bed dorms $20; cabins for 2 $83) or the basic rooms at the **Auski Roadhouse ❹**, on the northeastern corner of Karijini, just before the dusty turn-off to Wittenoom. (☎9176 6988. Budget singles $45; doubles $50; motel doubles $110.)

■ **HIKING.** The "hiking" trails listed in Visitors Centre, including the walk to the impressive lookout at **Junction Pool** and down into **Dales Gorge** to the natural steps that make up **Fortescue Falls,** cater mainly to the park's older visitors and the suggested times and difficulties are mostly overestimated for younger visitors. They tend to be short and well-maintained walks leading to peaceful spots above or within the gorges. Karijini, though, does offer more intrepid explorers a rare opportunity. Within the gorges are an abundance of **natural ledges.** Good balance and a sturdy grip are musts, but making your way to the deeper and more beautiful pools within the gorges, along the thin ledges that often lie meters above the rushing water and rocky floors below, can be the experience of a lifetime. Few natural parks offer this freedom to visitors; the reward for your willingness to test your bouldering techniques is total isolation and sights that won't appear on any postcards. There is considerable risk when blazing your own trails, so self-sufficiency and the use of *extreme care, strong footwear, wetsuits, and registering with the park ranger* are absolute musts.

THE KIMBERLEY

The Kimberley's 320,000 square kilometers of raw, semi-desert bush has hardly changed since its settlement by non-Aborigines a century ago. Pressed between the Indian Ocean and the Great Sandy Desert, entire sections of the vast open cattle land have remained uncharted until recent decades. Filled with boulder-stacked cliffs, unpredictable rivers and gorges, and proud pockets of settlement, the Kimberley is one of Australia's true remaining frontiers. This beautiful and untamed land is as rugged as it is awe-inspiring. Occupying the northernmost reaches of Western Australia, the Kimberley is accessible from the rest of the state by flights to Broome or via the long, lonely desert highway from Port Hedland. From the east, Routes 1 and 96 branch off the Stuart Hwy. of the Northern Territory. The region's only paved road is the Great Northern Hwy. Most others, including the Gibb River Rd. and its offshoots in the north, are unsealed 4WD tracks. Rainfall levels change drastically between the Kimberley's two seasons; flooded rivers during the Wet (Nov.-Mar.) often close these roads. Call ahead for road conditions (☎1800 013 314), and register with the police before leaving. The Kimberley's high season is the Dry (Apr.-Oct.).

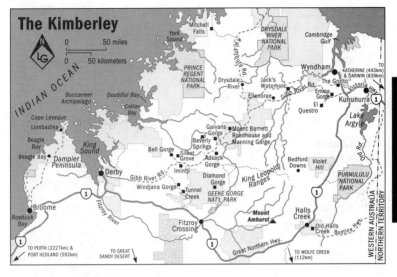

The Kimberley

WESTERN AUSTRALIA

WESTERN AUSTRALIA / NORTHERN TERRITORY

BROOME   ☎ 08

You know you're likely to enjoy a place when the airport bears a sign claiming, "Relax now, you're in Broome." Sprawling gracefully between the ocean and mangroves, Broome (pop. 14,000) has an immaculate shoreline and a carefree aura that feels surreal after driving through the Kimberley's dusty interior. The seaside mecca's fame grew as a result of a thriving pearling industry in the 1880s. Today, it attracts vacationers seeking to sink their toes into the cool sands of its pristine beaches. Visitors may find themselves lingering over an iced cappuccino or strolling at twilight down endless Cable Beach, reluctant to leave this romantic oasis.

▐ TRANSPORTATION

Airport: Broome International Airport (☎9193 5455). Follow the signs from Coghlan St. in the city center to McPherson St. **Qantas** flies direct to: Perth (3hr., around $650); Darwin (2hr., around $450); Alice Springs (2.5hr., around $500); Uluru (Ayers Rock) (2hr., around $500).

Buses: Bus station next door to Tourist Bureau. **Greyhound** (☎9192 1561) has service to **Perth** (32½hr., daily 8:30am, $268) and **Darwin** (27hr., daily 7:15pm, $230). **Integrity** (☎9226 1339) departs from Terri's Travel, 31 Carnavoran St., and offers a scenic bus to **Perth** (35hr., M and W 8am, $260).

Public Transportation: Town Bus (☎9193 6585) connects **Chinatown, Cable Beach,** and several hotels. (M-Sa 1 per hr. 7:10am-6:30pm, every ½hr. 10am-3pm.) First bus of the day reaches **Gantheaume Point** with no return service (prepare for the 5km walk to Cable Beach). $2.70, children $1; day pass $8.50, children $4.

Taxis: Broome Taxis (☎9192 1133). **Roebuck Taxis** (☎1800 880 330). 24hr. service.

Car Rental: Budget (☎9193 5355 or 1800 649 800; jbusby@budgetwa.com.au), at the airport; **Hertz,** 69 Frederick St. (☎9192 1428 or 1800 655 972; hertz.brm@bigpond.com); and **Broome Broome** (☎9192 2210), corner of Hamersley St. and Frederick St., each offer one-way rental options from $400. Broome Broome also has a YHA discount of $5 per day.

WESTERN AUSTRALIA

Broome

🏠 ACCOMMODATIONS
Broome Motel, **1**
Cable Beach Backpackers, **7**
Cable Beach Caravan Park, **5**
Kimberley Klub, **2**
Roebuck Bay Backpackers, **13**
Tarangau Caravan Park, **3**

🍎 FOOD
Blooms, **9**
Broome Fish and
Chips, **15**

Cable Beach Sand-
bar and Grill, **6**
Fong Sam's, **10**
Shady Lane, **14**

⭐ NIGHTLIFE
Divers Camp Tavern, **8**
Nippon Inn, **11**
Pearler's Bar, a.k.a "The
Roey", **12**
Sunset Bar, **4**

Broome Discount Car Hire (☎9192 3100), 100m from the airport on McPherson St., has no one-way option. If you're considering trying some of the Kimberley's 4WD tracks, try **Britz** (☎9192 2647; www.britz.com) on Clementson St., with campervans starting at $196 per day. All of the above prefer drivers 25+; all except Hertz will rent to 21+ for an additional fee. Book ahead in the high season from Apr.-Oct. **Note:** Car rentals vary drastically in prices, availability, and model due to weather concerns and road closures, especially during the Wet.

ORIENTATION

Broome occupies a peninsula, with the business area tucked on Roebuck Bay to the east and the beach sprawled on the Indian Ocean to the west. The **Great Northern Hwy.** (**Broome Hwy.** in town), curls into Roebuck Bay from the north, becoming **Hamersley St.** at its intersection with **Napier Tce.** This is **Chinatown,** the oldest part of Broome and the closest thing it has to a downtown. **Paspaley Shopping Centre, Johnny Chi Ln.,** and most restaurants and services are scattered on a few blocks of **Carnarvon St.** A block south of Napier Tce., Frederick St. heads west; going that way, a right on Cable Beach Rd. E., a right on Gubinge Rd., and then a left on Cable Beach Rd. W. will lead to **Cable Beach** on the other side of the peninsula. East of Broome, the Great Northern Hwy. enters Kimberley proper and commences its grueling haul toward the Northern Territory.

🛂 PRACTICAL INFORMATION

Tourist Office: Broome Tourist Bureau (☎9192 2222; www.ebroome.com/tourism). Well-marked on the corner of Broome Rd. and Bagot St. Open Apr.-Sept. M-F 8am-5pm, Sa-Su 9am-4pm; Oct.-Mar. M-F 9am-5pm, Sa-Su 9am-1pm.

Budget Travel: Harvey World Travel (☎9193 5599), Paspaley Shopping Centre in Chinatown. Serves as the broker for Qantas and other carriers. Open M-F 8:30am-5:30pm, Sa 9am-1pm. **Traveland,** 9 Johnny Chi Ln. (☎9193 7233), off Carnarvon St. across from the movie theater. Open M-F 8:30am-5pm, Sa 9am-1pm.

Currency Exchange: ANZ Bank, 16 Carnarvon St. (☎13 13 14). Open M-Th 9:30am-4pm, F 9:30am-5pm. **Commonwealth Bank** (☎9192 1103). On Hamersley and Barker St. Open M-Th 9:30am-4pm, F 9:30am-5pm. Both have a $7 charge for currency exchange.

Work Opportunities: Typically plenty of temporary food-service work in the dry season; check the message boards at hostels for postings and requests.

Books: Woody's Book Exchange (☎9192 8999), on Johnny Chi Ln. in Chinatown. Open M-F 9:30am-4:30pm, Sa 9:30am-2pm, Su 10am-1pm. **Kimberley Bookshop,** 6 Napier Tce. (☎9192 1944). Just east of Carnarvon St. Open M-F 10am-5pm, Sa 10am-2pm.

Markets: Courthouse Market, near the courthouse on the corner of Hamersley and Frederick St. Open Sa 8am-1pm. **Sunday Market** on Johnny Chi Ln. Open Su 9am-1pm.

Police: (☎9192 1212), at the corner of Frederick and Carnarvon St.

Internet Access: Telecentre, 40 Dampier Tce. (☎9193 7153). $5 per hr. Open M-F 9am-5pm, Sa 9am-1pm. **Munchies** (☎9192 5572), on the corner of Cable Beach and Murray Rd. $10 per hr. Open daily 7am-8pm.

Post Office: Australia Post (☎9192 1020), in Paspaley Shopping Ctr. Open M-F 9am-5pm. Poste Restante. **Postal Code:** 6725.

🏠🏕 ACCOMMODATIONS AND CAMPING

During the Dry (Apr.-Oct.), it is essential to book in advance, even at campgrounds. Most of Broome's backpackers have their own in-house bars, which means that BYO is strictly prohibited. All hostels in Broome are very communal and have the distinct feel of a refreshing tropical resort. The big decision when choosing a place to stay in Broome is whether you want to be close to Cable Beach or the shops and nightlife of Chinatown.

▧ Kimberley Klub (☎9192 3233; www.kimberleyklub.com), on Frederick St. between Robinson and Herbert St., a 5min. walk from Chinatown. Free pickup from Greyhound depot. Where luxury resort meets youth hostel. Social and family-friendly, with an enormous lagoon-shaped pool, full bar and snack counter, ping-pong, billiards, TV lounge, and sand volleyball court. Kitchen, laundry, coin operated A/C for some rooms, Internet, and tour booking desk. $10 deposit each for cutlery and linen. Reception daily 6:30am-8pm. Dorms $18; quint $20 per person; twins and doubles $70. NOMADS $1 discount or seventh night free. Extra $5 includes large breakfast. V/MC. ❷

■**Cable Beach Backpackers,** 12 Sanctuary Rd. (☎9193 5511 or 1800 655 022; meyo@tpg.com.au). An ideal location for those who can't get enough beach time. This intimate and lively hostel is run by friendly staff and offers kitchen, bar with fabulous happy hour, laundry, pool, billiards, Internet, and scooter rentals. A free shuttle makes rounds to Chinatown, Greyhound, and the airport. 4-bed dorms, some with A/C $19; twins with A/C $62. VIP/YHA $1 discount. V/MC. ❷

Roebuck Bay Backpackers (☎9192 1183; fax 9192 2390), on Napier Tce. This newly renovated and busy hostel is planted right next to Chinatown and the nightlife action, with 5 bars and a liquor store on premises. Luggage storage, kitchen, laundry, pool, and BBQ. Reception daily 7am-4pm and 5-8pm. 12-bed dorms $14; 8-bed with A/C $15; 4-bed with A/C $17; doubles $55. ❶

Broome Motel, 34 Frederick St. (☎9192 7775; www.broomemotel.com.au), opposite the junction with Robinson St. Just outside of Chinatown, total convenience with none of the late-night ruckus. Spacious ensuite rooms, all with A/C, are arranged bungalow-style around the parking lot, pool, BBQ, and laundry facilities. Reception 7am-8pm. Backpackers $70; standard $85-90; self-catering $110-115. Discounts for multi-night stays and during the Wet. Wheelchair accessible rooms available. V/MC. ❺

Camping ❶ is popular around Cable Beach, and most popular is the four-star **Cable Beach Caravan Park** on Millington Rd., where good location compensates for the crowds; it offers laundry, pool, and kitchen. (☎9192 2066; fax 9192 1997. 12min. to the beach. Sites $7.50-8.50 per person, powered sites for 2 $20-24. Handicap facilities available.) **Tarangau Caravan Park ❶**, 16 Millington Rd., at the corner of Millington and Lullfitz Dr., is quieter and much less crowded, but you should allow for a full 20min. walk to get to Cable Beach. Camping kitchen included. (☎9193 5084; fax 9193 7551. Sites for 2 $15.40, powered $22.)

◖ FOOD

Chinatown possesses only a smattering of Chinese **restaurants,** but the area is packed with tasty outdoor cafes and has two **supermarkets.** Coles (☎9192 6299), in the Paspaley Shopping Centre, is open daily 6am to midnight. Action Supermarket (☎9192 1611), in the Boulevard Shopping Centre, is open daily 8am-8pm.

■ **Cable Beach Sandbar and Grill** (☎9193 5090), on Cable Beach Rd. W., adjacent to pedestrian access to the beach. The sandy and sunburned patrons of Cable Beach come crawling for this super-snackbar. From tasty nachos ($10) to beef bourguignon pie ($15), the extensive menu includes light and hearty meals from around the world, vegetarian and otherwise, along with a kids menu. Grab a frozen mango daiquiri ($10) from the full bar and enjoy the stunning ocean view. Open daily 7am-9pm. ❷

Fong Sam's Cafe (☎9192 1030), on Carnarvon St. across from the cinema. Delicious baked goods, large portions, and reasonable prices make this street cafe in the heart of Chinatown a must for breakfast or lunch. Pasties run from 90¢. Fresh quiche and salad $11. Try a side of their amazing sautéed mushrooms ($2). Open daily 6:30am-5pm. ❶

Blooms Cafe and Restaurant, 31 Carnarvon St., (☎9193 6366) in Chinatown. Despite your best efforts to finish a meal, you'll find yourself thwarted by large portions. Choose from pastas, pizzas, and Thai curries, all in the $10-16 range. Lots of vegetarian options). BYO. Open 7am-9:30pm. ❷

Shady Lane Cafe (☎9192 2060), on Johnny Chi Ln. off Carnarvon St. A hidden treasure. Perfect breakfast or lunchtime oasis. Filling flapjacks ($8), toasted foccacia ($9), and smoothies ($5) make it both wallet- and tastebud-friendly. Open daily 7am-2:30pm. ❶

Broome Fish and Chips (☎9192 1280), at the corner of Frederick and Hamersley St. Cheap eats, huge portions, and more fried fish than you can shake a stick at. Brave the line at the counter then eat on the patio, because if it's not fresh, they don't serve it. Open daily 10:30am-2:30pm, 4:30-8:30pm. ❶

👁 🎣 SIGHTS AND ACTIVITIES

▨ **CABLE BEACH.** At Broome's paradise, 22km of clear Indian Ocean laps against the pearly white sand. Go for some fun in the sun; take a camel, sailing, or hovercraft tour; or indulge the voyeur in you at the clothing-optional portion of beach, past the rocks to the north. Whatever you do, be sure to stay for the sunset.

WATER ACTIVITIES. Surfboard rental *($8 per hr.)* is available on Cable Beach. Parasailing, jet skiing, and tubing operators work out of the vans that cruise the sand to rent out equipment. Would-be mermen visit **Workline Dive & Tackle** (☎9192 2233) on Short St. in Chinatown for all there is to know about scuba diving in Broome.

REPTILES OLD AND NEW. Ever wanted to stare death in face... through a chain link fence? Then get up-close and personal with aggressive saltwater crocodiles up to 5m long at **Malcolm Douglas Broome Crocodile Park.** *(200m from the beach access on Cable Beach Rd.* ☎9192 1489. *Feedings W-Su 3pm. Guided tours M-Tu 11am and 3pm. Open M-F 10am-5pm, Sa-Su 2-5pm. $15, concessions $12, children $8, families $38.)* These crocs' ancestors might be long gone, but pieces of them still reside at ▨**Gantheaume Point,** where a set of **dinosaur footprints** is preserved among the rocks. Found on the western tip of the Broome Peninsula about 5km from Cable Beach, the 120-million-year-old prints surface at very low tide (check at the tourist bureau) and can be difficult to find, so a plaster replica is at the top of the cliff. *(Take a left onto Gubinge Rd., where Cable Beach Rd. turns to the right.)*

OTHER BEACHES. Town Beach is farther south on the Roebuck Bay shore, at the end of Robinson St. To the left of the jetty, for three consecutive days each month from March to October (check at the tourist bureau for exact dates), Broome's massive 10m tide is so low that the exposed mudflats stretch for kilometers, reflecting the light of the full moon in a staircase pattern. The city celebrates with the **Staircase to the Moon Market** at Town Beach during these three days. At the lowest tides, the waters off Town Beach recede to uncover the skeletons of boats sunk in WWII. The **Mangrove Walk,** on the east coast between Chinatown and the Historical Society, weaves its way through a forest of mangroves.

BIRD OBSERVATORY. The **Broome Bird Observatory** is an excellent place to spy 40% of Australia's total bird species—it's one of only four such observatories in the country. *(25km outside of town. Take Broome Rd. for 9.2km and watch for the turn-off after the fire safety sign.* ☎9193 5600. *Open Apr.-Oct. daily 8am-5pm; Nov.-Mar. Tu-Su 8am-5pm. Self-guided tours by donation; half-day tours $35, with pickup $60. Book ahead June-Aug.)*

JAPANESE CEMETERY. Dating back to 1896, this solemn and utterly beautiful cemetery of over 700 graves stands as a tribute to the Japanese pearl divers of Broome. These entombed victims of drowning and diver's paralysis are a striking reminder of the dangers associated with pearling never mentioned at the innumerable pearl dealers or pearling-themed restaurants in town.

TOURS. Ride camels down Cable Beach at sunset, threading your way up the dunes to reach the hilltop at twilight. **Ships of the Desert** has morning, sunset, and

THE LOCAL STORY

OLD MACDONALD HAD A CROC

Brent Thoms is a career fireman who spends his holidays as a croc feeder at **Malcolm Douglas Broome Crocodile Park** *(see p. 715). Interview 6/9/02.*

Q: What do you do here?
A: I prepare the food for the farm crocodiles. We feed the crocodiles out at the farm and clean up after them. Me and three other guys also do the tours here at the park in Broome.

Q: Ever been bitten?
A: No, I don't put myself in a situation I this is dangerous. Out at the farm we're dealing in groups of probably 100 crocs, but they're all under 2 meters long. They're not really dangerous unless you provoke them. Keep a stick in your hand, and that'll fend one off just by hitting them on the nose.

Q: What role do crocodile farms play in the preservation of crocodiles?
A: They educate the public, but they also provide us a breeding stock for the sustainable farming operation. While you got commercial farms around, you've got a big stock of crocodiles. If some viral disease was going through the natural waterways to kill off the natural crocs, you've got a source of crocodiles that you can start stocking back up the natural waterways.

Q: What part of the crocodiles are usable?
A: Pretty much every part. The skin is the main thing—the belly skin—that's the big thing of value But every part of the skin is used. The teeth are sold as things to put in your hat to people who want to look like Crocodile Dundee. The meat is packaged up

twilight camel tours. (☎9192 6383. $30 per hr., full-day $75.) Also try **Red Sun Camel Safaris.** (☎9193 7423. *Tours 2:15pm and 4pm. $35 per hr.*) Without a strong 4WD, **land tours** may be your only way to see the rugged and beautiful Kimberley or northern shoreline, but the air-conditioned coaches and numerous stops at tourist traps may compromise the adventurousness of the experience. Be prepared to shell out for these expensive luxury tours. **Discover the Kimberley Tours** runs daytrips to the pristine beaches of the Dampier Coast, north of Broome. (☎1800 636 802. *8hr. tours depart W and F. $180, with Pearl Farm tour $215.*) **Over the Top Adventures** offers tours to the Dampier Peninsula and the Gibb River Rd. (☎9192 5211. *Dampier 1-day $205, 2-day $310; Windjana Gorge and Tunnel Creek 2-day $340; 5-day trip along the Gibb River Rd. $830.*) **Scenic flights,** some of which travel all the way to Mitchell Falls and the Buccaneer Archipelago, are pricey, but they offer a truly unique perspective on this natural wonderland. **Broome Aviation** (☎1300 136 629), **Seair Broome** (☎9192 6208), and **King Leopold Air** (☎1800 637 155) start at $285 for 2½hr-.

FESTIVALS. The **Easter Dragon Boat Regatta** is featured Saturday of Easter weekend at the Town Beach. Horse racing is big throughout July when the town starts hopping for the **Broome Cup** (July 26, 2003). For 10 days in early September, the **Shinju Matsuri Pearl Festival** celebrates the natural beauty of pearls. The **Mango Festival** (last weekend in November) pays homage to the mango harvest with a Mardi Gras celebration and a "Great Chefs of Broome Mango Cook Off.

◪ NIGHTLIFE

No visit to Broome is complete without catching a feature at the charming **◪Sun Pictures Outdoor Cinema,** on Carnarvon St., the oldest operating outdoor film theater in the world. It spun its first reel in 1916 and flicks still spin every night. Curl up on the distinctive benches under the stars. (☎9192 1077. $12, concessions $10.)

Brief affairs with beer and fellow backpackers are the staple of after-hours life in Broome, and many accommodations have in-house bars that encourage it. In town, **Pearler's Bar** a.k.a. **"The Roey,"** in the Roebuck Hotel on Carnarvon, is the spot for live music, beer, and partying backpackers. (☎9192 1221. Open M-W 10am-midnight, Th-Sa 10am-1am, Su noon-10:30pm.) **Nippon Inn,** on Dampier Tce. near Short St., is Broome's only nightclub. When the other bars wind down around midnight, this club is just getting started. Immerse yourself in purple walls and techno beats. (☎9192 1941. Open M, W, and F-Sa 9pm-4am.)

At Cable Beach, locals play pool at **Divers Camp Tavern,** on Cable Beach Rd., a bar and bistro where all the campers let loose on weekends. (☎9193 6066. Open M-Sa 10am-midnight, Su 10am-10pm. Brews from $2.20.) At the relaxed **Sunset Bar** at the Cable Beach Resort right on Cable Beach, grab a cocktail ($12) or beer ($4.50) and enjoy the gorgeous view. (☎9192 0400. Open daily 4pm-midnight.) The Cable Beach area clears out after sunset and is dead by 9pm, when great herds of campers and backpackers migrate to Chinatown for the late-night scene. Be prepared: Cable Beach bars may close earlier than posted hours if the night is slow.

EAST FROM BROOME

There are only two ways across the Kimberley to the Northern Territory: the sealed and tame Great Northern Highway, or the adventurous and unparalleled 4WD track known as the Gibb River Road. Both are long and lonely roads through isolated country. The Great Northern Highway, your only option during the wet season, is the fastest route to Purnululu and Kununurra, and the Gibb River Road takes you into the heart of the unique and wild Kimberley. These two routes split 167km west of Broome, near Derby, so pack your bags, put some petrol in the tank, and start trucking.

GREAT NORTHERN HIGHWAY

There is no question: it's a long, dry haul. The two major rest stops along the way are Fitzroy Crossing and Halls Creek. Just 208km after the highway split, **Fitzroy Crossing** offers a chance to stretch your legs on a 1-3 hour walk around nearby **Geeke Gorge** (GEEK-ee) or to take a **boat tour** from the gorge parking lot. (1hr.; June-Sept. 3 per day, Apr.-May and Oct.-Nov. 1-2 per day.) You can grab some grub at the **supermarket** on Forrest Rd. (Open M-F 8:30am-5:30pm, Sa-Su 8am-1pm.)

Another 287km down the highway is **Halls Creek.** If you have a spare minute, see the remains of **Old Halls Creek,** the site of the original gold rush in Western Australia. (16km down the unsealed Duncan Hwy.) Otherwise, hit the **grocery store** (☎9168 6186; open M-F 8am-6pm, Sa 8am-noon, Su 9am-noon) and the **Shell Station** (☎9168 6060; open daily 6am-10pm), and then hit the road. From Halls Creek it's 107km to the Purnululu turn-off and another 235km to Kununurra.

and sent to Asia. But there's starting to become quite a local market. You can go down to a Pizza Hut here and order a crocodile pizza.

Q: After working with crocs for so long, what do you think about them? Dangerous man-eaters, Italian belts waiting to happen, or just big dumb animals?

A: I suppose all three. They're not a very intelligent reptile, and reptiles are mainly instinctive. Their brain's the size of a golf ball. So there's not a lot to work with. But they are man eating. Anything that's over 3 meters long is quite capable of taking you and pulling you down and making you into his meal. It's quite easy to read what they're going to do, just by the way they're pulling their front legs back, ready to run at you. You're just watching that, that's really telegraphing their movements to you. And what they're looking on...they really do focus. But they're quiet predictable as well. When you're in a working environment with them, you sort of know they're going to be aggressive.

Q: What do you see as the biggest public misconception about crocodiles?

A: I think up this way people get a little bit blase. They come up here as probably a tourist and think that a lot of the signs are just there for show. But once they've started to go 'round the park here, they realize just what they (crocs) are and what they look like. I think it freaks people out to think these guys are inhabiting the waterways and estuaries right next door. People seem to think, "Oh, I'm in Broome, there are no crocs anywhere near here," but there are crocs everywhere.

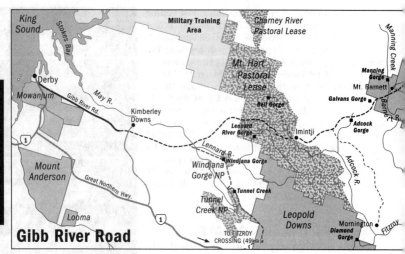

WESTERN AUSTRALIA

Gibb River Road

GIBB RIVER ROAD   ☎08

The Gibb River Road is a rugged and unforgettable 4WD track that crosses through the very center of the Kimberley. By day, wander the bumpy road to a series of national parks, gorges, Aboriginal camps, cattle stations, and waterholes. By night, sleep under the stars in isolated wilderness. For the true adventurers who long to conquer the bush first-hand, the challenge awaits.

GIBB RIVER ROAD AT A GLANCE

LENGTH: 647km.

FEATURES: Windjana Gorge, Tunnel Creek Nat'l Park, King Leopold Range.

HIGHLIGHTS: Dips into pristine, saltie-free gorges, unpopulated walks, and cliff jumping for the super-foolhardy.

GATEWAYS: Derby (p. 719), Kununurra (p. 724), Fitzroy Crossing (p. 717).

DURATION: In good conditions the road can take as little as 2 days, but it will take 4-5 days to enjoy the primary gorges, and longer to tackle the several turn-offs.

■♂ **ORIENTATION AND PRACTICAL INFORMATION.** The Gibb River Road begins 8km south of Derby off the Derby Hwy. and ends at the Great Northern Hwy. between Wyndham (48km from end) and Kununurra (45km from end). A series of access roads and tracks leads to the main attractions. The only through-road connection is at the Windjana/Tunnel Creek turn-off 119km from Derby, which eventually stretches to the Great Northern Hwy. and Fitzroy Crossing.

Guides: Tourist offices in Derby and Fitzroy Crossing sell copies of the *Traveller's Guide to the Gibb River and Kalumburu Roads,* which has detailed information on distances, limited services along the roads, and what to do in case you encounter a bush fire. ($3. Write to Derby Tourist Bureau, PO Box 48, Derby WA 6728. ☎9191 1426.)

Auto repairs: Neville Heron's Over the Range Repairs (☎9191 7471) is the only mechanical repair service that operates along the road.

Tours: Many people do the Gibb River Rd. via small group tours, which can be cheaper than renting your own 4WD. **Kimberley Adventure Tours** (☎1800 805 101; www.kim-

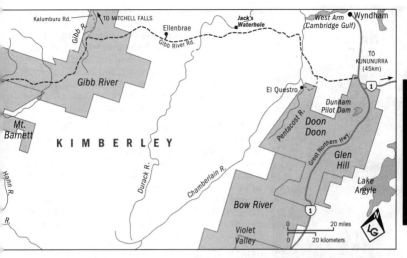

berleyadventure.com) offers a 5-day Gibb trek ($750) and a 13-day tour between Darwin and Broome ($2190). **Kimberley Wilderness Adventures** (☎ 1800 804 005; www.kimberleywilderness.com.au) has a 5-day ($1200) and 7-day ($1900) Gibb tour.

DERBY, GATEWAY TO THE GIBB. A west to east voyage along the Gibb starts at Derby. Check in at the **tourist office** at the end of Clarendon St. for the latest road conditions information. (☎ 9191 1426. Open Apr.-Sept. M-F 8:30am-4:30pm, Sa-Su 9am-1pm; Oct.-Mar. M-F 8:30am-4:30pm, Sa 9am-4pm.) The **West Kimberley Lodge ❺**, at the corner of Sutherland and Stanwell St., has quiet rooms with A/C and fridge. (☎ 9191 1031. Twins $65; suites $78.) The grassy **Kimberley Entrance Caravan Park ❶** on Rowan St., around the curve from the tourist office, overlooks mudflats. (☎ 9193 1055. Sites $9; powered $15, for 2 $22.) Be sure to register with the **Derby police** (☎ 9191 1444), on Loch St. near the Old Derby Gaol, before starting on the road. Get petrol on your way out of town at the **BP station**, on Loch St. across from Woolworth. (Open M-Sa 5:30am-7:30pm, Su 6am-7pm.)

HIKES, GORGES, AND CAMPING.

There are a seemingly infinite number of gorges along the Gibb River Rd. This section gives a sample of the different kinds of gorges you will find, but explore them all to find your favorite. Camping is allowed only in designated areas; much of the property along the road is privately owned. Listed after sight names are turn-off distances from Derby.

WINDJANA GORGE: THE HISTORICAL. *119km.* Pass through a natural stone archway into the ancient past. With bird calls echoing off the looming 100m tall limestone cliffs and freshwater crocodiles swimming in the Lennard River, you'll swear you just walked into Jurassic Park. This area is part of the 250-million-year-old Devonian Reef, and signs along the 3½km sandy walk explain the history of the reef and the fossils it contains. The walk can be tough going at parts, so wear solid shoes and bring plenty of water. (*Off a 21km access road. Camping with showers, toilets, and water $9.*)

TUNNEL CREEK: THE ADVENTUROUS. *119km.* So you want to be Indiana Jones? Training starts right here. Walk through this 850m cave… in total darkness… with

FROM THE ROAD

ROCK AND ROLL

It's funny how in an environment like the long and dusty Gibb River Road, the commonplace quickly becomes extreme, and the extreme very commonplace. Take for example rocks and Beatles. Rocks occupied most of my thoughts during the long days of driving. Since I was hundreds of miles from the nearest tow truck, I focused quite hard on steering around sharp rocks that might puncture a tire, lest I become one of those poor souls jacking up my car in the sweltering heat. It became a kind of war—me against the rocks. When I parked my Bushcamper at night, I would kick all the nearby pebbles away, just in case those feisty varmints decided to jump up and stab a tire when I turned my back. Eventually even my walks through picturesque gorges were partially tainted by the fact that these mammoth natural wonders were, in my eyes, large, sharp stone colonies just waiting to get out on the road.

On the other hand, finding an old, well worn Beatles tape under my car seat, a fairly mundane occurrence, seemed earth-shatteringly important given the total lack of radio on the Gibb. In a place where my most exciting diversion was deciding whether to salute the occasional passing car with one finger from each hand (the bull salute) or two fingers from one hand (the classic bunny-ears salute), a few tinny Beatles songs were the news of century. The good news is that I never had a flat tire, and driving the Gibb was the experience of a lifetime.

—Nick Horbaczewski

carnivorous ghost bats overhead... in thigh-deep water... filled with freshwater crocodiles. Not for the faint of heart, Tunnel Creek is an exhilarating experience, and the clearing at the far end, where Jandamarra, the famous Pigeon freedom-fighter of the Bunuba people was shot and killed in 1897, is well worth the trip. A good flashlight and enclosed shoes are essential for navigating the rocky floor. (A farther 35km down the access road from Windjana Gorge.)

BELL GORGE: THE BEAUTIFUL. *214km.* After a gentle 1km walk from the carpark, leave cars, caravans, and dirt roads behind and retreat to this deep, tranquil, perfectly bell-shaped gorge fed by an 8-tiered waterfall and surrounded by arrestingly colored cliffs. Go early and have it all to yourself, but be careful and stay well back from the cliff edges, as the rocks can be slippery or unstable. (Off a rough 29km on access road. Camping at Silent Grove or Bell Creek on the turn-off $9.)

IMINTJI STORE. *222km.* This brightly painted general store serves the Imintji Aboriginal community and Gibb River Road travelers. A reliable source of diesel fuel and a great place to grab a cold drink or supplies. Take care to drive slowly in the area, though, as children frequently cross the road.

GALVANS GORGE: THE TROPICAL. *286km.* This hidden gem may be the most heavenly spot along the road. An 800m walk takes you past lily-pond pools to a perfect blue lagoon complete with a waterfall. Swim in the crystal-clear water, or bathe under the fall's gentle spray. Try the rope swing on the lagoon's far side. If you do only one thing on the Gibb, visit this private paradise. (The entrance is unmarked; turn into the carpark—to your left if you're heading east—after a steep decline in the road, directly across from the scenic photo camera sign for westbound traffic.)

MT. BARNETT ROADHOUSE. *300km.* Owned and operated by the Kupungarri people, the roadhouse provides access to the Manning Gorge hike (1hr.), which warrants a stop. Full of groceries, hot food, and cold drinks, the roadhouse is the best facility on the road for getting petrol and supplies. Camping is available ($9).

KALUMBURU RD. *406km.* An entire 267km journey after its intersection with the Gibb River Rd., the Kalumburu branches north towards the Mitchell Plateau and Mitchell Falls (a four-cataract waterfall plunging into the Indian Ocean). This region is one of the most isolated and stunning sights in the Kimberley, but is even more bone-jarring than the Gibb—complete self-sufficiency is an absolute must.

SAFETY ON AND OFF THE ROAD. Traveling the Gibb River Road puts you a long way from help of any kind, so anyone planning to drive it should be well prepared. This list reviews some of the basic safety concerns, although is by no means all-encompassing. Consult with a tourist office, pick up a guide to the road, and check road conditions (☎ 1300 013 314) before heading out.

Your Vehicle: 4WD is essential. If you've never driven a 4WD before, ask your rental company for an explanation; many offer half- and full-day lessons. Ideally, your ride will be equipped with either a long-range fuel tank or 2 fuel tanks; if it isn't, bring at least 1 full tank's worth of extra fuel in fuel safe containers. Carry a minimum of 2 extra spare tires and a full set of tools. It is recommended that you get the highest level of insurance your rental car company offers, as vehicle damage is frequent due to the Gibb's extreme conditions.

What to Bring: Supplies are few and far between on the road, so self-sufficiency is a must. Water is the most important supply; you should carry at least 9L of water per person per day. Also bring ample amounts of food. You'll need light clothing to help you brave the midday sun, sturdy boots for the gorge walks, and warm clothing for the chilly nights, when the temperature can fall below freezing. In case of emergency, bring a first-aid kit and a fire extinguisher. Also, consider bringing an Electronic Position Indicator Radio Beacon (EPIRB) or a satellite phone, as cellular telephones do not work in these remote parts.

Tips on Driving: Speed is by far the number-one cause of accidents, so *slow down*. Check the road conditions before you go (☎ 1800 013 314), as most car insurance is invalidated by driving on closed roads. Don't drive at night, while tired, or after drinking. When you come across a waterway, wade in and check the conditions of the bottom, removing any logs. You should never cross water deeper than knee height. (Do not wade in if there is a risk of crocodiles in the area, most notably at the Pentecost River.) Also, drive with your headlights on to make yourself more visible to oncoming cars.

Signs: The signs along the road come in all shapes, sizes, and colors, but they all mean one thing: *slow down*. All of them refer to possible obstructions to driving and visibility. The most common are GRID, referring to a metal grate across the roadway, DIP, FLOODPLAIN, TRAFFIC HAZARD AHEAD, CREST, and 2 pictoral signs, curves and cattle crossing.

When to Go: The Gibb River Road is impassable during the Wet (Dec.-Apr.), so plan to drive it only during the Dry (May-Nov.).

Final Advice: The legendary Aussie friendliness extends onto the Gibb, so it is customary to wave at passing motorists. If you decide to stop, give passing cars a thumbs-up to let them know you're okay, and slow down as you pass other cars that have stopped to look for the thumbs-up.

ELLENBRAE. *475km.* This fabulous homestead has a small store and spacious camping ($9). The highlight of a night here is the outdoor, solid-rock shower with heated water courtesy of a wood-burning stove.

EL QUESTRO STATION: THE NUMEROUS AND VARIED. *614km.* You will need a Wilderness Park Permit ($12.50 per week) to get to the boat tours on Chamberlain Gorge and the 12 different bushwalks among the El Questro and Amalia Gorges. Many of the walks, including the El Questro Gorge trail and Chamberlain Gorge trail, feature Aboriginal rock art. Amalia Gorge trail offers a challenging hike among steep-sided cliffs, but the plunging pool at the end rewards hikers with a refreshing swim. *(Off a 16km access road. ☎ 9161 4318. Sites $12.50.)*

■**EMMA GORGE: THE SCENIC.** *623km.* The El Questro permit will get you into the Emma Gorge Resort. The 3.6km trail can be rocky at parts, but takes you to fern-covered crescent cliffs high above a perfect pool. A droplet waterfall gives the semblance of rain. No camping, but pricey cabins are available. *(Off a 2km access road; from here it is 24km to the end of the Gibb. Cabins ☎9169 1777. $66-91 per person.)*

PURNULULU (BUNGLE BUNGLE) NATIONAL PARK

A collection of beehives? A carton of eggs? The sight of Purnululu's striking and mysterious orange sandstone formations, striped with black bands of algae, regularly lends itself to such strange comparisons. Along with these amazing formations, which make up less than one-fifth of the Bungle Bungle Range, the park offers walks through deep chasms, down lush tropical valleys and even into the heart of these beautiful mountains. The inaccessibility and remoteness of Purnululu kept it hidden from the public until the 1980s, but the Kija Aboriginal people have inhabited the area for over 20,000 years, and the park is packed with Aboriginal cultural sites. The awkward name "Bungle Bungle" is thought to be either a corruption of the Kija word *purnululu,* meaning "sandstone," or a misspelling of a commonly found grass in the area, *Bundle Bundle.*

PURNULULU AT A GLANCE	
AREA: 209,000 hectares.	**GATEWAYS:** Kununurra (p. 724), Halls Creek (p. 724), Warmun (below).
FEATURES: Bungle Bungle Range, Ord River.	**CAMPING:** At Walardi and Kurrajong campsites, or registered overnight bush camping ($9 per night per person).
HIGHLIGHTS: Scenic helicopter flights, walks through gorges, Aboriginal sights.	
	FEES: Entry $9 per vehicle.

◨◪ TRANSPORTATION AND PRACTICAL INFORMATION. To drive to Purnululu, you need a high clearance 4WD (no caravans). Bring a spare tire, jack, water, food, and chutzpah. The unsealed access road, **Spring Creek Track,** is on the Great Northern Hwy. 250km south of Kununurra or 109km north of Halls Creek. For 53km, Spring Creek Track rumbles, splashes, bumps, and grinds its way to the Visitor Centre. Allow five hours driving time from Kununurra or four hours from Halls Creek to reach the park; the Spring Creek Track alone takes a solid two and a half hours. Go slowly, as road conditions change around every corner, and wildlife and oncoming traffic present a real hazard on this one-lane track. The vehicle **entry fee** is $9; fees are payable 24hr. at the **Visitors Center** near the entrance to the park. While you're there, reward your Herculean driving feat with a well-deserved "I survived the road to Bungle Bungle" bumper sticker.

Vehicular access to the park is closed during the Wet (Jan.-Mar.), but temporary closure due to rain is possible at other times. Call the **Department of Conservation and Land Management** (☎9168 4200) office in Kununurra for conditions. Topographic maps are available in Kununurra at the **Department of Land Administration** at the roundabout on Messmate Way. (☎9168 0255. Open M-F 8am-4:30pm.) **Camping ①** is $9 per person. The park has toilets and untreated water, but no food or fuel.

Warmun (formerly Turkey Creek) is less than 100km north of the Spring Creek Track on the Great Northern Hwy. to Kununurra. The **Turkey Creek Roadhouse ②** offers petrol and accommodations. (☎9168 7882. Key deposit $10. Reception daily 6am-8pm. Sites $6; on-site caravans $17, powered $22; dorms and singles $20.)

◪ TOURS. The best overview of the park's features is given at the ranger-led slide shows, 7:30pm nightly at the ranger station. This, however, requires getting to the park. Signing up for a tour can be cheaper than renting a car, but the options might be overwhelming. **Scenic flights** offer amazing views of the range.

BY AIR.

  Slingair Heliwork (☎9169 1300 or 1800 095 500; www.slingair.com.au). On-site helicopter $180. From Kununurra: 2hr. flight, no landing in the park $190; 4hr. helicopter $380; 8hr. helicopter and ground tour $580. From Warmun: 45min. flight, $165.

  Alligator Airways (☎9168 1333 or 1800 632 533). From Kununurra: 2¼hr. $190; full day air/ground $495; 2 gorges $575; overnight $700.

  East Kimberley Tours (☎9168 2213 or 1800 682 213; www.eastkimberleytours.com). Fly in and out from Kununurra: 1-day $415; 2-day $725; 3-day (2-night) $825.

BY LAND.

  East Kimberley Tours (☎9168 2213 or 1800 682 213). Drive in/drive out from Warmun: 1-day $165; overnight leaving M, W, F $375.

  Desert Inn 4WD Adventures (☎9169 1257 or 1800 805 010). Drive in and out from Kununurra or Warmun: 2-day $290; 3-day $430.

  Kununurra Backpackers Bungle Bungle Adventures (☎9169 1998 or 1800 641 998). 3-day self-guided canoe safari $135. Drive from Kununurra 2-day $295, 3-day $435.

ABORIGINAL FOCUS.

  Kimberley Dreamtime (☎9161 1288) offers highly personalized tours of Purnululu and other sites in the area that are privately owned and sacred to the Aboriginal people. Within Purnululu, they visit places restricted from public access through privately negotiated agreements with their traditional owners. Prices vary widely.

⛺🚶 **CAMPING AND WALKING TRAILS.** The only two legal campsites available within the park have untreated water, toilets, and firewood. Seven kilometers to the left of the **Visitors Center** is the bustling **Kurrajong campsite ❶**; 13km to the right is the quieter **Walardi campsite ❶**. (All sites $9.). These are the only sites where fires are allowed.

The **Bungle Bungle Range** is composed of fragile sandstone; to protect this natural wonder, people are not allowed to climb to the top. A handful of **walking tracks** wander along the edge of the range. All the walks are marked by pink surveyors tape or upright metal posts, painted white near the top. They can be difficult to follow at points, but nearly all the walks follow dry stream beds—when off the stream bed, take extreme care to stay on marked and well worn trails. Moving off the trail can cause considerable damage to the park's plant life. Always take 2L of water, solid hiking shoes, and a small medical kit.

Leaving from the Piccanninny Gorge carpark, 25km south of the Visitor Centre, three walks are available.

  Domes Walk. (1km) A sandy circuit trail that weaves among the beehive formations.

  Cathedral Gorge Walk. (3km return) Very flat and easy, heading along a dry riverbed into a gorge and ending at an astounding natural amphitheater known as the Cathedral. Although usually a quiet place of reflection, the acoustics are excellent and more than one visitor has been known to burst into song. The Domes Walk loops into the Cathedral Gorge Walk; the two are best done in conjunction.

  Piccanninny Creek and Gorge Trail. (30km return) The longest walk; hiking the entire length requires spending the night on the trail (register with the ranger station before departing). The first 7km is a smooth trail over bedrock and makes an nice day-hike. From there, the trail turns into the range and becomes rocky and much more difficult.

Starting from the carparks 21km north of the ranger station are three of the park's best hikes, despite their omission of the beehive formations.

WESTERN AUSTRALIA

TERMITE BE GIANTS When crossing through the lonely planes of the Kimberley, you may feel like you have intruded upon the barren fields of some distant planet when you cross through a curious array of upright stones, resembling an abandoned cemetery or our long-lost alien friends. You *are* on Earth, and those curious mounds are actually the work of colonies of hardworking termites. The mounds, which can measure up to 6m in height, serve as an essential part of the desert ecosystem, diligently consuming dead trees and other debris. Formed from a delicate mixture of termite food, saliva, feces, and round-the-clock efforts, we ask you: an architectural wonder or a big pile of shit? Either way, impressive for the little buggers.

Echidna Chasm Walk. (2km return) A thrilling voyage through a narrow crack in the range. Best seen at midday when the overhead sun brings the red cliff faces to life, this hike is a bad idea for the claustrophobic—it can get less than 1m wide at parts. The gravel floor makes it easy going. Don't be fooled by the false-end chamber or the seemingly boulder-blocked passageway; the trail doesn't end until the open chamber after the steel ladder.

Froghole Gorge. (1.4km return) This fairly technical walk requires a little finesse, leading through a lush valley to a pond filled with rockhole frogs. Follow the trail markers closely for the easiest and safest route around the many boulders. **Walanginjdji Lookout** (500m return), a short, sandy side trail to a peaceful spot, gives a great view of the range's western cliffs.

Mini Palms Gorge. (5km return) The park's most difficult day trail follows rocky river beds to a steep and boulder-strewn final ascent to a series of levels, the last of which is an observation platform. The view is less than spectacular, looking as much back over the trail as forward into an area of palms, but the hike is its own reward.

KUNUNURRA ☎08

Five-hundred kilometers west of Katherine, NT, the little pocket of civilization known as Kununurra (kuh-nah-NUR-ah; pop. 5000) sleeps beneath the sandstone formations of the eastern Kimberley. The name, meaning "big waters," is appropriate for a town that grew during the effort to reroute the Ord River for irrigation in the 1960s and 70s. Most travelers use Kununurra as a base to explore the dramatic attractions in the eastern Kimberley region, including Purnululu (Bungle Bungle) National Park, Lake Argyle, and the Gibb River Rd.

TRANSPORTATION

Flights: The airport is 5km down the Victoria Hwy. towards Wyndham. **Air North** (☎1800 627 474) flies twice daily to **Broome** ($312) and **Darwin** ($220).

Buses: Buses arrive at the tourist bureau at the corner of Coolibah Dr. and White Gum St. **Greyhound Pioneer** (☎13 20 30) departs for **Broome** (14hr., daily 5:30pm, $173) and **Darwin** (13hr., daily 9am, $129).

Cars: Budget, 947 Mango St. (☎9168 2033), and at the airport. **Avis,** 12 Coolibah Dr. (☎9169 1258), and at the airport. **Thrifty Territory Rent-a-Car,** 596 Bandicoot Dr. (☎9169 1911), at the BP service station. **Handy Rentals** (☎9169 1188), at the corner of Messmate Way and Bandicoot Dr. **Hertz** (☎9169 1424).

Taxis: Spuds Taxis (☎9168 2553). **Alex Taxi** (☎13 10 08).

✦ 🛈 ORIENTATION AND PRACTICAL INFORMATION

Messmate Way turns off the Victoria Hwy. at a petrol station and heads into town, where it crosses **Konkerberry Dr.** and ends at **Coolibah Dr.** The **Kununurra Shopping Centre** is on Konkerberry Dr. Most restaurants and the two hostels are on or near Konkerberry as it heads away from Messmate.

Tourist Office: Tourist Bureau (☎9168 1177), on Coolibah Dr. Open in the Dry (Apr.-Nov.) daily 8am-5pm; in the Wet (Dec.-Mar.) M-F 9am-4pm.

National Park Information: Conservation and Land Management (☎9168 4200), on Messmate Way at the traffic circle. Open M-F 8am-4:30pm. Sells park vehicle passes good at all parks in Western Australia. ($22.50 per month, $51 per year). Across the hall is the **Department of Land Administration** (☎9168 0255), which sells topographic maps of the Kimberley ($7.50). Open M-F 8am-4:30pm.

Banks: Commonwealth Bank (☎13 22 21), on the corner of Coolibah Dr. and Cotton Tree Ave., has a 24hr. **ATM**. Open M-Th 9:30am-4pm, F 9:30am-5pm.

Work Opportunities: Numerous short and long-term work opportunities in Kununurra. Within the city, asking at local establishments is often the most productive way to find employment, although the bulletin board at Coles and Tuckerbox are covered with postings looking for short-term help. Local melon growers regularly hire pickers Sept.-Dec.; some offer transport to and from Kununurra. Call to check availability: **Kane and Marie** (☎9169 1381); **Ord River Farming Company** (☎9169 3088); **PMS** (☎9168 1520); **Rocky Lerch Holdings** (☎9168 1216); **R.O. Smith & Sons** (☎9168 1774); **Tropical Sands** (☎9168 1878); **Barradale Farm** (☎9169 1386); **Bluey's Outback Farm** (☎9168 2177); **Ceres Farm** (☎9168 1613); and **Cummings Bros.** (☎9168 1400). Limited workers' accommodations at **Kununurra Backpacker Adventure Centre**.

Kimberley Road Conditions: ☎1800 013 314.

Police: (☎9166 4530, emergency ☎000), at Coolibah Dr. and Banksia St. 24hr.

Internet Access: Telecentre (☎9169 1868), at the corner of Banksia St. and Collibah Dr. $6 per hr. Open M-F 9am-5pm, Sa 10am-2pm. **Ruraltech** is behind the police station on Konkerberry Dr. $6 per hr. Open M-F 9am-5pm.

Post Office: (☎9168 1395), across from the police station at Coolibah Dr. and Banksia St. Open M-F 9am-5pm. **Postal Code:** 6743.

🏠 ACCOMMODATIONS

The options for backpackers are limited in Kununurra, so the motto during the Dry (Apr.-Nov.) is: "If you want a bed, book ahead."

Desert Inn (☎9168 2702), 2 blocks from the shopping center near the corner of Konkerberry and Tristania St. In addition to hip decorating feats with scrap metal and the color purple, this cozy place has a pool, patio, lounge areas, spacious kitchen, and laundry. Free pickup and drop-off. Dorms $18; doubles $45; triples and quads $19 per person. 7 night max. stay. VIP/YHA $1 discount. MC/V. ❷

Kununurra Backpackers Adventure Centre, 24 Nutwood Crescent (☎9169 1998). A 10min. walk from the tourist office; follow Konkerberry away from the highway, then turn right on Nutwood. In a quiet but social neighborhood; features A/C, pool, kitchen, VCR, full tour bookings desk, and laundry. Free pickup and drop-off. Key deposit $10. Dorms $18; twins and doubles $46. Some workers' accommodations. MC/V. ❷

Hotel Kununurra, 8 Messmate Way (☎9168 1344; hotelknx@wn.com.au), next to the BP station. Pool, spa, laundry, Internet, and a tasty restaurant. The well-maintained rooms vary between budget and luxury; all have A/C, fridge, and bath. Budget singles and doubles from $45; standard hotel $80-110. MC/V. ●

Camping is available along the Victoria Hwy. The **Red Gum Caravan Park** ● is a 10min. walk from town. (☎8972 2239. Laundry, pool, and BBQ. Sites $9, for 2 $18, powered $22; cabins $80, each extra person $7.) The **Riverview Caravan Park and Motel** ● near the hot springs, has a pool and spa. (☎8972 1011. Sites for 2 $17, powered $21; singles $61; doubles and twins $72; budget cabins for 2 $65-80.)

🔛 FOOD AND ENTERTAINMENT

Food options in Kununurra are limited. **Coles** in the shopping center has **groceries.** (☎9168 2711. Open daily 5am-midnight.) **Farmers Fruit and Vege-mart** ●, at the corner of Konkerberry Dr. and Ebony St., has sandwiches ($3.50) and $3 milkshakes. (☎9168 3583. Open M-F 6am-5:30pm, Sa 6am-noon.) (☎9168 2071. Open M-F 7am-5:30pm, Sa-Su 7am-4pm.) The main pub in town is **Gulliver's Tavern,** on Konkerberry Dr. at Cotton Tree Ave. (☎9168 1666. Open M-Th noon-11pm, F noon-1am, Sa noon-midnight, Su 1-9pm.)

🄖 SIGHTS AND ACTIVITIES

Kelly's Knob overlooks the stunning terrain of Kununurra. Take Konkerberry Dr. to its end; turn left on Ironwood, right on Speargrass, and right again at the large stone tablet. **Mirima (Hidden Valley) National Park,** 2km east of town, looks like a miniature Purnululu range, without the 6hr. drive. Three paths wind past the 350-million-year-old formations. The **Derdebe-Gerring Banan Lookout Trail** (400m) ascends a steep hill for a view of the Ord Valley and nearby sandstone ranges. The **Demboong Banan Gap Trail** (250m) heads through a gap in the range, then through a small valley, to a lookout over Kununurra. The **Looking at Plants Nature Trail** (400m) gives walkers an introduction to local plants and their use by Aborigines.

Ranger-led walks meet at the carpark at the end of Hidden Valley Rd. and at the lovely secluded retreat of Lily Pool in Hidden Valley. However, Lily Pool, along with the area that extends away from it down Lily Creek, are sacred men's places for the Miriwoong people—female travelers should respectfully avoid this part of the park. **Wild Adventure Tours** (☎0945 6643) offers travelers a more interactive and ecologically friendly take on the Kununurra area, with abseiling tours and instruction at local sites, including Kelly's Knob ($60) and the Grotto ($110).

The **Mirimon Dawang Woorlab-Gerring Language and Culture Centre** is more of an Aboriginal community center than a tourist sight, but the friendly staff welcomes visitors interested in local Aboriginal culture. (☎9169 1029. Head north of town and take the third left off Speargrass Rd., 10m before the sign for Kelly's Knob.)

🄓 DAYTRIP FROM KUNUNURRA: LAKE ARGYLE

Nestled between ancient orange sandstone hills and dotted with about 90 islands, the 850km² lake was created in the early 1970s as part of the ambitious Ord River Irrigation Project. Though it looks eerily out of place, Lake Argyle, the largest freshwater body in the Southern Hemisphere, is brilliantly blue and massive (it can hold 18 Sydney Harbours). Drive 35km south of Kununurra on the Victoria Hwy. and turn onto the access road. Another 35km leads to the **Lake Argyle Tourist Village.** Lake Argyle is a popular spot with locals and tourists alike, and is often touted by local tour organizations. What the many advertisements celebrating the lake and its role in the Ord River Valley development fail to mention, however, is the lake's darker secret: much of the land flooded in the river's rerouting was traditionally owned by the Miriwoong, who were in no way consulted in the planning of the project. Many of their sacred sites now rest at the lake's bottom.

Cruises are a popular way to see a fraction of the lake. **Lake Argyle Cruises** has a booking office at the Lake Argyle Tourist Village. (☎9168 7361. Tours May-Sept. daily, Oct.-Apr. by demand. 2hr. wildlife morning cruise $34; 2½hr. sunset cruise $43; 6hr. best of Lake Argyle cruise $98. Pickup in Kununurra $15.) **Ord Tours** explores other parts of the waterways heading to the Lower Ord River, famous for its salties and many species of birds. (☎9169 1165. 5hr. Tours Tu, Th, Sa, and Su 7am and 1pm. $45.) **Triple J Tours** has cruises of the lake and the Ord River. (☎9168 2682. Full-day from $85, including pickup.) **Kimberley Canoeing** offers a three-day self guided tour ($135, includes drop-off, pickup, canoe and camping gear; min. 2 persons.) The **Lake Argyle Tourist Village ❶** has accommodations. The **caravan park** has showers and laundry. (☎9167 1050. Sites $7, powered $11.50.) The **motel ❺** next door has a pool and restaurant. (☎9167 7360. Singles $72; doubles $77.)

WYNDHAM ☎08

A 20m-long crocodile statue welcomes you to Wyndham (pop. 800). The northernmost point on the Great Northern Hwy., this tiny port town is sleepy and isolated but more charming than Kununurra (100km south). Here the pioneer spirit thrives in the dramatic backdrop of the Bastion Range and the Cambridge Gulf.

Wyndham is neatly divided into two clusters. Most shops and services (and the big croc) are found in the southern section of town, including the **tourist office** in the Mobil station (☎9161 1281; open daily 6am-6pm) and **Internet** access at **Telecentre,** 6 O'Donnell St., opposite the Boab gallery. (☎9161 1161. Open M-Sa 9am-5pm.) The cheerful staff at the **Wyndham Caravan Park ❶,** near the Mobil station, will be more than glad to show you their giant 2000-year-old boab tree. (☎9161 1064. Sites $9, powered $12.) **Gulf Breeze Guest House ❷,** on the highway before the wharf, has a kitchen, TV, and shady patio. Reserve and pay for a room at the Wyndham Caravan Park. (☎9161 1401. Singles $20; doubles $45; families $50.)

Follow the signs east from the highway for the ◪**Five River Lookout,** 7km up a steep road with a tremendous view of the wharf, mudflats, and the Ord, Forrest, King, Durack, and Pentecost Rivers emptying into the gulf. At the **Wyndham Zoological Gardens and Crocodile Park,** just north of the wharf, you can munch on a croc-shaped fudge bar ($3) or get up close to the name-tagged crocs, whose placards read: "Hi! I'm David. I'm 6m long and I eat people and tip over boats. I mate with all the females." The park also houses six endangered Komodo Dragons. (☎9161 1124. Open in the Dry daily 8:30am-4pm; feedings at 11am. Call ahead in the Wet. $14.) The bronze **Dreamtime Statues,** across from the Mobil station, are a reminder of the heritage of Wyndham's Aboriginal population (currently over 50%).

Thirty kilometers south of Wyndham on the way to Kununurra, an unsealed 1km access road leads to ◪**The Grotto,** but you will have to descend 140 stone steps to reach the perfectly peaceful swimming hole. It is worth a trip at any time of year but looks best during the Wet when the waterfall is in full force.

WESTERN AUSTRALIA

APPENDIX

AUSSIE BEVERAGE GUIDE

TERMS OF EMBEERMENT. Nothing's more Australian than **beer,** and accordingly, the language used for it has an Aussie twist too. Because of the hot climate, Australian pubs generally eschew the British pint in favor of smaller portions, which stay cold until you're done. Thus, size is a major variable in the argot of ale. If you're too drunk to think of the proper terms, ordering by size, in ounces, usually works. On the mainland, try a "5," "7," "10," or "15." In Tasmania, order using the numbers "6," "8," "10," or "20." Most importantly, don't forget to **shout** your new-found mates a round—that is, to buy them all a drink.

REGION	BRING ME A...	STATE BEER
New South Wales:	**Pony** 140mL (5 oz.), **Beer / Glass** 200mL (7 oz.), **Middy** 285mL (10 oz.), **Schooner** 425mL (15 oz.)	Tooheys
Northern Territory:	**Darwin Stubbie** 1.25L (40 oz.) bottle	N/A
Queensland:	**Beer / Glass** 200mL (7 oz.), **Pot** 285mL (10 oz.), **Schooner** 425mL (15 oz.)	XXXX
South Australia:	**Butcher** 200mL (7 oz.), **Middy / Schooner** 285mL (10 oz.), **Pint** 425mL (15 oz., smaller than the British or American pint), **Real Pint** 560mL (20 oz.)	Coopers
Tasmania:	**Real Pint** 560mL (20 oz.)	Cascade, Boag's
Victoria:	**Beer / Glass** 200mL (7 oz.), **Pot** 285mL (10 oz.)	VB
Western Australia:	**Bobby / Beer** 200mL (7 oz.), **Middy** 285mL (10 oz.), **Pot** 425mL (15 oz.)	Emu Bitter
Australia:	**Handle** 285mL (10 oz.) glass with handle, **Long Neck** 750mL (25 oz.) bottle, **Stubbie** 375mL (12 oz.) bottle, **Tinny** 375mL (12 oz.) can, **Slab** case of 24 beers	

COOL BEANS. Coffee may not be Australia's specialty, to put it mildly, but there are plenty of great ways to get buzzed. Any of these drinks can be made weak, medium, or strong. Coffee drinks are all made with espresso, as opposed to those automatic-drip style brewing machines, so black coffee is quite a bit stronger in Oz. Whole milk is always used unless you specify something else, like cream or lowfat milk (referred to as "skinny").

WHAT TO ORDER...	...AND WHAT YOU'LL GET.
short black	60mL of espresso
long black	120-200mL of espresso
flat white	espresso with cold milk
cafe latte	espresso, hot milk, and froth
cappuccino	espresso, hot milk, and heaps of froth
macchiato	espresso with a bit of froth
vienna coffee	espresso, whipped cream, and powdered chocolate

GLOSSARY OF 'STRINE

'Strine is 'stralian for "Australian." The first trick to speaking Australian slang is to abbreviate everything: **Oz** for Australia, **brekkie** for breakfast, **cuppa** for cup of coffee, **sammy** for sandwich. The second, less ubiquitous aspect of Aussie slang is **rhyming. Noahs** are sharks (shark rhymes with ark, Noah built an ark), while **I'm on the dog** means "I'm on the phone" (bone rhymes with phone, and then the whole dog-bone thing). American travelers may be disturbed to be called **seppos,** for good reason: "Yanks" rhymes with "tanks," and the worst kind of tanks are septic tanks. Ouch! Australian **pronunciation** is harder to learn than the lingo—with Aboriginal words especially, but even with English-derived proper nouns, it can seem impossible. One rule to note: when Australians spell a word out or pronounce a number, they always use the expression "double" (or "triple"), as in the phone number "nine-three-double-seven-five-triple-one" (☎9377 5111).

ablution block: shower/toilet block at a campground
abseil: rappel
ace: awesome
aggro: aggravated
ANZAC biscuits: honey-oat cookies
arvo: afternoon
Aussie: Australian (pronounced Ozzie— thus, "Australia" is "Oz")
backpackers: hostel
bagged: criticized
banana bender: Queenslander
barbie: barbecue
bathers: bathing suit
belt bag: fanny pack (don't say "fanny" in Oz: it's a crude word for a part of the female anatomy)
beyond the black stump: *really* far away
billabong: a water hole
biro: pen
biscuit: cookie
bitumen: a rough black asphalt used to pave roads
bloke: guy, man (familiar)
bludger: moocher, grifter, lazy person; weak drinker
bluey: someone with red hair (seriously)
bonnet: hood of a car
boofhead: fool
book: make reservations
boot: trunk of a car
bottle shop: liquor store
brekkie: breakfast
Brizzy: Brisbane, QLD
bugger: damn
Bundy: Bundaberg, QLD, as in the rum
bush: wilderness
bush tucker: traditional Aboriginal wild foods
bushwalking: hiking
busk: to play music on the street for money
BYO: bring your own alcohol
campervan: mobile home, RV
capsicum: bell peppers
caravan: trailer, like a cabless campervan
carpark: parking lot
chap: guy, man; see bloke

chazzwazzer: bullfrog
chemist: pharmacy
chips: thick french fries, often served with vinegar and salt
chippers: fish and chips or fish and chips shops
chock-a-block: crowded
chook: chicken
chunder: vomit
coffee: beer
coldie: a cold beer
concession: discount; usually applies to students, seniors, or children, sometimes only to Australian students and pensioners
cordial: concentrated fruit juice
cossie: swimsuit
crook: sick
crow eater: South Australian
dag: one who is daggy (usage is common, often benevolent)
daggy: unfashionable, goofy
damper: traditionally unleavened bread
dear: expensive
Devonshire tea: tea and scones, often served in the late afternoon
dobber: tattle-tale
dodgy: sketchy
donk: power
doona, duvet: comforter, feather blanket
dramas: problems. "No dramas" = "no worries."
drink driving: driving under the influence of alcohol
drier than a dead dingo's donger: very thirsty
ensuite: with bath
entree: appetizer ("main" is a main dish)
esky: a cooler (originally from the brand name Eskimo)
excess: deductible (as in car insurance)
fair dinkum: genuine
fair go: equal opportunity
fairy floss: cotton candy
fancy: to like; as in "would you fancy...?"
feral: wild, punky, grungy
flash: fancy, snazzy

flat out like a lizard drinking: doing nothing
free call: toll-free call
franger: condom (colloquial, somewhat crude)
full on: intense
furphy: tall tale, exaggerated rumor (tell a furphy)
g'day: hello
give it a go: to try
good onya: good for you
glasshouse: greenhouse
grommet: young surfer
ground floor: American first floor ("first floor" is second floor, etc.)
grog: booze
hire: to rent
hitching: hitchhiking
holiday: vacation
hoon: loud-mouth, show-off
icy-pole: popsicle (sweet frozen treat on a stick)
jersey: sweater, sweatshirt
jackaroo: stationhand-in-training
jillaroo: female jackaroo
jumper: see jersey
keen: term of respect ("a keen surfer")
Kiwi: New Zealander
knackered: really tired
lad: guy, man; see chap
licensed: serves alcohol
like hen's teeth: rare
lollies: candies
magic: really wonderful, special
mate: friend, buddy (used broadly)
Mexican: Victorian
milk bar: convenience store
Milo: chocolate product in bar and drink varieities
mobile: cell phone
moke: an open-air, golf-cart-esque vehicle
mozzie: mosquito
nappy: diaper
newsagent: newsstand/convenience store
nibblies: snacks
no worries: sure, fine, or "you're welcome"
ocker: hick, Crocodile Dundee-type

odds and sods: odds and ends
off like a bucket of prawns: something has a bad smell
ordinary: bad; an "ordinary" road is full of potholes.
Owyergoin'?: How are you?
Oz: Australia
pavlova: a creamy meringue dessert garnished with fruit
pensioner: senior citizen
petrol: gasoline
piss: beer (usually)
pissed: drunk (usually)
pokies: gambling machines
Pom: person from England
powerpoint: power outlet
prawn: jumbo shrimp
pub: bar
publican: bartender
push bike: bicycle
raging: partying
return: round-trip
roadie: takeaway beer
'roo: as in kanga-
roobar: bumper protecting car from 'roo damage
roundabout: traffic rotary
rubber: eraser
sandgroper: a Western Australian (also Westralian)
sang or sanger: sausage
sauce: usually tomato sauce;

closest equivalent to ketchup.
serviette: napkin
sheila: slang for a woman
shout: buy a drink or round of drinks for others. Also a noun, as in an evening's worth of everyone buying rounds for each other.
side: team
singlet: tank top or undershirt
skivvie: turtleneck sweater
sook: crybaby (see winge)
spider: ice cream float or nasty arachnid (use context clues here)
squiz: a look (to take a squiz at something)
stone the crows!: an expression of surprise
'strine: Aussie dialect (from Australian)
'straya: Australia
swimmers: swimsuit
sunnies: sunglasses
suss: figure out, sort out
ta: short for thank you—usually muttered under breath.
ta ta: goodbye
TAB: shop to place bets, sometimes in pubs
takeaway: food to go, takeout
Tassie: Tasmania (TAZ-zie)
tea: evening meal

that's a boomerang: that's something very important to me I don't want you to steal
Tim Tams: chocolate covered graham-like cookie
torch: flashlight
touch wood: knock on wood
trackies: sweatpants
track suit: sweat suit, jogging suit
tucker: food.
uni: university (YOU-nee)
unsealed: unpaved roads, usually gravel, sometimes dirt
ute (yute): utility vehicle, pickup truck
upmarket: upscale, expensive
Vegemite: yeast-extract spread for toast and sammies
vejjo: vegetarian
walkabout: to spontaneously set off across the countryside
Walzking Matilda: Oz's unofficial national anthem
wanker: jerk (very rude term)
winge: to whine or complain
yakka: hard work
zed: Z (American "zee")

TEMPERATURE CHARTS

To convert from °C to °F, multiply by 1.8 and add 32. For a rough approximation, double the Celsius and add 25. To convert from °F to °C, subtract 32 and multiply by 0.55. For a rough approximation, subtract 25 and cut it in half.

°CELSIUS	-5	0	5	10	15	20	25	30	35	40
°FAHRENHEIT	23	32	41	50	59	68	77	86	95	104

Av. Temp. lo/hi Precipitation	January			April			July			October		
	°C	°F	mm	°C	°F	mm	°C	°F	mm	°C	°F	mm
Adelaide	16/28	61/82	19	12/22	54/72	43	7/15	45/59	65	10/21	50/70	43
Alice Springs	21/36	70/97	40	13/28	55/82	17	4/19	39/66	12	15/31	59/88	20
Brisbane	21/29	70/84	161	17/26	63/79	89	10/20	50/68	57	16/26	61/79	77
Cairns	24/31	75/88	407	22/29	72/84	200	17/26	63/79	27	20/29	68/84	38
Canberra	13/28	55/82	58	7/20	45/68	53	0/11	32/52	40	6/19	43/66	67
Darwin	25/32	77/90	393	24/33	75/91	103	20/31	68/88	1	25/34	77/93	52
Hobart	12/22	54/72	48	9/17	48/63	52	4/12	39/54	54	8/17	46/63	64
Melbourne	14/26	57/79	48	11/20	52/68	58	6/13	43/55	49	9/20	48/68	68
Perth	18/30	64/86	9	14/25	57/77	46	9/18	48/64	173	12/22	54/72	55
Sydney	18/26	64/79	98	14/23	59/72	129	8/16	46/61	100	13/22	55/72	79

OF MONOTREMES AND MEN
The Rise and Fall of the Mammals of Australia

The mammals of Australia are spectacularly unique. Some, such as kangaroos, koalas, and platypuses, are so memorable that they have become virtually synonymous with Australia in the minds of many people. What is it that makes Australia's mammal fauna so unusual? Living mammals of the world fall into three major groups (placentals, marsupials, and monotremes), and while other continental faunas are dominated by placentals, marsupials are the most prevalent group in Australia. Furthermore, Australia is the only continent where marsupials, placentals, and monotremes all co-exist.

Monotremes (which include the aquatic duck-billed platypus and the burrowing echidnas, or spiny anteaters) are the most primitive living mammals. Found only in Australia and the neighboring island of New Guinea, they represent an early offshoot on the mammal family tree and retain a number of rather reptilian characteristics; for example, they are the only mammals that lay eggs. However, like all mammals, monotremes have fur, maintain a relatively constant body temperature, and nurse their offspring with milk.

Placental mammals are so named because they give birth to well-formed offspring that have developed in a placenta for a relatively extensive period of time prior to birth. Placentals include most familiar mammals, such as dogs and cats, hoofed animals, whales and dolphins, and humans, among many others. In contrast to placentals, marsupials give birth to poorly-developed offspring following a very short pregnancy; after birth, offspring are usually nurtured to greater maturity in a maternal pouch, where they attach to a teat and are actively cared for by their mother.

Australia's native marsupials display a remarkably wide variety of appearances and lifestyles. Among the most famous are wallabies and kangaroos. Ranging in size from small-bodied bettongs (sometimes called "rat-kangaroos") to the 200 lb. red kangaroo (the largest living Australian mammal), these bounding bipeds are found throughout the continent and in Tasmania. Among the most remarkable are the beautifully-colored cliff-dwelling rock wallabies and the arboreal tree kangaroos of Queensland's tropical rainforests. Australia's forests and woodlands are also filled with possums of all shapes and sizes, including gliding possums that can soar from tree to tree like flying squirrels, brushtail and ringtail possums, which flourish even in suburban and urban environments, and mouse-sized honey possums, which pollinate some of Western Australia's most beautiful flowers. Slow-moving koalas can be spotted in eucalyptus trees throughout eastern Australia and on Kangaroo Island (where they have been introduced); their closest relatives, the wombats, are medium-sized, bear-like marsupials that live in underground burrows rather than trees.

Smaller Australian marsupials include bandicoots and bilbies—long-snouted, rabbit-like animals found in all habitats from desert to rainforest—and the beautifully-striped numbat, a marsupial anteater that lives only in southwestern Australia. While most marsupials eat plants or insects, a few are carnivorous; these include tiny, fast-moving "marsupial mice," cat-sized spotted quolls (or "tiger cats"), the voracious, black-and-white Tasmanian devil, and the wolf-sized thylacine (also called a Tasmanian tiger or wolf), the largest marsupial carnivore to survive to modern times. Tragically, thylacines became extinct in the 1930s after a concerted campaign of persecution. Unsubstantiated sightings are still periodically reported from Tasmania, but there is little chance that these marvelous creatures still survive. Finally, one of the most unusual marsupials of all is the rarely-seen marsupial mole; small, silky-furred, and blind, these remarkable animals dig tunnels underneath the vast deserts of central and western Australia.

Why are there so many marsupials in Australia, and why have monotremes survived there but nowhere else? Part of the explanation is Australia's long history of isolation. Long ago, the landmasses that now populate the globe south of the equator (including South America, Africa, Madagascar, Antarctica, Australia, and New Zealand) were united in a single, grand southern continent called Gondwanaland. Roughly 150 million years ago, this supercontinent began to break apart, the resultant fragments commencing an ever-so-slow march toward the positions they occupy today. Forty million years ago during the course of this journey, a lingering land connection between Australia and Antarctica was severed, beginning a long period of Australian isolation that would last until its drift northward finally brought it near the islands of far southeastern Asia. The marsupials and monotremes present in Australia when it separated from other continents diversified to dominate most of the terrestrial niches that today are occupied by placental mammals on other continents. Within the last several million years, two major groups of placentals—bats and rodents—have colonized Australia from Asia via flying or island-hopping, but no larger placentals are naturally present on the continent (the dingo, a close relative of the domestic dog, was brought to Australia by Asian seafarers about 3500 years ago).

Unfortunately, the mammals of Australia have suffered more devastating levels of extinction than have been seen on any other continent, both during human prehistory and in historical times. A massive extinction of large marsupials and monotremes (as well as giant birds and reptiles, collectively referred to as "megafauna") occurred in Australia about 50,000 years ago, broadly concurrent with the arrival of the ancestors of Aboriginal Australians to the continent. The first human colonizers would have seen (and hunted) rhinoceros-sized marsupials called diprotodons, which lumbered across Australia in the company of giant kangaroos, wombats, and echidnas, as well as (among other extraordinary creatures) the "marsupial lion" or Thylacaleo—a predator that probably ambushed large prey from trees like a modern leopard.

A second and considerably more recent spasm of extinction has gripped the continent since European exploration and colonization began; in the last 150 years alone, more than one-sixth of all native mammals have become extinct (including, among others, several wallabies, bandicoots, and jumping mice) and a much larger proportion of species have undergone drastic declines. Reasons for these widespread declines are as varied as they are tragic; they include the introduction of ecologically destructive non-native animals like foxes, cats, rabbits, and cane toads to the continent; conversion of natural habitats for agricultural and urban development; logging and (historically) active hunting; and the disruption of traditional land-burning practices of Aboriginal communities.

Today the world's most unique mammal fauna remains the most endangered, despite increased attention to conservation and sustainability on the part of Australians across the country. Long-term commitment to preservation of natural habitats, extermination of non-native pests, captive breeding of endangered species, and basic wildlife research will be necessary to halt ongoing declines among Australian mammals, which comprise a diverse, valuable, and irreplaceable component of Australia's natural heritage.

Kristofer M. Helgen is a research scientist at the South Australian Museum and is currently pursuing a Ph.D. in mammalogy at the University of Adelaide. His work focuses on the mammals of Australia, New Guinea, and the Pacific.

HOLLYWOOD DOWN UNDER
The Great Journey of the Australian Film Industry

What does everyone's favorite bit of bacon, Babe, have to do with the macho mayhem of Mad Max, or, for that matter, the outrageously campy antics of Priscilla, Queen of the Desert? And what on earth do Cate Blanchett, Geoffrey Rush, and Nicole Kidman have in common? They all hail from the same corner of the globe, and are part of Australia's rich and diverse film industry.

A number of successful international co-productions in the post-WWII economic boom triggered the intense debate that still characterizes the industry today. Since Australian films have often been financed through foreign money, the "Australian-ness" of movies has became an enduringly hot topic. Films like *The Shiralee*, a joint British-Australian production about a fancy-free wanderer forced to confront his responsibilities as a father, spurred questions about whether local productions should instead aspire for a national or more universal perspective.

Because of the crisis of confidence, between 1959 and 1966 no feature films were produced in Australia. The late 1960s saw little improvement; most "Australian" films were made by foreign directors, like Britain's Michael Powell, who examined Australian culture from a distance. Powell's 1966 *They're A Weird Mob*, for example, is a one-gag film relying on idiosyncrasies of Aussie "lingo" that were dated even when it was released.

Success in Australian cinema seems to come in waves, and the 1970s were a veritable renaissance for the film industry. Thanks to increased government support, budding filmmakers could now attend what was to become one of the world's finest film schools, the Australian Film, Television and Radio School, and film co-operatives thrived due to arts subsidies. The most successful films were inspired by European art-house in their slow narrative progression and emphasis on in-depth character studies. Notable examples include Bruce Beresford's Boer War epic *Breaker Morant*, Peter Weir's *Picnic at Hanging Rock*, a strange and eerie tale of schoolgirls lost in the bush, and Gillian Armstrong's *My Brilliant Career*, based on Miles Franklin's classic Australian novel.

After the critical successes of the 70s, the 1980s bought Australian films into commercial favor at the box office, both at home and abroad. George Miller's *Mad Max* began the trend, and then thanks to generous tax incentives set up by the federal government to encourage true-blue cinematic projects, hits like adolescent angst-fest *Puberty Blues* and Paul Hogan's *Crocodile Dundee* ensured Aussie accents aplenty on the big screen.

The so-called Post New-Wave films of the 1990s built upon these commercial successes while also gaining considerable critical acclaim. Directors emerging from Australia's top film schools produced personal, specific, and ultra-quirky movies that reflected a typically Australian blend of fatalism and irreverence—an intriguing blend seen at its best in *Muriel's Wedding* and *Priscilla, Queen of the Desert*. In addition, the Oscar-winning story of Australian pianist David Helfgott, *Shine*, and the adventures of Babe the talking pig, have heralded an era of unprecedented success for Australian films both domestically and on a global stage.

Most recently, Baz Luhrmann's tale of doomed love in a Paris nightclub has re-ignited debate over Australian cinema. On the surface, *Moulin Rouge*, like Luhrmann's preceding works, *Strictly Ballroom* and *Romeo+Juliet*, does not appear an overtly Australian film; it was, after all, funded by Fox and set in France. Paradoxically, *Moulin Rouge* is also the epitome of Australian cinematic innovation: in no way inward-looking or provincial, it was nevertheless directed by an Australian, was filmed down under, and features a Australian cast and crew. After winning a Golden Globe, Luhrmann reflected on why Australians are now enjoying such success: "There is this great love of the journey. When you feel you are on the edge of the world, which Australia is in a sense, looking out at the rest of the world, what better way to receive that story than through film?"

Amelia Lester, from Sydney, Australia, is a contributing writer to Australian Vogue *and has also worked on* The Sun Herald, *a major Australian newspaper.*

INDEX

A

AAA 48
Aboriginal
art 20, 79, 82, 141, 309,
310, 675
artists 282
bush fires 251
cultural centers 259, 278,
365, 410, 447, 531, 726
didgeridoos 263
Dreaming 13
Dreamtime Statues 727
history 12, 14
legends 13, 136, 346, 348,
373, 654, 709
music 19
plants 114, 576
reconciliation 256
rock art sites 229, 234,
255, 256, 257, 260, 269,
270, 283, 284, 366, 426,
531, 611, 615, 721
sacred sites 182
shell necklaces 537
tours 256, 260, 271, 279,
413, 420, 426, 434, 675,
697, 723
weapons 545
Abrolhos Islands, WA 699,
700
abseiling
Blue Mountains, NSW 132
Bright, VIC 645
Brisbane, QLD 311
Byron Bay, NSW 189
Coles Bay, TAS 544
Cradle Mountain, TAS 523
Grampians National Park,
VIC 616
Jindabyne, NSW 213
Katoomba, NSW 137
Launceston, TAS 537
Margaret River, WA 686
Noosa, QLD 345
Snowy River National Park,
VIC 658
Townsville, QLD 389
acacia 9
accommodations 53–57
bed and breakfasts 57

camping 57–61
hostels 53
hotels 54
university dorms 57
adapters 37
Adelaide Festival of Arts 450
Adelaide Hills, SA 452
Adelaide, SA 438–451
adventure trips 61
aerogrammes 50
AFL 21
Agnes Water, QLD 360
Airlie Beach, QLD 375–380
airplane travel
fares 38
Albany, WA 689
Albury, NSW 215–218
alcohol 34
drinking age 18, 34
drunk driving 34
Alexandra Heads, QLD 337
Alice Springs, NT 273–279
Alternatives to Tourism 66–
70
American Express 30, 46, 51
American Red Cross 35
Anakie, QLD 430
Angahook-Lorne State Park,
VIC 599
Anglesea, VIC 598
animals
dangerous 60
mammals 731
animals. See environment.
antipode of Washington,
D.C. 685
Anzac Day 15
Apollo Bay, VIC 599
Apsley and Tia Gorges, NSW
194
Aquarius Festival 182
Armidale, NSW 194
Armstrong, Gillian 733
Arnhem Land, NT 260–261
articles
Hollywood Down Under
733
Of Monotremes and Men
731
To Climb or Not to Climb
292
arts

literature 19
movies 20
music 19
visual arts 20
Asbestos Range National
Park, TAS 531
Ashes, the 21
Atherton Tablelands, QLD
412–416
Atherton, QLD 413
ATM cards 31
Augusta, WA 682
Austrail Pass 43
AustralAsia Railway 274
Australia and New Zealand
Army Corps (ANZAC) 15
Australia Rock, NSW 208
Australia Telescope 228
Australia Zoo, QLD 310
Australian Alps, VIC 653
Australian Automobile
Association (AAA) 48
Australian Capital Territory
71–82
Australian Football League
(AFL) 21
Brisbane, QLD 312
Darwin, NT 248
Melbourne, VIC 573
Sydney, NSW 117, 121
Australian Open 21, 573, 580
Australian sea lions 463
Australian Tourist
Commission 26
automobile assistance 48
Ayers Rock, NT 289

B

B&Bs 57
backpacks 59
Bairnsdale, VIC 653
Balancing Rock, QLD 336
Bald Rock National Park,
NSW 193, 336
Ballarat, VIC 619–623
Ballina, NSW 178
bandicoots 10
Bangalow, NSW 184
Barcaldine, QLD 430
Barmah State Park and

INDEX